Lecture Notes in Computer Science 13657

More information about this series at https://link.springer.com/bookseries/558

Yuan Xu · Hongyang Yan · Huang Teng ·
Jun Cai · Jin Li (Eds.)

Machine Learning for Cyber Security

4th International Conference, ML4CS 2022
Guangzhou, China, December 2–4, 2022
Proceedings, Part III

Springer

Editors
Yuan Xu
School of Computing and Informatics
University of Louisiana at Lafayette
Lafayette, IN, USA

Huang Teng
Institute of Artificial Intelligence
and Blockchain
Guangzhou University
Guangzhou, China

Jin Li
Institute of Artificial Intelligence
and Blockchain
Guangzhou University
Guangzhou, China

Hongyang Yan
Institute of Artificial Intelligence
and Blockchain
Guangzhou University
Guangzhou, China

Jun Cai
Guangdong Polytechnic Normal University
Guangzhou, China

ISSN 0302-9743 ISSN 1611-3349 (electronic)
Lecture Notes in Computer Science
ISBN 978-3-031-20101-1 ISBN 978-3-031-20102-8 (eBook)
https://doi.org/10.1007/978-3-031-20102-8

This Springer imprint is published by the registered company Springer Nature Switzerland AG
The registered company address is: Gewerbestrasse 11, 6330 Cham, Switzerland

Preface

The Fourth International Conference on Machine Learning for Cyber Security (ML4CS 2022) was held in Guangzhou, China, during December 2–4, 2022. ML4CS is a well-recognized annual international forum for AI-driven security researchers to exchange ideas and present their works.

The conference received 367 submissions. Committee accepted 100 regular papers and 46 short papers to be included in the conference program. It was single blind during the paper review process, and there are two reviews per paper at least. The proceedings contain revised versions of the accepted papers. While revisions are expected to take the referees comments into account, this was not enforced and the authors bear full responsibility for the content of their papers.

ML4CS 2022 was organized by Guangdong Polytechnic Normal University, Pazhou Lab, and Sun Yat-sen University. The conference would not have been such a success without the support of these organizations, and we sincerely thank them for their continued assistance and support.

We would also like to thank the authors who submitted their papers to ML4CS 2022, and the conference attendees for their interest and support. We thank the Organizing Committee for their time and effort dedicated to arranging the conference. This allowed us to focus on the paper selection and deal with the scientific program. We thank the Program Committee members and the external reviewers for their hard work in reviewing the submissions; the conference would not have been possible without their expert reviews. Finally, we thank the EasyChair system and its operators, for making the entire process of managing the conference convenient.

September 2022

Xiaochun Cao
Jin Li
Jun Cai
Huang Teng
Yan Jia
Min Yang
Xu Yuan

Organization

General Chairs

Xiaochun Cao	Sun Yat-sen University, China
Jin Li	Guangzhou University, China
Jun Cai	Guangdong Polytechnic Normal University, China
Teng Huang	Guangzhou University, China

Program Chairs

Yan Jia	Peng Cheng Laboratory, China
Min Yang	Fudan University, China
Xu Yuan	University of Louisiana at Lafayette, USA

Track Chairs

Machine Learning Based Cybersecurity Track

Wei Wang	Beijing Jiaotong University, China
Yu-an Tan	Beijing Institute of Technology, China

Big Data Analytics for Cybersecurity Track

Xuyun Zhang	Macquaire University, Australia
Wenchao Jiang	Guangdong University of Technology, China

Cryptography in Machine Learning Track

Xinyi Huang	Fujian Normal University, China
Joseph K. Liu	Monash University, Australia

Differential Privacy Track

Changyu Dong	Newcastle University, UK
Tianqing Zhu	University of Technology Sydney, Australia

Data Security in Machine Learning Track

Zheli Liu	Nankai University, China
Zuoyong Li	Minjiang University, China

Adversarial Attacks and Defenses Track

Qian Wang	Wuhan University, China
Kai Chen	Institute of Information Engineering, Chinese Academy of Sciences, China

Security and Privacy in Federated Learning Track

Lianyong Qi	Qufu Normal University, China
Tong Li	Nankai University, China

Explainable Machine Learning Track

Sheng Hong	Beihang University, China

Security in Machine Learning Application Track

Tao Xiang	Chongqing University, China
Yilei Wang	Qufu Normal University, China

AI/Machine Learning Security and Application Track

Hao Peng	Zhejiang Normal University, China

Workshop Chair

Wei Gao	Yunnan Normal University, China

Publication Chair

Di Wu	Guangzhou University, China

Publicity Chair

Zhuo Ma	Xidian University, China

Steering Committee

Xiaofeng Chen	Xidian University, China
Iqbal Gondal	Federation University, Australia
Ryan Ko	Waikato University, New Zealand
Jonathan Oliver	Trend Micro, USA
Islam Rafiqul	Charles Sturt University, Australia
Vijay Varadharajan	University of Newcastle, Australia
Ian Welch	Victoria University of Wellington, New Zealand
Yang Xiang (Chair)	Swinburne University of Technology, Australia
Jun Zhang (Chair)	Swinburne University of Technology, Australia
Wanlei Zhou	Deakin University, Australia

Program Committee

Silvio Barra	University of Salerno, Italy
M. Z. Alam Bhuiyan	Guangzhou University, China
Carlo Blundo	University of Salerno, Italy
Yiqiao Cai	Huaqiao University, China
Luigi Catuogno	University of Salerno, Italy
Lorenzo Cavallaro	King's College London, UK
Liang Chang	Guilin University of Electronic Technology, China
Fei Chen	Shenzhen University, China
Xiaofeng Chen	Xidian University, China
Zhe Chen	Singapore Management University, Singapore
Frédéric Cuppens	IMT Atlantique, France
Changyu Dong	Newcastle University, UK
Guangjie Dong	East China Jiaotong University, China
Mohammed EI-Abd	American University of Kuwait, Kuwait
Wei Gao	Yunnan Normal University, China
Dieter Gollmann	Hamburg University of Technology, Germany
Zheng Gong	South China Normal University, China
Zhitao Guan	North China Electric Power University, China
Zhaolu Guo	Chinese Academy of Sciences, China
Jinguang Han	Queen's University Belfast, UK
Saeid Hosseini	Singapore University of Technology and Design, Singapore
Chingfang Hsu	Huazhong University of Science and Technology, China
Haibo Hu	The Hong Kong Polytechnic University, Hong Kong
Teng Huang	Guangzhou University, China
Xinyi Huang	Fujian Normal University, China

Licheng Wang	Beijing University of Posts and Telecommunications, China
Lingyu Wang	Concordia University, Canada
Tianyin Wang	Luoyang Normal University, China
Wei Wang	Beijing Jiaotong University, China
Wenle Wang	Jiangxi Normal University, China
Sheng Wen	Swinburne University of Technology, Australia
Yang Xiang	Swinburne University of Technology, Australia
Run Xie	Yibin University, China
Xiaolong Xu	Nanjing University of Information Science & Technology, China
Li Yang	Xidian University, China
Shao-Jun Yang	Fujian Normal University, China
Zhe Yang	Northwestern Polytechnical University, China
Yanqing Yao	Beihang University, China
Xu Yuan	University of Louisiana at Lafayette, USA
Qikun Zhang	Beijing Institute of Technology, China
Xiao Zhang	Beihang University, China
Xiaosong Zhang	Tangshan University, China
Xuyun Zhang	Macquarie University, Australia
Yuan Zhang	Nanjing University, China
Xianfeng Zhao	Chinese Academy of Sciences, China
Lei Zhu	Huazhong University of Science and Technology, China
Tianqing Zhu	China University of Geosciences, China

Track Program Committee - AI/Machine Learning Security and Application

Hao Peng (Chair)	Zhejiang Normal University, China
Meng Cai	Xi'an Jiaotong University, China
Jianting Ning	Singapore Management University, Singapore
Hui Tian	Huaqiao University, China
Fushao Jing	National University of Defense Technology, China
Guangquan Xu	Tianjin University, China
Jun Shao	Zhejiang Gongshang University, China

Contents – Part III

Design of Active Defense System for Railway Communication Network Based on Deep Neural Network

Zheng guo Wu(✉)

Wuhan Railway Vocational College of Technology, Wuhan 430000, China
wzg1984109@163.com

Abstract. In order to improve the security of railway communication network, an active defense system of railway communication network based on deep neural network is proposed and designed. Through the design of railway communication network monitoring terminal, railway communication network alarm, railway communication network intrusion data parser and railway communication network active defense circuit, the hardware design of the system is completed. In the software part, based on the collected spatial data of railway communication network, the intrusion data characteristics of railway communication network are extracted by using deep neural network, and the active defense of railway communication network is realized by constructing the active defense model of railway communication network. The experimental results show that the function of the designed system meets the needs of users for the system function, and improves the performance of the system by reducing the memory occupancy, false alarm rate and packet loss rate.

Keywords: Deep neural network · Railway communication network · Active defense system · Data characteristics

1 Introduction

At present, the railway communication network attacks are escalating in terms of scale and attack means, and the security threats are becoming increasingly serious. Railway communication network is an important technical equipment and infrastructure to ensure transportation safety and improve efficiency. The railway communication network security protection technology is mainly based on the firewall and other passive defense means to extract the characteristics of known attacks. The management and control ability of network security is still relatively weak, lacking the technical means of centralized management and unified analysis of security management. Unable to timely and effectively respond to large-scale and highly targeted unknown malicious program attacks such as "Earthquake Network" and "flame" [1].

In domestic research, Miao Liren et al. [2] designed and implemented an IP address based on vector data packet processing acceleration for the first time, aiming at the problem that the IP address dynamic protection technology introduces additional overhead

Y. Xu et al. (Eds.): ML4CS 2022, LNCS 13657, pp. 1–14, 2023.
https://doi.org/10.1007/978-3-031-20102-8_1

and leads to the degradation of normal network transmission performance. The dynamic protection system enhances the data processing capability of the system while hiding the real IP address. Firstly, according to the difference in processing logic between the control plane and the data plane, the fast forwarding logic and the slow forwarding logic are designed respectively to reduce the data packet processing process. Secondly, for the frequent mapping between real IP and fake IP, an efficient IP address dynamic transformation mechanism with shared memory is proposed. Thirdly, using optimization and hash chain algorithm, IP hopping strategy and fake IP are formulated. The address pre-allocation mechanism minimizes system performance loss. Finally, the experimental results show that the system can effectively resist DoS attacks and control the hit rate of potential reconnaissance attacks below 16%, and the data processing performance also has a significant speed improvement. Liu Ni et al. [3] generally only consider one attack behavior for the traditional wireless sensor network attack and defense model, but in real situations, malicious nodes often take multiple attack methods at the same time in order to improve the attack success rate, and according to this situation, a wireless sensor attack and defense game model for multiple attacks is proposed. The game theory of complete information establishes three game models under attack respectively. Through the analysis and solution of the game model, the optimal strategy of both attackers and defenders is obtained, and the theoretical results are verified by numerical simulation method. The design of intrusion detection system has practical guiding significance.

In foreign research, Niu Z et al. [4] firstly identified and protected the key nodes of MANET IoT in order to enhance the robustness of the network to deliberate attacks. Most of the existing key node identification methods focus on a single topology snapshot in a static network or a dynamic network, do not consider the correlation between topology snapshots, and cannot effectively deal with the dynamic changes of MANET-IoT network topology. A dynamic key node identification method is proposed. Firstly, a comprehensive measurement method is used to measure the importance of nodes in the topology snapshot. Then, the sliding time window is introduced to filter out the topology snapshots closely related to the current snapshot, and the importance values of the same node in different topology snapshots are fused. Finally, the key nodes are selected according to the fusion importance ranking results. After that, the port hopping mechanism can be applied to key nodes to enhance the network defense capability. Simulation results show that in MANET-IoT networks, this method can identify key nodes more effectively than the existing static methods, and the port hopping mechanism can significantly improve the network's defense ability against denial of service attacks.

Based on the above research background, this paper uses deep neural network to design an active defense system to ensure the security of railway communication network. Deep neural network can accurately extract the intrusion characteristics of railway communication network, so as to accurately identify the intrusion threat and ensure the security of railway communication. The overall research technical route of the system is as follows:

(1) In the hardware part of the system, the railway communication network monitoring terminal, the railway communication network alarm, the railway communication network intrusion data parser and the railway communication network active defense circuit are designed to meet the use function of the system.

(2) In the system software part, according to the collected spatial data of railway communication network, the intrusion data characteristics of railway communication network are extracted by using deep neural network, and the active defense of railway communication network is realized by constructing the active defense model of railway communication network.
(3) Memory occupancy, false alarm rate and packet loss rate are the test indicators, and the system in this paper is compared with the traditional system.

2 Hardware Design of Active Defense System for Railway Communication Network

2.1 Design Railway Communication Network Monitoring Terminal

The hardware design of the railway communication network monitoring terminal can monitor whether the railway communication network is attacked by the outside world in advance, and make timely defense according to the monitoring results. The design of the railway communication network monitoring terminal depends on the rich peripheral resources of the railway communication network [5]. If divided according to the realized

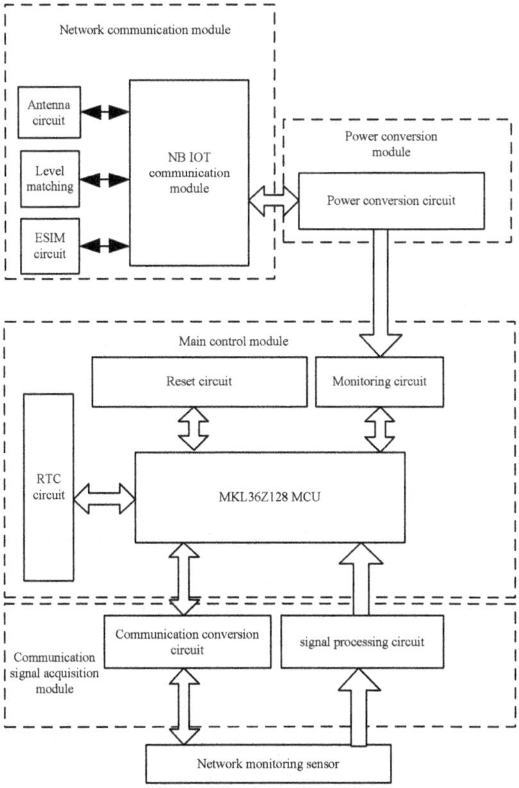

Fig. 1. Structure diagram of railway communication network monitoring terminal

functions, the hardware design of railway communication network monitoring terminal can be divided into main control module, network communication module, power conversion module and communication signal acquisition module [6]. The structure diagram of railway communication network monitoring terminal is shown in Fig. 1.

2.2 Design Railway Communication Network Alarm

The design of the railway communication network alarm is to combine the LED indicator light and the passive buzzer to alarm the intruded railway communication network. The working principle of the LED indicator light is that when the railway communication network is attacked, the intrusion risk signal is transmitted. To the sensor, trigger the LED indicator to turn on the power.

The alarm principle of the buzzer is to convert the intrusion signal of the railway communication network into a square wave, and output a clock signal through the interface of the single chip microcomputer, so as to control the buzzer alarm. The working principle of railway communication network alarm is shown in Fig. 2.

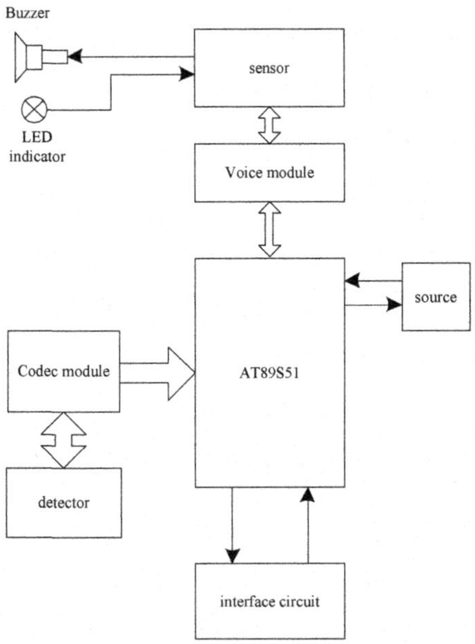

Fig. 2. Working principle of railway communication network alarm

When the buzzer sends out an alarm signal or the LED indicator lights up, it indicates that there is an intrusion risk in the railway communication network, and corresponding measures need to be taken at this time.

2.3 Designing a Railway Communication Network Intrusion Data Parser

The railway communication network intrusion data parser can parse according to the intrusion behavior of the railway communication network [7] and convert it into a data form suitable for the active defense of the railway communication network. The internal structure of the railway communication network intrusion data parser is shown in Fig. 3.

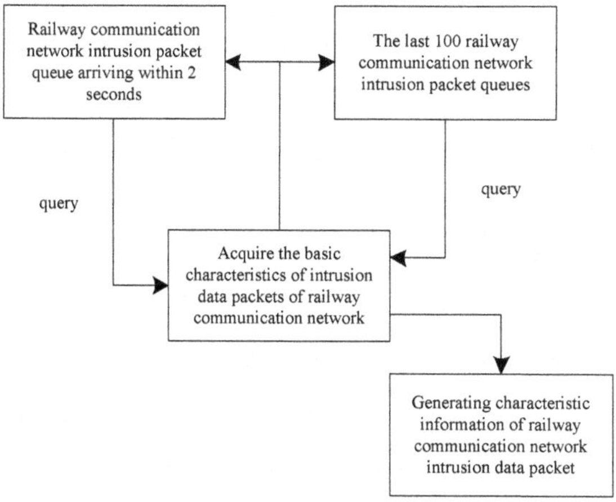

Fig. 3. The internal structure of the railway communication network intrusion data parser

The railway communication network intrusion data is obtained according to the data packets provided by the application layer. Through the packet processing of the 4-layer protocol in the railway communication network, the network intrusion data packets are transmitted to the TCP header, so that the intrusion data packets are transmitted from the transport layer to the network. At the same time, through IP in-depth analysis, the intrusion data packets are converted into data frames to complete the final transmission work. Then, the transmission data frame is parsed, and finally converted into a data form suitable for the analysis of intrusion data of the railway communication network through the analysis of the physical layer and the data link layer.

2.4 Design the Active Defense Circuit of Railway Communication Network

The design principle of the railway communication network active defense circuit is to filter the railway communication network data with security risks according to the output of the railway communication network intrusion data parser, so as to realize the active defense of the railway communication network. The railway communication network active defense circuit is shown in Fig. 4.

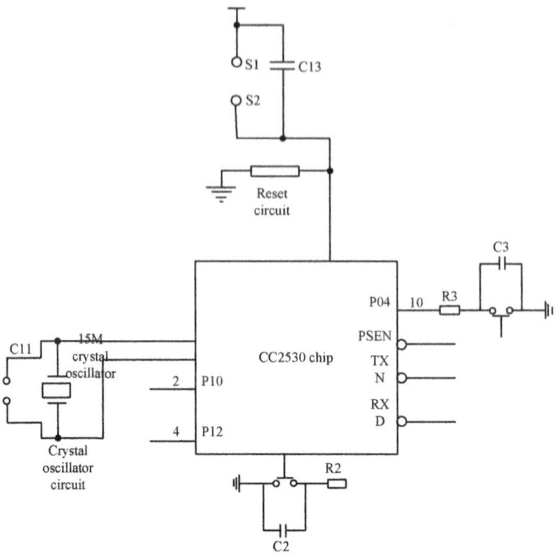

Fig. 4. The schematic diagram of the active defense circuit of the railway communication network

3 Software Design of Active Defense System for Railway Communication Network

3.1 Collecting Spatial Data of Railway Communication Network

The spatial data of railway communication network is collected mainly through firewall, intrusion detection system and virtual private network. Among them, the firewall sets the number of external connections of the railway communication network, which is the first layer of spatial data collection of the railway communication network. When the attacker attacks the railway communication network, the attack behavior data enters the network through the gateway. When the data stream Q passes through the firewall, the spatial data collection of the railway communication network will be carried out according to the set rules. Compare it with the set rules. If the match is successful, record the attack behavior data [8]. The process of firewall collecting attack behavior data is as follows:

$$A_i = \{a_1, a_2, \cdots, a_n\} \tag{1}$$

The intrusion detection system mainly detects the above attack behavior data that is not detected through the firewall. The spatial data of railway communication network collected by the intrusion detection system is expressed as:

$$B_i = Q - A_i = \{b_1, b_2, \cdots, b_n\} \tag{2}$$

The collection of the spatial data of the railway communication network by the virtual private network is mainly completed by the sebek tool, which is mainly divided into two parts, the client and the server [9]. The client is installed in the virtual private network part, and the server is installed in the gateway part. The sebek client mainly collects and saves the spatial data of the railway communication network flowing into the virtual private network, and then sends it to the sebek server. The railway communication network spatial data collected by the virtual private network is expressed as:

$$C_i = Q - A_i - B_i = \{c_1, c_2, \cdots, c_n\} \tag{3}$$

Among them, sebek client mainly realizes the collection of spatial data of railway communication network through function *read*(.).

3.2 Extraction of Railway Communication Network Intrusion Data Features Based on Deep Neural Network

According to the collected spatial data of the railway communication network, the following formula is defined by using the deep neural network to define the optimal solution of the intrusion data characteristics of the railway communication network, which is expressed as:

$$T_r = T_{r-1} p\left(\frac{M_r}{K_r}\right) \tag{4}$$

In the above formula, M_r represents the characteristic initial value of the railway communication network intrusion data, and T_{r-1} represents the weight of the railway communication network intrusion data.

When a deep neural network is constructed for the number of samples of railway communication network intrusion data, the position of the i neuron at $r + 1$ can be expressed as:

$$M_i(r+1) = \frac{M_i(r)}{M_j(r)} + J(M_i(r)) \tag{5}$$

In the above formula, $M_i(r)$ represents the input data of railway communication network intrusion data feature extraction, $J(\cdot)$ represents the location point of railway communication network intrusion data, and $M_j(r)$ represents the output data of railway communication network intrusion data feature extraction.

If the railway communication network intrusion data vector set contains y sample data, then the fuzzy mean vector of the railway communication network intrusion data sample χ_i is:

$$\chi_i = (\chi_{i1}, \chi_{i2}, \cdots, \chi_{is})^T \tag{6}$$

According to the fuzzy mean vector of the railway communication network intrusion data samples calculated above, the fitness value of the railway communication network intrusion data is calculated, which is expressed by the following formula:

$$\sum_{i=1}^{e} \psi_{ir} = 1, r = 1, 2, \cdots, n \tag{7}$$

In order to reflect the diversity characteristics of railway communication network intrusion data, the extraction expression of the characteristics of the sample set of railway communication network intrusion data can be obtained as follows:

$$J_g = \sum_{r=1i=1}^{n} \sum_{ir}^{e} \psi_{ir}^{l} \left(\frac{f_{ir}}{\chi_i} \right)^2 \tag{8}$$

In the above formula, l represents the sampling data of the railway communication network intrusion data feature, and f_{ir} represents the amplitude of the railway communication network intrusion data feature.

According to the confidence of the railway communication network intrusion data, the center vector of the i intrusion data in the railway communication network is obtained, and the training data feature extraction expression of the railway communication network intrusion data can be obtained as follows:

$$E = \{\psi_{ir} | i = 1, 2, \cdots, N\, k = 1, 2, \cdots, m\} \tag{9}$$

Among them, N represents the distribution characteristics of railway communication network intrusion data, and ψ_{ir} represents the distribution characteristics set of railway communication network intrusion data.

Suppose, X_e represents the training sample set of the entire railway communication network intrusion data, $\sum_s$ represents the railway communication network intrusion data sample set after training with deep neural network, D_{cn} represents the sample attribute of the railway communication network intrusion data, ϕB_f represents the railway communication network intrusion The information threshold of the data, the information threshold divided by the railway communication network intrusion data sample set Y_s corresponding to the attribute ϕ can be obtained by using the following formula:

$$F_n = \frac{h \times Y_s}{X_e} \times \frac{\{D_{cn} \times \phi B_f\}}{\{\xi_d\}} \tag{10}$$

Among them, ξ_d represents the total number of datasets of intrusion data of the entire railway communication network.

The deep neural network is used to represent the data vector of railway communication network intrusion data, namely:

$$d_{ir} = M_j(r) \| M_r - \chi_i \| \tag{11}$$

Assuming that Ω_{ir} represents the data set divided by network intrusion data attributes, the extraction of network intrusion data features can be completed by using the following formula:

$$F_w = \frac{Y_s \times \Omega_{ir}}{J_g} \times \chi_i \tag{12}$$

According to the above calculation steps, the intrusion data features of railway communication network are extracted by using deep neural network.

3.3 Constructing the Active Defense Model of Railway Communication Network

The railway communication network has certain propagation performance in the actual operation process, that is, message transmission between different vulnerable points. From the perspective of attack, the attacker comprehensively demonstrated the specific operation process of different vulnerability points in the implementation of the attack. In this process, new attack capabilities will be formed. The existence of these attacks will pose a certain degree of threat to the targets of the railway communication network [10]. These new attack capabilities will accurately reflect the specific propagation path and mode of attack. The specific operation process is as follows:

The calculation formula of railway communication network attack graph is:

$$G = (V_0 \cup C_d, T, \varsigma) \tag{13}$$

In the formula, V_0 represents the node set of initial conditions, C_d represents the node set of intermediate conditions, T represents the set of penetration nodes, and ς represents the set of attack tail results.

The railway communication network attack graph needs to satisfy the following constraints, namely:

$$\varsigma \subset ((T \times C_d) \cup ((V_0 \cup V) \times T)) \tag{14}$$

The attack graph can effectively identify the threats in the railway communication network. In order to effectively determine the conditional nodes, there are:

$$c_i \in V_0 \cup C_d \tag{15}$$

On the basis of the above, it is necessary to collect the corresponding basic data, which is actually the so-called condition node c_i and the penetration node e_i. At the same time, the specific occurrence probability $P(c_i)$ and $P(e_i)$ of each node in the attack graph are further calculated, and the following calculation formula can be obtained:

$$d(c_i) = \frac{P(c_i) + P(e_i)}{P(c_i)} \tag{16}$$

$$d(e_i) = \frac{P(c_i) + P(e_i)}{P(e_i)} \tag{17}$$

In the formula, $d(c_i)$ and $d(e_i)$ are expressed as the self-probabilities corresponding to the condition node c_i and the permeation node e_i, respectively. In the process of implementing the attack, the attacker will select the vulnerable nodes in the railway communication network to attack the network, which can effectively improve the system's control ability on the target network, and also effectively improve the anti-attack ability of the entire railway communication network.

On the basis of the above analysis, an active defense model of railway communication network is constructed, which is expressed as:

$$P(m_j) = \frac{P(c_i) \times P(e_i)}{P(c_i) + P(e_i)} \tag{18}$$

According to the above steps, the active defense model of railway communication network is constructed, and the active defense of railway communication network is realized.

4 Test Analysis

4.1 Test Plan

This paper verifies whether the system can meet the needs of users through functional testing and performance testing. The function test is mainly aimed at whether the user needs and the business logic of each function meet the expected design. It is expected that more codes of each function of the system can be tested to ensure that the system functions meet the expected results; The performance test mainly takes the number of user requests as the independent variable to test the memory occupancy, false alarm rate and packet loss rate of the system in the active defense of railway communication network.

4.2 Functional Testing

In the functional test of the system, this paper takes the user login registration function and the active defense function of railway communication network as examples to verify whether the system functions meet the requirements of users. The test results of user login and registration function are shown in Table 1.

Table 1. User login and registration function test results

Test steps	Expected outcome	Test results
Click the "Not yet registered" button on the login page	Unable to register, please contact the system administrator to register, you need to re-register a new account to log in	Pass
If one of the username, password, and verification code is empty, enter the username and password, and click the "Login" button	Unable to log in, a pop-up prompt that the username or password cannot be empty, can only log in normally when all are not empty	Pass
Enter the wrong verification code and click the "Login" button	Unable to log in, a verification code error message pops up. The verification code must be checked for consistency with the given verification code. Only when the verification code is consistent can the login be completed	Pass
Enter the correct username, password and verification code	The user name, password, and verification code all match those in the database. If you successfully log in to the system, you will be redirected to the main page of the system to display the user	Pass

The results in Table 1 show that the user login and registration function of the system can operate normally and meet the requirements of users.

4.3 Performance Test

In the performance test, in order to highlight the advantages of the system in this paper, the defense system based on vector packet processing is introduced and compared with the defense system for multiple attacks. The memory occupancy, false alarm rate, packet loss rate and active defense efficiency are tested. The results are as follows.

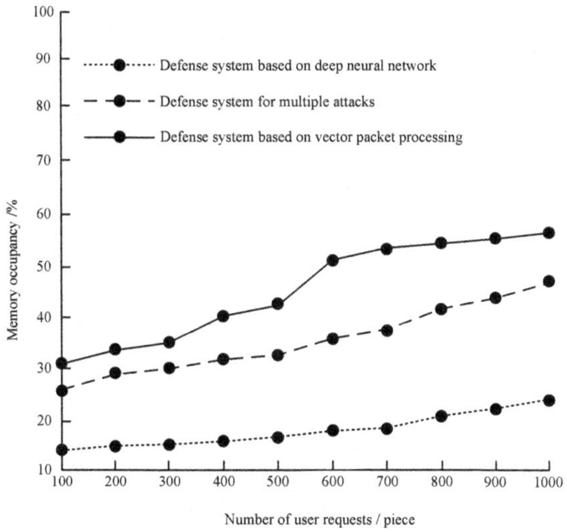

Fig. 5. Memory occupancy test results

It can be seen from the results in Fig. 5 that when the defense system based on vector packet processing and the defense system for multiple attacks are adopted, the memory occupancy of the system increases with the increase of the number of user requests. When the number of user requests reaches 1000, the memory occupancy is 57% and 48% respectively; When the system in this paper is used to actively defend the railway communication network, the memory occupancy rate is always within 25%. The memory occupancy rate of the system in the explanatory text can ensure the smoothness of the system operation.

It can be seen from the results in Fig. 6 that when the number of user requests is different, the false alarm rate of the defense system based on vector packet processing and the defense system for multiple attacks exceeds 30%. When the system in this paper is adopted, with the increase of the number of user requests, the false alarm rate of the active defense of the railway communication network can be controlled within 20%, which can realize the accurate defense of the railway communication network.

In Fig. 7, with the increase in the number of user requests, when the defense system based on vector data packet processing is used, the maximum packet loss rate reaches 57.5%. The change trend of the packet loss rate obtained by the defense system for various attacks and the system in this paper is compared. It is close, but the packet loss rate of the system in this paper is lower, which can be controlled within 25%, which avoids the loss of railway communication network data in active defense.

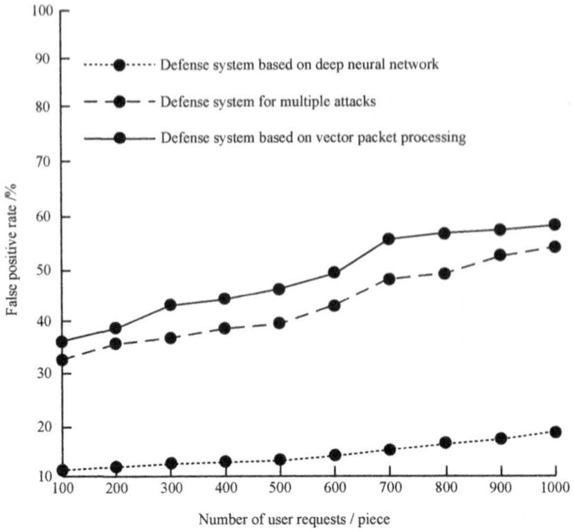

Fig. 6. False positive rate test results

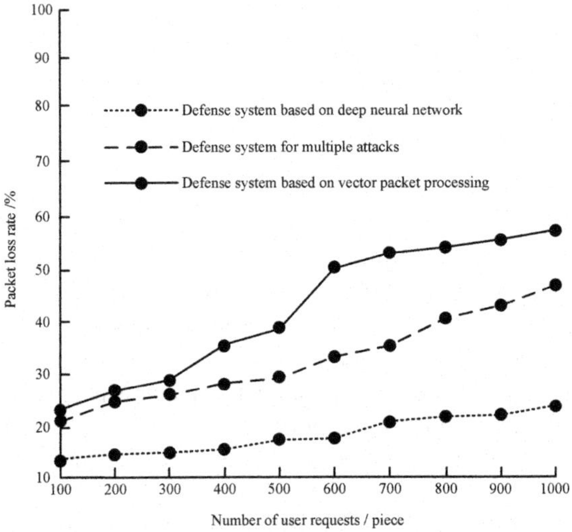

Fig. 7. Packet Loss Rate Test Results

According to the results in Fig. 8, when the defense system based on vector packet processing is adopted, the active defense efficiency of the railway communication network is less than 30%. When the defense system for multiple attacks is adopted, the active defense efficiency of the railway communication network is higher than that of the defense system based on vector packet processing, but it is also less than 55%. However, when the system in this paper is adopted, as users access the system more and more times, The active defense efficiency of the railway communication network gradually increases. When the number of users accessing the system reaches 100 times, the active

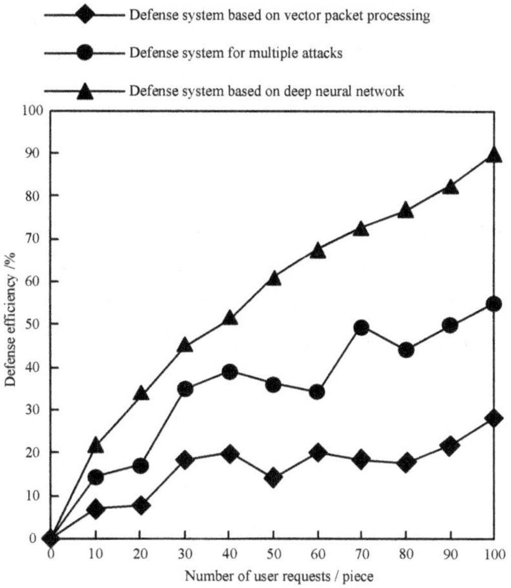

Fig. 8. Active defense efficiency of railway communication network

defense efficiency of the railway communication network reaches 90%, which can fully ensure the efficiency of the railway communication network in defense.

5 Conclusion

This paper presents the design and implementation of active defense system for railway communication network based on deep neural network. It is found that the functions and performance of the system can meet the needs of users. Although the research in this paper is in line with the expected design, there are still many deficiencies. In the future research, we hope to evaluate whether there are risks in the railway communication network in advance, and give timely warning against network abnormalities to ensure the normal operation of the railway communication network.

References

1. Zhaohui, D., Wei, Z., Guoyu, Y.: Research on network security defense system based on dynamic camouflage technology. Appl. Electronic Technique **48**(1), 129–132 (2022)
2. Li-ren, M.I.A.O., Hong-chao, H.U., Shu-min, H.U.O., et al.: The design and implementation of a vector packet processing accelerating dynamic protection system. Acta Electron. Sin. **47**(8), 1724–1730 (2019)
3. Liu, N., Zhou, H., Wang, B.: Attack-defense game models for multi-attack oriented wireless sensor network. Appl. Res. Computers **37**(8), 2491–2495 (2020)
4. Niu, Z., Li, Q., Ma, C., et al.: Identification of critical nodes for enhanced network defense in MANET-IoT networks. IEEE Access **8**, 183571–183582 (2020)

5. Sun, C.C.: An intuitionistic linguistic DEMATEL-based network model for effective national defense and force innovative project planning. IEEE Access **9**, 130141–130153 (2021)
6. Liu, S., et al.: Human memory update strategy: a multi-layer template update mechanism for remote visual monitoring. IEEE Transactions on Multimedia **23**, 2188-2198 (2021)
7. Liu, L., Zhang, L., Liao, S., et al.: A generalized approach to solve perfect Bayesian Nash equilibrium for practical network attack and defense. Inf. Sci. **577**, 245–264 (2021)
8. Shuai, L., Shuai, W., Xinyu, L., et al.: Fuzzy detection aided real-time and robust visual tracking under complex environments. IEEE Trans. Fuzzy Syst. **29**(1), 90–102 (2021)
9. Shaobo, Y., Qinghe, W., Xiaochun, W., et al.: Simulation of network space defense method based on virtual private technology. Computer Simulation **37**(05), 273–277 (2020)
10. Liu, S., Liu, D., Muhammad, K., Ding, W.: Effective template update mechanism in visual tracking with background clutter. Neurocomputing **458**, 615–625 (2021)

Human Resource Network Information Recommendation Method Based on Machine Learning

Xiao Wang(✉)

China University of Labor Relations, Beijing 100048, China
zhangjinsong65@163.com

Abstract. Human resource network information recommendation method is affected by similarity information, which leads to poor recommendation effect. A human resource network information recommendation method based on machine learning is proposed. The machine learning statistical model is established to filter the noise information. Temporal behavioral preference features were constructed to calculate the average number of information clicks. Data preprocessing is accomplished through data format conversion, data cleaning and data specification. The network information resources were retrieved, the pattern matching results were obtained, the loss function based on content association rules was constructed, and the recommendation model was constructed combined with hybrid genetic algorithm. The experimental results show that the highest recommendation accuracy of this method reaches 94%, and the highest recall rate is 0.90, which indicates that the application of research methods to recommend human resources network information has a good effect.

Keywords: Machine learning · Human resources network · Information recommendation · Genetic algorithm

1 Introduction

Although online recruitment has greatly facilitated the information transmission between job seekers and employers, with the growth of the size of job seekers and employers, the information resources in the recruitment platform have exploded, spurious recruitment information and invalid job search information have exploded, and it is also more difficult for both the supply and demand sides to obtain useful information from the platform, resulting in an increase in the time cost of enterprises and job seekers and a significant discount in the user experience. If the platform can realize accurate recommendation service according to the needs of users, it will not only help to improve users' loyalty to the platform, but also help enterprises break through the fierce industry competition. Therefore, how to mine information that may be of interest to different users and form personalized and accurate recommendations has become a hot spot in the industry. It is also a key way for today's major online recruitment platforms to improve service quality, seize customer traffic and enhance core competitiveness.

Y. Xu et al. (Eds.): ML4CS 2022, LNCS 13657, pp. 15–29, 2023.
https://doi.org/10.1007/978-3-031-20102-8_2

Literature [1] proposes a recommendation system architecture and optimization based on Boosting framework, and builds a Boosting framework, which integrates a strong recommendation system based on a variety of basic recommendation algorithms for the purpose of high-precision recommendation. The recommendation system integrated by this method can effectively improve the recommendation effect, but its recall rate is low. Literature [2] proposes an intelligent information recommendation model based on knowledge graph, which expands and improves the unit model, designs the domain knowledge model, dynamically updates the knowledge graph, and designs the learner model architecture. The Newton-Raphson iteration method is used to obtain the cognitive level, define the information recommendation achievement degree, and realize the intelligent information recommendation of the optimal path. However, when the method is applied in practice, its recommendation accuracy does not reach the expectation.

In order to improve the recommendation accuracy and recall rate of human resource network information recommendation method, a human resource network information recommendation method based on machine learning is proposed. In this method, machine learning algorithm is mainly introduced, and other algorithms are combined to make multiple algorithms combine with each other to achieve the purpose of high-precision recommendation information.

2 Filtering Based on Machine Learning Information

As a statistical model of pattern reasoning, machine learning can efficiently complete specific tasks without explicit instructions [3, 4]. The learning framework based on machine learning is shown in Fig. 1.

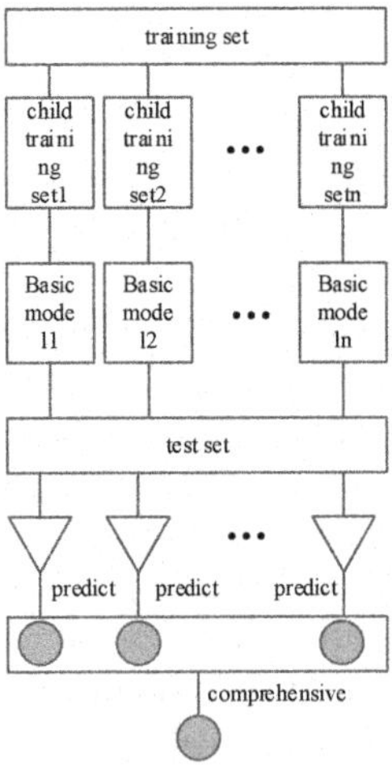

Fig. 1. Based on machine learning framework

Due to the lack of a clear task execution plan, the machine learning algorithm is based on sample learning, that is, "training data", for information filtering [5]. This information contains noise information. Therefore, it is also necessary to filter the noise information. The specific steps are as follows:

Step 1: Read in machine learning data and test data;

Step 2: Preprocess the learning data, and the processing content is word segmentation and stop word removal;

Step 3: Obtain the processed data from Step 2, and extract word features;

Step 4: Obtain the processed data from Step 3, and extract semantic features;

Step 5: serially fuse steps 3 and 4, extract text features, and obtain final text features;

Step 6: Pass the text features obtained in Step 5 to different classifiers, and obtain a classification model [6];

Step 7: Based on the model obtained in Step 6, adjust the model, and finally obtain the information after filtering the noise information.

The filtered information is discrete, heterogeneous and diverse, which is easy to cause data redundancy and information island. Therefore, it is necessary to integrate information resources.

The database connection pool technology is used to integrate heterogeneous data. The connection pool is the storage pool of connection objects. The amount of information is controlled through the internal connection mechanism, and the query interface in the system structure is used to provide the connection channel. Connecting with heterogeneous databases through Application Program Interface (API) functions on Java Database Connectivity (JDBC) can effectively convert query statements into specific databases, obtain various information of heterogeneous databases, and generate mapping information. In order to improve the efficiency of information mapping, it is necessary to reduce the delay. The delay of combinational logic is shown in Fig. 2.

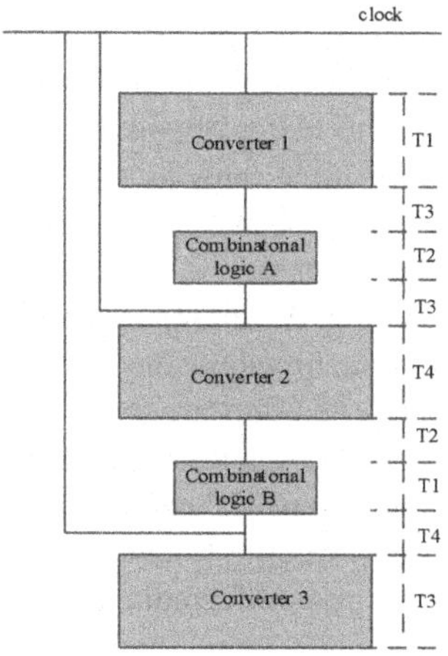

Fig. 2. Combination logic delay

In Fig. 2: $T1$ represents the mapping end time; $T2$ represents the network delay; $T3$ represents the timing logic setup time; $T4$ represents the mapping signal skew.

The information period for each mapping is:

$$T = T1 + T2 + T3 + T4 \tag{1}$$

When the mapping signal deviates, the network also delays. At this time, the minimum mapping period is:

$$T = T1 + T2 + T4 \tag{2}$$

Thereby, the minimum period for generating the mapping information is obtained, and the information mapping efficiency is improved. Fully combine personalized service mode, improve the boundary degree of user use, it is necessary to organically combine relevant majors and put them in different information folders to form integrated information.

3 Human Resource Network Information Recommendation Based on Machine Learning

Different recommendation tasks are designed for users interested in querying historical data. The following click behavior is the research goal. First, the user behavior is divided according to certain standards; Analyze the parallel structure of key data of diversity under different partition windows, and extract the characteristics of users' preference for information; Build recommendation model and preprocess data; According to the processing results, the research scheme of parallel recommendation algorithm is designed [7, 8].

3.1 Construction of Time-Series Behavior Preference Features

Select two behavior records from the data set, including clicking and collecting. The time is accurate to hours. In order to better obtain the time sequence characteristics of users, it is necessary to use every three days as the sample time window, and every eight hours as the statistical time window in this window to describe the user preference characteristics from different dimensions.

Take users as a sample for training. Assuming that users' browsing behavior needs to be predicted on October 19, select the first three days as the statistical window to analyze the sample data of that day. Sample features are extracted from the user behavior from October 15 to October 17, and whether the user tag information is selected on October 18 is used to establish the model training set. In order to better analyze the information hits, take the click behavior as an example to calculate the average number of users' clicks on the information. The calculation formula is as follows:

$$\overline{S}_{user} = \frac{S_{action\_count}}{S_{user\_unique\_item}} \tag{3}$$

In formula (3): S_{action_count} represents the number of user clicks in the time window; $S_{user\_unique\_item}$ represents the number of times the user clicks on different information in the time window. According to the constructed time series behavior preference characteristics, the data parallel structure is analyzed.

3.2 Data Preprocessing

Data collection refers to the process of collecting user attribute information, user behavior information and job attribute information data from human resources (HR) employment platform. The collected data mainly includes two parts: the attribute information of job seekers and positions stored in the business database of the employment platform, and the user behavior data from the employment platform. The former reflects the basic information of the applicant and the recruitment enterprise, while the latter reflects the applicant's preference behavior for the position. After collecting data, we need to preprocess the data, data preprocessing first needs to extract the relevant site data and analyze the user behavior data of a site; Filter useless data items, collect data sent to the server in a specific log format, and separate the data with "/h"; Confirm the recommended range and name the filtering rules according to the specific site Uniform Resource Locator (URL); After data preprocessing, we further analyze the diversity of key data parallel characteristics.

Data Format Conversion
The collected time series behavior preference features are sent to the server, and the preference features are simply analyzed through the data parallel structure. When the data is used as the input of the algorithm, the collected data needs to be preprocessed. The main purpose of preprocessing is to extract algorithm-related data from a large amount of data and convert it into the required format [9].

Data Cleaning
The collected data will contain more dirty data, including outliers, null values and meaningless special symbols. These data cannot be used as the input of the algorithm. They must be filtered out in the preprocessing step and filled in according to certain rules. Data cleaning is usually a two-step iterative process, including exception detection and data change.

The first step of data cleaning is to detect whether there are exceptions in the data. For the detection of data such as null values and special symbols, the regular expression method is used, and the identification code of this part is added to the kettle process. After identifying these dirty data, it is necessary to change and replace the data. Delete dirty data of text types such as null values and special symbols. For outliers, Lagrange interpolation method is used to solve the most filling value to replace the dirty data.

Data Protocol
The data specification is mainly a maintenance specification. By merging or deleting the same attributes, the number of attributes that need to be considered is reduced, and new attributes are also created to store eigenvalues that are meaningful to the algorithm, such as job ratings. Data reduction increases the dimension of data by creating new attributes through attribute construction, and reduces the dimension of data directly by deleting irrelevant attributes, thereby improving the efficiency of data mining and reducing computational costs.

When deleting an attribute, you need to select a subset of attributes. The objective of attribute subset selection is to find the minimum attribute set. The dimension of the minimum attribute subset should meet the minimum requirement of data mining algorithm for feature dimension, so that the results obtained by the algorithm on the minimum attribute subset are consistent with those obtained in the original attribute set. At the same time, mining on the reduced attribute set can make the discovered patterns easier to understand. Attribute construction can find the missing information about the relationship between data attributes, so as to improve the accuracy of data mining and facilitate developers' understanding of high-dimensional data structures.

The data specification will delete the data number attribute and note description attribute from different data sources, and add attributes to the scoring characteristics of the position.

3.3 Human Resource Network Information Recommendation Process

After data preprocessing, the data source is uploaded to the data warehouse. The algorithm reads the required data from the data warehouse as algorithm input. The HR network information recommendation process is shown in Fig. 3.

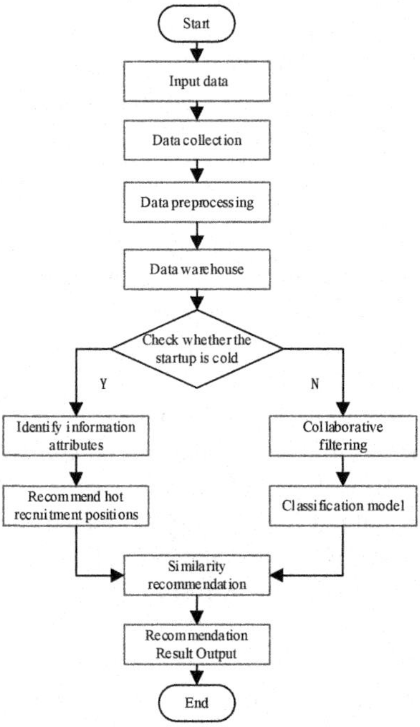

Fig. 3. Human resource network information recommendation process

The following five steps are implemented in conjunction with Fig. 3:

Step 1: Retrieval of network information resources.

According to the specific needs of a user, relevant information is collected, and the information is processed for users to query. Information resource retrieval is the premise of integration, and the advanced retrieval function of the database is deeply analyzed to increase the storage space of the database. Using the binary data conversion method to match the extracted information resources, the specific matching process is as follows:

①Through binary sequence between adjacent points, the convex growth or concave growth relationship between adjacent points is determined;
②The trend proportional data reduction method is used to reduce the candidate sequences and patterns between the adjacent points of the determined relationship to the same interval;
③The sequence similarity in the same interval is calculated to distinguish the amplitudes between convex growth or concave growth with different change amplitudes. According to the amplitude, each subsequence set is obtained, which is the pattern matching result.

In order to further improve the retrieval accuracy, it is necessary to use machine learning theory to filter the similarity of matching subsequence sets. If the total number of features of intermediate data in the big data set is greater than the total number of features of intermediate data in the reference set, it can be directly concluded that there is no similar information between the set and the reference set; On the contrary, it indicates that there is similar information, thus completing the information resource retrieval.

Step 2: Construction of loss function based on content association rules

Access information of the intelligent O&M platform is used as input information for mining association rules. Therefore, an association rule information mining method is proposed to obtain the information required by the user. Let X and Y be the recommended content item sets, Z be the association rule set, and X to Y is a basic association rule, which means that when the user accesses the X item set, the user also accesses the Y item set with the maximum probability. Basic content association rules are extracted based on information from the HUAWEI CLOUD Stack8.0 platform. Content association rules are the basis for information recommendation and have the following constraints: the actual support for the calculated information type is greater than the threshold and the highest support item set; each item set, there are non-empty subsets. An association rule is generated if the confidence is greater than a user-specified threshold confidence minimum. Information recommendation is implemented according to the above rules, and the recommendation results are displayed to users through display channels.

Assuming that there are K convolution kernels and N types of output layers, the feature obtained after sample pooling is an K-dimensional vector, and the resulting loss function based on content association rules can be expressed as:

The loss function can be obtained by maximizing the likelihood probability:

$$f = - \sum_{y}^{c} \log\left(P\left(c_y | x_y, \theta\right)\right) \tag{4}$$

In formula (4): c is the training data set, g_y is the real data type of the y sample; θ is the weight parameter of the output layer; x_y is the data type after sample pooling; P means that the sample is divided into the y type probability. In order to prevent over fitting, the neuron structure of the convolution layer needs to be simplified according to a certain probability to ensure that the weight does not work. After feature compression processing, on the basis of stable database storage space, the internal state and behavior control of data can be freely operated.

Step 3: classifier weight calculation based on Hybrid Genetic Algorithm

This part of the algorithm is responsible for obtaining the weights of ensemble learning based classifiers. The algorithm first randomly generates binary coded individuals to form the initial population, and then calculates the fitness of individuals in the population.

Calculation of individual fitness, the formula is:

$$Fit(x) = 1 + \left[\left|\frac{\alpha(x) - \beta}{\text{m}}\right|\right] \tag{5}$$

In formula (5), $\alpha(x)$ represents the individual fitness function; m represents the fitness; β represents the minimum value of the individual fitness function.

The basis of fitness calculation comes from the performance of the classification model generated by combining the base classifier with each generation of individuals on the test set. Calculate the proportion of individual fitness value in the total recommendation of human resources network information, the formula is:

$$c = \frac{Fit(x_i)}{\sum_{m}^{\text{i}} Fit(x_m)} \tag{6}$$

In formula (6), i represents the number of calculations.

Then judge whether the genetic algebra meets the cut-off conditions, and count the cumulative probability of individual selection. The formula is:

$$P' = \sum_{m \neq 1}^{\text{i}} c(x_m) \tag{7}$$

Set the threshold λ, , and compare the threshold with the cumulative probability result of formula (7) to select individuals. If $\lambda < T'$, select the m individual.

If the cut-off condition is not met, the self-adaptation in the genetic operation of the crossover operation, according to the dynamic crossover probability, crosses the genes between individuals to obtain a new individual. The new individual performs the adaptive mutation operation, and generates new individuals again according to the dynamically adjusted mutation probability cheap genes, and finally obtains a new population composed of new individuals.

Two random intersections of two generations are selected by sequence crossing method, and then two intersections are selected from the midpoint of the two intersections, which are crossed to the next generation, and then moved out to obtain two offspring. Using the fitness function, the maximum fitness value is determined, and it is used as an excellent child chromosome for further calculation.

The next step is to select new species based on simulated annealing. This step mainly simulates natural selection methods in nature, and combines simulated annealing to enhance the genetic ability of excellent individuals and maintain population diversity. After the selection operation, the population continues to enter the iteration of fitness calculation, cut-off condition judgment and genetic operation until the cut-off condition is met. The optimal individual is the optimal weight of the base classifier.

Step 4: Selective Integration and Hybrid Recommendations

In the recommendation process, the classification model and the matrix decomposition collaborative filtering algorithm based on implicit feedback form a hybrid recommendation, that is, the user's behavioral information on the post is used as implicit feedback, and the matrix decomposition method and the alternating least squares method are used to predict the position of the missing score. Score, build a complete scoring matrix, so as to get the user's scoring characteristics for all positions.

The fitness function is selected to represent the advantages and disadvantages of the recommendation, and the recommendation information is determined by the deviation between the classification result and the actual result. Therefore, the average absolute percentage error is adopted, and MAPE is used as the standard to measure the accuracy of prediction results, so as to meet the adaptability of genetic algorithm.

The MAPE formula is:

$$MAPE = \frac{1}{n}\sum_{i=1}^{n}\left|\frac{x_i - \hat{x}_i}{x_i}\right| \times 100\% \tag{8}$$

In formula (8), n represents the total number of recommendations; x_i, $\hat{x}_i$ represents ideal and actual recommended data respectively.

The optimal parameters are substituted into the recommendation model. The second-order adaptive coefficient method is used to analyze the human resource network information, and the trend items of the recommended human resource network information are obtained. The trend forecast is transformed into the original sequence forecast, so as to build a recommended model. The formula is:

$$T_n = T_n' * U_n \tag{9}$$

In formula (9), T_n' represents the trend item recommendation value; U_n represents the cycle index.

This feature is used as input to get the output of whether the user recommends the job, and then sorts the job data set marked as "recommended" in descending order, and recommends Top-N jobs to the user according to the scoring feature value.

4 Experiments

Experiment and analyze the data collected by the real human resources employment platform. The data scale of the experiment is as follows: the experimental data set contains 11900 candidates, 49700 jobs and 481400 user behavior records.

4.1 Experimental Setup

During the experiment, the experimental device shown in Fig. 4 was used to collect the information of the applicant and the applicant enterprise.

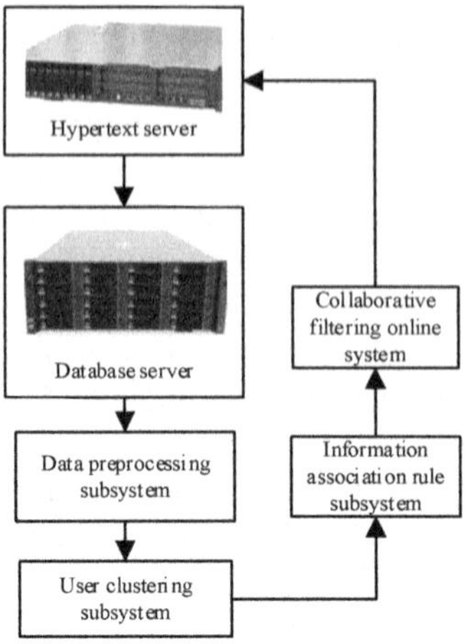

Fig. 4. Experimental setup

As can be seen from Fig. 4, the hardware structure of the system includes a data processing subsystem, a clustering subsystem, an association rule subsystem, and a recommendation subsystem. The online function of the collaborative filtering recommendation subsystem of the system can provide accurate information collection results for the experimental process.

Through the similarity of the target user feature model of the adjacent data set, the candidate information and the recruiting company information are collected, as shown in Table 1.

Table 1. Candidate information and recruiting enterprise information form

Candidate Information		Indicator A
Candidate characteristics	Graduation time	1
	Name	2
	Gender	3
	Graduated school	4
	Age	5
	With or without work experience	6
Recruitment company information		Indicator B
Recruiting company characteristics	Must be premised on human resource planning and job analysis	1
	Recruitment is an interactive choice between organizations and candidates	2
	Recruitment must consider cost	3

Analyze the relationship between related candidates according to the collection results of candidate information and recruitment enterprise information.

4.2 Experimental Indicators

After semantic classification association completes the analysis of keyword related content, you can obtain the level content related to it. The main purpose is to find relevant users in time and analyze according to the previous classification. According to the association results, each level of words can be classified to obtain a user set, as shown in Fig. 5.

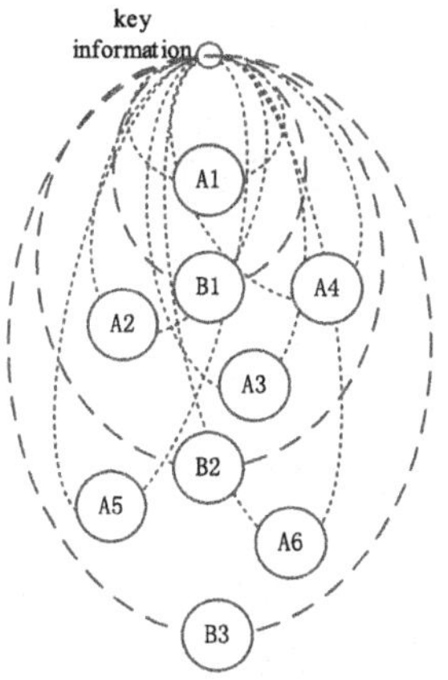

Fig. 5. Related user set discovery

Relevant user sets were obtained by this method, and the recommended evaluation indexes were formulated according to the user sets.

A reliable evaluation index is developed to measure the recommendation effect more accurately. The mean absolute deviation is the sum of the deviation between the single measured value and the mean value divided by the number of measurements. Therefore, the accuracy and recall are selected as the indicators for evaluating and recommending the results.

Let the user set be I, the recommended resource set obtained by the recommendation method for I users is $S(I)$, and the user's actual index behavior resource set is $U(I)$, then calculate the accuracy rate Precision and recall rate Recall, the formula is:

$$\text{Precision} = \frac{\sum_{\text{u}\in\text{I}} |S(I) \cap U(I)|}{\sum_{\text{u}\in\text{I}} |S(I)|} \tag{9}$$

$$\text{Recall} = \frac{\sum_{\text{u}\in\text{I}} |S(I) \cap U(I)|}{\sum_{\text{u}\in\text{I}} |U(I)|} \tag{10}$$

Through the above formulas, the construction of the experimental indicators is completed. The higher the calculation results of the two formulas, the better the recommendation effect.

4.3 Analysis of the Effectiveness of Information Collection

The Boosting algorithm, selective ensemble learning method and machine learning based recommendation method are used to analyze the effectiveness of information collection. The results are shown in Fig. 6.

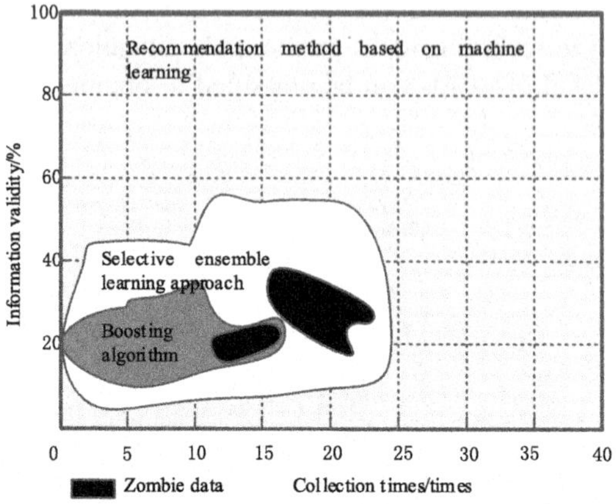

Fig. 6. Effectiveness of information collection by different methods

It can be seen from Fig. 6 that the information collected by the Boosting algorithm is less than 38% effective, and about 1/5 of the information is zombie information; the information collected by the selective ensemble learning method is less than 58% effective, and about 1/5 of the information is zombie information. /3 of the information is zombie information; the information collected using the machine learning-based recommendation method is 100% effective, and there is no zombie information. It can be seen from the above comparison results that the information collected by the machine learning-based recommendation method is effective.

4.4 Experimental Results and Analysis

Recommendation Accuracy

The recommendation accuracy determines the recommendation effect. The Boosting algorithm, the selective ensemble learning method, and the machine learning-based recommendation method are used to calculate the recommendation accuracy. The comparison results are shown in Fig. 7.

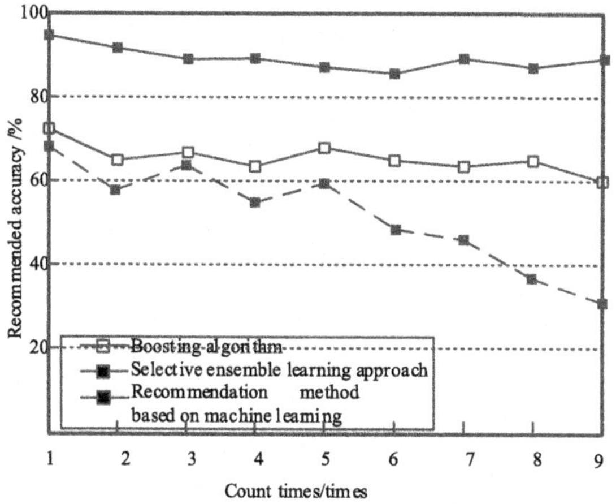

Fig. 7. Comparative analysis of recommendation accuracy of different methods

It can be seen from Fig. 7 that the recommended accuracy using the boosting algorithm reaches a maximum of 73% when the number of calculations is 1, and a minimum of 60% when the number of calculations is 9; Using the selective ensemble learning method, the recommended accuracy reaches a maximum of 69% when the number of calculations is 1, and a minimum of 30% when the number of calculations is 9; When machine learning-based recommendation methods are used, the recommendation accuracy reaches a maximum of 94% when the number of calculations is 1, and a minimum of 85% when the number of calculations is 6. According to the above comparison results, the recommendation accuracy based on machine learning is the highest.

Comparative Analysis of Recall Rate

In order to further verify the rationality of the research method, with three characteristics of the enterprise recruitment as experimental parameters, the indices 1, 2 and indicators respectively 3, and use the above three methods recommended the human resources information, analysis of the recommended method of recall rate and recall rate is higher, shows that the performance of the recommended method, the better, the higher its rationality, the results are shown in Table 2.

Table 2. Comparative analysis of indicators under different data sets of three methods

Enterprise recruitment indicators	Method	Recall
Indicator 1	Boosting algorithm	0.58
	Selective ensemble learning	0.68
	Recommendation method based on machine learning	0.88

(*continued*)

Table 2. (*continued*)

Enterprise recruitment indicators	Method	Recall
Indicator 2	Boosting algorithm	0.60
	Extreme Learning Machine	0.69
	Recommendation method based on machine learning	0.90
Indicator 3	Boosting algorithm	0.58
	Selective ensemble learning	0.66
	Recommendation method based on machine learning	0.85

It can be seen from Table 2 that using the Boosting algorithm, the highest recall rate is 0.60; using the selective ensemble learning method, the highest recall rate is 0.69; using the machine learning-based recommendation method, the highest recall rate is 0.90. The recall rate is higher than other methods by 0.30 and 0.21, respectively, which shows that the recall rate using the research method is higher.

5 Conclusion

In order to improve the recommendation performance of human resource network information, the proposed human resource network information recommendation method based on machine learning is applied to the field of human resource recommendation. With the help of the classification ability of association rules and hybrid genetic algorithm, the problem of data sparsity and "cold start" existing in the traditional recommendation algorithm are overcome, and the quality of human resources recommendation service is improved. The main innovations of the research work are as follows: data collection and preprocessing: collect the data of the online HR platform, and research and implement a data preprocessing method, which performs data cleaning, integration, protocol, transformation and other preprocessing operations on the collected HR data to ensure the quality of algorithm input data.

It has realized human resource network information recommendation and applied it to human resource recommendation service, but there are still aspects that need to be improved, mainly reflected in the following two aspects:

(1) The method is mainly for the job-seeking needs of the candidates, and provides job recommendation services to the candidates. However, in reality, not only job seekers need human resource recommendations, but employers also need recommendation services to recommend suitable job seekers to them when faced with a large number of job seekers' resumes. Therefore, the next step is to establish an employer-oriented human resources recommendation algorithm according to the application scenario of the employer to achieve two-way recommendation.

(2) The method uses the user's association rule, and obtains the user's browsing, collection, application and disinterested behavior information through this rule. Although normal recommendation services can be implemented, the scope of implicit feedback considered is relatively narrow. In practice, users' comments on posts and users' comments on enterprises can also be text-mined, and converted into useful implicit feedback information as the input of the algorithm. Therefore, how to mine and utilize these text-based implicit feedback information will become the next research goal.

Aknowledgement. School level undergraduate teaching reform project of China University of Labor Relations:Research on the teaching reform of collective negotiation system and Practice (Project No.: 2021JG07).

References

1. Yanbo, L., Xueyan, W., Kesheng, X.: Architecture and optimization of recommendation system based on Boosting framework. Modern Electronics Technique **43**(08), 19–21+28 (2020)
2. Yazhi, Y., Yong, Z., Jun, L.: Intelligent information recommendation model construction simulation based on knowledge graph. Computer Simulation **38**(01), 437–440+480 (2021)
3. Jihui, F., Shaohua, T.: Research on the application of improved machine learning collaborative recommendation algorithm in intelligent control. Machine Tool & Hydraulics **48**(18), 177–182 (2020)
4. Min, Z., Yixuan, Z.: Application of machine learning in human resource management. Human Resources Dev. China **39**(01), 71–83 (2022)
5. Yan, L.: Library bibliographic collaborative recommendation system based on machine learning algorithm. Modern Electronics Technique **43**(14), 180–182,186 (2020)
6. Yue, G., Dan, L., Kaihui, G.: Research on network traffic classification based on machine learning and deep learning. Telecommunications Science **37**(03), 105–113 (2021)
7. Daoheng, Z., Zhiqiang, L.: Parallel calculation method for maximum information coefficient. Science Technol. Eng. **21**(34), 14625–14633 (2021)
8. Jiaxing, W., Dapeng, T., Bin, C., et al.: Independent path-based process recommendation algorithm for improving biomedical process modelling. Electron. Lett. **56**(7), 531–533 (2020)
9. Haozheng, Z., Ming, H., Jingjing, Y., et al.: A data preprocessing method for automatic modulation classification based on CNN. IEEE Communications Letters: A Publication of the IEEE Communications Society **25**(4), 1206–1210 (2021)

Machine Learning Based Abnormal Flow Analysis of University Course Teaching Network

Shaobao Xu[1(✉)] and Yongqi Jia[2]

[1] Philippine Christian University, 1004 Manila, Philippines
xxsb202@126.com
[2] Jose Rizal University, 1552 Mandaluyong, Philippines

Abstract. Due to the influence of abnormal traffic of university course teaching network, the accuracy of analysis results is low, this paper presents a method for analyzing the network traffic of university course teaching based on machine learning. According to the process of encapsulating user data into Ethernet data frames, a network traffic identification model based on machine learning is constructed. The screening strength is controlled by the screening coefficient, and the model deviation is reduced by measuring the task. After data collection and sorting, data cleaning and pretreatment, model evaluation and unknown traffic detection, the network traffic analysis steps are designed to analyze the abnormal situation of teaching network traffic. The experimental results show that the highest F1 score is 98%, and the accuracy of the analysis results is high, which provides sufficient network traffic for college course teaching.

Keywords: Machine learning · University courses · Teaching network · Abnormal traffic analysis

1 Introduction

As a vital part of the Internet, the campus network should control its security and performance effectively and timely. Traditional network management methods mainly use traffic statistical analysis tools to detect traffic and record related logs, but this lack of a more in-depth analysis of the traffic behavior of the entire campus network, but less of the inherent characteristics of the study, so when abnormal network traffic can not be handled in a timely manner, so we need to study the traffic behavior and characteristics of the campus network, to help the entire network better operation and maintenance. The main network security threats faced by campus network can be summarized as follows: network security problems existing in wired network, campus local area network also faces; information transmitted through campus local area network is generally not encrypted, or its encryption degree is poor, which will lead to information interception and tampering with by hackers; some lawbreakers can bypass the firewall set up by campus network, thus illegally stealing the internal network; in addition to the malicious attack of lawbreakers, campus local area network personnel can also set up the mode of wireless network card, so that they can communicate with external personnel, which

Y. Xu et al. (Eds.): ML4CS 2022, LNCS 13657, pp. 30–43, 2023.
https://doi.org/10.1007/978-3-031-20102-8_3

aggravates the security problem of campus network; in addition to the security problem of wireless local area network itself, there are few special security measures and products for wireless network in the market at present, and the technical level is difficult to meet the requirements. If the network traffic can be predicted in advance, the precautionary measures can be taken in advance to ensure the stability and security of the campus network. Therefore, the study of network traffic forecasting model is a necessary means to solve the security problem of campus network.

Network traffic analysis technology in the process of continuous development, but also according to changes in the network environment and constantly improve the identification algorithm and extraction of traffic characteristics. The existing methods of network traffic identification can be divided into two parts: one is based on port number mapping, the other is based on net load. Among them, the concrete realization process of traffic analysis method based on port number mapping is as follows: First, grab the packet and extract the port number information of the packet head. Then, according to the mapping table of port numbers formulated by the IP address assignment agency, the corresponding network applications are found. For example, FTP applications correspond to 20 port numbers, SMTP applications to 25 port numbers, and HTTP applications to 80 port numbers. The method of port number mapping is used to analyze the type of traffic application in P2P application, and the technology of port identification is used to develop the traffic billing system [1]. Then, the net payload of each packet in the network data stream is retrieved by deep packet detection technology. If the characteristic field of an application layer protocol is found, the specific application type of the network data stream can be identified [2].

However, due to the popularity of P2P and passive FTP as well as the widespread use of random port and network address conversion and proxy technologies, the flow identification method based on port number mapping can not meet the needs of practical application gradually. The drawback of the flow identification method based on net load feature is that although the method is simple, effective and easy to maintain, and the identification accuracy is much higher than the flow identification method based on port number mapping, this method may violate the privacy of both sides of communication, can not identify encrypted data flow, need to update the feature segment library in time for new applications, and the net load of analytical flow needs a large amount of calculation. Therefore, with the widespread use of data encryption technology and various network applications, this traffic identification method will become increasingly unable to meet the actual needs.

Aiming at the problems mentioned above, this paper puts forward a traffic analysis method of university course teaching network based on machine learning. Analyze the process of user data encapsulated into Ethernet data frames, and build a network traffic identification model based on machine learning. Use the screening coefficient to screen the data, improve the accuracy of the data, reduce the error of the network traffic model by measuring the task, collect and sort out the data, improve the practicability of the model, clean and preprocess the data to ensure the consistency of the data, evaluate the model to determine the model parameters, analyze the unknown traffic to determine the abnormal network traffic and normal network traffic. Machine learning has the ability of data mining, which can extract the implicit and regular information from big data.

Using machine learning technology, the overall situation of network traffic is analyzed by extracting the statistical and behavioral characteristics of network traffic.

2 Construction of Network Traffic Identification Model Based on Machine Learning

The encapsulated data packet of university course teaching network consists of a packet head and a payload. The payload part is the data to be transmitted. Taking the TCP transport protocol as an example, the user data is encapsulated through the TCP/IP stack as shown in Fig. 1.

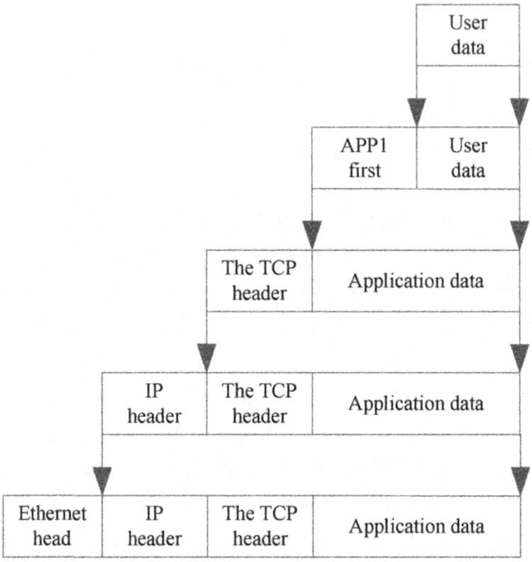

Fig. 1. Encapsulation of user data into Ethernet data frames

As can be seen from Fig. 1, when the source host sends data, the user data first passes through the application layer, adding the Appl header of the application layer, and obtains the application data transmitted in the network, that is, the load part of the packet; then, the application data is encapsulated through the transport layer, adding the TCP header, and obtains the TCP data segment transmitted in the transport layer; then, the TCP data segment is encapsulated through the network layer, adding the IP header, and obtains the IP datagram transmitted in the network layer; finally, the IP datagram is encapsulated through the link layer, adding the Ethernet header and tail, and obtains the Ethernet data frame transmitted in the link layer [3]. Ethernet data frame is the data transmitted directly on the physical link. When the destination host computer receives the data, it peels off the first part from the link layer to the application layer. In the encapsulated data packets described above, the applied data part is the payload, or the deep packet detection part, to be examined in depth [4]; the rest is the head part.

Network traffic identification model based on machine learning, as shown in Fig. 2.

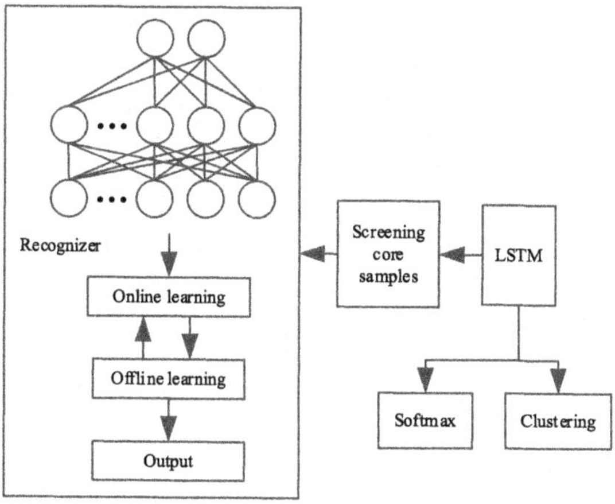

Fig. 2. Network traffic identification model based on machine learning

As can be seen from Fig. 2, the method combines the CNN -based incremental learning network traffic identification model and the LSTM -based semi-supervised network traffic clustering model. Based on the flow level semi-supervised network traffic clustering model, further filtering is added and the filtering results are fed back to the online learning model for updating training [5]. The model not only can give the result of traffic identification in time, but also can adapt to the change of network environment automatically. In addition, semi-supervision also can reduce the cost of traffic data annotation.

3 Traffic Analysis of University Course Teaching Network Based on Machine Learning

3.1 Data Screening

Because the filtered data is used for online learning model training, it is necessary to trade-off between the amount of data and the accuracy of the results. When the amount of data filtered is large, the accuracy of the data is relatively low. Although the amount of data filtered for updating the training online learning model is large and the number of training executions is large, the accuracy of the samples used for training is relatively low, which may lead to the false characteristics of the model [6]; conversely, when the amount of data filtered is small, the accuracy of the data is relatively high, although the accuracy of the data filtered for updating the training online learning model is very high, the number of samples available for training is small and the number of training executions is small, which may lead to the failure of the model to learn the new environment in a timely manner [7].

A screening coefficient is used to control the screening intensity, thereby controlling the trade-off between the amount of data and the accuracy. The formula can be as follows:

$$s_i = \lambda \cdot s_c \tag{1}$$

In formula 1, $\lambda > 0$ is the screening coefficient and s_c is the truncated distance. By adjusting the coefficient, we can control the range of density boundary, and then control the intensity of selecting sample data [8]. On the contrary, the smaller the screening coefficient is, the smaller the threshold value is, the larger the number of core samples is, and the lower the precision of core samples is. The setting of the filter coefficient is a trade-off between the amount and precision of the training data updated from the online learning model [9]. Setting appropriate coefficients can effectively improve the performance of online learning model.

3.2 Model Training

The analysis of normal network traffic and the analysis of abnormal network traffic are two closely related problems. From the point of view of machine learning, they both make some predictions based on the current network traffic (From this point of view, the detection of abnormal traffic can also be regarded as a special predictive problem). In learning, both of these problems rely on experience derived from historical traffic data over time; from the type of learning, the prediction of network traffic is a supervised learning problem, while the detection of abnormal traffic is an unsupervised learning problem [10].

Normal Network Traffic Analysis
In the process of analyzing normal network traffic, the task of learning is to predict the traffic at a certain time in the future according to the current observations of traffic. The improvement of task performance is measured by the deviation between the predicted result and the true value of traffic flow. The learning experience that relies on improving performance metrics comes from historical traffic data over time.

For normal network traffic analysis problems, offline training shall be adopted. The detailed steps are as follows:

Step 1: Collect network traffic data needed for training;
Step 2: Pre-training CNN model and LSTM-based encoder -decoder model:;
Step 3: Test CNN model and encoder -decoder model, if the test results do not meet the performance indicators;
Step 4: Output pre-trained CNN model and LSTM encoder model.

Analysis of Abnormal Network Traffic
In the process of analyzing abnormal network traffic, the task of learning is to judge whether the network traffic is abnormal according to the current observed value of traffic. The measure of performance improvement of a task is the deviation between the result of detection and the real traffic situation (normal or abnormal), and the learning process relies on the experience of improving the performance measure from the historical traffic data over time.

For the abnormal network traffic analysis problem, the online training mode is adopted, and the detailed steps are as follows:

Step 1: Receive a network packet;
Step 2: Extract the five-tuple information of the packet, i.e. Source IP, Destination IP, Source Port, Destination Port, Protocol >, as an identifier for a stream, if it exists in the database, go to Step 4;
Step 3: Increase the storage space for this identifier in the database;
Step 4: Store the packet header data of the packet in the corresponding position of the identifier, if the packet corresponding to the identifier has been stored P, go to step 5, perform packet level network traffic identification; otherwise go to step 6;
Step 5: Input the data of P packets into the packet level recognizer, get the recognition results, and output the recognition results, to step 6;
Step 6: If the flow for this identifier is complete, go to Step 7, otherwise go to Step 1;
Step 7: Input the data of the whole stream into the flow level recognizer, and get the recognition result. If the recognition result is the edge of the cluster, it indicates that the recognition is not very sure.
Step 8: If the sample is new, go to Step 9 and perform a structural update, otherwise go to Step 10;
Step 9: Increase the output node of the package level recognition model;
Step 10: Update the internal parameters of the package level identification model, including weights, offsets, and proficiency;
Step 11: Free up the storage space for this identifier and go to Step 1.

3.3 Design of Network Traffic Analysis Steps

The process of network traffic analysis based on machine learning can be divided into four steps: data collection and collation, data cleaning and preprocessing, model evaluation and unknown traffic detection.

In the network traffic analysis process, firstly, network traffic data will be collected and sorted, and the training set and the verification set will be separated after data cleaning and preprocessing; then the training set will be input into the machine learning model for parameter training, and after training, the verification set will be used to evaluate the performance of the model; if the model performs well on the verification set, the model will be saved; when there is any data with unknown traffic that needs to be detected, it will be cleaned and preprocessed as the input of the saved model, and finally the detection results of the traffic type will be output. The specific process is as follows:

Data Collection and Consolidation
There are two ways to obtain network traffic data, one is to use open traffic dataset, the quality of the data obtained in this way is high, do not need a lot of data cleaning operations, and the traffic type label is accurate. However, the difficulty of traffic detection using public data sets is that the characteristics of the current network environment are often different from those of the data sets. This method is based on the history of network traffic log or data frame to extract the available features manually, and then tag the data according to the real category of traffic. The data obtained by this way are noisy and

need more careful cleaning and preprocessing, but if we can ensure the accuracy of the training set and the training label, the model will be more practical.

Data Cleaning and Pretreatment

The effect of data cleaning and preprocessing has a great influence on the model. In order to shorten the system response time, the flow detection model with few parameters and simple structure is adopted in the current network environment. Network traffic logs or data frames contain a large amount of redundant information. Data cleaning mainly refers to extracting the original traffic features or statistical features needed from logs or available files; and preprocessing refers to the operation of removing and filling the extracted data to improve the data quality and transform them into structured data that meets the model input standards. Before model training, we need to divide the data set into training set and verification set. The training set is used for model training, and the verification set is used for model evaluation. In addition, the analysis of unknown flow also requires the same cleaning and preprocessing operations to ensure the consistency of training data.

Model Evaluation

In the model evaluation phase, a small size selector is used for feature selection and sample construction. Then these new samples are input into a stochastic forest and a limit tree model for evaluation. In addition, the size and number of selectors are dynamically determined. Larger feature sizes are used to combine features and build samples until the training loss function of the multigranularity traversal module is no longer reduced. Multi-granularity traversal is different from multi-granularity scan in deep forest model, the former is to search for different combinations of all features in structured data, and the latter is to construct new samples in image data by scanning pixels of different regions with a certain step size through a sliding window.

The traversal flow of the two combinations is shown in Fig. 3.

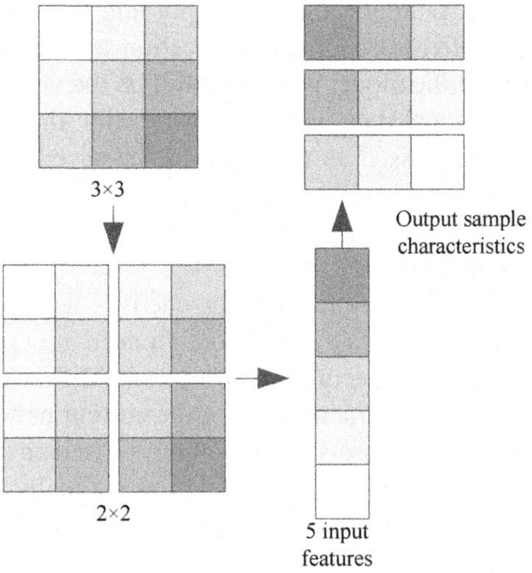

Fig. 3. Traversal flow of two combinations

As can be seen from Fig. 3, the input image of 3 × 3 size is taken as an example to illustrate the process of multi-granularity scanning. When the size of the sliding window is 2 × 2, when the step size is 1, the sliding window can slide down to the right until the right edge and the lower edge of the sliding window coincide with the original input image, resulting in four samples. With the structured data of 5 original features as an example, if the size of the selector is 3, then all possible combinations of 3 features can be traversed, resulting in ten samples according to the combination formula.

After the model is trained, the performance of the model needs to be evaluated with the help of the verification set. The common evaluation indexes are precision, recall, precision and F1 score. If the evaluation index of the model is lower than the expected value, it is necessary to analyze the reasons from feature validity, model validity, experimental environment setting and other aspects to find out the problem and make pertinent correction to the model; if the model performance meets the expected value, the model can be directly saved as the final network traffic analysis model.

Analysis of Unknown Flows

After the parameters of the model are determined, the detection of the unknown flow also needs to be washed and pretreated in the same way as the training set, and then input it to the trained model for detection. For the multi-classification problem of network traffic detection, the output of the model is the probabilistic vectors of each traffic type, and the traffic type corresponding to the highest one is the final analysis type.

The internal product matrix is constructed from the training data set, and the formula is:

$$E=\left(e\left(x_i, y_j\right)\right) \tag{2}$$

In formula (2), $e\left(x_i, y_j\right)$ represents some inner product of sample x_i and y_j through kernel function e. The eigenvalue decomposition of the inner product matrix is used to obtain the eigenspectrum. Calculate the large principal component vector of the sample to be tested, which is:

$$f_d = \sum_{j=1}^{x} \frac{\left(y_{telt}^1\right)^2}{\phi_j} \tag{3}$$

In formula (3), ϕ represents the characteristic spectrum, and y_{telt}^1 represents the principal component vector.

When calculating the small principal component vector of the sample to be tested, the formula may be:

$$f_x = \sum_{j=1}^{x} \frac{\left(y_{telt}^2\right)^2}{\phi_j} \tag{4}$$

In formula (4), y_{telt}^2 represents a small principal component vector.

Suppose there is a pair of false alarm parameters α_1 and α_2, if the calculation result of formula (3) and (4) is larger than the false alarm parameter, the network traffic shall be determined as abnormal traffic, otherwise it shall be deemed as normal traffic.

4 Experimental Analysis

4.1 Demand Analysis of University Course Teaching Network

A certain university course teaching network is a relatively large campus network, four campus is located in a relatively distant geographical location, the building to 100 trillion Ethernet network access, between the building by gigabit optical fiber connection, with more than 20 core and convergent switches, access to more than 600 switches, more than 60 network servers to undertake core services, distributed in the whole school more than 13000 information points, thousands of people at the same time. The network topology is shown in Fig. 4.

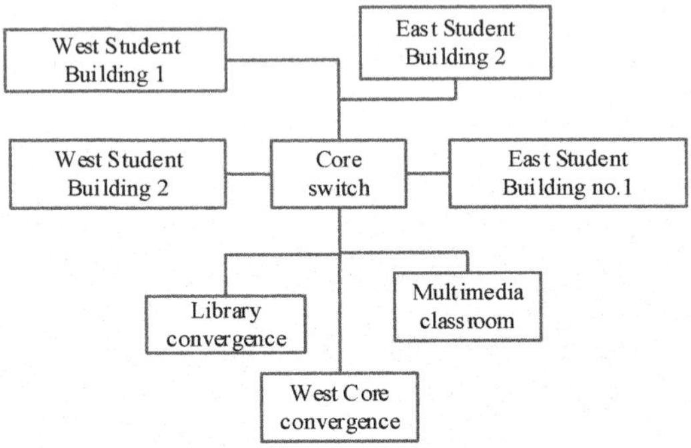

Fig. 4. University course teaching network topology

As a platform of teaching and scientific research, University Course Teaching Network must be able to provide a larger bandwidth, and it needs a long time network service. The main features of the university course teaching network are:

Multi-user, Wide Range
With the development and popularization of the network, campus network has been not only limited to the original computer room and classroom, but all over the teaching buildings, dormitories and so on. Today's campus network has covered the entire campus, the user base is also gradually expanding.

Frequent Traffic and Various Network Applications
In addition to the normal network applications of scientific research and teaching, there are quite a number of services also rely on the network, such as online games, campus network BBS, E-mails, etc. And some need high bandwidth, such as network game and FTP server.

Export Uniformity
Although the campus network covers a wide range of traffic types, but are basically

limited to a few exports, namely, telecommunications, Unicom and education network exports, mostly one or several routers connected to the external network.

Low Safety

Because the university curriculum teaching network's scope is big, the flow many characteristics, causes the university curriculum teaching network the security question to be day by day serious. Upgrading the operating system or installing firewalls and antivirus software for all the hosts of the University Course Teaching Network is a clear waste of manpower and resources. If you use the enterprise-class firewall policy, you may be part of the research nature of the application to shut out.

4.2 Experimental Indicators

The evaluation performance indicators include accuracy rate, precision, recall rate, F1 score, etc. F1 score is an index used to measure the accuracy of binary classification model in statistics. The accuracy rate is the most simple and commonly used performance indicator in classification problems, which is used to measure the percentage of correct samples identified against the total samples. The calculation formula is as follows:

$$N = \frac{M}{m} \tag{5}$$

In formula (5), M represents the total number of samples; m represents the number of samples correctly identified. Precision, recall rate and F1 score are commonly used performance indicators in traffic analysis problems. For traffic analysis problems, the performance indicators of each category should be calculated. When calculating the corresponding performance indicators of Z_0, Z_0 is regarded as a positive example, and the other categories are regarded as counterexamples. Based on the combination of the real results and the model identification results, the sample is divided into four cases: real case, false positive case, true negative case and false negative case. If the T_T, F_T, T_J, F_J represents the corresponding number of samples respectively, the following are:

$$T_T + F_T + T_J + F_J = m \tag{6}$$

$$T_T + F_T = M \tag{7}$$

According to the confusion matrix, the precision, recall and Fl fraction can be calculated. The precision represents the percentage of positive examples that are identified, also known as the precision ratio. The formula is:

$$P = \frac{T_T}{T_T + F_T} \tag{8}$$

The recall rate indicates how many of the samples that should be positive are correctly identified, also known as recall rate. The formula is:

$$R = \frac{T_T}{T_T + F_J} \tag{9}$$

F1 scores shall be defined as the harmonic average of precision ratio and recall ratio, and the calculation formula shall be:

$$\frac{1}{F1} = \frac{1}{2} \cdot \left(\frac{1}{P} + \frac{1}{R} \right) \tag{10}$$

In this experiment, the accuracy rate and F1 score were used as evaluation indexes.

4.3 Dataset Description

The correctness rate of traffic analysis of university course teaching network is verified from two aspects: one is the correctness rate of identifying normal network traffic and abnormal network traffic;

The specific experimental procedures are as follows:

①In the local area network, use the NetMate tool to collect network data packets and calculate the network traffic characteristics, according to the data flow grouping and marking is normal network traffic applications. The collected traffic is divided into 3 datasets named Al, A2 and A3 respectively.
②Extracting stream related information from data source files, vectorizing 3D feature vectors to form training and classification data sources.
③The traffic data collected and sorted from the core router exit of the University Course Teaching Network Center is shown in Table 1.

Table 1. Dataset/KB

Time/min	A1	A2	A3
2	20	35	42
4	20	30	44
6	18	32	46
8	18	35	44
10	−10	−38	−40
12	−15	−40	−42
14	−22	−42	−45

In Table 1, “-” represents a traffic exception. In each group, select 1000 data and divide them into 800 groups and 200 groups in 8: 2 ratio. Add 10% samples to the test set to verify the correctness of the machine learning-based traffic analysis method used in university course teaching network.

4.4 Experimental Results and Analysis

Accuracy Rate

In order to verify the effectiveness of the network traffic analysis method based on machine learning for university course teaching, it is compared with the traffic analysis method based on port number mapping and the traffic analysis method based on payload characteristics, as shown in Fig. 5.

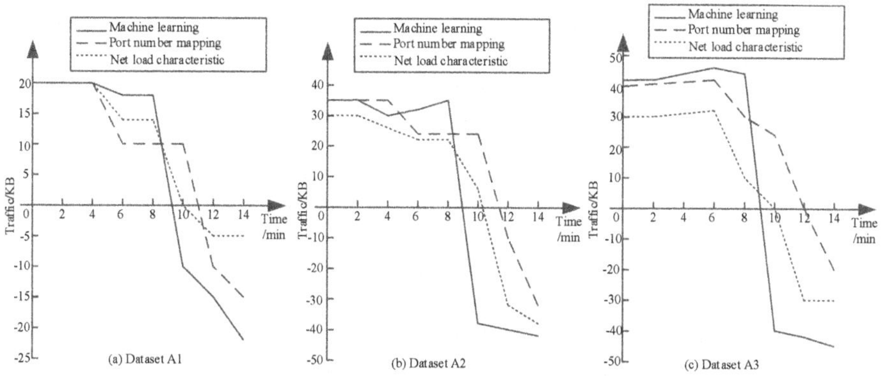

Fig. 5. Comparison of network traffic analysis results using three methods

As can be seen from Fig. 5 (a), the maximum value of network traffic analyzed using the port number-based traffic analysis method is 20 KB, and the minimum value of network traffic is −15 KB; the maximum value of network traffic analyzed using the traffic analysis method based on net load characteristics is 20 KB, and the minimum value of network traffic is −5 KB; the maximum value of network traffic analyzed using the network traffic analysis method based on machine learning -based teaching courses is 20 KB, and the minimum value of network traffic is −22 KB.

As can be seen in Fig. 5 (b), the maximum value of network traffic analyzed using the port number-based traffic analysis method is 35 KB and the minimum value of network traffic is −32 KB; the maximum value of network traffic analyzed using the traffic analysis method based on net load characteristics is 30 KB and the minimum value of network traffic is −38 KB; and the maximum value of network traffic analyzed using the network traffic analysis method based on machine learning -based teaching courses is 35 KB and the minimum value of network traffic is −42 KB.

As can be seen from Fig. 5 (c), the maximum value of network traffic analyzed using the port number-based traffic analysis method is 42 KB and the minimum value of network traffic is −20 KB; the maximum value of network traffic analyzed using the traffic analysis method based on net load characteristics is 32 KB and the minimum value of network traffic is −30 KB; and the maximum value of network traffic analyzed using the network traffic analysis method based on machine learning -based teaching courses is 46 KB and the minimum value of network traffic is −45 KB.

From the above analysis results, it can be seen that the result of the traffic analysis based on machine learning is consistent with the data in Table 1, and the accuracy is high.

F1 Score

Three methods of F1 score contrast analysis, the results are shown in Fig. 6.

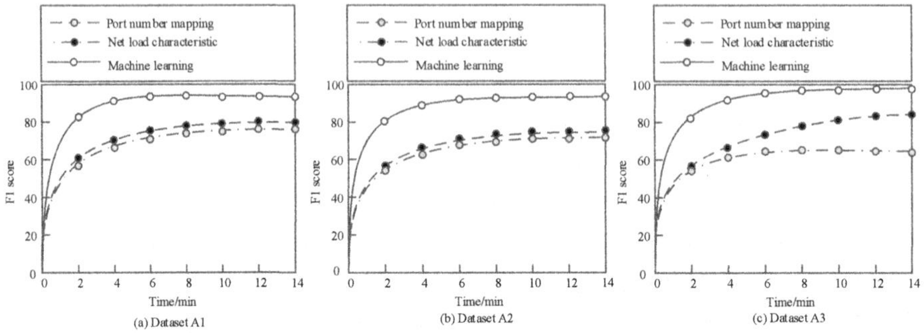

Fig. 6. Comparison of F1 score analysis results of three methods

As shown in Fig. 6 (a), using the port-number-based mapping approach to traffic analysis, the highest F1 score was 77 per cent; using the net-load character-based approach to traffic analysis, the highest F1 score was 80 per cent; and using the machine-learning -based approach to network traffic analysis for university courses, the highest F1 score was 96 per cent.

As shown in Fig. 6 (b), the maximum score of F1 is 70 per cent using the port-number-based mapping approach to traffic analysis; the maximum score of F1 is 73 per cent using the net-oad character-based approach to traffic analysis; and the maximum score of F1 is 94 per cent using the machine-learning -based approach to traffic analysis for university course teaching networks.

As shown in Fig. 6 (c), the maximum score of F1 was 64 per cent using the port-number-based mapping approach to traffic analysis; the maximum score of F1 was 82 per cent using the net-load character-based approach to traffic analysis; and the maximum score of F1 was 98 per cent using the machine-learning -based approach to traffic analysis for university course teaching networks.

Through the above analysis, it can be seen that the F1 score is the highest by using machine learning -based traffic analysis method.

5 Conclusion

Aiming at the problem of poor real-time performance of current traffic detection methods, this paper puts forward a traffic analysis method for university course teaching network based on machine learning. By constructing the traffic analysis model of university course teaching network, the original traffic features are filtered according to the importance scores of the features, and then a new sample is constructed into the model.

References

1. Yanan, W., Xue, Y., Haotao, Z., et al.: Algorithm of logical topology mapping for resource optimization based on reinforcement learning. Optical Communication Technol. **44**(06), 46–50 (2020)
2. Xiaowei, L., Yao, M., Yongle, C., et al.: Shodan traffic identification based on load characteristics and statistical characteristics. Comput. Eng. **47**(01), 117–122 (2021)
3. Liu, S., Liu, D., Muhammad, K., Ding, W.: Effective template update mechanism in visual tracking with background clutter. Neurocomputing **458**, 615–625 (2021)
4. Qilong, Z.: Short-term traffic prediction simulation of multi-scale network based on discrete variables. Computer Simulation **38**(05), 423–426+476 (2021)
5. Liu, S., et al.: Human memory update strategy: a multi-layer template update mechanism for remote visual monitoring. IEEE Trans. Multimedia **23**, 2188–2198 (2021)
6. Xue, B., Erbuli, N.: Research on visual analysis method based of multi-view collaboration on network traffic data. J. Chinese Computer Systems **41**(09), 1893–1897 (2020)
7. Meng, Y., Qin, T., Zhao, L., et al.: Network anomaly detection method based on residual analysis. J. Xi'an Jiaotong University **54**(01), 42–48+84 (2020)
8. Shuai, L., Shuai, W., Xinyu, L., et al.: Fuzzy detection aided real-time and robust visual tracking under complex environments. IEEE Trans. Fuzzy Syst. **29**(1), 90–102 (2021)
9. Xiaohui, L., Chaoyang, C., Huawei, Y., et al.: Large scale network traffic prediction based on cloud computing and big data analysis. J. Jilin University (Engineering edition) **51**(03), 1034–1039 (2021)
10. Huixiang, X., Min, C., Yingying, M.: Combined prediction model for nonlinear network flow based on big data analysis. J. Shenyang Univ. Technol. **42**(06), 670–675 (2020)

A Learned Multi-objective Bacterial Foraging Optimization Algorithm with Continuous Deep Q-Learning

Tianwei Zhou[1,2], Wenwen Zhang[1,2], Pengcheng He[1], and Guanghui Yue[3(✉)]

[1] College of Management, Shenzhen University, Shenzhen 518060, China
[2] Great Bay Area International Institute for Innovation, Shenzhen University, Shenzhen 518060, China
[3] School of Biomedical Engineering, Health Science Center, Shenzhen University, Shenzhen 518060, China
yueguanghui@szu.edu.cn

Abstract. Multi-objective bacterial foraging optimization (MBFO) algorithm is a kind of efficient swarm intelligence algorithm for multi-objective problems. However, both nested loop and the swimming step length setting are crucial to capability improvement for the specific problem. To deal with these two problems, this paper proposes learned multi-objective bacterial foraging optimization algorithm (LMBFO) which transforms nested loop between operations into a conditional selection and firstly combined multi-objective bacterial foraging optimization algorithm with continuous deep q-learning to realize adaptive parameter control. To verify the feasibility of LMBFO, it is trained and tested on classical multi-objective benchmark functions. Moreover, MBFO is utilized as the comparison to illustrate the superiority of our proposed MLBFO.

Keywords: Multi-objective bacterial foraging optimization · Continuous deep q-learning · Parameter control

1 Introduction

Multi-objective optimization problems (MOPs) have been of high profile, and the goal of MOPs is to find a set of solutions with mutually restrictive objective functions. Evolutionary algorithms (EAs) attract scholars' attentions for its high efficiency. A lot of multi-objective evolutionary algorithms (MOEAs) have been proposed and applied to real life problems, such as non-dominated sorting genetic algorithm II (NSGA-II) [1], multiobjective particle swarm optimization (MOPSO) [2], multi-objective bacterial foraging optimization (MBFO) [3] and so on.

Y. Xu et al. (Eds.): ML4CS 2022, LNCS 13657, pp. 44–53, 2023.
https://doi.org/10.1007/978-3-031-20102-8_4

Model free reinforcement learning (RL) has been favorably applied to abound tough problems. For most of the EAs, the choice of parameters and strategies is problem-oriented. Therefore, it has become a popular research topic to use RL to analyze the state in the EAs iteration process and make corresponding parameter and strategy choices. RL has been merged with different single objective evolutionary algorithms, such as bacterial foraging optimization [4,5], particle swarm optimization [6,7], and so on. In recent yeas, the popularity of combinations between MOEAs and RL are also increasing [8].

Except for the difference in the number of objectives, the combination of RL and EA can be divided into two categories: online learning [5] and offline learning [9]. Online learning means the RL learns from online information on an optimization task in a single iteration. For offline learning, unlike the previous type, offline learning utilizes the benefit of deep reinforcement learning algorithms. The parameters of deep reinforcement learning are firstly trained and optimized based on the training set. Then, the optimized parameters are applied to the test set or actual problems. Unlike online learning, offline learning can deal with more information from an iterative process and make decisions under continuous state spaces. Therefore, compared with online learning, offline learning is more robust. However, there is little research on the combination of offline learning and MOEAs. One potential reason is that the state of MOPs is hard to measure and forecast. However, reinforcement learning is a potential tool to improve the performance of MOEAs. For example, [10] utilized q-learning to choose parameters according to the state of individuals in decision space and solution space. Moreover, compared with the commonly utilized swarm intelligent algorithms, such as MOPSO and NSGA-II, MBFO is more powerful in multimodal problems since it is easy to jump out of local optimum. At the same time, MBFO also holds the disadvantages. The convergence speed is easily affected by how well the parameters and the problem match. Therefore, this paper tries to improve the performance of MBFO with the help of continuous deep q-learning algorithm.

In this paper, a learned multi-objective bacterial foraging optimization algorithm (LMBFO) is proposed to enhance the searching ability of MBFO. The main contributions are twofold. Firstly, MBFO is modeled as Markov decision process (MDP). Secondly, continuous deep q-learning algorithm is novelty embedded into MBFO to choose parameters according to the state of solutions and indicators automatically. Moreover, experimental results illustrate the superiority of our proposed LMBFO.

This paper is organized as follows. In Sect. 2, we introduce BFO, MBFO and double deep q-network in detail. In Sect. 3, the learned multi-objective bacterial foraging optimization algorithm (LMBFO) is proposed. Section 4 shows the experimental results and analyses, and the conclusions and discussions are presented in Sect. 5.

2 Pre-knowledge

2.1 Multi-objective Optimization

Multi-objective optimization problems involving m multiple, conflicting objectives with p constraints. In this paper, we try to get the Pareto set for MOPs, that is, solutions that cannot be improved in any of the objectives without degrading at least one of the other objectives.

$$\begin{aligned} &\min F(x) = f_1(x), \ldots, f_m(x), x \in \omega \\ &s.t. \begin{cases} g_i(x) \leq 0, \ i = 1, \ldots, q \\ h_j(x) = 0, \ j = q+1, \ldots, p \end{cases} \end{aligned} \tag{1}$$

2.2 Bacterial Foraging Optimization

Original Bacterial Foraging Optimization (BFO) tackles the problem by using three operators, including chemotaxis, reproduction, and elimination/dispersal. For more detailed information, please refer to [11].

2.3 Multi-objective Bacterial Foraging Optimization

Although BFO has been applied to many single objective optimization problems successfully, it cannot directly tackle MOPs with non-dominated solutions set. Thus, multi-objective bacterial foraging optimization (MBFO) was put forward by [3]. To extend BFO from single objective to multi-objective, this paper mainly raised health sorting and Pareto optimal method to realize the requirement of solving MOPs and diversity preservation scheme to improve search efficiency. In the typical MBFO, the following main processes are contained.

Chemotaxis. The ith individual in the population θ moves by the following equation:

$$\theta^i(j+1,k,l) = \theta^i(j,k,l) + c(i)\frac{\Delta(i)}{\sqrt{\Delta^T(i)\Delta(i)}} \tag{2}$$

where j, k, l are respectively the number of chemotaxis, reproduction and elimination process, and $c(i)$ is the length of unit walk and $\Delta(i)$ is the direction angle of the jth step.

Reproduction. In reproduction process, the better individual in the population will be kept, and the worse ones will be deleted.

Elimination and Dispersal. In the elimination and dispersal process, some individuals will be deleted and replaced with some probability to keep diversity of the whole population.

2.4 Continuous Deep Q-Learning

The continuous deep q-network was proposed by [12]. In this paper, normalized advantage function (NAF) was proposed, which firstly combined decomposing Q into an advantage term A with a state-value term V [13] and normalized action-value function [14]. It is simpler than DDPG [15] agents. The agent thus makes use of three models: the V_{model} learns the state value term, while the advantage term A is constructed based on the L_{model}. The μ_{model} always chooses the action that maximizes the Q function.

3 Framework of LMBFO

3.1 Model MBFO as MDP

To learn the parameters of the neural network, i.e., the agent or the controller, embedded in the MBFO, we firstly model the iteration procedure of the proposed MBFO as an MDP with the following definitions of environment, state, action, policy, reward.

Environment. For parameter control, an optimal controller is expected to be learned from optimization experiences obtained when optimizing a set of optimization problems. Therefore, the environment consists of a set of optimization problems (called training functions). They are used to evaluate the performance of the controller during learning process. Note that these training functions should have some common characteristics for which can be learned for a good parameter controller.
State. The indicators for MOPs are taken as states, and the details are listed as follows:

- Normalized generational distance(GD) $GD = \frac{(\sum_{i=1}^{n} d_i^p)^{1/p}}{n}$
- Normalized inverted generational distance (IGD) $IGD = \frac{\sum_{i=1}^{n} |\hat{d}_i|}{n}$
- Iteration stage till now $\frac{\text{NFE}}{\text{MAXNFE}}$, which respectively represents the number of fitness evaluations (NFE) and the maximum number of fitness evaluations (MAXNFE).
- The proportion of non-dominated solutions in the population $\frac{n_{nondominated}}{S}$
- Distance correlation between the fitness of the ith individual and other three randomly chosen Pareto solutions (when the number of the non-dominated solutions is less than three, copy randomly until the condition is satisfied).
- The ratio of the number of chemotaxis, reproduction and elimination and dispersal to the total number.

where d_i represents the Euclidean distance between the obtained i_{th} solution and the nearest reference point when $p = 2$, and $\hat{d}_i$ represents the distance from the Pareto solution set Z_i to the nearest reference point in population.

Action. In the MDP, given state S_t, the agent can choose (sample) an action from policy π defined as a probability distribution $p(A_t|S_t;\theta)$, where θ represents the parameters of the policy. Here, we define At as the control parameters, $\{C_i^j|C_i^j = action, 1 \leq j \leq Nc\ and\ 1 \leq i \leq S\} \in \mathbb{R}$.

Reward. Unlike single-objective optimization problems, the focus of multi-objective problems is the Pareto sets and solutions inside. On the one hand, after chemotaxis, reproduction or dispersal, the new solution dominates the original solution, then should be rewarded. Therefore, in this paper, one of the rewards is the number of new dominant solutions. On the other hand, the relationship between non-dominated solutions is also important. This can be measured by the IGD, GD, ϵ indicator and so on. When these metrics get better after iterations, the agent will also be rewarded.

3.2 Embedded CDQN into MBFO

To realize continuous control for swimming length for every individual, we embedded CDQN into MBFO after model it as MDP. Figure 1 shows the flowchart of embedded CDQN into MBFO. As discussed in the last subsection, the CDQN will be used to select swimming step length C in the chemotaxis process for each bacterium in the whole population. After apply C_i^j to generate new position of bacteria, the population will perform non dominated sorting. After that, the algorithm judges whether to perform reproduction or elimination process, then returns observation to CDQN.

The Algorithm 1 shows the details of LMBFO.

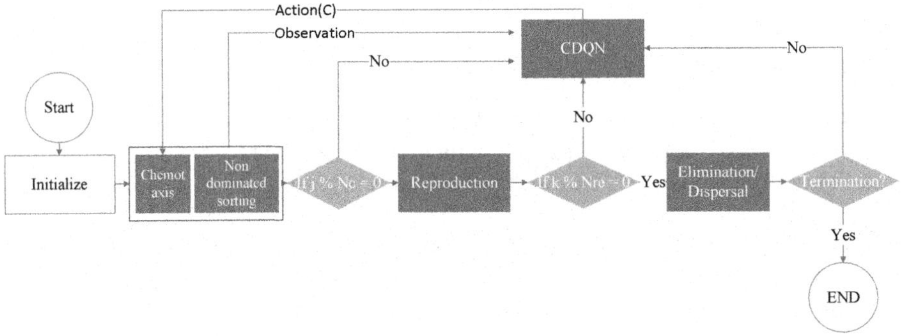

Fig. 1. The flowchart of LMBFO

4 Experiments

LMBFO was trained on DTLZ multi-objective benchmark and then tested on ZDT benchmark. The maximum number of fitness evaluation is 10000, the number of objective functions is 2, and the dimension of individual is set as 30. Moreover, MBFO [3] is chosen for comparison.

To make comparison fairly, 30 independent runs of each algorithm are conducted for the 22 testing functions. The operating experiment environment is listed as below.

- Platform: Python version 3.8.

Algorithm 1. LMBFO

Require: The times of elimination and dispersal N_{ed}, times of reproduction N_r, times of chemotaxisN_c, learning rate τ

Randomly initialize normalized Q network $Q(x, u|\theta^Q)$.
Initialize target network Q' with weight $\theta^{Q'} \leftarrow \theta^Q$.
Initialize replay buffer $R \leftarrow \emptyset$
for episode=1,M **do**
    Initialize a random process $\mathcal{N}$ for action exploration
    Receive initial observation state $x_1 \sim p(x_1)$
    for t=1,T **do**
        for ell=1,N_{ed} **do**
            for k=1,N_r **do**
                for j=1,N_c **do**
                    repeat
                        for i from 1 to S **do**
                            Select action $u_t = \mu(x_t|\theta^\mu) + \mathcal{N}_t$
                            Apply u_t to chemotaxis process
                            Observe r_t and x_{t+1}
                            Store transition (x_t, u_t, r_t, x_{t+1}) in R
                            Sample a random mini-batch of m transitions from R
                            Set $y_i = r_i + \gamma V'(x_{i+1}|\theta^{Q'})$
                            Update θ^Q by minimizing the loss L
                            Update the target network $\theta^{Q'} \leftarrow \tau\theta^Q + (1-\tau)\theta^{Q'}$
                        end for
                    until $N <$ MAXNFE
                end for
                Execute reproduction process
            end for
            Execute elimination/dispersal process
        end for
    end for
end for

- Processor: Intel Core i7 processor 2.70 GHz.
- Memory: 32 GB DDR3 ram.
- Operating System: Microsoft Windows 10, 64-bit.

4.1 Performance Measures

The quantitative performance of MLBFO can be measured by performance metrics. Two different metrics are introduced to evaluate the performance of the algorithm for multi-objective optimization problems in this paper.

Inverted Generational Distance (IGD). In order to evaluate the convergence and diversity of the algorithm, the IGD was computed as Eq. 3. The smaller the value is, the better the overall performance of the algorithm will be.

$$IGD = \frac{\sum_{i=1}^{n} |d_i|}{n} \tag{3}$$

Epsilon (ϵ). ϵ can give complete information about the relationship of two approximation sets. ϵ indicator is inexpensive to compute, and thus it represents a very viable alternative, specially when dealing with many objective problems.

4.2 Results and Analyses

The Table 1 shows the mean and standard deviation of the results for ZDT 1–4 and 6. For both metrics, the LMBFO outperforms MBFO. Numerically, the solution obtained by LMBFO is closer to the true Pareto solution.

The Fig. 2 shows the Pareto set obtained by MBFO and LMBFO. The figures in the first column are the results obtained by MBFO, which are shown by red dot. The figures in the second column are the results obtained by LMBFO, which are presented by green dot. For both columns, the Pareto sets are pictured in blue. For all test functions, the LMBFO performs better than the original MBFO. Specifically, for ZDT1-3, the solutions obtained by LMBFO are close to the real Pareto set. But for ZDT4 and ZDT6, there exists large room for improvement. One potential reason is the large difference between objection functions. Reinforcement learning requires more state features to learn better.

In summary, LMBFO outperforms MBFO on both diversity and stability with the same number of fitness evaluations.

Table 1. The mean and variance of IGD and Epsilon on ZDT

Fun.	MBFO				LMBFO			
	IGD		Epsilon(ϵ)		IGD		Epsilon(ϵ)	
	Mean	Std. Dev.	Mean	Std. Dev.	Mean	Std. Dev.	Mean	Std. Dev.
ZDT1	2.21E+00	2.74E−01	1.82E+00	2.24E−01	1.70E−01	1.74E−01	2.36E−01	1.82E−01
ZDT2	3.46E+00	2.69E−01	2.07E+00	4.52E−02	8.32E−03	2.01E−01	1.78E−02	2.03E−01
ZDT3	2.05E+00	2.53E−01	1.77E+00	2.01E−01	6.31E−02	2.53E−01	1.98E−01	2.43E−01
ZDT4	3.06E+02	9.56E+00	3.14E+02	2.27E+01	1.79E+02	1.30E+02	1.31E+02	1.57E+01
ZDT6	7.36E+00	8.84E−02	7.15E+00	3.28E−01	3.18E+00	1.01E−01	3.70E+00	1.01E−01

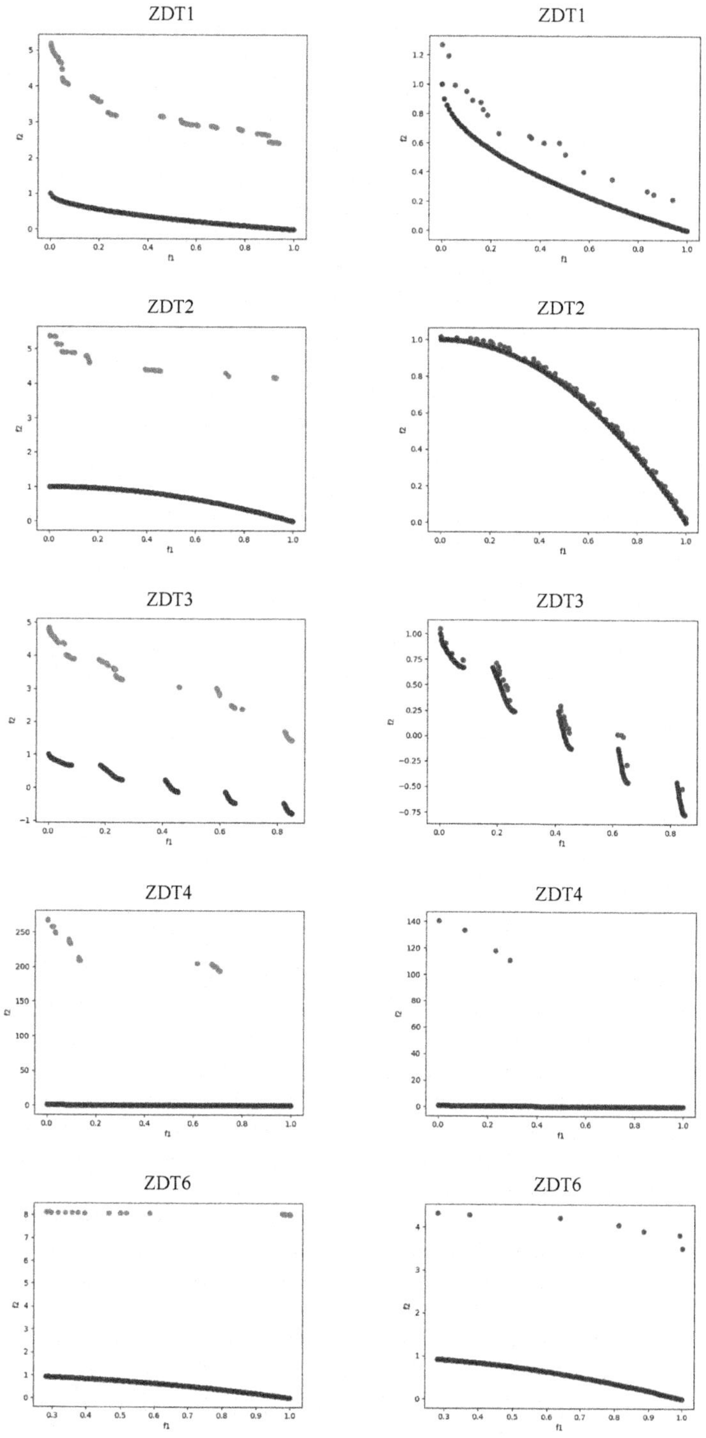

Fig. 2. The Pareto solutions of MBFO and LMBFO on ZDT

5 Conclusions and Discussions

In this paper, we propose LMBFO which firstly combines MBFO with DRL method to pursue a proper step length of chemotaxis in each iteration. After training on DTLZ benchmark functions, the LMBFO was tested on ZDT benchmark suits and achieved better performance compared against MBFO in limited number of evaluating fitness. In the future, we will pay attention to the application of this method in practical problems and the further combination of reinforcement learning and evolutionary algorithms.

Acknowledgments. The study was supported in part by the Natural Science Foundation of China Grant No. 62103286, No. 62001302, No. 71971143, in part by Social Science Youth Foundation of Ministry of Education of China under Grant 21YJC630181, in part by Guangdong Basic and Applied Basic Research Foundation under Grant 2021A1515011348, 2019A1515111205, 2019A1515110401, in part by Guangdong Province Philosophy and Social Science Planning Discipline Coconstruction Project under Grant GD22XGL22, in part by Natural Science Foundation of Guangdong Province under Grant 2020A1515010749, 2020A1515010752, in part by Natural Science Foundation of Shenzhen under Grant JCYJ20190808145011259, in part by Shenzhen Science and Technology Program under Grant RCBS20200714114920379, in part by Key Research Foundation of Higher Education of Guangdong Provincial Education Bureau under Grant 2019KZDXM030, in part by Guangdong Province Innovation Team under Grant 2021WCXTD002, in part by Special Projects in Key Fields of Ordinary Colleges and Universities in Guangdong Province under Grant 2022ZDZX2054.

References

1. Deb, K., Pratap, A., Agarwal, S., Meyarivan, T.: A fast and elitist multiobjective genetic algorithm: Nsga-ii. IEEE Trans. Evol. Comput. **6**(2), 182–197 (2002)
2. Coello Coello, C., Lechuga, M.: Mopso: a proposal for multiple objective particle swarm optimization. In: Proceedings of the 2002 Congress on Evolutionary Computation. CEC'02 (Cat. No.02TH8600), vol. 2, pp. 1051–1056 (2002). https://doi.org/10.1109/CEC.2002.1004388
3. Niu, B., Wang, H., Wang, J., Tan, L.: Multi-objective bacterial foraging optimization. Neurocomputing **116**, 336–345 (2013)
4. Niu, B., Zhang, C., Huang, K., Xiao, B.: A novel hybrid bacterial foraging optimization algorithm based on reinforcement learning. In: Huang, D.-S., Premaratne, P. (eds.) ICIC 2020. LNCS (LNAI), vol. 12465, pp. 567–578. Springer, Cham (2020). https://doi.org/10.1007/978-3-030-60796-8_49
5. Jiang, H., Dong, W., Ma, L., Wang, R.: Bacterial foraging algorithm based on reinforcement learning for continuous optimizations. In: Li, K., Li, W., Chen, Z., Liu, Y. (eds.) ISICA 2017. CCIS, vol. 873, pp. 41–52. Springer, Singapore (2018). https://doi.org/10.1007/978-981-13-1648-7_4
6. Liu, Y., Lu, H., Cheng, S., Shi, Y.: An adaptive online parameter control algorithm for particle swarm optimization based on reinforcement learning. In: 2019 IEEE Congress on Evolutionary Computation (CEC), pp. 815–822. IEEE (2019)
7. Wu, D., Wang, G.G.: Employing reinforcement learning to enhance particle swarm optimization methods. Eng. Optim. **54**(2), 329–348 (2022)

8. Wang, Y., et al.: Multi-objective workflow scheduling with deep-q-network-based multi-agent reinforcement learning. IEEE Access **7**, 39974–39982 (2019)
9. Sun, J., Liu, X., Bäck, T., Xu, Z.: Learning adaptive differential evolution algorithm from optimization experiences by policy gradient. IEEE Trans. Evol. Comput. **25**(4), 666–680 (2021)
10. Liu, Y., Lu, H., Cheng, S., Shi, Y.: An adaptive online parameter control algorithm for particle swarm optimization based on reinforcement learning. In: 2019 IEEE Congress on Evolutionary Computation (CEC), pp. 815–822 (2019). https://doi.org/10.1109/CEC.2019.8790035
11. Passino, K.: Biomimicry of bacterial foraging for distributed optimization and control. IEEE Control Syst. Mag. **22**(3), 52–67 (2002). https://doi.org/10.1109/MCS.2002.1004010
12. Gu, S., Lillicrap, T., Sutskever, I., Levine, S.: Continuous deep q-learning with model-based acceleration. In: International Conference on Machine Learning, pp. 2829–2838. PMLR (2016)
13. Baird, L.C., III.: Advantage updating. Tech. rep, WRIGHT LAB WRIGHT-PATTERSON AFB OH (1993)
14. Rawlik, K., Toussaint, M., Vijayakumar, S.: On stochastic optimal control and reinforcement learning by approximate inference. Proceedings of Robotics: Science and Systems VIII (2012)
15. Lillicrap, T.P., et al.: Continuous control with deep reinforcement learning. arXiv Preprint ArXiv:1509.02971 (2015)

Webpage Text Detection Based on Improved Faster-RCNN Model

Junling Gao[1], Moran Zhao[1], Jianchao Wang[1(✉)], Yijin Zhao[2], Lifang Ma[1], and Pingping Yu[1]

[1] College of School of Information Science and Engineering, Hebei University of Science and Technology, Shijiazhuang, Hebei, China
1299765852@qq.com

[2] College of Fedumi Information Engineering Institute, Hebei University of Science and Technology, Shijiazhuang, Hebei, China

Abstract. Under the new international situation, every country attaches great importance to the information security of the Internet, among which webpage anti-tampering is one of the top priorities. The premise of webpage tampering detection is to obtain webpages with different timestamps. Because of the diversity of website structure, it is necessary to make reasonable crawling strategy when using the traditional crawler method to obtain web pages, which leads to the problem of inflexible application. To address this, this paper adopts deep learning approach for detecting webpage text and thus acquiring web page information. The improved Faster-RCNN model is used to detect webpages and the resnet network is used to extract text features. In view of the feature of long text image font, the square convolution kernel of the traditional network is replaced by a rectangular convolution kernel to better fit the long and narrow features of the text; for the characteristics of dense text lines, the traditional NMS algorithm is replaced by the Soft-NMS algorithm to reduce the missed detection of dense regions. The experiments show that this algorithm has a better detection effect, which is important for network information security.

Keywords: Webpage tampering · Deep learning · Feature extraction · Network security

1 Introduction

As the speed of China's information construction accelerates, network and information security issues are becoming more and more prominent, which has attracted great attention from the state [1]. The websites of colleges and universities occupy an increasingly important position in the daily work of schools, which provides services for teaching and research, provides a platform for information exchange within colleges and universities, and also bridges communication between colleges and universities and external network information [2, 3]. The tampering of webpages on university websites will not only affect the normal operation of websites and cause significant economic loss, triggering information leakage security problems, but also cause serious damage to the image of

Y. Xu et al. (Eds.): ML4CS 2022, LNCS 13657, pp. 54–66, 2023.
https://doi.org/10.1007/978-3-031-20102-8_5

university websites and reduce their credibility. As the core technology to resist network attacks, webpage tampering identification technology can avoid the harm caused by malicious tampering and ensure safe network operation.

The prerequisite for webpage tampering detection is to obtain webpages with various timestamps. In terms of web crawling, most of the current research scholars use crawlers to obtain webpages. Generic crawlers are responsible for crawling from one website to another linked website only, regardless of the specific content of the website, until all the websites are crawled. There are differences in webpage structure due to different website categories, it is a tedious process to manually write parsing scripts for each webpage [4–6]. Also, the web structure of a website is not constant, which makes it expensive to maintain the crawler. The current distributed crawler systems for search engines are too complex and not very applicable [7]. Some stand-alone crawler frameworks can be improved to achieve distributed web crawling, but the constrained nature of the framework makes it inflexible to use. In the face of Internet data growing at an exponential rate, how to design and implement highly efficient and robust general-purpose crawler software is still one of the research hotspots nowadays. With the development of deep learning, this paper adopts the target detection method by detecting the text of webpages and then obtaining webpage information.

Deep learning-based methods have become a hot research topic for target detection. Based on the CNN (Convolutional Neural Network) algorithm, text detection algorithms developed by CNN include regression-based methods and segmentation-based methods. Based on the Faster-RCNN [8] framework, Tian et al. [9] proposed the CTPN(Connectionist Text Proposal Network) algorithm, which uses a set of anchor components with a fixed width to describe text lines, effectively solving the problem of detecting long text lines. Based on the one-stage detection SSD(Single Shot MultiBox Detector) [10] framework, Shi et al. [11] proposed the Seglink algorithm, which detects feature maps at different scales separately and introduces angle prediction for anchor, which has better robustness for text detection at different scales and angles. The regression-based method uses external rectangular boxes for localization, which is good for document text detection but cannot achieve accurate boundary envelopment for arbitrary shaped text, and the excess background noise will seriously interfere with the subsequent text recognition. Segmentation-based approaches usually learn from the ideas of classical semantic segmentation networks like FCN(Fully Convolutional Networks) [12] and FPN(Feature Pyramid Networks) [13] to build a network framework. Zhou et al. [14] proposed the EAST algorithm, which combines regression and segmentation to streamline the network process and end-to-end detection. Wang et al. [15] proposed the PSENet model, which uses a progressive scale expansion prediction algorithm to achieve detection of arbitrarily shaped text and also improves the separation of tight text instances.

To address the problems of complex structure of university websites, the crawler is constrained by the framework and inflexible to use, this paper uses deep learning to obtain web pages and crawl the information of web pages at each level by detecting the text of web pages. The Faster-RCNN algorithm is optimized by combining the defects and characteristics of the text. The original VGG16 network is replaced by a deeper network depth and less computationally intensive deep residual network (ResNet) to extract richer features;for the characteristics of text with lateral and varying length, a 1×5 shape convolution kernel is introduced on the deep convolution to adapt to the long and narrow shape of text lines; for the characteristics of dense text lines, the Soft-NMS algorithm is used instead of the traditional NMS algorithm to reduce the model complexity and improve the detection performance.

2 Traditional Faster-RCNN Algorithm

2.1 Faster-RCNN Algorithm Model

The Faster-RCNN network framework mainly consists of two subnetworks, namely, the region proposal network (RPN) and the Faster-RCNN detection network [16–18]. The RPN mainly generates high-quality region proposal candidate frames, judges and corrects the candidate frames by classification function and border regression function to initially locate the target. The input image is extracted by the convolutional neural network with features shared by the RPN and Faster-RCNN detection network. After entering the two subnets, the RPN is convolved by 3×3 convolutional kernels, and then the convolutional results are input to two 1×1 sized convolutional kernels for separate operations. One of the convolutional kernels converts the feature map into format by Reshape processing, and then the Softmax function determines whether there is a target object in the obtained anchor frame; the other convolutional kernel is followed by a regression function to determine the object coordinates. Faster-RCNN detects the region of interest (ROI) in the network, integrates the convolutional features with the proposed candidate frame information, and extracts the proposed feature blocks of uniform size for input to the fully connected layer. The classification function is used to calculate the class of the proposed feature block, and the border regression function is used to pinpoint the position of the detected frame.

Faster-RCNN unifies the four basic steps of target detection (candidate region generation, feature extraction, classification, and position correction) within a deep network framework [8, 19, 20]. The basic process is as follows: the image to be detected passes through the RPN network to generate candidate regions; the candidate region detection frames generated by the RPN network are highly overlapping and suppressed by the NMS algorithm; the candidate regions are detected using the Faster-RCNN network, which includes a CNN feature extraction network; the target is classified by the softmax regression algorithm to classify the target; the coordinates of the detection frame boundary are obtained by a multi-task lossy border regression algorithm. The Faster-RCNN model is shown in Fig. 1.

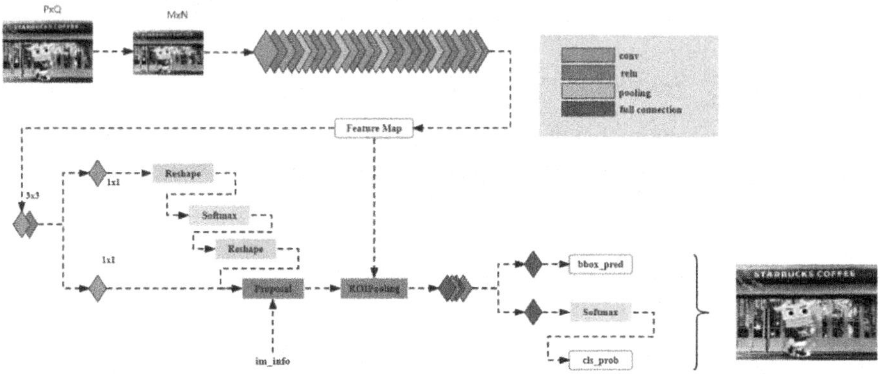

Fig. 1. Faster-RCNN model.

2.2 Region Proposal Network

RPN is essentially a convolutional neural network, centering on each point on the feature map, using a sliding window to traverse the incoming feature map and generate the corresponding anchor points, while mapping anchor boxes with different scales (128, 256, 512) and different proportions (1:1, 1:2, and 2:1 aspect ratio, respectively) on the original map, that is, three square boxes, three horizontal rectangular boxes, and three vertical rectangular boxes [21–23]. The structure of RPN is shown in Fig. 2. It consists of two branches. The classification layer classifies the target by outputting 2k scores from the classification function. The regression layer locates the coordinates of the target by outputting 4k vectors from the border regression function. The final output may contain rectangular candidate boxes for the target.

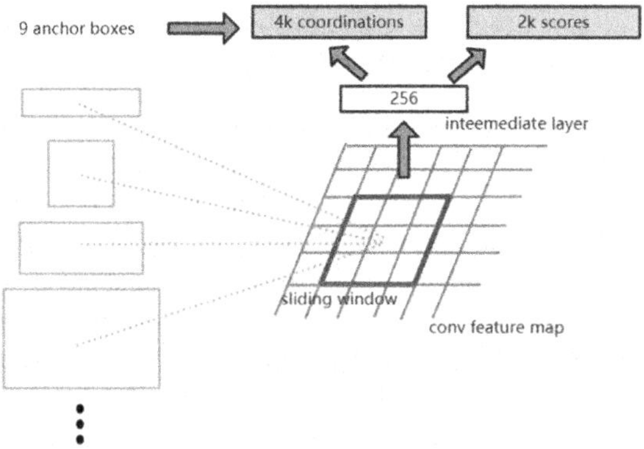

Fig. 2. RPN structure.

The classification loss function is used to train the classifier and its expression is:

$$L_{cls}(p_i, p_i^*) = -\lg(p_i p_i^* + (1 - p_i^*)(1 - p_i)) \tag{1}$$

where: p_i is the probability that the ith anchor point is predicted to be the target; p_i^* is a function to discriminate between positive and negative labels. The value of 1 indicating a positive anchor and the value of 0 indicating a negative anchor.

The regression loss function used to train the regressor, and its expression is:

$$L_{reg}(t_i, t_i^*) = \sum_{i \in (x,y,w,h)} M_{smoothL1}(t_i, t_i^*) \tag{2}$$

Among them,

$$M_{smoothL1}(x) = \begin{cases} 0.5x^2, |x| < 1 \\ |x| - 0.5, |x| \geq 1 \end{cases} \tag{3}$$

where: t_i is the predicted 4-D vector coordinate value of the target object; t_i^* is the actual 4-D vector coordinate value; $M_{smoothL1}$ is the loss error.

The loss function of the whole network is the sum of the classification loss function and the regression loss function, and its expression is:

$$L(p_i, t_i) = \frac{1}{N_{cls}} \sum_i L_{cls}(p_i, p_i^*) + \lambda \frac{1}{N_{reg}} \sum_i p_i^* L_{reg}(t_i, t_i^*) \tag{4}$$

where: λ, N_{cls}, N_{reg} is the coefficient of operation.

3 Improved Faster-RCNN Algorithm

3.1 Improved Faster-RCNN Algorithm Model

The algorithm proposed in this paper is improved on the basis of the Faster-RCNN target detection model: for the feature that the text font size is different and some text fonts are small, the original VGG16 network is replaced by a deeper network depth and a smaller operation depth residual network (ResNet) to extract richer features; for text with horizontal and variable length characteristics, 1 × 5 shape convolution kernels are introduced on deep convolution to accommodate the long and narrow shape of text lines; for the feature that some text lines are arranged compactly, the traditional NMS algorithm is replaced by the Soft-NMS algorithm to reduce the missed detection of dense regions. The architecture diagram of the Faster-RCNN model and the improved structure are shown in Fig. 3.

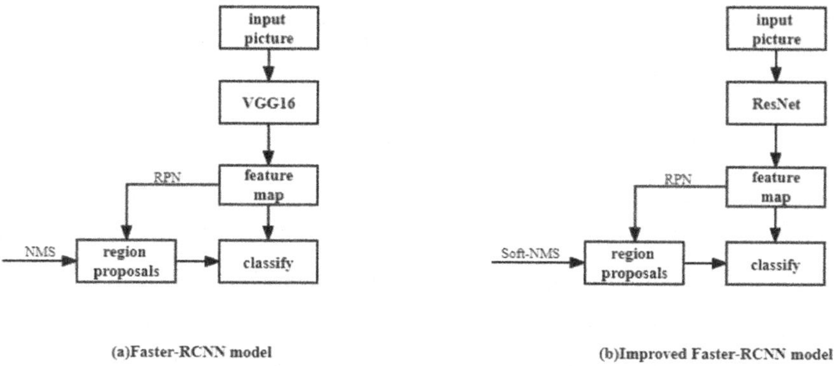

Fig. 3. Structure diagram of the improved model.

3.2 Residual Network Model

The structure of Resnet, which stands for Residual Network, is shown in the Fig. 4. Each residual component consists of two convolutional layers and a shortcut link, which is represented by the curved arrow.

The ResNet50 network is used in this study, and the main idea is to add a standard feedforward neural network to the jump which the connections of some layers, generating a residual block for each layer bypassed (Fig. 4). Thus, the goal of learning changes from learning the complete information to the residuals, and the difficulty of learning quality features is reduced greatly.

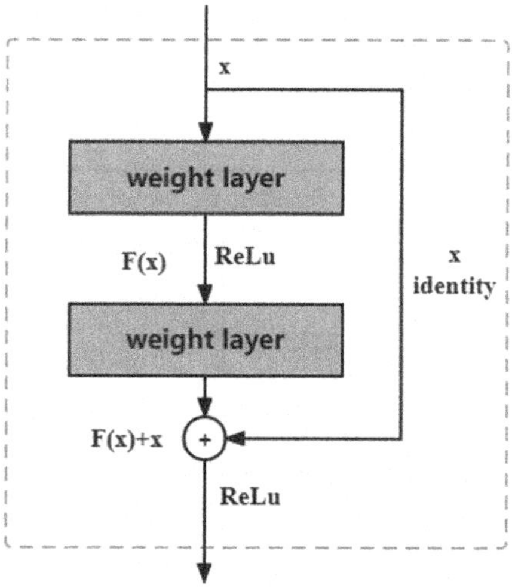

Fig. 4. Structure of ResNet residual block.

The residual block can be defined as:

$$y = F(x, \{W_i\}) + x \quad (5)$$

where: x, y are the inputs and outputs, $F(x, \{W_i\})$ is the learned residual mapping, and W_i is the weight of the ith layer.

If 2 layers are included, then.

$$F = W_{2\sigma}(W_{1x}) \tag{6}$$

where σ is the nonlinear function relu.

3.3 Regional Proposal Network Optimization

In the Faster-RCNN algorithm, although the RPN network generates nine different scales and ratios of anchor frames at each pixel position on the deep feature map by sliding window, corresponding to three scales (8, 16, and 32) and three aspect ratios (1:1, 1:2, and 2:1), the three scales and three aspect ratios set by the Faster-RCNN for text-based image datasets do not seem reasonable. The overall scale of the anchor frame is designed to favor medium and large targets, and each feature layer has a default frame with different sizes and ratios in order to be able to detect multi-scale text images. Each default box is traversed to match the IOU of the actual box. Due to the characteristics of text, this paper designed six aspect ratios of 1, 2, 3, 5, 7, and 10. But this will result in the default boxes behaving more densely in the horizontal direction and sparsely in the vertical direction. It will not match the best default box, or the best default box will not be able to return the whole text image, resulting in poor detection results in the vertical direction. Referring to the structure of textboxes, this paper set the vertical offset for each default box (as shown in Fig. 5). In the figure, only part of the aspect ratio is plotted. On top of the 4 × 4 grid, the square box indicates the default box with aspect ratio 1, and the rectangular box indicates the default box with aspect ratio 5. The dashed thickened square box is the vertical offset of the solid thickened square box. The dashed rectangular box is the vertical offset of the solid rectangular box.

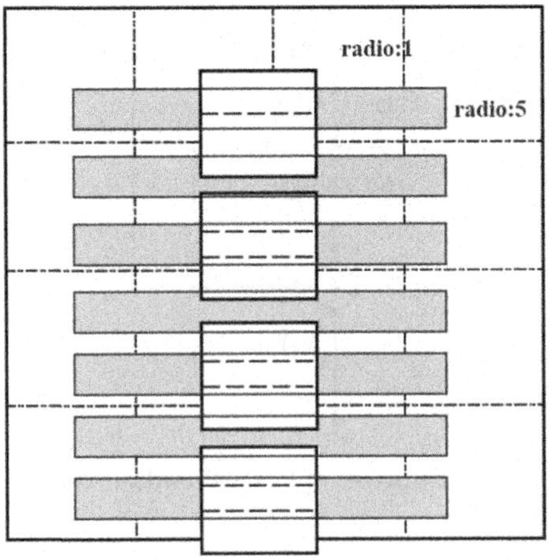

Fig. 5. Vertical offset.

For the generic target detection algorithm, the detection target has obvious boundaries. Set different aspect ratios for targets of different sizes, detect the object boundaries and then perform regression, finally, output the results. But for the text images in web pages, the image text does not have obvious boundaries, and the words in the text images have their own characteristics, such as English words and Chinese sentences, which are generally long, characterized by dense horizontal direction and sparse vertical direction. For this feature, to use a 1×5 convolution kernel (1×1 convolution kernel for the last layer) instead of the 3×3 convolution kernel used for general target detection. The rectangular convolutional filter produces a receiver domain that is better adapted to the characteristics of the image text and can avoid the effect of noise from the square filter.

3.4 Soft-NMS Algorithm

The general-purpose target detection algorithm usually uses non-maximum suppression (NMS) to post-process a large number of candidate frames to remove the redundant ones and obtain an optimal detection frame. This creates two problems:First, if there is a target in the box that is set to zero, it will cause the detection of the target to fail and reduce the detection rate. Second, the threshold value of NMS is not easy to determine; a small threshold setting will result in false deletion, and a large threshold setting will increase the risk of false detection and increase the false positive of the algorithm.

The detection frames generated by RPN network have high overlap due to the problems of the NMS algorithm. In order to less redundancy, we improve the post-processing using the Soft-NMS [24] algorithm. The principle of the Soft-NMS algorithm is that if the highest scoring detection frame has an IOU greater than a threshold with the remaining candidate frames, then that candidate frame will have a very low score and will not directly set the candidate frame to zero as in NMS algorithm. If the IOU of this detection box and the traversal of the remaining candidate boxes is lower than the set threshold, then it does not have a great impact on the detection score. The Soft-NMS algorithm is easy to implement as it does not add additional parameters or training. There are two ways to calculate the algorithm score reset function, which are the linear weighting function Eq. (7) and the Gaussian weighting function Eq. (8).

Linear weighting:

$$S_{\mathrm{i}} = \begin{cases} s_{i,} iou(M, b_i) < N_t \\ s_i(1 - iou(M, b_i), iou(M, b_i) \geq N_t \end{cases} \tag{7}$$

Gaussian weighting:

$$S_i = s_i e^{-\frac{iou(M, b_i)^2}{\sigma}}, \forall b_i \notin D \tag{8}$$

4 Simulation Performance Testing

4.1 Dataset

Most of the current research for text detection is conducted on natural scene datasets, and typical datasets include MLT-2017, ICDAR-2015, MSRA-TD500, etc. These datasets also contain images for Chinese text detection, but these currently available datasets are not well suited for the task of webpage text detection, mainly for the following reasons: first, the text in natural scenes is sparse, short and randomly distributed, while web pages are mostly long and concentrated; second, the background of natural scenes is complex, while the background of web pages is single. In summary, this paper selects the ICDAR2017 RCTW dataset and the homemade dataset for model validation and detection.

The International Conference on Document Analysis and Recognition (ICDAR) is the top conference in the field of text detection and recognition, and the datasets published by its Robust Reading Competion are widely used in the field of text. The datasets published by Robust Reading Competion are widely used in the field of text detection and recognition. To enrich the sample, the ICDAR2017 RCTW (Reading Chinese Text in the Wild) dataset is used in this paper.

The ICDAR2017 RCTW is mainly in Chinese and contains town street scenes, image screenshots, and indoor scenes, and the annotation format is four vertices of quadrilateral of a Chinese text lines, containing 12,263 images, including 8,034 images in the training set and 4,229 images in the test set.

The homemade dataset in this paper is mainly from university websites, and the annotation format is four vertices of a quadrilateral with Chinese text lines, containing 1200 images.

4.2 Training Details

The hardware platform used for the experiments is the Inter Core i7-8700K with a 6-core 3.7 GHz CPU, NVIDAGeForce GTX 1080Ti with an 11 GB GPU and 32 GB of RAM. The operating system of the software platform is Ubuntu 18.04. The deep learning tool is Pytorch, and the programming language is Python.

The Faster-RCNN model is used for testing and training, and Resnet50 is used as the base network for extracting image features in its framework. The dataset is divided into training and testing sets for the experiments, and the initial learning rate is set to 0.001. 60,000 rounds are trained, and the learning rate decays to 0.0001 after 10,000 rounds. Considering that the amount of text in an image is relatively large, the batch size of RPN is set to 64 to provide more samples for the training of Faster-RCNN.

4.3 Evaluation Metrics

The evaluation criteria parameters for the experiments in this paper rely on the following three parameters: accuracy (P), recall (R) and F-measure (F), which are calculated by the following equations.

$$P = \frac{TP}{TP + FP} \tag{9}$$

$$R = \frac{TP}{TP + FN} \tag{10}$$

$$F = 2 \times \frac{P \times R}{P + R} \tag{11}$$

where, TP denotes the number of positive samples predicted as positive samples, FP denotes the number of false positives predicted as negative samples, and FN denotes the number of missed positives predicted as negative samples. There may be a contradiction between accuracy (P) and recall (R), where one of the test metrics is high and the other is low. This is when it is necessary to consider both metrics together and just take the F-measure evaluation method.

4.4 Evaluation of Test Results

The performance of YOLOv5 [25], CenterNet [26], initial Faster-RCNN and the proposed algorithm in this paper were selected for performance comparison by testing on the ICDAR2017 RCTW dataset. The accuracy, recall and F-value performance of each algorithm are shown in Table 1 below, and the P-R curves are shown in Fig. 6.

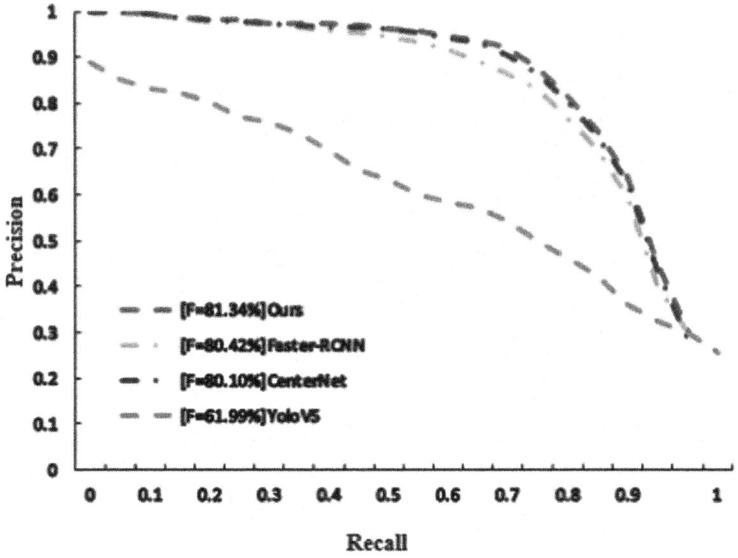

Fig. 6. Accuracy-recall curve.

As shown in Fig. 6, the improved algorithm proposed in this paper outperforms the other algorithms compared in any threshold case; as shown in Table 1, the accuracy, recall and F-measure values are higher than the other compared algorithms, and the F-measure reaches 81.34% (Fig. 7).

In this study, the target detection model Faster-RCNN is applied to the field of text detection to address the problem that traditional machine learning manually extracted features affect the recognition effect and counting accuracy due to human subjectivity. The Faster-RCNN target detection model is improved for text that mostly exists in the form of long rectangles. The original VGG16 is replaced by Resnet50, a deep residual network with deeper network depth and smaller operation, to extract richer features; for the feature that some text lines are arranged compactly, the traditional NMS algorithm is

Table 1. Performance comparison of the two algorithms.

Algorithms	The number of text	The number of detection	The number of truth	Precision	Reacll	Average F-measure
Yolov5	850	708	483	56.79%	68.24%	61.99%
CenterNet	850	923	710	83.51%	76.95%	80.10%
Faster-RCNN	850	870	705	82.94%	78.07%	80.42%
Improved Faster-RCNN	850	933	720	84.71%	77.20%	81.34%

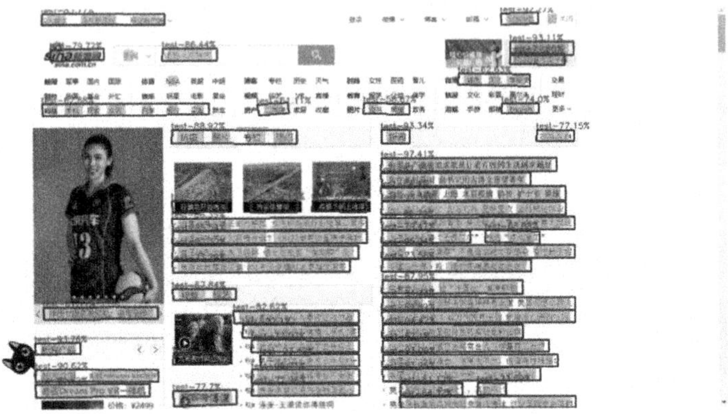

Fig. 7. Detection effect picture.

replaced by the Soft-nms algorithm to reduce the missed detection in dense regions. The experimental results show that the average accuracy of text detection reaches 84.71%, which is 1.79% higher than that of the original Faster-RCNN, indicating the effectiveness of the proposed algorithm in this paper.

5 Conclusion

In this paper, detect text in webpages according to the improved Faster-RCNN model, and use the simulated mouse to execute click commands on the detected text to open webpages at all levels in turn, and then obtain webpage information. The Faster-RCNN algorithm is improved to extract the network with Resnet50 as the backbone. The improved Faster-RCNN model is trained and tested on the ICDAR2017 RCTW dataset. The experiments show that the improved algorithm reduces the leakage rate and improves the detection accuracy. Webpage tampering detection is of great significance for network information security maintenance. We will continue to study the problem of segmenting dense text regions to improve the robustness of the algorithm.

Acknowledgements. We acknowledge funding from the sub project of national key R & D plan covid-19 patient rehabilitation training posture monitoring bracelet based on 4G network (Grant No.2021YFC0863200–6), the Hebei College and Middle School Students Science and Technology Innovation Ability Cultivation Special Project (Grant No.22E50075D), (Grant No.2021H011404) and (Grant No.2021H010203).

References

1. Lu, Y.H., Gao, J.: Design and implementation of anti-tampering monitoring system for campus secondary websites based on webpage comparison. Experimental Technol. Manage. **28**(06), 119–121+133 (2011)
2. Sun, L.W., He, G.F., Wu, L.F.: Research on web crawler technology. Computer Knowledge Technol. **6**(15), 4112–4115 (2010)
3. Chakrabarti, S., Van den Berg, M., Dom, B.: Focused crawling: a new approach to topic-specific Web resource discovery. Comput. Netw. **31**(11–16), 1623–1640 (2009)
4. Ma, J., et al.: Arbitrary-oriented scene text detection via rotation proposals. IEEE Trans. Multimedia **20**(11), 3111–3122 (2018)
5. He, T., Huang, W., Qiao, Y., Yao, J.: Text-attentional convolutional neural network for scene text detection. IEEE Trans. Image Process. **25**(6), 2529–2541 (2016)
6. Zhang, X., Zeng, Y., Jin., X.B., Yan, Z.W., Geng, G.G.: Boosting the phishing detection performance by semantic analysis. In: 2017 IEEE International Conference on Big Data, pp. 1063–1070. IEEE publisher, Piscataway (2017)
7. Yao, C., Bai, X., Liu, W.: A unified framework for multioriented text detection and recognition. IEEE Trans. Image Process. **23**(11), 4737–4749 (2014)
8. Ren, S., He, K., Girshick, R.: Faster R-CNN: towards real-time object detection with region proposal networks. IEEE Trans. Pattern Anal. Mach. Intell. **39**(6), 1137–1149 (2015)
9. Zhi, T., Huang, W., Tong, H.: Detecting text in natural image with connectionist text proposal network. In: 2016 14th European Conference on Computer Vision, pp. 56–72. Springer Science press, Amsterdam (2016). https://doi.org/10.1007/978-3-319-46484-8_4
10. Liu, W., Anguelov, D., Erhan, D.: SSD: single shot multi-box detector. In: 2016 14th European Conference on Computer Vision, pp. 21–37. Springer Science press, Amsterdam (2016). https://doi.org/10.1007/978-3-319-46448-0_2
11. Shi, B.G., Bai, X., Belongie, S.: Detecting oriented text in natural images by linking segments. In: 2017 IEEE Conference on Computer Vision and Pattern Recognition (CVPR), pp. 3482–3490. IEEE publisher, Honolulu (2017)
12. Long, J., Shelhamer, E., Darrell, T.: Fully convolutional networks for semantic segmentation. IEEE Trans. Pattern Analysis Machine Intelligence **39**(4), 640–651 (2015)
13. Lin, T.Y., Dollar, P., Girshick, R., He, K., Hariharan, B., Belongie, S.: Feature pyramid networks for object detection. In: IEEE Conference on Computer Vision and Pattern Recognition (CVPR), pp. 2117–2125. IEEE publisher, Honolulu (2017)
14. Zhou, X.Y., et al.: EAST: an efficient and accurate scene text detector. In: 2017 IEEE Conference on Computer Vision and Pattern Recognition (CVPR), pp. 2642–2651. IEEE publisher, Honolulu (2017)
15. Wang, W.H., et al.: Shape robust text detection with progressive scale expansion network. In: 2019 IEEE / CVF Conference on Computer Vision and Pattern Recognition (CVPR), pp. 9328–9337. IEEE publisher, Long Beach (2019)
16. Xie, Y., Lei, Y.: Image object detection based on deep convolutional neural network. Industrial Control Computer **30**(4), 96–97 (2017)

17. Razavian, A.S., Azizpour, H., Sullivan, J., Carlsson, S.: CNN features off-the-shelf: an astounding baseline for recognition. In: 2014 IEEE Conference on Computer Vision and Pattern Recognition Workshops, pp. 512–519. IEEE publisher, Columbus, OH, USA (2014)
18. Gu, J.X., et al.: Recent advances in convolutional neural networks. Pattern Recogn. **77**, 458–463 (2018)
19. Rong, X.J., Yi, C., Tian, Y.L.: Unambiguous text localization, retrieval, and recognition for cluttered scenes. In IEEE Trans. Pattern Analysis Machine Intelligence **44**(3), 1638–1652 (2022)
20. Liu, Y., Jin, L., Zhang, S., Luo, C., Zhang, S.: Curved scene textdetection via transverse and longitudinal sequence connection. Pattern Recogn. **90**, 337–345 (2019)
21. Patgiri, R., Katari, H., Kumar, R., Sharma, D.: Empirical study on malicious URL detection using machine learning. In: 15th International Conference on Distributed Computing and Internet Technology, pp. 380–388. IEEE publisher, India: Bhubaneswar (2019)
22. Ling, O.Y., Theng, L.B., Weiyen, A.C., Mccarthy, C.: Development of vertical text interpreter for natural scene images. IEEE Access **9**, 144341–144351 (2021)
23. Xu, Y., Wang, Y., Zhou, W., Wang, Y., Yang, Z., Bai, X.: Textfield: Learning a deep direction field for irregular scene text detection. IEEE Trans. Image Process. **28**(11), 5566–5579 (2019)
24. Bodla, N., Singh, B., Chellappa, R.: Soft-NMS-Improving object detection with one line of code. In: 2017 IEEE International Conference on Computer Vision, pp. 5562–5570. IEEE publisher, Venice, Italy (2017)
25. Liu, Y.F., Lu, B.H., Peng, J.Y.: Research on the use of YOLOv5 object detection algorithm in mask recognition. World Scientific Reaearch J. **6**(11), 377–383 (2020)
26. Duan, K.W., Song, B., Xie, L.: Center Net: keypoint triplets for object detection. In: Proceedings of 2019IEEE/CVF International Conference on Computer Vision (ICCV), pp. 6568–6577. IEEE publisher, Seoul, Korea (2019)

Turbo: A High-Performance and Secure Off-Chain Payment Hub

Jinchun He[1], Wangjie Qiu[2](✉), Rixin He[1], Shengda Zhuo[1], and Wanqing Jie[1]

[1] Institute of Artificial Intelligence and Blockchain, Guangzhou University, Guangzhou, China
[2] Beijing Advanced Innovation Center for Future Blockchain and Privacy Computing, Beihang University, Beijing, China
wjqiu86@gmail.com

Abstract. The scalability problems of blockchain systems are drastically amplified with the emergence of large-scale instantaneous transaction scenarios. Off-chain protocols are a prominent approach to alleviate these challenges. Payment channels allow two parties to lock funds inside the payment channel to enable instant transactions without involving the blockchain. The latest proposed payment hub (PH) allows off-chain transactions between multi-party through a tumbler. However, existing PH suffers from the problem of centralization, low throughput, and expensive challenge processes. We present Turbo, which allows direct, fast, and low-cost off-chain transactions between muti-party. Turbo allows any party to initiate arbitration against the guilty leader via the Immediate Fraud Proof Challenge (IFPC). Compared to NOCUST, Turbo increases throughput by approximately 30x and decreases the cost of the challenge by 50%. Moreover, Turbo reduces the complexity of the challenge process to O (1).

Keywords: Blockchain · Scalability · Off-chain payment · Layer2

1 Introduction

Blockchain technology is a revolutionary technique that enables cooperation between untrusted entities without a trusted third party [1]. With the boom in industries such as DAPPs (Decentralized Applications), DeFi (Decentralized Finance), NFT (Non-fungible tokens), and Metaverse, the market capitalization of cryptocurrencies has pushed to unprecedented heights (maximum total market capitalization is approximately $3 trillion). However, the major limitation of blockchain systems lies in their performance. For example, Bitcoin [2] can only handle to 7 transactions per second(tps) while Ethereum [3] supports up to 20tps, compared to over 47, 000 peak tps handled by Visa. Currently, scalability has become a significant problem for the development of the blockchain industry. On-chain (aka layer-1 main chain) scaling helps alleviate above problems. However, this technique requires modifying the underlying protocols, expanding block capacity [5], or replacing consensus algorithms [6], which may lead to fork or unanticipated costs. Moreover, the most promising Ether 2.0 [7, 8] could not be implemented in the short

Y. Xu et al. (Eds.): ML4CS 2022, LNCS 13657, pp. 67–75, 2023.
https://doi.org/10.1007/978-3-031-20102-8_6

term. Overall existing solutions for on-chain scaling based on existing blockchains have some degree of drawbacks.

Another advanced technique to solve the scalability problem is called off-chain scaling. The payment hub (PH) is one of the most promising solutions since it could offload the complex transaction process to off-chain to avoid expensive transaction fees and congested networks. But traditional PH face problems of centralization and low throughput, and expensive challenge processes.

In this paper, we present TURBO that achieves decentralization, high throughput, and efficiency to address the above problems.

Technical contributions:

1. For the first time, we introduce a decentralized leader-verifier mechanism to solve the single point of failure problem of NOCUST. Only one rational verifier is needed to provide security guarantees for Turbo.
2. Based on a new Interval State Merkle Tree structure, we design an efficient challenge process called Immediate Fraud Proof Challenge (IFPC), which has a shorter challenge period and less gas consumption for challenge process than NOCUST.
3. We design a concurrently supported off-chain transaction mechanism that allows users to make multiple transactions in a single epoch. In performance evaluation, the transaction throughput of Turbo is about 30x higher than that of NOCUST, and the transaction confirmation latency is at the millisecond level.
4. Turbo is compatible with all blockchain platforms with smart contract functionality. We implement smart contracts by solidity as a proof of concept and measure flexibility by gas consumption and computational complexity.

1.1 Paper Organization

The rest of the paper is organized as follows. Sect. 2 overviews the related work on off-chain protocols. In Sect. 3, we introduce the detailed design of Turbo. In Sect. 4, we describe our implementation and analyze the evaluation result. Finally, we conclude in Sect. 5.

2 Related Work

With the expansion of the cryptocurrency market and the popularity of DAPPs, scalability is considered a critical concern in academia and industry. A mass number of research and industry teams are dedicated to overcoming this critical limitation.

Payment channels were initially introduced by Spilman [16], and DMC [9] proposed the first duplex payment channel on Bitcoin. Payment Channel Networks (PCNs) [10, 11] allow two (or more) channels of transaction parties to make off-chain payments with the help of complex routing algorithms. However, PCNs suffer from two drawbacks: high failure rates of multi-hop payments [12] and channel imbalance problem [13].

The recently proposed Payment Hub (PH) [14, 15] constructs a star network topology which allows multiple parties to conduct off-chain transactions directly. TumbleBit [14] first proposed the concept of Bitcoin-compatible payment hub that anonymously links payers and recipients via a tumbler. It enables anonymous and fast transactions between multiple people. However, each participant needs to establish a channel with tumbler, which results in a complex transaction protocol and low collateral utilization. In addition, TumbleBit is only compatible with the Bitcoin network. NOCUST [15] is a multi-party payment hub with a degree of scalability and generality, which processes off-chain transactions through a non-custodial operator. This operator executes every coin transfer and periodically commits the checkpoint to the on-chain contract to keep consistency. However, it faces serious centralization problems, and its performance is still insufficient for high throughput payments scenarios.

In summary, none of the existing solutions achieve decentralized, efficient and high throughput to meet the requirements of large-scale instantaneous trading.

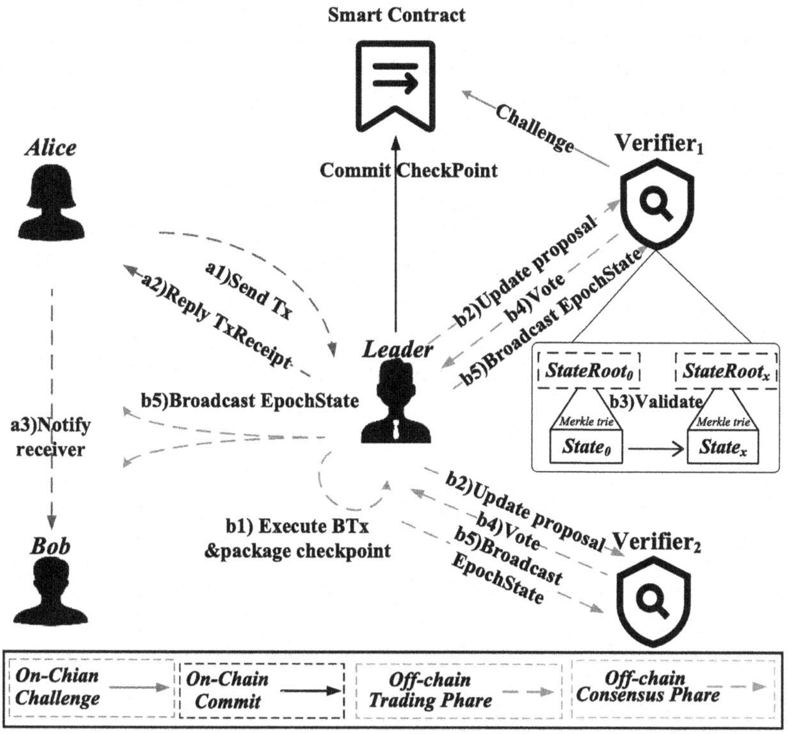

Fig. 1. Overview of turbo off-chain payments

3 TURBO Design

In this section, we present the design of Turbo. Setc. 3.1 is an introductory part about the overview of Turbo. Sect. 3.2 describes the election mechanism. In Sect. 3.3, we describe the details of off-chain transaction execution and on-chain checkpoint commits, respectively. In Sect. 3.4, we discuss how to resolve off-chain disputes through the challenge mechanism. Finally, we specify the exit process in Sect. 3.5.

3.1 Overview

Turbo is an account-based model payment protocol in which every participant has a user state representing their attributes (balance, collateral, identity, etc.). In a nutshell, Turbo can be considered a state machine. As shown in Fig. 1, the two basic modules of Turbo include on-chain smart contracts and off-chain transaction protocols. The smart contract maintains the assets, checkpoints, and the dispute resolver. The roles of Turbo protocol include participant, verifier, and leader with respective functions.

3.2 Collateral-Based Leader Election

The random leader election mechanism is critical for solving the centralization problem. The collateral-based election mechanism means that the more collateral assets are pledged, the greater the chance of being elected as a leader. Consequently, collateral has a significant constraining effect on the leader's behavior (i.e., the more collateral a leader pledges, the greater the cost of being evil). The probability p_i of election as a leader is defined as:

$$p_i = \frac{C_i}{\sum_{j=1}^{n+1} C_j}(p_i \in (0, 1)) \tag{1}$$

where c_i represents the amount of the collateral.

Generation of random numbers ζ:

$$\zeta = Radom\ Gernerate(State\ Root_{e-1}), \zeta \in \left(0, 2^{256}\right) \tag{2}$$

$$\zeta \in \sum_{j=1}^{i-1} V_j * 2^{256}, \sum_{j=1}^{i} V_j * 2^{256} \tag{3}$$

where *RadomGernerate* represents a random number generation function, we use the StateRoot_{e-1} as the seed for random number generation, and V_i is elected as the leader when ζ satisfies equation.

3.3 Off-Chain Transaction Execution

In our design, off-chain transaction information and specific balance states are not stored on chain. It is maintained by both the leader and the verifiers. The leader responds to transaction requests from participants and maintains off-chain global data as shown in Table 1.The verifier is responsible for verifying the validity and integrity of transaction execution.

Table 1. Global data for an epoch maintained by leader. Where n and j respectively denote the number of active and exiting participants, and x indicates the transaction volume.

Data	Description
$State_0\ (B_1, B_2, ..., B_n)$ $State_x\ (B_1, B_2, ..., B_n)$	Initial balance states of participants New balance states of participants
$Btx_e\ (Tx_1, Tx_2,..., Tx_x)$	Batch transactions for e epoch
$E_e\ (P_1, P_2, ..., P_n)$	List of enrolled participants for epoch e
$W_e\ (W_1, W_2,..., W_j)$	List of withdrawal participants for epoch e
$ISL_e\ (IS_1, IS_2, ..., IS_x)$	List of Interval States (IS)

Trading Phrase. During the trading phase, the payer initiates a transfer by sending a *Tx* to the leader, which is defined as follows:

$$Tx = \{\text{from, to, value, nonce}\}_{\sigma F} \tag{4}$$

where *from* and *to* represent the payer and recipient of the transaction, respectively. And *nonce* represents the unique identifier of the transaction. Finally, the signature of the transaction σ_F represents the payer's authorization of the transaction. The leader verifies the validity of the transaction Tx from the payer (signature validity, balance sufficiency, etc.), adds the transaction to the batch transaction sequence BTx_e, and replies a transaction receipt to both parties. This transaction receipt (*TxReceipt*) is defined as follows:

$$TxReceipt = \{Tx_{\sigma F},\ txid\}_{\sigma \mathrm{L}} \tag{5}$$

where σ_L indicates that this transaction is certified by the leader and *txid* indicates the execution order of this transaction.

Consensus Phrase. The consensus phase is mainly about the leader packaging consensus data and organizing verifiers to participate in the validation process. Firstly, the leader needs to process the batch of transactions generated in the trading phase, generate and broadcast the latest checkpoint of this epoch. The checkpoint (CP_e) is defined as follows:

$$CP_e = (LID,\ EON,\ PR,\ ISR,\ SR,\ ER,\ WR) \tag{6}$$

where *LID* represents the id of current leader, *EON* represents the epoch number, *PR*, *ISR*, *SR*, *ER* and *WR*, respectively, represent the Merkle roots of all transactions, Interval States, Final States, Enrollment Sets, and Withdrawal Sets for this epoch.

The verifier replies with a signature indicating an agreement to that *CP*, or initiates a challenge if there is fraud. The leaders cannot submit checkpoints to the intelligent system until all signatures have been collected. Finally, the leader broadcasts a new round of state and then enters a new epoch.

3.4 Challenge Mechanisms

Considering the possibility of the leader's behavior deviating from the expectation of the protocol, we offer a solution for solving disputes. When the leader acts in a malicious manner, for example by issuing arbitrary false BTx_e and CP_e, or the leader is offline, anyone could challenge it by the smart contract.

We propose the Instant Fraud Proof Challenge (IFPC) for the first two cases, which requires only an on-chain call to complete the challenge. Moreover, we use smart contracts to guarantee the integrity and correctness of the execution of the challenge process. For the third scenario, anyone can initiate a timeout challenge if the leader is out of service for more than a certain time. The leader must respond the challenge within a predefined time T, or the leader will be disqualified (i.e., a new leader will be elected).

3.5 Exit

Turbo allows dynamic withdrawals and exits. The participant should request a withdrawal from the leader at epoch e-2. The participant who applies for withdrawal should be frozen and moved to W_{e-1} by the leader. Finally, the participant can withdraw the balance to the on-chain blockchain wallet (e.g., ETH) in the epoch e.

4 Implementation and Evaluation

As a proof of concept, we implement a prototype of Turbo and evaluate its on-chain cost and performance. We deploy the smart contract on an Ethereum private chain by Truffle to validate the functionality and measure gas cost. In addition, we use Golang to build a prototype system for performance evaluation. The detailed evaluation process is described below.

On-Chain Cost. We use gas consumption to quantify the on-chain overhead. The evaluation metric GasPrice = 20 gwei (1 gwei = 10^−9 Ether). Table 2 shows the gas consumption of Turbo for each operation (averaged over 10 repeated runs). Each checkpoint commit consumes 363 Kgas when 10 verifiers are involved in the verification process. The gas consumption is kept at a low constant value for the rest of operations.

Leadership Election. We evaluate whether election depends on the percentage of the verifiers' collateral. To test our election algorithm, we instantiate 20 verifiers pledging a random number of collateral and participating in the election. We conducted 100 leadership elections. The frequency of verifiers winning elections roughly matches this deposit share (see Fig. 2). This demonstrates that the on-chain election mechanism achieves the expected fairness and usability.

Table 2. On-chain operation gas consumption (Kgas). SFC: State-Fraud Challenge. TFC: Tx-Fraud Challenge. n: the number of verifiers of Turbo. m: the number of participants of Turbo.

Operation		Cost	Complex
Join		76	O (1)
Commit		363	O(n)/n = 10
Challenge	**SFC**	51	O (1)
	TFC	143	O (1)
Withdraw		34	O (1)
Election		83	O (1)

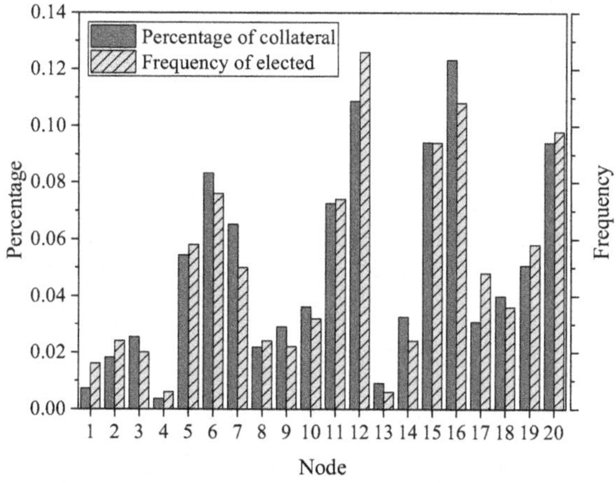

Fig. 2. Percentage of collateral vs. frequency of elected for 20 verifiers

Off-Chain transaction throughput. To evaluate the performance of Turbo, we deployed a payment hub on a PC and evaluated the off-chain transaction throughput through a series of stress tests. Our experimental environment is a PC with Intel Xeon Gold 6248R CPU and 32G RAM. We simulate a realistic network environment with 100Mbps bandwidth and 100ms latency. As shown in Fig. 3 the throughput of Turbo (around 9000) is 100x that of NOCUST (80) at 50 nodes. With the increasing number of nodes, Turbo (7300) is still 7x higher than NOCUST (950) with 600 nodes.

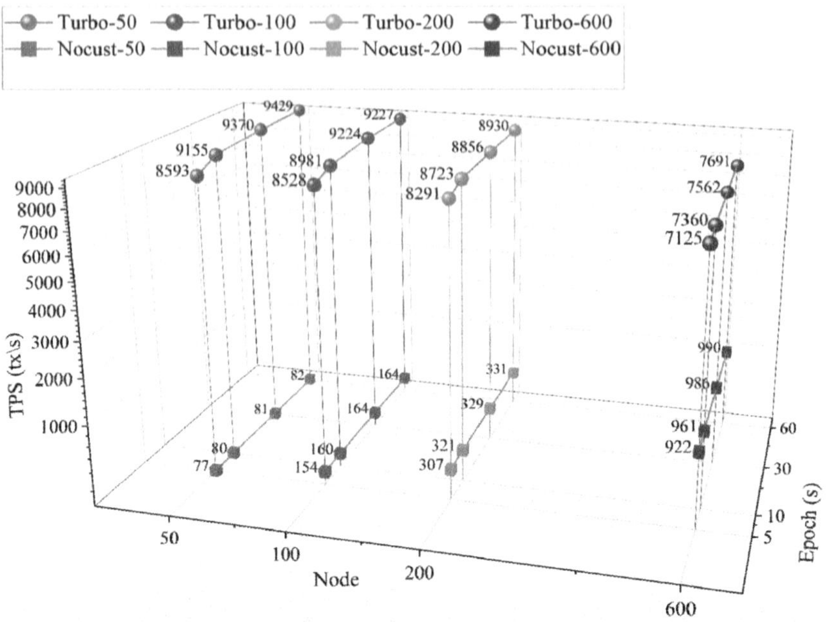

Fig. 3. Tps comparison between Turbo and NOCUST with different number of nodes and different durations epoch

5 Conclusion

We present a high-performance and secure off-chain payment hub called Turbo. It allows instant off-chain transactions between multi-party without the necessity to build channels separately. Combining the off-chain leader-verifier mechanism and the IFPC, only one rational verifier is required to provide security for the protocol.

The evaluation shows that Turbo outperforms NOCUST (SOA) work in terms of throughput and flexibility, with transaction throughput improving by 60x compared to ETH and about 30x compared to NOCUST. Turbo has better flexibility with a cost complexity of O (1) for join, challenge and exit operations, while challenge and exit operation complexity is O(log) in NOCUST.

In conclusion, Turbo offers a viable solution in the field of off-chain payment to meet the requirements of micro-payment scenarios with high throughput, low costs and security.

Acknowledgment. This work was funded by grants from the National Key Research and Development Program of China (Grant No. 2021YFB2700300).

References

1. Bonneau, J., Miller, A., Clark, J., Narayanan, A., Kroll, J.A., Felten, E.W.: Sok: research perspectives and challenges for bitcoin and cryptocurrencies. In: 2015 IEEE symposium on security and privacy. pp. 104–121. IEEE (2015)

2. Squarepants, S.: Bitcoin: a peer-to-peer electronic cash system. SSRN Electron. J. (2022). https://doi.org/10.2139/ssrn.3977007
3. Buterin, V.: Ethereum White Paper: A Next Generation Smart Contract & Decentralized Application Platform. Etherum. pp. 1–36 (2014)
4. Armknecht, F., Karame, G.O., Mandal, A., Youssef, F., Zenner, E.: Ripple: overview and outlook. In: Conti, M., Schunter, M., Askoxylakis, I. (eds.) Trust 2015. LNCS, vol. 9229, pp. 163–180. Springer, Cham (2015). https://doi.org/10.1007/978-3-319-22846-4_10
5. Bitcoin Cash - Peer-to-Peer Electronic Cash. https://bitcoincash.org/en/. Accessed 20 Apr 2022
6. Eyal, I., Gencer, A.E., Sirer, G., Van Renesse, R., Efe, A., Emin, G.: {Bitcoin-NG}: A Scalable Blockchain Protocol. usenix.org. 45
7. Kokoris-Kogias, E., Jovanovic, P., Gasser, L., Gailly, N., Syta, E., Ford, B.: Omniledger: a secure, scale-out, decentralized ledger via sharding. ieeexplore.ieee.org
8. Sharding on Ethereum – EthHub. https://docs.ethhub.io/ethereum-roadmap/ethereum-2.0/sharding/. Accessed 20 Apr 2022
9. Decker, C., Wattenhofer, R.: A fast and scalable payment network with bitcoin duplex micropayment channels. In: Symposium on Self-Stabilizing Systems. pp. 3–18. Springer (2015). https://doi.org/10.1007/978-3-319-21741-3_1
10. Poon, J., Dryja, T.: The bitcoin lightning network: Scalable off-chain instant payments
11. Raiden: Raiden Network (2020). https://raiden.network/
12. Mercan, S., Erdin, E., Akkaya, K.: Improving Transaction Success Rate in Cryptocurrency Payment Channel Networks. Elsevier (2021)
13. Khalil, R., Gervais, A.: Revive: rebalancing off-blockchain payment networks. In: Proceedings 2017 ACM SIGSAC Conference Computing Communications Security (2017). https://doi.org/10.1145/3133956
14. Heilman, E., AlShenibr, L., Baldimtsi, F., Scafuro, A., Goldberg, S.: TumbleBit: An untrusted bitcoin-compatible anonymous payment hub. In: Network and Distributed System Security Symposium (2017). https://doi.org/10.14722/ndss.2017.23086
15. Khalil, R.: NOCUST-A Non-Custodial 2 nd-Layer Blockchain Payment Hub (2018)
16. Spilman, J.: Anti dos for tx replacement. bitcoin-dev Mail. List (2013)

A Complete Information Detection Method for Vehicle CAN Network Gateway Based on Neural Network

Shen Jiang[1(✉)] and Hailan Zhang[2]

[1] School of Mechanical Electrical Engineering, Guangdong University Of Science & Technology, Dongguan 523000, China
gggsdf9@163.com

[2] School of Mechanical Electronic and Information Engineering, China University of Mining and Technology (Beijing), Beijing 100083, China

Abstract. Aiming at the problem of inaccurate bus anomaly detection due to the poor effect of information feature extraction in the complete information detection of automotive can network gateway, a new neural network-based complete information detection method of automotive can network gateway is proposed. Use high-speed CAN, low-speed CAN, LIN and central gateway to establish a vehicle CAN network architecture, calculate the information entropy of the vehicle CAN network gateway according to the probability of gateway information appearing in a specific time period, and extract the vehicle CAN network by establishing a structural model of the vehicle CAN network database. Introduce neural network, the information characteristic of CAN network gateway is substituted into the neural network, and the complete detection algorithm of vehicle CAN network gateway information is designed to realize the complete detection of vehicle CAN network gateway information. The experimental results show that the shorter the detection time of the detection method, the greater the difference between the information entropy value and the normal value, which is more conducive to the abnormal detection of the CAN bus. The detection method can effectively detect the bus anomalies at the time intervals of 15s, 10s, 5S, 3S, 1s and 0.5s, which is feasible and effective.

Keywords: Neural network · On board bus · CAN network · Gateway information · Complete detection

1 Introduction

Vehicle CAN bus [1] has been recognized by many international automobile manufacturers due to its advantages of low cost and high reliability. CAN bus CAN be seen even in the field of non-automobile manufacturing. Almost all key control systems related to body safety, such as engine control system, transmission control system, steering wheel control system and door control system, are implemented through the vehicle CAN bus. However, with the popularization of Internet of vehicles technology in recent years,

Y. Xu et al. (Eds.): ML4CS 2022, LNCS 13657, pp. 76–90, 2023.
https://doi.org/10.1007/978-3-031-20102-8_7

external nodes can access the original independent vehicle bus network through cellular data network, Bluetooth and WIFI as the media, resulting in the car in the driving process is easy to be remotely controlled by hackers, causing traffic chaos and even threatening life. Therefore, the security of vehicle bus network has been paid more and more attention [2, 3].

In domestic research, in order to detect network intrusion and protect the security of intelligent networked vehicles, Yu Tianqi et al. [4] proposed a mobile edge computing based in-vehicle CAN network intrusion detection method. The weighted self-information content of the CAN network gateway information ID and the normalized value of the ID are extracted as feature information, and the SVDD model is constructed and trained at the mobile edge computing server. The target vehicle identifies abnormal feature values based on the trained SVDD model, thereby Real-time vehicle CAN network intrusion detection is realized. When a small amount of gateway information is invaded, the accuracy of intrusion detection is significantly improved; Sheng Ming et al. [5] proposed a method to improve the network security of smart buses. A CAN bus gateway information anomaly detection method based on single-class support vector machine model, according to the characteristics of the gateway information data field of the CAN bus of the smart bus, the impact of the attack on the data field is analyzed, and the data field of the CAN gateway information is extracted into 8 training A large amount of driving data is used as the training set and test set, abnormal data is generated by random and simulation, and the parameters are adjusted by cross-validation. The test results show that the model can effectively detect the abnormal data of the bus CAN bus, improve Driving safety of smart buses.In foreign studies, Wang F et al. [6] proposed a new rollover index based on the position measurement of the center of mass. Firstly, the content integrator MCP is determined by estimating the position of the vehicle's center of mass. The MCP provides continuous rollover motion information before and after the tire is raised. Different standards are derived from the D'Alembert principle and the moment balance condition based on MCP. In addition to tire lifting, three new rollover states "rollover threshold", "rollover" and "in the air" jump of the vehicle are identified through the proposed standards. Compared with the existing representative lateral load transfer ratio of rollover index, the simulation results show that MCP index can successfully continuously and completely predict the vehicle rollover status, whether it is not rollover or tripped rollover.

Based on the above research background, in order to improve the information security detection effect of vehicle can network gateway, this paper uses neural network to design a complete information detection method of vehicle can network gateway, mainly introduces neural network algorithm, and combines other methods to realize information detection, so as to ensure the security of vehicle can network. The overall design scheme is as follows:

1) Establish vehicle can network structure. Through the vehicle can network, data is shared between on-board sensors, ECUs, actuators and other electronic devices, the network architecture is built, and each component is designed.
2) Calculate the information entropy of vehicle can network gateway. Taking the information entropy causing can bus as the index of CAN bus abnormality, the information entropy of CAN bus in time is calculated.

3) Extract the information characteristics of vehicle can network gateway. Information features are extracted through time decay function, the strength of gateway information and the composition of integrated gateway information.
4) A complete information detection algorithm of vehicle can network gateway based on neural network is designed. The neural network is introduced, and the information entropy calculation results are used as the input of the neural network. Combined with naive Bayesian hypothesis, the detection method is constructed and the detection results are output.
5) Experimental analysis. Build the experimental environment, calibrate the test indicators, and analyze the results.
6) Conclusion. Summarize the method of inductive design, explain the research purpose, and give the research results, conclusions and future research directions.

2 Design of Complete Detection Method for Vehicle CAN Network Gateway Information

2.1 Establish Vehicle CAN Network Architecture

Share the data between on-board sensors, ECUs, actuators and other electronic devices through the vehicle CAN network. Automobile manufacturers will adopt different on-board bus protocols according to the communication requirements of different on-board electronic devices and the relationship between different modules. Different on-board bus protocols need to be associated with each other through the central gateway. The vehicle CAN network architecture is shown in Fig. 1.

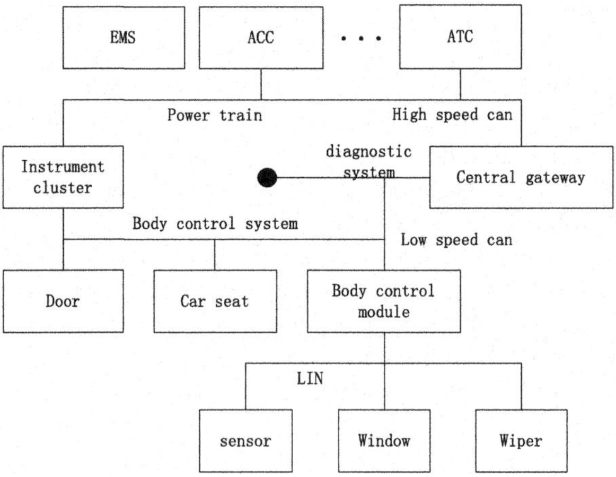

Fig. 1. Vehicle CAN network architecture

The vehicle CAN network architecture mainly includes the following parts:

(1) High-speed CAN: ISO (International Organization for Standardization, International Organization for Standardization) defines the high-speed communication CAN bus standard in the ISO11898 standard. The protocol stipulates that its communication speed is between 125 kbps and 1 Mbps, and the bus length can be up to 1 Mbps at the transmission speed. Up to 40 m, the high-speed CAN bus can meet the communication needs of up to 30 vehicle-mounted nodes at the same time. ACC (Adaptive Cruise Control, adaptive cruise control system), EMS (Engine Management System, engine management system) and ATC (Automatic Transmission Control, automatic transmission control system), etc. require frequent data communication.
(2) Low-speed CAN: ISO defines the low-speed communication CAN bus standard in the ISO11519 standard. The protocol stipulates that its communication speed is between 10 kbps and 125 kbps, and the bus length can be up to 1 km at a transmission speed of 40 kbps, which can meet up to 20 vehicles at the same time. The communication needs of the node. Among them, electronic equipment such as instrument panel, in the vehicular diagnosis system with low communication speed requirement, low speed CAN bus is generally used to realize data communication.
(3) LIN: the full name of LIN is Local Interconnect Network. In 2002, the first LIN bus protocol specification version V.1.3 was proposed. The biggest feature of LIN bus is that the cost is very low. In the environment where the bandwidth requirements for windows and wipers are not high, LIN bus is often used to realize data communication, which can greatly save the cost of building vehicles and improve the maintainability of vehicles to a certain extent.
(4) Central gateway: gateway is also called protocol converter. Data cannot be directly exchanged between different on-board bus protocols such as CAN, LIN, MOST and FlexRay, as well as between vehicle internal network and external network. As a "bridge", gateway is responsible for establishing interaction channels between different protocols and realizing data interaction between different protocols.

2.2 Calculate the Information Entropy of the Vehicle CAN Network Gateway

The appearance of data packets in the vehicle CAN network follows certain rules. When the car is no longer in a dormant state, the data packets in the bus are sent with certain rules. Some data packets in the in-vehicle network represent the state of the vehicle, some are sent periodically at a certain frequency, and some are only counted gateway information. When the car starts, the control information of the car will exist in the car CAN network. Therefore, in an in-vehicle CAN network, the kinds of CAN gateway information that appear in a specific vehicle state are limited.

The communication matrix of vehicle CAN bus determines the ID, transmission mode and signal mapping of CAN gateway information. The randomness of the gateway information packet in the CAN bus is far lower than that of the computer network. Under normal conditions, the gateway information in the CAN bus has a certain order, and its information entropy value should be low and stable within a certain period of time. When an attack occurs in the system, the random sequence of gateway information is disturbed, resulting in a change in the information entropy value of the CAN bus, which can be used as an indicator for detecting CAN bus anomalies.

According to the probability of gateway information in a specific time period, the information entropy of a single gateway information is calculated. According to the additivity of information entropy, the sum of information entropy of all gateways in this time period is the information entropy of the current CAN bus.

Let set B be the set of gateway information of a certain CAN bus in a period of time t, where $\{b_1, b_2, b_3, \ldots, b_n\}$ is the various gateway information that appears in the time of E, then the information entropy of the CAN bus in the time of t is:

$$H(B) = \sum_{b_i \in B} p(b_i) \log \frac{1}{p(b_i)} \tag{1}$$

where, $p(b_i), i = 1, 2, 3, \ldots, n$ represents the probability that each gateway information with different identifier b_i appears in t time.

Ideally, the period of CAN gateway information transmission is fixed, and the number of i gateway information transmitted in t time is $\frac{t}{b_i}$. Then the number of gateway information in CAN bus within t time is:

$$total = \left(\frac{t}{b_1} + \frac{t}{b_2} + \frac{t}{b_3} + \ldots + \frac{t}{b_n}\right) = t\sum_{i=1}^{n} \frac{1}{b_i} \tag{2}$$

Then the probability p of the i gateway information appearing in time t can be expressed as:

$$p(b_i) = \frac{n_i}{\text{total}} = \frac{t}{b_i} \times \frac{1}{t\sum_{i=1}^{n} \frac{1}{b_i}} = \frac{1}{b_i \sum_{i=1}^{n} \frac{1}{b_i}} \tag{3}$$

The information entropy $H(i)$ of message i is:

$$H(i) = P(b_i)I(b_i) = \frac{\log b_i \sum_{i=1}^{n} \frac{1}{b_i}}{b_i \sum_{i=1}^{n} \frac{1}{b_i}} \tag{4}$$

Then the information entropy of the CAN bus in time t is:

$$H(B) = \sum_{i=1}^{n} H_i \tag{5}$$

Then the function can be regarded as $f(x) = \frac{\log(x)}{x}$, and the function is a monotonically increasing function, that is, when new gateway information appears in the CAN gateway information, the function $f(x)$ increases and $H(B)$ also increases. That is to say, when new gateway information appears in the CAN bus, the information entropy of the CAN bus will ideally show an upward trend. Through theoretical analysis, it can be seen that the change trend of information entropy can be used as an indicator for detecting CAN bus anomalies.

2.3 Extraction of Vehicle CAN Network Gateway Information Features

In order to extract the information characteristics of automobile CAN network gateway, the structure model of vehicle CAN network database is established. The specific process is as follows:

Select the maximum value of the trust value obtained by querying the gateway information of the vehicle CAN network database at the current time, and the trust value with a long query interval has little impact on the current time, then, the time attenuation function queried by the gateway information of the CAN network database at the current time of the vehicle is:

$$f(t) = f(t-1) - \frac{1}{n} \tag{6}$$

where, $f(t-1)$ represents the attenuation function at time $t-1$, then the gateway information state equation integrated in the vehicle CAN network database at time $t-1$ can be expressed as:

$$p_i(t) = \sum_{n=1}^{N} \frac{A}{u} e^{-jkr} Q_{in} \frac{1}{u} e^{-jkr} \tag{7}$$

where, A represents the strength of the gateway information, u represents the length of the gateway information, e^{-jkr} represents the wavelength of the gateway information, and Q_{in} represents the instantaneous frequency of the gateway information generation.

According to the feedback coefficient of each storage node of the vehicle CAN network database gateway information [7], an integrated gateway information structure model is established:

$$p(y|\xi, \theta) = \sum_{t-1}^{t} \xi_t p_t(y|\delta_t, \Sigma_t) \tag{8}$$

where, ξ_k represents the scale of the gateway information, $p_k(y|\delta_k, \Sigma_k)$ represents the state prior distribution of the gateway information at the moment t, Σ_t represents the nonlinear recovery ability of the vehicle CAN network database, and δ_t represents the deviation function between the gateway information and other information points y. By setting $\{x_1, x_2, \cdots, x_N\}$ to represent the time series of the integrated gateway information in the vehicle CAN network database, and p_t represents the posterior probability estimation function of the gateway information, the composition form of the integrated gateway information in the vehicle CAN network database can be obtained:

$$p_{ij}^{n}(t) = \frac{\left[g_i(t) - g_j(t)\right]}{\sum_{j \in N} \left[g_i(t) - g_j(t)\right]} \tag{9}$$

where, $g_j(t)$ represents the occurrence probability of the t gateway information in the vehicle CAN network database with serial number j, and $g_i(t)$ represents the occurrence probability of the t gateway information in the vehicle CAN network database with serial number i.

This attribute approximately simplifies the gateway information extraction formula, resulting in:

$$E_{q\times r} = Y_{q\times U} H_{u\times u} Y^{U}_{u\times r} * p^{*}_{ij}(t) \tag{10}$$

where, $Y_{q\times U}$ represents the integrated dimension matrix, $H_{u\times u}$ represents the gateway information equilibrium probability, and $Y^{U}_{u\times r}$ represents the threshold value of the gateway information membership, and the gateway information is extracted:

$$E_n = \sum_{j=1}^{n} y_l \delta_l \tag{11}$$

where, y_l represents the number of gateway information in the vehicle CAN network, and δ_l represents the proportion of the number of gateway information in the number of vehicle CAN network databases.

2.4 Design a Complete Detection Algorithm of Vehicle CAN Network Gateway Information Based on Neural Network

In order to improve the detection effect of vehicle can network gateway [8], neural network is introduced [9], the calculation results of vehicle CAN network gateway information entropy are substituted into the neural network to detect the integrity of vehicle CAN network gateway information, and realize complete detection of vehicle CAN network gateway information with high precision and low missed detection rate. Among them, the neural network is used to process the vehicle CAN network gateway information test set, and a Bayesian probability expression is constructed to obtain the probability that the gateway information data in the vehicle CAN network belongs to a certain category. Obtain the objective function of gateway information data detection according to the probability calculation formula, calculate the prior probability value in the objective function, and use this value to complete the complete detection of vehicle CAN network gateway information.

Bayesian probability expression is constructed for each public opinion topic in the test set, and the probability that the record to be tested belongs to a certain category can be expressed as:

$$P(Category|f(t)) = \frac{P(\text{ Category }) \cdot P(f(t)| \text{ Category })}{P[f(t)]} \tag{12}$$

where, $P(Category|f(t))$ represents the probability that a record to be detected belongs to a certain category, $P(\text{ Category })$ represents the total number of vehicle CAN network gateway information data categories, $P(f(t)|\text{Category})$ represents the total number of filtered vehicle CAN network gateway information data occupying the total category, and $P[f(t)]$ represents the characteristic attribute value of vehicle CAN network gateway information data itself.

For each data record to be detected, its vector can be converted into content vector. Where the conversion expression is:

$$P(Category|f(t)) = \frac{[P(\text{Category}) \cdot P(a_{i1}, \cdots, a_{in})]}{P(a_{i1}, \cdots, a_{in})} \tag{13}$$

where, $P(a_{i1}, \cdots, a_{in})$ represents a constant sequence.

According to the calculation of formula (7), construct the objective function:

$$F_n = \text{argmax} P(Category) \cdot P(a_{i1}, \cdots, a_{in}) \tag{14}$$

According to the assumption of naive Bayes, the values of the internal component vectors of each record are independent of each other, so the joint probability is the product of the probabilities of each component. Therefore, the ultimate objective function expression is determined by the maximum value formula:

$$F_n = \text{argmax} P(Category) \prod P(a_{in} | \, Category) \tag{15}$$

where, $(a_{in} | \, Category)$ represents the prior probability of the training sample. The prior probability value can effectively improve the information data detection performance of the vehicle CAN network gateway. It can be obtained by using the statistics of the occurrence probability of each information data category in the training set:

$$P(a_{in} | \, Category) = \frac{\text{Frequency(Category)}}{\sum \text{Category}} \tag{16}$$

where, Frequency(Category) represents the number of occurrences of a certain data category, and $\sum$ Category represents the total number of samples in the training set.

Using formula (10), the classification results of positive and negative information data in the vehicle CAN network gateway information data can be obtained. Among them, the detection result of vehicle CAN network gateway information data can be expressed as:

$$S_n = \frac{P(a_{in} | \, \text{Category)}}{\sum \text{Category}} \tag{17}$$

where, S_n represents the detection result of vehicle CAN network gateway information data based on neural network.

So far, the design of a complete information detection method for vehicle can network gateway based on neural network has been completed. In the age of the Internet of Things and artificial intelligence [10], the difference between this method and the traditional method is that it introduces neural network algorithm, and on the basis of this method, it combines the structural model of vehicle can network database to extract information features, and combines information entropy. The combination of various methods improves the detection performance and accuracy, It has the advantages of many methods at the same time.

3 Experimental Analysis

3.1 Build the Experimental Environment

In the experiment, a real car of a certain brand was used as the experimental object, and Vehicle-Spy was used as the experimental tool to collect, send and analyze data.

Fig. 2. ValueCAN3

The hardware transceiver is ValueCAN3, which is the supporting hardware device of Vehicle-Spy. ValueCAN3 is shown in Fig. 2. The OBD interface end has two CAN interfaces, which can read the data of two CAN buses in the car at the same time, and the other end is connected to the PC The machine is connected via the USB port.

Find the CAN bus interface of the OBD-II port of the car with a multimeter and measure the car. Terminals 9 and 11 are one CAN bus, and terminals 6 and 12 are another CAN bus. Connect the vehicle OBD and ValueCAN3 through the OBD-II transfer interface, and connect the ValueCAN3 to the computer USB interface to complete the experimental connection.

When the vehicle is not started, run Vehicle-Spy and match the speed of the on-board CAN bus. After the matching is successful, you can view the received data in the data receiving interface. Since the experiment is connected to the two-way CAN bus of OBD-II at the same time, the data of SM CAN (low-speed CAN) and HS CAN (high-speed) CAN lines can be received in real time.

3.2 Calibration Test Indicators

According to the detection model established in the abnormal detection and calibration stage, the vehicle static state is taken as the detection state, and the information entropy of the vehicle CAN bus network in this state is calculated. Taking HS CAN as the detection object, the data collected from the HS CAN line is analyzed and collected as the data source.

By calculating about 50000 pieces of data collected randomly in the vehicle, it can be counted that there are 8 different ID data in the data source. The information entropy of different ids is calculated according to the information entropy calculation formula. The calculation results are shown in Table 1.

Table 1. Information entropy in normal state

ID	Number of occurrences	Frequency (p = number of times/50000)	Information entropy (p*log(1/p))
212	14216	0.28388	0.515868792
430	14221	0.28362	0.515836567
433	139	0.00296	0.024027097
612	1947	0.04900	0.182554901
619	1339	0.02728	0.140241744
627	1338	0.02684	0.140242644
431	16789	0.34190	0.528672768
			H (E) = 2.04744445

The results in Table 1 show that in this time period, the information entropy of HS CAN is about 2.047411511.

In order to analyze the influence of different detection time intervals on the information entropy of the vehicle CAN network gateway, the vehicle CAN network gateway information was collected at time intervals of 15s, 10s, 5s, 3s, 1s, and 0.5s, and 20 time slices were selected for each time interval., according to the calculation method in Table 1, calculate the information entropy value of the vehicle CAN network gateway in each time slice, and the calculation results are shown in Table 2.

Table 2. Information entropy at different time intervals

	15s	10s	5s	3s	1s	0.5s
1	2.052	2.051	2.049	2.050	2.052	2.062
2	2.043	2.043	2.045	2.044	2.052	2.030
3	2.051	2.043	2.049	2.050	2.040	2.062
4	2.044	2.051	2.045	2.045	2.052	2.030
5	2.052	2.051	2.049	2.050	2.040	2.062
6	2.052	2.043	2.046	2.050	2.040	2.062
7	2.043	2.043	2.046	2.045	2.052	2.030
8	2.052	2.051	2.049	2.045	2.040	2.062
9	2.043	2.051	2.049	2.050	2.052	2.030
10	2.043	2.043	2.045	2.050	2.040	2.062
11	2.052	2.051	2.045	2.044	2.040	2.030

(*continued*)

Table 2. *(continued)*

	15s	10s	5s	3s	1s	0.5s
12	2.052	2.043	2.049	2.044	2.052	2.030
13	2.044	2.043	2.049	2.050	2.052	2.062
14	2.044	2.051	2.045	2.044	2.040	2.062
15	2.052	2.051	2.045	2.050	2.052	2.030
16	2.043	2.043	2.049	2.044	2.040	2.030
17	2.043	2.043	2.049	2.044	2.052	2.062
18	2.052	2.051	2.046	2.050	2.040	2.030
19	2.043	2.043	2.049	2.050	2.052	2.062
20	2.052	2.051	2.046	2.044	2.040	2.030

The information entropy changes in Table 2 are shown in the figure. The information entropy values at different detection times under normal conditions are shown in Fig. 3.

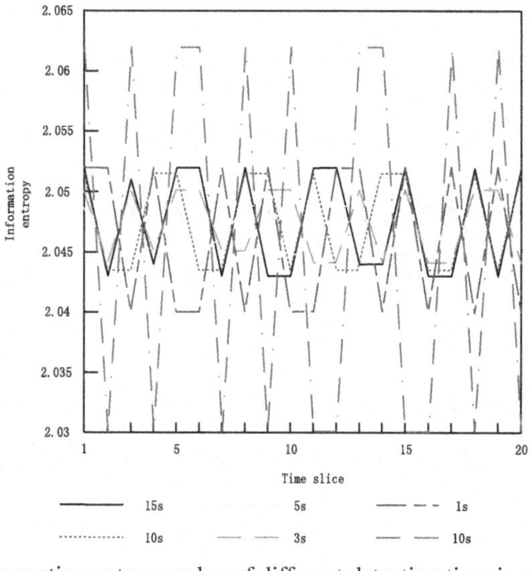

Fig. 3. Information entropy value of different detection time in normal state

It can be seen from Fig. 3 that the information entropy of the vehicle CAN network gateway always fluctuates within a certain range regardless of the value of the time interval, indicating that the information entropy of the vehicle CAN network gateway is maintained at a relatively stable value under normal conditions.

When the detection time is 3s and 5s, the fluctuation range of the curve is the smallest, and the information entropy value of the vehicle CAN network gateway is the most stable. When the detection time is 15s, 10s, and 1s, the results are not stable enough compared to the detection results of 3s and 5s, however, the results were much more stable than those of 0.5s interval.

It can be seen from the figure that when T is 0.5s, the information entropy of the vehicle CAN network gateway fluctuates greatly, indicating that the frequency of some gateway information in the vehicle CAN network bus is greater than 0.5s. When the detection time interval is 0.5s, the time length is not enough. Covering the complete cycle of the gateway information increases the entropy of the vehicle CAN network gateway information. By counting the information entropy of the vehicle CAN network gateway calculated at different time intervals T, the maximum entropy value, the minimum entropy value, the average entropy value and the maximum and minimum information entropy difference of the vehicle CAN network bus in different time intervals can be obtained. The information entropy statistical results are as follows: shown in Table 3.

Table 3. Information entropy statistical results

Time interval	Maximum entropy value	Minimum entropy value	Average entropy	Entropy difference
15s	2.052	2.043	2.0476	0.009
10s	2.051	2.043	2.047	0.008
5s	2.049	2.045	2.0472	0.004
3s	2.050	2.044	2.04715	0.006
1s	2.052	2.040	2.046	0.012
0.5s	2.062	2.030	2.046	0.032

It can be seen from the data in Table 3 that the value of information entropy fluctuates greatly at 0.5s and 1s. Considering that too short detection time T will increase the pressure on the system to process data, 0.5s and 1s can be temporarily omitted. The time interval between 15s and 10s is long. When a short-time attack attacks the vehicle CAN network gateway information, it is easy to cause insensitivity to short-time attack detection. It can be seen that when the time interval T is 5s or 3s, the information entropy of the CAN bus is the most stable, so 5s or 3s is used as the reference detection time interval. When an attack is detected with 5s as the time interval T, the change range of information entropy is between 2.049 and 2.045. This range is taken as the threshold range of information entropy detection. When the CAN bus information entropy is detected to be beyond this range in the static state of the vehicle, it CAN be determined that the current can bus is abnormal.

3.3 Analysis of Results

Edit a new gateway information to conduct a car attack experiment, and still choose to analyze the attack detection effect in the static state of the car. In the gateway information sending interface, edit a piece of CAN gateway information that does not exist in the car, its ID is set to 101 with a higher priority, the data field is set to the length of 8 fields, and sent to the car CAN bus at a fixed frequency of 0.05s data. The attack durations are 10s, 5s, 3s, 1s, and 0.5s respectively, and the corresponding information entropy values are stored and calculated at different time intervals T on the data receiving interface. The information entropy measured with different detection times is shown in Table 4.

Table 4. Information entropy of different attack durations

	15s	10s	5s	3s	1s	0.5s
10s	2.64	2.64				
5s	2.58	2.63	2.61			
3s	2.47	2.54	2.60	2.62		
1s	2.32	2.47	2.48	2.51	2.62	
0.5s	2.24	2.34	2.37	2.46	2.49	2.62
0.3s	2.12	2.15	2.32	2.35	2.43	2.57
0.1s	2.05	2.09	2.19	2.26	2.36	2.43

The results in Table 4 are shown in a graph. The change of information entropy is different under different attack duration and different detection time, as shown in Fig. 4.

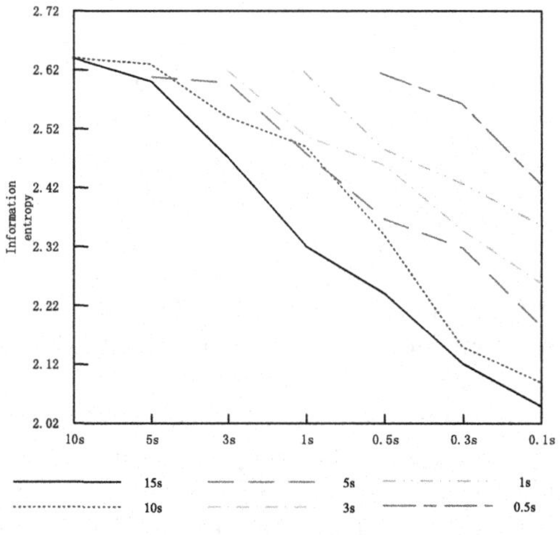

Fig. 4. Information entropy value under different attack duration and detection time

The solid line in Fig. 4 shows the maximum information entropy of CAN bus measured at different detection time intervals under normal conditions.

It can be seen from Fig. 4 that when attacking the car bus, under different attack durations and different detection times, the value of bus information entropy increases significantly, and compared with the maximum information entropy value under normal conditions, when encountering an attack, the information entropy of the CAN bus changes greatly, and the abnormality of the vehicle CAN bus can be effectively detected by detecting the change of the information entropy. And the shorter the detection time, the greater the difference between the information entropy value and the normal value, which is more conducive to the abnormal detection of the CAN bus. It can be seen from Fig. 4–10 that when the detection time interval T is 15 s and the intrusion time is 0.1 s, the CAN bus is The information entropy value is reduced to 2.0500, which is already in the normal information entropy threshold range. At this time, the system will not detect the abnormality of the bus. When the detection time interval T is 10s and the intrusion time is 0.1s, although the information entropy of the CAN bus does not enter the normal information entropy value range, it is very close to the normal information entropy range of the CAN bus, which is easy to cause the system to leak. This also verifies that the abnormal detection time interval should not be selected too long, but since it does not reach the normal range, the detection method determines that it is an abnormal state and effectively determines the attack.

4 Conclusion

In order to improve the completeness of vehicle CAN network gateway information and avoid information leakage, this paper proposes a complete detection method of vehicle CAN network gateway information based on neural network. This detection method introduces the neural network to construct the detection method, and before the construction, the information feature extraction and information entropy algorithm are constructed, which improves the effect of feature extraction and the determination of information entropy, so that the detection effect of the detection method based on neural network is better. Through the experimental test, it is found that this method can detect whether the CAN bus is abnormal at the time intervals of 15s, 10s, 5S, 3S, 1s and 0.5s, and the judgment result is accurate. It has certain feasibility in detecting the information of vehicle can network gateway. Although the research in this paper verifies the feasibility of fully detecting detecting the vehicle CAN network gateway information, the method still needs to be improved. In the real vehicle environment, the vehicle CAN network has many different states, and its state changes are many and complex. This paper proposed detection method can not cover all the complex states of the car. In the subsequent research, various states of vehicles are modeled and analyzed to achieve the purpose of applying the detection method to any state of the vehicles and improve the applicability of the detection method.

References

1. Yao, S., Xiaoni, W., Peng, L., et al.: Node authentication and encrypted communication mechanism for automotive CAN bus. Modern Electronics Technique **44**(9), 6–11 (2021)
2. Zhongwei, L., Kai, T., Yadong, G., et al.: In-vehicle CAN bus-off attack and its intrusion detection algorithm. J. Computer Appl. **40**(11), 3224–3228 (2020)
3. Li, F., Wu, X.: Intelligent network communication terminal information security simulation method. Computer Simulation **37**(5), 86-90 (2020)
4. Yu Tianqi, H., Jianling, J.J., et al.: Mobile EDGE computing based In-vehicle CAN network intrusion detection method. Computer Science **48**(1), 34–39 (2021)

5. Ming, S., Lingshan, C., Junjie, W., et al.: Abnormity detection method for In-vehicle CAN bus based on One-Class SVM. Automobile Technol. **5**, 21–25 (2020)
6. Wang, F., Chen, Y.: Vehicle rollover propensity detection based on a mass-center-position metric: a continuous and completed method. IEEE Trans. Vehicular Technol. **68**(9), 8652–8662 (2019)
7. Nannan, P., Yihuai, W., Wei, D., et al.: Design of CAN bus communication module in lithium battery management system based on MKE06Z64 chip. Chinese J. Power Sources **43**(5), 873–876 (2019)
8. Jiangpei, X., Jin, W., Chang, L., et al.: Security detection of CAN bus protocol for electric vehicle and charging pile. J. Shandong University (Natural Science) **55**(5), 95–104 (2020)
9. Xiaowei, W., Shoulin, Y., Hang, L., et al.: A network intrusion detection method based on deep multi-scale convolutional neural network. Int. J. Wireless Inf. Networks **27**(4), 503–517 (2020)
10. Liu,S., et al.: Human memory update strategy: a multi-layer template update mechanism for remote visual monitoring. IEEE Trans. Multimedia **23**, 2188–2198 (2021)

Optimization of Data Transmission Efficiency of Wireless Communication Network for Chemical Energy Monitoring

Chengmi Xiang(✉)

Xi'an Kedagaoxin University, Xi'an 710100, China
XM18292169558@163.com

Abstract. Due to the large amount of data in the wireless communication network, and the data transmission is easily affected by environmental factors, resulting in low data transmission efficiency. In order to reduce the data transmission delay and packet loss rate of wireless communication network and improve the data transmission efficiency, an optimization method of data transmission efficiency of wireless communication network for chemical energy monitoring is designed. In chemical energy monitoring, a perfect HTTP traffic model is established to simulate the data traffic behavior in the existing real monitoring process, so as to design a multicast wireless resource scheduling algorithm to implement wireless communication network data resource scheduling. Combined with the scheduling structure, an optimization model for data transmission efficiency of wireless communication network for chemical energy monitoring is established. The model can select the best link according to the different user experience requirements of upper layer applications and the current network environment. It can deal with the network interruption caused by network switching and realize the optimization of data transmission efficiency. The experimental results show that this method achieves low data transmission delay and packet loss rate in wireless communication network, and improves the data transmission efficiency.

Keywords: Chemical energy monitoring · Wireless communication network · HTTP traffic model · Data transmission efficiency optimization

1 Introduction

The energy problem is one of the three major problems in the world today, and is highly valued by all countries in the world. With the rapid advancement of the global industrialization process, all kinds of fossil fuels that human beings rely on will be exhausted, and the supply of oil, coal, natural gas, etc. will be exhausted, and the energy crisis is an unavoidable development trend [1]. The energy-saving work of the western market economy countries originated from the oil crisis caused by the Middle East war in 1973. Under the influence of the oil crisis, the western countries put energy conservation on the government's important agenda, and introduced various energy policies to improve energy utilization efficiency. Worldwide energy conservation efforts can be divided into two phases:

Y. Xu et al. (Eds.): ML4CS 2022, LNCS 13657, pp. 91–105, 2023.
https://doi.org/10.1007/978-3-031-20102-8_8

(1) From 1973 to the end of 1980s, countries around the world attached great importance to energy security due to the oil crisis. The main goal of this energy conservation campaign is to save energy, improve energy utilization, stabilize long-term energy supply, and meet the needs of national economic development [2].
(2) From the early 1990s to the present, marked by the "United Nations Environment and Development" conference held in Rio de Janeiro, Brazil in 1992, the "Framework Convention on Climate Change" was adopted at the conference, and the "Kyoto Protocol" was formed at the Kyoto Conference in Japan in 1997. Due to the deterioration of the ecological environment such as El Niño and global warming, the awareness of global green environmental protection has been raised. The goal of this energy-saving campaign is to save energy, reduce the release of greenhouse gases, promote sustainable development, and improve the living environment.

Industrial energy conservation is the top priority of energy conservation. Industrial energy consumption in the world generally accounts for about one third of the total energy consumption. In developed countries, such as Japan, Germany, France, the United Kingdom, the United States, Canada, Australia, etc., in order to solve the problem of rational energy use in industrial sectors and improve the efficiency of industrial energy use, remarkable achievements have been made in energy conservation and consumption reduction from various aspects, including the establishment of laws and regulations related to industrial energy conservation, the strengthening of energy supervision over high-energy consuming industrial enterprises, and the development of new energy conservation technologies, widely promote energy-saving products.

The rapid economic growth has brought huge material wealth, but at the same time, my country's economic growth has shown more and more obvious characteristics of high consumption and strong dependence on energy. The sector with the largest energy consumption, accounting for nearly 70% of energy consumption, is facing increasingly serious problems of energy demand and energy scarcity. My country attaches great importance to energy conservation and consumption reduction. The Outline of the Twelfth Five-Year Plan for National Economic and Social Development states: "Strengthen energy conservation management in key energy-consuming units." "Comprehensive Work Plan" (Guo Fa (2011) No. 26 document), it is pointed out: "By 2015, the national energy consumption per 10,000 yuan of GDP will be reduced to 0.869 tons of standard coal (calculated at the price in 2005), which is lower than that in 2010. During the 12th Five-Year Plan period, 670 million tons of standard coal have been saved." The 12th Five-Year Plan for Energy Conservation and Emission Reduction (2011–2015)" put forward a detailed goal: "By 2015, the energy consumption per unit of industrial added value (above scale) will be reduced by about 21% compared with 2010, and the proportion of the unit energy consumption indicators of major products (workload) reaching advanced energy-saving standards will be greatly increased, some industries and large and medium-sized enterprises have reached the world's advanced level of energy-saving indicators.

With the increasing pressure of energy conservation and emission reduction, the accuracy of energy conservation and emission reduction data is a major problem that has existed for a long time and needs to be solved urgently. Accurate and comprehensive energy conservation and emission reduction monitoring data is the basis of the entire energy conservation and emission reduction work. The "Twelfth Five-Year Plan for Industrial Energy Conservation" further proposes five safeguard measures. Among them, "Strengthening Industrial Energy Conservation Management" points out: establish an industrial energy conservation monitoring and early warning system, and step by step to promote the national, provincial, city (county) three-level industrial Construction of energy-saving monitoring system. The Implementation Plan for Strengthening Energy Conservation in Beijing further proposes to strengthen energy statistical monitoring and establish a city-wide energy conservation statistical system and energy conservation monitoring platform. The problem of energy consumption monitoring has been elevated to a strategic level, and the successful construction of an industrial enterprise energy consumption monitoring system has many advantages, such as promoting the development of the energy conservation and environmental protection service industry and ensuring the value of monitoring data [3]. Energy consumption monitoring is an indispensable preliminary work for enterprise energy-saving technological transformation, an important means to strengthen and urge enterprises to save energy and reduce consumption, and the basis for the formulation of national energy-saving measurement standards and the unification of testing standards. The establishment of an industrial energy consumption monitoring system must become the main task in the strategic deployment of energy conservation and emission reduction.

In the construction of industrial energy consumption monitoring system, the construction of wireless communication network for chemical energy monitoring is an important link. However, the traditional wireless communication network data transmission efficiency optimization method has the problems of high data transmission delay, high packet loss rate and low data transmission efficiency, and an optimization method of data transmission efficiency of wireless communication network is designed.

2 Optimization of Data Transmission Efficiency of Wireless Communication Network

2.1 Flow Model Design

In chemical energy monitoring, a perfect HTTP traffic model is established to simulate the data traffic behavior of existing real monitoring applications.

In order to establish a perfect HTTP traffic model, the existing mobile applications are classified according to the traffic characteristics of various monitoring applications, and a typical application is selected from each category for simulation. The classification is shown in Table 1 [4].

Table 1. Classification of typical monitoring mobile applications

Serial number	Monitoring application type	Data transmission flow characteristics
1	Always in class	RRC state switching generates a large amount of control signaling
2	Streaming audio and video	Large data flow, occupying independent channel resources for a long time
3	Download class	Large data flow and large network bandwidth
4	Mixed class	Mixed voice and browsing traffic characteristics

In order to describe the traffic behavior of different service types in detail, the configuration file method is adopted. The simulated traffic generator can simulate and generate HTTP data traffic of different service types by reading different configuration files.

Define Group as the basic unit of the traffic model. Each Group has a unique number and contains all HTTP requests corresponding to a specific user behavior. Each typical application is a combination of multiple user behaviors, that is, a group of Groups can describe the traffic behavior of a typical application. Therefore the configuration file is designed as a secondary mode. The first-level configuration file sets a single Group traffic model, and records all HTTP requests generated by the user behavior in detail through fields such as time, dependency flag, URI, total length of the request header, and additional attributes. The secondary configuration file is set to a combination of Groups, describing the traffic behavior of a typical application [5].

The field settings of the primary configuration file are shown in Table 2.

Table 2. Level 1 configuration file field settings

Serial number	Field	Explain
1	Response length	The length of the response returned by the request
2	Additional attributes	Properties in the request header to be set
3	Request body length	Request body length of post request
4	Total length of request header	Total length of request header, excluding request body
5	Method	Get or post
6	URI	Resource path
7	Dependency request number	Request sequence number that depends on the request

(*continued*)

Table 2. (*continued*)

Serial number	Field	Explain
8	Dependency flag	A value of −1 indicates that it does not depend on the response returned by any precursor request. Otherwise, it indicates the request number corresponding to the dependent response. That is, it can be sent only after receiving the response returned by the request
9	Time	The sending time of each request is set to −1 if the request depends on the response returned by the predecessor request

The secondary configuration file is used to set the comprehensive traffic model of each Group, and the field settings are shown in Table 3.

Table 3. Field settings of the secondary configuration file

Serial number	Field	Explain
1	Group number	Specify the group number to send
2	Time	Send time

The generation of the traffic model is done through the following steps:

(1) Use the smart terminal to simulate the user's behavior of using the monitoring application, and use the mobile phone packet capture software Shark to capture packets in this process to obtain the pcap file corresponding to this behavior.
(2) Parse the pcap file, analyze all HTP requests and responses contained in the file, and store them.
(3) Extract the corresponding parameters in the HTTP request and response and save them in the file, that is, get the first level of a certain behavior [6].
(4) Combine the Group files corresponding to an application to obtain a secondary configuration file and generate the traffic model of a typical application.

Key steps (2) and (3) are described in detail below.

There is 1 Pcap file header and multiple data packets in a Pcap file, each of which has its own data packet header and data packet content Pcap file header is 24 bytes, each data packet header is 16 bytes, followed by the data immediately following the packet.

The meaning of each field in the Pcap file header is:

(1) Magic is the file identification header, and pcap is fixed as: 0xA1B2C3D4. (4 bytes);
(2) Magor version is the main version number (2 bytes);
(3) Minor version is the minor version number (2 bytes);

(4) Timezone is the local standard time (4 bytes);
(5) Sigflags is the precision of the timestamp (4 bytes);
(6) Snaplen is the maximum storage length (4 bytes);
(7) Linktype is the link type (4 bytes);
(8) Each data packet of the Pcap file is a Packet, and each Packet consists of a Packet header and Packet data. The Packet header is 16 bytes, and the fields included are as follows:

(1) Timestamp: The timestamp is high, accurate to seconds;
(2) Timestamp: The low bit of the timestamp, accurate to micoscns;
(3) Caplen: The length of the data area, which can be used to calculate the position of the next data frame.
(4) Len: Offline data length, the length of the actual data frame in the network.
(5) Packet data: The specific content of the Packet (usually the data frame of the link layer), and the length is the size of the Caplen in the packet header. What is stored after the length of Caplen is the next Packet data packet in the PCAP file, that is to say: each Packet data packet in the Pcap file is not distinguished by the interval string, and the starting position of the next group of data in the file needs to be at the front. A Packet is ok. The format of the packet data part is in accordance with the standard protocol format of Ethernet frame, IP packet, TCP packet, etc. [7].

The parsing process of Pcap file is as follows:

(1) Read pcap file:
After reading a pcap file, extract the file header (the first 24 bytes) information of the Pcap file according to the format of the Pcap file header.
The pcap file header is followed by frame by frame packets. Each packet is divided into two parts: packet header and packet content. The contents of the packet can be determined according to the packet capture length in the packet header (the contents of the cap_len length from the packet header are the packet contents). In this way, the contents of all packages can be read out package by package. And store the contents of the packet in Raw_packets.
(2) Obtain pcap_packets from raw_ packets:
A raw_packets is just the 01 data of an Ethernet frame. According to the data format of the Ethernet frame, IP packet, and TCP packet, the specific information of these layers can be extracted in turn, and the objects of these three layers can be abstracted into pcap_packet. Object, and then group pcap_packets into an array of pcap_packets in order.
(3) There are recombined TCP packets to get HTTP packets:
MsS (maximum segment sizc) will be negotiated during TCP connection, which is generally 1460 bytes. If this size is exceeded, TCP packets need to be segmented. After the TCP packet is segmented and transmitted through the network, disorder, duplication, loss, etc. may occur. At this time, the TCP packet needs to be reassembled to obtain a complete http packet [8].
Because a Sockets (a set of IP, port pairs) intelligently uniquely identifies a TCP connection, and for TCP packets belonging to the same HTTP packet, their acks are the same. Therefore, sockets and ack are used together as a reassembly standard.

Among them, _tcp_buf stores tcp packets that have not been reassembled. If the ack of the tcp packet to be processed is the same as that of the TCP packet in _cp_buf, it will be placed in the same position pointed to by sockets in _tcp_buf, and the order will be arranged according to seq. When a different ack message arrives for the same socket, it means that the previous HTTP has been reorganized, and it is added to the http_list. Msg list and http_list are in one-to-one correspondence, and msg_list stores detailed information of an http package.

(4) Analyze the http package to get the http class object

The parsing steps of HTTP message are as follows:

An HTTP message is divided into http_header and http_content is divided into two parts by "/r/n/r/n"; Take an HTTP message as a string and segment "r/n/r/n" to get http_header and http_content two parts; Then to htp_ The header is divided by "/r/n" to get http_header the contents of each line.

http_header parsing:

(1) Determine whether it is http request or http response:
If the content of the first line of the http message is GET URI HTTP/1.1, it is an http request; if the content is HTTP/1.1 status_code status, it is an http response.
(2) Information carried by the http header:
The headers are all in the format of key: Use the split function to divide the ":", and then store it in a dictionary according to the key. Use a dictionary header_fields to store this information. It should be noted that the key needs to be converted to lowercase. Prevent some webpage headers from being irregular.
(3) Whether the content in the response has been compressed.

Judging the content-encoding field in the header (two values: deflate and gzip), if it is deflate, it is not compressed, and the content content can be processed directly. If it is gzip, it is compressed by gzip, and the content needs to be decompressed. Process the content. At this point, the work of analyzing the pcap file is completed, and the HTTP data obtained by the above process will be used as the basic data generated by the configuration file.

Through the parsing of the Pcap file parsing module, all HTTP requests are saved in a list. By traversing each request in the list, you can extract the time, url, method, header length, body length, response length and header change information respectively, and store them in the format of the configuration file to generate a level-1 configuration file. In addition, there are dependencies between HTTP requests. In many cases, the application receives a request response and finds that it needs to initiate more requests after parsing. Then these initiated requests depend on the response of the first request. This dependency is represented by a dependency field in the configuration file. The method to determine the dependency is as follows: in the process of parsing HTTP requests from front to back, record the links included in the response returned by each request. In the process of parsing subsequent requests, compare the URL of the request with the previously recorded links. If there is the same, it means that the request depends on the response returned by a previous request, and record this dependency in the configuration file.

According to the above steps, the flow model is generated. The main categories used are as follows:

Rd_pcap class, reads and parses the Pcap file and decomposes each data packet. The main functions are explained as follows:

rd_peapcap_file_name

Function description: Open the pcap file, decompose it according to the above steps, and get the following three data structures:

Pcap_header: the file header of the Pcap file;

Packet_headers: an array that stores the packet headers in order;

Raw_packets: An array that stores the contents of the data packets in order (excluding the header) one-to-one correspondence with the above data packet headers.

The Protocol class is the parent class of each protocol implementation class. It defines a function to convert the String stored in decimal to hexadecimal, which is used by the Ethernet class, IP class and other protocol implementation classes when analyzing fields.

The Ethernet class, which inherits the Protocol class, implements the parsing of Ethernet frames and the storage of data.

2.2 Radio Resource Scheduling

In wireless network transmission, wireless network resources are in RB units. In LTE, transmission is divided according to time and divided into each frame transmission. One LTE frame is divided into 10 LTE subframes, one frame is 10 ms, and one subframe is 1 ms. At the same time, a subframe is further divided into two time slots, and one slot is 0.5 ms. Since LTE uses OFDM technology, each symbol corresponds to an orthogonal sub-carrier, and the orthogonality of the carrier is used to counteract the interference between cells or noise. In the frequency domain, one subcarrier is 15 kHz. The definition of RB is composed of the concept of time-frequency two domains, that is, one slot in time and 12 subcarriers in frequency, which are called one radio resource block RB. The radio resource scheduler in the eNB uses RBs as resources to allocate radio resources to each UE.

At present, there are many scheduling algorithms for wireless resources, among which RR polling algorithm and PF proportional fairness algorithm are well-known. The polling algorithm provides services for the UE in the cell in turn for the eNB scheduler, and assigns RB to each UE in turn to ensure that each user can get services. However, this resource scheduling algorithm does not consider the specific situation of the user's wireless channel and will not achieve excellent system throughput. The principle of RR polling algorithm is to ensure the fairness of users at the expense of system throughput, which is usually regarded as the upper bound of time fairness. Since each resource scheduling has nothing to do with the previous scheduling results, the RR polling algorithm is memoryless. PF scheduling algorithm is a scheduling algorithm with memory, which takes into account the fairness of users and system throughput, and is a compromise between the two. The PF scheduling algorithm calculates the priority of each user for each RB. The priority of the user is determined by the ratio of the instantaneous rate that the current RB can generate on the current user to the average historical throughput of the user. The higher the current instantaneous rate, the lower the average historical throughput, the higher the priority of the user, and the higher the probability of sharing RB resource blocks. As the name suggests, the proportional fairness algorithm ensures the fairness of each user in a certain proportion, but it also takes into account the current channel state of the user and ensures that the throughput of the system is in a relatively good state. Therefore, PF scheduling algorithm is the mainstream wireless resource scheduling algorithm at present.

However, in the multicast transmission system, the scheduling algorithm is different from that of the unicast system. Because multicast transmission only needs to consume one radio resource to provide multicast services for all multicast users, the allocation of multicast radio resources is rarely involved in multicast transmission. However, in our transmission optimization scheme, multiple multicast groups need to be involved, and multicast radio resources need to be allocated to multiple multicast groups, so a multicast radio resource scheduling and allocation algorithm is needed to allocate radio resources to each multicast group resource. The flow of the multicast radio resource scheduling algorithm we designed is as follows. The MBMS-GW sends the multicast data to the eNB of each SFN cell, and the multicast radio resource scheduler in the MCE multicast transmission synchronization entity is based on the worst UE of each multicast group. Channel resources allocate RBs to each multicast group, and then deliver the multicast radio resource allocation result to each eNB in the SFN domain, and then the eNB performs corresponding allocation actions. As mentioned above, the wireless air interface resources are in units of RBs and have a certain number. A reasonable and efficient multicast wireless resource scheduling algorithm can improve the transmission efficiency of the system. Since multicast scheduling is different from unicast scheduling, a multicast group only needs to consume one wireless resource, so the resource scheduling for multicast transmission is actually the scheduling for multicast groups. Combined with the PF proportional fair scheduling algorithm in the unicast system, the following multicast radio resource scheduling algorithm is designed.

(1) If there is only one multicast group in the current SFN domain, allocate all multicast radio resources to the multicast group;
(2) When the number M of multicast groups m in the SFN domain is greater than or equal to 2, perform the following steps in combination with the PF scheduling algorithm.

Calculate the current data transmission rate V_i that can be generated on each multicast group for each RB. The data transmission rate of the multicast group is determined by the user with the worst channel quality in the multicast group. The lower the channel quality, the higher the corresponding MCS selection. Low, the lower the rate that each RB can generate;

Calculate the average throughput W_i of each multicast group in the past period of time;

Take the following formula as the judgment criterion.

$$p = \frac{2V_i}{W_i} \tag{1}$$

In formula (1), p refers to the data transmission bandwidth [9].

Prioritize each multicast group by p, and assign RB to the largest multicast group;

When the number of RBs allocated to a multicast group is sufficient to satisfy the current data transmission, the multicast group no longer participates in resource allocation;

Repeat the above steps until all multicast wireless resource allocations are exhausted or all multicast groups have sufficient wireless resources.

2.3 Data Transmission Efficiency Optimization

A wireless communication network data transmission efficiency optimization model for chemical energy monitoring is designed. This model can select the best link for the application according to the different user experience requirements of the upper-layer application and the current network environment, and can also deal with the network interruption caused by network switching. Model students should design and implement the following design goals.

(1) Ensure the user experience of different types of applications through intelligent link selection. The designed model should be flexible and must be able to adapt to diverse user experience requirements. The model should be able to adapt to the dynamically changing network environment and implement fine-grained link selection strategy. Link selection should be application granularity rather than terminal granularity. For example, traffic of different applications on the same terminal should be allocated to different interfaces to ensure user experience of different applications.
(2) Seamless and efficient network exception handling. When network exceptions occur, the model should be able to seamlessly and quickly recover from network exceptions, and should not add additional development burden to the application developers.
(3) Compatible with existing systems and application interfaces. The model must be compatible with existing operating systems and programming interfaces. At the same time, the deployment of this model does not want to modify the existing application interface, operating system kernel, or network infrastructure.
(4) Adapt to a variety of network exceptions. In reality, network anomalies can be divided into long disconnection and short disconnection according to the duration. A short disconnect is defined as a short interruption that occurs when a network is quickly switched from one network to another. The long broken chain is defined as the long-term network interruption caused by the complete loss of the network. The system should be able to automatically handle short chain breaks, and notify the user of long chain breaks that are difficult to recover [11].

In general, the model runs in the form of system services in practical applications, located between the application and the operating system, and selects the best wireless link for different applications according to real-time network conditions and application types. In order to achieve the above design goals, the model mainly includes three parts. The application adaptive strategy, the link selector and the local flow manager, which reasonably, fully and intelligently utilize the lower-layer network interface to ensure the user experience of the upper-layer application.

The model designs an application-granularity adaptive strategy to describe the user experience requirements of different applications. At the same time, the model provides users with a customizable interactive interface through a visual graphical interface, which is used to set the user experience requirements of the application. The design of the adaptive strategy follows the following principles [12].

(1) The designed adaptive strategy must cover a variety of application types, such as delay sensitive applications, bandwidth sensitive applications, etc.;
(2) The adaptive strategy should be adapted to the different states of the application. For example, the same application may run in the foreground or background;
(3) The user interface of the adaptive strategy should be simple and easy to use.

In order to be applicable to many types of applications, the model designs three types of adaptive strategies.

(1) The traffic sensitive strategy is used to optimize the wireless network traffic overhead of the application. This strategy is suitable for delay insensitive applications.
(2) The delay sensitive strategy is used to optimize the user perceived delay and is suitable for real-time interactive applications.
(3) Bandwidth intensive applications are used to optimize the network bandwidth available to applications, and are suitable for applications such as streaming media. For each policy, the model allows users to set performance requirements (defined as high, medium and low levels) to control the performance requirements of traffic, delay and bandwidth [10].

In the actual running process, the model will monitor various status information, such as network type, network connection, application running in the foreground or background, etc. The model monitors various states of the current model through an environment monitoring module. The monitoring uses the network status listener, which is used to monitor the real-time status information of all currently available networks.

The link selection algorithm used in the model is as follows.

In principle, the link selection shall meet the following three principles.

(1) The link switching delay introduced by the algorithm should be as low as possible.
(2) Since link handoff always brings fixed overhead or loss, the algorithm should not be too sensitive to the accidental decline of link quality to avoid frequent handoff.

As for the second principle, consider the following situation: when the equipment accidentally experiences a very short-term link signal dip, signal interference, etc. during the user's movement, the more appropriate approach should be to maintain the current connection and do not switch the interface, rather than immediately switch to another interface.

In order to satisfy the first principle, a pre-switching threshold T, which is slightly higher than the value P_R is designed, which can be expressed by the following formula.

$$Thb = 2(1+\alpha) * P_R \tag{2}$$

α in formula (2) refers to a positive number.

The design reasons are as follows: in practice, there is a hardware delay of 1–3 s from opening an interface to its actual use. In order to reduce the switching delay, a solution that is easy to think of is to always open the two interfaces at the same time, but this obviously introduces a large energy consumption overhead. At this point, the pre-switching threshold T we set comes into play.

To satisfy the second principle, the pre-handover threshold can come into play again. When the performance is lower than T for the first time, the model does not immediately perform the interface switching operation, but starts a Timer and starts timing; if within the set threshold time period, the performance of the current interface satisfies the following formula.

$$W_E < T \tag{3}$$

In formula (3), W_E refers to the performance of the current interface.

Then switch to the standby interface. Due to the buffer mechanism of time threshold, this method can reduce the sensitivity of the model to the low-quality performance of the link.

The optimization process of data transmission efficiency of wireless communication network for chemical energy monitoring is shown in Fig. 1.

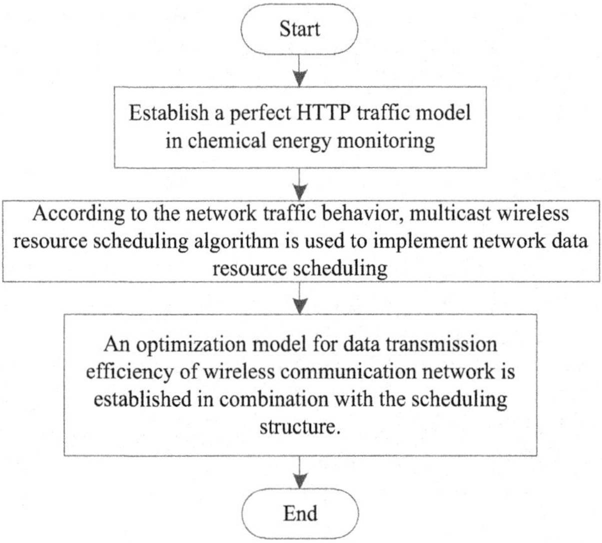

Fig. 1. Optimization process of wireless communication network data transmission efficiency

3 Performance Test

3.1 Building an LTE Multicast Test Environment

Test the performance of a designed method for optimizing data transmission efficiency in a wireless communication network for chemical energy monitoring. The LTE multicast test environment built in the test includes a base station and two UEs, both of which are multicast UEs and belong to the same eNB cell. On the right is the core network part, including pGW, MME, server and MCE. PGW is the abbreviation of SGW/PGW, which is the unity of the two. The function of MBMS-GW is similar to that of pGW, and it is no longer implemented separately, but the function of MBMS-GW is completed on the PGW. MCE is a multicast scheduling entity, and we implement the corresponding multicast scheduling in the eNB multicast scheduler. The server is an Internet server set up on the network service side to provide network content services. In the simulation, we installed a UDP application on the server. The UDP application only generates UDP data packets for delivery. One UDP data packet is generated every second, and a total of 9 UDP data packets are generated for delivery. LTE multicast transmission the system sends these UDP data packets to each multicast UE in a multicast transmission mode.

3.2 Network Parameter Settings

The parameter settings of the wireless communication network for chemical energy monitoring in the experiment are shown in Table 4.

Table 4. Network parameter settings

Serial number	Simulation parameters	Numerical value
1	Number of nodes	200
2	Average packet length/kbits	45
3	Channel transfer rate/MB	3
4	Minimum interest value	0.5–0.8
5	Maximum hops	8
6	Node cache size/MB	85–125
7	Node moving speed (m/s)	2–2.5

Optimize the data transmission efficiency of the network, and test the performance improvement of the optimized network.

Test items include delay and packet loss rate.

3.3 Analysis of Test Results

Delay Comparison Test

Figure 2 shows the data transmission delay of wireless communication network for experimental chemical energy monitoring after and before optimization of data transmission efficiency.

According to the data transmission delay comparison test data in Table 5, after using the design method to optimize the data transmission efficiency of the experimental network, the network delay is greatly reduced.

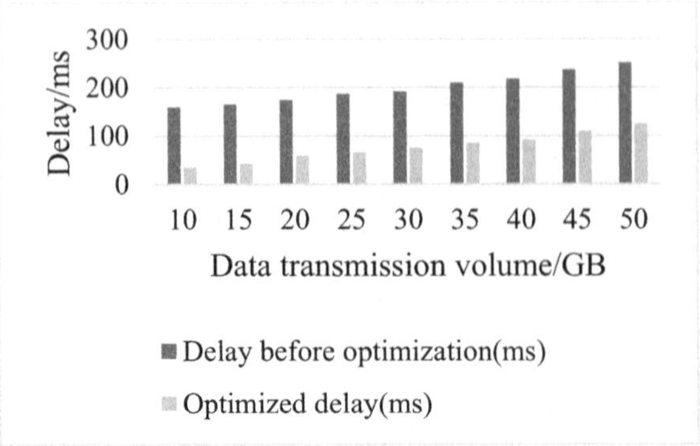

Fig. 2. Delay comparison test data

Comparison Test of Packet Loss Rate

The comparison test results of the packet loss rate of the experimental chemical energy monitoring wireless communication network after and before the optimization of data transmission efficiency are shown in Fig. 3.

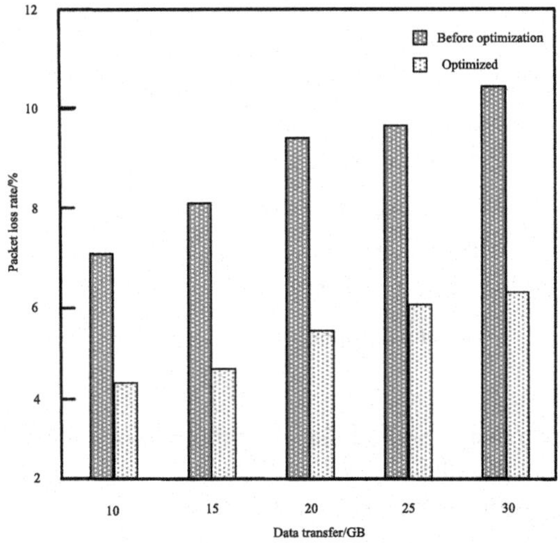

Fig. 3. Packet loss rate comparison test results

According to the comparison test results of packet loss rate in Fig. 3, after the data transmission efficiency is optimized by using the design method, the packet loss rate of the experimental chemical energy monitoring wireless communication network is greatly reduced, which proves the performance of the design method.

4 Conclusion

In the research of wireless communication network for chemical energy monitoring, a data transmission efficiency optimization method is designed to realize the effective optimization of data transmission efficiency, which is of great significance for the development of chemical energy monitoring.

Acknowledgement. Special Project of Shaanxi Provincial Education Department: Research on Energy Monitoring Network, No.: 14JK2055.

References

1. Mariappan, S.M., Selvakumar, S.: A novel location pinpointed anti-jammer with knowledged estimated localizer for secured data transmission in mobile wireless sensor network. Wireless Pers. Commun. **118**(4), 2073–2094 (2021)
2. Zhou, Y., Zhang, Z., Dong, P., et al.: Simultaneous wireless power and data transmission based on unsymmetrical current waveforms with duty cycle modulation. IEEE Access **8**, 16495–16504 (2020)
3. Azad, M., Chi, T.N., Oh, H.: A two-channel slotted sense multiple access protocol for timely and reliable data transmission in industrial wireless sensor networks. Int. J. Distrib. Sens. Netw. **16**(4), 1391–1412 (2020)
4. Ji, W., Zhu, W.: Profit maximization for sponsored data in wireless video transmission systems. IEEE Trans. Mob. Comput. **19**(8), 1928–1942 (2020)
5. Liu, S., et al.: Human memory update strategy: a multi-layer template update mechanism for remote visual monitoring. IEEE Trans. Multimed. **23**, 2188–2198 (2021)
6. Xin, W., Jiang, Z., Lin, G., et al.: Stochastic optimization of data access and hybrid transmission in wireless sensor network. IEEE Access **8**, 62273–62285 (2020)
7. Liu, S., Wang, S., Liu, X., et al.: Fuzzy detection aided real-time and robust visual tracking under complex environments. IEEE Trans. Fuzzy Syst. **29**(1), 90–102 (2021)
8. Berbakov, L., Dimic, G., Beko, M., et al.: Collaborative data transmission in wireless sensor networks. IEEE Access **8**, 39647–39658 (2020)
9. Gao, P., Li, J., Liu, S.: An introduction to key technology in artificial intelligence and big data driven e-learning and e-education. Mob. Netw. Appl. **26**, 2123–2126 (2021)
10. Yan, F.Q., Liu, Y.T., Wang, Y.C., et al.: Short-term network traffic prediction based on mawilab data set. Comput. Simul. **36**(5), 407–411 (2019)
11. Hong, S., Zhang, X., Zhu, J., Zhoa, T., Wang, B.: Suppressing failure cascades in interconnected networks: considering capacity allocation pattern and load redistribution. Mod. Phys. Lett. B **30**(5), 1650049 (2016)
12. Hong, S., Zhu, J., Braunstein, L.A., Zhoa, T., You, Q.: Cascading failure and recovery of spatially interdependent networks. J. Stat. Mech.: Theory Exp. **2017**(10), 103208 (2017)

Deep Spatio-Temporal Decision Fusion Network for Facial Expression Recognition

Xuanchi Chen[1,2], Heng Yang[1], Xia Zhang[3], Xiangwei Zheng[1,2(✉)], and Wei Li[4(✉)]

[1] School of Information Science and Engineering, Shandong Normal University, Jinan, China
xwzhengcn@163.com
[2] Shandong Provincial Key Laboratory for Distributed Computer Software Novel Technology, Jinan, China
[3] Internet Diagnosis and Treatment Center, Taian City Central Hospital, Taian, China
[4] Shandong Normal University Library, Shandong Normal University, Jinan, China
liww72@sdnu.edu.cn

Abstract. Facial expression recognition (FER) becomes research focus in affective computing, as it already plays an important role in public security application scenarios such as urban safety management and safety driving assistance systems. Modeling the spatiotemporal information of facial expression sequences in a targeted manner, integrating and utilizing them appropriately is challenging. In this paper, a facial expression recognition method based on spatial-temporal decision fusion network (STDFN) is proposed. Firstly, the facial expression sequences are divided into four sub-sequences according to face regions, and BiLSTM are used for each of sub-sequences to extract local temporal features. The local morphological features of facial expressions can be captured in more detail to maximize the utilization of the temporal features of dynamic facial expressions. Then, VGG19 is utilized to extract the shallow spatial features of peak expression frame, and the channel weights of spatial features is assigned by squeeze-and-excitation module to attain the weighted spatial features. This allows valid spatial features to be purposefully retained to avoid overfitting. Finally, temporal features and spatial features are used separately calculating expression classification results. And a decision-level fusion module is designed to fuse the two results to obtain the final FER result. Extensive experimental results demonstrate that on three FER datasets CK+, Oulu-CASIA and MMI, achieves 98.83%, 89.31% and 82.86% accuracy, which proved that STDFN effectively improved the recognition accuracy of FER.

Keywords: FER · BiLSTM · SENet · Decision fusion

1 Introduction

Facial expressions, as the most commonly used fashion in human affective interaction, are the key factor for machines to perceive human emotions. With the exponential increase of computer computing power, facial expression recognition (FER) has gradually become a highlight in human-computer interaction and is widely used in areas such

Y. Xu et al. (Eds.): ML4CS 2022, LNCS 13657, pp. 106–120, 2023.
https://doi.org/10.1007/978-3-031-20102-8_9

as urban safety management, criminal investigation assistance and safety driving assistance [1, 2]. Due to previous ground-breaking research, FER can be classified into two types: static image-based approach that focuses more on spatial features and dynamic sequence-based approach that focuses more on temporal features [3]. The static image-based FER methods can effectively extract spatial information, but cannot model the dynamic information of facial expressions. Dynamic sequence-based methods extract temporal features by capturing the evolution of facial expressions and usually achieve good performance. However, FER is a rather complex facial analysis task, and even humans are unable to recognize the emotions of others by focusing only on a single facial feature information. It is difficult to improve the performance of FER based on spatial or temporal features only. Hence, a key challenge for FER is to extract the spatiotemporal features in a targeted manner and integrate the information of both complementarily.

To this end, a FER method based on spatial-temporal decision fusion network (STDFN) is proposed. In order to get the utmost out of the temporal and physical features of dynamic facial expression, we designed temporal feature extraction module to capture the expression evolution information between frames. The bi-directional long short-term memory (BiLSTM) [19] is used to learn the mode between frames in two directions, pay more attention to the context relationship between frames to obtain more accurate temporal information. In addition, the occurrence of facial expressions is often coupled with dynamic changes in the combination of facial parts [4]. For capture the morphological features of facial expressions in a more detailed way, our model first divides each frame of image sequence into four parts and produces four groups of sub-sequences. Then, using sub-sequence training four groups of BiLSTM to obtain local temporal features, and spliced to globe temporal features. At the same time, we designed spatial feature extraction module based on VGG [18] and SENet [5] (VGG-S). The shallow spatial feature maps of peak expression images are extracted by VGG19, channel weights are assigned to the shallow spatial feature maps using SENet, the obtained weighted feature maps are used to calculate the classification results of face expressions. Finally, an adaptive decision fusion module is designed to integrate the expression classification results of the two modules to obtain the final face expression classification results.

The main works of this paper are as follows:

(1) We peoposed FER method based on spatial-temporal decision fusion network, temporal and spatial feature extraction module were designed separately to capture spatiotemporal information, and an adaptive decision fusion module to integrate spatiotemporal information.
(2) We designed temporal feature extraction module based on BiLSTM, with divided facial landmarks into different areas to learn the details of facial expression evolution, which effectively utilizes the information before and after expression changes in various facial regions;
(3) We designed spatial feature extraction module based on VGG19-S, adopting VGG19 extract shallow features maps and SENet assign weight to shallow feature channels, which is helpful for accurate collection of useful spatial information.
(4) Numerous experiments have shown that STDFN achieved 98.83%, 89.31% and 82.86% accuracy on three FER datasets include CK+, Oulu-CASIA and MMI, demonstrating the effectiveness of the proposed method.

The rest of this paper is organized as follows. Section 2 presents the research progress of FER methods. Section 3 describes STDFN in detail, and Sect. 4 presents our experimental results. Finally, in Sect. 5 we summarize the conclusions and point out the direction of our future work.

2 Related Works

2.1 Facial Expression Recognition

As an essential task in computer vision, early FER methods extracted features by handcrafted and designed classifiers to classify the features to obtain expression recognition results. Klaser et al. [6] extended the traditional hand-designed feature approach by designing a local descriptor to model the temporal information contained in facial expression sequences, and effectively improves FER performance. Liu et al. [7] proposed STM-ExpLet for streaming modeling of videos, which models each video clip as a spatiotemporal streaming module (STM) to improve feature discrimination. However, most handcrafted features are susceptible to the external environment and has poor characterization capability. With the rapid development of deep learning algorithms, deep neural networks can draw on large amounts of data to learn the required features autonomously, effectively bypassing complex manual feature extraction.

2.2 Deep FER Based on Spatio-Temporal Features

The occurrence of facial expressions as a continuous human action possesses an innate temporal correlation, so researchers have proposed deep spatiotemporal networks based on expression sequences to model the more capable spatiotemporal features. Jung et al. [8] proposed a FER approach containing two sub-networks, which were used to extract the appearance features and temporal geometric features, and features were integrated for the expression recognition task, which effectively improved the expression recognition accuracy. Zhang et al. [9] proposed a temporal-spatial recurrent neural network to effectively improve the accuracy of FER tasks by building multiple RNNs to capture spatiotemporal information with high discriminative power by scanning from different angles. Zhao et al. [10] proposed a peak-piloted deep network (PPDN) for learning the evolutionary information between peak expressions and non-peak expressions, which improves models' generalization ability when facial differences between individuals are larger. However, existing methods do not capture the dynamic information of critical areas of the face in a targeted manner, and most of them are commonly based on the spatiotemporal information of facial expressions at the image level, which results in increased computational complexity of models and vulnerability to noise during image transmission.

3 The Proposed Method

Figure 1 shows the framework of our proposed approach. Our model starts from the input of the original image sequence and preprocesses the data first. To minimize the complexity of the calculation, 16 key frames are selected from original sequences to represent the dynamic evolution of the whole sequence and these 16 images contain the first and last frames. For the sequences with insufficient frames, the last frame is used to fill backward until they are sufficient. Then, facial clipping is performed for the key frames, and the gray processing is to avoid the influence of light and facial color on the classification results. To avoid overfitting due to the small amount of data, rotation and flipping are used to expanding the dataset. The sequence data is divided into two modules, one is directly used to extract temporal information and the other selects a peak expression frame (the last frame) from the sequence data to extract spatial information. The two modules are used to predict facial expression classification respectively. In the end, classification by integrating the predicted values from two modules. In the following, we will introduce the details of the two modules and the method of decision fusion.

3.1 Temporal Feature Extraction Based on BiLSTM

The occurrence of facial expressions is coupled with the dynamic evolutionary process of key facial parts. For instance, happiness can be expressed as the corner of the mouth up and eyebrows open; sadness is the corner of the mouth down, eyes smaller; surprise is characterized that the eyes become larger and mouth opens. In fact, facial landmarks can well reflect these dynamic evolution processes. Therefore, the facial landmarks are divided into four parts for model training to attain four local features, which is employed to focus more on a particular part of the face over time. Local features of the four parts are fused to ensure the integrity of the extracted facial expression information. Then, BiLSTM is adopted to learn temporal feature, which can not only effectively avoid the gradient disappearance in long-term learning, but effectively capture the context information between image frames.

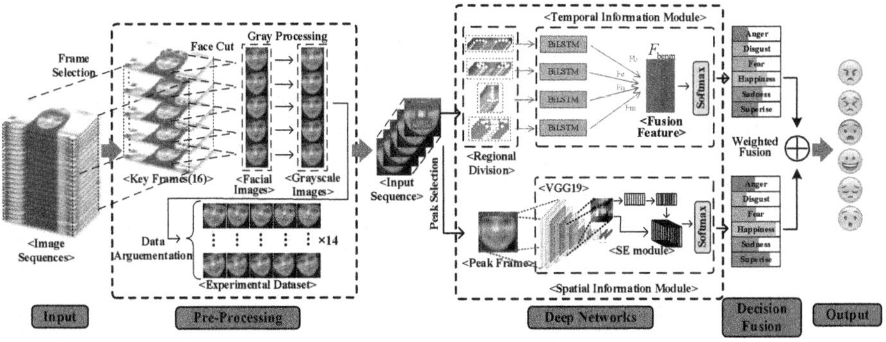

Fig. 1. Framework of spatial-temporal decision fusion network.

As shown in Fig. 2, the evolution process between image frames is abstracted as the coordinate change process of facial landmarks. First of all, the input layer of the network maps the facial landmark points of each frame into a one-dimensional vector, so that each facial region is represented as a matrix, which is respectively used as the input of the corresponding BiLSTM. Four partial local features are extracted by the corresponding BiLSTM and the local features are stitched and fused to obtain the global features. Finally, Softmax is used as the classification layer.

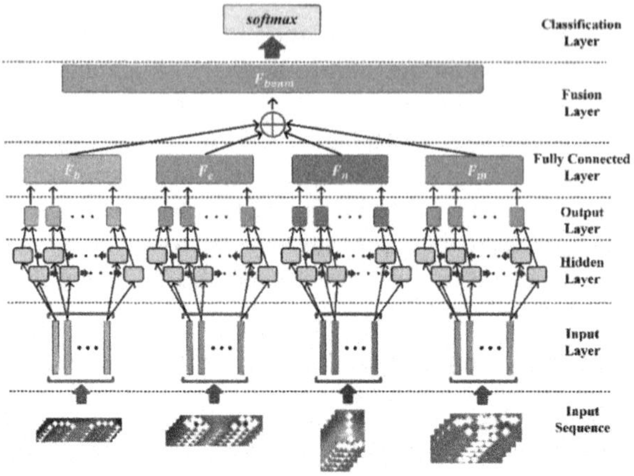

Fig. 2. BiLSTM structure for extracting temporal information.

BiLSTM extends the single-way LSTM by introducing a second layer, in which the connections between the hidden layer flow in reverse chronological order, exploiting the temporal information of "past" and "future". In our model, the original images are divided into four parts, including eyebrows, eyes, nose, and mouth, and they are represented as one-dimensional vectors as the input of BiLSTM. Partial based local features F_b, F_e, F_n, F_m are obtained from the output layer. Then the local features are combined by Formula (1), which obtain the global features F_{benm}:

$$F_{benm} = [F_b \oplus F_e \oplus F_n \oplus F_m] \tag{1}$$

where $F_b, F_e, F_n,$ *and* F_m are the features of eyebrows, eyes, nose and mouth, respectively, and $\oplus$ denotes the *concat* operation

Take F_b as an example to explain the hidden layer process of BiLSTM, the formula of forward propagation cell structure in BiLSTM is as Formula (2–7):

$$f_{bt} = \sigma\left[w_{bf}(h_{bt-1}, x_{bt}) + b_{bf}\right] \tag{2}$$

$$i_{bt} = \sigma\left[w_{bi}(h_{bt-1}, x_{bt}) + b_{bi}\right] \tag{3}$$

$$\hat{c}_{bt} = tanh(w_{b\hat{c}}(h_{bt-1}, x_{bt}) + b_{b\hat{c}}) \tag{4}$$

$$c_{bt} = \hat{c}_{bt} * i_{bt} + f_{bt} * c_{bt-1} \tag{5}$$

$$o_{bt} = \sigma\left[w_{bo}(h_{bt-1}, x_{bt}) + b_{bo}\right] \tag{6}$$

$$\vec{h_{bt}} = o_{bt} * tanh(c_{bt}) \tag{7}$$

where, t denotes the number of frames, w denotes the weight matrix,x_{bt} is the input vector, f_{bt} is the oblivion gate, which decides to discard the information in the previous state. i_{bt} is the input gate, which determines the information currently to be retained. σ denotes the *sigmoid* activation function, *tanh* denotes the hyperbolic tangent activation function. $\hat{c}_{bt}$ expresses the alternative update units, and c_{bt} is the updated cell state, which multiplied by the old cell state and forgetting gate and added to the new candidate values. c_{bt} uses an *sigmoid* layer to determine the output of updated cell state. The cell states are processed by *tanh* and the multiplied with the output of the sigmoid layer to obtain $\overrightarrow{h_{bt}}$, where $\overrightarrow{h_{bt}}$ denotes the embedding representation of the forward-LSTM. The backward calculation process is similar to the forward process, and $\overleftarrow{h_{bt}}$ denotes the embedding representation of the backward-LSTM.

Then, the forward and backward outputs of the BiLSTM are combined by Formula (8–10):

$$\overrightarrow{h_{bt}} = \overrightarrow{LSTM}\left(h_{bt-1}, w_{bt}, c_{bt-1}\right) \tag{8}$$

$$\overleftarrow{h_{bt}} = \overleftarrow{LSTM}\left(h_{bt+1}, w_{bt}, c_{bt+1}\right) \tag{9}$$

$$F_b = h_{bt} = \overrightarrow{h_{bt}} \oplus \overleftarrow{h_{bt}} \tag{10}$$

where $\overrightarrow{LSTM}$ represents the forward LSTM and $\overleftarrow{LSTM}$ represents the backward LSTM. h_{bt} denotes the BiLSTM hidden layer output and is taken as F_b.

Finally, global feature F_{benm} is fed to *Softmax* for estimate the facial expression. The calculation process of *Softmax* is shown in Formula (11).

$$y_i = S(Z)_k = \frac{e^{z_k}}{\sum_{j=1}^{K} e^{z_j}} \tag{11}$$

Among them, y_i represents the calculated softmax value and $k \in [1, K]$, K denotes the number of expression categories, Z represents the output of the previous layer.

The loss function uses cross entropy calculated by Formula (12), where $T_k \in [0, 1]$.

$$Loss = -\sum_{k=1}^{K} T_k \ln y_k \tag{12}$$

3.2 Spatial Feature Extraction Based on VGG19-S

To extract the spatial information of facial expressions, the peak frame from the sequence is selected as the input of VGG19-S. The shallow convolutional layer of pre-trained VGG19 is used to extract shallow features, and then SENet is employed to learn the channel weights of the shallow features, assign the weights to the shallow features to obtain a weighted feature map, and use Softmax for classification.

As shown in Fig. 3, the structure of the spatial feature extraction model VGG19-S is illustrated. The input dimension is $64 \times 64 \times 1$ gray image, and the shallow features are obtained after convolution operations with two $3 \times 3 \times 64$ layers, two $3 \times 3 \times 128$ layers, four $3 \times 3 \times 256$ layers and one $3 \times 3 \times 512$ layer. Next, SENet is used to explicitly model the interdependence among feature channels, and the significance degree of each one is automatically obtained through learning. Then, according to this importance degree, channels with higher scores are promoted and those channels with lower scores are suppressed. With squeeze operation, feature compression is performed and each 2D feature channel is turned into a 1D constant, which has a global receptive domain. This is achieved by using the global average pool to generate channel statistics. For a shallow feature U, each channel has a spatial dimension $m \times n$, and a statistic V is generated for each channel, such that the c th element of V is calculated with Formula (13).

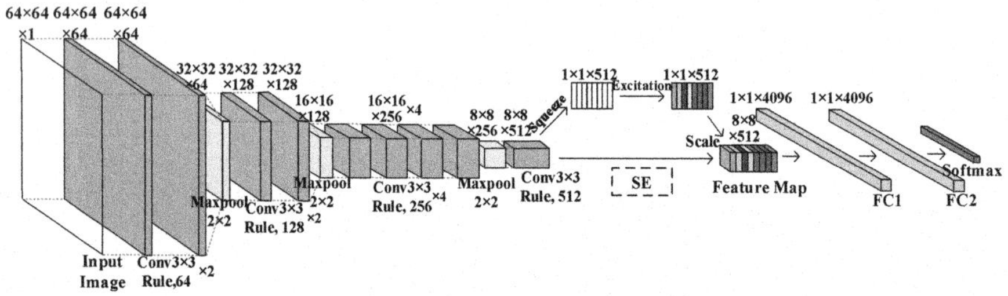

Fig. 3. VGG19-S structure for extracting spatial information.

$$V_C = Squeeze(U) = \frac{1}{m \times n}\sum\nolimits_{a=1}^{m}\sum\nolimits_{b=1}^{n} u_c(a, b) \tag{13}$$

Next, the *Excitation* is required to fully capture the channel dependencies. Weights are assigned to each feature channel by w to simulate channel correlation information. The calculation process as Formula (14).

$$S = Excitation(V, w) = \sigma(w_2\delta(w_1 V)) \tag{14}$$

where δ denotes the ReLU function, and $w_1 \in R^{\frac{C}{r}\times C}$, $w_2 \in R^{C\times\frac{C}{r}}$, r is a hyperparameter, usually $r = 16$.

Finally, S is treated as the significance of each feature channel. The weighted result f_c of the feature channel c is calculated as Formula (15).

$$f_c = Scale(U_c, S_c) = S_c \cdot U_c \tag{15}$$

$$F_S = \{f_1, f_2, \ldots, f_c\} \tag{16}$$

where $Scale(U_c, S_c)$ denotes the channel-wise multiplication between S_c and U_c, and F_S denotes the spatial features of the peak frame.

3.3 Weighted Decision Fusion

For sequence images of facial expressions, there are two kinds of information: temporal domain and spatial domain. We use the two kinds of information to analyze facial expressions respectively. However, better results are often obtained by integrating the two kinds of information. A weighted fusion method of decision levels is used to integrate the two dimensions. In order to facilitate fusion, *Softmax* is used for classification of the two networks, $P_T(0 \le P_T(k) \le 1) = [P_T(1), P_T(2), \ldots, P_T(K)]$ represents the classification of the temporal network and $P_S(0 \le P_S(k) \le 1) = [P_S(1), P_S(2), \ldots, P_S(K)]$ represents the classification of the spatial network. The prediction results are calculated by Formula (17). Where α is the parameter.

$$Prediction = argmax(\alpha P_T(k) + (1 - \alpha)P_S(k)) \tag{17}$$

3.4 Algorithmic Description

The description of STDFN is shown in Algorithm 1.

Algorithm 1. **STDFN**($Lb, Lb, Ln, Lm, Peak, label, \lambda, \alpha, num\_cell, r$)

Input: Landmark points set $\{Lb|0 \leq Lb \leq BS\}$, $\{Le|0 \leq Le \leq ES\}$, $\{Ln|0 \leq Ln \leq NS\}$, $\{Lm|0 \leq Lm \leq MS\}$; Peak frame image set $\{Peak|0 \leq Peak \leq S\}$; Lable set $\{lable|0 \leq lable \leq S\}$; Larning rate λ; **Fusion weight** α; Number of LSTM neurons num_cell; Hyperparameter r.
Output: Prediction result set $Prediction\{\}$.
Initialization: Initialize the parameters to be learned in the STDFN model.
Process:

For i =1 to I
  Temporal features are extracted by BiLSTM:
    $Lb^{i*} = \left(Lb_1^{i*}, Lb_2^{i*}, \ldots, Lb_B^{i*}\right)$
    $Le^{i*} = \left(Le_1^{i*}, Le_2^{i*}, \ldots, Le_E^{i*}\right)$
    $Ln^{i*} = \left(Ln_1^{i*}, Ln_2^{i*}, \ldots, Ln_N^{i*}\right)$
    $Lm^{i*} = \left(Lm_1^{i*}, Lm_2^{i*}, \ldots, Lm_M^{i*}\right)$
    $\{F_b^i, F_e^i, F_n^i, F_m^i\} = \text{BiLSTM}(Lb^{i*}, Le^{i*}, Ln^{i*}, Lm^{i*})$
    $F_{benm}^i = [F_b^i \oplus F_e^i \oplus F_n^i \oplus F_m^i]$
  Spatial features are extracted by VGG-S:
    $U^{m \times n \times c} = VGG19(Peak(i))$
    $V_C = Squeeze(U) = \frac{1}{m \times n} \sum_{a=1}^{m} \sum_{b=1}^{n} u_c(a, b)$
    $S = Excitation(V, w) = \sigma(w_2 \delta(w_1 V))$;
    $f_c = Scale(U_c, S_c) = S_c U_c$ // SENet to assign channel weights to shallow features.
    $F_S^i = [f_1, f_2, \ldots, f_c]$ // get the spatial features
  Calculate classification results:
    $P_T^i = \left[P_T^i(1), P_T^i(2), \ldots, P_T^i(K)\right] = softmax(F_{benm}^i)$;
    $P_S^i = \{P_S^i(1), P_S^i(2), \ldots, P_S^i(K)\} softmax(F_S^i)$
    $Prediction(i) = argmax(\alpha P_T(k) + (1 - \alpha) P_S(k))$
End For
$Prediction = \{Prediction(i)\}_{i=1}^{I}$
return $Prediction$

4 Experiments and Discussion

4.1 Datasets

TO extensively and objectively evaluate the performance of STDFN, we experimented on three widely used sequences collected under laboratory control facial expression datasets: the CK+ [12], the Oulu-CASIA [13], and the MMI [17]. The expression sequences are the evolution of neutral face frames to peak expression frames, where 6-class basic expression recognition tasks of anger, surprise, disgust, fear, happiness, and sadness are performed on both Oulu-CASIA and MMI datasets. In the CK+ dataset, contempt was added to perform the 7-class classification task. To ensure fairness, random 5-fold cross-validation was used on datasets to obtain the evaluation performance of the models.

4.2 Data Preprocessing

Face Clipping and Gray Processing. FER database is uncropped, and removing background can eliminate the influence of the surrounding environment in the image on the accuracy of FER. The dlib tool is used to crop the facial image out to 64 × 64 pixels. Then, to prevent the effects of factors such as illumination intensity on the prediction results, we convert the facial images to gray images.

Data Augmentation. FER based on deep learning algorithm needs enough effective training data, which can prevent overfitting in deep neural network training and ensure the generalization performance of FER. However, the current open FER database lacks sufficient training data. Therefore, data augmentation becomes an indispensable part of deep learning algorithm-based FER. as shown in Fig. 4, We use an off-line data augmentation method, rotated each pre-processed training image at angle of {−15°, −10°, −5°, 0°,15°, 10°, 15°}, then the rotated image is flipped on the X-axis. in the end, a single original image will produce a 14-fold image sample.

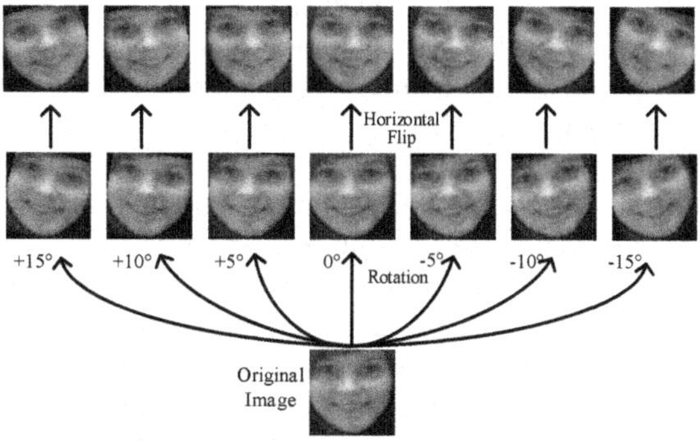

Fig. 4. Data augmentation in CK+. The first batch of images were obtained by rotation of 0°, 5°, 10°, 15°, −5°, −10°, −15°, then the second batch of images were obtained by inversion of the first batch.

4.3 Results and Analysis

Implementation Details and Parameters. We marked the whole face with 68 coordinates points, which were divided into 4 facial regions: eyebrows with 10 coordinates; eyes with 12 coordinates; nose with 9 coordinates; mouth with 19 coordinates. All the LSTM modules used 3 × 256 structure, which is three layers of LSTM subnet, each layer is set with 256 neurons. After learning each sequence, update weights. On the VGG-S model, SGD is used to optimize the parameters. The momentum is 0.9, the weight decay is 0.004, and the initial learning rate is 0.001.

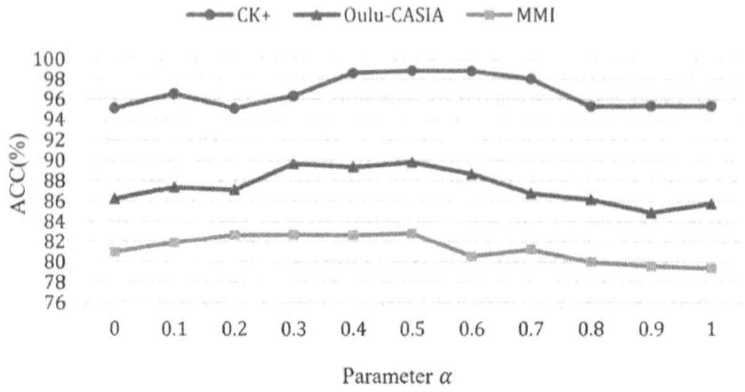

Fig. 5. The accuracy under different parameters α on three datasets.

In order to balance the information provided by the time network and the space network, we study the weight by changing the hyperparameter α of formula (16) from 0 to 1. When $\alpha = 0$, only the information provided by the spatial network is retained, when $\alpha = 1$, only the information provided by the temporal network is retained, and the change step of α is set to 0.1. Figure 5 shows the changes in the accuracy of FER on the CK+, Oulu-CASIA and MMI datasets with the change of α. In order to prevent the contingency of the experiment, the figure shows the average accuracy obtained by the 5-fold cross-validation method.

Ablation Experiments. The performance of the spatial-temporal information decision fusion network is mainly determined by the respective performance of the temporal network and the spatial network. In order to evaluate the respective functions of the two networks, we conducted ablation experiments on three datasets. Table 1 summarizes the ablation experimental results. The experimental results show that both the spatial network and the temporal network can complete the facial expression recognition task separately. However, due to the limited integrated feature information, a single network cannot achieve high recognition accuracy. After the decision fusion method, our model achieves the best performance.

Table 1. Ablation experiments on three datasets.

Method	Descriptor	CK+	Oulu-CASIA	MMI
Temporal network	BiLSTM	96.56%	85.76%	79.37%
Spatial network	VGG19-S	95.71%	86.21%	80.95%
Ours	**STDFN**	**98.83%**	**89.31%**	**82.86%**

Comparative Experiments. Table 2 shows the performance comparison of the proposed method with the SOTA method on three datasets. Most researchers chose to implement the 7-class recognition task on the CK+ dataset. The current known best performance for 7-class is PHRNN-MSCNN, which achieved 98.50% accuracy. On the

7-class classification task, our method achieved 98.83% recognition accuracy, surpassing the existing methods. Moreover, the PPDN achieved 99.30% accuracy on 6-class classification task for the CK+ dataset. We also performed a 6-class classification task by removing contempt, achieved recognition accuracy by 99.39%.

Table 2. FER accuracy (%) of various methods on CK+, Oulu-CASIA and MMI database.

Method	Descriptor	CK+	Oulu-CASIA	MMI
Klaser et al. [6]	HOG 3D	91.44	70.63	60.89
Liu et al. [7]	STM-Explet	94.19	74.59	75.12
Zhang et al. [9]	STRNN	95.40	–	–
Ding et al. [16]	FN2EN	96.80	87.71	–
Jung et al. [8]	DTAGN	97.25	81.46	70.24
Yang et al. [11]	DeRL	97.30	88.00	73.23
Hu et al. [14]	CTSLSTM	–	–	78.40
Zhang et al. [4]	PHRNN-MSCNN	98.50	86.25	81.18
Liu et al. [15]	MIC	–	–	81.29
Zhao et al. [10]	PPDN	99.30 (6)	–	–
Spatial-temporal networks	**STDFN (6-class)**	**99.39**	–	**–**
Spatial-temporal networks	**STDFN (7-class)**	**98.83**	**89.31**	**82.86**

Previously, the best performance was achieved the 88.00% accuracy by DeRL on Oulu-CASIA dataset. They trained a generating model to generate roughly neutral faces for pictures of facial expressions, and learned to recognize facial expressions by learning the residual information from the generating model. STDFN achieves the highest recognition accuracy of 89.31%, which is better than the most advanced methods at present. In addition, compared with PHRNN-MSCNN, which is based on spatial-temporal network, our model achieves a relatively satisfactory performance improvement. And our STDFN achieves 82.86% FER accuracy on the MMI dataset, which indicates that the method has a strong generalization capability. Our method has surpassed among currently known methods, both manual feature-based and spatiotemporal network-based methods.

As shown in Fig. 6 (a), on CK+, STDFN has achieved very high accuracy in recognizing the five expressions of happiness, anger, disgust, fear and surprise, which indicates that our model has been able to fully recognize these labels. However, contempt and sadness are still less effective, perhaps because the facial changes in some samples of both expressions are too slight. The confusion matrix results of STDFN in Oulu-CASIA dataset are shown in Fig. 6 (b). STDFN has high accuracy in identifying happiness, anger and surprise, and low accuracy in identifying fear, sadness and disgust. Especially for disgust, our method has a low recognition accuracy, most of which will be confused with anger, indicating that our method is still unable to accurately capture the subtle changes of facial expressions. It is worth mentioning that although the recognition accuracy of disgust is low, our method does not appear serious confusion in expression recognition, and is generally more balanced. This shows that our method has a certain robustness. Figure 6 (c) shows the distribution of samples with classification errors in STDFN on the MMI dataset, and the two expression classes with low classification accuracy are disgust and fear. This is because some of the sample labels of these two classes in the original dataset are inaccurate.

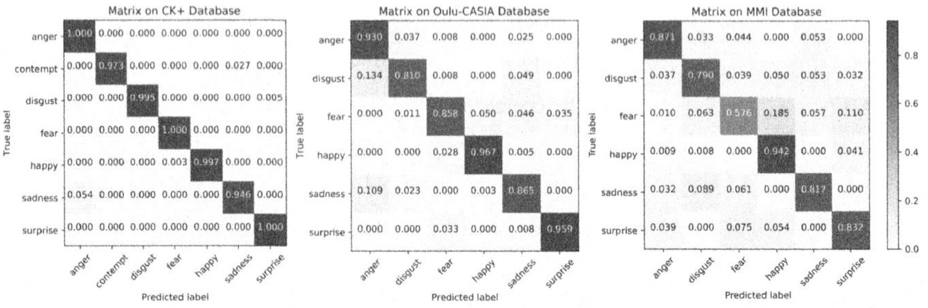

(a) CK+ (b) Oulu-CASIA (c) MMI

Fig. 6. Confusion matrix for STDFN implements the facial expression recognition task on three datasets. (a) Confusion matrix for the CK+ dataset; (b) Confusion matrix for the Oulu-CASIA dataset; (c) Confusion matrix for the MMI dataset.

5 Conclusion and Future Works

In this paper, a FER method based on spatial-temporal decision fusion network is proposed. From the perspective of temporal information, we use BiLSTM to consider the time correlation between the frames before and after the image sequence, and integrate the local features of facial expressions through the division of facial regions. To the spatial information, VGG19 is used to obtain the shallow spatial features of the peak frames, and SENet is applied to module to learn the weight between feature channels. Finally, a decision fusion method is used to successfully combine the temporal and spatial dimension information of facial expression images. We not only implemented a spatial-temporal network-based FER method, but effectively improved the accuracy of the FER system. Finally, we discuss the parameter selection of decision fusion method, and compared our method with the current SOTA method. The experimental results show that our method has achieved an accuracy of 98.83%, 89.31% and 82.86% respectively on the most commonly used datasets CK+, Oulu-CASIA and MMI.

In future, we will focus on more extensive research on consciousness recognition and emotion recognition to further explore valuable information, and set out to develop more powerful methods to capture subtle evolution in facial expressions to further improve the accuracy of FER. We further intend to integrate physiological signals data into the FER system to realize the human emotion analysis system of multi-modal information fusion.

Acknowledgments. This work is supported by the Natural Science Foundation of Shandong Province (No. ZR2020LZH008, ZR2021MF118, ZR2019MF071), the Shandong Provincial Key Research and Development Program (Major Scientific and Technological Innovation Project) (NO. 2021CXGC010506, NO. 2021SFGC0104).

References

1. Tayibnapis, I.R., Koo, D.Y., Choi, M.K., et al.: A novel driver fatigue monitoring using optical imaging of face on safe driving system. In: 2016 International Conference on Control, Electronics, Renewable Energy and Communications (ICCEREC), pp. 115–120 (2016)
2. Poria, S., Cambria, E., Bajpai, R., et al.: A review of affective computing: from unimodal analysis to multimodal fusion. Inf. Fusion **37**, 98–125 (2017)
3. Li, S., Deng, W.: Deep facial expression recognition: a survey. IEEE Trans. Affect. Comput. (2020)
4. Zhang, K., Huang, Y., Du, Y., et al.: Facial expression recognition based on deep evolutional spatial-temporal networks. IEEE Trans. Image Process. **26**(9), 4193–4203 (2017)
5. Hu, J., Shen, L., Sun, G.: Squeeze-and-excitation networks. In: Proceedings of the IEEE Conference on Computer Vision and Pattern Recognition (CVPR), pp. 7132–7141. IEEE (2018)
6. Klaser, A., Marszałek, M., Schmid, C.: A spatio-temporal descriptor based on 3D-gradients. In: BMVC 2008-19th British Machine Vision Conference (BMVC), vol. 275, pp. 1–10. British Machine Vision Association (2008)
7. Liu, M., Shan, S., Wang, R., et al.: Learning expression lets on spatio-temporal manifold for dynamic facial expression recognition. In: Proceedings of the IEEE Conference on Computer Vision and Pattern Recognition (CVPR), pp. 1749–1756. IEEE (2014)
8. Jung, H., Lee, S., Yim, J., et al.: Joint fine-tuning in deep neural networks for facial expression recognition. In: Proceedings of the IEEE International Conference on Computer Vision (ICCV), pp. 2983–2991. IEEE (2015)
9. Zhang, T., Zheng, W., Cui, Z., et al.: Spatial–temporal recurrent neural network for emotion recognition. IEEE Trans. Cybern. **49**(3), 839–847 (2018)
10. Zhao, X., et al.: Peak-piloted deep network for facial expression recognition. In: Leibe, B., Matas, J., Sebe, N., Welling, M. (eds.) ECCV 2016. LNCS, vol. 9906, pp. 425–442. Springer, Cham (2016). https://doi.org/10.1007/978-3-319-46475-6_27
11. Yang, H., Ciftci, U., Yin, L.: Facial expression recognition by de-expression residue learning. In: Proceedings of the IEEE Conference on Computer Vision and Pattern Recognition (CVPR), pp. 2168–2177 (2018)
12. Lucey, P., Cohn, J.F., Kanade, T., et al.: The extended Cohn-Kanade dataset (ck+): a complete dataset for action unit and emotion-specified expression. In: 2010 IEEE Computer Society Conference on Computer Vision and Pattern Recognition-Workshops (CVPRW), pp. 94–101 (2010)
13. Zhao, G., Huang, X., Taini, M., et al.: Facial expression recognition from near-infrared videos. Image Vis. Comput. **29**(9), 607–619 (2011)
14. Hu, M., Wang, H., Wang, X., et al.: Video facial emotion recognition based on local enhanced motion history image and CNN-CTSLSTM networks. J. Vis. Commun. Image Represent. **59**, 176–185 (2019)
15. Liu, X., Jin, L., Han, X., et al.: Mutual information regularized identity-aware facial expression recognition in compressed video. Pattern Recogn. **119**, 108105 (2021)

16. Ding, H., Zhou, S.K., Chellappa, R.: Facenet2expnet: regularizing a deep face recognition net for expression recognition. In: 2017 12th IEEE International Conference on Automatic Face & Gesture Recognition (FG), pp. 118–126. IEEE (2017)
17. Valstar, M., Pantic, M.: Induced disgust, happiness and surprise: an addition to the mmi facial expression database. In: Proceedings of 3rd International Workshop on EMOTION (Satellite of LREC): Corpora for Research on Emotion and Affect, p. 65 (2010)
18. Simonyan, K., Zisserman, A.: Very deep convolutional networks for large-scale image recognition. arXiv preprint arXiv:1409.1556 (2014)
19. Zhou, P., Shi, W., Tian, J., et al.: Attention-based bidirectional long short-term memory networks for relation classification. In: Proceedings of the 54th Annual Meeting of the Association for Computational Linguistics (ACL), vol. 2, pp. 207–212 (2016)

A Tabu-Based Multi-objective Particle Swarm Optimization for Irregular Flight Recovery Problem

Tianwei Zhou[1,2], Yichen Lai[1], Xiaojie Huang[1], Xumin Chen[1], and Huifen Zhong[1,3](✉)

[1] College of Management, Shenzhen University, Shenzhen 518060, China
zhonghf510520@163.com

[2] Great Bay Area International Institute for Innovation, Shenzhen University, Shenzhen 518060, China

[3] Faculty of Business and Administration, University of Macau, Macau 999078, China

Abstract. Air transportation is eminent for its fast speed and low cargo damage rate among other ways. However, it is greatly limited by emergent factors like bad weather and current COVID-19 epidemic, where irregular flights may occur. Confronted with the negative impact caused by irregular flight, it is vital to rearrange the preceding schedule to reduce the cost. To solve this problem, first, we established a multi-objective model considering cost and crew satisfaction simultaneously. Secondly, due to the complexity of irregular flight recovery problem, we proposed a tabu-based multi-objective particle swarm optimization introducing the idea of tabu search. Thirdly, we devised an encoding scheme focusing on the characteristic of the problem. Finally, we verified the superiority of the tabu-based multi-objective particle swarm optimization through the comparison against MOPSO by the experiment based on real-world data.

Keywords: Crew recovery · Irregular flight · Tabu-based multi-objective particle swarm optimization · Tabu search

1 Introduction

In the third year of facing COVID-19, the world is still suffering under the highly infectious variant Omicron. Though the dynamic clearing policy adopted by Chinese government reduces the loss greatly, the following lockdown and quarantine lead to flight circuit breaker mechanism. Moreover, weather anomaly generated by global warming may also cause irregular situation.

According to the Normal Statistical Method of Civil Aviation Flight [1] released by Civil Aviation Administration of China, normal flights can be defined as follows "flights depart 10 min or shorter after scheduled departure time without sliding back, veering or preparing for landing, or arrive within 10 min before scheduled arrival time." And irregular flights refer to those do not obey above conditions. Usually, the occurrence of irregular flight happens days or even hours before takeoff, which requires airline to

Y. Xu et al. (Eds.): ML4CS 2022, LNCS 13657, pp. 121–132, 2023.
https://doi.org/10.1007/978-3-031-20102-8_10

recover it correctly and timely. The recovery is composed of route, flight, aircraft and crew recovery. And only crew recovery problem takes humanistic factors into account amongst them, which is a channel to exhibit airline's corporate responsibility and also a crucial means to improve onboard services. Hence the main question addressed in this paper is crew recovery problem.

Plenty of scholars have studied the irregular flight recovery problem from a wide variety of angles. Chutima et al. [2] considered cost, workload and pilots' preference at the same time. Wen et al. [3] took flight flying time variability into account. Zeighami et al. [4] and Zhou et al. [5] separately developed an algorithm based on alternating Lagrangian decomposition and ant colony algorithm in solving the problem. Doi et al. [6] and Quesnel et al. [7] respectively studied the impact of fair working time and crews' preferences on crew recovery problem. Antunes et al. [8] emphasized the robustness of schedule. Wen et al. [9] studied the relationship between manpower availability and crew scheduling strategies. Evler et al. [10] and Jin et al. [11] adopted rolling horizon algorithm and column generation method respectively in cope with the recovery problem. However, each of them indeed had come up with a way to either actualize the problem or speed the convergence velocity. In this paper, we introduced crew's satisfaction of work time to the previous single objective model of cost, which was highly associated with the efficiency and effectiveness of rearrangement. In addition, it also enriched the diversity of the original recovery problem.

When solving models with more than one objective, it usually fails to meet the demand of accuracy and timeliness by merely changing the multi-objective problem into single-objective one. And multi-objective algorithms, like MOPSO, can satisfy the needs of multiple objectives and show their merits like fewer adjustment parameters. However, it also inherits the shortcomings like easily falling into local optimum, which is the main focus of recent studies. Zhang et al. [12] developed a competitive mechanism to further improve the global and personal best particles. Luo et al. [13] introduced an indicator and direction vectors to enhance the capability of local exploration and maintain the non-dominated solution. Cui et al. [14] proposed a two-archive mechanism to emphasize convergence and diversity separately. Devaraj et al. [15] hybridized MOPSO and firefly algorithm to minimize the search space. Qu et al. [16] and Liang et al. [17] both introduced a self-organized based MOPSO to locate multiple Pareto optimal solutions. Liu et al. [18] used objective space division method to find Pbest and Gbest. Mohd et al. [19] hybridized dynamic boundary search method with MOPSO. Goyal et al. [20] came up with a hybrid algorithm of RSM (Response Surface Methodology) and MOPSO. Mahapatra et al. [21] introduced a hesitant fuzzy MOPSO algorithm to MORRA problem. Sellami et al. [22] suggested a MOPSO combined with MATPOWER toolbox. Whereas, recent studies in the field of MOPSO have only focused on the improvement of its internal mechanism and search methods, but few attempt to integrate other algorithms into MOPSO. Therefore, in this paper, we combined MOPSO with tabu search to improve the local optimum problem.

The main contributions of this paper include three parts. First, the crew recovery model would be closer to real-world situation after we considered the satisfaction of crew members besides recovery cost. Secondly, we proposed a tabu-based multi-objective particle swarm optimization enabling the primary algorithm to overcome the local optimum problem. Thirdly, we established a coding scheme based on the characteristics of the problem.

The paper has been organized in the following way. Section 2 states the multi-objective model. Section 3 describes the tabu-based multi-objective particle swarm optimization. Section 4 explains the encoding scheme. Section 5 presents the simulation results against comparative algorithms. Section 6 concludes the paper and points out the future directions.

2 Model of Multi-objective Crew Recovery Problem

This section describes the model of crew recovery problem. The model considering cost and satisfaction is listed below. Table 1 explains the meaning of parameters displayed in the mathematical model.

Table 1. Definition of symbols

Symbols	Meaning of symbols
F	Set of flight
K	Set of crew member's number
A	Set of crew base
P	Set of crew task pairing
i	Subscripts of flight, $i \in F$
j	Subscripts of crew task list, $j \in P$
a	Subscripts of airport, $a \in A$
k	Superscripts of crew, $k \in K$
p	Subscripts of flight sequence executed by crew $k, p = 1, 2, \cdots n$
c_i	Cost of canceling flight i
h_a	Number of flights for airport a executing original schedule after recovery
d_j^k	Cost of crew k executing crew task list j
s_j, f_j	Start and finish time of crew task list j
PVN	Sum of vacation of all members
x_j^k	Whether crew k executes task list j
y_i	Whether flight i is canceled
a_{ij}	Whether flight i is contained in crew task list j
b_{pa}, e_{pa}	Whether the pth task is started or ended at airport a
x_j^k	The jth task executed by crew k
t_j^k	Working time possessed by the jth task executed by crew k
$\overline{t^k}$	Average working time executed by crew k, $\overline{t^k} = \sum_{j \in P} x_j^k t_j^k / \sum_{j \in P} x_j^k$

$$\min Z_1 = \sum_{k\in K}\sum_{j\in P} d_j^k x_j^k + \sum_{i\in F} c_i y_i \tag{1}$$

$$\min Z_2 = \sum_{k\in K}\sum_{j\in P} \left(x_j^k t_j^k - x_j^k \overline{t^k}\right)^2 \tag{2}$$

Our model includes two objective functions. Objective function (1) demands the lowest executing cost and canceling cost. Objective function (2) requires the minimum of crew member's worktime variance, which means the fairness of the worktime of each crew is preferred.

$$s.t. \sum_{k\in K}\sum_{j\in P} a_{ij} x_j^k + y_i = 1 \; \forall i \in F \tag{3}$$

$$\sum_{k\in K} x_j^k \le 1, \; \forall j \in P \tag{4}$$

$$\sum_{j\in P} x_j^k (f_j - s_j) \le 100, \; \forall k \in K \tag{5}$$

$$\left| x_{j+1}^k s_{j+1} - x_j^k f_j \right| \ge x_j^k x_{j+1}^k \; \forall k \in K, j \in P \tag{6}$$

$$x_p^k b_{pa} = x_{p+1}^k e_{(p+1)a}, \; \forall k \in K, \; \forall a \in A, \; p \in Z \tag{7}$$

Constraint (3) ensures each flight can only be executed by single crew, or canceled. Constraint (4) guarantees each crew can execute at most one task list. Constraint (5) requires the duration of crew executing task every month is less than 100 h. Constraint (6) restricts the rest time of crew between two consecutive tasks is more than 1 h. Constraint (7) ensures the ending airport of preceding task is the same as the following task's airport.

3 Improved Multi-objective Particle Swarm Algorithm

In this section, we present our tabu-based multi-objective particle swarm algorithm, abbreviated as MOPSO-TS, which combining the primary MOPSO and tabu search.

3.1 Primary MOPSO

Multi-objective particle swarm optimization is based on single-objective PSO, finding global excellent solution set through establishing non-dominant solution set and selecting one particle in non-dominant set as guiding solution. Through randomizing the location of each point, iterating and updating towards different directions and broadly exploring the unknown space, a Pareto front will be obtained finally.

3.2 Tabu-Based Multi-objective Particle Swarm Algorithm

Due to MOPSO's drawback of prematurity and local optima, we introduced tabu search to the primary MOPSO.

Tabu search algorithm is an iterative search algorithm simulating human intelligence. It can avoid roundabout searching by setting up tabu list and tabu principle, therefore escape from local optimal point and enhance the ability of global search.

Targeting at the shortcoming of MOPSO, we combine the MOPSO with tabu search. Since the initial solution shows a great impact on the effectiveness of tabu search algorithm, firstly, we introduce tabu search algorithm after optimizing iteratively by MOPSO. Then updating the tabu list on the basis of comparatively excellent group which is constituted by non-dominant solution and partly dominant solution. And searching in the neighborhood until the terminal condition is met. The process in detail is presented in Fig. 1 and the improvement is circled in red.

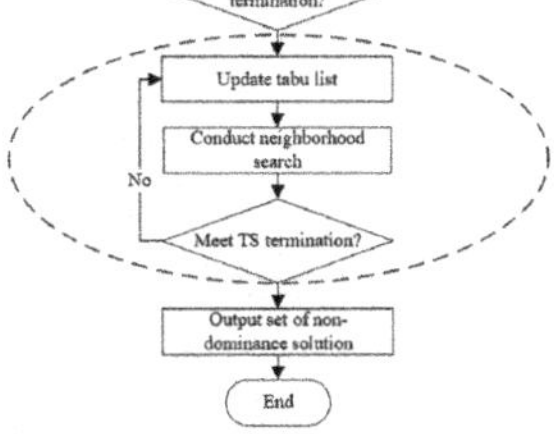

Fig. 1. Flow chart of MOPSO with tabu search

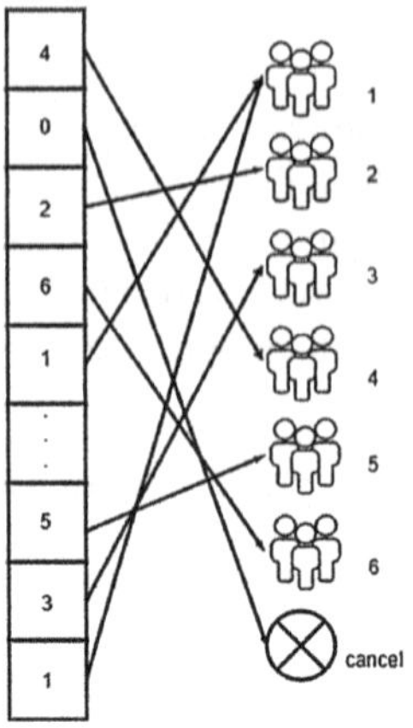

Fig. 2. Encoding scheme of crew recovery problem

3.3 Tests and Results

Intending to verify the performance of MOPSO-TS, we adopted the ZDT1, ZDT2 and ZDT3 as test functions forwarded by famous scholar Deb [23].

This paper compared MOPSO-TS with primary MOPSO under the same test functions and conditions, and evaluated these algorithms through IGD and HV. Table 2 shows the average number of each index after 30 times of independent experiments.

Table 2. Results of test functions

Test function	Index	MOPSO	MOPSO-TS
ZDT1	IGD	9.57E−03	6.56E−03
	HV	7.11E−01	7.15E−01
ZDT2	IGD	9.21E−03	6.54E−03
	HV	4.17E−01	4.40E−01
ZDT3	IGD	1.21E−02	8.18E−03
	HV	5.95E−01	5.97E−01

According to the table, the Pareto fronts concluded by MOPSO-TS in the three test functions are all better than MOPSO. And among the algorithms, MOPSO-TS has the smallest IGD and biggest HV, indicating that MOPSO-TS is better in convergency, diversity and overall performance.

4 Encoding Scheme

According to the model and the characteristic of the problem, we adopted the encoding scheme in Fig. 2.

Each particle in the group represents one scheduling scheme. The number of particle's dimension refers to the total number of flights. For each dimension which equals to k, it represents the corresponding flight is executed by the kth crew. If the dimension value is 0, it means the flight is canceled.

Table 3. Primary flight schedule

Flight	Departure airport	Arrival airport	Departure time	Arrival time	Flying time
1481	BOS	CLE	730	930	158
1519	BOS	GSO	1015	1210	155
1687	CLE	BOS	740	940	156
789	CLE	EWR	1100	1225	119
1867	CLE	GSO	1335	1450	113
1609	CLE	GSO	1650	1805	112
1568	CLE	GSO	2150	2305	110
1601	EWR	GSO	700	843	117
1779	EWR	GSO	830	1015	121
1690	EWR	CLE	955	1134	124
1531	EWR	GSO	1155	1330	130
1431	EWR	GSO	1300	1440	136
1626	GSO	EWR	1220	1353	129
1670	GSO	CLE	1240	1355	124
1678	GSO	CLE	1545	1700	108
1591	GSO	CLE	1630	1758	121
1720	GSO	CLE	1725	1843	116
1698	GSO	EWR	1825	1957	130

5 Experiments and Results

In this section, we simulated the rescheduling process due to the cancelation of certain flight under the force majeure like inclement weather and natural disaster on MATLAB2020a, while balancing the minimal recovery cost and even worktime.

Table 4. Primary crew schedule

Crew	Flight number	Departure airport	Arrival airport	Departure time	Arrival time	Flying time
E1	1601	EWR	GSO	700	843	117
	1626	GSO	EWR	1220	1353	129
E2	1779	EWR	GSO	830	1015	121
	1670	GSO	CLE	1240	1355	124
	1609	CLE	GSO	1650	1805	112
E3	1690	EWR	CLE	955	1134	124
	1867	CLE	GSO	1335	1450	113
	1678	GSO	CLE	1545	1700	108
E4	1531	EWR	GSO	1155	1330	130
	1591	GSO	CLE	1630	1758	110
	1568	CLE	GSO	2150	2305	110
E5	1687	CLE	BOS	740	940	156
	1519	BOS	GSO	1015	1210	155
	1698	GSO	EWR	1825	1957	130
E6	1481	BOS	CLE	730	930	158
	789	CLE	EWR	1100	1225	119
	1431	EWR	GSO	1300	1440	136
	1720	GSO	CLE	1725	1843	116

5.1 Parameter Setting

This paper used data in Table 3 and Table 4 [24] to verify the performance of MOPSO-TS in solving irregular flight recovery problem, involving 18 flights and 6 crews. The total flying time must be less than 100 h and the gap between two continual flights is ought to be longer than one hour. The canceling cost is 100 thousand yuan and switching cost is 20 thousand yuan. Table 5 is the detailed parameter setting of MOPSO-TS. To simulate abnormal situation, we assume that flight 1720 is canceled due to epidemic.

Table 5. Parameters of algorithm

Symbols	Meaning	Value
	MOPSO-related	
I	Maximum iteration time	2000
D	Dimension of particle	17

(*continued*)

Table 5. (*continued*)

Symbols	Meaning	Value
NP	Number of particles	100
NR	Number of repository	100
NC	Number of candidate	150
W	Inertia weight	0.9
Wdamp	Inertia weight damping rate	0.9
v_{max}; v_{min}	Lower and upper bound of variables	6;0
c_1	Personal learning coefficient	1.5
c_2	Global learning coefficient	1.5
	Tabu Search-related	
TI	Maximum iteration time of tabu search	500
mu	Mutation rate	0.7
nGrid	Number of grid per dimension	7
Alpha	Inflation rate	0.1
Beta	Leader selection pressure	2
Gamma	Deletion selection pressure	2
TL	Tabu length	9

5.2 Experiment Result

We adopted MOPSO-TS and MOPSO to solve the problem independently for thirty times, and compared the Pareto Front of them. Pareto front has many points, and we

Table 6. Recovered crew schedule

Crew	Flight number	Departure airport	Arrival airport	Departure time	Arrival time	Flying time
E1	1601	EWR	GSO	700	843	117
	1670	GSO	CLE	1240	1355	129
	1609	CLE	GSO	1650	1805	112
E2	1779	EWR	GSO	830	1015	121
	1626	GSO	EWR	1220	1353	124
E3	1690	EWR	CLE	955	1134	156
	1867	CLE	GSO	1335	1450	155
	1678	GSO	CLE	1545	1700	108
E4	1531	EWR	GSO	1155	1330	124
	1591	GSO	CLE	1630	1758	110

(*continued*)

Table 6. *(continued)*

Crew	Flight number	Departure airport	Arrival airport	Departure time	Arrival time	Flying time
	1568	CLE	GSO	2150	2305	110
E5	1687	CLE	BOS	740	940	130
	1519	BOS	GSO	1015	1210	116
	1698	GSO	EWR	1825	1957	136
E6	1481	BOS	CLE	730	930	158
	789	CLE	EWR	1100	1225	119
	1431	EWR	GSO	1300	1440	136

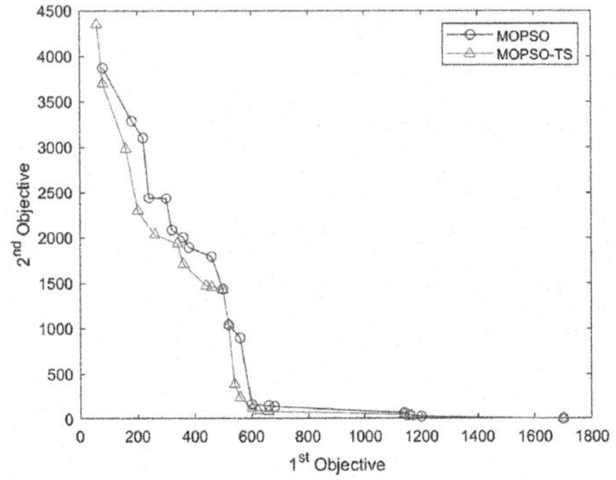

Fig. 3. The Pareto Front of MOPSO-TS, MOPSO

choose one of the point with the lowest cost to exhibit the specific recovery scheme, which is shown as Table 6.

According to the Pareto Front curves in Fig. 3, the front of MOPSO-TS was closer to the bottom left of target space than MOPSO, which demonstrated MOPSO-TS performed better in the solution of our model.

6 Conclusions and Future Directions

In this paper, we studied irregular flight recovery problem, created a multi-objective model considering the fare and satisfaction concurrently and proposed an improved multi-objective particle swarm optimization hybridizing tabu search. In the future, we will apply our algorithm to other problems with multiple objectives and come up with new elements to enrich our model.

Acknowledgment. The study was supported in part by the Natural Science Foundation of China Grant No. 62103286, No. 71971143, No. 62001302, in part by Social Science Youth Foundation of Ministry of Education of China under Grant 21YJC630181, in part by Guangdong Provincial Philosophy and Social Sciences Planning Project under Grant GD22XGL22, in part by Guangdong Basic and Applied Basic Research Foundation under Grant 2019A1515110401,

2021A1515011348, 2019A1515111205, in part by Guangdong Province Philosophy and Social Science Planning Discipline Co-construction Project under Grant GD22XGL22, in part by Natural Science Foundation of Guangdong Province under Grant 2020A1515010749, 2020A1515010752, in part by Key Research Foundation of Higher Education of Guangdong Provincial Education Bureau under Grant 2019KZDXM030, in part by Natural Science Foundation of Shenzhen under Grant JCYJ20190808145011259, in part by Shenzhen Science and Technology Program under Grant RCBS20200714114920379, in part by Guangdong Province Innovation Team Intelligent Management and Interdisciplinary Innovation under Grant 2021WCXTD002, in part by Special Projects in Key Fields of Ordinary Colleges and Universities in Guangdong Province under Grant 2022ZDZX2054.

References

1. Notice on the issuance of Normal Statistical Method of Civil Aviation Flight[R]. Communique of Civil Aviation Administration of China (2003)
2. Chutima, P., Arayikanon, K.: Many-objective low-cost airline cockpit crew rostering optimisation. Comput. Ind. Eng. **150**, 106844 (2020)
3. Wen, X., Ma, H.L., Chung, S.H., et al.: Robust airline crew scheduling with flight flying time variability. Transp. Res. Part E: Logist. Transp. Rev. **144**, 102132 (2020)
4. Zeighami, V., Saddoune, M., Soumis, F.: Alternating Lagrangian decomposition for integrated airline crew scheduling problem. Eur. J. Oper. Res. **287**(1), 211–224 (2020)
5. Zhou, S.Z., Zhan, Z.H., Chen, Z.G., et al.: A multi-objective ant colony system algorithm for airline crew rostering problem with fairness and satisfaction. IEEE Trans. Intell. Transp. Syst. **22**(11), 6784–6798 (2020)
6. Doi, T., Nishi, T., Voß, S.: Two-level decomposition-based matheuristic for airline crew rostering problems with fair working time. Eur. J. Oper. Res. **267**(2), 428–438 (2018)
7. Quesnel, F., Desaulniers, G., Soumis, F.: Improving air crew rostering by considering crew preferences in the crew pairing problem. Transp. Sci. **54**(1), 97–114 (2020)
8. Antunes, D., Vaze, V., Antunes, A.P.: A robust pairing model for airline crew scheduling. Transp. Sci. **53**(6), 1751–1771 (2019)
9. Wen, X., Chung, S.H., Ji, P., et al.: Individual scheduling approach for multi-class airline cabin crew with manpower requirement heterogeneity. Transp. Res. Part E: Logist. Transp. Rev. **163**, 102763 (2022)
10. Evler, J., Lindner, M., Fricke, H., et al.: Integration of turnaround and aircraft recovery to mitigate delay propagation in airline networks. Comput. Oper. Res. **138**, 105602 (2022)
11. Jin, H., Chen, S., Ran, X., et al.: Column generation-based optimum crew scheduling incorporating network representation for urban rail transit systems. Comput. Ind. Eng. **169**, 108155 (2022)
12. Zhang, X., Zheng, X., Cheng, R., et al.: A competitive mechanism based multi-objective particle swarm optimizer with fast convergence. Inf. Sci. **427**, 63–76 (2018)
13. Luo, J., Huang, X., Yang, Y., et al.: A many-objective particle swarm optimizer based on indicator and direction vectors for many-objective optimization. Inf. Sci. **514**, 166–202 (2020)
14. Cui, Y., Meng, X., Qiao, J.: A multi-objective particle swarm optimization algorithm based on two-archive mechanism. Appl. Soft Comput. **119**, 108532 (2022)
15. Devaraj, A.F.S., Elhoseny, M., Dhanasekaran, S., et al.: Hybridization of firefly and improved multi-objective particle swarm optimization algorithm for energy efficient load balancing in cloud computing environments. J. Parallel Distrib. Comput. **142**, 36–45 (2020)

16. Qu, B., Li, C., Liang, J., et al.: A self-organized speciation based multi-objective particle swarm optimizer for multimodal multi-objective problems. Appl. Soft Comput. **86**, 105886 (2020)
17. Liang, J., Guo, Q., Yue, C., Qu, B., Yu, K.: A self-organizing multi-objective particle swarm optimization algorithm for multimodal multi-objective problems. In: Tan, Y., Shi, Y., Tang, Q. (eds.) ICSI 2018. LNCS, vol. 10941, pp. 550–560. Springer, Cham (2018). https://doi.org/10.1007/978-3-319-93815-8_52
18. Liu, J., Zhang, H., He, K., et al.: Multi-objective particle swarm optimization algorithm based on objective space division for the unequal-area facility layout problem. Expert Syst. Appl. **102**, 179–192 (2018)
19. bin Mohd Zain, M.Z., Kanesan, J., Chuah, J.H., et al.: A multi-objective particle swarm optimization algorithm based on dynamic boundary search for constrained optimization. Appl. Soft Comput. **70**, 680–700 (2018)
20. Goyal, K.K., Sharma, N., Dev Gupta, R., et al.: A soft computing-based analysis of cutting rate and recast layer thickness for AZ31 alloy on WEDM using RSM-MOPSO. Materials **15**(2), 635 (2022)
21. Mahapatra, G.S., Maneckshaw, B., Barker, K.: Multi-objective reliability redundancy allocation using MOPSO under hesitant fuzziness. Expert Syst. Appl. **198**, 116696 (2022)
22. Sellami, R., Farooq, S., Rafik, N.: An improved MOPSO algorithm for optimal sizing & placement of distributed generation: a case study of the Tunisian offshore distribution network (ASHTART). Energy Rep. **8**, 6960–6975 (2022)
23. Deb, K., Pratap, A., Agarwal, S., et al.: A fast and elitist multi-objective genetic algorithm: NSGA-II. IEEE Trans. Evol. Comput. **6**(2), 182–197 (2002)
24. Wei, G., Yu, G., Song, M.: Optimization model and algorithm for crew management during airline irregular operations. J. Comb. Optim. **1**(3), 305–321 (1997)

A Robot Foreign Object Inspection Algorithm for Transmission Line Based on Improved YOLOv5

Zhenzhou Wang[1], Xiaoyue Xie[1], Xiang Wang[1(✉)], Yijin Zhao[2], Lifang Ma[1], and Pingping Yu[1]

[1] College of School of Information Science and Engineering, Hebei University of Science and Technology, Shijiazhuang, Hebei, China
wangxiang@hebust.edu.cn
[2] College of Feduni Information Engineering Institute, Hebei University of Science and Technology, Shijiazhuang, Hebei, China

Abstract. Aiming at the problems of slow detection rate and low accuracy of traditional transmission line inspection methods, a transmission line target detection model based on improved YOLOv5 is proposed in this paper. Firstly, the Bottleneck module in the Backbone network is replaced to improve the lightweight of the model; then the coordinate attention (CA) module is introduced to design the Backbone network to improve the performance of model detection; finally, the frame regression loss function is changed to improve the accuracy of detection. After the transmission line images are further expanded, the foreign object data sets of transmission line are constructed. Experiments on the above data sets show that: Compared with YOLOv5, the detection accuracy of the optimized model is improved by 6.7%, the mean average precision (mAP) reaches 87.0%, and the detection speed is improved by 16.0%. The YOLOv5 lightweight model proposed in this paper reduces the power consumption of the platform and improves the model detection speed and accuracy. It is more conducive to the deployment of the target detection model in the mobile terminal.

Keywords: Transmission line inspection · Target detection · YOLOv5 · The lightweight of the model · The coordinate attention

1 Introduction

Transmission lines are characterized by large capacity, long transmission distance, wide coverage and large demand. In the open-air environment for a long time, foreign bodies like kites, balloons and falling plastic films will hang on the transmission lines. This has a great impact on the normal transmission of power, so it is very necessary to inspect the transmission line. The traditional manual inspection method has low efficiency and complicated working process, and the result is easily affected by the external environment. It has high requirements for the professional ability of the staff and it is unable to meet the daily inspection needs of the transmission line. With people's attention to the

Y. Xu et al. (Eds.): ML4CS 2022, LNCS 13657, pp. 133–147, 2023.
https://doi.org/10.1007/978-3-031-20102-8_11

safety of high voltage transmission lines and the development of science and technology, robot inspection is widely used to inspect high-voltage transmission lines.

In order to realize the detection of transmission lines, many scholars have tried many ways, in the early days, mainly through the traditional image processing methods. Reference [1] showed a fusion algorithm based on contour feature and gray similarity matching, which realized high-precision insulator contour extraction and accurate separation of insulator pieces, and established an insulator defect detection model based on insulator piece spacing and gray similarity. Reference [2] used the moving edge technology, designed the edge data processing layer, extracted the image features of transmission line inspection by image projection, and abstracted the obtained features into a two-dimensional plane to realize the image recognition of power grid transmission line inspection. However, the image feature extraction process of the above methods was very complex and slow, and the algorithm performance was easily affected by the geographical background difference of transmission lines and various weather, so the generalization ability was not high.

With the improvement of computer hardware level, deep learning algorithm also has rapid development. At present, the representative target detection algorithms are roughly divided into two categories: one is the two-stage algorithm based on candidate regions. The main representative algorithms are Region Convolutional Neural Network (RCNN) [3], Faster-RCNN [4], etc. After generating candidate regions that may contain detection targets, Convolutional Neural Networks (CNN) [5] is used to classify and regress the candidate blocks, and then the detection frame is obtained. Reference [6] showed a new layered architecture of a deep convolution neural network to locate and detect insulator defects. The cascaded network used CNN which based on a layered network to transform the defect detection problem into a two-level target detection problem. Reference [7] firstly used Faster-RCNN to quickly locate the insulator and then classified the location area, finally semantic segmentation judges whether the insulator is burst. Although the detection accuracy of the two-stage algorithm is high, this method firstly extracts the potential location of the target through the candidate area generation network, then carries out detection and recognition. As a result, the detection speed is slow and the real-time effect cannot be achieved. Therefore, the performance of target detection algorithm in embedded devices is greatly limited.

The other is a single-stage algorithm based on regression calculation. Representative algorithms include Single Shot MultiBox Detector (SSD) [8], You Only Look Once (YOLO) [9], YOLOv3 [10] and YOLOv5 [11]. This kind of algorithm uses the idea of regression to directly return the position of the target frame and the target category at multiple positions of the image. In recent years, scholars have applied it to the detection of different objects. Reference [12] designed a fault method based on single-stage SSD detection algorithm for insulator with multi-level perception in aerial images. Reference [13] completed the training of the insulator database by using the YOLO network model and achieved a good recognition effect. Reference [14] proposed an improved YOLOv3 model, which used SPP network and multi-scale prediction network to improve the accuracy of insulator fault detection.

To sum up, in this paper, the YOLOv5 recognition model is improved and applied to the field of transmission line inspection. Firstly, Ghost Bottleneck module is replaced with the Bottleneck module in the YOLOv5 network [15]; then the coordinate attention (CA) module [16] is introduced; and finally, efficient intersection over union loss (EIOU Loss) is used as the loss function. On the basis of ensuring the lightweight of the detection model, the high detection speed is considered. The inspection robot will take a large number of real-time pictures of high-voltage lines, and accurately identify and analyze these pictures by using the deep convolutional neural network in the training stage. Then, the deep semantic features of line foreign objects are automatically extracted in the test stage, which can reduce the rate of false detection and missed detection.

2 YOLOv5 Network Structure

In June 2016, Joseph Redmon et al. [13] proposed the YOLO deep learning framework. The YOLOv5 network structure inherits the extremely high detection speed of previous versions of YOLO, by introducing the concept of residual block in the residual neural network, the hierarchical relationship of the network and the logic of existing prediction modules are dynamically optimized to improve the performance for detecting small targets. YOLOv5 has four network structures, namely YOLOv5s, YOLOv5m, YOLOv5l, and YOLOv5x [5]. Due to the differences in the depth and width of the network structure, the size and precision of the four versions of the model increase successively. The research content of this paper is transmission line inspection. Compared with the detection accuracy, it has higher requirements for the detection speed of network structure, therefore, this paper selects YOLOv5s as the network structure. The YOLOv5 network structure is mainly divided into four parts: Input, Backbone, Neck, and Prediction [17], as shown in Fig. 1.

The Input network mainly includes data enhancement, adaptive picture scaling, adaptive anchor box calculation and other functions. Mosaic data enhancement is mainly carried out by randomly selecting four images for random scaling, distribution and splicing. The detection data set is enriched, the robustness of the algorithm is strengthened, and the model can better detect small target objects in the image. A small number of black edges are added to the original image, which are uniformly scaled to a standard size of $608 \times 608 \times 3$ and then sent to the neural network. Adaptive anchor frame calculation is trained on the initial anchor frame to get the prediction frame, calculate the gap between the prediction frame and the real frame, the gap between the prediction frame and the real frame can be calculated, then the network update parameters in reverse, which can make the pre-diction result more reasonable.

The Backbone network is mainly used to extract network features, containing Focus, CSP [18], SPP [19], etc. The Focus module performs four slice operations and a convolution operation of thirty-two convolution kernels. The original image of $608 \times 608 \times 3$ becomes the characteristic diagram of $304 \times 304 \times 32$, which reduces the loss of feature information caused by convolution. The CSP module solves the problem of large computation of network structure. It is mainly used to extract the network features in the samples and fuse the feature information of different layers to form a richer feature map. The SPP structure is a spatial feature pyramid pool structure, which is mainly used to expand the receptive field, integrate local and global features, and enrich the information of the feature map.

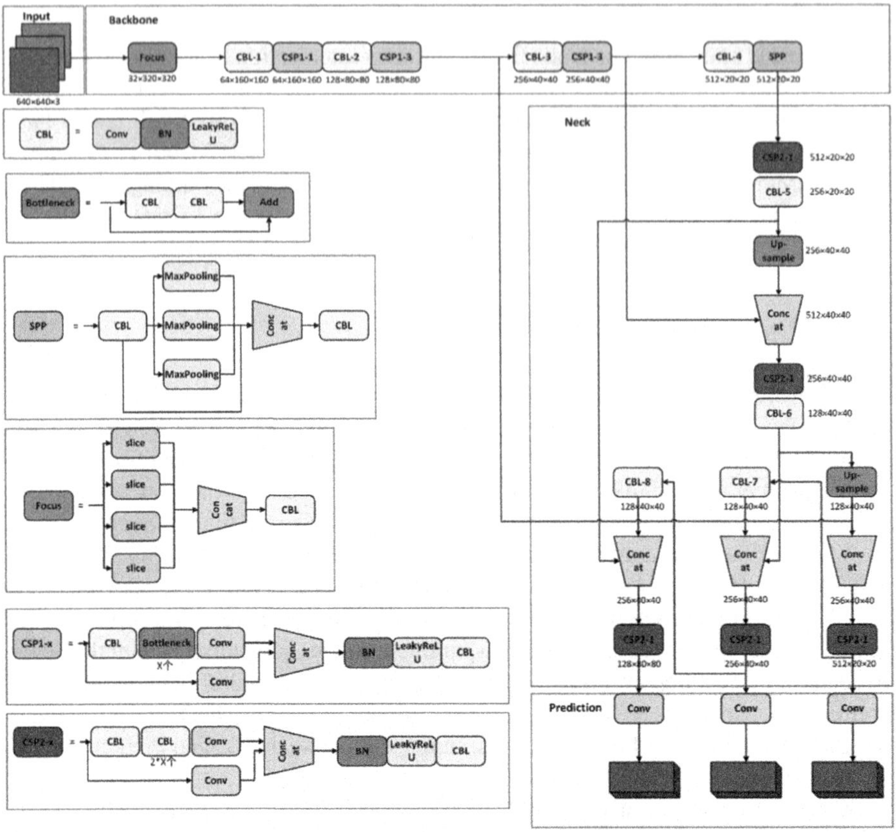

Fig. 1. YOLOv5 network structure.

The Neck network is mainly used to fuse different size feature maps and extracts high-level semantic features. It adopts the structure of FPN+PAN [20]. The FPN structure transmits the high-level feature information of the detected target from top to bottom through down-sampling. Then, the feature pyramids of two PAN structures are used for up-sampling, the shallow features are transmitted from bottom to top, and the information is transmitted to the prediction layer.

The Prediction network mainly includes loss function and Non Maximum Suppression (NMS) [21]. GIOU Loss [22] is used as a loss function in YOLOv5, which increases the measurement of the intersection scale and solves the problem of disjoint boundary boxes that IOU Loss [23] cannot handle. The NMS is used to filter the optimal target box, which solves the problem that a target has multiple candidate boxes. The NMS performs non-maximum suppression on the last detection box of the target, selects the prediction box with high score for retention, and removes the corresponding candidate box with low score.

3 Improvement of YOLOv5 Network Structure

The backbone network in YOLOv5 algorithm has more Bottleneck structures, and the convolution kernel in convolution operation contains a large number of parameters, which increases the deployment cost of the model. In this paper, the lightweight Ghost Bottleneck module is used to replace some standard volume layers in the YOLOv5 backbone network. Since the YOLOv5 network structure uses the same weighting method to extract feature information of different importance, there is a problem of no attention preference in the extraction process of the position coordinates and categories of the regression target frame in the output layer. By establishing the interdependence between channels, The CA module can adaptively calibrate the corresponding characteristics between channels. It is difficult for GIOU Loss to optimize the prediction frame in the horizontal or vertical direction, resulting in slow convergence. Therefore, EIOU Loss with better performance is adopted in this paper, the improved network model is called YOLOv5-GCE.

The improved process is divided into three steps and the steps are as follows. The improved YOLOv5 network structure is shown in Fig. 2 and the algorithm flow is shown in Fig. 3.

1. The residual components of the first CSP1-1 structure in the Backbone part of YOLOv5 are replaced with one Ghost Bottleneck module. The second and third CSP1-3 residual components in the Backbone of YOLOv5 are replaced with three Ghost Bottleneck components, which can reduce the network scale and improve the calculation speed;
2. On the basis of step 1, the attention mechanism is embedded into the CSP module of the Backbone network to help the model to better extract the features of the target of interest, which well obtains the global receptive field and encodes accurate location information, greatly enhancing the accuracy of model training.
3. On the basis of step 2, EIOU Loss is used to improve the accuracy of detection.

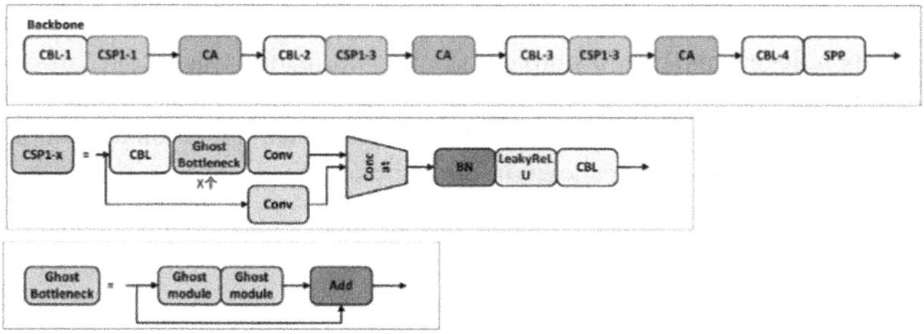

Fig. 2. Improved network structure diagram.

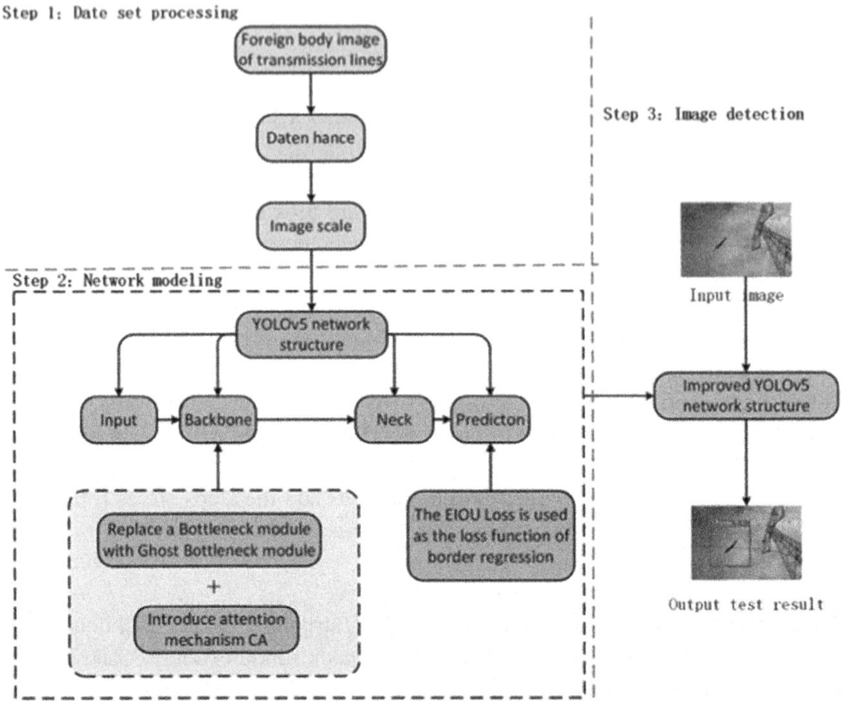

Fig. 3. Flow chart of improved YOLOv5 model.

3.1 Ghost Bottleneck

The original Bottleneck module in YOLOv5 generates too many redundant feature maps in the process of feature extraction, which not only occupies hardware memory, but affects the running speed of the network. In order to further reduce the demand for hardware resources, this paper uses the idea of the Ghost Net [16] structure for reference and replaces the heavy Bottleneck module in YOLOv5 with the Ghost Bottleneck module. Compared with the direct conventional convolution, the computation of Ghost convolution is greatly reduced, and only a simple linear transformation can produce most of the feature information. The module is mainly composed of two Ghost modules stacked. The Ghost module uses fewer parameters and low-cost linear operation to generate rich feature diagrams. Its principle is shown in Fig. 4 below.

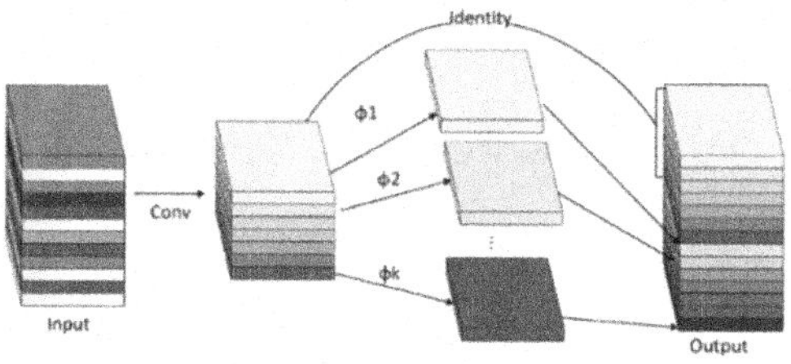

Fig. 4. Ghost module.

As can be seen from Fig. 4 above, the implementation of the module is divided into two parts. One part is obtained by ordinary convolution, the other part is generated by linear operation, and finally the two groups of feature maps are spliced together in the specified dimension. In this case, obtaining the same number of feature maps is only half of the computation. Ghost structure operation can be expressed as:

$$Y' = X * f' + b \tag{1}$$

This equation is a traditional convolution layer that outputs a small number of characteristic maps. Where, X is the input characteristic diagram, * is the convolution operation, f' is the convolution kernel of the convolution operation, Y′ is the characteristic diagram of channels, and b is the offset term.

$$y_{ij} = \Phi_{i,j}(y_i'), \ \forall i = 1, \cdots, m, \ j = 1, \cdots, s \tag{2}$$

This equation is a linear transformation operation for generating redundant features, where, y_i is the ith channel feature of Y′, $\Phi_{i,j}$ is the linear operation of the jth Ghost feature map generated by y_i'. It can be seen that each y_i' can generates s Ghost feature maps. Therefore, m*s characteristic graphs can be obtained by linear operation of m feature graphs.

3.2 Coordinate Attention

Due to the irregular shape of the kite and the thin film on the transmission line, the detection rate of foreign matters on the transmission line is not accurate. In recent years, the attention mechanism module has been widely used in the deep neural network in order to improve the performance of the model. Therefore, this paper introduces the CA module to improve the accuracy of the network. By splitting the two-dimensional global pool operation into two one-dimensional coding processes, the attentional mechanism can capture not only the cross-channel information but the direction perception and position perception information, so that the module can locate and recognize the target of interest more accurately. The structure of the CA module is shown in Fig. 5.

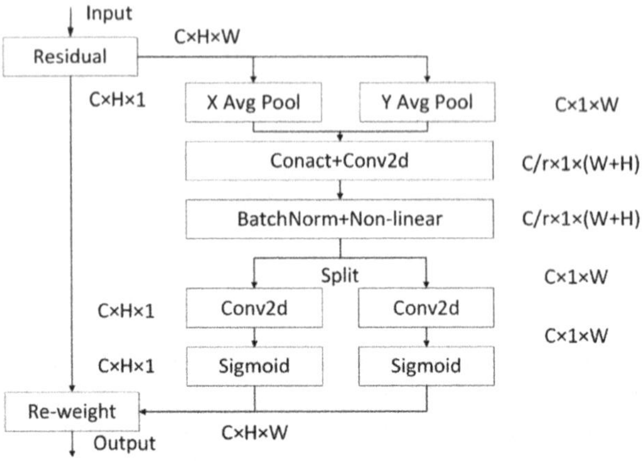

Fig. 5. Coordinate attention.

As can be seen from the above Fig. 5, the CA module firstly divides the input feature map into the horizontal direction and vertical direction. The average pooling of dimensions (H, 1) and (1, W) are used to encode each channel along with horizontal and vertical coordinates respectively. That is the output of the c channel with height H and the c channel with width W. The equation is as follows:

$$Z_c^h(h) = \frac{1}{W}\sum_{0\leq i\leq W} x_c(h, i) \tag{3}$$

$$Z_c^{\mathrm{w}}(\mathrm{w}) = \frac{1}{H}\sum_{0\leq i\leq H} x_c(\mathrm{j,w}) \tag{4}$$

Then, the two transformations in the above formula are combined with two spatial directions, and two feature maps Z^h and Z^{w} are generated in a cascade. The feature maps in the two directions which obtain the global receptive field are spliced together, the 1 × 1 convolution module is used to transform them:

$$f = \delta(F_1([Z^h, Z^w])) \tag{5}$$

In this equation, [,] is the splicing operation along with the spatial dimension, δ is a nonlinear activation function, and f is the intermediate feature mapping of spatial information encoded in horizontal and vertical directions.

Along the dimension of space, it will decompose into two separate tensors f^{h} and f^{w}. The feature graph f is transformed by 1 × 1 convolution which obtains the characteristic graphs F_h and F_{w} with the same number of channels as the original. The attention weights $\mathrm{g^h}$ and $\mathrm{g^w}$ in height and width of feature images are obtained by Sigmoid activation function σ, and the equation is as follows:

$$g^h = \sigma(F_h(f^h)) \tag{6}$$

$$g^w = \sigma(F_w(f^w)) \tag{7}$$

Finally, the final feature map with attention weight in the width and height direction is obtained through multiplication weighting calculation on the original feature map, and its final output is shown in Eq. (8):

$$Yc = (i,j) = x_c(i,j) \times g_c^h(i) \times g_c^w(j) \tag{8}$$

3.3 Loss Function

As the loss function of YOLOv5 network structure, GIOU Loss improves the existing problems when the real frame does not intersect with the prediction frame, but when the prediction frame is in the real frame of the target, its loss value will not change and its relative position relationship cannot be distinguished. It is also difficult to optimize the prediction frame in the horizontal or vertical direction, resulting in slow convergence. Therefore, EIOU Loss is introduced which clearly measures the differences of three geometric factors in the boundary box, namely overlapping area, center point and side length. EIOU Loss disassembles influence factors of aspect ratio on the basis of CIOU Loss and calculates the length and width of the target frame and anchor frame respectively. The loss function includes three parts: overlap loss, center distance loss and width height loss. The width and height loss minimizes the difference between the width and height of the target box and the anchor box, which make the convergence faster. EIOU Loss is shown in Eq. (9):

$$L_{EIOU} = L_{IOU} + L_{dis} + L_{asp} = 1 - IOU + \frac{\rho^2(b, b^{gt})}{c^2} + \frac{\rho^2(w, w^{gt})}{c_w^2} + \frac{\rho^2(h, h^{gt})}{c_h^2} \tag{9}$$

In this equation, c_w and c_h are the width and height of the smallest external frame covering the prediction frame and the real frame. Therefore, EIOU Loss frame regression loss function with better performance was adopted in this paper.

4 Experimental Results and Comparative Analysis

4.1 Experimental Data Set

In this paper, 340 transmission line images are taken in real-time by camera. It includes single target images and multi-target images, close-up images, long-range images and complex sample data in different weather, different time and different places. Due to a large amount of background information and noise in the sample images, it is a great challenge to the target detection network. In order to enhance the generalization ability of the model and make the model learn deeper feature information, firstly the data set is expanded. By rotating, clipping or converting brightness and contrast based on the original image data, the target detection image has different forms and scales. Finally, a total of 1500 data sets are obtained, and the training sets, test sets and verification sets are distinguished according to the ratio of 8:1:1. Some data samples are shown in Fig. 6.

Fig. 6. Partial data samples.

LabelImg, an annotation tool for image data set, is used to select the target line image, including the category and position of the target frame, and generates the corresponding XML file format for training and testing. After labeling, the sample data sets are made into the standard PASCAL VOC2012 format according to the data sets format of YOLO series algorithm. There are 2000 instances in 1500 images.

4.2 Experimental Environment

The experimental environment in this paper is shown in Table 1 below.

Table 1. Experimental environment.

Operating system	CPU	GPU	Memory	CUDNN	CUDA	Frame platform	Compiling language
Windows x64	i5-12500H	RTX3050	16 GB	7.6	10.1	Pytorch 1.6	Python 3.8

During all training and testing, the model parameters are configured as follows: the initial learning rate is 0.01 and the weight-decay is 0.0001, the momentum is 0.9, and the batch size is set to 32. According to the multiple training result of the model, it is found that the effect is the best when the epoch setting is 270.

4.3 Evaluation Criterion

The performance and detection effect of the experimental model in this paper is evaluated by the following five aspects: the recall(R), the precision (P), and mAP @0.5 [24], model size and detection speed frames per second (FPS) [9]. The specific calculation process is as follows:

$$\text{Precision} = \frac{TP}{TP + FP} = \frac{TP}{N} \tag{10}$$

$$\text{Recall} = \frac{TP}{TP + FP} = \frac{TP}{P} \tag{11}$$

$$\mathrm{mAP} = \frac{1}{c}\sum_{i=1}^{c}\int_{0}^{1} p(r)dr \tag{12}$$

4.4 Comparative Experiment

Data Set Experimental Results. In deep learning, the loss function value can reflect the error between the final prediction result of the target detection model and the actual real value, and it also can be used to analyze and judge the advantages and disadvantages of the training process, the convergence degree of the model and whether it is over fitted. The original model and the improved model are trained with epochs on the same data set for comparative analysis to verify whether the improved YOLOv5-GCE model can improve the performance of the network model. The transformation curves of loss function value with epoch are shown in Fig. 7.

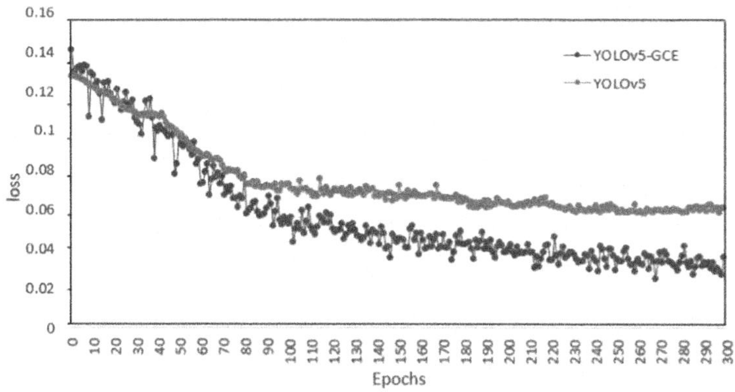

Fig. 7. Variation curve of loss function value with the number of training rounds.

As can be seen from Fig. 7, during the training process, both of them decline rapidly in the early stage and eventually level off, but the loss function of the YOLOv5-GCE model declines faster than the original YOLOv5 model. The GIOU Loss curve of the network model before and after the improvement tends to be stable when they train to 270 epochs, and the model converges when the loss value reaches 0.02. The improved model has a lower loss function value under the same number of training rounds, indicating that the improved model has less loss of details and stronger feature learning ability.

Training and evaluation parameters usually reflect the model training process and the effect of target detection. In this paper, the value of mAP@0.5 is used to judge the model performance, and the performance changes are shown in Fig. 8 below.

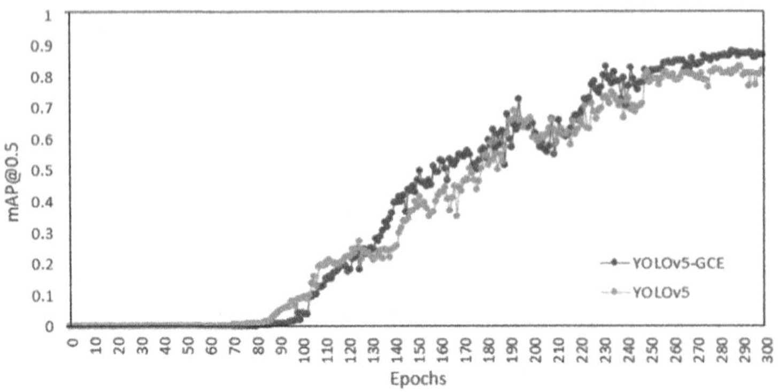

Fig. 8. mAP change curve.

As can be seen from Fig. 8, the mAP parameters of YOLOv5 and the improved model YOLOv5-GCE fluctuate in different degrees, and the overall smooth rise gradually converges at 270 epoch. After the parameter values of the YOLOv5-GCE model are relatively stable, they are higher than YOLOv5. It can be seen that the improved optimization model is significantly better than the original model YOLOv5.

Comparative Experimental Analysis. For the evaluation of model performance, ablation experiments are carried out on different models to verify the performance of different network structures by comprehensively considering the three aspects of mAP, FPS and model size. The ablation Experiment of the four network models is shown in Table 2.

Table 2. Ablation experiment.

Experiment	Ghost	CA	EIOU	R	P	mAP	FPS	Model size
1				82.4	80.8	81.5	36.3	12.5
2	√			81.5	79.4	80.2	43.5	8.8
3	√	√		86.0	85.6	85.8	40.5	9.1
4	√	√	√	87.2	86.9	87.0	42.1	9.7

It can be seen from the experimental data in Table 2 that after replacing the Bottleneck module in YOLOv5 with the Ghost Bottleneck module, the size of the model is only 70.4% of the original model, and the detection speed is 43.5 f/s. Compared with the original model, it is improved obviously. But at the same time, the accuracy of the model is flawed. In experiment 3, after adding the CA module to the network module, the loss of the data sets in the training process are reduced and more learning features are retained. The mAP is improved by 7.0% based on the model of the experiment 2, but it has no significant impact on the detection speed. In experiment 4, although the detection speed decreased slightly, the mAP was improved after replacing the frame regression loss function. To sum up, compared with other structures, the lightweight structure in this paper can achieve higher accuracy, better reasoning speed and better model performance.

In order to further verify the efficiency of the network proposed in this paper, the classical network structures of YOLOv3 and YOLOv4 are added for multiple comparisons. They are trained with the same amount of epochs, and the results are shown in Table 3 below:

Table 3. Comparison of test results of different network structures.

Model	R	P	mAP	FPS	Model size
Faster RCNN	84.6	81.7	83.5	14.7	48
SSD	73.3	70.9	72.6	30.3	16.1
YOLOv3	74.3	72.4	73.8	31.5	16.6
YOLOv4	80.0	78.9	79.1	34.3	14.7
YOLOv5	82.4	80.8	81.5	36.3	12.5
YOLOv5-GCE	87.2	86.9	87.0	42.1	9.7

By analyzing the dates in Table 3, the detection accuracy of the YOLOv5-GCE model has absolute advantages over SSD, YOLOv3 and YOLOv4, and has been improved compared with the YOLOv5 network. The SSD algorithm has a detection speed of 30.3 FPS, but its average accuracy is low. The two-stage detection algorithm Faster R-CNN has a higher average accuracy of 83.5%, but the detection speed is the lowest. Not only the mAP is improved by 5.4%, but the model size is only 77.6% of the original model. The detection speed is also greatly improved. FPS is 5.8 higher than YOLOv5, 10.6 and 7.8 higher than YOLOv3 and YOLOv4 respectively.

The actual operation effect of YOLOv5s and YOLOv5-GCE is shown in Fig. 9 below.

(a) YOLOv5 (b) YOLOv5-GCE

Fig. 9. Comparison of detection results between YOLOv5 and improved YOLOv5.

By comparing the detection results of different scenes in Fig. 9 (a) and (b), it can be seen that the original YOLOv5 model misses the detection of small targets, while the improved YOLOV5-GCE model misses less. Some edge targets and fuzzy targets are more likely to be detected. At the same time, the improved YOLOV5-GCE model is easier to detect some edge and fuzzy tar-gets. For larger and clearer targets, both the original model and the improved network model can be detected accurately, but the improved network is slightly accurate. This shows that the improved network reduces the loss of image information, obtains more information and improves the integrity of effective information.

5 Conclusion

Aiming at the existing problems in the current transmission line inspection task, this paper proposes an improved line detection algorithm based on the YOLOv5 network structure. The computation is reduced, the model is compressed and the feature information extraction ability of the model is enhanced. Experimental results show that the new model is more simplified and its complexity is significantly reduced, which accelerates the detection speed of the model and improves the adaptability of the model to mobile devices. The method presented in this paper has some limitations in foreign body detection, further research is still needed to improve the detection accuracy on the premise of ensuring the detection efficiency of the algorithm. The YOLOv7 network model will be considered for classification and detection of all kinds of foreign objects to improve the detection accuracy.

Acknowledgments. We acknowledge funding from the Special Project of Cultivating Scientific and Technological Innovation Ability of University and Middle School Students (Grant No. 2021H011404), the Special Project of Cultivating Scientific and Technological Innovation Ability of University and Middle School Students (Grant No. 2021H010203), the Hebei College and Middle School Students Science and Technology Innovation Ability Cultivation Special Project (Grant No. 22E50075D) and the Sub Project of National Key R&D Plan Covid-19 Patient Rehabilitation Training Posture Monitoring Bracelet Based on 4G Network (Grant No. 2021YFC0863200-6).

References

1. Tan, P., Li, X.F., Xu, J.M., Ma, J.E., Wang, F.J., Ding, J., et al.: Catenary insulator defect detection based on contour features and gray similarity matching. J. Zhejiang Univ. – Sci. A: Appl. Phys. Eng. **21**(1), 64–73 (2020)
2. Jalil, B., Moroni, D., Pascali, M., Salvetti, O.: Multimodal image analysis for power line inspection. In: International Conference on Pattern Recognition and Artificial Intelligence, Beijing, pp. 13–17 (2018)
3. Jubayer, F., et al.: Detection of mold on the food surface using YOLOv5. Curr. Res. Food Sci. **4**, 724–728 (2021)
4. Yan, B., Fan, P., Lei, X.Y., Liu, Z.J., Yang, F.Z.: A real-time apple targets detection method for picking robot based on improved YOLOv5. Remote Sens. **13**(9), 1619 (2021)
5. Jalil, B., Leone, G.R., Martinelli, M., Moroni, D., Berton, A.: Fault detection in power equipment via an unmanned aerial system using multi modal data. Sensors **19**(13), 3014 (2019)
6. Tao, X., Zhang, D., Wang, Z., Liu, X., Zhang, H., Xu, D.: Detection of power line insulator defects using aerial images analyzed with convolutional neural networks. Trans. Syst. Man Cybern.: Syst. **5**(4), 1486–1498 (2020)

7. Wang, Y., Wang, J., Gao, F., Hu, P., Li, J.: Detection and recognition for fault insulator based on deep learning. In: 2018 11th International Congress on Image and Signal Processing. Bio Medical Engineering and Informatics, Beijing, pp. 1–6 (2018)
8. Zhao, J.Q., Zhang, X.H., Yan, J.W., Qiu, X.L., Yao, X., Tian, Y.C., et al.: A wheat spike detection method in UAV images based on improved YOLOv5. Remote Sens. **13**(16), 3095 (2021)
9. Perera, R., Guzzetti, D., Agrawal, V.: Optimized and autonomous machine learning framework for characterizing pores, particles, grains and grain boundaries in microstructural images. Comput. Mater. Sci. **196**, 110524 (2021)
10. Chowdhury, P.N., Shivakumara, P., Nandanwar, L., Samiron, F., Pal, U., Lu, T.: Oil palm tree counting in drone images. J. Pre-proof **153**, 1–9 (2021)
11. Ning, Z.X., Wu, X.J., Yang, J., Yang, Y.Q.: MT-YOLOv5: mobile terminal table detection model based on YOLOv5. Conf. Ser. **1978**(1), 012010 (2021)
12. Jiang, H., Qiu, X.J., Chen, J., Liu, X., Zhuang, S.: Insulator fault detection in aerial images based on ensemble learning with multi-level perception. IEEE Access **7**, 61797–61810 (2019)
13. Wang, J.H., Xiao, T., Gu, Q.Y., Chen, Q.: YOLOv5_CSL_F: YOLOv5's loss improvement and attention mechanism application for remote sensing image object detection. In: 2021 International Conference on Wireless Communications and Smart Grid, pp. 197–203 (2021)
14. Liu, J.J., Liu, C.Y., Wu, Y.Q., Xu, H.J., Sun, Z.: An improved method based on deep learning for insulator fault detection in diverse aerial images. Energies **14**(14), 4365 (2021)
15. Han, K., Wang, Y.H., Tian, Q., Guo, J., Xu, C.: Ghost net: more features from cheap operations. In: 2020 IEEE/CVF Conference on Computer Vision and Pattern Recognition, Washington, pp. 1580–1589 (2020)
16. Zha, M.F., Qian, W.B., Yi, W.L., Hua, J.: A lightweight YOLOv4-based forestry pest detection method using coordinate attention and feature fusion. Entropy **23**(12), 1587 (2021)
17. Zou, Z., Shi, Z., Guo, Y., Ye, J.: Object detection in 20 years: a survey. IEICE Transactions on Fundamentals of Electronics. Communications and Computer Sciences (2019)
18. Wang, C.Y., Liao, H.Y.M., Wu, Y.H., Chen, P.Y., Yeh, I.H.: CSP net: a new backbone that can enhance learning capability of CNN. In: 2020 IEEE/CVF Conference on Computer Vision and Pattern Recognition Workshops, Washington, pp. 390–391 (2020)
19. He, K.M., Zhang, X.Y., Ren, S.Q., Sun, J.: Spatial pyramid pooling in deep convolutional networks for visual recognition. IEEE Trans. Pattern Anal. Mach. Intell. **379**(9), 1904–1920 (2014)
20. Liu, S., Qi, L., Qin, H., Shi, J., Jia, J.: Path aggregation network for instance segmentation. In: 2018 IEEE/CVF Conference on Computer Vision and Pattern Recognition, Utah, pp. 8759–8761 (2018)
21. Tang, J.L., Liu, S.B., Zheng, B., Zhang, J., Wang, B., Yang, M.K.: Smoking behavior detection based on improved YOLOv5s algorithm. In: The 9th IEEE International Symposium on Next-Generation Electronics, Changsha, pp. 1–4 (2021)
22. Rezatofighi, H., Gwak, N., Gwak, J.Y., Sadeghian, A., Savarese, S.: Generalized intersection over union: a metric and a loss for bounding box regression. In: 2019 IEEE/CVF Conference on Computer Vision and Pattern Recognition, California, pp. 658–666 (2019)
23. Redmon, J., Divvala, S., Girshick, R., Farhadi, A.: You Only Look Once: unified, real-time object detection. In: Proceedings of the IEEE Conference on Computer Vision and Pattern Recognition, New York, pp. 779–788 (2016)
24. Wang, X.Z., Wei, J.Y., Liu, Y., Li, J.H., Zhang, Z., Chen, J.Y., et al.: Research on morphological detection of FR I and FR II radio galaxies based on improved YOLOv5. Universe **7**(7), 211 (2021)

Path Planning Algorithm Based on A_star Algorithm and Q-Learning Algorithm

Xiaodong Zhao[1], Mengying Cao[1], Jingfang Su[1](✉), Yijin Zhao[2], Shuying Liu[1], and Pingping Yu[1]

[1] College of School of Information Science and Engineering, Hebei University of Science and Technology, Shijiazhuang, Hebei, China
sujingfang1980@hebust.edu.cn

[2] College of Feduni Information Engineering Institute, Hebei University of Science and Technology, Shijiazhuang, Hebei, China

Abstract. The path planning algorithm is one of the most important algorithms in indoor mobile robot applications. As an integral part of ground mobile robot research, the path planning problem has greater research and application value. Based on machine learning, the mobile robot is continuously tried and trained in the simulation environment to eventually achieve the optimal path planning requirements for real-time obstacle avoidance, resulting in a new path planning algorithm. To make the planning goal smoother, after optimizing the global path planning A_star algorithm, it is necessary to combine the Q-learning algorithm, so this paper proposes the HA-Q algorithm. Under the HA-Q algorithm, the mobile robot can smoothly move from the specified starting point to the target point where the specified function is designated, to realize the functions of obstacle avoidance and path selection. After some simulation experiments, the HA-Q algorithm is more consistent with the ground mobile robot movement in the actual scene compared to the traditional algorithm. At the same time, these experimental results also show that the algorithm can be used to obtain a short and smooth path, avoid obstacles in real time, and effectively avoid the problem of falling into a locally optimal solution.

Keywords: Path planning · Mobile robot · A_star · Q-learning

1 Introduction

With the rapid development of artificial intelligence, indoor mobile robots have entered people's lives [1]. Path planning is an indispensable part of the autonomous navigation process of mobile robots [2]. Path planning means designing the desired path for mobile carriers to avoid obstacles and arrive at the designated destination when there are obstacles in the space [3–5]. It can be divided into global path planning and local path planning.

The A_star algorithm is a very effective path optimization algorithm, which is faster than the Dijkstra algorithm [6]. It first appeared in 1968, and the overall framework of

Y. Xu et al. (Eds.): ML4CS 2022, LNCS 13657, pp. 148–157, 2023.
https://doi.org/10.1007/978-3-031-20102-8_12

the algorithm is a graph traversal search algorithm [7]. Unlike most other graph search algorithms, it uses a heuristic function to estimate the distance between any point on the map and the target point. Through this heuristic, it is possible to coordinate the search in the best direction. In an unknown environment, the reward and punishment mechanism of the Q-learning reinforcement learning algorithm can apply incentives at the target node, so that the incentives are transmitted along the path. Rewards and punishments are interdependent throughout the learning process [8]. Finally, the mobile robot will get closer and closer to the target point.

The A_star algorithm is well mature and has the advantage that it is fully capable of capturing the solution. However, the resulting disadvantage is that the algorithm is complicated in the dynamic moving obstacle environment. Therefore, the improved A_star algorithm has been widely studied. Xin Yu et al. proposed the improved A_star algorithm that adjusts the number of searchable neighborhoods from eight discrete ones to infinite ones [9]. Chen Guangrong et al. [10] proposed a path planning method based on the combination of convex optimization [11] and the A_star algorithm. This method allows the A_star algorithm to use a large-scale grid to plan the general trend of an optimal path to improve efficiency. Then the ir-SDP method is used to solve A maximum convex polygon barrier-free area for the position of the mobile robot so that the robot can carry out motion planning and obstacle avoidance processing in this area.

Zhu Zhibin et al. used system data to iteratively solve the control method that minimizes a given objective function in order to achieve consistency in multi-intelligent systems [12]. Later Osmankovic D et al. [3] proposed a fuzzy neural network so that the mobile robot can avoid static and dynamic obstacles autonomously after making full use of sensor information and information collection of the surrounding environment for navigation. Feng Shuo et al. [13] nested deep learning into the Q-learning framework for robot path planning in 3D disaster relief environments. But the A_star algorithm cannot guarantee that the search path is optimal when there are multiple minima, and its space growth is exponential, which will cause too many redundant points. The method of adding the direction cost to the cost function of the A_star algorithm is adopted to reduce the number of raster searches. Therefore, it is necessary to use the improved A_star algorithm. At the same time, to optimize the effect of path planning, this paper takes the environmental information based on learning prior knowledge as the research condition and performs reinforcement learning on this.

2 A_star Algorithm

2.1 Traditional A_star Algorithm

The traditional A_star algorithm mainly consists of the Dijkstra algorithm and the greedy algorithm. To some extent, it retains the ability of the Dijkstra algorithm to find the shortest path, whereas the greedy algorithm can restrict its blind iterative operation. The main idea of the traditional A_star algorithm is to select the next node by using a heuristic search method based on the global map information. At the same time, it is necessary to evaluate the cost consumed by the initial node to the current node and the cost expected to be consumed by the current node to the destination. The output of the evaluation function is used to evaluate the input of all nodes in a neighborhood of the current node. The evaluation function can be expressed as:

$$f(n) = g(n) + h(n) \quad (1)$$

In the formula, $g(n)$ is the rollback cost, which indicates the consumption cost generated from the initial node to the current node; $h(n)$ is the forward cost, which is the cost expected to be consumed from the current node to the destination; $f(n)$ is an evaluation function, which represents the global substitution value integrating two different costs. Its main function is to evaluate the size of the function and to determine whether the planned path is convenient. $g(n)$ and $h(n)$ are mutually restricted [14]. $g(n)$ is the traversed set in the whole process and its size will not change because of subsequent operations. Therefore, if $f(n)$ is to be sufficiently small, the main goal of the study should be to minimize $h(n)$. Just like the Dijkstra algorithm, the A_star algorithm also maintains an Open List and a Closed List [13], where the Open List stores adjacent grids which already been searched grids and they are the nodes that will be searched by the algorithm. Closed List stores nodes, which is the smallest node of $f(n)$ in the Open List for each sort.

The implementation process of the traditional A_star algorithm is as follows:

(1) First, the starting point of the ground mobile robot is denoted as node S, and it is put into the Open List. At this point, Closed List is an empty table;
(2) Nodes in the area covered by obstacles in the known environment or nodes in the unknown environment need to be recorded as obstacle nodes and stored in the Closed List;
(3) Search for reachable nodes around S, which are also nodes whose value is 0 in the cost grid map, and place them in Open List;
(4) Ejecting the node S in the Open List and adding the node S to the Closed List. At the same time, the value of $f(n)$ about each reachable node needs to be calculated, and the node with the smallest value of $f(n)$ should be taken as the next moving node of the ground mobile robot. The search will fail if the Open List is empty at this point and a viable path cannot be found;
(5) It is necessary to judge whether there is a target node in the Closed List. The algorithm will successfully search for the path if there is one. Instead, go to step (6);
(6) Traverse all the grids in the neighborhood of the current node n, select a grid, in which the value of f(n) is the smallest, and set the node m as the next moving node. Then pop the current node n from the Open List and put it into the Closed List;
(7) Determine whether node m is in the Open List and Closed List:

    1) If the node m is not in the Open List and Closed List, add it to the Open List;
    2) If node m is in the Open List, it is necessary to compare the calculated value of node m in $f(n)$ with the value of node m in $f_{pre}(n)$ stored in the Open List. The stored value of $f_{pre}(n)$ should be replaced by the value of $f(n)$ if $f(n)$ is less than $f_{pre}(n)$, and the m node is will be added to the Closed List;

3) The node will be skip if the node m exists in Closed List, which indicates that the node is on the current optimal path, then return to the previous step and continue to compare other child nodes;

(8) Repeat steps (5) to (7) until the target node is searched or the Open List is empty.

2.2 Hybrid A_star Algorithm

The A_star algorithm doesn't take into account the direction of motion of the object, but the Hybrid A_star algorithm considers the actual situation of the object movement. The mobile robot starts from a specific position and can only reach the position where can be possible. When the A_star algorithm is used to search, another path is finally obtained because of the algorithm itself or environmental influences. In this paper, the Hybrid A_star algorithm is considered under the premise of considering the moving direction of the object. In the Hybrid A_star algorithm, the actual motion constraints of the object are considered, so the mobile robot can appear at any position in each grid, which is more in line with the actual planning situation. The Hybrid A_star algorithm takes into account an additional theta compared to the A_star algorithm for grid search, in which case the continuous 3D state space (x, y, θ) becomes a grid.

The heuristic function of the A_star algorithm search efficiency is crucial, and it also is important to have reasonable and effective research to estimate the target price of the extended node. The function is divided into two kinds in the Hybrid A_star algorithm: no obstacle of integrity constraints inspired the cost and the integrity of the heuristic cost have obstacles.

The Hybrid A_star algorithm is similar to the A_star algorithm, the key difference is that the Hybrid A_star state transformation occurred in the continuous space (extended node), rather than a discrete space. Although the Hybrid A_star algorithm search in discrete grid map building, each path point is not limited by the grid, and the excess of similar path points are pruned with the help of the grid.

2.3 Simulation Experiment

This simulation experiment will be simulated in MATLAB, the rendering shown in Fig. 1 is the simulation result in the platform. The blue curve is the path planning of the traditional A_star algorithm and the red color curve is the Hybrid A_star algorithm in the figure. The Hybrid A_star algorithm makes the integral path planning algorithm smooth. The traditional A_star algorithm is shown in Fig. 1. And Fig. 2 and Fig. 3 show the application effect of the Hybrid A_star algorithm in path planning.

3 Q-Learning Algorithm

3.1 Q-Learning Algorithm

The Q-learning algorithm is a stand-alone control algorithm as one of the reinforcment learning methods [15, 16]. It can be applied to any Markovian decision process to obtain

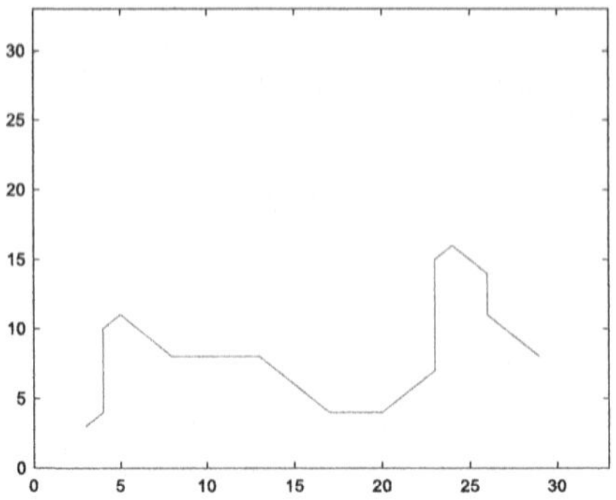

Fig. 1. The traditional A_star algorithm.

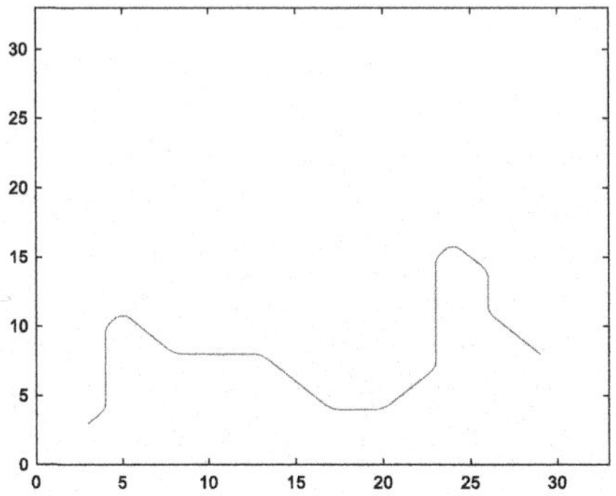

Fig. 2. The hybrid A_star algorithm.

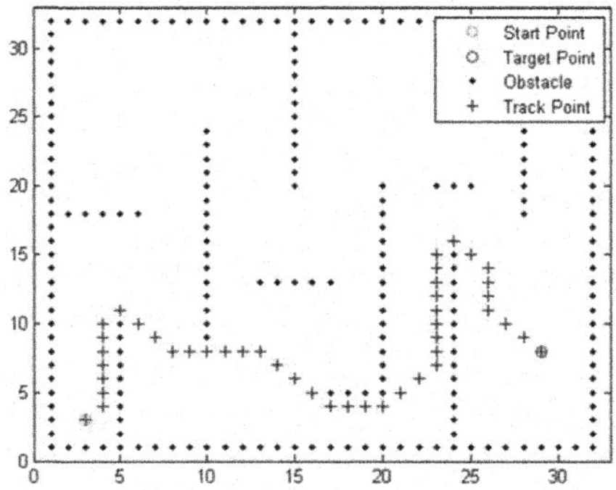

Fig. 3. Application of the hybrid A_star algorithm in path planning.

an optimal policy. The Q-learning algorithm [17] is a general reinforcement learning algorithm that uses iterative computation to approximate the optimal value. The robot will tend to choose the path again if the environment gives a positive reward ($+r$) for this choice; conversely, the tendency will decrease if the environment gives a negative reward ($-r$) for this choice. The Q-learning algorithm continuously adjusts the previous strategy through the feedback result information, so that the algorithm realizes a process of dynamic allocation [18].

$$r_t = r(s_t, a_t, s_{t+1}) \tag{2}$$

From Eq. 2, it can be seen that the probability distribution is determined by the state-action estimate at the beginning of the moment t. The update rule for the optimal value function obtained by iterative calculation is varied according to Eq. 3.

$$Q(s, a) = r(s, a) + \gamma \max_{a'} Q(\delta(s, a'), a') \tag{3}$$

In the above equation $\gamma \in (0, 1)$ is the commutation factor, the reward obtained from the execution of the action a by the state s is $r(s, a)$, and the function to determine the state s from the next action a' and the action to be performed is δ. The definition of the Q-function is the basis of the Q-learning algorithm [19]. The combination of the Q-learning algorithm with the robot path planning algorithm continuously selects and updates the Q-value. Also, its exploration coefficients keep decreasing with the training time of the algorithm, i.e., the optimal is selected to the maximum extent (Table 1).

3.2 Simulation Experiment

Table 1. Q-learning algorithm pseudo-code.

Q-learning algorithm
Initialize $Q(s,a)$ arbitrarily
Repeat (for each episode)
Initialize s
Repeat (for each step of the episode)
Choose a from s using policy derived from $Q(e.g., \varepsilon - greedy)$
Take action a, observe r, s'
$Q(s,a) \leftarrow Q(s,a) + \alpha\left[r + \gamma \max_{a'} Q(s',a') - Q(s,a)\right]$
$s \leftarrow s'$
Until s is terminal

In the MATLAB software simulation of the robot walking room when the room number is from 0 to 5, from the beginning of the room to the target room, the output of the optimal strategy is shown in Table 2.

4 Mixed Algorithm

The HA-Q algorithm is guided by the global path mainly based on the A_star algorithm, and the Q-learning algorithm is used to adjust the local path in real-time. A compound

Table 2. Q-learning algorithm optimal strategy.

Q-learning algorithm optimal strategy
Initialized state 1
the robot goes to 5
the robot goes to 6

path planning strategy is developed according to the ground mobile robot's attributes and motion characteristics, which effectively solves the path planning and real-time obstacle avoidance problems of mobile robots in complex indoor environments, and ensures that the robot can safely and smoothly reach the target point.

The HA-Q algorithm absorbs the advantages of global path planning algorithm and machine learning algorithm, which is more efficient and practical compared with single path planning. The following steps shows the flow chart of the HA-Q algorithm:

1. Initialization of the exploration factor, maximum number of iterations, termination state parameters, target state parameters, maximum count threshold, start update moment, number of iterations, the current moment, action-value function, number of visits to the state-action pair, success path, and success path storage table for the single robot system;
2. Determine whether the number of iterations is greater than the maximum number of iterations, if yes: execute step 3; if not: initialize the current state parameters and then execute step 3;
3. Generating a random number, comparing the random number with the exploration factor and selecting an action command, and calculating the parameters of the robot's running state and the reward function after executing this action command based on this action command;
4. Determine whether the run state parameter is equal to the termination state parameter, if yes: continue to determine whether the run state parameter is equal to the target state parameter. If equal, store the success path into the success path storage table, execute the iteration count self-add one, and then return to step 2; if not equal, execute the iteration count self-add one, and then return to step 2; if not: execute the next step;
5. Determine whether the start update moment is less than or equal to the current moment. If yes: store the reward function, execute the visit count of the state-action pair since plus one, and then execute the next step; if not: determine whether the visit count of the state-action pair is equal to the maximum count threshold, if yes, update the action value function, and then execute the next step, if not, then execute the next step;
6. Store the run status parameters into the success path, execute the current moment self-add one, and return to step 3;
7. After the action value function is obtained, the action command is selected from the action value function according to the preset initial state parameters, and repeated to obtain the optimal path for the single-robot system.

The experiments in this subsection will be conducted in the simulation platform MATLAB. As can be seen from the results of Fig. 4 and Fig. 5, the proposed HA-Q algorithm in this paper can obtain a complete planning path, which combines the characteristics of the improved A_star algorithm and the Q-learning algorithm. At the same time, the HA-Q algorithm makes up for the shortcomings of these two algorithms to a certain extent, which further analyzes and verifies the obstacle avoidance technology to meet the requirements of safety and stability, and can ensure that the indoor mobile robot can quickly and smoothly reach the target point.

This experiment will be simulated in MATLAB. The Q-learning algorithm finds the trajectory process as shown in Fig. 4. And the trend of the planned path length is shown in Fig. 5.

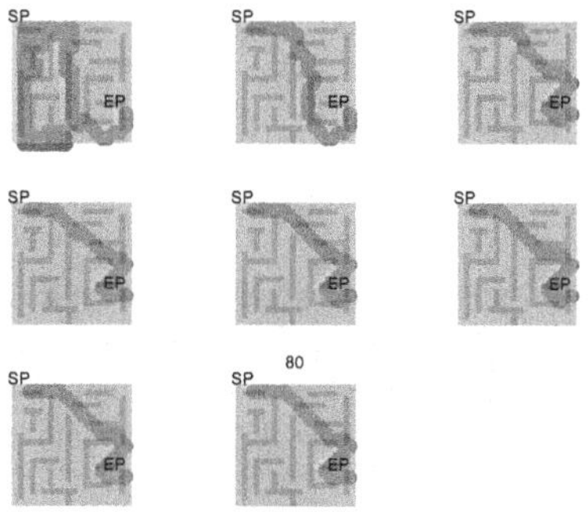

Fig. 4. The Q-learning algorithm finds the trajectory process.

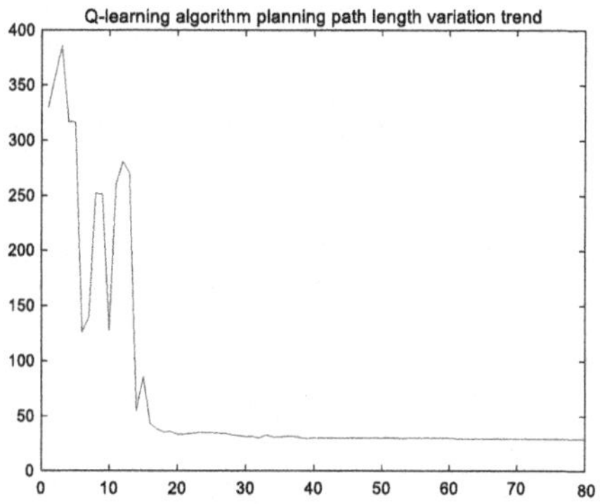

Fig. 5. Trend of the planned path length.

From the above experiments, it can be proved that the trend of path planning effect based on the Q-learning algorithm gradually becomes better, the path length for conducting search path gradually becomes shorter, and the planning process also becomes smooth under the planning of the Hybrid A_star algorithm.

5 Conclusion

The path planning system of ground mobile robots is mainly divided into two kinds, one is a global path planning system, and the other is a machine learning system. In this paper, a real-time obstacle avoidance strategy based on an improved A_star algorithm and Q-learning algorithm is proposed. Experiments further verify that the HA-Q algorithm meets the requirements of obstacle avoidance technology and can ensure the indoor mobile robot reaches the target smoothly.

Acknowledgements. We acknowledge funding from the sub project of national key R & D plan covid-19 patient rehabilitation training posture monitoring bracelet based on 4G network (Grant No. 2021YFC0863200-6), the Hebei College and Middle School Students Science and Technology Innovation Ability Cultivation Special Project (Grant No. 22E50075D), (Grant No. 2021H010206), and (Grant No. 2021H010203).

References

1. Zhang, H.D., Zheng, R., Cen, Y.W.: Present situation and future development of mobile robot path planning technology. Acta Simulata Systematica Sinica **17**, 439–443 (2005)
2. Zi, B., Lin, J., Qian, S.: Localization, obstacle avoidance planning and control of a cooperative cable parallel robot for multiple mobile cranes. Robot. Comput. Integr. Manufact. **34**, 105–123 (2015)
3. Osmankovic, D., Tahirovic, A., Magnani, G.: All terrain vehicle path planning based on D* lite and MPC based planning paradigm in discrete space. In: 2017 IEEE International Conference on Advanced Intelligent Mechatronics (AIM), pp. 334–339. Munich, Germany (2017)
4. Liang, C.L., Zhang, X.K., Han, X.: Route planning and track keeping control for ships based on the leader-vertex ant colony and nonlinear feedback algorithms. Appl. Ocean Res. **101**(1), 102239 (2020)
5. Yuan, Q., Han, C.S.: Research on robot path planning based on smooth A* algorithm for different grid scale obstacle environment. J. Comput. Theor. Nanosci. **13**(8), 5312–5321 (2016)
6. Kang, H.I., Lee, B., Kim, K.: Path planning algorithm using the particle swarm optimization and the improved Dijkstra algorithm. In: 2008 IEEE Pacific-Asia Workshop on Computational Intelligence and Industrial Application, pp. 1002–1004. Wuhan, China (2009)
7. Sudhakara, P., Ganapathy, V.: Trajectory planning of a mobile robot using enhanced A-star algorithm. Indian J. Sci. Technol. **9**(41), 1–10 (2016)
8. Hong, S., Zhu, J.X., Braunstein, L.A., et al.: Cascading failure and recovery of spatially interdependent networks. J. Stat. Mech: Theory Exp. **10**, 103208 (2017)
9. Xin, Y., Liang, H., Du, M., et al.: An improved A* algorithm for searching infinite neighbourhoods. Robot **36**, 627–633 (2014)
10. Chen, G.R., Guo, S., Wang, J.Z., et al.: Convex optimization and A-star algorithm combined path planning and obstacle avoidance algorithm. Control and Decision **35**, 2907–2914 (2020)
11. Stephen, B., Lieven, V.: Convex Optimization. Cambridge University Press, England (2004)
12. Zhu, Z.B., Wang, F.Y., Yin, Y.H.Z., et al.: Consensus of discrete-time multi-agent system based on Q-learning. Control Theory Appl. **38**(07), 997–1005 (2021)
13. Feng, S., Shu, H., Xie, B.Q., et al.: 3D Environment Path Planning Based On Improved Deep Reinforcement Learning. Comput. Appl. Softw. **38**(01), 250–255 (2021)

14. Zhang, H.T., Cheng, Y.H.: Path finding using A*algorithm. Microcomput. Inf., Control and Decision **24**, 238–239+308 (2007)
15. Qiao, J.F., Hou, Z.J., Ruan, X.G.: Neural network-based reinforcement learning applied to obstacle avoidance. J. Tsinghua Univ. (Sci. Technol.) **48**, 1747–1750 (2008)
16. Geng, X.J.: Self-Organizing Collaborative Target Search of Mobile Multi-Agent Based on Reinforcement Learning. Nanjing University of Posts and Telecommunications (2020)
17. Huang, B.Q., Cao, G.Y., Wang, Z.Q.: Reinforcement learning theory, algorithms and application. In: 2011 International Conference on Mechatronic Science, Electric Engineering and Computer (MEC), pp. 34–38 (2006)
18. Hong, S., Yang, H., Zhao, T., et al.: Epidemic spreading model of complex dynamical network with the heterogeneity of nodes **47** (9–12), 2745–2752 (2016)
19. Watkins, C.J.C.H.: Learning from delayed rewards. Robot. Auton. Syst. **15**(4), 233–235 (1989)

Belief χ^2 Divergence-Based Dynamical Complexity Analysis for Biological Systems

Lang Zhang and Fuyuan Xiao(✉)

School of Big Data and Software Engineering, Chongqing University, Chongqing 401331, China
xiaofuyuan@cqu.edu.cn,doctorxiaofy@hotmail.com

Abstract. Physiological signals contain the information of physical state in healthy systems. Especially, the complexity of dynamical time series data is a valid indicator to measure the pathological states. However, how to quantify the complexity of physical signals is still an open issue. In this paper, a novel complexity analysis algorithm based on divergence, called DCA, is proposed to figure out the complexity of biological system time series. Specifically, DCA algorithm splits biological systems time series data into different slices with boundaries. In addition, the feature of each time series data is extracted by converted into the basic probability assignments (BPAs) based on the Dempster-Shafer (D-S) evidence theory. DCA algorithm considers that the average divergence of BPAs indicates the complexity in a piece of time series. Moreover, an application in cardiac inter-beat interval time series is carried out to demonstrate the effectiveness of the proposed algorithm, which performs well in a pathological states analysis issue.

Keywords: D-S evidence theory · Belief χ^2 divergence · Dynamical complexity analysis · Biological system

1 Introduction

Biological systems produce valuable information with time series data, which contributes to the field of pathological researches. Specifically, complexity analysis of biological system time series reflects the changing environment of the patients physical state [1–3]. The complexity of the biological systems data can be measured effectively with entropy of information [4,5]. In time series, the more information there is, the larger complexity it should be. Moreover, it means that the information is more uncertain. So, the complexity of a piece of time series can

Supported by the National Natural Science Foundation of China (No. 62003280), Chongqing Talents: Exceptional Young Talents Project (No. cstc2022ycjh-bgzxm0070), and Chongqing Overseas Scholars Innovation Program (No. cx2022024).

Y. Xu et al. (Eds.): ML4CS 2022, LNCS 13657, pp. 158–167, 2023.
https://doi.org/10.1007/978-3-031-20102-8_13

be measured by figuring out the uncertainty of the information. Besides, uncertainty measure is widely applied in multi-source information fusion for decision making [6], fault analysis [7], and so on [8]. Nevertheless, it is still a challenge to measure the uncertainty of information which may be conflicting [9]. Hence, several well-known works has been proposed to manage multi-source information, including Deng entropy [10], belief entropy [11], Z-network [12], TDBF [13], information quality [14], and so on [15–17].

In this study, it is considered that D-S evidence theory [18–20] addresses a uncertainty problem in a flexible way [21–23]. In this case, the D-S evidence theory is taken into account to process the biological systems time series data by means of presenting them in the format of BPAs. BPAs are able to illustrate the uncertainty feature of data points by assigning probabilities to different categories [24,25]. In order to measure the discrepancy of BPAs, following aspects are investigated by scholars, including distance [26], correlation coefficient and divergence. Particularly, Xiao et al. [27] proposed a uniform BJS divergence-based method to consider both subjective weights and objective weights. Zhu et al. [28] considered the number of possible hypotheses with Rényi divergence. Wang et al. proposed IVIFJS divergence [29] to take the weight of membership and non-membership into account. Recently, Zhang and Xiao [30] proposed $SEB\chi^2$ divergence to measure the difference between belief function by focusing the discrepancy and correlationship of both singleton sets and multi-element sets. As for time series of biological systems, they often have more sophisticated structure. Hence, there is a limitation that it is difficult to measure the complexity of time series effectively. In this case, $SEB\chi^2$ is taken into account to be applied to process the time series data points whether they are on the boundaries of time slices. At the same time, the inner feature of biological systems can be illustrated.

In this work, a novel complexity analysis algorithm based on $SEB\chi^2$ divergence, called DCA, is proposed to measure the complexity of time series in biological systems. DCA algorithm divides biological systems data into multiple BPAs with different time scales. Then, the complexity of time series is obtained by averaging the divergence of corresponding BPAs. Furthermore, a specific application in cardiac inter-beat interval time series is carried out to demonstrate the effective performance in analyzing the complexity in a real issue.

Main contributions are presented as follows:

- Biological systems time series data is converted into mass function by using the D-S evidence theory, where feature of data can be extracted.
- The proposed DCA algorithm proposes an effective way to figure out the complexity of time series data in biological systems by generating BPAs and measure the average divergence of them.
- An application for pathological states analysis in cardiac inter-beat interval time series is carried out to illustrate the effectiveness of DCA algorithm.

The structure of this work shows as follows: In Sect. 2, the basic concepts of D-S evidence theory and divergence are introduced. A novel DCA algorithm in complexity analysis for biological systems is derived in Sect. 3. Section 4 puts forward an implement to illustrate the effective performance of the proposed algorithm in a real issue. Section 5 makes a conclusion of this paper.

2 D-S Evidence Theory and Divergence Measure

Some fundamental concepts are briefly presented in this section, including D-S evidence theory [18,19] and $SEB\chi^2$ divergence measure [30].

Definition 1. (Framework of discernment). Let the discernment Θ be a finite set which can be defined as:

$$\Theta = \{f_1, f_2, \ldots, f_n\}. \tag{1}$$

Then, its power set 2^Θ can be defined as [31]:

$$2^\Theta = \{\varnothing, \{f_1\}, \ldots, \{f_n\}, \{f_1, f_2\}, \ldots, \{f_1, f_2, \ldots, f_h\}, \ldots, \Theta\}, \tag{2}$$

where $\varnothing$ indicates the empty set.

Definition 2. (Mass function). Based on discernment Θ, the mass function m [32,33] can be defined as:

$$m : 2^\Theta \rightarrow [0, 1], \tag{3}$$

with the rule of

$$\sum_{E \in 2^\Theta} m(E) = 1 \quad \text{and} \quad m(\varnothing) = 0. \tag{4}$$

If $m(E) > 0$, E is a focal element.

Definition 3. *(SEBχ^2* **divergence measure).** Let m_1 and m_2 be two BPAs. The $SEB\chi^2$ divergence measure [30] can be defined as:

$$D_{SEB\chi^2}(m_1, m_2) = \frac{1}{2}\left[D_{EB\chi^2}\left(m_1, \frac{m_1 + m_2}{2}\right) + D_{EB\chi^2}\left(m_2, \frac{m_1 + m_2}{2}\right)\right]. \tag{5}$$

where

$$D_{EB\chi^2}(m_1, m_2) = \sqrt{\left(\frac{m_1(\theta)}{\sqrt{m_2(\theta)}} - \sqrt{m_2(\theta)}\right)' \Psi \left(\frac{m_1(\theta)}{\sqrt{m_2(\theta)}} - \sqrt{m_2(\theta)}\right)}, \tag{6}$$

with $\theta \in \Theta$, and

$$\Psi(F_i, F_j) = \frac{2^{|F_i \cap F_j|} - 1}{2^{|F_i|} - 1} \cdot \frac{2^{|F_i \cap F_j|} - 1}{2^{|F_j|} - 1}. \tag{7}$$

F_i and F_j represent m_1 and m_2 $(i, j = 1, 2, \ldots, 2^{n-1})$. $|\cdot|$ indicates the cardinality of a BPA. Ψ can be regarded as correlation coefficient [34].

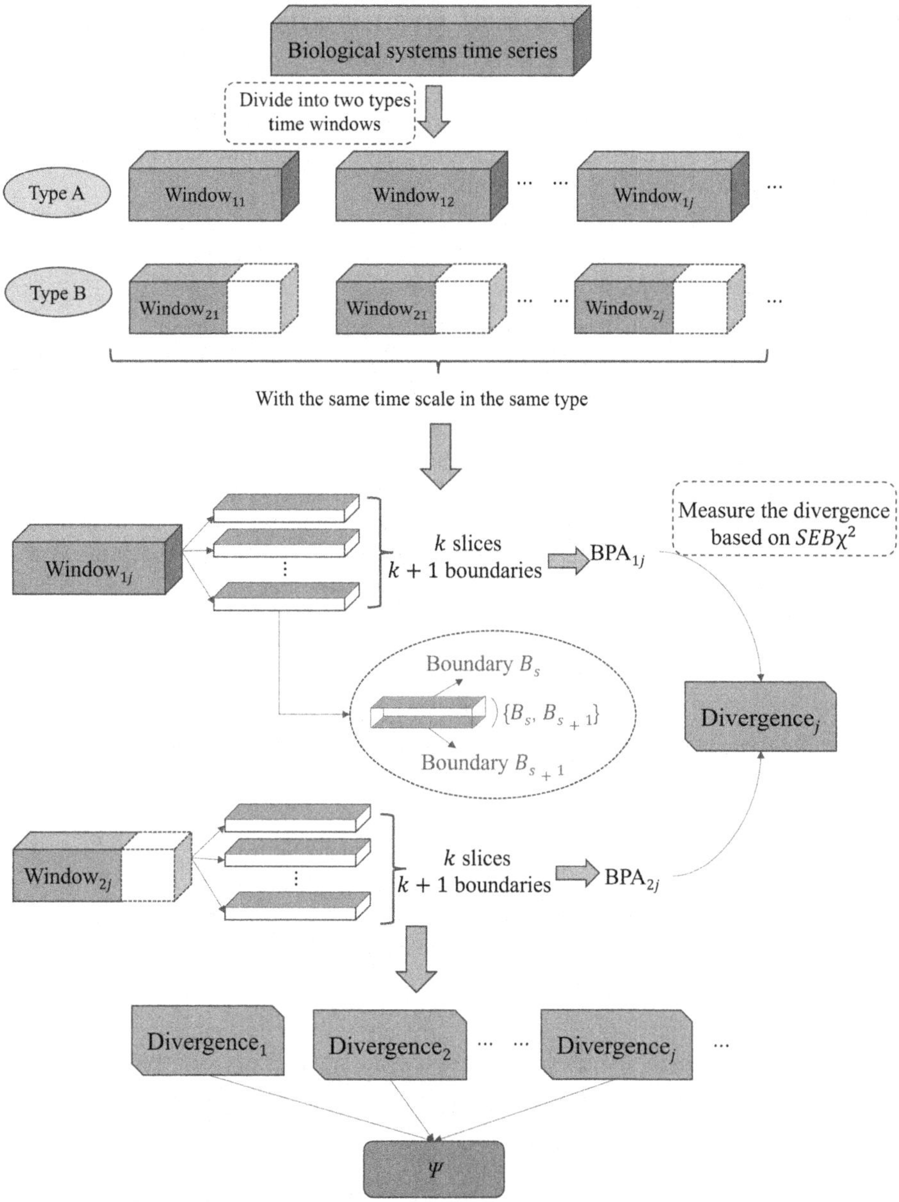

Fig. 1. Flowchart of the DCA algorithm for biological systems.

3 $SEB\chi^2$-Based Dynamical Complexity Analysis Algorithm for Biological Systems

The dynamical complexity analysis algorithm based on $SEB\chi^2$ divergence is introduced in this section which consists two steps. The flowchart of DCA algorithm for biological systems is shown in Fig. 1.

In the first step, biological systems time series $\{x_i\} = \{x_1, \ldots, x_N\}$ with length N is divided into two lists of consecutive non-overlapping time windows as type A $\left\{w_{Aj}^{(\tau)}\right\}$ and Type B $\left\{w_{Bj}^{(\tau)}\right\}$. Type A $w_{Aj}^{(\tau)} = \left\{x_{(j-1)\tau+1}, \ldots, x_{(j-1)\tau+\tau}\right\}$ is of length τ. Besides, j is the window index which ranges from 1 to N/τ. It can be regarded that type B is the truncation of type A in each window as $w_{Bj}^{(\tau)} = \left\{x_{(j-1)\tau+1}, \ldots, x_{(j-1)\tau+v}\right\}$, where $v < \tau$.

The time interval of each window ranges from x_{min} to x_{max} where x_{min} and x_{min} indicate the lower and the upper boundaries, respectively, of time series $\{x_i\}$. The time interval is equally split into k slices. Each slice contains two boundaries as B_s and B_{s+1}, which represents the specific state. If data points are in the same slice, then it can be considered that they are in the same state.

Let the total number of x_i over w_{Aj} or w_{Bj} between B_s and B_{s+1} be p. Then, the focal element of BPA based on each time window can be defined as:

$$m_{ij}(\{B_s, B_{s+1}\}) = \frac{p}{|w_{ij}|}, \qquad i \in \{A, B\}, \tag{8}$$

where indicates the length of time series. In addition, if data points of length q fall on the border B_s coincidentally, the focal element can be defined as follows:

$$m_{ij}(\{B_s\}) = \frac{q}{|w_{ij}|} \qquad i \in \{A, B\}. \tag{9}$$

In the second step, the divergence Div_j in each corresponding window is figured out based on $SEB\chi^2$ divergence measure:

$$Div_j = D_{SEB\chi^2}(m_{Aj}, m_{Bj}). \tag{10}$$

Finally, the average divergence represents the complexity of a biological system time series Ψ:

$$\Psi = \frac{\sum_{i=1}^{N/\tau} Div_i}{N/\tau}. \tag{11}$$

The pseudocode of dynamical complexity analysis algorithm for biological systems based on $SEB\chi^2$ divergence is shown in Algorithm 1.

4 Application

In this section, the biological systems time series data is described, which shows the way of selecting valid data points. Next, an implement of DCA algorithm for biological systems is carried out to shows the effective performance in specific time series.

Algorithm 1: Complexity analysis algorithm for biological systems based on $SEB\chi^2$ divergence

---

Input: Biological systems time series $\{x_i\} = \{x_1, \ldots, x_N\}$;
Output: Complexity result Ψ

Split the time series $\{x_i\}$ into two types of windows $\left\{w_{Aj}^{(\tau)}\right\}$ and $\left\{w_{Bj}^{(\tau)}\right\}$;
Determine the lower and upper sides of time interval $\{x_{min}, x_{max}\}$;
Divided each time window into k slices;
Count the number of data points on or between boundaries;
for i=1;$i \leq N/\tau$ **do**
    Figure out the BPAs m_{1i} and m_{2i} of each time window by using the Eq. (8) and Eq. (9);
end
for i=1;$i \leq N/\tau$ **do**
    Calculate the divergence Div_i in each corresponding window by using Eq. (10);
end
Calculate the complexity of biological systems time series Ψ by using Eq. (11);
return Ψ.

4.1 Data Description

In this study, cardiac inter-beat interval time series is applied to demonstrate the feasibility of DCA algorithm for biological systems complexity analysis. The data is selected from the databases on PhysioNet [35] as follows:

- BIDMC Congestive Heart Failure Database (CHF);
- MIT-BIH Normal Sinus Rhythm Database (Healthy);
- Long Term AF Database (AF).

All the above databases are long-term ECG (Electrocardiography) databases with 20–24 h record. Specifically, the numbers of subject are 15, 18 and 84. As for CHF and Healthy databases, each subject is truncated into 5 sets inter-beat interval time series by utilizing the first 500 data points from 10,000 data points. As for AF data base, 75 records are adopted according to the annotation in PhysioNet. Because the lengths of them exceed 500 data points. Hence, there are 240 sets inter-beat interval time series. Specifically, 75, 90 and 75 records are from CHF Healthy and AF, respectively.

Next, the time series is processed. First, the data points $\{x_i\}$ are ranked and split into 1000 segments. To release the influence of noise and detection error, the 1_{st} and 999_{th} 1000-quantiles of the ranked segments are regarded as $x_{min} = 0.3$ and $x_{max} = 1.6$.

4.2 Implement of DCA Algorithm for Biological Systems

Three specific instances are carried out to demonstrate the process of DCA algorithm for biological systems. Three representative biological systems time series from CHF, Healthy and AF are taken into consideration. To simplify the experiment, each time series is analyzed with 140 data points, whose parameters are at $\tau = 10$, $\upsilon = 5$ and $k = 55$. In this case, each time series will be split into 14 time windows.

Table 1 shows the 14 divergence values for each time window of data sets, respectively. Figure 2 shows the three original time series and divergence series, respectively. The resulting complexity values Ψ of the three sets above are obtained as 0.1704 of CHF, 0.3637 of Healthy and 0.5094 of AF.

From the original time series of three data sets, it shows that the CHF subject has the lowest fluctuation while AF subject has the highest fluctuation in cardiac inter-beat interval time series. As divergence illustrates the inner difference of a single time window, the divergence of three sets should follows: CHF subject < Healthy subject < AF subject. In this case, divergence can be used as an indicator of complexity.

From the information above, DCA algorithm can effectively analyze the complexity of biological systems time series data of different types.

Table 1. The divergence value of CHF, Healthy and AF in each time window.

Subject	Win_1	Win_2	Win_3	Win_4	Win_5	Win_6	Win_7
CHF	0.4201	0.0000	0.0000	0.2335	0.0000	0.3464	0.1633
Healthy	0.3651	0.3342	0.3237	0.1309	0.2725	0.4320	0.5033
AF	0.5773	0.5164	0.4472	0.5164	0.4000	0.4472	0.5773
Subject	Win_8	Win_9	Win_{10}	Win_{11}	Win_{12}	Win_{13}	Win_{14}
CHF	0.2582	0.0000	0.2182	0.0000	0.3464	0.2000	0.2000
Healthy	0.4761	0.5164	0.5164	0.3651	0.2981	0.2093	0.4381
AF	0.4472	0.5773	0.5773	0.5164	0.5071	0.5773	0.4472

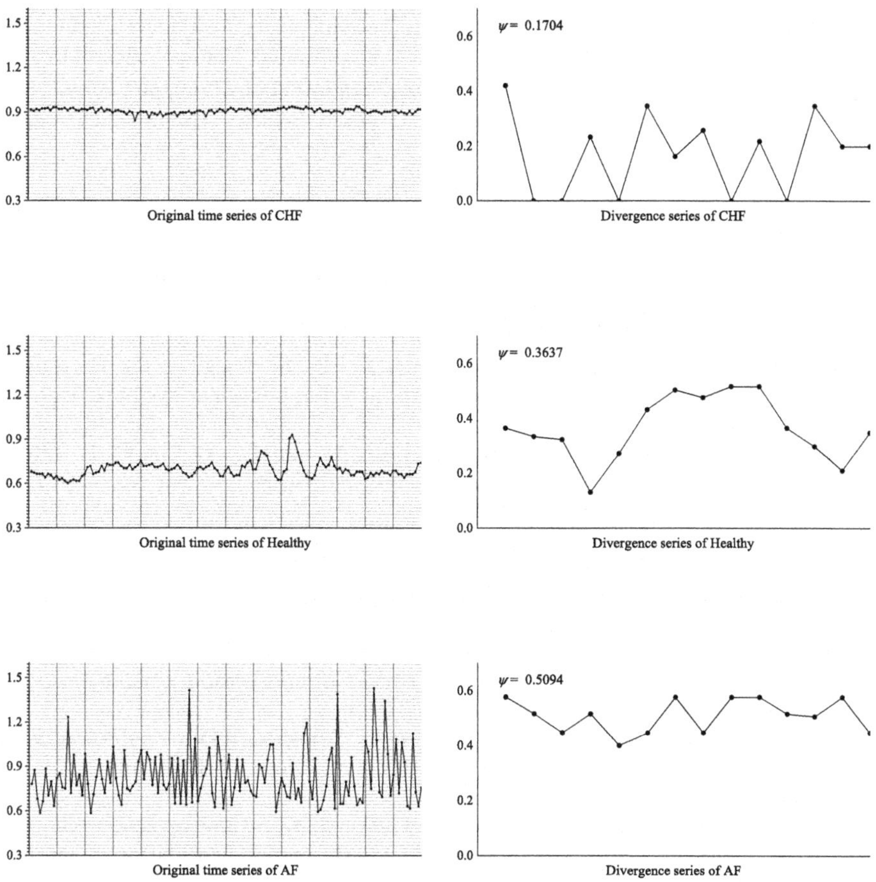

Fig. 2. Demonstration of DCA algorithm for biological systems on specific instances.

5 Conclusion

As biological systems usually produces time series, the complexity analysis on time series are significant. This research shed new light on the dynamical complexity analysis based on $SEB\chi^2$ divergence for biological systems. The main innovation point of the proposed method was that it took inner divergence of a time series into consideration. Also, the data points on boundaries and in slices were dealt differently by generating BPAs. In addition, the effectiveness of DCA algorithm for biological systems was demonstrated by applying it in cardiac inter-beat interval time series. Moreover, DCA algorithm provided a novel way to address the biological systems problems in physical state analysis. In summary, DCA algorithm had considerable abilities in dynamical complexity analysis for biological systems. In the future study, the time complexity of the DCA algorithm for biological systems should be addressed to adapt to real-time data flexibly.

Funding. This research is supported by the National Natural Science Foundation of China (No. 62003280), Chongqing Talents: Exceptional Young Talents Project (No. cstc2022ycjh-bgzxm0070), Natural Science Foundation of Chongqing, China (No. CSTB2022NSCQ-MSX0531), and Chongqing Overseas Scholars Innovation Program (No. cx2022024).

References

1. Cui, H., Zhou, L., Li, Y., Kang, B.: Belief entropy-of-entropy and its application in the cardiac interbeat interval time series analysis. Chaos Solitons Fractals **155**, 111736 (2022)
2. Hsu, C.F., Wei, S.-Y., Huang, H.-P., Hsu, L., Chi, S., Peng, C.-K.: Entropy of entropy: Measurement of dynamical complexity for biological systems. Entropy **19**(10) (2017)
3. Cao, Z., Ding, W., Wang, Y.-K., Hussain, F.K., Al-Jumaily, A., Lin, C.-T.: Effects of repetitive ssveps on eeg complexity using multiscale inherent fuzzy entropy. Neurocomputing **389**, 198–206 (2020)
4. Cao, Z., Lin, C.-T.: Inherent fuzzy entropy for the improvement of eeg complexity evaluation. IEEE Trans. Fuzzy Syst. **26**(2), 1032–1035 (2017)
5. Cao, Z., Prasad, M., Lin, C.-T.: Estimation of ssvep-based eeg complexity using inherent fuzzy entropy. In: 2017 IEEE International Conference on Fuzzy Systems (FUZZ-IEEE), pp. 1–5. IEEE (2017)
6. Fu, C., Chang, W., Yang, S.: Multiple criteria group decision making based on group satisfaction. Inf. Sci. **518**, 309–329 (2020)
7. Meng, D., Wang, H., Yang, S., Lv, Z., Hu, Z., Wang, Z.: Fault analysis of wind power rolling bearing based on EMD feature extraction. CMES-Comput. Model. Eng. Sci. **130**(1), 543–558 (2022)
8. Meng, D., Lv, Z., Yang, S., Wang, H., Xie, T., Wang, Z.: A time-varying mechanical structure reliability analysis method based on performance degradation. Structures **34**, 3247–3256 (2021)
9. Shang, Q., Li, H., Deng, Y., Cheong, K.H.: Compound credibility for conflicting evidence combination: an autoencoder-K-Means approach. IEEE Trans. Syst. Man Cybern. Syst. (2021). https://doi.org/10.1109/TSMC.2021.3130187
10. Deng, Y.: Uncertainty measure in evidence theory. Sci. China Inf. Sci. **63**(11), 210201 (2020)
11. Zhou, M., Zhu, S.-S., Chen, Y.-W., Wu, J., Herrera-Viedma, E.: A generalized belief entropy with nonspecificity and structural conflict. IEEE Trans. Syst. Man Cybern. Syst. (2021). https://doi.org/10.1109/TSMC.2021.3129872
12. Jiang, W., Cao, Y., Deng, X.: A novel Z-network model based on Bayesian network and Z-number. IEEE Trans. Fuzzy Syst. **28**(8), 1585–1599 (2020)
13. Li, Y., Pelusi, D., Cheong, K.H., Deng, Y.: The arithmetics of two dimensional belief functions. Appl. Intell. **52**(4), 4192–4210 (2022)
14. Li, D., Deng, Y., Cheong, K.H.: Multisource basic probability assignment fusion based on information quality. Int. J. Intell. Syst. **36**(4), 1851–1875 (2021)
15. Wang, Z., Li, Z., Wang, R., Nie, F., Li, X.: Large graph clustering with simultaneous spectral embedding and discretization. IEEE Trans. Pattern Anal. Mach. Intell. **43**(12), 4426–4440 (2021). https://doi.org/10.1109/TPAMI.2020.3002587
16. Wang, Z., Wang, C., Li, X., Gao, C., Li, X., Zhu, J.: Evolutionary Markov dynamics for network community detection. IEEE Trans. Knowl. Data Eng., 1 (2020). https://doi.org/10.1109/TKDE.2020.2997043

17. Song, Y., Fu, Q., Wang, Y.-F., Wang, X.: Divergence-based cross entropy and uncertainty measures of Atanassov's intuitionistic fuzzy sets with their application in decision making. Appl. Soft Comput. **84**, 105703 (2019)
18. Dempster, A.P.: Upper and lower probabilities induced by a multivalued mapping. In: Classic works of the Dempster-Shafer Theory of Belief Functions, pp. 57–72. Springer, Heidelberg (2008). https://doi.org/10.1007/978-3-540-44792-4_3
19. Shafer, G.: A mathematical theory of evidence. In: A Mathematical Theory of Evidence. Princeton University Press (1976)
20. Yager, R.R.: Generalized Dempster-Shafer structures. IEEE Trans. Fuzzy Syst. **27**(3), 428–435 (2019)
21. Xiong, L., Su, X., Qian, H.: Conflicting evidence combination from the perspective of networks. Inf. Sci. **580**, 408–418 (2021)
22. Liu, Z., Liu, Y., Dezert, J., Cuzzolin, F.: Evidence combination based on credal belief redistribution for pattern classification. IEEE Trans. Fuzzy Syst. **28**(4), 618–631 (2020)
23. Xu, X., Zhang, D., Bai, Y., Chang, L., Li, J.: Evidence reasoning rule-based classifier with uncertainty quantification. Inf. Sci. **516**, 192–204 (2020)
24. Liu, Z., Zhang, X., Niu, J., Dezert, J.: Combination of classifiers with different frames of discernment based on belief functions. IEEE Trans. Fuzzy Syst. **29**(7), 1764–1774 (2021)
25. Song, X., Xiao, F.: Combining time-series evidence: a complex network model based on a visibility graph and belief entropy. Appl. Intell. (2022). https://doi.org/10.1007/s10489-021-02956-5
26. Han, D., Dezert, J., Yang, Y.: Belief interval-based distance measures in the theory of belief functions. IEEE Trans. Syst. Man Cybern. Syst. **48**(6), 833–850 (2018)
27. Xiao, F., Wen, J., Pedrycz, W.: Generalized divergence-based decision making method with an application to pattern classification. IEEE Trans. Knowl. Data Eng. (2022). https://doi.org/10.1109/TKDE.2022.3177896
28. Zhu, C., Xiao, F., Cao, Z.: A generalized Rényi divergence for multi-source information fusion with its application in EEG data analysis. Inf. Sci. (2022). https://doi.org/10.1016/j.ins.2022.05.012
29. Wang, Z., Xiao, F., Ding, W.: Interval-valued intuitionistic fuzzy Jenson-Shannon divergence and its application in multi-attribute decision making. Appl. Intell. (2022). https://doi.org/10.1007/s10489-022-03347-0
30. Zhang, L., Xiao, F.: A novel belief $\chi 2$ divergence for multisource information fusion and its application in pattern classification. Int. J. Intell. Syst. (2022). https://doi.org/10.1002/int.22912
31. Deng, Y.: Random permutation set. Int. J. Comput. Commun. Control **17**(1), 4542 (2022). https://doi.org/10.15837/ijccc.2022.1.4542
32. Deng, Y.: Information volume of mass function. Int. J. Comput. Commun. Control **15**(6), 3983 (2020)
33. Chen, L., Deng, Y., Cheong, K.H.: Probability transformation of mass function: a weighted network method based on the ordered visibility graph. Eng. Appl. Artif. Intell. **105**, 104438 (2021)
34. Pan, L., Deng, Y.: An association coefficient of a belief function and its application in a target recognition system. Int. J. Intell. Syst. **35**(1), 85–104 (2020)
35. Bidmc congestive heart failure database, mit-bih normal sinus rhythm database, and long term af database. http://www.physionet.org/physiobank/database. Accessed 5 Dec 2016

Local Feature Acquisition Method of Multi-layer Vision Network Image Based on Virtual Reality

Jinzhu Liu(✉) and Shuai Zheng

XiaMen HuaXia University, XiaMen 361024, China
liuwenping74@163.com

Abstract. As an important part of image features, local image features reflect the changes of local information in the image, which are not easily disturbed by various changes such as noise, illumination, scale, and rotation. Faced with this situation, this paper proposes a method for local feature acquisition of multi-layer visual network images based on virtual reality. Based on virtual reality technology, the multi-layer visual network image is reconstructed in layers, and the reconstructed images are preprocessed by histogram equalization and denoising. The SUSAN algorithm and the SIFT algorithm are combined to realize the acquisition of local image features. The results show that compared with the original SUSAN algorithm and the original SIFT algorithm, the average running time of the researched method is shorter and the overlap error is smaller, which indicates that the researched method has lower time complexity and higher acquisition accuracy.

Keywords: Virtual reality technology · Multi-layer visual network image · Layered reconfiguration · Pretreatment · SUSAN algorithm · SIFT algorithm · Image local feature acquisition

1 Introduction

How to obtain a more discriminative image local feature descriptor is an important hotspot in the field of computer vision. It plays an important role in image modeling and reconstruction. Image local feature descriptor has a good effect on maintaining the invariance of image rotation. The scale invariant feature transform descriptor proposed by Lowe can efficiently detect key points in images because of its scale invariance. It is the most widely used descriptor in image recognition. These feature descriptors have different design and implementation methods, but their purpose is to optimize the general performance of image local features. However, the advantages of human visual system for extracting image local features have not been taken into account in the implementation of existing algorithms. The purpose of computer vision is to extract meaningful descriptive information from images or image sequences. Traditional methods establish algorithm models with the help of geometry, physics, learning theory and statistical methods, sample and process visual information, and achieve some results, but they are still far from the cognitive ability of biological visual system [1]. Some researchers

Y. Xu et al. (Eds.): ML4CS 2022, LNCS 13657, pp. 168–181, 2023.
https://doi.org/10.1007/978-3-031-20102-8_14

have proposed an improved SUSAN corner detection algorithm to extract image features through corner detection. After Canny edge detection, SUSAN corner detection is performed on the detected edge pixels, and then Euclidean distance is used to make the detected corners more accurate. However, because the modified algorithm requires layered reconstruction of multi-layer vision network images, it may increase the time of image feature extraction [2]. Other researchers have done image feature matching by improving SIFT algorithm. By reducing the vector dimension, the selection range of the neighborhood around the feature points is reduced, the matching time of the image feature points is accelerated, and the matching error rate is reduced to a certain extent [3]. In order to solve this problem, this paper will combine SUSAN algorithm and sift algorithm to design a multi-layer visual network image local feature acquisition method based on virtual reality, in order to improve the accuracy of image local feature acquisition.

2 Research on Local Feature Acquisition of Multi-layer Visual Network Images

Local feature acquisition is usually the first step for many problems in computer vision and digital image processing, such as image classification, image retrieval, wide baseline matching, etc. the quality of feature extraction directly affects the final performance of the task [4]. Therefore, the local feature extraction method has important research value. However, the image often changes in scale, translation, rotation, illumination, angle of view and blur. Especially in practical application scenarios, the image will inevitably have large noise interference, complex background and large target attitude changes. This brings more challenges to the problem of image local feature acquisition. Therefore, the research on local feature acquisition method still has important theoretical significance and application value, which is worthy of researchers' continued attention.

2.1 Layered Reconstruction of Multi-layer Visual Network Images Based on Virtual Reality

Virtual reality, also known as spiritual environment technology, is a lifelike three-dimensional virtual reality environment built by people using computer technology, which provides users with a new technology that can independently interact with them through computer input devices [5]. Based on many characteristics of virtual reality technology and the rapid development of computer technology and virtual reality technology, virtual reality technology has made great achievements. While changing people's lifestyle, it is also considered as one of the major technologies that may cause great changes in the world in the 21st century.

At present, the interactivity in the virtual reality system is mainly realized through nine aspects. Conceptuality is the rationality of the existence of various things (real or imagined) in the virtual environment, and most other digital media also have this feature, such as animation, movies, etc. The rapid development of digital processing, display technology and media acquisition technology has led to the explosive growth of 3D image data. As a new type of multimedia image mode, 3D image mainly provides images with different viewing angles for the left eye and right eye of the human, so as to use the human perception ability to create a three-dimensional perception scene for the viewer. Therefore, 3D images have attracted more and more attention in the multimedia field. It has an increasingly broad market demand [6]. However, with the continuous development of 3D images, there are still many technical problems that need to be solved urgently, among which the most urgent problem is the layered reconstruction of 3D images. The layered reconstruction of 3D images is directly related to the compression quality of the images. However, there are certain problems in the traditional methods of layered reconstruction of 3D images, which lead to a great decrease in the quality of images during compression.

For the above situation. In this chapter, virtual reality technology is used to realize layered reconstruction of 3D images: firstly, 3D images are layered based on virtual reality technology, and then layered reconstruction of 3D images is realized by triangulation algorithm. The specific steps of hierarchical reconfiguration are as follows:

1) Firstly, the virtual reality technology is used to layer the 3D image;
2) Set a point corresponding to the minimum value and the maximum value, and extract a total of four maximum values. The four maxima extracted represent the quadrangular coordinates of the corresponding containment rectangle of the scattered point set, and the circumscribed circle radius value and center coordinates of the containment rectangle are obtained to obtain the circumscribed circle coordinates of the containment rectangle;
3) Obtain the vertex coordinates of the circumscribed triangle corresponding to the circumscribed circle of the containing rectangle, and obtain the specific coordinates of the circumscribed triangle;
4) Taking the vertex coordinates of the circumscribed triangle as additional points, the three vertices are placed in the points group of the layered 3D image in a counterclockwise direction, and the circumscribed triangle is placed in the triangle array of the layered 3D image;
5) Insert data points point by point: Initialize the triangulation and insert data points point by point. First, the relationship between the three sides a, b, c and the insertion point V is judged by the CCW judgment method.
6) Find the triangles that the insertion point V can insert until a triangle mesh is formed, so as to realize the hierarchical reconstruction of the 3D image.

2.2 Image Preprocessing

When an image is sent to the computer as input information for processing, there is often noise due to various reasons, which is not suitable for the recognition of the machine vision system. Generally, the image will be preprocessed before entering the vision system. The preprocessing process is not a complete denoising process. Its main purpose is to enhance the useful information of the image and eliminate the unnecessary information as much as possible. In fact, Image preprocessing is the enhancement of useful information.

Histogram Equalization

Histogram equalization is a kind of point processing. The gray value distribution of most images is uneven, and there is often a phenomenon of centralized gray value distribution. The uneven distribution of gray values is very unfavorable for image segmentation and image comparison. The result of image equalization is that the number of pixels of each gray level is basically the same, so that the upper limit value of the histogram obtained does not have much difference, showing a horizontal state [7]. Histogram equalization can be done in the following ways:

$$S_{D(x,y)} = N \cdot \frac{\sum_{a=1}^{A} h(a) \cdot D(x, y)}{A} \tag{1}$$

In the formula, $S_{D(x,y)}$ represents the image output after histogram equalization processing, A represents the number of pixels, N represents the number of gray levels, $D(x, y)$ represents the input image, and $h(a)$ represents the histogram of the input image.

This method is relatively simple, but after the histogram is extended, the new histogram is still unbalanced, so the new histogram should be modified.

Image Denoising

Image information inevitably carries noise in the process of transmission, which will affect image recognition, so the process of denoising in image processing is essential [8]. Gaussian noise is a kind of noise with normal distribution. Linear filter can select the desired frequency from many frequencies, and it is also suitable for removing the unwanted frequency from many frequencies. It has an obvious effect on Gaussian noise.

Mean Filter

The mean filter is a relatively simple linear filter, which belongs to the local spatial domain algorithm. The value of each pixel is replaced by the average pixel value of its surrounding points to achieve the purpose of smoothing the image [9]. The specific formula is as follows:

$$G(x, y) = \frac{\sum_{(x,y) \in F} H(x, y)}{n} \tag{2}$$

In the formula, $H(x, y)$ represents the original image, $G(x, y)$ represents the filtered image, F is a neighborhood set generated around (x, y), and n is the number of all points in the neighborhood F. The size of F determines the value of n, and also determines the radius of the neighborhood. The mean filter will blur the image while eliminating noise, and the size of its radius will have a proportional impact on the blurriness of the image.

Gaussian Filter

The function of Gaussian filter is to eliminate Gaussian noise. It is a process of weighted average of image. For each pixel, the convolution template is used to weighted average the pixel gray values in the neighborhood to determine its value. Gaussian filtering can be realized by discrete window sliding window convolution or Fourier transform. The former is commonly used, but with the increase of the amount of calculation, the latter should be considered when it causes great pressure on time and space.

The discrete window sliding window convolution is completed by a separable filter, which is the one-dimensional decomposition of multidimensional convolution. Generally, two-dimensional zero mean discrete Gaussian function is used for noise removal. Equation (3) is the specific formula of two-dimensional zero mean Gaussian function.

$$E(x, y) = e^{-\frac{x^2+y^2}{2d^2}} \tag{3}$$

In the formula, d is the standard deviation; $E(x, y)$ is the Gaussian function; (x, y) is the point coordinate.

Gaussian filter belongs to low-pass filter, which plays an important role in machine vision. Its wide application is inseparable from the characteristics of Gaussian function: two-dimensional Gaussian function has rotational symmetry; Gaussian function is a single valued function; The Fourier transform spectrum of Gaussian function is single lobe; The adjustability of Gaussian filter width makes a compromise between image features and abrupt variables; Gaussian function is separable.

2.3 Realization of Image Local Feature Acquisition

Local feature acquisition is a necessary step before local feature description. After the collected feature points or feature areas are described by description operators, corresponding processing is carried out according to the characteristics of different application algorithms. For example, in the image mosaic and matching algorithm, feature points or feature regions are matched [10].

There is no general or precise definition of image features so far. For different problems, different application objects and application scenarios, the definitions of features will be different to varying degrees. Simply put, a feature is the interesting part of a digital image, which is the basis of many image processing algorithms. Therefore, the success of an algorithm has a lot to do with the features it defines, selects, and uses.

Some basic concepts related to image features are edges, corners, regions, features, and ridges.

- Edge is the set of pixels that constitute the boundary (or edge) between two regions in the image. It can be summarized as line feature or point feature. It mostly exists in places where the gray information of the image changes dramatically. Generally, the shape of the edge may be arbitrary, and may even include crossed pixels. In the practical operation of feature detection, the edge is usually defined as a set of points with large gradient amplitude in the image, and the gradient angle of these points is the orthogonal direction of the edge. When describing edges, because discrete point sets are extracted, and "false edges" are often detected (shadows in images form edge like features under different illumination). Therefore, some algorithms often filter the points with high gradient amplitude (select some points and eliminate some points) and use a certain way to connect them to form a perfect description of edge features.
- A corner is a point feature in an image, which is different from the one-dimensional structure of the edge, and has a two-dimensional structure in the local corner. It

generally occurs where the direction of the boundary changes drastically, where the edges of multiple straight lines intersect, or where the grayscale of the image changes drastically. Therefore, several early corner detection algorithms usually first perform edge detection on the image, and then find the place where the edge direction changes abruptly, that is, the position of the corner. The subsequent corner detection algorithm removes the step of detecting the edge, but directly finds the point with large curvature value in the image gray gradient information, so as to obtain the corner information more accurately. Compared with other image features, corner points are easier to detect, and at the same time, it has good stability for various image transformations, noise interference, changes in external conditions and other factors.

- The regional feature is different from the corner, but it is also composed of point and line features, and the information contrast between the sub blocks of the image is high.
- The local feature points obtained from the local feature description reflect the local characteristics of the image. Local features are not easy to be affected by image rotation, scale, angle of view and other change factors, but also try to avoid the shortcomings of some global features, such as easy to be affected by factors such as target occlusion or complex background. Therefore, local features can better solve the problem of image recognition in the case of translation, scaling, angle change, rotation, scale transformation, noise or occlusion. At the same time, they are widely used in image matching, image mosaic, image registration and three-dimensional reconstruction, which is a hot issue in recent years.

The local feature points of an image are mainly divided into two categories: blobs and corners. Spots represent areas that are different from the surrounding color or grayscale; corners usually refer to the corners of objects in the image or the intersections between edge lines. Correspondingly, the local image feature description methods include blob detection and corner detection.

SUSAN Algorithm

The local gradient method is sensitive to the influence of noise and has a large amount of calculation, while SUSAN corner point is a morphological-based corner point feature acquisition method, which is directly calculated based on the image gray value. The method is simple and the calculation efficiency is high. The idea of the SUSAN corner point algorithm is to use a circular template with a fixed radius to slide on the image. The center pixel of the template is called the kernel. If the difference between the gray value of other points in the template and the gray value of the kernel is less than the threshold, it is considered that The point and the nucleus belong to a similar gray level, and the area composed of all pixels that satisfy this condition is called the nucleus value similarity area (USAN). In this way, the local neighborhood of the core pixel is divided into two parts, that is, the similar area and the dissimilar area, and the image texture structure of the local area is reflected by counting the size of the similar area of the core value, that is, the number of points that make up the USAN area. When the USAN area is large, it is generally a smooth area, and when the USAN area is small, it is generally a corner point.

SIFT Algorithm

SIFT algorithm has scale invariance and rotation invariance, and is widely used in image matching. The algorithm mainly includes four steps: scale space extreme value detection, key point location, direction assignment and key point description.

Step 1: scale space extreme value detection. In order to ensure the scale invariance, the concept of scale space is introduced. The scale space has a parameter that controls the change of scale, so as to construct different scale spaces. The scale space function $P(i, j, z)$ is obtained by convolution of the input image $Q(i, j)$ and the variable scale Gaussian kernel function $T(i, j, z)$, expressed as follows:

$$P(i, j, z) = Q(i, j) \otimes T(i, j, z) \tag{4}$$

In,

$$T(i, j, z) = \frac{1}{2\pi z^2} e^{-\frac{i^2+j^2}{2z^2}} \tag{5}$$

where $\otimes$ represents the convolution operation, (i, j) represents the pixel coordinates in the image, and z is the scale factor.

The size of z determines the clarity of the image. The large-scale factor corresponds to the overall features of the image, and the small-scale factor corresponds to the detailed features of the image. Therefore, the large z value corresponds to the low resolution (blur), and the small z value corresponds to the high resolution (clarity). To establish the scale space, firstly, Gaussian pyramid is constructed, which is completed by fuzzy filtering and down sampling. The pyramid consists of multiple sets of images. Each group of images has multiple sub images with the same size. The first group is the original image, and the next group of images are obtained from the down sampling of the previous group of images. These images are arranged from bottom to top, from large to small, forming a Gaussian pyramid. The number of groups n of Gaussian pyramid image should not be too large, otherwise the image size on the top of the tower is very small, and the significance of feature point detection will be lost.

The Laplacian of Gaussian (LoG) takes the second-order derivation of the image to complete the detection of feature points at different scales, but there is a problem of low detection efficiency, so the SIFT algorithm uses the difference of Gaussian (DoG) image instead of the Laplacian of Gaussian image., and DoG has better stability and stronger anti-interference than LoG. The difference image can be obtained by subtracting two adjacent sub-images in each group of images, and the extreme value detection is performed on the basis of the difference image. The difference image is represented as

$$\begin{aligned} L(i, j, z) &= \left[T(i, j, kz) - T(i, j, z)\right] \otimes Q(i, j) \\ &= P(i, j, kz) - P(i, j, z) \end{aligned} \tag{6}$$

where k is the multiplicative factor of two adjacent scale spaces.

Step 2: Keypoint positioning. After the extreme points are detected in the scale space, they are used as keypoint candidates. For each candidate location keypoint, its stability will be evaluated to decide whether to retain the detection result. The detection of extreme points in the previous step is carried out in discrete space. In order to obtain a more accurate extreme value position, the sampling points are fitted with a three-dimensional quadratic function, and the unstable and low-contrast key points at the edge are eliminated at the same time. So as to find the real feature points.

Step 3: key orientation matching. After the position information of feature points is determined, SIFT algorithm counts the gradient direction distribution of pixels in the neighborhood of each key point, so as to determine the direction for them, so that the final extracted features meet the rotation invariance. The gradient and amplitude of each feature point are solved as follows.

$$\phi(i,j) = \sqrt{\frac{[P(i+1,j) - P(i-1,j)]^2}{[P(i,j+1) - P(i,j-1)]^2}} \tag{7}$$

$$\varphi(i,j) = \arctan\frac{P(i+1,j) - P(i-1,j)}{P(i,j+1) - P(i,j-1)} \tag{8}$$

In the formula, $\phi(i,j)$ and $\varphi(i,j)$ represent the magnitude and direction of the gradient, respectively, and $P(i,j)$ is the value in the space of the scale where the feature point is located.

The gradient amplitude and direction of each pixel in the neighborhood of key points are counted, and then histogram statistics are carried out. The direction 3600 is equally divided into 8 sub intervals, and the sum of gradient amplitudes of all surrounding pixels falling into the corresponding interval is counted. The angle with the largest cumulative amplitude is taken as the main direction of the key point, and the angle with an amplitude greater than 80% of the maximum value is taken as the auxiliary direction of the key point.

Step 4: Description of key points. The SIFT feature descriptor is the result of statistics on the Gaussian image gradient in the neighborhood of the feature point. The algorithm first divides the neighborhood of the feature point into blocks, and counts the gradient histogram in each block to generate the feature vector descriptor. The description Symbol is an abstract representation and is unique. Take the main direction of the feature point as the direction axis and the feature point as the origin to establish a new coordinate. In the 16×16 neighborhood of each feature point, the SIFT algorithm calculates the gradient direction histogram for 4×4 4×4 regions. There are 8 statistical directions, and a statistical interval is set every 45°, thereby forming For an 8-dimensional vector, 4×4 such vectors can be generated in a 16×16 neighborhood, thus finally forming a 128-dimensional feature vector in the SIFT feature extraction algorithm. Finally, in order to make the feature extraction algorithm have good illumination invariance, the generated feature vector descriptor is normalized, and the processing process is as follows.

$$v_j = \frac{l_j}{l_1 + l_2 + \ldots + l_{128}} \tag{9}$$

where, $L = (l_1, l_2, \ldots, l_j, \ldots, l_{128})$ is the currently obtained 128 dimensional eigenvector descriptor, and $V = (v_1, v_2, \ldots, v_j, \ldots, v_{128})$ is the normalized eigenvector descriptor.

Image Local Feature Acquisition Based on SUSAN + SIFT

The SUSAN algorithm is combined with the SIFT algorithm to realize the acquisition of local image features. The specific process is shown in Fig. 1 below.

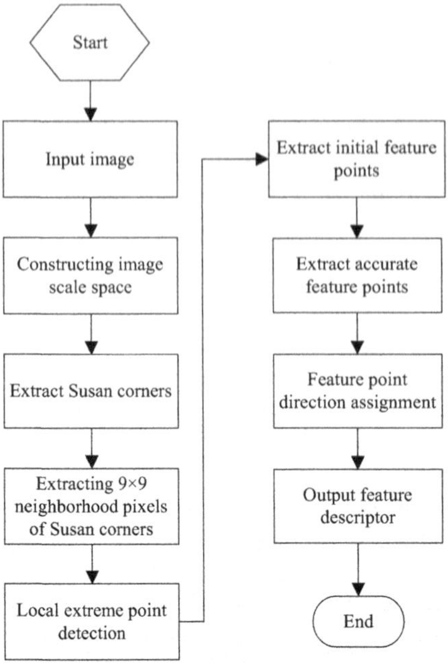

Fig. 1. The process of image local feature acquisition based on SUSAN + SIFT

The implementation process of the improved SIFT feature extraction algorithm is divided into the following five steps.

Step 1: SUSAN corner detection. The input original image is filtered using a 37-pixel circular template to count the area of the USAN area at all pixels. When the area is less than the threshold, it is determined as the initial corner point, and then the initial corner point is subjected to local non-polarization. A large value is suppressed to obtain SUSAN corner points, and the position and grayscale information of the corner points are saved.

Step 2: construct the scale space. The operation of constructing scale space is completely consistent with the original operation of SIFT algorithm. Through continuous downsampling of images and Gaussian filtering of different scales for each size of images, a Gaussian pyramid is formed, and then the images of adjacent two layers in each group in the Gaussian pyramid are differed to form a Gaussian difference pyramid to complete the construction of scale space.

Step 3: Extremum detection in scale space. Map the positions of the detected SUSAN corners to the corresponding positions of each group and each layer (the mapping method is to downsample the SUSAN corners), and remove the edge SUSAN corners in each group of images, Then, each pixel in the 9×9 neighborhood of the corner point in each layer of the image is detected by the local maximum value of 26 neighborhoods. If the point is a local maximum value, it is determined as the initial feature point.

Step 4: Location of key points. First, through the fitting function, the position and scale information of the initial feature points are corrected, and the points with too low contrast are eliminated. Then, the edge response points are eliminated by judging the relationship between the two eigenvalues of the Hessian matrix, and finally each feature point is calculated. Harris's corner response value CRF, eliminates the feature points less than 1/10 of the absolute value of the absolute value of all feature points, so as to obtain the final accurate feature points.

Step 5: determine the key direction. The main and secondary directions of feature points are obtained by statistical gradient direction histogram of pixels in the neighborhood of feature points.

Step 6: generation of feature descriptor. Feature descriptors are generated according to the formation process of feature descriptors, and normalized to generate feature descriptors with scale invariance, rotation invariance and illumination invariance.

3 Method Test

3.1 Sample Preparation

For the multi-layer visual network image local feature acquisition method based on virtual reality, when it has not been tested, it is only limited to the theoretical significance, and has no practical value for the actual scene. Therefore, it is necessary to carry out a series of algorithm tests, and compare and analyze with the original algorithm that has not been improved, so as to comprehensively and objectively evaluate the improved algorithm. In this paper, a large number of data tests are carried out for the multi-layer visual network image local feature acquisition method based on virtual reality. 20 images are selected as the original test set to test the performance of this method, the original SUSAN algorithm and the original SIFT algorithm, and the relevant experimental data are obtained. Thus, the experimental evaluation indexes are calculated, displayed and analyzed, and the final evaluation results are obtained. Some image samples are shown in Fig. 2 below.

Fig. 2. Partial image sample

3.2 Image Hierarchical Reconstruction Results

The images in the samples are reconstructed in layers with the help of 3ds Max software of virtual reality technology. Taking one of the samples as an example, the image layer reconstruction results are shown in Fig. 3 below.

Fig. 3. Image layered reconstruction results

3.3 Image Feature Collection Results

The method based on virtual reality is used to collect local features of 20 sample images. The results are shown in Table 1 below.

Table 1. Image feature collection results

Image samples	Number of eigenvectors
1	244
2	584
3	423
4	756
5	1244
6	357
7	844
8	654

(continued)

Table 1. (*continued*)

Image samples	Number of eigenvectors
9	578
10	424
11	365
12	772
13	201
14	585
15	1255
16	418
17	842
18	427
19	624
20	515

3.4 Evaluation Indicators

(1) For feature extraction of such large-scale and complex images, the time complexity of the algorithm is the primary evaluation standard. If the time complexity is too high, the image processing time is too long, and the computational memory is also very large. Even if the performance of the algorithm in other aspects is very good, it is also very limited in application scenarios. Therefore, this paper first analyzes the time complexity of the method for the research method. The analysis method is: use the original SUSAN algorithm, the original SIFT algorithm and the research method to test 30 images in the image test set, count the average running time of the three algorithms, and then compare the time complexity of the method.

(2) Use the overlap error between regions to measure the acquisition accuracy of the method. Let μ and η denote local features detected from two images with the same scene but with affine changes, O denote the homography matrix between the two images, and O_η denote the mapping of regions to regions through the homography matrix In the image where it is located, ξ_μ represents the ellipse fitting region corresponding to the region, and the overlap error $\Phi(\mu, \eta)$ between the two regions is expressed as:

$$\Phi(\mu, \eta) = 1 - \frac{\xi_\mu \cap O_q}{\xi_\mu \cup O_q} \tag{10}$$

If the overlap error between two regional features is less than a set threshold, the two regional features are considered to be related.

3.5 Method Test Results

Among the 20 sample images, one image is randomly selected and compared with the original SUSAN algorithm, the original SIFT algorithm and the studied method. The effect of image local feature acquisition is shown in Fig. 4.

(a) Original SUSAN algorithm

(b) Original SIFT algorithm

(c) Research methods

Fig. 4. Image local feature acquisition effect of different methods

It can be seen from Fig. 4 that the local feature points of the image that can be collected by the research method in this paper are far more than those of the two methods, which proves that the local feature collection effect of the image of the research method in this paper is better.

At the same time, the process of image local feature acquisition is recorded, and the overlapping error between the collected running time and the image area is compared. The test results are shown in Table 2 below.

Table 2. Method test results

Method	Average running time (s)	Overlap error (%)
Research methods	5.25	2.25
Original SUSAN algorithm	8.32	5.87
Original SIFT algorithm	7.31	5.66

As can be seen from Table 2, the running time of the original SUSAN algorithm is 8.32 s, the running time of the original SIFT algorithm is 7.31 s, while the running time of the method studied in this paper is 5.25 s, which is shorter. In terms of error, the overlap error of the original SUSAN algorithm is 5.87%, the overlap error of the original SIFT algorithm is 5.66%, while the overlap error of the research method in this paper is 2.25%, the overlap error is smaller, and the acquisition accuracy is higher.

4 Conclusion

This paper studies the local feature acquisition method of multi-layer visual network image based on virtual reality, and extracts the local feature of the reconstructed multi-layer visual network image. Combining the existing SUSAN algorithm with SIFT algorithm, the ability of image feature acquisition of multi-layer visual network is enhanced. The experimental test proves that the research method can effectively speed up the running time of image local feature acquisition, reduce the overlapping error between image regions, and improve the accuracy of acquisition.

However, due to time constraints, this paper did not consider the threshold problem in SUSAN algorithm when studying the new image local feature acquisition method, so we can continue to improve the design method in the next research to enhance the adaptability of the algorithm.

References

1. Liu, S., et al.: Human memory update strategy: a multi-layer template update mechanism for remote visual monitoring. IEEE Trans. Multimedia **23**, 2188–2198 (2021)
2. Zheng, H., Lin, Y.: An improved SUSAN corner detection algorithm. Computer Knowledge and Technology, Academic Edition **16**(22), 3 (2020)
3. Cheng, J., Zhang, J., Hu, J.: Improvement of SIFT algorithm in image feature matching environment. J. Heilongjiang Univ. Sci. Technol. **30**(4), 4 (2020)
4. Liu, S., Liu, D., Muhammad, K., Ding, W.: Effective template update mechanism in visual tracking with background clutter. Neurocomputing **458**, 615–625 (2021)
5. Shuai, L., Shuai, W., Xinyu, L., et al.: Fuzzy detection aided real-time and robust visual tracking under complex environments. IEEE Trans. Fuzzy Syst. **29**(1), 90–102 (2021)
6. Saad, E., Hirakawa, K.: Improved photometric acceptance testing in image feature extraction tasks. J. Electron. Imaging **29**(4), 1 (2020)
7. Ramkumar, B., Laber, R., Bojinov, H., et al.: GPU acceleration of the KAZE image feature extraction algorithm. J. Real-Time Image Proc. **17**(5), 1169–1182 (2020)
8. Classification of wood knots using artificial neural networks with texture and local feature-based image descriptors. Holzforschung **76**(1), 1–13 (2022)
9. Wang, Y., Song, X., Gong, G., et al.: A multi-scale feature extraction-based normalized attention neural network for image denoising. Electronics **10**(3), 319 (2021)
10. Wang, Y., Yang, Y., Zhang, P.: Gesture feature extraction and recognition based on image processing. Traitement du Signal **37**(5), 873–880 (2020)

Channel Selection for EEG Emotion Recognition via an Enhanced Firefly Algorithm with Brightness-Distance Attraction

Ben Niu, Gemin Liang, Bang Tao, Chao Fu, Shuang Geng(✉), Yang Wang, and Bowen Xue

College of Management, Shenzhen University, Shenzhen 518060, China
lianggemin2021@email.szu.edu.cn, {gs,wangyanghim}@szu.edu.cn

Abstract. Accurate recognition of human emotions through EEG data is of great significance in human-computer interaction, mental health, intelligent medical care and other fields. EEG signal contains a large number of meaningful and extractable features. Therefore, effective feature selection plays an essential role in reducing feature dimensions and avoiding redundancy. In order to select the emotion related features from hundreds of features and achieve better emotion recognition results, we propose an enhanced firefly algorithm (EFA) for EEG emotion recognition, which is based on brightness-distance based attraction and roulette-based local search strategies. Then, we apply EFA to select features for EEG emotion recognition and provide a novel encoding method of fireflies to distinguish the importance of channels and bands respectively. We conduct comparative experiments to evaluate the performance of EFA on DEAP database. The experimental results confirm the superiority of the proposed method in AUC score.

Keywords: Emotion recognition · Feature selection · Swarm intelligence · Fire-fly algorithm · EEG

1 Introduction

Emotion plays an important role in human life. With the development of human-computer interaction (HCI) technology, there are many researches on emotion recognition in recent years. Generally, emotion recognition is mainly based on two kinds of signals: physical signals such as facial expression [1] and speech [2], and physiological signals such as electroencephalogram (EEG) [3] and respiration (RSP) [4]. Among them, EEG has attracted extensive attention of researchers because it is more objective and handier than other signals.

EEG-based emotion recognition usually involves the following steps: preprocessing, feature extraction, feature selection and classification. There are different kinds of features can be extracted from EEG signals, such as time-domain features, frequency-domain features, time-frequency features and nonlinear features [5]. Since most EEG signals are collected in the form of time domain, and it need to transform the signals

Y. Xu et al. (Eds.): ML4CS 2022, LNCS 13657, pp. 182–196, 2023.
https://doi.org/10.1007/978-3-031-20102-8_15

from time domain to frequency domain by some algorithms, like fast Fourier transfer (FFT) [6], short-time Fourier transform [7] and wavelet transform [8]. Furthermore, band power, power spectral density and differential entropy can be calculated from the frequency bands.

Since hundreds of features can be extracted from EEG signals, it is necessary to select features before classification to reduce the feature dimension and avoid redundancy. Principal component analysis (PCA) is the most commonly used dimension reduction technique, which decomposes EEG signals into independent components and removes interference [9, 10]. Swarm intelligence (SI) algorithms have been proposed to solve the problem of feature selection and achieved good results. Particle swarm optimization (PSO) is utilized to select the emotion related features for EEG emotion recognition [11]. Nakisa et al. [12] apply ant colony optimization and PSO for the feature selection of EEG datasets.

Recently, Firefly Algorithm (FA) [13] has been applied in various fields due to its advantages of less parameters and simple operation. In the aspect of distance-based attraction mechanism, FA can automatically divide the whole colony into multiple sub-colonies, which can naturally and effectively deal with nonlinear and multi-modal optimization problems [14]. However, it has the limitations of slow convergence speed, early maturity and low accuracy in the late iterations.

To tackle the limitations of FA and achieve better emotion recognition results for EEG data, we propose an enhanced FA for emotion recognition. Firstly, we transform signals from time domain to frequency domain by FFT and calculate their band power characteristics. Then, we propose an enhanced FA with brightness-distance based attraction and roulette-based local search strategy. Subsequently, we apply this enhanced FA to select the most important features for EEG emotion recognition. In brief, the main contributions of this work are as follows:

1. We propose an Enhanced Firefly Algorithm (EFA) with two strategies: brightness-distance based attraction (BDA) and roulette-based local search strategy (RLS).
2. We apply the enhanced firefly algorithm to select features for EEG emotion recognition and provide a novel encoding method of fireflies to distinguish the importance of channels and bands respectively.
3. We conduct extensive experiments on a public database DEAP [15] to demonstrate the effectiveness of proposed method. The results show that EFA based feature selection algorithm outperforms other competitive feature selection algorithms in EEG-based emotion recognition.

2 Related Work

2.1 EEG Feature Extraction and Selection

Feature extraction and selection play an important role in EEG-based emotion recognition. Feature extraction is mainly to reduce the dimension of EEG data and extract emotion related features from EEG data to study the emotional state of subjects. As a key component of emotion recognition, the quality of features directly determines the performance of emotion recognition model.

EEG Feature Extraction. In the existing research on EEG emotion recognition, there are four kinds of extracted EEG signal features: time-domain features, frequency-domain features, time-frequency features and nonlinear features [5]. Frequency domain features are the most widely used features in emotion recognition based on EEG, such as band power, power spectrum and power spectral density. FFT is used to decompose the EEG signals into five bands: delta, theta, alpha, beta and gamma, and then extract the log band energy of these five bands as features [6]. Li et al. [7] adopt short-time Fourier transform for time-frequency transformation and calculate the power spectral density of four frequency bands respectively.

EEG Feature Selection. In the research of EEG emotion recognition, more electrodes are usually placed on the subject's scalp to obtain more abundant emotional information. However, with the increase of the number of electrodes, the number of features rises sharply, which will lead to excessive calculation and reduce the real-time performance of the system. PCA is used for dimensionality reduction of high-dimensional data, which projects the data onto the principal components, so as to generate the main features of emotion-related EEG and remove useless or noisy information [9, 10]. ReliefF-based channel selection algorithm is applied to reduce the number of channels used in classification task [16]. SI algorithm is widely used in feature selection and its effectiveness has been proved. In the recent years, researchers have applied SI algorithm to feature selection for EEG-based emotion recognition and achieved satisfactory results, such as PSO [11], FA [17], grey wolf optimizer [18] and cuckoo search [19].

2.2 Firefly Algorithm

FA [13] is a heuristic swarm intelligence approach inspired by the flashing behavior of fireflies. The optimization problem is solved by simulating the mutual attraction and movement of fireflies caused by foraging and communication in nature. Fireflies with less brightness are attracted to the brighter one. The brightness of a firefly is determined by the objective function. For the maximum optimization problem, the brightness of a firefly can be simply proportional to the fitness of the objective function. Mutual attraction depends on the light intensity perceived by the firefly, which diminishes with distance. If there is no firefly brighter than a specific firefly, it will move randomly.

As the attractiveness of a firefly is proportional to the light intensity which decrease by distance, the attraction of fireflies is defined as:

$$\beta = \beta_0 e^{-\gamma {r_{ij}}^2} \tag{1}$$

where β_0 is is the attraction of the firefly itself when $r = 0$, γ is light absorption coefficient and r_{ij} is the distance between the fireflies.

The distance between two fireflies can be calculated by Euclidean distance as follow:

$$r_{ij} = \|x_i - x_j\| = \sqrt{\sum\nolimits_{k=1}^{d} \left(x_{i,k} - x_{j,k}\right)^2} \tag{2}$$

where x_i and x_j are the position of firefly i and j respectively, $x_{i,k}$ is the k-th component of the firefly i and d is the dimension of the problem.

Each firefly i compares its brightness with that of other firefly j. If firefly j is brighter than i, firefly i moves toward firefly j as Eq. (3). Otherwise, firefly i move randomly as Eq. (4).

$$x_i(t+1) = x_i(t) + \beta\left(x_j(t) - x_i(t)\right) + \alpha r \tag{3}$$

$$x_i(t+1) = x_i(t) + \alpha r \tag{4}$$

where α is a parameter that determines the random search and it decreases with the increase of the number of iterations t, and r is a d-dimensional Gaussian random vector.

For EEG emotion recognition, it is significant to select features highly correlated to emotion from hundreds of extracted features. Although FA has been used in feature selection, it has the limitations of slow convergence speed, early maturity and low accuracy in the late iterations. To achieve better emotion recognition results for EEG data, this paper develops an enhanced FA for feature selection of EEG signals.

3 Enhanced Firefly Algorithm for Emotion Recognition

3.1 General Framework

In this section, we propose an enhanced FA feature selection for EEG emotion recognition. The general framework is presented in Fig. 1. At the first step, we transform signals from time domain to frequency domain by FFT and calculate their band power characteristics. Then, we propose an enhanced FA with brightness-distance based attraction (BDA) and roulette-based local search strategy (RLS). Subsequently, we apply this enhanced FA to select the most important features for EEG emotion recognition. More details are explained as follows.

3.2 Feature Extraction

Data Preprocessing. We leverage DEAP emotion database and its processed EEG signals data of 32 subjects to recognize emotion in the two dimensions of valence and arousal. Each subject participated in 40 trials, and 63 s signals data were collected in each trail. To expand the number of samples per subject without breaking the time continuity, we segment each 63 s trial into 30 samples (4 s long) by sliding window. The size and the step of the window are set 4 s and 2 s respectively. Finally, we get a total of 1200 samples (40 trials $\times$ 30 segments) for each subject. The labels of 30 samples extended from one trail are the same.

Fast Fourier Transform. After data preprocessing, we obtain 1200 samples for each subject, and each sample contains 32 channels of 4-s EEG signals. For each channel of a sample, we use FFT [20] to transform EEG data from time domain to frequency domain, and then use band-pass filter to decompose it into five frequency bands closely related to people's psychological activities, namely theta (4–8 Hz), alpha (8–12 Hz), low beta (12–16 Hz), high beta (16–25 Hz) and gamma (25–45 Hz). Since the collected EEG

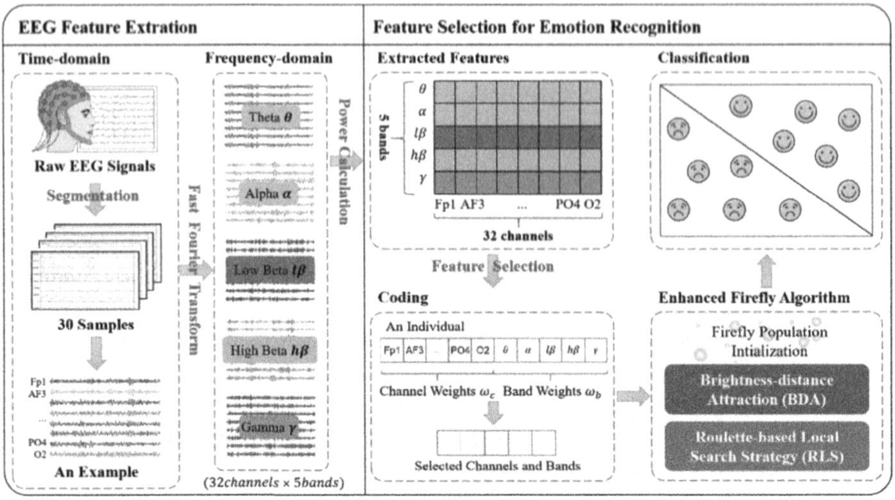

Fig. 1. General framework of proposed method

signal is a discrete sequence $s(n)$, , discrete Fourier transfer (DFT) is often applied to the transformation of EEG data as follow:

$$S(k) = DFT[s(n)] = \sum_{n=0}^{N-1} s(n) W_N^{nk} = \sum_{n=0}^{N-1} s(n) e^{-j\left(\frac{2\pi}{N}\right)nk} (k = 0, 1, \ldots, N-1) \tag{5}$$

where N represents the number of sample points and $W_N = e^{-j\left(\frac{2\pi}{N}\right)}$ is a transform matrix. Due to the high computational complexity of DFT, FFT improves its efficiency by replacing the computation of one larger DFT with the computation of several smaller DFTs.

Band Power. Band Power, a common feature extracted from EEG signals is used to recognize the emotion [5]. The power of a specific frequency band corresponding to channel T in sample i is calculated as

$$p_{iT} = \frac{1}{N} \sum_{k=1}^{N} \left| X_N^{iT}(k) \right|^2 \tag{6}$$

where $X_N^{iT}(k)$ is the FFT of the EEG signals for channel T in sample i, N is the length of FFT and equals the sample length 512 points (4 s).

A 512-point fast Fourier transform (FFT) is used to compute the power of each frequency band and 160 (32 channels × 5 bands) features are obtained for each sample. In order to eliminate the influence of scale differences between features and treat each feature equally, Z-score normalization is applied to each feature. For the feature f_i belonging to sample i, the Z-score normalized value was computed as

$$f_i^{norm} = \frac{f_i - \mu_f}{\sigma_f} \tag{7}$$

where μ_f and σ_f are the mean and the standard deviation of the feature f across all samples respectively.

3.3 Enhanced Firefly Algorithm

FA has the advantages of less parameters, simple operation and easy implementation. However, conventional FA updates its location by moving towards the brighter one and their attractiveness just depends on the light intensity which decrease with the distance as presented in Eq. (1) and (3). In brief, the attraction between two fireflies only depends on their distance. However, we think that the attraction between fireflies depends not only on their distance, but also on their brightness difference. On the other hand, FA has the limitations of slow convergence speed, early maturity and low accuracy in the late iterations. Therefore, we propose two strategies to tackle these challenges, namely brightness-distance based attraction (BDA) and roulette-based local search strategy (RLS). The flow chart of the algorithm is shown in Fig. 2.

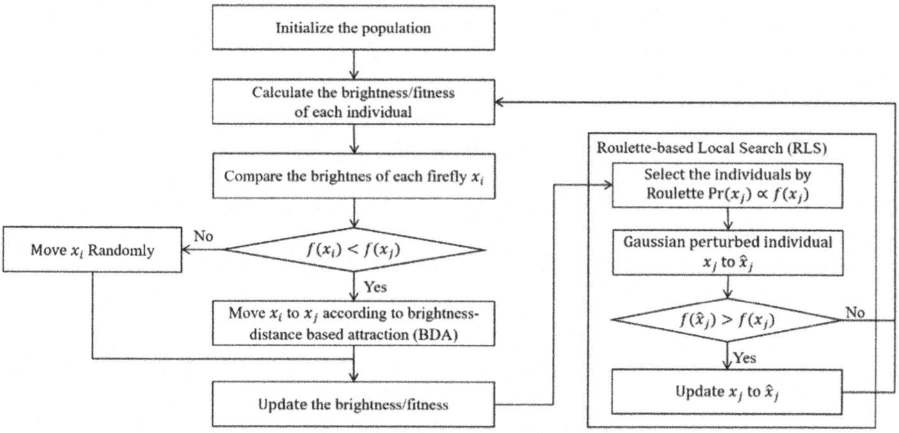

Fig. 2. Flow chart of enhanced firefly algorithm for maximum problem

Brightness-Distance Based Attraction (BDA). For conventional FA, the firefly will move toward the brighter one and their attraction depends on the light intensity which decrease with the distance as presented in Eq. (1) and (3). We think that the attraction between fireflies depends not only on their distance, but also on their brightness difference. If firefly j is much brighter than firefly i, their attraction will be stronger.

To depict this, we propose a relative brightness influence factor c to represent the brightness difference of mutual attraction between fireflies.

$$c = \frac{f(x_j) - f(x_i)}{max[f(x)] - min[f(x)]} \tag{8}$$

where $f(x_i)$ is the brightness value of the firefly i, $max[f(x)]$ and $min[f(x)]$ are the maximum and minimum brightness values of the current population respectively. Therefore, the movement of fireflies as Eq. (3) can be modified as:

$$x_i(t+1) = x_i(t) + c \cdot \beta\left(x_j(t) - x_i(t)\right) + \alpha r \tag{9}$$

Roulette-Based Local Search Strategy (RLS). To tackle the limitations of slow convergence speed, early maturity and low accuracy of firefly algorithm, we propose Roulette-based Local Search Strategy (RLS). Firstly, we apply Roulette algorithm to select the individuals with higher fitness values. The probability of an individual being selected is proportional to its fitness $\Pr(x_j) \propto f(x_j)$. The selection strategy of roulette algorithm is shown as follow:

$$P(x_j) = \frac{f(x_j)}{\sum_{j=1}^{n} f(x_j)} (j = 1, 2 \ldots n) \tag{10}$$

where $P(x_j)$ is the probability of individual x_j selection, $f(x_j)$ is the fitness value of individual x_j and n is the total number of fireflies.

After selecting a subset of fireflies that perform well, we take Gaussian perturbations on these individuals and move them around themselves. The position of the movement can be expressed as:

$$\hat{x}_j = x_j + \alpha r \tag{11}$$

where x_j is the current position of firefly j, $\hat{x}_j$ is the position after the update, r is an n-dimensional Gaussian random vector and α is a parameter that determines the random search. Finally, we choose the position with the best performance as follow:

$$new\_x_j = best(\hat{x}_j, x_j) \tag{12}$$

3.4 Enhanced Firefly Algorithm for Feature Selection

Encoding of Fireflies. As presented in Sect. 3.2, each sample contains 32 channels, including Fp1, AF3,..., PO4 and O2. Each channel can be transformed from time domain to frequency domain by FFT, and then decomposed into five frequency bands. After that, we calculate the band power of each frequency band. Therefore, we can obtain 160 features (32 channels × 5 bands) for each sample. We adopt enhanced FA to select some important features from these 160 features. Due to this specific method of feature extraction, each firefly can be decoded into 37 dimensions, of which 32 dimensions are channel importance weights $\omega_c \in R^{1\times 32}$, and 5 dimensions are band importance weights $\omega_b \in R^{1\times 5}$.

The encoding of a firefly x is presented in Fig. 3. We can obtain importance weights W for 160 features as follow:

$$W = {\omega_b}^T \cdot \omega_c \tag{13}$$

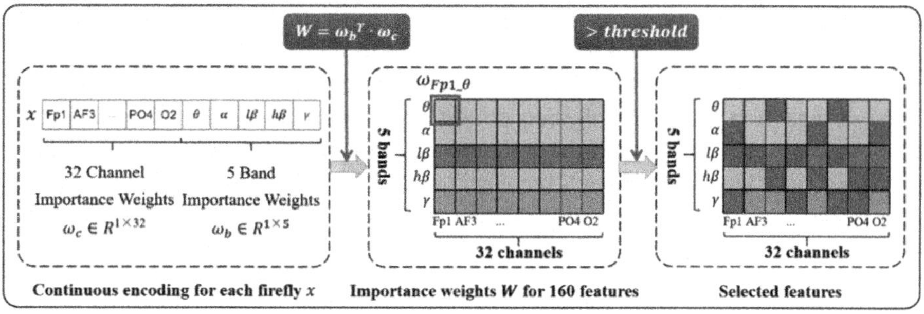

Fig. 3. Encoding scheme for a firefly

where ω_{Fp1_θ} represent the importance weight for band power that extracted from frequency bands θ of channel Fp1.

After that, we select features whose important weights are higher than the threshold, and the threshold is set to the average of all feature weights. The selection coefficient of feature f is calculated as:

$$C_f = \begin{cases} 0, w_f < \overline{w} \\ 1, w_f \geq \overline{w} \end{cases} \tag{14}$$

where w_f is the weight of the feature f and $\overline{w}$ is the average of all feature weights. The strategy for choosing the features as follow:

$$feature\_list = \{f | C_f = 1\} \tag{15}$$

Fitness Function. Fitness function is used to evaluate the performance of classification practice after selecting the most important features. We select K-Nearest Neighbor algorithm [21] as the classifier because of its advantages of simplicity and high precision. We adopt widely used area under ROC curve (AUC) as model performance measurement metrics. Therefore, the fitness is as follows:

$$fitness = AUC = \frac{1}{m^+ m^-} \sum\nolimits_{x^+ \epsilon D^+} \sum\nolimits_{x^- \epsilon D^-} I(x^+, x^-) \tag{16}$$

$$I(x^+, x^-) = \begin{cases} 1, & P_{x^+} > P_{x^-} \\ 0.5, & P_{x^+} = P_{x^-} \\ 0, & P_{x^+} < P_{x^-} \end{cases} \tag{17}$$

where m^+ and m^- are the number of positive samples and negative samples respectively, D^+ and D^- represent the set of positive samples and negative samples respectively and P_x is the prediction of sample x.

4 Experiments

4.1 Experimental Settings

Datasets. We conducted experiments on DEAP, a database for emotion analysis using physiological signals, which was published by Koelstra [15]. DEAP is based on the three-dimensional emotion model of Valence-Arousal-Dominance (VAD), and its EEG data can be used for emotion recognition research. In the process of data collection, a total of 32 subjects were selected for the experiment, including 16 males and 16 females, ranging in age from 19 to 37. In the data collection experiment, the physiological signals of the subjects were collected through 40 channels, among which the top 32 were EEG channels and the last eight channels were peripheral physiological signals. As this paper is about the correlation analysis of EEG data, our analysis is mainly based on the EEG data collected from the first 32 EEG channels.

Evaluation Protocols. We conducted subject-dependent experiments on DEAP database. Since each subject participated on 40 trials that was not enough for our experiments, we segmented each trial into 30 samples with the sliding window (size of 4 s and step of 2 s). Therefore, we totally obtained 1200 samples (40 trials $\times$ 30 segments) for each subject. The labels of 30 samples segmented from one trail are the same. For each subject, 960 samples were taken as training set and 240 samples as testing set. We evaluated our proposed model on 2 dimensional emotions, namely Valence and Arousal, and the threshold to divide samples into two classes was set to 5. We applied AUC as a criterion to evaluate the accuracy of the algorithm in emotion recognition.

Comparison Algorithms. In order to evaluate the performance of enhanced FA (EFA), we selected three heuristic algorithms as our comparison algorithms, namely PSO, GA and FA. We selected features by these four SI-based algorithms and then adopted KNN algorithm for emotion classification. Additionally, ReliefF-PNN [16], an algorithm that selected channels by ReliefF algorithm and classified the emotion by probabilistic neural network (PNN), was selected as a comparison algorithm to verify the effectiveness of SI-based feature selection in classification tasks.

Parameter Settings. For four SI-based algorithms, the candidate solutions were initialized between 0 and 1, and the lower and upper boundaries were set to 0 and 1. The population size of SI-based algorithms was set to 50 and the maximum number of iterations was set to 100. We searched the existing literature and found the most commonly used and recommended parameter settings for SI algorithms. EFA and FA shared the same parameters. For ReliefF-PNN, we traversed the sigma values from 0.1 to 0.9 with a step size of 0.1, and finally selected 0.1 with the highest accuracy.

4.2 Experimental Results

Classification Results and Number of Selected Features. We conducted 10 independent runs for all methods, and calculate average AUC as overall performance. Figure 4 displays the overall performance of our proposed EFA and the other four algorithms. It can be seen that four SI-based algorithms perform better than ReliefF-PNN in most subjects. It confirms the effectiveness of SI-based feature selection for emotion recognition. Among the four SI-based algorithms, EFA achieves the highest accuracy on both Valence and Arousal, evident from the positive effect of our proposed BDA and LRS strategies of EFA. Figure 5 depicts the number of features selected by five algorithms for each subject. As shown in the figure, the feature numbers of GA and ReliefF-PNN for all subjects are the least, followed by EFA and FA algorithm, and the number of features of PSO is much more than that of other algorithms. Table 1 shows the average performance (AUC) of 10 runs for each subject in more details. It can be found that EFA achieves the best accuracy in almost all subjects.

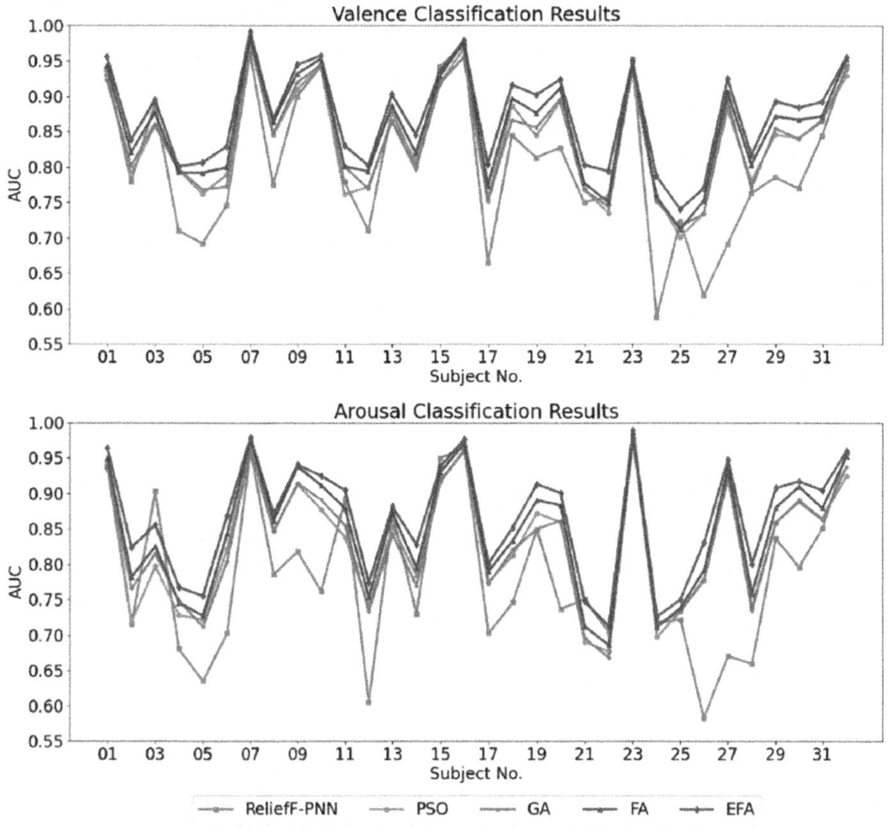

Fig. 4. Testing performance (AUC) of comparison algorithms in valence and arousal

Optimization Results. Figure 6 shows the fitness optimization for subject 01 and 32 with iteration process. Compared with FA, EFA is featured by the faster convergence speed in the first 10 iterations and converge to higher fitness. We believe that the improved performance of EFA benefits from the BDA and RLS strategies. For BDA strategy, the attraction of fireflies depends on brightness and distance, which help fireflies move faster to the brighter position. For RLS strategy, it provides opportunity for fireflies with higher fitness to achieve the better results. Furthermore, PSO has fast convergence while it obtains the lower AUC value, which may be caused by trapping into local optimum. The convergence of GA is slow and converge to lower fitness.

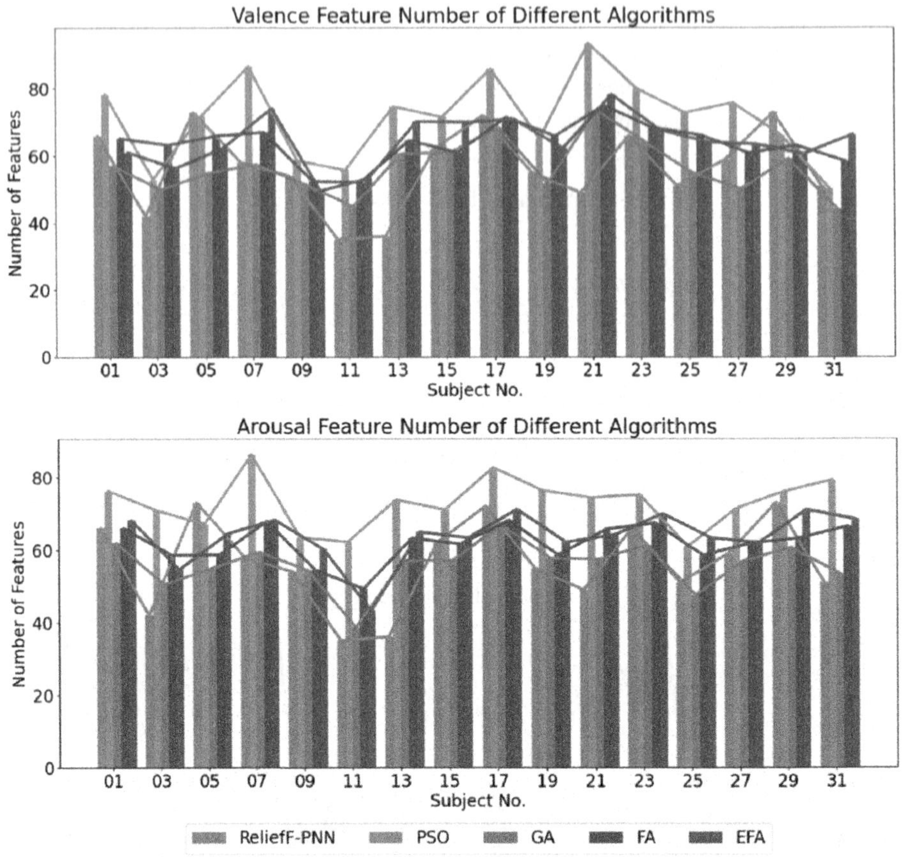

Fig. 5. The number of selected features in valence and arousal

Table 1. Average AUC performance (%) of 10 runs for each subject

Sub	Valence					Arousal				
	ReliefF	PSO	GA	FA	EFA	ReliefF	PSO	GA	FA	EFA
01	93.83	92.97	92.31	94.38	**95.61**	93.82	94.51	93.38	95.05	**96.43**
02	77.88	78.96	80.15	82.05	**83.85**	71.54	71.89	76.57	78.18	**82.38**
03	88.99	85.86	86.11	87.74	**89.55**	**90.31**	79.70	81.46	82.52	85.61
04	70.99	79.57	79.71	79.20	**80.06**	68.03	72.83	74.86	74.56	**76.75**
05	69.25	76.20	76.82	79.19	**80.60**	63.51	72.24	71.17	72.75	**75.51**
06	74.59	78.88	77.21	79.95	**82.87**	70.26	82.14	80.39	84.34	**86.94**

(continued)

Table 1. *(continued)*

Sub	Valence					Arousal				
	ReliefF	PSO	GA	FA	EFA	ReliefF	PSO	GA	FA	EFA
07	96.14	97.81	97.88	98.63	**99.17**	96.15	96.59	96.47	97.72	**97.97**
08	77.49	84.51	84.67	86.44	**86.78**	78.59	84.82	84.66	86.21	**87.21**
09	90.01	91.00	92.00	93.25	**94.50**	81.79	91.31	91.49	93.81	**94.09**
10	94.37	94.50	94.51	95.33	**95.79**	76.17	87.78	89.14	91.18	**92.51**
11	77.92	76.16	80.09	80.11	**83.04**	89.31	83.83	85.54	87.93	**90.49**
12	71.03	77.21	76.94	79.42	**80.24**	60.48	74.03	73.36	75.35	**77.39**
13	87.98	86.62	86.47	88.75	**90.30**	87.19	85.36	84.25	87.36	**88.20**
14	80.22	81.03	79.65	81.99	**84.55**	73.02	78.44	76.94	79.47	**82.81**
15	**94.21**	91.89	91.77	92.87	93.42	**95.03**	91.90	91.66	93.00	93.81
16	97.16	96.73	95.59	97.69	**97.92**	96.48	96.00	96.19	97.13	**97.70**
17	66.52	75.41	75.10	77.37	**80.36**	70.26	77.45	77.23	78.98	**80.08**
18	84.47	88.73	86.70	89.75	**91.66**	74.57	81.23	82.02	83.36	**85.22**
19	81.34	84.45	85.66	87.70	**90.27**	84.96	87.27	85.06	89.09	**91.34**
20	82.75	89.31	89.64	91.21	**92.42**	73.70	86.02	86.21	88.37	**90.11**
21	75.03	76.86	76.82	77.75	**80.32**	**75.07**	69.08	69.61	71.25	74.73
22	75.81	73.55	74.43	75.05	**79.44**	70.46	67.72	66.84	68.62	**71.31**
23	**95.30**	94.25	93.82	95.08	94.99	98.29	97.90	97.72	98.65	**98.94**
24	58.84	76.02	75.15	75.84	**78.77**	71.80	69.72	71.54	71.12	**72.61**
25	72.39	70.13	71.63	71.25	**74.04**	72.23	73.40	73.36	73.86	**75.03**
26	61.83	73.42	73.42	75.23	**76.99**	58.26	77.66	77.95	79.14	**83.10**
27	69.16	88.23	89.57	90.74	**92.58**	67.06	92.26	92.64	93.61	**94.79**
28	76.31	78.07	77.03	80.32	**81.69**	65.98	73.98	73.43	75.84	**80.00**
29	78.57	84.63	85.49	87.26	**89.37**	83.67	85.88	85.97	88.03	**90.81**
30	77.02	84.08	84.07	86.78	**88.49**	79.59	89.07	88.85	91.01	**91.72**
31	84.43	86.77	86.55	87.27	**89.29**	85.07	86.52	86.34	87.97	**90.51**
32	94.41	92.97	93.80	95.35	**95.63**	95.84	92.50	93.83	95.31	**96.06**
Ave	80.51	83.96	84.09	85.65	**87.33**	78.70	82.84	83.00	84.71	**86.63**

Channel Importance and Band Importance. We obtained the optimal solution for each subject through 4 SI-based algorithms. According to our encoding method, the optimal solution contains 37 dimensions, among which the top 32 are the importance weights for channels and the last 5 dimensions are the importance weights for bands. Table 2 shows the average importance of five frequency bands of all subjects in Valence and Arousal classification tasks. It reveals that frequency bands with higher frequency

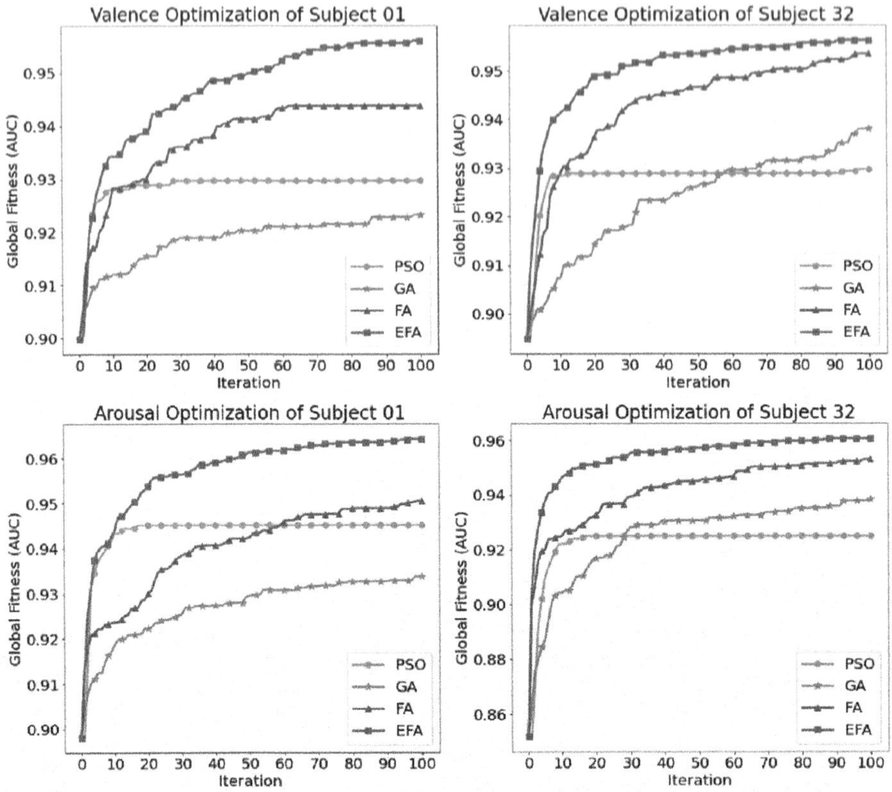

Fig. 6. Fitness optimization for subject 01 and 32 in valence and arousal

are more significant for predicting emotion classification. We calculated the average importance of channels of all subjects and found out the top 10 important channels as shown in Fig. 7. It shows that the top 10 channels of valence are mainly located in frontal and parietal brain regions related to emotion processing, while top 10 channels of arousal are mainly located in parietal and occipital brain regions.

Table 2. The importance of different bands in valence dimension

Band name	Valence				Arousal			
	PSO	GA	FA	EFA	PSO	GA	FA	EFA
Theta	0.4449	0.1421	0.1977	0.2010	0.4358	0.1477	0.1996	0.1840
Alpha	0.5563	0.2316	0.3192	0.3116	0.5732	0.2316	0.3000	0.3004
Low-beta	0.7590	0.4312	0.4859	0.4843	0.7510	0.4306	0.4861	0.4949
High-beta	0.9012	0.5233	0.6333	0.6216	0.7943	0.5383	0.5720	0.5556
Gamma	**0.9246**	**0.7125**	**0.7582**	**0.8305**	**0.8847**	**0.7518**	**0.7433**	**0.8058**

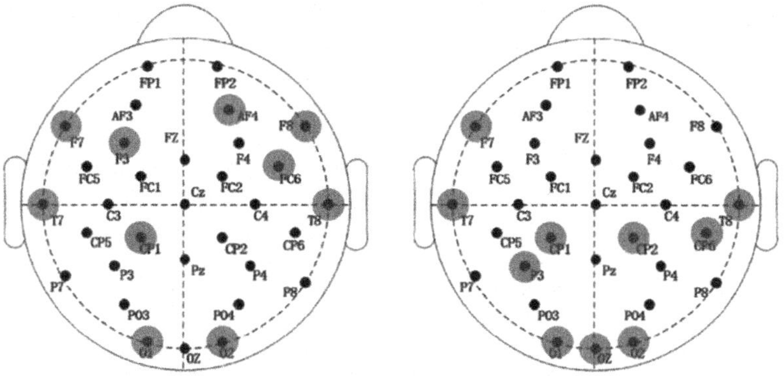

Valence Classification Task Arousal Classification Task

Fig. 7. Top 10 important channels in valence and arousal

5 Conclusion

In this work, we propose Enhanced Firefly Algorithm (EFA) with brightness-distance based attraction (BDA) and roulette-based local search strategy (RLS), which provide faster convergence and higher accuracy. We apply EFA to EEG-based emotion recognition and provide a novel encoding method of fireflies, which can distinguish the importance of channels and bands respectively. We conducted subject-dependent experiments on DEAP database, and the experimental results show that the EFA achieves the highest accuracy among the competitive feature selection methods in emotion classification of arousal and valence. Our proposed algorithm requires further improvement to reduce the number of selected features. In future studies this problem will be handled by considering multi-objective optimization for feature selection.

Acknowledgement. This study is supported by National Natural Science Foundation of China (71901150, 71901143), Natural Science Foundation of Guangdong (2022A1515012077), Guangdong Province Innovation Team "Intelligent Management and Interdisciplinary Innovation" (2021WCXTD002), Shenzhen Higher Education Support Plan (20200826144104001).

References

1. Ko, B.C.: A Brief review of facial emotion recognition based on visual information. Sensors. **18**(2), 401 (2018)
2. Ingale, A.B., Chaudhari, D.S.: Speech emotion recognition. Int. J. Soft Comput. Eng. (IJSCE). **2**(1), 235–238 (2012)
3. Bos, D.O.: EEG-based emotion recognition. The Influence of Visual and Auditory Stimuli **56**(3), 1–17 (2006)
4. Wei, C.Z.: Stress emotion recognition based on RSP and EMG signals. In: Advanced Materials Research, vol. 709, pp. 827–831. Trans Tech Publications Ltd. (2013)

5. Jenke, R., Peer, A., Buss, M.: Feature extraction and selection for emotion recognition from EEG. IEEE Trans. Affect. Comput. **5**(3), 327–339 (2014)
6. Nie, D., Wang, X.W., Shi, L.C., Lu, B.L.: EEG-based emotion recognition during watching movies. In: 2011 5th International IEEE/EMBS Conference on Neural Engineering, pp. 667–670 (2011)
7. Li, D., Wang, Z., Wang, C., et al.: The fusion of electroencephalography and facial expression for continuous emotion recognition. IEEE Access. **7**, 155724–155736 (2019)
8. Piho, L., Tjahjadi, T.: A mutual information based adaptive windowing of informative EEG for emotion recognition. IEEE Trans. Affect. Comput. **11**(4), 722–735 (2018)
9. Zhang, Q., Lee, M.: A hierarchical positive and negative emotion understanding system based on integrated analysis of visual and brain signals. Neurocomputing **73**(16–18), 3264–3272 (2010)
10. Rahman, M.A., Hossain, M.F., Hossain, M.F.: Employing PCA and t-statistical approach for feature extraction and classification of emotion from multichannel EEG signal. Egypt. Inform. J. **21**(1), 23–35 (2020)
11. Li, Z., Qiu, L., Li, R.: Enhancing BCI-based emotion recognition using an improved particle swarm optimization for feature selection. Sensors **20**(11), 3028 (2020)
12. Nakisa, B., Rastgoo, M.N., Tjondronegoro, D.: Evolutionary computation algorithms for feature selection of EEG-based emotion recognition using mobile sensors. Expert Syst. Appl. **93**, 143–155 (2018)
13. Yang, X.S.: Nature-inspired Metaheuristic Algorithms. Luniver Press (2010)
14. Yang, X.-S., Deb, S., Zhao, Y.-X., Fong, S., He, X.: Swarm intelligence: past, present and future. Soft. Comput. **22**(18), 5923–5933 (2017). https://doi.org/10.1007/s00500-017-2810-5
15. Koelstra, S., Muhl, C., Soleymani, M.: Deap: a database for emotion analysis; using physiological signals. IEEE Trans. Affect. Comput. **3**(1), 18–31 (2011)
16. Zhang, J., Chen, M., Hu, S.: PNN for EEG-based emotion recognition. In: 2016 IEEE International Conference on Systems, Man, and Cybernetics (SMC), pp. 002319–002323. IEEE (2016)
17. He, H., Tan, Y., Ying, J., Zhang, W.: Strengthen EEG-based emotion recognition using firefly integrated optimization algorithm. Appl. Soft Comput. **94**, 106426 (2016)
18. Yildirim, E., Kaya, Y., Kiliç, F.: A channel selection method for emotion recognition for EEG based on swarm-intelligence algorithms. IEEE Access **9**, 109889–109902 (2021)
19. Sreeshakthy, M., Preethi, J.: Classification of human emotion from deap EEG signal using hybrid improved neural networks with cuckoo search. BRAIN Broad Res. Artif. Intell. Neurosci. **6**(3–4), 60–73 (2016)
20. Nussbaumer, H.J.: The fast Fourier transform. In: Fast Fourier Transform and Convolution Algorithms. Springer, Berlin, Heidelberg (1981). https://doi.org/10.1007/978-3-662-00551-4_4
21. Cover, T., Hart, P.: Nearest neighbor pattern classification. IEEE Trans. Inf. Theory **13**(1), 21–27 (1967)

Security Risk Assessment Method of High Voltage Power Communication Network Based on Fuzzy Clustering

Zhengjian Duan(✉) and Xingguo Li

School of Management, Hefei University of Technology, Hefei 230009, China
duanzhengjian46896@163.com

Abstract. Due to the lack of preprocessing of evaluation index data in the process of high-voltage power communication network security risk evaluation, the evaluation effect is poor. Therefore, a high-voltage power communication network security risk evaluation method based on fuzzy clustering is proposed. By determining the influencing factors and evaluation indicators, the operation data of high-voltage power communication network are collected and preprocessed. According to the preprocessing results, the similarity of the operation data of high-voltage power communication network is measured, and the fuzzy clustering method is used to realize the safety risk assessment of high-voltage power communication network. The experimental results show that the security risk assessment results of the proposed method are consistent with the actual results, and the evaluation effect is good.

Keywords: Fuzzy clustering · High voltage · Electric power communication network · Safety risks · Evaluation · Indicators

1 Introduction

The power communication network came into being to ensure the safe and stable operation of the power system. Together with the safety and stability control system and dispatching automation system of the power system, it is collectively referred to as the three pillars of the safe and stable operation of the power system. At present, it is the basis for grid dispatch automation, network operation marketization and management modernization; it is an important means to ensure the safety, stability and economic operation of the grid; it is an important infrastructure of the power system.

Improving the communication quality and increasing the reliability of the power communication network are the consistent requirements and expectations of the State Grid Corporation of China and the provincial, municipal and local power supply companies for the power communication network. Improving the communication quality and increasing its reliability is a continuous process throughout the life cycle of the power communication network. Improving the reliability of the power communication network and reducing the occurrence of risk events can not only rely on the design and optimization of the network structure in the design stage of the communication network, but also

Y. Xu et al. (Eds.): ML4CS 2022, LNCS 13657, pp. 197–211, 2023.
https://doi.org/10.1007/978-3-031-20102-8_16

need to find the unreliable problems, risk events and potential risk threats in the power communication network through effective evaluation of the reliability and risk events of the power communication network during the operation of the power communication network, and take corresponding improvement and improvement measures, Strengthen the inspection, maintenance and management of the existing network, reduce the risk of the power communication network and improve the reliability, so as to provide more safe and reliable services for the power system. From the process of improving reliability, the risk assessment of power communication network is the key. Only effective assessment can identify the unreliable factors in the operation of power communication network, namely potential risk events and threats, and prevent the occurrence of disastrous risk events. Therefore, it is very important to evaluate the risk of power communication network.

Reference [1] proposes a safety and reliability evaluation method of power communication network based on bowtie model. By calculating the importance of data links, the link associated risk value is obtained as the main basis for data link risk identification of power communication network; The fault tree and fault tree structure are used to obtain the data information of network faults. Based on bowtie model, the causes of risks are identified, classified according to the nature of risks, and the risk assessment matrix of power communication network is established to achieve the goal of safety and reliability assessment. However, this method has low accuracy in reliability evaluation of power communication network, resulting in poor evaluation effect. In view of the problems existing in the above methods, this paper proposes a High-Voltage Ionization communication network security risk evaluation method based on fuzzy clustering. By determining the influencing factors of the power communication network, the High-Voltage Ionization communication network security risk evaluation index is obtained, and the evaluation index data is preprocessed. According to the preprocessing results, the similarity measurement of the evaluation index data is carried out, The split K-means clustering method is used to evaluate the security risk of high-voltage power communication network. Through simulation experiments, it is verified that this method can accurately evaluate the security risk of high-voltage power communication network, and solve the problems existing in the traditional methods.

2 Determination of Influencing Factors and Evaluation Indicators

The determination of the influencing factors of the power communication network is directly related to the concept of security risk assessment. Only by understanding the relevant concepts of security risk assessment can the corresponding influencing factors be determined. Since the power communication network is a huge information system, this paper only analyzes the influencing factors of the power optical fiber protection channel and conducts a security risk assessment for it. Based on the principles of international standards and index establishment, we can obtain the following factors influencing the safety risk assessment of power optical fiber protection channels:

(1) System environment safety risk

The natural environment around the optical fiber, disasters and engineering construction often cause serious damage to the optical fiber. Natural disasters include: lightning current causes serious damage to optical fiber materials and structures, leading to optical fiber fracture and short circuit and burnout of communication equipment circuit board; In the heavy ice area, the optical cable jumps and dances due to de icing in spring, resulting in optical fiber deformation and fracture; The cable is damaged by wind, and the long-term breeze vibration and unstable high-frequency galloping will cause serious harm; In recent years, with the rapid development of China's economy and society, the incidents that lead to optical cable breakage often occur during construction.

(2) Network transmission security risks

The quality of network transmission mainly depends on its transmission speed and accuracy. The optical fiber transmission delay is a phenomenon that exists in all transmissions. Generally, it should not be greater than 5/s km μ. If the delay is too large, the transmission signal will be distorted. During the manufacturing process of the optical fiber, due to the difference in temperature and tensile force, the optical fiber will have some defects. A certain loss, this is the intrinsic loss, generally this loss is not large; the optical fiber will also have a certain loss in the process of connection and installation; the quality of the network structure mainly depends on its self-healing ability, which includes the use of It can dynamically adjust the information transmission by changing the corresponding path, etc., to ensure the completion of its tasks.

(3) Physical equipment security risk

As a large number of network equipment are used in the optical fiber protection channel, such as optical transceiver, multiplexing equipment, PCM equipment, special optical core for protection, power supply, etc., the safety of these equipment will also directly affect the normal operation of the system and network applications [2]. For example, the communication power supply is the heart of the communication system. In recent years, the communication circuit interruption caused by the communication power supply failure has accounted for a large proportion of the communication failures, so there are risks in the communication power supply.

(4) Human management of security risks

Safe network equipment is inseparable from human management. A good security strategy ultimately depends on people to implement. Therefore, management plays an important role in network security. Therefore, it is necessary to carefully analyze the security risks brought by management. Insufficient management system, insufficient security inspection of communication system, unreasonable analysis of communication system accident, incomplete testing of communication equipment and incomplete communication data, etc. may cause management security risks; insufficient training of communication personnel, unreasonable staffing and harmonious degree of communication personnel It also poses a management security risk.

The first step to evaluate the importance of the business is to establish an evaluation index system. The evaluation index reflects the difference in the impact of the business on the power grid. The selection of the evaluation index should fully consider the business characteristics.

Based on the analysis of the characteristics of the power communication network business in the previous section, the business characteristics are reflected in the requirements of the business on the communication network and the impact of the business on the power grid. The establishment of the business importance evaluation index system should grasp the business characteristics, that is, it needs to start from the above two influencing factors of the business. Therefore, this paper establishes two evaluation index systems of business importance, namely, the evaluation index system of business importance of communication network factors and the evaluation index system of business importance of power grid factors, from the perspective of the requirements of business on communication network and the impact of business on Power Grid.

The analytic hierarchy process is used to quantify the indicators and determine the corresponding weight of the risk assessment indicators. Analytic hierarchy process mainly decomposes the index elements into objectives, criteria and schemes, and determines the weights of network risk fuzzy evaluation indicators on this basis [3].

Firstly, the evaluation object set is determined as follows:

$$O = \{u_1, u_2, u_3, \ldots, u_n\} \tag{1}$$

In the above formula, the risk evaluation object set, u_1, u_2, u_3 and u_n respectively represent the evaluation factor indicators.

Then the weight distribution vector of the evaluation factor is established, and its expression is as follows:

$$V = \{v_1, v_2, v_3, \ldots, v_n\} \tag{2}$$

In formula (2), v_1, v_2, v_3, and v_n represent the network risk assessment level respectively.

On this basis, a judgment matrix is constructed to judge the relative importance of each index reflected by the values of matrix elements [4]. The scaling method of numbers 1–9 and their reciprocal is adopted. The scaling meaning of each data is as follows (Table 1):

Table 1. Scale meaning

Serial number	Scale value	Relationship between the two
1	1	Both are equally important
2	3	The former is more important than the latter
3	5	The former is slightly more important than the latter
4	7	The former is more important than the latter

(continued)

Table 1. (*continued*)

Serial number	Scale value	Relationship between the two
5	9	The former is extremely important than the latter
6	2, 4, 6, 8	Report the intermediate state of the above adjacent judgments

Finally, the hierarchical ranking is carried out to determine the weights of network risk fuzzy evaluation indicators, and the expression is:

$$R = \frac{G}{M}/a \tag{3}$$

In formula (3), M represents the eigenvector of the indicator, G represents the importance weight of the indicator, and a represents the order of the judgment matrix.

In this way, the determination of the weight of the fuzzy evaluation index of network risk is completed through the above process.

3 High-Voltage Power Communication Network Operation Data Collection

Based on the above determined influencing factors, collect the relevant data of influencing factors. Due to the diversity of data, it is difficult to mine, so it is necessary to design the actual state of each group of samples in the model, so that the nodes between the grids can be optimized at the same time, so as to ensure the normal training of massive data. The multi-dimensional structure of the equipment will lead to inaccurate output data. The state of the data should be corrected immediately after it is input into the network model, so that the data can find the best position in the process of in-depth learning. This will enhance the depth of learning, flexibly describe the characteristics of the data, and strengthen the stability of the structure [5]. For the High-Voltage Ionization communication network data, we should not blindly continue to learn. We should establish a standard and keep closer to the goal. Only when the neural network model is improved more concretely, the in-depth learning is carried out more deeply, the more representative the data mining is, the higher the accuracy is. A well-designed network model is the core of data mining.

Assuming that a random data set is $\left\{\left(x^{(1)}, y^{(1)}\right), \ldots, \left(x^{(n)}, y^{(n)}\right)\right\}$, n represents the index, which represents the number of samples, and the research shows that the set shows a gradual upward trend, so the established function expression is:

$$F(a, b; x, y) = \frac{1}{2}\left\| h_{a,b}(x) - y^2 \right\| \tag{4}$$

In the formula, (x, y) represents the data sample, (a, b) represents the learned data sample, and $h_{a,b}$ represents the number of depth iterations.

This function is the loss function of a single data [6], which cannot represent the whole set. The rules obtained are not representative. It is necessary to add more samples to predict the change of the function. The loss function of all samples can be expressed as:

$$\frac{1}{4}\sum_{i=1}^{m}\left(\frac{1}{2}h_{a,b}\left(x^{(i)}\right)-y^{(i)2}\right)\Bigg]+\frac{\sigma}{2}\left(W^{(n)}\right)^2 \tag{5}$$

Among them, m represents the number of sample sets, i represents the multiple, W represents the deep learning matrix, σ represents the feature vector, and k represents the coefficient.

It can be seen from the function that as long as the variation range of an eigenvector is obtained, the network model law of a set can be inferred. The results obtained according to the classification of data categories are iterated [7] and input into the system. Each element in the matrix can be clustered according to the model. The specific steps are as follows:

(1) First, reset all elements of the matrix to zero, make the matrix an empty set, and re-receive the parameters after grid classification, that is, $\Delta W = 0$;
(2) For the initial data sample (x, y), obtain the previous data samples in descending order, denoted as $\Delta F(a-1, b-1; x-1, y-1)$;
(3) Disrupt the original position and state of the grid model, re optimize, design a grid with the same window size, and input data samples;
(4) Calculate the weight of the neural network, and the expression is:

$$\omega^{(i)} = \omega^{(n)} - \alpha\left[\left(\frac{1}{m}\Delta\omega^{(n)}\right) + \sigma\omega^{(i)}\right] \tag{6}$$

In the formula, ω represents the weight coefficient, $\Delta\omega$ represents the average weight, and α represents the falling angle.

With the gradual decline of the model, the lost data samples are gradually reduced, and the required data network is retained.

After the above training, the data mining rules [8] are formulated. The specific mining rules are:

(1) The information to be processed is processed in blocks, the processed results are input into the cluster nodes, and the support of each data node is calculated. The support calculation formula is expressed as:

$$m_j = N * \sum_{i=1}^{m} x_{ij} \cdot h \tag{7}$$

In the above formula, N represents the number of data, and h represents the data node support calculation parameter.
(2) Execute the map program, obtain the local data set from the network file, accumulate all the extracted data sets, and integrate them into a whole;
(3) Enter another numerical record information in the mapper, compare the information with the previous information, if there is the same data, send it to the same node, dig frequently, and get the final mining result;
(4) Unify different data information into data nodes and summarize all results.

4 Preprocessing of the Evaluation Data

Since the dimensions of the attributes of the power communication network samples are different, they should be normalized before risk assessment. Attribute types generally include benefit type, cost type, fixed type, deviation type, interval type, deviation interval type, etc. [9]. Among them, the benefit attribute refers to the attribute whose value is larger the better, the cost attribute refers to the attribute whose attribute value is smaller, the better attribute, and the fixed attribute refers to the attribute whose value is closer to a certain fixed value α_j and the better the attribute. The type attribute refers to the attribute whose value deviates from a certain fixed value β_j, the better. The interval type attribute refers to the attribute whose attribute is closer to a certain fixed interval $\left[q_1^j, q_2^j\right]$, the better. Let $I_i(i = 1, 2, \cdots 6)$ represent benefit type, cost type, fixed type, and deviation type respectively. Set of subscripts for type, interval, and deviation interval attributes. In order to eliminate the influence of different physical dimensions on the evaluation results, the sample attribute matrix can be normalized according to the following formula during evaluation:

$$r_{ij} = \frac{a_{ij}}{\max\limits_{i} a_{ij}} i = N, j \in I_1 \tag{8}$$

5 Data Similarity Metrics

Before data clustering, it is necessary to ensure that the measurement of data is effective, and the similarity can still be preserved after successive measurements. Assuming that the sample data is xi and $xi \in X$, when the similar set X is in the multi-dimensional space, and the adjacent data before and after have the same characteristics, the sequence can be called heterogeneous data. In fact, the principle of data clustering is to measure the distance based on the original data, and determine the cluster center according to the attributes of the sample, so as to achieve the purpose of analysis. The dissimilarity measure is the definition of data attributes [10]. In order to simplify the calculation and more accurately describe the deep meaning of data clustering, the dissimilarity measure can be expressed as:

$$w\left(x_i, x_j\right) = \sum_{p=1}^{n} \beta\left(x_{ip}, x_{jp}\right) \tag{9}$$

$$\beta\left(x_{ip}, x_{jp}\right) = \begin{cases} 1, & x_{ip} = x_{jp} \\ 0, & x_{ip} \neq x_{jp} \end{cases} \tag{10}$$

Among them, v represents the spatial dimension, w represents the measurement coefficient, $\left(x_i, x_j\right)$ represents the i or j data sample, β represents the angle of rotation, p represents the similarity factor, and $\left(x_{ip}, x_{jp}\right)$ represents the clustered sample. It seems that the measurement results are the same, but In the process of deep learning, there are data samples with different semantics, so the distance between the two can be expressed as:

$$d_n(x_i, x_j) = \left(d\left(x_{i1}, x_{j1}\right)\ldots, d\left(x_{in}, x_{jn}\right)\right)^2 \tag{11}$$

It can be seen from the formula that the total distance is accumulated through many small distances, that is, as long as the order of data distribution remains unchanged, the distance will also remain unchanged. Therefore, determining the dissimilarity measurement is selective and meets the traditional triangle principle. Similarly, the distance between heterogeneous data is calculated based on the formula. The formula is:

$$x_i - x_j = \left(x_{i(l+1)} - x_{j(l+1)}, \ldots, x_{i(l+N)} - x_{j(1+N)}\right)^p \tag{12}$$

The distance between the data shows the distance of the entire structure, and the small pushes the big. With the penetration of deep learning, the heterogeneous data gradually finds its own state and position, and the weight established in the formula will be rewritten according to the main characteristics of the data. Construct a network model, and the weighted data will be input into the device in a clustered manner, then the formula of distance d_m becomes:

$$d_m(x_i, x_j) = \sqrt{\left(x_i - x_j\right)^n \sum^{-1} \left(x_i - x_j\right)} \tag{13}$$

Among them, $\sum^{-1}$ represents the squared difference after reconstructing the model.

Put all the obtained distances into the matrix, and all the internal parameters contain specific information. Divide the primary and secondary according to the content of the information, which fully reflects the flexibility of the data. However, no matter how the data are matched and combined, they do not break away from the neural network change rules, and all meet the standard of deep learning.

6 Implementation of Risk Assessment Based on Fuzzy Clustering

After filtering data mining candidate sets, cluster big data. The split K-means clustering method is easy to implement and has a low computational cost. However, this method has a greater impact on the initial classification center. When the initial classification points are not good enough, the global optimal convergence of the clustering algorithm will become difficult. Therefore, the initial clustering center must be optimized. At the same time, in the process of processing, the number of classification clusters is uncertain. If the time complexity exceeds the overflow node, it will increase the time complexity. Based on the above problems, the objective function for setting the search classification center is written as:

$$f\left(p_\mu\right) = \sum_{i=1}^{N} \max\left\{d_k^i - p_\mu - p_i^2\right\} \tag{14}$$

In the above formula, d_k^i represents the distance from node k to the classification center to which it belongs, p_μ represents the initial classification center, and p_i represents the number of iterations of the i mean algorithm.

If the clustering result of class k is known to be F_k, in the clustering process of class F_{k+1}, the estimated results of $k+1$ initial classification centers are expressed as:

$$m_{k+1}^* = \arg\max_{p_u} f(p_u) \tag{15}$$

During the classification process, there will be more data distributed around F_k. Therefore, during the retrieval process, each reference point is in its own category. Constructing a plane in the direction of the first main unit and dividing the corresponding categories into two subsets on this plane further narrows the search range. Based on the above analysis, an incremental K-means algorithm based on principal component analysis is proposed. The specific process is as follows:

(1) Initialization, select the category with the largest variance in F_k and record it as V;
(2) For the covariance matrix of V, the eigenvector decomposition of singular value to maximum eigenvalue is used;
(3) Taking x as the initial center and combining with the classification center, the $k+1$ clustering result is obtained.

Repeat the above steps, iterate the algorithm continuously, complete the clustering of information, and then use the business importance to further measure the security risk of the power communication network.

The business importance indicates the degree to which the power system is affected after the power business is interrupted. The greater the degree of influence, the higher the degree of importance. Since the power service is carried on the power communication network and plays a functional role in the power system, the evaluation of the importance of the power service should not only analyze the factors of the communication network, but also consider the influence of the power grid.

From the analysis of communication network factors, the power business has certain transmission requirements for the communication network it carries, such as time delay, bit error rate, reliability, security, etc. the impact of the business on the power system is reflected in the transmission requirements of the business on the power communication network. Therefore, using the requirements of the business on the communication network to evaluate the importance of the business can reflect the impact of the business on the power system from the factors of the power communication network. From the analysis of power grid factors, the impact of power business interruption on the power grid is different, such as the power grid function and scope of influence. The more core and scope of the influence, the higher the importance of the business. Therefore, using the business impact on the power grid to evaluate the business importance can reflect the impact of the business on the power system from the power grid factors.

The factor business importance matrix is expressed as:

$$P = \begin{pmatrix} \begin{pmatrix} C_1 \\ G_1 \end{pmatrix} & 0 & 0 & \cdots & 0 \\ 0 & \begin{pmatrix} C_2 \\ G_2 \end{pmatrix} & 0 & \cdots & 0 \\ 0 & 0 & \begin{pmatrix} C_3 \\ G_3 \end{pmatrix} & \cdots & 0 \\ \vdots & \vdots & \vdots & \ddots & \vdots \\ 0 & 0 & 0 & \cdots & \begin{pmatrix} C_I \\ G_I \end{pmatrix} \end{pmatrix} \quad (16)$$

In the above matrix, C_1 and G_1 respectively represent the feature of factor business importance.

The network is composed of nodes and edges, and the security risk of the network depends on the security risks of the nodes and edges in the network. From the perspective of topology structure, the status and influence of nodes and edges in the network are not the same. After the failure of a node or edge with a higher status, the impact on the communication network will be greater, so its risk is higher. In the power communication network, the running services directly affect the power grid equipment, involving power production. The failure of nodes or edges will lead to service interruption and cause security risks. Therefore, the importance of the services carried by nodes or edges is also a major measure of security risks. Index.To sum up, the establishment of the security risk assessment model of power communication network should be based on the nodes and edges in the network, and the comprehensive assessment should be carried out according to its topology characteristics and the services carried. Suppose the network model is $G = (V, L)$, where $V = \{v_1, v_2, \ldots, v_n\}$ is the set of network nodes and $L = \{l_1, l_2, \ldots, l_m\}$ is the set of network edges.

Specifically in the power communication network, the "loss of event" represents the loss caused by the failure of a component (node, edge) in the power communication network, which can be expressed by the importance of the unit. The higher the importance of the unit, the failure of the unit The greater the loss; the "event probability" represents the failure probability of the unit in the power communication network. Therefore, the unit safety risk assessment method in the power communication network is expressed as:

$$R = I \times p \quad (17)$$

In the above formula, R represents unit risk, I represents unit importance, and p represents unit failure probability.

The determination of unit failure probability involves the device layer. For example, for the evaluation of edge failure probability, factors such as the material, type, environment, service life, and fault statistics of the transmission link need to be considered, while the node failure probability needs to consider the type of node equipment, Factors such as years of operation, redundant configuration, and fault statistics. The research focus of this paper is to evaluate the security risk of power communication network from the business layer and topology layer, and does not involve the vulnerability analysis of the equipment layer. Therefore, the failure probability of nodes and links is set to be the same, and no differentiated treatment is performed. The unit security risk assessment method in the communication network can be expressed as:

$$R = I \tag{18}$$

As a special network of power and communication intersection, power communication network will bring certain losses to the communication network and the power grid when failure events occur. Therefore, to evaluate the loss caused by the failure of network units, we should start from the two aspects of power and communication. The loss of nodes or edges in the power system can be measured and evaluated by the importance of services. With the failure of a unit, the interruption of the services carried by the unit will occur. The more the number of services carried on the unit and the more important the services are, the more serious the loss caused by the failure to the power grid will be; The unit has different positions in the communication network topology and has different influence on the network. The higher the topological position, the more obvious the transmission function of the unit in the communication network, and the stronger the network's dependence on the unit. The failure of the unit will bring greater losses to the communication network. Therefore, the unit topology importance can be used to measure the loss of the unit failure to the communication network.

$$SI = \sum_{k=1}^{S} n_k Q_k \tag{19}$$

In the above formula, SI represents the importance of unit services, n_k represents the number of k-type services, and Q_k represents the importance of k-type services.

After the above calculation, the business importance and business importance are obtained, and on this basis, the contribution coefficients of each business are evaluated, and then the business importance evaluation model is used to complete the comprehensive risk evaluation.

The determination of contribution coefficient is very important. It is related to the fusion results of multiple factors, and it is the finishing touch in the whole process of comprehensive business importance evaluation. The contribution coefficient of a factor represents the degree to which the business importance of the factor can reflect the comprehensive business importance. The larger the contribution coefficient is, the closer the influence of this factor on the power system is, and the more the business importance of this factor can represent the comprehensive business importance. In the whole evaluation model, whether the contribution coefficient is reasonable is directly related to the accuracy of the comprehensive evaluation results, so it is of great importance to determine the contribution coefficient. As the evaluation index of this section, the contribution coefficient belongs to an external objective thing. The external conditions have strong interference and complexity. Moreover, human consciousness also has fuzziness for objective things, so it is impossible to directly and accurately assign values to the evaluation index. Therefore, a systematic method is needed to evaluate and assign the evaluation index accurately. At present, the common methods are AHP (analytic hierarchy process) and expert evaluation.

The determination of the contribution coefficient requires the comparison of two factors, the power grid and the communication network, which involves the interdisciplinary evaluation of power and communication. Therefore, the traditional AHP, expert assignment and other methods will bring greater impact to the evaluation results due to the different subjective opinions of experts. It is difficult to correctly characterize the significance of the contribution coefficient. In this paper, a method of comprehensive evaluation by experts is adopted, and the two factors are scored by multiple experts, and all expert opinions are compared and summed to calculate the contribution coefficient. This evaluation method integrates all expert opinions, obtains moderate value results, and reduces the difference of results caused by subjective scoring.

The process of determining contribution coefficient by expert comprehensive evaluation method is as follows, and the evaluation steps are as follows:

1) Firstly, the corresponding assignment rules are established before the expert makes a judgment;
2) Secondly, use experts to score, and make statistics to establish a scoring table;
3) Thirdly, the relative contribution matrix is established according to the scoring table in step 2;
4) Then, the relative contribution matrix is summed to obtain the relative contribution sum matrix;
5) Finally, the relative contribution and the elements in the matrix are processed to extract the contribution coefficient.

Using the contribution coefficient to integrate the importance of single-factor business can not only reflect the common characteristics of the impact of the two factors on the power system, but also reflect the difference in the proportion of the two factors on the power system. The method of comprehensive evaluation by experts calculates the contribution coefficient, which makes the evaluation of the contribution coefficient more accurate and objective. Therefore, the final business importance can comprehensively, fully and objectively reflect the influence of the business on the power system. After obtaining the network element risk degree, comparatively analyze the network risk distribution. The higher the risk, the greater the security risk that the unit bears. It is necessary to implement necessary security protection measures or focus on monitoring to control the loss caused by the occurrence of risks. The establishment of the power communication network security risk assessment model provides a quantitative standard for the assessment of network unit risk, and more directly shows the vulnerability of the communication network, which is of great significance for the security protection of communication and even the stable operation of the power grid.

To sum up, the specific process of the high-voltage power communication network security risk assessment method based on fuzzy clustering proposed in this paper is shown in Fig. 1.

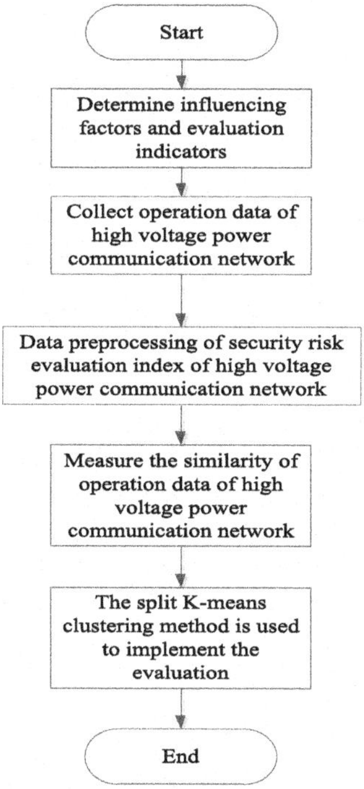

Fig. 1. Specific flow chart of high voltage power communication network security risk assessment method based on Fuzzy Clustering

7 Experimental Comparison

In order to verify the effectiveness of the proposed High-Voltage Ionization communication network security risk assessment method, experimental comparison is carried out. In order to ensure the preciseness of the experiment, the proposed method is compared with the traditional method. The comparison results are as follows.

The evaluation accuracy is selected as the experimental index to test the safety risk evaluation accuracy of the High-Voltage Ionization communication network of this method and the traditional reference [1] method. The test results are shown in Table 2.

Table 2. Comparison results of safety risk assessment accuracy of high voltage ionization communication network of the two methods /%

Number of experiments/time	Method in this paper	Reference [1] method
10	92.6	85.2
20	93.4	85.6
30	94.0	86.7

(*continued*)

Table 2. (*continued*)

Number of experiments/time	Method in this paper	Reference [1] method
40	94.8	87.2
50	95.2	87.9
60	96.7	88.5
70	98.6	89.2

According to the data in Table 2, the accuracy of this method for the safety risk assessment of High-Voltage Ionization communication network can reach 98.6%, and the accuracy of reference [1] method for the safety risk assessment of High-Voltage Ionization communication network is only 89.2%. The accuracy of this method for the safety risk assessment of High-Voltage Ionization communication network is the highest, and the evaluation effect is the highest.

8 Conclusion

The power communication network plays a vital role in the safe and stable operation of the power system. This paper proposes a security risk assessment method for high-voltage ionization communication network based on fuzzy clustering. By applying this method, the security of the power communication network can be evaluated, and the security risks of the ionization network can be detected, prevented, and dealt with early to ensure the safe and stable operation of the power system.

References

1. Shi, F.: Power communication network security reliability evaluation algorithm based on BowTie model. Telecom Power Technology **38**(24), 54–56, 61 (2021)
2. Yang, J., Luo, J., Zhang, H.: Fuzzy neural network based optimal and fair real power management for voltage security in distribution networks with high pv penetration. J. Electr. Eng. Technol. **15**(6), 2471–2478 (2020)
3. Velusamy, D., Pugalendhi, G., Ramasamy, K.: A cross-layer trust evaluation protocol for secured routing in communication network of smart grid. IEEE J. Sel. Areas Commun. **38**(1), 193–204 (2020)
4. Kong, P.Y., Song, Y.: Joint consideration of communication network and power grid topology for communications in community smart grid. IEEE Trans. Industr. Inf. **16**(5), 2895–2905 (2020)
5. Zhang, H., Zhao, X., Geng, S., Lu, W., Ma, Y.: Selection of indoor relay node positions for a three-hop low-voltage broadband power line communication system. IET Commun. **14**(5), 746–751 (2020)
6. Velusamy, D., Pugalendhi, G.K.: Water cycle algorithm tuned fuzzy expert system for trusted routing in smart grid communication network. IEEE Trans. Fuzzy Syst. **28**(6), 1167–1177 (2020)

7. Hu, J., Yang, H.: Multi-point power load forecasting method based on outlier data mining. Computer Simulation **38**(12), 66–69, 93 (2021)
8. Liu, S., et al.: Human memory update strategy: a multi-layer template update mechanism for remote visual monitoring. IEEE Trans. Multimedia **23**, 2188–2198 (2021)
9. Liu, S., Wang, S., Liu, X., Lin, C.T., Lv, Z.: Fuzzy detection aided real-time and robust visual tracking under complex environments. IEEE Trans. Fuzzy Syst. **29**(1), 90–102 (2021)
10. Liu, S., Liu, D., Khan, M., Ding, W.: Effective template update mechanism in visual tracking with background clutter. Neurocomputing **458**, 615–625 (2021)

Trimodal Fusion Network Combined Global-Local Feature Extraction Strategy and Spatial-Frequency Fusion Strategy

Danyang Yao[1], Jinyu Wen[1], Amei Chen[2], Meie Fang[1](✉), Xinhua Wei[2], and Zhigeng Pan[3]

[1] School of Computer Science and Cyber Engineering, Guangzhou University, Guangzhou, China
{1692009112,1361120721}@qq.com, fme@gzhu.edu.cn
[2] Department of Radiology, Second Affiliated Hospital of South China University of Techonology, Guangzhou, China
17690189@qq.com, eyxinhuawei@163.com
[3] School of Artifical Intelligence, Nanjing University of Information Science and Technology, Nanjing, China
003443@nuist.edu.cn

Abstract. Two or more images are fused into one to complement each other's information, which is conducive to assisting doctors in locating disease types, conditions, and lesions. Most of the existing methods focus on the fusion of two modalities, and in fact, it is very common for the disease that requires the fusion of trimodal to assist diagnosis. This paper proposes a high-precision trimodal medical image fusion network. According to the information characteristics of anatomical images and functional images in medical images, we designed the global texture module (GTM) and the local detail module (LDM) for feature extraction simultaneously. The fusion strategy fully combined the advantages of spatial domain and frequency domain to retain more complete texture detail information and global contour information. At the same time, the multi-attention mechanism is adopted to extract more effective depth features and more accurate location information. Experimental results show that the proposed method is effective in both subjective vision and objective index evaluation.

Keywords: Trimodal · Image fusion · Deep learning · Fourier transform

This work was supported by the National Natural Science Foundation of China (Nos. 62072126, 61772164), the Fundamental Research Projects Jointly Funded by Guangzhou Council and Municipal Universities (No. 202102010439), Zhejiang Provincial Natural Science Foundation of China (No. L221F020008), and Postgraduate Innovation Project of Guangzhou University (No. 2021GDJC-D16). Danyang Yao and Jinyu Wen contributed equally to this work.

Y. Xu et al. (Eds.): ML4CS 2022, LNCS 13657, pp. 212–226, 2023.
https://doi.org/10.1007/978-3-031-20102-8_17

1 Introduction

Medical images play an important role in the diagnosis and treatment of diseases by doctors. Due to the characteristics of medical image multi-modality and the limitations of each modal, multimodal medical image fusion came into being. The purpose is to extract and synthesize information from multiple source images to obtain a more accurate, comprehensive, and reliable description of a certain area or target. The proportion of key information in medical images is small and the same part and body state in most of medical images are very similar. Different from natural images, subtle changes in the background tissues with high similarity may represent a certain lesion. Therefore, it is important to pay attention to the key medical information and features for medical image fusion.

Computed tomography (CT), magnetic resonance imaging (MRI), positron emission tomography (PET) and single-photon emission computed tomography (SPECT) are commonly used modalities of medical images for computer aided design (CAD). CT has high resolution with clear bone imaging, which provides a good reference for locating lesion, but the lesion itself is poorly displayed. While SPECT and PET provide functional information about the human body, but the description of anatomical structures is poor. MRI's spatial resolution is lower than that of CT, but soft-tissue imaging is clear and facilitates the determination of lesion extent. Further, MRI can be classified into MRI-T1 and MRI-T2 etc. MRI-T1 are mostly used to observe anatomical structures, and MRI-T2 can clearly show tissue lesions. Therefore, it's important to comprehensive use of the patient's information from multimodal medical image to reflect the detection site of the anatomical structure, tissue metabolism, and other aspects of the information, which facilitates doctors to diagnose and treat diseases.

Image fusion algorithms can be broadly divided into two categories: traditional methods [19] and deep learning-based methods [27]. Traditional methods are mainly to use a variety of mathematical and statistical tools to optimize algorithms [1–3,12–17,20,21,23,24,26,28]. Different traditional methods have their advantages, but it is hard to obtain deep features of the images for traditional methods. In recent years, DL-based methods have been rapidly developed and widely used [4,8–11,18,25,29]. Most of existing models are effective for fusing specific types of images and limited in two-modal fusion task.

This paper focuses on key medical information of different modals and proposes a trimodal fusion framework concerned several kinds of often-used anatomical images and functional images. The main contributions are as follows:

1. Construct a DL-based trimodal fusion framework for anatomical medical images and functional medical images, which is designed for the fusion of MRI/MRI-T2, PET/SPECT and CT/MRI-T1.
2. According to the different imaging characteristics of anatomical images and functional images, we propose GTM and LDM to extract respectively distinguished spatial domain features from different modalities.

3. Combine spatial and frequency information to build fusion strategy, which converts the pixel-level high and low-frequency information into energy gradients to retain valid information and remove periodic noise.
4. Both channel and spatial attention mechanism are adopted to respectively locate key information and dig information aggregation as far as possible on the direction of the channel in order to extract more effective depth features.

2 Related Work

DL-Based Fusion Methods: Neural networks have been applied to a variety of fusion problems [9]. [18] propose a dual discriminator adversarial generation network to fuse multi-resolution images without causing blurring of thermal radiation information and loss of visible texture details. [8] used structural similarity as loss function during training, and applied color-coding to visualize fusion images by quantifying the contribution of each input image in partial derivative of the fusion image. [29] propose an end-to-end trained full convolutional fusion model that uses two convolutional layers to extract salient features of images from multiple input images, then selects appropriate fusion rules according to the image type. [10] propose a fusion network based on nested connectivity and spatial/channel attention models. Networks based on nested connections can save a lot of information in the input data from a multi-scale perspective, and describe the importance of each spatial location and the depth characteristics of each channel. [4] propose a convolutional neural network based on Laplace pyramid decomposition, which decomposes the source images into different spatial frequency bands, fuses them separately on each spatial frequency layer. Due to the specificity of medical images themselves and the difference from natural images, we select convolutional neural networks to handle the fusion problem.

Trimodal Fusion Methods: Most of the multimodal image fusion on medical images is limited in two modals, [22] demonstrate that CT-PET fused image brought greater observer-significant differences than CT only when applied to outline large volume tumors in the head and neck. In contrast, trimodal fusion can simultaneously generate multiple parameters such as discriminated tissue, blood flow, metabolism, and location. [6] demonstrate that CT-MRI-PET fused image can better distinguish postoperative changes from residual tumors in gliomas of the brain and improve the accuracy of tumor outlining than CT-MRI. [5] demonstrate that CT-MRI-PET fused image can achieve accurate target localization and reduce differences between observers in stereotactic fractional radiation therapy for meningiomas. [9] propose a real-time image fusion method, which uses a pre-trained neural network to generate a single image containing multi-modal source features, extracts the depth feature map of the source image based on convolutional neural network, and generates the fusion weights that drive the multimodal image fusion process to obtain the weight map. [7] propose a two-stage image fusion strategy based on non-downsampled shear wave transform and a simplified pulse-coupled neural network, which is implemented in HSV space. In the image processing software and radiotherapy planning system of practical clinical applications, it is also limited to fusion two modals images.

In fact, the fusion of trimodal medical images is particularly important. We take an example from the results of the trimodal fusion experiment to describe this point, as shown in Fig. 1. In the source CT, there are two white circles of different sizes near the vermis, which turn into small gray circles in the part indicated by the red arrow in MRI, indicating that the part is not swollen, but the edge is not clear enough. The blue arrow indicates that the white circle is contained in the surrounding highlighted tissue and cannot be identified. In the source SPECT image, the sites indicated by the two arrows are less active than the surrounding tissue, indicating no metabolic abnormalities. First, when CT and MRI were fused, the fusion result (Fig. 1(d)) included anatomical information and tissue information. But the site indicated by the arrow was only different from the original CT in contrast, and the tissue information in the MRI had no obvious diagnostic effect on doctors. Then, when MRI and SPECT were fused (Fig. 1(e)), the shape and contour of the two arrows were the same as that of the original MRI, and the functional information was not obvious. However, when the trimodal images were fused (Fig. 1(f)), the information of tissue metabolism and other information are added, and the shapes of the two parts are significantly different from the original image, which is clear enough for doctors to accurately diagnose the location and degree of lesions.

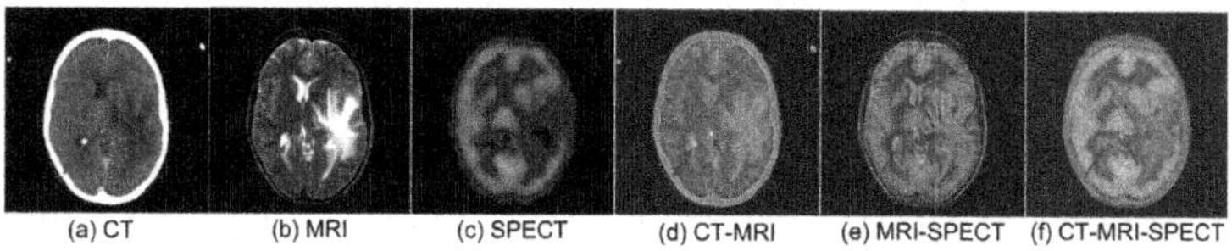

Fig. 1. Take an example to illustrate that trimodal medical image fusion is necessary and important for CAD.

3 Methodology

We propose a novel trimodal medical image fusion network, which can fuse trimodal images covering anatomical images and functional images with high accuracy. In the process of feature extraction, we designed GTM and LDM to extract feature information for different modal characteristics of medical images. We adopt the channel and spatial attention mechanism method to find the channel location of the key information in the image and then find the spatial location with the most information aggregation based on the direction of the channel to capture the location information, which is convenient to extract more effective depth features. Fourier transform is added in the fusion strategy to transform image feature information from spatial domain to frequency domain for processing. High and low-frequency information at the pixel level is converted into an energy gradient to retain effective information and remove periodic noise. It is

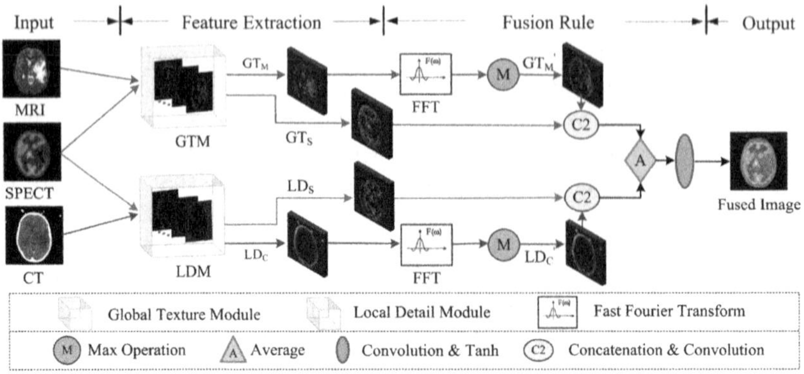

Fig. 2. Trimodal medical image fusion framework, which including two feature extraction modules and fourier transform for feature frequency domain transformation.

the first time to combine spatial domain and frequency domain transform in the medical image fusion methods. We fully combine the advantages of spatial domain and frequency domain transformation to retain more complete texture details and global contour information. The fusion framework is shown in Fig. 2.

GTM and LDM were designed to extract feature information for CT and MRI respectively. SPECT provides functional information about the human body. It is a pseudo-color image, and the metabolic intensity information of tissues in various parts is expressed by color contrast, but its texture information is weak. Therefore, GTM and LDM are used to extract its characteristic information simultaneously, and the location and degree of lesions are determined by combining with the features of anatomical images. CT have high resolution, clear bone imaging, and can reflect bleeding of tissues and organs, which can be used to locate the location of lesions. Therefore, the LDM is used to extract its high-frequency information. MRI is not as clear as CT, but soft tissue imaging is clearer, which is suitable for observing soft tissue structure to determine the scope of the lesion. Therefore, the GTM is used to extract its low-frequency information. Finally, the feature information is fused to obtain the fusion result. Through the targeted information extraction, the important information in the source image can be obtained with a simple network framework.

3.1 Global Texture Module

The global texture feature extraction module structure is shown in Fig. 3, in this module, the operation of convolution feature extraction is mainly to capture global information of context by changing the number of channels in different layers. First, without changing the size of the input image, we extract features by increasing the dimension to 64 dimensions through some series of CBR and then taking the dimension to 16 dimensions as the output. GTM extracts the low-frequency information in the image, that is, the large flat area where the

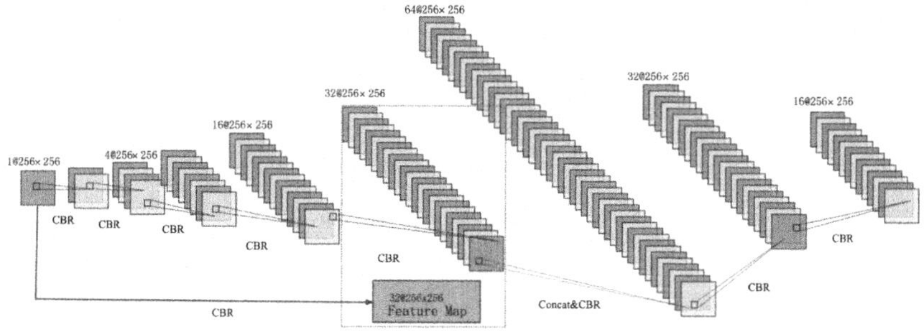

Fig. 3. The process of GTM: extracting low frequency information from images.

brightness and gray value change slowly in the image, which is a comprehensive measure of the intensity of the whole image and can obtain a large range of information in the image. The blocks represent the feature map stack diagram, and the number at the top indicates the number of channels and the size of the image. CBR is a set of operations, specifically representing the convolution operation, batch normalization, and ReLU activation function.

3.2 Local Details Module

The local detail feature extraction module structure is shown in Fig. 4. This module mainly obtains feature maps through convolution operation and raises feature dimensions to 128 dimensions through up sampling and a series of CBR operations. In the CBR after max pooling and dimension reduction, the dimension is reduced to 16 dimensions as the output dimension. CBR operation, namely convolution operation, batch normalization, and ReLU activation function. At the same time, up sampling and maximum pooling are added to extract the local details of the input image. LDM extracts the high-frequency information in the image, which can be understood as the detail signal. It is mainly used to measure the edge and contour of the image and can obtain specific details information. Adding two cascade operations can capture long-distance dependencies and link up and down convolutional layers to reduce losses.

3.3 Fusion Strategy with Frequency Domain Transformation

In this paper, fourier transform is added to the fusion strategy to transform the spatial high and low-frequency information extracted from anatomical images into the frequency domain, and the spatial signals are converted into amplitude and phase at different frequencies. Amplitude covers the global information of the image, such as texture and color. Phase contains the local information of the image, that is, the contour, shape, and other information. After feature centralization processing, it is beneficial to distinguish high and low-frequency information. The discrete Fourier transform (DFT) of the function $F(x, y)$ with

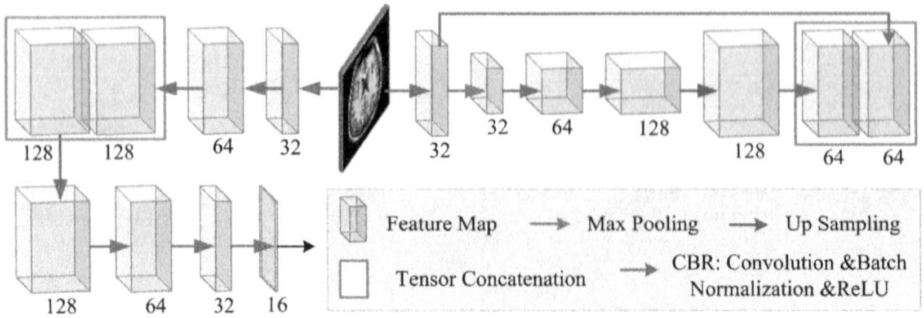

Fig. 4. The process of LDM: extracting high frequency information from images.

the image size of $M \times N$ is:

$$F(u,v) = \frac{1}{MN} \sum_{x=0}^{M-1} \sum_{y=0}^{N-1} f(x,y)\, e^{-j2\pi(ux/M+vy/N)} \tag{1}$$

Given $F(u,v)$, the inverse Fourier transform can be obtained by inverse DFT $f(x,y)$:

$$f(x,y) = \sum_{u=0}^{M-1} \sum_{v=0}^{N-1} F(u,v)\, e^{j2\pi(ux/M+vy/N)} \tag{2}$$

where u and v are frequency variations, x and y are spatial domain image variables, and the value range is $x/u = 0, 1, ..., M-1, y/v = 0, 1, ..., N-1$.

Then the feature information is transformed from the frequency domain to the spatial domain and the high and low-frequency information of the functional image for feature fusion. The high and low frequency information after Fourier transform was maximized, and then fused with the high and low-frequency information of SPECT respectively by concatenation and convolution operations. After averaging the output high and low-frequency information, convolution and Tanh operation are performed, and the final fusion result is output, as shown in Fig. 2.

3.4 Loss Function

The loss function calculation in this paper is shown by Eq. (3), λ according to the fusion effect, 0.8 is the best fusion effect.

$$L = \lambda L_s + L_p, \tag{3}$$

$$\begin{aligned} L_s = & [\alpha(1 - SSIM(I_F, I_1)) + \beta(1 - SSIM(I_F, I_2))\& \\ & + \gamma(1 - SSIM(I_F, I_3)) + \epsilon)]^{\frac{1}{2}}, \end{aligned} \tag{4}$$

$$L_p = [\alpha L_2(I_F, I_1) + \beta L_2(I_F, I_2) + \gamma L_2(I_F, I_3) + \epsilon]^{\frac{1}{2}}, \tag{5}$$

where α, β and γ set to 0.3, 0.3, 0.4. To reduce the error, ϵ is set to 10^{-6}. By the way, When using the proposed network for two-modal image fusion, we reset α, β and γ as 0.5, 0, 0.5. I_1, I_2 are anatomical images, corresponding to CT and MRI. I_3 is functional image, corresponding to SPECT and PET.

4 Experiments

We collected medical images from the whole brain atlas of the open dataset, and selected CT, MRI-T1, MRI-T2, SPECT and PET, all images in the dataset are pre-registered. MRI-T1, MRI-T2 and PET were used during training. The MRI-SPECT input is used to test the fusion of two modal medical images, and the CT-MRI-SPECT is used to test the fusion of trimodal medical images. The images used in this experiment are all brain images, with a size of 256×256.

Experiments were conducted in a single RTX 2080Ti GPU. In the training process, the initial learning rate is 0.001, 101 epoch, batch size is 2. We adopted an adaptive loss adjustment strategy to update the learning rate to 0.1 times of its original value every 20 epochs.

Entropy (EN), mutual information (MI), spatial frequency error ratio (rSFe), standard deviation (SD), and visual information fidelity (VIFF) were used to quantitatively evaluate results. EN is used to quantify how much average information in discrete gray level from all source images are retained in the fused image. MI is used to quantify the amount of information transmitted from each source image to the fused image, a measure of the correlation between two images. SD provides a measure of the dispersion intensity of the fused image. VIFF assesses the fidelity of visual information. Larger value of these indicators means better fusion effect.

rSFe (as Eq.(6)) is a relative measurement, and is used to reflect local intensity changes in picture information, which is determined by the sum of squares of four spatial frequencies (Row, Column, Main Diagonal, Secondary Diagonal) and four first order gradients (Horizontal, Vertical, Main Diagonal, Secondary Diagonal). Its computational formula are listed as Eq.(6). Smaller absolute value of this indicator means better fusion effect.

$$\text{rSFe} = \frac{\sqrt{\sum_{k\in\Omega_1} SF_k^2} - \sqrt{\sum_{l\in\Omega_2} Grad_l I_F}}{\sqrt{\sum_{l\in\Omega_2} Grad_l I_F}}, \tag{6}$$

where $\Omega_1 = \{\text{RF, CF, MDF, SDF}\}, \Omega_2 = \{\text{H, V, MD, SD}\}$, I_F is the fused image. And SF_k are calculated according to the following formulas:

$$SF_k = \begin{cases} \sqrt{\frac{1}{MN}\sum_{i=1}^{M}\sum_{j=2}^{N}[I_F(i,j) - I_F(i-k+1, j+k-2)]^2}, & k = 1, 2, \\ \\ \sqrt{w_{\text{d}} \cdot \frac{1}{MN}\sum_{i=2}^{M}\sum_{j=2}^{N}[I_F(i,j) - I_F(i-1, j+2k-7)]^2}, & k = 3, 4, \end{cases} \tag{7}$$

$$Grad_l I_F = \max_{l \in \Omega_2} \{\text{abs}(Grad_l I_1), \text{abs}(Grad_l I_2), \text{abs}(Grad_l I_3)\} \quad (8)$$

where the image size is M × N, w_d represents the distance weight, and its value is $1/\sqrt{2}$. I_1, I_2 and I_3 represent the three source images.

4.1 The Fusion of Three Input Images

Medical image fusion has less work based on trimodal, so we have selected the progressive experimental comparison of the two trimodal fusion methods proposed so far. We compare the fusion results with those of Zero-LF [9] and Jin et al. [7]. Authors of these two papers haven't opened their source codes. So we reproduced their work according to the procedures described in their papers to obtain test results for comparisons.

4.1.1 Experiment on CT-MRI-SPECT Images

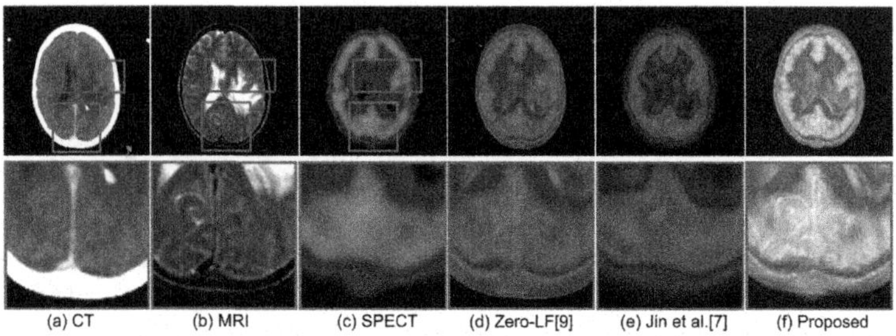

Fig. 5. Left: Source images (CT/MRI/SPECT) and their corresponding amplified images of ROIs; Right: Trimodel fusion results obtained by Zero-LF [9], Jin et al. [7] and the proposed method. (Color figure online)

For the experimental results, we focus on the two parts marked by the color box, as shown in Fig. 5. The blue frame contains the caudal nucleus head, transparent septum, middle sail cavity, central anterior gyrus, central groove, and other parts; the red frame contains the callosum pressure part, straight sinus, wedge leaf, superior sagittal sinus, parietal occipital groove, and other parts. From the fusion result graph, it can be seen that the fusion results of the [7] retain the functional information in SPECT to a large extent, but the information in the original CT and MRI are not retained enough, and the contrast is not clear, and the visual effect is poor. Zero-LF and our method are not far behind in visuals, and we will analyze them from the details. We enlarged the red box part for ROI detail comparison, the result of the [7] is missing the texture information in the CT and MRI, from which only a large amount of functional information can be obtained, which is not conducive to the accurate positioning of the lesion. Both

Zero-LF and our method preserve the anatomical and functional information of the three source images to a large extent. From the perspective of subjective visual quality, the contrast of the proposed method is clearer.

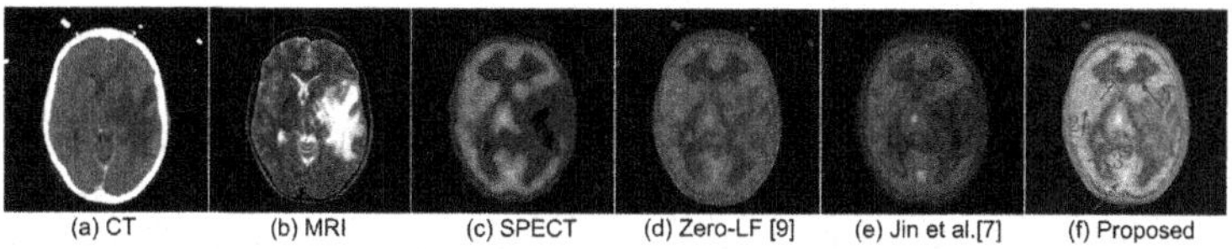

Fig. 6. An example for comparing the performance of different methods on the fusion of CT-MRI-SPECT from the perspective of subjective visual quality.

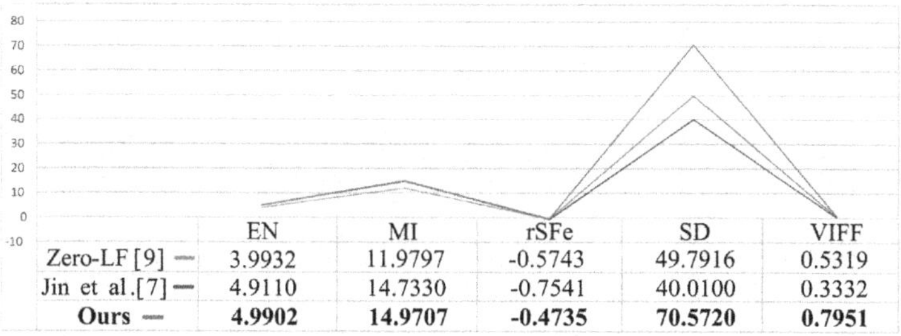

Fig. 7. The chart for comparing the performance of different methods on the fusion of CT-MRI-SPECT from the perspective of objective index evaluation, including En, MI, rSFe, SD, and VIFF.

Another set of experimental results is shown in Fig. 6. Compared with source images, after the fusion of the three images, Zero-LF and the fusion results of our method well retained important anatomical information in CT, tissue information in MRI, and functional information in SPECT. But the fusion result of the [7] only retain much more functional information in the SPECT, missing important information in other two modalities. In Fig. 6(f), Arrow 1 to Arrow

Table 1. Evaluation index values of ablation studies

Methods	EN	MI	rSFe	SD	VIFF
w/o fft	4.5019	13.5058	−0.5267	69.0023	0.9470
I1+gtm	4.4250	13.2750	−0.5690	73.5940	1.1924
I2+ldm	4.3809	13.1426	−0.5286	**77.7885**	1.1987
Ours	**4.5041**	**13.5122**	**−0.5128**	75.5713	**1.5891**

5 respectively point to the knees of the corpus callosum and the anterior feet of the lateral ventricles, the insulae and lateral fissures, the cerebellar worms and hippocampal paracosm, the superior sagittal sinuses and wedges, and the caudal nucleus and globus pallidus. Compared with the source images, the fusion image obtained by our method shows a distinct outline of the white matter edge in the regions pointed by Arrow 1, Arrow 2, and Arrow 4. And these regions show higher brightness, which means that our method retains more complete tissue information from source MRI. Compared with Zero-LF, clearer functional information is retained around Arrow 5, and the contrast is obvious. Compared with [7], less functional information but more organizational information is retained by our method. And the obvious black edge can be seen where the arrow points in the fusion result of our method. On the upper side pointed by Arrow 3, two black circles can be clearly seen. From the perspective of subjective visual quality, the contrast of the proposed method is clearer.

Further, from the perspective of objective index evaluation, the proposed method is also better than the other two methods in EN, MI, rSFe, SD, and VIFF. The indicators are shown in Fig. 7.

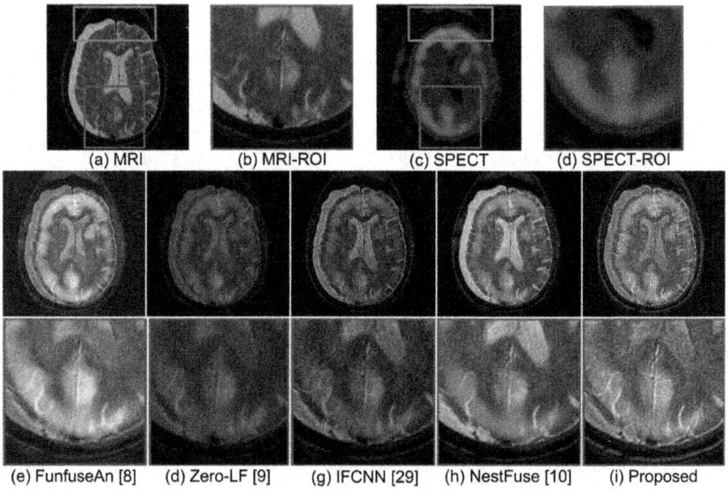

Fig. 8. Top ((a)–(d)): Source images (MRI/SPECT) and their corresponding amplified images of ROIs; Bottom ((e)–(i)): the two-modal fusion results obtained by FunfuseAn [8], Zero-lf [9], IFCNN [29] and NestFuse [10] and the proposed method.

4.2 Experiment on Two Input Images

When the inputs are two modalities, the feature map of I_1 is regarded as its low-frequency information, which obtained through a simple one-step convolution operation is equivalent to the global texture information of I_1. We selected

FunfuseAn [8], Zero-LF [9], IFCNN [29] and NestFuse [10] for test and comparison. The parameters of these methods are set to the default values in their source codes.

Table 2. Evaluation index values of MRI-SPECT fusion results obtained by different methods

Methods	EN	MI	rSFe	SD	VIFF
FunfuseAn [8]	6.0903	12.1806	−0.5955	60.2307	0.2679
Zero-LF [9]	5.2478	10.4956	−0.7620	42.8846	0.1538
IFCNN [29]	5.5447	11.0893	−0.5485	51.9171	0.1674
NestFuse [10]	5.7672	11.5343	−0.5575	**71.1673**	0.2587
Ours	**6.2961**	**12.5921**	**−0.4493**	64.4565	**0.3272**

4.2.1 Experiment on MRI-SPECT Images

In this section, the test results are stored and displayed in grayscale. As shown in Fig. 8, the blue box shows the superior frontal gyrus, middle frontal gyrus, inferior frontal gyrus, cingulate gyrus, cingulate sulcus, etc. In the red frame are the lateral ventricle, the posterior foot of the lateral ventricle, the inferior sagittal sinus, the straight sinus, the middle sail cavity, and the superior sagittal sinus. Image contrast is slightly worse in Zero-LF and IFCNN. FunfuseAn, NestFuse, and the method proposed by us have similar image contrast. FunfuseAn and NestFuse retain more functional information but less organizational information. Carefully comparing the amplified ROIs in the red box, we can see that the fused image obtained by the proposed method better retain both functional and organizational information from source images, with more obvious texture information. We can see matched black ellipses and white textures.

The objective evaluation indexes of experimental results are shown in Table 2. It can be seen that our proposed method outperforms the other four methods in EN, MI, rSFe and VIFF. Only SD is slightly worse than the value of the NestFuse. Therefore, we propose that the method of two modals fusion still has advantages over the other four methods.

4.3 Ablation Studies

We design three groups of ablation experiments to illustrate the effectiveness of frequency domain transform and the rationality of GTM and LDM in the proposed fusion framework. Figure 9 illustrates one group of experimental results.

w/o FFT Experiment: Remove the fourier transform from the fusion strategy. As shown in Fig. 9(d), the information integrity of the fusion result decreases. The feature centralization processing in the frequency domain is missing, and the

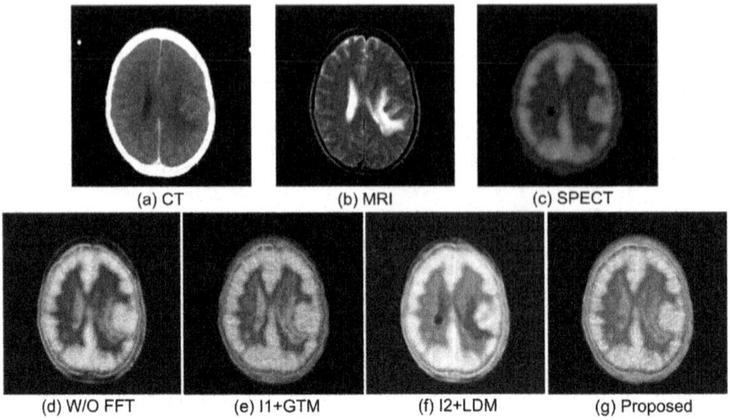

Fig. 9. Comparison of fusion results from ablation experiments. (a)–(c): source images; (d)–(g): fused images obtained by three kinds of ablation experiments and the proposed method.

information of the fused image is in a discrete state. Meanwhile, edge information of CT and texture detail of MRI are also partially lost.

I_1+GTM Experiment: Extract the characteristics of I_1 through both LDM and GTM, instead of only LDM in the proposed method. As shown in Fig. 9(e), the tissue information and functional information in MRI and SPECT were well fused. But key information from CT is missing. For example, the clear contour of source CT image became a little fuzzy and the outer edges of the image show the contour morphology of the SPECT.

I_2+LDM Experiment: Extract the characteristics of I_2 through both LDM and GTM, instead of only GTM in the proposed method. As shown in Fig. 9(f), some textural distortions produced in the fused image. And there existed the phenomena of overlap, artifact and obscure contour information, which is disadvantage for clinically observing organization information and locating lesions.

In terms of objective indicators, the proposed method is better than the above three sets of ablation experiments in EN, MI, rSFe and VIFF. So the fusion strategy and the conversion strategy from spatial domain to frequency domain work well, as shown in Table 1 and Fig. 10.

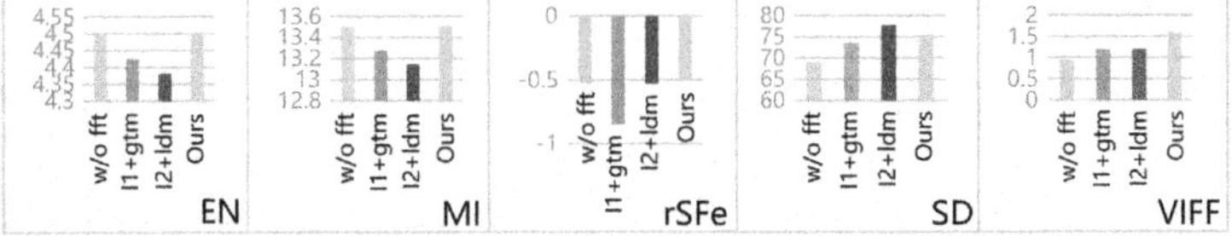

Fig. 10. Histogram of five commonly-used evaluation indicators for fused images obtained by three kinds of ablation methods and the whole proposed method.

5 Conclusion

Trimodal medical image fusion is important for CAD of many diseases. While few researchers focus on this topic. In this paper, we propose a novel trimodal medical image fusion network (also suitable for two-modal fusion), which is mainly designed for fusing MRI/MRI-T2, PET/SPECT and CT/MRI-T1. Combining global-local feature extraction strategy and spatial-frequency fusion strategy, the novel fusion network achieved trimodal fusion and reached satisfied fusion effect. Compared with representative two-modal fusion and three-modal fusion methods, the proposed method has higher image quality, has better results in the subjective visual evaluation and objective indicators, and is more generalized and robust. We'll devote to apply it in CAD in the future.

References

1. Bhatnagar, G., Wu, Q.M.J., Liu, Z.: Directive contrast based multimodal medical image fusion in nsct domain (2013)
2. Bhatnagar, G., Wu, Q.J., Liu, Z.: Directive contrast based multimodal medical image fusion in nsct domain. IEEE Trans. Multimedia **15**(5), 1014–1024 (2013)
3. Du, J., Li, W., Xiao, B., Nawaz, Q.: Union laplacian pyramid with multiple features for medical image fusion. Neurocomputing **194**, 326–339 (2016)
4. Fu, J., Li, W., Du, J., Xiao, B.: Multimodal medical image fusion via laplacian pyramid and convolutional neural network reconstruction with local gradient energy strategy. Comput. Biol. Med. **126**, 104048 (2020)
5. Grosu, A.L., et al.: 11c-methionine pet improves the target volume delineation of meningiomas treated with stereotactic fractionated radiotherapy. Int. J. Radiation Oncology Biol. Phys. **66**(2), 339–344 (2006)
6. Grosu, A.L., et al.: L-(methyl-11c) methionine positron emission tomography for target delineation in resected high-grade gliomas before radiotherapy. Int. J. Radiation Oncology Biol. Phys. **63**(1), 64–74 (2005)
7. Jin, X., Chen, G., Hou, J., Jiang, Q., Zhou, D., Yao, S.: Multimodal sensor medical image fusion based on nonsubsampled shearlet transform and s-pcnns in hsv space. Signal Process. **153**, 379–395 (2018)
8. Kumar, N., Hoffmann, N., Oelschlägel, M., Koch, E., Kirsch, M., Gumhold, S.: Structural similarity based anatomical and functional brain imaging fusion. In: Zhu, D., Yan, J., Huang, H., Shen, L., Thompson, P.M., Westin, C.-F., Pennec, X., Joshi, S., Nielsen, M., Fletcher, T., Durrleman, S., Sommer, S. (eds.) MBIA/MFCA -2019. LNCS, vol. 11846, pp. 121–129. Springer, Cham (2019). https://doi.org/10.1007/978-3-030-33226-6_14
9. Lahoud, F., Süsstrunk, S.: Zero-learning fast medical image fusion. In: 2019 22th International Conference on Information Fusion (FUSION), pp. 1–8. IEEE (2019)
10. Li, H., Wu, X., Durrani, T.S.: Nestfuse: an infrared and visible image fusion architecture based on nest connection and spatial/channel attention models. CoRR abs/2007.00328 (2020)
11. Li, H., Wu, X.J., Kittler, J.: Infrared and visible image fusion using a deep learning framework. In: 2018 24th International Conference on Pattern Recognition (ICPR), pp. 2705–2710. IEEE (2018)
12. Li, S., Kang, X., Fang, L., Hu, J., Yin, H.: Pixel-level image fusion: a survey of the state of the art. Inf. Fusion **33**, 100–112 (2017)

13. Li, S., Kang, X., Hu, J.: Image fusion with guided filtering. IEEE Trans. Image Process. **22**(7), 2864–2875 (2013)
14. Li, T., Wang, Y.: Biological image fusion using a nsct based variable-weight method. Inf. Fusion **12**(2), 85–92 (2011)
15. Liu, Y., Chen, X., Ward, R.K., Wang, Z.J.: Image fusion with convolutional sparse representation. IEEE Signal Process. Lett. **23**(12), 1882–1886 (2016)
16. Liu, Y., Liu, S., Wang, Z.: A general framework for image fusion based on multi-scale transform and sparse representation. Inf. Fusion **24**, 147–164 (2015)
17. Liu, Y., Yang, J., Sun, J.: Pet/ct medical image fusion algorithm based on multi-wavelet transform. In: 2010 2nd International Conference on Advanced Computer Control, vol. 2, pp. 264–268 (2010)
18. Ma, J., Xu, H., Jiang, J., Mei, X., Zhang, X.P.: Ddcgan: a dual-discriminator conditional generative adversarial network for multi-resolution image fusion. IEEE Trans. Image Process. **29**, 4980–4995 (2020)
19. Manchanda, M., Sharma, R.: An improved multimodal medical image fusion algorithm based on fuzzy transform. J. Vis. Commun. Image Represent. **51**, 76–94 (2018)
20. Mertens, T., Kautz, J., Van Reeth, F.: Exposure fusion. In: 15th Pacific Conference on Computer Graphics and Applications (PG 2007), pp. 382–390. IEEE (2007)
21. Qu, G., Zhang, D., Yan, P.: Medical image fusion by wavelet transform modulus maxima. Opt. Express **9**(4), 184–190 (2001)
22. Riegel, A.C., Berson, A.M., Destian, S., Ng, T., Tena, L.B., Mitnick, R.J., Wong, P.S.: Variability of gross tumor volume delineation in head-and-neck cancer using ct and pet/ct fusion. Int. J Radiation Oncology Biol. Phys. **65**(3), 726–732 (2006)
23. Singh, R., Khare, A.: Fusion of multimodal medical images using daubechies complex wavelet transform-a multiresolution approach. Inf. Fusion **19**, 49–60 (2014)
24. Wang, L., Li, B., Tian, L.f.: Multi-modal medical image fusion using the inter-scale and intra-scale dependencies between image shift-invariant shearlet coefficients. Inf. Fusion **19**, 20–28 (2014)
25. Xiang, L., et al.: Deep-learning-based multi-modal fusion for fast MR reconstruction. IEEE Trans. Biomed. Eng. **66**(7), 2105–2114 (2019)
26. Yang, B., Li, S.: Multifocus image fusion and restoration with sparse representation. IEEE Trans. Instrum. Meas. **59**(4), 884–892 (2009)
27. Ying, C., Yu, N., Wu, L.: Image feature training and fusion algorithm based on deep learning representation. J. Jiangsu Normal Univ. (Natural Sci. Edition) (2018)
28. Yu, N., Qiu, T., Bi, F., Wang, A.: Image features extraction and fusion based on joint sparse representation. IEEE J. Sel. Top. Signal Process. **5**(5), 1074–1082 (2011)
29. Zhang, Y., Liu, Y., Sun, P., Yan, H., Zhao, X., Zhang, L.: Ifcnn: a general image fusion framework based on convolutional neural network. Inf. Fusion **54**, 99–118 (2020)

Data Security Risk Prediction of Labor Relationship Rights Protection Network Platform Based on Machine Learning

Min Yu(✉)

China University of Labor Relations, Beijing 100048, China
jhfg5413@163.com

Abstract. In order to improve the effect of data security risk prediction of labor relations rights protection network platform, this paper introduces machine learning algorithm into this field, and designs a new network platform data security risk prediction method. Determine the data risk index of the network platform of labor relationship rights protection, calculate the weight of the risk data in the website data, and find the risk data characteristics in the website. Build the decision tree, calculate the data entropy involved in the decision tree, summarize the characteristics of the risk data, create the nodes of the decision tree, and get the status of the risk data of the labor relationship rights protection network platform. The obtained risk data status is brought into the Bayesian network probability definition to analyze the risk degree of the risk data. The experimental results show that the design method can effectively shorten the evaluation time and improve the risk prediction accuracy.

Keywords: Machine learning · Labor relations rights and interests · Rights protection · Network platform · Data security · Risk forecast

1 Introduction

Employees are an important component of the production of social wealth, and the life object growing in the social environment. Any employee engaged in production and operation activities has their own rights and interests, and relies on these rights and interests to maintain their own operation and development. If employees lack the pursuit of rights and interests, they will lose the internal motivation to engage in production and operation [1].

To protect the rights and interests of workers is a responsibility entrusted by law, to safeguard the legitimate rights and interests of workers, is conducive to the establishment and maintenance of a labor system adapted to the socialist market economy, and to promote economic development and social progress. In order to discover the data security risks of the labor relations rights protection network platform in time and improve the data security of the labor relations rights protection network platform, it is necessary to predict the data security risks of the labor relations rights protection network platform.

Y. Xu et al. (Eds.): ML4CS 2022, LNCS 13657, pp. 227–241, 2023.
https://doi.org/10.1007/978-3-031-20102-8_18

At present, some scholars have studied this, but there are problems of poor prediction effect and low accuracy. Machine learning is an algorithm and statistical model used by computer systems. It relies on patterns and reasoning to effectively perform specific tasks. It is regarded as a subset of artificial intelligence. Machine learning algorithm can establish a mathematical model based on sample data, called "training data", and make predictions or decisions to perform tasks without explicit programming. Because it can obviously overcome the weakness of data analysis and prediction, in order to improve the effect of data security risk prediction of network platform, this paper introduces it into this field, a new data security risk prediction method is designed by using machine learning algorithm. Determine the data risk indicators of the labor relations rights protection network platform, calculate the weight of risk data in the website data, and find out the characteristics of risk data in the website. The decision tree is constructed, the data entropy in the decision tree is calculated, the characteristics of risk data are summarized, the decision tree nodes are generated, and the risk data status of the labor relations rights protection network platform is obtained, so as to complete the design of the data security risk prediction method of the labor relations rights protection network platform. Finally, the effectiveness of the design method is proved by experiments.

2 Risk Data Extraction of the Network Platform Based on Machine Learning

The risk data analysis process of the network platform based on machine learning is shown in Fig. 1 below:

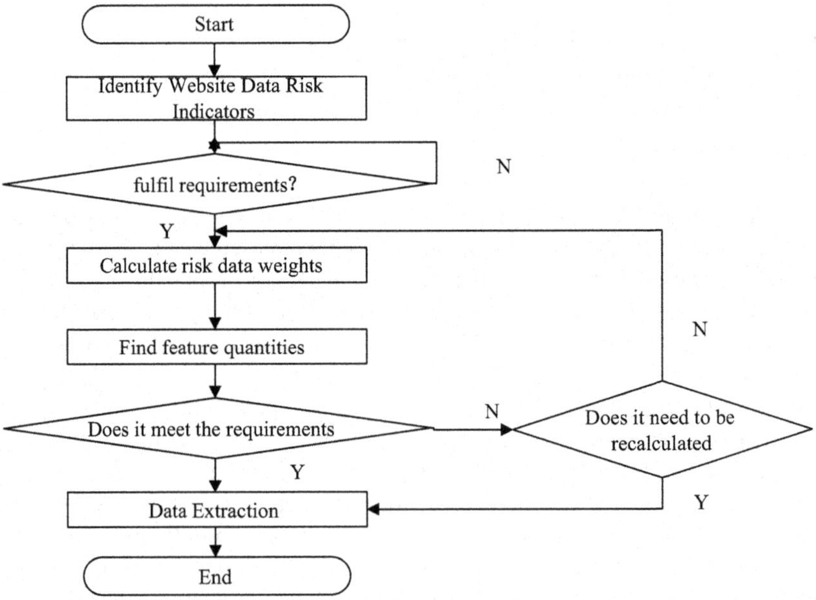

Fig. 1. Analysis process of risk data extraction method based on machine learning

Set risk source, hidden risk and joint risk characteristics as risk data characteristics of network platform, respectively with A, B, C, risk source index sample is risk level, risk probability, risk attribute; hidden risk index sample of network platform is change data information risk and hidden data risk sample; website joint risk sample is risk effect [4–7]. According to the above description of the risk indicators of the network platform, the evaluation index matrix is constructed, as follows:

$$e_j = -k \sum_{i=1}^{s} y_{ij} \ln y_{ij} \tag{1}$$

When it represents the entropy weight of the index data of the network platform, the website is the most, and the measure of the risk sample is a constant. In formula (1), k represents the entropy weight of the index data of the labor relations rights and interests protection network platform. When it is taken as 1, it represents that the risk confusion degree of the website is the largest and the risk degree is serious; y_{ij} represents the measurement value of the risk sample, which is a constant.

The index system is shown in Fig. 2 below:

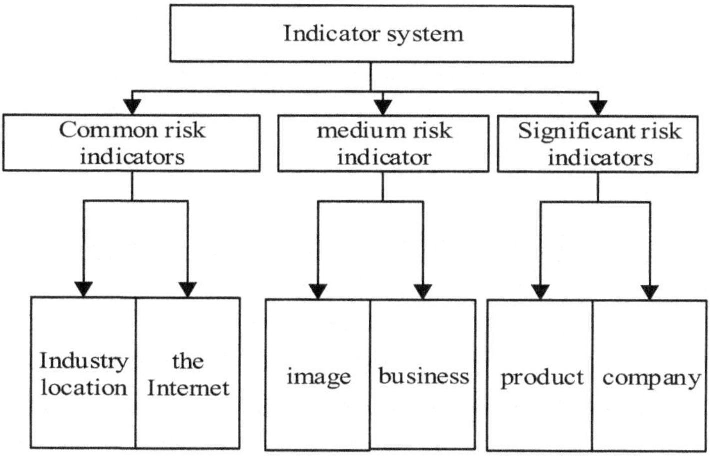

Fig. 2. Index system

There is a large amount of information data on the labor relations rights and interests protection network platform. In order to search quickly and not omit to retrieve the risk data containing risk factors, it is necessary to compress the site data first. In this paper, the vector data compression method is used to filter the risk data of e-commerce websites. First, the multidimensional data is used, and the calculation formula is as follows:

$$c = \varphi * P_1 \tag{2}$$

In formula (2), P_1 represents the power eigenvector of the actual website data information; φ represents the n-dimensional column vector whose data is converted to vector format. The middle component of the actual power feature vector of each type of the network platform is replaced by the corresponding constant, and the safe data in the risk data set of the network platform is excluded, and the risk data set is obtained, which is shown as follows:

$$\mathrm{x} = \sum_{i=1}^{n} h p_i j_i \tag{3}$$

In formula (3), h represents the random vector of data; j_i represents the error of risk data eigenvector compression; p_i represents the actual data compression balance coefficient [8, 9].

Of labor relations rights protection network platform of risk data compression, can reduce the risk data feature extraction process and workload, then the labor relations rights protection network platform risk feature vector extraction, the compression of successful labor relations rights protection network platform risk data feature classification of all data collection, and then weighted the data, extract the characteristics of different risk data, the calculation formula is as follows:

$$0 = x\{\|\Delta x(m)\|^2\} = \sum_{i=m+1}^{n} p_i - b_{ij} \tag{4}$$

In formula (4), m represents the number of iterations for calculating the risk data vector of the labor relations rights and interests protection network platform; b_{ij} represents the initial center position of risk characteristic data vector calculation; $\Delta x(m)$ represents the weighted value of risk data characteristics [10].

3 Data Security Risk Prediction of the Network Platform Based on Machine Learning

3.1 Network Platform for Protecting Labor Relations Rights and Interests

The IOT monitoring service platform is mainly divided into on-site information level and centralized control level. The on-site information level is mainly to set up multiple fixed monitoring points on the labor relations rights and interests protection network platform. Through the sensor time, the data information during real-time operation can be decoded, edited and transmitted anywhere. By setting the monitoring time and monitoring the collection of data records, through machine learning data sharing and real-time reporting, the collected data can be compressed, encoded and transmitted to the central control level.

The network platform of labor relations rights protection is shown in Fig. 3 below:

The information-level data acquisition formula is described in (5):

$$U_n = E\delta^{-2}[\tau_{an}\partial_n(T_n)] \tag{5}$$

In formula (5), U_n represents the value of different monitoring points at different times and converted into numerical value; $E\delta^{-2}$ is a constant value; τ_{an} represents real-time data section; ∂_n represents real-time data; T_n refers to the distance between

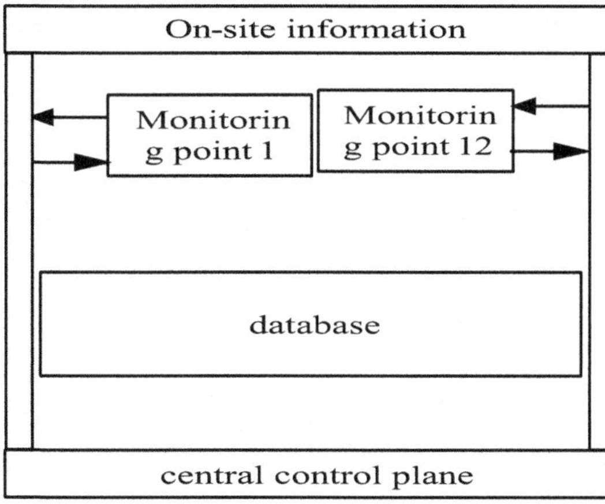

Fig. 3. Network platform for labor relations rights and interests protection

monitoring points. Through the information of different labor relations rights and interests protection network platforms monitored in different time periods, the converted values in different time periods can be calculated, and the values can be sorted out for subsequent statistical monitoring [5].

The central control level, as the central monitoring module of the whole system, integrates and stores the compressed and coded data transmitted by the sensors, analyzes and judges the data, and determines whether the labor relationship rights and interests at different time points and different monitoring points are stable and safe. The labor relations rights protection network platform based on machine learning will display the information and data transmitted from the field information layer in real time, so as to realize the regional positioning of risk positions.

Based on machine learning the rights and interests of labor relations protection network platform data security risk prediction architecture can realize hydropower station monitoring data collection, online monitoring data collection, provide data for digital cases, built a comprehensive integration of big data link platform, for the security and stability of information risk early warning system. Central control level can show different time running data of different monitoring points, at the same time when the abnormal value generated automatically alarm, operators through alarm warning and screen abnormal values and risk points, to track to preliminary judge risk situation and risk area, risk judgment data instructions to record and storage, so that in the future work to past risk query and determine whether will affect the future work process, can be timely prediction and regular maintenance.

3.2 Protection of Labor Relationship Rights and Interests Data Security Risk Prediction of the Network Platform

Machine learning is through the algorithm protocol for data depth analysis, in order to achieve some demand, this paper adopts machine learning technology decisions and Bayesian network algorithm to the labor relations rights protection network platform risk data risk assessment, using Bayesian network algorithm to improve the accuracy of decision tree data analysis. The decision tree is shown in Fig. 4 below:

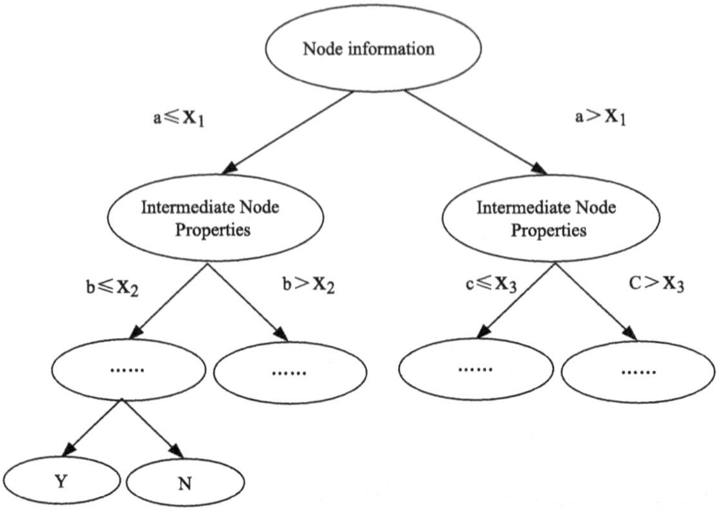

Fig. 4. Decision tree

Decision tree algorithm is one of the important methods of data risk analysis. As the name suggests, decision tree is to reasonably divide the overall data into similar state charts according to the hierarchy structure, state and data to complete the in-depth analysis of data. Each fulcrum in the decision tree structure is the key point connecting each data. In the data analysis, the data tree needs a data entropy for data judgment guidance. The calculation formula of data entropy is shown as follows:

$$E(S) = \sum_{i=1}^{n} (m_i + n_i)/(m + n) \tag{6}$$

In formula (6), S represents the root of the decision tree and the set of data to be analyzed m, n represents the number of data sets n_i, m_i represents possible nodes in the decision tree structure [14]. The directed acyclic diagram of Bayesian networks is shown in Fig. 5 below:

When the decision tree algorithm analyzes the risk data, its nodes will divide the binary nodes according to the actual situation, but the decision tree has a chance to the data analysis of the binary nodes, which reduces the analysis effect of the decision tree, so the accuracy of the decision tree analysis data is improved through the Bayesian network algorithm.

The essence of Bayesian network algorithm is to complete the forward analysis and reverse analysis based on conditional probability. On the one hand, it is to check the data analysis, and on the other hand, to ensure the depth and accuracy of the data analysis.

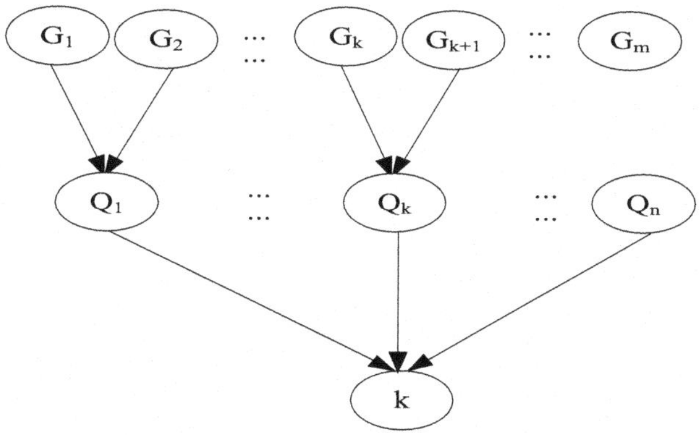

Fig. 5. Directed acyclic graph of Bayesian networks

That is, the formula of the Bayesian network algorithm, which is defined as:

$$p(A|B) = \frac{p(B|A)p(A)}{p(B)} \tag{7}$$

In formula (7), $p(B)$ represents the prior probability of data analysis; $p(B|A)$ represents the posterior probability of data analysis. The Bayesian network algorithm decision tree is shown in Fig. 5 below (Fig. 6):

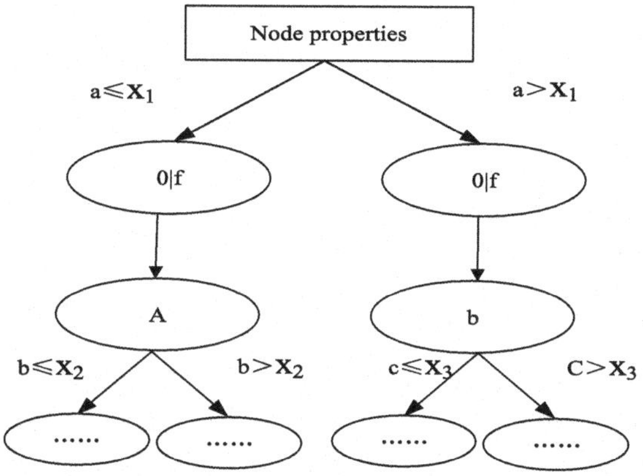

Fig. 6. A Bayesian network algorithm decision tree

According to the multiple states of the data analyzed by the decision tree, it can be brought into the Bayesian network probability algorithm, and the full probability of each state is obtained. The formula is as follows:

$$P(Y) = \sum_{i=1}^{n} p(B|A = a_i) \tag{8}$$

To sum up, summarized based on the decision tree and Bayesian network probability algorithm based on the rights and interests of labor relations network platform data security risk prediction analysis process, the research of machine learning risk data extraction method as the basis, this paper build based on data mining technology website risk assessment model, specific steps are as follows (Fig. 7):

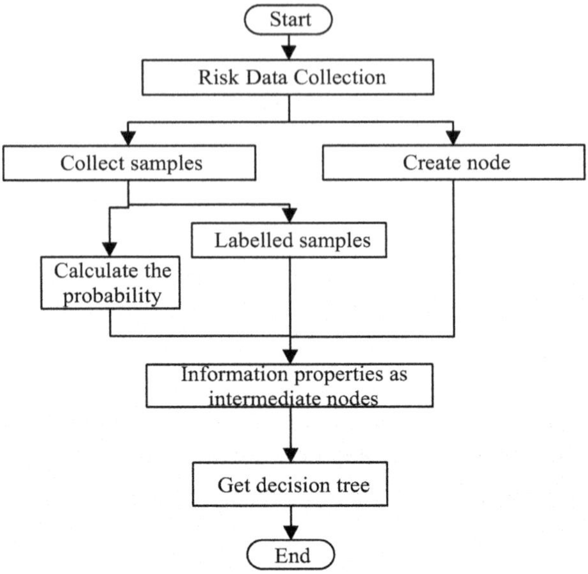

Fig. 7. Data security risk prediction process of the network platform based on machine learning

(1) First, define the collection of risks existing in the network platform of labor relationship rights protection, and the collection form is as follows:

$$Y = F_{vt} * loss \quad F \in \{F1, F2, F3, F4, F5\} \tag{9}$$

In formula (9), $F1$ means that there is a risk vulnerability in the confidentiality of the data of the labor relations rights and interests protection network platform; $F2$ indicates that there is a risk vulnerability in the data integrity of the labor relations rights and interests protection network platform; $F3$ indicates that there is a risk vulnerability in the reliability of the data of the labor relations rights and interests protection network platform; $F4$ indicates that there is a risk vulnerability in the principle of the data of the labor relations rights and interests protection network platform; $F5$ indicates that there is a risk vulnerability in the data defense of the labor relations rights and interests protection network platform; F_{vt} represents the probability of data risk caused by website attack; *loss* the loss in the process of the risk of the labor relations rights and interests protection network platform is affected by the amount of website data risk;

(2) Then complete the data in the labor relationship rights protection network platform for risk data extraction, compress the extracted risk data according to the decision tree algorithm, and simplify the workload of risk assessment on the website;
(3) Secondly, in the compressed website risk data set, the website data risk state is calculated according to the decision tree theory and the Bayesian network probability algorithm;
(4) Finally, the risk probability of the data risk status and the hidden risk probability of the data risk of the network platform is calculated, and the risk assessment model of the e-commerce website is shown as follows:

$$F(t) = 1 - \lim_{2} F_{vt} + e_j * x \tag{10}$$

In formula (10), the unknown significance is shown above.

The results of data security risk prediction of the network platform are presented in the form of 100%. The evaluation result is 0–30%, and the low-risk website; the evaluation result is 30–60%, 30% −60%; the evaluation result is 60% and high-risk website.

The key network information is first extracted. The number of network information searched by network users is huge, and the variety of information is various and complex, so it is easy to be mixed together during transmission. If the prediction is made at the same time in a certain period of time, the efficiency of the prediction results will be greatly reduced, and the real needs of network users cannot be accurately predicted. Therefore, when predicting the search target of network information, the first thing to do is to extract the key network information. This paper uses clustering technology to extract the target mask, identify the candidate box, filter and extract the user search data, update the extracted target mask, and update the results in the text information, which reduces the difficulty of extraction. Due to the high complexity of the network transmission layer, in order to meet its needs, it is necessary to constantly update the target mask and strengthen the refresh of the network. When extracting and analyzing the key network information, the time is recorded and analyzed in real time to complete the set extraction target.

Then you filter the target information. The network information search target is iteratively classified to obtain the phased target information classified for the first time. If the uncoordinated information appears in the target information, store the lower right and left corner of the target box, store the first information screening results in the upper left and right corners of the candidate box, and move the central target information to the edge of the candidate box during secondary screening to filter the last information at any time. In the final screening of target information, control the time of classification and screening, and try to get the final target information in the shortest time, while the accuracy of the results and the timeliness of screening must be guaranteed.

Finally, get the network information that users search. Find specific network information from coarse to fine. The information content searched by users can be divided into many aspects. From different positioning angles, analyze the edge information of the target information according to the central content, move the central target information to the edge of the candidate box, overlap with the edge information, and accurately predict the location through the overlapping information. Traditional software can only use density based detection methods, Through iterative classification of different aspects of loose network information, to improve the accuracy of network information search targets.

So far, the design of data security risk prediction method based on network platform has been completed.

4 Experimental Research

In order to verify the effectiveness of the data security risk prediction method of the labor relations rights protection network platform based on machine learning designed in this paper, the flow change trend of network information will be detected. When the information of the network platform is in the normal state, the flow change trend is shown in Fig. 8 below:

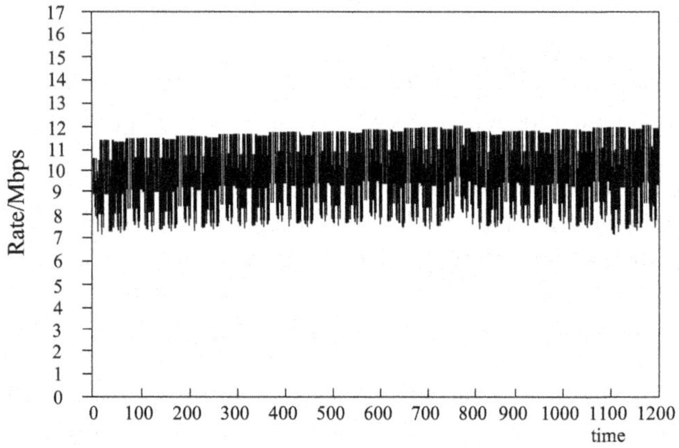

Fig. 8. Trend of flow rate under normal condition

According to the above figure above, in the case of no attack or the network receives normal requests, the fluctuation of network traffic is relatively stable, basically at 9 – 12 Mbps.When there is a network information leakage point, the change trend of the network throughput is detected, and the resulting network throughput change is shown in Fig. 9 below:

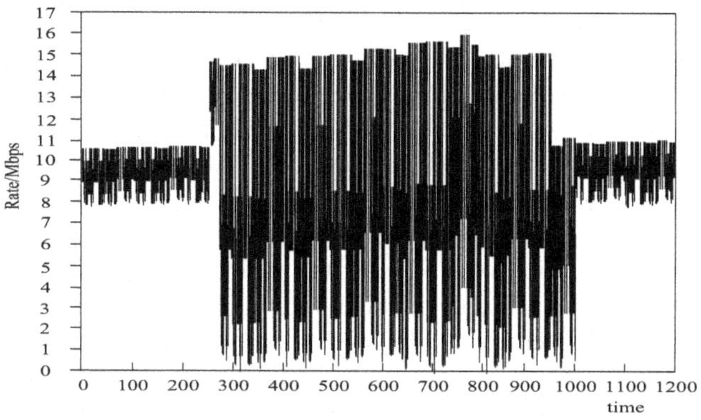

Fig. 9. Changes in network throughput during information leakage

According to the figure above, when information leakage occurs, the network throughput decreases significantly, and the information throughput rate decreases by about 72%. It can be seen that the network information node leakage has a great impact on the normal work of the network platform for the protection of labor relations rights and interests. After verifying the working ability of the detection method, choose the traditional hidden Markov model of labor relations protection network platform data security risk prediction method and the Fourier algorithm data security risk prediction method comparison experiment, after the network information attack efficiency experiment results as shown in Fig. 10:

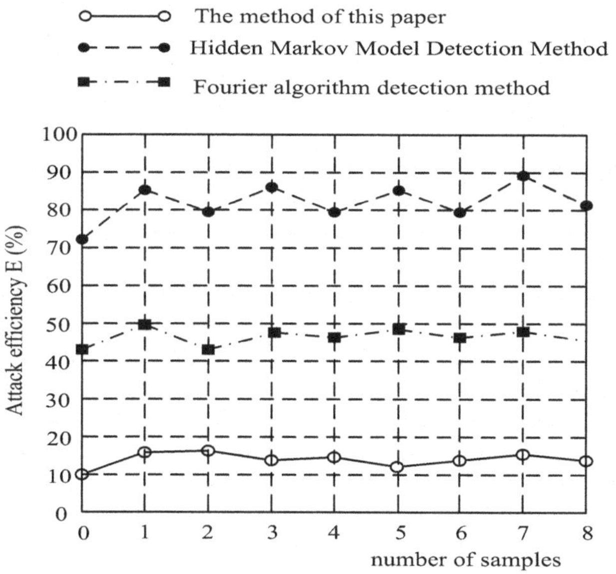

Fig. 10. Experimental results of the postdetected network information attack rate

According to the figure above, after using the detection of the detection method proposed herein, the attack efficiency of external attacks is significantly reduced, always between 10% and 20%. After using the detection method based on Fourier algorithm, the attack efficiency is between 40% and 50%, while after using the Markov model detection method, the attack efficiency is between 70% and 80%.Thus, the detection method proposed has the highest attack detection capability, which can effectively reduce the external attack efficiency and improve the network security after detection.

The cause of this phenomenon is based on the hidden Markov model Ad hoc network information leakage point of labor relations rights protection network platform data security risk prediction method and Fourier algorithm Ad hoc network information leakage point of labor relations rights protection network platform data security risk prediction method, the two methods have certain limitations, only suitable for continuous network signal.

Based with wavelet reconstruction, greatly improves the security of network information transmission. Machine learning has its own advantages and fast transmission rate. Because machine learning is not connected, it is disconnected after each response, so the possibility of information leakage is low. This paper enables machine learning to optimize the server mode of traditional network information transmission and determine the appropriate detection parameters. Based on the classical Fourier algorithm, the paper improves and proposes the rapid detection method for wavelet reconstruction, so the overall detection ability is stronger.

The data security risk prediction model of labor relations security network platform studied in this paper has certain logic, but in order to verify whether the model has application significance and achieve the expected purpose, this paper conducts comparative testing, and verifies and analyzes according to the test conclusion. In order to avoid the chance of comparison results, this paper selects data security risk prediction method and data testing network security platform data security risk prediction method as the traditional control risk assessment model, collaboration to complete the test. Before the experiment, two network platforms of labor relationship rights protection were randomly selected as the trial subjects, and the evaluation efficiency of different risk assessment models was determined to combine the average accuracy of the two experimental results.

Before the start of the trial, the randomly selected labor relationship rights protection network platform is risk assessed according to the professional software, and the evaluation results are encrypted and stored, which are the important reference data for the results of the risk assessment model after the trial. In the process of the test, the data analyzer recorded the evaluation process and important data of the three models on the labor relationship rights protection network platform in real time. All the three evaluation models submitted two evaluation results respectively. After the test, the staff verifies the data, summarizes the data, draws the test conclusion, and arranges the test site and test equipment. Since the test operation eliminates possible external interference factors, the test conclusion has credibility and authenticity. The obtained experimental results are shown in Table 1 below:

Table 1. Evaluates the risk index

	Assess the risk index	
	Squirrel selling book net	Daily E-commerce website
Professional evaluation software	55%	30%
Data security risk prediction method based on data mining	54.5%	30%
Data security risk prediction method based on data analysis	50%	27%
Data security risk prediction method based on machine learning	53%	26%

According to the traditional prediction method and the actual prediction effect of the prediction method of this paper, record the accuracy of two methods, the traditional prediction method and the network information search target prediction, the target information and real target information comparison results, the accuracy results as shown in Fig. 11:

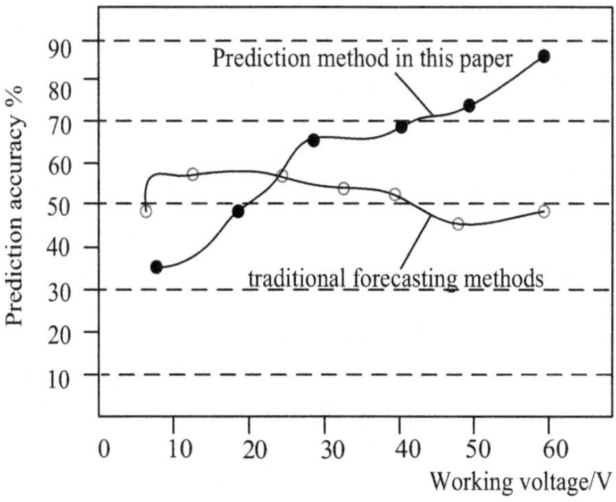

Fig. 11. Accuracy experiment results

According to Fig. 11, the two prediction methods classify the network information search target, but the prediction results are very different. The traditional prediction method, the accuracy of the target information is 70%, while the prediction method designed in this paper is 88%, 18% higher than the traditional method, indicating that the prediction method designed in this paper has a higher accuracy of the target information. The results of the prediction time experiment are shown in Table 2 below:

Table 2. Prediction time for the experimental results

Experimental times / times	Prediction time, / min	
	Conventional method	The method of this paper
1	15.22	5.23
2	16.04	5.42
3	15.87	5.07
4	15.44	5.88
5	15.96	5.09

According to the above table, the text mining network information prediction method proposed in this paper takes much less time than the traditional methods and has better prediction ability.

Traditional prediction methods have low power to predict uncoordinated information data, The capability value is only 0.1, Much different from the standard capacity value of 1.5. However, the prediction method designed in this paper has a strong ability to predict uncoordinated information data. The capability value reaches 1.8, It is also 0.3 higher than the standard capability value. Although both the traditional prediction methods and the prediction methods designed in this paper can predict the network information search targets. However, the traditional prediction method is poor. The accuracy of the prediction results is much lower than the prediction method designed in this paper. And the prediction performance is poor. Therefore, the target prediction method based on network information search based on text mining is better than the traditional prediction method. The prediction effect is better, Higher effectiveness and feasibility.

5 Conclusion

This paper studies a machine-based network platform data security risk prediction method, first according to the characteristics of the risk data, and then according to the risk assessment characteristics of the decision tree algorithm and Bayesian network algorithm of labor relations security network platform risk assessment model, complete the study of this paper. Finally, through comparative test analysis, prove that the assessment of risk assessment method high efficiency, can achieve the expected effect of this paper, shorten the data risk in the labor relations rights and interests protection network platform data time, ensure the rights and interests of labor relations network platform data transaction security, has certain application value.

References

1. Li, Y., Zhang, Z.: Network security risk loss assessment method based on queuing model. Comput. Simul. **4**, 258–262 (2021)
2. Cui, S.Y., Li, C., Chen, Z., Wang, J., Yuan, J.: Research on risk prediction of dyslipidemia in steel workers based on recurrent neural network and lstm neural network. IEEE Access **3**(99), 1–1 (2020)
3. Wang, S., et al.: Human short-long term cognitive memory mechanism for visual monitoring in IoT-assisted smart cities. IEEE Internet of Things J. **9**, 7128–7139 (2021). https://doi.org/10.1109/JIOT.2021.3077600
4. Zhou, X., Li, W., Wen, Z.: Data analysis for risk prediction of cervical cancer metastasis and recurrence based on DCNN-RF. J. Phys. Conf. Ser. **1813**(1), 012033 (2021)
5. Liu, S., He, T., Dai, J.: A survey of CRF algorithm based knowledge extraction of elementary mathematics in Chinese. Mob. Netw. Appl. **26**(5), 1891–1903 (2021). https://doi.org/10.1007/s11036-020-01725-x
6. Silva, G.M., Leo, L.D.S., Eller, C.C., et al.: Similar gaps, different paths? Comparing racial inequalities among BA holders in Brazil and the United States. Int. J. Comp. Sociol. **62**(5), 359–384 (2021)
7. Gao, P., Li, J., Liu, S.: An introduction to key technology in artificial intelligence and big data driven e-learning and e-education. Mob. Netw. Appl. **26**(5), 2123–2126 (2021). https://doi.org/10.1007/s11036-021-01777-7
8. Lee, S., Kim, J.H., Park, J., Oh, C., Lee, G.: Deep-learning-based prediction of high-risk taxi drivers using wellness data. Int. J. Environ. Res. Public Health **17**(24), 9505 (2020)
9. Li, D., Xu, J., Li, L.: Research on network lending risk analysis based on platform efficiency. J. Finan. Risk Manag. **10**(4), 453–472 (2021)
10. Liang, H., et al.: Data mining-based model and risk prediction of colorectal cancer by using secondary health data: a systematic review. Chin. J. Cancer Res. **32**(02), 124–133 (2020)

Research on LSTM Based Traffic Flow Prediction Adaptive Beacon Transmission Period and Power Joint Control

Botao Tu, Guanxiang Yin, Guoqing Zhong, Nan Jiang, and Yuejin Zhang(✉)

School of Information Engineering, East China Jiaotong University, Nanchang 330013, China
zyjecjtu@foxmail.com

Abstract. In vehicle-to-vehicle communication, each vehicle regularly broadcasts its own status information in its beacon broadcast to create awareness of the surrounding vehicles. Moreover, most security applications in vehicular ad hoc networks are based on periodic security information. However, vehicular ad hoc networks are characterized by large node density changes, fast network topology changes, diverse wireless channel quality changes and so on, which makes it difficult to guarantee real-time and reliable beacon message transmission. Therefore, we want to predict the future traffic flow to improve the beacon transmission performance. Among many prediction models, we choose the LSTM prediction model with higher stability and accuracy. In this paper, based on the short-time traffic flow prediction model of the improved LSTM network, the traffic flow time data is taken as the input sample, and the LSTM network is used to predict the traffic flow. Then, the combined control algorithm of the adaptive beacon transmission period and transmission power is realized through the predicted parameters. Experimental simulation and analysis show that this algorithm can significantly reduce the distribution delay and improve the packet delivery rate, which proves that our method can effectively reduce channel congestion and improve the performance of vehicle network.

Keywords: Internet of vehicles · V2V communication · Traffic flow prediction · Adaptive transmission · Joint control

1 Introduction

The core part of vehicular ad hoc network is security application. Through the safety application, the vehicle can predict the danger in advance and get the information such as accident warning, so the acquisition of safety information is very important. In v2v communication, safety information can be divided into emergency safety information driven by events and basic safety information periodically broadcast by vehicle nodes [1]. Basic safety information is also known as beacon message, which periodically broadcasts its own basic state information, such as position, speed, acceleration, etc., to adjacent vehicles. But vanets is a discrete, self-organizing network with little infrastructure that

Y. Xu et al. (Eds.): ML4CS 2022, LNCS 13657, pp. 242–250, 2023.
https://doi.org/10.1007/978-3-031-20102-8_19

treats vehicles like nodes in a lan, each communicating with each other over multiple wireless network connections [2].

Vehicular ad hoc network has the characteristics of high node density, fast network topology and diverse wireless channel quality [3]. As a result, real-time and reliable transmission of beacon message is difficult to be guaranteed, so it is necessary to find appropriate optimization basis and optimization method to improve the performance of beacon message transmission. In the current optimization research, most of the existing channel state or traffic state are used as the basis of optimization, but this lag information is easy to lead to beacon message transmission is not timely, resulting in channel congestion and other consequences.

Therefore, we consider predicting the traffic flow to improve the beacon transmission performance.

Traffic flow index is an important means to understand the operation status of traffic network and measure the effectiveness of congestion mitigation strategies [4]. There are many traditional prediction models, such as Kalman filter model, Autoregressive Integrated Moving Average model, etc. [5]. Taking the relevant knowledge of artificial intelligence technology as the theoretical framework and LSTM as the core of the model, this paper establishes a model for prediction. Because LSTM can learn traffic flow data from time series and improve the prediction accuracy of traffic flow [6, 7].

In this paper, an adaptive combined control of transmission period and power of beacons based on traffic flow prediction is proposed. Firstly, the existing traffic state data is used to predict the future traffic parameters. In this paper, the short-term traffic flow prediction model based on the improved long and short-term memory network is adopted. The traffic flow time data is taken as the input sample, and the LSTM network is used to predict the traffic flow. After the predicted parameters are obtained, the transmission performance of beacon message is optimized by combining the signal generation frequency and transmission power.

The structure of this paper is as follows: In Sect. 2, we introduce the improved traffic flow prediction based on LSTM. In Sect. 3, we introduce the implementation of the joint control algorithm. In Sect. 4, it is mainly the setting of simulation parameters and the analysis of experimental results. The last part is the conclusion.

2 Traffic Flow Prediction

The prediction of traffic flow can be regarded as a learning problem. First, we learn basic flow patterns based on existing historical traffic flow data, then build a suitable prediction model, and finally output forecast data. It is found that short-term traffic flow data is a kind of time series data with strong nonlinearity and randomness. LSTM is very effective in processing time series data. Therefore, this paper chooses LSTM as the basic model of short-term traffic flow prediction.

LSTM is a branch of RNN, and unlike RNN, the hidden layer nodes of RNN become memory modules in LSTM. With the addition of memory module, LSTM has memory ability, which can solve the problem of gradient disappearance and long-term dependence to a certain extent. However, LSTM, like most neural networks, is prone to local optimization due to the use of neural network gradient descent algorithm and suffers from high computational overhead in the parameter tuning process, so there is still room for improvement in LSTM prediction [8] (Fig. 1).

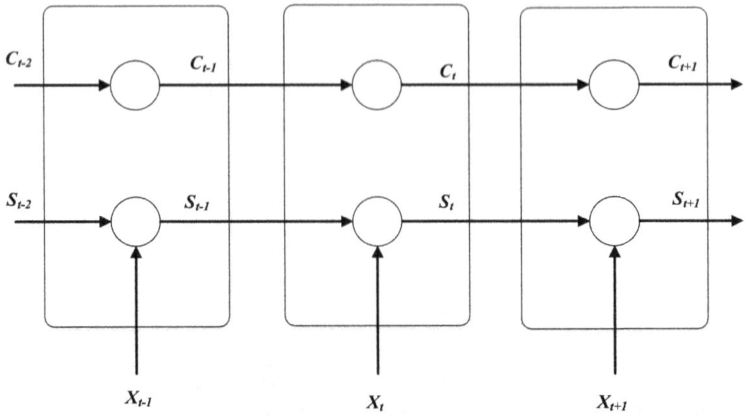

Fig. 1. Basic structure diagram of LSTM

Training of short-term and long-term memory networks is also an important process. As a recurrent neural network, the training algorithm of short - and long-term memory network is backpropagation algorithm. The training process of short - and long-term memory network consists of three steps.

(1) Firstly, the values of five neurons, namely forgetting gate ft, input gate it, unit status update Ct, output gate ot and St vector, are calculated by forward calculation. The calculation formulas are as follows:

$$f_t = \sigma(W_f[s_{t-1}, x_t] + b_f) \tag{1}$$

$$i_t = \sigma(W_i[s_{t-1}, x_t] + b_i) \tag{2}$$

$$\tilde{c}_t = \tanh(W_c[s_{t-1}, x_t] + b_c) \tag{3}$$

$$c_t = f_t * c_{t-1} + i_t * \tilde{c}_t \tag{4}$$

$$o_t = \sigma(W_o[s_{t-1}, x_t] + b_o) \tag{5}$$

$$s_t = o_t * \tanh(c_t) \tag{6}$$

(2) The results of input and output are processed by gated structure and cell unit, and then the output data is sent to the next output layer or hidden layer.

(3) The value of the error term of each neuron is obtained by reverse calculation. The calculation method of the error term transmitted from the current layer L to the

previous layer L-1 according to the structure is the derivative of the weighted input of the activation function to layer L-1, and the calculation formula is shown in Formula 7.

$$\delta_t^{l-1} \overset{def}{=} \frac{\partial E}{net_t^{l-1}} = \left(\delta_{f,t}^T W_{fx} + \delta_{i,t}^T W_{ix} + \delta_{\tilde{c}t}^T W_{\tilde{c}x} + \delta_{o,t}^T W_{ox}\right) * f'\left(net_t^{l-t}\right) \tag{7}$$

(4) Calculate the gradient of each weight according to the corresponding error term. Figure 2 is obtained by adding data set for experiment.

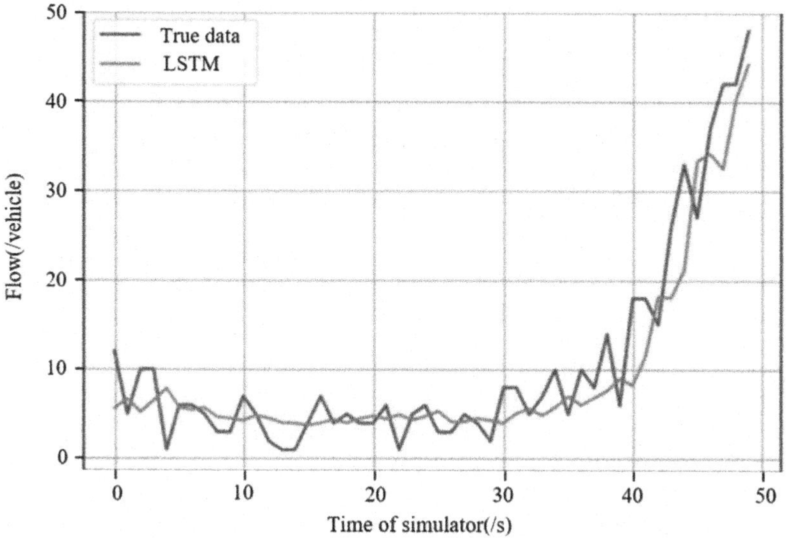

Fig. 2. LSTM traffic flow forecast

Thus, we can obtain the vehicle density d_{i+1} of the predicted future traffic state.

3 Joint Control Algorithm

As is known to all, the high-speed mobility of vehicles and V2V communication links are often very short. The rapid change of traffic density from sparse to dense may lead to rapid channel saturation and congestion. In VANETS, traffic accidents and other emergencies need to be timely and reliably transmitted to surrounding vehicles. Based on the above considerations, one strategy to increase the duration of communication links in VANETS is to increase transmission power to increase transmission range. However, increasing transmission power may cause serious interference and high network overhead under high density communication conditions. Therefore, dynamically adjusting power to changing traffic flow density is a key requirement. Another strategy is to reduce its beacon load transfer rate to reduce channel, because too fast rate of beacon message will result in a short time with a large amount of data transmitted in the channel, could channel congestion problem, especially in the node density larger this problem is particularly prominent in the traffic environment, channel congestion will lead to beacon message collision rate increase, the delivery rate of decline. However, under the condition of sparse traffic flow, too small transmission rate will lead to poor information accuracy, so the design of adaptive beacon transmission rate is also a key requirement.

Based on the above consideration, this paper designs an adaptive beacon transmission rate and power joint control algorithm based on traffic flow prediction. Considering the lag of the optimization parameters in the traditional method, we predicted the future traffic state parameters according to the existing traffic state data, and then carried out the joint control optimization based on the predicted parameters. From the above, we define an adaptive factor Δ as follows:

$$\Delta = \left(\frac{\lambda}{\mathrm{d}_{i+1}} + 1\right)^{-1} \tag{8}$$

where, λ is set according to the state parameters of vehicle nodes, which is related to the speed and acceleration, and d_{i+1} is the predicted vehicle density mentioned above.

Therefore, we can finally get the adaptive rate and power control algorithm as follows:

$$R_{\mathrm{i}+1} = \max(R_{\mathrm{i}} \cdot e^{-\alpha\Delta}, R_{\min}) \tag{9}$$

$$P_{i+1} = \min(P_i \cdot e^{-\beta\Delta}, P_{\max}) \tag{10}$$

$$\alpha + \beta = 1 \tag{11}$$

where Ri + 1 represents the transmission rate at moment i + 1, R_i is the transmission rate at moment i, Δ is the adaptive factor, represents the current traffic state of vehicle node, R_{min} represents the minimum transmission rate allowed by beacon message. Similarly, P_{i+1} represents the transmission power at time i + 1, P_i is the transmission power at time i, and P_{max} represents the maximum transmission power allowed by beacon messages.

We all know that channel resources are limited, and it is difficult to achieve the most ideal situation of transmission rate and transmission power at the same time, so we set α and β to carry out the weight ratio of speed and power.

4 Simulation Experiment

4.1 Simulation Parameter Setting

This section is mainly about the simulation analysis of the joint control algorithm designed by us. We design two groups of vehicle nodes, which are configured with the same communication mode, vehicle position, speed and acceleration. But the difference is that one group has a fixed transmission period and transmission power, and the other group allocates the period and power according to our adaptive joint control algorithm. In order to simulate the urban vehicle operation model more realistically, we use NS2 as the network simulator and SUMO as the mobility generator. Therefore, we can import the real urban map into NS2 for the topology environment of network simulation. Figure 3 shows part of urban road network in Xinjian District of Nanchang city, Jiangxi Province.

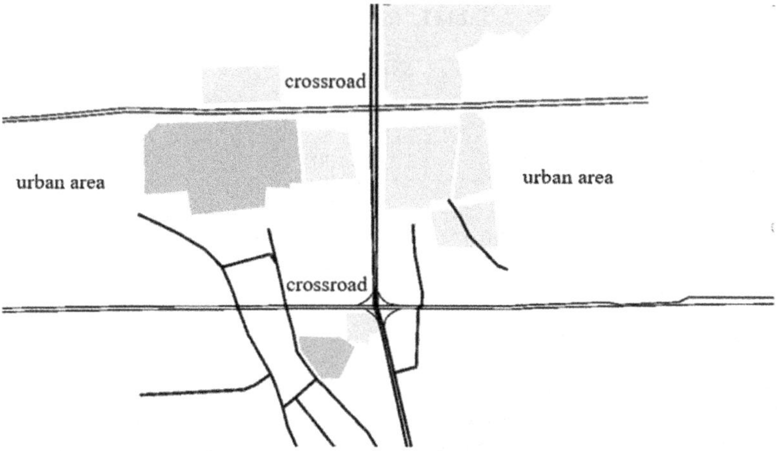

Fig. 3. The simulation network

We set the size of the simulation area as 1000 m × 1000 m and the number of vehicle nodes as 0–100. The physical layer protocol is IEEE802.11p, the transmission distance is 550 m, and the routing protocol is DSDV. Internet of vehicles security applications tend to use lower data transfer rates [9]. In practical application, factors such as signal-to-noise ratio, transmission time and packet conflict probability need to be considered comprehensively. Jiang et al. [10] carried out simulation research to determine the most robust data transmission rate for broadcast communication. The results show that a data transfer rate of 6 Mbps is the best choice for security-related communication. Other simulation parameters are shown in Table 1.

Table 1. Simulation parameter settings

Parameter	Value
Carrier frequency	5.89 Ghz
MAC protocol	IEEE 802.11p
Bit rate	6 Mbps
Beacon size	500 Bytes
Propagation model	Two-ray ground model
Transmission range (m)	550
Transport layer protocol	DSDV
Antenna gain	4 dB

(*continued*)

Table 1. (*continued*)

Parameter	Value
Antenna height	1.5 m
Number of vehicles	0–100
Fixed transmission power	10 mw
Fixed transmission rate	10 Hz

4.2 Analysis of Experimental Results

The experiment in this paper is simulated in the SUMO + NS2 environment. The number of vehicles ranges from 0 to 100. The simulation time starts from 0 s and ends in 100 s.

Figure 4 shows the change of PDR with vehicle density. When the vehicle density is low, the delivery rate of the fixed transmitting power and period is close to that of the proposed algorithm. However, with the increase of vehicle density, the joint control algorithm dynamically adjusts the period and power to make the delivery rate higher than that of the fixed transmitting power and period.

Figure 5 shows the variation of distribution delay with density. In the case of fixed transmission power and period, the distribution delay increases rapidly with the increase of vehicle density, because at this time, the number of nodes participating in channel competition increases, and the network congestion is serious. However, when using the algorithm in this paper, we dynamically control the power and period to cope with congestion, so the delay growth is relatively gentle. After comparison, we find that

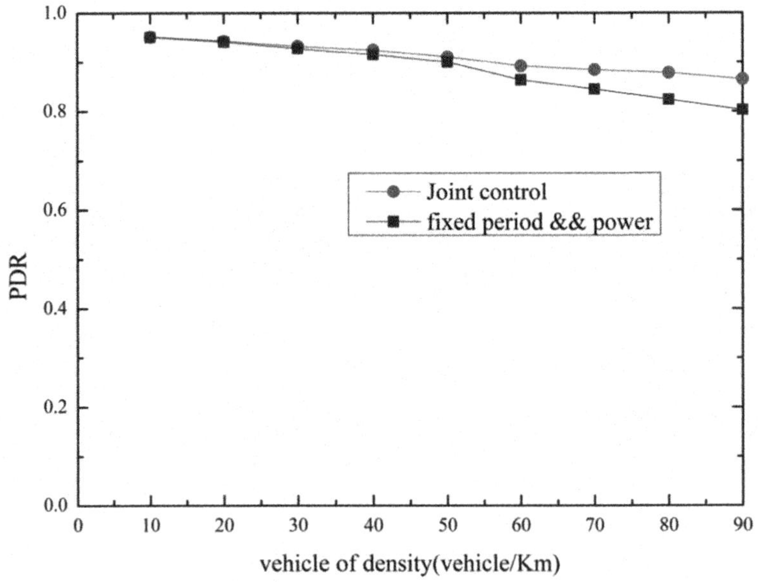

Fig. 4. Packet transfer rate under different vehicle density

the algorithm in this paper has significantly improved the packet transmission rate and significantly reduced the distribution delay compared with the algorithm with fixed power and period.

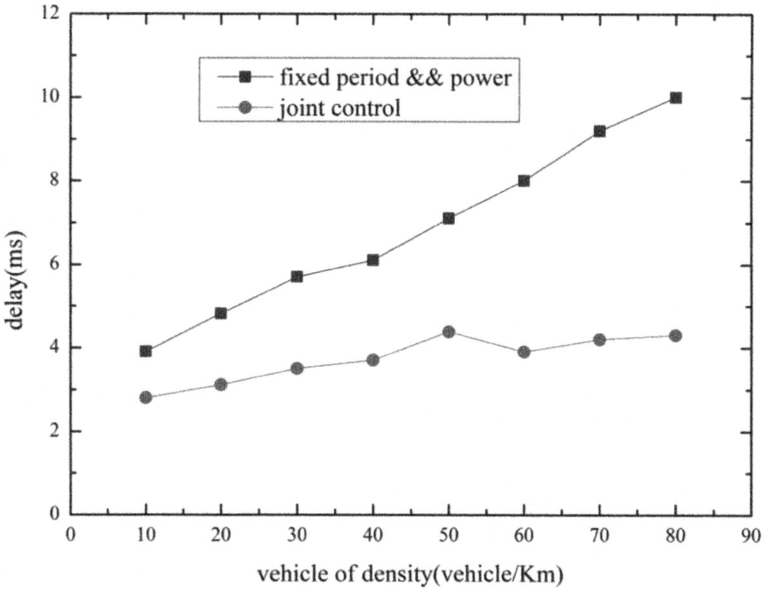

Fig. 5. Comparison between fixed period and power and distribution delay of the proposed algorithm

5 Conclusion

This paper presents a power and period control algorithm for combined beacons based on vehicle position prediction. By analyzing the traffic flow prediction parameters of vehicles, we dynamically control the transmission power and period of beacons. Considering the limited channel resources, we carry out the weight ratio of transmission power and period, so as to realize the adaptive adjustment of beacon period and power under different traffic conditions. After simulation analysis, the algorithm in this paper further improves the stability of communication link. Experimental results show that compared with fixed period and power, the proposed algorithm can significantly reduce the distribution delay and improve the packet delivery rate. Ensure the effective transmission of safety information. This paper proposes a possible solution to the beacon transmission problem using deep learning method and believes that the solution will have greater practical value after further study.

However, the experiment in this paper does not consider the test in high-speed environment, and the selection of vehicle nodes is too few. In addition, our next work can also consider the weight of dynamic distribution period and power.

Acknowledgements. This work was supported in part by the National Natural Science Foundation of China under Grant 92159102, Grant 11862006, Grant 61862025.

References

1. Wang, M., Chen, T., Du, F., Wang, J., Yin, G., Zhang, Y.: Research on adaptive beacon message transmission power in VANETs. J. Ambient. Intell. Humaniz. Comput. **13**(3), 1307–1319 (2020). https://doi.org/10.1007/s12652-020-02575-x
2. Ali, A.K., Phillips, I., Yang, H.: Evaluating VANET routing in urban environments. In: 39th International Conference on Telecommunications and Signal Processing, pp. 60–63. IEEE (2016)
3. Belamri, F., Boulfekhar, S., Aissani, D.: A survey on QoS routing protocols in Vehicular Ad Hoc Network (VANET). Telecommun. Syst. **78**(1), 117–153 (2021). https://doi.org/10.1007/s11235-021-00797-8
4. Tu, B., Zhao, Y., Yin, G., Jiang, N., Zhang, Y.: Research on intelligent calculation method of intelligent traffic flow index based on big data mining. Int. J. Intelli. **37**(2), 1186–1203 (2022)
5. Yuan, H., Zhu, X.N., Hu, Z.: Deep multi -view residual attention network for crowd flows prediction. Neurocomputing **404**, 198–212 (2020)
6. Ma, Q., Huang, G.H., Ullah, S.: A multi-parameter chaotic fusion approach for traffic flow forecasting. IEEE Access. **8**, 222774–222781 (2020)
7. Lu, Z.L., Lv, W.F., Cao, Y.B.: LSTM variants meet graph neural networks for road speed prediction. Neurocomputing **400**, 34–45 (2020)
8. Zhou, J., Chang, H., Cheng, X., et al.: A multiscale and high-precision LSTM-GASVR short-term traffic flow prediction model. Complexity **2020**, 1–17 (2020). https://doi.org/10.1155/2020/1434080
9. Javadi, M.S., Habib, S., Hannan, M.A.: Survey on inter-vehicle communication applications: current trends and challenges. Information Technology Journal **12**(2), (2013)
10. Jiang, D., Chen, Q., Delgrossi, L.: Optimal data rate selection for vehicle safety communications. In: Proceedings of the fifth ACM international workshop on Vehicular Internet working, pp. 30–38. DBLP (2008)

Construction of Color Network Model of Folk Painting Based on Machine Learning

Rong Yu and Bomei Tan(✉)

Nanning University, Nanning 530200, China
yyrr22@yeah.net

Abstract. In order to more accurately explore and reflect the color design thinking of folk paintings, and provide more reference and inspiration for the current design with Chinese characteristics and ethnic characteristics, a research on the construction of color network model of folk paintings based on machine learning was proposed. By calculating the folk painting color feature point set, the concentric circles coordinate system, constructing the corresponding feature points according to the folk painting color main curvature, the tectonic pattern of folk painting color description factor, combined with folk drawing design of color invariants, matching the folk painting color, the introduction of image histogram constraint, nonlinear histogram transformation model is set up, According to the contrast distortion adjustment algorithm, the model is solved, and the folk painting color network model is constructed. The case shows that the color network model can accurately reflect the color characteristics and color matching design logic of Ansai folk paintings.

Keywords: Machine learning · Folk painting · Painting color · Network model · Color matching

1 Introduction

In the long history of the development of Chinese art, folk art, as the source of the formation of art form, contains a unique historical color and the practical significance of continuous development [1]. The folk art created by the working people in the production and labor mostly reflects their spiritual pursuit of a better life, condenses their simple aesthetic taste, and has a unique national character and strong local color.

A comprehensive review of the relevant literature on the color of folk paintings shows that the existing research methods and conclusions are more empirical, qualitative and sporadic, and slightly inadequate in scientific and systematic aspects. In domestic research, Yan Yao and others [2] in order to more accurately explore and reflect the color design thinking of Ansai folk painting, and provide reference and inspiration with more Chinese and national characteristics for the current design, they took Ansai folk painting as the research object and carried out research on the construction of digital network model. First, they used K-means clustering algorithm to calculate image color clustering, and obtained the local contribution of color network nodes and nodes. Then,

Y. Xu et al. (Eds.): ML4CS 2022, LNCS 13657, pp. 251–264, 2023.
https://doi.org/10.1007/978-3-031-20102-8_20

The efficiency matrix of node contribution degree is constructed by expert evaluation method, and it is combined with the calculation of node local contribution degree to obtain the global contribution degree of the node, so as to realize the optimization of basic color network and the construction of color model. Finally, the reliability of the model is verified by randomly selecting case samples. The proposed new color network model comprehensively considers the node contribution degree, It can optimize the calculation method of node degree of color network. The case verification shows that the color network model can accurately reflect the color characteristics and color design logic of Ansai folk paintings; Yangmei et al. [3] put forward a method of constructing Dunhuang mural color network model and its application in product design to assist designers in color culture decoding design activities. Through the establishment of Dunhuang mural image database, Extract image feature colors, based on the principle of graph theory and the co-occurrence relationship between feature colors, establish color network model and main and auxiliary color network model, use VBA language and CorelDRAW platform to develop color extraction system and automatic color matching population generation engine, and assist designers to generate graphic design schemes and product development that can reflect color images in batches in combination with color network model, Finally, the innovative color matching of Dunhuang caisson pattern and its application in product design are tested. The results show that this method can highly restore the color image of Dunhuang murals, and can be used as a new idea for the innovative application of Dunhuang murals.

Folk painting art is more brilliant because of its unique culture, the color is unified and harmonious, and has a clear color tendency. At the same time, the contrast of complementary colors makes the color full of law and motion, which is of great research value and is often used as a reference for color matching by designers. At present, the domestic research on color focuses on the discussion of painting, artistic style and decorative language. The unique style of folk painting and its color harmony relationship are mostly summarized. The subjective description of the color distribution law is usually carried out by using the "formal aesthetic principle", "six methods" or "decorative color structure" method, and the colors are perceptually combined and matched according to the order of decorative colors [4]. Based on experience and cognition, it lacks systematic research on "colorology" and "iconology". It is only a simple imitation and repetition of the ancestors, which is not enough as a scientific basis for the expression of designer culture. The construction of color network model can help designers to rationally mine the color characteristics and relationships of folk paintings, and objectively restore the color images of folk paintings.

Based on the above research background, this paper uses machine learning to build a color network model of folk painting, so as to restore the regional and cultural characteristics of folk painting. The unique artistic language of folk art is particularly striking in color. On the whole, most of the colors used in folk art are matched with primary colors with high purity. While emphasizing color contrast, they often like to use gold and silver lines for harmonic treatment. This emphasis on harmony and unity in color contrast has formed a unique decorative meaning of folk art, which is more prominent in folk paintings. The excavation and application of color aesthetic taste in folk painting is not only reflected in the field of painting, but also penetrated into modern art design.

2 Design of Color Network Model for Folk Painting

2.1 Match the Color of Folk Painting

In the process of matching the colors of folk paintings, the color feature point set of folk paintings is extracted, the corresponding concentric coordinate system is constructed respectively, the principal curvature of the color feature points is calculated, the color descriptor is constructed, and the color invariants of folk paintings are extracted, based on which the color matching of folk paintings is completed [5]. The specific steps are detailed as follows:

Assuming that x_h represents the color feature point set of folk painting, l_j represents the n color feature, h_f represents the color space scale of folk painting, then x_h is calculated by using the following formula, namely:

$$x_h = \frac{\{g_k \times l_j\}^n}{h_f \times g_j} + \frac{\{sg_j \times k_i\}}{g_k} \tag{1}$$

In formula (1), g_j represents the category number of color features, sg_j represents the vector of each color feature, k_i represents the distribution probability of each color in folk painting, and g_k represents the maximum observed value of each color distribution state in folk painting. Assuming that f_v represents the center of l_j, and σ_n represents the scale corresponding to the feature point, the corresponding concentric coordinate system is constructed by using the following formula:

$$E_r(x, y) = \frac{\sigma_n \times g_i}{f_v \times l_j} \tag{2}$$

where g_i represents the sub ring area in the concentric circle.

Assuming that σ_p represents the initial folk painting color pattern, the principal curvature of folk painting color feature points is calculated by using the following formula:

$$H_i(x, y) = \frac{\sigma_p \times k_p}{l_p} \times \{g_h, g_y, g_x\} \tag{3}$$

In formula (3), l_p and k_p represent the second-order partial derivative of Gaussian function respectively, g_h, g_y and g_x represent convolution function. Assuming that $|e(x, y)|$ represents the coordinates of the largest color feature points in the folk painting pattern, and k_o represents the J_i feature points contained in the i ring, the color descriptor of the folk painting pattern is constructed by using the following formula:

$$E_u = \frac{J_i \otimes k_o}{|e(x, y)|} \tag{4}$$

Assuming that μ_p represents the approximate relationship between the color RGB component of the folk painting pattern and its Gaussian distance weighting, and $l(dg)$ represents the color invariant of the j color feature point in the i ring, the color invariant of the folk painting pattern is extracted by using the following formula:

$$E_i = \frac{\mu_p}{l(dg)} \times E_u \tag{5}$$

Assuming that d_s represents the Euclidean distance of the feature descriptor, u_o represents the 32-dimensional color information descriptor, and l_p represents the weight parameters of the descriptor, the color matching of folk paintings is completed by using the following formula:

$$E_r = \frac{l_p \times d_s}{l_p} \times u_o \tag{6}$$

By calculating the color feature points set of folk painting, the corresponding concentric coordinate system is constructed. According to the principal curvature of the color feature points of folk painting, the color description factors of folk painting patterns are constructed. Combined with the color invariants of folk painting patterns, the colors of folk painting are matched.

2.2 Adjust the Color of Folk Painting

According to the limitations of conventional histogram equalization methods, the visual perception characteristics of human eyes are analyzed, and the constraints of image histogram are introduced to establish a nonlinear histogram transformation model. From the perspective of optimal correction results, the evolutionary optimization of genetic algorithm is used to optimize the model of nonlinear histogram [6], and the optimized model is solved according to the contrast distortion adjustment algorithm, so as to realize the automatic color adjustment of folk paintings. The specific process is as follows:

Assuming a folk painting pattern with size $x \times y$ is given, the gray level mapping expression of histogram equalization method is:

$$\begin{cases} q(i) = \frac{f_i}{xy} \\ T(i) = (J-1)\sum\limits_{j=0}^{i} q(j) \end{cases} \tag{7}$$

where J represents the gray level of folk painting patterns, f_i represents the number of occurrences of gray level i in folk painting patterns, $q(j)$ represents the probability function, and $T(i)$ represents the mapping transformation function.

To sum up, in the process of adjusting the color of folk painting patterns, we can better adjust the color by introducing the constraints of image histogram, establishing a nonlinear histogram model and optimizing the model.

2.3 Extracting Invariant Features of Folk Painting Colors

Color is a very important core factor in the pattern design of folk painting, and occupies a very core position in visual art. Color is the visual sensory effect of the eyes stimulated by external light. At present, most folk painting patterns are too simplistic in color matching and pay too much attention to unity and coordination in their decorative design, so they cannot give the visual pleasure that color should have [7]. Therefore, in the process of color matching of folk painting patterns, the affine invariant region of folk painting patterns is constructed by using machine learning algorithm, the autocorrelation matrix of each pixel in folk painting patterns is obtained, the response function of each pixel is given, the relevant affine invariant parameters are calculated, and all colors in the color space are clustered. The specific steps are detailed as follows:

Assuming that M represents the Gaussian window, F_d represents the convolution symbol, and M_g represents the autocorrelation matrix of each pixel (x, y) in the folk painting pattern, the affine invariant region of the folk painting pattern is constructed by using the following formula:

$$R_o = \frac{(x, y) \oplus F_d}{M_g \times j_g \times M} \oplus E_g \tag{8}$$

where j_g represents the response function of the corner and E_g represents the measure of the corner.

Assuming that $C(x, y)$ represents the non maximum value of the corner response function, M_g is calculated by using the following formula:

$$M_g = \frac{C(x, y) \times K_g}{Y_k \times R_o} * o_j \tag{9}$$

where Y_k represents a constant and o_j represents a given measurement threshold.

To sum up, it can be explained that in the process of constructing the color network model of folk painting patterns, we first use the basic visual elements of folk painting patterns to obtain the pixel weights in the neighborhood window, obtain the visual characteristics of the HSV color component distribution of the pixels of folk painting patterns, and extract the invariant visual characteristics of the colors of folk painting patterns.

2.4 Compensation for Color Brightness of Folk Paintings

By analyzing the color of folk painting patterns, the corresponding relationship between the brightness and color of folk painting patterns is obtained, and the optimal value of the brightness and color relationship of folk painting patterns is calculated. The histogram is introduced to obtain the brightness histogram of the corresponding area of folk painting patterns [8]. The brightness and color of folk painting patterns are transformed to complete the color brightness compensation of folk painting patterns. The specific process is as follows:

By analyzing the color of folk painting patterns, the corresponding relationship between brightness and color of folk painting patterns is obtained, which is expressed as:

$$f_{r,y}(x, y) \approx k_y + h_y \times f_{l,y}(\Delta x + \Delta y) \tag{10}$$

where $f_{r,y}(x, y)$ is the color component value of folk painting pattern at (x, y) position, $f_{l,y}(\Delta x + \Delta y)$ is the value of color corresponding point in folk painting pattern, h_y and k_y are the brightness factor and color factor in folk painting pattern respectively.

When h_y and k_y are the most appropriate, the brightness and color correspondence of folk painting patterns is the most accurate. The optimal value of brightness and color correspondence of folk painting patterns is given by using the following formula:

$$W = \sum_{x=1}^{M-1} \sum_{y=1}^{N-1} f_{r,y}(x, y) - h_y \times f_{l,y}(\Delta x + \Delta y) + k_y \tag{11}$$

where, M and N are the width and height of folk painting patterns respectively [9]. The histogram after color brightness compensation of folk painting patterns is given by using the following formula:

$$H_{l,y}(i)h_y k_y = H_{l,y} \frac{h_y + k_y}{h_y} \tag{12}$$

To sum up, it can be explained that in the process of building the color network model of folk painting patterns, brightness compensation is carried out for the missing part of folk painting patterns, which improves the overall sense of hierarchy of folk painting patterns, reduces the complexity of calculation, and lays a foundation for building the color network model of folk painting patterns.

2.5 Constructing the Color Network Model of Folk Painting

By building a color library to extract the feature colors of murals, it can provide color selection for designers and obtain the frequency and proportion of feature colors, but it can not let designers understand the relationship between feature colors. In order to restore the image beauty of folk painting colors, it is also necessary to find the connection between characteristic colors. Therefore, the concept of machine learning is introduced to express the relationship between extracted colors, which is based on which to assist designers in color creative activities. In the color matching process, it is necessary to determine the theme color of the design scheme, that is, the main color, to lay the foundation of the overall style image of the scheme, and then collocation of several or more

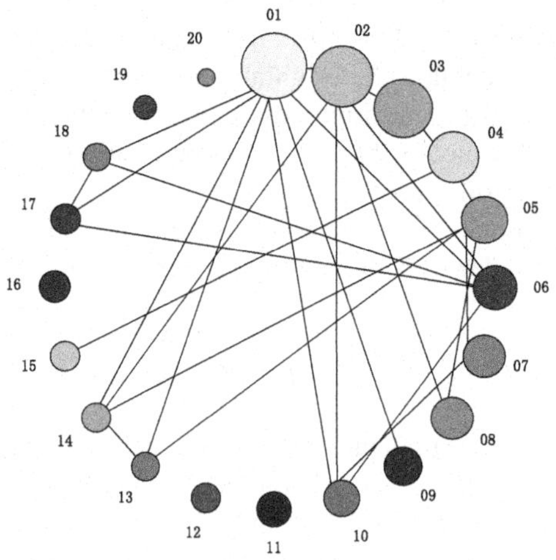

Fig. 1. Construction of color relation network

auxiliary colors, simple but not monotonous, showing the unique gorgeous Dunhuang color. Therefore, the complex network of the relationship between the characteristic colors of the architecture is needed first when constructing the architecture color network. Then, based on the relationship network, the primary color is determined, and the relationship network between the primary color and its secondary color is constructed [10, 11]. Color relation network construction is shown in Fig. 1.

In the color relation network of Fig. 1 architecture, 20 nodes represent the 20 feature colors extracted by clustering. The size of nodes, namely the size of the circular color block, represents the weight of each feature color (color weight in the main color mode). The connection line between nodes represents the co-occurrence of two feature color fusion color library maps at a certain frequency, and the co-occurrence frequency threshold is set in advance. When the threshold is exceeded, co-occurrence is achieved. After several tests, it is found that the network construction with a threshold of 0.4 is the most stable, so the threshold is set as 0.4. The determination of the main color needs to consider the color relationship and the weight of the characteristic color. Therefore, an expert team was formed to screen the four characteristic colors 01, 02, 03 and 04 with the largest weight. After discussion, because the lightness of the characteristic color 01 is higher than the other three characteristic colors, it can better highlight the design, and the weight is the largest, which most conforms to the image of folk painting. Therefore, the characteristic color 01 is the main color and the auxiliary color is selected.

After the primary color is determined, in order to select the appropriate color combination, the selected auxiliary color should have a strong connection with the primary color. According to the definition of strong and weak relation group in the closure principle of graph theory, if two nodes are connected, a strong relation group will be formed. The stronger the embeddedness is, the greater the trust relation is, that is, the closer the color relation is. Therefore, multiple feature color nodes of primary and secondary colors need to be connected in pairs. If not, the threshold of node connection relationship should be reduced and the network should be reconstructed. According to the final design

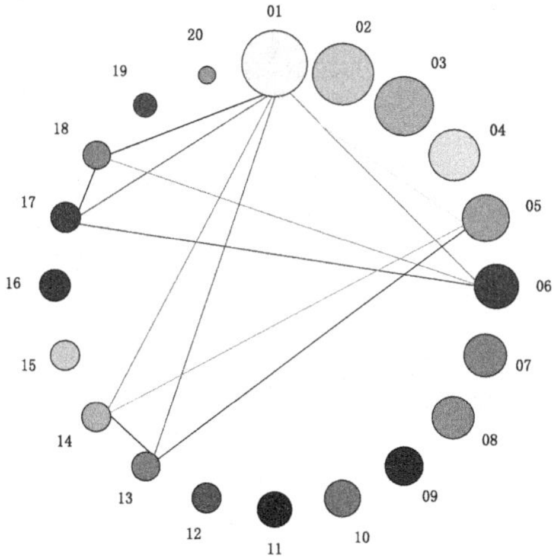

Fig. 2. Main and auxiliary feature color selection network

requirements, determine the number of auxiliary colors, generally no less than two auxiliary colors, this paper chooses three auxiliary colors; The 01 feature color is used as the main color to select three auxiliary colors, including (05,13,14) and (06,17,18), which are distinguished by black and red connection lines respectively. The main and auxiliary feature color selection network is shown in Fig. 2.

According to the above process, the color network model of folk painting is constructed, and its process is shown in Fig. 3.

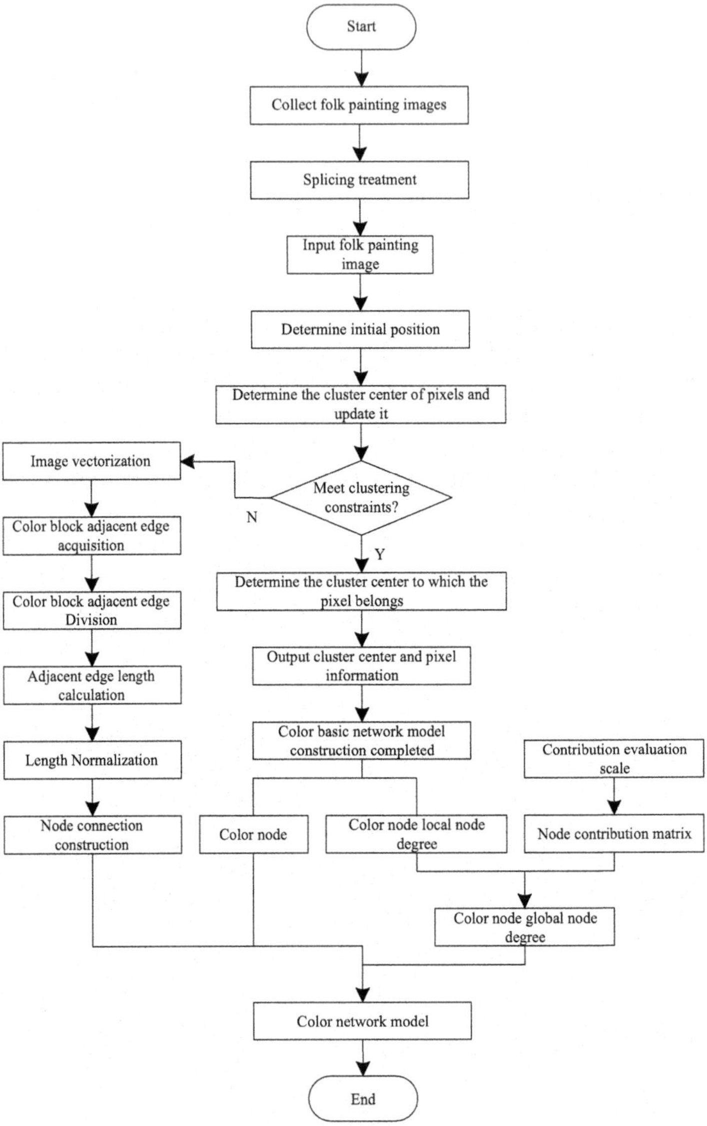

Fig. 3. Model building process

For the convenience of understanding, the construction process of folk painting color network model is summarized as follows:

Step1: Collect a large number of images of folk paintings, combine multiple images into one format by using the existing graphic design software, and input the images;
Step2: Specify the number of clustering centers and the initial position of clustering, and use K clustering algorithm to cluster the colors of folk paintings, so as to determine the node and local node degree of the network model;
Step3: Vectorize the folk painting, use vector software to measure the adjacent length between color blocks, determine the connection thickness, and establish node connections, so as to realize the construction of the basic network model of folk painting;
Step4: Rating and scoring the contribution between colors to obtain the contribution matrix between color nodes;
Step5: Finally, the contribution matrix of nodes and local node degrees are integrated to optimize the basic network model and finally realize the construction of folk painting color network model.

3 Case Analysis

Taking Ansai folk painting as the research object, this paper verifies and demonstrates the construction method of color network model. In this paper, four graduate students were assigned to collect images of Ansai folk paintings, and a total of 134 classic paintings of Ansai folk paintings were collected. Seven Ansai painting inheritors and four senior color design researchers analyzed the representativeness of the collected works and believed that the collected painting samples could accurately reflect the color characteristics and color design thinking of Ansai folk paintings.

In order to ensure the accuracy of the color extraction results of the painting pixel points and the adjacent edge length of the two color nodes, Photoshop software is used

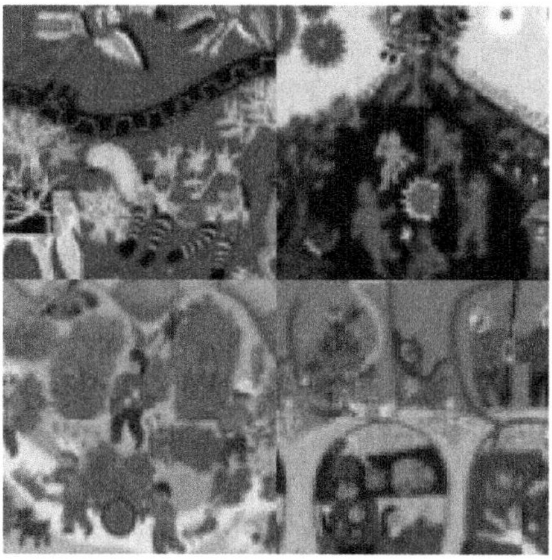

Fig. 4. Mosaic results of Ansai folk painting image samples

to scale and assemble 134 works in the same proportion according to the size of the original painting. The partial display effect of the mosaic results of the painting samples is shown in Fig. 4.

Through the research on the actual painting process of Ansai painting, it is found that the pigments used in Ansai painting are usually 12 kinds of advertising colors, and most of them use uncoordinated solid colors, and most of the techniques are flat painting. Further visual analysis of the picture color shows that the final presentation of the color basically conforms to the painting law. Therefore, the number of color clustering centers is specified, and the initial clustering position is randomly specified on each feature color. Using machine learning algorithm, RGB values of 12 color network nodes and local node degrees of color nodes are obtained. To facilitate observation, the local node degree of color nodes is normalized. The final results are shown in Table 1.

Table 1. RGB values of color network nodes and their normalized local node degrees

Node number	R value	G value	B value	Local node degree value
1	138	57	39	1.00
2	269	214	0	0.74
3	233	101	63	0.54
4	0	0	0	0.53
5	101	180	39	0.35
6	217	116	175	0.33
7	56	49	106	0.32
8	216	218	197	0.31
9	27	174	194	0.29
10	204	202	87	0.26
11	0	140	114	0.21
12	69	84	56	0.17

The adjacent edge length of two color nodes is counted by pixels, and the results are normalized.

The node contribution matrix is used to optimize the color basic network model:

A 5-level evaluation scale of color node contribution degree "{almost no contribution, slight contribution, general contribution, large contribution, great contribution}" is constructed by using Likert quantity, and the corresponding score is "{0.2, 0.4, 0.6, 0.8, 1.0}". Seven Ansai painting inheritors were selected to score the mutual contributions of color nodes one by one, and the total score of a single node was taken as the contribution of the node. Based on this, the contribution matrix of color nodes can be constructed. The normalized contribution of nodes is shown in Table 2.

Table 2. Normalized color node contribution data

Node number	Contribution value	Node number	Contribution value
1	1.00	7	0.83
2	1.00	8	0.76
3	0.96	9	0.74
4	0.93	10	0.70
5	0.91	11	0.69
6	0.89	12	0.63

The optimized color network model, i.e. the final model, is shown in Fig. 5.

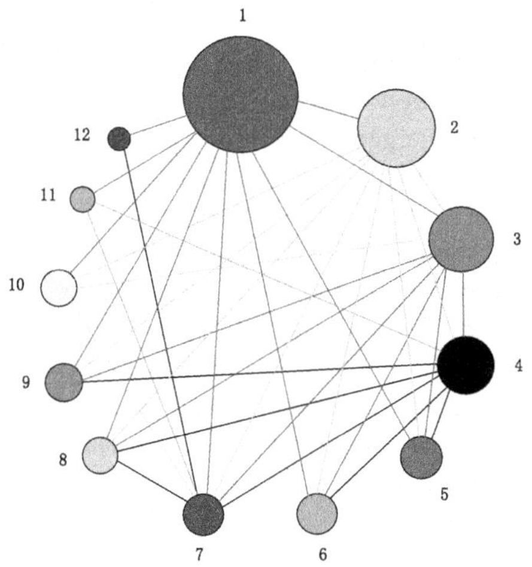

Fig. 5. Ansai folk painting color network model

In order to evaluate the reliability of Ansai folk painting color network model, two Ansai paintings were verified and analyzed. Random selection is carried out in the library to obtain an original experimental sample Fig. 6 (a) and a newly selected sample Fig. 6 (b).

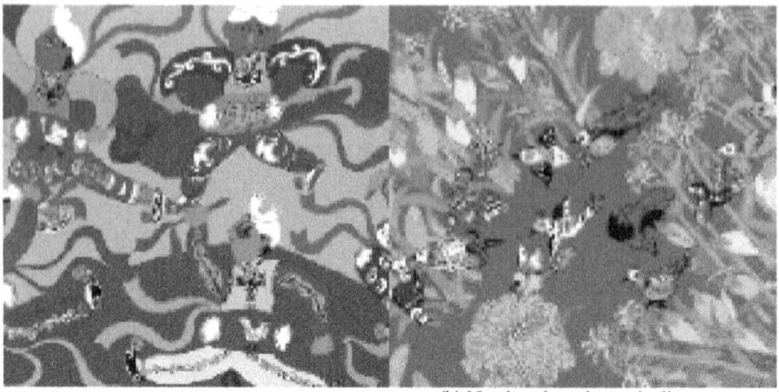

(a) Original experimental sample diagram (b) Newly selected sample diagram

Fig. 6. Ansai paintings

The Fig. 6 shows that the original experimental samples are mainly composed of characters, new selected samples are mainly composed of animals, to the colour of independent network model validation sample build, and the colours of the selected sample network model and the proposed ansai folk painting color, comparing the network model to verify the model to the generalization of ansai folk painting color ability and reliability. The color network model of the two works is shown in Fig. 7.

As can be seen from Fig. 7, since the color relationship of a single work is relatively simple, it is not of practical significance to simply calculate the error between the models, and more attention should be paid to the accuracy of the model's generalization of the color relationship during the comparative analysis of color models. Therefore, after comparing the models, it is found that the color network model of Ansai folk paintings can completely summarize the sample color model, that is, the model has a good reliability in describing the color relationship characteristics of Ansai paintings.

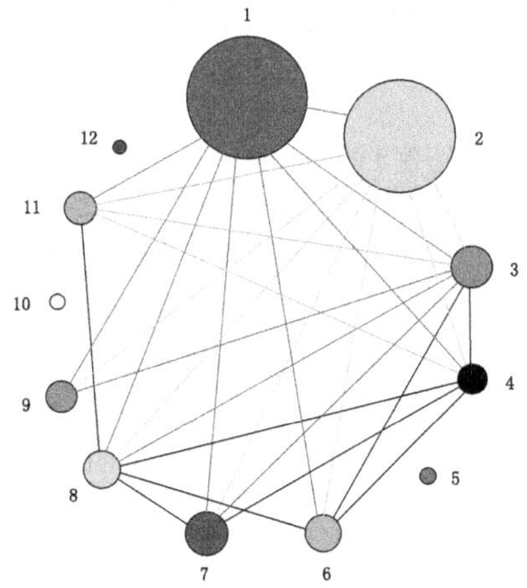

(a) Color network model of original experimental sample graph

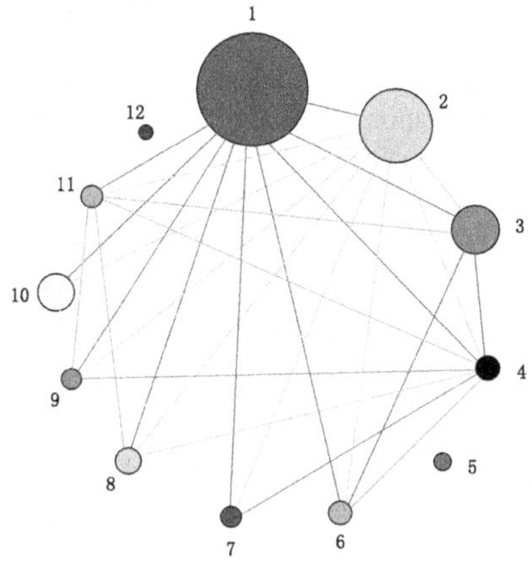

(b) Color network model of newly selected sample map

Fig. 7. Two sample color network models

4 Conclusion

As an intangible cultural heritage, folk painting has unique regional cultural characteristics. Its strong and unrestrained color and color matching techniques can provide unique color design inspiration and basis for the design fields of clothing and products. Therefore, to study the color system of folk painting, grasp its unique color characteristics and color design logic, and reuse its color design thinking in modern clothing and household articles can effectively endow products with unique color emotion and cultural connotation, and realize product design innovation and differentiation. This paper presents a research on the construction of folk painting color network model based on machine learning. The example results show that the model has certain reliability. Although the research of this paper can show the color characteristics of folk painting, there are still many areas that need to be improved. In the future research, in order to further assess the reliability and application scope of this technology, it is also expected that relevant research peers can carry out more extensive verification of this technology and model.

Acknowledgement. "A study on the cultural and creative design and artistic creation of the unique landscape resources in Weizhou Island" by Professor 2021 of Nanning University, project number: 2021 JSGC22.

References

1. Liu, S., Liu, D., Muhammad, K., Ding, W.: Effective template update mechanism in visual tracking with background clutter. Neurocomputing **458**, 615–625 (2021)
2. Yan, Y., et al.: Research on the construction of Ansai folk painting color network model. J. Silk **57**(11), 120–125 (2020)
3. Mei, Y., Jin-song, L., Yi-yan, W.: Construction and application of color network model of Dunhuang traditional fresco. Packag. Eng. **41**(18), 22–228 (2020)
4. Kim, M., Kang, D., Lee, N.: Feature extraction from oriental painting for wellness contents recommendation services. IEEE Access **7**, 59263–59270 (2019)
5. Jiang, Y., Zheng, L.-B.: Application research of chinese traditional painting coloring mode in poster design. Packaging Eng. **42**(18), 321–325 (2021)
6. Liu, S., Wang, S., Liu, X., Lin, C.-T., Lv, Z.: Fuzzy detection aided real-time and robust visual tracking under complex environments. IEEE Trans. Fuzzy Syst. **29**(1), 90–102 (2021). https://doi.org/10.1109/TFUZZ.2020.3006520
7. Qian, W., et al.: Artistic paintings classification based on information entropy. J. Graph. **40**(6), 991–999 (2019)
8. Zhu, M., Jiao, H., Zhao, X.: A color transfer method based on neighborhood-first searching and texture similarity matching. Imaging Sci. Photochem. **38**(6), 935–940 (2020)
9. Weiwei, C., Yan, C.: Color space matching analysis of clothing colors and clothing styles based on PCCS color system. J. Silk **56**(1), 66–72 (2019)
10. Shuai, L., et al.: Human memory update strategy: a multi-layer template update mechanism for remote visual monitoring. IEEE Trans. Multimedia **23**, 2188–2198 (2021)
11. Wen, M.Y., Liao, W.G.: Incremental mining algorithm for uncertain data based on machine learning. Comput. Simul. **38**(11), 290–294 (2021)

Research on Intrusion Prevention Optimization Algorithm of Power UAV Network Communication Based on Artificial Intelligence

Gebiao Hu(✉), Zhichi Lin, Zheng Guo, Ruiqing Xu, and Xiao Zhang

Construction Branch of State Grid Jiangxi Electric Power Co., Ltd, Nanchang 330001, China
z0220dd@163.com

Abstract. Aiming at the problem of poor intrusion prevention in power UAV network communication, this paper proposes an optimization algorithm for power UAV network communication intrusion prevention based on artificial intelligence. Detect the abnormal data of power UAV network communication, strengthen the data filtering and management, and carry out adaptive filtering for abnormal areas to achieve effective data preprocessing. Furthermore, it captures communication intrusion data, transmits data filter signal, adjusts detection algorithm, monitors internal signal and avoids bad signal. The optimal intrusion threshold is calculated, and the collected data is adjusted on the basis of artificial intelligence algorithm to obtain the final parameters of the algorithm. Experimental results show that the convergence value of the algorithm is 3×10^5, which has low convergence. Strong anti invasion ability and good practical application prospects. The results show that the algorithm based on artificial intelligence has good performance.

Keywords: Artificial intelligence · Electric UAV · UAV network · Network Communications · Anti intrusion optimization · Optimization algorithm

1 Introduction

The power UAV network has been deeply rooted in people's life. The current power UAV network environment is very complex, and the attack means are more and more diverse. At present, the single technology can not meet the demand of network security. Firewall can effectively catch external attacks and ensure network communication security. In recent years, the optimization technology of power UAV network communication anti-intrusion technology and intrusion detection technology have been effectively integrated to ensure network security through a new industrial mode. When there are external attacks, the anti-intrusion optimization algorithm screens the data of external attacks through detection and judgment to ensure that user information will not be lost.

Some scholars have studied this. Chen et al. [1] proposed an intrusion detection method for UAV network based on spatiotemporal convolution network. The spatiotemporal graph convolution network is composed of graph convolution network and gated recursive unit, and the spatiotemporal evolution characteristics of the network are

Y. Xu et al. (Eds.): ML4CS 2022, LNCS 13657, pp. 265–278, 2023.
https://doi.org/10.1007/978-3-031-20102-8_21

extracted from complex and changeable data. Intrusion detection is completed by extracting features related to intrusion detection through attention mechanism. This method can detect it, but the amount of calculation is large. Cao et al. [2] proposed a relay cooperative UAV assisted cognitive radio network security communication method. The secondary transmitter is used to decode and forward confidential messages, and the UAV is used as a mobile jammer to send interference noise, so as to reduce the eavesdropper's decoding ability, but this method takes a long time to transmit information.

To sum up, this paper studies a new optimization algorithm of power UAV network communication intrusion prevention based on artificial intelligence.

2 Abnormal Detection of Network Communication Data of Electric UAV

2.1 Data Collection

The collected data will have some data quality problems, in the preprocessing process, the original time scale alignment, filling missing values and a series of operations. The main purpose of this process is to refine the data, and to input the high quality data into the module for calculation and analysis data modeling. After the data are processed preliminarily, the correlation is calculated, different time series are determined by data segmentation, the sequence is redesigned, the matrix is obtained, and the time sequence correlation graph is established [3]. Firstly, the correlation is calculated. Secondly, the abnormal data is divided into sequential clusters and extracted again. Finally, the abnormal data is processed and detected. In this process, the big data must be sensed, the big data must be diagnosed according to the different characteristics of the signal and the big data fusion method, the original data must be collected, and then the big data detected by the big data must be analyzed to get the distribution spectrum. The data structure is reconstructed by association mapping, and the fuzzy statistic amplitude is obtained. Finally, according to the collected data, the initial sample of big data output can be obtained by calculating the result in the time-frequency plane [4].

2.2 Adaptive Filtering Processing

Adaptive filtering is a kind of best filtering method developed in recent years. It has strong adaptability and can process information better. Therefore, it can be applied in many fields such as control, image processing, etc. [5]. Set up a new big data distribution structure, get the big data eigenvalue by correlation method, determine the estimated value, extract the eigenvalue from the estimated value, and get the correlation relation.

The system gets the best sampling eigenvalue of power UAV network communication data, divides several points dynamically, constructs adaptive filter, realizes wireless dynamic compression sensing industrial big data to get filter output function, realizes dynamic parameter adjustment, gets adaptive learning eigenvector, and completes the processing.

2.3 Abnormal Data Detection

After the completion of adaptive filtering processing, anomaly data detection, the main task of anomaly detection is to identify those anomaly data that last a long time [6]. In the process of detection, the time series group is used as the basic analysis to test the single dimension. A set of anomaly sequence data is determined, and anomaly detection is carried out in two steps. In this process, the value of edge weights is detected to ensure that edge weights are lower than correlation threshold.

3 Network Communication Intrusion Data Acquisition of Power UAV Based on Artificial Intelligence

Artificial intelligence is a new technological science that studies and develops theories, methods, technologies and application systems for simulating, extending and expanding human intelligence. Artificial intelligence has a wide range of fields, including robots, language recognition, image recognition and so on. When using artificial intelligence technology to process data, it can not only improve the accuracy, but also divide the data into levels. At the same time, it also has integration, which can combine the two concepts to produce more benefits. In this paper, artificial intelligence is used to collect intrusion communication data.

Start the cloud task inside, detect, control and filter the packets through SPI, start the filtering rules, the data from UAV need to complete the data matching through different personalized rules, when the packets can not determine the appropriate filtering rules, we need to start the query program. If the user is identified as standard, the user data needs to be reset, and detailed filtering rules are established to ensure that each data is filtered [7].

A intelligent meta-classifier is used to label intrusive data. Assuming a representation of data as a, the result of marking the rth intelligent meta-classifier as a may be represented as:

$$G(a) = b\sum_{r=1}^{R} sign\left(g_{r(a)} = b\right) \tag{1}$$

where, $G(a)$ represents the marking result; $sign$ means indicating function; $g_{r(a)}$ means unmarked data; b is the marking coefficient. When $g_{r(a)} = b$, the value of $sign$ is 1, and it is zero anyway.

The host detector collects the running data of the host operating system and the log of the application program, and the network detector obtains the network data packet, identifies the intrusion data according to the corresponding intrusion rules, and processes the data simply. When the intrusion data is detected, the alarm mechanism is activated and the intrusion information is sent to the central processor [8, 9].

After receiving the alarm signals and intrusion data from different detectors, the CPU divides the intrusion data into R data sets X based on the principle of elastic search.

Calculate the confidence of the marked intrusion data a as follows:

$$con(a) = \frac{1}{R}\sum_{r=1}^{R} sign\left(g_{r(a)} = b\right) \tag{2}$$

Starting from the random solution, the scheduling reliability of particle location is analyzed. In order to ensure the reliability of computing resources, the heterogeneous characteristics of different data in the artificial intelligence environment are analyzed to determine whether the data is intrusion information.

$$w^t = Suc^t \cdot (w_{\max} - w_{\min}) + w_{\min} \tag{3}$$

where, Suc^t represents the success rate of data operation process; $w_{\max}$ represents the maximum value of inertia weight; $w_{\min}$ represents the minimum value of inertia weight; w^t represents the information weight obtained during the operation of t time.

Considering the noise pollution carried by the intrusion data, the generalization error algorithm is introduced to estimate the generalization error of the confidence error. The calculation method is as follows:

$$u = \frac{1}{n} \sum_{(a,b)} nsign(con(a)) \tag{4}$$

Among them, n indicates that the data set X contains the number of data; u indicates the generalization error; according to the above error estimate, if the error value is more than 1, the confidence calculation shall be reconstructed; if the error value is less than 1, the error is not enough to affect the final calculation result, and can be ignored for the next step.

Select the confidence threshold. According to the above results, the optimal thresholds of high confidence and low confidence are represented by ε_1^r and ε_2^r. The selection of confidence threshold affects the efficiency of data analysis. The optimal threshold of high confidence and low confidence should satisfy the following relations:

$$\varepsilon_1^r = \frac{1}{\varepsilon_2^r} \tag{5}$$

According to the confidence threshold of the data, the intrusion data whose confidence is higher than the highest confidence threshold are divided into training samples, which are trained and analyzed. For intrusion data whose confidence is below or between low confidence optimal thresholds, replay data set X for next data calculation[10].

According to the result of intrusion data identification, the appropriate defense mechanism is matched from the database, and the control unit of the central processor sends out control instructions to control the operation of the corresponding defense mechanism, and the data results and information are stored in the memory to realize data analysis and facilitate the next intrusion signal detection.

4 Anti Intrusion Optimization Algorithm

4.1 Battery Optimization of Electric UAV System

Battery discharge is carried out by the nodes at the two ends of the battery. Therefore, the two poles of the battery are also important positions for measuring the remaining battery power.

In order to ensure the validity and reliability of the data monitoring of battery residual power in the power UAV system, the relationship between battery resistance and current is calculated.

After the level of the remaining battery power is determined, the remaining battery power shall be monitored in real time by the implemented power of the battery and the capacity consumed in unit time, and the other data parameters in the battery shall be calculated according to all calculable variables [11].

First, calculate the remaining power inside the battery by using the formula as follows:

$$H = \sum Q_i * t - \frac{u_i}{I} + g * j_i + |w_i * \partial| \tag{6}$$

Of which, H represents the remaining amount of the battery; t represents the amount of time consumed by the battery in a certain period of time; g represents the number of times the battery voltage has been adjusted; ∂ represents a constant with a range of values of [0,3], and Q_i represents the relationship between the battery capacity and the resistance; u_i represents the voltage output of the battery at the last moment of the effective time; j_i represents the voltage output of the battery at the first time of the calculation period; I represents the initial current value of the battery; and w_i represents the instantaneous current.

Finally, the parameter value of battery residual power data is continuously monitored by using the power accumulation algorithm. The battery has great uncertainty for the external conditions. In order to eliminate the influence of these two errors on the monitoring of battery residual power, the nonlinear Kalman filter state observation equation is introduced to control the system. The equations are as follows:

$$x_k = \frac{f[X_{K-1}, K-1] + T_{K-1} * D_w}{w_s(t)} + \frac{y(t)}{\beta} \tag{7}$$

where, D_w represents the signal state vector of the monitoring system at a certain time; X_{K-1} represents the observation signal vector of the monitoring system at a certain time; T_{K-1} and $y(t)$ respectively represent the state transition matrix and observation matrix of the system signal; β represents the noise of monitoring system and observation noise respectively; $K-1$ is constant; $w_s(t)$ indicates output filtering of the battery.

4.2 Optimal Monitoring of Network Communication Intrusion Prevention for Electric UAV

There are many parameters in power UAV network communication. In this paper, we can directly calculate the parameters of communication anti-intrusion as the key data for monitoring. The optimized monitoring model of power UAV network communication against intrusion based on artificial intelligence is composed of system capacity monitoring module, ohm internal resistance monitoring module, system voltage monitoring module and polarization effect monitoring module. Each module monitors different parameters in the UAV system, and finally finishes the monitoring of optimized data against intrusion by calculation [12].

The capacity model mainly monitors the power consumption of the anti-intrusion system. If the battery capacity is too low, it will lead to excessive battery consumption. The standard capacity of the battery model is 2.6 A * h, and the temperature of the battery will lead to the consumption of the battery energy.

The task of the Ohmic Internal Resistance Model based on artificial intelligence is to monitor the output resistance of the system in real time. Once the resistance is too high, will disturb the battery internal current and voltage of the normal work, according to Ohm's law, circuit resistance sudden rise or fall, will affect the battery power pulse. The curve of ohmic resistance variables with temperature is shown in Fig. 1:

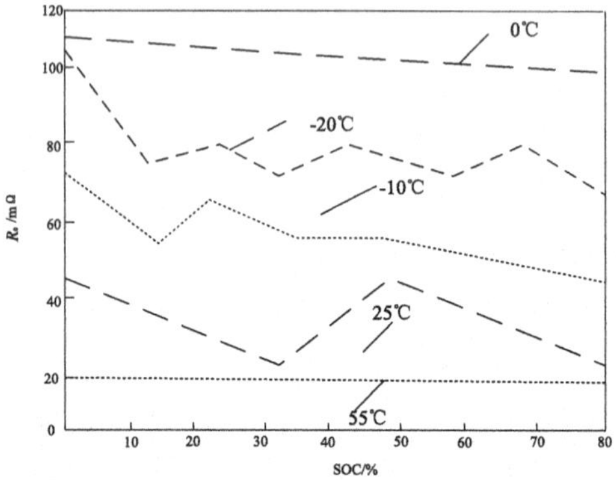

Fig. 1. Variation curve of ohmic internal resistance variable with temperature

The main task of the system monitoring model is to monitor the open-circuit voltage of the battery. The open-circuit voltage of the battery will affect the consumption of the battery. When the temperature is constant, the open circuit voltage fluctuation of the battery is in a slowly fluctuating state, the energy consumption speed of the battery will be faster; When the temperature changes, the open circuit voltage changes slowly, the battery energy consumption will be increased on the basis of. Therefore, not only the temperature of battery itself but also the interference of SOC should be taken into account when monitoring the open circuit voltage of battery.

The monitoring principle of the polarization effect parameter monitoring model is that the main data in the model is the RC parameter of the system, and the parameter is a variable. The RC parameter is directly related to the residual power parameter in the battery, and the less battery power available, the greater the RC parameter value. Moreover, the range of RC parameters is different at different stages.

The fundamental of calculating the internal polarization effect parameters of the battery residual power data enables to calculate the RC parameters of the battery. The calculation formula is as follows:

$$G = \frac{U_{OC} - \zeta * e^{\frac{i}{R_i C_1}} - U_2 * e^{\frac{i}{R_2 C_2}}}{\eta + W} \tag{8}$$

where, ζ represents the size of the internal pulse wave of the battery; U_{OC} represents the terminal voltage at the beginning of battery standing; R_i represents the internal resistance at the moment when the battery is standing; η refers to the polarization coefficient of the battery; W refers to battery output discharge; The meaning of other unknowns is the same as above.

When the range of RC parameters is between 1 and 10, the remaining battery power is between 100% and 85%; when the range of RC parameters is between 20 and 30, the remaining battery power is between 84% and 60%; when the range of RC parameters is between - 1 and - 20, the remaining battery power is between 59% and 20%; when the range of RC parameters is between - 30, the remaining battery power is less than 10%.

The change in the electrochemical polarization resistance of a specific cell is shown in Fig. 2:

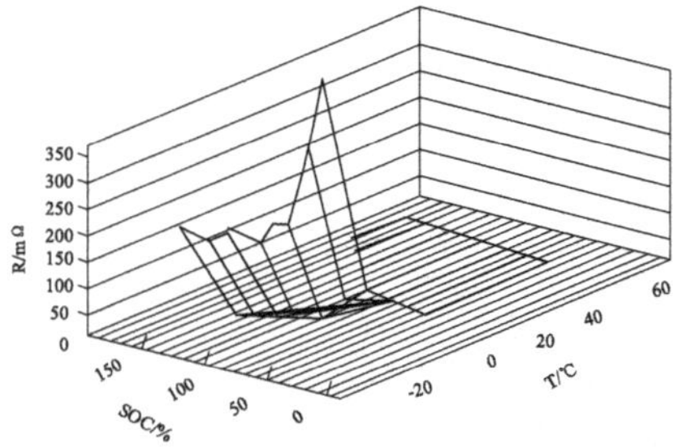

Fig. 2. Variation of electrochemical polarization resistance in the battery

Intrusion Prevention Optimization Monitoring and Inspection of Electric UAV Network Communication

Through the above discussion, the optimization of anti-intrusion data of electric power UAV network communication based on artificial intelligence is completed. The instruments to be prepared for the test are a controllable test platform, 3 thermostat devices, 3 generator devices, 3 battery application devices and 2 A * h/3.7 V, 6 A * h/3.7 V, 12 A * h/3.7 V batteries.

In order to ensure the fairness and reliability of the experiment, the variable gain coefficient and the constant temperature environment of the battery are verified in three small experiments. To avoid the damage to the test system caused by each test, each test is performed on a new battery of the same model [13].

In the experiment of variable gain coefficient, the test period is 5 min. In order to avoid accidental test, the same test is repeated for five times and the average value is calculated. During test time, the current data waveforms and cell variable gain ripple diagrams corresponding to each moment are shown in Figs. 3 and 4:

In order to ensure the reliability of the optimized data, the current variable gain data are generated in noiseless environment.

Figure 4 shows that the current of battery has nothing to do with the service life of battery, but the variable gain coefficient of battery. The bigger the variable gain coefficient is, the closer the current of battery is to normal value. If the variable gain coefficient of battery is smaller or larger, the current of battery will be affected. In addition, when the variable gain of the battery is reduced, the convergence speed is also reduced, which

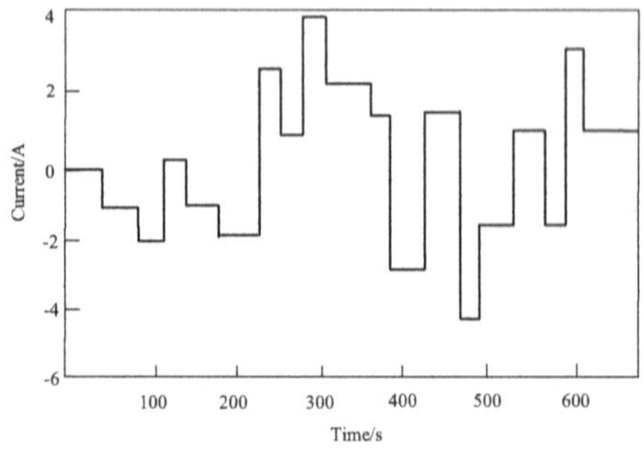

Fig. 3. Battery current feedback waveform

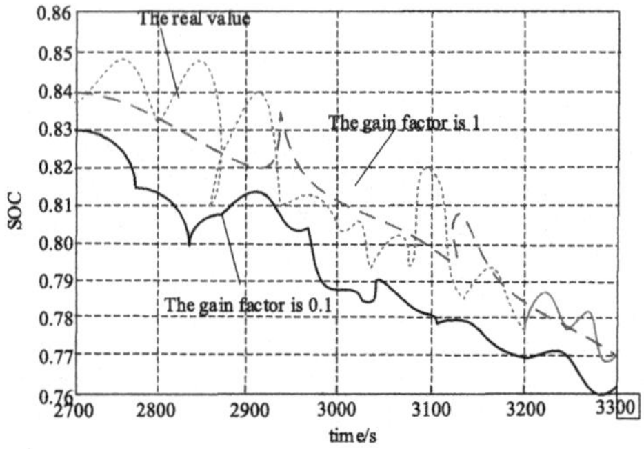

Fig. 4. Variation of variable gain coefficient of battery

leads to the higher probability of the error in the calculation. Therefore, the convergence speed of the intrusion prevention system can be adjusted by adjusting the variable gain of the battery to improve the monitoring accuracy of the method.

In order to verify whether the data monitoring of the optimization algorithm is effective, we need to prepare a current tester based on the test platform. The principle of

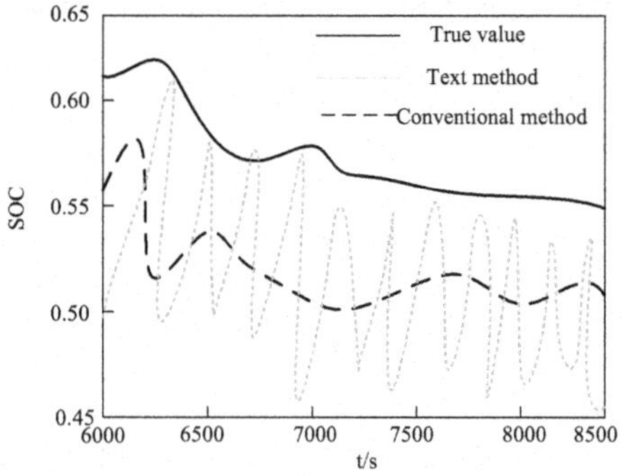

Fig. 5. Comparison between the actual remaining quantity of battery and the test method results at −25 °C

the test is to compare the battery temperature, residual power and battery current with the data of the optimized algorithm, and the test time is set to 30 min. The test data are shown in Figs. 5 and 6:

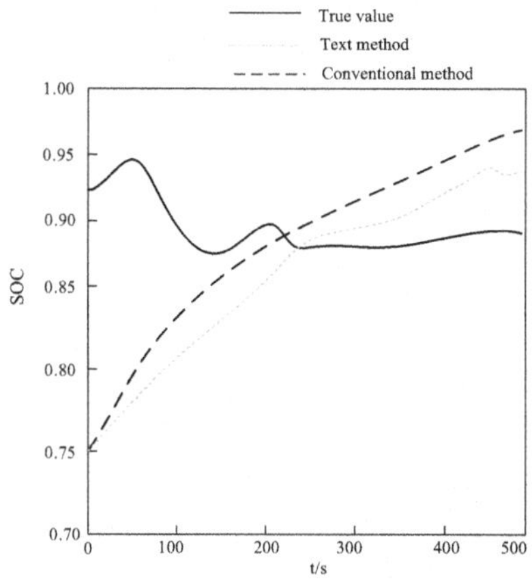

Fig. 6. Comparison between the actual remaining quantity of the battery at 25 °C and the results of the test method

Figures 5 and 6 show the variation of the actual battery residual capacity at different temperatures and the variation of the battery residual capacity monitored by the two test methods.

Compared with the above figure, the errors of the two methods are 0.0012 and 0.0034 for 25 °C and −25 °C respectively, so it can be proved that the monitoring efficiency is not affected by the battery temperature.

5 Experimental Study

5.1 Research on Anti Intrusion Performance

In order to verify the effectiveness of the proposed optimization algorithm for power UAV network communication intrusion prevention, a comparative experiment is designed. Setting up experimental parameters: the selected data center is the data center of artificial intelligence, and the physical machine is set a total of 1,100. The physical machine can connect with the access layer, the aggregation layer and the core layer, so as to ensure that the communication link speed can be stable at 2–10 Mbit/s during the communication process, and the distribution is carried out in the manner of Weibull, and the communication link failure interval during the acquisition process is counted to obtain the number of particles.

In order to determine the reliability of communication intrusion prevention optimization algorithm in artificial intelligence environment and determine the impact of different failure recovery rates on intrusion data capture system, the number of cloud tasks generated is 5000, the communication rate CCR ratio in the communication process is 1.0, and the task takes 150 s to execute. By analyzing the influence of failure recovery rate on the success rate of task execution, the experimental results are shown in Fig. 7:

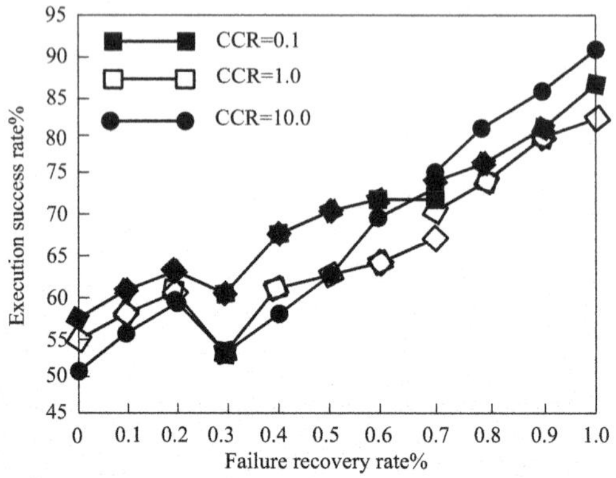

Fig. 7. Experimental results of the effect of failure recovery rate on task execution success rate

According to Fig. 7, the recovery mechanism does not work when the network communication anti-intrusion system proposed in this paper starts up. In this process, the success rate of communication task is very low. The higher the CCR is, the more intensive the computation is, and the heavier the computation is. It can be found from the graph that when the recovery ratio of failure is more than 0.5, the work capacity of the network communication intensive task is higher than that of the computational intensive task, and when the recovery ratio is more than 0.5, the work capacity of the network communication intensive task is improved rapidly and exceeds that of the communication-intensive task. Thus, after joining the network communication anti-intrusion system designed in this paper, the working ability of the system increases, and the failure recovery rate increases to 1. Although the types of tasks are different, the success rate of the three tasks is not 100%.

This research method is compared with spatiotemporal convolution network intrusion detection method and relay cooperative secure communication method to analyze the convergence of different calculation methods when the number of tasks is different. The experimental results are shown in Table 1:

Table 1. Convergence test results

Number of tasks	Iterations		
	Spatiotemporal convolution network intrusion detection method	Relay cooperative secure communication method	This research method
1000	85	21	10
2000	88	15	20
3000	96	28	30
4000	100	46	40
5000	105	52	50
6000	114	58	60
7000	118	62	70
8000	126	68	80
9000	138	76	90

According to Table 1, this paper's network communication anti-intrusion system iterates in a regular mode, which has a good support for information capture operation.

Summarizing the iterations in Table 1, the convergence curves for different task numbers are shown in Fig. 8:

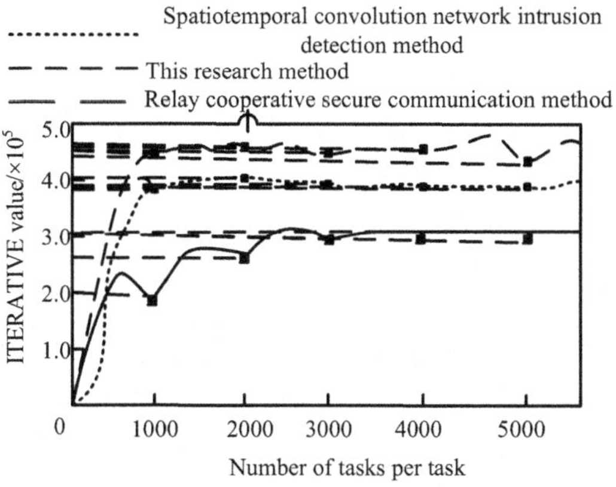

Fig. 8. Convergence curve of different tasks

According to Fig. 8, the convergence curve gradually increases with the increase of the number of tasks. When the convergence value reaches 3×10^5, the convergence value does not increase. The convergence value of the traditional method is between 4×10^5–5×10^5, and the anti-intrusion performance of the system proposed in this paper is always better than the traditional method. Experimental results show that the proposed system can analyze the failure recovery mechanism and failure control strategy, determine the failure law of different resource terminals, and ensure the effectiveness of the system. The traditional network communication anti-intrusion system can not fully consider the reliability of artificial intelligence in the process of task scheduling, and the quality of anti-intrusion greatly decreases.

5.2 Study on Practical Application Effect

In order to verify the practical application effect of the proposed network anti intrusion optimization algorithm based on artificial intelligence, the following experiments are designed. The method in this paper, the spatiotemporal convolution network intrusion detection method and the relay cooperative security communication method are used to process the same set of data samples, and the application effect of the system is evaluated. By comparing the distribution of this method with traditional methods and original data, the distribution of data samples is verified.The experimental results are shown in Fig. 9.

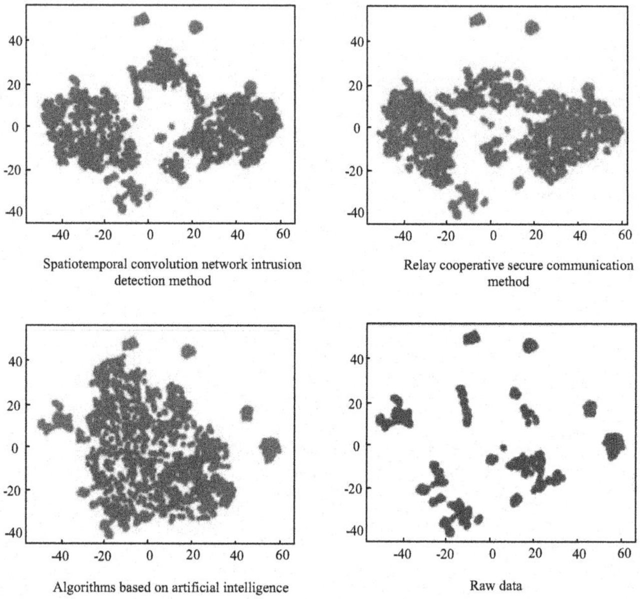

Fig. 9. Schematic diagram of data distribution generated after 200 training sessions

As can be seen from Fig. 9, compared with the other two traditional detection systems. The data distribution of the communication data anomaly detection studied in this paper is highly similar to the data distribution of the original sample after 200 times of training, while the data distribution of the traditional method is relatively messy. It shows that the research method in this paper has higher coincidence rate and more uniform distribution, so the data analysis and classification detection ability of this paper is stronger.

The research method in this paper is combined with the spatiotemporal convolution network intrusion detection method and the relay cooperative security communication method to detect and analyze the characteristics and anomalies of the data set. By comparing the number of detected feature points with the corresponding F1 value, the accuracy of data detection of three classification algorithms is analyzed.

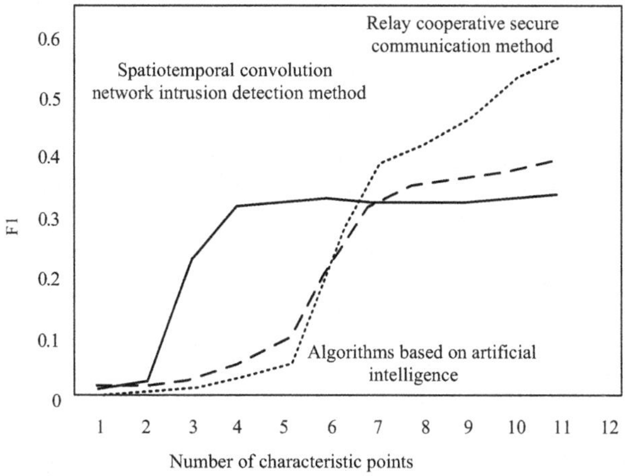

Fig. 10. Comparison results of F1 values of three algorithms

As shown in Fig. 10, when the number of feature points is 4, the F1 value of the traditional detection system is between 0.1–0.3. The research method of this paper is below 0.1. When the number of feature points exceeds 5, the F1 value of the research method in this paper gradually increases, and the F1 value of the traditional method. Because the higher the F1 value, the better the classification performance. Therefore, the system has strong classification performance and strong ability to detect and extract feature points. The accuracy of data classification detection and feature extraction for the same data set is higher than that of the traditional detection system, which not only reduces the difficulty of data analysis and processing, but also improves the overall efficiency of the detection system and accelerates the process of data detection. To sum up, the algorithm based on artificial intelligence has better data classification performance and higher data detection accuracy, which is conducive to the intrusion detection of electric UAV network communication.

6 Conclusion

There are a lot of data resource nodes in AI operation, and more communication nodes can be allocated reasonably through large-scale complex system, and different tasks can be performed well on data resource nodes. Applying trustworthy artificial intelligence to power UAV network communication intrusion prevention optimization system can ensure the task to be carried out. In this paper, the failure recovery mechanism is used to complete the information modeling, and the anti-intrusion ability of this system is determined by the experimental platform. Experimental results show that the optimized algorithm can analyze the parameters of intrusion information in communication process, and determine quantitatively the effect of recovery rate and maximum failure times on scheduling performance. Future in-depth study should be more in-depth analysis when communication data failure, how to carry out quantitative analysis, after confirming the security factors, give more effective anti-intrusion methods.

References

1. Chen, Z., et al.: UAV network intrusion detection method based on spatio-temporal graph convolutional network. J. Beijing Univ. Aeronaut. Astronaut. **47**(5), 1068–1076 (2021)
2. Cao, S., et al.: Secure communication in cognitive radio network assisted by cooperative relay and UAV. Comput. Eng. **47**(6), 203–209 (2021)
3. Liu, S., He, T., Dai, J.: A survey of CRF algorithm based knowledge extraction of elementary mathematics in Chinese. Mob. Netw. Appl. **26**(5), 1891–1903 (2021). https://doi.org/10.1007/s11036-020-01725-x
4. Husnain, G., Anwar, S.: An intelligent probabilistic whale optimization algorithm (i-WOA) for clustering in vehicular ad hoc networks. Int. J. Wireless Inf. Netw. **29**(2), 143–156 (2022)
5. Liu, B., Zhu, Q., Zhu, H.: Trajectory optimization and resource allocation for UAV-assisted relaying communications. Wireless Netw. **26**(1), 739–749 (2020)
6. Gao, P., Li, J., Liu, S.: An introduction to key technology in artificial intelligence and big data driven e-learning and e-education. Mobile Netw. Appl. **26**(5), 2123–2126 (2021). https://doi.org/10.1007/s11036-021-01777-7
7. Zahra, M., Ibrahim, Z., Al-Safi, A.: Using a hybrid algorithm and feature selection for network anomaly intrusion detection. J. Mech. Eng. Res. Dev. **44**(4), 253–262 (2021)
8. Wang, Y., et al.: Aerodynamic optimization of a SCO2radial-inflow turbine based on an improved simulated annealing algorithm. Proc. Inst. Mech. Eng., Part A: J. Power Energy **235**(5), 1039–1052 (2021)
9. Liu, S., et al.: Human memory update strategy: a multi-layer template update mechanism for remote visual monitoring. IEEE Trans. Multimedia **23**, 2188–2198 (2021)
10. Aledhari, M., Razzak, R., Parizi, R.M.: Machine learning for network application security: empirical evaluation and optimization. Comput. Electr. Eng. **91**(16), 107052 (2021)
11. Wang, J.F., Jia, G.W., Lin, J.C., Hou, Z.: Cooperative task allocation for heterogeneous multi-UAV using multi-objective optimization algorithm. J. Cent. South Univ. **27**(2), 432–448 (2020)
12. Cong, J., Wang, X., Wan, L., Huang, M.: Neural network-aided sparse convex optimization algorithm for fast DOA estimation. Trans. Inst. Meas. Control **44**(8), 1649–1655 (2022). https://doi.org/10.1177/01423312211049067
13. Li, S.S., Wang, X.K., Fu, Z.Q.: Construction of an extended target echo platform based on FEKO and MATLAB. Comput. Simul. **39**(1), 5.10–13+33 (2022)

Design of Network Big Data Anti Attack System for Carbon Emission Measurement Based on Deep Learning

Sida Zheng[1(✉)], Shuang Ren[2], Jun Wang[3], Chang Wang[3], and Yaoyu Wang[1]

[1] State Grid Jibei Eelectric Power Company Limited Metrology Center, Beijing 100045, China
yagus14@126.com

[2] School of Computer and Information Technology, Beijing Jiaotong University, Beijing 100044, China

[3] State Grid Jibei Eelectric Power Company Limited Metrology Center Internet Affairs Department, Beijing 100045, China

Abstract. In order to ensure the integrity and security of carbon emission measurement data, a big data anti attack system design of carbon emission measurement network based on deep learning is proposed. Using the deep learning algorithm, the anti attack system of carbon emission measurement network big data is optimized from two aspects of hardware and software functions. Refit the network traffic collector, parallel processor, memory and other hardware equipment, and adjust the connection mode between the communication network and the system circuit. With the support of the hardware system, the corresponding model is established according to the carbon emission measurement principle and network structure, and the standard characteristics of different types of network attacks are set. Collect the real-time data of carbon emission measurement network, extract the network data features by using the deep learning algorithm, and detect the current network attack type through feature matching, so as to realize the big data anti attack function of the system. Through the system test experiment, it is concluded that compared with the traditional anti attack system, under the function of the optimized design system, the amount of successful data of carbon emission measurement network attack is reduced by 2.12 GB, and the response speed is significantly improved.

Keywords: Deep learning · Carbon emission measurement · Network big data · Anti attack system

1 Introduction

Carbon emission is a general term for greenhouse gas emission. Unless otherwise specified, carbon and carbon dioxide are equivalent. Carbon emission is a general concept, and there is no distinction between carbon emission and carbon dioxide emission. Any human activity may cause carbon emissions. For example, ordinary people can cause carbon emissions by simply burning a fire and cooking. The exhaust gas from any object

Y. Xu et al. (Eds.): ML4CS 2022, LNCS 13657, pp. 279–293, 2023.
https://doi.org/10.1007/978-3-031-20102-8_22

after burning will produce carbon emissions [1]. The government recognizes that greenhouse gases have brought and will continue to bring disasters to the earth and mankind, so the terms "carbon emissions" and "carbon neutrality" have become the cultural basis for most people to understand, accept and take action. The research on carbon emission mainly focuses on carbon emission measurement, carbon emission prediction, carbon emission factor analysis, etc. In order to alleviate the greenhouse effect and provide auxiliary tools for carbon neutralization, a carbon emission measurement network is proposed.

Some illegal users will attack and tamper with the data in the carbon emission measurement network for some purposes. In order to ensure the integrity and security of the carbon emission measurement network data, the carbon emission measurement network big data anti attack system is designed and developed. The anti attack system detects the network behavior and makes certain decisions on the network behavior according to the security policy, such as alarm, discarding, blocking, etc. The anti attack system consists of two parts: firewall and intrusion detection. Although the anti attack system consists of these two modules, the anti attack system does not simply combine these two modules.

Deep learning is a kind of representation learning technology developed on the basis of artificial neural network. It is also a branch of machine learning that has developed most rapidly in recent years. Deep learning is an adaptive learning model that can simulate the human brain for analysis by using neural network technology. Its purpose is to simulate or learn the working mechanism of the human brain for data interpretation or analysis. When a traditional machine learning method is used in a task, it needs to extract the features of the data used in the task first, so as to give full play to the ability of the machine learning algorithm. However, it takes a lot of time to extract the features manually, and the emergence of the model based on neural network makes this part of the work possible for the machine to learn automatically. The deep learning algorithm is applied to the optimization design of the anti attack system of carbon emission measurement network big data, in order to improve the anti attack effect of the system and improve the operation performance of the system at the same time.

2 Design of Network Big Data Anti Attack Hardware System

2.1 Network Traffic Collector

The purpose of the design and installation of network traffic collector is to realize the collection of network operation data for carbon emission measurement and provide data support for the judgment of network attack status. The network traffic collector is designed based on netfpga hardware platform. The structure adopts a top-down approach. The internal logic of FPGA is divided into five functional modules, which are sampling module, timing module, address mapping module, flow management module and PCI interface module [2]. The basic structure of the network traffic collector is shown in Fig. 1.

The network traffic collector is the basic part of the entire netfpga flow statistical processing. According to the NetFlow protocol method, it samples and extracts the front-end data packets to reduce the statistical traffic. The module implements two standard sampling methods according to Cisco net protocol: periodic sampling and random

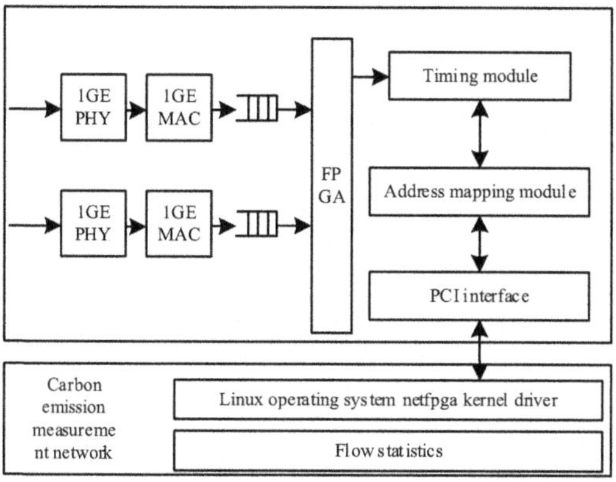

Fig. 1. Structure diagram of network traffic collector for carbon emission measurement

sampling. Periodic sampling is to extract data packets at fixed intervals. After selecting the first data packet, the next data packet is extracted every n data packets. Random sampling is to randomly select n data packets with the same sampling probability, and the probability of each data packet being sampled is the same. The time tag refers to the protocol standard of NetFlow, and uses a 32-bit timer as the statistical time tag, which can meet the range requirements of measurement time in the actual carbon emission measurement network environment [3]. The address mapping module uses the flow identification information to establish the mapping relationship between the flow and the storage address. Generally, the network uses five tuples to identify a stream. Because hash operation will inevitably lead to hash conflicts, and a large number of conflicts will reduce the accuracy of statistics, a two-stage hash method is used to reduce the probability of hash collision. The two-stage hash method can not eliminate the hash conflict. In order to ensure the correctness of the flow information statistics, it is necessary to determine the timeout of the data flow, delete the aging and timeout data flow statistics in time, and then effectively update, manage and maintain the storage space of the table item information. The PCI interface module uses high-speed stream statistical information transmission between platforms by using high-bandwidth PCI bus protocol and high-performance DMA controller to realize hardware communication between the service host and netfpga platform. In order to complete the correct and effective processing of data stream, the Gigabit MAC core of XilinxFPGA is used to generate four Gigabit Ethernet network cards as transceivers for network data stream processing.

2.2 Parallel Processor

Network processor is a kind of processor specially used to process network application packets, which belongs to a kind of integrated circuit. The optimized design of the carbon emission measurement network big data anti attack system parallelizes the traditional processor. The optimized concurrent processor is composed of 9 RISC processors, several memory control units, MFS interfaces and PCI bus interfaces encapsulated in one chip. The design structure of the concurrent processor in the system is shown in Fig. 2.

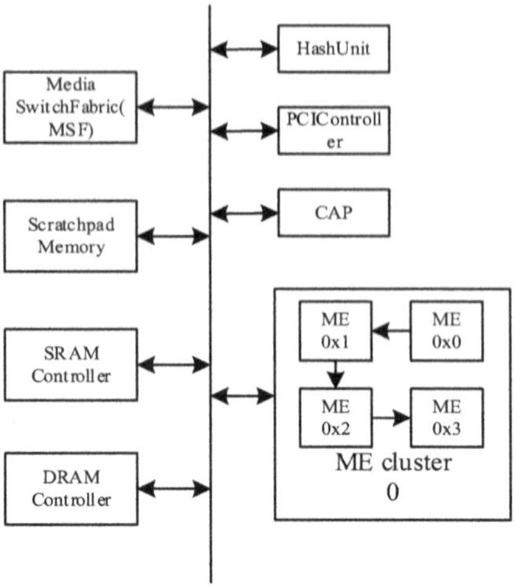

Fig. 2. Internal structure diagram of system parallel processor

The 32-bit programmable micro engine in the parallel processor operates at 400 MHz. Each micro engine can support 4 to 8 threads, and each thread has an independent program counter. It undertakes most of the network packet processing work. One intelxscale core processor with operating frequency of 400 MHz [4]. The MSF interface is used to connect the physical layer devices and the switch fabric. It consists of several independent interfaces, which can be configured separately to support Utopia, pos-phy or csix protocols. The clock frequency of the interface bus is 25–125 MHz.

2.3 Communication Network

The system communication transmission network can adopt the network topology of optical fiber self-healing ring, or the backbone network topology of dual ring tangent and multi ring tangent. The configuration intersection mechanism is perfect. Both the intersecting ring and the tangent ring can realize the service protection when a section of optical fiber is interrupted in each of the two SNCP rings [5]. At the same time, the intersecting ring can protect the business when a single intersecting node fails, which is applicable to scenarios that require failure protection for a single intersecting node in the ring. In addition, the SDH complex network structure can also be adjusted by means of shared optical fiber virtual path protection, shared optical path protection of multiplexing section, DNI networking, etc., which can be reasonably planned according to the specific situation to form the SDH complex network and improve the rationality of the SDH transmission network structure. Through the optimization of the system communication network, the transmission between the data collection results of the real-time carbon emission measurement network and the processor is realized.

2.4 Carbon Emission Measurement Network System Memory

In order to improve the running speed and flexibility of the big data anti attack system of carbon emission measurement network, it can be improved on the basis of the basic

Harvard structure by providing multiple program and data memories, which adopt this enhanced Harvard structure. The system memory includes one program code memory and two data memories. The program code memory only stores instructions, the program data memory stores program data, and the data memory stores general data. The access to these memories is independent of each other. The system can provide two operands while fetching instructions, which can greatly improve the execution efficiency of the system. The access address needs to be converted and expanded to 15 bits, which is divided into four pages for management [6]. The data memory is divided into on-chip and off-chip parts. The on-chip capacity is 16k*16, and the access address is 14 bits. It is divided into two pages for management. The address space 0x2000-ox3fdf of the data memory is reserved for the system, and the top 32 addresses ox3feo-ox3fff are occupied by the control register of the memory image.

The clock circuit and reset circuit in the system are optimized, and the optimization results are shown in Fig. 3.

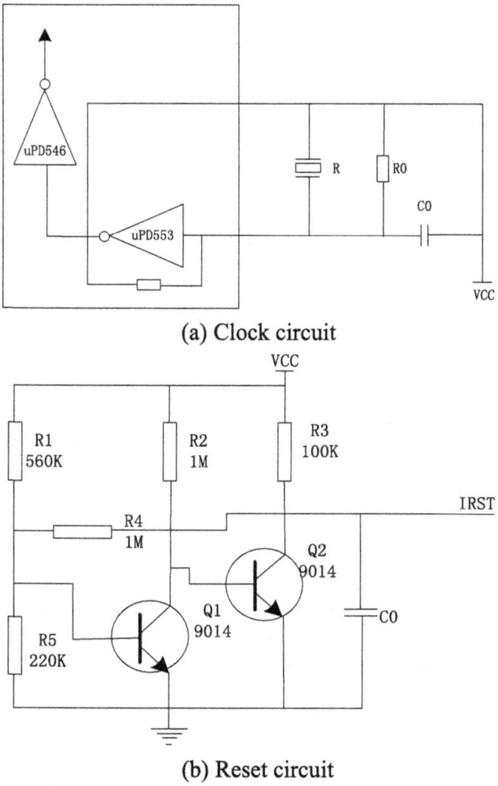

Fig. 3. System circuit diagram

The optimized design of carbon emission measurement requires different clock frequencies for equipment components in the network big data anti attack hardware system. All clocks of the platform are provided by FPGA. The reset module can effectively ensure the normal operation of the platform and the ability to correct errors, which is very important to ensure the normal operation of the platform. For the reset control of the system, a reset management module is specially designed in FPG to ensure the normal and orderly reset of all devices.

3 Software Function Design of Network Big Data Anti Attack System

3.1 Construction of Carbon Emission Measurement Network Model

The energy consumption of power generation in power system is mainly high carbon emission fossil fuels such as gasoline and diesel. In order to facilitate the calculation of carbon emission of power system, the fuel consumption method is used to calculate the carbon emission of power system. The calculation model can be quantitatively expressed as:

$$C_1 = \sum_{i=1}^{3} A_i \times \kappa_p \times Q_i \times 10^{-10} \tag{1}$$

where, variables A_i, κ_p and Q_i are the fuel consumption, carbon emission coefficient and power generation of power system respectively. The specific value of variable Q_i can be expressed as:

$$Q_i = P_{\text{generation}} \times t_{\text{generation}} \tag{2}$$

where $P_{\text{generation}}$ and $t_{\text{generation}}$ are the generation power and generation duration respectively. By substituting the calculation results of formula 2 into Formula 1, the carbon emission calculation results of any power station in the power system can be obtained [7]. In the above way, the location and carbon emissions of power stations are marked in the power grid environment, and the construction results of the carbon emission measurement network model are obtained in combination with the power grid topology.

3.2 Set Network Attack Standard Characteristics

In order to obtain a good anti attack effect of network big data for carbon emission measurement, it is necessary to determine the types of attacks suffered by the current network big data. The victims are unable to provide services and communicate with other hosts, and their attacks are often many to one. Figure 4 shows the principle of DDoS attack.

The process of DDoS attack generally includes three stages: collecting information, occupying the puppet machine and implementing the attack. The most important thing to launch a DDoS attack in the stage of collecting information is to establish a botnet. After fully obtaining the information of the attacker, the attacker will select the host with security vulnerabilities and good network conditions, and control it by bottling it [8]. When an attacker controls a large number of puppet machines, it becomes very simple to launch a DDoS attack. It only needs to send commands to the controller to attack

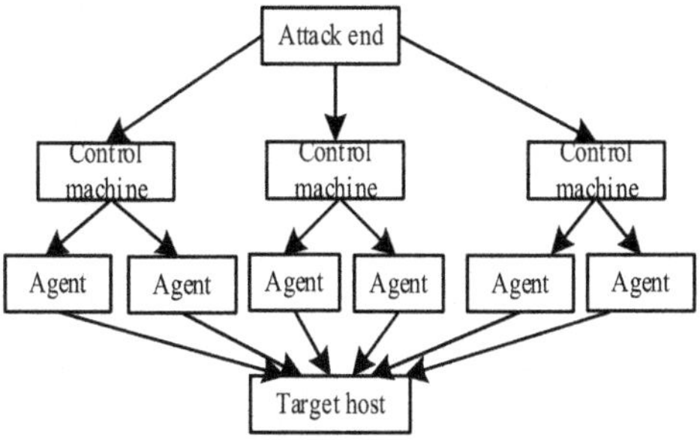

Fig. 4. Schematic diagram of DDoS attack

the victim.According to the above DDoS attack principle, the change characteristics of network operation parameters under the action of this attack can be obtained and marked as $\tau_{\text{standard},DDoS}$. Similarly, the action principles and corresponding characteristics of other network attack types can be obtained, which can be used as the evaluation standard to judge whether there is an attack on the network and the type of attack.

3.3 Collect Real-Time Data of Carbon Emission Measurement Network

The network real-time data acquisition module mainly carries out the functions of web application traffic capture, protocol analysis and traffic recording. The function of this part is realized by using the socket library in Python. Socket is a network communication library integrated in Python for sending network requests and responses. It can access all methods of the socket interface of the operating system. In the actual implementation, the socket is used to monitor the specific port of the host, and all the data sent to the port is obtained, so as to achieve uninterrupted access to real-time traffic. The minimum and maximum normalization method is used to perform linear transformation on the original collected data. The processing process can be expressed as follows:

$$x = \frac{x_{\text{collection}} - x_{\text{Min}}}{x_{\text{Max}} - x_{\text{Min}}} \tag{3}$$

where $x_{\text{collection}}$ is the initial collected data of the carbon emission network, x_{Min} and x_{Max} correspond to the minimum and maximum values of the initial collected data. According to the above process, the carbon emission measurement network data collection and processing are realized.

3.4 Extracting Network Data Features Using Deep Learning Algorithm

In the optimized emission measurement network big data anti attack system, the cyclic neural network is selected as the execution object of the deep learning algorithm. Cyclic neural network is generally used to analyze the data associated with time, fully mine the sequence information between the data, and has the ability to trace the source. Cyclic neural network has memory, parameter sharing and Turing completeness, so it has certain advantages in learning the nonlinear characteristics of sequences.Figure 5 shows the basic structure of the recurrent neural network.

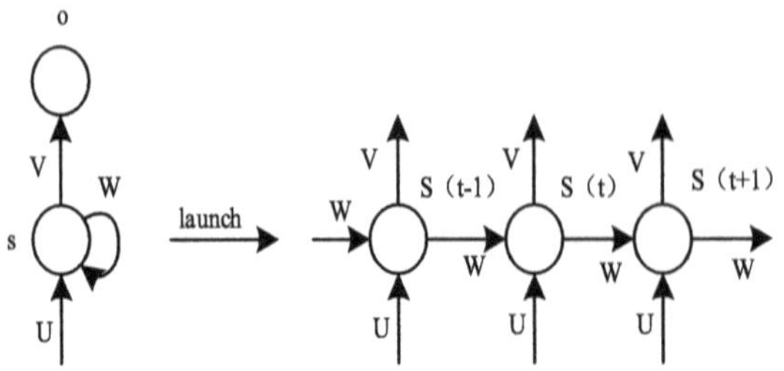

Fig. 5. Structure diagram of cyclic neural network

Cyclic neural networks usually assume that the input data are independent of each other and have no time dependence. The output of the recurrent neural network model depends on the sum of the current input information and the previous memory information. The value of the recurrent neural network at time t depends not only on the current input value, but also on the memory value at time T-1 [9]. The feedback loop of the recurrent neural network and the time sequence information of its input data, the recurrent neural network can perform tasks that the feedforward network cannot perform, and the sequence information of different time steps is stored in the hidden state of the recurrent neural network. Mathematically, the process of carrying memory can be described as:

$$h_t = g(\mathrm{W}x_t + Uh_{t-1}) \tag{4}$$

where W and U are the weighting matrix and state matrix of the recurrent neural network respectively, h_{t-1} and h_t are the hidden states at time t and time $t-1$ respectively, x_t is the input value at time t, and $g()$ is the activation function. Using the cyclic neural network represented by formula 4, the deep learning algorithm is implemented to extract the features of the carbon emission measurement network. The extraction results of statistical characteristics of IP packets can be expressed as:

$$\tau_{IPDCF} = \sum \{ \mathrm{N}_{Packet} \}_{\Delta t} \tag{5}$$

where N_{Packet} is the number of network packets and Δt is the sampling time of packets. By substituting the real-time collected and processed carbon emission measurement network data into formula 4, the feature extraction results of network traffic peak value, valley value, average value and other features can be obtained.

3.5 Detecting Carbon Emissions and Measuring Cyber Attacks

In the process of carbon emission measurement and network DDoS attack detection, it is considered that the packets generated by the puppet host's DDoS attack on the network_ The in message will be much higher than the normal one. According to this feature, a modified attribution function is constructed for the traffic. The function construction results are as follows:

$$\varphi(t) = \begin{cases} 0 & F(\Delta t) < Avg(f) \\ \frac{[F(\Delta t) - Avg(f)]^2}{[F(\Delta t)]^2} & Avg(f) \le F(\Delta t) \le Max \\ 1 & F(\Delta t) \ge \mathrm{Max} \end{cases} \tag{6}$$

where $F(\Delta t)$ is the packet generated by openflow switch in unit time_ In and notify the controller of the number. f is the number of packetin messages generated. $Avg(f)$ and Max are the lower limit traffic and upper limit traffic. When the specific value of $F(\Delta t)$ is lower than the lower limit of traffic or higher than the upper limit of traffic, it is determined that there is an attack on the current carbon emission measurement network, and the attack type is DDoS attack.In addition, formula 7 is used to calculate the similarity between the current network data features and the set standard features, so as to judge the current network attack status and attack type.

$$\psi(i) = \sqrt{\left(\tau_{\text{standard},i} - \tau_{com}\right)^2} \tag{7}$$

where $\tau_{\text{standard},i}$ is the standard feature of type i attack set, and τ_{com} is the comprehensive network feature extracted by the deep learning algorithm. If the calculation result of formula 7 is higher than ψ_0, it is determined that the current carbon emission measurement network has attack behavior and the attack type is i. otherwise, the next attack type needs to be matched until the detection result is obtained. If the matching results do not meet the threshold requirements, it is determined that the current network has no attack behavior.

3.6 Realize the Anti Attack Function of Carbon Emission Measurement Network Big Data

The anti attack program is executed for the carbon emission measurement network with attack behavior. The anti attack principle is shown in Fig. 6.

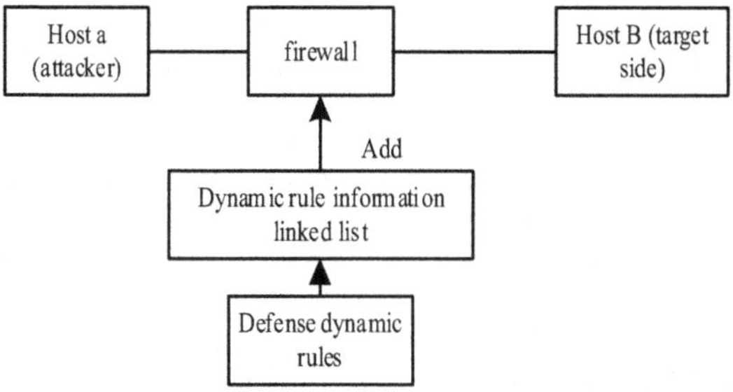

Fig. 6. Anti attack schematic diagram of network big data for carbon emission measurement

The optimized anti attack system adopts a two-layer defense mechanism. The netfilter/iptables firewall with intrusion detection function is placed in the gateway to complete the first layer of defense from the external network to the internal network. The firewall host is connected to the internal and external network, and is equipped with two network cards: network card 1 is connected to the external network, and network card 2 is connected to the internal network. The firewall not only stores its own static filtering rules, but also iptables intrusion detection rules transformed from CVE based snort rules, as well as dynamic filtering rules generated by the interaction of an attack and the firewall [10]. The second layer of defense is completed by cooperation between Snort and firewall. Snort Intrusion detection system is deployed in the intranet. After discovering the attack, it immediately notifies the firewall to block it. Snort and firewall transmit blocking information to each other based on client/sever mode. The dynamic rule information linked list in the following figure stores the control information of the dynamic rules that have been added to the firewall.

4 System Test

In order to test the feasibility of the network big data anti attack system for carbon emission measurement based on deep learning, a system test experiment is designed. System test refers to the test of the whole system, taking hardware, software and operators as a whole to check whether it does not conform to the system specification. This test can find errors in system analysis and design. By testing the anti attack function of the system, the optimization effect of the system is verified.

4.1 Configure System Development and Operation Environment

There are certain requirements for memory and graphics card in the hardware environment of the system test experiment. A total of 6 pieces of 16GB memory and NVIDIA geforcegtx1660super graphics card are used in the experiment. This configuration can improve the efficiency in processing data and model training. The software environment uses Python language to implement the model code, and pytoch machine learning library to implement the deep learning model. The carbon emission measurement network is selected as the function object of the system. The carbon emission measurement network includes 2 hosts, which respectively simulate LV and convert to IV, and AI, 1 openflow switch and 1 opendaylight controller. The IP network includes 1 router and 1 test server.

4.2 Prepare a Network Attack Tool for Carbon Emission Measurement

The tfn2k tool is used to simulate the network attack behavior. The tfn2k uses the distributed client/server function, stealth and encryption technology and various functions to control any number of remote computers to generate anonymous denial of service attacks and remote shell access on demand. IP switching technology is used in tfn2k. At the same time, tfn2k can generate most types of attacks: UDP flooding, tcp/syn flooding, ICMP flooding and mixed attacks, including various attacks. In this experiment, a number of different types of attack programs were set up to constitute the attack scenarios of the experiment.

4.3 Prepare Network Data Samples

Select the data in HTTP dataset CSIC 2010 data set,Use the flow generator to synthesize the carbon emission measurement network data and the attack program to generate the system test data samples. Table 1 shows the preparation of carbon emission measurement

Table 1. Sample of carbon emission measurement data

Year	2018	2019	2020	2021
Area A	36.95	36.43	35.24	35.67
Area B	23.65	24.04	21.84	19.88
Area C	90.42	90.73	88.43	84.23
Area D	21.16	21.60	20.75	20.14
Area E	54.66	54.95	53.85	51.39

data samples in a certain region.Divide a certain area into five areas: A area, B area, C area, D area and E area.

Under the function of traffic generator, the size of data packets and the rate of generating traffic can obey different distributions, such as uniform distribution, exponential distribution, normal distribution, Poisson distribution, Pareto distribution, Cauchy distribution, gamma distribution and Weibull distribution, and even the distribution law can be customized. Figure 7 shows the data samples of the carbon emission measurement network under DDoS attacks.

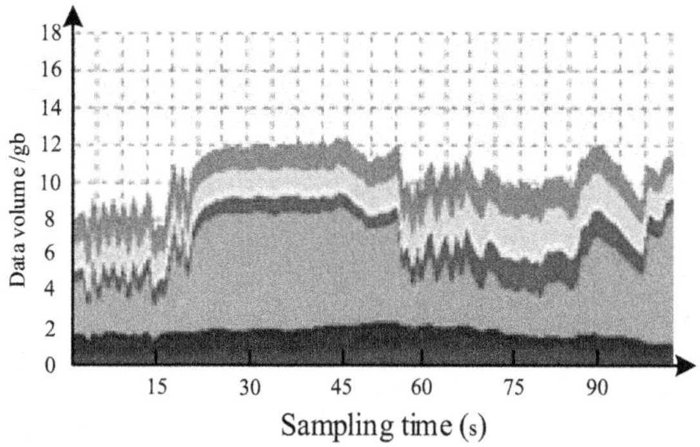

Fig. 7. Schematic diagram of carbon emission measurement network data sample

The above implementation capabilities can be used to test subsequent system attacks with different flow rates and sizes.

4.4 Set Operation Parameters of Deep Learning Algorithm

As the optimized carbon emission measurement network big data anti attack system applies the deep learning algorithm, it is necessary to set the relevant operating parameters in the experimental environment. Common super parameters include: number of hidden layers, number of hidden layer nodes, learning rate, regularization, dropout rate, optimizer, activation function, etc. Different super parameters have different effects on the detection ability of the model. The ability of neural network can be greatly improved by setting appropriate super parameters. In the actual parameter adjustment process, this experiment adopts the method of phased parameter adjustment to optimize the super parameters. Phase by phase parameter adjustment: first conduct a preliminary range search, and then narrow the range to conduct a more detailed search according to the place where the good results appear. Or fix other superparameters according to the empirical value, test one of them purposefully, and iterate step by step until all the superparameters are selected. The advantage of this method is that it can get better results in the number of priority attempts. After initializing the super parameters according to the empirical parameters, perform parameter tuning in the order of hidden layer size, learning rate, batchsize and dropout rate. The learning rate is set to 0.001, the batchsize and dropout rates are 256 and 0.75 respectively, and the maximum number of iterations is 200.

4.5 System Test Process and Result Analysis

Under the cooperative operation mode of hardware equipment and software program, the set operation parameters and prepared data samples are imported into the system operation environment, and the network attack program is started at the same time. The function realization results are obtained by optimizing the operation of the anti attack system, as shown in Fig. 8.

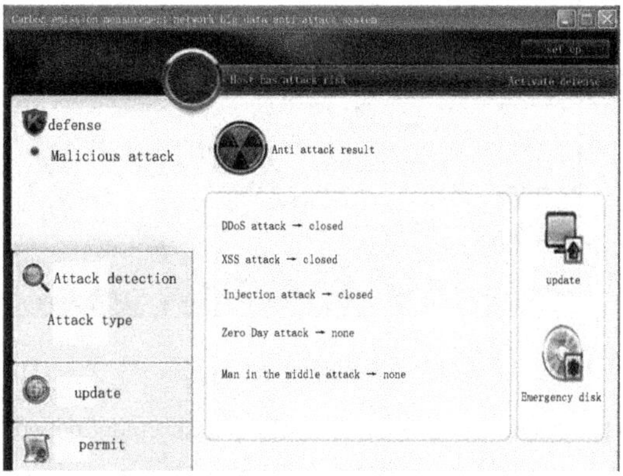

Fig. 8. Operation results of network anti attack system for carbon emission measurement

The system test experiment set the traditional host based anti attack system as the comparison system. In order to realize the quantitative comparison of the anti attack function of the system, two quantitative test indicators, namely, the number of successful attacks hitting the active port and the anti attack response time, are set. The numerical results of the data volume indicator of successful attacks are as follows:

$$N_{\text{attack}} = N_{in} - N_{\text{receive}} \tag{8}$$

where N_{in} and N_{receive} are the actual amount of data generated and received in the carbon emission measurement network respectively. Finally, it is calculated that the larger the value of N_{attack}, the worse the anti attack function of the corresponding system. In addition, the numerical results of the anti attack program response time index are as follows:

$$\Delta T_{response} = t_{defense} - t_{attack} \tag{9}$$

In formula 9, the variable $t_{defense}$ represents the time when the system attack task is completed, and t_{attack} is the time when the attack program acts on the carbon emission measurement network. The larger the calculation result of the response time index of the anti attack program, the worse the anti attack function of the corresponding system. Through the statistics of relevant data, the test results of successful data volume of system attack are obtained, as shown in Table 2.

Table 2. Test results of data volume of successful system attack

Number of experiments	Actual data volume of carbon emission measurement network /GB	Actual amount of data received by host based anti attack system/GB	Carbon emission measurement based on in-depth learning actual data received under the action of network big data anti attack system/GB
1	15.0	13.5	14.5
2	15.0	14.3	15.0
3	15.0	12.2	15.0
4	15.0	13.4	14.8
5	15.0	14.1	15.0
6	15.0	10.2	14.6
7	15.0	12.8	15.0
8	15.0	11.4	15.0

By substituting the data in Table 2 into formula 8, it is calculated that the average amount of successful attack data under the action of host based anti attack system is 2.26GB, while the average amount of successful attack data under the action of optimized design system is 0.14GB. In addition, through the calculation of formula 9, the test and comparison results of the response time of the system's anti attack program are obtained. The shorter the response time is, the faster the system's anti attack response speed is, as shown in Fig. 9.

As can be seen from Fig. 9, the response time of the host based carbon emission measurement network big data anti attack system is generally 4-5s, while the response time of the optimized network big data carbon emission measurement anti attack system based on deep learning is 1-2s. The response time of the optimized design system is shorter and the response speed is faster. This proves that the optimized network big data

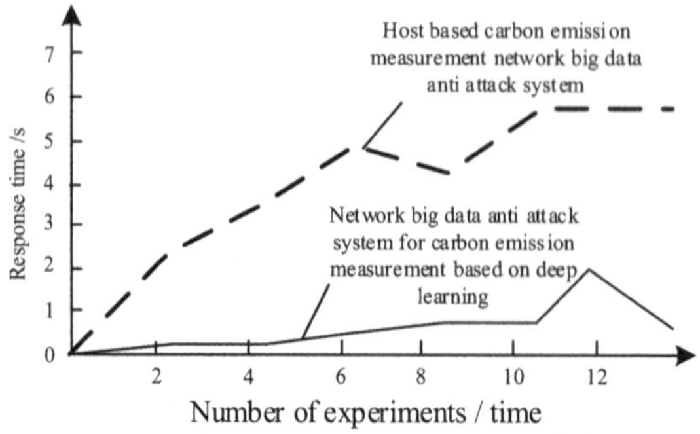

Fig. 9. Test results of network data anti attack response speed

anti attack system for carbon emission measurement based on deep learning has better anti attack effect.This is because this paper uses deep learning algorithm to optimize the design of carbon emission measurement network big data anti attack system from two aspects of hardware and software functions. According to the carbon emission measurement principle and network structure, the corresponding model is established to set the standard characteristics of different types of network attacks.

5 Conclusion

The carbon emission measurement network is of great significance to improve the air environment. Through the optimization design of the carbon emission measurement network big data anti attack system based on in-depth learning, the integrity and security of the carbon emission measurement network data are guaranteed to the greatest extent, which is conducive to the smooth development of carbon emission management.

Aknowledgement. 1. Project Name: Research on key technologies of air pollution control based on power big data, science and Technology Project Supported by State Grid Corporation of China (Contract No.: 5200-202114093A-0-0-00).

2. NSFC FUNDED PROJECT: Research on mission safe unloading and reliable scheduling system for multi-modal and multi-user edge vehicular cloud services (No. 62072025).

References

1. Wang, C.-M.: Mathematical modeling and simulation of network attack detection based on incremental learning. Comput. Simul. **38**(01), 273–306 (2021)
2. Bosah, C.P., Li, S., Ampofo, G.K.M., Liu, K.: Dynamic nexus between energy consumption, economic growth, and urbanization with carbon emission: evidence from panel PMG-ARDL estimation. Environ. Sci. Pollut. Res. **28**(43), 61201–61212 (2021). https://doi.org/10.1007/s11356-021-14943-x
3. Liu, S., Liu, D., Muhammad, K., Ding, W.: Effective template update mechanism in visual tracking with background clutter. Neurocomputing **458**, 615–625 (2021)

4. Yang, C.-T., Chan, Y.-W., Liu, J.-C., Kristiani, E., Lai, C.-H.: Cyberattacks detection and analysis in a network log system using XGBoost with ELK stack. Soft Comput. **26**(11), 5143–5157 (2022). https://doi.org/10.1007/s00500-022-06954-8
5. Wang, S., Pei, Q., Zhang, Y., Liu, X., Tang, G.: A hybrid cyber defense mechanism to mitigate the persistent scan and foothold attack. Secure. Commun. Network. **2020**, 1–15 (2020)
6. Liu, S., Wang, S., Liu, X., Lin, C.-T., Lv, Z.: Fuzzy detection aided real-time and robust visual tracking under complex environments. IEEE Trans. Fuzzy Syst. **29**(1), 90–102 (2021)
7. Liu, S., et al.: Human memory update strategy: a multi-layer template update mechanism for remote visual monitoring. IEEE Trans. Multimedia **23**, 2188–2198 (2021)
8. Zhan, K.: Design of computer network security defense system based on artificial intelligence and neural network. J. Intell. Fuzzy Syst. **9**, 1–13 (2021)
9. Hao, W., Yao, P., Yang, T., Yang, Q.: Industrial cyber–physical system defense resource allocation using distributed anomaly detection. IEEE Internet Things J. **9**(22), 22304–22314
10. Sengupta, S., Chowdhary, A., Sabur, A., Alshamrani, A., Huang, D., Kambhampati, S.: A survey of moving target defenses for network security. IEEE Commun. Surv. Tutorials **22**(3), 1909–1941 (2020)

An Efficient Particle YOLO Detector for Urine Sediment Detection

Zejian Chen[1], Rong Hu[1], Fukun Chen[2], Haoyi Fan[2], Fum Yew Ching[3], Zuoyong Li[4], and Shimei Su[5](✉)

[1] Fujian Provincial Key Laboratory of Big Data Mining and Applications, School of Computer Science and Mathematics, Fujian University of Technology, Fuzhou 350118, Fujian, China

[2] School of Computer and Artificial Intelligence, Zhengzhou University, Zhengzhou 450001, Henan, China

[3] School of Computer Sciences, Universiti Sains Malaysia, Penang 11800, Malaysia

[4] Fujian Provincial Key Laboratory of Information Processing and Intelligent Control, College of Computer and Control Engineering, Minjiang University, Fuzhou 350121, Fujian, China

[5] School of Electrical Engineering, Zhengzhou University, Zhengzhou 450001, Henan, China

smsu@zzu.edu.cn

Abstract. Urine sediment detection is an essential aid in assessing kidney health. Traditional machine learning approaches treat urine sediment particle detection as an image classification task, segmenting particles for detection based on information such as edges or thresholds. However, the segmentation of sediment particles is complex due to the low contrast and weak edge characteristics of urine sediment images. In this paper, we consider urine sediment particle detection as a object detection task and propose the YOLOv5s-CBL, a detector dedicated to particle detection. Specifically, to mitigate the impact of background noise on detection accuracy, we inherit CBAM on the YOLOv5s model to help the network filter useless noise information and find regions of interest to extract target features. Then, we expand the original three-scale feature layer to improve the sensitivity of the model to larger-scale target sediment particles. Finally, we use the BiFPN structure instead of the original PANet combined with the FPN structure, which can more effectively fuse multiple different scales of information to improve the detection performance of the model. We compared state-of-the-art methods on two real-world datasets, and the experimental results demonstrated the effectiveness of YOLOv5s-CBL.

Keywords: Urine sediment detection · Deep learning · YOLOv5

Y. Xu et al. (Eds.): ML4CS 2022, LNCS 13657, pp. 294–308, 2023.
https://doi.org/10.1007/978-3-031-20102-8_23

1 Introduction

Kidney disease is a major threat to human health and affects millions of people worldwide [20]. As an important method in analyzing kidney diseases, urine sediment detection can reflect the health of patients' kidneys through the changes in sediment particles, which is an important basis for subsequent clinical diagnosis. However, the diagnostic accuracy of urine sediment detection is dependent on the professionalism and clinical experience of the medical personnel. Meanwhile, it is easily affected by external factors such as visual bias and equipment malfunction. Therefore more and more automated urine analyzers based on machine learning methods are developed for the detection of urine deposits [9,13,15,19,30].

Traditional machine learning algorithms regard urine sediment detection as an image classification task. First, the data is preprocessed to segment the sediment particles from the urine image. Then the main features of the sediment are extracted by a CNN network. Finally, the extracted features are fed into a trained classifier for classification. However, most urine sediment images have low contrast and weak edge features. Therefore, segmenting the entire image's urine sediment particles is not easy. Recently, deep learning-based urine sediment detection has started to be used to solve the segmentation problem and achieved excellent results. So, similar to Liang et al. [10,11,26], we also consider urine sediment inspection as an object detection task.

In this paper, we propose the YOLOv5s-CBL model, an end-to-end object detection model that is more suitable for urine sediment detection. Specifically, we first considered the sparsity of urine images. To mitigate the impact of background noise on detection accuracy, we integrated CBAM [24] on top of the YOLOv5s model to help the network filter the noisy information from urine images to find the region of interest to extract target features. Then to improve the sensitivity of the model to larger-scale target sediment particles, we extended the original three-scale feature layer by using the added 64x downsampling as a fourth feature layer to detect larger-scale sediment particles in the urine images. Finally, to obtain better feature representation capability, we replace the original PANet [12] combined with the FPN [21] structure with the BiFPN [21] structure to fuse feature information of different scales in a targeted manner. The comparison with state-of-the-art methods on two urine sediment particle detection datasets demonstrates the effectiveness of the YOLOv5s-CBL.

The main contributions of this paper are as follows:

- We propose a urine sediment detection method based on an improved YOLOv5 model. By introducing a larger scale detection head and CBAM to help the network capture sediment particle targets at different scales in sparse urine images and using a BiFPN feature aggregation structure to fuse feature information at different scales to obtain better representation capability.
- We add a larger scale prediction head to detect larger sediment objects in the dataset, and filter the effect of background noise information with the integrated CBAM to help the network find the target region of interest from the whole image.

- We optimize the feature aggregation structure of the neck network by replacing the structure of PANet in YOLOv5 with BiFPN. While reducing the number of parameters, the network can learn the importance of distribution weights of each feature in a targeted manner to obtain better representation capability.
- We have conducted extensive experiments on two real-world datasets comparing DFPN, BCPNet, PVANet, YOLOv3-tiny, YOLOv3 and YOLOv5s models, and the experimental results demonstrate the effectiveness of the proposed method.

Our paper is structured as follows. We first discuss related work (Sect. 2) and present YOLOv5s-CBL in Sect. 3. Experimental results are presented in Sect. 4. Sections 5 and 6 are the conclusion and acknowledgements, respectively.

2 Related Work

2.1 Urine Sediment Detection

Traditional urine sediment detection uses manual microscopy to count the sediment of centrifuged urine samples. However, the accuracy of detection depends on the skill level of the cytologist and increases the amount of labor. Therefore it cannot be applied on a large scale. Machine learning methods have been widely used for urine sediment image analysis to improve standardization and detection accuracy. Ranzato et al. [15] developed a simple and generalized bioparticle identification system. Using a hybrid Gaussian classifier to identify 12 urine sediment particles achieved 93% accuracy. Liu et al. [13] used an SVM classifier to classify a variety of urine sediment particles, including RBC, WBC, Cast, and Crystal, and achieved 91% accuracy. Liang et al. [9] used SVM and decision tree to construct a classification filter, which improved the detection accuracy to 93.72%. Shen et al. [19] constructed a multiclass classifier based on the AdaBoost learning algorithm and SVM, which effectively used Harr wavelet features to improve the recognition accuracy. Zhou et al. [30] used an artificial neural network model to classify 12 classes of sediment images after segmentation, and the recognition accuracy of red blood cells reached 96.19%. Although traditional machine learning methods achieve excellent performance, they can only detect limited types of urine sediment particles. Moreover, the low contrast and weak edge features of urine sediment images make segmentation to extract features more difficult.

Recently deep learning-based urine sediment detection has been proposed to solve the problem mentioned above. Zhang et al. [28] used a pre-trained Faster R-CNN [18] model to detect blood cells in urine sediment images and achieved an F1 score of 91.4%. However, only two classes of red blood cells and white blood cells could be detected. Pan et al. [14] used convolutional neural networks to identify three classes of urine sediment particles and achieved 98.07% accuracy. Ji et al. [7] developed a particle recognition system based on AlexNet and the area feature algorithm (AFA). The network was trained by 300,000 images and finally achieved 97% accuracy. Liang et al. [10] identified urine sediment particles in an end-to-end manner based on trimmed-SSD, Faster R-CNN [18], PVANet [8], vand Multi-Scale Faster R-CNN [4] models. The mAP reached 84.1% in 7 categories of urine sediment particles. Liang et al. [11] proposed DFPN based on FPN [21] by combining DenseNet, which can effectively eliminate the category confusion problem in urine sediment images and achieved 86.9% mAP. Yan et al. [26] used the bidirectional context propagation network BCPNet [2] for urine sediment particle detection, improving the localization and classification ability of the model. However, although the deep learning-based approach effectively overcomes the problem of complex segmentation and feature extraction, it requires a large number of images with manual annotation. In addition, these methods have many problems in practical application, such as operation speed and endpoint deployment.

2.2 Object Detection

Object detection is a core problem in the field of computer vision, where the goal is to isolate a specific object from the input image and obtain both the corresponding class and location information. Compared with classification tasks, object detection requires more stringent recognition ability of deep learning models, which need to fully understand the foreground and background information of the image to find the target of interest in the background.

To solve the above problem, Ross Girshick et al. [1] proposed a representative two-stage object detection model, R-CNN. R-CNN [1] divides the detection process into two independent phases, first extracting several candidate regions from the target image and then scaling each candidate region to a fixed size and feeding it into the CNN network for classification and recognition. Although R-CNN [1] significantly improves the performance of target detection tasks, the complex detection process and slow inference speed prevent it from being applied to terminals for real-time detection.

To achieve end-to-end object detection and improve detection speed, Joseph Redmon et al. [16] proposed the one-stage target detection model YOLO. It treats the object detection task as a regression problem, predicting the position and class of the object directly from the entire input image through a unified framework, significantly improving the detection speed. Compared to other object detection models, the YOLO series is faster and more scalable for a wider range of applications. Wang et al. [23] proposed a YOLOv5-CHE model dedicated to leukocyte image recognition based on YOLOv5, which achieved 99.3% mAP. Wang et al. [22] used the improved YOLOv5-P2 model to detect rebar ends, significantly improving detection accuracy on dense small targets. Yang et al. [27] developed a face recognition system using the YOLOv5 model to screen whether a mask is worn. The results substantially outperformed other classical object detection models to achieve 97.90% accuracy. Although the YOLO series is widely used in industrial and medical fields, there is still a gap in the study of YOLOv5-based urine sediment detection. Therefore, we improved the YOLOv5 model on two urine sediment particle datasets to make it suitable for urine sediment detection.

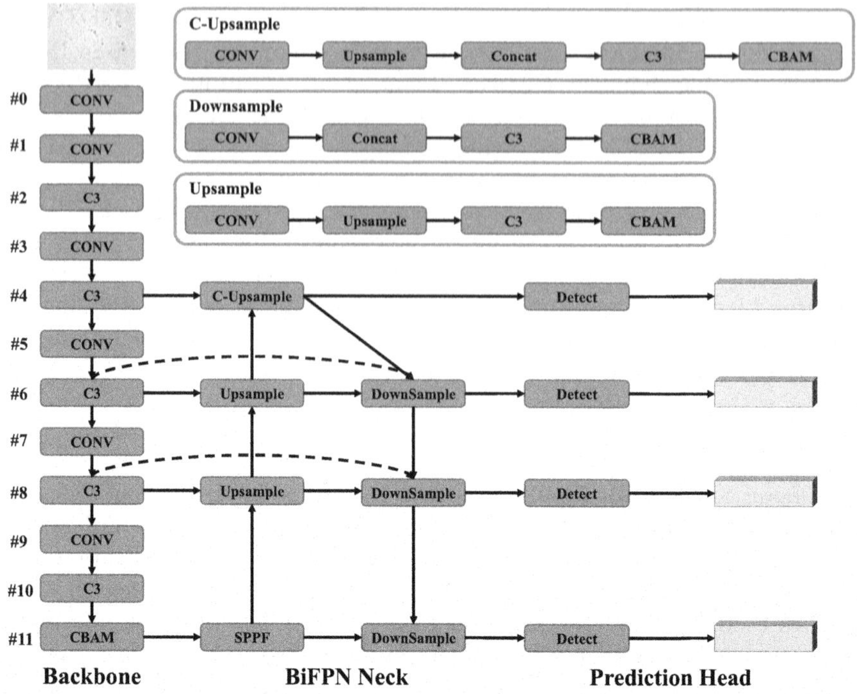

Fig. 1. The architecture of the proposed YOLOv5s-CBL. (1) CSPDarknet53 backbone with a CBAM module. (2) Neck using the structure of the BiFPN. (3) Feature map of four prediction heads using the CBAM module in neck.

3 Method

3.1 Overview of YOLOv5s-CBL

This work aims to develop an end-to-end urine sediment detection system. Therefore, we optimized the YOLOv5s model based on two urine sediment particle examination datasets and proposed a YOLOv5s-CBL model that is more suitable for urine sediment detection. The structure of YOLOv5s-CBL is shown in Fig. 1.

Prediction Head for Larger Object. The original YOLOv5 uses a three-scale feature layer to detect large, medium, and small targets in the dataset. However, we found that Dataset1 contains many larger-scale urine sediment particles. Therefore, the detection performance of YOLOv5 on these targets is not satisfactory. To improve the detection accuracy, we extended the original three-scale feature layer. We added 64x downsampling after 32x downsampling as a fourth prediction head to detect urine sediment particles at a larger scale. Figure 1 shows that the prediction head has a larger perceptual field and is more sensitive to larger-scale targets. With the four-scale feature layer, our model makes full use of both shallow feature information and high-level semantic information to improve the detection performance significantly.

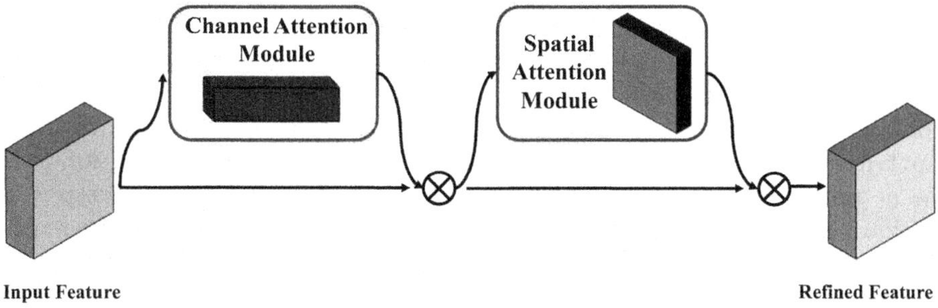

Fig. 2. The overview of CBAM.

CBAM. We found that urine sediment particles occupy only a tiny area of the image, so a large amount of background information would negatively affect the detection accuracy of the model. We integrated the CBAM [24] into YOLOv5 to help the model extract useful target information from the whole image and filter the interference of noisy information.

CBAM [24] is a simple and effective lightweight attention module that can be integrated into any CNN architecture for end-to-end training. As shown in the Fig. 2, CBAM [24] contains two submodules, CAM (Channel Attention Module) and SAM (Spatial Attention Module), which perform attention operations in the channel and spatial dimensions, respectively. The CAM module compresses the input image in the spatial dimension to make the model more focused on the meaningful information part of the image. The channel attention is calculated as follows:

$$\begin{aligned} M_c(F) &= \sigma(MLP(AvgPool(F)) + MLP(MaxPool(F))) \\ &= \sigma(W_1(W_0(F^c_{avg})) + \sigma(W_1(W_0(F^c_{\max})) \end{aligned} \tag{1}$$

where σ denotes the sigmoid activation function, $W_0 \in R^{C/r \times C}$ and $W_1 \in R^{C \times C/r}$ denote the two weights of the MLP, respectively. Unlike the CAM module, the SAM module compresses the image in the channel dimension to obtain the target's location information and help the model find the region of interest from the whole image. The spatial attention is calculated as follows.

$$\begin{aligned} M_s(F) &= \sigma(f^{7\times 7}([AvgPool(F); MaxPool(F)])) \\ &= \sigma(f^{7\times 7}([F^s_{avg}; F^s_{\max}])) \end{aligned} \tag{2}$$

where σ denotes the sigmoid activation function and $f^{7\times 7}$ represents the convolution kernel size of 7×7.

BiFPN. Although the feature fusion approach of PANet [12] combined with FPN [21] has been widely used in deep learning models, it simply sums features at different scales after fixing them to a specific size. This approach ignores the difference in the degree of contribution of different resolutions to feature fusion. Inspired by EfficientDet, we replace the feature aggregation structure of YOLOv5 with the BiFPN [21] structure. Similar to PANet [12], BiFPN [21] is also based on a bidirectional feature aggregation path structure. By fusing the features of both bottom-up and top-down paths to enhance the characterization ability of the backbone network. Moreover, to differentially learn different input features, BiFPN [21] introduces an additional weight for each input to the network, removes nodes with only one input edge, and adds a jump connection between the input and output nodes at the same scale. Based on such improvements, the model can learn the importance of different input features in a targeted manner and obtain better feature representation capability. The results on two urine sediment particle detection datasets show that BiFPN [21] has better performance in urine sediment detection. The BiFPN [21] structure is shown in Fig. 3.

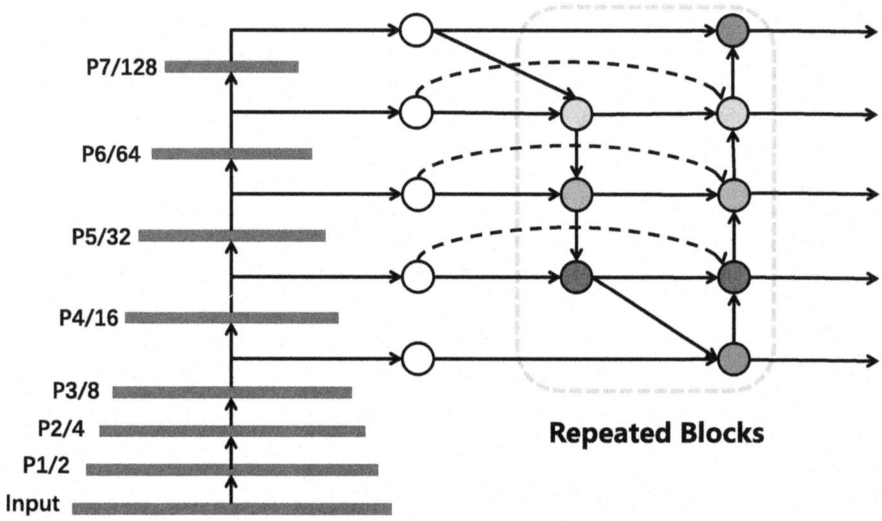

Fig. 3. The structure of BiFPN.

4 Experimental Results and Analysis

In this section, we first present the dataset, evaluation metrics, baseline methodology, and implementation details. Then, we compare with the latest baseline on Dataset1 and Dataset2 to validate the effectiveness of the proposed method.

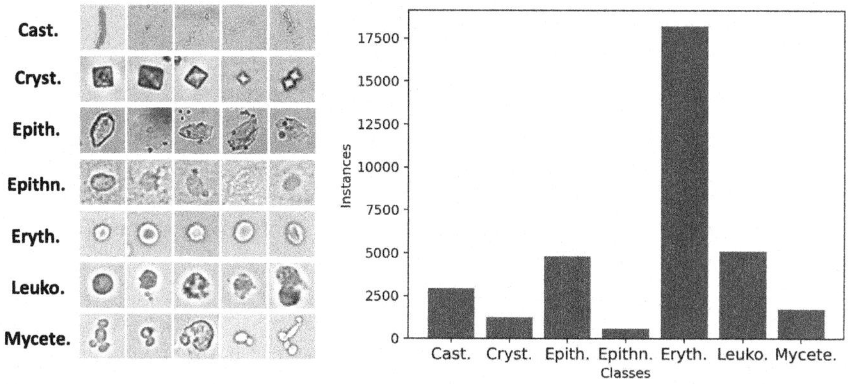

Fig. 4. Samples images and the number of labels of each category in Dataset1.

4.1 Dataset and Evaluation Metric

We evaluate the performance of the proposed method by using two real-world urinary sediment datasets, termed Dataset1 and Dataset2. Dataset1 was from the USE public dataset. [10,11,25] and consisted of 5646 images with a resolution of 800×600, containing seven cell categories: cast, cryst, epith, epithn, eryth, leuko, and mycete. The images and the corresponding number of labels of each category in Dataset1 are shown in Fig. 4; Dataset2 was from a self-built corporate dataset that contains 3200 urinary sediment images with the image size of 1024×1024 and 8 predefined example categories: RBC, WBC, SQEP, CAOX, OCRY, BACI, FUNGI, and MUCS. Figure 5 shows the eight categories of Dataset2 and the number of labels of each category.

In this paper, we use the mAP (mean Average Precision) as the evaluation metric. The mAP is the mean value of the average precision of all categories, which is often used to evaluate the detection accuracy of a model in object

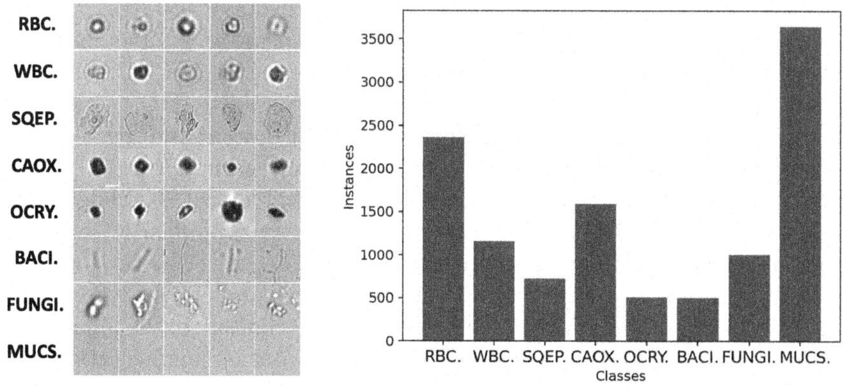

Fig. 5. Samples images and the number of labels of each category in Dataset2.

detection tasks, which is defined as follows:

$$mAP = \frac{\sum_{i=1}^{C} AP_i}{C} \tag{3}$$

where AP denotes the average precision, defined as the area enclosed by the PR curve and the coordinate axis, C denotes the total number of categories detected.

4.2 Baseline Methods

We compare the proposed YOLOv5-CBL with the following state-of-the-art methods:

- **DFPN** [11] is an FPN [21] network with DenseNet as the backbone network, which is used to detect sediment particles in urine images.
- **BCPNet** [2] is a bi-directional context propagation network for real-time semantic segmentation, which enhances the localization and differentiation ability of the model by building a hybrid feature pyramid architecture that complements the spatial information of the higher-level features and the semantic information of the bottom-level features.
- **PVANet** [8] is an improved end-to-end model based on Faster R-CNN [18], which further improves the speed of detection while maintaining the accuracy of Faster R-CNN [18].

We also conducted experimental comparisons with YOLOv3 [17], YOLOv3-SPP [17], and YOLOv5s mainstream object detection models to validate the effectiveness of the YOLOv5s-CBL further.

4.3 Implement Details

In this paper, the experimental environment is Windows 11 64-bit operating system with the 12th Gen Intel(R) Core(TM) i9-12900H@2.50 GHz,1TB SSD, and NVIDIA GEFORCE RTX 3070Ti with 8 GB memory. All our models are based on Python 3.7 runtime environment, Pytorch 1.11.0, CUDA 11.6, and CUDNN 8.3.

In the training phase, we used stochastic gradient descent and cosine learning rate decay strategies to train the network, with initial learning rate 0.01, weight decay factor 0.0005, momentum factor 0.937, and batch size 16. Depending on the dataset we used a different number of epochs and input sizes, where the number of epochs and input size on Dataset1 is 200 and 800×800, while the number of iterations and input size on Dataset2 is 70 and 1024×1024.

In addition, we used Mosaic and image perturbation data enhancement strategies such as HSV-Hue augmentation, HSV-Saturation augmentation, HSV-Value augmentation, translate, scale, and flip during the training of all models.

Table 1. The comparison of the performance in Dataset1.

Method	mAP	Eryth	Leuko	Epith	Cryst	Cast	Mycete	Epithn
PVANet [8]	84.10	88.40	84.30	87.10	87.70	76.50	89.00	76.00
DFPN [11]	86.90	93.80	92.70	87.10	83.90	75.90	90.40	84.40
BCPNet [2]	88.20	**94.85**	**94.38**	87.99	84.66	74.57	90.71	90.21
YOLOv3-tiny [17]	88.50	76.10	90.70	88.60	86.20	91.10	95.70	90.90
YOLOv3 [17]	90.20	80.20	93.20	88.60	89.80	91.40	96.50	91.70
YOLOv5s	90.60	81.20	91.40	90.50	**90.80**	91.70	96.60	91.70
YOLOv5s-CBL	**91.70 0.17**	83.10 0.50	**91.970.45**	**92.67 0.32**	89.93 1.03	**91.87 0.25**	**97.40 0.10**	**95.00 0.96**

Table 2. The comparison of the performance in Dataset2.

Method	mAP	RBC	WBC	SQEP	CAOX	OCRY	BACI	FUNGI	MUCS
YOLOv3-tiny [17]	60.60	78.60	66.20	91.90	80.40	36.60	44.20	48.20	38.70
YOLOv3 [17]	66.50	76.80	**75.00**	92.7	**85.70**	39.40	56.60	59.10	46.40
YOLOv5s	67.4	**82.40**	67.50	90.50	83.60	40.90	**63.70**	**59.30**	51.10
YOLOv5s-CBL	**68.40 0.62**	80.53 1.01	73.60 1.47	**93.37 0.21**	81.53 0.38	**45.37 1.63**	63.57 3.43	56.9 3.36	**52.50 1.14**

4.4 Experimental Results and Analysis

In this section, we show the results of YOLOv5s-CBL on two real-world datasets and compare them with the state-of-the-art methods to demonstrate the effectiveness of the proposed method. The results of the comparison experiments are shown in Table 1 and Table 2. We conducted several experiments on Dataset1 and Dataset2 and took the average value as our final result.

Comparisons with the State-of-the-Art. Table 1 shows the results of state-of-the-art methods on Dataset1. It can be seen that the detection accuracy of the YOLOv5s-CBL is better than the existing state-of-the-art methods on Dataset1, reaching 91.7% mAP. Compared with PVANet [8], DFPN [11], and BCPNet [2], the mAP of YOLOv5s-CBL is improved by 7.6%, 4.8%, and 3.5%, respectively, while the mAP is improved by 1.1% compared with YOLOv5s. Note that the results in PVANet [8], DFPN [11], and BCPNet [2] were copied from the original papers.

To further verify the effectiveness of YOLOv5s- CBL, we compare YOLOv3-tiny [17], YOLOv3 [17], and YOLOv5s on Dataset 2. Unlike Dataset 1, Dataset 2 contains more small objects and the feature information is more difficult to capture, which poses a greater challenge to the model's performance. As can be seen from the results in Table 2, our method still achieves the best performance even on the tiny target urine sediment particle dataset. Compared with YOLOv5s, the mAP improved by 1.0%, proving that YOLOv5s-CBL performs more accurately and robustly than other models. We show the confusion matrix on Dataset1 and Dataset2 respectively, as shown in Fig. 6.

Ablation Studies. We evaluated the importance of each component by ablation experiments on Dataset1, as shown in Table 3.

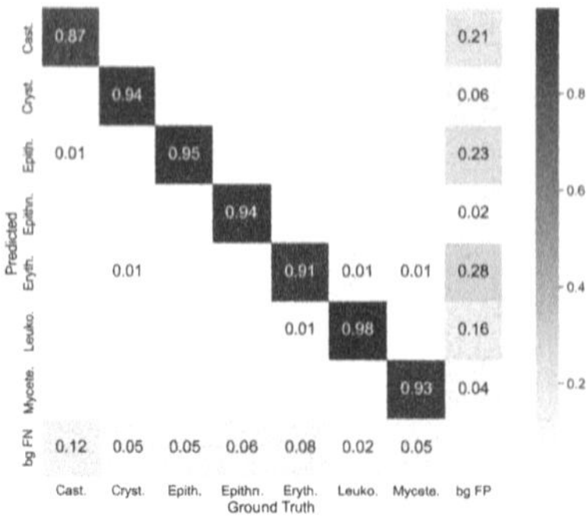

(a) Confusion martix of Dataset1.

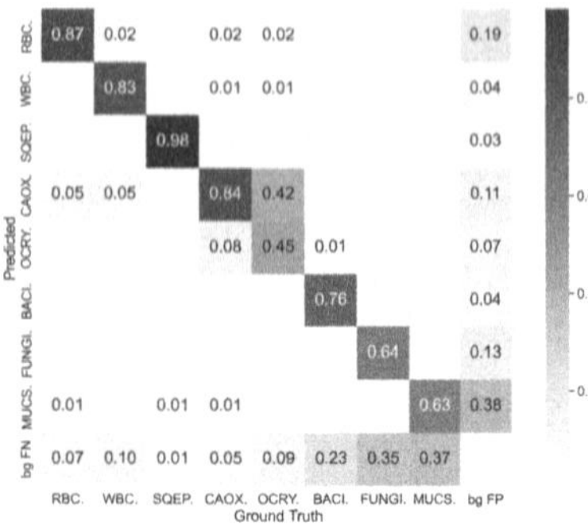

(b) Confusion martix of Dataset2.

Fig. 6. Confusion matrix. (a)Confusion martix of Dataset1. (b)Confusion martix of Dataset2.

Table 3. Ablation on dataset1 with YOLOv5s.

larger-head	BiFPN	CBAM	mAP	cast	cryst	epith	epithn	eryth	leuko	mycete
			90.60	81.20	91.40	90.50	90.80	91.70	96.60	91.70
✓			91.40	83.20	**91.90**	92.30	88.80	91.90	97.00	94.40
	✓		90.80	80.50	92.00	91.30	89.10	91.60	97.20	93.90
		✓	91.30	80.80	90.70	92.00	**92.00**	**92.20**	96.40	95.30
✓	✓		91.50	82.30	91.50	**93.00**	89.70	92.10	97.50	94.60
✓		✓	91.40	82.70	91.20	91.70	90.30	91.70	97.40	94.60
	✓	✓	91.50	82.60	90.80	92.40	89.90	92.00	97.50	95.00
✓	✓	✓	**91.90**	**83.60**	91.50	92.90	90.20	92.10	**97.40**	**95.70**

Effect of Extra Prediction Head. We added 64x downsampling to YOLOv5s to extract deeper semantic information and used it as a larger-scale prediction head to capture larger-size urine sediment particles in the input image. As can be seen from Table 3, the larger-scale prediction head improves the mAP of the model by 0.7% and outperforms the YOLOv5s in almost all categories.

Effect of BiFPN. We replaced the feature aggregation structure of YOLOv5s with a lightweight BiFPN [21]. BiFPN [21] optimizes the feature fusion and enables the network to learn more critical feature information in a targeted manner by increasing the corresponding weights. The results in Table 3 show that the mAP of YOLOv5s with BiFPN [21] improves by 0.2% compared to YOLOv5s without BiFPN [21].

Effect of Attention Module. To reduce the impact of redundant background information on the detection accuracy of the model, we added the CBAM [24] to the YOLOv5s network for extracting the region of interest on the input image. The results proved that the CBAM [24] could effectively reduce the interference of background information and improve the mAP of the model, as shown in Table 3.

To further explore the impact of attention modules on the network, we compared the current mainstream attention modules SE [6] and Coordinate Attention (CA) [5]. The results in Table 4 show that CBAM [24] can locate and identify objects of interest in urine images more effectively than SE [6] and CA [5].

Table 4. The comparison of the performance in different attention module.

Method	mAP	Cast	Cryst	Epith	Epithn	Eryth	Leuko	Mycete
YOLOv5s-SE	91.30	**82.80**	**93.40**	92.10	89.10	92.10	97.30	92.20
YOLOv5s-CBAM	**91.50**	82.60	90.80	**92.40**	**89.90**	92.00	**97.05**	**95.00**
YOLOv5s-CA	90.90	81.10	90.50	92.00	88.80	91.80	97.30	94.90

Table 5. The comparison of the performance in different IoU loss function.

Method	mAP	Cast	Cryst	Epith	Epithn	Eryth	Leuko	Mycete
YOLOv5s-CBL+CIoU	**91.90**	**83.60**	91.50	**92.90**	90.20	**92.10**	**97.40**	**95.70**
YOLOv5s-CBL+EIoU	91.40	82.70	90.90	92.50	90.30	91.50	97.10	94.80
YOLOv5s-CBL+α-IoU	91.00	81.80	90.50	90.70	91.90	91.50	97.00	93.60
YOLOv5s-CBL+α-CIoU	91.40	82.20	**92.20**	90.10	**92.50**	91.60	97.20	93.90
YOLOv5s-CBL+α-EIoU	90.60	80.30	90.80	91.30	**92.50**	91.80	96.80	90.80

Effect of IoU. We explored the impact of IoU Loss on the network detection accuracy, and compared CIoU Loss, EIoU Loss [29], α IoU-Loss, α CIoU Loss, and α-EIoU Loss on the YOLOv5s-CBL, respectively, where α-CIoU Loss and α-EIoU Loss are replacing the IoU Loss in α-IoU Loss with CIoU Loss and EIoU Loss [29]. CIoU Loss is the default bounding box regression loss in the YOLOv5s, which further considers the overlapping area, centroid distance, and aspect ratio of the bounding box based on DIoU Loss, effectively improving the regression accuracy of the bound box; EIoU Loss [29] splits the aspect ratio influence factor based on CIoU Loss and calculates the width-height difference value separately, optimizing the problem of the difference between the width-height of the bounding box and the confidence; α-IoU is a Power IoU loss function proposed by Jiabo He et al. [3] at NeurIPS 2021, which contains a Power IoU term, a Power canonical term, and a Power parameter α. By adjusting α, the detector can adaptively increase the loss of high IoU objects and the weighting of the gradient to improve bounding box regression accuracy. Experiments on multi-target detection benchmarks and models show that α-IoU Loss [3] can significantly outperform existing IoU-based losses. Note that the Power parameter α of α-IoU Loss [3] is taken as 3 for all experiments in this paper. The results of the IoU Loss comparison experiments are shown in Table 5.

We found that the detection accuracy of YOLOv5-CBL based on CIoU Loss outperformed the models based on EIoU Loss [29] and α IoU Loss [3] on Dataset1. Therefore, we finally use CIoU Loss as the bounding box regression loss function.

Detection Result on Dataset1 and Dataset2. We have selected some images from the test set as the display of the detection results, as shown in Fig. 7.

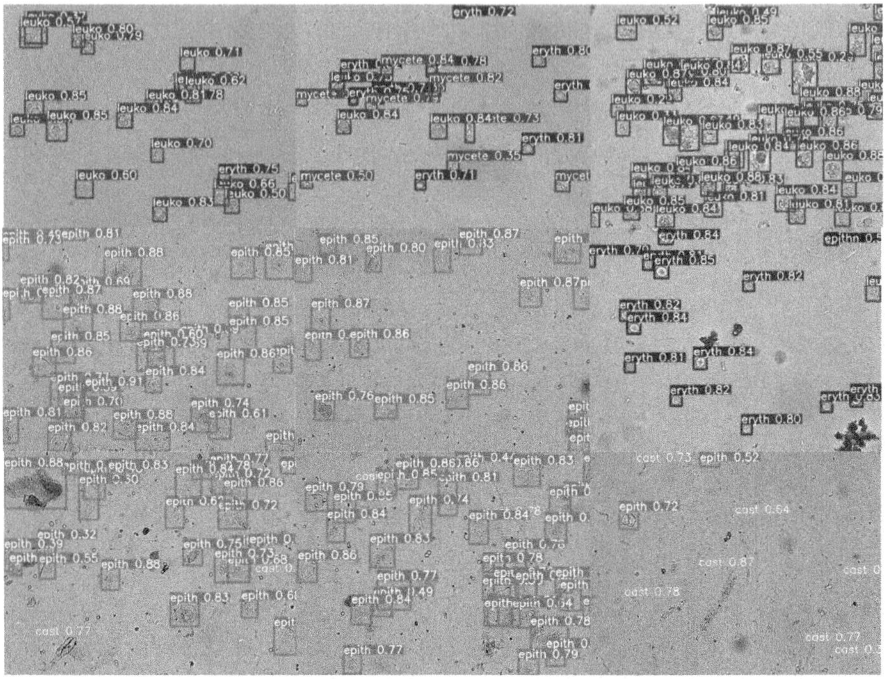

Fig. 7. Some visualization results from our YOLOv5s-CBL.

5 Conclusion

In this paper, we present the YOLOv5s-CBL model dedicated to urine sediment detection. The model integrates a larger-scale prediction head and CBAM to capture sediment particles in urine images. The features at different scales are then fused by BiFPN to improve the accuracy of urine sediment detection. We compared state-of-the-art methods on two urine sediment particle datasets, and the experimental results demonstrated the effectiveness of YOLOv5s-CBL.

Acknowledgements. This work is partially supported by National Natural Science Foundation of China (61972187), Natural Science Foundation of Fujian Province (2020J02024).

References

1. Girshick, R., Donahue, J., Darrell, T., Malik, J.: Rich feature hierarchies for accurate object detection and semantic segmentation. In: Proceedings of the IEEE Conference on Computer Vision and Pattern Recognition (CVPR), June 2014
2. Hao, S., Zhou, Y., Guo, Y., Hong, R.: Bi-direction context propagation network for real-time semantic segmentation. arXiv preprint arXiv:2005.11034 (2020)
3. He, J., Erfani, S., Ma, X., Bailey, J., Chi, Y., Hua, X.S.: α-iou: a family of power intersection over union losses for bounding box regression. In: Advances in Neural Information Processing Systems 34 (2021)
4. Hoang Ngan Le, T., Zheng, Y., Zhu, C., Luu, K., Savvides, M.: Multiple scale faster-rcnn approach to driver's cell-phone usage and hands on steering wheel detection. In: Proceedings of the IEEE Conference on Computer Vision and Pattern Recognition Workshops, pp. 46–53 (2016)
5. Hou, Q., Zhou, D., Feng, J.: Coordinate attention for efficient mobile network design. In: Proceedings of the IEEE/CVF Conference on Computer Vision and Pattern Recognition, pp. 13713–13722 (2021)
6. Hu, J., Shen, L., Sun, G.: Squeeze-and-excitation networks. In: Proceedings of the IEEE Conference on Computer Vision and Pattern Recognition, pp. 7132–7141 (2018)
7. Ji, Q., Li, X., Qu, Z., Dai, C.: Research on urine sediment images recognition based on deep learning. IEEE Access **7**, 166711–166720 (2019)
8. Kim, K.H., Hong, S., Roh, B., Cheon, Y., Park, M.: Pvanet: deep but lightweight neural networks for real-time object detection. arXiv preprint arXiv:1608.08021 (2016)
9. Liang, Y., Fang, B., Qian, J., Chen, L., Li, C., Liu, Y.: False positive reduction in urinary particle recognition. Expert Syst. Appl. **36**(9), 11429–11438 (2009)
10. Liang, Y., Kang, R., Lian, C., Mao, Y.: An end-to-end system for automatic urinary particle recognition with convolutional neural network. J. Med. Syst. **42**(9), 165 (2018)
11. Liang, Y., Tang, Z., Yan, M., Liu, J.: Object detection based on deep learning for urine sediment examination. Biocybernetics Biomed. Eng. **38**(3), 661–670 (2018)
12. Liu, S., Qi, L., Qin, H., Shi, J., Jia, J.: Path aggregation network for instance segmentation. In: Proceedings of the IEEE Conference on Computer Vision and Pattern Recognition, pp. 8759–8768 (2018)
13. Liu, X., Sun, Z.: A kind of computer microscopic urinary sediments analyzer by svm. In: 2008 International Workshop on Education Technology and Training & 2008 International Workshop on Geoscience and Remote Sensing, vol. 1, pp. 483–486. IEEE (2008)
14. Pan, J., Jiang, C., Zhu, T.: Classification of urine sediment based on convolution neural network. In: AIP Conference Proceedings, vol. 1955, p. 040176. AIP Publishing LLC (2018)
15. Ranzato, M., Taylor, P., House, J.M., Flagan, R., LeCun, Y., Perona, P.: Automatic recognition of biological particles in microscopic images. Pattern Recogn. Lett. **28**(1), 31–39 (2007)
16. Redmon, J., Divvala, S., Girshick, R., Farhadi, A.: You only look once: unified, real-time object detection. In: Proceedings of the IEEE Conference on Computer Vision and Pattern Recognition, pp. 779–788 (2016)
17. Redmon, J., Farhadi, A.: Yolov3: an incremental improvement. arXiv preprint arXiv:1804.02767 (2018)

18. Ren, S., He, K., Girshick, R., Sun, J.: Faster r-cnn: Towards real-time object detection with region proposal networks. In: Advances in Neural Information Processing Systems 28 (2015)
19. Shen, M.l., Zhang, R.: Urine sediment recognition method based on svm and adaboost. In: 2009 International Conference on Computational Intelligence and Software Engineering, pp. 1–4. IEEE (2009)
20. Suhail, K., Brindha, D.: A review on various methods for recognition of urine particles using digital microscopic images of urine sediments. Biomed. Signal Process. Control **68**, 102806 (2021)
21. Tan, M., Pang, R., Le, Q.V.: Efficientdet: scalable and efficient object detection. In: Proceedings of the IEEE/CVF Conference on Computer Vision and Pattern Recognition, pp. 10781–10790 (2020)
22. Wang, C., ZHANG, Y., Sun, S., Zhang, H.: Steel-bar end face detection based on improved yolov5 algorithm. Computer Systems and Applications, pp. 68–80 (2022)
23. Wang, J., Sun, Z., Guo, P., Zhang, L.: Improved leukocyte detection algorithm of yolov5. Computer Engineering and Applications, pp. 134–142 (2022)
24. Woo, S., Park, J., Lee, J.-Y., Kweon, I.S.: CBAM: Convolutional Block Attention Module. In: Ferrari, V., Hebert, M., Sminchisescu, C., Weiss, Y. (eds.) ECCV 2018. LNCS, vol. 11211, pp. 3–19. Springer, Cham (2018). https://doi.org/10.1007/978-3-030-01234-2_1
25. Yan, M., Liu, Q., Yin, Z., Wang, D., Liang, Y.: A bidirectional context propagation network for urine sediment particle detection in microscopic images. In: ICASSP 2020–2020 IEEE International Conference on Acoustics, Speech and Signal Processing (ICASSP), pp. 981–985 (2020)
26. Yan, M., Liu, Q., Yin, Z., Wang, D., Liang, Y.: A bidirectional context propagation network for urine sediment particle detection in microscopic images. In: ICASSP 2020–2020 IEEE International Conference on Acoustics, Speech and Signal Processing (ICASSP), pp. 981–985. IEEE (2020)
27. Yang, G., Feng, W., Jin, J., Lei, Q., Li, X., Gui, G., Wang, W.: Face mask recognition system with yolov5 based on image recognition. In: 2020 IEEE 6th International Conference on Computer and Communications (ICCC), pp. 1398–1404. IEEE (2020)
28. Zhang, X., Chen, G., Saruta, K., Terata, Y.: Detection and classification of rbcs and wbcs in urine analysis with deep network (2018)
29. Zhang, Y.F., Ren, W., Zhang, Z., Jia, Z., Wang, L., Tan, T.: Focal and efficient iou loss for accurate bounding box regression. arXiv preprint arXiv:2101.08158 (2021)
30. Zhou, X., Xiao, X., Ma, C.: A study of automatic recognition and counting system of urine-sediment visual components. In: 2010 3rd International Conference on Biomedical Engineering and Informatics, vol. 1, pp. 78–81. IEEE (2010)

Evolutionary Factor-Driven Concise Bacterial Foraging Optimization Algorithm for Solving Customer Clustering Problems

Lijing Tan[1], Kuangxuan Qing[2,3], Chen Guo[2(✉)], and Ben Niu[2,3]

[1] School of Management, Shenzhen Institute of Information Technology, Shenzhen 518172, China

[2] College of Management, Shenzhen University, Shenzhen 518060, China
chen.guo@connect.um.edu.mo

[3] Greater Bay Area International Institute for Innovation, Shenzhen University, Shenzhen 518060, China

Abstract. To mitigate the disadvantages of the K-means algorithm, an evolutionary factor-driven concise bacterial foraging optimization algorithm is proposed to handle customer data clustering tasks (EFCBFOK). First, to decrease the computing complexity of BFO, a concise BFO with a simplified structure is used. Second, driven by the evolutionary factors, a modified step size strategy is designed. Third, evolutionary factor-driven chemotaxis operation is proposed to make the bacteria select the learning objects from multiple generations of personal historical best and global best; it can expand the search space and enhance the population diversity. To evaluate the performance of the EFCBFOK, EFCBFOK is compared with the other three algorithms on three validity indexes of five customer datasets. Experimental results show that EFCBFOK outperforms the other three clustering algorithms in terms of solution quality, three validity indexes, and computing time.

Keywords: Evolutionary factor · Bacterial foraging optimization · K-means · Customer clustering

1 Introduction

Data clustering is the process of dividing data into multiple clusters or groups based on similarity. Clustering has applications in many fields, including exploratory data analysis, image segmentation, and mathematical programming [1]. Many traditional clustering algorithms have been proposed, and K-means is one of the important algorithms. However, K-means is sensitive to the initialization, which greatly impacts the clustering results; once the quality of initial cluster centers is poor, effective clustering results may not be obtained and easily fall into local optimum [2].

Y. Xu et al. (Eds.): ML4CS 2022, LNCS 13657, pp. 309–320, 2023.
https://doi.org/10.1007/978-3-031-20102-8_24

To improve the quality of traditional clustering methods, researchers have started to study the combination of swarm intelligence and clustering algorithms. Swarm intelligence is a computational technique based on the behavioral rules of biological groups. It is inspired by social insects and swarming vertebrates, which have the characteristics of autonomy and robustness and are used to solve distributed problems. Various swarm intelligence algorithms have been proposed, and these algorithms have been used to solve data clustering tasks. For example, cohesive hierarchical clustering is introduced into the brainstorming algorithm [3], particle swarm algorithm (PSO) is efficiently mixed with fuzzy clustering [4], fireworks algorithm is combined with hard clustering technique [5], brainstorming algorithm is combined with K-means for numerical optimization [6], etc.

The bacterial foraging optimization algorithm (BFO), as a new member of the swarm intelligence, mimics the foraging behaviors of bacteria. It has received much attention recently and has been combined with clustering techniques to solve practical problems [7, 8]. To further explore the potential of BFO in solving data clustering problems, in this paper, an evolutionary factor-driven concise bacterial foraging optimization algorithm (EFCBFO) is proposed to solve the customer data clustering problems (EFCBFOK). Due to the original BFO having high computing complexity, a concise BFO (CBFO) [9] with a simplified structure is employed. The main improvements of this paper are as follows. (1) Based on the evolutionary factor [10], a modified step size updating strategy is proposed to make it change with the evolutionary states, which can better balance exploration and exploitation. (2) To guide the bacteria to find global optimum and escape local optimum, an improved chemotaxis operation is designed that integrates the delayed information. Based on this, during each iteration, bacteria can select learning objects from multiple generations of personal historical best and global best individuals, expanding the search space and enhancing the population diversity. (3) Combining the EFCBFO with K-means, EFCBFOK is designed to handle the customer data clustering problems. Comparative experiments verify that EFCBFOK has better performance than its competitors in terms of solution quality, three validity indexes, and computing time.

The remaining parts of this paper are organized as follows. Section 2 briefly introduces the traditional BFO and the K-means algorithm; Sect. 3 presents and discusses the EFCBFOK in detail. Section 4 presents the experiments and analyses. Section 5 concludes the whole paper and provides an outlook for future work.

2 Background

2.1 Bacterial Foraging Optimization Algorithm

The BFO is a stochastic search algorithm proposed by Passino in 2002 that mainly simulates the food searching behaviors of *E. coli* in the human intestine [11]. In this paper, three operations of BFO, chemotaxis, reproduction, and elimination-dispersal, are included [12] and described in detail.

Chemotaxis is the essential operation in the BFO, which includes two actions: swimming and tumbling. In this stage, the bacterial swarm moves to high nutrients places or away from low nutrients through these two actions. The chemotaxis operation is shown as Eq. (1),

$$\theta^i(j+1,k,l) = \theta^i(j,k,l) + C(i)\phi(i) \tag{1}$$

where $\theta^i(j, k, l)$ represents the position of bacteria i during the jth chemotaxis, kth reproduction, and lth elimination-dispersal operations. $C(i)$ is the step size taken during the chemotaxis process and $\phi(i)$ represents a unit length of the random direction.

The chemotaxis operation is followed by a reproduction operation. At this stage, the bacteria in poor health conditions are deleted, and bacteria in good health split into two bacteria at their current position.

For each elimination-dispersal operation, a fixed probability is used to determine whether a bacterium performs this operation; if the operation is performed, the current bacterium will die, and then a new bacterium is randomly generated in the solution space.

2.2 K-means Algorithm

The K-means is a common and simple clustering technique [13]. K-means randomly initializes a set of k cluster centers, then proceeds by alternating between two steps: assignment and update [14]. Given a dataset X with n data points, $X = \{x_1, x_2, \ldots, x_n\}(i = 1, 2, \ldots, n)$. M is the set of cluster centers, $M = \{m_1, m_2, \ldots, m_k\}(1 \le p, q \le k)$. $S_p^{(t)}$ is the set of data points belonging to pth cluster at the tth generation. The assignment and update steps are presented as follows.

Assignment Step: compute the Euclidean distances between the data points and cluster centers, and each data point x_i is assigned to the cluster with the least square Euclidean distance, which is presented in Eq. (2),

$$S_p^{(t)} = \left\{x_i : \left\|x_i - m_p^{(t)}\right\|^2 \le \left\|x_i - m_q^{(t)}\right\|^2, \forall p, 1 \le p \le k\right\} \tag{2}$$

where $m_p^{(t)}$ and $m_q^{(t)}$ imply the pth and qth cluster centers at the tth generation, respectively.

Update Step: recalculate the average values of the data points assigned to each cluster,

$$\mathrm{m}_\mathrm{p}^{(t+1)} = \frac{1}{\left|\mathrm{S}_\mathrm{p}^{(t)}\right|} \sum_{\mathrm{x}, \in \mathrm{S}_\mathrm{p}^{(t)}} \mathrm{x}_\mathrm{ip} \tag{3}$$

where $\left|S_p^{(t)}\right|$ is the number of data points belonging to the pth cluster at the tth generation. $m_p^{(t+1)}$ is the pth cluster center at the $(t + 1)th$ generation.

Usually, the objective of K-means algorithm is to minimize the sum of squared errors (SSE), which is presented in Eq. (4),

$$SSE^{(t)} = \sum_{p=1}^{k} \sum_{x_i \in S_p^{(t)}} D\left(x_i, m_p^{(t)}\right)^2 \tag{4}$$

where $D(,)$ is the Euclidean distance, $SSE^{(t)}$ is the SSE at the tth generation.

3 The Proposed Algorithm

To improve the performance of traditional BFO, this paper proposes an evolutionary factor-driven concise bacterial foraging optimization algorithm (EFCBFO). Then, the EFCBFO is combined with K-means (EFCBFOK) to solve customer data clustering tasks. In the EFCBFOK, based on the evolutionary factors proposed in [10], evolutionary factor-driven step size and evolutionary-driven chemotaxis are designed. The details of EFCBFOK are described as follows.

3.1 Evolutionary Factors

Evolutionary factor (E_f) [10] is the indicator of the discovery of the exploration and exploitation states of the population. During the evolution process, the population distribution characteristics change not only with the number of iterations but also according to the E_f [10]. In [10], the E_f can be predicted by the average distance between each individual. Concretely, at the beginning of the iteration, when the population is more dispersed, the average distance between each individual will be relatively large; this is the exploration stage. When the individuals reach the local or global optimal region, the average distance between each individual will be relatively small; this is the exploitation stage.

Based on this concept, the E_f is calculated as follows. The first step is to calculate the average distance between the *ith* individual and the other individuals in the population by using the Euclidean distance. The equation is as follows.

$$d_i = \frac{1}{S-1}\sum_{j=1, j\neq i}^{S}\sqrt{\sum_{d=1}^{D}\left(\theta^{id} - \theta^{jd}\right)^2} \tag{5}$$

where d_i is the average distance of the *ith* individual. S and D are the number of population and dimensions, respectively. θ^{id} and θ^{jd} are the position vectors of *ith* and *jth* individual in the *dth* dimension.

Based on the average distances of all the individuals, three important distances, d_g, d_{min}, and d_{max}, are defined. Specifically, d_g is the average distance of the global best individual. d_{min} and d_{max} are the minimal and maximal average distances in all the average distances, respectively. After getting these distances, the E_f is calculated as,

$$E_f = \frac{d_g - d_{min}}{d_{max} - d_{min}} \tag{6}$$

It can be seen that the E_f is located in the range [0,1]. It will be relatively small when the average distance between bacteria is relatively close and relatively large when the average distance between bacteria is relatively far.

According to the E_f, evolutionary states can be obtained [10, 15]. In [15], four types of evolutionary states are exploration state, exploitation state, convergence state, and jump-out state. These states denoted $\xi(k)$ can be acquired by dividing the E_f into four equal intervals, which is presented in Eq. (7),

$$\xi(k) = \begin{cases} 1, & 0 \leq E_f < 0.25 \\ 2, & 0.25 \leq E_f < 0.5 \\ 3, & 0.5 \leq E_f < 0.75 \\ 4, & 0.75 \leq E_f \leq 1 \end{cases} \tag{7}$$

When $\xi(k)$ is equal to 1, 2, 3, and 4, it is the convergence, exploitation, exploration, and jumping-out states, respectively.

3.2 Evolutionary Factors-Driven Step Size

In the original BFO, the step size $C(i)$ is the length of each step during the swimming action, which is a constant. However, if $C(i)$ is too small, the bacteria focus on local search/exploitation, and it may take a long time to find the optimal value; if $C(i)$ is too lager, the bacteria focus on global search/exploration, and the optimal value may be missed. Based on these analyses, it can be observed that E_f shares some characteristics with the $C(i)$, i.e., E_f is relatively large in the exploration and jump-out states and relatively small in the convergence state [10]. Therefore, $C(i)$ can be defined based on the E_f, which is presented in the following equation,

$$C(i) = (C_{max} - C_{min})E_f + C_{min} \tag{8}$$

where C_{max} and C_{min} are the maximal and minimal step sizes, respectively. This paper sets C_{max} as 0.1 and C_{min} as 0.01. The step size varies with the E_f, and a larger $C(i)$ will be more favorable for global search in the jump-out and exploration states; the smaller $C(i)$ in the convergence state favors the local search.

3.3 Evolutionary Factors-Driven Chemotaxis Operation

To make better use of the historical information, delayed information of bacterial swarm is used to guide the bacteria to move to the optimal directions. Concretely, two indicators denoted $\varepsilon_i(k)$ and $\varepsilon_g(k)$ are employed. Among them, k is the information delay interval, which implies that the personal historical best and global best of recent k generations should be recorded and used. $\varepsilon_i(k)$ and $\varepsilon_g(k)$ are two uniformly generated integers in the range of $[1, k]$. i and g represent the indexes of personal best and global best, respectively.

Additionally, another two indicators denoted as $s_i(k)$ and $s_g(k)$ are used in this paper. Combining the evolutionary states, the values of $s_i(k)$ and $s_g(k)$ are shown in Table 1. In the convergence state, the bacteria are expected to reach the region near the global optimum, so the value of $s_i(k)$ and $s_g(k)$ is taken as 0. In the exploitation state, as much local information as possible needs to be used, so the value of $s_i(k)$ is taken as $E_f(k)$. In the exploration state, more global information needs to be used, so the value of $s_g(k)$ is taken as $E_f(k)$. In the jump-out state, the bacterial subsets desire to jump out from the region near the local optimum, so the value of $E_f(k)$ needs to be taken at the same time to provide more information for the bacteria to jump out from the local optimum.

Table 1. Values of indicators.

Modes	States	$s_i(k)$	$s_g(k)$
$\xi(k)=1$	Convergence	0	0
$\xi(k)=2$	Exploitation	$E_f(k)$	0
$\xi(k)=3$	Exploration	0	$E_f(k)$
$\xi(k)=4$	Jumping-out	$E_f(k)$	$E_f(k)$

Based on the aforementioned analysis, an improved chemotaxis operation is designed, which is shown as follows,

$$\begin{aligned} \theta^i(j+1,k,l) &= \theta^i(j,k,l) + C(i)\phi(i) \\ &+ s_i(k)C(i)r_1\big(p_i(k-\varepsilon_i(k)) - \theta^i(j,k,l)\big) \\ &+ s_g(k)C(i)r_2\big(p_g\big(k-\varepsilon_g(k)\big) - \theta^i(j,k,l)\big) \end{aligned} \tag{9}$$

where r_1 and r_2 are the uniformly generated numbers in [0,1]. $p_i(k-\varepsilon_i(k))$ And $p_g\big(k-\varepsilon_g(k)\big)$ are the selected personal historical best and global best individuals, respectively. It can be seen that the designed chemotaxis operation includes four parts. The first and second parts are the same as the original BFO. The third and fourth parts are the self-learning and global learning parts with delayed information. Based on the evolutionary states, the bacteria can learn from different individuals.

3.4 The Framework of EFCBFOK

Combining EFCBFO and K-means, EFCBFOK is designed to handle customer clustering tasks. In EFCBFOK, SSE is the objective function. The framework of EFCBFOK is described as follows (Fig. 1).

Step 1. Initialize the position of the population and the parameters of the algorithm.
Step 2. Evaluate the fitness values of the population, and store their personal historical best and global best.
Step 3. Iteration loop.
Step 3.1. Obtain the evolutionary factors according to Eq. (6), and obtain Table 1 according to Eq. (7).
Step 3.2. Update the positions of the population by implementing evolutionary factors-driven chemotaxis operation.
Step 3.3. If the iteration number is a multiple of reproduction frequency (F_{re}), implement the reproduction operation.
Step 3.4 If the iteration number is a multiple of elimination-dispersal frequency (F_{ed}), implement the elimination-dispersal operation.
Step 4. Repeat step 3 until the conditions are met.

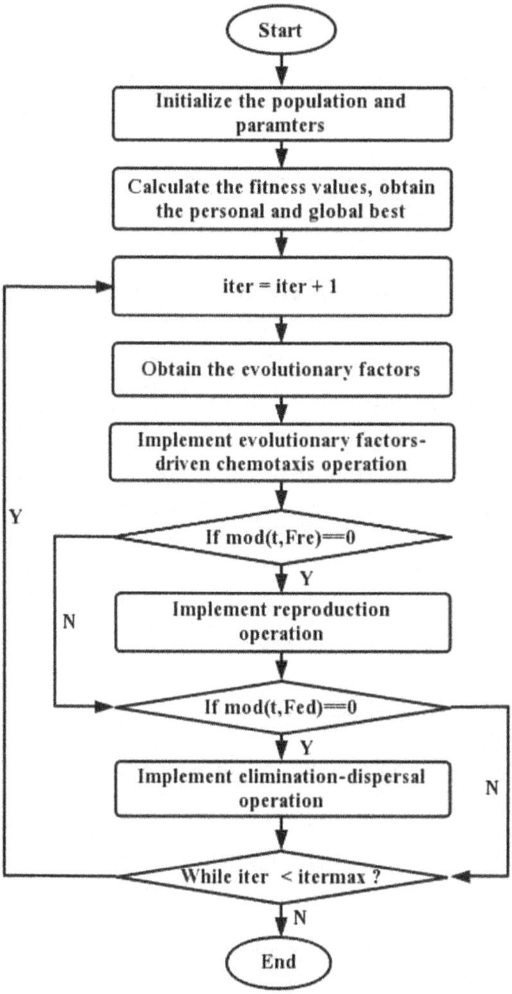

Fig. 1. The framework of EFCBFOK.

4 Experiments and Analyses

4.1 Datasets and Experimental Parameters

To demonstrate the superiority of the EFCBFOK, five datasets, Taiwan, German, Australian[1], Marketing, and Hotel[2], are selected as the testing datasets. The missing and invalid data are deleted before clustering. The description of the five testing datasets is shown in Table 2.

[1] Data source: https://archive.ics.uci.edu/ml/datasets.php.

[2] Data source: https://www.kaggle.com/

Table 2. The description of the testing datasets.

Dataset	Samples	Features	Clusters
German	1000	24	2
Marketing	2216	25	2
Australian	690	14	2
Taiwan	30000	23	2
Hotel	6665	9	4

Additionally, three algorithms are selected as the competitors, which are K-means, PSO-based clustering technique (PSOK) [16], and CBFO-based clustering algorithm (CBFOK) [9]. The parameters of EFCBFOK, PSOK, and CBFOK are listed as follows. The population size is 100; the number of independent runs and iterations are 10 and 100, respectively. For EFCBFOK and CBFOK, the reproduction frequency is 5, and the elimination-dispersal frequency is 2. For PSOK, the $C_1 \text{and} C_2$ are 2. These algorithms are coded using PyCharm Community Edition 2021. To evaluate the clustering quality of all the algorithms, inter-cluster distance, Silhouette [17], and F-measure [18] are selected as validity indexes.

4.2 Experimental Results and Analysis

Table 3 gives the average optimal solutions of three validity indexes over 10 runs. Table 3 also gives the computation times for the four algorithms. This paper uses boldface with underline and boldface to highlight the best and second-best values of the four algorithms on different metrics. Figure 2 shows the SSE convergence curves for all algorithm traversals in the five datasets, respectively. From Table 3 and Fig. 2, three observations can be concluded.

- The EFCBFOK algorithm performs well than its competitors regarding to the three validity indexes on all five datasets, especially on German and marketing datasets. As for the F-measure, EFCBFOK obtains overwhelming advantages over its peers. This implies that the EFCBFOK algorithm effectively improves the clustering quality of customer datasets. Conversely, PSOK has the worse performance among these four algorithms, which only gets several second ranking on some datasets regarding one validity index.
- In terms of computing time, although K-means performs optimally, the EFCBFOK uses less time on the five data sets compared to the swarm intelligence-based clustering algorithms. This implies that the proposed EFCBFOK has a faster convergence speed than that of CBFOK and PSOK.
- From the iterative curves, it can be seen that the iterative curve of EFCBFOK is below the other algorithms. This means that the EFCBFOK outperforms the other three algorithms in terms of global optimality regardless of the dataset.

Table 3. The experimental results of EFCBFOK and its competitors on five datasets.

Datasets	Metrics	EFCBFOK	CBFOK	PSOK	K-means
German	Inter-cluster distance	**5.00E−01**	2.55E−01	2.53E−01	**3.60E−01**
	Silhouette	**4.76E−02**	4.74E−02	4.14E−02	**1.18E−01**
	F-measure	**5.80E−01**	5.76E−01	**5.80E−01**	5.38E−01
	Time(s)	**8.30E+01**	8.90E+01	8.88E+01	**8.22E+01**
Marketing	Inter-cluster distance	**4.20E−01**	**3.23E−01**	2.78E−01	3.08E−01
	Silhouette	**1.62E−01**	7.67E−02	7.86E−02	**8.18E−02**
	F-measure	**6.28E−01**	6.04E−01	6.03E−01	**6.12E−01**
	Time(s)	**2.26E+02**	2.37E+02	2.29E+02	**2.23E+02**
Australian	Inter-cluster distance	4.01E−01	**4.08E−01**	3.54E−01	**4.96E−01**
	Silhouette	**1.87E−01**	1.38E−01	**1.76E−01**	1.70E−01
	F-measure	**6.65E−01**	6.26E−01	6.43E−01	**6.49E−01**
	Time(s)	**3.93E+01**	4.02E+01	4.03E+01	**3.40E+01**
Taiwan	Inter-cluster distance	4.55E−01	**5.03E−01**	**5.00E−01**	3.38E−01
	Silhouette	**3.34E−01**	**3.39E−01**	2.55E−01	2.67E−01
	F-measure	**6.01E−01**	**5.79E−01**	5.61E−01	5.77E−01
	Time(s)	**2.27E+02**	2.30E+02	2.30E+02	**2.06E+02**
Hotel	Inter-cluster distance	1.67E+00	1.62E+00	**1.69E+00**	**1.72E+00**
	Silhouette	**1.64E−01**	1.52E−01	1.60E−01	**2.33E−01**
	F-measure	**3.36E−01**	3.26E−01	**3.35E−01**	3.16E−01
	Time(s)	**9.71E+01**	9.72E+01	9.85E+01	**8.46E+01**

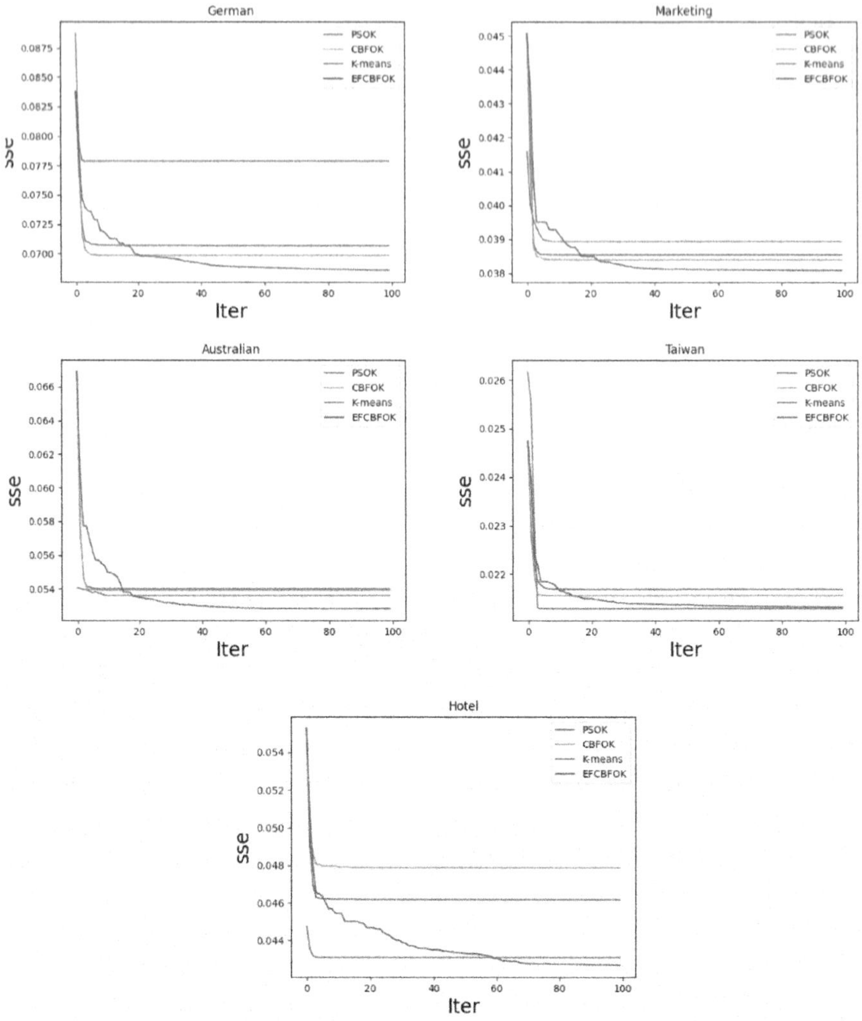

Fig. 2. SSE iterative curves of four algorithms on five datasets

5 Conclusion

This paper proposes a concise evolutionary factor-driven bacterial foraging optimization algorithm to solve the customer clustering problem (EFCBFOK). First, the concise BFO with a simplified structure is used to decrease the computing complexity of BFO. Then, a modified step size strategy is proposed according to the evolutionary factors. Additionally, driven by the evolutionary factor, an improved chemotaxis operation is proposed to let the bacteria select the learning individuals from multiple generations of personal historical best and global best; it can expand the search space and enhance the diversity. To validate the effectiveness of the EFCBFOK, EFCBFOK is compared with the other three algorithms on three validity indexes of five customer datasets. Experimental results demonstrate that EFCBFOK has better performance than its competitors regarding solution quality, three validity indexes, and computing time.

In future work, EFCBFOK will be used to solve multi-objective data clustering tasks. Furthermore, more strategies should be designed to enhance the performance of BFO.

Acknowledgments. The work described in this paper was supported by The Natural Science Foundation of Guangdong Province (Grant No. 2020A1515010752, 2020A1515010749), Key Research Foundation of Higher Education of Guangdong Provincial Education Bureau (Grant No. 2019KZDXM030), University Innovation Team Project of Guangdong Province (Grant No. 2021WCXTD002).

References

1. Madhulatha, T.S.: An overview on clustering methods. arXiv preprint arXiv (2012)
2. Atabay, H.A., Sheikhzadeh, M.J., Torshizi, M.: A clustering algorithm based on integration of K-Means and PSO. In: 2016 1st Conference on Swarm Intelligence and Evolutionary Computation (CSIEC), pp. 59–63. IEEE (2016)
3. Chen, J., Wang, J., Cheng, S., Shi, Y.: Brain storm optimization with agglomerative hierarchical clustering analysis. In: Tan, Y., Shi, Y., Li, L. (eds.) ICSI 2016. LNCS, vol. 9713, pp. 115–122. Springer, Cham (2016). https://doi.org/10.1007/978-3-319-41009-8_12
4. Mehdizadeh, E.: A fuzzy clustering PSO algorithm for supplier base management. Int. J. Manage. Sci. Eng. Manage. **4**, 311–320 (2009)
5. Misra, P.R., Si, T.: Image segmentation using clustering with fireworks algorithm. In: 2017 11th International Conference on Intelligent Systems and Control (ISCO), pp. 97–102. IEEE (2017)
6. Zhu, H., Shi, Y.: Brain storm optimization algorithms with k-medians clustering algorithms. In: 2015 Seventh International Conference on Advanced Computational Intelligence (ICACI), pp. 107–110. IEEE (2015)
7. Guo, C., Tang, H., Niu, B.: Evolutionary state-based novel multi-objective periodic bacterial foraging optimization algorithm for data clustering. Expert. Syst. **39**, e12812 (2022)
8. Bhaladhare, P.R., Jinwala, D.C.: A clustering approach for the-diversity model in privacy preserving data mining using fractional calculus-bacterial foraging optimization algorithm. In: Advances in Computer Engineering 2014 (2014)
9. Ben, N., Qiqi, D., Hong, W., Jing, L.: Simplified bacterial foraging optimization with quorum sensing for global optimization. Int. J. Intell. Syst. **36**, 2639–2679 (2021)
10. Zhan, Z.-H., Zhang, J., Li, Y., Chung, H.S.-H.: Adaptive particle swarm optimization. IEEE Trans. Syst. Man Cybern. Part B **39**, 1362–1381 (2009)
11. Passino, K.M.: Biomimicry of bacterial foraging for distributed optimization and control. IEEE Control Syst. Mag. **22**, 52–67 (2002)
12. Liu, Y., Passino, K.: Biomimicry of social foraging bacteria for distributed optimization: models, principles, and emergent behaviors. J. Optim. Theory Appl. **115**, 603–628 (2002)
13. Phillips, S.J.: Acceleration of k-means and related clustering algorithms. In: Mount, D.M., Stein, C. (eds.) ALENEX 2002. LNCS, vol. 2409, pp. 166–177. Springer, Heidelberg (2002). https://doi.org/10.1007/3-540-45643-0_13
14. MacKay, D.J., Mac Kay, D.J.: Information theory, inference and learning algorithms. Cambridge university press (2003)

15. Song, B., Wang, Z., Zou, L.: On global smooth path planning for mobile robots using a novel multimodal delayed PSO algorithm. Cogn. Comput. **9**, 5–17 (2017). https://doi.org/10.1007/s12559-016-9442-4
16. Van der Merwe, D., Engelbrecht, A.P.: Data clustering using particle swarm optimization. In: The 2003 Congress on Evolutionary Computation, 2003. CEC 2003, pp. 215–220. IEEE (2003)
17. Rousseeuw, P.J.: Silhouettes: a graphical aid to the interpretation and validation of cluster analysis. J. Comput. Appl. Math. **20**, 53–65 (1987)
18. Taha, A.A., Hanbury, A.: Metrics for evaluating 3D medical image segmentation: analysis, selection, and tool. BMC Med. Imaging **15**, 1–28 (2015)

Brain Storm Optimization Algorithm with Multiple Generation Strategies for Patient Data Clustering

Chen Guo[1], Xikun Liu[1,2], and Keqin Yao[3](✉)

[1] College of Management, Shenzhen University, Shenzhen 518060, China
[2] Greater Bay Area International Institute for Innovation, Shenzhen University, Shenzhen 518060, China
[3] Shenzhen Health Development Research and Data Management Center, Shenzhen 518060, China
szhealth-yao@163.com

Abstract. To alleviate the shortcomings of the K-means algorithm, this paper employs an improved brain storm optimization algorithm (BSO) to solve data clustering issues. Specifically, to enhance the performance of BSO, an improved BSO with three generation strategies (BSOMGS) is proposed to increase the diversity of the algorithm. Then, the BSOMGS integrates with K-means (BSOMGSK) to handle patient data clustering tasks. To verify the performance of the BSOMGSK, BSOMGSK is compared with the other four algorithms on two evaluation indexes of six patient datasets. Additionally, three variants of BSOMGSK, namely BSOMGSK-V1, BSOMGSK-V2 and BSOMGSK-V3, are also presented to test the effectiveness of the new strategies. Experimental results demonstrate that the BSOMGSK is markedly better than its competitors regarding clustering performance. These results also validate the effectiveness and usefulness of the three generation strategies designed in the BSOMGSK.

Keywords: Brain storm optimization algorithm · Multiple generation strategies · K-means · Patient data clustering

1 Introduction

Data clustering aims to divide the objects into different clusters based on the similarity, which is one of the important unsupervised learning techniques [1]. After clustering, the objectives in the same cluster has the highest similarity, and the objectives in the different clusters has the lowest similarity [2]. Generally, distance is used to measure the similarity between objectives. Thus, good clustering partitions mean a small intra-cluster distance and a big inter-cluster distance. Various data clustering techniques have been proposed, such as partition-based, hierarchical-based, density-based, model-based [3], to name a few. Among them, partition-based clustering techniques have been widely studied and applied [4].

Y. Xu et al. (Eds.): ML4CS 2022, LNCS 13657, pp. 321–333, 2023.
https://doi.org/10.1007/978-3-031-20102-8_25

K-means, due to its simple implementation and fast convergence, is a popular partition-based clustering technique [4]. Thus far, K-means has been successfully applied in many fields, such as image segmentation [5], customer segmentation [6], wireless sensor networks [7], healthcare [8], social tags [9], etc. Although K-means obtain these achievements, it has some shortcomings. On one hand, K-means is sensitive to the initialization. Different initialization methods will obtain different clustering results. On the other hand, K-means is susceptible to noise. The cluster centers will be affected if the dataset has noise, leading to low-quality clustering results.

To alleviate the initialization and noise sensitivity issue of K-means, researchers investigate the evolutionary computation-based algorithms [10]. These algorithms mainly include two categories, that is evolutionary algorithms and swarm intelligence optimization algorithms [11]. Evolutionary algorithms are inspired by the biological evolution in nature, and swarm intelligence optimization algorithms get inspiration from the searching behaviors of bird block, fish swarm, bacteria colonies, etc. Genetic algorithm (GA) [12] and particle swarm optimization algorithm (PSO) [13] are representatives of these two categories, respectively. Due to these algorithms have the characteristics of self-adaptive, self-organizing, flexible, and robust, they have been applied to solve many data clustering problems [2, 14]. For example, PSO is used to cluster customer datasets [6], GA and differential evolution algorithm (DE) [15] are employed to handle benchmark data clustering tasks [16, 17], bacterial foraging optimization algorithm is used to deal with credit risk assessment tasks [18].

Brain storm optimization algorithm (BSO) [19] is a member of swarm intelligence optimization algorithms, which gets the ideal from the behavior of the human brainstorming process. Since its inception, BSO has been employed in various applications, like electric power systems [20], wireless sensor networks [21], finance [22], and so on. To further enhance the performance of BSO and extend its application, this paper first proposes an improved BSO with three generation strategies (BSOMGS). Concretely, these generation strategies are intracluster crossover generation strategy, intercluster crossover generation strategy, and Cauchy generation strategy. Then, BSOMGS combines the K-means (BSOMGSK) to cluster six patient datasets. The experimental results demonstrate that BSOMGSK outperforms its competitors and also verify that the new generation strategies have a positive effect on the performance enhancement of BSO.

The remaining parts of this paper are organized as follows. Section 2 presents the background of this paper, covering the brain storm optimization algorithm and K-means clustering algorithm. Section 3 introduces the brain storm optimization algorithm with multiple generation strategies for patient data clustering. Section 4 presents the experimental studies, including the testing datasets, evaluation indexes, and experimental results. Section 5 gives the conclusion of this paper.

2 Background

2.1 Brain Storm Optimization Algorithm

The brain storm optimization (BSO) algorithm is an excellent swarm intelligence paradigm inspired by the behavior of the human brainstorming process [19]. The BSO algorithm has two main operators: the convergence operator and the divergence operator. The process of BSO is shown in the following steps in detail.

First, generate n individuals randomly and calculate the fitness values.

Second, divide n individuals into m clusters $(C = \{c_1, ..., c_p, ..., c_m\}(p = 1, 2, \ldots, m))$ by using K-means clustering algorithm. Then, choose the individuals with the best fitness value in each cluster as the cluster center.

Third, generate a new individual and use it to replace a randomly selected cluster center if $rand(0, 1)$ is less than the preset probability.

Fourth, generate I_{old} by choosing from two methods by comparing the $rand(0, 1)$ and preset probability P_1. If the former one less than the second one, method 1 is selected; otherwise, method 2 is selected.

Method 1. Select a cluster p with certain probability. If $rand(0, 1)$ is less than the preset probability P_2, cluster p's center c_p is chosen as the I_{old}; otherwise, randomly choose an individual from this cluster (denoted as I_p) as I_{old}. The process is shown in Eq. (1),

$$I_{old} = \begin{cases} c_p \; if rand(0, 1) < P_2 \\ I_p \end{cases} \tag{1}$$

Method 2. Select two clusters p and q. If $rand(0, 1)$ is less than the predefined probability P_3, the cluster centers c_p and c_q is combined to generate I_{old}; otherwise, randomly choose two individuals from these two clusters (denoted as I_p and I_q) to generate I_{old}. The process is shown in Eq. (2),

$$I_{old} = \begin{cases} w * c_p + (1 - w) * c_q \; if rand(0, 1) < P_3 \\ w * I_p + (1 - w) * I_q \end{cases} \tag{2}$$

Fifth, generate I_{new} according to I_{old}, the process is shown in Eq. (3),

$$I_{new} = I_{old} + \delta \cdot G(0, 1) \tag{3}$$

where $G(0, 1)$ is a random value in (0,1) generated by Gaussian. δ is shown in as below,

$$\delta = logsig\left(\frac{0.5maxt - curt}{k}\right) * rand(0, 1) \tag{4}$$

where $logsig()$ is a sigmoid transfer function, $maxt$ is the maximum iteration number, $curt$ is the current iteration number, and k is the changing slope of $logsig()$ function.

Sixth, compare the fitness values of I_{new} and I_{old} and leave the better individual.

2.2 K-means Clustering

The K-means is the basic and simplest data clustering approach. As for K-means algorithm, the first K clusters are randomly chosen, and then each data is divided into one cluster based on the similarity. Generally, Euclidean distance is employed to evaluate the similarity. The sum of the squared error (SSE) is the objective function, and the smaller value means the better partition. Given a dataset O with N data points, marked as $O = \{o_1, ..., o_i, ..., o_N\}(i = 1, 2, \ldots N)$. C denotes the set of all K clusters, marked as $C = \{c_1, ..., c_p, ..., c_K\}(p = 1, 2, \ldots, K)$. $dist(,)$ denotes the distance of the data points. The SSE is shown in Eq. (5–6),

$$SSE = \sum_{p=1}^{K} \sum_{o_i \in c_p} dist^2(c_p, o_i) \tag{5}$$

$$c_p = \frac{1}{|c_p|} \sum_{\forall o_i \in c_p} o_i \tag{6}$$

where c_p is the cluster center of cluster p, which is the mean values of data points in the cluster p. $|c_p|$ is the total number of data points in cluster p.

3 Proposed Algorithm

3.1 Brain Storm Optimization Algorithm with Multiple Generation Strategies

To enhance the performance of the original BSO algorithm, the BSO with multiple generation strategies (BSOMGS) is proposed. These generation strategies are intracluster crossover generation strategy, intercluster crossover generation strategy, and Cauchy generation strategy. The details about these three strategies are introduced as follows.

Intracluster Crossover Generation Strategy. In the method 1 of original BSO (see Sect. 2.1), for selected cluster p, its cluster center (c_p) or a randomly selected individual I_p is needed to generate I_{old}. To increase the diversity of the selected individual, the intracluster crossover generation strategy is proposed to produce I_{old} when $rand(0, 1)$ is bigger than P_2. This strategy originates from the crossover operation in GA. First, set a crossover point, and divide the c_p and I_p into two parts. Then, two new individuals, cI_{cross1} and cI_{cross2}, are generated. cI_{cross1} combines the first part of c_p and the second part of I_p, cI_{cross2} combines the first part of I_p and the second part of c_p. Therefore, the Eq. (1) can be changed to Eq. (7),

$$I_{old} = \begin{cases} c_p & if rand(0, 1) < P_2 \\ w * cI_{cross1} + (1 - w) * cI_{cross2} & \end{cases} \tag{7}$$

Intercluster Crossover Generation Strategy. In the method 2 of orginal BSO (see Sect. 2.1), two cluster centers (c_p and c_q) or individuals belonged to these two clusters (I_p and I_q) are needed to generate I_{old}. Similarly, to enhance the diversity of selected cluster centers or individuals, the intercluster crossover generation strategy is proposed. Take two cluster centers p and q as an example. Concretely, based on the crossover operation, set a crossover point that divide the two individuals into two parts, then two new individuals, c_{cross1} and c_{cross2} (I_{cross1} and I_{cross2} for two selected individuals belonging to clusters p and q), are generated: the first individual combines the first part of c_p and the second part of c_q; the second individual combines the first part of c_q and the second part of c_p. Thus, the Eq. (2) can be changed to Eq. (8),

$$I_{old} = \begin{cases} w * c_{cross1} + (1 - w) * c_{cross2} \; if rand(0, 1) < P_2 \\ w * I_{cross1} + (1 - w) * I_{cross2} \end{cases} \tag{8}$$

Cauchy Generation Strategy. In the original BSO, Gaussian distribution is used to generate new individual. However, Cauchy distribution can generate more diverse individual than Gaussian distribution [23]. Compared with the Gaussian mutation, the Cauchy mutation will produce a larger variation asynchronous length to help the individuals escape from the local optimum. Hence, to further increase the diversity of individuals and search more potential areas, the Cauchy generation strategy is employed to replace the Gaussian distribution. The Eq. (3) can be changed to Eq. (9),

$$I_{new} = I_{old} + \delta \cdot Cauchy(0, 1) \tag{9}$$

3.2 Objective Functions

To obtain a clustering result that is compact within clusters and separated between clusters, the compactness-separation index (C-S) proposed in [16] is used as the objective function of this paper. With the help of C-S, high-quality cluster partitions can be obtained. The C-S is shown in Eqs. (9–11),

$$comp_p = \frac{\sum_{o_i \in c_p} dist(c_p, o_i)}{|c_p|} \tag{10}$$

$$sep_p = \min_{\forall p \neq q} \{d(c_p, c_q)\} \tag{11}$$

$$C - S = \sum_{p=1}^{K} (comp_p - sep_p) \tag{12}$$

where $comp_p$ is the compactness of cluster p, and sep_p is the separation of cluster p. $C - S$ is the compactness-separation index of all the clusters. Other symbols appeared in Eqs. (9–11) are the same as in Sect. 2.2. For the C-S, the smaller the better.

3.3 The Framework of BSOMGSK

Based on the introduction above, BSOMGSK is proposed by using the BSOMGS to optimize the C-S. The framework of BSOMGSK is depicted in Algorithm 1.

Algorithm 1. BSOMGSK

Input: a dataset, parameters of BSOMGS
Output: final clustering results
for $run = 1{:}\,maxrun$
  Initialize the position of all individuals and calculate their fitness function using equation (12)
    for $curt = 1{:}\,maxt$
      Implement the first, second, and third steps of BSO
      Implement the fourth step of BSO using equations (7) or (8) to generate I_{old}
      Implement the fifth step of BSO using equations (9) and (4)
      Implement the sixth step of BSO
    end
    Store the best clustering results of each run;
end
Store all the best clustering results of all the runs
Obtain a final clustering results

4 Experimental Studies

In this paper, original BSO [19], PSO [13], DE [15], and GA [12] are selected to combine with K-means as the competitors to test the performance of BSOMGSK regarding two evaluation indexes on six testing datasets. These competitors are named BSOK, PSOK, DEK, and GAK, respectively. In addition, three variants of BSOMGSK, namely BSOMGSK-V1, BSOMGSK-V2 and BSOMGSK-V3, are designed to investigate the effectiveness of the proposed strategies.

All experiments implement 20 independent runs and 500 iterations. The population size of all the evolutionary algorithms and swarm intelligence algorithms is 50. For BSOMGSK and BSOK, the corresponding parameters refer to [24]. For PSOK, W_{max} and W_{min} are 0.9 and 0.4, the C_1 and C_2 are 2. For DEK, the crossover probability is 0.2. For GAK, the crossover percentage is 0.8 and the mutation percentage is 0.3. All experiments are conducted on a PC with 2.20 GHz CPU and 16.0 GB memory using MATLAB R2021b.

4.1 Testing Datasets

To test the performance of proposed algorithm, this paper employs six patient stratification datasets[1] as the testing datasets. The description of the datasets is shown in Table 1, including the tissues, number of samples, number of features, and number of clusters.

[1] Data source: https://schlieplab.org/Static/Supplements/CompCancer/datasets.htm.

4.2 Evaluation Indexes

Various evaluation indexes have been proposed to estimate the quality of clustering partitions obtained by different clustering algorithms. This paper selects two indexes, that is Accuracy (ACC) [25] and Fmeasure (FM) [3], to evaluate the performance of BSOMGSK and its comparative algorithms. For the ACC and FM, the higher the better. For further information, please refer to the corresponding references.

Table 1. The description of testing datasets.

Dataset	Tissues	Samples	Features	Clusters
Singh-2002 (D1)	Prostate	102	339	2
Khan-2001 (D2)	Multi-tissue	83	1069	4
Armstrong-2002-v1 (D3)	Blood	72	1081	2
Dyrskjot-2003 (D4)	Bladder	40	1203	3
Bhattacharjee-2001 (D5)	Lung	203	1543	5
Nutt-2003-v1 (D6)	Brain	50	1377	4

4.3 Experimental Results of BSOMGSK and Its Competitors

The experimental results, that is mean values and standard values, of BSOMGSK and its competitors are shown in Table 2. The best mean values of two evaluation indexes on six datasets are shown in bold and underlines, and the mean values ranked second are shown in bold only. The total number of first ranking and second ranking are presented in the last row of Table 2.

It can be seen from the last row of Table 2 that the number of first/second ranking of BSOMGSK, BSOK, PSOK, DEK, and GAK are 12/3, 1/6, 1/5, 2/2 and 4/1. Concretely, BSOMGSK obtains two first rankings on datasets D1, D3, D4, D5 and D6. On the contrary, BSOK performs relatively poorly on dataset D3 regarding to all the evaluation indexes. PSOK has poor performance on D1 and D2 datasets, DEK on D2, D4, and D5 datasets, and GAK on D4 and D6 datasets, respectively. Combining the above analysis, the proposal BSOMGSK has the overwhelming performance than its competitors and other four algorithms have inconsistent performance on different datasets. Additionally, the average C-S, ACC and FM of BSOMGSK and its competitors on six datasets are shown in Fig. 1. It can be observed that BSOMGSK outperforms its peer algorithms over C-S of six datasets. As for ACC, except for Khan-2001 dataset, BSOMGSK has the outstanding performance than other four algorithms. As for FM, BSOMGSK also has better performance. In brief, the experimental results confirm the potential and effectiveness of the BSOMGSK compared to its counterparts.

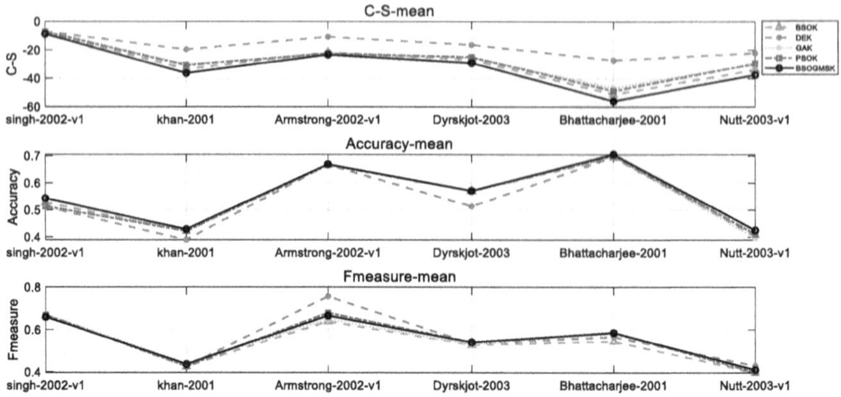

Fig. 1. Mean evaluation indexes of BSOMGSK and its competitors on six datasets.

4.4 Experimental Results of BSOMGSK and Its Variants

To verify the effectiveness of three improvements designed in BSOMGSK, ablation experiments are conducted. Three variants of BSOMGSK are proposed: BSOMGSK-V1 is the variant of BSOMGSK without Cauchy generation strategy, BSOMGSK-V2 is a variant of BSOMGSK without intercluster crossover generation strategy, and BSOMGSK-V3 is a variant of BSOMGSK without intracluster crossover generation strategy. The experimental results are shown in Table 3.

For Table 3, the last row is the total number of first and second ranking. It can be observed that the number of first/second ranking of BSOK, BSOMGSK-V1, BSOMGSK-V2, BSOMGSK-V3 and BSOMGSK are 1/2, 2/2, 1/10, 1/1 and 16/1, respectively. Comparing BSOMGSK with its three variants and BSOK, it verifies that the designed strategies in BSOMGSK has the positive effect on the performance enhancement. Additionally, the intercluster crossover generation strategy improves the performance of BSOK best. In a nutshell, the strategies designed in BSOMGSK are feasible and effective.

Table 2. The experimental results of BSOMGSK and its competitors on six datasets.

Dataset	Evaluation index		BSOK	PSOK	DEK	GAK	BSOMGSK
D1	C-S	Mean	**−7.4261**	−7.2433	−6.9284	−6.9410	**<u>−8.7278</u>**
		Std.	0.7387	1.4069	0.0198	0.0216	1.1403
	ACC	Mean	**0.5270**	0.5132	0.5113	0.5098	**<u>0.5422</u>**
		Std.	0.0244	0.0092	0.0048	0.0000	0.0169
	FM	Mean	0.6656	0.6683	**0.6697**	**<u>0.6699</u>**	0.6597
		Std.	0.0104	0.0067	0.0065	0.0063	0.0060

(continued)

Table 2. (*continued*)

Dataset	Evaluation index		BSOK	PSOK	DEK	GAK	BSOMGSK
D2	C-S	Mean	**−33.4916**	−30.7936	−19.5624	−29.9604	<u>**−36.3627**</u>
		Std.	1.1416	1.5778	0.0859	1.7607	0.7485
	ACC	Mean	0.4211	0.4217	0.3892	<u>**0.4295**</u>	**0.4283**
		Std.	0.0411	0.0298	0.0546	0.0355	0.0563
	FM	Mean	0.4257	0.4272	0.4259	<u>**0.4402**</u>	**0.4365**
		Std.	0.0418	0.0347	0.0460	0.0432	0.0435
D3	C-S	Mean	−21.6050	−22.3026	−10.7129	**−22.5096**	<u>**−23.2914**</u>
		Std.	0.3548	0.4012	0.0394	0.3355	0.3083
	ACC	Mean	0.6667	0.6667	**0.6674**	0.6667	<u>**0.6688**</u>
		Std.	0.0000	0.0000	0.0031	0.0000	0.0093
	FM	Mean	0.6390	**0.6798**	<u>**0.7571**</u>	0.6482	0.6659
		Std.	0.0483	0.0038	0.0430	0.0319	0.0269
D4	C-S	Mean	**−26.7416**	−24.9402	−16.2825	−25.3221	<u>**−29.0805**</u>
		Std.	0.6622	3.0435	0.0482	1.1982	0.5232
	ACC	Mean	<u>**0.5713**</u>	<u>**0.5713**</u>	0.5138	0.5700	<u>**0.5713**</u>
		Std.	0.0515	0.0475	0.0250	0.0426	0.0383
	FM	Mean	0.5282	**0.5402**	0.5346	0.5308	<u>**0.5409**</u>
		Std.	0.0691	0.0421	0.0605	0.0464	0.0432
D5	C-S	Mean	**−51.2421**	−48.7587	−27.1149	−46.5592	<u>**−55.9246**</u>
		Std.	1.2536	1.1368	0.0583	1.8884	1.2835
	ACC	Mean	0.6941	**0.7005**	0.6958	0.6990	<u>**0.7054**</u>
		Std.	0.0130	0.0119	0.0142	0.0114	0.0168
	FM	Mean	0.5454	**0.5861**	0.5663	<u>**0.5901**</u>	0.5852
		Std.	0.0727	0.0459	0.0873	0.0426	0.0460
D6	C-S	Mean	**−33.8734**	−29.3924	−22.1076	−29.8861	<u>**−37.4413**</u>
		Std.	1.4967	3.8883	0.1222	2.3501	0.9390
	ACC	Mean	0.4080	**0.4100**	0.4020	0.3950	<u>**0.4250**</u>
		Std.	0.0278	0.0287	0.0531	0.0317	0.0435
	FM	Mean	0.3970	0.3987	<u>**0.4294**</u>	0.4034	**0.4107**
		Std.	0.0325	0.0353	0.0478	0.0249	0.0377
First/Second			1/6	1/5	2/2	4/1	12/3

Table 3. The experimental results of BSOMGSK and its variants on six datasets.

Dataset	Evaluation Index		BSOK	BSOKMGS-V1	BSOMGSK-V2	BSOMGSK-V3	BSOMGSK
D1	C-S	Mean	−7.4261	−8.1177	**−8.6604**	−7.6640	**−8.7278**
		Std.	0.7387	1.0490	1.2826	0.9005	1.1403
	ACC	Mean	0.5270	**0.5417**	0.5382	0.5304	**0.5422**
		Std.	0.0244	0.0264	0.0182	0.0215	0.0169
	FM	Mean	**0.6656**	0.6604	0.6622	**0.6663**	0.6597
		Std.	0.0104	0.0108	0.0079	0.0094	0.0060
D2	C-S	Mean	−33.4916	−34.2748	**−36.1868**	−35.0320	**−36.3627**
		Std.	1.1416	0.8837	1.0708	1.0580	0.7485
	ACC	Mean	0.4211	0.4199	**0.4235**	0.4205	**0.4283**
		Std.	0.0411	0.0492	0.0332	0.0331	0.0563
	FM	Mean	0.4257	0.4196	**0.4320**	0.4274	**0.4365**
		Std.	0.0418	0.0420	0.0257	0.0306	0.0435
D3	C-S	Mean	−21.6050	−22.1207	**−23.2134**	−22.5772	**−23.2914**
		Std.	0.3548	0.2377	0.2685	0.2486	0.3083
	ACC	Mean	0.6667	**0.6688**	0.6681	0.6674	**0.6688**
		Std.	0.0000	0.0093	0.0062	0.0031	0.0093
	FM	Mean	0.6390	0.6551	**0.6573**	0.6567	**0.6659**
		Std.	0.0483	0.0273	0.0294	0.0345	0.0269
D4	C-S	Mean	−26.7416	−27.5409	**−28.9581**	−27.7334	**−29.0805**
		Std.	0.6622	0.5979	0.3953	0.5195	0.5232
	ACC	Mean	**0.5713**	**0.5713**	0.5650	0.5675	**0.5713**
		Std.	0.0515	0.0569	0.0384	0.0381	0.0383
	FM	Mean	0.5282	0.5323	0.5344	**0.5380**	**0.5409**
		Std.	0.0691	0.0537	0.0332	0.0472	0.0432
D5	C-S	Mean	−51.2421	−51.4897	**−55.4426**	−53.3046	**−55.9246**
		Std.	1.2536	1.1263	1.6555	1.8451	1.2835
	ACC	Mean	0.6941	**0.7034**	0.7025	0.7032	**0.7054**
		Std.	0.0130	0.0189	0.0085	0.0132	0.0168

(*continued*)

Table 3. (*continued*)

Dataset	Evaluation Index		BSOK	BSOKMGS-V1	BSOMGSK-V2	BSOMGSK-V3	BSOMGSK
	FM	Mean	0.5454	0.5845	**0.5928**	0.5765	**0.5852**
		Std.	0.0727	0.0684	0.0414	0.0583	0.0460
D6	C-S	Mean	−33.8734	−34.9688	**−37.2989**	−36.2124	**−37.4413**
		Std.	1.4967	1.5678	0.8493	0.9025	0.9390
	ACC	Mean	**0.4080**	0.3980	0.4060	0.3970	**0.4250**
		Std.	0.0278	0.0430	0.0495	0.0374	0.0435
	FM	Mean	0.3970	0.3991	**0.4071**	0.3908	**0.4107**
		Std.	0.0325	0.0323	0.0431	0.0343	0.0377
First/Second			1/2	2/2	1/10	1/1	16/1

5 Conclusion

This paper hybrids an improved BSO with multiple generation strategies with K-means (BSOMGSK) to deal with patient data clustering tasks. Concretely, first, BSOMGS is designed by integrating the intracluster crossover generation strategy, intercluster crossover generation strategy, and Cauchy generation strategy into original BSO. Then, BSOMGSK is proposed by combining the BSOMGS with K-means. To validate the clustering ability of BSOMGSK and validate the effectiveness of proposed strategies, experiments are conducted to compare BSOMGSK with the other four evolutionary computation-based algorithms and also with its three variants. Comparative experiments demonstrate that the BSOMGSK outperforms its four competitors and also verify the effectiveness and feasibility of three generation strategies.

In the future work, BSOMGSK will be employed to solve multi-objective data clustering tasks. In addition, more improvements should be developed to further enhance the performance of BSO.

Acknowledgments. The work described in this paper was supported by The Natural Science Foundation of Guangdong Province (Grant No. 2020A1515010749), Key Research Foundation of Higher Education of Guangdong Provincial Education Bureau (Grant No. 2019KZDXM030), University Innovation Team Project of Guangdong Province (Grant No. 2021WCXTD002).

References

1. José-García, A., Gómez-Flores, W.: Automatic clustering using nature-inspired metaheuristics: A survey. Appl. Soft Comput. **41**, 192–213 (2016)
2. Saxena, A., et al.: A review of clustering techniques and developments. Neurocomputing **267**, 664–681 (2017)
3. Han, J., Pei, J., Kamber, M.: Data mining: concepts and techniques. Elsevier (2011)

4. Jain, A.K.: Data clustering: 50 years beyond K-means. Pattern Recogn. Lett. **31**, 651–666 (2010)
5. He, L., Zhang, H.: Kernel K-means sampling for Nyström approximation. IEEE Trans. Image Process. **27**, 2108–2120 (2018)
6. Li, Y., Chu, X., Tian, D., Feng, J., Mu, W.: Customer segmentation using K-means clustering and the adaptive particle swarm optimization algorithm. Appl. Soft Comput. **113**, 107924 (2021)
7. Qin, J., Fu, W., Gao, H., Zheng, W.X.: Distributed k-means algorithm and fuzzy c-means algorithm for sensor networks based on multiagent consensus theory. IEEE Trans. Cybern. **47**, 772–783 (2016)
8. Adapa, B., Biswas, D., Bhardwaj, S., Raghuraman, S., Acharyya, A., Maharatna, K.: Coordinate rotation-based low complexity k-means clustering architecture. IEEE Trans. Very Large Scale Integr. Syst. **25**, 1568–1572 (2017)
9. Yang, J., Wang, J.: Tag clustering algorithm LMMSK: improved K-means algorithm based on latent semantic analysis. J. Syst. Eng. Electron. **28**, 374–384 (2017)
10. Hancer, E., Karaboga, D.: A comprehensive survey of traditional, merge-split and evolutionary approaches proposed for determination of cluster number. Swarm Evol. Comput. **32**, 49–67 (2017)
11. Al-Sahaf, H., et al.: A survey on evolutionary machine learning. J. R. Soc. N. Z. **49**, 205–228 (2019)
12. Sumathi, S., Hamsapriya, T., Surekha, P.: Evolutionary intelligence: an introduction to theory and applications with Matlab. Springer Science & Business Media (2008)
13. Shi, Y., Eberhart, R.: A modified particle swarm optimizer. In: 1998 IEEE international conference on evolutionary computation proceedings. IEEE world congress on computational intelligence (Cat. No. 98TH8360), pp. 69–73. IEEE (1998)
14. Nanda, S.J., Panda, G.: A survey on nature inspired metaheuristic algorithms for partitional clustering. Swarm Evol. Comput. **16**, 1–18 (2014)
15. Fatih Tasgetiren, M., Liang, Y.-C., Sevkli, M., Gencyilmaz, G.: Particle swarm optimization and differential evolution for the single machine total weighted tardiness problem. Int. J. Prod. Res. **44**, 4737–4754 (2006)
16. Rahman, M.A., Islam, M.Z.: A hybrid clustering technique combining a novel genetic algorithm with K-Means. Knowl.-Based Syst. **71**, 345–365 (2014)
17. Sheng, W., Wang, X., Wang, Z., Li, Q., Zheng, Y., Chen, S.: A differential evolution algorithm with adaptive niching and k-means operation for data clustering. IEEE Trans. Cybern. (2020)
18. Guo, C., Tang, H., Niu, B.: Evolutionary state-based novel multi-objective periodic bacterial foraging optimization algorithm for data clustering. Expert. Syst. **39**, e12812 (2022)
19. Shi, Y.: Brain storm optimization algorithm. In: International conference in swarm intelligence, pp. 303–309. Springer (2011)
20. Jadhav, H., Sharma, U., Patel, J., Roy, R.: Brain storm optimization algorithm based economic dispatch considering wind power. In: 2012 IEEE International Conference on Power and Energy (PECon), pp. 588–593. IEEE (2012)
21. Chen, J., Cheng, S., Chen, Y., Xie, Y., Shi, Y.: Enhanced brain storm optimization algorithm for wireless sensor networks deployment. In: International Conference in Swarm Intelligence, pp. 373–381. Springer (2015)
22. Sun, Y.: A hybrid approach by integrating brain storm optimization algorithm with grey neural network for stock index forecasting. In: Abstract and Applied Analysis. Hindawi (2014)

23. Wang, F., Zhang, H., Zhou, A.: A particle swarm optimization algorithm for mixed-variable optimization problems. Swarm Evol. Comput. **60**, 100808 (2021)
24. Cheng, S., Chen, J., Lei, X., Shi, Y.: Locating multiple optima via brain storm optimization algorithms. IEEE Access **6**, 17039–17049 (2018)
25. Yang, Y.: An evaluation of statistical approaches to text categorization. Inf. Retrieval **1**, 69–90 (1999)

TGPFM: An Optimized Framework for Ordering and Transporting Raw Materials for Production

Dongni Hu[1(✉)], Wenjun Li[2], Yada Yu[3], Junhao Li[4], and Hongyang Yan[5]

[1] School of Computer Science and Cyber Engineering, Guangzhou University, Guangzhou 510006, China
3174272866@qq.com

[2] Institute of Artificial Intelligence and Blockchain, Guangzhou University, Guangzhou 510006, China
wenjun1999@e.gzhu.edu.cn

[3] School of Economics and Statistics, Guangzhou University, Guangzhou 510006, China
123688916@qq.com

[4] School of Computer Science and Cyber Engineering, Guangzhou University, Guangzhou 510006, China
975984240@qq.com

[5] Institute of Artificial Intelligence and Blockchain, Guangzhou University, Guangzhou 510006, China
hyang_yan@gzhu.edu.cn

Abstract. Developing efficient raw material ordering and transshipment strategies for companies with uncertain supply has attracted extensive interests from both academic and industrial researchers. Some methods have been proposed, such as obtaining a strategy using a heuristic algorithm, or developing an ordering scheme and a transportation scheme separately. These methods can work in some cases, but they can also lead to local optimization. To address this problem, we proposed the TGPFM framework, which takes raw material ordering, transshipment, and inventory into account. The TGPFM is made up of a supply capacity grey cycle prediction model, a transporter time series prediction model, a supplier PCA evaluation model, a multi-objective ordering scheme planning model, and a transshipment planning model. As a result, the problem of local optimization, which is induced by considering each process separately, can be effectively avoided. We conducted experiments on data from national competitions to verify the framework's validity. The results show that putting a weight limit on inventory and material types in the ordering model, as well as using a PCA-based supplier ranking table, can help get a better overall plan. The time series of transit loss outperforms the grey prediction, and the grey prediction model combined with the excess fluctuation function can better predict supplier supply quantity.

This work was supported by National Natural Science Foundation of China (No.62102107, 62072132, 62002074, 62072127, 62002076).

Y. Xu et al. (Eds.): ML4CS 2022, LNCS 13657, pp. 334–349, 2023.
https://doi.org/10.1007/978-3-031-20102-8_26

Keywords: Principal components analysis · Grey-prediction · Multi-objective programming · Prediction of time series · Periodic fluctuation

1 Introduction

Thanks to the global economy's integration and the development of the Internet, supply chains, and other technologies, people can now choose from a growing number of manufacturer brands when purchasing goods. As a result, the number of suppliers available to manufacturers is steadily growing. Manufacturers would prefer to spend the majority of their costs on the product and avoid the costs of ordering, forwarding, and stocking the goods in order to maximize profits. The cost composition varies by segment; for example, when ordering raw materials, consider the supply and demand balance, cost price, supplier selection, and so on. The importance of an effective materials ordering plan and supplier selection strategy has been revealed by [10]. The choice of supplier, according to [5], can affect the project schedule. Failure to choose the right supplier, according to [6], will increase the cost of ordering as well as the cost of implementing the project. The volume of goods being forwarded, the forwarder chosen, and other factors should all be considered when evaluating forwarding. Stock capacity, the amount of goods arriving, and other factors should all be taken into account when planning inventory. Although [17] takes into account both project scheduling and material procurement, it neglects to account for warehouse capacity, which does not correspond to reality. At the same time, the aforementioned connections are interconnected. According to [16], if the project schedule and material procurement are not taken into account as a whole, the total project cost will rise. Consequently, the better the coordination, the lower the total project cost.

The following sub-problems have been refined to reduce the total cost of goods in the ordering, forwarding, and warehousing processes while still meeting business needs.

- RQ1: How to measure the supplier's ability to supply?
- RQ2: How can historical data be used to forecast a supplier's ability to supply over time in order to arrive at a good ordering solution when supply and demand are uncertain?
- RQ3: How to set the cost-cutting objective function and constraints for ordering and forwarding solutions?
- RQ4: How to maximize total cost savings by combining ordering, forwarding solutions, and inventory restrictions?
- RQ5: How can attrition rates for forwarders be accurately predicted?

To address the aforementioned sub-problems, we proposed the TGPFM framework, which takes into account the ordering and transportation of raw materials in its entirety. To forecast future availability over a given time horizon, a grey forecasting model and a fluctuating model of excess output were first combined. Second, using time series weighted shifts, the forwarders' weekly attrition rates were predicted. The order plan for the next 24 weeks is created by using the multi-objective programming model to add the ratio of material A and B as a preference in the objective function with the goal of minimizing cost. By establishing 11 supplier indicators, the PCA-based supplier evaluation form was created. The predicted forwarder attrition rate was used to establish a forwarder ranking table. The forwarding scheme was implemented by substituting the ordering scheme and the two ranking tables into the 0–1 planning model.

In summary, this article makes the following contributions.

- We propose a TGPFM framework that includes a time series forecasting model, a grey forecasting model, a PCA, an excess volatility function, and a multi-objective planning model for picking the optimal strategy for minimizing raw material costs throughout ordering, transportation, and storage.
- We used a functional approximation to forecast supply capacity and a grey forecasting model to forecast supply fluctuations. Ultimately, the weighted and summed results were used to determine the final supplier supply.
- To obtain the forwarding scheme, we created a supplier and forwarder ranking table and substituted the obtained ordering scheme into the planning model with the two ranking tables.
- Inventory weights and raw material weights were added to the ordering scheme's objective function to balance inventory and ordering costs, as well as to limit stock levels.
- We conducted extensive experiments on the Mathematical Modelling National Competition dataset to validate the effectiveness of our proposed framework. Experiments have shown that TGPFM can develop lower-cost ordering and transshipment schemes for raw materials in the face of supply and demand uncertainty.

2 Background

The globalization of the economy has resulted in the formation of dynamic supply chain alliances. Companies can use supply chain management to cut costs, such as procurement, distribution, and storage, and thus gain a competitive advantage in the marketplace. However, many businesses are concerned about how to achieve quality management; one of the challenges is supply chain uncertainty, which manifests itself in supply, demand, articulation, and business operations. The uncertainty of supply (variations in the number of available suppliers) and the uncertainty of convergence are discussed in this paper (losses in transit). See Fig. 1 for the specific process.

Heuristic algorithms and planning models are the two main types of solutions that have been developed for the ordering scheduling problem in enterprises.

For very large data sets, intelligent algorithms are required, but recent research has revealed that there is still a risk of falling into a local optimum. The Resource-Constrained Project Scheduling Problem (RCPSP) has a wide range of applications, and its research is both academically and practically important. Large-scale, strongly constrained, multi-objective, uncertain, and NP-hard are

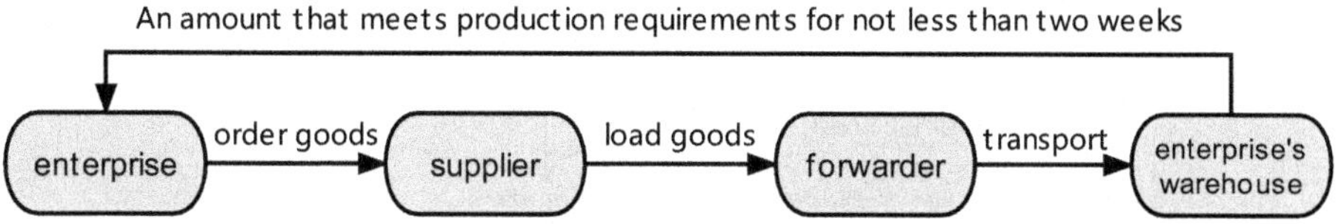

Fig. 1. Ordering and shipping process

some of the complexities. As a result, a variety of heuristic and meta-heuristic algorithms to solve it have been proposed. [14] proposed a multi-stage stochastic mixed-integer programming with endogenous uncertainty and a heuristic search for feasible solutions, lowering the total cost significantly. [2] proposed a method for project scheduling that took into account material ordering, procurement, and supplier selection all at the same time in order to maximize profit and improve the heuristic algorithm with a restart mechanism. However, there is no single heuristic or meta-heuristic algorithm that can solve the RCPS-DC problem in a reasonable amount of time.

Although methods that use planning models to solve the ordering transit problem can produce optimal results, none of them have produced more specific scheduling and ordering solutions. The use of a mixed-integer programming model to obtain optimal ordering solutions under multiple constraints was proposed by [7], and computational experiments showed that large computers are not required to solve problems with relatively large data sizes. To find the ordering solution, [23] used linear programming with value-at-risk as the objective function. The above schemes, as can be seen, do not take into account ordering, transshipment, and inventory as a whole.

3 Methodology

This section delves into the specifics of the components that make up the framework provided in this paper. Specifically, the TGPFM model is composed of time series prediction, grey prediction, multi-objective programming, PCA, and periodic wave function. Grey forecasting and periodic fluctuation constitute the supplier quantity forecasting model. The supplier multi-objective model is combined with the supplier quantity forecasting model to solve the ordering scheme. The ordering scheme combines supplier ranking table (PCA algorithm), transportation loss prediction (time series), and a multi-objective programming model of forwarder to get the transportation scheme. The specific steps are shown in Fig. 2.

3.1 Problem Definition

Assume that different raw materials are ordered at varying prices, but that transportation and storage costs are the same per unit. A manufacturing company requires N raw materials in a certain quantity. How to establish a strategy for

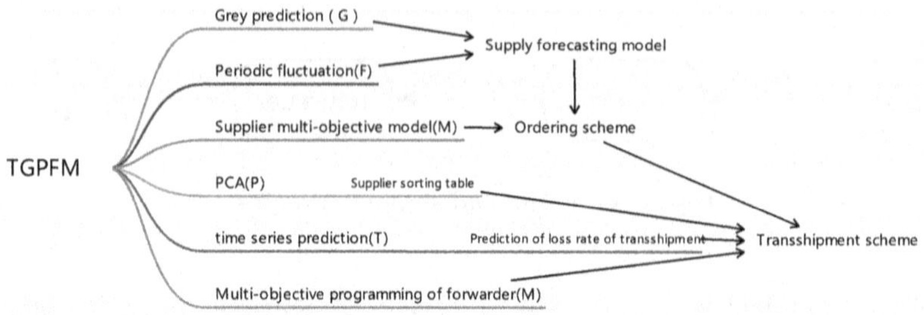

Fig. 2. The framework of TGPFM model

ordering and moving raw materials over the following T weeks. In this study, we suppose that there are three types of raw materials and that T equals 24 weeks.

3.2 Supplier Supply Forecast Based on Historical Data

The 240 weeks are divided into ten stages, with an average supply quantity determined for each stage. Furthermore, to reflect the supply rule of providers over time, it was integrated into the grey prediction model.

Grey System Prediction. This paper uses the GM(1, 1) model [22] to expand. The model's prediction premise is as follows: by accumulating a given data series, a collection of new data series with a clear trend is formed. Next, for prediction, a model is created based on the new data series' developing tendency. The original data series is then recreated using the accumulation and subtraction approach, resulting in the predicted result. The modeling process is rough as follows:

Step 1: Let a set of original data be $x^{(0)} = \left(x^{(0)}(1), x^{(0)}(2), \ldots x^{(0)}(n)\right)$, n is the number of data. Accumulate $x^{(0)}$ to weaken the volatility and randomness of the random sequence, and get a new sequence as follows:

$$x^{(1)} = \left(x^{(1)}(1), x^{(1)}(2), \ldots x^{(1)}(n)\right) \tag{1}$$

$$x^{(1)}(k) = \sum_{i}^{k} x^{(0)}(i), k = 1, 2, \ldots, n \tag{2}$$

Step 2: Generate adjacent mean equal weight column of $x^{(1)}$:

$$z^{(1)} = \left(z^{(1)}(2), z^{(1)}(3), \ldots z^{(1)}(k)\right), k = 2, 3, \ldots, n \tag{3}$$

$$z^{(1)}(k) = 0.5x^{(1)}(k-1) + 0.5x^{(1)}(k), k = 2, 3, \ldots, n \tag{4}$$

Step 3: Establish a first-order unitary differential equation of the whitening form of t for $x^{(1)}$ according to grey theory:

$$GM\left(1,1\right):\frac{dx^{(1)}}{dt}+ax^{(1)}=u \tag{5}$$

Among them, a, u are the coefficients to be solved, which are called development coefficient and grey action quantity, respectively. The effective interval of a is $(-2, 2)$, and the matrix formed by a,u is grey parameter $\hat{a}=\begin{pmatrix} a \\ u \end{pmatrix}$ As long as the parameters a, u are obtained, $x^{(1)}(t)$ can be obtained, and then the predicted value of $x^{(0)}$ can be obtained.

Step 4: Average the accumulated generated data to generate B and a constant term vector Y_n:

$$B=\begin{bmatrix} -z^{(1)}\left(2\right) & 1 \\ -z^{(1)}\left(3\right) & 1 \\ \vdots & \vdots \\ -z^{(1)}\left(n\right) & 1 \end{bmatrix}=\begin{bmatrix} -\frac{1}{2}\left(x^{(1)}\left(1\right)+x^{(1)}\left(2\right)\right) & 1 \\ -\frac{1}{2}\left(x^{(1)}\left(2\right)+x^{(1)}\left(3\right)\right) & 1 \\ \vdots & \vdots \\ -\frac{1}{2}\left(x^{(1)}\left(n-1\right)+x^{(1)}\left(n\right)\right) & 1 \end{bmatrix} \tag{6}$$

Step 5: Use the least square method to solve the grey parameter $\hat{a}$, then

$$\hat{a}=\left(B^TB\right)^{-1}B^TY_n \tag{7}$$

Step 6: Substitute grey parameter $\hat{a}$ into $\frac{dx^{(1)}}{dt}+ax^{(1)}=u$, and solve $\frac{dx^{(1)}}{dt}+ax^{(1)}=u$ to get

$$\hat{x}^{(1)}\left(t+1\right)=\left(x^{(1)}\left(1\right)-\frac{u}{a}\right)e^{-at}+\frac{u}{a} \tag{8}$$

Step 7: Subtract and restore the above results to get the predicted value.

Periodic Wave Function. We apply the function fitting and averaging to acquire the basic supply capacity of 402 providers in the next 24 weeks because the supplier's supply amount given in the table is related to the orderer's ordering quantity as well as its own supply capacity. We consider every 24 weeks to be an ordering cycle because this company orders and transships raw goods every 24 weeks [8].

Firstly, the average supply quantity r_1 is calculated, and the data of supply quantity greater than two times of average r_1 is regarded as oversupply. After deleting the over-supply data, the average r_2 of the remaining data is calculated, that is, calculating the number of times m of excess supply, and the average r_2 is taken as the basic supply capacity of each supplier.

$$\begin{cases} r_1=\frac{\sum x}{240} \\ r_2=\frac{\sum x}{m}, x\leq 2r_1 \end{cases} \tag{9}$$

For the oversupply data, we get the mean r_3 and the times t. Divide the number t by 10 to get the frequency T of oversupply in each order cycle.

$$\begin{cases} r_3 = \frac{1}{t}\sum x, x > 2r_1 \\ T = \frac{t}{10} \end{cases} \tag{10}$$

The sine function is used to construct a 24-week fluctuation function, and the probability of overproduction fluctuation is introduced.

$$\sin\left(\frac{\pi}{12} * T * i\right) > 0.95, i \in (1, 24) \tag{11}$$

After adding the excess supply fluctuation, the supply capacity of the current week is:

$$G = r_2 + r_3 + \varepsilon, \varepsilon \sim N\left(r_1, \sigma^2\right) \tag{12}$$

Finally, add the general error ε of normal distribution based on historical data, and we can get the forecast supply in the next 24 weeks. Where ε^2 is the variance of the supplied sample.

Supplier Supply Quantity Prediction

The average value of function fitting was given 4/5 weight, the grey prediction model was given 1/5 weight, and the final prediction result was solved after adding.

3.3 Ordering Scheme Model Based on Multi-objective Programming

Preliminary Analysis of ABC Raw Material Supplier

In normal circumstances, businesses purchase raw materials at a lower unit price and utilize fewer raw resources. The Table 1 shows that Class A materials use less energy and are less expensive. Because Class B raw materials have the greatest cost per unit price for finished products, firms will choose to use Class A raw materials, followed by Class C. In addition, fitting historical data reveals that just 24% of weekly orders of Class B materials can meet capacity requirements. Therefore, we limited the weight of C and B products in the objective function [4].

Table 1. Cost performance of raw materials

Type of raw materials	The unit price	Unit consumption of finished products	Unit cost of finished products
A	1.2	0.6	0.72
B	1.1	0.66	0.726
C	1.0	0.72	0.72

Establishment of Ordering Scheme Model

As far as practicable, each supplier selects just one forwarder per week, and each forwarder's transshipment capacity is limited to 6,000 cubic meters. When each provider's volume is greater than 6,000 per week, the organization receives just 6,000 per week from each supplier. If it is less than 6,000, the supplier is responsible for providing the real supply to the company. The accumulated items of suppliers are carried to the enterprise warehouse as soon as feasible to simplify the examination of difficulties and practical problems. As a result, the untransported items of suppliers are estimated and will arrive at the enterprise warehouse the following week.

We used a single week as an example to build a multi-objective programming model with the most cost-effective ordering strategy. The overall weekly supply of raw materials must fulfill the production needs. To keep the steel industry's costs down, that is, to keep the purchase and warehouse inventory costs as low as possible [21].

Since the storage volume needs to meet the enterprise's capacity demand, xx_i is obtained by converting the material volume into the enterprise's capacity. Write E_t as the storage volume of week t, which is determined by the storage volume of last week E_{t-1}, the usage of raw materials in production this week L and the new transportation volume.

$$E_t = E_{t-1} - L + \sum xx_i \tag{13}$$

$$min\ Cost = q \cdot (1.2a + 1.1b + 1.0c) + 2000 \cdot b + 100 \cdot c + p \cdot E_t \tag{14}$$

$$s.t. \begin{cases} a = \sum 0.6x_i, x \in A \\ xx_i = x_i/0.6, x \in A \\ b = \sum 0.66x_i, x \in B \\ xx_i = x_i/0.66, x \in B \\ c = \sum 0.72x_i, x \in C \\ xx_i = x_i/0.72, x \in C \\ L = 28200 \\ E_t > 28200, E_t = E_{t-1} - L + \sum xx_i \end{cases} \tag{15}$$

In the formula, a,b and c represents the purchased quantity of three types of raw materials (unit: cubic meter), p is the weight of purchase cost, q is the weight of storage quantity, p is 2/5 and q is 3/5. Assume that $E_1 = 56400$.

In the formula, Cost is the cost of purchasing all raw materials, a,b,c is the volume of purchasing three kinds of raw materials, where x_i is the supply quantity of the supplier i and L is the consumption of raw materials in stock in the current week.

Following the acquisition of the supply situation, it is vital to minimize transportation loss in order to save money on purchases, ensure that goods are not lost, and reduce the number of selected transporters. The results of the ordering scheme model were used to fill in the gaps in the above-mentioned transportation scheme model.

3.4 Measuring Supplier's Importance

To measure the importance of suppliers, we define the following indicators (Fig. 3).

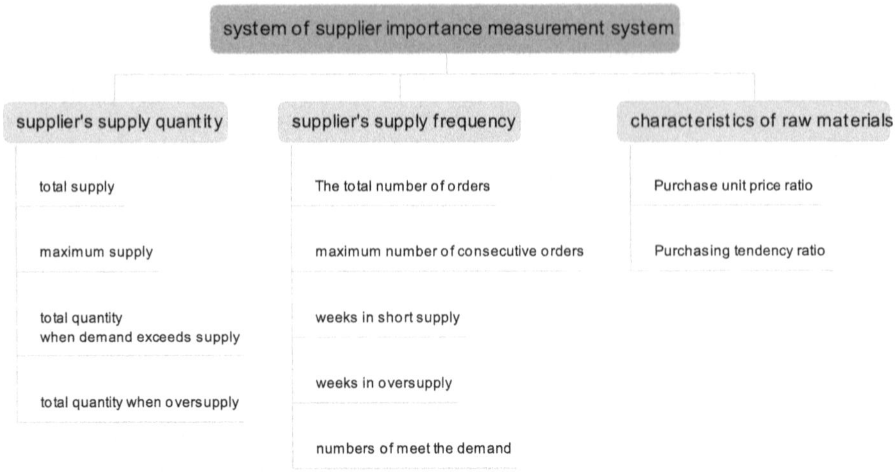

Fig. 3. Index system diagram of supplier's importance

(1) Unit purchase ratio [20]

Definition: With the purchase price of Class C raw materials as the unit purchase price, the purchase price of Class A raw materials: the purchase price of Class B raw materials: the purchase price of Class C raw materials = 1.2:1.1:1.

(2) Procurement propensity ratio

Definition: Consumption of all kinds of raw materials per cubic meter of products, class A: class B: class C = 0.6:0.66:0.72.

Supplier Importance Evaluation Model Based on PCA

The method of determining the relevance of a supplier is multi-cause and one-effect. PCA is a statistical analysis method that divides a large number of variables into a few comprehensive indices. Its aim is to reduce the dimension of the original data characteristics and limit information loss following dimensionality reduction while guaranteeing that as little "information is lost" as possible. As a result, we opted to employ 11 index data to construct a principal component analysis-based evaluation of supplier importance. The specific process shows in Fig. 4.

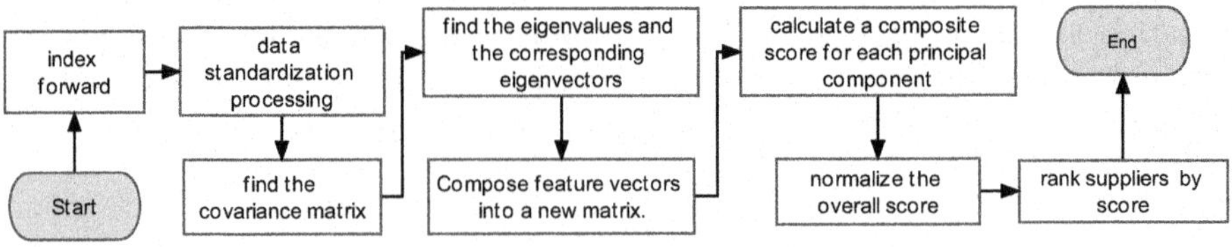

Fig. 4. The process of PCA

The quantitative definition in this model is based on the data in Annex 1, and it is clear that the higher the final comprehensive score, the larger the importance.

3.5 Prediction of Loss Rate of Transporters

Firstly, the 240-week data was divided into ten cycles, with the data of the corresponding week in each cycle being processed using the weighted moving average approach. Since the most recent facts carried more weight in predicting the future [15,18].

Let the time series be $f_1, f_2...$, the formula of weighted moving average method is

$$Mean = \frac{w_1 f_t + w_2 f_{t-1} + w_3 f_{t-2} + \cdots + w_N f_{t-N+1}}{w_1 + w_2 + w_3 + \cdots + w_N} \tag{16}$$

$Mean$ was the weighted moving average, $w_i$was the weight of f_{t-i+1}, $w_1 > w_2 > \cdots > w_N$ shows that recent data is more important to mean, and Mean was used as the prediction of the loss rate.

3.6 Establishment of Transport Scheme Model

The weekly is also used as an example for multi-objective programming with the lowest attrition rate transshipment system. The raw materials must be transferred once a week, but the transporter's weekly transport capacity must not exceed 6000. Furthermore, since each transporter has the same turnover volume and transportation cost, transportation losses should be avoided, and the number of transporters should be reduced to save costs [11,13].

$$min\ loss = \sum x_{ij} \cdot t_j \tag{17}$$

$$s.t. = \begin{cases} \sum_{i=1} x_{i1} \leq 6000 \\ \vdots \\ \sum_{i=1} x_{i8} \leq 6000 \\ \sum_{j=1} x_{1j} \geq X_1 \\ \vdots \\ \sum_{j=1} x_{kj} \geq X_k \end{cases} \tag{18}$$

where loss was the total loss rate of all transport schemes.x_{ij} represents the number of goods from supplier i to be moved by the shipper j.t_j is the loss rate of the j forwarder and X_i is the order quantity of the i supplier. Please refer to the Fig. 5 for details.

The forwarder ranking table is rated according to the expected weekly loss of forwarders, while the supplier ranking table is ranked according to the supplier ranking table derived by PCA.

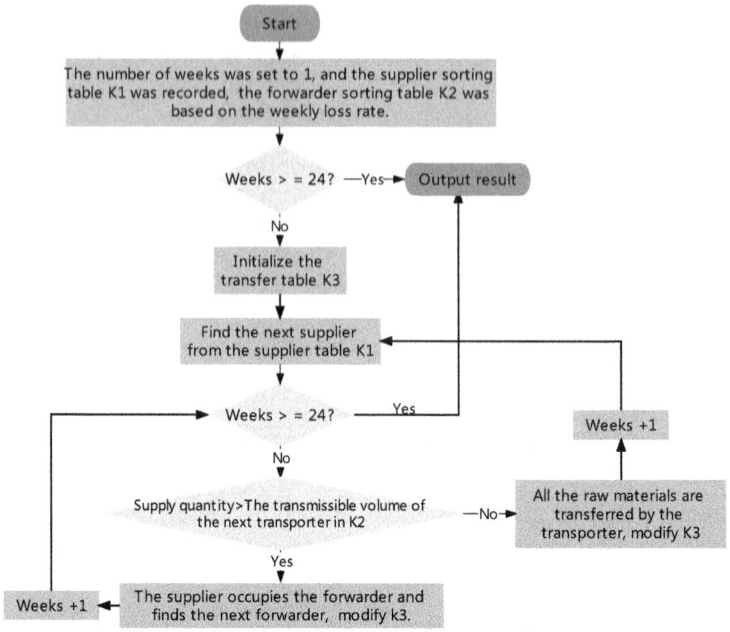

Fig. 5. Transfer scheme algorithm

4 Experimental Results

The difference between a multi-objective programming model and an intelligent algorithm is that it is the optimal solution obtained by traversing all combinations, while the optimal solution obtained by an intelligent algorithm is a random combination, which may fall into the local optimum. Therefore, the optimal solution in this paper does not need to be proved, and the calculation in this paper is basic addition and subtraction, and the multiplication is simple, so the speed of lingo operation is sufficient.

From the supplier proportion result in Fig. 6, it can be seen that Class A suppliers account for the most, followed by Class B suppliers. A total of 202 suppliers were selected, and the inventory was more than 28200.

4.1 Inspection Experiment of the Ordered Scheme

If the objective function didn't add the setting of the weight of material types, the result was that 402 companies were selected, which was obviously unreasonable. Moreover, the purchased quantity was small in the first week and the goods were purchased from all suppliers in the next 23 weeks, which obviously couldn't meet the demand in reality.

If the objective function didn't add weight to the warehouse cost and purchase cost, the purchase cost was higher than the result of this paper and the total

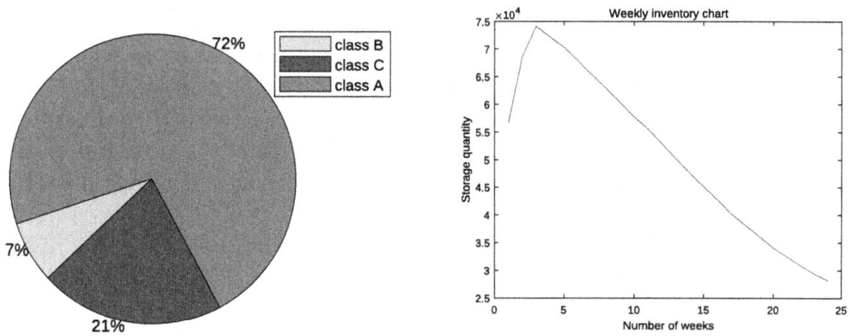

(a) Supplier Category Proportion (b) Weekly Inventory

Fig. 6. Forecast order result.

inventory was lower by 9074. Although more inventory will increase the storage cost. However, from the historical data, it is known that the supplier's supply capacity is limited, which actually can't reach the expected inventory. Moreover, the inventory cost is generally much lower than the purchase cost, and more inventory can make the enterprise run normally.

4.2 Prediction Accuracy Test of Transporter

The loss of the last cycle was predicted by using the historical data of forwarders in the first 9 cycles (24 weeks per cycle). And the error was compared with the tenth cycle.

Table 2. The comparison of different prediction results

Algorithm	Time series prediction	Grey prediction
MAE	0.4304	0.6034
RMSE	0.7626	0.8943

The results in Table 2 show that the prediction accuracy of time series prediction is better than that of grey prediction, and the overall deviation of data is small.

4.3 Test Experiment of Transport Scheme

The characteristics of forwarders' loss rate change obviously and the prediction accuracy is high, so the predicted loss was used for ranking. Because the forwarding scheme was made in advance, the risk of later prediction was taken into account, for example, the supplier that buys the most in the current week may be unable to supply goods due to its insufficient supply capacity, and the forwarder with the lowest loss will waste resources, resulting in more actual losses. Therefore, we did not adopt the optimal transshipment scheme, but adopted the supplier allocation table, and assigned the forwarder with the lowest loss to the supplier with the most likely large supply. Therefore, the question becomes whether to use the supplier ranking of materials or the supplier capability ranking table of PCA [12].

The predicted supply scale in the next 24 weeks, the order decision, and the predicted loss rate table were substituted into the transshipment scheme model. The difference was only the supplier ranking table.

Table 3. Comparison of results of PCA and material category

	Consumption of goods	Destination volume	Attrition rate
Ranking table result of PCA	2252.60	650714.0543	0.00346
Result of material category	2237.35	648604.9477	0.00344

It can be seen from the Table 3 that the supplier ranking in the transshipment scheme is the best according to PCA ranking, which not only had a large final destination transportation volume but also had a low loss rate.

4.4 Comparative Experiment of Supplier Ranking Algorithm

It can be concluded from the Table 4 that Suppliers selected by PCA based on ranking results and historical data are superior to TOPSIS comprehensive evaluation in terms of supply and supply frequency [9].

Table 4. Top 10 suppliers

Ranking	1	2	3	4	5	6	7	8	9	10
Pca ID	229	108	140	282	329	275	361	151	348	308
Topsis ID	151	229	361	108	374	348	140	330	308	282

4.5 Inspection of Supply Capacity Forecast and Ordering Scheme

Substitute the data of the first nine cycles into the order quantity forecasting model to obtain the supply of the tenth cycle, and put it into the objective function to get the order result, which was compared with the original order result of the tenth cycle. The results are in Fig. 7.

By observing the actual supply data of suppliers, it can be found that the inventory does not reach 56400 at the end of nine cycles. So it was assumed that

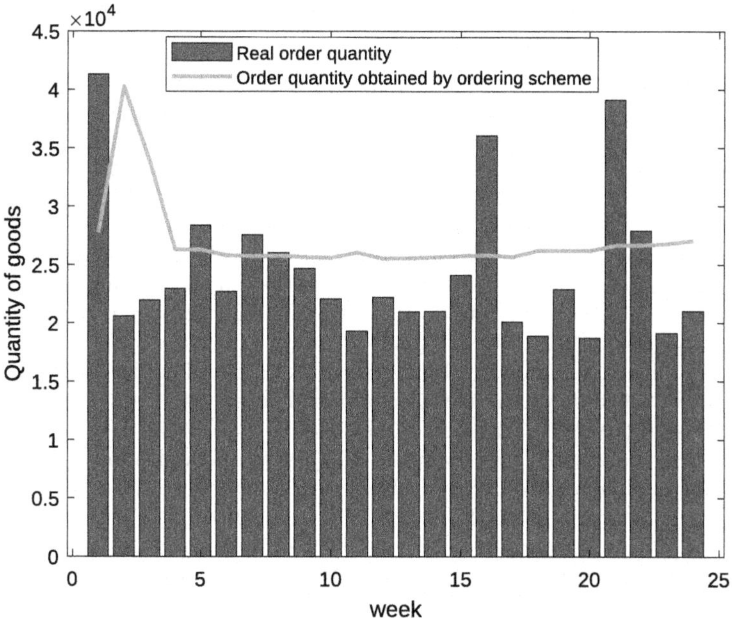

Fig. 7. Order quantity forecast inspection

there was an initial inventory of 35,000. The ordering plan table was obtained after the supplier prediction model and multi-objective model, with an average difference of 5932.244, which was acceptable relative to the supply quantity of 10,000 units. Moreover, the actual supply quantity obtained from the actual order quantity from the actual supply data cannot meet the inventory requirements. If the order quantity is larger, the supplier can provide more goods [1].

5 Conclusion

The TGPFM framework proposed in this paper is composed of a grey cycle prediction model of supply capacity, a time series prediction model of transporters, a PCA evaluation model of suppliers, a multi-objective ordering scheme planning model, and a transshipment planning model. The experimental results show that: 1. The objective function of the ordering scheme should limit the weight of inventory and material type value. 2. PCA-based supplier evaluation table in the transshipment strategy is superior to the supplier material ranking table and TOPSIS comprehensive evaluation Table 4. The prediction of supply capacity should be combined with the grey prediction model and the excess fluctuation function. 5. The prediction and planning effect of the model in this paper is good. However, the drawback of this paper is that the experimental data used is only the national competition data set. In the future, the amount of data should be increased for experiments. Our future research direction is to consider multi-supplier ordering and transshipment schemes [3] and stock sharing [19].

References

1. The commitment conundrum of inventory sharing. Prod. Oper. Manag. **29**(2), 353–370 (2020)
2. Asadujjaman, M., Rahman, H.F., Chakrabortty, R.K., Ryan, M.J.: Resource constrained project scheduling and material ordering problem with discounted cash flows. Comput. Ind. Eng. **158** (2021)
3. Basappa, M., Jallu, R.K., Das, G.K., Nandy, S.C.: The Euclidean k-supplier problem in ir2. Oper. Res. Lett. J. Oper. Res. Soc. Am. **49**(1), 48–54 (2021)
4. Chaume, K., Chiadamrong, N.: Meta-prediction model for introducing lateral transshipment policies in a retail supply chain network through regression analysis. Eur. J. Ind. Eng. **12**(2), 199–232 (2018)
5. Chen, W., Lei, L., Wang, Z., Teng, M., Liu, J.: Coordinating supplier selection and project scheduling in resource-constrained construction supply chains. Int. J. Prod. Res. **56**(19/20), 6512–6526 (2018)
6. Habibi, F., Barzinpour, F., Sadjadi, S.J.: A mathematical model for project scheduling and material ordering problem with sustainability considerations: a case study in Iran. Comput. Ind. Eng. **128**, 690–710 (2019)
7. Haksever, C., Moussourakis, J.: A model for optimizing multi-product inventory systems with multiple constraints. Int. J. Prod. Econ. **97** (2005)
8. Jiangming, J., Zhigang, B., Baoli, D., Kaisheng, Z.: Bayesian network forecasting of key material supply in uncertain environment. In: 2010 First International Conference on Networking and Distributed Computing, pp. 81–85. Hangzhou, Zhejiang, China (2010)
9. Kaya, S.K., Aycin, E.: An integrated interval type 2 fuzzy AHP and Copras-G methodologies for supplier selection in the era of industry 4.0. Neural comput. Appl. **33**(16), 10515–10535 (2021)
10. Khoshjahan, Y., Najafi, A.A., Afshar-Nadjafi, B.: Resource constrained project scheduling problem with discounted earliness-tardiness penalties: mathematical modeling and solving procedure. Comput. Ind. Eng. **66**(2), 293–300 (2013)
11. Naderi, S., Kilic, K., Dasci, A.: A deterministic model for the transshipment problem of a fast fashion retailer under capacity constraints. Int. J. Prod. Econ. **227**(Sep.), 107687.1–107687.14 (2020)
12. Piechota, S., Glas, A.H., Essig, M.: Questioning the relevance of supplier satisfaction for preferred customer treatment: antecedent effects of comparative alternatives and multi-dimensionality. J. Purchas. Supply Manag. **27**(1), 100672.1–100672.17 (2021)
13. Salhi, S., Gutierrez, B., Wassan, N., Wu, S., Kaya, R.: An effective real time grasp-based metaheuristic: application to order consolidation and dynamic selection of transshipment points for time-critical freight logistics. Expert Syst. Appl. **158**(Nov.), 113574.1–113574.17 (2020)
14. Sha, Y., Zhang, J., Cao, H.: Multistage stochastic programming approach for joint optimization of job scheduling and material ordering under endogenous uncertainties. Eur. J. Oper. Res. **290**(3), 886–900 (2021)
15. SONG, Y., Li, Y., Yang, H., Xu, J., Luan, Z., Li, W.: Adaptive watermark generation mechanism based on time series prediction for stream processing, **15**(6), 58–72 (2021)
16. Tabrizi, B.H., Ghaderi, S.F.: Simultaneous planning of the project scheduling and material procurement problem under the presence of multiple suppliers. Eng. Optim. 1474–1490 (2015)

17. Tabrizi, B.H., Ghaderi, S.F., Haji-Yakhchali, S.: Net present value maximisation of integrated project scheduling and material procurement planning. Int. J. Oper. Res. **34**(2), 285–300 (2019)
18. Von Schleinitz, J., Graf, M., Trutschnig, W., Schroeder, A.: VASP: an autoencoder-based approach for multivariate anomaly detection and robust time series prediction with application in motorsport. Eng. Appl. Artif. Intell. Int. J. Intell. Real-Time Autom. **104** (2021)
19. Wang, Z., Dai, Y., Fang, S.C., Jiang, Z.Z., Xu, Y.: Inventory transshipment game with limited supply: trap or treat. Naval Res. Logist. **67**(6), 383–403 (2020)
20. Wei, C., Wu, J., Guo, Y., Wei, G.: Green supplier selection based on codas method in probabilistic uncertain linguistic environment. Technol. Econ. Dev. Econ. **27**(3), 530–549 (2021)
21. Xu, F., Wang, H.: Ordering and transferring model of dual-channel supply chain with delivery time difference. Adv. Eng. Inform. **49** (2021)
22. Yang, W., Li, B.: Prediction of grain supply and demand structural balance in china based on grey models. Grey Syst. Theory Appl. **11**(2), 253–264 (2021)
23. Ju Zhou, Y., Hong Chen, X., Run Wang, Z.: Optimal ordering quantities for multi-products with stochastic demand: return-CVAR model. Int. J. Prod. Econ. **112**(2), 782–795 (2008)

Visual Analysis of Facial Expression Recognition Research Based on Knowledge Graph

Yuan Bo, Fan Jiajia, and Jin Zhuang(✉)

College of Computer, Guangdong University of Science and Technology, Dong Guan 523066, People's Republic of China
jinzhuang@gdust.edu.cn

Abstract. The change of facial expression is the external form of human inner activity, and the change of facial expression in the process of interaction is also a medium of communication. The same is true in teaching. Researchers have conducted a lot of research on how to obtain facial expressions, and how to identify and analyze them after obtaining them. In future research, it is very important how to quickly find the facial recognition methods and technologies suitable for the scene, how to quickly find the existing problems on the basis of existing research, and to optimize and carry out follow-up research. This paper mainly analyzes the research literature on facial expression recognition collected by CNKI in the past 10 years, and uses the knowledge graph technology to display it visually, so as to provide reference and theoretical support for users to choose methods when conducting research on facial expression recognition.

Keywords: Knowledge graph · Facial expression recognition · Visual analysis

1 Introduction

Facial expressions are one of the important ways of human emotion expression [1]. In the teaching process, the communication between teachers and students is generally done in the form of dialogue. However, in most cases, students' psychological activities and learning status will not be organized into natural language. At this time, teachers need to supplement the exchange of information by observing students' facial expressions. In order to realize the reading and analysis of students' facial expressions, teachers need to continuously observe the facial expressions of multiple students in the teaching process, which undoubtedly greatly increases the work intensity of teachers and is not conducive to organizing teaching. Based on this, a variety of facial expression recognition technologies have emerged, but how to find the technology you need in a short period of time and apply it in the teaching process has become a new problem.

This paper mainly used the literature about facial expression recognition methods collected in the CNKI database to organize the corpus, extract the abstract part, and use the knowledge map tool to visualize the data after the preliminary screening of the data, which is convenient for later selection. Suitable technology. This will provide future researchers with a more intuitive display of the research status.

Y. Xu et al. (Eds.): ML4CS 2022, LNCS 13657, pp. 350–357, 2023.
https://doi.org/10.1007/978-3-031-20102-8_27

2 Relevant Research Basis

2.1 Facial Expression Recognition

When Dang Hongshe and others studied facial expression recognition, they made the following summaries and reflections on the existing problems in the process of expression recognition: First, the classification of expressions is not detailed enough, and there is a lack of data on facial expressions of characters in complex scenes. The expression labels in the dataset need to be expanded. Secondly, the influence of factors such as illumination and occlusion on the data source. Thirdly, the lack of composite expressions makes it impossible to judge the complex diversity of features in the process of feature extraction. Fourth, for multi-modal recognition, the complementation of multiple feature information will improve the accuracy of recognition [2]. In the process of studying facial expression recognition, Jiang Bin et al. [1]. Studied the recognition of non-frontal face images, mainly thinking about the following aspects: First, most of the current standard face databases are not real enough, and in the process of feature extraction, there will be certain data impact. Second, the cost of researching algorithms for feature extraction and expression classification is too high, which is mainly reflected in the deep model. And high complexity. Third, in the process of researching facial expression recognition, the main data type is single, most of which are still images. In the study of facial expressions, Hong Huiqun et al. [3]. Pointed out that the current multimodal data research mainly has the following problems: First, there are differences in the acquired data sources, which are mainly reflected in angles, occlusion, light, etc. Second, the number of public data sources for multimodal datasets has decreased, which greatly hindered the research on the development of facial expression technology. Thirdly, the number of types of expressions in the dataset is not concentrated, some expression images are more, and some have fewer images. Fourth, in the process of recognition, the correlation between modalities is not deeply connected, and there are cases where features are lost or feature correlation is not high. Fifth, in the process of studying multimodal facial expressions, if there is no considering the research of fusion algorithm, it will lead to the problem that the algorithm is too difficult and the research threshold is too large.

In summary, in the process of facial expression recognition, it is also necessary to improve the quality of the images originally collected in the data set. If there are problems such as inappropriate light sources, occlusions, and inappropriate angles, it needs to be standardized during the collection process. In the process of collecting different types of expressions, it is necessary to collect more different micro-expressions to improve the acquisition of feature points; in the process of realizing the recognition model, a multi-modal method can be used to add information from different feature sources.

For researchers, in the face of numerous literatures, it is difficult to quickly find existing problems and related literature, so that they cannot efficiently determine their research direction, and they will spend too much time in literature search. In response to this problem, this study uses knowledge graph technology to visualize relevant literature, so that researchers can quickly complete literature analysis.

This research uses the knowledge graph technology to visualize many documents including the above, so as to establish the links within the documents, help researchers to quickly discover existing problems in the field and determine their own research direction.

2.2 Knowledge Graph Visualization

In the process of researching knowledge graph visualization, Wang Yongchao et al. [4]. Pointed out that the application of knowledge graph needs to be optimized in the following three points: the filtering and sampling methods of data sources also need to be adjusted according to the characteristics of the corresponding data domain. When combining deep learning methods, to quickly train the effect and improve the rate of real-time visualization, when implementing multi-dimensional data sources, it is also necessary to visualize the three-dimensional data. In the research of knowledge graph visualization, Wang Xin et al. [5]. Pointed out the following research directions: realizing unified visual query language management for knowledge graphs of various data types, secondly, using cutting-edge technology and the data model of knowledge graph, visualization technology can better show the relationship between data, thirdly, in different fields, the cross-domain integration of knowledge graphs can be realized, and visualization technology can be applied to them, fourthly, expand the source of knowledge map data, use visual technology to display query and analysis of multiple data structures, fifth, Combined with the use of visual query combination technology of cross -domain knowledge graphs to achieve the unity of multiple visual tools for different data sources. In the process of researching knowledge graphs, Ma Ruixin et al. [6]. Proposed that multi-sample knowledge graphs need to be researched in a variety of ways, including research on hybrid reasoning, multi-relationship, dynamic update, and neural network reasoning, which need to combine the data generated by the application scenarios to construct the knowledge system in real time. This is a phased work. While enriching the resource library, it is also necessary to combine the updated technology to improve the quality of the map. Regarding the construction of the knowledge graph model, Dong Xiaoxiao [7] and others have made method innovations for the knowledge graph in the field of education, and proposed a theory oriented by the core literacy and literacy development of the discipline. Its core is to decompose the application requirements and the establishment of boundaries according to the target of the corresponding knowledge field, and construct the knowledge graph combing the entity types, attributes, and relationships of knowledge content.

In summary, knowledge graph visualization still needs to be displayed around data in different fields, and it needs to integrate multiple data types and more cutting-edge technologies for cross-study.

3 The Experimental Test

The experimental test part of this research was mainly divided into four steps:

1) First, obtain the literature information on "Facial Expression Recognition" in China National Knowledge Infrastructure (Abbreviated as CNKI), the main method was to use Spider-based crawler technology to obtain the label structure of CNKI pages, and used automatic processing to collect and save data. A total of 861 related documents were obtained. As shown in Fig. 1.

In this step, this study implemented a step-by-step method of collecting literature content, in order to avoid the impact of network interruption and frequent access. The first step is to crawl the title, network address and author of documents related to "facial expression

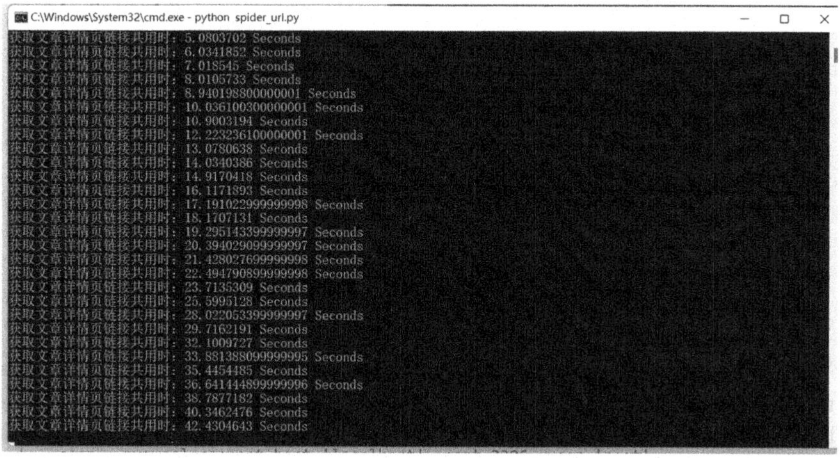

Fig. 1. Process diagram for obtaining literature

Fig. 2. Screenshot of the process of obtaining document information for the first time

recognition" on CNKI, as shown in Fig. 2. The second step is to classify and collect the data in the network address, including: title, literature link, author, year, journal name, abstract and keywords, as shown in Fig. 3.

NUM	PaperName	PaperUrl	Author	Year	Journal	Abstracts	Keywords
844	基于多层融合方	//cdmd.cnki	张艳华	2014	北京工业大	【摘要】:	在 人脸表情识别;
845	基于动态模期神	//cdmd.cnki	王赛	2012	西南大学	【摘要】:	人 表情识别;特征
846	面向中学化学虚	//cdmd.cnki	郝明阳	2021	淮阴工学院	【摘要】:	化 实验课堂管理;
847	动态人脸表情识	//cdmd.cnki	应伟	2005	湖南大学	【摘要】:	新 表情识别;特征
848	基于儿童视觉认	//cdmd.cnki	朱诗喊	2018	湘潭大学	【摘要】:	随 视觉认知儿童
849	基于动态序列的	//cdmd.cnki	王洋	2017	沈阳工业大	【摘要】:	人 主动外观模型;
850	基于双线性模型	//cdmd.cnki	徐欢	2014	北京工业大	【摘要】:	近 三维表情识别;
851	基于局部关键区	//cdmd.cnki	卢冰	2019	河南理工大	【摘要】:	微 微表情识别;局
852	城市开放空间视	//cdmd.cnki	胡雪筠	2020	哈尔滨工业	【摘要】:	城 城市开放空间;
853	基于深度残差网	//cdmd.cnki	张瑞军	2020	西安邮电大	【摘要】:	随 人脸表情识别;
854	基于深度学习的	//cdmd.cnki	陈慧萍	2019	河北科技大	【摘要】:	随 人脸表情识别;
855	云计算环境下人	//www.cnki.	谢文达	2017	计算机测量	【摘要】:	随 云计算环境;人
856	基于二元模式的	//cdmd.cnki	付晓峰	2008	浙江大学	【摘要】:	人 人脸识别;人脸
857	基于双值韦伯算	//www.cnki.	郝晓丽;田音	2017	中北大学学	【摘要】:	针 面部表情识别;
858	基于注意力机制	//cdmd.cnki	徐志鹏	2021	南京邮电大	【摘要】:	人 人脸表情识别;
859	3-5岁幼儿表情i	//cdmd.cnki	王军利	2012	浙江师范大	【摘要】:	幼 幼儿表情标签
860	人脸表情识别算	//cdmd.cnki	孙雯玉	2006	北京交通大	【摘要】:	人 人脸表情识别;
861	仿入头像机器人	//cdmd.cnki	孟庆梅	2009	哈尔滨工业	【摘要】:	随 仿入头像机器.

`SELECT * FROM `cnki`.`detail_info` LIMIT 0, 1000`   第 861 条记录 (共 861

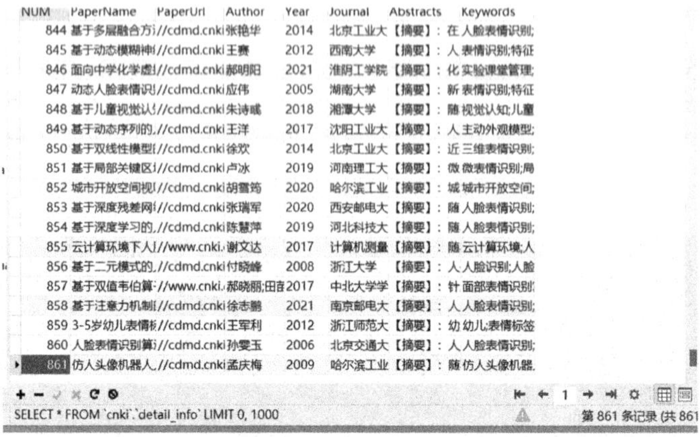

Fig. 3. Screenshot of the process of obtaining document details

2) Visual display based on Neo4j graph database, use "CALL apoc.load.jdbc()" statement to import data table, Neo4j can display various attributes for nodes and edges [8]. This study used MATCH statement to achieve graph matching, WHERE statement to achieve Filter conditions, RETURN statement to achieve result return. As shown in Fig. 4.

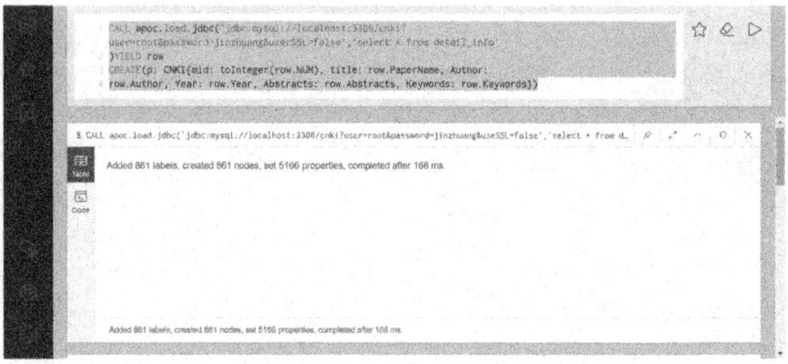

Fig. 4. Process diagram of importing data

3) Finally, using neo4j to visualize the triple relationship between documents, the document name is used as an entity, other characteristics of the document are used as

attributes, and similar keywords between documents are used as links. Here, the keyword similarity calculation is performed based on the python third-party library difflib, and the similarity value greater than 0.5 is identified as the association type, and the associated literature number is recorded, as shown in Fig. 5.

Fig. 5. Example graph of document similarity correlation

4) Finally, used the results of neo4j visual display to construct the knowledge graph, and obtained the results that the method and technology are related between each entity scene. The results can help to provide a reference for the selection of research directions, technology types, and models in different facial expression recognition scenarios in the later stage. The specific results are shown in Fig. 6.

Fig. 6. Visual analysis results of "Facial Expression Recognition".

4 Conclusion

The main work of this paper includes: we discussed the current research status of facial expression recognition and knowledge graph. Based on this, we used CNKI's Chinese and English literature on "facial expression recognition" as research data, extracted the text information in the corresponding literature content and save the results, used the neo4j graph database to construct triples, in which the relationship between entities and entities was calculated by using the literature keywords to calculate the similarity value. The final visualized knowledge graph can help researchers effectively and quickly select research directions and corresponding technologies and models. In the process of facial expression recognition in small scenes, an appropriate method can be selected for experiments, and there is no need to perform model calculations for simple recognition requirements in complex scenes.

Of course, in this study, there are certain deficiencies, mainly reflected in: keywords and abstracts may not completely cover the content of the entire literature. In view of this situation, when dealing with the relationship between documents, the main content of the article can also be added to increase the influence on the characteristics of the documents.

Acknowledgment. The research is supported by the 2021 school level project "Under the analysis and research of university students online learning behavior" of Guangdong University of science and Technology (Project No.: GKY-2020KYZDK-11).

References

1. Jiang, B., Zhong, R., Zhang, Q., Zhang, H.: Survey of non-frontal facial expression recognition by using deep learning methods. Comput. Eng. Appl. **57**(08), 48–61 (2021)
2. Dang, H., Wang, M., De Zhang, X.: A survey of facial expression recognition methods based on deep learning. Sci. Technol. Eng. **20**(24), 9724–9732 (2020)
3. Hong, H., Shen, G., Huang, F.: Summary of expression recognition technology. J. Frontiers Comput. Sci. Technol. 1–16 (2022)
4. Wang, Y., Luo, S., Yang, Y., Zhang, H.: A survey on knowledge graph visualization. J. Comput.-Aided Des. Comput. Graph. **31**(10), 1666–1676 (2019)
5. Wang, X., Fu, Q, Wang, L., Xu, D., Wang, H.: Survey on visualization query technology of knowledge Graph. Comput. Eng. **46**(06) (2020)
6. Ma, R., Li, Z., Chen, Z., Zhao, L.: Review of reasoning on knowledge graph. Comput. Sci. **49**(S1), 74–85 (2022)
7. Dong, X., Zhou, D., Huang, X., Gu, H., Li, Z.: Research on method of constructing knowledge graph mode in educational field oriented by subject core literacy. e-Educ. Res. **43**(05), 76–83 (2022)
8. Wei, J., Minghua, W., Jinming, C., Liu Jiangdong, P., Zhiqi, S.X.: Calculation of power supply reliability of distribution network based on Neo4j graph database. Autom. Electr. Power Syst. **43**(05), 1–17 (2022)

Brainstorming-Based Large Scale Neighborhood Search for Vehicle Routing with Real Travel Time

Jia Liu[1], Nanqing Guo[1,2], and Bowen Xue[1(✉)]

[1] College of Management, Shenzhen University, Shenzhen 518060, China
isxuebowen@163.com

[2] Greater Bay Area International Institute for Innovation, Shenzhen University, Shenzhen 518060, China

Abstract. It is vital to improve the efficiency of urban distribution with severe traffic congestion problems. However, few studies on urban distribution consider the impact of road conditions, which leads to less instructive results to the real-world problems. This paper considers the real travel time of the vehicles to minimize the total distribution time. Furthermore, hybrid brain storm optimization and large neighborhood search algorithm (BSO-LNS) are designed to solve this problem. The experimental results show that the proposed BSO-LNS algorithm is superior to peer competitors. The optimized routes are easier to obtain the global optima, which is suitable for solving the urban distribution problem under such complex road conditions.

Keywords: Real-time road conditions · Urban distribution · Crawler · Brain storm optimization · Large neighborhood search

1 Introduction

As an essential part of the last-mile distribution in the logistics chain, urban distribution plays a significant role in the entire supply chain. With the increasing prominence of urban governance problems, the role of urban distribution has become more prominent. Urban distribution is an important part of the Vehicle Routing Problem (VRP). Since Solomon and Desrosiers [1] put forward the concept of the time window in VRP, there is increasing research on Vehicle Routing Problem With Time Windows (VRPTW). Furthermore, Jabali [2] proposed the concepts of the soft time window and hard time window, and introduced the penalty function into the objective function to solve the VRPTW, thus giving birth to considerable research on urban distribution [3–7]. At the present stage, with the acceleration of the urban process, the road traffic conditions are becoming more and more complex, which puts forward higher requirements for urban distribution. The traditional path planning represented by Euclidean distance can no longer meet the current distribution demand. At this stage, urban distribution needs to consider the impact of road conditions and develop a more efficient algorithm to solve the problem of urban distribution better in reality.

Y. Xu et al. (Eds.): ML4CS 2022, LNCS 13657, pp. 358–370, 2023.
https://doi.org/10.1007/978-3-031-20102-8_28

In recent years, there has been more research on real-time road conditions. Some scholars consider the dynamics of travel time through the system's design to receive real-time road network information in the distribution process, automatically adjust the distribution route and upload it to the distribution driver [8]. Thanks to the development of big data collection technology, obtaining historical road condition data is no longer challenging. We can collect real-time road condition information in the process of a vehicle driving through the electronic map platform [9]. By collecting road condition data in a specific time range, the designed algorithm is used to predict the driving speed of each road section [10] to realize the route change. As the problem becomes more and more complex, some scholars choose to design a more efficient algorithm [11] through reasonable planning of the departure time of each car to avoid congested roads [12] effectively.

In this paper, we use crawler technology to obtain the real travel time through Amap API and choose a hybrid algorithm (BSO-LNS) that combines brainstorming optimization algorithm (BSO) and large neighborhood search algorithm (LNS) to solve this kind of distribution optimization problem. The large neighborhood search algorithm is an excellent local search algorithm, which is proposed by Shaw [13] and is often used to solve VRPTW. Although the brainstorming algorithm is relatively young, it has received widespread attention since it was proposed by Shi [14] in 2011, and it has also been used to solve the VRPTW in recent years. However, few papers use BSO alone to solve VRPTW [15,16], and more often, they are hybrids with other algorithms [17–20], all achieving better results than BSO algorithm.

The next section of this paper is organized as follows. Section 2 focuses on the basic process of combining the BSO and the LNS algorithm, Sect. 3 develops a VRPTW model to find the shortest total time spent, Sect. 4 gives the comparison results of the experiments, and the last section is used to conclude and look ahead.

2 BSO-LNS for VRPTW

2.1 Problem Description

Based on real-time road conditions, the urban distribution problem can be described as follows: a department store distribution center located in an urban area needs to deliver goods to several supermarkets in the surrounding area, and the geographic location information of the distribution point can be obtained from Amap, the number of goods required to be delivered by each supermarket on that day is prepared by the distribution center at least one day in advance, and the vehicles loaded with their respective responsibilities for the distribution of supermarkets set off from the distribution center toward the planned route, when arriving before the left time window of supermarkets, they need to wait until the service start time to unload the goods, and if they exceed the right time window, they will be penalized in the target function. At the same time, under the influence of considering the actual road conditions, the constant speed of each vehicle and the distance between the two is no longer assumed here to be counted as the Euclidean distance, still, the passage time and distance between the two are obtained in real-time through Amap, the corresponding passage time and distance matrix is obtained, aiming for the optimized delivery solution with the least total driving time to be closer to the actual delivery scenario under the urban congestion environment. In addition, the following assumptions are made for the problem to be solved.

(1) Each vehicle serves only one route, each node can only be served once by one vehicle, the vehicle type is the same and the load capacity is known, the total number of vehicles, the maximum mileage is not limited.
(2) The vehicle departs from the distribution center and finally returns to the distribution center within the time window.

2.2 Model Building

The VRPTW model considering the road conditions is constructed as follows:

$$\begin{aligned} \min Z = \sum_{k=1}^{K}\sum_{i=0}^{n}\sum_{j=0}^{n} x_{ijk}t_{ij} &+\alpha \cdot \sum_{k=1}^{K} \max[(\sum_{i=0}^{n}\sum_{j=0}^{n} x_{ijk} - G),0] \\ &+\beta \cdot \sum_{i=1}^{n} \max[(l_{ik} - b_i),0] \end{aligned} \tag{1}$$

$$\sum_{k=1}^{K}\sum_{i=0}^{n} x_{ijk} = 1; \forall j \in N \tag{2}$$

$$\sum_{i=0}^{n} x_{0ik} = 1; \forall \mathrm{k} \in \mathrm{K} \tag{3}$$

$$\sum_{i=0}^{n} x_{ijk} - \sum_{i=0}^{n} x_{ijk} = 0; \forall j \in n, k \in K \tag{4}$$

$$\sum_{i=0}^{n} x_{i0k} = 1; \forall \mathrm{k} \in \mathrm{K} \tag{5}$$

$$a_0 \le u_{0k} \le b_0; \forall k \in K \tag{6}$$

$$x_{ijk} = 0 or 1 i, j = 0,1,...n; \forall k \in K \tag{7}$$

The variables used in the model are shown in Table 1.

In the model, (1) is the objective function, which indicates the minimum total vehicle travel time and penalty cost for late arrival and overloading [17]; the constraint (2) indicates that each customer point can only be distributed by one vehicle; constraint (3) (4) (5) indicates that the input and output of distribution vehicles must satisfy the flow balance constraints; constraint (6) indicates that each vehicle starts from the distribution center and returns to the distribution center within the time window of the distribution center after completing the distribution; constraint (7) denotes the corresponding 0–1 constraint.

Table 1. Variable description.

Symbols	Description
i, j	$i, j = 0, 1, ..., n$. 0 means the distribution center,1∼n denotes supermarkets
k	Vehicle no. $k = 1,2,...,K$
G	Maximum loading capacity of vehicle
t_{ij}	The actual passage time of vehicles between nodes, obtained by the crawler
a_i	The earliest service time of supermarket i
b_i	The latest closing time of supermarket i
s_i	Receiving service time of supermarket i
a_0	The earliest departure time of a vehicle at a distribution center
b_0	The latest time for the vehicle to return to the distribution center
g_i	The demands of supermarket i
M	denotes a large enough positive number for the penalty constraint
x_{ijk}	If truck k from node i to node j, then $x_{ijk} = 1$, else $x_{ijk} = 0$
l_{ik}	The time of vehicle k arrives at supermarket i
u_{ik}	The time of supermarket i began to accept the service of vehicle k, which i = 1, 2, ..., N

2.3 Coding Analysis

In this paper, integer coding is used for distribution schemes to code individuals. To indicate simplicity, if there are now nine supermarkets to be delivered and there are at most three vans available in the distribution center at present, the individual codable schemes can be roughly divided into three cases according to the number of vehicles used.

(1) If three vehicles are dispatched to perform distribution tasks at the same time, one possible way for an individual to behave is as Fig. 1. Where numbers 1–9 denote supermarkets to be delivered, 10 and 11 denote distribution centers.

Fig. 1. One of situation with three vehicles.

Then, from Fig. 1, it can be seen that distribution centers 10 and 11 divide all individuals into 3 distribution routes and the distribution scheme can be expressed as follows, where 0 denotes the distribution center.
Distribution route 1: $0 \rightarrow 1 \rightarrow 3 \rightarrow 5 \rightarrow 6 \rightarrow 0$
Distribution route 2: $0 \rightarrow 2 \rightarrow 7 \rightarrow 9 \rightarrow 0$
Distribution route 3: $0 \rightarrow 4 \rightarrow 8 \rightarrow 0$

(2) If only two vehicles are assigned to the distribution task, one possible representation of the individual is as Fig. 2

Fig. 2. One of situation with two vehicles.

Then, as can be seen from the Fig. 2, the distribution scheme is expressed as follows.
Distribution route 1: $0 \rightarrow 1 \rightarrow 3 \rightarrow 5 \rightarrow 6 \rightarrow 0$
Distribution route 2: $0 \rightarrow 2 \rightarrow 7 \rightarrow 9 \rightarrow 8 \rightarrow 4 \rightarrow 0$

(3) If only 1 vehicle is assigned to the distribution task, one possible way for an individual to behave is as Fig. 3

Fig. 3. One of situation with one vehicle.

Then, as can be seen from the Fig. 3, the distribution scheme is as follows.
Distribution route: $0 \rightarrow 3 \rightarrow 5 \rightarrow 6 \rightarrow 1 \rightarrow 2 \rightarrow 7 \rightarrow 9 \rightarrow 8 \rightarrow 4 \rightarrow 0$

From the above coding method, it can be seen that if the number of supermarkets to be delivered is N and the distribution center can arrange at most K vehicles for delivery, then the individual coding can be expressed as a permutation of $N + K - 1$ numbers. Next, a population consisting of individuals according to the above encoding can be randomly generated. The fitness function chosen for this algorithm is the reciprocal of the objective function value.

3 Brain Storm Optimization with Large Neighborhood Search

3.1 Brain Storm Optimization

Inspired by the brainstorming session, an act of human brainstorming and bursting with creative inspiration, the brainstorming optimization algorithm was first proposed by shi [14] in 2011. The algorithm received much attention once it was proposed because it has the advantages of simple structure and few hyperparameters, which are ideal for solving high-dimensional multi-peak problems.

The basic idea of the BSO algorithm is to map each person's idea to each individual in the population and represent it as a feasible solution in the problem-solution set. The specific steps are as follows:

Step 1: Random initialization. Generate n individuals as the initial solution for the population. Step 2: Evaluation. The fitness function values are calculated for these n individuals. Step 3: Clustering. The initially generated populations are clustered and grouped into m categories using the K-means method. And each individual in these m categories is ranked according to the fitness function value, and the best individual in each category is selected as the class center. Step 4: Generate new individuals. The generated new individuals follow the Eqs. (8) and (9) are updated, and the better individuals among them are saved. Step 5: Update the population. Determine whether the iteration termination condition is satisfied. If not, continue iterating and updating until the loop termination condition is satisfied.

$$X^d_{new} = X^d_{select} + \xi f(\mu, \sigma) \tag{8}$$

$$\xi = \log sig((0.5 \cdot \max\_iter - cur\_iter)/k) \cdot rand() \tag{9}$$

where $f(\mu, \sigma)$ is the normal distribution function, $\log sig$ is the logarithm of the sigmoid, and max_iter and cur_iter are the maximum number of iterations and the current number of iterations.

3.2 Large Neighborhood Search

Large Neighborhood Search(LNS) is an algorithm that uses two core ideas, "destroy" and "repair" [13]. The two core ideas of LNS are "destroy" and "repair", which simply means that the destroy operator destroys some individuals in the current solution, and then the repair operator is used to repair the destroyed solution. The advantage is that after destroying and repairing, we can get the full ordering of the initial solution and traverse the solution space of more problems.

The destroy steps are as follows:

Step 1: Firstly, we construct two sets, one is the set S for storing customers of distribution routes, and the other is the set V for temporarily storing removed customers. Step 2: First select a customer i from the set S at random and deposit it in the set V. Step 3: Choose any customer j from the set V, and then calculate the correlation between the remaining customers in the set S (denoted as S') and customer j are calculated separately, and then sorted according to the relevance from largest to smallest, and finally according to the formula $\text{int}(rand^D \cdot S')$ to decide the next customer to move out, the general value of D between 5 and 20, used to control the value is not exactly the way to maximize relevance. This process is repeated until the number of customers removed reaches a predetermined value.

The repair steps are as follows:

Step 1: Each insertable customer has an uncertain number of insertion positions, and the fitness difference is calculated for each possible case and the solution after being destroyed, and recorded. Step 2: Sort the fitness difference from largest to smallest, choose the insertion position with the largest difference to insert the customer back, and repeat the process until all the removed customers are inserted back.

3.3 BSO-LNS

The basic idea of combining BSO and LNS algorithm is that after BSO performs the individual update operation, it selects some of the worse individuals to "destroy" and "repair" according to the fitness so that the selected solutions are at least no worse than the original ones. Finally, the two parts of individuals are merged and iterated until the end of the cycle. More details are shown in Algorithm 1.

Algorithm 1: BSO-LNS Algorithm

```
Initialize parameters;
Initialize population;
while not terminated do
    evaluating individuals;
    k-means for population;
    update individuals;
    evaluating individuals;
    select poor individuals in top n% fitness;
    perform destory and repair for selected individuals;
    merge the updated individual with the original remaining individual;
    evaluating individuals;
    perform global individual update;
end
```

4 Experiments

4.1 Experimental Description

The data used in this experiment are provided by a distribution company, as shown in Table 2 and Table 3 (the contents not listed in the table are the same as Table 2.), which represent the order data of two days, respectively, where node 1 denotes the distribution center and nodes 2 to node 21 denote the supermarkets to be delivered, and the delivery vehicles are known to have a capacity of 7 tons, allowing a maximum of 10 vehicles for delivery. All experiments were conducted using MATLAB (R2018b) on an Intel(R) Core(TM) i7-8565U CPU @ 1.80 GHz with 8.00 GB of RAM.

4.2 Experimental Setup and Analysis of Results

In order to study the effect of road conditions on distribution, three experiments were carried out. In Experiment 1 and Experiment 2, the asymmetric passage time matrices of vehicles between nodes were obtained from AMap via Python program at 6:00 pm on 5.28 and 6.10, respectively, under the scenario of considering road conditions, and the acquisition was set to consider road conditions;

Table 2. Data set of Experiment 1.

Node	1	2	3	4	5	6	7
Longitude	115.971	115.9379	115.9028	115.838	115.9170	115.9053	115.8417
Latitude	28.6959	28.5315	28.6161	28.7578	28.6548	28.6310	28.6653
Demand /t	0	1.4269	0.3998	0.7220	3.2	1.1348	0.58
Service	0	21.40395	5.997345	10.8309	25	17.022	8.7
Left time	7:00	8:00	8:30	9:00	8:30	8:00	8:00
Right Time	21:00	16:00	17:00	16:00	11:00	17:00	17:00
Node	8	9	10	11	12	13	14
Longitude	115.807	115.9618	115.8104	115.9291	115.8936	115.9038	115.9107
Latitude	28.6752	28.6633	28.6959	28.5575	28.5852	28.6762	28.7476
Demand /t	0.22723	0.55351	1.528	3.4688	1.05399	0.49	3.28
Service	6.40854	8.30274	22.92	21.6262	15.80994	7.35	29.2
Left time	8:00	9:30	8:00	8:00	8:30	8:00	8:00
Right Time	17:00	16:00	17:00	16:00	17:00	16:00	16:00
Node	15	16	17	18	19	20	21
Longitude	115.948	115.8066	115.9469	116.1404	115.8710	115.8996	115.9192
Latitude	28.85	28.6923	28.6345	28.6558	28.6172	28.6739	28.6853
Demand /t	0.74466	2.16381	1.6	3.98634	3.21517	0.6	2.2077
Service	11.1699	32.45718	24	29.7951	28.22755	9	23.1167
Left time	8:00	8:00	8:00	8:00	8:00	10:00	8:00
Right Time	17:00	16:00	17:00	17:00	17:00	17:00	16:00

Table 3. Data set of Experiment 2 and 3.

Node	1	2	3	4	5	6	7
Demand /t	0	1.36	1.78	0.73	0.8	0.69	0.54
Service time	0	15	20	10	7	6	5
Node	8	9	10	11	12	13	14
Demand /t	2.38	0.56	2.59	1.56	0.87	1.49	0.36
Service time	24	5	25	16	8	15	5
Node	15	16	17	18	19	20	21
Demand /t	1.56	0.56	1.08	0.71	1.94	2.28	1.97
Service time	17	5	10	8	20	28	20

Experiment 3, on the other hand, did not consider road conditions, but used the traditional straight-line distance for calculation.

Meanwhile, to better reflect the performance of the BSO-LNS algorithm, the original BSO, GA-LNS and PSO-LNS algorithms are used for comparison in each experiment, and the common parameter settings for these experiments are shown in Table 4. The parameters in the BSO algorithm are set as follows: $m = 5, p1 = 0.1, p2 = 0.5, p3 = 0.5, p4 = 0.3, p5 = 0.2$. The parameters in the GA algorithm are set as follows: $pc = 0.9, pm = 0.05$. The parameters in the PSO algorithm are set as follows: $c1 = 1.5, c2 = 2.0, w = 1$.

Table 4. Common parameter setting for these algorithms.

Algorithm	N	Max iter	α	β	D
BSO-LNS	60	400	20	100	15
BSO	60	400	20	100	–
GA-LNS	60	400	20	100	15
PSO-LNS	60	400	20	100	15

Table 5. Simulation results of BSO-LNS with BSO, GA-LNS and PSO-LNS of 10 runs.

Data	Opt.	Alg.	Best	Worst	Avg	Var
Experiment1	461	BSO-LNS	461	461	461	0
		BSO	464.81	491.5	475.97	71.33
		GA-LNS	464	480	470.8	18.16
		PSO-LNS	463	505.87	487.04	150.85
Experiment2	578	BSO-LNS	578	581	578.7	1.21
		BSO	585	610.2	598.34	46.7
		GA-LNS	588	605	595.6	33.64
		PSO-LNS	583	610.6	595.38	49.88
Experiment3	3974.64	BSO-LNS	3974.64	3974.64	3974.64	0
		BSO	4038.59	4194.59	4112.41	2030.5
		GA-LNS	3974.64	3974.64	3974.64	0
		PSO-LNS	3995.52	4132.11	4050.15	1485.64

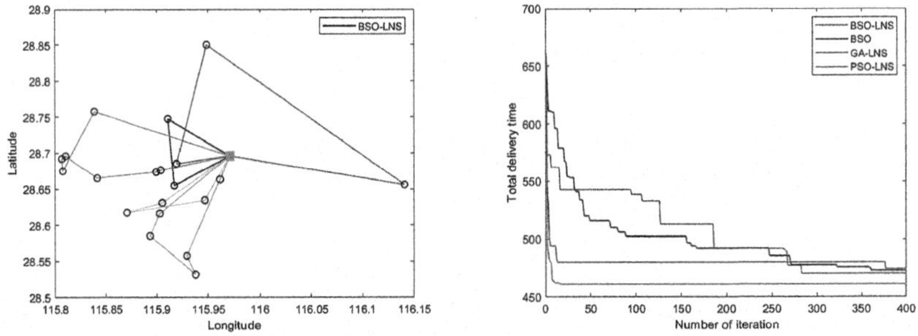

(a) BSO-LNS algorithm optimal solution

(b) Performance comparison

Fig. 4. Experiment 1.

We run the four algorithms each 10 times for each experiment, and show the results in Table 5. From Table 5, Fig. 4(b), Fig. 5(b) and Fig. 6(b), it can be seen that in the three experiments, the solution obtained by the BSO-LNS algorithm is the smallest and requires only a small number of iterations to converge to the optimal solution, and the variance of the results of the multiple experiments is 0 or very close to 0. This indicates that the performance and robustness of the

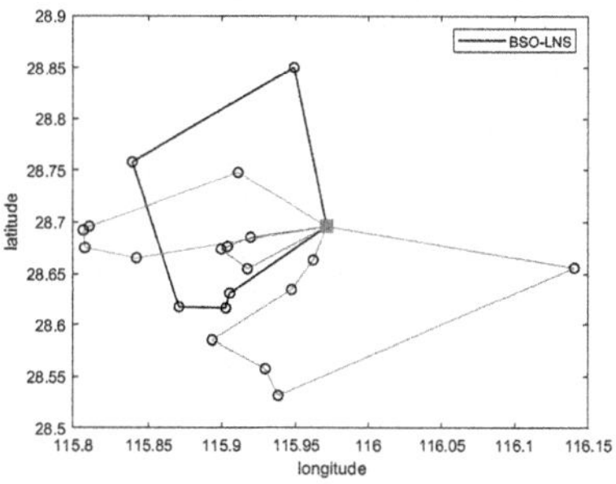

(a) BSO-LNS algorithm optimal solution

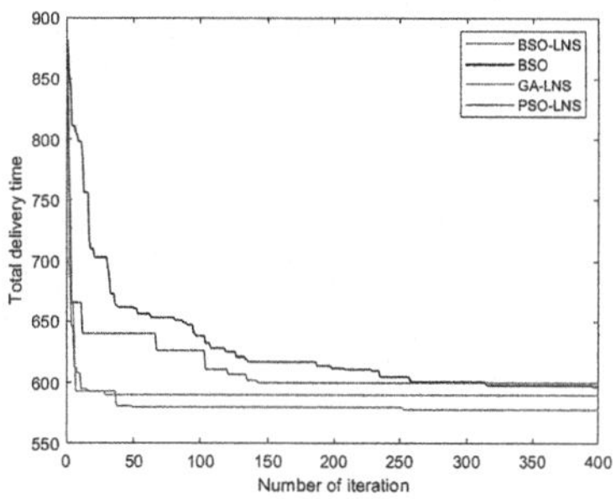

(b) Performance comparison

Fig. 5. Experiment 2.

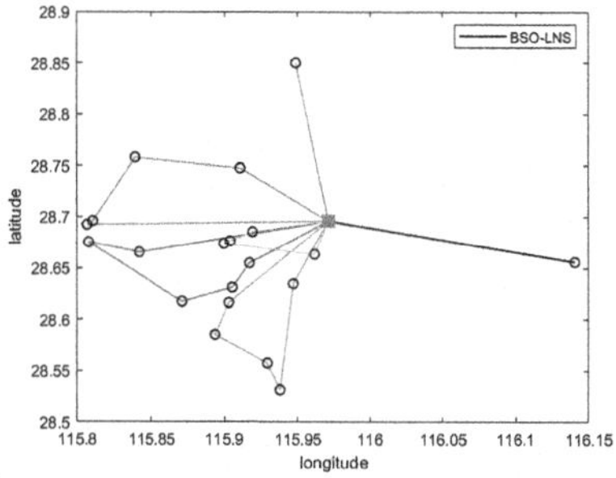

(a) BSO-LNS algorithm optimal solution

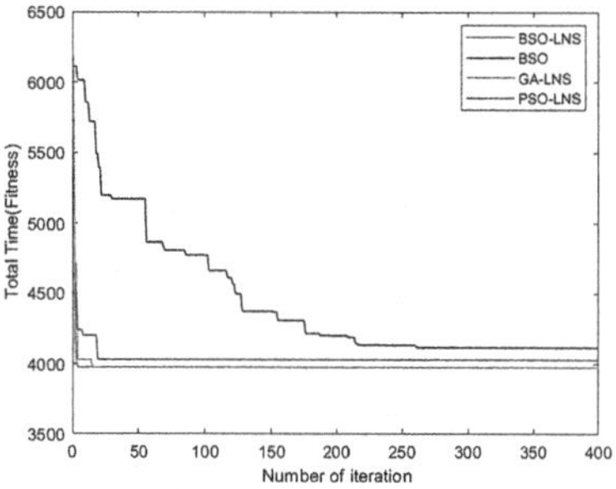

(b) Performance comparison

Fig. 6. Experiment 3.

BSO-LNS algorithm are very good, and compared with GA and PSO, the BSO is more suitable to be mixed with LNS algorithm to solve VRPTW.

Many experiments have found that the total delivery time of Experiment 2 is higher than that of Experiment 1, which shows that the road conditions under Experiment 2 conditions are more congested than Experiment 1, indicating that road conditions have an impact on urban distribution efficiency. The optimal solution of Experiment 3 is very different from Experiment 2, and combined with Fig. 5(a) and Fig. 6(a), BSO-LNS only needs to arrange 4 vehicles in Experiment 2, while the same distribution data needs to arrange 6 vehicles in Experiment 3, which shows that the traditional calculation of straight-line distance without considering road conditions does not have great reference significance for distribution in real scenarios.

From Table 6, it can be found that the solution obtained by the original BSO algorithm in Experiment 1 will have the situation that the actual vehicle load exceeds the rated vehicle load, such as route $0 \rightarrow 16 \rightarrow 10 \rightarrow 1 \rightarrow 8 \rightarrow 0$ is a violation of the loading capacity constraint (the maximum vehicle load is 7

Table 6. Random result of experiment 1.of 10 runs.

Alg	Distribution route	Loading(t)	Loading rate (%)	Value
BSO-LNS	0-12-19-6-9-15-7-3-0	6.311108	90.15869	Time of use: 461 min
	0-2-11-1-10-8-0	6.903115	98.61593	
	0-16-18-5-0	5.94997	84.99957	
	0-20-14-17-0	6.938785	99.1255	
	0-4-13-0	6.48	92.57143	
GA-LNS	0-14-3-7-6-18-5-0	6.623931	94.62759	Time of use: 464 min
	0-16-17-0	5.58634	79.80486	
	0-2-11-10-1-8-0	6.903115	98.61593	
	0-20-12-19-4-0	6.49778	92.82543	
	0-9-15-13-0	6.971812	99.59731	
BSO	0-20-14-17-0	6.938785	99.1255	Time of use: 484 min
	0-3-9-15-7-11-2-0	6.094927	87.07039	
	0-19-6-18-5-0	5.52997	78.99957	
	0-16-10-1-8-0	7.049296	100.7042	
	0-12-4-13-0	6.97	99.57143	
PSO-LNS	0-11-10-1-2-0	6.349599	90.70855714	Time of use: 470 min
	0-12-19-6-9-15-7-3-0	6.311108	90.15868571	
	0-20-14-17-0	6.938785	99.1255	
	0-8-16-18-5-0	6.503486	92.90694286	
	0-4-13-0	6.48	92.57142857	

tons), which is undesirable in real life. This can be avoided by mixing LNS in the BSO algorithm, which makes the global search and local search capability of the hybrid algorithm further enhanced.

5 Conclusion

In this paper, based on the real time road conditions, we abandon the traditional VRPTW, which is often calculated by the straight line distance between two points and assuming a constant speed, and use a web crawler to automatically obtain the actual passage time of vehicles between two points from AMap. The efficient hybrid BSO-LNS algorithm is used for the solution and the results are compared with PSO-LNS, GA-LNS and the original BSO algorithm. The obtained results are better than the other three algorithms and are more robust. The experimental results also show that the impact on realistic urban distribution is significant in the case of considering road conditions and not considering road conditions. In future work, we will consider acquiring more real-time road condition data and taking travel time dynamics into account with time series prediction.

Acknowledgment. The work described in this paper was supported by Natural Science Foundation of Guangdong Province (Grant No. 2020A1515010749), Key Research Foundation of Higher Education of Guangdong Provincial Education Bureau (Grant No. 2019KZDXM030), University Innovation Team Project of Guangdong Province (Grant No. 2021WCXTD002).

References

1. Solomon, M.M., Desrosiers, J.: Survey papertime window constrained routing and scheduling problems. Transp. Sci. **22**(1), 1–13 (1988)
2. Jabali, O., Leus, R., Van Woensel, T., De Kok, T.: Self-imposed time windows in vehicle routing problems. Or Spectrum **37**(2), 331–352 (2015)
3. Berov, T.D.: A vehicle routing planning system for goods distribution in urban areas using google maps and genetic algorithm. Int. J. Traffic Transp. Eng. **6**(2), 159–167 (2016)
4. Liu, J., Hu, X., Chen, J., Chen, X., Wen, X.: Research on urban distribution optimization under point-based billing on simulated annealing with variable neighborhood. J. Uncertain Syst. **15**(01), 2250005 (2022)
5. Wang, J., Pu, K., Shen, Z.: Urban distribution vehicle routing optimization and empirical analysis under the influence of carbon trading policy. In: 2018 3rd International Conference on Politics, Economics and Law (ICPEL 2018), pp. 411–416. Atlantis Press (2018)
6. Zheng, W., Wang, Z., Sun, L.: Collaborative vehicle routing problem in the urban ring logistics network under the Covid-19 epidemic. Math. Probl. Eng. **2021** (2021)
7. Leng, K., Li, S.: Distribution path optimization for intelligent logistics vehicles of urban rail transportation using VRP optimization model. IEEE Trans. Intell. Transp. Syst. **23**(2), 1661–1669 (2021)
8. Taniguchi, E., Shimamoto, H.: Intelligent transportation system based dynamic vehicle routing and scheduling with variable travel times. Transp. Res. Part C Emerg. Technol. **12**(3–4), 235–250 (2004)
9. Kritzinger, S., Doerner, K.F., Hartl, R.F., Kiechle, G., Stadler, H., Manohar, S.S.: Using traffic information for time-dependent vehicle routing. Procedia-Soc. Behav. Sci. **39**, 217–229 (2012)
10. Falek, A.M., Gallais, A., Pelsser, C., Julien, S., Theoleyre, F.: To re-route, or not to re-route: impact of real-time re-routing in urban road networks. J. Intell. Transp. Syst. **26**(2), 198–212 (2022)
11. Yu, G., Yang, Y.: Dynamic routing with real-time traffic information. Oper. Res. **19**(4), 1033–1058 (2019)
12. Liu, C., Kou, G., Zhou, X., Peng, Y., Sheng, H., Alsaadi, F.E.: Time-dependent vehicle routing problem with time windows of city logistics with a congestion avoidance approach. Knowl.-Based Syst. **188**, 104813 (2020)
13. Shaw, P.: A new local search algorithm providing high quality solutions to vehicle routing problems, p. 46. APES Group, Department of Computer Science, University of Strathclyde, Glasgow, Scotland, UK (1997)
14. Shi, Y.: Brain storm optimization algorithm. In: Tan, Y., Shi, Y., Chai, Y., Wang, G. (eds.) ICSI 2011. LNCS, vol. 6728, pp. 303–309. Springer, Heidelberg (2011). https://doi.org/10.1007/978-3-642-21515-5_36
15. Ke, L.: A brain storm optimization approach for the cumulative capacitated vehicle routing problem. Memetic Comput. **10**(4), 411–421 (2018)

16. Song, M.X., Li, J.Q., Han, Y.Y., Zheng, Z.X.: Solving the vehicle routing problem with time window by using an improved brain strom optimization. In: 2019 IEEE Congress on Evolutionary Computation (CEC), pp. 1306–1313. IEEE (2019)
17. Wu, L., He, Z., Chen, Y., Wu, D., Cui, J.: Brainstorming-based ant colony optimization for vehicle routing with soft time windows. IEEE Access **7**, 19643–19652 (2019)
18. Shen, Y., Liu, M., Yang, J., Shi, Y., Middendorf, M.: A hybrid swarm intelligence algorithm for vehicle routing problem with time windows. IEEE Access **8**, 93882–93893 (2020)
19. Liang, X., Yang, J., Xiang, Z., Chen, Y.: Two-stage brain storm optimization-simulated annealing algorithm for constrained vehicle routing problem. In: 2021 3rd International Academic Exchange Conference on Science and Technology Innovation (IAECST), pp. 1357–1362. IEEE (2021)
20. Liu, M., Shen, Y., Zhao, Q., Shi, Y.: A hybrid BSO-ACS algorithm for vehicle routing problem with time windows on road networks. In: 2020 IEEE Congress on Evolutionary Computation (CEC), pp. 1–8. IEEE (2020)

A SAR Image Preprocessing Algorithm Based on Improved Homomorphic Wavelet Transform and Retinex

Jianchao Wang[1], Hainan Cheng[1], Xiang Wang[1](✉), Yijin Zhao[2], Shuying Liu[1], and Pingping Yu[1]

[1] College of School of Information Science and Engineering, Hebei University of Science and Technology, Shijiazhuang, Hebei Province, China
wangxiang@hebust.edu.cn

[2] College of Feduni Information Engineering Institute, Hebei University of Science and Technology, Shijiazhuang, Hebei Province, China

Abstract. Synthetic Aperture Radar (SAR) imaging technology is gradually applied in the field of security inspection. However, the existence of speckle noise in SAR image will seriously affect its image interpretation and post-processing. To solve this problem, a SAR image preprocessing algorithm based on improved homomorphic wavelet transform (HWT) and Retinex is proposed. Firstly, the HWT is improved. The SAR images obtained after denoising by homomorphic wavelet threshold denoising method and total variation (TV) model denoising method were decomposed by $coif4$ wavelet basis, and the low-frequency parts obtained by homomorphic wavelet threshold denoising method and the high-frequency parts obtained by TV model denoising method are recombined; Then, the recombined sub-image is reconstructed by inverse wavelet transform to achieve better denoising effect while retaining the effective boundary information; Finally, the single-scale Retinex (SSR) algorithm is used to enhance the reconstructed SAR image to further improve the image quality. Experimental results show that the proposed algorithm can effectively remove noise while enhancing the edge and detail information of the image, and improve image readability and the accuracy of security check target detection and recognition.

Keywords: Noise removal · Image enhancement · SAR-image · SSR · HWT

1 Introduction

Millimeter wave (MMW) imaging technology is a method to obtain images by receiving the scattered echo radiation data of background environment and target objects using high-frequency radio waves [1]. Compared with X-rays which use ionizing radiation [2, 3], MMW are harmless to the human body and safer [4, 5]. In addition, MMW can penetrate clothes, plastics and other materials, and detect objects hidden in clothes [6, 7].

Scanning SAR (ScanSAR) is adopted in this paper as shown in Fig. 1. SAR is a new type of high-resolution imaging radar, which has the characteristics of strong

Y. Xu et al. (Eds.): ML4CS 2022, LNCS 13657, pp. 371–384, 2023.
https://doi.org/10.1007/978-3-031-20102-8_29

penetration and is not affected by weather. In the process of image gather, acquisition and transmission, SAR imaging system will be "polluted" by visible and invisible noise in varying degrees, and the strong scattering point shadowing effect of the target will lead to low contrast of SAR image [8, 9]. In order to get a clear and high-quality image, it is necessary to de-noise and enhance the image quality of the collected SAR image, filter out the noise in areas other than the target to be identified, and highlight the image edges and details of the target to be identified, thereby improving the accuracy of security check target recognition. In various active imaging systems, such as SAR, laser or ultrasonic imaging, the signal to be recovered is often polluted by multiplicative noise, unlike ordinary visible images, which are polluted by additive noise [10, 11]. At present, SAR image denoising methods mainly include speckle suppression, background clutter suppression and target enhancement.

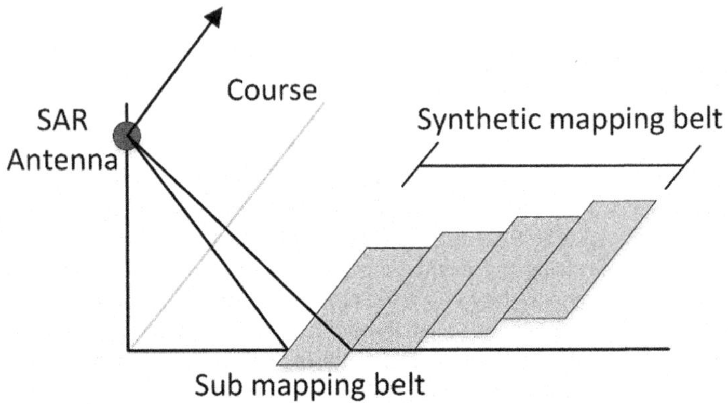

Fig. 1. ScanSAR.

In recent years, a large number of experts and scholars at home and abroad have tried a variety of algorithms to remove noise in SAR images and improve image quality to obtain clearer and more effective images. For example, the improved Retinex algorithm adopted in reference [12] not only enhances the local contrast of the image, but also suppresses the "contour effect", but the average gray value of the processed image is relatively large and the subjective effect is poor. HWT algorithm is proposed in reference [13], which is mainly aimed at multiplicative noise. It has a good effect of removing speckle noise, but it also blurs the edge information, resulting in the loss of edge and detail information. The method of nonlocal vector TV denoising model proposed in reference [14] can maintain the edge and other details of multi-channel SAR image while denoising, but it is easy to be affected by large noise points and can't distinguish texture and noise well.

To solve the above problems, according to the characteristics of SAR image, which contains not only Gaussian noise but also speckle noise [15]. Papers first improves the HWT, then combines the improved HWT with Retinex algorithm, and finally proposes a SAR image preprocessing algorithm based on improved HWT and Retinex. This algorithm can retain the edge and detail information of the target image needed to be recognized on the basis of better filtering out the mixed noise, improve image contrast and quality, and make the accuracy of target recognition higher. After many experiments, the comparison of five denoising algorithms shows that the proposed method can effectively remove SAR image noise, preserve image edge and detail information, and enhance image quality.

2 Retinex Image Enhancement Algorithm

According to Retinex theory, the SSR algorithm first constructs a Gaussian surround function to filter the image, and then subtracts the illumination component from the original image in the logarithmic domain to obtain the reflection component, which is used as the output result image [16].

The concrete expression is as follows:

$$r_i(x, y) = Log\left[I_i(x, y)\right] - Log\left[I_i(x, y) * G(x, y)\right] \tag{1}$$

where $r_i(x, y)$ is the image enhancement output, the subscript i $\in R, G, B$, and $I_i(x, y)$ represents the distribution of the original image $I(x, y)$ in the ith spectrum, and $*$ is the convolution, and $G(x, y)$ is the Gaussian kernel function, whose function is constructed as follows:

$$G(x, y) = \lambda e^{-\left(x^2+y^2\right)/c^2} \tag{2}$$

where λ is the normalization constant, and c is the scale constant of Gaussian filtering. And the larger the scale constant, the more the gray dynamic range is compressed, which means the more image sharpening [17].

The Retinex enhancement algorithm is mainly used to estimate the noise at different positions in the image and remove them, which can compress the dynamic range of the image, maintain the image edge and detail information to a certain extent, and enhance the image color. However, due to the uneven distribution of each component of the whole image and the lack of pertinence of the algorithm, the overall gray value of the processed image is dark and the denoising effect is poor.

3 Wavelet Transform (WT) Image Denoising Algorithm

3.1 Homomorphic Wavelet Threshold Denoising

HWT can observe signals on multiple scales, and scale changes are reflected in the transformation of scale parameters [18, 19]. The mathematical model of multiplicative noise can be expressed as:

$$y(t) = s(t) \cdot e(t) \tag{3}$$

where $y(t)$ is the noisy observation signal, and $s(t)$ is the real signal, and $e(t)$ is the noise.

Homomorphic wavelet threshold denoising, firstly, the noise-containing signal $y(t)$ is subjected to homomorphic transformation, that is, logarithmic transformation, and the multiplicative noise is transformed into additive noise, which can be expressed as [20]:

$$G(t) = \ln(s) + \ln(e) \tag{4}$$

Secondly, through wavelet threshold denoising, the transformed signal $G(t)$ containing additive noise is decomposed in multiple scales, the threshold is selected to quantify the wavelet coefficients, the wavelet coefficients belonging to noise are removed at each scale, the wavelet coefficients belonging to the signal are retained and enhanced, and finally the signal after wavelet threshold denoising is reconstructed and the inverse exponential transform is used to recover the real signal.

The reconstructed signal obtained by homomorphic wavelet threshold denoising has better smoothness, but the error is relatively large.

3.2 Homomorphic Wavelet Threshold Denoising

Since the TV of the noisy image is larger than that of the normal image, image denoising is equivalent to optimizing the image, and its expression is:

$$E(f) = \int \Omega |\nabla f| pdxdy + \lambda_2 \int \Omega (f - f_0) pdxdy \tag{5}$$

where the definition domain is Ω, and the pixel point $(x, y) \in \Omega$, and $f(x, y)$ is the original image, and $f_0(x, y)$ is an image with noise, and the regular term parameter is p, and the gradient of the image is ∇f. The former term of the formula is the regular term mainly used for denoising, and the latter term is the fidelity term to make the image undistorted as much as possible, so that the denoised image can be closer to the original image [21].

4 Algorithm Proposed in This Paper

4.1 Improver HWT

Since the SAR image has the characteristics of both additive noise and multiplicative noise, it is necessary to use HWT to convert the multiplicative noise in the SAR image into additive noise, so that the smooth area can be better denoised, but the HWT has a better denoising effect and blurs the edge information, resulting in a lot of loss of details and reducing the overall quality of the image; while the TV model denoising can well preserve the edge and detail information of the image. This paper mainly uses the advantages of the two methods to reconstruct the images obtained by the two methods. The reconstruction principle is shown in Fig. 2.

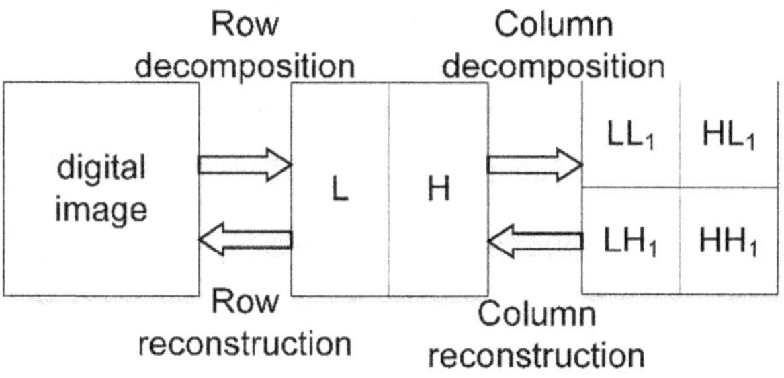

Fig. 2. Refactoring schematic diagram.

Based on the advantages of the two algorithms, this paper reconstructed the image obtained by TV denoising with good edge denoising effect and the image obtained by homomorphic wavelet threshold denoising with good smooth region denoising effect, and then constituted a new denoised image, which the improvement process is shown in Fig. 3. Compared with the previous HWT denoising image and TV denoising image, the new denoising image can achieve better denoising effect in smooth areas while retaining effective boundary information.

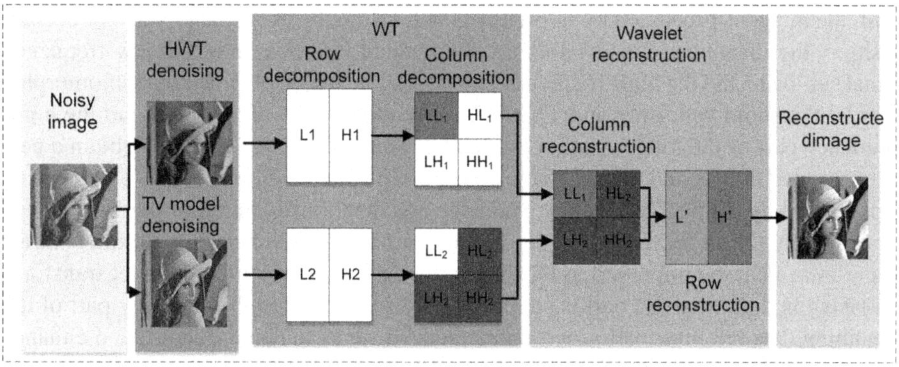

Fig. 3. Improvement process.

The steps are as follows:

Step1: Row decomposition. Based on *coif* 4 wavelet basis [22], the image denoised by homomorphic wavelet threshold and the image denoised by total variation model are decomposed into two parts: low-frequency L and high-frequency H respectively;

Step2: Column decomposition. Then, on the basis of two row decomposition images, the *coif* 4 wavelet basis is used for column decomposition respectively. The final homomorphic wavelet threshold denoising image is decomposed into low-frequency sub-images LL_1 and three high-frequency sub-images HL_1, LH_1 and HH_1; and the image denoised by the TV model is decomposed into a low-frequency sub-image LL_2 and three high-frequency sub-images HL_2, LH_2, and HH_2;

Step3: Column reconstruction. The LL_1 with better effect after homomorphic wavelet threshold processing is used as the low-frequency sub-image, and the HL_2, LH_2 and HH_2 3 sub-images with better edge information processing after TV denoising are used as high-frequency sub-images, and then 4 sub-images Reconstitute a new high-frequency sub-image H' and low-frequency sub-image L';

Step4: Row reconstruction. The new high-frequency sub-image H' and low-frequency sub-image L' obtained by column reconstruction are finally recombined into a new image.

4.2 Improver HWT Combined with Retinex Algorithm

Based on the principle of wavelet transform, it can be seen that wavelet denoising has a big disadvantage, that is, denoising reduces the contrast of the image at the same time, which leads to poor recognition of the image.

According to the SSR algorithm, removing the low-frequency part from the original image will leave the high-frequency component in the original image. The SSR algorithm further enhances the high-frequency information such as image edge and detail information to improve the image contrast, but the noise removal is not complete.

Aiming at the advantages and disadvantages of the above two algorithms, a SAR image preprocessing algorithm based on improved HWT and Retinex is finally proposed. First, the image is processed by improved HWT. Using the principle of wavelet decomposition, the image can be described as the detailed information of the low-frequency signal sub-band and the high-frequency sub-band. The image obtained by homomorphic wavelet threshold denoising and TV the low-frequency part of the noise and the high-frequency part of the total variation model denoising are reconstructed to obtain a new reconstructed image; and then, the new image fused after the improved HWT processing is processed by the SSR algorithm. The edge and detail information of the SAR image processed by the improved HWT algorithm can be further enhanced, and the contrast of the image can be improved at the same time and the problem of wavelet transform denoising is that the noise part is suppressed again, and the high frequency part of the remaining detailed information is again enhanced, so as to better denoise and enhance the image at the same time. The overall process is shown in Fig. 4.

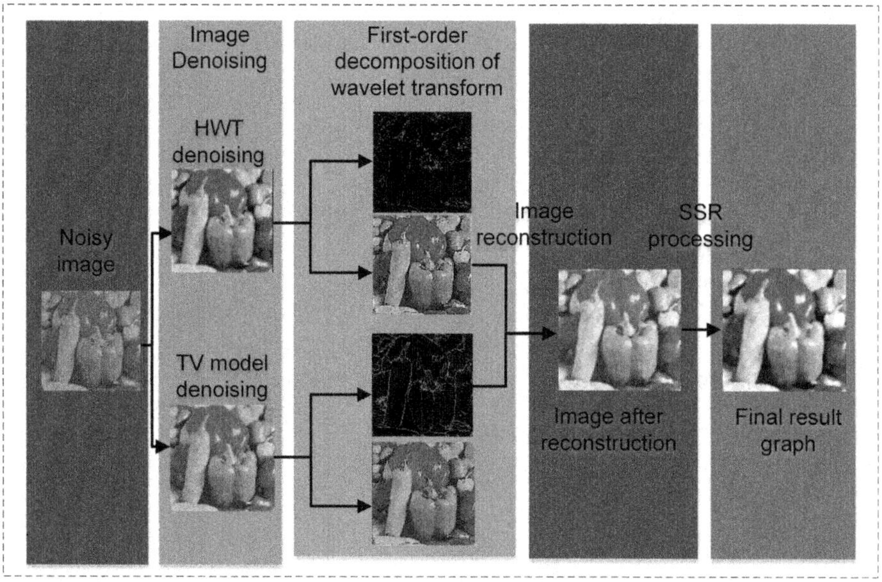

Fig. 4. Overall process block diagram.

4.3 Improver HWT Combined with Retinex Algorithm

Step1: Image denoising. Firstly, the original image with noise is denoised by homomorphic wavelet threshold and total variation model respectively, and two denoised images are obtained;

Step2: WT decomposition. Since the *coif* 4 wavelet base has a good denoising effect and can prevent new noise after image decomposition and fusion, this paper selects the *coif* 4 wavelet base to perform a first-level wavelet transform decomposition on the two images obtained after two different methods of denoising. The two images are respectively decomposed into high-frequency sub-images and low-frequency sub-images;

Step3: Image reconstruction. Through the comparison of the various details of the image in the wavelet transform domain, Select LL_1, which has a better effect after homomorphic wavelet threshold denoising, as the low-frequency sub-image, and select HL_2, LH_2, and HH_2 three sub-images with better edge information processing after TV denoising as high-frequency sub-images. Fusion is achieved on different scales, and important wavelet coefficients are extracted;

Step4: Image acquisition. Through the inverse wavelet transform (IWT), the fused image is obtained;

Step5: Image enhancement. SSR processing is performed on the denoised SAR image obtained after fusion to realize the improvement of image quality and obtain the final result image (Fig. 5).

4.4 Flow Chart of Algorithm

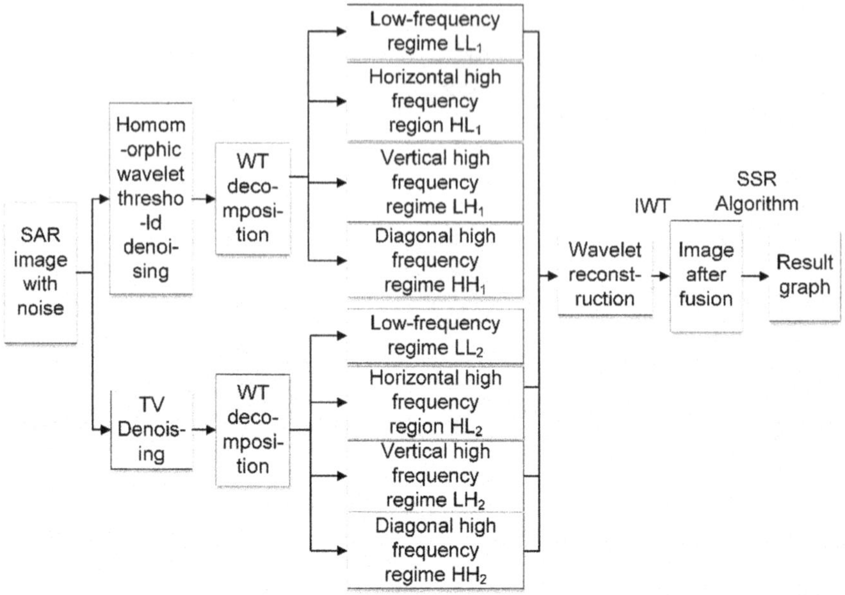

Fig. 5. The algorithm flow of this paper.

5 Experimental Results and Comparative Analysis

In order to verify the effectiveness of the algorithm in this paper, the images collected by the SAR system are verified by examples, and compared with the four algorithms of HWT, improved Retinex algorithm, TV model, and improved HWT, from both subjective visual effects and objective quantitative evaluation.

5.1 Subjective Visual Effect Analysis

Image data usually has clear texture features and reasonable gray-scale effects. From a subjective point of view, the HWT has a better denoising effect, but the loss of details is more serious; the improved Retinex algorithm has no obvious denoising effect, and the image is excessively blurred; the denoising effect of the TV model is average, and the noise cannot be effectively suppressed; the improved HWT has a good denoising effect, but the image contrast needs to be strengthened. The algorithm in this paper uses a combination of improved homomorphic wavelet transform and Retinex algorithm. This method can perform image denoising and enhancement at the same time, and the denoising effect is significant, and the edge and detail area will not be excessively smooth, and the edge and detail information of the object can be effectively retained. The comparison results are shown in Fig. 6 and Fig. 7, where SAR image 1 is an image acquired under normal conditions; SAR image 2 is acquired under clothing occlusion.

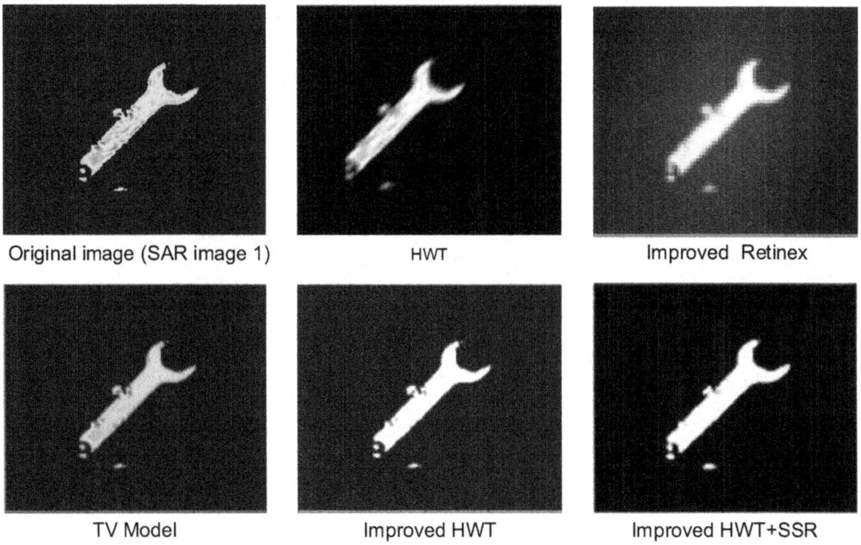

Fig. 6. The result graph of SAR image 1 processed by different algorithms.

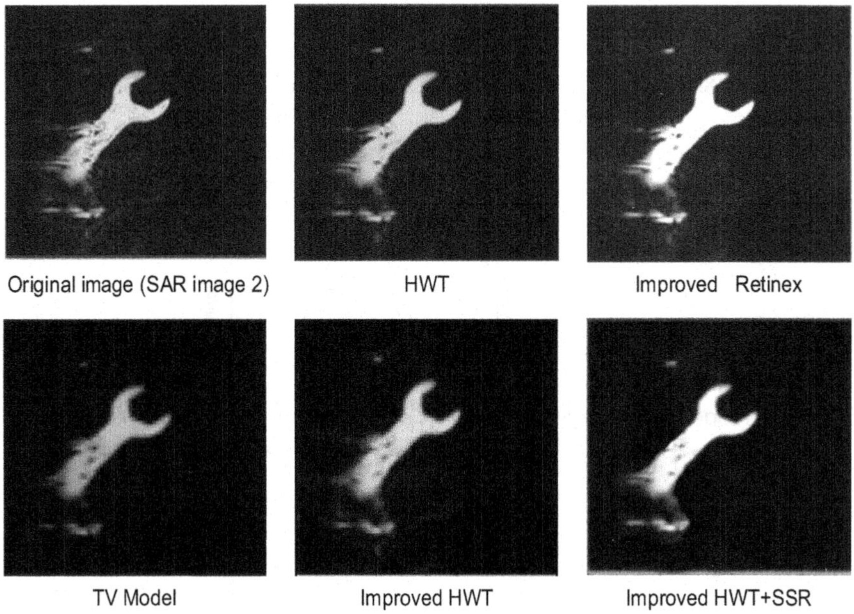

Fig. 7. The result graph of SAR image 2 processed by different algorithms.

The histogram can intuitively see the contrast of the image. Comprehensive comparison of 5 algorithms, the low grayscale area of the algorithm in this paper, that is, the grayscale area around 0–10, has relatively more pixels, and the middle grayscale pixels are few and almost negligible. The rightmost area, that is, the area around 245–255 has the largest number of pixels. From this, it can be concluded that the image processed by the algorithm in this paper has the best contrast effect, which is convenient for the identification of the target image, as shown in Fig. 8 and in Fig. 9.

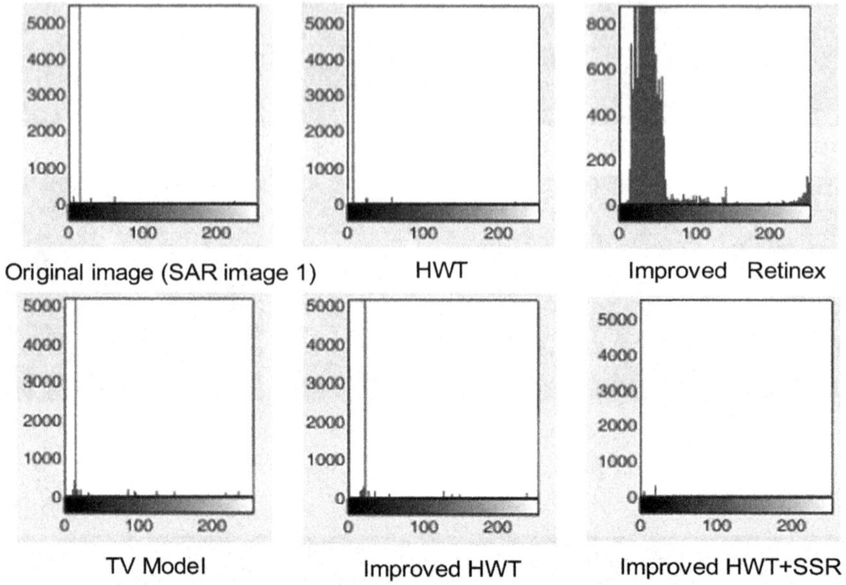

Fig. 8. (SAR image 1) histogram comparison of different algorithms.

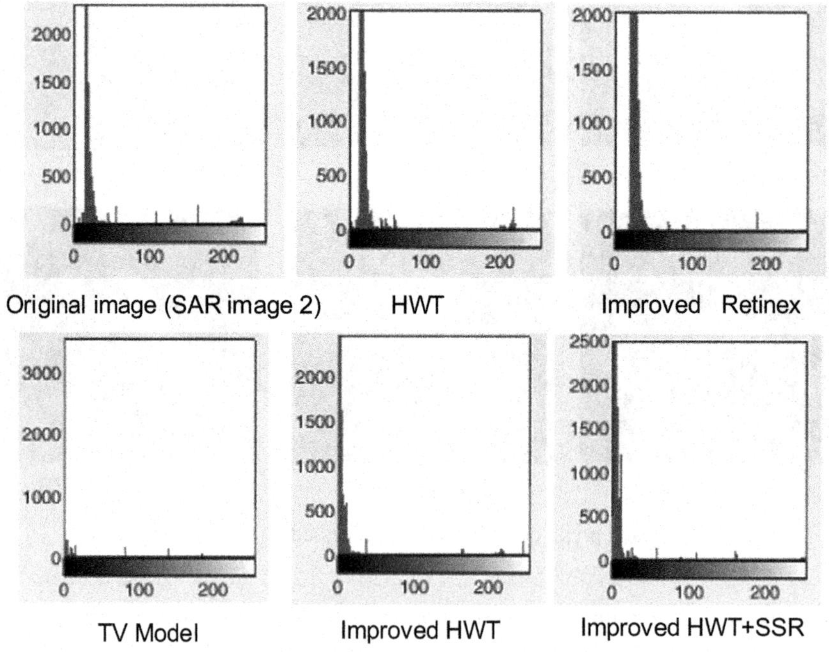

Fig. 9. (SAR image 2) histogram comparison of different algorithms.

5.2 Objective Quantitative Evaluation

In order to objectively evaluate different algorithms, four evaluation indicators are selected for verification, including RMSE, PSNR, ENL, EPI. Where RMSE is the difference between the denoised image and the original image, the smaller the better [23]; the PSNR represents the ratio of the maximum possible power of the signal to the destructive noise power that affects its representation accuracy, and the larger the PSNR, the stronger the denoising ability of the algorithm [24]; the ENL is the ratio of the mean and the standard deviation, reflecting the relative intensity of the noise, and the higher the ENL larger indicates the better the visual effect of the algorithm after denoising [25, 26]; the EPI is a full-reference image evaluation index used to evaluate the degree of similarity between the filter result and the original image, and the higher the EPI the better the filter algorithm retains the edge, which its range is [0,1] [27].

Where RMSE is defined as:

$$RMSE(M,N) = \sqrt{\frac{1}{M \times N}\sum_{i=1}^{M}\sum_{j=1}^{N}\left(\hat{f}(i,j) - f(i,j)\right)^2} \tag{6}$$

PSNR is defined as:

$$PSNR = 10 \cdot \lg\left(\frac{255^2}{\frac{1}{M \times N}\sum_{i=1}^{M}\sum_{j=1}^{N}\left(\hat{f}(i,j) - f(i,j)\right)^2}\right) \tag{7}$$

ENL is defined as:

$$ENL = \frac{\mu^2}{\sigma^2} \tag{8}$$

EPI is defined as:

$$EPI = \frac{\sum_{i=1}^{M}\sum_{j=1}^{N}\left(\left|\hat{f}(i,j) - \hat{f}(i-1,j)\right| + \left|\hat{f}(i,j) - \hat{f}(i,j-1)\right|\right)^2}{\sum_{i=1}^{M}\sum_{j=1}^{N}\left(\left|f(i,j) - f(i-1,j)\right| + \left|f(i,j) - f(i,j-1)\right|\right)^2} \tag{9}$$

where $f(i,j)$ is the original SAR image, $\hat{f}(i,j)$ is the image after denoising, the image size is $M \times N$, μ is the average value of the image [25, 26], and σ is the corresponding standard deviation [25, 26].

The comparison results of evaluation indicators of different algorithms are shown in Table 1 and Table 2. Through these data, we can find that the five methods can basically play a role in denoising and improving image quality. Among them, the algorithm proposed in this paper is in terms of image retention (RMSE), uniform area noise suppression (ENL), edge detail preservation (EPI) in texture area, or noise suppression performance from a global perspective (PSNR) are all optimal.

Table 1. (SAR image 1) Comparison of evaluation indexes between different algorithms.

Method	RMSE	PSNR	ENL	EPI
Original image (SAR image 1)	0.1288	65.9378	0.3191	1
HWT	0.0504	74.0848	0.4211	0.6715
Improve Retinex	0.0922	68.8093	0.9024	0.6863
TV Model	0.0700	71.1950	0.6562	0.8565
Improve HWT	0.0424	75.6735	0.9418	0.8849
Improve HWT + SSR	**0.0141**	**84.9299**	**1.1901**	**0.9210**

Table 2. (SAR image 2) Comparison of evaluation indexes between different algorithms.

Method	RMSE	PSNR	ENL	EPI
Original image (SAR image 2)	0.1631	63.8877	0.4216	1
HWT	0.0728	70.9003	0.4913	0.8012
Improve Retinex	0.1277	65.9927	0.8134	0.7824
TV Model	0.0943	68.6269	0.6054	0.8516
Improve HWT	0.0624	72.2174	0.8445	0.8912
Improve HWT + SSR	**0.0332**	**77.7676**	**0.9822**	**0.9042**

6 Conclusion

This paper proposes a SAR image preprocessing method based on improved HWT and Retinex. First, the HWT is improved, the improved algorithm has better denoising effect on the smooth area and edge area of the image. And it also improves the integrity of the edge and detail information; and then, perform Retinex processing on the improved HWT-processed image to improve image quality, increase image contrast, enhance image clarity, and highlight image edges and details. This method has obvious improvement in both subjective and objective evaluation, which lays a foundation for subsequent target recognition. However, the combination of the two algorithms is time-consuming in processing, so further research is needed to improve the efficiency of image processing while improving image quality.

Acknowledgments. We acknowledge funding from the sub project of national key R & D plan covid-19 patient rehabilitation training posture monitoring bracelet based on 4G network (Grant No.2021YFC0863200-6), the Hebei College and Middle School Students Science and Technology Innovation Ability Cultivation Special Project (Grant No.22E50075D), (Grant No.2021H010206), and (Grant No.2021H010203).

References

1. Nüßler, D., Heinen, S., Sprenger, T., Hübsch, D., Würschmidt, T.: T-SENSE a millimeter wave scanner for letters. In: Millimetre Wave and Terahertz Sensors and Technology VI, vol. 8900, pp. 890000M. International Society for Optics and Photonics (2013)
2. Xin, L., et al.: An adaptive filtering method for millimeter wave human security inspection image. Journal of Microwaves **36**(05), 29–35 (2020)
3. Alotaibi, M., Alotaibi, B.: Detection of covid-19 using deep learning on x-ray images. Intelligent Automation & Soft Computing **29**(3), 885–898 (2021)
4. Saraereh, O.A., Ali, A.: Beamforming performance analysis of millimeter-wave 5g wireless networks. CMC-Computers Materials & Continua **70**(3), 5383–5397 (2022)
5. Prabhu, T., Pandian, S.C.: Design and implementation of t-shaped planar antenna for mimo applications. Computers Materials Continua **69**(2), 2549–2562 (2021)
6. Küter, A., Schwäbig, C., Krebs, C., Brauns, R., Kose, S., Nüßler, D.: A stand alone millimetre wave imaging scanner: System design and image analysis setup. In: 2018 15th European Radar Conference (EuRAD), pp. 485–488. IEEE Press, Madrid (2018)
7. Yocky, D.A., West, R.D., Riley, R.M., Calloway, T.M.: Monitoring surface phenomena created by an underground chemical explosion using fully polarimetric video SAR. IEEE Trans. Geosci. Remote. Sens **57**(5), 2481–2493 (2019)
8. Yanik, M.E., Torlak, M.: Near-field MIMO-SAR millimeter-wave imaging with sparsely sampled aperture data. IEEE Access **7**, 31801–31819 (2019)
9. Zuo, F., Min, R., Pi, Y., Li, J., Hu, R.: Improved method of video synthetic aperture radar imaging algorithm. IEEE Geosci. Remote Sens. Lett. **16**(6), 897–901 (2019)
10. Yu, X.K., Li, J.X.: Adaptive kalman filtering for recursive both additive noise and multiplicative noise. IEEE Transactions on Aerospace and Electronic Systems, 1 (2021)
11. Artyushenko, V.M., Volovach, V.I.: The effect of multiplicative noise on probability density function of signal and additive noise. In: 2018 Moscow Workshop on Electronic and Networking Technologies (MWENT), pp. 1–5. IEEE Press, Moscow (2018)
12. Dan, L. D., Rui, T. C.: The denoising method of SAR image based on Retinex. In: 2010 2nd International Conference on Future Computer and Communication, pp. V3-625-V3-628. IEEE Press, Wuhan (2010)
13. Wang, M.K., Zhou, S.J., Li, Z.N., Wang, F.W.: Research of multiplicative noise removal method based on homomorphic wavelet. Plant Maintenance Engineering **13**(7), 38–40 (2018)
14. Xi, R.B., Wang, Z.M., Zhao, X., Xie, M.H., Wang, X.L.: A non-local means based vectorial total variational model for multichannel SAR image denoising. In: 2013 6th International Congress on Image and Signal Processing (CISP), pp. 234–239. IEEE Press, Hangzhou (2013)
15. Buades, A., Coll, B., Morl, J.M.: A review of image denoising algorithms, with a new one. Multiscale Model. Simul. **4**(2), 490–530 (2005)
16. Fu, Q., Xu, K., Jung, C.: Retinex-based perceptual contrast enhancement in images using luminance adaptation. IEEE Access **6**, 61277–61286 (2018)
17. Feng, W., Zhu, X.F., Xiang, R.X., Sun, Y.Y., Zhen, Z.: Design of cloud and mist removal system from remote sensing images based on dual-tree complex wavelet transform. Journal of Applied Optics **39**(1), 64–70 (2018)
18. Khare, P., Srivastava, V. K.: Image Watermarking Scheme using Homomorphic Transform in Wavelet Domain. In: 2018 5th IEEE Uttar Pradesh Section International Conference on Electrical, Electronics and Computer Engineering (UPCON), pp. 1-6. IEEE Press, Gorakhpur (2018)
19. Chen, X., Zhang, Y., Lin, L., Wang, J., Ni, J.: Efficient anti-glare ceramic decals defect detection by incorporating homomorphic filtering. Comput. Syst. Sci. Eng. **36**(3), 551–564 (2021)

20. Rezaei, H., Karami, A.: SAR image denoising using homomorphic and shearlet transforms. In: 2017 3rd International Conference on Pattern Recognition and Image Analysis (IPRIA), pp. 80–83. IEEE Press, Shahrekord (2017)
21. Lv, D.H., Yan, D., Zhang, Y., Ren, Y.: Study on Total Variational Denoising Algorithm Based on Penalty Term of Exponential Function. In: 2021 40th Chinese Control Conference (CCC), pp. 3295–3298. IEEE Press, Shanghai (2021)
22. Daniel, E.: Optimum wavelet-based homomorphic medical image fusion using hybrid genetic–grey wolf optimization algorithm. IEEE Sens. J. **18**(16), 6804–6811 (2018)
23. Dubey, P., Dubey, P.K., Soni, C.: A hybrid technique for digital image edge detection by combining second order derivative techniques log and canny. In: 2nd International Conference on Data, Engineering and Applications (IDEA), pp. 1-6. IEEE Press, Bhopal (2020)
24. Bouhlel, N.: Parameter estimation of multilook polarimetric SAR data based on fractional determinant moments. IEEE Geosci. Remote Sens. Lett. **16**(7), 1075–1079 (2019)
25. Yuan, X.H., Liu, T.: Texture invariant estimation of equivalent number of looks based on log-cumulants in polarimetric radar imagery. J. Syst. Eng. Electron. **28**(1), 58–66 (2017)
26. Alenezi, F.: Image dehazing based on pixel guided cnn with pam via graph cut. Computers, Materials & Continua **71**(2), 3425–3443 (2022)
27. Andreozzi, E., Pirozzi, M.A., Fratini, A., Cesarelli, G., Cesarelli, M., Bifulco, P.: A novel image quality assessment index for edge aware noise reduction in low-dose fluoroscopy: preliminary results. In: 2020 International Conference on e-Health and Bioengineering (EHB), pp. 1–5. IEEE Press, Iasi (2020)

Medical Data Clustering Based on Multi-objective Clustering Algorithm

Shilian Chen, Yingsi Tan, Junkai Guo, Yuqin He(✉), and Shuang Geng

College of Management, Shenzhen University, Shenzhen 518060, China
heyuqin2021@email.szu.edu.cn, gs@szu.edu.cn

Abstract. With the development of massive medical data, clustering algorithm becomes an effective way for medical data processing and data mining. On the one hand, it helps medical learners find effective information patterns from massive data; on the other hand, it promotes the development of medical technology and increase productivity. For traditional clustering algorithm, a single clustering index is difficult to meet people's needs of diversity and comprehensiveness. In contrast, multi-objective clustering (MOC) considers multiple objectives at the same time, and comprehensively deals with various clustering problems and standards, such as compactness, diversity of feature selection and high data dimension. Artificial bee colony algorithm (ABC) has a faster speed and embodies the idea of swarm intelligence. It imitates the optimization process of bees, and finally obtains the global optimal value. On this basis, this paper proposed a multi-objective artificial bee colony clustering algorithm (MOC-NABC) that is combined with current better-performed clustering algorithm. It takes normalized mutual information (NMI), Calinski-Harabasz (CH), Fowlkes-Mallows index (FMI) and silhouette coefficient (SC) of clustering as the final evaluation indexes. The experiment on UCI mouse protein gene dataset shows that the overall performance effect is greatly improved, e.g. compact clustering and the effective utilization of data features.

Keywords: Multi-objective optimization problem · Multi-objective artificial bee colony algorithm · Clustering algorithm · Medical data

1 Introduction

The large scale of medical informatization and the development of artificial technology enhance medical diagnosis technology. Artificial intelligence medical has a wide range of applications in medical imaging, auxiliary diagnosis, drug research and other contexts. Artificial intelligence technology can quickly find the internal relationship diagnosis method in hundreds of data set, bear large workload and work non-stop operation, which better liberates the productivity of doctors. At the same time, when the stock of data is large enough, the efficiency and practicability of artificial intelligence technology will be more extensive. Therefore, it has important significance and application prospects for the overcoming the diseases, as well as for diagnosing various physical problems of patients. In 2019, the State Council issued instructions on the use of medical data

Y. Xu et al. (Eds.): ML4CS 2022, LNCS 13657, pp. 385–399, 2023.
https://doi.org/10.1007/978-3-031-20102-8_30

[1]. Then, Ji Ping and others scholars [2] combined the guidance of State Council and existing medical health data, suggested that we need to pay more attention to artificial intelligence and improve the generalization ability for various practical needs.

Clustering algorithm is an important method in data mining, and medical data clustering is widely used in medical field. It is employed to classify patients or other medical subjects into groups by leveraging their physical data, assisting doctor to make the initial judgment. For medical data analysis, clustering algorithm not only improves the processing speed and effective use of massive data, but also contributes to discover the hidden patterns and information in the data. Therefore, it further benefits the diagnosis of biomedical phenomena. In recent years, based on the characteristics of medical data, a variety of clustering methods have been proposed. Typical examples include gene expression data analysis, genome sequence analysis, biomedical document mining and nuclear magnetic resonance image analysis.

Traditional clustering algorithms often optimize only one clustering criterion, this may not find all the clusters with different data structures [3], or the shape hidden in the subspace of the original feature space. At the same time, because of the disastrous dimensionality and poor interpretability of data, it has been a long-standing challenge to construct grouping models with high diagnostic capability and good generalization ability. Multi-objective clustering (MOC) is a type of clustering algorithm that considers simultaneous optimization of multiple objectives to integrate various clustering problems, such as closeness, diversity of solutions and other characteristics. Artificial bee colony algorithm (ABC) is proposed by Karaboga [4]. This algorithm has the characteristics of strong comprehensive ability, and maintains excellent results in jumping off local optimization, as well as showing convergence and diversity.

Many scholars have researched the field of multi-objective clustering and gained certain achievement in recent years. Hancer [5] proposed a variable-string length based multi-objective differential evolution approach for simultaneous clustering and feature selection. In the meantime, Kuo [6] suggested analyze cluster by vector updating and jumping which involves Pareto rank assignment. Dutta [7] designed context-sensitive and cluster-orient genetic operators for an unknown number of clusters to deal with continuous and categorical data.

In order to solve the problem of data dimension disaster and poor interpretability, and get rid of the traditional single clustering index, this paper proposed a novel multi-objective clustering algorithm that is combined improved bee colony algorithm with excellent clustering algorithm This algorithm takes the standard information difference of clustering, Calinski-Harabasz index, Fowlkes-Mallows index and Silhouette Coefficient as the final evaluation indexes of multi-objective algorithm, and combines four effective clustering methods: Clustering Hierarchy (AHC) [8], K-means [9], Birch [10] and Gaussian Mixed Model (GMM) [11]. Experiments on UCI mouse protein gene dataset show that the overall performance of clustering has been improved, which makes contributions to the selection of high-dimensional medical data and the clustering pattern recognition of medical data. This paper has several achievements. Firstly, we improved artificial bee colony algorithm by adding a new learning method in the stage of leading bees and scout bees. Second, this paper proposed a MOC-NABC algorithm that combined with excellent clustering algorithm. Compared with common clustering methods, it enhances the clustering accuracy of medical item datasets. Third, we combined four clustering algorithms with different swarm intelligence algorithms (BFO, PSO, ABC) and evolutionary strategies (ES) to adjust the feature selection. We found that NABC performs well in SC and CH indicators among these algorithms, and it is relatively equal in NMI and FMI indicators with the strongest comprehensive ability.

2 Methodology

2.1 Clustering Algorithms

IN terms of clustering process, two general types of basic clustering are considered: hierarchical-based clustering algorithms and partition-based clustering algorithms. This paper will focus on four clustering algorithms as the basic clustering algorithms, including Agglomerative Hierarchical Clustering (AHC), K-means, Birch and Gaussian Mixture Model (GMM) [12].

Agglomerative Hierarchical Clustering (AHC): Hierarchical methods use a series of nested groupings of the data set to cluster a set of data objects, from a single cluster to a cluster containing all individuals, and vice versa. The former is called agglomerative hierarchical clustering, and the latter is called divisive hierarchical clustering.

K-means: IN the initialization process of K-means, randomization is usually used to determine the initial number and cluster centers. The next step is to select an appropriate heuristic algorithm, and use the iterative merging process to calculate the distance metric of the points to determine the cluster center of the data merging, until the cluster is sufficiently compact and the clusters are sufficiently separated.

Birch: Birch's idea is to use a clustering feature tree to store the statistical summary of the original data, which captures important clustering information of the original data. It calculates the similarity between nodes by a certain similarity measure, sorts them from high to low, and gradually reconnects each node.

Gaussian Mixture Model (GMM): The theoretical basis of the Gaussian mixture model is on the assumption that the data obeys the Gaussian distribution as a prior probability, which can be understood as the data generated by the Gaussian distribution. By continuously increasing the number of Gaussian distributions in the model, it is possible to continuously approximate the original form of the data.

2.2 Evaluation Metrics for Clustering Algorithms

Four objective clustering factors [13] including Silhouette Coefficient, calinski-harabasz Index, Fowlkes–Mallows index and Normalized Mutual Information are considered in the proposed in the multi-objective bee colony clustering algorithm.

Silhouette Coefficient: The silhouette coefficient is a measure of cluster validity, and if the actual labels of the clustering results are unknown, it must be evaluated using the model itself. Under the similarity measure, the silhouette coefficient represents the relationship between the intra-cluster distance and the inter-cluster distance, and it is suitable for situations where the actual category information is unknown.

Calinski-Harabasz Index: Calinski-Harabasz, known as the Variance Ratio Criterion, calculates the score by evaluating the between-class variance and the within-class variance, which is defined as the ratio of the mean dispersion within a cluster to the dispersion between clusters, and scores are higher when clusters are compact and well-separated.

Fowlkes–Mallows Index: Fowlkes-Mallows score (FMI) is a comparison number between two value, using the geometric mean of precision and recall rate, which are TP (label = true and predict label = true), FP (label = true and predict label = false, or predict label = false and label = true) and FN (label = false and predict label = false). FMI scores range from 0 to 1. Higher values closer to 1 indicate good similarity between the two clusters.

Normalized Mutual Information: Standardized mutual information uses entropy as the denominator to standardize and adjust the mutual information value, so that information sets of different magnitude units can be compared and returned. Standard mutual information is often used to compare the degree of similarity between two sets of information, which can objectively evaluate the accuracy of a set partition compared with a standard partition.

2.3 Artificial Bee Colony Optimization Algorithm

Artificial Bee Colony Optimization Algorithm (ABC) is provided by Karaboga. ABC model can be used to effectively deal with multi-variable and multi-function optimization problems. ABC algorithm is very similar to many other swarm optimization algorithms, and it is also an another mature, effective and excellent theoretical application of swarm intelligence. The algorithm simulates the behavior of bees, measures the current target, constantly updates itself and completes the iteration of artificial bees' self-updating.

The main components of bee colony optimization algorithm to realize heuristic thought are as follows: honey source (solution in solution space), leading bee (the subject of solution), following bee (the main way of information exchange), and scout bee (the key of jumping out of local optimum). The process of bee searching for high-quality honey source has the following three steps.

The position of the leading bee represents the search position. At the beginning, the moving mode of the leading bee is defined by the following formula:

$$V_{id} = x_{id} + \Phi(x_{id} - x_{jd}) \tag{1}$$

where Φ is a random number evenly distributed in [0,1], determining the interference degree of the following bees in the search process. When the fitness of the new honey source V_{id} is better than x_i, the fit is calculated by using the feedback of fitness function.

If the current fit ratio is better than the old honey source position, the new honey source position will be determined to replace the old solution x_i, otherwise, x_i will be kept.

When the following bee completes a round of position update, it will get a new round of honey source information. At this time, the leading bee will dance and share information with the following bee, and the following bee will make a choice by roulette. $P(i)$. . Formula (2)describes the cumulative fitness of per iteration.

$$p_i = \frac{fit_i}{\sum_{i=1}^{Np} fit_i} \tag{2}$$

After the following bee completes the search process, if the x_i has not been updated or changed under the limit cycle, the system will determine that it is trapped in the local optimum, the task of following bees is finished after x_i is abandoned, and at the same time, it will be transformed into reconnaissance bees. The scout bee generates a new honey source by the following formula to jump out of the local solution (honey source) and enters a new cycle. L_d, U_d describes the lower and upper limit of optimization. *trial* describes Current optimization times.

$$X_i^{t=1} \begin{cases} L_d + rand(U_d - L_d), & trial \geq \lim it \\ X_i^t, & trial < \lim it \end{cases} \tag{3}$$

2.4 Enhanced Multi-objective Clustering Framework with Improved ABC

In this paper, four representative algorithms, AHC, Birch, GMM and K-means, are used in the gene dataset of mouse protein expression. In order to better measure the clustering effect, we choose four clustering indexes (SC, FMI, SC and CH) in two categories (supervised and unsupervised) to measure the clustering effect. There are 72 feature dimensions in the dataset after processing.

In this paper, 8, 16, 24, 36 and 48 feature dimensions are selected for comparison, and the rule is applied to determine the number of cluster centers for K-means and other algorithms that need to be determined, and finally 36 feature dimensions and 8 cluster centers are selected. For the parameter settings of other clustering algorithms, we choose the default values. Figure 1 shows the steps of the improved multi-objective optimization clustering algorithm. Usually, in the optimization process of ABC algorithm or other optimization algorithms, we will simply and randomly learn from other global solutions or optimal solutions to improve the particle optimization ability. In NABC, we added a new learning method in the stage of leading bee and scout bee. The object of bee learning and information transmission is no longer the global one, but the honey source and bees with the top 10% fitness value and the global optimal solution.

The following equation describes the improvement. Rand(x_j) stands for the top 10% outstanding bees, Φ_1, Φ_2 represents the speed at which bees learn from the global optimal solution and the top 10% solution.

$$V_{id} = x_{id} + \Phi_1\left(x_{gbest} - x_{id}\right) + \Phi_2\left(rand\left(x_j\right) - x_{id}\right) \tag{4}$$

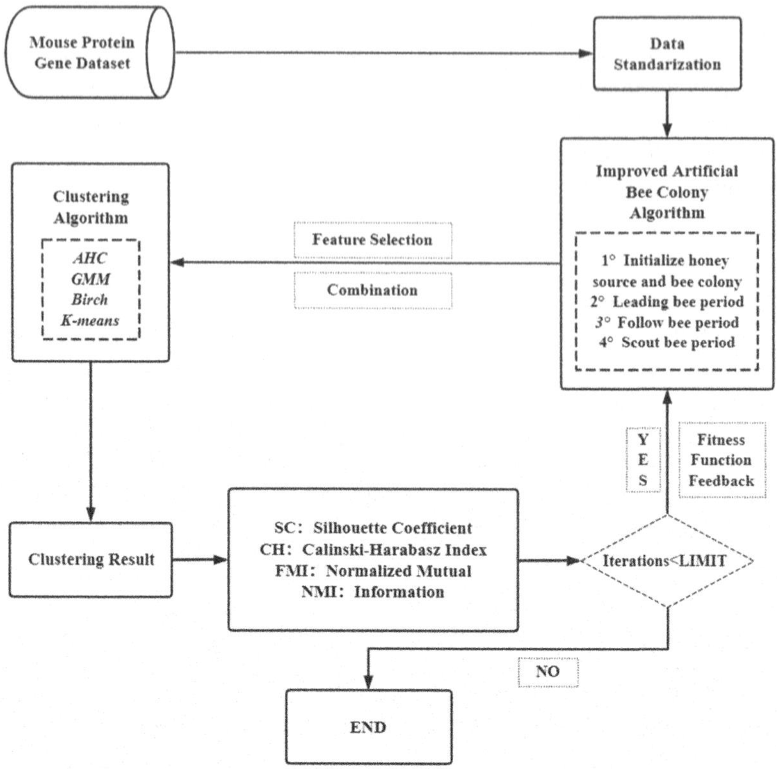

Fig. 1. The overall flow of the enhanced ABC

Under this condition, the algorithm makes use of the better solution in the whole world to make fast convergence. At the same time, it enables to promote the global search ability and avoid local optimization, therefore improve optimization efficiency.

The selected features are transferred to the clustering algorithm for model training. In the following bee stage, each following bee will use Eq. (5) to calculate its selection probability $Ps(i)$. $\sum_{i=0}^{pN} Fitness$ describes the cumulative probability of each iteration. Fitness represents the fitness value of the objective function which measured the honey source that the bee have found. Using this method to determine the object followed by the following bees ensures that the better leading bees have more probability to spread information and speed up the convergence speed. In the meantime, bees at a temporary disadvantage also have opportunities, which helps to avoid local optimal solution. Lastly, once the NABC algorithm reaches the maximum number of iterations, the method will output the best feature selection dimension and the corresponding clustering index.

$$Ps(i) = \frac{Fitness}{\sum_{i=0}^{pN} Fitness} \tag{5}$$

3 Experiments and Results

3.1 Data Set

This paper used the gene dataset of Mice Protein Expression Dataset [14] in UCI. The data compared mouse protein gene expression with the treatment effect of the Down syndrome drug "Memantine" in a biological control experiment. In today's research on Down syndrome, the overexpression of normal chromosomal genes and chromosomal duplication have been used as a very important detection method for "Down syndrome". Therefore, in order to detect the effect of "memantine" on the corresponding genes, the therapeutic effect of protein expression was evaluated by using mouse gene expression to evaluate drug efficacy. The dataset contains 1077 mouse samples and finally obtained 72 gene expression contents, describing eight types of mice according to characteristics such as genotype, behavior and treatment.

3.2 Experiment Settings

As shown in the below figures, the final output of the multi-objective clustering algorithm is the data feature selection and sample clustering results obtained from multiple sets of multi-index (target) training optimization. The output of each optimization algorithm is a set of Pareto solutions, in which the optimal feature combination is selected and input to the corresponding clustering algorithm to output a set of sample clustering results.

In this paper, the hardware condition is Intel (r) core (TM) i7-8550u CPU @ 1.80 ghz 2.00 ghz; The experimental environment is Python3.9. The experimental dataset is the mouse protein gene dataset from UCI. We directly use this data and extract useful information, delete a large number of missing dimensions in the data, fill in the mean of a few missing dimensions, and apply it to the experimental test of the designed multi-objective clustering algorithm.

We also selected the above multi-objective bee colony optimization algorithm and compared it with the other three common optimization algorithms, including multi-objective bacterial optimization algorithm (MOBFO) [15], multi-objective particle swarm optimization algorithm (MOPSO) [16]and multi-objective evolutionary algorithm (MOES) [17]. As the comparison algorithm in this section, the experimental parameters of the algorithm are consistent with the third section of the fourth part. The parameters were set in the clustering experiment of mouse protein gene traits (Table 1).

Table 1. Algorithm parameter setting.

Method	Value
MOC-PSO	Weight (inertia weight) = 0.8
	L1 (learning speed) = 2
	L2 (learning speed) = 2

(continued)

Table 1. (*continued*)

Method	Value
	Rand1 (random constant) = 0.6
	Rand2 (random constant) = 0.3
	Part_num (number of particles) = 50
	Np = feature number = 36
	Iteration = 50
MOC-NABC	Part_num (number of particles) = 50
	Fb (number of leading bee and follow bees) = 50
	Ub(upper bound of abandoning) = round(0.6*nVar*pN))
	Iteration = 50
	Np = feature number = 36
MOC-ES	N_kid (number of offspring) = 25
	pN (number of gene) = 50
	Gene_size = Feature number = 36
	Generation = 50
MOC-BFO	pN (number of bacteria) = 50
	Np = feature number = 36
	Nc (chemotaxis time) = 24
	Ns (swimming time) = 4
	Nre(reproduction time) = 2
	Ned(number of elimination) = 1
	Iteration (Nc*Nre*Ned) = 48

3.3 Experiment Results

As shown in the below figures, the final outputs of the multi-objective clustering algorithm are the data feature selection and sample clustering results obtained from multiple sets of multi-index (target) training optimization. The outputs of each optimization algorithm are a set of Pareto solutions, then select the optimal feature combination and input them into the corresponding clustering algorithm to get a set of sample clustering results.

To evaluate the final clustering performance, this paper uses 4 performance metrics for comparison. In the figures below, in order to better reflect the gradient descent clustering optimization effect, "score" is the numerical result of the index.

From the final Pareto result and the optimization curve of each index, it can be seen that NABC performs very well on SC and CH, with NABC exceeding the second BFO by 8% and NABC also performing well in CH. This shows that NABC is outstanding in the distance between cluster cohesion and cluster center in clustering effect, and in supervised learning, NABC is equal to other excellent algorithms in NMI and FMI indexes, reaching 0.5 and 0.4. At the same time, considering that NABC's optimization time and algorithm complexity are lower than BFO's, it shows greater superiority (Table 2 and Figs. 2, 3, 4 and 5).

Table 2. Experimental results of multi-objective clustering algorithm optimization.

Algorithm		SC	SC	FMI	CH
MOC_NABC	K-means	0.4136	0.5879	0.3753	**8276.9225**
	GMM	0.4861	0.5915	0.4247	5349.4911
	AHC	**0.4657**	0.5802	0.4057	7085.2524
	Birch	0.4649	**0.6370**	0.4048	**8746.6796**
MOC_ABC	K-means	0.4262	0.3671	0.3595	1499.7507
	GMM	**0.5169**	0.2072	0.4283	1401.2700
	AHC	0.4601	0.1872	0.4171	543.0246
	Birch	0.4779	0.1849	0.4142	773.2166
MOC_BFO	K-means	0.3578	0.5285	0.3578	6485.3938
	GMM	0.4629	0.5626	0.4629	6128.1491
	AHC	0.3974	0.5181	0.3974	5553.4811
	Birch	**0.4918**	0.5425	0.4106	3249.1321
MOC_PSO	K-means	0.3924	0.1763	0.3370	177.2404
	GMM	0.4586	0.1576	0.3980	158.0333
	AHC	0.4432	0.1649	0.4187	166.7836
	Birch	0.4461	0.1577	0.3923	156.7215
MOC_ES	K-means	0.3980	0.1724	0.3263	170.7654
	GMM	0.3889	0.1582	0.3727	144.5454
	AHC	0.4461	0.1561	0.3692	138.4147
	Birch	0.4355	0.1553	0.3955	138.6880

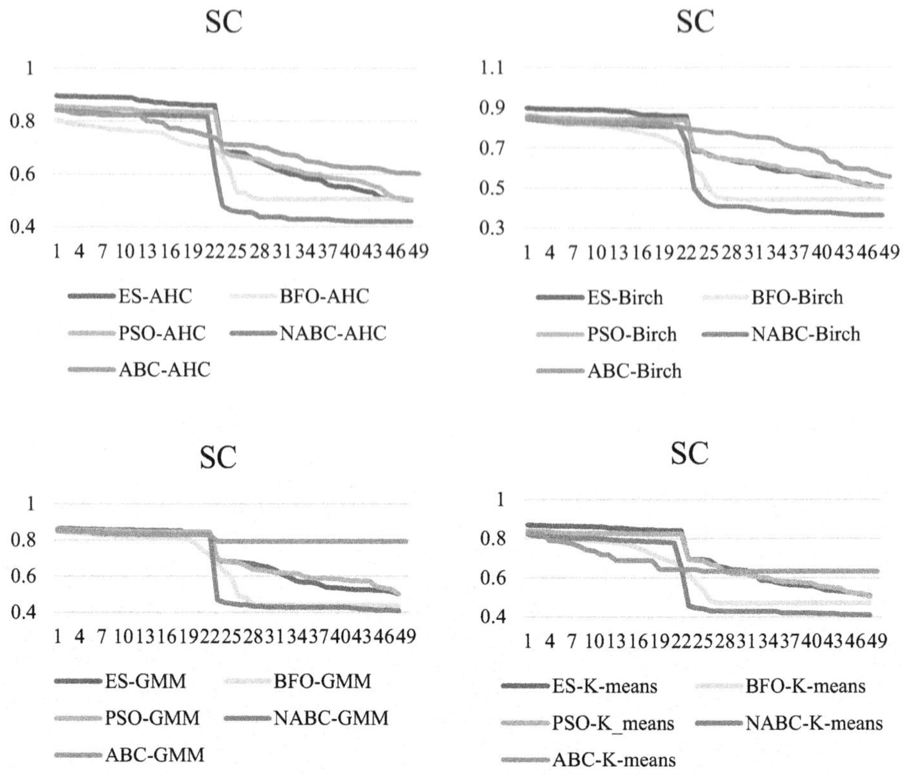

Fig. 2. The results of SC comparative experiment.

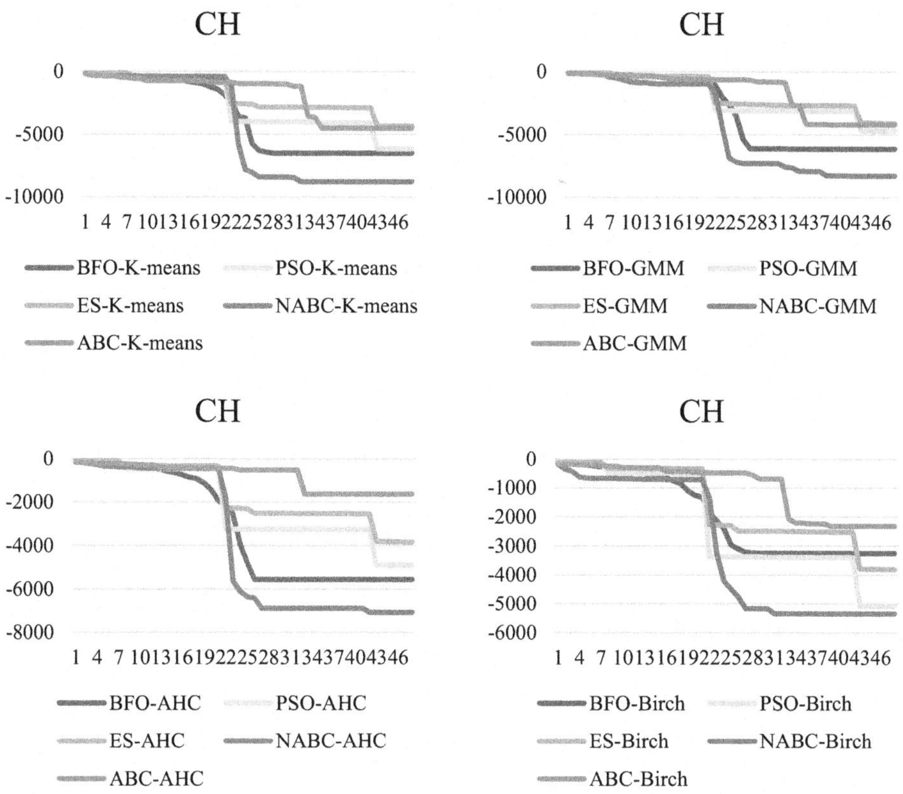

Fig. 3. CH comparative experimental results.

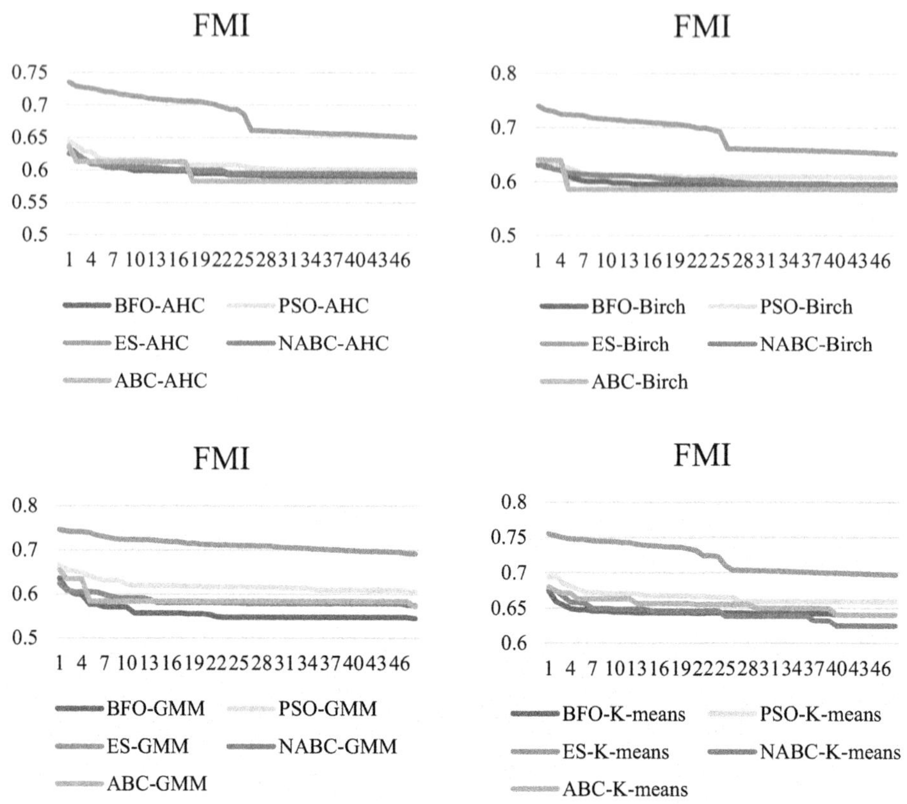

Fig. 4. FMI comparative experiment results.

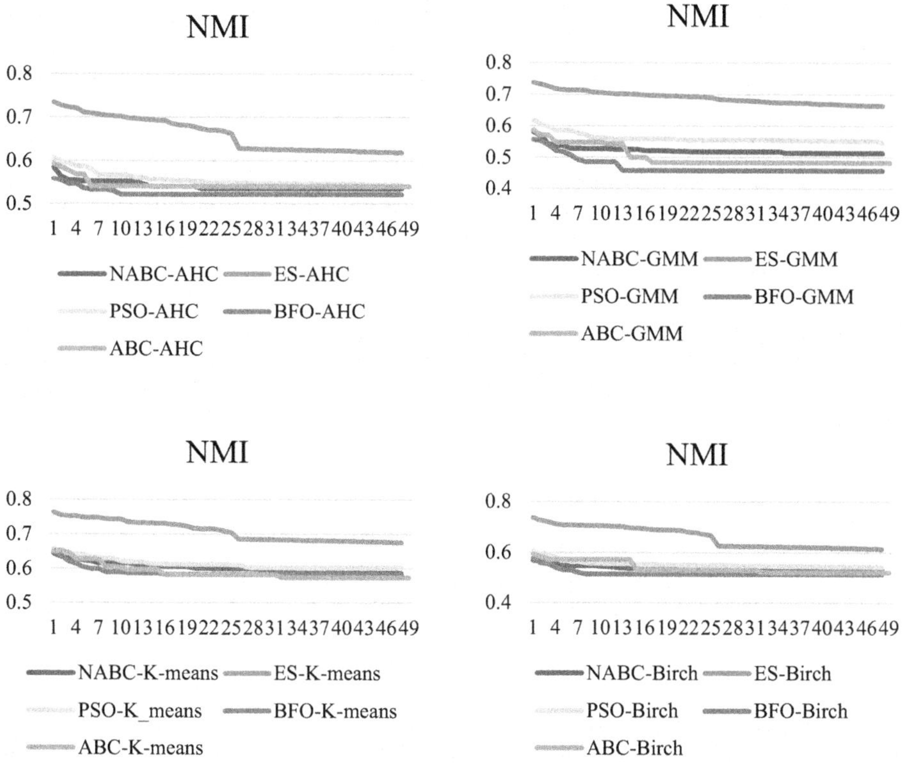

Fig. 5. NMI comparative experiment results.

4 Conclusion

In order to improve the accuracy of medical data prediction, an improved ABC (NABC) algorithm was proposed, and it is combined with four clustering algorithms and clustering indexes to form a multi-objective clustering algorithm. For ABC algorithm, the learning method of bee colony in the stage of leading bee and scout bee are improved. Besides learning the global solution, the bee colony randomly learns the top 10% solution set of the global best. In addition, in the process of following bees, selection probability is introduced to improve the performance of bee. Compared with ABC, PSO, ES, BFO and other algorithms, the performance of NABC is obviously better. This paper has several achievements. Firstly, we improved artificial bee colony algorithm by adding a new learning method in the stage of leading bees and scout bees. Second, this paper proposed a MOC-NABC algorithm that combined with excellent clustering algorithm. Compared with common clustering methods, it enhances the clustering accuracy of medical item datasets. Third, we combined four clustering algorithms with different swarm intelligence algorithms (BFO, PSO, ABC) and evolutionary strategies (ES) to adjust the feature selection. We found that NABC performs well in SC and CH indicators among these algorithms, and it is relatively equal in NMI and FMI indicators with the strongest comprehensive ability.

There are some limitations in this proposed algorithm. Firstly, after optimizing ABC's follow-up bee and scout bee stage, NABC increases additional computation, but overall, NABC's excellent effect and cost from the experiment become relatively reasonable. Secondly, the improved NABC is designed to be tested on UCI mouse protein gene dataset, and the application ability of generalization algorithm in many aspects remains to be tested. Our further research is to test and apply NABC in multiple data sets. Finally, the algorithms compared with NABC in this paper are all classic optimization algorithms. With the progress of research, there may be more excellent multi-objective clustering algorithms, and the comparison between these algorithms needs to be tried.

Acknowledgement. This study is supported Natural Science Foundation of Guangdong (2020A1515010749, 2022A1515012077), Guangdong Province Innovation Team "Intelligent Management and Interdisciplinary Innovation" (2021WCXTD002), Shenzhen Higher Education Support Plan (20200826144104001).

References

1. Office of the State Council: Guiding Opinions of the General Office of the State Council on Promoting and Regulating the Development of Health Medical Person Data Application (2021)
2. Ji, P., Zhu, D., Xie, Y.X.: Reflections on the application of scientific research sharing of health and medical data. Medicine and Philosophy **43**(1), 5–8 (2022)
3. Andreopoulos, B., An, A., Wang, X., Schroeder, M.: A roadmap of clustering algorithms: Finding a match for a biomedical application. Briefings in Bioinformatics **10**(3), 297–314 (2009)
4. Karaboga, D., Basturk, B.: Artificial bee colony (ABC) optimization algorithm for solving constrained optimization problems. Springer, International fuzzy systems association world congress (2007)
5. Hancer, E.: A new multi-objective differential evolution approach for simultaneous clustering and feature selection. Eng. Appl. Artif. Intell. **87**, 103307 (2020)
6. Kuo, R.J., Zulvia, F.E.: Multi-objective cluster analysis using a gradient evolution algorithm. Soft. Comput. **24**(15), 11545–11559 (2020)
7. Dutta, D., Sil, J., Dutta, P.: Automatic clustering by multi-objective genetic algorithm with numeric and categorical features. Expert Syst. Appl. **137**, 357–379 (2019)
8. Day, W.H.E., Edelsbrunner, H.: Efficient algorithms for agglomerative hierarchical clustering methods. J. Classif. **1**(1), 7–24 (1984)
9. MacQueen, J.: Some methods for classification and analysis of multivariate observations. In: Proceedings of the fifth Berkeley symposium on mathematical statistics and probability. Oakland, CA, USA (1967)
10. Zhang, T., Ramakrishnan, R., Livny, M.: BIRCH: an efficient data clustering method for very large databases. ACM SIGMOD Rec. **25**(2), 103–114 (1996)
11. Reynolds, D.A.: Gaussian mixture model. Encyclopedia of biometrics **41**, 659–663 (2009)
12. Jain, A.K., Dubes, R.C.: Algorithms for Clustering Data. Prentice-Hall Inc, Upper Saddle River, NJ, USA (1988)
13. Rai, P., Singh, S.: A survey of clustering techniques. International Journal of Computer Applications **7**(12), (2010)
14. Higuera, C., Gardiner, K.J., Cios, K.J.: Self-organizing feature maps identify proteins critical to learning in a mouse model of down syndrome. PLoS ONE **10**(6), e0129126 (2015)

15. Majhi, R., Panda, G., Majhi, B., Sahoo, G.: Efficient prediction of stock market indices using adaptive bacterial foraging optimization (ABFO) and BFO based techniques. Expert Syst. Appl. **36**(6), 10097–10104 (2009)
16. Zhao, L., Yang, Y.: PSO-based single multiplicative neuron model for time series prediction. Expert Syst. Appl. **36**(2), 2805–2812 (2009)
17. Kang, H.I.: A fuzzy time series prediction method using the evolutionary algorithm. In International Conference on Intelligent Computing. 530–537. Springer, Berlin, Heidelberg (2005)

Self-supervised Visual-Semantic Embedding Network Based on Local Label Optimization

Zhukai Jiang and Zhichao Lian(✉)

Nanjing University of Science and Technology, Nanjing, China
lzcts@163.com

Abstract. Image-text retrieval has always been an important direction in the field of vision-language understanding, which is dedicated to bridging the semantic gap between two modalities. The existing methods are mainly divided into global visual-semantic embedding and local region-word alignment. Although the local region-word alignment method has achieved remarkable results, this method based on fine-grained features often leads to low retrieval efficiency. At the same time, the method based on global embedding lacks extra semantic information, resulting in insufficient accuracy. In this paper, we propose a novel self-supervised visual-semantic embedding network based on local label optimization. Specifically, we generate a label for the entire image-text pair from the local information and use this label to optimize our embedding network, which can not only affect the retrieval efficiency but also significantly improve the retrieval accuracy. Experimental results on two benchmark datasets validate the effectiveness of our method.

Keywords: Visual-semantic embedding · Self-supervised · Local label · Image-text retrieval

1 Introduction

With the rapid growth of various modal data in the Internet, information processing between cross-modal data is urgently needed. In all modalities of data, images and text dominate, so vision-language understanding has naturally become a hot research direction. With the progress of deep learning technology in recent years, many vision-and-language tasks have achieved remarkable results, such as image caption [1], text-to-image synthesis [19] and image-text retrieval [5]. In this paper, we focus on the image-text retrieval task, which refers to returning a similarity ranking of data from another modal in a database based on input image or text modal data. Obviously, bidirectional image-text retrieval has a wide range of applications. People often need to enter a text description to search for the most relevant image or enter an image to search for news corresponding to the image. The current popular image-text retrieval approaches

Y. Xu et al. (Eds.): ML4CS 2022, LNCS 13657, pp. 400–412, 2023.
https://doi.org/10.1007/978-3-031-20102-8_31

can be roughly divided into two classes, global visual-semantic embedding and local region-word alignment.

Global visual-semantic embedding refers to mapping the data of two different modalities into the common representation space to obtain the global representation, and calculate the image-text similarity in this space. Traditional methods use statistical correlation analysis to learn linear projections by optimizing target statistics. One of the most representative works is Canonical Correlation Analysis [6], which learns common spaces by maximizing associations between cross-modal data. Thanks to advances in deep learning technology, many methods have emerged to learn public spaces through deep neural networks [5,11,13,15,22].For example, Faghri et al. [5] use classical feature extraction networks such as ResNet [7] and GRU [3] to extract global features for image-text pairs, and fully exploit the potential information between image and text pairs through the triple loss function based on the most negative sample. This loss function has also become the basis of subsequent work. For labeled data, DSCMR [22] designed a new loss function to minimize the discriminative loss in two representation spaces so as to preserve the semantic difference and intra-modal invariance.

The visual-semantic embedding methods mentioned above all input the image as a whole into the network, and the use of the overall feature has indeed achieved certain results. But gradually people found that if you want to further improve the accuracy of retrieval, the use of overall features is far from enough. In fact, when people describe what they see, they often describe objects or other key areas in the image, and the words in the text correspond to a specific area in the image. Therefore, people began to study fine-grained local region-word alignment methods. In these methods, the overall similarity is computed by the correlation between image local regions and text words. SCAN [10] proposed a cross-modal stack attention module (Stack Cross Attention) for region-text alignment, and then used the aligned image region features and text word features for similarity

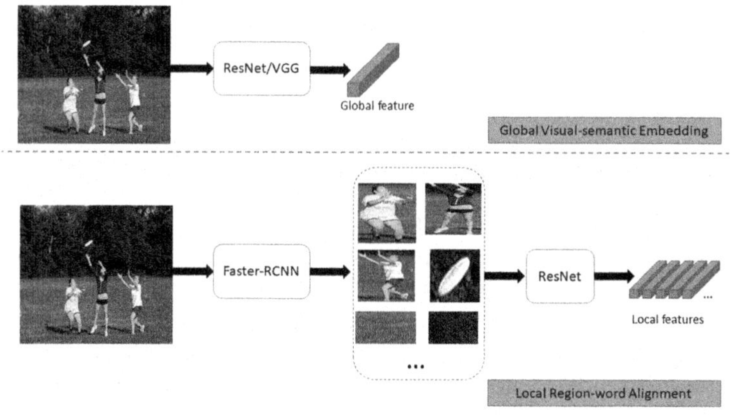

Fig. 1. Two methods of image feature extraction.

calculation. Later, people carried out further research [12,17,21] on this basis, and the local region-word alignment method achieved remarkable success.

But the drawbacks of the local region-word alignment method are equally obvious. As shown in Fig. 1, to extract the region features, it is necessary to first detect the salient regions of the image through the Faster-RCNN [14] model, and then use the ResNet101 [7] network to extract the deep semantic features of these regions. In addition, the process of calculating similarity by local region-word alignment method during retrieval is more complicated, and it will consume a lot of time when the retrieval data set is too large. When performing large-scale retrieval in practical applications, the visual-semantic embedding method with high efficiency but insufficient accuracy is the mainstream choice. Based on the above discussion, in order to improve retrieval accuracy while maintaining retrieval efficiency, this paper proposes a self-supervised visual-semantic embedding network (S-VSE) based on local label optimization. During network training, we simultaneously extract global and local features of images and text. Besides the key main global embedding branch, we augment the pseudo-label generation branch with image local information to provide additional supervision information. Using additional supervision information, the network can learn a better common embedding space, and only need to extract global features and use the main branch to obtain the global representation for similarity calculation during testing, so that the retrieval time will not be increased. Our main contributions can be summarized as follows:

(1) We propose a novel self-supervised visual-semantic embedding network based on local label optimization(S-VSE), which uses the local information of image text to obtain the labels of image-text pairs, and uses this label information to optimize the embedding space.

(2) We use the self-attention module to obtain the text global representation, and the self-attention module can effectively select important parts of the entire text.

(3) We conduct experiments on two benchmark image-text retrieval datasets, and the experimental results demonstrate the effectiveness of our method.

2 Related Work

2.1 Global Visual-Semantic Embedding

The essence of global visual semantic embedding is to embed cross-modal data into a latent space in which the similarity of heterogeneous data can be directly calculated. The main challenge of this type of method is to bridge the "heterogeneous gap" between the cross-modal data. Initially, people tried to use some traditional methods to study. For example, CCA [6] uses linear projection to encode cross-modal data into a highly correlated common subspace. Later, people began to apply deep neural networks to projection. DCCA [2] builds multiple stacked non-linear transformation layers and learns to maximize the correlation of visual and textual representations.

Driven by the wave of artificial intelligence, the fields of natural language processing and computer vision have made tremendous progress. People have begun to use classical feature extraction networks and pre-trained models on large-scale datasets for cross-modal retrieval research. VSE++ [5] uses the pre-trained model of ResNet network on ImageNet [4] and the GRU [3] network with strong ability in the direction of natural language processing to extract the image-text pair global features, and firstly proposes a triplet based on the most negative sample loss. This loss function has also become the basis for subsequent research. DAN [13] uses a two-stream convolutional neural network to extract image and text features, treats each image-text pair as a different instance, and uses additional instance loss to optimize the common space, which can not only mine the intra-modality The subtle differences can also maintain the differences between modalities. DSCMR [22] uses the weight sharing strategy to eliminate the cross-modal differences in the public representation space and learn the modality invariant features. SSAH [11] incorporates adversarial learning into cross-modal hashing research in a self-supervised manner. The main contribution of this work employs several adversarial networks to maximize semantic relevance and representation consistency between different modalities. In addition, the self-supervised semantic network is used to discover high-level semantic information in the form of multi-label annotations. PRDH [20] considers the similarity of different instances within the same modality and utilizes a matrix to constrain the generated hash codes.

All the methods mentioned above can be summarized as global visual-semantic embedding methods, because these methods embed the whole image and text into a common representation space, using a vector to represent the whole image or text. However, there are more complex correspondences between image and text. Text often selectively describes the content of an image, and the same text or area also has complex semantic information in different image-text pairs. To mine complex relationships, coarse-grained global features are not enough, and people gradually begin to use fine-grained local features for related research.

2.2 Local Region-Word Alignment

Karpathy and Fei-Fei [8] first extract local features for each image and text, and compute image-text similarity by aggregating local similarities. SCAN [10] proposes a stacked cross-attention mechanism that aligns each region with all words and aligns each word with all regions, and accurate local similarity can be obtained through the aligned local features. On the basis of SCAN, PFAN [16] further considers the location information of the region, and designs a location information aggregation strategy for accurate retrieval. Considering contextual information, CAAN [21] exploits both global inter-modal alignment and intra-modal correlation to find underlying correlation. Although local region-word alignment methods have achieved remarkable results, local alignment methods consume more time in both the feature extraction stage and retrieval stage.

Therefore, more efficient global visual-semantic embedding methods still have research value.

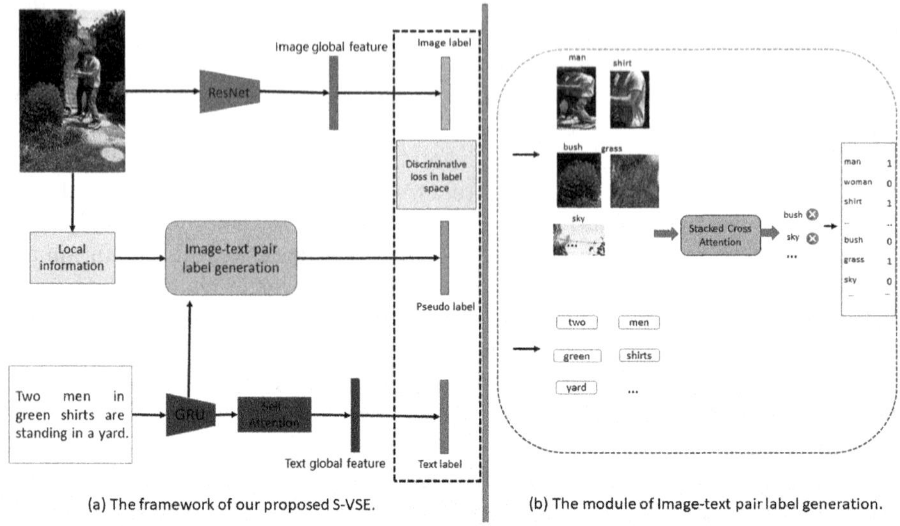

Fig. 2. (a) is the framework of S-VSE, which mainly consists of the main visual-semantic embedding branch and the image-text label generation module. (b) describes the flow of image-text label generation module, which is to eliminate irrelevant regions through the alignment of local information.

3 Method

The overall network framework of our proposed method is shown in Fig. 2(a). The network is mainly divided into a visual-semantic embedding branch and a image-text pair label generation module. Regarding the visual-semantic embedding branch, we add a self-attention module based on VSE++ to obtain a better global representation of the text. The general framework of the image-text label generation branch is shown in Fig. 2(b). We use Stack Cross Attention to calculate the correlation of image regions with a given text, so as to select important regions for label generation. We will detail our approach from the following five sections.

3.1 Feature Extraction

Image Representation. For each input image I, we follow VSE++ [5] to extract image global feature $V_0 \in \mathbb{R}^{4096}$ using a pretrained ResNet152 model. Regarding image local information, we follow DSRAN [18] to first detect K salient regions of the input image using the Faster-RCNN model pre-trained on the Visual Genomes [9] dataset, and then extract the feature vectors and label probability vectors of these regions. For regional feature vectors, we need to go through a fully connected layer for dimensionality reduction, and finally we get the local feature set $V = \{v_1, v_2, ..., v_K\} \in \mathbb{R}^{1024\ timesK}$ and the local label probability vector set $C = \{c_1, c_2, ..., c_K\} \in \mathbb{R}^{1600 \times K}$.

For each input text T, we follow VSE++ [5] to divide the text into M words, and then use a bidirectional GRU network to extract the feature representation of each word. In this way, we get the local feature set $T = \{t_1, t_2, ..., t_M\} \in \mathbb{R}^{1024 \times M}$. Since the text itself consists of several words, the mean feature of the local feature set of the text is often used as the global representation of the text. In my approach, we use a self-attention part to mine inter-word relations (we will introduce this module in detail in Sect. 3.3) to suppress unimportant information in the text and obtain a more accurate global text representation T_g.

3.2 Image-Text Pair Label Generation

First we convert the obtained image local label probability set C into one-hot labels. For each local region of the image, we have obtained a 1600-dimensional probability vector, i.e. the total number of categories is 1600. We set the class with the largest probability value as 1 to indicate the class the region belongs to, and the rest of the values are 0. In this way, we get the local label set $L = \{l_1, l_2, ..., l_K\} \in \mathbb{R}^{1600 \times K}$, but such a simple image local label obviously cannot meet our needs. In fact, the text description corresponding to the image is often a description of some specific content of the image, and not all important areas will appear in the text description. Also, different regions have different semantics in different texts. Therefore, when generating the label of the entire image-text pair, we need enough interaction between the image and text to mine complex correspondences.

We use Stack Cross Attention [10] for local region-word alignment. For K regions and M words, first calculate the cosine similarity between image regions and text words:

$$s_{ij} = \frac{v_i^T t_j}{\|v_i\| \, \|t_i\|}, i \in [1, K], j \in [1, M], \tag{1}$$

where s_{ij} represents the similarity between the i-th region and the j-th word. The local similarity is then normalized using the following formula:

$$\overline{s}_{ij} = \frac{[s_{ij}]_+}{\sqrt{\sum_{i=1}^{K} [s_{ij}]_+^2}}, \tag{2}$$

where $[x]_+ \equiv max(x, 0)$.

Then, to attend on words with respect to each image region, we use a weighted combination of word representations. For example for the j-th word, the definition is as follows:

$$a_i^t = \sum_{j=1}^{M} \alpha_{ij} t_j, \tag{3}$$

where

$$\alpha_{ij} = \frac{exp(4\overline{s}_{ij})}{\sum_{j=1}^{M} exp(4\overline{s}_{ij})}. \tag{4}$$

We still use cosine similarity to calculate the correlation between each region and the aligned words, i.e.

$$R_i = \frac{v_i^T a_i^t}{\|v_i\| \, \|a_i^t\|}, i \in [1, K]. \tag{5}$$

The label $\hat{L}$ of the entire image-text pair is defined as:

$$\hat{L} = \sum_{i=1}^{K} R_i^* l_i, \tag{6}$$

where

$$R_i^* = \begin{cases} 1, R_i \geq \beta \\ 0, R_i < \beta \end{cases} \tag{7}$$

. β represents the threshold of correlation, when the correlation of the region is less than β, we consider the region to be irrelevant to the content of the text.

3.3 Self-attention Module

For the obtained text local features T, we calculate the mean value of text local features $q = \frac{1}{M}\sum_{j=1}^{M} t_j$, and use q as the query in the self-attention module. That is to calculate the attention score of q about all word features:

$$w = (W_1 q)^T (W_2 T), \tag{8}$$

where W_1 and W_2 are learnable parameter matrices. Then use the Softmax function to normalize the score w to get the attention weight of each word $\overline{w} = \{\overline{w}_1, \overline{w}_2, .., \overline{w}_M\}$.

Finally we use this weight to get the text global representation T_g:

$$T_g = \sum_{j=1}^{M} \overline{w}_j t_j. \tag{9}$$

3.4 Visual-Semantic Embedding

For the image global feature V_0, we normalize it and let it into a 1024-dimensional common representation space to get the global representation V_g:

$$V_g = W^T V_0, \tag{10}$$

where W is a learnable embedding matrix. In this way, for the input image-text pair (I, T), we use the cosine similarity function to calculate their similarity $S(I, T)$, i.e.

$$S(I,T) = \frac{V_g^T T_g}{\|V_g\| \, \|T_g\|}. \tag{11}$$

3.5 Loss Function

We adopt a hinge-based triplet ranking loss with emphasis on hard negatives [5] as our main loss. This loss function is defined as:

$$L_{embed} = [\mu + S(I,\widehat{T}) - S(I,T)]_+ + [\mu + S(\widehat{I},T) - S(I,T)]_+, \tag{12}$$

where $[x]_+ \equiv max(x, 0)$, μ is a margin parameter, $\widehat{T} = argmax_{t \neq T} S(I, t)$ and $\widehat{I} = argmax_{i \neq I} S(i, T)$ stand for hardest negatives in a mini-batch.

In addition, drawing on the idea of DSCMR, we also add a fully connected layer as the label space after the embedding layer of the image and text, so that the discriminative loss in the label space can be obtained:

$$L_{label} = \left\| P_1 V_g - \widehat{L} \right\|_F + \left\| P_2 T_g - \widehat{L} \right\|_F, \tag{13}$$

where P_1 and P_2 are the parameter matrices of the fully connected layer, $\| * \|_F$ represents the F-norm. The total loss is defined as follows:

$$Loss = L_{embed} + \lambda * L_{label}, \tag{14}$$

where λ is a constant value that balances the impact of two loss terms.

4 Experiments

4.1 Dataset and Evaluation Metric

We evaluated our model on MS-COCO and Flickr30K datasets. MS-COCO contains 123,287 images, each with five text annotations. According to VSE++ [5], we divide the dataset into 25000 image-text pairs for validation, 25000 image-text pairs for testing, and the remaining image-text pairs for training. Flickr30K contains 31,000 images, each with five text annotations. We also follow VSE++ [5] to divide the dataset into 5000 image-text pairs for validation, 5000 image-text pairs for testing, and the remaining image-text pairs for training. We follow DSRAN [18] to adopt R@1, R@5, R@10 and Rsum as our evaluation metrics.

4.2 Implementation Details

We follow the VSE++ approach and divide the model into two types: finetune (ft) and no finetune. No fine-tuning refers to freezing the parameters in the pre-trained ResNet152 model used to extract the global features of the image during training, and only training the parameters of the embedding layer. Fine-tuning is to train all parameters used to extract global image features without fine-tuning the model. In addition, in the label generation part of the image and text, the parameters in the SCAN model that we have trained are used in the extraction of local features of images and texts. On both datasets, we set the number of image regions K to 36, the parameter $\mu to 0.2$, the parameter β to 0.4 and λ to 10. The maximum number of epochs for model training without fine-tuning is 25, the initial learning rate is 0.0002, the learning rate is reduced to 0.00002 after 15 epochs, and the batch size is 128. The maximum number of epochs for fine-tuning model training is 25, the initial learning rate is 0.00002, and the learning rate is reduced to 0.000002 after 15 epochs, and the batch size is 64. All experiments are performed on an NVIDIA 3090 GPU, and the Adam optimizer is used for training.

Table 1. Results on Flickr30k

Method	Image-to-text			Text-to-image			Rsum
	R@1	R@5	R@10	R@1	R@5	R@10	
DSPE	40.3	68.9	79.9	29.7	60.1	72.1	351.0
VSE++	43.7	71.9	82.1	32.3	60.9	72.1	363.0
VSE++(ft)	52.9	80.5	87.2	39.6	70.1	79.5	409.8
DAN	55.6	81.9	89.5	39.1	69.2	80.9	416.2
S-VSE	52.1	77.0	86.5	36.3	66.3	76.6	394.7
S-VSE(ft)	**62.9**	**85.3**	**91.5**	**45.8**	**75.4**	**83.6**	**444.5**

Table 2. Results on MS-COCO

Method	Image-to-text			Text-to-image			Rsum
	R@1	R@5	R@10	R@1	R@5	R@10	
DSPE	50.1	79.7	89.2	39.6	75.2	86.9	420.7
VSE++	58.3	86.1	93.3	43.7	77.6	87.8	446.8
VSE++(ft)	64.6	90.0	95.7	52.0	84.3	92.0	478.6
DAN	65.6	89.8	95.5	47.1	79.9	90.0	467.9
S-VSE	60.9	87.7	94.2	44.8	79.0	89.1	455.7
S-VSE(ft)	**66.2**	**90.6**	**96.0**	**54.9**	**86.0**	**93.6**	**487.2**

4.3 Experimental Results and Analysis

We compare our proposed S-VSE network with three classic global visual-semantic embedding methods (DSPE [15], VSE++ [5], DAN [13]). Tables 1 and 2 are our experimental results on Flickr30k and MS-COCO.

Looking at Table 1, we can find that our proposed S-VSE model achieves the best retrieval performance on the Flickr30k dataset. With fine-tuning, compared with the current best model DAN, we achieve a significant improvement of 28.3% in the Rsum metric, and the improvement in other detail metrics is also very obvious. For example, we can also achieve significant improvements of 7.3% and 6.7% on the R@1 metric for text retrieval and image retrieval. Without fine-tuning, the S-VSE model is able to achieve a huge 31.7% improvement on the Rsum metric compared to our base model VSE++. Looking at Table 2, we can find that on the MS-COCO dataset, our S-VSE model can achieve 8.9% and 8.6% improvement in Rsum without fine-tuning and fine-tuning, respectively, compared with VSE++. Clearly, our model does not improve as well on MS-COCO dataset as it does on Flickr30k. The reason may be that the MS-COCO dataset has far more training data than Flcikr30k. With the support of a large number of samples, the network itself has the ability to mine latent semantic information, but the additional supervision information provided by our method cannot cause significant improvement.

In addition, we also mentioned above that retrieval efficiency is also a very important indicator in the retrieval field. Taking testing on the Flickr30k dataset as an example, we compare our S-VSE model with the global embedding model VSE++ and the local alignment model SCAN. Table 3 shows the results of experiments. The "Feature Extraction Time" in the table refers to the total time (second) used to calculate the image global representation and text global representation of the 5000 image-text pairs on the Flickr30k test set. "Retrieval Time" in the table refers to the total time taken to calculate the similarity of 5,000 image-text pairs using the obtained image-text representations and then perform bidirectional retrieval based on the similarity. It is worth noting that our S-VSE model does not need to extract the local features of the image text during testing, and only extracts the global representation of the image text to calculate the similarity.

Table 3. Retrieval efficiency comparison

Method	Feature extraction time	Retrieval time	Rsum
VSE++	24.3	13.2	409.8
S-VSE	25.4	13.2	444.5
SCAN	–	67.5	465.0

Our S-VSE model is equivalent to adding a self-attention module on the basis of VSE++ for the acquisition of text global representation after removing the image-text pair label generation branch. Observing Table 3, it can also be found that the feature extraction time of the VSE++ and S-VSE models is close, and both use the cosine similarity to obtain the similarity between the image representation and the text representation, so their retrieval time is the same. In contrast, SCAN calculates the final similarity through the interaction

Table 4. Results of ablation studies

Method	Image-to-text			Text-to-image			Rsum
	R@1	R@5	R@10	R@1	R@5	R@10	
VSE++	43.7	71.9	82.1	32.3	60.9	72.1	363.0
VSE++(ft)	52.9	80.5	87.2	39.6	70.1	79.5	409.8
S-VSE-1	45.6	74.2	83.6	33.8	63.4	74.7	375.3
S-VSE-1(ft)	57.0	81.0	88.5	44.0	73.7	82.4	426.6
S-VSE-2	48.0	77.8	85.9	36.0	66.2	76.8	390.4
S-VSE-2(ft)	60.3	84.0	90.6	45.1	75.3	83.2	438.5
S-VSE	52.1	77.0	86.5	36.3	66.3	76.6	394.7
S-VSE(ft)	**62.9**	**85.3**	**91.5**	**45.8**	**75.4**	**83.6**	**444.5**

between the local features of the image and text, so SCAN spends a lot of time for retrieval. Although the retrieval accuracy of our proposed S-VSE is 20.5% lower than that of SCAN, our retrieval efficiency is higher and more suitable for practical production.

4.4 Ablation Study and Analysis

We perform some ablation studies in this section to prove the effectiveness of our proposed method. Specifically, we remove the image-text pair label generation branch in the S-VSE network, and denote the network that only contains the global embedding branch as S-VSE-1. Then remove the self-attention module in the S-VSE network, directly use the mean vector q as the final text representation, and denote the network as S-VSE-2. Table 4 shows the results of our ablation experiments on the Flickr30k dataset. Comparing VSE++ and S-VSE-1, it can be seen that the introduction of self-attention module can bring significant improvement without label information optimization. Comparing S-VSE-1 and S-VSE we can find that additional label information can also significantly improve model performance. However, comparing S-VSE-2 and S-VSE, it can be seen that removing the self-attention module under the action of supervision information does not cause a significant reduction in performance.

5 Conclusion

In this paper, we propose a novel self-supervised visual-semantic embedding network (S-VSE) based on local label optimization. Our S-VSE network uses the label information of the image regions and the interaction between the image-text pairs to obtain the label of the entire image-text pair, and uses this supervision information to optimize the embedding space. Furthermore, we also introduce a self-attention module for enhancing feature representation. The experimental results on two benchmark datasets also demonstrate that our method can significantly improve the retrieval performance of the global visual-semantic embedding model while ensuring the retrieval efficiency.

References

1. Anderson, P., et al.: Bottom-up and top-down attention for image captioning and visual question answering. In: 2018 IEEE/CVF Conference on Computer Vision and Pattern Recognition, pp. 6077–6086 (2018)
2. Andrew, G., Arora, R., Bilmes, J.A., Livescu, K.: Deep canonical correlation analysis **28**, 1247–1255 (2013)
3. Cho, K., et al.: Learning phrase representations using RNN encoder-decoder for statistical machine translation (2014)
4. Deng, J., Dong, W., Socher, R., Li, L., Li, K., Fei-Fei, L.: ImageNet: a large-scale hierarchical image database, pp. 248–255 (2009)
5. Faghri, F., Fleet, D.J., Kiros, J.R., Fidler, S.: VSE++: improving visual-semantic embeddings with hard negatives (2018)
6. Hardoon, D.R., Szedmák, S., Shawe-Taylor, J.: Canonical correlation analysis: an overview with application to learning methods. Neural Comput. **16**(12), 2639–2664 (2004)
7. He, K., Zhang, X., Ren, S., Sun, J.: Deep residual learning for image recognition. In: 2016 IEEE Conference on Computer Vision and Pattern Recognition (CVPR), pp. 770–778 (2016)
8. Karpathy, A., Fei-Fei, L.: Deep visual-semantic alignments for generating image descriptions, pp. 3128–3137 (2015). https://doi.org/10.1109/CVPR.2015.7298932
9. Krishna, R., et al.: Visual genome: connecting language and vision using crowdsourced dense image annotations. Int. J. Comput. Vision **123**, 32–73 (2016)
10. Lee, K.H., Chen, X., Hua, G., Hu, H., He, X.: Stacked cross attention for image-text matching. arXiv abs/1803.08024 (2018)
11. Li, C., Deng, C., Li, N., Liu, W., Gao, X., Tao, D.: Self-supervised adversarial hashing networks for cross-modal retrieval, pp. 4242–4251 (2018)
12. Liu, C., Mao, Z., Liu, A., Zhang, T., Wang, B., Zhang, Y.: Focus your attention: a bidirectional focal attention network for image-text matching. In: Proceedings of the 27th ACM International Conference on Multimedia (2019)
13. Nam, H., Ha, J.W., Kim, J.: Dual attention networks for multimodal reasoning and matching. In: 2017 IEEE Conference on Computer Vision and Pattern Recognition (CVPR), pp. 2156–2164 (2017)
14. Ren, S., He, K., Girshick, R.B., Sun, J.: Faster R-CNN: towards real-time object detection with region proposal networks. IEEE Trans. Pattern Anal. Mach. Intell. **39**, 1137–1149 (2015)
15. Wang, L., Li, Y., Lazebnik, S.: Learning deep structure-preserving image-text embeddings, pp. 5005–5013 (2016)
16. Wang, Y., et al.: Position focused attention network for image-text matching, pp. 3792–3798 (2019)
17. Wang, Z., et al.: Camp: cross-modal adaptive message passing for text-image retrieval. In: 2019 IEEE/CVF International Conference on Computer Vision (ICCV), pp. 5763–5772 (2019)
18. Wen, K., Gu, X., Cheng, Q.: Learning dual semantic relations with graph attention for image-text matching. IEEE Trans. Circuits Syst. Video Technol. **31**, 2866–2879 (2021)

19. Xu, T., et al.: AttnGAN: fine-grained text to image generation with attentional generative adversarial networks. In: 2018 IEEE/CVF Conference on Computer Vision and Pattern Recognition, pp. 1316–1324 (2018)
20. Yang, E., Deng, C., Liu, W., Liu, X., Tao, D., Gao, X.: Pairwise relationship guided deep hashing for cross-modal retrieval, pp. 1618–1625 (2017)
21. Zhang, Q., Lei, Z., Zhang, Z., Li, S.: Context-aware attention network for image-text retrieval. In: 2020 IEEE/CVF Conference on Computer Vision and Pattern Recognition (CVPR), pp. 3533–3542 (2020)
22. Zhen, L., Hu, P., Wang, X., Peng, D.: Deep supervised cross-modal retrieval. In: 2019 IEEE/CVF Conference on Computer Vision and Pattern Recognition (CVPR), pp. 10386–10395 (2019)

A New Deep Network Model for Stock Price Prediction

Min Liu, Hui Sheng, Ningyi Zhang, Yu Chen, and Longjun Huang(✉)

School of Software, Jiangxi Normal University, Nanchang, China
{liumin1,202140100843,zny,003721}@jxnu.edu.cn,
chenyu7825@163.com

Abstract. Over the recent past, many stock price prediction models that rely on deep neural networks have been developed. However, each has unique characteristics that cause variations in performance between models. With the existing deep neural network models, we propose a novel deep neural network-based stock price prediction model in this paper in order to predict stock prices more accurately. Specifically, this paper presents a method for extracting stock price series data based on the auto-encoder (AE) technique, which has strong non-smoothness and non-linear characteristics. Furthermore, the bi-directional long short-term memory (BiLSTM) module is imported as the primary unit structure in AE so that the historical and future important information of stock price series data can be sufficiently mined. Attention mechanisms are also investigated to make the extracted features more valuable for predicting stock prices. Lastly, the prediction is implemented by multi-layer, fully connected network work. The prediction results of the proposed method on two stock datasets are more prominent than other methods.

Keywords: Stock price prediction · Auto-encoder · Bi-directional LSTM · Attention mechanism

1 Introduction

The rapidly developing Internet technology has allowed a huge mass of financial information to be collected from various financial websites and has had a large impact on our daily lives. How to make full use of financial data to provide investors with valuable information for decision-making has become a significant task during the era of big data. The stock market is an important place in the emerging financial activities in the increasingly active financial market. It offers a high rate of return, attracts all types of investors, and allows for forecasting through financial data, thus reducing the risk of investment decisions [1]. Nevertheless, there are many factors that can affect the movement of stock prices, such as the macro-economic development of the country, the formulation of relevant laws and regulations, the operating and financial conditions of the company, the psychology of investors, the guidance of public opinion, and so on. The above reasons make stock prices have high irregularity and volatility, therefore there is a great uncontrollable risk for investors to invest in stocks. To enable investors

Y. Xu et al. (Eds.): ML4CS 2022, LNCS 13657, pp. 413–426, 2023.
https://doi.org/10.1007/978-3-031-20102-8_32

to reduce investment risks and make correct investment decisions, it is of great practical significance to study the technology or quantitative method [2] of stock price prediction.

At present, many stock price prediction models [2] have been developed and achieved excellent performance. There are many econometric statistical based traditional models, such as the autoregressive (AR), moving average (MA), autoregressive moving average (ARMA), autoregressive integrated moving average (ARIMA), linear exponential smoothing (LES), generalized autoregressive conditional heteroscedasticity (GACH), which aim to explore the relationship among variables to find the best prediction result. Moreover, the above models still have some limitations. First, these methods rely heavily on the assumptions of linearly structured models, making it difficult to capture non-linear changes in stock prices. These methods assume that changes in the data are invariant, while financial time series contain features [3] such as high noise, time variation, and dynamics.

To address the above issues, this paper uses a machine learning approach to perform nonlinear analysis of financial time series. Artificial neural network (ANN) differs from econometric statistical models, which does not require a rigorous model structure and additional assumptions. In addition, it has been extensively applied to financial time series due to its powerful nonlinear mapping capability and generalization properties [3, 9, 10].

In latest years, long short-term memory (LSTM) networks are frequently utilized in time series prediction tasks [4, 5], and problems such as gradient disappearance or gradient explosion, which exist in recurrent neural networks (RNN) [6], can be overcome by LSTM using memory units and gating units. To make full use of historical and future information, a bi-directional LSTM (BiLSTM) [7] network is developed, which contains both forward LSTM and backward LSTM, and its final prediction result is better than LSTM.

The attention mechanism [8] can utilize finite resources to quickly filter out valuable target information from the vast amount of information. The attention mechanism originates from human vision, where the human eye can rapidly scan the target area to acquire helpful information and repress other meaningless details speedily. Currently, attention mechanisms have been broadly applied to computer vision, natural language processing, and speech recognition, and have succeeded in studies related to time series.

Due to the successful use of deep learning and attention mechanism in image analytics [11, 12], a prediction model based on time series is developed in this paper for predicting the stock closing price. First, BiLSTM is integrated into AE to extract the characteristics of the stock and combine them with the characteristics of the attention mechanism algorithm to finally obtain a deep density network for predicting stock prices. In the experimental section, the proposed model is compared with other models on two stock data sets, Shanghai Composite Index and CSI 300, to test the validity of the presented model.

2 Related Works

Recently, a variety of stock price prediction methods have put forward, which includes traditional machine learning and deep learning methods. Multiple machine learning methods includes k-nearest neighbor (KNN), support vector machine (SVM), support vector regression (SVR), random forest (RF), general algorithm (GA) and neural network (NN) have been explored and fused for stock price prediction [13, 14]. For example, Nayak et al. [15] combined SVM and KNN to implement the Indian stock market forecasting. Then, the weighted SVM is combined with KNN for the development trend of Chinese stock market [16]. Zhang et al. [17] fused AdaBoost, GA, and probabilistic SVM to predict stock and obtained better prediction performance. Picasso et al. [18] integrates RF, SVM and NN to predict the stock trend.

Deep learning is an essential offshoot of machine learning that extracts higher-level abstract characteristics for data representation and is broadly adopted in image processing and computer vision [19]. Lately, financial time series such as stock price data are analyzed through deep learning methods [20, 21]. For instance, Rather et al. [22] combined the traditional machine learning methods (i.e., ARMA and LSE) and recurrent neural networks (RNN) to realize stock return prediction. Stock price prediction using the LSTM model can address the gradient vanishing and gradient exploding problems in RNN [23]. Subsequently, many methods have been developed that combine traditional machine learning techniques with LSTMs to analyze financial series data. For example, Kim et al. [24] combined LSTM with GACH model to determine the fluctuation of stock price. Li et al. [25] combined feature selection and LSTM method to build a prediction model. Zhao et al. [6] integrated AM into RNN to propose two different prediction models, which can select and pay attention to the key information of stock data.

Recently, many CNN-based methods have been proposed to predict stock trends and achieve good results [26, 27]. This is because of CNN has two characteristics, i.e., local perception and parameter sharing, which lead to the reduction of parameters. For example, Sezer et al. [28] first obtained the 2D images converted from stock indicators, and secondly designed a new method to make predictions through CNN. Moreover, 2D images were obtained from time series data using the gram angle field technology, and then the U.S. market trends were predicted through the integrated learning framework of CNN [29]. Since the temporal data contains noise, the sequence reconstruction method is used to denoise it first, and then in order to predict the stock price, the spatial structure is extracted from the denoised data through the CNN model [30]. The description of trading behavior patterns have been defined by utilizing three matrices, including transaction, sale and purchase quantity matrices. Then, in order to effectively extract the deep features of transaction behavior, a CNN model is explored [31].

3 Preliminary

The model presented in this paper is designed by a comprehensive analysis considering self-encoders, bi-directional long and short-term memory networks, and attention mechanisms. In that section, we will briefly outline the above approach.

Autoencoder is a category of artificial neural networks used in semi-supervised and unsupervised learning, and its function is to acquire representations of the input information by taking it as a learning target. The role of the encoder is to encode the high-dimensional input into low-dimensional hidden variables, thus forcing the neural network to learn the most informative features; the role of the decoder is to restore the hidden variables in the hidden layer to the initial dimension, and the optimal state of the autoencoder is that the output of the decoder can be ideally or approximately recovered from the original input.

LSTM is a kind of temporal recurrent neural network specially designed to solve the long-term dependence problem in recurrent neural networks. The LSTM has two kinds of gates: the input gate, the forgetting gate, and the output gate. The information of the previous state is input to the LSTM as input. First, the LSTM receives the input information and calculates the value of the input gate, which is used to control the current data input's effect on the memory unit's value. All gate calculations are influenced by the current input data and the last moment LSTM cell output value, in addition to the previous memory cell value. Then, the forgetting states information, which information coming from the previous cell needs to be discarded from the cell state. Then the state information is updated. It is decided which new information in the cell state needs to be stored. Finally, the new information is output through the output gate. Due to the unique design structure of LSTM, LSTM is suitable for processing and predicting important events with very long intervals and delays in the time series. The two-way LSTM is an extension of the LSTM model where two LSTMs are applied to process the input data, divided into a forward and a backward layer. In the forward layer, one LSTM is used for the input sequence, and in the backward layer, the reverse form of the input sequence is fed into the LSTM model. Two applications of the LSTM lead to improved learning of long-term dependencies, thus improving the model's accuracy.

The attention mechanism has two main aspects, deciding which part of the input needs to be attended to and allocating limited information processing resources to the essential parts. In this paper, we use channel attention. Firstly, the input feature map is subjected to a global average pooling operation, followed by a 1-dimensional convolution operation with a convolution kernel of size k, and the weights of each channel are obtained after the activation function. The weights are multiplied with the corresponding elements of the original input feature map to obtain the final output feature map. The attention mechanism used in this paper is effortless in thought and operation and has minimal impact on the network processing speed.

4 The Proposed Method

Deep Neural Networks are used in combination with a large number of methods to predict stock prices, but there are some differences on the performance of different models because the stock prices are affected by many factors. This paper presents a new deep network prediction model to forecast stock prices more accurately. Initially, the Auto-Encoder is introduced in the model to extract the effective features of the stock data to deal with the stock price series due to its strong non-stationary and non-linear characteristics. Moreover, the BiLSTM module is considered as the main unit structure of the auto-encoder, which can fully mine the important information of historical data and future data for stock price series data. Then, attention theory is introduced to feature extraction from stock series data, which allows for a more accurate prediction of stock prices. Finally, a multi-layer fully connected network is employed to accomplish the prediction. The general structure of the model is shown in Fig. 1.

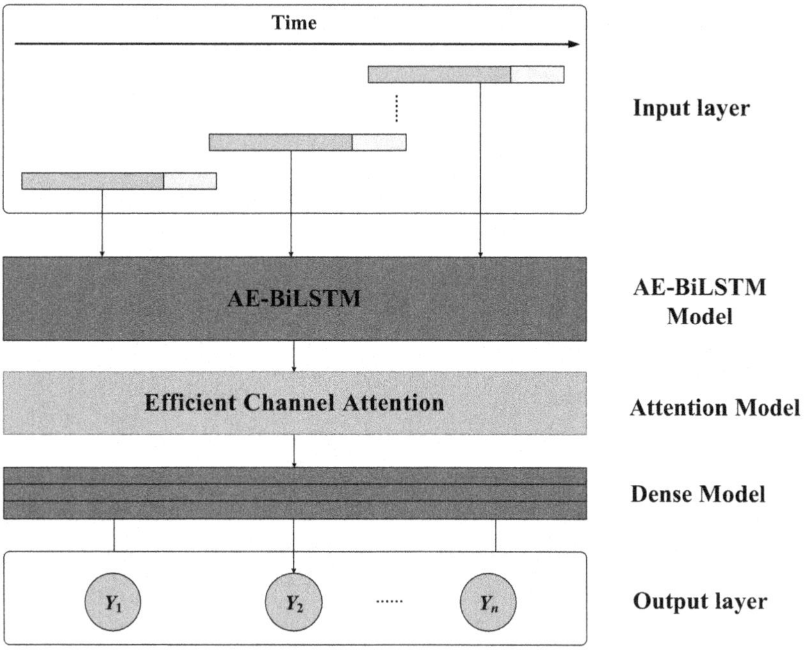

Fig. 1. The general structure of the proposed model

The auto-encoder (AE) is an unsupervised neural network model that consists of two parts: encoding and decoding [32]. The encoder is mainly responsible for learning the hidden features from the input sample data, while the decoder is mainly responsible for reconstructing the original input data from the hidden features. Assuming D-dimensional samples $x^{(n)} \in R^D,\ n = 1, 2, ..., N$, the AE maps the data to the feature space and obtains an encoding $z^{(n)} \in R^d,\ n = 1, 2, ..., N$ for each sample. It is expected that this set of encodings can reconstruct the original samples. The objective function can be defined as follows:

$$\varphi = \min \sum_{n=1}^{N} ||x^{(n)} - g(f(x^{(n)}))||_F^2 \tag{1}$$

where $f(\bullet)$ and $g(\bullet)$ denote as activation function. The three-layer neural network is the simplest auto-encoder and shown in Fig. 2, consisting of an input layer, a hidden layer, and an output layer. The amount of neurons in both input and output layers is identical. The encoding process is performed between the input layer and the hidden layer, the decoding process is performed between the hidden layer and the output layer, and the layers are fully connected to each other.

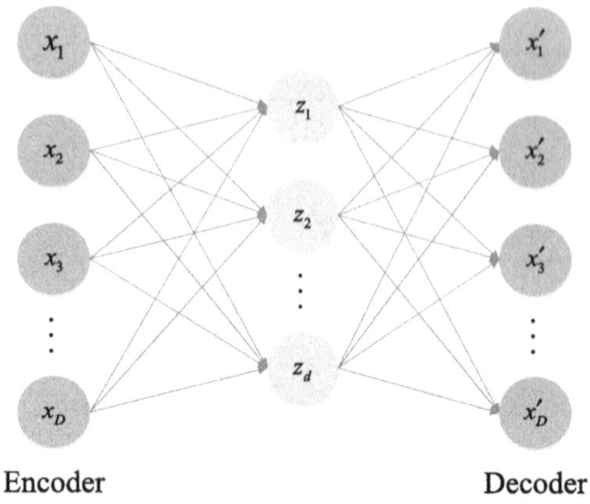

Fig. 2. The structure of auto-encoder with three-layer network

Considering the characteristics of stock time series data, BiLSTM as a unit is introduced into the auto-encoder, and the structure of BiLSTM is shown in Fig. 3.

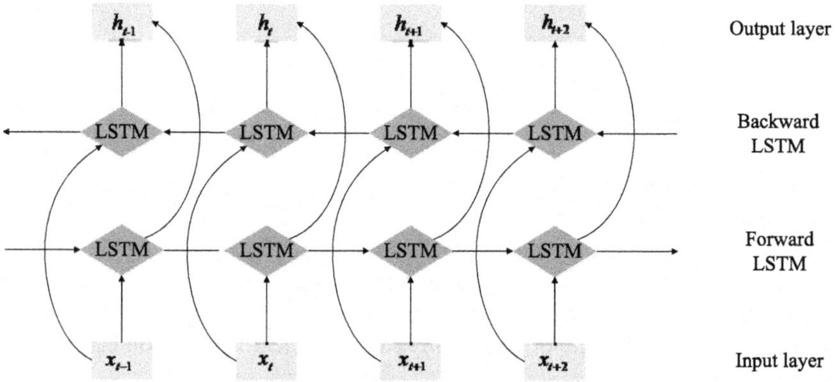

Fig. 3. The structure of BiLSTM

The channel attention mechanism (CAM) is one of the most widely used methods in computer vision, such as image classification and image segmentation, and achieves better performance. Nevertheless, in order to achieve better model performance, most methods are devoted to designing more complex attention models, which will inevitably increase the computational complexity of the model. To prevent model overfitting and reduce computational effort, Efficient Channel Attention (ECA) as a lightweight and low-complexity module is integrated into our proposed method [33]. ECA learns the relevance of each channel and generates different weights according to the magnitude of the correlation. In multidimensional stock price statistics, ECA assigns more weight to the most crucial components and generates less weight in the irrelevant components. This allows the network model to focus on more valuable information and enhances the sensitivity to key functions. The ECA structure is shown in Fig. 4.

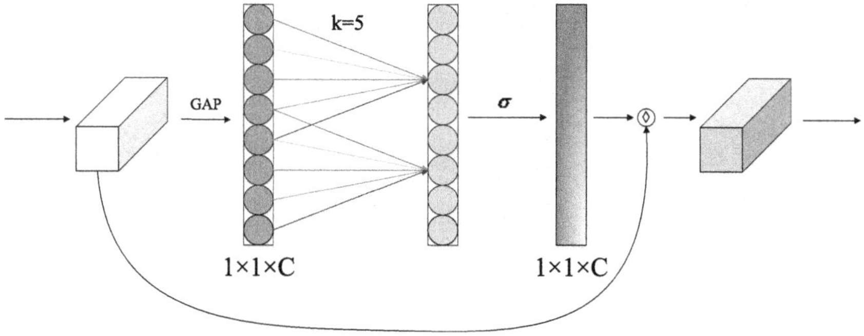

Fig. 4. Architecture of ECA model

From the Fig. 4, after channel global average pooling (GAP), local cross-channel interactions are captured by each channel of ECA and its *k* neighbors. At the same time, the channel weights are generated using a one-dimensional fast convolution of size *k*. To avoid manually adjusting *k* by cross-validation, the mapping of channel dimension C adapts to determine the value of *k*, that is:

$$\omega = \sigma(C1D_k(y)) \tag{2}$$

where C1D represents 1-D convolution. Since the kernel diameter *k* of the one-dimensional convolution is in proportion to the channel dimension *C*, the correspondence is as follows:

$$C = \varphi(k) = 2^{(\gamma \times k - b)} \tag{3}$$

Thus, the kernel size *k* can be adaptively determined according to Eq. (4) for a given channel dimension *C*.

$$k = \psi(C) = |\frac{\log_2(C) + b}{\gamma}|_{odd} \tag{4}$$

where $|t|_{odd}$ denotes the odd number closest to t. In all experiments, γ and b are set to 2 and 1, respectively. Markedly, non-linear mapping increases the interaction range of higher dimensional channels and shortens the interaction range of lower dimensional channels

Finally, using the fully connected (Dense) model, the correlations among the features are obtained and mapped to the outcome space. In the proposed AE-BiLSTM-ECA's network model, to solve the nonlinear problem better, a multi-layer full connection layer is introduced, which can achieve accurate prediction according to many different factors. The structure diagram of the fully connected layer with three layers is represented in Fig. 5.

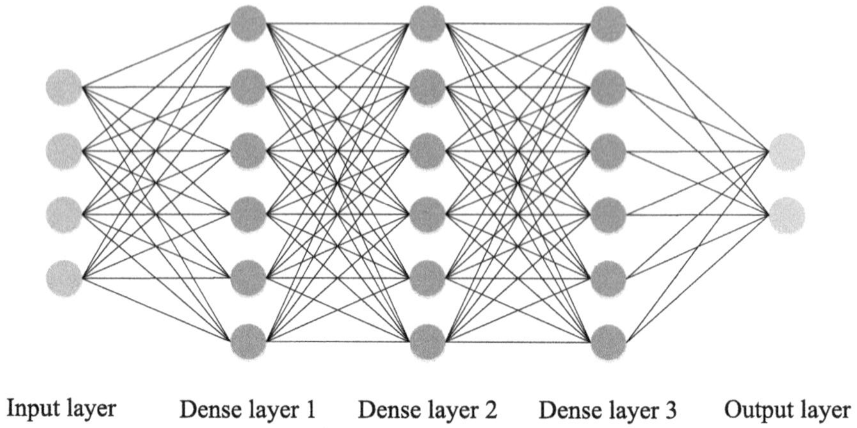

Fig. 5. The structure diagram of dense model

5 Experiments

5.1 Dataset Description and Pre-processing

The experimental data were obtained from NetEase Finance, including Shanghai Stock Composite Index (referred to as SSCI, stock code: 000001), and CSI 300 (stock code: 399300).The data of each stock contains seven characteristics, such as closing price (CP), highest price (HP), lowest price (LP), opening price (OP), previous day's closing price (PCP), up or down amount (UDA), and up or down rate (UDR). Since these seven attributes are obtained from actual stock market transactions and can reflect the most basic information about stock prices, they are selected as the inputs to the model. The specific information of the two stock data is summarized in Table 1. Tables 2 and 3 displays selected data from each stock as well as descriptive statistical information about the data, where descriptive statistics include mean, median, plurality, standard deviation, variance, maximum value, minimum value, and quantity for each attribute. We can clearly see that there are large variances and fluctuations in the stock data.

Table 1. Specific information on the two types of stock data

Stock	The time periods	Total data/group
SSCI	1990/12/20–2020/11/23	7304
CSI 300	2002/01/07–2021/03/17	4657

5.2 Evaluation Functions

The mean squared error (MSE) stands for the expected value of the square of the difference between the parameter estimate and the true value of the parameter. The degree of

Table 2. Partial information on SSCI stock data

Date	CP	HP	LP	OP	PCP	UDA	UDR
1990/12/20	104.390	104.390	99.980	104.300	99.980	4.410	4.411
1990/12/21	109.130	109.130	103.730	109.070	104.390	4.740	4.541
...	...	...	...	...	...	...	...
2000/12/28	2053.704	2061.051	2047.742	2054.517	2058.244	−4.540	−0.221
2000/12/29	2073.477	2073.878	2055.505	2055.828	2053.704	19.773	0.963
...	...	...	...	...	...	...	...
2020/11/20	3377.727	3380.149	3356.309	3359.597	3363.088	14.639	0.435
2020/11/23	3414.490	3431.653	3377.986	3384.104	3377.727	36.763	1.088
Average	1986.648	2004.091	1965.175	1985.333	1986.221	0.442	0.071
Median	1909.716	1927.174	1892.712	1911.063	1909.408	0.855	0.067
Mode	134.240	134.740	134.190	125.270	134.240	−0.460	0.997
Standard deviation	1072.439	1081.367	1059.720	1071.066	1072.504	40.963	2.439
Variance	1150125	1169355	1123006	1147182	1150266	1677.959	5.948
Minimum	104.390	104.390	99.980	104.300	99.980	−354.684	−16.394
Maximum	6092.057	6124.044	6040.713	6057.428	6092.057	649.500	105.269
Quantity	7304	7304	7304	7304	7304	7304	7304

variation of the data can be evaluated by calculating the MSE. If the MSE is smaller, it means that the prediction model describes the experimental data with better accuracy, and is calculated as below:

$$MSE = \frac{1}{n}\sum_{t=1}^{n}(X_t - X_t')^2 \tag{5}$$

The Root Means Squared Error (RMSE) represents the expected value of the squared error, which is the deviation between the predicted and actual values in the range of [0, + ∞). If the prediction result is consistent with the actual situation, the RMSE is 0, and the model can be called ideal. Thus the numerical result of RMSE varies with the predicted result. The formula for calculating RMSE is:

$$RMSE = \sqrt{\frac{1}{n}\sum_{t=1}^{n}(X_t - X_t')^2} \tag{6}$$

The Mean Absolute Error (MAE) refers to the average distance between the model predicted value and the true value of the sample. MAE can avoid the problem of errors canceling each other out and is used to express the severity of the deviation of the predicted values compared to the true values. A more petite MAE means that the deviation

Table 3. Partial information on CSI 300 stock data

Date	CP	HP	LP	OP	PCP	UDA	UDR
2002/01/07	1302.080	1302.080	1302.080	1302.080	1316.460	−14.380	−1.092
2002/01/08	1292.710	1292.710	1292.710	1292.710	1302.080	−9.370	−0.720
…	…	…	…	…	…	…	…
2012/01/04	2298.753	2365.988	2298.298	2361.499	2345.742	−46.989	−2.003
2012/01/05	2276.385	2316.657	2272.153	2290.780	2298.753	−22.368	−0.973
…	…	…	…	…	…	…	…
2021/03/16	5079.362	5084.309	5009.951	5054.409	5035.544	43.818	0.870
2021/03/17	5100.858	5123.545	5020.126	5062.771	5079.362	21.496	0.423
Average	2762.711	2785.604	2734.602	2760.160	2761.898	0.813	0.043
Median	2851.915	2888.093	2818.248	2848.155	2850.829	1.339	0.069
Mode	1221.760	1221.760	1221.760	1221.760	1221.760	−17.370	−0.487
Standard deviation	1187.877	1201.201	1171.218	1187.380	1187.571	52.682	1.653
Variance	1411051	1442883	1371753	1409871	1410325	2775	2.731
Minimum	818.033	823.860	807.784	816.546	818.033	−391.866	−9.240
Maximum	5877.202	5930.912	5815.609	5922.071	5877.202	378.179	9.390
Quantity	4657	4657	4657	4657	4657	4657	4657

of the predicted value from the actual value is minor. The formula of MAE is shown as follows:

$$MAE = \frac{1}{n}\sum_{t=1}^{n}\left|X_t - X_t'\right| \tag{7}$$

Mean Absolute Percentage Error (MAPE), which represents the sum of each absolute error divided by the actual value, is one of the most commonly used metrics to assess prediction accuracy. In fact, it is the average of the error percentages. The formula of MAPE is shown as follows:

$$MAPE = \frac{1}{n}\sum_{t=1}^{n}\frac{\left|X_t - X_t'\right|}{\left|X_t'\right|} \tag{8}$$

where X_tX_t represents the predicted value and $X_t'X_t'X_t'$ represents the true value. The smaller the value of the above evaluation index, the more accurate the prediction result.

5.3 Results and Discussions

In this section, we will perform a calibration verification of the model described in this paper, CNN, LSTM, BiLSTM, CNN-LSTM, AE-LSTM, CNN-BiLSTM, AE-BiLSTM,

BiLSTM-ECA, AE-LSTM-ECA, CNN-LSTM-ECA are used and compared with the AE-BiLSTM-ECA model proposed.

Table 4. Forecast results of different models on the SSCI stock data

Model	MSE	RMSE	MAE	MAPE
CNN	8447.149	91.908	79.914	2.426
LSTM	4222.102	64.978	50.585	1.805
BiLSTM	2603.726	51.027	35.419	1.239
CNN-LSTM	2603.726	51.027	35.419	1.239
AE-LSTM	2590.940	50.901	37.692	1.296
CNN-BiLSTM	2321.235	48.179	32.289	1.129
AE-BiLSTM	2455.008	49.548	36.147	1.249
BiLSTM-ECA	2184.278	46.736	32.737	1.116
AE-LSTM-ECA	2025.349	45.004	29.624	1.025
CNN-LSTM-ECA	2200.705	46.911	32.353	1.142
AE-BiLSTM-ECA	**1935.398**	**43.993**	**28.940**	**1.019**

Table 5. Forecast results of different models on the CSI 300 stock data

Model	MSE	RMSE	MAE	MAPE
CNN	6218.092	78.855	63.981	1.843
LSTM	5809.153	76.217	58.679	1.662
BiLSTM	5091.610	71.356	52.119	1.446
CNN-LSTM	4905.472	70.039	52.457	1.431
AE-LSTM	4908.142	70.058	53.112	1.525
CNN-BiLSTM	4643.541	68.144	51.143	1.410
AE-BiLSTM	4288.830	65.489	48.640	1.335
BiLSTM-ECA	4161.203	64.507	46.453	1.289
AE-LSTM-ECA	3225.251	56.791	37.473	1.037
CNN-LSTM-ECA	4568.808	67.593	51.061	1.395
AE-BiLSTM-ECA	**3158.452**	**56.200**	**36.681**	**1.020**

Tables 4 and 5 shows the prediction results of two stock datasets using different methods. Because of the different amounts of data contained in each dataset and the volatility of the stock data, which leads to considerable differences in the data, the results obtained by applying the same evaluation metrics to the two datasets also differ significantly. According to the experimental results, we can draw the following conclusions:

1) For a single model (i.e., CNN, LSTM, and BiLSTM), initially, the CNN model has the lowest prediction performance because it does not utilize the historical stock price information more effectively. Thne, the BiLSTM utilizes bi-directional information from historical data, so the BiLSTM model is able to further improve the prediction ability compared to the LSTM.
2) Since CNNs and AEs are good at extracting effective features from data, combining them with traditional recurrent neural networks (LSTM and BiLSTM networks) can improve the predictive performance of the models. However, since AE combined with a single model is using the recurrent neural network as the core unit in the AE model, the model performance of AE combined with recurrent neural is higher than that of CNN combined with the recurrent neural network model.
3) The sensitivity of this network to the main features is improved due to the addition of the attention module ECA. Therefore the prediction effect of the network model incorporating the attention module is significantly better than the prediction effect of the original network model. The results show that the introduction of the attention module ECA in this paper helps the model to focus more on the impact on the stock price.
4) Of all methods compared, the AE-BilSTM-ECA model was optimal on all four indicators. In particular, the results of the proposed model are significantly better than the traditional single model (i.e. CNN, LSTM and BiLSTM). A recurrent neural network model that combines feature extraction with attention mechanism outperforms the model that contains only features or attention. The results show that the prediction of stock data using AE-BiLSTM-ECA method is correct.

6 Conclusions

In this paper, a novel deep network forecasting model, that is AE-BilSTM-ECA model, is presented to predict stock prices. The network which introduces the bi-directional LSTM module as the primary cell in the autoencoder can sufficiently mine the historical and future critical information of the stock price series data. And the ECA module is also implemented in this network to weight the extracted characteristics, which enables more reliable prediction of stock prices. The experiments in this paper are conducted on two stocks, SSE Composite Index, China Unicom and CSI 300. Among the ten comparative methods, the AE-BilSTM-ECA model performs the most optimally, and in particular, the results of this model are remarkably superior to the conventional single models (i.e., CNN, LSTM, and BiLSTM). The future research can explore whether the introduction of sparse self-attentiveness can enhance the prediction performance and effectiveness of this model.

Acknowledgment. This work is supported in part by grants from the National Natural Science Foundation of China (No. 62062040), the Outstanding Youth Project of Jiangxi Natural Science Foundation (No. 20212ACB212003), the Jiangxi Province Key Subject Academic and Technical Leader Funding Project (No. 20212BCJ23017).

References

1. Cavalcante, R.C., Brasileiro, R.C., Souza, V.L.F., et al.: Computational intelligence and financial markets: A survey and future directions. Expert Syst. Appl. **55**, 194–211 (2016)
2. Thakkar, A., Chaudhari, K.: Fusion in stock market prediction: a decade survey on the necessity, recent developments, and potential future direction. Information Fusion **65**, 95–107 (2021)
3. Sezer, O.B., Gudelek, M.U., Ozbayoglu, A.M.: Financial time series forecasting with deep learning: A systematic literature review: 2005–2019. Appl. Soft Comput. **90**, 106181 (2020)
4. Ding, G., Qin, L.: Study on the prediction of stock price based on the associated network model of LSTM. Int. J. Mach. Learn. Cybern. **11**(6), 1307–1317 (2019). https://doi.org/10.1007/s13042-019-01041-1
5. Baek, Y., Kim, H.Y.: ModAugNet: a new forecasting framework for stock market index value with an overfitting prevention LSTM module and a prediction LSTM module. Expert Syst. Appl. **113**, 457–480 (2018)
6. Zhao, J., Zeng, D., Liang, S., Kang, H., Liu, Q.: Prediction model for stock price trend based on recurrent neural network. J. Ambient. Intell. Humaniz. Comput. **12**(1), 745–753 (2020). https://doi.org/10.1007/s12652-020-02057-0
7. Lu, W., Li, J., Wang, J., et al.: A CNN-BiLSTM-AM method for stock price prediction. Neural Comput. Appl. **33**(10), 4741–4753 (2020). https://doi.org/10.1007/s00521-020-05532-z
8. Niu, Z., Zhong, G., Yu, H.: A review on the attention mechanism of deep learning. Neurocomputing **452**, 48–62 (2021)
9. Hu, J., Zheng, W.: A deep learning model to effectively capture mutation information in multivariate time series prediction. Knowl.-Based Syst. **203**, 106139 (2020)
10. Torres, J.F., Hadjout, D., Sebaa, A., et al.: Deep learning for time series forecasting: a survey. Big Data **9**(1), 3–21 (2021)
11. Chong, E., Han, C., Park, F.C.: Deep learning networks for stock market analysis and prediction: Methodology, data representations, and case studies. Expert Syst. Appl. **83**, 187–205 (2017)
12. Nti, I.K., Adekoya, A.F., Weyori, B.A.: A systematic review of fundamental and technical analysis of stock market predictions. Artificial Intelligence Review **53**(4), 3007–3057 (2020)
13. Ahmed, N.K., Atiya, A.F., Gayar, N.E., et al.: An empirical comparison of machine learning models for time series forecasting. Economet. Rev. **29**(5–6), 594–621 (2010)
14. Henrique, B.M., Sobreiro, V.A., Kimura, H.: Literature review: Machine learning techniques applied to financial market prediction. Expert Syst. Appl. **124**, 226–251 (2019)
15. Nayak, R.K., Mishra, D., Rath, A.K.: A Naïve SVM-KNN based stock market trend reversal analysis for Indian benchmark indices. Appl. Soft Comput. **35**, 670–680 (2015)
16. Chen, Y., Hao, Y.: A feature weighted support vector machine and K-nearest neighbor algorithm for stock market indices prediction. Expert Syst. Appl. **80**, 340–355 (2017)
17. Zhang, X., Li, A., Pan, R.: Stock trend prediction based on a new status box method and AdaBoost probabilistic support vector machine. Appl. Soft Comput. **49**, 385–398 (2016)
18. Picasso, A., Merello, A., Ma, Y., et al.: Technical analysis and sentiment embeddings for market trend prediction. Expert Syst. Appl. **135**, 60–70 (2019)
19. Shrestha, A., Mahmood, A.: Review of deep learning algorithms and architectures. IEEE access **7**, 53040–53065 (2019)
20. Han, Z., Zhao, J., Leung, H., et al.: A review of deep learning models for time series prediction. IEEE Sens. J. **21**(6), 7833–7848 (2019)
21. Li, A.W., Bastos, G.S.: Stock market forecasting using deep learning and technical analysis: a systematic review. IEEE access **8**, 185232–185242 (2020)

22. Rather, A.M., Agarwal, A., Sastry, V.N.: Recurrent neural network and a hybrid model for prediction of stock returns. Expert Syst. Appl. **42**(6), 3234–3241 (2015)
23. Bathla, G., Rani, R., Aggarwal, H.: Stocks of year 2020: prediction of high variations in stock prices using LSTM. Multimedia Tools and Applications, pp. 1–17 (2022)
24. Kim, H.Y., Won, C.H.: Forecasting the volatility of stock price index: A hybrid model integrating LSTM with multiple GARCH-type models. Expert Syst. Appl. **103**, 25–37 (2018)
25. Li, H., Hua, J., Li, J., et al.: Stock forecasting model FS-LSTM based on the 5G Internet of things. Wireless Communications and Mobile Computing, 2020 (2020)
26. Hoseinzade, E., Haratizadeh, S.: CNNpred: CNN-based stock market prediction using a diverse set of variables. Expert Syst. Appl. **129**, 273–285 (2019)
27. Chen, Y., Fang, R., Liang, T., et al.: Stock price forecast based on CNN-BiLSTM-ECA Model. Scientific Programming, 2021 (2021)
28. Sezer, O.B., Ozbayoglu, A.M.: Algorithmic financial trading with deep convolutional neural networks: Time series to image conversion approach. Appl. Soft Comput. **70**, 525–538 (2018)
29. Barra, S., Carta, S.M., Corriga, A., et al.: Deep learning and time series-to-image encoding for financial forecasting. IEEE/CAA Journal of Automatica Sinica **7**(3), 683–692 (2020)
30. Wen, M., Li, P., Zhang, L., et al.: Stock market trend prediction using high-order information of time series. Ieee Access **7**, 28299–28308 (2019)
31. Long, J., Chen, Z., He, W., et al.: An integrated framework of deep learning and knowledge graph for prediction of stock price trend: An application in Chinese stock exchange market. Appl. Soft Comput. **91**, 106205 (2020)
32. Mohanty, D.K., Parida, A.K., Khuntia, S.S.: Financial market prediction under deep learning framework using auto encoder and kernel extreme learning machine. Appl. Soft Comput. **99**, 106898 (2021)
33. Guo, C., Szemenyei, M., Hu, Y., et al.: Channel attention residual u-net for retinal vessel segmentation. In: IEEE International Conference on Acoustics, Speech and Signal Processing. IEEE, pp. 1185–1189 (2021)

A Method for Residual Network Image Classification with Multi-scale Feature Fusion

Guo Ru[1,2], Peng Sheng[1,2(✉)], Anyang Tong[1,2], and Zhenyuan Li[1,2]

[1] School of Artificial Intelligence and Big Data, Hefei University, Hefei, China
ruguo0809@163.com, cppjava@163.com

[2] Hefei Economic and Technological Development Zone, Jinxiu Avenue No.99. Shushan District, Hefei City, Anhui Province, China

Abstract. The traditional convolutional neural network (CNN) only focuses on the features of the last layer of the network, ignoring those of other layers. The detailed information of the shallow network can improve the accuracy of classification to some extent. With the deepening of the network, the problems such as gradient disappearance and explosion are obvious. In order to alleviate this problem, a method for residual network image classification with multi-scale feature fusion is proposed in the paper. First of all, the Random Image Cropping and Patching (RICAP), a data augmentation method, is adopted to cut and splice the new training samples from the training set, based on which feature maps of different sizes are obtained by residual modules. Secondly, after reducing the dimension of high-level feature maps, all the feature maps with the same dimension are processed by the multi-scale fusion. Finally, these feature vectors are input into the Softmax classifier for training and classification, and the method of learning rate decay is used in the training process. The experiment results indicate that this method has a good performance on image classification based on the public datasets of MNIST and CIFAR-10.

Keywords: Multi-scale feature fusion · Residual network · Data augmentation · Image classification

1 Introduction

Image classification is one of the basic tasks of computer vision. Traditional image classification algorithms extract the color, texture and spatial features of images, which perform well in simple tasks while output unsatisfactory results in complex tasks. As a typical representative of deep learning, Deep Convolutional Neural Network (DCNN) has excellent performance in computer vision tasks. Compared with traditional image classification algorithms that manually extract features, DCNN, extracting features from input images via convolution operation, can effectively learn representations from a large number of samples, and has stronger model generalization ability. However, it remains the following problems: (1) As the network becomes more complex and the parameters increase, the risk of over-fitting in the process of training also grows, and the generalization ability becomes poor. (2) In practice, due to insufficient quantity or poor

Y. Xu et al. (Eds.): ML4CS 2022, LNCS 13657, pp. 427–438, 2023.
https://doi.org/10.1007/978-3-031-20102-8_33

quality of samples, the training model has poor effect and generalization ability. (3) Most networks only focus on the features of the last layer, ignoring the feature information in different layers.

In view of the above problems, the method we propose in the paper can be divided into three parts: ResNet-18 Network, RICAP [1], and FPN. Firstly, RICAP is used to randomly crop four images from the training dataset, and patch them to generate new training images which are mixed with the class labels of the four images. Secondly, feature maps of different sizes are obtained by successive and fixed down-sampling in ResNet-18, and then the high-level feature maps are downscaled by 1×1 convolution, followed by multi-scale fusion of feature maps with the same dimensionality in the high and low layers using bilinear interpolation, so as to improve the representational capacity of the feature vectors. Finally, the fused feature vectors are input into the Softmax classifier for training and classification, and meanwhile the learning rate is decayed by constant segment. The contributions of this paper are as follows:

- We adopt RICAP to randomly select four images from the training samples for cropping, and the cropped images are patched to produce a new training sample. Under the condition of the original label unchanged, features of samples can be changed according to prior knowledge, so that the new sample approximately conforms to the real distribution of the data. In the era of deep learning, the scale and quality of data determine the upper limit of model learning, and therefore large-scale and high-quality data will greatly improve the generalization ability of the model. Data augmentation technique can increase the number of training samples on a limited dataset, thus prevent over-fitting to a certain extent.
- We use ResNet-18 Network and Shortcut Connect to transmit part of the original input information to the next network layer without matrix multiplication and non-linear transformation. This method effectively reduces the difficulty of deep network training, protects the integrity of information, and solves such problems as gradient disappearance or explosion.
- We use Feature Pyramid Network (FPN) as the network structure and improve the network. It is often used in object detection, which can achieve multi-scale detection without increasing the computational load of the model. In this paper, its characteristic of multi-scale feature fusion is applied for image classification with ResNet-18 as the backbone network, thus establishing a feature pyramid with strong semantic information on all scales. In this way, the multi-scale feature fusion is completed by the fusion of high and low level features through up-sampling.

2 Related Research

The purpose of image classification [2] is to determine the category to which the image belongs by using some classification algorithms given a pair of input images, and its main process usually includes three steps: image preprocessing, feature extraction and classifier design. As one of the popular research directions in the field of computer vision, image classification based on vision has a wide range of applications, including unmanned driving [3], object detection[4, 5], attitude estimation [6], facial recognition [7], etc. Therefore, the technique has very high value in research and application.

2.1 Data Augmentation

Data augmentation has always been a hot spot in the field of image classification, and rich data is an important guarantee to solve computer vision problems. Traditional data augmentation methods are based on a series of known affine transformation and image processing, which can greatly improve the generalization ability of models, reduce the risk of over-fitting, and improve robustness. Random erasing [8] can correctly classify the object even part of it is covered, forcing the network to use partially uncovered data for recognition, which increases the difficulty of training and improves the generalization ability of the network to a certain extent. Cutout [9] is used to randomly select a square area of a fixed size in the image and set the pixel value in this area to 0 or other uniform values. Similar to Random erasing, the latter method allows the network to better utilize the global information of the image, rather than relying on a small set of specific features. Mixup [10] can mix two images to form a new one and also has the function of soft labels which can mix the class labels of two images and enhances the linear expression between training samples. These new data augmentation techniques have been applied to deep CNNs and made a great breakthrough. Compared with Mixup, the method used in this paper is RICAP has three obvious differences: (1) It selects four images to synthesize; (2) It synthesizes images from space through splicing.; (3) It adds the operation of crop before splicing.

2.2 Convolutional Neural Network

Yann LeCun et al. [11] put forward the LeNet-5 neural network, which is based on the gradient back propagation algorithm for training. By successively alternating connected convolutional and down-sampling layers, the input image can be transformed into a series of feature maps passed to the fully connected neural network, and the final step is to use the Sigmoid function for activation. However, disadvantages of the method include weak generalization ability and small size of training dataset. Krizhevsky et al. [12] again proposed AlexNet neural network, which introduced Dropout technique and ReLU activation function, in order to speed up the gradient descent and alleviate the problem of network over-fitting. Based on the method, Simonyan et al. [13] introduced VGG network, which studied the relationship between performance and depth of CNN and was equipped with excellent generalization ability, but network degradation will be caused with the increase of network depth. To solve the problem, He et al. [14] proposed the ResNet neural network, which can greatly speed up the training of deep network and greatly improve the accuracy of classification. Its greatest contribution is to put forward the residual structure, which can fitting the input and output of each layer through the residual connection, thus retains the characteristic information of the input image to the maximum extent. But the Image classification method based on ResNet neural network only focuses on the features of the last layer of the network, ignoring those of other layers. Although the high-level features are equipped with strong semantic information, the resolution ratio is low and the perception ability of the detailed features is poor. In view of the fact that the detailed information can improve the detection accuracy to a certain extent, this paper proposes a method for residual network image classification with multi-scale feature fusion, so as to study how to efficiently fuse the high and low-level features, to further improve the representational capacity of the network model, as well as to further improve the accuracy of image classification. Firstly, RICAP is used to randomly crop four images from the training dataset, and patch them to generate new training images which are mixed with the class labels of the four images. Secondly, feature maps of different sizes are obtained by successive and fixed down-sampling, and then the high-level feature maps are downscaled by 1 × 1 convolution, followed by multi-scale fusion of feature maps with the same dimensionality in the high and low layers using bilinear interpolation, so as to improve the representational capacity of the feature vectors. Finally, the fused feature vectors are input into the Softmax classifier for training and classification, and meanwhile the learning rate is decayed by constant segment, which is helpful to the convergence of the algorithm and easier to approach the optimal solution. The experiment results indicate that this method has a good performance on image classification based on the public datasets MNIST and CIFAR-10.

3 Methodology

3.1 RICAP

In recent years, with CNN having achieved excellent results in different fields, the main reason is that it contains a large number of parameters capable of fitting a wide variety of data distributions. However, smaller data with too many parameters will suffer from a certain degree of overfitting. Data augmentation by increasing samples of the dataset can effectively alleviate the problem. As shown in Fig. 1, the data augmentation technique RICAP [1] is performed by firstly selecting four images from the training set randomly, and then clipping each image, and finally patching the clipped images into a new training image and inputting into CNN.

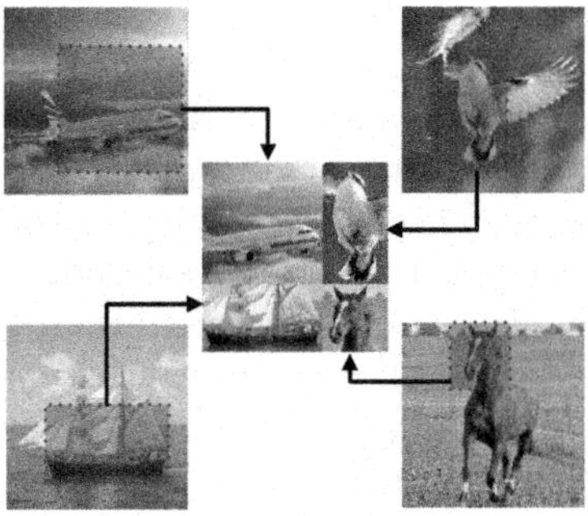

Fig. 1. The concept of RICAP

As shown in Fig. 2, detailed steps by RICAP are as follows:

1) Randomly select four images k ($k \in \{1, 2, 3, 4\}$) from the training set, and paste them to the top left, top right, bottom left and bottom right respectively.

2) With I_x and I_y denoting the width and height of the original training images, boundary positions (w, h) of the four images k $(k \in \{1, 2, 3, 4\})$ are drawn by obeying the uniform distribution. Therefore, (w_k, h_k) represents the size of image k:

$$w_1 = w_3 = w,$$

$$w_2 = w_4 = I_x - w,$$

$$h_1 = h_2 = h,$$

$$h_3 = h_4 = I_y - h. \tag{1}$$

3) The position of the top left corner of each image k is determined as (x_k, y_k):

$$x_k \sim u(0, I_x - w_k),$$

$$y_k \sim u(0, I_y - h_k). \tag{2}$$

4) In the process of image classification, the new image combined by the four images k is blended with the unique thermal encoding class labels c_k, whose scale is proportional to the area of the new image, thus defining the target label c as follows:

$$c = \sum_{k \in \{1,2,3,4\}} W_k c_k \mathrm{for} \mathrm{W_k} = \frac{\mathrm{w_k h_k}}{\mathrm{I_x I_y}} \tag{3}$$

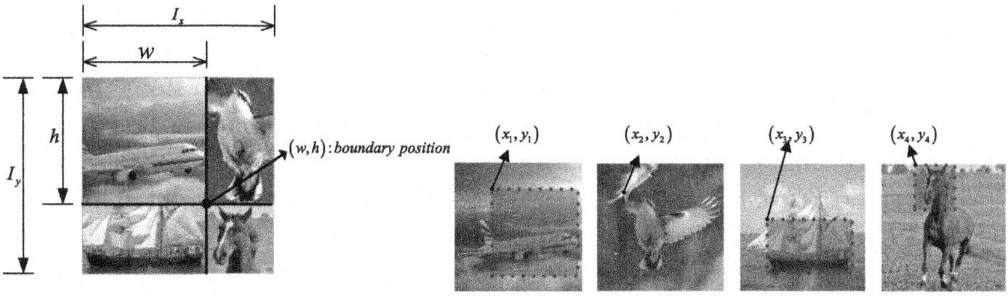

Fig. 2. Graphical Representation of RICAP

3.2 ResNet-18

The feature extraction network in the proposed method is combined by ResNet-18 and FPN. The specific parameters of ResNet-18 are shown in Table 1, and its network structure is shown in Fig. 3. Four residual modules denoted as C2 to C5 are included, each of which contains two residual structures. Each structure needs to be convoluted

Table 1. Network structure of ResNet-18

Layer name	Convl	Conv2		Conv3	Conv4	Conv5	
output size	32×32	32×32		16× 16	8× 8	4 × 4	1 × 1
18-layer	7 × 7,64 Stride 2	7 × 7 max *pool* Stride 2	$\begin{bmatrix} 3\times3, & 64 \\ 3\times3, & 64 \end{bmatrix} \times 2$	$\begin{bmatrix} 3\times3, & 128 \\ 3\times3, & 128 \end{bmatrix} \times 2$	$\begin{bmatrix} 3\times3, & 256 \\ 3\times3, & 256 \end{bmatrix} \times 2$	$\begin{bmatrix} 3\times3, & 512 \\ 3\times3, & 512 \end{bmatrix} \times 2$	Average pool, 10-d fc,softmax

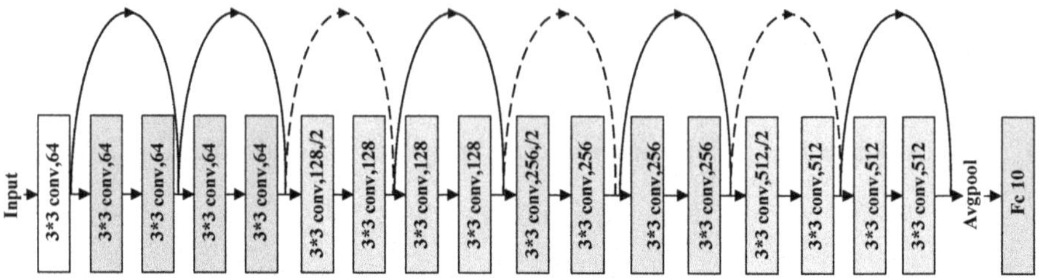

Fig. 3. ResNet-18 Structure Diagram

twice, and the size of the convolution kernels is 3 × 3. For C2 to C5, the number of each convolution kernel is 64, 128, 256, and 512 respectively. The whole network consists of 18 layers, including 17 convolutional layers and 1 pooling layer.

The images processed by RICAP are input to ResNet-18, and the feature maps with half the size of the previous residual module are obtained, thus completing the bottom-up process in the feature pyramid fusion network structure. Subsequently, multi-scale feature fusion will be conducted by FPN.

3.3 FPN

FPN changes the number of 512 channels at the highest level of C5 in ResNet-18 to the number of 64 channel with a 1 × 1 convolutional kernel, thus obtaining the new feature map P5. Bilinear interpolation is adopted to up-sample P5 twice, and then connected horizontally to Conv64 of C4 with a 1 × 1 convolutional layer, thus obtaining P4. P3 is obtained by the same way. Figure 4 shows the whole process of multi-scale feature fusion of at high and low levels. The up-sampling of bilinear interpolation is conducted as follows:

Bilinear transformation will happen in the process. Given the value of the four points $Q_{12} = (x_1, y_2)$,$Q_{21} = (x_2, y_1)$,$Q_{22} = (x_2, y_2)$ at the known function f, to get the value of interpolation point $P = (x, y)$ at the unknown function f, we have:

$$f(x, y) \approx \frac{f(Q_{11})}{(x_2 - x_1)(y_2 - y_1)}(x_2 - x)(y_2 - y) + \frac{f(Q_{21})}{(x_2 - x)(y_2 - y)}(x - x_1)(y_2 - y)$$
$$+\frac{f(Q_{12})}{(x_2 - x_1)(y_2 - y_1)}(x_2 - x)(y - y_1) + \frac{f(Q_{22})}{(x_2 - x)(y_2 - y)}(x - x_1)(y - y_1) \tag{4}$$

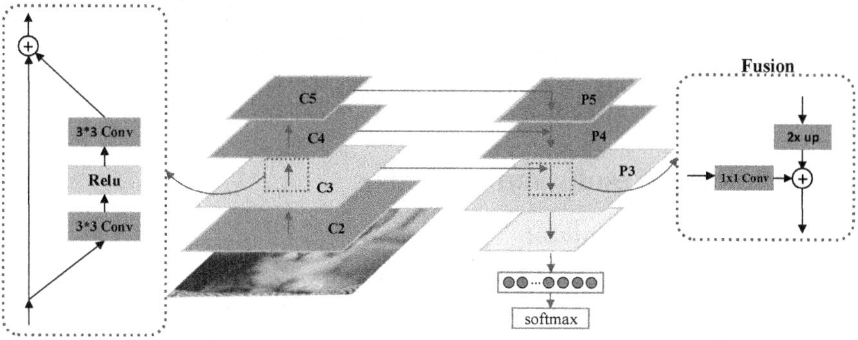

Fig. 4. Feature pyramid network

Finally, the fused feature vectors are input to the Softmax classifier for training and classification, and the learning rate is decayed by constant segments in the process. Afterwards, the Cross Entropy Loss (CEL) function is used to calculate the loss values. The detailed steps are as follows:

1) RICAP randomly select four images from the training dataset for clipping and patching, and the new training image, the size of which is specified to 32 × 32, will be output.
2) After inputting the image to ResNet-18, the feature maps of each residual module will be obtained, size of which is half of the previous residual module.
3) The convolution kernel of 11 is used to change the number of channels, and the bilinear interpolation is used for up-sampling, thus obtaining the multi-scale fusion features.
4) The activation layer is the ReLU function, which has a relatively wide excitation boundary that allows the network to introduce sparsity on its own, and can overcome the problem of gradient disappearance, thus speeding up the training, i.e.:

$$f(x) = \max(0, x) \tag{5}$$

5) The pooling layer aims at dimension reduction of features, in order to obtain feature invariance and prevent over-fitting to some extent. In this paper, the average pooling method is adopted.
6) The CEL function is used to measure the variability between the true and predicted distributions to calculate the loss values:

$$Loss = -\sum_{i=1}^{n} p(x_i)\ln(\mathrm{q(x_i)}) \tag{6}$$

   In this equation, $p(x_i)$ represents the true probability distribution corresponding to the variable $p(x_i)$, while $q(x_i)$ represents its predicted probability distribution. n is the number of categories in the sample.
7) The learning rate is gradually decayed by constant segments while training, which helps the algorithm to converge and approach the optimal solution more easily.

8) After multi-scale feature fusion, the images enter full connection through the averaging pooling layer. The fully connected layer forms the complete image through the weight matrix, which takes the local features extracted by the feature extractor [15], and then finish the process of image classification.

4 Experimental Results and Analysis

4.1 Experimental Environment

The experimental environment of this paper is: Windows, AMD Ryzen 7 4800H CPU, NVIDIA GeForce GTR 1650 Ti GPU, Pytorch-based deep learning framework, Python programming language. Experiments were carried out on the commonly used datasets of MNIST and CIFAR-10 [16] to prove the effectiveness of the proposed method.

The following recognition accuracy is used as the evaluation criteria:

$$Accuracy = \frac{TP}{Total} \times 100\% \tag{7}$$

In the formula, *TP* denotes the number of correctly classified samples and *Total* the total number of classified samples.

4.2 Introduction to Datasets

MNIST Dataset. The MNIST dataset was proposed by the National Institute of Technology and Standards. Its training set consists of handwritten digits from 250 people, 50% of which are census Bureau employees and 50% high school students, and its test set contains the same proportion of handwritten digits. A total of 70,000 grayscale images of 1-channel with the size of 28 × 28 are included, 60,000 of which are used as the training set and 10,000 as the test set.

In the experiment, in order to improve the generalization ability of the model, RICAP is introduced in the training process based on the data augmentation technique of random flipping. In terms of parameter settings, the batch size is set to 64 with the help of SGD optimizer. The learning rate decay strategy is used in the process with the initial learning rate $\eta = 0.01$, and η will decrease to 0.1 times of the original learning rate when the accuracy reaches its peak.

Cifar-10 Dataset. The cifar-10 dataset is also a more commonly used image classification dataset for recognizing real objects in a small dataset. It contains 60,000 RGB images of size 32 × 32, of which 50,000 images are the training set and 10,000 images are the test set, divided into 10 categories: airplane, automobile, bird, cat, deer, dog, frog, horse, ship, truck. unlike the MNIST dataset, the cifar-10 dataset is more challenging than the MNIST dataset because all the images are in color and the objects to be recognized are more complex.

In the experiment, in order to improve the generalization ability of the model, the RICAP method is introduced in the model training process based on the data enhancement technique using brightness variation, random flip. In terms of parameter settings, the batch size is set to 128, the SGD optimizer is used, and the learning rate decay strategy is used during the training process, with the initial learning rate, which decreases to 0.1 times of the original learning rate when the accuracy reaches the peak.

4.3 Comparative Experiment

Based on the MNIST dataset, Table 2 shows the comparison between the experimental results of other algorithms and the method proposed in the paper. It can be seen that the recognition accuracy of ResNet on the test set is 94.0%, CNN-SVM (PSO) 96.0%, VGG-16 97.89%, the method in paper [17] 98.1%, and the method in this paper 99.42%, which shows that the last one has the best result on the MNIST dataset.

Table 2. Recognition accuracy on MNIST dataset

Network Models	Accuracy (%)
ResNet	94.0
CNN-SVM(PSO)	96.0
VGG-16	97.89
Paper [17]	98.1
Method of this Paper	99.42

Based on the Cifar-10 dataset, Table 3 demonstrates the comparison between the experimental results of other algorithms as follows and the method of this paper. The recognition accuracy of ResNET-CE on the test set is 90.41%, WideResNet 95.03%, DSENet(depth = 40) 92.52%, and the method in this paper 96.25%, which also shows that the method in this paper has the best effect on the CIFAR-10 dataset.

Table 3. Recognition accuracy on CIFAR-10 dataset

Network Models	Accuracy (%)
ResNet-CE	90.41
SqueezeNet	90.26
WideResNet	95.03
DSENet(depth = 40)	92.52
Method of this Paper	96.25

The confusion matrices of the method of this paper on both MNIST and Cifar-10 datasets are shown in Tables 4 and 5 respectively. As the most basic and intuitive means to measure the recognition accuracy of the image classification model, the confusion matric describes the correspondence between the true category in the horizontal direction and the predicted category in the vertical direction.

Table 4. Confusion MATRIX for MNIST dataset based on the method of this paper

MNIST Type	The Method of this Paper									
	0	1	2	3	4	5	6	7	8	9
0	996	0	0	2	0	0	0	0	2	0
1	0	998	0	0	0	0	0	2	0	0
2	0	0	994	0	0	0	0	5	1	0
3	0	0	0	995	0	3	0	0	1	1
4	0	0	0	0	994	0	0	0	1	5
5	0	0	0	6	0	992	2	0	0	0
6	6	0	0	0	1	0	993	0	0	0
7	0	0	5	0	0	0	0	993	0	2
8	3	1	0	0	0	0	0	0	996	0
9	0	0	0	0	7	2	0	0	0	991

Table 5. Confusion matrix for Cifar-10 dataset based on the method of this paper

Cifar-10 Type	The Method of this Paper									
	Airplane	Automobile	Bird	Cat	Deer	Dog	Frog	Horse	Ship	Truck
Airplane	97	1	1	0	0	0	0	0	0	1
Automobile	1	97	0	0	0	0	0	0	0	2
Bird	1	0	98	0	0	0	1	0	0	0
Cat	0	0	1	96	0	2	1	0	0	0
Deer	0	0	2	0	97	0	0	1	0	0
Dog	0	0	0	2	0	96	2	0	0	0
Frog	1	0	2	2	0	2	92	0	1	0
horse	0	0	1	0	2	1	0	96	0	0
Ship	0	1	0	0	0	0	0	0	97	2
Truck	1	3	0	0	0	0	0	0	1	95

The test results of the model in this paper on MNIST dataset are plotted into Table 4, which shows that its accuracy is higher for number 0, 1, 8 and lower for numbers 5, 7, 9. The reason lies in the fact that some numbers are so visually similar that the model is unable to distinguish them accurately. For example, the number 5 may be incorrectly identified as 3 or 6, the number 7 as 2 or 9, and the number 9 as 4 or 5. Similarly, Table 5 shows the result on the Cifar-10 dataset. Due to the high similarity in visual category, the Frog category is easily misidentified as Bird, Cat or Dog, and Truck as

Automobile and Ship. By comparison, the recognition accuracy of the method in this paper is significantly improved on both datasets.

5 Conclusion

This paper introduces a method for residual network image classification with multi-scale feature fusion. Based on the residual neural network, the author adopts RICAP and FPN to fuse the features extracted from high and low layers, and meanwhile uses the method of learning rate decay for training. In order to validate the effectiveness of the method, the classification results on MNIST and Cifar-10 datasets serves as the proof. It is suggested that the method of this paper should be applied to more complex and large-scale datasets in the future, such as Cifar-100 and ImageNet. The data augmentation technique RICAP in this method only uses mixed new images in the training process where the original images are not involved, which requires more time to achieve better results. What's more, this method utilizes the fusion of low-level high-resolution and high-level strong semantics, resulting in spending a lot of time training the network. Therefore, further study is needed to improve the method in the near future.

Acknowledgment. This work was supported by "the Scientific Research Foundation of HEFEI University" (Grant No. 20RC19) and "Graduate Science Research Project of Anhui Universities"(No.YJS20210564).

References

1. Takahashi, R., Matsubara, T., Uehara, K.: Data augmentation using random image cropping and patching for deep CNNs. IEEE Trans. Circuits Syst. Video Technol. **30**(9), 2917–2931 (2020)
2. Rawat, W., Wang, Z.H.: Deep convolutional neural networks for image classification: a comprehensive review. Neural Comput. **29**(9), 2352–2449 (2017)
3. Radwell, N., Johnson, S.D., Edgar, M.P., Higham, C.F., Murray-Smith, R., Padgett, M.J.: Deep learning optimized single-pixel LiDAR. Appl. Phys. Lett. **115**(23), 5 (2019)
4. Qiang, B.H., Chen, R.D., Zhou, M.L., Pang, Y.C., Zhai, Y.J., Yang, M.H.: Convolutional neural networks-based object detection algorithm by jointing semantic segmentation for images. Sensors **20**(18), 14 (2020)
5. Hamouda, M., Ettabaa, K.S., Bouhlel, M.S.: Smart feature extraction and classification of hyperspectral images based on convolutional neural networks. IET Image Proc. **14**(10), 1999–2005 (2020)
6. Wu, C.R., Chen, L., Wu, S.Q.: A novel metric-learning-based method for multi-instance textureless objects' 6D pose estimation. Applied Sciences-Basel **11**(22), 12 (2021)
7. Niu, J.-Y., Xie, Z.-H., Li, Y., Cheng, S.-J., Fan, J.-W.: Scale fusion light CNN for hyperspectral face recognition with knowledge distillation and attention mechanism. Appl. Intell. **52**(6), 6181–6195 (2021). https://doi.org/10.1007/s10489-021-02721-8
8. Zhong, Z., Zheng, L., Kang, G.L., Li, S.Z., Yang, Y.: Assoc Advancement Artificial, I.: Random Erasing Data Augmentation. In: 34th AAAI Conference on Artificial Intelligence. Assoc Advancement Artificial Intelligence. New York (2020)

9. Devries, T., Taylor, G.W.: Improved Regularization of Convolutional Neural Networks with Cutout (2017)
10. Zhang, H., Cisse, M., Dauphin, Y.N., Lopez-Paz, D.: mixup: Beyond Empirical Risk Minimization (2017)
11. Lecun, Y., Bottou, L., Bengio, Y., Haffner, P.: Gradient-based learning applied to document recognition. In: Proceedings of the IEEE 1998, vol. **86**(11), pp. 2278–2324 (1998)
12. Krizhevsky, A., Sutskever, I., Hinton, G.E.: ImageNet classification with deep convolutional neural networks. Commun. ACM **60**(6), 84–90 (2017)
13. Simonyan, K., Zisserman, A.J.C.S.: Very deep convolutional networks for large-scale image recognition. Computer Science (2014)
14. He, K., Zhang, X., Ren, S., Sun, J.J.I.: Deep residual learning for image recognition. In: IEEE Conference on Computer Vision and Pattern Recognition (CVPR) 2016 (2016)
15. Sainath, T.N., Mohamed, A.R., Kingsbury, B., Ramabhadran, B.: Deep convolutional neural networks for LVCSR. In: IEEE International Conference on Acoustics, Speech, and Signal Processing (ICASSP). Ieee. Vancouver, Canada (2013)
16. Krizhevsky, A., Hinton, G.J.H.o.S.A.D.: Learning multiple layers of features from tiny images. Computer Science **1**(4) (2009)
17. Zhao, H.H., Liu, H.J.G.C.: Multiple classifiers fusion and CNN feature extraction for handwritten digits recognition. Granular Computing (2019)

Face Morphing Detection Based on a Two-Stream Network with Channel Attention and Residual of Multiple Color Spaces

Min Long[1](✉), Cheng-kun Jia[1], and Fei Peng[2]

[1] School of Computer and Communication Engineering, Changsha University of Science and Technology, Changsha 410114, China
caslongm@aliyun.com

[2] Institute of Artificial Intelligence and Blockchain, Guangzhou University, Guangzhou 510000, Guangdong, China

Abstract. Aiming at the performance improvement of face morphing detection, a novel method is proposed by using a two-stream network with channel attention and residual of multiple color spaces. This method first obtains H, S, V, Y, Cb, Cr six color channel image, then use the bilateral filter for filtering the six color channel to get the corresponding residual noise image, then the combined six channel image and the residual noise image as input to the designed two-stream network for training, so as to detect the morphed face image. In addition, an efficient channel attention module is proposed to improve the expressiveness of the model. Experiments are conducted on the standard databases, and the performance of the proposed method is compared with that of 9 state-of-the-art morphing attack detection methods. The results show that the proposed method can achieve better detection performance than the existing works.

Keywords: Face recognition · Face morphing detection · Deep learning · Residual noise

1 Introduction

With the development of biometric technology, facial biometric systems are widely used in law enforcement, surveillance, national ID card, border control and other fields. However, the latest research found that the face recognition system is vulnerable to face morphing attack [1], and its effectiveness has been verified in commercial face recognition systems. The difficulty of detecting facial fusion was further demonstrated by analyzing the recognition ability of observers including facial recognition experts on morphed faces [2].

Therefore, face morphing attack poses a serious security threat to the face recognition system, especially to the issuance and verification of electronic travel documents [3]. In a facial morphing attack, a criminal can use a similar-looking conspirator to generate a morphed face image. As long as the morphed face image is true enough, the inspectors and commercial face recognition systems can be deceived, and both the criminal and

Y. Xu et al. (Eds.): ML4CS 2022, LNCS 13657, pp. 439–454, 2023.
https://doi.org/10.1007/978-3-031-20102-8_34

the conspirator can use the morphed image stored in the electronic passport to achieve legal identity verification.

At present, face morphing attack detection methods are mainly divided into the following four types: texture based methods [4–6], image quality based methods [7–11], deep learning-based methods [12–14], and multiple features based methods [15, 16]. However, these methods still have problems of high error rate, poor robustness, and high system complexity.

To this end, the paper proposes a face morphing detection method based on a two-stream network with channel attention and residual of multiple color spaces. The main contributions are summarized as follows.

- A face morphing detection method based on residual noise of multiple color spaces is proposed. This method uses the difference of residual noise images in H, S, V, Y, Cb, and Cr color channels to detect morphed face. The use of multi-color space can better capture the different features of real and morphed face images.
- An improved channel attention module is proposed. Compared with the original multi-spectral attention module, avoids the negative impact of dimension reduction on channel attention prediction and the loss of location information caused by multispectral operation, and further improves the expression ability of the model.
- The features of the multi-space residual noise image are fused with the multi-space image features. The image information in HSV and YCbCr space is used to locate abnormal texture, and the residual noise information is used to highlight the difference between real face and morphed face. The fusion of the two contributes to a more comprehensive feature representation and can further improve detection performance.

The rest of the paper is organized as follows: the related work is introduced in Sect. 2, the proposed method is depicted in Sect. 3, and experimental results and analysis are provided in Sect. 4. Finally, some conclusions are drawn in Sect. 5.

2 Related Work

With the texture difference between the real face and the morphed face, a morphed face can be detected by the texture difference. Raja *et al.* proposed a morphed face detection method based on the features of color space [3]. It extracts texture features from color channels and uses probabilistic collaborative representation classifier for classification. Raghavendra *et al.* proposed to use binarized statistical image feature (BSIF) to detect morphed face images [4]. It uses a BSIF filter to extract texture features from an image and uses a linear support vector machine (SVM) for classification. It shows superior performance compared with some existing texture methods. Scherhaget *et al.* combined and evaluated the deep features of LBP, BSIF, HOG, Scale-invariant feature transform (SIFT), Speeded Up Robust Features (SURF) and Openface [5].

Image quality-based methods detect morphed faces by quantifying the difference in compression artifacts and noise introduced during the morphing process. Makrushin *et al.* proposed a morphed face detection method based on JPEG compression features [6]. It uses Benford features calculated from quantized discrete cosine transform coefficients to detect morphed face images. Debiasi *et al.* proposed a morphing attack detection system based on Photo Response Non-Uniformity (PRNU) [7]. It detects the morphed face based on the change of PRNU caused by the morphing process. Peng *et al.* proposed a face morphing detection method using the Fourier spectrum of sensor pattern noise [8]. It uses the noise difference of the sensor pattern of the image to detect the morphed face. The experimental results show that it can accurately detect complete morphing and splicing morphing.

Currently, deep learning has been extensively implemented for face morphing detection, and some pre-trained CNN architectures such as AlexNet, VGG, ResNet, GoogleNet, and InceptionV3 *et al.* are utilized. Seibold *et al.* proposed a morphing attack detection method based on deep learning [9]. Three widely used network architectures are studied, and it is found that the pre-processed VGG19 network can obtain the best performance. Raghavendra *et al.* proposed to use a pre-trained deep convolutional neural network to detect morphed face images [10]. The features on the first fully connected layer of two D-CNNs (VGG19 and AlexNet) are implemented for morphed face detection.

At present, there are a variety of texture-based detection methods and deep learning-based detection methods. If the features extracted are complementary, they can be combined to improve the accuracy. Venkatesh *et al.* proposed to ensemble features to detect morphed face images [11]. It simultaneously extracts BSIF, HOG and LBP features from two different color spaces HSV and YCbCr. Scherhag *et al.* proposed the first multi-algorithm fusion method for face morphing attack detection [12]. The method uses texture descriptors, key point extractors, gradient estimators and deep learning methods to for face morphing detection.However, it increases the complexity.

From the above analysis, although texture-based detection methods are is simple, it only uses the features of the surface of an object, and it cannot obtain high-level image content; For deep learning-based methods, its performance is highly depended on the size of dataset, and small number of samples generally lead to poor accuracy. While for multiple features-based methods, it still has the defect of high complexity. To strike a balance between complexity and detection performance, the residual noise in the multiple color spaces is used to detect the morphed face in this paper.

3 The Proposed Method

The block diagram of the scheme proposed in this paper is shown in Fig. 1. The proposed method is mainly composed of pre-processing, multiple color spaces decomposition, denoising color channels based on bilateral filtering, and two-stream neural network design.

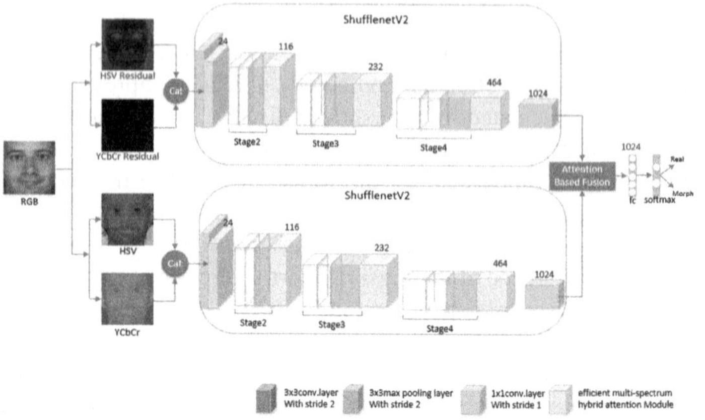

Fig. 1. Framework of the proposed face morphing detection method.

3.1 Pre-processing

In face morphing attack, the face region is generally located in the center of the image. To accurately extract features from the image, only the largest central area of the image is retained. In the preprocessing stage, the face of the given image is segmented and normalized according to the eye coordinates detected by the dlib landmark detector [13]. Subsequently, the normalized area is cropped to 224 × 224 pixels to ensure that the algorithm is only applied to the face area.

3.2 Multiple Color Spaces Decomposition

Since noise consists of both color and brightness, the relative amount of chrominance noise and brightness noise can vary significantly between camera models. Since HSV and YCbCr color spaces can separate strong color and brightness information, these information can provide complementary data for detection. Therefore, six color channels of HSV and YCbCr are selected to extract residual noise. Given face image I, the color channel images are

$$HSV(I) = [I_H, I_S, I_V], \tag{1}$$

$$YCbCr(I) = [I_Y, I_{Cb}, I_{Cr}], \tag{2}$$

where the six color channel images are $I_{Ci} = \{I_H, I_s, I_V, I_Y, I_{Cb}, I_{Cr}\}$, $i = \{1, 2, 3, 4, 5, 6\}$.

3.3 Denoising Based on Bilateral Filtering

Bilateral filtering considers the spatial information and the similarity of gray level to achieve the purpose of edge preservation and denoising. It is simple, non-iterative and partial. The denoising of H, S, V, Y, Cb and Cr color channels was carried out by bilateral filter to obtain the corresponding denoising image: I_{H0}, I_{S0}, I_{V0}, I_{Y0}, I_{Cb0}, I_{Cr0}, Then calculate the residual noise on the six channels: $R_H = I_H - I_{H0}$, $R_s = I_s - I_{s0}$, $R_v = I_v - I_{v0}$, $R_Y = I_Y - I_{Y0}$, $R_{Cb} = I_{Cb} - I_{Cb0}$, $R_{Cr} = I_{Cr} - I_{Cr0}$. Figure 2 shows the residual noise image of the six color channels H, S, V, Y, Cb and Cr, which clearly shows the differences between the real image and the morphed image in edge, texture, intensity, color saturation and brightness.

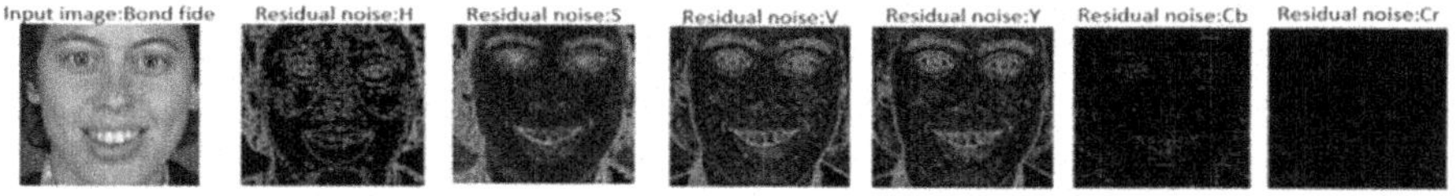

(a) Residual noise images of real faces of six channels

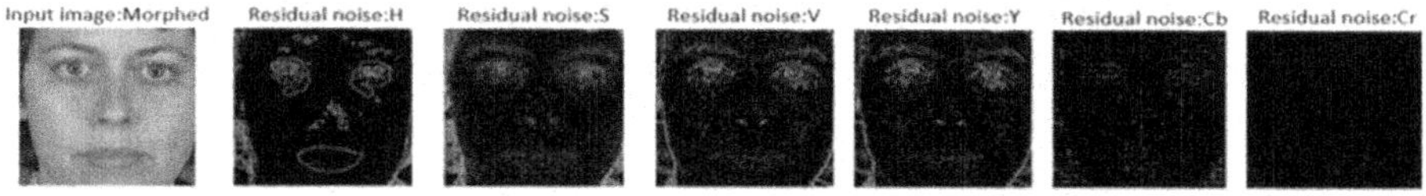

(b) Residual noise images of morphed faces of six channels

Fig. 2. Residual noise image obtained by using the proposed method on (a) Bona fide face (b) morphed face.

3.4 Two-Stream Neural Network Framework (TSCNN)

Images in HSV and YCbCr spaces can better capture facial texture features and locate abnormal textures, but the disadvantage is that taking them as input will make the convolutional neural network biased towards specific textures [14], resulting in generalization problems. The residual noise image can remove the color texture, reveal the morph trace, and expose the difference between the real region and the morph region. The fusion of the two can make the model pay more attention to the fusion trace, and promote the representation learning mutually, thereby improving the detection performance.

As mentioned above, the images in HSV and YCbCr are complementary to the residual noise images in HSV and YCbCr. Therefore, a two-stream network is proposed (as shown in Fig. 1). In this network, the image information input1 of HSV and YCbCr spaces and the multi-space residual noise information input2 are respectively input into two streams for end-to-end training. In the feature fusion stage, the most advanced AFF module [15] (as shown in Fig. 3) is used to fuse the two learned features (multi-space image feature and multi-space residual noise feature). Then the fused features are sent to the Softmax layer for classification. Each of these streams is based on the same network.

Lightweight convolutional neural network ShuffleNetV2 is an efficient CNN architecture. It utilizes two new operation methods of grouping point convolution and channel shuffling, which greatly reduces the computational cost while maintaining the accuracy, and has the advantages of low complexity and few parameters. This paper uses two ShuffleNetV2 as the backbone network.

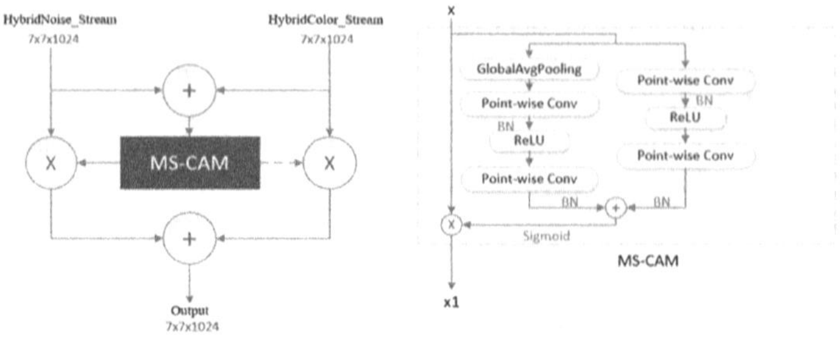

Fig. 3. The structures of AFF module.

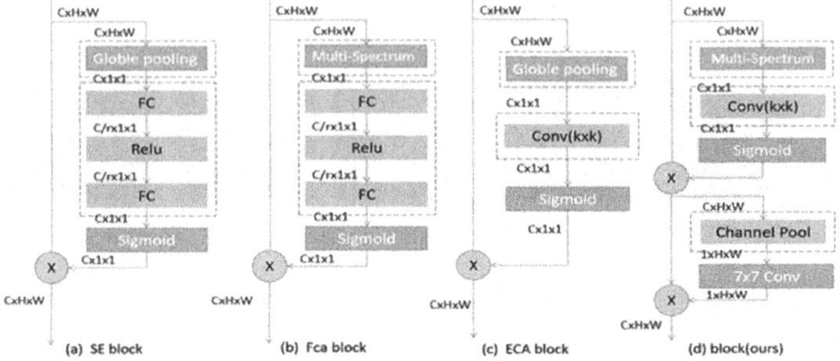

Fig. 4. The attention block (d) proposed in this paper is compared with SE [16] (a), Fca [17] (b) and ECA[18] (c).

Attention mechanisms have been widely used in natural language processing and computer vision. To this end, this paper designs an efficient channel attention mechanism module to further improve the expressiveness of the model. The channel attention mechanism improves the expressive ability of the network by paying attention to the importance of each channel in the image and learning the dependencies of each channel. In terms of channel attention mechanism, the most representative network is SENet [16], and the basic structure of SE block is shown in Fig. 4(a).

The SE module helps the neural network learn the importance of each feature channel through the two-step operation of Squeeze and Excitation. The first step is the Squeeze operation. GAP is used to compress the features in the spatial dimension, and the global spatial features of each channel are used as the representation of the channel to form a $1 \times 1 \times$ C channel descriptor. Described as follows:

$$Sc = Fgap(UC) = \frac{1}{H \times W} \sum_{i=1}^{H} \sum_{j=1}^{W} UC(i, j), \tag{3}$$

where H and W represent the length and width of the feature map, and Uc represents the input feature map. The second step is the Excitation operation. After obtaining the global spatial features, the dependencies between each feature channel are learned through two fully connected layers. Described as follows:

$$Z = F2(\mathrm{Re}LU(F1(S))), \tag{4}$$

Here, F1 and F2 represent two linear transformations that can be learned to capture the importance of each channel. Accompanied by a deep learning algorithm based on frequency domain, FcaNet [17] (see Fig. 4(b) for the basic structure) is the first to generalize GAP to a more general representation form from the perspective of frequency domain, namely 2-dimensional discrete cosine transform DCT. To better compress the channel and capture rich input representations, a multispectral channel attention module is proposed (see Fig. 5(b)). The module firstly divides X into multiple parts along the channel dimension, denoted as $[X^0, X^1, \ldots, X^{n-1}]$, where $C^I = C/n$. For each part, a two-dimensional DCT component is assigned as follows:

$$Freq^i = 2DDCT^{ui,vi}(X^i) = \sum_{h=0}^{H-1}\sum_{w=0}^{W-1} X^i_{:,h,w} B^{ui,vi}_{h,w}, \tag{5}$$

In the above formula, $[u_i, v_i]$ represents the component subscript of two-dimensional DCT, and $Freq^i$ is the vector of C^I dimension, corresponding to the frequency component of each part. The multispectral vector can be obtained by splicing the $Freq^i$ of each part:

$$Freq = cat([Freq^0, Freq^1, \ldots, Freq^{n-1}]), \tag{6}$$

In the above formula, *Freq* represents the obtained multispectral vector. The attention map can be obtained by passing *Freq* through Eq. (8). However, studies [18, 19] show that dimensionality reduction in Eq. (8) brings side effects to channel attentional prediction, and it is inefficient and unnecessary to capture all dependencies between channels. After Eq. (11), although richer feature representations are captured, it squeezes global spatial information into channel descriptors, so it is difficult to preserve positional information, which is critical for capturing spatial structure in visual tasks. In order to solve the above two problems, this paper proposes an efficient attention mechanism module (see Fig. 4(d) for the basic structure). To avoid dimensionality reduction and effectively capture cross-channel interaction information, it is considered to capture local cross-channel interaction information from each channel and its K neighbors. For this purpose, the multi-spectral vector obtained above is subjected to a fast $1D$ convolution with kernel size of k, as described below:

$$Z = \sigma(C1Dk(Freq)), \tag{7}$$

where C1D represents $1D$ convolution, and the convolution kernel size k represents the coverage of local cross-channel interactions, that is, how many neighbors near the channel participate in the attention prediction of this channel.

In order to solve the problem of position loss caused by formula (11), this paper uses the spatial relations of features to generate a spatial attention diagram. Different from channel attention, spatial attention focuses on the information part of "where", which is a supplement to channel attention. In order to calculate spatial attention, the average pooling operation was firstly carried out to generate effective feature descriptors, and then a 7×7 convolution operation was carried out to reduce the dimension to one channel, namely $H \times W \times 1$. Then the spatial attention feature is generated by sigmoid. Finally, the feature is multiplied with the input feature of the module to obtain the final generated feature. The process is described as follows:

$$Ms(Z) = \sigma(f^{7\times7}(AvgPool(Z))) = \sigma(f^{7\times7}(Z^{s}_{avg})), \tag{8}$$

$$Uz = Ms(Z) \otimes Z, \tag{9}$$

where ⊗ denotes element-wise multiplication, where σ denotes the sigmoid activation function, $f^{7\times7}$ denotes the convolution operation with a filter size of 7, and Uz is the final output. Figure 5 depicts the computational process of the spatial attention mechanism module.

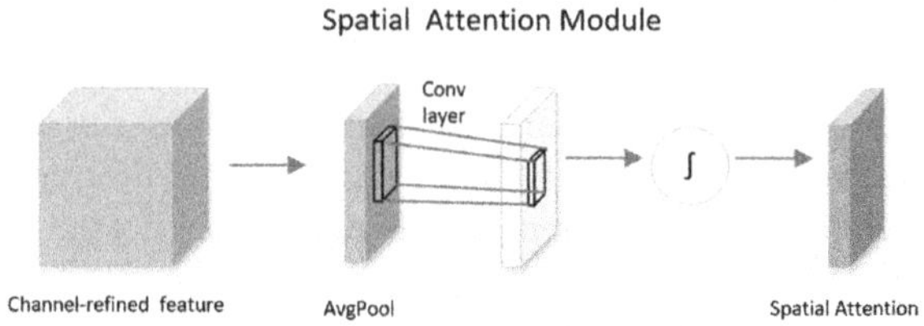

Fig. 5. Spatial attention module.

In order to further improve the expressive ability of the neural network, the designed and efficient attention mechanism modules are inserted after the three stages of stage2, stage3, and stage4 in ShufflenetV2 as the backbone network.

4 Experimental Results and Analysis

4.1 Datasets and Evaluation Criteria

The experiments are performed on Pytorch v1.6.0 and implemented on the GeForce GTX 1060Ti GPU. All experiments on different datasets follow the same settings. The standard datasets FEI_M and HNU(FaceMDB1, FaceMDB2, FaceMDB3, FaceMDB4) used in the experiments are from paper [8] and [20]. The basic information of the datasets is listed in Table 1 and Table 2. Among them, the pixel fusion factor and position fusion factor in FEI_M and HUN(FaceMDB1) are fixed at 0.5. However, in practical application, the morphed image may fuse pixels and positions in different proportions. In order to simulate the real scene, random values of 0.1–0.9 are used for pixel fusion factor and position fusion factor respectively by HNU(FaceMDB2) and HNU(FaceMDB3). In HNU(FaceMDB4), these two factors are randomly selected.

To evaluate the effectiveness of the proposed method, the experimental results of the method are compared with four traditional methods BSIF [4], FS-SPN [8], LBP [25] and HOG [26] and five deep learning methods VGG19 [9], ResNet18 [21], SqueezeNet [22], ShuffleNetV2 [23], MobileNetV2 [24]. Meanwhile, the standardized ISO metrics [27] attack presentation classification error rate (APCER), bona fide presentation classification error rate (BPCER), average classification error rate (ACER), accuracy(ACC) and

Table 1. HNU dataset

Dataset	Subset	# Bona fide	# Splicing morphing
FaceMDB1	Training set	1121	1121
	Development set	564	330
	Testing set	566	377
FaceMDB2	Training set	1121	1125
	Development set	564	567
	Testing set	566	567
FaceMDB3	Training set	1121	1125
	Development set	564	567
	Testing set	566	567
FaceMDB4	Training set	1121	1125
	Development set	564	567
	Testing set	566	567

Table 2. FEI_M dataset

Dataset	Subset	# Bona fide	# Splicing morphing
FEI_M	Training set	81	6480
	Development set	20	380
	Testing set	99	9702

equal error rate (EER) are used to evaluate the detection performance. APCER, BPCER, ACER and EER are defined as:

$$APCER = MCR/M, \tag{10}$$

$$BPCER = RCM/R, \tag{11}$$

$$ACER = (APCER + BPCER)/2, \tag{12}$$

$$ACC = 1 - \frac{MCR + RCM}{M + R}, \tag{13}$$

where MCR represents the number of morphed face image which is classified as the real face image, RCM represents the number of real face image that is classified as morphed face image, M and R represent the number of the morphed face image and the number of the real face image, respectively. Besides, the results with EER when APCER = BPCER is also provided.

4.2 Implementation Details

The network is trained end-to-end. For each dataset, SGD is used for optimization, and the model is trained with the cross-entropy loss function. The description function is defined as follows:

$$Loss = -\frac{1}{N}\sum_{i}^{N}[yiIn\hat{_{yi}} + (1 - yi)In(1-\hat{_{yi}})], \tag{14}$$

In the formula, i is the index of the training sample, N is the number of training samples, $\hat{y_i}$ is the predicted value of the ith sample, and y_i is the label of the ith sample. During training and validation, the batch size is 4, and during testing, the batch size is 16. In the setting of learning parameters, momentum is set as 0.9, learning rate as 0.001, and 30 epochs are trained.

4.3 Experimental Results and Analysis

4.3.1 Single Dataset Experiment and Analysis

To effectively evaluate the performance of the morphing attack detection method, the performance is evaluated on a single dataset, and the results are listed in Table 3.

For the proposed method, the EERs on FEI_M and HNU (MDB1) datasets are 1.04% and 0.88% respectively, and it can obtain the best performance on FEI_M and HNU (MDB1) datasets compared with BSIF [4], FS-SPN [8], LBP [25], HOG [26], VGG19 [9], ResNet18 [21], SqueezeNet [22], ShuffleNetV2 [23], and MobileNetV2 [24]. From an overall, the performance of the deep learning-based methods is generally better than that of the traditional methods on two datasets. For deep learning-based methods, ShuffleNetV2 and ResNet18 can achieve better detection performance than the other networks; while for traditional methods, FS-SPN can achieve the best detection performance. Compared with the existing 9 different methods, the proposed method can achieve good performance. Furthermore, the performance of different methods evaluated on the HNU database with different pixel fusion factors are tested, and the results are listed in Table 4. From Table 4, the EERs of the proposed method on HNU MDB2, MDB3, MDB4 are 0.98%, 1.21% and 1.16%, respectively. Compared with BSIF [4], FS-SPN [8], LBP [25], HOG [26], VGG19 [9], ResNet18 [21], SqueezeNet [22], ShuffleNetV2 [23], and MobileNetV2 [24], the proposed method achieves the best detection performance on HNU MDB2, MDB3, MDB4. From an overall, the performance of the deep learning-based methods is better than that of the traditional methods on three datasets with different pixel fusion factors.The method is still robust under the conditions of different fusion factors and position factors.

4.3.2 Cross-Dataset Experiments and Analysis

To test the generalization ability of the proposed method, cross-dataset experiments are performed. Here, the FEI_M and HNU((MDB1)) datasets are selected for cross-validation, and the results are listed in Table 5. From Table 5, the EERs of the proposed method in cross-datasets are 4.48% and 7.95%, which are 2.15% and 3.27% higher than

Table 3. Performance comparison of different methods on FEI_M, HNU (MDB1) datasets

Algorithm	FEI_M			HNU(FaceMDB1)		
	EER (%)	BPCER@APCER		EER (%)	BPCER@APCER	
		=5%	=10%		=5%	=10%
BSIF [4]	8.13	8.67	4.79	20.80	22.60	19.82
LBP [25]	9.01	10.13	7.01	23.28	25.04	22.00
HOG [26]	11.01	13.13	9.33	24.84	62.90	48.39
FS-SPN [8]	**1.01**	2.02	0.98	1.93	1.53	1.21
VGG19 [9]	7.07	10.10	6.06	15.06	18.06	13.98
ResNet18 [21]	3.03	2.02	1.01	2.47	4.18	2.03
SqueezeNet [22]	10.20	14.14	11.11	13.42	21.11	14.49
ShuffleNetV2 [23]	4.04	2.02	1.01	4.01	3.98	1.89
MobileNeV2 [24]	4.04	5.05	3.13	3.53	3.36	1.41
Proposed method	1.04	**1.09**	**0.66**	**0.88**	**1.31**	**0.37**

Table 4. The performance of different methods on HNU(FaceMDB2, FaceMDB3, FaceMDB4) datasets

Algorithm	HNU(FaceMDB2)			HNU(FaceMDB3)			HNU(FaceMDB4)		
	EER (%)	BPCER@APCER		EER (%)	BPCER@APCER		EER (%)	BPCER@APCER	
		=5%	=10%		=5%	=10%		=5%	=10%
BSIF [4]	20.39	20.27	18.17	19.38	21.67	17.79	21.36	23.67	18.08
LBP [25]	22.12	20.18	20.01	23.70	23.00	20.88	22.99	21.76	20.18
HOG [26]	22.72	61.02	46.91	21.16	47.09	31.92	23.46	59.61	48.50
FS-SPN [8]	1.56	2.02	1.01	1.49	**1.01**	0.49	1.69	**1.41**	0.18
VGG19 [9]	14.08	19.21	12.88	17.78	19.41	15.16	18.96	19.06	16.13
ResNet18 [21]	1.41	**0.53**	0.18	2.65	1.24	**0.35**	3.53	2.65	0.88
SqueezeNet [22]	5.64	7.95	1.77	13.23	20.14	15.37	20.09	35.34	27.92
ShuffleNetV2 [23]	4.06	3.53	1.41	9.19	14.66	8.66	7.60	14.49	4.42
MobileNeV2[24]	4.59	4..59	2.65	5.65	6.18	2.83	4.94	4.77	2.30
Proposed method	**0.98**	0.59	**0.12**	**1.21**	**1.01**	0.57	**1.16**	**1.41**	**0.16**

the best results among the existing methods. From an overall, the generalization ability of the deep learning-based methods is better than that of the traditional methods, and the proposed method can achieve the best generalization ability among them.

Table 5. Quantitative performance of the MAD algorithms on cross-dataset

Training dateset	Test dateset	Algorithms	EER (%)	BPCER@APCER	
				=5%	=10%
HNU (MDB1)	FEI_M	BSIF [4]	30.27	87.77	63.16
		LBP[25]	31.11	41.90	21.93
		HOG [26]	40.01	60.01	50.33
		FS-SPN [8]	37.37	85.69	75.02
		VGG19 [9]	10.28	14.14	11.11
		ResNet18 [21]	6.63	8.08	3.03
		SqueezeNet [22]	12.15	14.14	10.10
		ShuffleNet [23]	12.63	24.24	15.15
		MobileNet[24]	15.87	35.35	23.23
		Proposed method	**4.48**	**2.02**	**1.01**
FEI_M	HNU (MDB1)	BSIF [4]	42.09	70.68	49.25
		LBP[25]	49.72	82.16	53.14
		HOG [26]	35.48	87.10	80.97
		FS-SPN [8]	27.09	56.17	32.14
		VGG19 [9]	17.14	24.54	16.45
		ResNet18 [21]	11.88	42.29	24.25
		SqueezeNet [22]	31.63	65.27	52.27
		ShuffleNet [23]	12.12	20.20	16.16
		MobileNet [24]	11.22	**12.01**	5.04
		Proposed method	**7.95**	12.54	**4.77**

4.3.3 Ablation Experiment and Analysis

(1) Channel ablation experiment

To highlight the effectiveness of the designed two-stream network, ablation studies are conducted on two datasets, and the experimental results are shown in Table 6.

Table 6. Experimental results on single-stream and two-stream networks

	FEI_M			HNU(MDB1)		
	ACER (%)	EER (%)	ACC (%)	ACER (%)	EER (%)	ACC (%)
MultipleNoise-CNN	1.23	1.59	**99.96**	0.89	**0.88**	99.13
MultipleColor-CNN	6.08	2.59	99.26	7.07	3.00	94.16
TSCNN(ours)	**0.86**	**1.04**	99.87	**0.65**	**0.88**	**99.66**

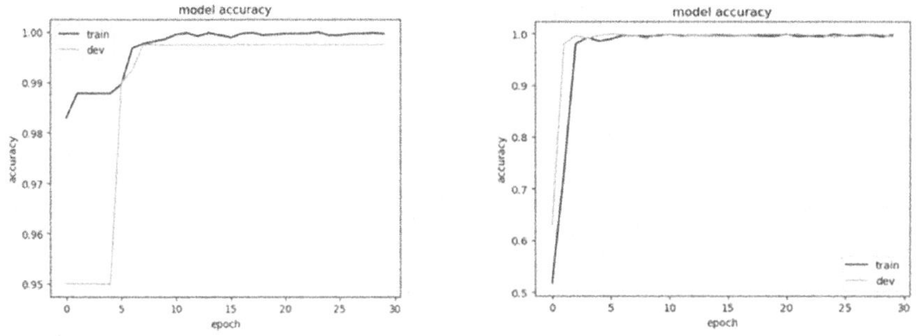

(a) training and validation loss curves in FEI_M (b) training and validation loss curves in HNU(MDB1)

Fig. 6. Loss curves of TSCNN model on two datasets

It can be seen that the ACERs of TSCNN on the two datasets are 0.86% and 0.65%, the EERs are 1.04% and 0.88%, and the ACCs are 99.87% and 99.66%, respectively. Compared with multi-space images, the ACERs increased by 5.22% and 6.42%, the EERs increased by 1.55% and 2.12%, and the ACCs increased by 0.61% and 5.50%, respectively. Compared with the multi-space residual noise, the ACERs are increased by 0.37% and 0.24%, respectively, and the EER is increased by 0.55% on FEI_M, which obtained good performance on both datasets. This is attributed to the fact that the image information in HSV and YCbCr spaces is used to locate abnormal textures. Multi-space residual noise information is used to highlight the differences between real faces and morphed faces, and the fusion of the two contributes to a more comprehensive feature representation.

Figure 6(a) and Fig. 6(b) show the loss curves of the TSCNN model on the FEI_M and HNU(MDB1) datasets, respectively. 99.95% and 99.40% training and validation accuracy were achieved on FEI_M dataset, and 99.82% and 99.89% training and validation accuracy were achieved on HNU(MDB1) dataset.

(2)Attention Mechanism Ablation Experiment

Table 7 shows the experimental results of different attention methods on the FEI_M and HUN(MDB1) datasets.

From Table 7, it can be seen that compared with other attention methods, using the method of classification model has better transferability, which is attributed to the improvement of the method based on the multispectral attention method. The improved module solves the side effects of channel attention prediction caused by dimensionality reduction and the loss of position information caused by multispectral operation without increasing parameters.

(3) Channel ablation experiment

In addition, to highlight the effectiveness of the selected color channels, comparative experiments are conducted to different color spaces, and the results are listed in Table 8. From the results, for the proposed method, the ACERs are 1.23% and 0.89%, the EERs are 1.59% and 0.88%, and the ACCs are 99.96% and 99.13%, respectively. Compared with RGB, HSV and YCbCr, the residual noise in HSV and YCbCr multiple color spaces achieves good results. This may be attributed to the fact that HSV and YCbCr

Table 7. Experimental results of different attention methods

	FEI_M			HNU(MDB1)			Param (M)
	ACER (%)	EER (%)	ACC (%)	ACER (%)	EER (%)	ACC (%)	
ShufflenetV2 [30]	5.91	4.04	99.18	4.15	4.01	96.28	1.255654
ShufflenetV2_SE	**5.16**	3.92	**99.58**	3.93	**2.12**	96.62	1.264597
ShufflenetV2_ECA	5.07	3.15	99.07	3.80	2.83	96.71	1.255667
ShufflenetV2_FCA	5.48	3.30	99.05	4.51	2.39	96.28	1.290686
ShufflenetV2_Ours	5.37	**3.02**	**99.58**	**3.18**	**2.12**	**97.13**	1.255814

Table 8. Experimental results based on each color channel

Channel	FEI_M			HNU(FaceMDB1)		
	ACER (%)	EER (%)	ACC (%)	ACER (%)	EER (%)	ACC (%)
R G B	2.05	2.31	98.90	1.68	1.41	97.98
H S V	4.21	2.14	99.58	1.21	**0.88**	98.72
YCbCr	1.31	**1.43**	99.77	1.72	1.06	98.09
HSV + YCbCr	**1.23**	1.59	**99.96**	**0.89**	**0.88**	**99.13**

color spaces can separate strong color information and brightness information, which can provide complementary data for face morphing detection.

5 Conclusion

In this paper, a face morphing detection method based on a two-stream network with channel attention and residual of multiple color spaces is proposed. It is based on the exploration of multiple color spaces, and the residual noise features in *H*, *S*, *V*, *Y*, *Cb*, *Cr* color channels and the original image features are utilized to detect morphed faces. The use of multiple color spaces can better capture the different features of the bona fide and morphed face images, which helps to reliably detect morphed faces. The fusion of multi-space residual noise features and multi-space image features contributes to a more comprehensive feature representation, which can further improve the detection performance. Experiments verify the robustness and generalization of the proposed method on morphed face datasets. Future work will try to use a two-stream network with channel attention and residual of multiple color spaces to detect differential morphing attacks.

Acknowledgement. This work was supported in part by project supported by National Natural Science Foundation of China (Grant No. 62072055, U1936115, 92067104).

References

1. Scherhag, U., Raghavendra, R.: On the vulnerability of face recognition systems towards morphed face attacks. In: International Workshop on Bio metrics and Forensics, pp. 1–6 (2017)
2. Ferrara, M., Franco, A., Maltoni, D.: On the effects of image alterations on face recognition accuracy. In: Bourlai, T. (ed.) Face Recognition Across the Imaging Spectrum, pp. 195–222. Springer, Cham (2016). https://doi.org/10.1007/978-3-319-28501-6_9
3. Ramachandra, R., Raja, K., Venkatesh, S.: Face morphing versus face averaging: vulnerability and detection. In: International Joint Conference on Biometrics (IJCB), pp. 555–563 (2017)
4. Raghavendra, R., Raja, K.B., Busch, C.: Detecting morphed face images. In: IEEE International Conference on Biometrics: Theory, Applications, and Systems, pp. 1–8 (2016)
5. Scherhag, U., Rathgeb, C., Busch, C.: Morph detection from single face images: a multi-algorithm fusion approach. In: Proceedings of the International Conference on Biometrics Engineering and Application (ICBEA), pp. 6–12 (2018)
6. Makrushin, A., Neubert, T., Dittmann, J.: Automatic generation and detection of visually faultless facial morphs. In: International Joint Conference on Computer Vision, Imaging and Computer Graphics Theory and Applications, pp. 39–50 (2017)
7. Debiasi. L., Scherhag, U., Rathgeb, C., Uhl, A., Busch, C: Prnu-based detection of morphed face images. In: International Workshop on Biometrics and Forensics (IWBF), pp. 1–7 (2018)
8. Zhang, L., Peng, F., Long, M.: Face morphing detection using fourier spectrum of sensor pattern noise. In: IEEE International Conference on Multimedia and Expo (ICME), pp. 1–6. San Diego, CA (2018)
9. Seibold, C., Samek, W., Hilsmann, A., Eisert, P.: Detection of face morphing attacks by deep learning. In: International Workshop on Digital Watermarking, pp. 107–120 (2017)
10. Raghavendra, R., Raja, K.B., Venkatesh, S., Busch, C.: Transferable Deep-CNN features for detecting digital and print-scanned morphed face images. In: IEEE Conference on Computer Vision and Pattern Recognition Workshops, pp. 1822–1830 (2017)
11. Venkatesh, S., Ramachandra, R., Raja, K., Busch, C.: Single image face morphing attack detection using ensemble of features. In: IEEE International Conference on Information Fusion (FUSION), pp. 1–6. Rustenburg, South Africa (2020)
12. Scherhag, U., Rathgeb, C., Busch, C.: Morph deterction from single face image. In: Biometric Engineering and Applications, pp. 6–12 (2018)
13. King, D.E.: Dlib-ml: a machine learning toolkit. J. Mach. Learn. Res. 1755–1758 (2009)
14. Luo, Y., Zhang, Y.: Generalizing face forgery detection with high-frequency features. In: IEEE Conference on Computer Vision and Pattern Recognition, pp. 16312–16321 (2021)
15. Dai, Y., Gieseke, F., Oehmcke, S., Wu, Y., Barnard, K.: Attentional feature fusion. In: IEEE Winter Conference on Applications of Computer Vision (WACV), pp. 3559–3568 (2021)
16. Hu, J., Shen, L., Sun, G.: Squeeze-and-excitation networks. In: IEEE Conference on Computer Vision and Pattern Recognition, pp. 7132–7141 (2018)
17. Qin, Z., Zhang, P., Wu, F.: FcaNet: Frequency Channel Attention Networks. ArXiv (2020)
18. Wang, Q., Wu, B., Zhu, P., Li, P., Zuo, W., Hu, Q.: ECA-Net: efficient channel attention for deep convolutional neural networks. In: IEEE Conference on Computer Vision and Pattern Recognition (CVPR), pp. 11531–11539 (2020)0
19. Woo, S., Park, J., Lee, J.-Y., Kweon, I.S.: Cbam: convolutional block attention module. In: Ferrari, V., Hebert, M., Sminchisescu, C., Weiss, Y. (eds.) ECCV 2018. LNCS, vol. 11211, pp. 3–19. Springer, Cham (2018). https://doi.org/10.1007/978-3-030-01234-2_1
20. Peng, F., Zhang, L.-B., Long, M.: FD-GAN: face de-morphing generative adversarial network for restoring Accomplice's facial image. In: IEEE Access, pp. 75122–75131 (2019)

21. He, K., et al: Deep residual learning for image recognition. In: IEEE Conference on Computer Vision & Pattern Recognition IEEE Computer Society, pp. 770–778 (2016)
22. Iandola, F.N., Han, S., Moskewicz, M.W., Ashraf, K., Dally, W.J., Keutzer, K.: Squeezenet: alexnet-level accuracy with 50x fewer parameters and 1mb model size. CoRR, abs/1602.07360 (2016)
23. Zhang, X., Zhou, X., Lin, M., et al.: ShuffleNet: an extremely efficient convolutional neural network for mobile devices. In: IEEE Conference on Computer Vision and Pattern Recognition, pp. 6848–6856 (2018)
24. Sandler, M., Howard, A., Zhu, M., Zhmoginov, A., Chen, L.C.: Mobilenetv2: Inverted residuals and linear bottlenecks. In: CVPR, pp. 4510–4520 (2018)
25. Chingovska, I., Anjos, A., Marcel, S.; On the effectiveness of local binary patterns in face anti-spoofing. In: Biometrics Special Interest Group, pp. 1–7 (2012)
26. Scherhag, U., Rathgeb, C., Busch, C.: Towards detection of morphed face images in electronic travel documents. In: IAPR Workshop on Document Analysis Systems, pp. 1–6 (2018)
27. Information Technology –Biometric presentation attack detection–Part 3: Testing and reporting, JTC 1/SC 37, Geneva, Switzerland, ISO/IEC FDIS 30107-3:2017 (2017)

DU-Net: A Novel Architecture for Retinal Vessels Segmentation

Yan Jiang[1], Ziji Zeng[2], Lingxia Chen[1], Jiyong Hu[1], and Ping Li[1](✉)

[1] School of Software, Jiangxi Normal University, Nanchang, China
{202040100754,201926701128,202040100749,003173}@jxnu.edu.cn
[2] School of Management and Engineering, Capital University of Economics and Business, Beijing, China

Abstract. Early diagnosis is fundamental for ophthalmic diseases which may cause deterioration of the human vision system, such as hypertension, glaucoma, and diabetic retinopathy. Ophthalmologists usually examine fundus images to evaluate the clinical condition of retinal blood vessels, which becomes a significant indicator for diagnosing various ophthalmic diseases. Whereas, manually labeling retinal vessels is a time-consuming and burdensome task, and it is also required extensive clinical experience. Therefore, it is necessary to implement automatic segmentation for retinal vessels. This paper integrates the dense-block into a U-Net to propose a novel network structure called DU-net, which can improve the accuracy of blood vessel segmentation by alleviating the problems of gradient disappearance and image structure feature loss. Related experiments are conducted on one publicly available fundus image dataset (DRIVE). The results demonstrate that the proposed DU-net outperforms most comparison methods in terms of different evaluation metrics.

Keywords: Segmentation · Retinal vessel · U-Net · Dense-block · DU-Net

1 Introduction

Early diagnosis is a key measure for ophthalmic diseases, such as glaucoma [1], hypertension [2], and diabetic retinopathy [3], which may reduce the performance of human vision. In clinical testing, ophthalmologists usually assess clinical conditions of retinal vessels by examining fundus images. However, segmenting blood vessels of fundus retinal images is a time-consuming task. And it requires high comprehensive skills for label markers. Therefore, real-time and automatic segmentation of retinal vessels is very crucial for paramedics to diagnose ophthalmic diseases. And it has drawn much attention in recent decades [4].

Y. Xu et al. (Eds.): ML4CS 2022, LNCS 13657, pp. 455–468, 2023.
https://doi.org/10.1007/978-3-031-20102-8_35

With the rapid development of computer technology, computer-aided diagnosis (CAD) technologies have been widely applied to clinical diagnosis [5], which utilizes computer technologies to analyze medical images for improving diagnostic efficiency. To achieve precise segmentation results of retinal vessels to assist doctors during the diagnosis and treatment, many methods have been conducted by combining image processing and deep learning techniques, and they are broadly categorized into unsupervised and supervised methods.

For unsupervised segmentation methods, Chaudhuri et al. [6] applied the Gaussian-shaped curve and matched filter detection to segment retinal vessels automatically, which extracted many features of fundus images. Subsequently, many other methods have been derived, including morphological based methods [7, 8], and matched filter-based methods [9]. They firstly were designed to extract features of blood vessels from preprocessed fundus images, and then further separated blood vessels from the background. Therefore, the results heavily depend on the feature design and feature extraction to a certain extent.

Different from unsupervised learning methods, supervised learning-based segmentation methods first design the feature extraction to obtain structure features from fundus images, then they construct a classification model with a pre-prepared dataset, and finally utilize the trained classification model to segment retinal vessels. For instance, discrete wavelet transform [10], Gaussian filtering [11], and vascular filtering [12], have been developed for extracting retinal structural features. Meanwhile, how to design a classifier is also a critical step in supervised learning methods. K-nearest neighbor (KNN) [13], support vector machine (SVM) [14], and artificial neural networks (ANN) [15] have been exploited to build classification models. For example, Staal et al. [16] built a supervised model with the ridgeline to segment retinal vessel images, which first applied a sequential forward selection algorithm to obtain the optimal features, and then the k-nearest neighbor was adopted to classify pixel points. Soares et al. [17] employed a two-dimensional Gabor filter to extract features of retinal images, and utilized a Bayesian classifier for the classification of retinal images. Ricci et al. [18] exhibited a kind of retinal vessel segmentation method, which combined two orthogonal detectors and gray pixel values on the preprocessed green channel images to extract feature images, then used the support vector machine to complete the classification. Fraz et al. [19] combined AdaBoost and Bagging algorithms to integrate the results of different feature extractions and classification models. Compared with unsupervised learning methods, these supervised methods can improve the accuracy dramatically. However, because they are sensitive to the changes in vessel scale, vessel morphology, and geometric transformations of vessel images, they still suffer the problems of insufficient precision or mis-segmentation of tiny vessels, which is far from the requirements of intelligent vascular segmentation and clinical application.

For the past few years, deep learning has made significant breakthroughs in computer vision fields, such as image classification [20] and object detection [21]. Many deep learning methods have also been applied to fundus retinal vessel segmentation. For example, Ronnerberger et al. [22] exhibited a U-shaped network (U-Net) on the basis of fully convolutional networks (FCNs) [23], which adopted the structure of encoder, decoder, and skip-connection. Compared with other previous work, the experiment results have shown that U-Net has significant superiority in medical image segmentation. However, with the expansion of the training set and the deepening of the network, it may be suffered some problems, such as failure to segment micro-vessels, fracture at the intersection of micro-vessels, loss of the details of complex morphological vessels, and insensitivity to pathological information.

To overcome problems of the existed deep learning methods in retinal vessel segmentation, in this paper, we introduce a dense-block into U-Net to build a network structure named DU-Net, which fully takes advantage of U-Net and Dense-Net. In our proposed DU-Net, we replace the original convolution module with a dense-block during down-sampling and up-sampling, which can strengthen feature reuse, decrease the number of parameters and alleviate the problem of gradient disappearance to some extent. Extensive experiments are performed on one publicly available fundus image dataset (DRIVE). The results imply that our DU-Net outperforms most comparison methods according to different evaluation metrics.

The remainder of this paper is organized as follows: Sect. 2 reviews the related works including U-Net and Dense-Net. Section 3 expounds on the proposed DU-Net model. Section 4 conducts experiments to evaluate the performance. Finally, the conclusions are given in Sect. 5.

2 Related Works

2.1 U-Net

U-Net is a semantic segmentation network on the basis of a fully connected convolutional neural networks (FCNs) [23], containing an encoder and a decoder. The encoder is responsible for extracting features from an input image, while the decoder is responsible for up-sampling to recover the original image from extracted features. The network structure of U-Net is shown in Fig. 1. In this figure, the blue arrow represents a convolution operation with kernel size 3×3 for feature extraction. The red arrow is a pooling operation with kernel size 2×2 to decrease the dimension of features and the computational cost, which can also prevent overfitting and enhance the generalization ability. The green arrow indicates an upsampling operation, which can recover a downsampled feature map to the same resolution as the original feature. The gray arrow denotes the skip-connection, which can implement the feature reuse in decoding stages. The orange arrow represents a convolution operation with kernel size 1×1, which can reduce the number of feature channels.

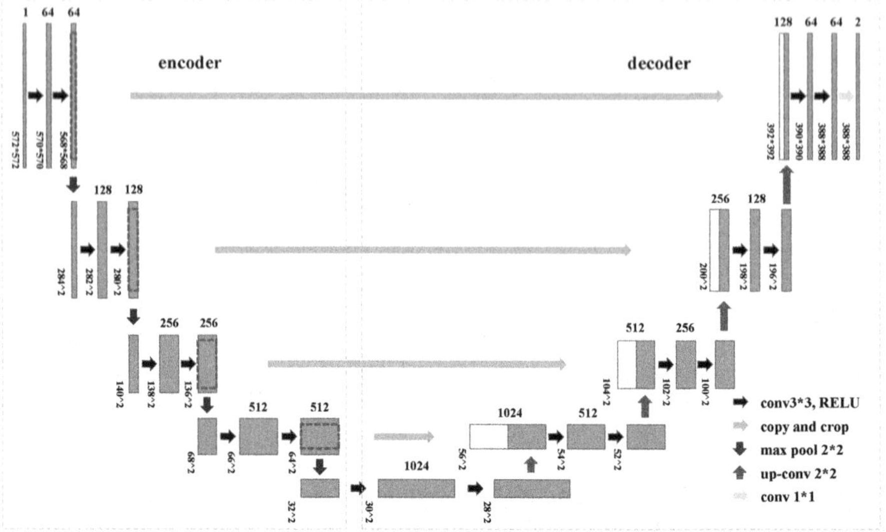

Fig. 1. Traditional U-Net network structure

2.2 DenseNet

To achieve better performance for the convolutional neural network, it is necessary to design a more complex neural network architecture. However, how to alleviate gradient disappearance and degradation has become an attractive problem. To solve this problem, ResNet [24] and Highway Networks [25] have been designed by introducing an identity mapping. Unlike ResNet and Highway Networks, Fractual Nets built parallel network architecture to ensure the gradient propagation with a deep structure [26]. A common of the mentioned methods is that their feature maps are connected across network layers. In order to enhance the feature reuse and decrease the number of parameters, the concept of dense-block was first proposed and then a deep neural network named DenseNet was developed [27].

The Dense-Block with three Dense-Layers is displayed in Fig. 2, in which the input of the Lth layer is not only related to the input of the L-1th layer but also related to the output of all previous network layers. It can be expressed as:

$$X_L = H_L([X_0, X_1, \ldots, X_{L-1}]) \tag{1}$$

where $[\cdot]$ denotes a concatenation operation, which combines all output feature maps from X_0 to X_{L-1} together, and H is a nonlinear transformation.

To extend the network structure and extract more valuable features, DenseNet adopts a feature reuse strategy to merge feature maps obtained from different Dense-Block layers. However, since the sizes of each feature map are inconsistent, the downsampling operation in DenseNet is performed by introducing a conversion layer between different dense-blocks and the output is used as the input of the next dense-block. The structure of the DenseNet containing two dense-blocks is displayed in Fig. 3.

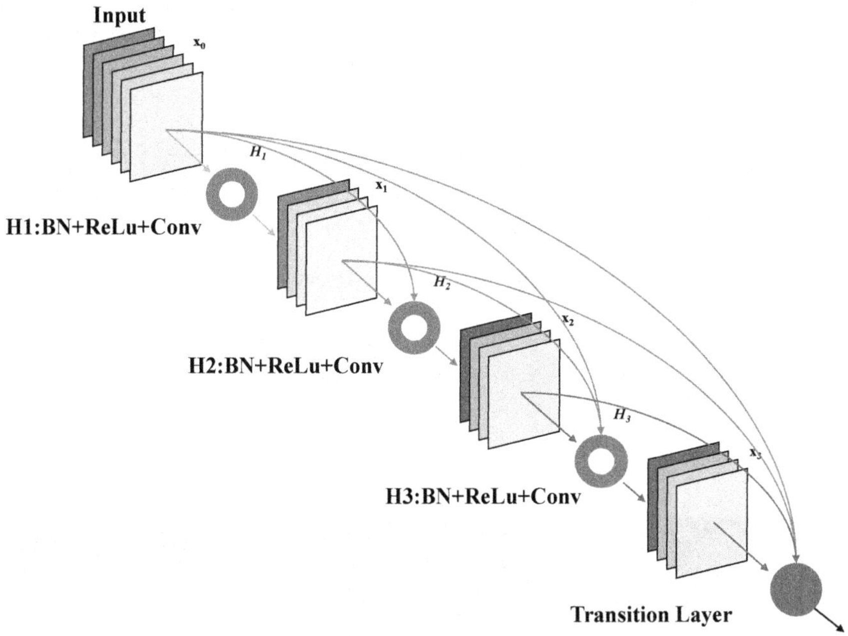

Fig. 2. Dense-block with 3 dense-layers

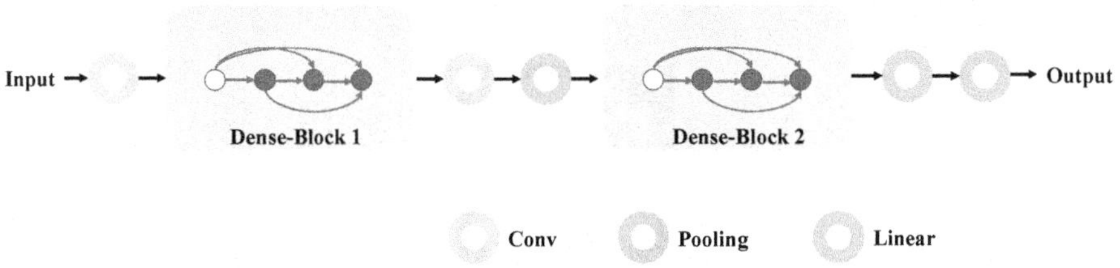

Fig. 3. The structure of the DenseNet network with 2 dense-blocks

3 DU-Net Based Retinal Vessel Segmentation

In this section, we first provide the procedures of the retinal vessel segmentation, and then the framework of the proposed DU-Net model is described.

3.1 Procedure of Retinal Vessel Segmentation

The automatic segmentation of blood vessels for retinal fundus images is helpful for early screening and diagnosis of ocular diseases. With the rapid development of deep learning, many deep learning models have been widely generated and applied to medical image segmentation tasks. The flowchart of segmentation for retinal vessels is shown in Fig. 4, which is consisted of the training stage and testing stage.

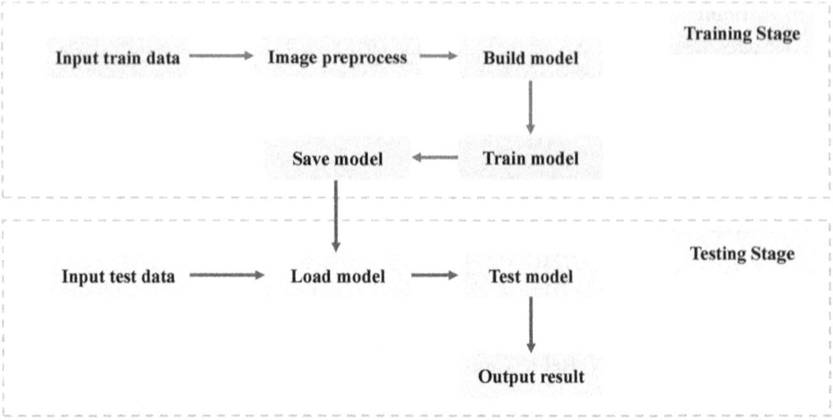

Fig. 4. The flowchart of retinal vessel segmentation

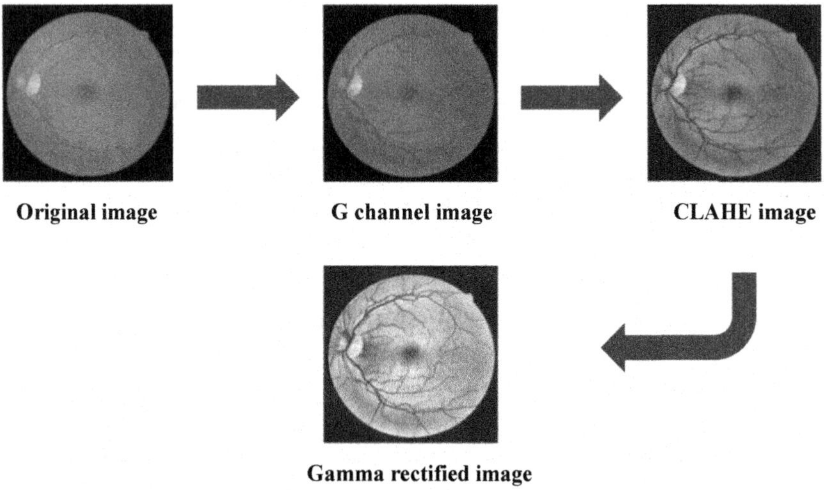

Fig. 5. The each stage of image preprocessing

The image preprocessing is a fundamental step in the training stage, which includes three steps. In the first step, it readjusts input images to a uniform size. Then, different structures of G-channel images with high contrast are extracted from the original images, and the contrast histogram equalization is carried out to improve the image contrast further. Finally, local adaptive Gamma correction [28] is used to perform Gamma value matching operations in terms of the different features of the fundus image background and blood vessel pixels. Hence, the image preprocessing can be reduced the interference of other parts on blood vessel segmentation. The each stage of image preprocessing is shown in Fig. 5.

3.2 The Proposed DU-Net Model

TO solve the existing deep learning network's problems of retinal vessel segmentation, such as insufficient accuracy, loss of details, and missegmentation, this paper designs the DU-Net network architecture by incorporating the core idea of U-Net and DenseNet. The proposed network replaces the original convolutional module with a Dense-Block in the encoder and decoder, which can strengthen the reuse of features and reduce the number of parameters. And it makes the network easier to train and alleviates the problem of gradient disappearance.

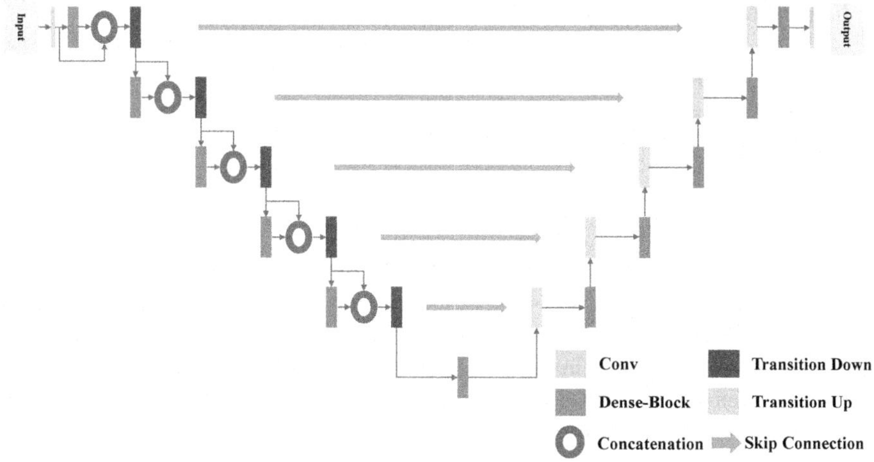

Fig. 6. The structure of the DU-Net

The structure of the proposed DU-Net model consists of a downsampling and an upsampling path, displayed in Fig. 6. The downsampling module is denoted as a dark purple rectangle, containing Batch Normalization (BN), ReLU, Convolution layer, Dropout, and Maximum pooling layer. The specific structure of downsampling is illustrated in Fig. 7 (a). The blue rectangle indicates dense-block, which can enhance the feature reuse. The dense-layer of denseblock contains Batch Normalization, ReLU, Convolutional layer, and Dropout, which is listed in Fig. 7 (b). An orange rectangle represents an upsampling module, which performs a 3×3 deconvolution layer with a step of 2 to restore the size of the original image. The specific structure of the up-sampling part is displayed in Fig. 7 (c). The green of hollow circle denotes the concatenation operation, which concatenates the extracted features by dense-block with the features before dense-block. The gray arrows indicate skip-connection, which combines the feature maps from a downsampled path to its corresponding upsampled path. The green rectangle represents the convolution operation.

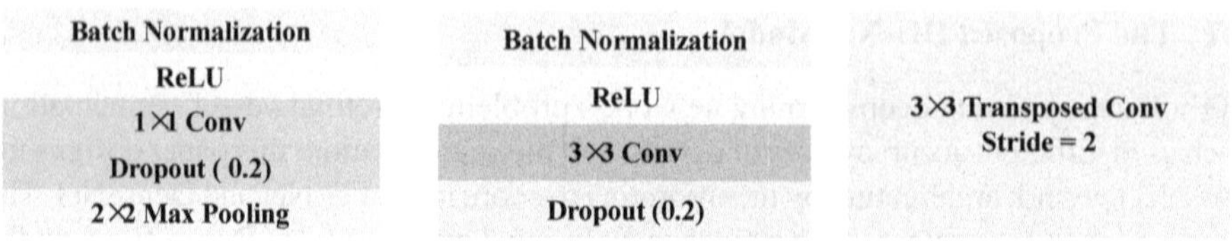

(a) (b) (c)

Fig. 7. The structure of difference modules in the DU-Net

4 Experimental Results and Analysis

This section evaluates the effectiveness of the proposed DU-Net model. Firstly, the dataset and several criteria used in the experiments are introduced. Then, the experimental results are obtained, and analyzed in detail.

4.1 Dataset

The used dataset is a publicly common DRIVE dataset [16], which contains 40 images. The dataset is classified into two subsets, the training set and the test set, and each set contains 20 images. In addition, each image consists of a masked image and a hand-segmented vessel image. The masked image is used to mark the segmentation area, and the latter is taken as a standard to evaluate the segmentation effect. Some of the images of the DRIVE dataset are displayed in Fig. 8.

4.2 Evaluation Criteria

To verify the effectiveness of the proposed model, three indicators such as Sensitive (*Sen*), Specificity (*Spe*) and Accuracy (*Acc*), are adopted to measure the performance, defined as Eqs. (2)–(4):

$$Sensitive = \frac{T_p}{T_p + F_N} \tag{2}$$

$$Specificity = \frac{T_N}{T_N + F_P} \tag{3}$$

$$Accuray = \frac{T_p + T_N}{T_p + T_N + F_P + F_N} \tag{4}$$

where T_p, T_N, F_p and F_N denote true positive, true negative, false positive, and false negative, respectively. In this experiment, Sensitive (*Sen*) is a ratio of vascular pixels accurately classified to all the vascular pixels in one image. Specificity (*Spe*) is a proportion of the proper classification of vascular pixels and blood vessels of pixels in one image. Accuracy (*Acc*) represents the ratio of vascular and non-vascular pixels correctly classified to all pixels in the image.

Besides, the ROC curve is also utilized to validate the comprehensive segmentation performance of the proposed model in our work. The vertical axis of a ROC curve is the true positive rate (TPR) and the horizontal axis is a false positive rate (FPR), which can reflect the changing trend of the true positive rate and the false positive rate under different thresholds. The larger its value is, the better the model performance is. In addition, AUC represents an area of the ROC curve. If the value of AUC is close to 1 or the area of AUC is large, it stands for the model has excellent performance.

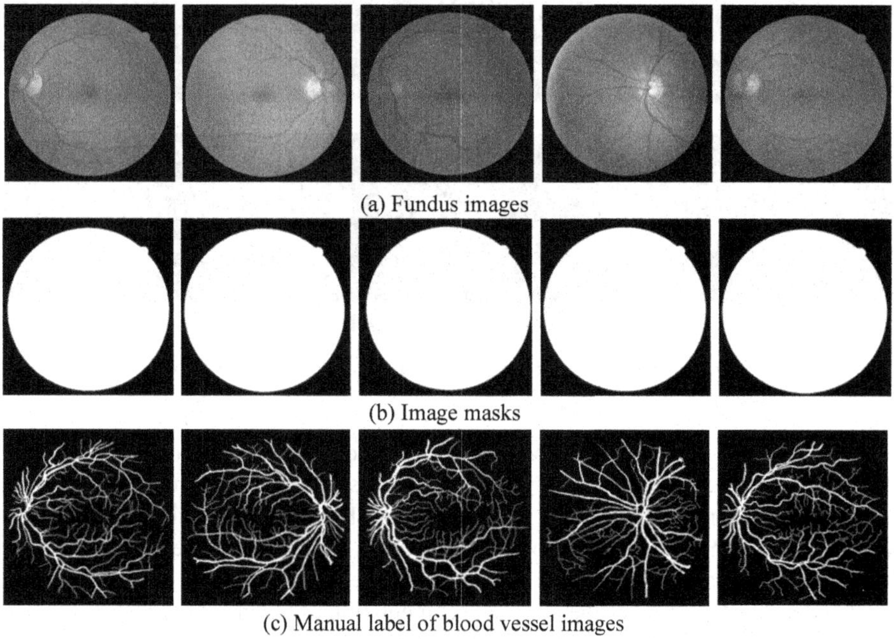

Fig. 8. Some images of the DRIVE dataset

4.3 Experimental Setting

The proposed DU-Net model uses PyCharm as Integrated Development Environment (IDE) and is implemented by using the deep learning framework named PyTorch. The PC machine runs on the Windows 10 operating system with Intel(R) CoreTM i7-7700 CPU@3.6 GHz, RAM 16 GB, and GPU Nvidia GeForce GTX 1080.

4.4 Experimental Results

Firstly, to visually demonstrate the excellent performance of the proposed DU-Net model for fundus retinal vessel segmentation, the obtained segmentation results of partial images on the test set are illustrated in Fig. 10.

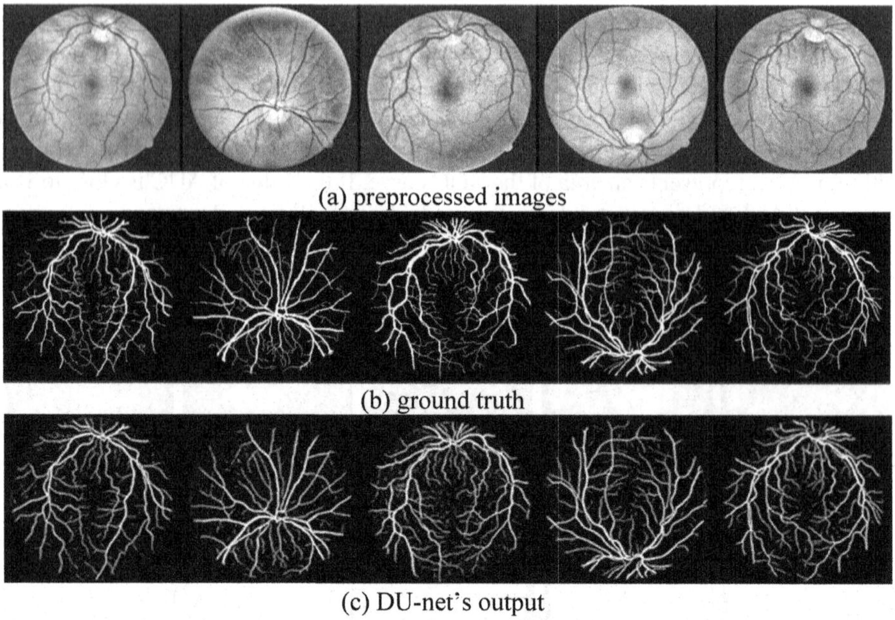

Fig. 9. The visualization results of the proposed DU-Net model

As we can see in Fig. 9, the proposed DU-Net model not only can accurately segment the thicker blood vessels, but also guarantees high segmentation accuracy for delicate blood vessels. Moreover, it does not missegment the obvious non-vascular structures such as the optic disc and optic cup into blood vessels in the retinal image. The experiment results indicate that the segmentation accuracy of the proposed model is relatively high.

Then, to further indicate the accurate segmentation of the proposed DU-Net in fundus retinal images, we test the image patches with blood vessels and without blood vessel structures. And the segmentation results of these image patches are displayed in Fig. 10, the presented DU-Net model can accurately segment blood vessels and effectively distinguish vascular from non-vascular structures.

Finally, the comparison results of the proposed DU-Net model and the other state-of-the-art methods are listed in Table 1. The literature [29] used a set of B-COSFIRE filters to select blood vessels and blood vessel ends. The literature [30] regarded the segmentation task as a multi-label problem, and it combined Gaussian matching filters and U-Net to generate a vessel segmentation framework. The literature [31] combined modified morphology and Otsu to design an unsupervised segmentation algorithm. The literature [32] suggested a retinal vessel segmentation method via the multiscale Gaussian filtering and phase stretch transform (PST). The literature [33] proposed an R2U-Net method, which used cyclic residual blocks instead of convolutional blocks in each layer of the encoding stage. The literature [34] presented a new segmentation loss function, which integrated the segmentation level and pixel-level weights to balance the loss share of coarse and fine vessels.

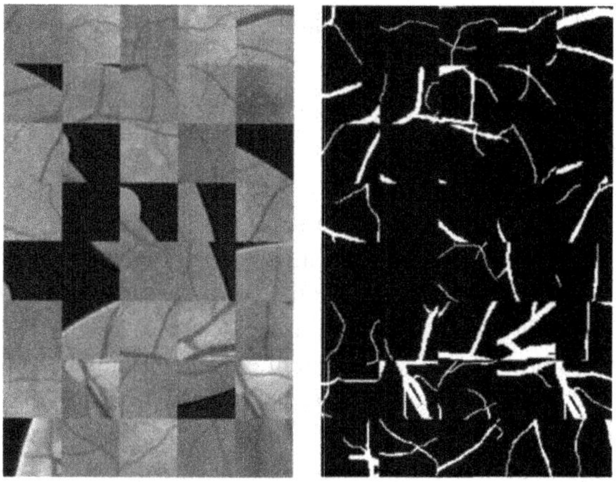

Fig. 10. The segmentation results of the image patches of the proposed DU-Net model

Table 1. Performance comparison of different models on the DRIVE dataset

Method	Sen	Spe	Acc	AUC
U-Net [22]	0.7537	0.9820	0.9531	0.9755
B-COSFIRE [29]	0.7731	0.9724	0.9467	0.9588
GU-Net [30]	0.7802	0.9876	0.9636	**0.9772**
Otsu [31]	0.5686	**0.9926**	0.9382	------
PST-MSGF [32]	0.7410	0.9894	0.9502	------
R2U-Net [33]	0.7799	0.9813	0.9556	0.9784
Yan et. al. [34]	0.7653	0.9818	0.9542	0.9752
DU-Net	**0.7822**	0.9841	**0.9651**	0.9739

Seeing from the Table 1, we can summarize as:

(1) Since these methods of [29] and [30] are unsupervised methods, the performances are lower than the other compared methods. The experiment results prove that introducing the label information to the procedure of training can improve the segmentation performance.
(2) The evaluation indicators of U-Net based methods (i.e., GU-Net [30], R2U-Net [33], and DU-Net) are better than that of the traditional U-Net method in most cases, which demonstrates that combining the dense block or residual blocks with the traditional U-Net network can strengthen feature reuse and alleviate the problem of gradient disappearance.
(3) Although the Specificity (Spe) value is inferior to Otsu [31], GU-Net [30], and PST-MSGF [32], and AUC values are only superior to B-COSFIRE [29]. The Accuracy (Acc) and Sensitive (Sen) values of the proposed DU-Net model outperform the

other compared algorithms. The phenomenon reflects that DU-Net can segment more delicate vessels and increase the sensitivity of vessel segmentation.

5 Conclusions

Automatic segmentation of retinal blood vessels is a significant procedure for preventing and treating ocular diseases. This paper designs an original framework to overcome the disadvantages of existing deep learning methods for segmenting retinal blood vessels. In the proposed framework, a series of pre-processes are performed on the fundus retinal images. Then, we propose a DU-Net architecture to segment retinal blood vessels by incorporating the advantages of the DenseNet and U-Net network. Since DU-Net integrates the dense-block, it not only can enhance the feature reuse and reduce the number of parameters, but also contributes to the improvement of sensitivity. However, the proposed model still suffers some limitations for the extremely thin vessels in some fundus images, which will be further studied to improve the segmentation accuracy for thin blood vessels in future work.

Acknowledgment. This work is supported in part by grants from the National Natural Science Foundation of China (No. 62062040), the Outstanding Youth Project of Jiangxi Natural Science Foundation (No. 20212ACB212003), the Jiangxi Province Key Subject Academic and Technical Leader Funding Project (No. 20212BCJ23017).

References

1. Pathan, S., Kumar, P., Pai, R.M., et al.: Automated segmentation and classifcation of retinal features for glaucoma diagnosis. Biomed. Signal Process. Control **63**, 102244 (2021)
2. Jin, Q., Meng, Z., Pham, T.D., et al.: DUNet: a deformable network for retinal vessel segmentation. Knowl.-Based Syst. **178**, 149–162 (2019)
3. Salamat, N., Missen, M.M.S., Rashid, A.: Diabetic retinopathy techniques in retinal images: a review. Artif. Intell. Med. **97**, 168–188 (2019)
4. Badar, M., Haris, M., Fatima, A.: Application of deep learning for retinal image analysis: a review. Comput. Sci. Rev. **35**, 100203 (2020)
5. Wang, S., Ouyang, X., Liuang, T., et al.: Follow my eye: using gaze to supervise computer-aided diagnosis. IEEE Trans. Med. Imaging (2022). https://doi.org/10.1109/TMI.2022.3146973
6. Chaudhuri, S., Chatterjee, S., Katz, N., et al.: Detection of blood vessels in retinal images using two-dimensional matched filters. IEEE Trans. Med. Imaging **8**(3), 263–269 (1989)
7. Rodrigues, L.C., Marengoni, M.: Segmentation of optic disc and blood vessels in retinal images using wavelets, mathematical morphology and Hessian-based multi-scale filtering. Biomed. Signal Process. Control **36**, 39–49 (2017)
8. Imani, E., Javidi, M., Pourreza, H.R.: Improvement of retinal blood vessel detection using morphological component analysis. Comput. Methods Programs Biomed. **118**(3), 263–279 (2015)
9. Singh, N.P., Srivastava, R.: Retinal blood vessels segmentation by using Gumbel probability distribution function based matched filter. Comput. Methods Programs Biomed. **129**, 40–50 (2016)

10. Ramani, G., Menakadevi, T.: Detection of diabetic retinopathy using discrete wavelet transform with discrete Meyer in retinal images. J. Med. Imaging Health Infor. **12**(1), 62–67 (2022)
11. Ramos-Soto, O., Rodriguez-Esparza, E., Balderas-Mata, S.E., et al.: An efficient retinal blood vessel segmentation in eye fundus images by using optimized top-hat and homomorphic filtering. Comput. Methods Programs Biomed. **201**, 105949 (2021)
12. Haq, I.U., Nagoaka, R., Makino, T., et al.: 3D Gabor wavelet based vessel filtering of photoacoustic images. In: 2016 38th Annual International Conference of the IEEE Engineering in Medicine and Biology Society (EMBC), pp. 3883–3886. IEEE (2016)
13. Zhao, Y., Xie, J., Pan, S., Zheng, Y., Liu, Y., Cheng, J., Liu, J.: Retinal artery and vein classification via dominant sets clustering-based vascular topology estimation. In: Frangi, A.F., Schnabel, J.A., Davatzikos, C., Alberola-López, C., Fichtinger, G. (eds.) MICCAI 2018. LNCS, vol. 11071, pp. 56–64. Springer, Cham (2018). https://doi.org/10.1007/978-3-030-00934-2_7
14. Balasubramanian, K., Ananthamoorthy, N.P.: Robust retinal blood vessel segmentation using convolutional neural network and support vector machine. J. Ambient. Intell. Humaniz. Comput. **12**(3), 3559–3569 (2019). https://doi.org/10.1007/s12652-019-01559-w
15. Preethy Rebecca, P., Allwin, S.: Detection of DR from retinal fundus images using prediction ANN classifier and RG based threshold segmentation for diabetes. J. Ambient. Intell. Humaniz. Comput. **12**(12), 10733–10740 (2021). https://doi.org/10.1007/s12652-020-02882-3
16. Staal, J., Abramoff, M.D., Niemeijer, M., et al.: Ridge-based vessel segmentation in color images of the retina. IEEE Trans. Med. Imaging **23**(4), 501–5091 (2004)
17. Soares, J.V.B., Leandro, J.J.G., Cesar, R.M., et al.: Retinal vessel segmentation using the 2-D Gabor wavelet and supervised classification. IEEE Trans. Med. Imaging **25**(9), 1214–1222 (2006)
18. Ricci, E., Perfetti, R.: Retinal blood vessel segmentation using line operators and support vector classification. IEEE Trans. Med. Imaging **26**(10), 1357–1365 (2007)
19. Fraz, M.M., Remagnino, P., Hoppe, A., et al.: An ensemble classification-based approach applied to retinal blood vessel segmentation. IEEE Trans. Biomed. Eng. **59**(9), 2538–2548 (2012)
20. Gu, J., Wang, Z., Kuen, J., et al.: Recent advances in convolutional neural networks. Pattern Recogn. **77**, 354–377 (2018)
21. Zhao, Z.Q., Zheng, P., Xu, S., et al.: Object detection with deep learning: a review. IEEE Trans. Neural Netw. Learn. Syst. **30**(11), 3212–3232 (2019)
22. Ronneberger, O., Fischer, P., Brox, T.: U-net: Convolutional networks for biomedical image segmentation. In: International Conference on Medical Image Computing and Computer-Assisted Intervention, pp. 234–241. Springer, Cham (2015)
23. Long, J., Shelhamer, E., Darrell, T.: Fully convolutional networks for semantic segmentation. In: Proceedings of the IEEE Conference on Computer Vision and Pattern Recognition, pp. 3431–3440 (2015)
24. He, K., Zhang, X., Ren, S., et al.: Deep residual learning for image recognition. In: Proceedings of the IEEE Conference on Computer Vision and Pattern Recognition, pp. 770–778 (2016)
25. Srivastava, R.K., Greff, K., Schmidhuber, J.: Highway networks. arXiv preprint arXiv:1505.00387 (2015)
26. Larsson, G., Maire, M., Shakhnarovich, G.: Fractalnet: Ultra-deep neural networks without residuals. arXiv preprint arXiv:1605.07648 (2016)
27. Huang, G., Liu, Z., Van Der Maaten, L., et al.: Densely connected convolutional networks. In: Proceedings of the IEEE Conference on Computer Vision and Pattern Recognition, pp. 4700–4708 (2017)

28. Rahman, S., Rahman, M.M., Abdullah-Al-Wadud, M., Al-Quaderi, G.D., Shoyaib, M.: An adaptive gamma correction for image enhancement. EURASIP J. Image Video Process. **2016**(1), 1–13 (2016). https://doi.org/10.1186/s13640-016-0138-1
29. Strisciuglio, N., Azzopardi, G., Vento, M., et al.: Supervised vessel delineation in retinal fundus images with the automatic selection of B-COSFIRE filters. Mach. Vis. Appl. **27**(8), 1137–1149 (2016)
30. Gao, X., Cai, Y., Qiu, C., et al.: Retinal blood vessel segmentation based on the Gaussian matched filter and U-net. In: 2017 10th International Congress on Image and Signal Processing, BioMedical Engineering and Informatics. IEEE, pp. 1–5 (2017)
31. Wang, W.H., Zhang, J.Z., Wu, W.Y.: Improved morphology combined with Otsu for retinal vessel segmentation. Comput. Appl. Res. **07**, 2228–2231 (2019)
32. Cai, Z.Z., Tang, P., Hu, J.B., et al.: Segmentation of retinal vessels based on PST and multiscale Gaussian filtering. Appl. Res. Comput. **36**(06), 1893–1896 (2019)
33. Alom, M.Z., Hasan, M., Yakopcic, C., et al.: Recurrent residual convolutional neural network based on u-net (r2u-net) for medical image segmentation. arXiv preprint arXiv:1802.06955 (2018)
34. Yan, Z., Yang, X., Cheng, K.T.: Joint segment-level and pixel-wise losses for deep learning based retinal vessel segmentation. IEEE Trans. Biomed. Eng. **65**(9), 1912–1923 (2018)

Sub-pixel Level Edge Extraction Technology for Industrial Parts for Smart Manufacturing

Bowen Zhang(✉) and Yingjie Liu

Shandong Normal University, Jinan, Shandong, China
910681156@qq.com

Abstract. With the development of science and technology, image edge detection and extraction technology, which is one of the most basic and important aspects of digital image processing, is gradually being applied to life science. Currently, image edge detection and extraction for sub-pixel lacks accuracy, which suffers from image noise such as shadow burrs or distortions. To address such challenges, in this paper, we use histogram equalization, bilinear interpolation, and progressive and least-squares fitting methods to extract the high-precision edge contour at a sub-pixel level from complex images with interference noise and aberrations in the edge contour and analyze it. Thus, we obtain a new image with uniform grayscale distribution, and no shadow interference or distortion, to extract subpixel images with higher accuracy compared with the original image using bilinear interpolation. And then we extract subpixel edge contours and obtain contour data (number of contour subpixels, contour length) by the improved Canny operator and the FindContours function of the OpenCV library. In this way, the edge information of parts can be extracted from the original fuzzy boundary in smart manufacturing.

Keywords: Subpixel · Bilinear interpolation · Canny operator

1 Introduction

The edges of a target object are significant for image recognition and computer analysis, which contain rich intrinsic information (such as orientation, step properties, and shape) and are important attributes for extracting image features in image recognition. Image edge contour extraction is a very important process in boundary segmentation and a classical problem in image processing. The purpose of both contour extraction and contour tracking is to obtain the external contour features of an image. Applying certain methods to characterize the contours when necessary to prepare the image shape analysis is significant for performing advanced processing such as feature description, recognition, and understanding.

Subpixels are virtual pixels defined between two physical pixels of the image acquisition sensor and image sub-pixel edge extraction is a more accurate method than traditional pixel edge extraction. If the accuracy is increased to 0.1 pixels using the subpixel technique, it is equivalent to 10 times higher resolution for image system analysis, which

Y. Xu et al. (Eds.): ML4CS 2022, LNCS 13657, pp. 469–483, 2023.
https://doi.org/10.1007/978-3-031-20102-8_36

meets the increasing measurement accuracy required by technological developments for various workpieces and parts.

Existing methods for extracting edge contours of sub-pixel precision images suffer from the following problems:

Image Noise. Images are often affected by different types of noise during acquisition, storage, and transmission. Even data sets collected by various image acquisition devices are contaminated with noise. Image noise, i.e., common burr shadows, etc., can interfere with the extraction of image edge contours, which is unpredictable.

Image Distortion. Deviations in the lens manufacturing accuracy as well as in the assembly process can introduce image distortions that cause distortion in the original image and interfere with the accuracy of the analysis of image edge data.

Holistic Analysis. Current edge detection algorithms such as Sobel and canny can detect image edge pixel boundaries based on the difference in image gray values, but cannot analyze the contours as a whole.

Therefore, we will address this problem in this paper: *how to break the above problems one by one, integrate and apply them, extract sub-pixel image contour edges and analyze them as a whole without noise and distortion interference?*

We study the principle of image noise and distortion and minimize the interference of uncertainties to the image by methods such as histogram equalization algorithm or distortion correction. Based on this, we extract sub-pixel images with 1/16 accuracy and analyze the image edge contour extraction using the linear interpolation method. The specific process is as follows.

- For image noise, the three images are deburred in turn using functions such as MATLAB's Fspecial and Imfilter. Also considering that some images are taken under complex lighting conditions with more interference information, they are processed separately by histogram equalization algorithm and hole-filling expansion operation to get new images with uniform grayscale distribution and no shadow interference.
- For image distortion, we processed the three calibration plate images with MATLAB to obtain the camera's internal reference matrix and distortion coefficients. The undistort function of the OpenCV library is used to correct the image distortion to obtain the new images.
- Using the bilinear interpolation algorithm [1], the width and height of each pixel point of the three images were enlarged by 4 times the original, i.e., the images were enlarged by 16 times, thus extracting sub-pixel images with 1/16 accuracy relative to the original images.

2 Preliminary

2.1 Assumptions

To eliminate some unnecessary factor interference, we made assumptions about the equipment and various image data used in the experimental process.

- Assume that all the circles of the calibration plate are symmetric circles and all the symmetric circles are equally spaced and of the same size.
- Assume that the edge contour of the given original image is determined and there is no dichotomy.
- Assume that there are no external factors influencing when taking photos of product parts, and the given images are all valid.
- Assume that the image plane in the geometry is a continuous surface, i.e., each pixel point no longer has an actual size except for the indicated coordinates

2.2 Description of Symbols

This article uses a large number of computer-specific symbols, flags, acronyms, specialized units of measurement, custom nouns and terms, etc., so we have written a compilation table of notes to help readers better understand the content of the article (Table 1).

Table 1. Description of symbols

Symbols	Definition
k	Gaussian function kernel vector
$P_{[i,j]}$	The first-order partial derivative matrix in the x-direction
$Q_{[i,j]}$	The first-order partial derivative matrix in the Y-direction
$M_{[i,j]}$	Gradient amplitude
$\theta_{[i,j]}$	Gradient direction
$S_x(S_y)$	The convolution operator in the x(y) direction
$x_{corrected}$	Radial factor in the x-direction
$y_{corrected}$	Radial factor in the y-direction
f_x, f_y	Camera focal length
(c_x, c_y)	Optical Center
$Distortion_{coefficients}$	The convolution operator in the x(y) direction
C	Calibration plate symmetry circumference

3 Methodology

3.1 Image Pre-processing

To extract sub-pixel edge contours with an accuracy of 1/16 and above, first, it is necessary to eliminate edge burr, shadow, and interference from complex light as well as image distortion generated during camera imaging. For the edge burr and shadow interference, they are eliminated by MATLAB's Fspecial function and Imfilter function; for images under complex light, they are first processed by the histogram equalization algorithm of the MATLAB toolbox, and then filled with holes and expanded to get a new image without interference. For images with distortion, the MATLAB processing calibration plate is used to obtain the camera's internal reference matrix and distortion coefficient. Based on this, the undistort function of the OpenCV library is used to correct the distortion of the images to obtain the new images.

Eliminate Edge Burrs and Shadows. For an image with burrs and shadow interference, it is converted to a grayscale image and then to a binary image. The Fspecial function is then called to generate the filter template, and the Gaussian low-pass filter gaussian, the standard deviation of the filter sigma is used for the operation. Then, the image is denoised by using the Imfilter function to realize the convolution of a 3-channel RGB image and a single-channel filter and return the 3-channel image. After that, the binary image is subjected to ossification, which extracts the skeleton but keeps the objects in the image unbroken and does not change the image Euler number. Finally, the deburring operation of the original image is completed by removing small branches.

For images with complex light interference, the original image is transformed by the Hist function of MATLAB. Since the gray levels are integers between 1 and 256, the expanded gray levels are rounded to obtain a matrix of size 1*256, which represents the gray levels before expansion. The value of the corresponding element of each level is the value of the gray level after the expansion of the gray level, and finally, a new image with uniform distribution of the gray histogram is obtained.

After that, to obtain a new image without shadow interference, image morphology processing erosion and expansion [2] are performed on the image (Fig. 1).

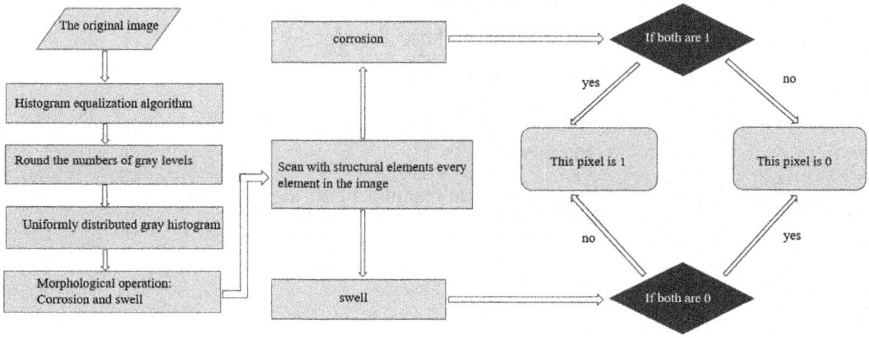

Fig. 1. Removal of light interference operation process

Image Distortion Correction. In practice, the camera in the imaging often produces a variety of problems, such as radial aberration and tangential distortion [3], which makes people see the image appears "stretched" or "distorted" intuition. To ensure accuracy, it is necessary to restore the image as much as possible, i.e., to correct the image distortion.

To achieve image correction and get a relatively small distortion image, it is necessary to first complete the calibration with MATLAB, get the camera's internal reference matrix and distortion coefficient, and then use the OpenCV library's correction function. After considering the effect of the combination of the undistort function of the OpenCV library with InitUndistortRectifyMap and remap functions, we chose the undistort function [4].

Camera Parameters Calibration. In the process of aberration correction, we need to care about the camera parameters for the internal reference matrix and aberration coefficients. Calibration will have five aberration coefficients change, including three radial aberrations (k_1, k_2, k_3) and two tangential aberrations (p_1, p_2), where k_1, k_2 and k_3 is the radial aberration coefficient, r is the radial distance from the center of the image to the pixel point. The relationship between the aberrations and the parameters is as follows.

Radial distortion:

$$x_{corrected} = x\left(1 + k_1r^2 + k_2r^4 + k_3r^6\right) \tag{1}$$

$$y_{corrected} = y\left(1 + k_1r^2 + k_2r^4 + k_3r^6\right) \tag{2}$$

Tangential distortion:

$$x_{corrected} = x + \left[2p_1xy + p_2\left(r^2 + 2x^2\right)\right] \tag{4}$$

$$y_{corrected} = y + \left[p_1\left(r^2 + 2y^2\right) + 2p_2xy\right] \tag{5}$$

Experiments show that due to the higher power distance nonlinearity corresponding k_3 is more drastic and prone to great distortion if the model is not well estimated, so we use two parameters in Matlab, set k_3 to 1, and choose miscut and barrel distortion to enhance the robustness of the model.

The final training of the three given calibration plate image information yielded the camera's internal reference matrix as follows:

$$\text{Ans} = \begin{matrix} 2.7077 \times 10^4 & 0 & 0 \\ 0.0117 \times 10^4 & 2.7116 \times 10^4 & 0 \\ 0.1706 \times 10^4 & -0.023 \times 10^4 & 0.0001 \times 10^4 \end{matrix}$$

And it yielded the distortion coefficients as follows (Table 2):

Calibration Analysis. With the known internal reference matrix and distortion coefficients, we correct the distortion of the given image by the undistort function of the OpenCV library [5] (Fig. 2).

Table 2. DistCoeffs.

Coefficient	Numeric
k_1	−0.10875063
k_2	−0.1550688
k_3	−0.00261486
k_4	−0.001547705
k_5	0

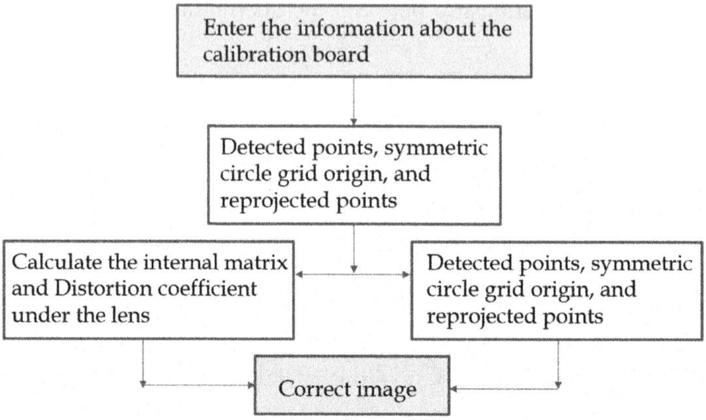

Fig. 2. Calibration analysis process

The internal reference matrix obtained from MATLAB is transposed with OpenCV, and for the unit conversion we use the following formula:

$$\begin{bmatrix} x \\ y \\ z \end{bmatrix} = \begin{bmatrix} f_x & 0 & c_x \\ 0 & f_y & c_y \\ 0 & 0 & 1 \end{bmatrix} \begin{bmatrix} X \\ Y \\ Z \end{bmatrix} \tag{6}$$

The presence of w here is interpreted by the unit coordinate system. The unknown parameters f_x,f_y are the camera focal lengths, and (c_x, c_y) is the optical center represented by the pixel coordinates. If the two axes use α common focal length with an aspect ratio, then

$$f_y = f_x * \alpha \tag{7}$$

Aspect ratio is the relative length of the data unit of the coordinate axis, where α is usually equal to 1.

The five distortion coefficients are also represented in OpenCV as a 5-column row matrix:

$$Distortion_{coefficients} = \begin{bmatrix} k_1 \; k_2 \; p_1 \; p_2 \; k_3 \end{bmatrix} \tag{8}$$

Therefore, for the old pixel point at the coordinates in the (x, y) input image, its position on the output image after the correction of Eq. 6, Eq. 7 and Eq. 8 will be: $(x_{corrected}, y_{corrected})$.

3.2 Improving Image Accuracy and Extracting Edge Contours

A bilinear interpolation algorithm is used to extract subpixel images, and then an improved Canny operator is used to detect the edge contours of the images. Since the image height and width are enlarged equally after bilinear interpolation, the horizontal and vertical coordinates are artificially reduced separately in the program to obtain the X and Y coordinate data of each pixel point on each contour relative to the original image. Finally, the extracted contour data are output as the corresponding color edge contour images using the DrawContours function in the OpenCV library to observe the overall relationship of the contours more intuitively.

Bilinear Interpolation Method to Improve Image Resolution. The bilinear interpolation method, also known as quadratic linear interpolation, means that one linear interpolation is performed in each of the two directions. The core idea of the algorithm is to calculate the floating-point coordinate pixel value using the four pixels around the target pixel point.

The bilinear interpolation is calculated in two directions respectively a total of 3 times single linear interpolation, first in the x-direction for 2 times single linear interpolation to obtain two temporary points $R_1(x, y_1)$, $R_2(, y_2)$, and then in the y-direction for 1-time single linear interpolation to obtain $P(x, y)$.

Regarding the single linear interpolation in the x-direction, the final equation of the single linear interpolation in the previous step is directly brought in;

$$f(R1) = \frac{x_2 - x}{x_2 - x_1} f(Q_{11}) + \frac{x - x_1}{x_2 - x_1} f(Q_{21}) \tag{9}$$

$$f(R2) = \frac{x_2 - x}{x_2 - x_1} f(Q_{12}) + \frac{x - x_1}{x_2 - x_1} f(Q_{22}) \tag{10}$$

Regarding the monoclinic difference in the y-direction:

$$f(P) = \frac{y_2 - y}{y_2 - y_1} f(R_1) + \frac{y - y_1}{y_2 - y_1} f(R_2) \tag{11}$$

Substitute the result of the first step into the second step.

$$\begin{aligned} f(x, y) = & \frac{f(Q_{11})}{(x_2-x_1)(y_2-y_1)}(x_2 - x)(y_2 - y) + \frac{f(Q_{21})}{(x_2-x_1)(y_2-y_1)}(x - x_1)(y_2 - y) \\ & + \frac{f(Q_{12})}{(x_2-x_1)(y_2-y_1)}(x_2 - x)(y - y_1) + \frac{f(Q_{22})}{(x_2-x_1)(y_2-y_1)}(x - x_1)(y - y_1) \end{aligned} \tag{12}$$

To summarize, it can be seen that there is this relationship in the calculation: $x_2 = x_1 + 1, y_2 = y_1 + 1$.

Then the denominators in the above equation are all 0, as follows

$$\begin{aligned} f(x,y) = & f(Q_{11})(x_2 - x)(y_2 - y) + f(Q_{21})(x - x_1)(y_2 - y) \\ & + f(Q_{12})(x_2 - x)(y - y_1) + f(Q_{22})(x - x_1)(y - y_1) \end{aligned} \tag{13}$$

That is the value of the target point is obtained:

$$f(x,y) = f(Q_{11})\omega_{11} + f(Q_{21})\omega_{21} + f(Q_{12})\omega_{12} + f(Q_{22})\omega_{22} \tag{14}$$

A subpixel is a subdivision of the basic unit of the pixel, thus increasing the image resolution. Typically, subpixel edge points exist in areas of the image where excessive changes occur gradually.

Improved Canny Operator to Detect Subpixels. The edges of an image are a set of pixels that change step or roof in pixel grayscales at the image location (Fig. 3).

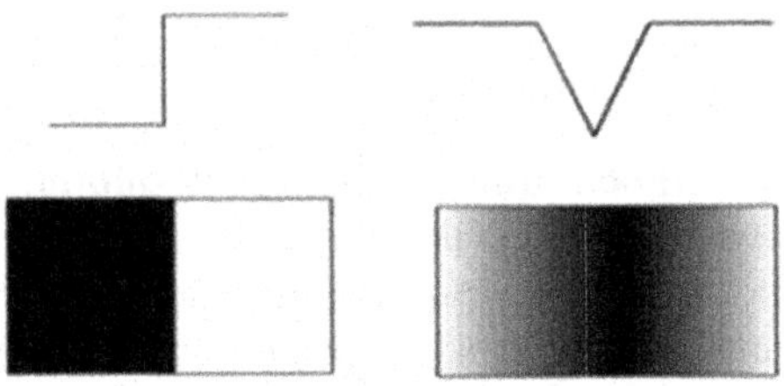

Fig. 3. Step-like and roof-like.

The basic idea of image edge detection is to calculate the local differential operator of an image based on the apparent change in pixel grayscale at the edge location of the image.

The algorithm used by the Canny operator to determine the edges of an image is as follows:

Algorithm 1 Canny operator edge detection

```
Input cv2                                                #cv2 is the original image
Output Image edge
IMG = cv2.imread('zxp.jpg')
lenna_img = cv2.cvtColor(IMG, cv2.COLOR_BGR2RGB)
gray image = cv2.cvtColor(IMG, cv2.COLOR_BGR2GRAY)
gaussian = cv2.GaussianBlur(gray image, (5, 5), 0)
Canny = cv2.Canny(gaussian, 50, 150)                     #Canny operator
plt.rcParams['font.sans-serif'] = ['SimHei']
titles = [u'original image', uncanny operator']
images = [lenna_img, Canny]
for i in range(2) do
        plt.subplot(1, 2, i + 1), plt.imshow(images[i], 'gray')
      plt.title(titles[i])
      plt.xticks([]), plt.yticks([])
end for
return Image edge                                        # Displays the image edge
```

First, Gaussian filtering is applied to the image. A discrete Gaussian function is used to generate a set of normalized Gaussian kernels to effectively filter the high-frequency noise superimposed in the ideal image, and then a weighted summation is applied to each point of the image grayscale matrix based on the Gaussian kernel function.

The following is the discrete 1D Gaussian function, and the 1D kernel vector can be obtained by determining the parameters:

$$K = \frac{1}{\sqrt{2\pi}\sigma} e^{-\frac{x^2}{2\sigma^2}} \tag{17}$$

The following is the discretized two-dimensional Gaussian function, and the two-dimensional kernel vector can be obtained by determining the parameters:

$$K = \frac{1}{2\pi\sigma * \sigma} e^{-\frac{x^2+y^2}{2\sigma^2}} \tag{18}$$

A finite difference with first-order partial derivatives is used to calculate the magnitude and direction of the gradient. The image gray value gradient can be approximated using first-order finite differences so that two matrices of the image partial derivatives in the x and y directions can be obtained. The calculation is as follows:

The formula for calculating the gradient amplitude is:

$$|\nabla f(x, y)| = \sqrt{\nabla_x^2 f + \nabla_y^2 f} \tag{19}$$

The gradient direction is calculated as:

$$\Theta(x, y) = \arctan \frac{\nabla_y f}{\nabla_x f} \tag{20}$$

The convolution operators used in the x and y directions are as follows:

$$s_x = \begin{bmatrix} -1 & 1 \\ -1 & 1 \end{bmatrix}, s_y = \begin{bmatrix} 1 & 1 \\ -1 & -1 \end{bmatrix} \tag{21}$$

Finally, the first-order partial derivative matrix in the x- and y-directions, the gradient amplitude and the gradient direction are given by:

$$P[i,j] = \frac{\begin{pmatrix} f[i,j+1] - f[i,j] + \\ f[i+1,j+1] - f[i+1,j] \end{pmatrix}}{2} \tag{22}$$

$$Q[i,j] = \frac{\begin{pmatrix} f[i,j] - f[i+1,j] + \\ f[i,j+1] - f[i+1,j+1] \end{pmatrix}}{2} \tag{23}$$

$$M[i,j] = \sqrt{P[i,j]^2 + Q[i,j]^2} \tag{24}$$

$$\theta[i,j] = \arctan(\frac{Q[i,j]}{P[i,j]}) \tag{25}$$

After getting the global gradient, the maximum local gradient value pixel points need to be filtered out by suppressing the non-extreme value, and the gray value corresponding to the non-extreme value points is set to 0. This can eliminate a large part of the non-edge ones, so that the image edges can be initially extracted.

Canny's non-maximal value suppression. The first step is to determine the direction of the gradient: as shown in Figure x below, X is the pixel point to be discussed, and each quarter-circle of the gradient vector is divided into two cases by the 45° line, one tends to be horizontal and the other tends to be vertical, with a total of 8 directions, but due to the existence of Centro symmetry, the directions corresponding to 1 and 5 are the same, so we only consider 4 of them for non-maximal suppression. T (Fig. 4)

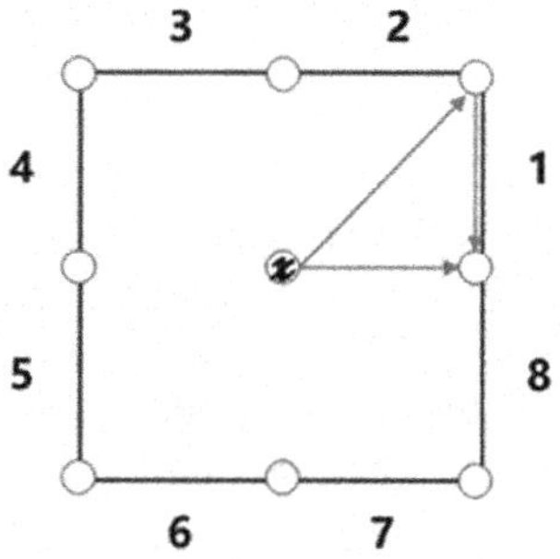

Fig. 4. Linear interpolation interval to determine the gradient direction

The next step is to perform the linear interpolation. If the gradient extremes are not on the pixel points, but at a point between them, i.e. sub-pixel points the calculation needs to be linearly interpolated. Take the interval in direction 1 below as an example, the gradient value of the red point is calculated from the gradient values of the green and yellow points. As for which point the red point is closest to, it needs to be calculated.

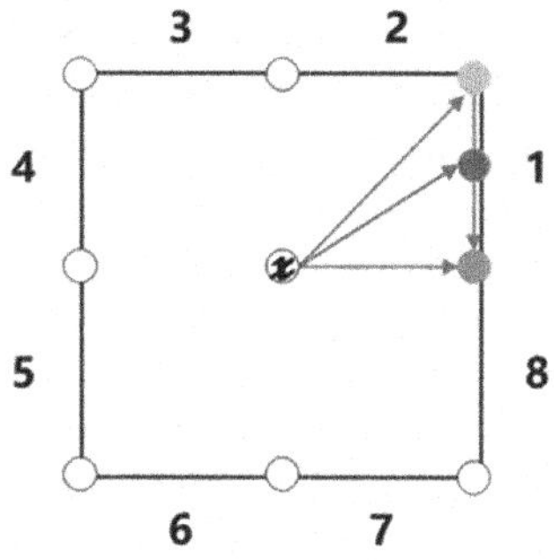

Fig. 5. Linear interpolation interval

The distance between the yellow point and the green point, which we name as the weight d (Fig. 5).

The gradient value of the red point in the interval $d = \frac{i_y}{i_x}$, in direction 1:

$$mag1 = mag(i_x + m) * (1 - d) + mag(i_x + m - 1) * d \tag{26}$$

Finally, the non-maximal suppression is accomplished by using the maximal points with pixel values larger than the low threshold as weak edges.

The Canny algorithm reduces the number of false edges by double thresholding method, using two thresholds selected, θ_1 andθ_2, generally, the high threshold is 2 to 3 times the low threshold, and an edge image is obtained according to the high threshold so that an image contains few false edges. Iterate through the whole gray matrix, if the gradient of a point is higher than the high threshold, set 1 in the result, if the gradient value of the point is lower than the low threshold, set 0 in the result, if the gradient value of the point is between the high and low threshold, the following judgment is needed: check the 8 neighboring points of the point (consider it as the center point) to see if there is a point with gradient value higher than the high threshold if it exists, it means that the center point and the determined edge point connected, so set 1 in the result, otherwise set 0 until the whole image edge is closed.

3.3 Sub-pixel Edge Profile Data Analysis

Based on the completion of sub-pixel edge contour extraction and the known calibration plate data, the number of sub-pixel points contained in the edge contour and the number of pixels in the symmetric circle contour of the calibration plate are obtained using the FindContours function of the OpenCV library.

The ratio of the number of pixels is the length ratio of the contour, which means that there is a correlation between the contour length and the symmetric circle circumference of the calibration plate, and this correlation means that the ratio of the number of pixels of both is equal to the ratio of the length of both, which can be expressed as:

$$\frac{C}{C_i} = \frac{N}{n_i} = \frac{1}{\lambda_i} \tag{27}$$

where λ_i is the scaling factor between c_i and c, C is the perimeter of the symmetric circle of the calibration plate; C_i is the physical length of the ith edge contour; N denotes the number of pixel points contained in the symmetric circle contour, and n_i is the number of pixel points in the ith contour.

So Eq. 26 is the required proportional relationship between the edge contour and the circumference of the symmetry circle.

After the distortion correction of the image, the new image obtained has a small error with the actual size of the object. On this basis, the number of pixel points per contour can be calculated using the FindContours function of the OpenCV library. The length of the circle and the number of pixels in the calibration plate image are certain values, and thus the length of each edge contour can be determined using the known symmetric garden perimeter of the calibration plate. It is difficult to calculate the pixel points of a certain symmetric circle edge contour of the calibration plate, so we calculated the number of pixel points of the contour of 22 × 17 symmetric circles in the image of the calibration plate.

$$N = \frac{1}{n}\sum\nolimits_{1}^{n} N_i \tag{28}$$

where N denotes the final number of pixel points of the symmetric circle edge contour. To obtain the length of each contour it is also necessary to calculate the data of the perimeter of the symmetric circle using the data of the calibration plate, i.e., the diameter of each symmetric circled is 1 mm.

$$\mathrm{C} = \prod d \tag{29}$$

So in the contour length, the actual physical length C_i is obtained by substituting the number of pixel points n_i for each edge contour in turn into Eq. 27.

4 Experiment

4.1 Datasets

We used two sets of images to complete this experiment.

One set of images is a representative set of images containing image noise that we selected to test the effectiveness of the image noise removal technique used in this thesis and the results of subpixel edge contour extraction. To show the overall relationship of the extracted edge contours more intuitively, the content of the images was chosen to be relatively simple.

Another set of images contains three images of the calibration plate at different angles and one image of the product. The diameter of the dots on the calibration plate is 1mm and the center distance between the two dots is 2 mm. This set of images is used to check the effect of image distortion correction, further extract edge contours from the product image, and analyze the number of pixel dots and the length of the contours of each contour.

4.2 Experimental Details

For the edge burr and shadow of Pic1_1 and Pic1_2, interference is operated by MATLAB's Fspecial function and Imfilter function.

The following figure shows the comparison between the original image and after the deburring operation, it can be seen that the effect of the processing is very obvious and the purpose of pre-processing is achieved (Fig. 6).

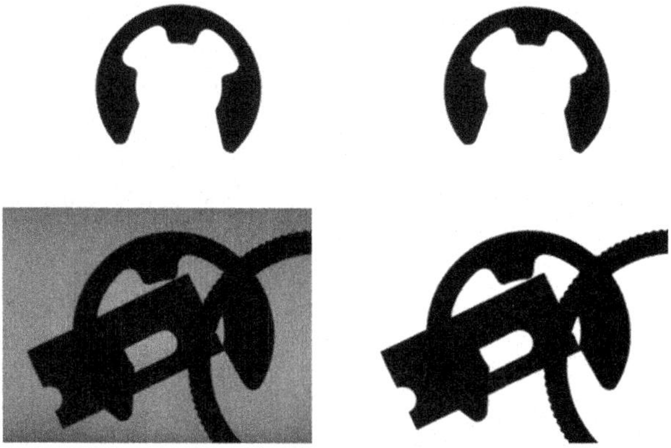

Fig. 6. Comparison of the original image and deburred image

For the complex light interference of this, the histogram equalization algorithm of MATLAB toolbox is used to process it, and the original image is transformed by Hist function to obtain a new image with uniform distribution of gray histogram, and further image morphology processing erosion and expansion is applied to the image to eliminate shadow interference.

The following figure shows the comparison between the original image and the processed light, which shows that the effect of the processing is very obvious and achieves the purpose of pre-processing (Fig. 7).

Fig. 7. Comparison of the original image and adjusted brightness

To perform aberration correction for the product images, the three calibration plate images are first processed in MATLAB to calculate and obtain the camera's internal reference matrix and aberration coefficients. After that, the undistort function of the OpenCV library is used to correct the image distortion to get the new image (Fig. 8).

Fig. 8. New image after distortion correction

4.3 Results and Analysis

After linear interpolation of the above two sets of pre-processed images to improve the accuracy (to 1/16 accuracy in this experiment), the sub-pixel edge contours were extracted and the contour data were obtained by the improved Canny operator and the FindContours function of the OpenCV library. To observe the edge relationship of the first set of images more visually, the extracted edge contours are drawn on the images in different colors using the DrawContours function of the OpenCV library, and the output is a color edge contour image (Fig. 9).

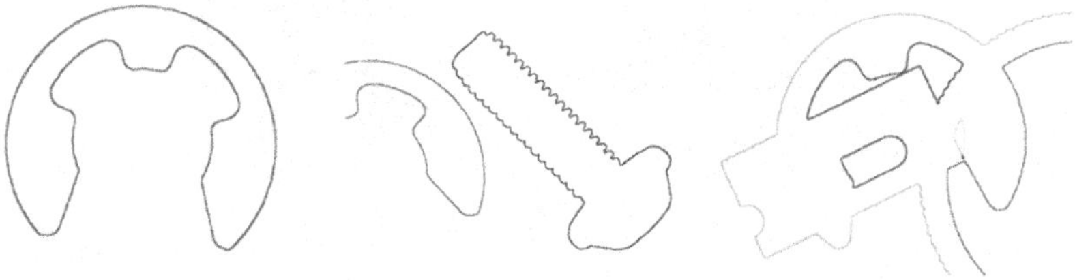

Fig. 9. Extracted edge contour map

And the length of each contour is calculated using the correlation that exists between the length of each contour of the product image in the second set of images and the length of the symmetric circle circumference of the calibration plate, i.e., the ratio of the number of pixels of both is equal to the ratio of the length of both.

High Signal-to-Noise Ratio. This criterion indicates that a good detection effect should have a high signal-to-noise ratio, the edges of the image should be detected realistically, and the non-edge parts of the image should not be detected as edges. We use a signal-to-noise ratio (SNR) as a more objective criterion, but the larger the value of the parameter, the better.

$$SNR(f) = \frac{\left|\int_{-W}^{W} G(-x)f(x)dx\right|}{\delta\sqrt{\int_{-W}^{W} f^2(x)dx}} \tag{30}$$

$G(x)$ in the formula is used to express the edge function of the image, $f(x)$ is used to denote the smoothing operation used in the filter function, and δ is used to represent the mean squared difference of the noise in the image.

Control the Accuracy of the Edge Detection. This is the basic requirement of the edge detection algorithm. The detection accuracy directly reflects the goodness of an algorithm, and the larger the evaluation parameter Location, the better.

$$Location = \frac{\left|\int_{-w}^{w} G'(-x)f'(x)dx\right|}{\delta\sqrt{\int_{-w}^{w} f'^{2}(x)dx}} \tag{31}$$

Reduce the Corresponding Number of Times for the Same Edge. For the detected image edges, the edge points should be detected accurately to avoid pseudo-edges. If we use the function D(f) to denote the average of the distances between the zero-crossing points of the impulse response derivatives of the detection operator, then there are:

$$D(f') = \pi\left\{\frac{\int_{-\infty}^{\infty} f'^{2}(x)dx}{\sqrt{\int_{-\infty}^{\infty} f(x)dx}}\right\}^{\frac{1}{2}} \tag{32}$$

It is tested that the method of subpixel edge contour detection and analysis in this paper can suppress the noise well and detect the overall contour, and the sensitivity of the algorithm to detect the edge pixel points is greatly improved, Analysis of the ROC curve generated by MATLAB shows that the image tends to the upper left corner, and the calculated AUC is 0.5586, which is larger than other existing experiments, indicating that the stability and accuracy of the subpixel edge contour extraction technique used in this paper are high.

5 Conclusion

In this paper, we proposed how to extract and analyze image edge contours based on sub-pixel accuracy from images in complex cases. Based on bilinear interpolation to improve the image resolution, we use grayscale processing and distortion correction to minimize the noise and distortion of the image, and then extract the edge contours by an improved Canny operator. The experimental data show that our method is robust and minimizes the influence factors such as image noise, and solves the problem of extracting accurate edge contours in complex situations.

References

1. Le, T.: Fisheye Image Correction Practice and Comparison. China University of Mining and Technology (2021)
2. Han, W., Hong, Y.: Research and implementation of binocular camera calibration based on OpenCV. Fujian Computer (2018)
3. Jiawei, Y., Bin, X., Lei, Y.: Camera distortion correction method based on opencv. Science and Technology Prospect (2015)
4. Ye, Z., Jiamei, W., Jiyong, Z., Zhiyong, Y.: An improved edge detection algorithm based on the canny operator. Electronic World (2013)
5. Ben, N.: Subpixel Edge Detection and Automatic Recognition of Geometric Features. Hefei University of Technology (2014)

USDSE: A Novel Method to Improve Service Reputation Based on Double-Side Evaluation

Jianmao Xiao[1], Jia Zeng[1], Xu Miao[2], Yuanlong Cao[1], Jing Zhao[1(✉)], and Zhiyong Feng[3]

[1] School of Software, Jiangxi Normal University, Nanchang, China
{jm_xiao,ylcao}@jxnu.edu.cn, jia_zeng_jxnu@163.com, zhaojinghaze@163.com
[2] China Unicom Software Research Institute, Beijing, China
miaox1@chinaunicom.cn
[3] College of Intelligence and Computing, Tianjin University, Tianjin, China
zyfeng@tju.edu.cn

Abstract. Fair evaluation of users is the basic guarantee for the healthy development of the service ecosystem. However, existing methods do not provide an indicator of when can get fair evaluation and how to reduce the proportion of malicious users from the root. This paper proposes a "user-service" double-side evaluation(USDSE) model to solve the problem above. Firstly, we start with getting the reputation of users by using the evaluation of service. Normal and malicious users are distinguished by their reputation. Secondly, we use the minimum number of normal users as the indicator to show when we can get fair evaluation. Finally, the revenue of employing collusive users has been analyzed to reduce the proportion of collusive users indirectly. The simulation experiments show that USDSE effectively improves the accuracy of identifying malicious users and reduces the revenue of employing collusive users.

Keywords: Evaluation of users · Evaluation of services · Reputation · Unfair rating filtering · Minimum user

1 Introduction

Evaluation of users, indicating the user's view of the service, can reflect the quality of service. Therefore, referencing evaluations from other users to decide whether to use a particular web service has become a common method. However, for fame or interest, many service providers will employ malicious collusive users to improve their reputation or reduce the reputation of their competitors [6,18], leading to the creation of certain blackmarket services [4], which will seriously damage the credibility of evaluation. Meanwhile, there are many unreasonable evaluations such as zombie users never evaluating services [2]; Some of the comments are fake and may not reflect spontaneous opinions [16]; irresponsible users

Y. Xu et al. (Eds.): ML4CS 2022, LNCS 13657, pp. 484–498, 2023.
https://doi.org/10.1007/978-3-031-20102-8_37

always give random evaluations [22]. Due to user preferences and ecosystem environmental changes, normal users may have biased judgments on the quality of services. And an online review site typically hosts millions and billions of products and ratings [19,27]. These will make it difficult for users to find high-quality services according to the evaluation. Worse still, that will lead to the loss of users, which will damage the healthy development of the service ecosystem.

Many studies consider how to remove malicious evaluations in order to improve the fairness of user evaluations [1,2,5,24] and detect fake reviews [10, 14,16,23]. However, there are some key limitations in the previous study.

- Many previous methods mainly collect the information from the evaluation of users [1,24]. However, they ignore that the service itself also has a cognitive process for the user, i.e., the evaluation of service.
- Previous studies have either ignored detecting random and malicious users [11,17] or characterized behavior malicious users too clearly [22].
- To the best of our knowledge, no indicator has been provided to show when a user can get fair evaluation [2,17]. We hope the indicator will help users to choose the service from the evaluation at a proper time.
- Existing models fail to consider analyzing the revenue of employing malicious collusive users [22,24]. The behavior of malicious users will also evolve as the detection mechanism changes.

In order to solve the problem mentioned above, a "user-service" double-side evaluation (USDSE) model that considers both users and services are proposed to improve the fairness of evaluation.

The main contributions of this work are listed as follows:

- By adding the evaluation of the service to the user, the double-side evaluation between the service and the user is established. USDSE effectively improves the accuracy of identifying malicious users compared with HMRep [22].
- USDSE considers multiple behaviors of malicious users. For example, malicious users may give random evaluations, malicious users may collude with each other, and service providers that employ malicious users may collude with each other to enhance their reputation.
- A proof has been given by using the Chernoff Bound and Bayes formula to get fair evaluation with minimum normal users. For cases where some malicious users are not detected or normal users mutate into malicious users, a solution has been given by taking the proportion of different user types as input.
- As far as we know, we are the first to make a revenue analysis after identifying malicious users. The experiment shows that USDSE can effectively reduce the revenue of employing collusive users and indirectly reduce the proportion of employing collusive users in the ecosystem.

2 USDSE Mechanism

2.1 Basic Framework

We envision a service ecosystem that can meet all user's requirements. Figure 1 shows the framework of getting fair evaluation of users. In USDSE, the service

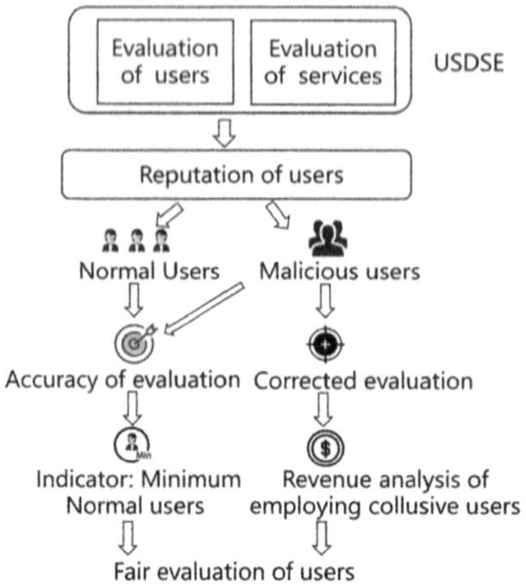

Fig. 1. Framework of getting fairness evaluation

would evaluate the user based on the user's behavior. The user's reputation will be calculated by the service's evaluation of the user. Furthermore, we divide users into normal users and malicious users by their reputation. We will take the following two steps to get fair evaluation of users.

On the one hand, by using the accuracy of normal users, we can solve the problem that how many normal users are required to get fairness evaluation when a new service enters the ecosystem. On the other hand, the USDSE model will do the revenue analysis of the service providers who employ the collusive users, and compares the revenue after establishing USDSE. Intuitively, after removing the malicious user's evaluation, the service provider's revenue from employing collusive users will be reduced.

Figure 2 shows our user-service double-side evaluation model. The model can be divided into two parts: the evaluation of users and the evaluation of service. The user will choose the service he needs. After the service is consumed, the user reports the feedback rating regarding the level that he evaluates on the service. The service that users have evaluated would also evaluate the user in USDSE.

2.2 The Evaluation of Users

The user's evaluation of the service reflects his satisfaction with the service, including both the satisfaction of the functional requirements and non-functional requirements, such as response time and availability. In this section, we will introduce users' evaluation of services in USDSE.

Definition 1: For $\forall u_i \in U$, the evaluation of u_i can be defined as a tuple:

$$E_i = (WS_i, \tau_i)$$

where WS_i is the collection of services that u_i has evaluated. WS_i $=\{ws_{i1}, ws_{i2}, ..., ws_{im}\}$, $|WS_i| = m$, m is the size of service collection; τ_i is

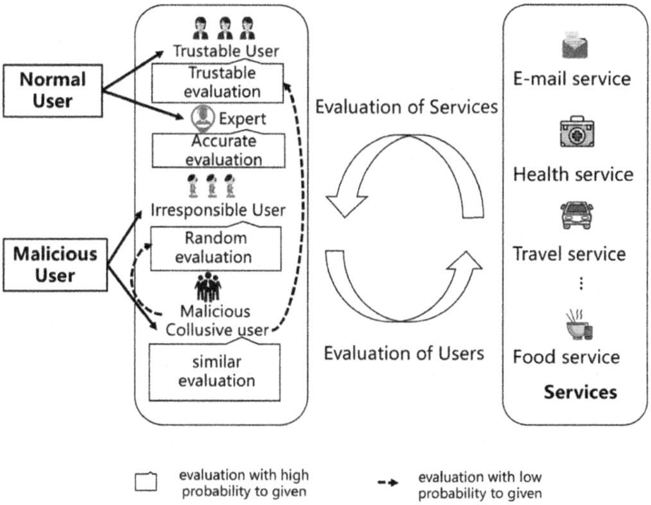

Fig. 2. Procedures of the USDSE

the function that u_i give evaluations : for $\forall ws_{ij} \in WS_i, \tau_i(ws_{ij}) = r_{ij}(r_{ij} \in [0,5], j \in [1,m])$ $r_{ij}$is the feedback rating given by u_i on service ws_{ij}.

Definition 2: Users in the system can be divided into :

$$U = \{NU, MA\}$$

$NU = \{Exp, Tu\}$ is a set of experts and trustable users. $Exp = \{ex_1, ex_2, ..., ex_p\}$, $|Exp| = p$, p is the size of experts collection, $Tu = \{tu_1, tu_2, ..., tu_q\}$, $|Tu| = q$, q is the size of trustable users collection. $MA = \{Cou, Ir\}$ is a set of collusive users and irresponsible users. $Cou = \{cou_1, cou_2, ..., cou_s\}$, $|Cou| = s$, s is the size of collusive users collection. $Ir = \{ir_1, ir_2, ..., ir_t\}$, $|Ir| = t$, t is the size of irresponsible users collection. We should notice that $p + q + s + t = n$, n is the total number of users.

Definition 3: For $\forall tu_i \in Tu$, his rating function on the service can be defined as following:

$$\tau_i(ws_{ik}) = N(\mu_k, \sigma^2)$$

$N(\mu, \sigma^2)$ is a normal distribution function, where μ_k is the true quality of ws_{ik}, σ^2 represents the user's deviation on services caused by users bias.

Definition 4: For $\forall ex_i \in Ex$, his rating function on the service can be expressed as

$$\tau_i(ws_{ik}) = \mu_k$$

Definition 5: For $\forall cou_i \in Cou$, his rating function on the service can be defined as following

$$\tau_i(ws_{ik}) = f(flag_k)$$

If $flag_k = 0$ means that ws_{ik} is the service owned by employer, then $\tau_i(ws_{ik}) = highest\ score$. If $flag_k = 1$,then $tau_i(ws_{ik}) = N(\mu_k, \sigma^2)$. It means that the collusive user will disguise as a trustable user when evaluating the current service.

Definition 6: For $\forall ir_i \in Ir$, his rating function on the service can be expressed as:

$$\tau_i(ws_{ik}) = Random(minscore, maxscore)$$

where $Random(minscore, maxscore)$ is a random function raging from minimum score to maximum score.

2.3 The Evaluation of Services

Definition 7: The service's evaluation on the user can be modeled as a tuple:

$$SE_k = (UE_k, \zeta_k)$$

where $UE_k = \{ue_{k1}, ue_{k2}, \ldots, ue_{kn}\}$ is the set of users who have evaluated the service ws_k. ζ_k is the rating function of service:for $\forall ue_{kj} \in UE_k, \zeta_k(ue_{kj}) = r_{kj}, r_{kj} \in [0, 5], j \in [1, n]$.$r_{kj}$ means that the feedback rating on ue_{kj} given by the servicews_k.

Definition 8: For service ws_k, its evaluation function on the user can be expressed as:

$$\zeta_k(ue_{kj}) = \begin{cases} top\ score - |ws_k - \tau(ws_k)|, T(ws_k) \geq \tau_j(ws_k) \\ top\ score, \\ T(ws_k) < \tau_j(ws_k) \end{cases}$$

where $\zeta_k(ue_{kj})$ is the feedback rating of u_j given by ws_k. $\tau_j(ws_k)$ is the rating given by u_j, $T(ws_k)$ is the cognitive function of the service based on its quality, and will return the true quality of the service itself. We assume that the service has a clear understanding of its own quality. If the evaluation given by the user is higher than its true quality, it will give the highest score $maxscore$ as feedback rating. If the evaluation given by the user is lower than the true quality of the service itself, the feedback ratings of the users will be determined according to the deviation between the true quality of service and the evaluation of users.

2.4 Reputation Calculation and Identification of Different Types of Users

In this section, we will introduce how to calculate the reputation of users and identity different types of users.

Definition 9: For $\forall u_i \in U$, his reputation is calculated as follows:

$$r_j^i = (\sum_{k=1}^{m} \zeta_k(ue_{kj}))/m$$

$$r_j = (1 - \lambda) * r_j + (\lambda * r_j^i)$$

where r_j^i is the average reputation given by all the services which u_j has evaluated. r_j is the current reputation of u_j. λ is the learning rate which can reflect the effect of history to the reputation.

Definition 10: We can use (1) to distinguish different users.

$$g(u) = \begin{cases} Nu, if\ r_j > K \\ MA, else \end{cases} \tag{1}$$

$g(u)$ is the function to judge the types of user. When the reputation of user is greater than the specified threshold, the model considers it as a normal user. Moreover, we identity experts by the following inequality

$$r_j > T(T \geq K)$$

Definition 11: We identify collusive users through evaluation similarity clustering. The collusion detection process is as follows: Firstly, we will calculate the evaluation similarity among users in MA

$$s_{ef} = 1 - \sqrt{((\sum_{i=1}^{l}(\tau_e(ws_{ei}) - \tau_f(ws_{fi}))^2)/(l+1))}$$

l is the size of service collection where the service is the common service evaluated by u_e and u_f. Then we will construct the maximum spanning tree of fuzzy graph in the collection of malicious users, where V denotes the set of vertices and E denotes the set of undirected edges. The weight of an edge is the evaluation similarity of the two connected vertices calculated by the above equation. Then we will cut the edges with the weight below φ to perform clustering [22]. Moreover, remove collusive users from malicious users, the remaining users are irresponsible users.

2.5 Minimum Number of Normal Users to Get Fair Evaluation

In order to get fair evaluation, we use the minimum number of users as an indicator to show when can get fair evaluation. For a given accuracy of service evaluation A, the minimum number of normal users to get the fair evaluation can be calculated as:

$$n = \frac{-In\,(1-A) * 2 * (\theta * \alpha + \nu * (1-\alpha))}{(\theta * \alpha + \nu * (1-\alpha) - 1/2)^2} \tag{2}$$

where θ is the mean accuracy of normal users, while ν is the mean accuracy of malicious users. α is the proportion of users who will perform fair evaluation on services in the normal user. α can reflect the normal user. When α is equal to 100%, which means that we think all the normal users detected in USDSE will make the correct evaluation of the service. When αequals 10%, it means that only 90% of the normal users detected in USDSE will give the correct rating. The proof is as follows: we assume that the normal users are more likely to give a correct evaluation. p_i is the probability that u_i will give correct evaluation of the service. Further, at least $n/2$ normal users in the system will give fair evaluation. The probability of at least $n/2$ normal users will give fair evaluation on service can be calculated as:

$$P_{\frac{n}{2}} = \sum_{\xi \subseteq U, |\xi| \geq \lceil n/2 \rceil} \prod_{u_i \in \xi} p_i \prod_{u_j \notin \xi} (1 - p_j)$$

The mean value of $P_{n/2}$ is:

$$\begin{aligned} E\left(P_{\frac{n}{2}}\right) &= E\left(\sum_{\xi \subseteq U, |\xi| \geq \lceil n/2 \rceil} \prod_{u_i \in \xi} p_i \prod_{u_j \notin \xi} (1 - p_j)\right) \\ &= E\left(\sum_{k=\lceil n/2 \rceil}^{n} \left(\sum_{\xi \subseteq U, |\xi| = k} \left(\prod_{u_i \in \xi} p_i \prod_{u_j \notin \xi} (1 - p_j)\right)\right)\right) \\ &= \left(\sum_{k=\lceil n/2 \rceil}^{n} \left(\sum_{\xi \subseteq U, |\xi| = k} \left(\prod_{u_i \in \xi} E(p_i) \prod_{u_j \notin \xi} E(1 - p_j)\right)\right)\right) \end{aligned} \tag{3}$$

We can see that $E(u_i) = \mu$, then the above user mean value is:

$$\begin{aligned} E\left(P_{\frac{n}{2}}\right) &= \left(\sum_{k=\lceil n/2 \rceil}^{n} \left(\sum_{\xi \subseteq U, |\xi| = k} \left(\prod_{u_i \in \xi} \mu \prod_{u_j \notin \xi} (1 - \mu)\right)\right)\right) \\ &= \left(\sum_{k=\lceil n/2 \rceil}^{n} \left(\sum_{\xi \subseteq U, |\xi| = k} \left(\mu^k (1 - \mu)^{n-k}\right)\right)\right) \\ &= \sum_{k=\lceil n/2 \rceil}^{n} C_n^k \mu^k (1 - \mu)^{(n-k)} \end{aligned} \tag{4}$$

According to Chernoff bound[1],

$$\sum_{k=\lceil n/2 \rceil}^{n} C_n^k \mu^k (1 - \mu)^{(n-k)} \geq 1 - e^{\left(-\frac{1}{2\mu} n (\mu - 1/2)^2\right)} \tag{5}$$

In this paper, we use the average accuracy of users $u_i$to replace the $E(u_i)$, the following will be used to calculate μ.

$$E(u_i) = \frac{\sum_{j=1}^{m} \frac{r_{ij} - \bar{r}_j}{Max(\bar{r}_j - minscore, maxscore - \bar{r}_j)}}{m} \tag{6}$$

$\bar{r}_j$ is the real quality of ws_{ij} which could be calculated using the average rating of all normal users. $Max(\bar{r}_j - minscore, maxscore - \bar{r}_j)$ is the maximum deviation between $\bar{r}_j$ and user could give. Assume that the accuracy of the evaluation is required to be A, as long as the above formula is made larger than A. We can get minimum of users to get fair evaluation. However, the malicious user may gain trust through camouflage, and suddenly launch an attack at a certain time,

[1] https://en.wikipedia.org/wiki/Chernoff_bound.

causing damage to the credibility of the service. Therefore, we need to consider the situation in which some users suddenly become malicious collusive users. The user type in the system is $U = \{NU, MA\}$, then for the u_i , his probability of giving the fair evaluation is:

$$\begin{aligned} P(u_i) &= P(fair\ evaluation|NU) * P(NU) \\ &+ P(fair\ evaluation|MA) * P(MA) \end{aligned} \tag{7}$$

when the user is normal, $E(p_N)$ is the probability that a normal user gives fair evaluation on the service; when the user is malicious, $E(p_M)$ is the probability that a malicious user gives fair evaluation on the service. Based on the historical data of the USDSE, we can see calculate that $E(p_N) = E(P(fairevaluation|NU)) = \theta$ from normal users detected in USDSE. $E(p_M) = E(P(fairevaluation|MA)) = \nu$ from malicious users. Notice that $E(P(u_i)) = \theta * \alpha + \nu * (1 - \alpha)$. Finally, the minimum number of normal user to get the fair service evaluation can be shown as (2).

2.6 Revenue Analysis of Employing Collusive Users

The basic purpose of the general service provider to employ collusive user is to improve its own revenue. Figure 3 shows two scenarios in which service providers employ collusive users. In scenario 1, service providers employ collusive users respectively to improve their reputation. In USDSE, the services provided by the service provider will also give these collusive users a good evaluation and help them improve their reputation. In scenario 2, the service providers will collaborate with others to employ collusive users, and the collusive users will evaluate all the services of these cooperative service providers. The following equation can be used to calculate the revenue of employing collusive users.

$$\begin{aligned} net\_revenue &= rre - \ totalCost \\ rb &= \frac{1}{1 + e^{-increase\_rating}} \\ totalCost &= \sum_{i=1}^{cnum} \sum_{j=1}^{en} cost\_onetime + \ cc \\ cost\_onetime &= \beta * eq(\beta \ > \ 0) \\ cc &= \ k * \ costofColluding(k \ > \ 0) \end{aligned} \tag{8}$$

The $net\_revenue$ is the total revenue obtained by employing collusive users. rre is the revenue obtained by the raise of users' evaluation with the help of collusive users. $increase\_rating$ is the increase of service's rating after employing malicious collusive users. $totalCost$ is the total cost of employing collusive users. $cnum$ is the total number of collusive users. en is total evaluation number for a collusive user. $cost\_onetime$ is the cost of one evaluation for a collusive user which depends on the quality of evaluation(eq). Intuitively, when the malicious user pretends to evaluate the service as normal users, the cost will increase compared with random evaluation. λ is the parameter describing the relation between the quality of evaluation and the cost at one time. cc is the communication

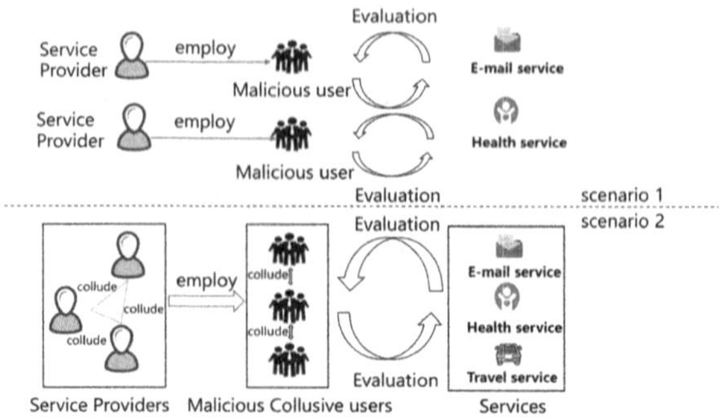

Fig. 3. Two scenarios for collusive user

cost among service providers. $costofColluding$ is the cost of colluding a service provider. k is the number of service providers who collude together to employ users.

3 Experimental Evaluation

Because of the current limited availability of evaluation data, many existing methods [15,22,24] used simulation data for performance evaluation. The simulated malicious and subjective evaluation can reflect the real situations by setting the magnitude (e.g. 1, 2, . . . , 10) of subjective feedback ratings and the density (e.g. 10, 20, . . . , 100%) of malicious feedback ratings [13,22]. Hence, in our experiments, we also employ simulation to generate malicious and biased feedback ratings to evaluate the proposed approach.

3.1 Dataset

In the simulation experiment, the number of users is 1000, the number of services is 50. To evaluate our scheme's capability of detecting malicious users, the collusive user ratio varies from 0% to 100%. For example, if the collusive user ratio is 50%, that means half of the malicious users are irresponsible and give random ratings and half of the malicious users are colluding. We simulated three scenarios in the experiment.

- 700 normal users, 300 malicious users, the percentage of normal users is high (HNU)
- 500 normal users, 500 malicious users, the percentage of normal users is medium (MNU)
- 300 normal users, 700 malicious users, the percentage of normal users is low (LNU)

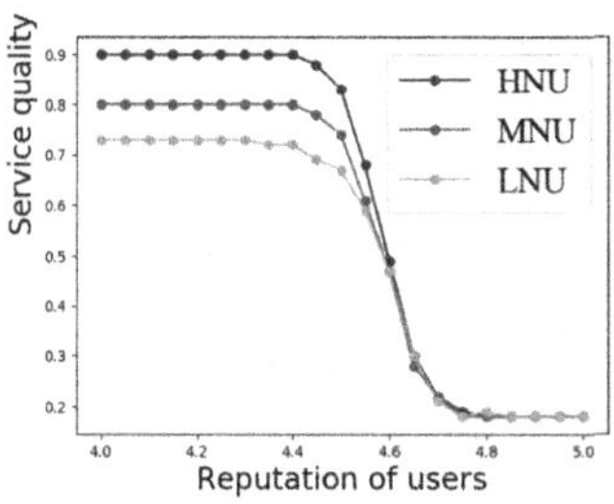

Fig. 4. F1-score in three scenarios

For simplicity, we set the ratio of trusted users to experts to be 1: 9. We use NS, CS, and IS to represent the set of normal users, collusive users, and irresponsible users, respectively, to allow DNS, DCS, and DIS to represent the set of normal users, collusive users, and irresponsible users detected in USDSE. The evaluation index is F1-Score, F1-score is the weighted sum of model precision and recall rate, taking into account the precision and recall rate of the model, as defined below:

$$\begin{aligned} F1 - score &= \frac{2 * Precision * Recall}{Precision + Recall} \\ Precision &= \frac{||DGS \cap GS||}{(||DGS \cap GS|| + ||DGS \cap (CS \cup IS)||)} \\ Recall &= \frac{||DGS \cap GS||}{(||DGS \cap GS|| + ||(DIS \cup DIS) \cap GS||)} \end{aligned} \tag{9}$$

3.2 Studies on Parameters

The reputation of users can be obtained based on the evaluation of services. When the reputation of the user is greater than K, it is considered a normal user. In order to find a reasonable K to achieve better performance, we set the user reputation ranging from 4 to 5 and use F1-score as the evaluation index. In the above three scenarios, the ratio of the collusive user and the irresponsible user is 50% (the result is the same with the change of the ratio of collusive user ratio in HNU, MNU, LNU). Figure 4 shows the variation of F1-score in three different scenarios. When the K value is set between 4 to 4.4, F1-score is the highest, in other words, the model works best; when the K is greater than 4.4, the F1-score decreases. That is because there is a certain bias in the evaluation of the services for some normal users caused by the environment and subjective preferences.

3.3 Malicious User Detection

In order to test the effect of the USDSE mechanism to identify normal users, we compare the USDSE with HMRep [22]. HMRep uses the deviation of rating

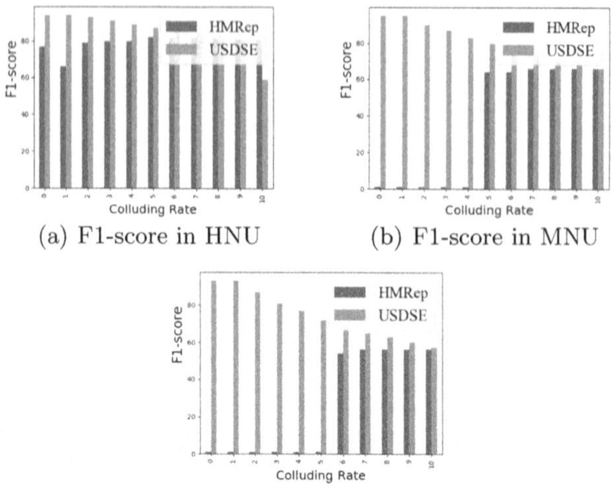

(a) F1-score in HNU

(b) F1-score in MNU

(c) F1-score in LNU

Fig. 5. F1-score compared with HMREp

to identify different types of users. Figure 5 shows the effect of USDSE and HMRrep in three scenarios. USDSE can maintain a high F1-score value in all three scenarios, up to 95%. This is mainly due to the use of services on the evaluation of users which can better reflect the true quality of users; when the proportion of malicious users is less than 60%, USDSE is more efficient than HMRep. This is because the proportion of irresponsible users is high and the characteristics of evaluation behavior are easy to distinguish.

3.4 Response to Service Quality Change

In this section, we will detect the ability of the USDSE to respond to the change of service quality. We tested it in the HCU scenario, a service whose quality oscillates between 1 (low quality) and 5 (high quality). Specifically, the quality of service was 1 in the first 5 cycles and then rose to 5 in another 5 cycles and keep repeating this pattern, we consider two scenarios,

1) the service's quality swing from 1 to 5
2) the service's quality swing from 5 to 1

From Fig. 6, we can see that USDSE is sensitive to the change of service quality. When the services swing from high quality to poor quality, the obtained results are more accurate. When the quality of the service changes from high to low or low to high, the evaluation of the service of normal users and experts will change, but their reputation will not be changed with the change of service quality. So even if the service Quality changes, our models can quickly monitor changes in service and give a fair assessment of service.

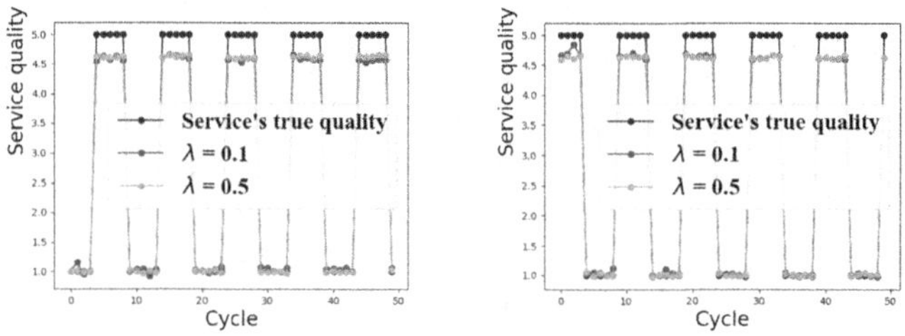

(a) Beginning with low quality (b) Beginning with high quality

Fig. 6. Response to service quality change

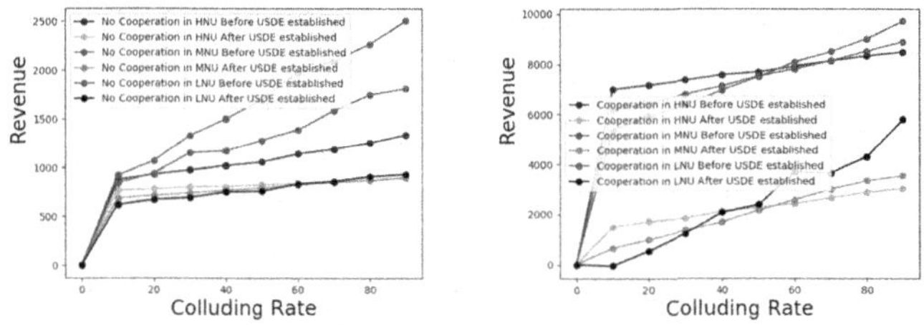

(a) No Cooperation (b) Cooperation

Fig. 7. Revenue analysis of employing malicious users

3.5 Revenue Analysis of Employing Malicious Collusive Users

Figure 7 shows the revenue of employing the collusive users in three scenarios (HNU, MNU, LNU) when no cooperation(Fig. 7(a))and cooperation (Fig. 7(b))among service providers (the procedure could be seen in Fig. 3).

With the proportion of collusive users increasing, the revenue is gradually increasing. At the same time, we can see from Fig. 7(a) that in the three scenarios, after the USDSE filter out the malicious user's evaluation, the revenue is almost the same in the end. The reason why the revenue starts to decline at the beginning in Fig. 7(b) is that the correction of evaluation in USDSE and increase of communication cost caused by cooperation. We noticed that the revenue in LNU is higher than in HNU to the end. That's because some collusive users aren't been identified with the increase of the collusive users.

4 Related Work

At present, researchers mainly obtain fair evaluation of users from two aspects: comment and rating of users. Some studies judge the correctness of comment by a single feature of the comment. Wu et al. [26] believe that consumers are more likely to accept recommendations from reviewers when historical ratings in a product area vary widely. [9] present a novel method called DeFrauder to detect and rank fraud reviewer groups. There are studies that use sentiment analysis to judge false comments. Li J et al. [12] analyze the emotional words in user comments and analyze the semantics of the text from the perspective of emotional polarity, indicating that the false comment contains more emotional words. Franklin et al. [21] propose a method to determine the polarity of comments based on CIAA(confidentiality, integrity, availability, and authentication) related keywords. [20] propose a method called SentiDraw that uses star ratings of reviews to develop domain-specific emotional dictionaries to determine polarity.

Due to the diversity of the comment, it is necessary to determine which factors will affect the quality of the user's comment and speculate on these factors in advance. [3] present a new reputation system using machine learning to predict the reliability of consumers from their profile, which may be a potential solution for future reputation systems.

Many studies use feedback ratings to get fair reviews, so researchers often need to filter malicious feedback ratings. A.Josang et al. [8] assume that the user feedback score follows the beta distribution. They use the sensitivity coefficient q to roughly indicate the percentage of dishonest feedback. The smaller the q value, the lower the false positive rate, and the more false negatives in dishonest feedback. However, the method of A.Josang assumes that user feedback follows a specific distribution, and Weng [25] proposes a new entropy-based method to measure the quality of evidence and further filter unfair evaluations. The proposed method does not require assumptions about the distribution of ratings. Considering the aggregation of malicious user comment time, Yang et al. [28] use statistical methods to detect the time interval of malicious feedback. Considering the complex attack scenarios, the performance of these methods has some limitations. Cai et al. [7] propose a two-phase approach for fraudulent rater detection.

5 Conclusion

The proposed model utilizes the service to evaluate the users, establishes the users' reputation, filters the malicious users, and provides a fair evaluation of users. Experimental results show that our model can effectively identify malicious users compared with HMRep and we can see that USDSE is sensitive to the change of service quality. The USDSE can reduce the revenue of employing collusive users in different scenarios. In essence, USDSE is to improve the objectivity and fairness of users' evaluation from two different dimensions: evaluation of users and evaluation of services.

In the future, we will establish a user-service double-side evaluation model in the ecosystem and verify the validity of the model through real data. At the same time, we will consider the impact of silent users when getting fair evaluation and use more user information to help the service evaluate users.

Acknowledgements. This work is supported by the Foundation of Jiangxi Educational Committee under Grant No. GJJ210338, the National Natural Science Foundation of China (NSFC) under Grant No. 61962026, the National Natural Science Key Foundation of China grant No. 61832014 and No. 62032016, the Natural Science Foundation of Jiangxi Province under Grant No. 20192ACBL21031.

References

1. Akoglu, L., Chandy, R., Faloutsos, C.: Opinion fraud detection in online reviews by network effects. In: ICWSM, vol. 13, pp. 2–11 (2013)
2. Allahbakhsh, M., Ignjatovic, A.: An iterative method for calculating robust rating scores. IEEE Trans. Parallel Distrib. Syst. **26**(2), 340–350 (2015)
3. Alqwadri, A., Azzeh, M., Almasalha, F.: Appl. Mach. Learn. Online Reput. Syst. **18**(3), 11 (2021)
4. Arora, U., Dutta, H.S., Joshi, B., Chetan, A., Chakraborty, T.: Analyzing and detecting collusive users involved in blackmarket retweeting activities. ACM Trans. Intell. Syst. Technol. **11**(3) (2020). https://doi.org/10.1145/3380537https://doi.org/10.1145/3380537
5. Baek, H., Jang, M., Kim, S.: Who leaves malicious comments on online news? An empirical study in Korea. Journal. Stud. **23**(4), 432-447 (2022). https://doi.org/10.1080/1461670X.2022.2031258
6. Byun, H., Jeong, S., kwon Kim, C.: SC-COM: spotting collusive community in opinion spam detection. Inf. Process. Manag. **58**(4), 102593 (2021). https://doi.org/10.1016/j.ipm.2021.102593, https://doi.org/10.1080/1461670X.2022.2031258
7. Cai, Y., Zhu, D.: Who can we trust: A new approach for fraudulent rater detection in reputation systems. Decis. Sci. **51**(1) (2020)
8. Commerce, B.E., Jøsang, A., Ismail, R.: The beta reputation system. In: In Proceedings of the 15th Bled Electronic Commerce Conference (2002)
9. Dhawan, S., Gangireddy, S., Kumar, S., Chakraborty, T.: Spotting collective behaviour of online frauds in customer reviews. In: Proceedings of the Twenty-Eighth International Joint Conference on Artificial Intelligence (IJCAI-2019 (2019)
10. Hajek, P., Barushka, A., Munk, M.: Fake consumer review detection using deep neural networks integrating word embeddings and emotion mining. Neural Comput. Appl. **32**(1) (2020)
11. Li, B., Song, R., Liao, L., Liu, C.: A user-oriented trust model for web services. In: 2013 IEEE Seventh International Symposium on Service-Oriented System Engineering, pp. 224–232. IEEE (2013)
12. Li, J., Ott, M., Cardie, C., Hovy, E.: Towards a general rule for identifying deceptive opinion spam. In: Proceedings of the 52nd Annual Meeting of the Association for Computational Linguistics, vol. 1, pp. 1566–1576 (014). https://doi.org/10.3115/v1/P14-1147
13. Limam, N., Boutaba, R.: Assessing software service quality and trustworthiness at selection time. IEEE Trans. Softw. Eng. **36**(4), 559–574 (2010). https://doi.org/10.1109/TSE.2010.2
14. Liu, M., Shang, Y., Yue, Q., Zhou, J.: Detecting fake reviews using multidimensional representations with fine-grained aspects plan. IEEE Access **9**, 3765–3773 (2021). https://doi.org/10.1109/ACCESS.2020.3047947
15. Maarouf, I., Baroudi, U., Naseer, A.R.: Efficient monitoring approach for reputation system-based trust-aware routing in wireless sensor networks. IET Commun. **3**(5), 846–858 (2009)

16. Martens, D., Maalej, W.: Towards understanding and detecting fake reviews in app stores. Empir. Softw. Eng. **24**(6), 3316–3355 (2019)
17. Nguyen, H.T., Zhao, W., Yang, J.: A trust and reputation model based on Bayesian network for web services. In: 2010 IEEE International Conference on Web Services, pp. 251–258. IEEE (2010)
18. Oh, H.K., Jung, J., Park, S., Kim, S.W.: A robust reputation system using online reviews? Comput. Sci. Inf. Syst. **17**, 7–7 (2020)
19. Rezvani, M., Rezvani, M.: A randomized reputation system in the presence of unfair ratings. ACM Trans. Manage. Inf. Syst. **11**(1) (2020). https://doi.org/10.1145/3384472, https://doi.org/10.1145/3384472
20. Sharma, S.S., Dutta, G.: Sentidraw: Using star ratings of reviews to develop domain specific sentiment lexicon for polarity determination. Inf. Process. Manag. **58**(1), 102412 (2021)
21. Tchakounté, F., Pagor, A., Kamgang, J.C., Atemkeng, M.: Ciaa-repdroid: a fine-grained and probabilistic reputation scheme for android apps based on sentiment analysis of reviews. Fut. Internet **12**(9), 145 (2020)
22. Wang, M., Wang, G., Zhang, Y., Li, Z.: A high-reliability multi-faceted reputation evaluation mechanism for online services. IEEE Trans. Serv. Comput. **12**, 836–850 (2016)
23. Wang, N., Yang, J., Kong, X., Gao, Y.: A fake review identification framework considering the suspicion degree of reviews with time burst characteristics. Exp. Syst. Appl. **190**, 116207 (2022). https://doi.org/10.1016/j.eswa.2021.116207https://www.sciencedirect.com/science/article/pii/S0957417421015219
24. Wang, S., Zheng, Z., Wu, Z., Lyu, M.R., Yang, F.: Reputation measurement and malicious feedback rating prevention in web service recommendation systems. IEEE Trans. Serv. Comput. **8**(5), 755–767 (2015)
25. Weng, J., Miao, C., Goh, A.: An entropy-based approach to protecting rating systems from unfair testimonies. IEICE Transactions 89-D, 2502–2511 (09 2006). https://doi.org/10.1093/ietisy/e89-d.9.2502
26. Wu, X., Jin, L., Xu, Q.: Expertise makes perfect: How the variance of a reviewer's historical ratings influences the persuasiveness of online reviews. J. Retail. **97**(2), 238-250 (2021). https://doi.org/10.1016/j.jretai.2020.05.006, https://www.sciencedirect.com/science/article/pii/S0022435920300270
27. Yang, B., Liu, Y., Liang, Y., Tang, M.: Exploiting user experience from online customer reviews for product design. Int. J. Inf. Manag. **46**, 173-186 (2019). https://doi.org/10.1016/j.ijinfomgt.2018.12.006, https://www.sciencedirect.com/science/article/pii/S0268401218305437
28. Yang, Y., Sun, Y., Kay, S., Yang, Q.: Defending online reputation systems against collaborative unfair raters through signal modeling and trust. In: SAC '09: Proceedings of the 2009 ACM Symposium on Applied Computing, pp. 1308–1315 (2009). https://doi.org/10.1145/1529282.1529575

Morphology-Based Soft Label Smoothing Strategy for Fine-Grained Domain Adaptationming

Kangshun Li[1], Yi Wang[1](✉), Tian Feng[2], Hassan Jalil[2], and Huabei Nie[3]

[1] College of Computer Science, Guangdong University of Science and Technology, Dongguan 523000, Guangdong, China
gust312@163.com

[2] School of Mathematics and Information, South China Agricultural University, Guangzhou 510642, Guangdong, China

[3] School of Computer and Informatics, Dongguan City University, Dongguan 523808, Guangdong, China

Abstract. Semantic segmentation algorithms are the cornerstone of the autonomous driving algorithm. The implementation of these algorithms requires a lot of data. However, due to the complex and changeable production environment, the differences in image style, illumination and weather conditions not only significantly degrade the performance of network models under development environment data, but also cause costly data annotation. This paper proposes a dilation-corrosion soft label smoothing strategy. This strategy utilizes the existing self-supervised learning soft label generation strategy and overcomes the premise assumption defect of the fine-grained adversarial model on the target domain model. Our strategy evaluates its effectiveness on the domain adaptation task of **GTA5 → Cityscapes**. At the same time, we reduce the amount of source domain data by half and the number of domain classification training iterations by half, the resulting in the comprehensive evaluation index is 1.5% higher, and the individual category is 10 percentage points higher. Our strategy shortens the time and improves the efficiency of segmentation.

Keywords: Semantic segmentation · Domain adaptive learning · Self-supervised learning · Soft label smoothing

1 Introduction

In the target segmentation task, training and test datasets are drawn from an identical distribution. While the training and test data do not conform to the independent identical distribution (IID), most neural network models need to re-collect data and train from scratch to conform to the assumption of the IID assumption of the training set and test set. At present, the main reason why many academic achievements are difficult to obtain that the data in the laboratory development environment is different or even far from the objective world data in the production environment. The phenomenon caused by this

Y. Xu et al. (Eds.): ML4CS 2022, LNCS 13657, pp. 499–506, 2023.
https://doi.org/10.1007/978-3-031-20102-8_38

distribution mismatch is similar as the model is trained from dataset A, but the dataset B needs to be verified and tested. By labeling the dataset in the production environment, we can make the data set conform to the IID to improve the performance of the model, but this performance is often expensive and even impossible to achieve, which is the curse of dataset labeling. Usually, in order to obtain accurate dataset labels, some experts of this field need to do a lot of tedious manual operations on the data set. For example, in the medical image segmentation field [1], Annotation of the dataset is performed exclusively by experienced physicians, so the acquisition of dataset labels is very difficult. In the field of autonomous driving, the objective real-world weather conditions, urban style, weather conditions are complex and changeable [2].

The domain adaptive algorithm is proposed in this context. This algorithm focuses on the assumption of independent and identical distribution, and aims to learn new unlabeled data in the production environment through the training model, so that the network model can learn the domain invariance characteristics between different datasets, such as shape, style, size, etc. Domain adaptive algorithm also absorbs the latest algorithm technology in other fields, and its performance has been greatly improved. For example, TransDA [3] network introduces SWIN component into feature extractor, and improves the domain adaptive algorithm by improving the structure of feature extractor. DeepLabv3 [4] segmentation network is improved at the classifier level and deleted the CRF; introduced the self-supervised learning strategy into the self-supervised learning network of domain adaptive algorithm [5]; the distillation learning strategy in the model compression algorithm is introduced into the domain adaptive learning. Even if the source domain model is used as the teacher model, knowledge can be extracted by its strong model expression ability, and the target domain model is used as the student model [6].

2 Related Work

2.1 Domain Adaptive

Domain adaptive algorithm is a sub-algorithm of transfer learning algorithm. The problem of this algorithm is how to train unlabeled data, which belongs to a part of unsupervised learning field. When the data used for forward propagation of the network model come from two different datasets: A and B, these two datasets usually do not conform to the independent identical distribution assumption, and the performance of the neural network model on the dataset without labels is unsatisfactory. The traditional training set and test set expression terms have some errors in the domain adaptive algorithm, so there is another set of related terms to express in the domain adaptive algorithm. Areal label of training set, called the source domain $\mathcal{S}$. In the problem of target detection, the source domain usually refers to a dataset with a label, and the test set to be used for target detection is called the target domain $\mathcal{T}$, corresponding to a dataset without a label. The premise of traditional deep learning is that $\mathcal{S}$ and $\mathcal{T}$ are independent and identically distributed. The problem of domain adaptive algorithm is that the $\mathcal{S}$ and $\mathcal{T}$ are distributed differently, so that the trained network model can reduce the domain offset between $\mathcal{S}$ and $\mathcal{T}$. Therefore, the purpose of the migration learning algorithm is to learn the same commonness among different datasets, so that the same model can have better detection effect in $\mathcal{S}$ and $\mathcal{T}$.

Under the conventional target detection framework, the data set is generated by collecting relevant data and forming R (where the dataset is expressed in mathematical form of D), and then the data set R is calibrated and segmented by Label marking software to form a training set T and a test set V. There may be several test sets t_1, t_1. The relationship between data sets can be expressed in mathematical form as shown in formula $\mathbb{R} = \{\mathbb{T}, \mathbb{V}, \mathbb{t}_1, \mathbb{t}_2 \cdots\cdot\}$, $\mathbb{T} \cap \mathbb{V} = \emptyset$. Any picture can be expressed by the given distribution function formula [7]: $P(C, B, I)$, where B is the target box to confirm the object position; C is the name of object's specific class; I represent the overall style attribute of picture. The corresponding object detection problem is expressed by the following formula: $P(C, B|I)$, represent the picture I, the location B of the object and the corresponding target name C need to be found. Due to the different distribution between source domain and target domain, there is a certain domain offset between source domain and target domain, namely: $P_S(C, B|I) \neq P_T(C, B|I)$. On this basis, a binary domain discriminator D is added to distinguish which domain the image comes from, represented by following formula: $P(D|B, I)P(B|I) = P(B|D, I)P(D|I)$.

2.2 Self-supervised Learning

When there is no manually constructed label data, the supervised learning method cannot calculate the error through the loss function, nor can it update the weight value of the neural network through back propagation. The self-supervised learning method solves this problem; in the other words, where does the knowledge come from? After introducing the self-supervised learning training strategy into the domain adaptive algorithm, the neural network model can generate pseudo tags by iteration, and then rely on these pseudo tags to retrain the network to enhance the performance of the network, such as BDL [8], CAG [10], CBST [11], TranDA [8]. However, after adding the self-supervised learning module, the problems will emerge one by one, i.e., how to ensure the false labels submitted to the network are strictly classified and must be correct. The existing approach use the model trained by the source domain data to forward the target domain data in the network, and then directly performed hard pruning regularization for each prediction confidence in the data to prevent the target domain model from overfitting. Hard pruning regularization reduce the confidence of pixels whose confidence exceeds the threshold, but even after many experiments, carefully set threshold pruning will still produce noisy false labels after self-supervised training.

2.3 Datasets

In algorithmic studies of domain adaptation, some public datasets are usually used and are presented here: the Cityscapes [5] dataset, which comes from different cities in Europe and consists of a large series of images of street traffic, the dataset officially provides labeled files for target detection and instance segmentation, and is usually used as a migration learning because it reflects real-world street scenes algorithm because it reflects real-world street scenes. The dataset contains 19 categories such as universal cars, people, and roads, and there exists a mirror set Cityscape Foggy [5], which is a Cityscapes fog synthetic dataset to simulate model robustness under foggy weather conditions, and the GTA5 [6] dataset, which is from the well-known video game Grand

Theft Auto V, which has a large number of images available because it is set in Los Angeles, USA and is more realistic, and is usually used as a source domain in migration learning algorithms. Therefore, the task of the domain adaptive algorithm is usually to train on the GTA5 dataset and validate on the Cityscapes dataset. However, due to the standard type of Cityscapes dataset, other datasets usually exist as source domains , and the category labels will be consistent with the Cityscapes dataset. The experiments conducted in this paper precisely utilize GTA5 → Cityscapes. i.e., the GTA5 dataset is used for training and the Cityscapes dataset is used for validation. The image samples can be seen in Fig. 1.

GTA5Source Datasets Cityscapes Target Datasets

Fig. 1. Network needs to learn the commonality between the two.

3 FFADA Neural Network

3.1 FADA Neural Network

The verification effect of the model with the two-class domain identifier is significantly improved as compared with the model without the addition of the two-class domain identifier,. However, the binary classification model also has some defects. When performing the pixel-by-pixel target segmentation task, the simple binary classifier is obviously too extensive. For tasks that need some fine-grained, extending the original binary classifier to the C-class classifier is a good improved algorithm. In addition to the fine-grained improvement in the domain classifier component, the FADA network [9] also introduces the self-supervised learning strategy into the domain adaptive algorithm. In self-supervised learning, and in the face of small sample labels or even no sample labels, the strategy of using the good ability of existing models to generate pseudo labels is usually adopted to help the model training. The model trained from the source domain data is used to detect the target domain data, and the test results with high confidence output by the source domain model are used as ''labels'' help to train the target domain network model. Because the 'tag' comes from the output of the source domain network model, it becomes a pseudo tag. The mathematical expression can be seen in Formula 1.

$$\mathcal{L}_{ce} = -\sum_{i=1}^{H\times W}\sum_{k=1}^{K}\hat{y}_t^{(i,k)}\log\left(p_t^{(i,k)}\right) \tag{1}$$

$\mathcal{L}_{ce}$ represents the cross-entropy loss function, H, W is the height and width of the input image, $\hat{y}_t^{(i,k)}$ represents the input of the target domain data from the pseudo label obtained by the model, $p_t^{(i,k)}$ is the label output value of the target domain model. K represents K class. The cross-entropy function is a loss function for the classification.

As a domain discriminator of binary classification, if $\hat{y}_t^{(i,k)}$ is used as the label of the source domain and the target domain of binary classification, $p_t^{(i,k')}$ in formula (1) represents the output of the domain classification result of each pixel after the softmax function, the task of the domain classifier is to identify the binary classification domain of each pixel, and the formula is expressed as follows:

$$\hat{y}_t^{(i,k)} = \begin{cases} 1, ifk = argmax_{k'}p_t^{(i,k')} \\ 0, otherwise \end{cases} \tag{2}$$

when the domain classifier is fine-grained, the softmax can be improved to conform the fine-grained, and the output of each category can be normalized. The normalization formula is defined as Eq. (3):

$$\hat{y}_t^{(i,k)} = \frac{\exp\left(\frac{z_k}{T}\right)}{\sum_{j=1}^{K}\exp\left(\frac{z_j}{T}\right)} \tag{3}$$

3.2 FFADA Neural Network

The domain adaptive algorithm mainly works in the domain classifier module. The classifier will output the pixel classification of source domain and target domain data, and input them into the domain classifier module together. Through the domain classification of source domain data and target domain data, the domain invariance characteristics between the two domains are learned. In the state-of-the-art (SOTA) model designed by the FADA network, the output of the classifier are pruned by regularization threshold, and the unified confidence level higher than the threshold ζ is replaced by a specific value φ to avoid the lack of target domain model learning caused by the over-hard soft label output by the source domain model network. The formula is:

$$\begin{gathered} \hat{y}_t^{(i,k)} > \zeta = \varphi \\ (\mathrm{i} = 1, 2, \ldots, H \times W; k = 1, 2, \ldots, K) \end{gathered} \tag{4}$$

However, when this method is also applied to the target domain network model, it will cause of some problems: there are some deficiencies in the classification ability of the target domain network model, because it is not trained by the supervised data. For a model network that lacks its own classification ability, and the assumption of 'cutting confidence in order to prevent over-fitting' is somewhat arbitrary.

The algorithm proposed in this paper is based on the defects described above: the classification ability of the target domain model classifier without supervised training is insufficient, so the traditional soft label generation strategy has defects. This strategy is to input the classification result y after the classifier classifies the feature map directly into domain classifier D for domain classification. While the FFADA network model using the soft label smoothing strategy of expansion corrosion work differently. After the classifier obtains the target domain data, the classification result y_t is not directly input into the domain classification module D, but a threshold binarization B:

$$B = \begin{cases} 1, & \hat{y}_t^{(i,k)} > 0.5\ (i = 1, 2 \ldots, H \times W; i = 1, 2 \ldots, K) \\ 0, & otherwise \end{cases} \tag{5}$$

After the threshold binarization, the classification result y_t will be a tensor with the same shape as y_b, it can be clearly seen that the binary classification results show a more obvious body category contour. It can be seen in Fig. 2, the object category contour displayed after binarization. It is natural to think the morphological operations on the original classification results, such as expansion, corrosion, opening and closing operation. The confidence of the smooth region is replaced by the average value.

$$r_t^{(i,k)} = \frac{\sum_i^{r_t^{(i,k)}=1} \hat{y}_t^{(i,k)}}{\sum_{i=1}^{H \times W} r_t^{(i,k)}} (k = 1, 2, \ldots, K) \tag{6}$$

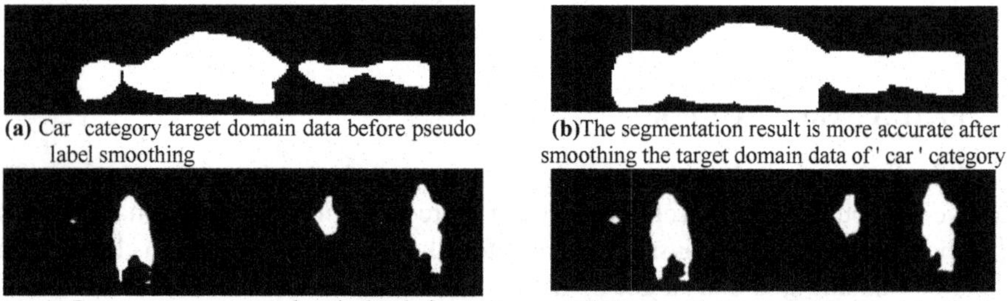

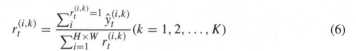

(a) Car category target domain data before pseudo label smoothing

(b) The segmentation result is more accurate after smoothing the target domain data of ' car ' category

(c) Person category target domain data before pseudo label smoothing

(d) Person category target domain data after pseudo label smoothing

Fig. 2. Pseudo-labels after our strategy

4 Experiment

The implementation strategies of domain adaptive experiments are usually as follows: first, train the network on the source domain model, and then load the source domain model weight file into the target domain model for domain classification confrontation training. The abscissa is the number of iterations selected by the model, and the ordinate is the evaluation index mIoU. Only source domain data participate in training, and mIoU is 0.3388. According to Fig. 3, the soft label smoothing strategy can increase by 10–20% in individual categories (the only-src used as a reference).

In this experiment, the best result of 40,000 iterations is 46.32%. After using the soft label smoothing strategy, the best result of FFADA network in the same equipment and the same variable is 47.88%, which is 0.9% higher than the result claimed by the FADA network, and nearly 1.5%higher than the FADA model. In terms of speed, when the number of iterations is set to 24,000, then FFADA network can achieve the highest accuracy of the model, which is almost twice the speed of 40,000 iterations designed by FADA network. According to the Fig. 2, the oscillation problem of mIoU in FADA network during the training coincides with the oscillation problem that described in TransDA model, and FFADA can effectively solve the oscillation problem.

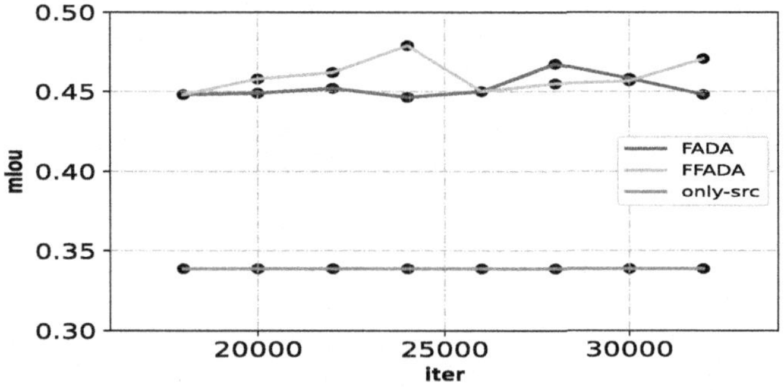

Fig. 3. Comparison of three network verification results

5 Conclusion

The FFADA model can not only reduce the number of iterations but also improve the accuracy. In addition, there is a vibration problem after the FADA model is trained to 25000 iterations. According to the joint paper of Tsinghua University and Tencent AI Laboratory, they improved the model based on the FADA network and also has a vibration problem.

Acknowledgements. This work was supported by Natural Science Foundation of Guangdong Province (2020A1515010784), the Key Field Special Project of Guangdong Provincial Department of Education (2021ZDZX1029), the Guang dong Youth Characteristic Innovation Project (2021KQNCX120), and the Natural Science Project of Guangdong University of Science and Technology (GKY-2021KYYBK-20).

References

1. Wang, R., et al.: Medical image segmentation using deep learning: a survey. IET Image Proc. **16**(5), 1243–1267 (2022)

2. Pan, S.J., Yang, Q.: A survey on transfer learning. IEEE Trans. Knowl. Data Eng. **22**(10), 1345–1359 (2009)
3. Liu, Z., et al.: Swin transformer: hierarchical vision transformer using shifted windows. In: Proceedings of the IEEE/CVF International Conference on Computer Vision, pp. 10012–10022 (2021)
4. Chen, L.-C., Zhu, Y., Papandreou, G., Schroff, F., Adam, H.: Encoder-decoder with atrous separable convolution for semantic image segmentation. In: Ferrari, V., Hebert, M., Sminchisescu, C., Weiss, Y. (eds.) ECCV 2018. LNCS, vol. 11211, pp. 833–851. Springer, Cham (2018). https://doi.org/10.1007/978-3-030-01234-2_49
5. Zbontar, J., et al.: Barlow twins: self-supervised learning via redundancy reduction. In: International Conference on Machine Learning, pp. 12310–12320. PMLR (2021)
6. Mirzadeh, S.I., et al.: Improved knowledge distillation via teacher assistant. Proceedings of the AAAI Conference on Artificial Intelligence **34**(04), 5191–5198 (2020)
7. Chen, Y., et al.: Domain adaptive faster R-CNN for object detection in the wild. In: Proceedings of the IEEE Conference on Computer Vision and Pattern Recognition, 3339–3348 (2018)
8. Li, Y., Yuan, L., Vasconcelos, N.: Bidirectional learning for domain adaptation of semantic segmentation. In: Proceedings of the IEEE/CVF Conference on Computer Vision and Pattern Recognition, pp. 6936–6945 (2019)
9. Wang, H., et al.: Classes matter: a fine-grained adversarial approach to cross-domain semantic segmentation. In: European conference on computer vision, pp. 642–659. Springer, Cham (2020)
10. Zhang, Q., et al.: Category anchor-guided unsupervised domain adaptation for semantic segmentation. Adv. Neural Inf. Process. Syst. **32** (2019)
11. Zou, Y., et al.: Unsupervised domain adaptation for semantic segmentation via class-balanced self-training. In: Proceedings of the European conference on computer vision (ECCV), 289–305 (2018)

MOOC Performance Prediction and Online Design Instructional Suggestions Based on LightGBM

Yimin Ren[1], Jun Wang[1,2(✉)], Jia Hao[1,2], Jianhou Gan[1,2], and Ken Chen[1]

[1] Key Laboratory of Education Informatization for Nationalities, Ministry of Education, Yunnan Normal University, Kunming 650500, China
dongling1988@126.com

[2] Yunnan Key Laboratory of Smart Education, Yunnan Normal University, Kunming 650500, China

Abstract. Recently, the research on the teaching effectiveness of online teaching has gradually become the focus of people's attention. As a well-known learning platform, MOOC has also become the main front for many learners to conduct online learning. However, some students are not clear about their own learning situation during the learning process, so that they can't get a qualifying grade in a MOOC course. Thus, In order to make the teachers and learners to anticipate the learning performance and then check the gaps as early as possible, we propose a MOOC performance prediction model based on the algorithm of LightGBM, and then compare its results with the others state-of art machine learning algorithms. Experimental results show that our proposed method outperform than the others. Research also leverages LightGBM's interpretability, Analyzed the external environment and existing cognitive structure, two factors that affect online learning. And this is the basis for suggestions on online instructional design.

Keywords: Performance prediction · LightGBM · Online instructional design

1 Introduction

Since the 21st century, blending learning has created a new wave of learning internationally, learners are no longer limited to the courses and time offered by the school, and can learn according to their own circumstances. An epidemic in 2020 has brought online education into the spotlight at an alarming rate, followed by researchers' enthusiasm for online education researches. At present, there are many types of online education platforms, but the quality is uneven. One of the most widely used courses in universities is the Massive Open Online Course (MOOC), which is set up by top international universities and provides free courses from various schools on-line. Since its inception in 2013, MOOCs in China have gradually established a unique development model. At present, the number and scale of application of MOOCs in China ranks first in the world. If we can explore the student management method of MOOC and then apply it to domestic MOOCs. Maybe it can help Chinese MOOCs develop better.

Y. Xu et al. (Eds.): ML4CS 2022, LNCS 13657, pp. 507–519, 2023.
https://doi.org/10.1007/978-3-031-20102-8_39

Because today's MOOCs are used by learners from all fields of life, everyone learns for different purposes and in different ways. So, many learners may fail to achieve excellent or qualified grades, or even dropout. There are many reasons for this, such as objective reasons like the inability to squeeze out time and the network environment does not allow. As well as subjective reasons like lack of self-control, inability to interact with teachers and give up because of lack of attention. If the MOOC designers can anticipate learners' final grade, they can send some warning based on the prediction results, and then pay attention to check the gaps as soon as possible to avoid failing the course. Teachers can also get certain early warnings and adjust the teaching design as soon as possible to help learners better acquire knowledge.

Although some researchers [1–3] are currently conducting related research on MOOC student performance prediction. However, there are a large number of MOOC learners, they generate a large amount of learning behavior data and feature dimensions. Therefore, researchers need to spend a lot of time and storage costs when building a performance prediction model. On the other hand, in the process of online learning, in addition to learners, there are also important members, namely teaching organizers. As one of the components of human resources in learning resources, teachers are ignored by some researchers. After some researchers predict MOOC scores, they only feedback the results to students, allowing students to explore ways to improve their academic performance. They don't understand some machine learning algorithms that provide a ranking of features in the process of building a performance prediction model. It is the ranking of the importance of the features to the prediction results. Corresponding analysis of this ranking can provide new ideas for the teaching design of online education. The fundamental purpose of instructional design is to create a variety of effective teaching systems through the systematic arrangement of teaching processes and teaching resources to promote learners' learning. Unlike traditional teaching, the learners of online teaching may have different a prior knowledge and are in different external environments, but the fundamental purpose of the instructional design is to facilitate learners' learning. Therefore, it is worthwhile to pay attention to how to improve traditional instructional design according to the characteristics of online teaching and learning.

In terms of prediction, The Gradient Boosting Decision Tree (GBDT) in machine learning already has high accuracy and interpretability, and has advanced performance in many tasks. However, when faced with massive data, its shortcomings are also obvious. Because GBDT needs to traverse all instances of each feature to calculate the information gain and find the optimal split point, it is very time-consuming. To make up for this shortcoming of GBDT, LightGBM was proposed. LightGBM proposes two new algorithms from reducing the number of samples and reducing the feature dimension. Experiments show that LightGBM can reduce the prediction time and still have high accuracy.

According to this situation, first of all, this study selects the Open University Learning Analysis Dataset (OULAD), which has a huge amount of data, to build an online performance prediction model based on the LightGBM algorithm. And use Decision Tree (DT), Random Forest (RF), Support Vector Machine (SVM), Adabo-ost (Ada) four machine learning algorithms to build a performance prediction model and compare it with the LightGBM algorithm. The experiment found that the prediction error of the

MOOC performance prediction model based on the LightGBM algorithm is smaller. Then, the second work done in this study is, Using the interpretability of LightGBM, the importance ranking table of the influence of features on the prediction results is obtained. According to this ranking, two factors that can provide reference for online teaching design are obtained, namely, the influence of the external environment and the influence of the learner's original cognitive structure. Finally, two online teaching design suggestions are given.

2 Related Research

2.1 MOOC Performance Prediction

The research on performance prediction has become one of the research hotspots in the field of educational technology, but in the process of research, many scholars have to face the problem of excessive time cost caused by the large amount of data. Some researchers avoid this by selecting a small number of subjects. Hasan [4] et al. Collected course data from only 22 students and used three types of data characteristics, namely, GPA, pre-course grades, and online module quizzes, to predict the final grade level; Zhao [5] et al. selected 38 students of education technology in Northeast Normal University as the research object, and used 13 variables of learning activity as the characteristics of the dataset, designed and constructed an online learning intervention model based on data mining algorithm and learning analysis technology. In addition to the large amount of data generated by learners, another feature of online learning is that learners have many feature dimensions. For example, Li Shuang et al. [6]. Selected 150 students from four courses at the National Open University as the study population and collected 26 learning variables about their four courses as features to construct the assessment model. Therefore, the author believes that the achievement prediction for MOOC cannot get around the difficult problem of wide data volume and many data set features. Therefore, finding algorithms that can reduce time and storage costs can effectively solves this challenge.

2.2 Analysis of Relevant Factors Affecting the Prediction Results of Online Performance

Soon after the rise of online learning, some researchers focused on the analysis of factors affecting online learning. However, at that time, due to technical limitations, researchers could only use statistical and data mining methods to simply analyze students' learning behaviors to derive relevant factors affecting online learning. For example, Wei et.al [7] studied three types of behavioral data generated by 9369 new students studying the online course as an example, and used data mining methods to derive the characteristics of several online learning behaviors and their influencing factors. However, today, the analysis of factors affecting online learning can be incorporated into the study of online learning performance prediction. Because some of the machine learning algorithms are interpretable in the process of building performance prediction models, researchers can use this interpretable component to give suggestions for instructional design enhancements for online learning after the models are built. For example, Qing Wu et al. [8].

Chose Bayesian networks for student performance prediction and analyzed the model, and then gave suggestions that learners should be more motivated in the learning process. Although Bayesian algorithm is also interpretable, it requires all data to be discretized, so using Bayesian algorithm for grade prediction is more suitable for scenarios where the grade result is a classification problem, such as predicting a pass or fail result.

2.3 Lack of Recommendations for Instructional Organizers at the End of Online Performance Prediction

In order for the study to have a landing point, i.e., a specific application in an educational scenario, the researcher typically uses the prediction results as a reminder to the teachers and learners at the end of the prediction, acting as an early warning. For example, Xu et al. [9] predicted student performance and provided early warning of student performance based on a Heterogeneous information network. Some scholars have also made performance predictions early in students' learning so that learners can gain an understanding of their learning early and adjust their learning early [10–12]. However, simple warnings only provides the limited positive guidance for teachers to change their instructional design.

However, there are still many shortcomings in the current study, including a small number of research subjects so it cannot provide guidance for MOOC courses with a large amount of data, a lack of analysis of explainable factors in the regression prediction process, and some of the studies only serve as an early warning and cannot suggest improvements for teachers and students. Starting from these problems, this study selects the LightGBM algorithm to construct a performance prediction model for a MOOC dataset with a large amount of data: OULAD. Because the online learning dataset has a large amount of data and many feature dimensions, the LightGBM algorithm can take advantage of its own advantages to reduce the amount of data and feature dimensions. This not only ensures the accuracy, but also saves the time and memory overhead of the experiment. Moreover, we can also use the interpretability of the LightGBM algorithm to analyze the prediction results. And propose instructional design improvements to the instructional organizer.

3 Construction of MOOC Learning Performance Prediction Model Based on LightGBM

LightGBM is an algorithm improved on GBDT. GBDT uses a decision tree as a base learner to improve the performance of the model through the idea of integration. The specific workflow of GBDT is shown in Fig. 1 below. It will input the training data into the weak learner to calculate the gradient through the loss function, and then input the result to the next weak learner. In this process, the weights of the parameters are adjusted, and each prediction result is finally added to obtain the final prediction result.

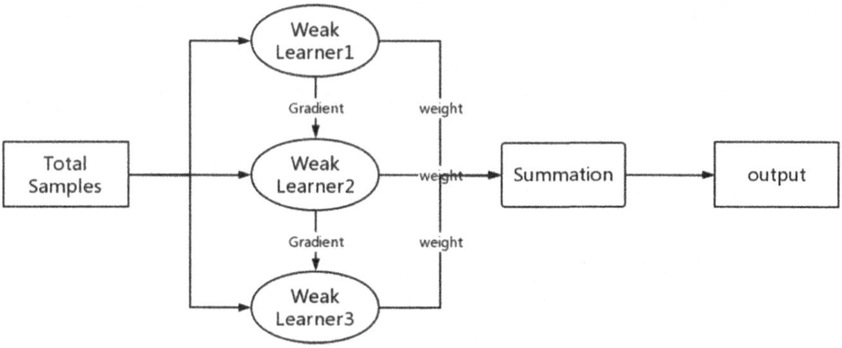

Fig. 1. The gradient boosting flow chart of GBDT

Although GBDT has high accuracy, when selecting split points, it needs to traverse each data to calculate the information gain of all possible split points, so this algorithm is time-consuming when processing massive data. Because its computational complexity is proportional to the amount of data and feature dimension On the basis of GBDT, LightGBM adds two new algorithms to solve this problem, namely Gradient-based One-Side Sampling (GOSS) and Exclusive Feature Bundling (EFB). This not only ensures the high accuracy of the algorithm, but also greatly reduces the consumption of time and storage costs.

3.1 Introduction to the Experimental Data Set

The UK Open University Learning Analytics Dataset (OULAD) was released by the OUAnalyse research group led by Professor ZdenekZdrahal at the Open Data 7 Quintessence Challenge Day on November 17, 2015. The uniqueness of the dataset lies in the richness of the data, which describes student behavior in a virtual learning system. It contains over millions of records generated from 22 courses and more than 32,000 students. The construction of the performance prediction model in this study is centered on the "StudentInfo" worksheet, which is a student information table in the OULAD dataset. This worksheet covers data such as student demographic information and past learning experiences. The features in the dataset provide a more complete description of the student's basic condition and provide a solid foundation for the accuracy of grade prediction. After removing the information that has less relevance to students' grades, such as academic number, we finally get 10 features including "code_module", "gender", "region", "highest_education", "imd_band", "age_band", "num_of_prev_attempts", "studied_credits", "disability", "final_result" are involved in the construction of the MOOC performance prediction model, where final_result is the target variable, and the prediction results will be compared with it to find the error between the prediction results and the true value.

3.2 Preprocessing of the Dataset

In order to make the data meet the usage conditions of the algorithm LightGBM, it is necessary to encode the required features in the dataset. The specific encoding method is shown in Table 1 below.

Table 1. Feature code table

Features	Range of values	Code
code_module	[AAA, BBB, CCC, DDD, EEE, FFF, GGG]	[1–7]
code_presentation	[2013J, 2013B, 2014J, 2014B]	[1–4]
Gender	[F,M]	[1, 2]
Region	[East Anglian Region, Scotland, North Western Region, South East Region…]	[1, 2, 3, 4,…, 13]
highest_education	[HE Qualification, A Level or Equivalent, Lower Than A Level…]	[1, 2, 3,…, 5]
imd_band	[90%–100%, 20%–30%, 30%–40%,…]	[1, 2, 3,…, 8]
age_band	[0–35,35–55, > = 55]	[1–3]
Disability	[Yes, No]	[1,0]

3.3 Construction of MOOC Performance Prediction Model Based on LightGBM

LightGBM has a faster training speed, lower memory consumption and better accuracy because the algorithm improves the gradient boosting decision tree algorithm in two steps. The former one is the GOSS, and the latter is the EFB. GOSS and EFB can optimize the data processing steps, and then help to reduce the amount of data and the related features. The construction of the LightGBM-based MOOC performance prediction model consists of four core steps, and the details are listed as follow.

Converting Features in a Dataset into a Histogram
Take the feature "imd_band" as an example, this feature represents the economic status of the learner. If the previous integrated learning algorithm is used, the economic status of each learner needs to be traversed, and the time overhead required is O (data*feature). Such a time overhead is undoubtedly too high for a data set with a large amount of data. And using the Histogram-based decision tree algorithm can cut the data in a feature into several different bins, and then put the data into the corresponding bins. Therefore, the economic status of the students will be divided into 3 different bins: "1–3", "4–6", and "7–8", and then put the corresponding economic status of each student in the data set into the corresponding bin middle. Then the time over-head will be reduced from the original O(data*feature) to O(feature*bins).

Leaf-wise Algorithm with Depth Limit
LightGBM's leaf growth strategy is a vertical growth strategy, This vertical leaf growth

strategy is called leaf-wise. Leaf-wise will find the leaf with the largest splitting gain from all the current leaves each time, then split, and so on [13]. For example, after splitting the dataset with the feature "gender = F", there are two leaves with the features "disability = YES" and "imd_band = 90%–100%", then the algorithm will choose the one with the greater splitting gain for the next split, and the other one will not be split. Therefore, compared with the previous leaf-wise strategy, leaf-wise can reduce more errors and get better accuracy with the same number of splits. However, leaf-wise also has the disadvantage that using this leaf-growing strategy may grow deeper decision trees and produce overfitting. To avoid this problem, the LightGBM algorithm adds a maximum depth limit to the leaf-wise to ensure high efficiency and prevent overfitting at the same time.

Use GOSS to Reduce the Number of Samples
GOSS is a balanced algorithm to reduce the amount of data and ensure the accuracy by excluding most of the samples with small gradients and using only the remaining samples to calculate the information gain [13]. Taking the feature "imd_band" as an ex-ample, the GOSS algorithm has the following steps.

Sort all samples of the feature "imd_band" to be split according to the gradient size, define two constants a and b. And a represents the value ratio of samples with large gradients, b represents the value ratio of samples with small gradients;

Select a*data_num("imd_band") samples with large gradients, and then select b*data_num("imd_band") samples with small gradients from the remaining samples;

In order not to change the distribution of the data, it is necessary to weight the samples with small gradients and multiply by a constant $\frac{(1-a)}{b}$ to enlarge the weights of the samples with small gradients;

Finally this $(a + b) \times 100\%$ data is used to calculate the information gain.

Use EFB Algorithms for Feature Reduction
High-dimensional data is often sparse, and this sparsity inspires us to design a lossless method to reduce the dimensionality of features. In the LightGBM algorithm, this method of reducing the feature dimension is the mutually exclusive feature bundle EFB [13]. EFB mainly includes the following steps: ranking the features according to the number of non-zero values;

Calculate the conflict ratio between different features;

Iterate through each feature and try to merge features to minimize the conflict ratio.

The mutually exclusive feature bundle can reduce the time complexity of the histogram from O(#data*feature) to O(#data*bundle), and since the number of bundles is much smaller than the number of features, we are able to greatly accelerate the training process of GDBT without losing accuracy.

4 Experimental Results

4.1 Experimental Setup

Evaluation Metrics
The student performance prediction problem in this experiment is a regression problem,

so the root mean square error (RMSE), mean square error (MSE), and mean absolute error (MAE) were chosen to evaluate the LightGBM-based MOOC performance prediction results. These three indicators reflect the distance between the predicted value and the actual value, so the closer the values are, the smaller the gap between the predicted value and the groundtruth. And their expressions are shown in Eq. (1), Eq. (2), and Eq. (3), respectively. Where, n denotes the number of students, y_{pre} denotes the predicted grade of the ith student, and y denotes the true grade of the ith student.

$$\sqrt{\frac{1}{n}\sum\nolimits_{i=1}^{n}\left(y_{pre}-y\right)^2} \tag{1}$$

$$\frac{1}{n}\sum\nolimits_{i=1}^{n}\left(y-y_{pre}\right) \tag{2}$$

$$\frac{1}{n}\sum\nolimits_{i=1}^{n}\left|\left(y-y_{pre}\right)\right| \tag{3}$$

Parameter Setting

The parameters setting of the LightGBM are listed in Table 2, and it took several iterations of the data using the GridSearchCV function to arrive at this optimal set of parameters. Through practical experiments, it was found that the best results were achieved by using the parameters after tuning the parameters for model construction.

Baseline Methods

The LightGBM algorithm can also work quickly in the face of a huge amount of data, and the prediction accuracy is high. In order to verify the LightGBM-based MOOC performance prediction results, we compared it with the other four machine learning algorithms which were commonly used in the other field, namely Decision Tree (DT), Random Forest (RF), Support Vector Machine (SVM), and Adaboost (Adaptive Boosting).

Table 2. Parameter setting table

Parameter name	Parameter value	Parameter name	Parameter value
Estimator	gbdt	objective	Regression
learning_rate	0.1	n_estimators	188
max_depth	4	num_leaves	5
max_bin	35	min_data_in_leaf	1
bagging_fraction	0.8	bagging_freq	40
feature_fraction	0.6	lambda_l1	0.3
lambda_l2	0.1	param_grid	params_test5
cv	5	n_jobs	– 1

4.2 Experimental Results

Experimental Results

MOOC performance prediction models were constructed based on each of the five algorithms on the jupyter notebook in the Python platform. In terms of the experimental process, the LightGBM algorithm takes the shortest time and occupies the least storage space. In terms of the experimental metric results, the LightGBM algorithm predicts the least error between student grades and final student grades, and the specific performance of each algorithm is shown in Table 3 below.

Table 3. Parameter setting table

	Light GBM	DT	RF	SVM	Ada
RMSE	0.97	1.34	1.07	0.99	0.98
MSE	0.95	1.81	1.15	0.98	0.96
MAE	0.79	1.02	0.88	0.80	0.81

This experiment is enough to prove that the LightGBM algorithm has superior performance in the prediction work with large amount of data. Because the three indicators of LightGBM are the lowest, that is to say, the value error predicted by LightGBM is the smallest (see Fig. 2). It shows that GOSS and EFB in the LightGBM algorithm can effectively help MOOC performance prediction to solve the problem of large amount of data and many feature dimensions.

Ranking of Feature Importance

Taking advantage of the interpretability of the LightGBM algorithm, a ranking table of the importance of features affecting the prediction results can be derived during its prediction work (see Fig. 3).

According to this graph, the top 5 factors affecting predicted performance are: "region", "code_module", "studied_credits", "highest_education", and "imd_band". Analyzing the first five factors, "studied_credits" and "highest_education" can be attributed to the learners' existing cognitive structure level, while "region" and "imd_band" can be categorized as the influence of the external environment. Since "code_module" is a factor that cannot be changed objectively, so the next step of this study is to suggest the instructional design of online teaching from two aspects: learners' existing cognitive structure level and external environmental factors.

Analysis of the Advantages of Using Lightgbm for Prediction

According to theoretical analysis and experimental results, the advantages of using LightGBM for prediction mainly include the following two aspects: First, LightGBM greatly reduces the computational complexity of prediction. This benefits from the GOSS algorithm and the EFB algorithm. They reduce the amount of data and feature dimension. Second, the LightGBM algorithm is interpretable, and this interpretability can help us

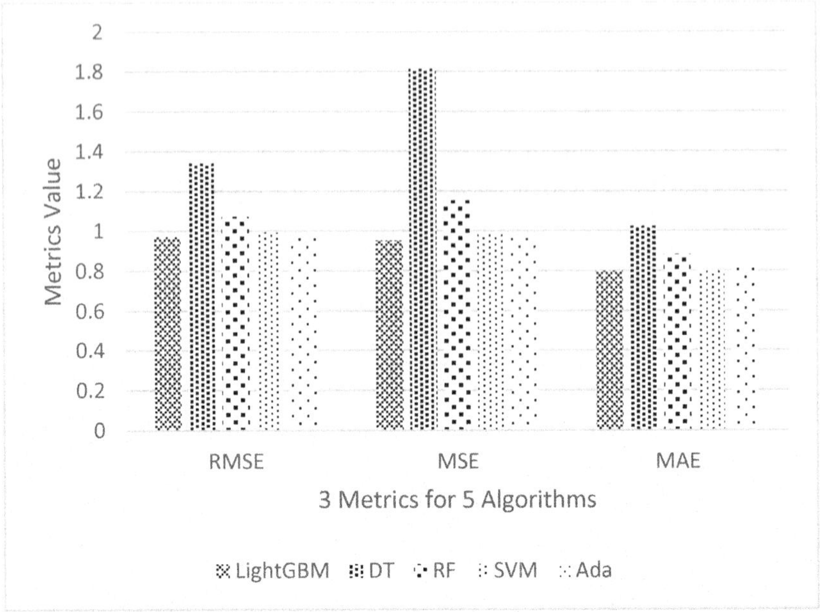

Fig. 2. Performance graph of 3 metrics for 5 algorithms

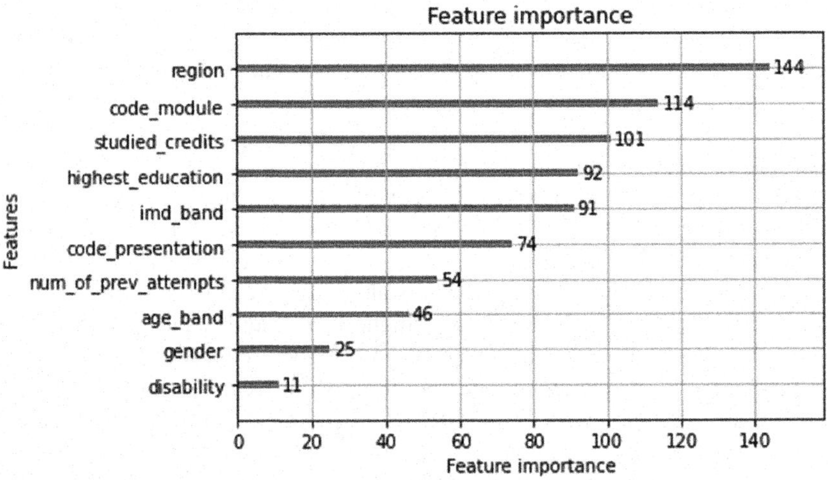

Fig. 3. Map of important features affecting prediction results

find regularities in the data, and these regularities can usually reflect the problems existing in online teaching. Help teachers and students solve problems as soon as possible to improve learning effect.

5 Suggestions for Online Instructional Design Based on Experimental Results

5.1 Different Instructional Designs for Learners in Different External Environments

The learning process of students is a dynamic process, which is affected and restricted by many factors. The external environment is one of the factors affecting students' learning. For example, in the MOOC performance prediction work conducted in this study, "region" and "imd_band" represent the learner's region and the learner's economic status, respectively. These two characteristics, as external environment characteristics, have a great influence on the prediction results. And the mutual information experiment of these two features found a strong correlation between the two features. That is to say, in different regions with different economic conditions, the effectiveness of learners receiving online education is also different. Analyzing the reasons, one cannot be ignored is that the network environment in underdeveloped areas is obviously weaker than that in economically developed areas. The network environment is extremely important for online education, for example, during an epidemic online class, learners with a good network environment can learn without hindrance. However, students in many areas have poor network environments, and they have to spend a lot of time and effort in finding a network environment that can meet the conditions of online classes. Therefore, the delay and lag of the network makes this group of students miss a lot of learning content.

Therefore, according to the different external environments of different learners, the adjusted instructional design can help learners to solve some of the learning difficulties from the external environment. For example, for learners in less developed areas of the network environment, an inquiry-shaped instructional design can be considered, the structure of which is illustrated in Fig. 4 below. The inquiry-shaped instructional design has strong self-feedback, and learners can obtain information through manipulating media and conduct discovery learning through a series of learning activities such as observation, hypothesis, experimentation, verification, and adjustment. This requires a strong ability to integrate teaching resources and a strong information literacy. In such online teaching, the real-time requirements for the network environment can be

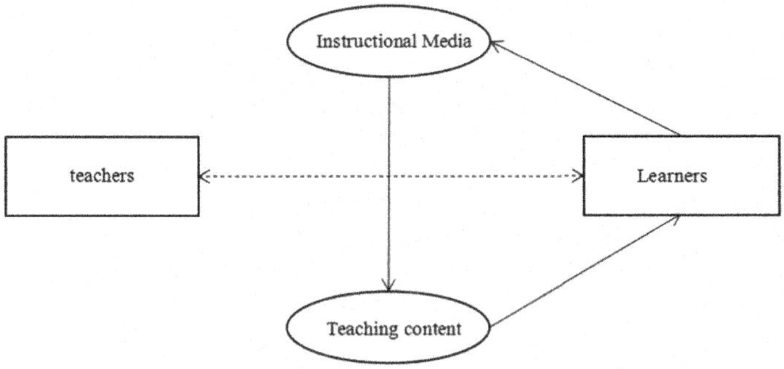

Fig. 4. Illustration of inquiry-shaped teaching structure

appropriately reduced, and the instructor mainly plays the role of guiding and answering questions in the learning process of the learners. Moreover, this way of online teaching allows learners to learn as many times as they want, because the teaching resources developed by the instructor are always available.

5.2 Different Online Instructional Designs for Learners with Different Pre-existing Cognitive Structures

Pre-existing cognitive structure is a key factor in the occurrence and maintenance of learning and is one of the main factors governing the learning process. Important features that affect the prediction results in this study: "studied_credits" and "highest_education", which represent learners' credits and their highest educational level, respectively. Also illustrate the important influence of pre-existing cognitive structures on learners. Before designing an online course, the organizer should understand the learners' existing cognitive structure, which will help to set the starting point of the online course, which is an important prerequisite for tailoring the teaching to the students' needs.

Students are the object of online teaching, and without this element, teaching loses its meaning. In the teaching process, individual differences in student learning are related to the individual student's original knowledge structure, intelligence level, and also to the student's subjective effort. For online teaching organizers, students' intelligence level and effort cannot be easily changed, but they can design different instruction for the same knowledge point according to learners' original cognitive structure. Therefore, it is suggested that online teaching organizers can design different teaching methods and assign different tasks based on learners' education, age, and existing knowledge reserves, so that different learners can reasonably choose the online learning courses according to their actual situations.

Acknowledgements. This work is supported by Yunnan Normal University Graduate Research Innovation Fund (Grant No. YJSJJ22-B88), Yunnan Innovation Team of Education Informatization for Nationalities, and Scientific Technology Innovation Team of Educational Big Data Application Technology in University of Yunnan Province.

References

1. Luo, Y., Xibin, F., Han, S.: Exploring the interpretability of a student grade prediction model in blended courses. Distance Educ. China, 46–55 (2022)
2. Xian, Wei, F.: The evaluation and prediction of academic performance based on artificial intelligence and LSTM. Chinese J. ICT Educ. 123–128 (2022)
3. Hao, J.F., Gan, J.H.: MOOC performance prediction and personal performance improvement via Bayesian network. Educ. Inf. Technol. 1–24 (2022)
4. Hasan, F., Palaniappan, S., Raziffar, T.: Student academic performance prediction by using decision tree algorithm. In: IEEE 2018 4th International Conference on Computer and Information Sciences (ICCOINS), pp. 1–5 (2018)
5. Zhao, H.Q., Jiang, Q., Zhao, W., Li, Y., Zhao, Y.: Empirical research of predictive factors and intervention countermeasures of online learning performance on big data-based learning analytics. e-Educ. Res. 62–69 (2017)

6. Li, S., Li, R., Yu, C.: Evaluation model on distance student engagement: based on LMS data. Open Educ. Res. **24**(01), 91–102 (2018)
7. Wei, S.F.: An analysis of online learning behaviors and its influencing factors:a case study of students' learning process in online course open education learning guide in the open university of China. Open Educ. Res. 81–90+17 (2012)
8. Qing W, Ru-guo L.: Predicting the students' performances and reflecting the teaching strategies based on the e-learning behaviors. Modern Educ. Technol. 6, 18–24 (2017)
9. Xu Xiaoyu, F.: Research on the prediction and early warning model of student achievement based on heterogeneous information network. Inf. Technol. Netw. Secur. 84–89 (2022)
10. Márquez, C., Vera, F.: Early dropout prediction using data mining: a case study with high school students. Expert Syst. **31**(1), 107–124 (2016)
11. Lykourentzou, F., Giannoukos, S., Nikolopoulos, T.: Dropout prediction in e-learning courses through the combination of machine learning techniques. Comput. Educ. **53**(3), 950–965 (2009)
12. Ke, G., Qi, F., Thomas, M.S., Finley, T.: LightGBM: A Highly Effificient Gradient Boosting Decision Tree. Curran Associates Inc, Neural Information Processing Systems (2017)
13. Ke, G., et al.: LightGBM: a highly efficient gradient boosting decision tree. Adv. Neural Inf. Process. Syst. **30** (2017)

MOOC Dropout Prediction Based on Bayesian Network

Shuang Shi[1,2], Shu Zhang[1,2](✉), Jia Hao[2,3], Ken Chen[2], and Jun Wang[2,3]

[1] School of Information Science and Technology, Yunnan Normal University, Kunming 650500, China
zhangshu@ynnu.edu.cn

[2] Key Laboratory of Education Informatization for Nationalities, Ministry of Education, Yunnan Normal University, Kunming 650500, China

[3] Yunnan Key Laboratory of Smart Education, Yunnan Normal University, Kunming 650500, China

Abstract. High dropout rates and unsatisfactory learning outcomes have become the main problems of MOOC platforms, and the intervention of dropout prediction at the early stage is an effective way to solve these problems. To this end, we propose a dropout prediction model based on Bayesian networks (Dropout Prediction Bayesian Network, DPBN), which uses mutual information and the pruning to construct the structure of DPBN, and then the parameters are learned by the maximum likelihood estimation (MLE). The model can represent the influence of each feature on the dropout rate and enhance the interpretability of the model. Based on the constructed DPBN, we adopt the exact inference method to predict the dropouts successfully. The experimental results demonstrate the accuracy and validity of our proposed method.

Keywords: MOOC · Dropout prediction · Bayesian network · Mutual information

1 Introduction

Along with the outbreak of COVID-19 epidemic, a great number of online courses and users is going to flourish. With the ability to provide learners with massive learning resources and encourage students to learn independently without the limitation of time and space, Massive Open Online Courses (MOOC) has become a main online learning trend. However, the MOOC platform also has some problems that hinder its development, such as high registration but low completion rate, high dropout rate, and unsatisfactory learning effect. These problems not only reduce the value of using catechism courses, but also cause some wastage of learning resources. Thus, it is important for MOOC platforms to accurately predict dropouts early in the learning process, so as to identify the students who are at high risk of dropout, and then intervene in a timely manner.

However, the vast majority of current dropout predictions are dedicated to discovering the metrics, models, and algorithms with the best predictive accuracy. As more

Y. Xu et al. (Eds.): ML4CS 2022, LNCS 13657, pp. 520–532, 2023.
https://doi.org/10.1007/978-3-031-20102-8_40

metrics are adopted and more complex algorithms are used, the simplicity and interpretability of the model is declining. On the other hand, previous research has mostly ignored the practicality of machine learning algorithms in solving the problem, blindly pursuing the complexity and accuracy of the models. Besides, there are many factors that influence student dropout, and it is a major challenge for dropout prediction model researchers to use dropout prediction models to well characterize these associations and to identify the major factors that influence student dropout in order to design subsequent interventions.

To address these difficulties, a dropout prediction model based on Bayesian networks (Dropout Prediction Bayesian Networks, DPBN) is proposed in this paper. BN, a graphical model that can express causal relationships and associated uncertain knowledge, are suitable for solving problems which has multiple control factors. Bayesian network has the advantages of clear and intuitive problem solving, and has become a research hotspot in academia. It has been widely used in pattern recognition, decision support, medical diagnosis, data mining, sensor fusion, and automatic control, etc., but it has no application in online learning dropout prediction. The application of Bayesian network for dropout prediction can well describe the direct association of relevant factors affecting dropout, as well as the influence probability of each factor on the prediction result, which strengthens the interpretability of the prediction model. So this paper uses a Bayesian network for dropout prediction.

Bayesian networks is consisted of directed acyclic graphs (Directed Acyclic Graph, DAG) and conditional probability tables (Conditional Probability Tables, CPTs). Therefore, the learning of Bayesian networks includes structure learning and parameter learning. For the former, we adopt the Mutual Information based method, and for the latter, we use the maximum likelihood estimation method.

In the feature processing part, it includes data integration, cleaning, discretization and coding. The structure of BN is constructed by first calculating the mutual information between every two nodes, then determining whether there are edges between two nodes according to the formulated mutual information threshold, and finally removing unreasonable edges by pruning. The parameter calculation part of BN, this paper uses the maximum likelihood estimation method to calculate the CPT of each node.

The research in this paper is summarized as follows.

(1) In this paper, the important factors affecting dropout were firstly screened based on mutual information and then the structure of the network model was constructed using mutual information combined with pruning. Finally, the model parameters were calculated with the maximum likelihood estimation.
(2) Based on the constructed dropout prediction model (DPBN), network inference is used to accurately predict the probability of students' dropout.
(3) Our proposed DPBN is compared with several methods on the OULAD dataset, and the experimental results verify the effectiveness of the algorithm proposed in this paper.

Structure of this paper: Sect. 2 provides an overview of the current status of dropout prediction research at home and abroad, Sect. 3 introduces the data set used in the experiment and the process of data pre-processing, Sect. 4 describes the process of

DPBN construction, Sect. 5 shows the experimental results, and Sect. 6 presents the study conclusions and future prospects.

2 Related Work

2.1 Current Status of Foreign Dropout Prediction Research

The high dropout rate of MOOC has been a concern in the field of online education, and many domestic and international scholars have conducted studies in this field. Foreign research includes analysis and prediction of MOOC learners' behavioral characteristics, interactions, course completion rates, as well as improving course construction and intervening in the teaching process based on learners' behavioral. For example, in terms of modeling, Panagiotakopoulos et al. [1] used nine classification algorithms to predict dropouts and concluded that LightGBM was the best performing model with an accuracy of 96%. Blundo et al. [2] developed a data-driven decision support system (DSS) to identify students at risk of dropping out of school based on FCA (formal concept analysis) and temporal concept analysis. Adnan et al. [3] selected the machine learning algorithm with the best metrics in each aspect for creating predictive models at different percentages of course length. Finally, students' assessment scores, engagement intensity (i.e., clickstream data), and time-related variables were found to be important factors in online learning. Youssef et al. [4], proposed a method based on a feature selection approach and an integrated machine learning algorithm to predict learners at risk of dropping out, learners who are likely to fail, and learners who are on their way to success. Goopio et al. [5] found that factors such as learning experience, interactivity, course design, technology, language, time, and context affect learners' dropout rates. Lacave [6] used the K2 algorithm to identify dropout factors in the course Computer Science Research through Bayesian network modeling.

2.2 Current Status of Dropout Prediction Research in China

Domestic dropout research focuses on several aspects such as learning behavior analysis, outcome prediction, analysis of influencing factors. Wang et al. collated data from the XuetangX platform, and then analyzed users' learning behaviors to grasp their learning characteristics. And the extracted learning behavior features were used to train a random forest model to predict the dropout situation. Wang et al. [7] compared and analyzed the learning behavior of Chinese and American online learners in terms of courses, learners, and platforms, and pointed out the factors influencing the high dropout rate of MOOC and other platforms. Guo et al. [8] selected five learning behaviors and used a binary logistic regression model to model and predict participants' dropout based on the principle of less correlation. To predict the dropout rate of Beijing University courses on Coursera platform, Lu et al. [9] used predicted the dropout rate based on nine features and found that the long-short memory network and support vector machine models worked better. Lin et al. [10] predicted learners' performance based on linear regression and Deep Neural Network (DNN). Yang Lu et al. used the AdaBoost to predict whether learners would drop, and the results showed that two learning behaviors, "completing homework" (problem) and "watching video" (video) had a significant effect on the dropout prediction.

Wei et al. [11] established an RFLP index system for predicting MOOC users' learning behaviors and attrition by improving the RFM model, and determined the characteristic variables influencing MOOC users' attrition by histogram test and chi-square test, and finally combined with the (GMDH) network to build a MOOC user attrition prediction model. In addition, the construction of dropout prediction models has been studied in several dissertations from 2016 to the present, using a wide variety of methods, with algorithms transforming from simple single algorithms (Logistic Regression, Support Vector Machine, Decision Tree) to dynamic algorithms connecting time series (Hidden Markov Models, Neural Networks) and the integration of multiple complex algorithms (e.g., Decision Tree and Support Vector Machine e hybrid algorithms, ELM, etc.) [12].

However, the current state of research on the MOOC dropout prediction problem still has some limitations. Most current dropout prediction methods are dedicated to pursuing the best prediction accuracy, but ignore the pedagogical principles behind the predictors and the technical limitations of teachers in actual teaching. Another limitation is the lack of model interpretability. Existing prediction models cannot explain existing results in terms of the specific causes that lead to specific outcomes. When providing educators with decisions and learners with interventions, targeted advice cannot be given in terms of the behavioral patterns that lead to that outcome.

3 Data Preprocessing

3.1 Dataset Description

OULAD is a current international publicly shared learning analytics dataset, the uniqueness of this dataset lies in the richness of the data, which describes student behavior in the Virtual Learning System (VLE) [13]. It contains several data such as basic information, registration, and learner activity records of more than 32,000 students from 7 modules, 22 online courses, and more than millions of records from the UK Open University between 2013 and 2014. In order to protect personal data, the dataset is anonymized, using the latest technology k-anonymity model and L-diversity, which reflects the dropout rate of MOOC, and the dataset has a large course span and data volume, which is suitable for the construction of dropout prediction model, so the dataset is selected for this study. OULAD contains seven data tables.

Among them, the student information table mainly contains students' demographic information and course learning results (whether they passed or not); the course information table contains course modules and course information; the student registration table contains students' registration and deregistration dates; the task table contains information about tasks and assessment types in the course; the student task table records students' scores in the corresponding tasks and the date of submitting tasks, with a total of 173912 rows The Student Interaction table contains information about the interactions that students perform on the platform, including the type of interaction (understood as the type of learning activity), time and number of interactions; the Interaction Behavior table contains the type of interaction and the date of the start and end of the activity [14].

3.2 Data Preprocessing

The data processing involved in this paper is as follows.

Calculate Total Number of Sumclick. First, the columns sum_click and id_student in the StudentVle.csv data table are used to find the total number of clicks for each student as one of the features of the dropout prediction model.

Calculate the Lastcore. First, we merge the two tables, assessments.csv and studentAssessment.csv, by the column id_assessment, and then remove the data whose assessment_type belongs to Exam, because we are only concerned with the calculation of the usual score, not the final score. Then multiply each test score by the corresponding weight as each student's score for each quiz, and finally add up each student's score for each quiz by the column id_student as each student's usual score.

Data Encoding and Discretization. Since the constructed Bayesian network model is based on discrete data, the data needs to be discretized before the network is constructed. Therefore, in this paper, the total number of hits and hours, as well as the number of credits, for each student are discretized with equal width. The discretized data reduces the number of parameters computed for the Bayesian model. The pre-processed dataset has 23,387 data and 11 attributes.

4 Construction of a Dropout Prediction Model

4.1 Feature Selection

Firstly, based on the summary of previous studies and data in the dataset, i feature variables were selected as the features of this study, and the feature set was set as $\{V_1, V_2, V_n\}$, $V_i(i \in$ {sumclick, lastscore, gender, region, imd_band, age_band, disability, highest_education, studied_credits, num_of_prev_attempted}), represent either the demographic or student participation characteristics. V_{ij} is the jth value of the i-th feature. Mutual information is then applied to analyze the learner's features. Complex correlations among the factors and between the influencing factors and dropout were analyzed to further identify behavioral indicators that have a significant impact on dropout.

4.2 Structural Learning

Based on the basic concept of BN, the definition of Dropout Predictive Bayesian Network (DPBN) is given below.

Definition 1. The DPBN model is a DAG $G = (X, E, \theta)$, where: $X = \{X_1, X_2, \ldots, X_n\}$ is the set of nodes in G, E is the set of directed edges between nodes in G, and θ is the set of nodes CPT in G. Let the parent set of $X_i \rightarrow X_j (1 \leq i, j \leq n, i \neq j)$ denote that X_j depends on X_i. If the set of parent nodes of X_i is $P_a(X_i)$, the CPT of node X_i is $P(X_i|P_a(X_i))$. Given the set of parent nodes of X_i $P_a(X_i)$, X_i is conditionally independent from all its non-descendant nodes.

According to the information theory, two discrete variables X_i and X_j have joint probability function $P(X_i, X_j)$ and marginal probability functions $P(X_i)$, $P(X_j)$, then the mutual information between variables X_i and X_j is:

$$I(X_i, X_j) = \sum_{X_i, X_j} P(X_i, X_j) \log \frac{P(X_i, X_j)}{P(X_i)P(X_j)} \tag{1}$$

The mutual information is non-negative, i.e., $I(X_i, X_j) \geq 0$. The equal sign holds when and only when X_i and X_j are independent of each other. The more X_i and X_j tend to be independent, the results of $I(X_i, X_j)$ is closer to 0, which is the base of independence tests between two random variables. The mutual information can also describe the correlation between two random variables.

In this paper, we use a combination of mutual information and pruning for Bayesian network construction based on the third method. First, we use MI to test the correlation between individual features and dropouts. The MI values between nodes are calculated to determine whether there are edges between them, and then the initial structure is pruned and de-looped. Finally, the parameters of all nodes are calculated by MLE. The structure specific process is shown in Algorithm 1.

Algorithm 1 Structural construction of DPBN

Input: OULAD dataset D, dropout related attributes and predictor dropout, $X = \{X_1, X_2, \ldots, X_n\}$, node order ρ and threshold e
Output: DAG structure of DPBN: $G = (X, E)$

1) Determine the initial structure of the network
   $G \leftarrow$ an unbounded graph consisting of nodes $X_1, X_2, \ldots, X_n$, $H \leftarrow \emptyset, E \leftarrow \emptyset$
   /*H is a list of node pairs and E is a set of directed edges */
   For any two different variables in ρ Do
     If $I(X_i, X_j)$>e Then$H \leftarrow H \cup (X_i, X_j)$
   End For
2) Pruning
   For for each directed edge $(X_i, X_j) \in E$ Do
     If the edge between X_i and X_j is not reasonableThen
       Delete(X_i, X_j)permanently
     End If
   End For
   Return G

Time Complexity of Algorithm 1:

Algorithm 1 performs the mutual information formula $O(n^2)$ times for a DAG containing m data instances and n nodes, and each computation time is O(m); the number of executions of pruning is much smaller than $O(n^2)$. Therefore, Algorithm 1 can construct DPBN in $O(mn^2)$ time.

4.3 Parameter Calculation

The parameters of DPBN are the combinations of the conditional probability tables (CPT). For parameter learning, the commonly used methods are maximum likelihood estimation (MLE) and expectation maximization method (EM). Because the MLE can well solve the problem of learning Bayesian network parameters with known network structure in the case of sufficient sample size, this paper uses the maximum likelihood estimation method to build conditional probability tables. MLE treats the parameters θ of the Bayesian network as independent variables. Using the likelihood function with respect to the parameter θ as the optimization objective.

Based on the complete BN structure, when the set of parents of the predicted nodes is $Pa(V_i)$ and the predicted node V_i takes the value of v_{ij}, we calculate the conditional probability θ_{ijk} corresponding to the predicted node by maximum likelihood estimation (MLE), as shown in Eq. (2).

$$\theta_{ijk} = \frac{Num\big(V_i = v_{ij}, Pa(V_i) = k\big)}{Num(Pa(V_i) = k)} \tag{2}$$

where $Num\big(V_i = v_{ij}, Pa(V_i) = k\big)$ denotes the number of instances in the dataset when the value of V_i is v_{ij} and its parent node takes the value k. $Num(Pa(V_i) = k)$ denotes the number of instances in the dataset when the parent node of V_i is k.

4.4 Model-Based Dropout Prediction

Given the value of the parent node, we can calculate the probability value when the dropout case is 1 or 0, respectively, and then choose the value with the highest probability as the final measure. Algorithm 2 describes in detail how we predict whether a learner drops out of school and obtain the final prediction result. Given a complete DPBN, we predict whether a student drops out of school or not based on a probabilistic inference method.

The reasoning based on Bayesian network is how to realize the result prediction, which mainly includes the following steps:

First enter the value of the given evidence variable into the model, $V = \{V_1 = V_{11}, V_2 = V_{21}, V_n = V_{n1}\}$.

The inference part of the model is the specific values of the query variable q derived from the inference of the evidence variables, and the probability of each value.

Finally, the specific value of the maximum probability and its probability value are output, and a label is defined for the value for output.

The specific procedure is shown in Algorithm 2.

Algorithm 2 DPBN-based dropout prediction

Input: Set of features: $V = \{V_1 = V_{11}, V_2 = V_{21}, V_n = V_{n1}\}$
Output: The dropout prediction results: p
1.Probability value of the predicted label: $value$
2.$value_1 \leftarrow P(q = 0|V_1 = V_{11}, V_2 = V_{21}, \ldots V_n = V_{n1})$
3.$value_2 \leftarrow P(q = 1|V_1 = V_{11}, V_2 = V_{21}, \ldots V_n = V_{n1})$
4.If $value_1 = \max\{value_1, value_2\}$ then $value \leftarrow value_1, p \leftarrow 0$
5.else $value \leftarrow value_2, p \leftarrow 1$
6.return $value$ and p

For example, if the student is from South East Region, gender is Male, her highest educational background is "A Level or Equivalent", and he clicks on the study material in the range of 60 to 80, with usual scores in the range of 0 to 20. According to the constructed DPBN, the conditional probability P (q = 1|region = South East Region, gender = Male, sumclick = 60–80, lastscore = 0–20, highest_education = A Level or Equalent) is the maximum. Therefore DPBN predicts that this student will drop out of school.

5 Experiment

5.1 Experiment Setup

Dataset. Firstly, the pre-processed OULAD dataset is divided into a training set and a test set with a ratio of (8:2) with the five-fold cross-validation method. All data preprocessing codes and methods presented in this paper are implemented on Jupyter notebook bas- ed on Python 3.0.

Evaluation Metrics. Accuracy (Accuracy): It refers to the ratio of the number of correctly predicted samples to the total number of predicted samples, it does not consider whether the predicted samples are positive or negative cases, and reflects the overall performance of the model algorithm, and its formula is Eq. (3).

$$Accuracy = \frac{TP + TN}{TP + TN + FP + FN} \tag{3}$$

where TP (True Positives) refers to the number of instances that are correctly classified as positive, i.e., the number of instances that are actually dropouts and classified as dropouts by the classifier; FP (False Positives) refers to the number of instances that are incorrectly classified as positive, i.e., the number of instances that are actually non-dropouts but classified as dropouts by the classifier. FN (False Negatives) refers to the number of instances that are incorrectly classified as negative, i.e., the number of instances that are actually dropouts but are classified as no dropouts by the classifier; TN (True Negatives) refers to the number of instances that are correctly classified as negative, i.e., the number of instances that are actually no dropouts and are classified as no dropouts by the classifier.

F1-Score (F1-Score) is defined as the summed average of the precision and recall rates, its maximum value is 1 and its minimum value is 0. The formula is Eq. (4).

$$F1 - Score = 2\frac{Precision \times Recall}{Precision + Recall} \tag{4}$$

AUC: (Area Under Curve): the area under the ROC curve, whose value usually ranges from 0.5 to 1, and the larger the value is, the better the performance of the model algorithm.

To validate our predictions, this paper is also compared with five other baselines.

- Logistic Regression (LR), a typical dichotomous classification method, uses gradient descent to solve for parameters to achieve the purpose of dichotomizing data.
- Naive Bayes (NB) is a statistical classification method based on Bayes' theorem and the assumption of conditional independence of features. It uses Bayesian formula to find the conditional probability of a sample for each category, and the category corresponding to the largest conditional probability is the category corresponding to the sample.
- Decision Tree (DT) is based on a tree structure for decision making. Each non-leaf node in the tree represents a test on a feature attribute, each branch represents the output of this feature attribute on a value domain, and each leaf node stores a category.
- Random Forest (RF) further introduces random attribute selection in the training process of decision tree to improve the generalization performance of the final integrated classifier, based on the decision tree as the base learner to build Bagging integration.
- Support Vector Machine (SVM), Support Vector Machine is a supervised machine learning method commonly used in binary classification applications.
- Multilayer Perceptron (MLP), Multilayer Perceptron is also called Artificial Neural Network (ANN) to solve nonlinear separable problems by increasing the number of layers.

Based on the idea of five-fold cross-validation, we randomly selected the corresponding proportions from the data set and the test results were noted as T1, T2,…, T5. The specific parameter values are shown in Table 1.

Parameters of the random forest, "n_ estimators" is the number of subtrees, "max_ depth" is the maximum depth of the tree, usually between 10–100. "min_samples_ split" is the minimum number of samples required for internal nodes, and is the default value of 2. The parameters of SVM are set, first is the kernel function, choose "rbf". "C" is the penalty coefficient, "gamma" is a parameter that comes with the function after choosing rbf function as kernel. The larger the gamma is, the smaller the support vector is, and the smaller the gamma value is, the more support vectors are. The number of support vectors affects the speed of training and prediction. In SVC, if the data is unbalanced (e.g.many positive numbers and few negative numbers), set class_weight = 'balanced', probability = True, which sets the randomness of the underlying implementation. Logistic regression with penalty = '11, for penalty, C = 0.001, mainly regulates the strength of the regularization, the smaller the value, the stronger the regularization. Solver = 'saga' is the optimization algorithm used inside the logistic regression. The maximum depth of the decision tree max_depth = 10, the minimum number of samples of leaf nodes min_samples_leaf = 1, this value limits the minimum number of samples of leaf nodes, if the number of a leaf node is less than the number of samples, it will be pruned together with its siblings. Min_samples -_split = 2, the minimum number of samples required for internal node re-division, the default is 2. Parameters of the multilayer perceptron: solver = 'lbfgs', alpha = 1e-5, hidden_layer_sizes = (10,4), random_state = 1.

Table 1. Experimental parameter setting.

Method	Parameters
DPBN	None
RF	n_ estimators = 10, max_ depth = 13, min_ samples_ split = 2
SVM	kenel = 'rbf', class_ weight = 'balanced', gamma = 1, C = 1, probability = True
LR	C = 0.001, penalty = 'l1', solver = 'saga'
NB	None
DT	max_depth = 10, min_samples_leaf = 1, min_samples_split = 2
MLP	solver = 'lbfgs', alpha = 1e-5, hidden_layer_sizes = (10,4), random_state = 1

5.2 Experimental Results

We calculated the accuracy, F1 scores, and AUC values for T1, T2,..., and T5, as shown in Fig. 1, and the mean values of the results after five 5-fold cross-validation are presented in Table 2.

As can be seen from Fig. 1.(a), the experimental results are converging gradually after five five-fold cross-validation. The dropout prediction model in this paper achieves an accuracy rate of about 84.7% in the test results, which is the highest compared to several other algorithms. Next is the random forest algorithm, which were the second greatest algorithm. In this experiment, the Bayesian network algorithm has higher prediction accuracy than RF, which shows the effectiveness of our proposed model. The third place is MLP. The deep learning algorithm is slightly inferior in processing tabular data. This is because the characteristics of the data have many categorical variables, and the effect is not particularly good for deep learning algorithms that specialize in processing continuous variables. This is followed by the decision tree algorithm, which is a particularly common algorithm for classification tasks. Finally, the results of the NB and logistic regression algorithms are slightly worse, which is reasonable.

F1 values and AUC are often used to judge the quality and stability of a model, with larger values indicating a better model. It is obvious from Fig. 1. (b) and Fig. 1. (c) that the model in this paper is convincing in terms of stability. The largest value belongs to our model. Next is the logistic regression, which has the same AUC values as the model in this paper. This is related to the powerful performance of its own algorithm. The

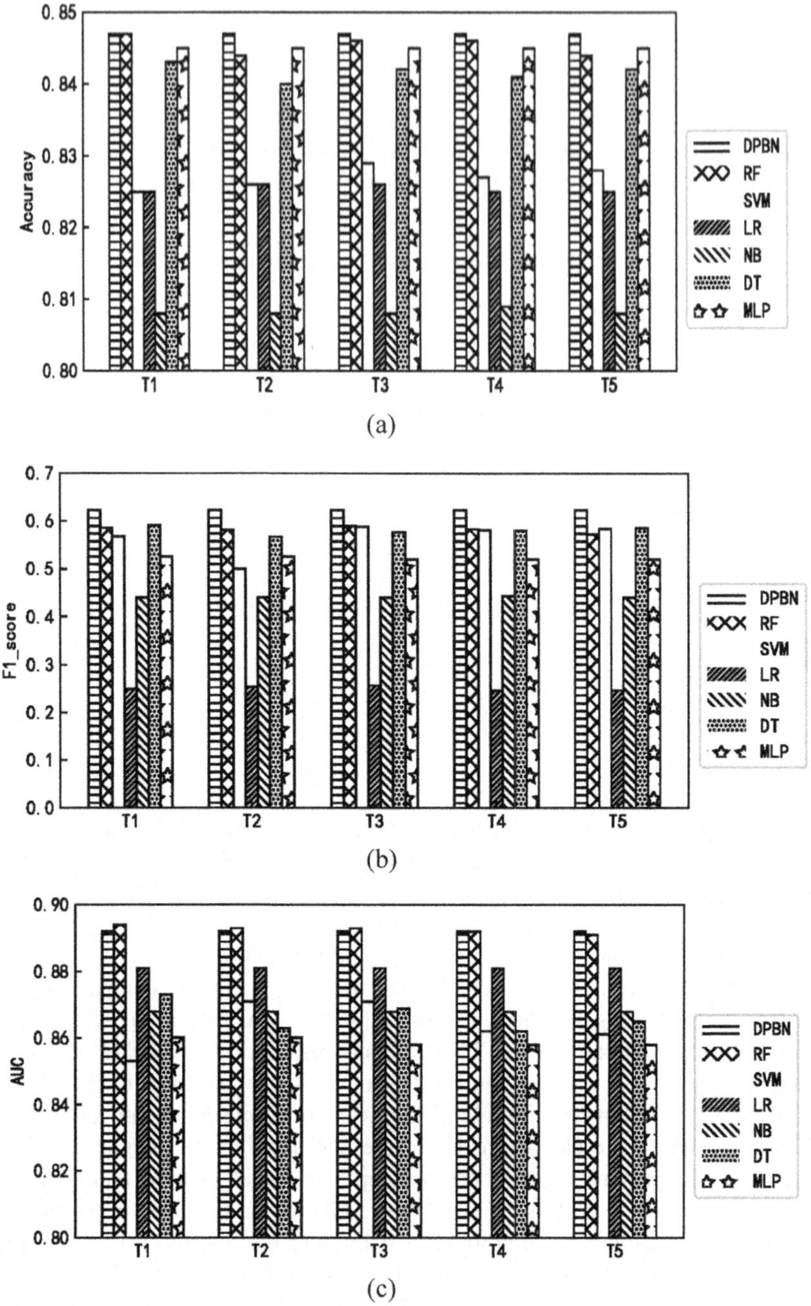

Fig. 1. The three subplots (a), (b) and (c) show the accuracy, F1 scores and AUC values for T1-T5, respectively.

logistic regression algorithm belongs to linear model, which is suitable for regression analysis and less suitable for classification problems.

Table 2 shows the average values of the experimental results. Overall, it can be observed that DPBN outperforms other methods in terms of accuracy, F1 and AUC values due to its not only can express the uncertain dependence between multiple MOOC-related features, but also easier the inference of the final grades in the form of probabilities, thus making predictions more valid and enhancing the interpretability of the model.

Table 2. Mean value of experimental results.

Method	Accuracy	F1-Score	AUC
DPBN	**0.847**	**0.623**	**0.892**
RF	0.845	0.582	0.892
SVM	0.827	0.564	0.862
LR	0.825	0.25	0.811
NB	0.808	0.441	0.868
DT	0.842	0.579	0.866
MLP	0.845	0.522	0.859

6 Conclusion

In this paper, we propose a dropout prediction model in MOOC, which can predict the dropout status of students in MOOC from their personal background information as well as engagement data. When we use the proposed model to predict the predicted status of MOOC learners, we first collect the individual learning data of learners and form a feature vector to perform dropout prediction using Bayesian network inference. Experimental results based on the OULAD dataset show that this dropout prediction model outperforms others.

However, the research in this paper has many areas that can be expanded, such as attribution analysis based on the Bayesian network model, or adding the current deep learning algorithm specializing in processing tabular data on the basis of this model, while improving the accuracy of the model, Enhancing the interpretability of deep learning. Therefore, future research should start with addressing the high dropout rate of MOOCs, exploit the interpretability of the Bayesian network model, and then improve the model to dig deeper into the reasons behind MOOC dropout. From the point of view of reasons, the solution strategies and intervention measures to reduce the dropout rate of MOOC platform are proposed.

Acknowledgment. This work is supported by School of Information Science and Technology, Yunnan Normal University Graduate Research Innovation Fund (NO. CIC2022011),Scientific research foundation of Yunnan Provincial Department of Education (Grant No. 2022Y180), Yunnan Innovation Team of Education Informatization for Nationalities, and Scientific Technology Innovation Team of Educational Big Data Application Technology in University of Yunnan Province.

References

1. Panagiotakopoulos, T., Kotsiantis, S., Kostopoulos, G., Iatrellis, O., Kameas, A.: Early dropout prediction in MOOCs through supervised learning and hyperparameter optimization. Electronics **10**, 1701 (2021). https://doi.org/10.3390/electronics10141701
2. Blundo, C., Fenza, G., Fuccio, G., Loia, V., Orciuoli, F.: A time-driven FCA-based approach for identifying students' dropout in MOOCs. Int. J. Intell. Syst. **37**(4), 2683–2705 (2021)
3. Adnan, M., et al.: Predicting at-risk students at different percentages of course length for early intervention using machine learning models. IEEE Access **9**, 7519–7539 (2021)
4. Youssef, M., Mohammed, S., Hamada, E.K., Wafaa, B.F.: A predictive approach based on efficient feature selection and learning algorithms' competition: Case of learners' dropout in MOOCs. Educ. Inf. Technol. **24**(6), 3591–3618 (2019). https://doi.org/10.1007/s10639-019-09934-y
5. Goopio, J., Cheung, C.: The MOOC dropout phenomenon and retention strategies. J. Teach. Travel Tour. **21**(2), 177–197 (2021)
6. Lacave, C., Molina, A.I., Cruz-Lemus, J.A.: Learning analytics to identify dropout factors of computer science studies through Bayesian networks. Behav. Inf. Technol. **37**(10–11), 993–1007 (2018)
7. Wang, X.Y., Gang, Z., Xiao, L.: Research on the learners dropout prediction based on the MOOC data. Mod. Educ. Technol. **27**(06), 94–100 (2017)
8. Guo, W.F., Chao, F., Guo, X.D.: Predicting the MOOC dropout rate with binary logistic regression model. Comput. Era **12**, 50–53 (2017)
9. Lu, X.H., Wang, S.Q., Huang, J.J., Chen, W.G., Yan, Z.W.: Predicting dropout rates of MOOCs with sliding window model. Data Anal. Knowl. Discov. **1**(04), 67–75 (2017)
10. Lin, P.F., He, X.Q., Chen, T.T., Wu, H.J., He, J.H.: Prediction of loss and teaching intervention for learners in MOOC from perspective of deep learning. Comput. Eng. Appl. **55**(22), 258–264 (2019)
11. Ling, W., Guo, X.Y.: Using adapted RFM and GMDH algorithms to predict MOOC user attrition rate. Distance Educ. China **09** (2020)
12. Chang, L.Y., Jing, L., Chong, H.: Research on MOOC dropout. Library Tribune 1–14 (2021)
13. Kuzilek, J., Hlosta, M., Zdrahal, Z.: Open university learning analytics dataset. Sci. Data **4**(1), 1–8 (2017)
14. Shi, W.R., Niu, X.J., Zheng, Q.H.: Empirical study on the influencing factors of activity-centered online courses learning outcomes: take OULAD as an example. J. Open Learn. **23**(06), 10–18 (2018)

Knowledge Enhanced BERT Based on Corpus Associate Generation

Lu Jiarong[1], Xiao Hong[1(✉)], Jiang Wenchao[1,2], Yang Jianren[2], and Wang Tao[1]

[1] School of Computer Science and Technology, Guangdong University of Technology, Guangzhou 510006, China
wh_red@163.com

[2] Guangzhou Yun Shuo Technology Development Co., Ltd, Guangzhou 511458, China

Abstract. The pre-training model represented by BERT has limited accuracy due to a lack of professional domain knowledge support. The knowledge-enhanced BERT model effectively improves the lack of knowledge in downstream tasks in different fields by introducing external professional knowledge and has achieved better results than the BERT model. However, the knowledge-enhanced BERT injected large-scale external knowledge, resulting in a sharp increase in computing resource requirements and training time. To solve this problem, a knowledge enhancement method based on corpus associate generation (CAG) is proposed. The input text corpus is disassembled into a sequential sequence of word sets and entity noun sets through entity noun recognition, and the word sets are associated with external knowledge triples through entity nouns. Using semantic splicing to generate corpus with external knowledge. Finally, the original BERT model structure is used to inject the corpus containing knowledge into the downstream tasks for knowledge enhancement, avoiding the introduction of additional model structures to increase the model complexity, to achieve the purpose of reducing the amount of calculation. Experimental analysis with 6 public data sets such as LCQMC and XNLI, the results show that compare to K-BERT, the average calculation time of knowledge introduction and training is reduced by 53.5% and 37.4% .

Keywords: Natural language processing · Pre-training models · Knowledge enhanced · Corpus generation · Training acceleration

1 Introduction

Natural language processing is an important branch of computer science. In recent years, with the development of artificial intelligence and the rapid improvement of hardware performance, there are many neural network models for natural language processing had been proposed, such as ELMo [1], OpenAI GPT [2], BERT [3]. These models have excellent natural language understanding and information processing capabilities, far exceeding traditional models such as N-Gram [4], Decision tree [5], Maximum entropy model [6, 7].

Y. Xu et al. (Eds.): ML4CS 2022, LNCS 13657, pp. 533–547, 2023.
https://doi.org/10.1007/978-3-031-20102-8_41

As a mainstream natural language understanding model in recent years, BERT has shown good performance in many open domain tasks. BERT is composed of Encoder of Transformer and self-attention mechanism of Self-Attention [8]. The Base and Large models of BERT have 12 and 24 layers of the above structure respectively, which constitutes a deep neural network. The main contribution of BERT is to propose and extend the two-step method of the pre-trained model. Firstly, a large number of the corpus is used to train the model parameters to obtain the knowledge and language cognitive ability in the universal context, and then the pre-training parameters are used to fine-tune the downstream tasks. The two-step strategy of pre-training and fine-tuning makes BERT the best model for many open field tasks in 2018.

However, BERT still does not solve some common problems of the pre-training model. For example, limited by the scale and characteristics of the pre-training corpus and the learning ability of the model, its application still has limitations. To improve the accuracy and performance of BERT, many studies have adjusted and optimized based on Bert. The specific optimization directions include adjusting the pre-training process, modifying the model structure or injecting external knowledge. The knowledge that used for enhancing the model comes from the knowledge graph. The knowledge modeling is a key problem of the knowledge graph construction, Yun et al. [9] proposed a survey of knowledge modeling and techniques to build a knowledge graph so that we could utilize the knowledge information better.

In adjusting the pre-training process, Baidu-ERNIE [10] and BERT-WWM [11] had improved the work in the pre-training stage. They changed the way of masking a single character to masking a complete Chinese word and trained the model with the help of a larger Chinese corpus. RoBERTa [12] deleted the NSP training of BERT and used longer training time and longer sentences for model training. In the direction of model structure improvement, XLNet [13] used transformer-XL to replace the transformer structure of BERT [14] and added more data for pre-training. T5 [15] model used decoder-encoder structure to replace encoder structure of BERT,then training the model with Colossal Clean Crawled Corpus data set, which with larger scale and purer data than BERT, so as to become the best model in a series of downstream tasks. In the direction of introducing external knowledge, compared with clear and structured explicit knowledge, pre-training allowed the model to obtain vague implicit knowledge from a large number of corpuses. To solve the problem that BERT lacks explicit knowledge, incorporating explicit knowledge into the model can improve the generalization ability and robustness of the model [16] such as THU-ERNIE [17], KnowBERT [18], K-BERT [19], KSGKT [20].

In addition, the optimization methods for injecting extra knowledge can be divided into pre-training and fine-tuning according to the different stages of knowledge introduction. THU-ERNIE and KnowBERT injecting knowledge in the pre-training phase of the model, encoded knowledge entities through word2vec [21] and TransE [22], input their respective fusion layer structure, and superimposed them on the deep neural network to achieve knowledge injection. Compared to THU-ERNIE and KnowBERT, K-BERT added explicit knowledge in the Fine-tune phase with a replaceable knowledge database for different domains and gained performance improvements in downstream tasks in various specific domains [23] K-BERT does not import knowledge in the pre-training phase so that reduces the additional compute resources requirements for knowledge embedding. However, in order to inject knowledge from the knowledge graph, K-BERT also has its own problems that mention below.

1) The structure of sentence tree with explicit knowledge cannot be directly trained by the original BERT model.
2) Analysis sentence tree by using the visible matrix create too much information redundancy.
3) Visible matrix expands exponentially with the length of input sentences, and it takes longer to inject knowledge and training.

To solve these problems, this paper proposed a Corpus Associate Generation based Knowledge Enhanced BERT(CAGBETR). CAGBERT transforms the heterogeneous data from the knowledge graph into a sequence structure then embedding to the model. Explicit knowledge is injected on the basis of semantic association. By this method we effectively reduce model training cost and calculation time both in knowledge enhancement and fine-tuning training.

The experiment was carried out on six open datasets, such as LCQMC and XNLI. The results show that the accuracy of CAGBERT is equal to K-BERT in downstream tasks, but the average time spent in knowledge introduction and training phases is 53.5% and 37.4% lower than K-BERT respectively.

2 Corpus Associate Generation Based Knowledge Enhanced BERT

2.1 Symbol Definition

We denote a sentence $S = \{c_0, c_1, c_2, ..., c_n\}$ as a sequence of token combinations, n represents the length of the sentence. English tokens are taken at the word-level, while Chinese tokens are at character-level. Each token is included in the vocabulary, represent as $c_i \in \mathbb{V}$. The Knowledge Graph is defined as $\mathbb{K}$, which contains all triples $\tau = (e_i, r, e_j), \tau \in \mathbb{K}$. e_i and e_j represent two different entity's names, while r represents the relationship between the two different entities. All nouns of the entities from corpus represented as $Noun \in \mathbb{K}$.

2.2 Model Overview

The structure of the CAGBERT is shown in Fig. 1. It consists of four parts, the knowledge layer for querying the knowledge entity, corpus generator for connecting the knowledge entity and the related text, embedding layer which contains token embedding, position embedding, segment embedding, and the 12 layers encoder of Transformer. External knowledge comes from the replaceable knowledge base, so as to enhance the knowledge of tasks in different professional fields.

The extra knowledge from knowledge base and sentences from the dataset will be applied to downstream tasks through the following process.

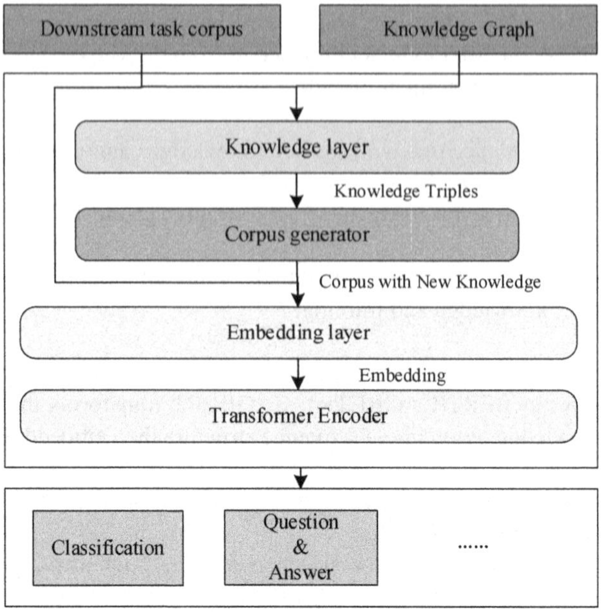

Fig. 1. Model structure and operation process.

(1) The original sentences will be copied after input into the model, one copy will directly enter the embedding layer waiting for data embedding.
(2) Another data copy will be handed over to the knowledge layer, which connected to the external knowledge base, querying for the knowledge entities of the sentences, and the query result will be sent to the corpus generator.
(3) The corpus generator fuses the knowledge triples with its relevant sentences, and transmits the newly generated corpus to the Embedding layer.
(4) The copy of the original sentence and the new corpus for knowledge enhancement are send to the embedding layer for Embedding at the same time, and finally handed over to the Transformer encoder layer for model training.

2.3 Corpus Associate Generation Method for Knowledge Injection

The pre-training model is training on large-scale unlabeled corpus, which contains human natural language to obtain information hidden in the corpus. This concept has been implemented in different engineering applications and has been demonstrated in a number of natural language tasks such as GLUE, SQuAD, etc. However, such knowledge injected by such traditional methods will have a lot of redundancy and noise, which will increase the computational load of model training. To overcome this problem, a Corpus Associate Generation (CAG) method is proposed to generate corpus with domain semantics-related knowledge to fine-tune the model. In order to achieve better performance in downstream tasks in different domains, this part of explicit knowledge is injected into the pre-training model so that the model can obtain knowledge related to the downstream task semantics from the external knowledge base.

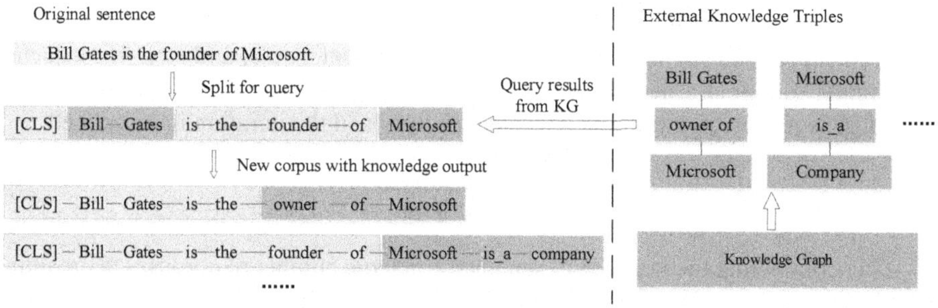

Fig. 2. Associating external knowledge and original corpus to generate new corpus.

As we shown in the Fig. 2, the process of knowledge injection by the CAG method required the knowledge triples $\mathcal{T}$ and the entity noun set $\mathbb{E}$ which both obtained from the knowledge layer. The model uses external knowledge base for knowledge enhancement and entity retrieval for entity selection. In order to obtain the entity nouns from its original input corpus, the knowledge layer needs to distinguish the entity noun contained in the original sentence $S = \{c_0, c_1, c_2, ..., c_n\}$ of the input, as shown in Formula (1).

$$\mathbb{E} = \text{Seg(S, Noun)} \tag{1}$$

The entity noun set $\mathbb{E} = \{Noun_0, Noun_1, ..., Noun_n\}$ identified above is for query the external knowledge base, and the matching triple sets $\mathcal{Q} = \{\tau_0, \tau_1, \tau_2, ..., \tau_n\}$,$\tau = \left(e_i, r, e_j\right)$ are obtained from the external knowledge base, as shown in formula (2).

$$\mathcal{Q} = \text{Query}(\mathbb{E}, \mathbb{K}) \tag{2}$$

Through the above two-step calculation, the knowledge triples set $\mathcal{T}$ and the entity nouns set $\mathbb{E}$ for the subsequent corpus generation are prepared. Then, the knowledge triples set $\mathcal{T}$ is randomly sorted by Top-K algorithm shown in formula (3), and the knowledge triples are extracted according to the number of configured in the model.

$$T = TopK(Q) \tag{3}$$

After Top-K running with the parameters set above, the Top-2 knowledge triple $\mathcal{T}$ returned by the algorithm. This knowledge belongs to the external knowledge graph $\mathbb{K}$, which is a subset of $\mathbb{K}$ and is symbolized as $\mathcal{T} \in \mathbb{K}$.

After the corpus generator obtains the knowledge triple set $\mathcal{T}$ and the entity noun set $\mathbb{E}$, the input sentences will be segment and reconstituted into sentences in left-to-right order, as shown in Formula (4). This operation is intended to distinguish the knowledge entities in the input sentences. The entity nouns which required knowledge enhance will be explicitly identified from the sentence sequences for the next CAG operations.

$$\mathcal{s} = \{Noun_0, c_1, c_2, Noun_3, \ldots, c_n\} \tag{4}$$

Then select the knowledge triple $\tau = \left(e_i, r, e_j\right)$ which matches the entity from the knowledge triple set $\mathcal{T}$ and convert it to the knowledge short sentence $\mathcal{w}_i$through the transform operation. Replace the previously marked entity noun with the knowledge short sentence $w_i$during the constituting process of sentence s, and stop the sequence $s$generation to output a new sentence t. This process is described as formula (5), the procedure is repeated until the sentence $s$converges and the iteration is completed.

$$\begin{cases} w_i = \text{Transform}(\tau_i) \\ t_i = s_i + w_i \end{cases} \tag{5}$$

After completing the iteration of sentence t, a large number of corpuses Scontaining explicit knowledge will be prepared. Then, as shown in Fig. 1, these data will be used as input data for the transformer layer along with the original input sentence S.

2.4 Transformer and Embedding Layer

Once the data enters the Embedding layer, the Embedding operation on the data will follow the BERT design, including Token Embedding, Position Embedding, and Segment Embedding. Token embedding denotes word embedding. In order to solve the problem that sentence sequence position information may be lost during word embedding, it must be supplemented by position embedding. Finally, Segment Embedding is used to distinguish between multiple sentences in a single input during the embedding process.

The Token Embedding operation is executed with reference to BERT, following its model parameters and vocabulary. The label [CLS] is used at the beginning of a sentence, and the label [SEP] is used to distinguish between different sentences in a single input in which each token is converted to an embedded vector with a dimension $\mathcal{H}$ by preset parameters provided by BERT.

To prevent the model from degenerating into a word bag model due to lack of sequence information, Position Embedding embeds data for each word in a sentence in a left-to-right order, giving the model some relative location information.

Segment Embedding uses Boolean value pairs (0,1) as segment markers. For example, when sentences $\{c_0, c_1, c_2, ..., c_n\}$ and $\{w_0, w_1, w_2, ..., w_n\}$ need to be input into the model at the same time for training or fine-tuning, they will be stitched together to form a long sentence $\{[CLS], c_0, c_1, c_2, ..., c_n, [SEP], w_1, w_2, ..., w_n\}$. In order to distinguish them within the model, two clauses in the sentence are distinguished by (0,1), which is represented as $\{0, 0, 0, ..., 0, 1, 1, ..., 1\}$ of segment tags. Token Embedding, Position Embedding, and Segment Embedding form the basic input structure layer of the model and perform preliminary operations on the input data.

The Transformer layer follows the transformer structure of BERT, and its encoder consists mainly of a multi-head attention mechanism, a fully connected feed-forward neural network, residual linking and normalization. The result $e = e_0, e_1, e_2 \dots\dots e_n$of the Embedding layer is used as input to the model. The multi-head attention mechanism is composed of eight self-Attention modules. The input vector $e$is multiplied by matrix based on matrix W^Q, W^K and W^V to get the query matrix Q, the key matrix K and the value matrix V. Then the self-attention is calculated using Q, K and V, as shown in formula (6).

$$Attention(Q, K, V) = softmax\left(\frac{QK^T}{\sqrt{dk}}\right)V \tag{6}$$

Unlike K-BERT, the Attention calculation in this model still uses the traditional calculation formula, rather than the modified Mask-Self-Attention method in K-BERT, as shown in Formula (7). The knowledge enhancement method proposed in this paper does not need to modify the structure of the Transformer layer, and self-Attention reduces the size of the operation by reducing the SoftMax operation of the visible matrix VM compared with Mask-Self-Attention.

$$S = softmax\left(\frac{QK^T + VM}{\sqrt{dk}}\right) \tag{7}$$

The output at the Transformer layer uses the cross-entropy loss function [24] as shown in formula (8), which trains the neural network structure in backward propagation as the target function for downstream tasks.

$$\mathcal{H}(y, \hat{y}) = \sum\nolimits_i y_i \log \frac{1}{\hat{y}_i} \tag{8}$$

Formula (8) y_i represents the true distribution probability of the input data, corresponding to the label in the data set, and $\frac{1}{\hat{y}_i}$ represents the prediction distribution probability, corresponding to the classification probability of the model output. In subsequent experiments, this loss function is used to train the model.

2.5 Time Complexity Analysis

FLOPs represent the number of floating-point operations used to measure the complexity of the model calculation and as an indirect measure of the speed of the neural network model. The larger the FLOPs value, the more operations the model needs in actual operation and is positively related to the actual operation time [25].

The sentence tree data structure used by the K-BERT requires two additional computations: (1) a visible matrix for interpreting the sentence tree data structure; (2) Mask-Self-Attention calculation to prevent BERT model from confusing input information. The quantity of computations used to calculate the VM during the introduction of knowledge is shown in formula (9).

$$FLOPs_{VM} = \mathcal{N} + \mathcal{M}^2 + \mathcal{P} \tag{9}$$

For example, a sentence with length $\mathcal{N}$ is injected with knowledge, assuming it additionally injects knowledge of $\mathcal{M}$. It needs to be computed in K-BERT to get a visible matrix for interpreting its sentence tree data structure, whose matrix dimension is $\mathcal{N} + \mathcal{M}$. Due to the sparseness of the generated matrix and the degree of data association, additional computational times consuming number $\mathcal{P}$ are needed to supplement the visible matrix information.

If the scale of operation mentioned above is expressed as n, the functional operation of this part can be expressed as (10). This part involves matrix operation with dimension $\mathcal{N} + \mathcal{M}$ and needs to be supplemented by a selective assignment operation whose scale $\mathcal{P}$ is positively related to $\mathcal{N} + \mathcal{M}$, which is treated as approximation here. The time complexity of this operation can be described by a big O notation. In the worst case, the time complexity of the calculation is shown in formula (11). The calculation time of the VM algorithm in K-BERT is shown in formula (12) and the time complexity is $O(n^2)$.

$$f(n) = n^2 + n \tag{10}$$

$$T(n) = O(f(n)) \tag{11}$$

$$T(n) = O\left(n^2\right) \tag{12}$$

The knowledge injection method proposed in this paper based on CAG uses a lighter way to inject knowledge into downstream tasks without importing additional data structures and interpreting the injected knowledge. The input data will be directly embedded by the Embedding layer in the model structure. The amount of corpus generation calculation for knowledge injection is shown in formula (13).

$$FLOPs_{CK} = \mathcal{N} + \mathcal{M} \tag{13}$$

After knowledge injection into a sentence of length $\mathcal{N}$, assuming that it additionally inject a knowledge triple of number $\mathcal{M}$, it combines the knowledge triple of length $\mathcal{N}$ with the knowledge triple of number $\mathcal{M}$, outputs a corpus containing external knowledge of number $\mathcal{N} + \mathcal{M}$. Similarly, when the above operation n is expressed as its size, the function operation of this part can be expressed as formula (14), its time complexity can be described by big O notation in formula (15) which as O(n). Meanwhile the time complexity of calculating VM algorithm in K-BERT can be obtained by calculating the time complexity in the worst case as formula (12).

$$f(n) = 2n \tag{14}$$

$$T(n) = O(n) \tag{15}$$

Relative to the time complexity $O(n^2)$ of VM algorithm in the knowledge introduction process of K-BERT, the time complexity of the model proposed in this paper reaches $O(n)$, which can effectively reduce the time complexity of its model training and theoretically reduce the time consumption of model training.

3 Experiment and Analysis

3.1 Experimental Data Set

In order to verify the performance of the model, we set up experiments including Question-and-Answer tasks and text classification tasks. Six data sets were introduced into the experiment:

Book review: The dataset contains 20,000 positive and 20,000 negative comments collected from Douban, and the task is to discern the sentiment tendency from the sentences given.

XNLI: The dataset is a cross-linguistic language comprehension dataset that contains two sentences per input, and the task is to determine the relationship between the two sentences, distinguishing them as either "inclusive", "neutral" or "contradictory".

LCQMC: LCQMC is a large-scale Chinese question matching corpus whose task goal is to determine whether two questions have a similar intent.

NLPCC-DBQA [26]: NLPCC-DBQA is a task to predict answers to each question from the given document.

Law_QA: It contains a sample of 36,000 questions and answers in the legal field, including questions, answers from users, and the best answers, with the task of selecting the best answer for the question from the responses.

Insurance_QA: More than 8,000 insurance industry Q&A data, including user questions, user answers, and best answers, with the task of choosing the best answer for the question from the answers.

Among them, Book review, XNLI, LCQMC, and NLPCC-DBQA are open domain datasets, Law_QA and insurance_QA are specific domain datasets. The metrics that use for valuation include include accuracy and time consumption.

WikiZh is a Chinese Wikipedia corpus, which was used to train Google BERT in the experiment. It contains 1 million formatted Chinese entries, a total of 120 million sentences, and the total data size is 1.2 GB. CN-DBpedia [27] is a large-scale open-domain encyclopedic knowledge base developed by the Knowledge Work Lab of Fudan University, which covers tens of millions of entities and hundreds of millions of relational attributes. The experiments are conducted using CN-DBpedia for knowledge enhancement with some simplification of CN-DBpedia. Referring to the data processing of CN-DBpedia in K-BERT, the official CN-DBpedia is refined by eliminating the triads with entity names less than 2 in length or containing special characters in the experimental data preprocessing, and the streamlined CN-DBpedia contains a total of 5.17 million triples.

3.2 Baseline and Experimental Environment

In order to verify the performance of the proposed model, we designed two comparative experiments. In the comparative experiment, we set Google BERT Base and K-BERT as the baseline. Google Bert base is a model published by Google with pre-training using WikiZH corpus. The model parameters of the Google Bert base are as follows: L = 12, A = 12, and H = 768. Where L represents the number of layers of the attention mechanism, A represents the number of heads of the multi-head attention mechanism, and H represents the dimension of the hidden layer. In addition, the neural network parameters of the model are 110M. The neural network parameters of K-BERT and Google BERT are compatible with each other, and their numbers are both 110M. Therefore, we use the same model parameters as Google BERT in the experiment of K-BERT.

To maintain the preciseness and comparability of the experimental data, K-BERT experiments were conducted using the same experimental setting as the original model parameters, and CAGBERT was conducted using the same parameters as the Google Bert base. The simplified version of CN-DBpedia is adopted for the knowledge base introducing external knowledge to ensure that the experimental environment is consistent

Table 1. Experimental environment.

Experimental environment	
Operating system	Ubuntu 20.04.1 LTS
CPU	AMD Ryzen Threadripper 3970X 32-Core Processor
GPU	TITAN RTX
Memory size	64 GB
Deep learning framework	Pytorch
CUDA version	11.0

with the K-BERT. The experimental environment is shown in Table 1. The learning rate is $5 * 10^{-5}$, single experimental task is run for 5 epochs, and the batch size is set to 32.

3.3 Evaluation Metrics

In order to quantify the performance of the model, accuracy is used to evaluate the performance of the model in dealing with downstream tasks. The confusion matrix used to calculate the accuracy is shown in Table 2.

Table 2. Confusion matrix.

	Positive	Negative
True	True positive (TP)	True negative (TN)
False	False positive (FP)	False negative (FN)

Accuracy rate (ACC) refers to the proportion of correctly predicted samples in the total samples, and it could be described as formula (16).

$$Acc = \frac{TP + FN}{TP + TN + FP + FN} \tag{16}$$

In the comparative experiment of downstream tasks, Speedup and Time-count are introduced. The time consumption is counted by the accurate timing of the system clock, and the calculation formula of speedup is described in (17).

$$Speedup_p = \frac{Time_1}{Time_p} \tag{17}$$

p represents the number of processors and $Time_1$ represents the execution time of the current sequential execution algorithm. $Time_p$ represents the execution time of parallel algorithms when there are p processors. In order to strictly compare the execution time, we set $p = 1$, the calculation result represents the speedup of the two algorithms. $Time_1$ represents the time-consuming of K-BERT, $Time_p$ represents the time-consuming of CAGBERT. The larger the speedup, the better the acceleration effect of the CAGBERT model.

3.4 Experimental Results and Analysis

The experimental data set is divided into training data set, Dev data set and test data set. The train training set is used to fine-tune the model, and Dev dataset and test dataset are used to verify the accuracy improvement of the model in downstream tasks.

Table 3. Model achievements in different domain tasks (Acc. %).

Dataset\Model	Google BERT	K-BERT	CAGBERT
	Dev Test	Dev Test	Dev Test
Book_Review	88.28 87.05	88.60 87.30	88.39 87.21
LCQMC	88.07 85.98	88.91 87.10	88.80 87.22
XNLI	76.0 75.4	76.5 76.0	76.6 76.2
Law_QA	86.08 86.09	86.33 87.17	86.17 87.06
Insureace_QA	81.28 75.67	83.73 77.64	83.58 77.59
NLPCC-DBQA	93.40 93.30	97.63 95.22	97.99 95.54

As shown in Table 3, the experimental results show that CAGBERT achieves 1.24% higher accuracy than Google BERT on LCQMC data set in the text classification task, and improves the accuracy of 0.8% and 0.16% on XNLI and Book Review data sets respectively. In the Question-and-Answer task, benefit by the enhancement of external knowledge, CAGBERT's accuracy on the NLPCC-DBQA [25] data set is 2.24% higher than that of Google Bert, and in Law_QA and Insurance_QA accuracy is 0.97% and 1.92% higher than Google Bert respectively.

Experiments show that the accuracy of CAGBERT in text classification tasks and Question-and-Answer tasks is close to K-BERT. In order to further compare the time-consuming of knowledge injection, NLPCC-DBQA, Law_QA, Insurance_ QA, and book review datasets were used for the time-consuming comparative experiment of fine-tune and knowledge injection. In the experiment, a high-precision system timer is equipped to record the time-consuming process of fine-tune and knowledge injection of K-BERT and CAGBERT. The results are retained to three decimal places. The smaller the value of the result, the less time it takes in the training phase, which indicates less demand for computational resources.

The fine-tune time-consuming experimental results of CAGBERT and K-BERT models are shown in Table 4. The experimental results show that the time-consuming of CAGBER in the above six data sets is less than that of K-BERT. As can be seen from Table 4, all the speedup ratio of CAGBERT compared to K-BERT is greater than 1 on all six datasets, indicating that CAGBERT generally takes less time than K-BERT in Fine-tune phase and achieves a maximum speedup of 1.87 times on the LCQMC dataset and a minimum speedup of 1.10 times on Law_QA dataset.

In the experiments, the FLOPs counters were used to accumulate the FLOPs of K-BERT and CAGBERT during the knowledge injection phase. The measurement data results of K-BERT and CAGBERT are shown in Table 5. From Table 5, it can be seen

Table 4. Time counts for fine-tuning each model in the 6 NLP tasks (Time s).

Dataset\ Model	LCQMC	Book Review	NLPCC-DBQA	XNLI	Insurance QA	Law QA
K-BERT	6629.974	558.849	5033.878	6606.774	137.067	797.971
CAGBERT	**3537.393**	**319.336**	**3261.797**	**4427.781**	**96.128**	**723.065**
Speedup	**1.87x**	**1.75x**	**1.54x**	**1.49x**	**1.42x**	**1.10x**

Table 5. FLOPs of K-BERT and CAGBERT in the knowledge injection (M = Million).

Modle\Dataset	NLPCC-DBQA	Law QA	Insurance QA	Book Review
K-BERT	61.2 M	43.7 M	6.5 M	4.4 M
CAGBERT	10.3 M	5.70 M	0.9 M	0.5 M

that the FLOPs of CAGBERT are significantly smaller than K-BERT, which indicates that CAGBERT operates less than K-BERT in the knowledge injection process. For example, on the Book Review and NLPCC-DBQA datasets, CAGBERT reduces FLOPs by 3.9 M and 50.9 M respectively compared with K-BERT, which verifies the model we proposed requires fewer computing resources.

The CAG method reduces the computational resources requirement for knowledge injection in downstream tasks by reducing the number of operations in the knowledge injection stage.

The time-consuming test results are shown in Table 6. It can be seen from Table 6 that CAGBERT has achieved different degrees of acceleration in the experiments. It reduces the knowledge injection operation time by 73.33% on the Law_QA dataset compared to K-BERT, achieving a speedup of 3.75 times that of K-BERT.

Table 6. Time consumption of K-BERT and CAGBERT in the knowledge injection (Time s).

Modle\Dataset	NLPCC-DBQA	Law QA	Insurance QA	Book Review
K-BERT	276.618	552.988	83.533	21.670
CAGBERT	250.707	147.472	22.396	13.377
Speedup	**1.10x**	**3.75x**	**3.73x**	**1.62x**

In summary, the above experiments demonstrate that CAGBERT achieves a significant speedup over K-BERT in both Fine-tune and knowledge injection phase, proving that the CAGBERT model has a significant advantage in training speed.

3.5 Ablation Experiments

To validate the effectiveness and robustness of CAGBERT, ablation experiments were constructed to demonstrate the effectiveness of the CAG-based knowledge enhancement approach for downstream tasks.

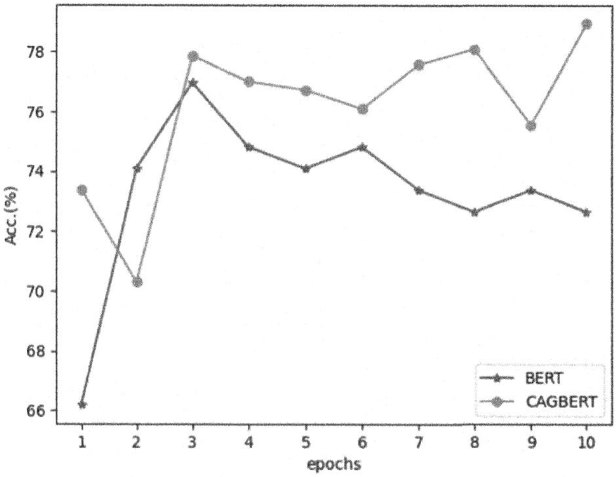

Fig. 3. Experimental on the finance field dataset.

As show in the legend in Fig. 3, CAGBERT indicates the BERT model apply with the knowledge enhancement method, BERT indicates the original Google BERT base. After the analysis of Fig. 3 we could have these conclusions below:

(1) CAGBERT can achieve the best effect result among the experiment object.
(2) The model without CAG method shows obvious accuracy degradation in the experiment.

From the above experimental results, it can be seen that the CAG method can improve the accuracy performance of the model on downstream tasks by providing external knowledge for the model.

4 Conclusion

For the lack of professional domain knowledge support for the BERT, which lead to accuracy compromise in the professional filed, K-BERT injects external knowledge to improve the accuracy but brings the problem of computing resources and training time increasing. This paper proposes a knowledge-enhanced BERT model based on corpus associate generation named CAGBERT. CAGBERT does not need to invasively modify BERT original neural network structure and has better robustness and model compatibility. The lightweight and rapid knowledge introduction method has lower requirements on computing resources and is convenient for large-scale industrial applications and system integration. Experiments show that CAGBERT achieves the same accuracy as K-BERT on six public data sets but the knowledge introduction and training calculation is way faster, the average time consumption of CAGBERT is 53.5% and 37.4% lower than K-BERT respectively.

In the future, we will continue the research on better precision query and semantic relevance to conduct high-quality screening of knowledge to improve the accuracy of the model. And research on how the distillation technology used for improve the speed of model, and achieve lightweight model construction will be appropriate.

Acknowledgments. This study is funded by the Guangdong Science and Technology Plan Project (2021B1212100004).

References

1. Peters, M.E., Neumann, M., Iyyer, M., et al.: Deep contextualized word representations. In: Proceedings of NAACL-HLT, pp. 2227–2237 (2018)
2. Radford, A., Narasimhan, K., Salimans, T., et al.: Improving language understanding by generative pre-training (2018)
3. Devlin, J., Chang, M.W., Lee, K., et al.: Bert: Pre-training of deep bidirectional transformers for language understanding. arXiv preprint arXiv:1810.04805 (2018)
4. Cavnar, W.B., Trenkle, J.M.: N-gram-based text categorization. In: Proceedings of SDAIR-94, 3rd Annual Symposium on Document Analysis and Information Retrieval, p. 161175 (1994)
5. Quinlan, J.R.: C4. 5: Programs for Machine Learning. Elsevier (2014)
6. Berger, A., Della Pietra, S.A., Della Pietra, V.J.: A maximum entropy approach to natural language processing. Comput. Linguist. **22**(1), 39–71 (1996)
7. Chen, D.G., Ma, J.L., Ma, Z.P., Zhou, J.: Summary of natural language processing pre-training technology. J. Front. Comput. Sci. Technol. **15**(08), 1359–1389 (2021)
8. Vaswani, A., Shazeer, N., Parmar, N., et al.: Attention is all you need. Adv. Neural Inf. Process. Syst. 5998–6008 (2017)
9. Yun, W., Zhang, X., Li, Z., et al.: Knowledge modeling: a survey of processes and techniques. Int. J. Intell. Syst. **36**(4), 1686–1720 (2021)
10. Sun, Y., Wang, S., Li, Y., et al.: Ernie: enhanced representation through knowledge integration. arXiv preprint arXiv:1904.09223 (2019)
11. Cui, Y., Che, W., Liu, T., et al.: Pre-training with whole word masking for chinese bert. arXiv preprint arXiv:1906.08101 (2019)
12. Liu, Y., Ott, M., Goyal, N., et al.: Roberta: a robustly optimized bert pretraining approach. arXiv preprint arXiv:1907.11692 (2019)
13. Yang, Z., Dai, Z., Yang, Y., et al.: Xlnet: generalized autoregressive pretraining for language understanding. Adv. Neural Inf. Process. Syst. **32** (2019)
14. Dai, Z., Yang, Z., Yang, Y., et al.: Transformer-XL: attentive language models beyond a fixed-length context. In: Proceedings of the 57th Annual Meeting of the Association for Computational Linguistics, pp. 2978–2988 (2019)
15. Raffel, C., Shazeer, N., Roberts, A., et al.: Exploring the limits of transfer learning with a unified text-to-text transformer. J. Mach. Learn. Res. **21**, 1–67 (2020)
16. Sun, Y., Qiu, H.P., Zheng, Y., Zhang, C.R., He, C.: A survey of knowledge enhancement methods for natural language pre-training models. J. Chin. Inf. Process. **35**(07), 10–29 (2021)

17. Zhang, Z., Han, X., Liu, Z., et al.: ERNIE: enhanced language representation with informative entities. In: Proceedings of the 57th Annual Meeting of the Association for Computational Linguistics, pp. 1441–1451 (2019)
18. Peters, M.E., Neumann, M., Logan, R., et al.: Knowledge enhanced contextual word representations. In: Conference on Empirical Methods in Natural Language Processing and the 9th International Joint Conference on Natural Language Processing (EMNLP-IJCNLP) (2019)
19. Liu, W., Zhou, P., Zhao, Z., et al.: K-bert: Enabling language representation with knowledge graph. In: Proceedings of the AAAI Conference on Artificial Intelligence, vol. 34, no. 03, pp. 2901–2908 (2020)
20. Gan, W., Sun, Y., Sun, Y.: Knowledge structure enhanced graph representation learning model for attentive knowledge tracing. Int. J. Intell. Syst. **37**(3), 2012–2045 (2022)
21. Mikolov, T., Chen, K., Corrado, G., et al.: Efficient estimation of word representations in vector space. arXiv preprint arXiv:1301.3781 (2013)
22. Bordes, A., Usunier, N., Garcia-Duran, A., et al.: Translating embeddings for modeling multi-relational data. Adv. Neural Inf. Process. Syst. **26** (2013)
23. Yuze, L., Xin, L., Zunwang, K., Zhe, L., Slam, W.S.: A survey of pre-training language models for knowledge perception. Comput. Eng. 1–21 [2021–11–11] (2021).https://doi.org/10.19678/j.issn.1000-3428.0060823
24. De Boer, P.T., Kroese, D.P., Mannor, S., et al.: A tutorial on the cross-entropy method. Ann. Oper. Res. **134**(1), 19–67 (2005)
25. Molchanov, P., Tyree, S., Karras T, et al.: Pruning convolutional neural networks for resource efficient inference. In: 5th International Conference on Learning Representations, ICLR 2017-Conference Track Proceedings (2019)
26. Duan, N., Tang, D.: Overview of the NLPCC 2017 shared task: open domain chinese question answering. In: Huang, X., Jiang, J., Zhao, D., Feng, Y., Hong, Yu. (eds.) NLPCC 2017. LNCS (LNAI), vol. 10619, pp. 954–961. Springer, Cham (2018). https://doi.org/10.1007/978-3-319-73618-1_86
27. Xu, B., Xu, Y., Liang, J., Xie, C., Liang, B., Cui, W., Xiao, Y.: CN-DBpedia: a never-ending Chinese knowledge extraction system. In: Benferhat, S., Tabia, K., Ali, M. (eds.) IEA/AIE 2017. LNCS (LNAI), vol. 10351, pp. 428–438. Springer, Cham (2017). https://doi.org/10.1007/978-3-319-60045-1_44

Multi-objective Particle Swarm Optimization Based on Archive Control Strategy

Meilan Yang[1], Fei Chen[1], Qian Zhang[1], Jie Yang[2], Xiaoli Shu[3], and Yanmin Liu[2](✉)

[1] School of Mathematics and Statistics, Guizhou University, Guiyang 550025, China
[2] Zunyi Normal University, Zunyi 563002, China
yanmin7813@163.com
[3] School of Data Science and Information Engineering, Guizhou Minzu University, Guiyang 550025, China

Abstract. In recent years, many improved multi-objective particle swarm optimization algorithms have been proposed to solve multi-objective optimization problems, but there are still some shortcomings. Therefore, in order to enhance the convergence and diversity of the algorithm, the multi-objective particle swarm optimization based on archive control strategy (ACMOPSO) is proposed. Firstly, by introducing the objective extreme optimal solution of particles in the population as the learning sample, the search ability of the particles and the diversity of the population can be enhanced. Secondly, the regional division control strategy is used in the algorithm to control the external archive, which effectively improves the quality of the solutions in the external archive and the search ability of the population. Finally, the numerical experiments of the proposed ACMOPSO and MOEAIGDNS, SPEA2, NSGA-II, MOPSO, and MPSOD are carried out on five test functions. The numerical experiments show that the overall performance of the proposed ACMOPSO is better than that of the other five algorithms.

Keywords: Multi-objective optimization · Multi-objective particle swarm optimization · Objective extreme value

1 Introduction

Multi-objective optimization problems (MOPs) [1] are very common in real life, and they are different from single-objective optimization problems. When solving a MOP, a set of solutions is usually obtained rather than a single solution. At present, the MOP is one of the research hotspots in the artificial intelligence

Supported by the Key Laboratory of Evolutionary Artificial Intelligence in Guizhou (Qian Jiaoji [2022] No. 059) and the Key Talens Program in digital economy of Guizhou Province.

Y. Xu et al. (Eds.): ML4CS 2022, LNCS 13657, pp. 548–562, 2023.
https://doi.org/10.1007/978-3-031-20102-8_42

neighborhood. In order to deal with such problems effectively, researchers have proposed various improved multi-objective particle swarm optimization algorithms (MOPSOs) [2] and multi-objective evolutionary algorithms (MOEAs). In recent decades, various MOEAs based on population evolutionary computation have been used to solve MOPs, such as non-dominated sorting genetic algorithm (NSGA) [3], improved NSGA (NSGA-II) [4], and strength Pareto evolutionary algorithm (SPEA2) [5] and so on.

In order to improve the diversity and convergence of the MOPSO, researchers have proposed a series of improved MOPSOs. Li et al. [6] used explicit difference and crowding density estimation methods to update the external archive in the MOPSO. This method effectively speeded up the convergence velocity of the algorithm and avoided particles falling into local optimum. Sharma et al. [7] adopted a reference line-based diversity preference method to update the external archive in the MOPSO, which effectively improved the diversity of the population. Lin et al. [8] proposed a new velocity update equation in the MOPSO, which improved the search ability of the population. A series of improved MOPSOs have been proposed to solve MOPs, but there is still room for improvement.

In the work, the multi-objective particle swarm optimization based on archive control strategy (ACMOPSO) is proposed. This algorithm introduces two improved strategies in the traditional MOPSO [2]. The ACMOPSO achieves good overall performance in solving selected MOPs. The main contributions of this algorithm are as follows:

(1) A novel velocity update strategy is adopted in the MOPSO. Because the traditional PSO has fast convergence speed, so it has fallen into local optimum. Therefore, this strategy uses the objective extreme optimal solution in the current population as a new learning sample, which helps to enhance the diversity of the population and improve the search ability of particles.

(2) In the aspect of external archive control of MOPSO, the ACMOPSO proposes an improved external archive control strategy. When the size of the external archive reaches the upper limit, the most dense lattice in the grid is selected according to the distribution of the non-dominated solutions in the archive on the grid. Secondly, the selected densest lattice is divided into 2^m regions on average, and then the most dense region of non-dominated solutions is selected from all regions. Then, the distance between the objective function value of all non-dominated solutions in the densest region and the left end point of the lattice is calculated, and the non-dominated solution with the largest distance value is deleted. This helps to improve the quality of solutions in the external archive and enhance the search capability of the population.

The rest of this paper is organized as follows. The second section is related work, introducing MOP and particle swarm optimization. The third section introduces the multi-objective particle swarm optimization based on archive control strategy. The fourth section presents the numerical experiments and comparison results. Finally is the summary.

2 Related Work

2.1 Multi-objective Optimization

In general, the multi-objective optimization problem (taking the minimization problem [9] as an example) can be described as:

$$Min\overrightarrow{y} = (f_1(\overrightarrow{x}), f_2(\overrightarrow{x}), ..., f_m(\overrightarrow{x})) \tag{1}$$

where, $\overrightarrow{x} = (x_1, x_2, ..., x_D)(\overrightarrow{x} \in \Omega \subseteq R^D)$ is the vector in the decision space; m represents the number of objectives in the objective space; $f : \overrightarrow{x} \longrightarrow \overrightarrow{y}$ represents the mapping relationship; and $\overrightarrow{y}(\overrightarrow{y} \in R^m)$ represents the vector in the objective space.

The definition of the non-dominated relation, Pareto optimality, and Pareto front [2] in the MOP (1) is as follows:

Definition 1. *Let $\overrightarrow{x}_u$ and $\overrightarrow{x}_v$ be two solutions of the MOP (1). If*

$$\forall i \in 1, 2, ..., m : f_i(\overrightarrow{x}_u) \leq f_i(\overrightarrow{x}_v) \bigwedge \exists j \in 1, 2, ..., m : f_j(\overrightarrow{x}_u) < f_j(\overrightarrow{x}_v) \tag{2}$$

Then the$\overrightarrow{x}_u$ dominates $\overrightarrow{x}_v$.

Definition 2. *Let $\overrightarrow{x}^*$ be the solution of the MOP (1). If*

$$\neg\exists\overrightarrow{x} \in \Omega : f(\overrightarrow{x}) \preceq f(\overrightarrow{x}^*) \tag{3}$$

Then $\overrightarrow{x}^*$ is called the Pareto optimal.

Definition 3. *In the decision space, the Pareto optimal set (Pareto optimal set, P^*) is defined as:*

$$P^* = \{\overrightarrow{x}^* | \neg\exists\overrightarrow{x} \in \Omega : f(\overrightarrow{x}) \preceq f(\overrightarrow{x}^*)\} \tag{4}$$

Definition 4. *In P^*, the Pareto front (Pareto front, PF) is defined as:*

$$PF = \{\overrightarrow{y} = (f_1(\overrightarrow{x}^*), f_2(\overrightarrow{x}^*), ..., f_m(\overrightarrow{x}^*)) | \overrightarrow{x}^* \in P^*\} \tag{5}$$

2.2 Particle Swarm Optimization

Particle swarm optimization (PSO) [10] is an optimization algorithm that simulates the behavior of swarm intelligence proposed by Kennedy and Eberhart. Its ideas are inspired by the foraging behavior of groups such as birds and fish. In PSO, each individual is a candidate solution in the population, and the individuals in the population are usually called particles. The flight velocity of the particles is affected by the optimal historical solutions of the individuals and the optimal historical solutions of the population. Therefore, the particles in the population will adjust according to their current flight state and approach the optimal solutions as close as possible. The velocity and position update equations for each particle are as follows:

$$v_{ij}(t+1) = w \cdot v_{ij}(t) + c_1 \cdot r_1 \cdot (p_{ij}(t) - x_{ij}(t)) + c_2 \cdot r_2 \cdot (g_{ij}(t) - x_{ij}(t)) \quad (6)$$

$$x_{ij}(t+1) = x_{ij}(t) + v_{ij}(t+1) \quad (7)$$

where, $v_{ij}(t)$ represents the j th dimension element of the i th particle velocity vector in the t th iteration; w represents inertia weight, $w = 0.4$; c_1 and c_2 represent learning factors, $c_1 = c_2 = 2.0$; r_1 and r_2 represent random numbers uniformly distributed in the range $[0, 1]$; $x_{ij}(t)$ represents the j th dimension element of the i th particle position vector in the t th iteration; $p_{ij}(t)$ represents the j dimensional element of the individual historical optimal position vector of the i th particle at the t th iteration; and $g_{ij}(t)$ represents the j dimensional element of the population history optimal position vector of the i th particle at the t th iteration.

3 Multi-objective Particle Swarm Optimization Based on Archive Control Strategy

In the traditional MOPSO [2], a new extreme optimal solution archive is introduced to store the objective extreme optimal solutions in the population. Then, selecting objective extreme optimal solutions from the archive as learning samples to make them new search direction for particles, so as to enhance the search ability of particles. In addition, a new control strategy is adopted for the external archive that stores non-dominated solutions. This method can maintain the quality of non-dominated solutions in external archive, and can also improve the search ability of particles. The specific working conditions are as follows:

3.1 Specific Steps of the ACMOPSO

Step 1: Initialization. Initialize parameter settings; Initialize the positions and velocities of particles;

Step 2: Set current iteration t = 1;

Step 3: Calculate the objective function value of the particles in the population;

Step 4: The particles in the population are sorted by using the non-dominated sorting method, and then the non-dominated solutions in the population are stored in the external archive;

Step 5: Use the strategy in Sect. 3.2 to determine the individual historical optimal position and population historical optimal position of particles;

Step 6: Use the strategy of Sect. 3.2 to store objective extreme optimal solutions, as well as to determine and update objective extreme optimal solutions of the particle;

Step 7: Update the velocities and positions of particles in the population using Eq. (8) and Eq. (7);

Step 8: Implement mutation strategy on new particles in the population;

Step 9: Update and control external archives using Sect. 3.3;

Step 10: Update the individual historical optimal position and the population historical optimal position of the particle;

Step 11: Judge whether the function evaluation times reach the maximum evaluation times. If it is reached, stop the loop work; otherwise, return to the Step 6.

The flow chart of ACMOPSO is shown in Fig. 1:

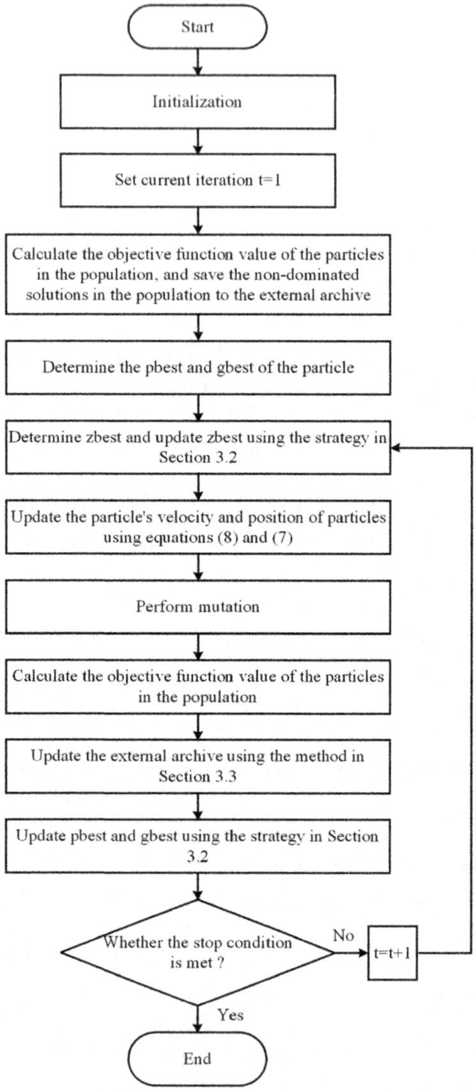

Fig. 1. ACMOPSO's flowchart.

3.2 Novel Velocity Update Strategy

Initially, in the traditional PSO [10], the velocities and positions of particles are usually updated according to the information of optimal historical solutions of the individuals and optimal historical solutions of the population. Due to the fast convergence velocity of particles, it is easy to lead to premature convergence of the algorithm. In order to enhance the diversity and search ability of the population, a new search direction is designed in this paper.

First, an extreme optimal solution archive is established to store the objective extreme optimal solutions in the population. Find the minimum value of each objective from the objective function values of all particles, and call the particle corresponding to the minimum value of each objective as the objective extreme optimal solution. As the number of iterations increases, the extreme optimal solution archive will be continuously updated. The update of the extreme optimal solution archive can effectively increase the diversity of the population. Then, from a set of objective extreme optimal solutions in the archive, the random method is used to select the objective extreme optimal solution as the learning sample and record its position as *zbest*. By cooperating the new learning sample with the optimal historical position of the individual (*pbest*) and the optimal historical position of the population (*gbest*) to guide the particle to search for the optimal solution, which can improve the particle's search ability. The particle's new velocity update equation is as follows:

$$v_{ij}(t+1) = w \cdot v_{ij}(t) + c_1 \cdot r_1 \cdot (p_{ij}(t) - x_{ij}(t)) + c_2 \cdot r_2 \cdot (g_{ij}(t) - x_{ij}(t)) + c_3 \cdot r_3 \cdot (z_{ij}(t) - x_{ij}(t)) \quad (8)$$

where, c_3 represents the learning factor, $c_3 = 2.0$; r_3 represents a random number uniformly distributed in the range $[0, 1]$; $z_{ij}(t)$ represents the j th dimension element of the objective extreme optimal position vector of the i th particle in the t th iteration.

The size of the population is fixed in ACMOPSO, but the *pbest*, *gbest*, and *zbest* of the particles are updated as the number of iterations increases. In each iteration, the *pbest*, *gbest*, and *zbest* selection method for each particle is as follows:

Choose *pbest*: In each iteration, the rank of the current particle is compared with the rank of *pbest* (the rank is obtained by the Pareto sort [11] method. This method is mainly based on the Pareto sorting obtained by comparing the objective function values). If either of the two is better, its position is taken as the *pbest* of the current particle; If the two do not dominate each other, a solution is randomly selected as the optimal historical solution of the individual and its position is recorded as *pbest*.

Choose *gbest*: In each iteration, the external archive will obtain a set of non-dominated solutions. Then, the roulette strategy is used to select the optimal historical solution of the population from a set of non-dominated solutions, and its position is recorded as *gbest*.

Choose *zbest*: A set of objective extreme optimal solutions obtained in the extreme solution archive at each iteration. Then, the objective extreme optimal solution of the population is selected from a set of objective extreme optimal solutions by random method, and its position is recorded as *zbest*.

3.3 External Archive Control Strategy

The external archive is used to store some non-dominated solutions in the population, which are the candidate solutions of the optimal historical solution of the population used to guide the particles search direction. Set a threshold in the external archive to limit the size of the external archive. As the number of evaluations increases, the number of non-dominated solutions also increases. If the number of non-dominated solutions in the external archive reaches the threshold, the scale of the external archive needs to be controlled. The ACMOPSO uses regional division control strategy to control external archive.

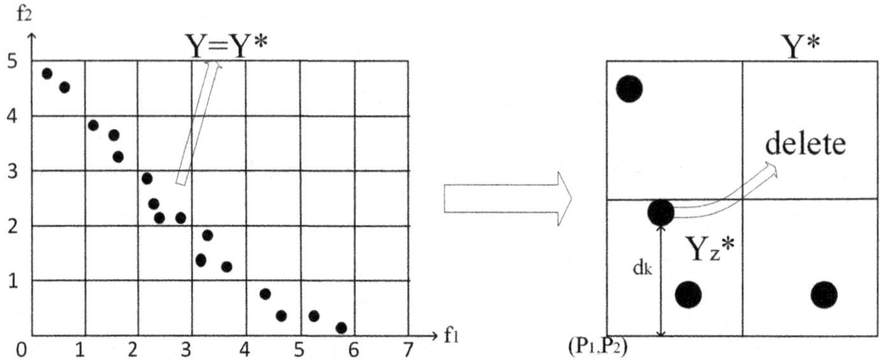

Fig. 2. The first case of controlling external archive.

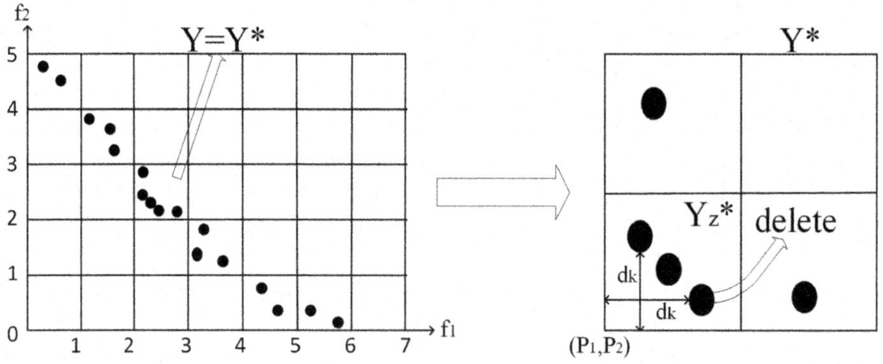

Fig. 3. The second case of controlling external archive

The adaptive grid method [12] is adopted when the capacity in the external archive is full. This method assigns the non-dominated solutions to the grid according to the objective function values of the non-dominated solutions. Then, find the lattice with the largest number of non-dominated solutions from the grid, and record it as the most dense lattice Y. The traditional MOPSO [2] uses a random method to remove non-dominated solutions in the densest lattice Y. The random deletion method is blind, which may delete the more guiding non-dominated solutions in the external archive, and affect the search ability of the algorithm. Compared with the traditional MOPSO, the ACMOPSO proposed in this paper adopts the regional division control strategy. The densest lattice Y may not be unique. If lattice Y is unique, directly select lattice Y to implement the control strategy and record it as Y^*; If lattice Y is not unique, first measure the number of non-dominated solutions in each dense lattice Y, and then select the lattice with the largest number of non-dominated solutions and record it as Y^*; If the number of non-dominated solutions in each dense lattice Y is equal, a lattice is randomly selected and record it as Y^*. This strategy divides the grid Y^* into 2^m (m represents the number of objectives) equal regions according to 1/2 of the unit length of the grid. Find the densest region among the 2^m regions and denote it as Y_z^*. The distance d from the function value of each objective of all non-dominated solutions in the region Y_z^* to the left endpoint in the lattice Y^* is solved by Eq. (9). However, the largest distance d_k among all d is found by Eq. (10) and Eq. (11), and denote the position of d_k corresponding to the non-dominated solution as $\overrightarrow{x}_k$. If $\overrightarrow{x}_k$ is unique, delete the non-dominated solution corresponding to $\overrightarrow{x}_k$ directly (take tow objectives as an example, as shown in Fig. 2). If there are multiple $\overrightarrow{x}_k$, select one $\overrightarrow{x}_k$ randomly and delete its corresponding non-dominated solution (take tow objectives as an example, as shown in Fig. 3). Then go back to judging whether the lattice Y is unique, and continue to execute the control strategy. This loop stops when the number of deletions reaches 40% of the total number of non-dominated solutions in lattice Y. This method helps to maintain the quality of non-dominated solutions in external archive.

$$d_{ij} = f_{ij} - p_{ij} \tag{9}$$

$$d_k = max(d_{11}, ..., d_{r1}, ..., d_{1m}, ..., d_{rm}) \tag{10}$$

$$\overrightarrow{wbest}(t+1) = \begin{cases} \overrightarrow{x}_k(t), & d_k \quad is \quad one \\ \overrightarrow{x}_{k(l)}(t), & d_k \quad is \quad more \end{cases} \tag{11}$$

where, f_{ij} represents the objective function value of the j th objective of the i th particle, $j = 1, 2, ..., m$; p_{ij} represents the coordinate value of the j th objective at the left endpoint in the ith lattice Y^*; d_{ij} represents the distance from the j th objective of the i th particle to the objective corresponding to the left endpoint of the lattice Y^*; d_k represents the maximum distance from the k th solution to the left endpoint of lattice Y^* among all non-dominated solutions; r represents the total number of non-dominated solutions in the region Y_z^*, i=1,2,...,r; and $\overrightarrow{x}_k$ represents the position of d_k corresponding to the non-dominated solution. If there is only one d_k, directly find the position corresponding to d_k and record it as *wbest*; If there are more than one d_k, randomly find a position corresponding to $d_{k(l)}$ from d_k and record it as *wbest*.

4 Numerical Experiment Results and Analysis

4.1 Test Functions and Parameter Settings

In order to verify the effectiveness of the ACMOPSO, five test functions are used to verify the overall performance of the ACMOPSO, two typical MOPSOs and the competitive MOEAs. The five test functions have ZDT1, ZDT2, ZDT3, ZDT4, and ZDT6 [13], which are all bi-objective test functions. The Pareto front of ZDT1 is convex and its dimension is set to 30. The Pareto front of ZDT2 is non-convex and its dimension is set to 30. The Pareto front of ZDT3 is discontinuous and its dimension is set to 30. The Pareto front of ZDT4 is convex and its dimension is set to 10. The Pareto front of ZDT6 is uneven and its dimension is set to 10. This five test functions is a typical bi-objective test function.

In this paper, two typical MOPSOs and three competitive MOEAs are used to compare the performance with ACMOPSO, including MOEAIGDNS [14], MOPSO [15], MPSOD [16], NSGA-II [4], and SPEA2 [5]. The total number of evaluations of the objective function value is set to 10000. The size of the population is set to 200. The size of external archive is set to 200. All algorithms run independently on each test function for 30 times. In order to fairly verify the effectiveness of the ACMOPSO, the parameter settings of the other five algorithms are referred to the original text. The original codes of these five algorithms are all from the PlatEMO platform [17].

4.2 Performance Index

In order to quantitatively evaluate the performance of these six algorithms, inverted generational distance (IGD) [18] index and hypervolume (HV) [19] index are adopted. The specific description is as follows:

Inverted generational distance (IGD) index: The IGD is an index commonly used to evaluate the performance of algorithms. It is mainly used to calculate the mean distance from the true Pareto front point to its close solution. The smaller the IGD index value obtained by the algorithm, the better the convergence and diversity of the algorithm.

Hypervolume (HV) index: The HV is also an index commonly used to evaluate the performance of algorithms. It is mainly used to calculate the area volume of the control reference point in the objective space, but it is used to evaluate the convergence and diversity of the algorithm. The larger the HV index value obtained by the algorithm, the better the convergence and diversity of the algorithm. The reference point of the HV index is set as (1.1 ,..., 1.1).

Table 1. On the ZDT series of test functions, the mean and standard deviation results of the IGD index values obtained by running 30 independent runs of MOEAIGDNS, SPEA2, NSGA-II, MOPSO, MPSOD, and ACMOPSO.

Problem	IGD	MOEAIGDNS	SPEA2	NSGA-II	MOPSO	MPSOD	ACMOPSO
ZDT1	Mean	8.2546e–2	4.2590e–2	4.0219e–2	6.9127e–1	9.5837e–2	**8.3470e–03**
	Std	(9.21e–3)	(9.06e–3)	(8.05e–3)	(1.80e–1)	(3.37e–2)	**(1.29e–03)**
ZDT2	Mean	1.5075e–1	7.5357e–2	6.8550e–2	1.4408e+0	1.5149e–1	**1.1038e–02**
	Std	(3.30e–2)	(1.49e–2)	(1.55e–2)	(4.32e–1)	(1.08e–1)	**(3.77e–03)**
ZDT3	Mean	6.5717e–2	3.8070e–2	1.1501e–02	7.9818e–1	1.9941e–1	**4.9591e–03**
	Std	(1.22e–2)	(1.23e–2)	(7.79e–3)	(2.35e–1)	(5.03e–2)	**(1.18e–03)**
ZDT4	Mean	2.0255e+0	**7.6251e–1**	8.9436e–1	1.2780e+1	3.5780e+1	2.6911e+01
	Std	(6.24e–1)	**(2.73e–1)**	(3.43e–1)	(4.75e+0)	(7.48e+0)	(6.99e+00)
ZDT6	Mean	1.1776e+0	6.0743e–1	6.0291e–1	8.4724e–2	1.6334e–2	**9.7368e–03**
	Std	(2.05e–1)	(1.62e–1)	(1.13e–1)	(2.10e–1)	(1.06e–2)	**(7.42e–03)**

Table 2. On the ZDT series of test functions, the mean and standard deviation results of the HV index values obtained by running 30 independent runs of MOEAIGDNS, SPEA2, NSGA-II, MOPSO, MPSOD, and ACMOPSO.

Problem	HV	MOEAIGDNS	SPEA2	NSGA-II	MOPSO	MPSOD	ACMOPSO
ZDT1	Mean	6.1298e–1	6.6567e–1	6.6890e–1	9.9029e–2	5.8131e–1	**7.1272e–1**
	Std	(1.10e–2)	(1.22e–2)	(1.06e–2)	(8.28e–2)	(4.51e–2)	**(2.66e–3)**
ZDT2	Mean	2.5595e–1	3.4245e–1	3.5152e–1	2.2876e–3	2.6800e–1	**4.3694e–1**
	Std	(3.16e–2)	(2.03e–2)	(2.13e–2)	(1.25e–2)	(1.04e–1)	**(4.50e–3)**
ZDT3	Mean	5.5698e–1	5.7287e–1	5.7605e–1	1.0386e–1	4.6045e–1	**5.9852e–1**
	Std	(7.59e–3)	(8.40e–3)	(5.43e–3)	(1.06e–1)	(4.58e–2)	**(1.44e–3)**
ZDT4	Mean	0.0000e+0	**8.2981e–2**	5.7130e–2	0.0000e+0	0.0000e+0	0.0000e+0
	Std	(0.00e+0)	**(1.04e–1)**	(8.43e–2)	(0.00e+0)	(0.00e+0)	(0.00e+0)
ZDT6	Mean	0.0000e+0	1.7772e–2	1.1657e–2	3.3934e–1	**3.7597e–1**	3.5277e–1
	Std	(0.00e+0)	(2.38e–2)	(1.77e–2)	(1.05e–1)	**(9.43e–3)**	(2.77e–2)

4.3 Numerical Comparison Results of Algorithms

In Tables 1 and 2, the numerical results show that the algorithm runs independently for 30 times on each test function to obtain the mean value and standard deviation of IGD and HV index values. In Tables 1 and 2, the algorithm results with the best performance on each test function are bold. From the data in Table 1, the performance between ACMOPSO and the other five algorithms can be effectively verified. It can be seen from Table 1 that the ACMOPSO proposed in this paper performs better than the other five algorithms in the ZDT1, ZDT2, ZDT3, and ZDT6 test functions. In ZDT4 test function, the ACMOPSO, MOPSO, and MPSOD perform slightly worse than the other three algorithms.

In Table 1, the performance of ACMOPSO proposed in this paper is verified to be superior to the other five algorithms by IGD index. In order to further verify the effectiveness of ACMOPSO, the HV index is introduced in Table 2 for verification. The HV index is used to verify the diversity and convergence of each algorithm. It can be seen from Table 2 that the HV value obtained by ACMOPSO is the best among the ZDT1, ZDT2, and ZDT3 test functions. On the ZDT6 test function, the overall performance of ACMOPSO is slightly worse than that of MPSOD. But in terms of IGD index, ACMOPSO has the best IGD value compared to the other five algorithms. The performance of the ACMOPSO, MOPSO, MPSOD, and MOEAIGDNS is slightly worse than the other two algorithms on the ZDT4 test function. To sum up, the ACMOPSO proposed in this paper has better performance in terms of convergence and diversity than the other five algorithms.

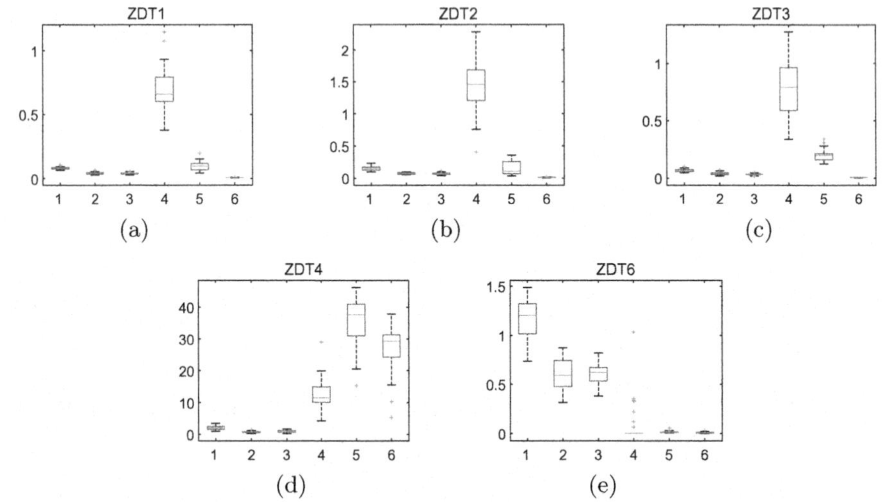

Fig. 4. On the ZDT series test function, a boxplot of the IGD indicator results obtained by running the six algorithms independently for 30 times is drawn (1, 2, 3, 4, 5, and 6 on the abscissa are represented as MOEAIGDNS, SPEA2, NSGA-II, MOPSO, MPSOD, and ACMOPSO respectively).

In order to visually see the convergence of the six algorithms, a boxplot of the IGD index results obtained by running the algorithm independently for 30 times is drawn in Fig. 4. It can be seen from Fig. 4 that the convergence of ACMOPSO is significantly better than the other five algorithms on the ZDT1, ZDT2, and ZDT3 test functions, and the convergence of MOPSO is the worst. On the ZDT6 test function, ACMOPSO, MOPSO, and MPSOD have similar convergence, and they significantly outperform the other three algorithms. On the ZDT4 test function, ACMOPSO, MOEAIGDNS, and MPSOD perform slightly worse than the other three algorithms. On ZDT1, ZDT2, and ZDT3 test functions, ACMOPSO has the smallest IGD value and the smallest box spacing. This shows that the ACMOPSO proposed in this paper performs better in terms of convergence accuracy and stability.

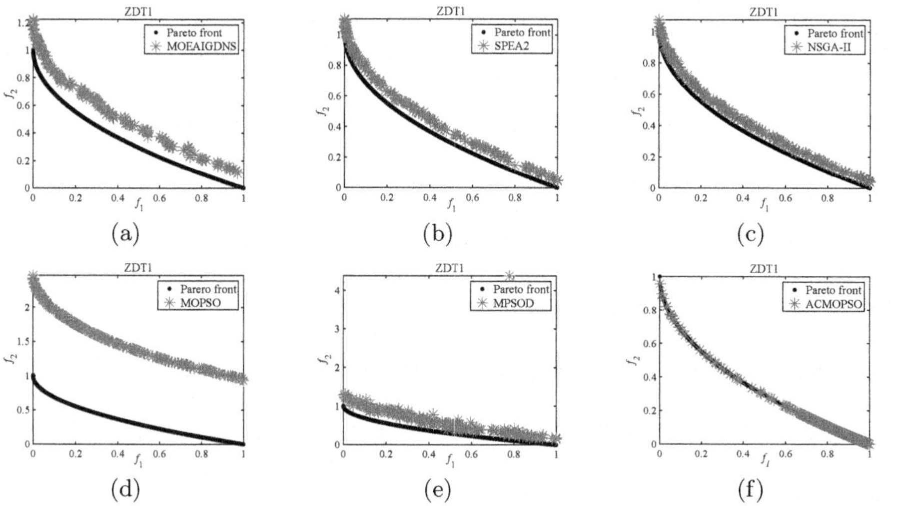

Fig. 5. The solutions obtained by MOEAIGDNS, SPEA2, NSGA-II, MOPSO, MPSOD, and ACMOPSO approximate the situation on the true Pareto front of ZDT1.

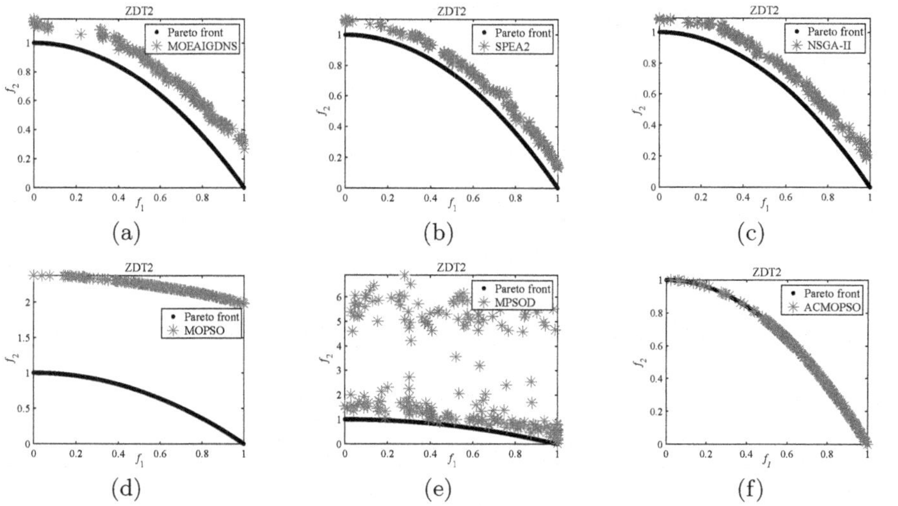

Fig. 6. The solutions obtained by MOEAIGDNS, SPEA2, NSGA-II, MOPSO, MPSOD, and ACMOPSO approximate the situation on the true Pareto front of ZDT2.

In Figs. 5, 6, and 7, the convergence graphs of the Pareto front of the six algorithms on ZDT1, ZDT2, and ZDT3 test functions are plotted, and the convergence and distribution effect of the algorithms can be seen intuitively. It can be seen from Fig. 5 that the solution obtained by the ACMOPSO has good convergence on the true Pareto front of ZDT1. However, the solutions obtained by the other five algorithms have poor convergence on the true Pareto front of ZDT1, and almost none of them converge to the true Pareto front. As shown in Fig. 6, the solution obtained by the ACMOPSO has better convergence on the true Pareto front of ZDT2, and the solution distribution on the true Pareto front is relatively uniform. The solutions obtained by MOEAIGDNS, SPEA2, NSGA-II, and MOPSO have poor convergence on the true Pareto front of ZDT2, but the solutions obtained by MPSOD have poor convergence and distribution on the true Pareto front of ZDT2. As shown in Fig. 7, the solution obtained by ACMOPSO has optimal convergence and distribution on the true Pareto front of ZDT3. The solutions obtained by MOEAIGDNS, SPEA2, NSGA-II, and MOPSO are more uniformly distributed on the true Pareto front of ZDT3, but their convergence is poor. The solution obtained by the MPSOD has the worst convergence and distribution performance on the true Pareto front of ZDT3. All in all, compared with the other five algorithms, the solution obtained by ACMOPSO proposed in this paper has better convergence and distribution on the true Pareto front of the test function.

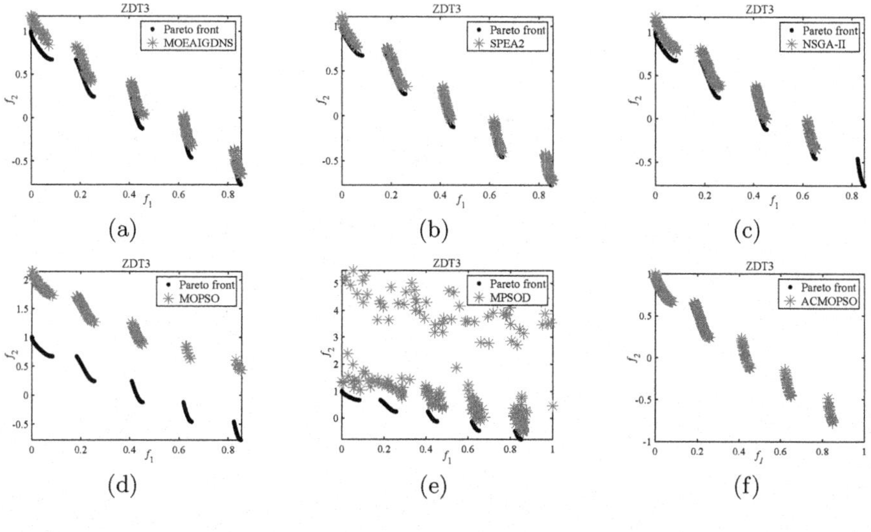

Fig. 7. The solutions obtained by MOEAIGDNS, SPEA2, NSGA-II, MOPSO, MPSOD, and ACMOPSO approximate the situation on the true Pareto front of ZDT3.

5 Conclusion

This paper presents the multi-objective particle swarm optimization algorithm based on archive control strategy (ACMOPSO), which effectively improves the convergence and diversity of algorithm. Add new learning sample to guide the particle's search direction, thereby enhancing the particle's search ability. The external archive control strategy effectively maintains the quality of non-dominated solutions in external archive. In numerical experiments, the ACMOPSO proposed in this paper is compared with two typical MOPSOs and three competitive MOEAs to verify the effectiveness of ACMOPSO. At the same time, it is verified that the two strategies can effectively improve the convergence and diversity of the algorithm.

Acknowledgements. This work was supported in part by Key Laboratory of Evolutionary Artificial Intelligence in Guizhou (Qian Jiaoji [2022] No. 059) and the Key Talens Program in digital economy of Guizhou Province.

References

1. Tian, Y., Cheng, R., Zhang, X., Cheng, F., Jin, Y.: An indicator based multi-objective evolutionary algorithm with reference point adaptation for better versatility. IEEE Trans. Evol. Comput. **22**(4), 609–622 (2017)
2. Coello Coello, C.-A., Toscano Pulido, G., Lechuga, M.-S.: Handling multiple objectives with particle swarm optimization. IEEE Trans. Evol. Comput. **8**(3), 256–279 (2004)
3. Srinivas, N., Deb, K.: Multiobjective function optimization using non-dominated sorting genetic algorithms. Evol. Comput. **2**(3), 221–248 (1994)
4. Deb, K., Agarwal, S., Pratap, A., Meyarivan, T.: A fast and elitist multiobjective genetic algorithm: NSGA-II. IEEE Tran. Evol. Comput. **6**(2), 182–197 (2002)
5. Zitzler, E., Laumanns, M., Thiele, L.: SPEA2: improving the strength Pareto evolutionary algorithm for multi-objective optimization. In: Proceeding of 5th Conference on Evolutionary Methods for Design, Optimization and Control with Applications to Industrial Problems, pp. 103, 95–100 (2001)
6. Li, L., Chang, L., Gu, T., Sheng, W., Wang, W.: On the norm of dominant difference for many-objective particle swarm optimization. IEEE Trans. Cybern. **51**(4), 2055–2067 (2021)
7. Sharma, D., Vats, S., Saurabh, S.: Diversity preference-based many-objective particle swarm optimization using reference-lines-based framework. Swarm Evol. Comput. **65**(4), 100910 (2021)
8. Lin, Q.-Z., et al.: Particle swarm optimization with a balanceable fitness estimation for many-objective optimization problems. IEEE Trans. Evol. Comput. **22**(1), 32–46 (2018)
9. Deb, K.: Multiobjective Optimization Using Evolutionary Algorithm: An Introduction. John Wiley and Sons, Chichester (2001)
10. Kennedy, J., Eberhart, R.: Particle swarm optimization. In: Proceedings of the IEEE International Conference on Neural Networks (ICNN 1995), vol. 4, pp. 1942–1948, December (1995). http://doi.org/10.1109/ICNN.1995.488968
11. Goldberg, D.-E.: Genetic Algorithms in Search, Optimization and Machine Learning. Addison-Wesley, Reading (1989)
12. Knowles, J.-D., Corne, D.-W.: Approximating the nondominated front using the Pareto archived evolution strategy. Evol. Comput. **8**(2), 149–172 (2000)
13. Zitzler, E., Deb, K., Thiele, L.: Comparison of multiobjective evolutionary algorithms: empirical results. Evol. Comput. **8**(2), 173–195 (2000)
14. Tian, Y., Zhang, X.-Y., Cheng, R., Jin, Y.-C.: A multi-objective evolutionary algorithm based on an enhanced inverted generational distance metric. In: 2016 the IEEE Congress on Evolutionary Computation (CEC 2016), pp. 5222–5229, August (2016). http://doi.org/10.1109/CEC.2016.7748352

15. Coello, Coello, C.-A., Lechuga, M.-S.: MOPSO: a proposal for multiple objective particle swarm optimization. In: Proceedings of the 2002 Congress on Evolutionary Computation (CEC 2002), vol. 2, pp. 1051–1056, February (2002). http://doi.org/10.1109/CEC.2002.1004388
16. Dai, C., Wang, Y., Ye, M.: A new multi-objective particle swarm optimization algorithm based on decomposition. Inf. Sci. **325**, 541–557 (2015)
17. Tian, Y., Cheng, R., Zhang, X., Jin, Y.: PlatEMO: a matlab platform for evolutionary multi-objective optimization. IEEE Comput. Intell. Mag. **12**(4), 73–87 (2017)
18. Zhou, A., Jin, Y., Zhang, Q., Sendhoff, B., Tsang, E.: Combining model-based and genetics-based offspring generation for multi-objective optimization using a convergence criterion. In: Proceedings of IEEE Congress on Evolutionary Computation (CEC 2006), pp. 892–899, July (2006). http://doi.org/10.1109/CEC.2006.1688406
19. While, L., Hingston, P., Barone, L., Huband, S.: A faster algorithm for calculating hypervolume. IEEE Trans. Evol. Comput. **10**(1), 29–38 (2006)

A Hybrid Multi-objective Genetic-Particle Swarm Optimization Algorithm for Airline Crew Rostering Problem with Fairness and Satisfaction

Tianwei Zhou[1,2], Xuanru Chen[1], Xusheng Wu[3(✉)], and Chen Yang[1,2]

[1] College of Management, Shenzhen University, Shenzhen 518060, China
[2] Great Bay Area International Institute for Innovation, Shenzhen University, Shenzhen 518060, China
[3] Shenzhen Health Development Research and Data Management Center, Shenzhen 518028, China
1257451869@qq.com

Abstract. With the continuous development of today's air transport industry, the size of airline crew and flight volume increase continuously. At the same time, crew scheduling becomes increasingly complex and important. The rationality of flight crew scheduling scheme affects flight operation cost and crew satisfaction. Therefore, this paper focuses on the crew scheduling problem aimed at improving crew satisfaction and fairness of work allocation. First, an improved crew scheduling model is established with constraints. Second, a new hybrid multi-objective genetic algorithm is proposed in which a barebones particle swarm optimization (BBPSO) based mutation operator is fused to the framework of non-dominated genetic algorithms. Finally, the experimental results verify the superiority of proposed algorithm based on the actual data of three routes. Moreover, the scheduling scheme could improve market competitiveness and strengthen operation management.

Keywords: Crew rostering · Barebones particle swarm optimization · Nondominated sorting genetic algorithm · Multi-objective swarm intelligence optimization algorithm

1 Introduction

Affected by the policy of restricting travel due to epidemic, the whole civil aviation industry is facing serious challenges. In particular, as an important part of operating costs, crew labor costs affect the market competitiveness of the airline. Moreover, the disruption of circadian rhythms usually leads to a decrease in crew alertness along with weakened decision abilities [1]. Therefore, airlines should try to take into account the preferences of the crew and balance their workload. This paper tries to present the crew rostering problem (CRP) from the crews' perspective by balancing the relationship between crew satisfaction and fairness.

Many studies have previously explored fairness and satisfaction metrics. Fairness refers to the balanced distribution of all crews and pairings. Doi *et al.* [2] regarded the sum of the deviation of each crew members' working hours from the standard working

Y. Xu et al. (Eds.): ML4CS 2022, LNCS 13657, pp. 563–575, 2023.
https://doi.org/10.1007/978-3-031-20102-8_43

hours as a evaluation of fairness. De Armas *et al.* [3] also used working hours as a metric of work balance and introduced three criteria. However, simply using flight time to measure fairness is not comprehensive. Therefore, two attributes were additionally considered in Zhou *et al.* [4], including duty time and overnight time far away from base, to better reflects the degree of balance in workload distribution. In terms of satisfaction, Gamache *et al.* [5] argued that a series of weighted bids reflecting crew preferences should be added when obeying the relevant regulations. Dawid *et al.* [6] suggested taking crew members' preferences such as days off when setting work lines. Kasirzadeh *et al.* [7] set a constraint on the lower limit of the number of crews' preferred flights and vacations. Based on the above analysis, this paper tries to utilize crews' preferred flights and vacations to describe satisfaction.

Since CRP is a NP-hard problem, evolutionary algorithm is one of the potential solvers. For example, Ezzinbi *et al.* [8] proposed to use PSO algorithm to build CRP model and it had better relatively performance compared to GA algorithm. Banerjee *et al.* [9] extended the existing non-dominated ranking genetic algorithm (NSGA-II) with interval fitness and column exchange crossover and mutation. Nevertheless, single improved algorithm is limited by the underlying theoretical and algorithmic framework. It is difficult to present an optimization algorithm based on natural mechanisms. Therefore, algorithm hybridization is the preferred method to improve algorithm performance. Shi *et al.* [10] used the hybrid PSO-GA optimization algorithm in determining biomass pyrolysis kinetics. Sun *et al.* [11] proposed a distributed cooperative evolutionary algorithm for the flexible job shop scheduling problem by combining GA and PSO. The chromosome crossover and mutation of GA are employed to update individual particles.

However, the above two hybrid strategies have some defects. They ignore the relationship between information sharing among particles and the convergence speed acceleration. Moreover, in some variants of PSO, barebones particle swarm optimization (BBPSO) [12] only utilized to update the position of particles without velocity. In this study, we tried to add BBPSO algorithm in the framework of NSGA-II to accelerate convergence speed. The contributions of this study are listed as follows:

(1) The initial solutions are generated randomly according to one of the important time constraints of CRP. And a penalty function is added to the two fitness functions to reduce the feasible domain boundary.
(2) The hybrid multi-objective genetic-particle swarm optimization algorithm, abbreviated as hMOBBPSO-GA, is proposed based on BBPSO. Selection operation is improved to avoid premature maturation of individuals. And BBPSO is embedded in NSGA-II as a mutation operator to accelerate convergence speed.
(3) We bridge the gap between problem and algorithm through integer and binary encoding.

The remaining of this paper is arranged as follows. In Sect. 2, we introduce CRP mathematical model containing the definition of CRP, airline regulations and the objective function. In Sect. 3, we specify the improved algorithm process and coding methods. Section 4 presents the simulation experiments and the experimental results compared with other algorithms. Finally, in Sect. 5, we provide the conclusion and point out the directions for future research improvements.

2 Problem Definition and Formulation

In this section, CRP model is thoroughly studied. Firstly, the relative definitions of models are explained. Then a specific expression is presented according to the definition of the objective function. Finally, the time constraints are proposed based on the requirements of CCAR121-R5 document [13].

2.1 Notations

The definitions of symbols used in CRP are listed as follows:

Table 1. The definition of symbols

Symbol	Definition	Symbol	Definition
p_j	j^{th} of pairing	c_i	i^{th} of crews
s_j	Start time of pairing p_j	pf_i	Preferred flights of crew c_i
e_j	End time of pairing p_j	pv_i	Preferred vacations of crew c_i
f_j	Flight time of pairing p_j	PN	Total number of pairings
d_j	Duty time of pairing p_j	CN	Total number of crews
o_j	Overnight time of pairing p_j	X	The assignment table for pairings
PPN	Sum of pairings corresponding to all crew preferred flights	APN	Sum of pairings that want to avoid during the vacations
$sppn$	Sum of pairings to which all crews are assigned for the preferred flights	$sapn$	Sum of pairings on preferred vacations successfully avoided by all crews
ep	Entry preparation time	et	Exiting time
cf_i	Total flight time of crew c_i	co_i	Total overnight time of crew c_i
cd_i	Total duty time of crew c_i	n_i	Sum of pairings performed by crew c_i
$cfd_{d,i}$	Flight time of crew c_i on day d	$cdd_{d,i}$	Duty time of crew c_i on day d
P	Set of all pairings	E	Set of all crews in the base

2.2 Problem Description

We use $(s_j, e_j, f_j, d_j, o_j)$ as the attributes of pairings, where j denotes the number of pairings. In this model, the other three attributes need to be preprocessed to gain the flight time f_j, duty time d_j, and departure overnight time o_j. The required attribute values can be calculated according to the related definitions in Fig. 1.

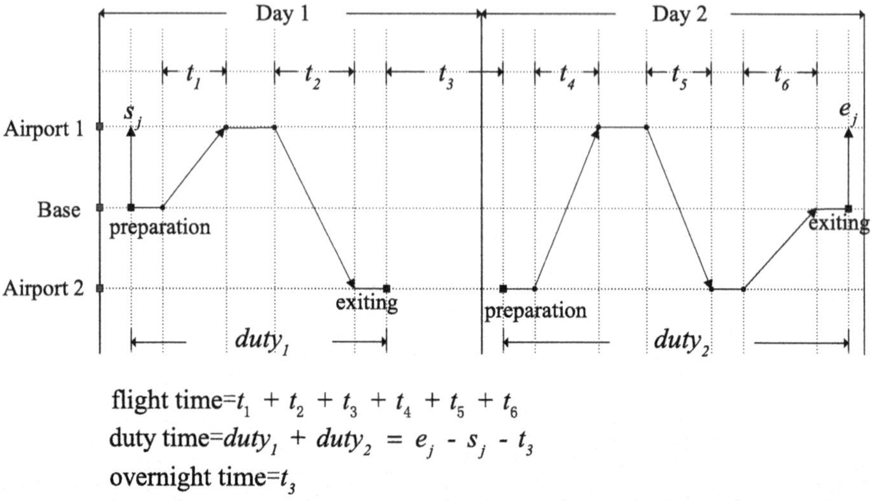

Fig. 1. Schematic diagram of attribute calculation for the pairing

In the CRP model, $(pf_i, pv_i, cf_i, cd_i, co_i)$ represents the attributes of the crew members. The first two attributes denote the crew members' preferred flights and preferred holidays, respectively. In this study, crew members' preferred flights are associated with their bases, which generally means that crew members prefer flights that are based at the departure or arrival airport. It saves time for positioning and avoids additional workload. There are two ways to improve crew satisfaction. One is to assign pairings of the preferred flight to the corresponding crew member. The other is to avoid assignments during preferred holidays.

2.3 Objective Formulation

Unlike most existing crew rostering problem models that consider cost in the airline's perspective, we propose a model that takes into account both fairness and satisfaction goals in the crews' perspective [4]. Since standard deviation is the most commonly used index to measure the workload balance of different members, we calculate the deviation of three time indicators from the average values of crews to determine the fairness and is expressed as:

$$g_1(X) = \sqrt{\frac{1}{E}\sum_{i\in E} dev_i} \tag{1}$$

where

$$dev_i = (cf_i - \overline{f})^2 + (cd_i - \overline{d})^2 + (co_i - \overline{o})^2 \tag{2}$$

$$cf_i = \sum_{j=1}^{n_i} \hat{f}_{i,j} \tag{3}$$

$$cd_i = \sum_{j=1}^{n_i} \hat{d}_{i,j} \tag{4}$$

$$co_i = \sum_{j=1}^{n_i} \hat{o}_{i,j} \tag{5}$$

$$\overline{f} = \frac{1}{\mathrm{E}} \sum_{i \in E} cf_i \tag{6}$$

$$\overline{d} = \frac{1}{E} \sum_{i \in E} cd_i \tag{7}$$

$$\overline{o} = \frac{1}{E} \sum_{i \in E} co_i \tag{8}$$

In this manuscript, the sum of the percentage of preferred flights and preferred vacation being satisfied is applied to represent the satisfaction of the pairing assignments of the crews. And the satisfaction function is expressed as:

$$g_2(X) = \frac{sppn}{PPN} + \frac{sapn}{APN} \tag{9}$$

To facilitate subsequent model evaluation as well as calculation, it is turned into two minimization bi-objective problems. The specific objectives are defined as:

$$optimize\ G(X) = \begin{cases} \min\ g_1(X) \\ \min 2 - g_2(X) \end{cases} \tag{10}$$

2.4 Constraints Formulation

As we known, the scheduling must meet the regulations of CAAC and airlines. And the assignments distributed to each set of crew should meet the requirements of transit time connection and the limit of worktime, which ensures the best working condition of the crew for rest and related preparations.

(1) Specifically, the rest time between two backward and forward connected pairings assigned to the same crew member should not be less than 10 h.

$$\hat{s}_{i,j+1} - \hat{e}_{i,j} \geq 10, \forall i \in \{1, 2, ..., CN\} \forall j \in \{1, 2, ..., n_i - 1\} \tag{11}$$

(2) No crew member can fly more than 100 h in any one natural month.

$$\sum_{d=1}^{30} cfd_{d,i} \leq 100, \forall i \in \{1, 2, ..., CN\} \tag{12}$$

(3) The cumulative time on duty cannot exceed 60 h in any seven consecutive natural days.

$$\sum_{d=1+k}^{7+k} cdd_{d,i} \leq 60, \forall i \in \{1, 2, ..., CN\} \forall k \in \{1, 2, ..., 23\} \tag{13}$$

(4) Cumulative duty time cannot exceed 210 h in any one natural month.

$$\sum_{d=1}^{30} cdd_{d,i} \leq 210, \forall i \in \{1, 2, ..., CN\} \tag{14}$$

(5) Each crew member should be scheduled for at least 48 consecutive hours of rest during 144 h prior to the flight mission. The constraint formula is Eq. (15), where $checkRest_{i,j}$ is an indicator of whether the crew member's j^{th} pairing satisfies this requirements and $rest_{i,j,k}$ is used to check whether the rest time of crew member satisfies a minimum of 48 consecutive hours during the 144-h period prior to the start of the jth pairing.

$$\sum_{j=2}^{n_i} checkRest_{i,j} = 0, \forall i \in \{1, 2, ..., CN\} \tag{15}$$

where

$$checkRest_{i,j} = \begin{cases} 1, \text{ if } \sum_{k=0}^{j-1} rest_{i,j,k} = 0 \\ 0, \text{ if } \sum_{k=0}^{j-1} rest_{i,j,k} \neq 0 \end{cases} \tag{16}$$

$$rest_{i,j,k} = \begin{cases} 1, \text{ if } \min(\hat{s}_{i,k+1} - \hat{e}_{i,k}, \hat{s}_{i,k+1} - (\hat{s}_{i,j} - 144)) \geq 48 \\ 0, \text{ if } \min(\hat{s}_{i,k+1} - \hat{e}_{i,k}, \hat{s}_{i,k+1} - (\hat{s}_{i,j} - 144)) < 48 \end{cases} \tag{17}$$

3 Proposed Algorithm for Solving CRP

In this paper, the NSGA-II algorithm is suitably improved to meet the features of the CRP model, including population initialization, genetic operation and coding method.

3.1 Algorithm Flow of NSGA-II

The specific computational process is shown in Fig. 2. And the algorithm runs as follows:

Step 1 Population initialization: Generate the initial population.
Step 2 Fitness calculation: Calculate the fitness of each chromosome according to the relevant parameters.
Step 3 Non-dominated sorting and calculation of crowding degree: The parent population is non-dominated to obtain the frontier sorting value and crowding degree.

Step 4 Selection operation: Half of the chromosomes are selected from the parent population according to the tournament mechanism.
Step 5 Crossover operation: Generate offspring by randomly generating crossover points.
Step 6 Mutation operation: Randomly select a certain number of offspring and randomly change the gene values with a certain probability.
Step 7 Merge operation: merge the offspring population with the parent population.
Step 8 Fast non-dominated sorting and calculation of crowding degree: Fast non-dominated sorting of the entire population to obtain the frontier sorting value and crowding degree.
Step 9 Pareto filtering operation: Based on the ranking value and crowding degree, half of the population is selected to form a sub-population to replace the original population.
Step 10 Termination condition: If the number of iterations does not exceed the maximum number of iterations, then go to Step 5; If not, then terminate the evolutionary process.

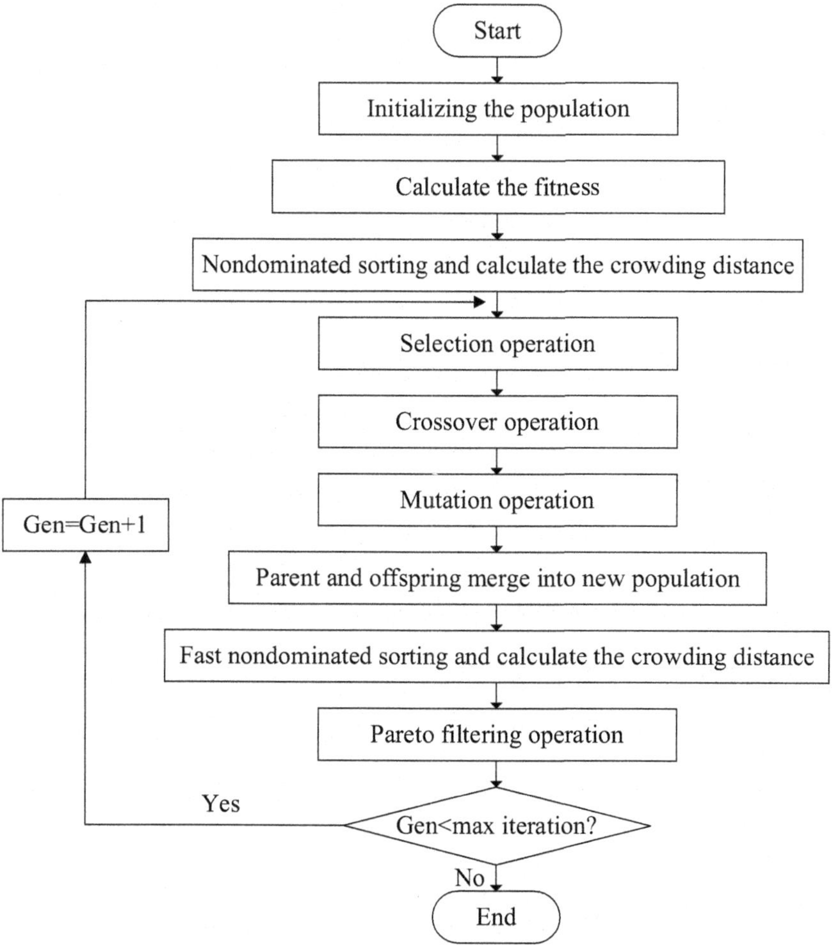

Fig. 2. Algorithm process of NSGAII

3.2 Proposed Algorithm

The flow of hMOBBPSO-GA is shown in Fig. 3. The red part indicates the improved steps.

3.2.1 Population Initialization

In order to satisfy the constraints related to the solution of the crew rostering problem, the random generation method was not adopted. Instead, we first randomly assign crew members to the first few pairings and ensure that each crew member is matched with one pairing. After that, we roughly select feasible crews for subsequent pairings based on the constraints of Eq. (11). This contributes to the speed and the probability of converging into a feasible solution.

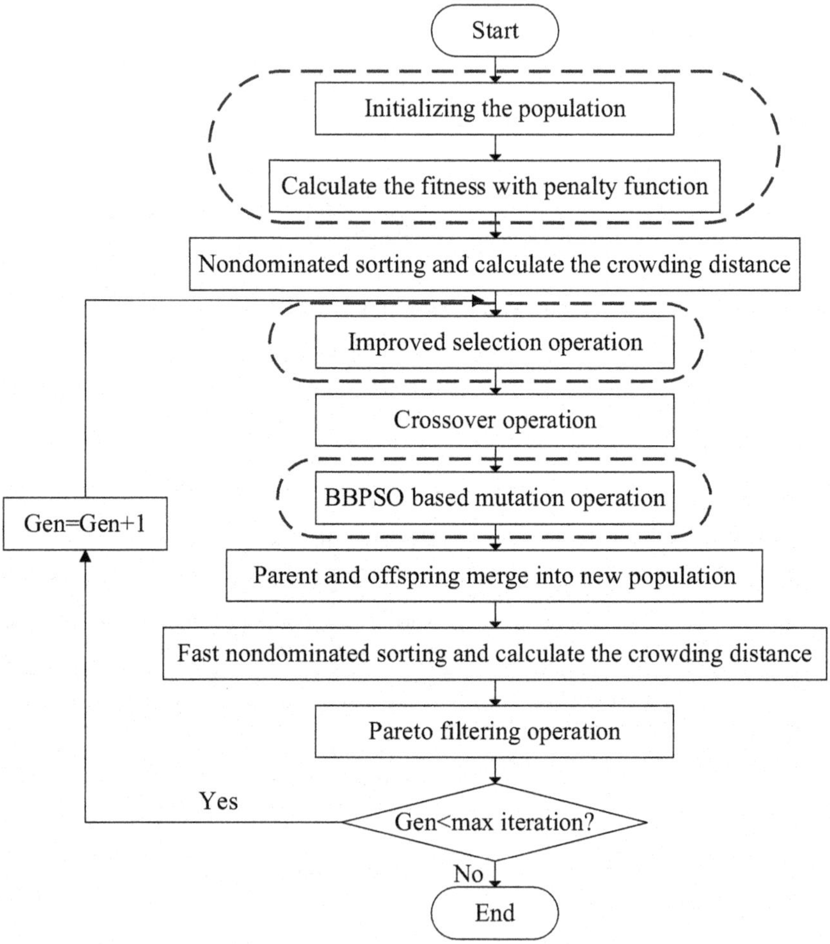

Fig. 3. Algorithm process of hMOBBPSO-GA

3.2.2 Selection Operator

The purpose of selection is to pick superior individuals from the exchanged population so that they have the opportunity to act as parents to reproduce offspring for the next generation. However, in order to avoid premature convergence and choose individuals with more chances of survival, the following strategy is adopted in this study [14]. First, two individuals are randomly selected from the population. If the random number generated between 0 and 1 is less than the probability r which is usually set to 0.8, then we select the better one; otherwise, we select the worse one. Next the selected individual is released back into the population and can be selected as a parent again.

3.2.3 BBPSO-Based Mutation Operator

Based on the idea that position updating of particle swarm can be treated as a mutation operation [15], together with the fact that the velocity vector in the standard PSO cannot match with the individuals after the genetic operation, position update is designed in Eq. (18) according to the idea of BBPSO.

$$P_i(k+1) = g_{best}(k) + \alpha \times C(1,0) \times |\, p_{best}(k) - g_{best}(k)\,|, \quad if\ rand(0,1) < P_m \tag{18}$$

where $p_{best}(k)$ denotes the individual historical optimal position; $g_{best}(k)$ represents the global best particle; $C(1,0)$ is the random number generated by the standard Cauchy distribution; k shows the number of current iterations of the population.

$$\alpha = \alpha_{\min} + (\alpha_{\max} - \alpha_{\min}) \times k/Gn \tag{19}$$

where α ($\alpha \in (0, 1)$) is a control factor. Gn is the maximum number of iterations. α_{max} is the maximum of control factor, while α_{min} is the minimum of control factor. Larger or smaller values of α correspond to more discrete or more clustered particle populations, respectively. In this study, a linearly decreasing value of $\boldsymbol{\alpha}$ is employed to accelerate the convergence at the early stage of evolution and to improve the probability of escaping the local optimum at the late stage of evolution.

3.3 Coding

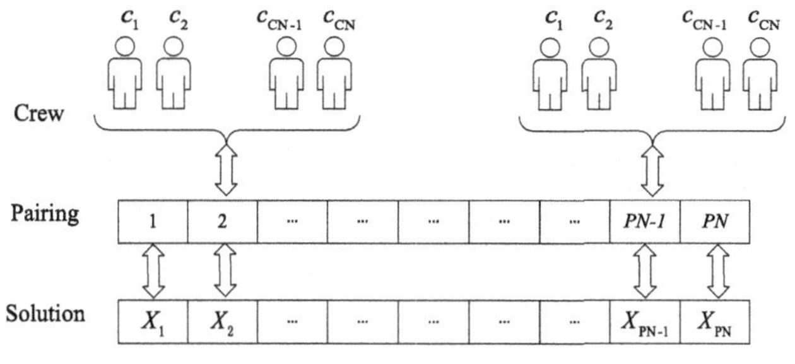

Fig. 4. Coding of crew rostering problem

To simplify the model, we consider only the allocation of pilots and assume that only one pilot is needed for each flight in our model. For each pairing, only one crew member can be selected among the executable crews. Combining the problem with the characteristics of the genetic algorithm, the solution of the crew rostering problem can be viewed as a sequence of crew members selected for each pairing from the set of available duty crews, as shown in Fig. 4. Each chromosome in the population represents a feasible solution.

In the part algorithm solving steps, we also convert the integer encoding to a fixed-length binary encoding for convenience, as shown in Eq. (20). Specifically, the binary variable expresses whether a crew performs the pairing or not.

$$x = \begin{bmatrix} x_{1,1} & x_{2,1} & \cdots & x_{CN,1} \\ x_{1,2} & x_{2,2} & \cdots & x_{CN,2} \\ \cdots & \cdots & \ddots & \cdots \\ x_{1,PN} & x_{2,PN} & \cdots & x_{CN,PN} \end{bmatrix} \tag{20}$$

4 Experiments and Comparisons

4.1 Experimental Settings

In this paper, experimental tests are conducted to verify the performance of hMOBBPSO-GA to solve the crew rostering problem based on a real data set. All algorithms are implemented in MATLAB R2021b and run on a computer with an eight-core processor R7-5700U and 16.0 GB RAM. We collected flight data for three routes of China Southern Airlines based at Shenzhen Airport in December 2021. And Table 2 shows a summary of the collected flight data. Meanwhile, the relevant parameters in the improved model are listed in Table 3.

Table 2. Size of instance data

No. of flights	No. of pairings(*PN*)	No. of pilots(*CN*)
264	95	6

Table 3. Parameters setting

Symbol	Definition	Value
N	Population size	200
D	Particle dimension	95

(*continued*)

Table 3. (*continued*)

Symbol	Definition	Value
P_c	Probability of crossover	0.9
P_m	Probability of mutation	0.5
G_n	Maximum number of generations	100
α_{max}	Maximum of control factor	0.5
α_{min}	Minimum of control factor	0.8

4.2 Experimental Results

To illustrate the efficiency of our proposed algorithm, MOPSO and NSGA-II are utilized as comparison algorithms. Each of these three algorithms are iterated for 100 generations. We pick out the non-dominated solutions from the results obtained from 10 independent runs and draw Pareto front comparisons against the other algorithms in Fig. 5. Two performance metrics, including hypervolume (HV) and C-metric, are employed for performance evaluations in Table 4 and Table 5. The HV value of hMOBBPSO-GA is significantly higher compared with MOPSO and NSGA-II, which reflects the better convergence and wider range distribution between its non-dominated solutions. In addition, C(hMOBBPSO-GA, NSGA-II) = 1.000 and C(hMOBBPSO-GA, MOPSO) = 1.000 mean that all the non-dominated solutions in NSGA-II and MOPSO are dominated by the non-dominated solutions of hMOBBPSO-GA. The comparisons indicate that solution set from hMOBBPSO-GA covers a wider range and the improved algorithm has better performance.

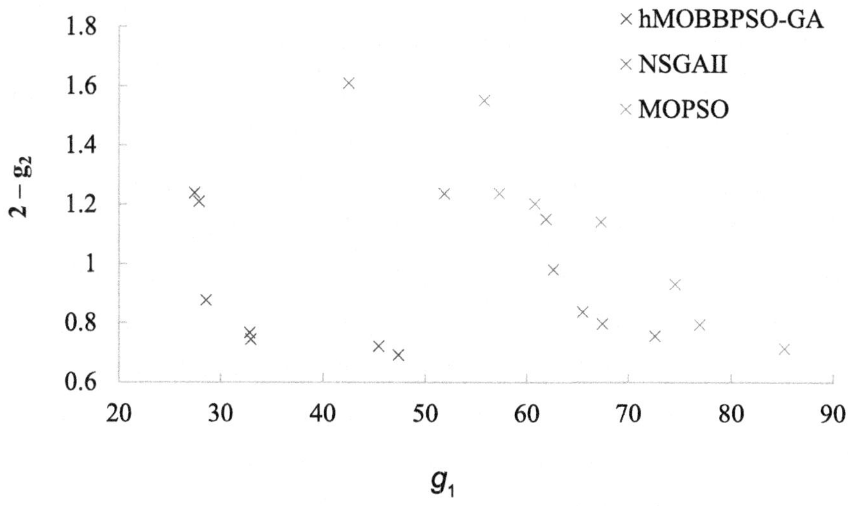

Fig. 5. Performance of hMOBBPSO-GA, NSGA-II and MOPSO

Table 4. Comparison between hMOBBPSO-GA and other algorithms on C-metric

NSGA-II		MOPSO	
C(hMOBBPSO-GA,-)	C(-,hMOBBPSO-GA)	C(hMOBBPSO-GA,-)	C(-,hMOBBPSO-GA)
1.000	0.000	1.000	0.000

Table 5. Comparison of hMOBBPSO-GA with other algorithms on HV

Metrics	hMOBBPSO-GA	NSGA-II	MOPSO
HV	9.842	16.746	17.580

5 Conclusion

We propose an improved hybrid algorithm hMOBBPSO-GA based on the idea of BBPSO to solve the crew rostering problem with satisfaction and fairness objectives. The initial solution are generated randomly according to one of the important time constraints of CRP, which efficiently avoids some infeasible solutions and improves the quality of the initial solution. The selection operation of the genetic algorithm is modified to avoid falling into local optimum prematurely. Furthermore, depending on the basic idea of BBPSO, the learning direction is provided for the individual mutation operation to accelerate the convergence of the algorithm. Experiments are conducted on a real-world monthly instance. The results verify the superiority of hBBPSO-GA in solving multi-objective CRP compared against NSGA-II and MOPSO. In the future, we will further consider flight crews with different classes and cabin crews in CRP.

Acknowledgment. The study was supported in part by the Natural Science Foundation of China Grant No. 62103286, No. 62001302, No. 71971143, in part by Social Science Youth Foundation of Ministry of Education of China under Grant 21YJC630181, in part by Guangdong Basic and Applied Basic Research Foundation under Grant 2021A1515011348, 2019A1515111205, 2019A1515110401, in part by Guangdong Province Philosophy and Social Science Planning Discipline Co-construction Project under Grant GD22XGL22, in part by Natural Science Foundation of Guangdong Province under Grant 2020A1515010749, 2020A1515010752, in part by Natural Science Foundation of Shenzhen under Grant JCYJ20190808145011259, in part by Shenzhen Science and Technology Program under Grant RCBS20200714114920379, in part by Key Research Foundation of Higher Education of Guangdong Provincial Education Bureau under Grant 2019KZDXM030, in part by Guangdong Province Innovation Team under Grant 2021WCXTD002, in part by Special Projects in Key Fields of Ordinary Colleges and Universities in Guangdong Province under Grant 2022ZDZX2054.

References

1. Badánik, B., Le Duc, M., Kandera, B.: Understanding scheduling preferences of airline crews. Transp. Res. Procedia **59**, 223–233 (2021)
2. Doi, T., Nishi, T., Voß, S.: Two-level decomposition-based matheuristic for airline crew rostering problems with fair working time. Europ. J. Oper. Res. **267**(2): 428–438 (2018)

3. De Armas, J., Cadarso, L., Juan, A.A., et al.: A multi-start randomized heuristic for real-life crew rostering problems in airlines with work-balancing goals. Ann. Oper. Res. **258**(2), 825–848 (2017)
4. Zhou, S.Z., Zhan, Z.H., Chen, Z.G., et al.: A multi-objective ant colony system algorithm for airline crew rostering problem with fairness and satisfaction. IEEE Trans. Intell. Transp. Syst. **22**(11), 6784–6798 (2020)
5. Gamache, M., Soumis, F., Villeneuve, D., et al.: The preferential bidding system at Air Canada. Transp. Sci. **32**(3), 246–255 (1998)
6. Dawid, H., König, J., Strauss, C.: An enhanced rostering model for airline crews. Comput. Oper. Res. **28**(7), 671–688 (2001)
7. Kasirzadeh, A., Saddoune, M., Soumis, F.: Airline crew scheduling: models, algorithms, and data sets. EURO J. Transp. Logist. **6**(2), 111–137 (2017)
8. Ezzinbi, O., Sarhani, M., El Afia, A., et al.: Particle swarm optimization algorithm for solving airline crew scheduling problem. In: 2014 International Conference on Logistics Operations Management. IEEE, pp. 52–56 (2014)
9. Banerjee, T., Biswas, A., Shaikh, A.A., et al.: An application of extended NSGA-II in interval valued multi-objective scheduling problem of crews. Soft. Comput. **26**(3), 1261–1278 (2022)
10. Shi, L., Gong, J., Zhai, C.: Application of a hybrid PSO-GA optimization algorithm in determining pyrolysis kinetics of biomass. Fuel **323**, 124344 (2022)
11. Sun, L., Lin, L., Li, H., et al.: Large scale flexible scheduling optimization by a distributed evolutionary algorithm. Comput. Ind. Eng. **128**, 894–904 (2019)
12. Krohling R A, Mendel E. Bare bones particle swarm optimization with Gaussian or Cauchy jumps. In: 2009 IEEE Congress on Evolutionary Computation. IEEE, pp. 3285–3291 (2009)
13. Ministry of Transport of the People's Republic of China. 14th Ministerial Meeting (Aug. 29, 2017). Large Aircraft Public Air Transport Carrier Operation Certification Rules. http://www.caac.gov.cn/XXGK/XXGK/MHGZ/201710/P020171009385743667633.pdf
14. Wang, X., Gao, L., Zhang, C., et al.: A multi-objective genetic algorithm based on immune and entropy principle for flexible job-shop scheduling problem. Int. J. Adv. Manufact. Technol. **51**(5), 757–767 (2010)
15. Angeline, P.J.: Evolutionary optimization versus particle swarm optimization: philosophy and performance differences. In: International Conference on Evolutionary Programming. Springer, Berlin, Heidelberg, pp. 601–610 (1998)

Plant Leaf Area Measurement Using 3D Imaging: A Comparative Study Between Dynamic Structured Light Stereo and Time-of-Flight

Yi Wang and KangShun Li(✉)

College of Software Engineering, Guangdong University of Science and Technology, Dongguan 532000, China
likangshun@sina.com

Abstract. Leaf area measurement is essential for various plant-related sciences. Two common 3D imaging modalities were utilized to measure plat leaf areas: a commercially available time-of-flight camera and a dynamic structured light stereo camera constructed with an optical MEMS-based micro projector. A joint point cloud segmentation and repairing method were developed to reduce the impact of holes (missing pixels) and significant noise (flying pixels) in point clouds. Results from dummy and real leaves showed that dynamic structured light stereo produced much more accurate outputs than time-of-flight, and the latter tended to overestimate leaf areas.

Keywords: Leaf area measurement · Dynamic structured light stereo camera · 3D imaging

1 Introduction

Leaves are responsible for photosynthesis and evapotranspiration in plants. They are the most visible portion of a plant and the most responsive to the environment. As such, leaf area measurement is important for various plant-related sciences, such as botany, agriculture, and ecology.

Traditionally, plat leaf area is measured by grid count, gravimetric, and planimeter. 2D imaging and computer vision technology have been employed for noncontact leaf area measurement [1–4]. However, the accuracy of 2D image-based leaf area measurement is highly dependent on leaf surface geometry and camera position and orientation. Various 3D imaging methods have also been utilized for the same purpose, such as laser scanning [5], time-of-flight [6, 7], and passive stereo vision [8, 9]. Laser scanning can produce an accurate leaf 3D model, thus providing precise leaf area measurement results. However, merging line scanning point clouds to create a 3D surface requires complex motor control and is time-consuming. On the other hand, time-of-light (TOF) and passive stereo vision are snapshot 3D imaging and do not rely on spatial scanning, but their convenience and efficiency come at the cost of accuracy.

Y. Xu et al. (Eds.): ML4CS 2022, LNCS 13657, pp. 576–584, 2023.
https://doi.org/10.1007/978-3-031-20102-8_44

This report combines optical MEMS-based digital light projector and stereo vision to capture 3D leaf surface information via dynamic structured light patterns. This approach combines the advantages of the laser mentioned above scanning with snapshot ToF and passive stereo vision as it does not need time-consuming scanning and hardware-dependent point cloud fusion while acquiring highly accurate 3D leaf surfaces. Leaf area measurement errors were compared between in-house-built, dynamic structured light stereo and a commercial TOF 3D camera (Azure Kinect DK, Microsoft) using the same data processing process.

2 Methods

2.1 Dynamic Structured Light Stereo Imaging

Structured light 3D imaging usually employs a projector to artificially generate one or more patterns on a target surface to be measured. A camera captures the surface with the projected patterns. The distortions of the projected patterns on the target surface are related to the surface profile, and accurate 3D geometric surface shapes can be recovered using the triangulation principle. The projected patterns can be coded in the spatial or time domains. The former typically utilizes diffractive optical elements (DOE) and lasers to produce pseudo-random prints, as in Intel RealSense and Apple FaceID cameras. The latter typically employs optical MEMS (Micro-Electro-Mechanical System) or LCoS (Liquid Crystal on Silicon) and LEDs to generate various dynamic patterns [10].

This report uses Litemaze DST300 3D camera (Fig. 1a) to capture leaf 3D surface information. This camera consists of a micro projector with DLP4500 optical MEMS (1140 * 912 array) from Texas Instruments to generate sequential coded patterns at the center and two cameras with Sony IMX250 global shutter CMOS image sensors (2448 × 2048 array, pixel size 23.45 μm * 3.45 μm) on the two sides. The default baseline of the stereo cameras is 15cm, which can be adjusted via rotating the two cameras in the X direction in a small range.

The stereo cameras are calibrated using the widely used Zhang method [11]. The calibration board is a square glass (H = 24.0 cm) with a 7 × 7 pattern of circles (Fig. 1 bottom) (R = 1.5 cm, D = 3.0 cm), the orientation of the calibration board can be determined with the single unique corner (top-left in the image shown).

For 3D reconstruction, images from the two cameras were rectified using the calibration output. For each sequence of projected patterns, a time domain code is generated for the images from each camera, and the code from one camera is matched to the same code from the other camera by searching. The disparity is obtained and further converted to depth using the stereo camera parameters (Eq. 1).

$$Z = \frac{\mathrm{Bf}}{\mathrm{D}} \tag{1}$$

where Z is depth, B is the stereo baseline, f is the stereo camera focal length, and D is disparity. As stereo matching utilizes time domain coding, it does not go through the inherent lowpass filtering in spatial domain codings such as semi-global stereo matching [12] and other dense stereo matching methods, thus producing highly accurate dense depth information.

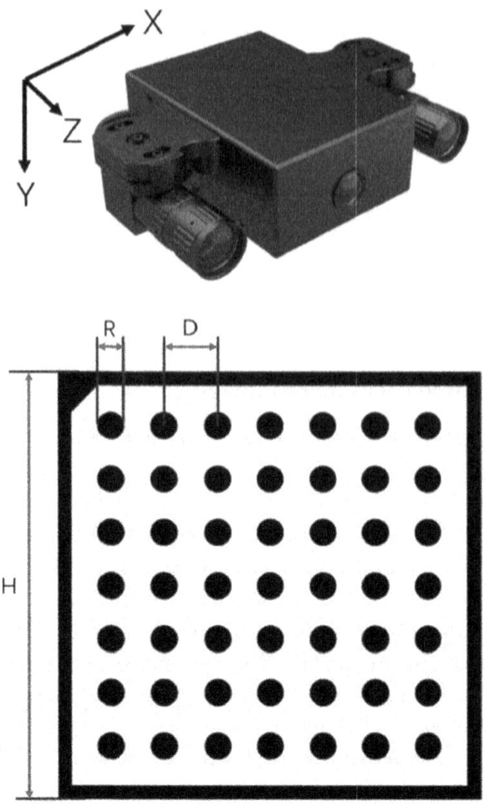

Fig. 1. Dynamic structured light stereo camera and calibration board

Fig. 2. A leaf captured by the left sensor of the Litemaze DTS300. Left: as in the original state; Right: cut into two pieces and flattened.

2.2 Image Acquisition and Leaf Samples

The Litemaze DST300 and Microsoft Azure Kinect DK cameras were mounted on a custom metal frame back-to-back about 50cm on top of a flat surface, such that their front edges were roughly aligned with their working distances were similar. Leaves were placed on the flat surface. This way, images from the two 3D cameras were captured in the same environmental conditions.

The Litemaze DST300 captured 2D images at the native sensor resolution, while the reconstructed depth images resolution of 2048 * 1536. The Kinect DK depth image resolution was set to the narrow field of view (NFOV) mode (640 * 576). Though the Kinect DK depth sensor has a native resolution of 1280 * 720, it can only be fully employed at 1200 * 1200 wide field of view (WFOV) mode [13].

White printing papers were clipped into circles, squares, rectangles, and isosceles triangles of different sizes with known parameters as dummy plant leaves for verification purposes. Each such dummy flat leaf was placed in various positions in the FOVs of the two 3D cameras to capture images. In addition, each dummy leaf was artificially morphed into a non-flat surface to simulate acting as a plant leaf.

40 Real plant leaves were collected from 4 different types of plants (Epipremnum aureum, Schefflera arboricola Hay, Ligustrum japonicum Thumb, and Radermachera). The images were captured while each leaf was in its natural state on the flat Table. To obtain the ground truth areas of real leaves, they were placed under a glass panel to be flattened so that their images were captured in a way like dummy flat leaves. For leaves that the glass panel cannot easily find flat, they were cut into multiples along the most curved places so that each piece could be appropriately flattened. The total area of a leaf processed this way is the sum of the areas of each flattened piece. Figure 2 shows an example of the flattening of a leaf as captured by a black-and-white sensor of the Litemaze DST300 as it was illuminated by uniform blue light from the DLP4500 micro projector.

2.3 Joint Point Cloud Segmentation and Repairing

To segment out leaf area from the background, we operate on the leaf depth map, which is essentially a 2D image. The 2D leaf image was obtained by segmenting the image from the same primary sensor (usually the left one) in the dynamic structured light stereo camera using normalized Graph Cut [14]. The binarized leaf mask was applied to the leaf depth map to remove the background. The processed depth map was converted to a point cloud using camera parameters. Due to leaf light absorption, specular reflection, or noise, the depth information of certain parts of the leaf surface may be missing (holes in a point cloud), and some pixels outside of the leaf region may have erroneous depth values (flying pixels in a point cloud). Simple filtering or smoothing cannot fully repair points that could hole or remove a large number of connected flying pixels.

We employed two different methods for point cloud repairing. The first uses combinations of morphological operations (erosion, dilation, open and close) to remove flying pixels and gradient-based inpainting to fill holes in the point cloud directly. The second utilizes iterative image inpainting [15]. We modified the original image inpainting technique and termed it as 2D image-guided depth map inpainting: first, a 2D image mask is used to constrain the depth map inpainting process; second, the gradients used for determining the values inpainting new pixels are a mixture of image gradients from both the 2D image and the depth map. Figure 3 shows an example of a raw leaf depth map, the corresponding 2D image, the segmented leaf mask, and the depth map inpainting output.

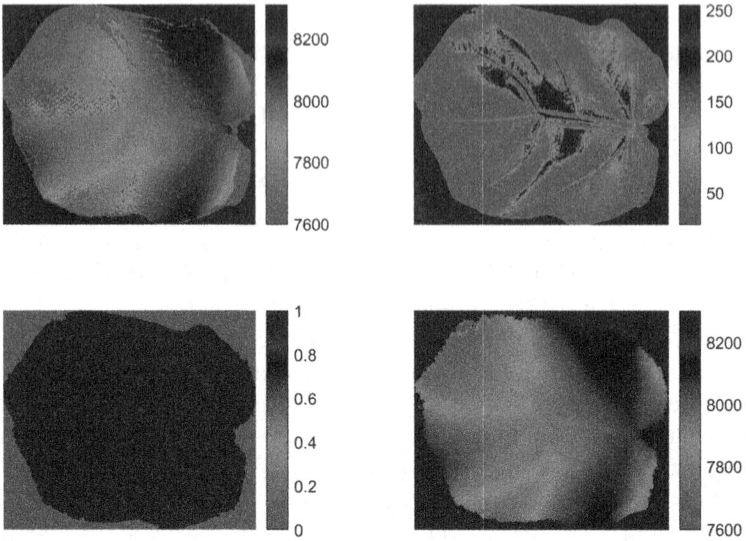

Fig. 3. 2D image-guided depth map inpainting example. (1) Top left: original leaf depth map; (2) top right: 2D leaf image; (3) bottom left: leaf segmentation mask; (4) bottom right: leaf depth map inpainting output.

2.4 Leaf Area Calculation

For 2D images, they are rectified using camera calibration results, and the total number of pixels in the segmented mask is proportional to the area. This relationship was calibrated using clipped plat papers of different geometric shapes with known ground truth.

For 3D images, segmentation and filtering were done as described above. Depth maps were converted to point clouds, which were further converted to meshes using various methods. For simplicity, we used triangular meshes in this report. The area of a leaf mesh was calculated as the sum of the areas of all the triangles in the mesh.

3 Results

3.1 Dummy Leaves

As shown in Table 1a, b, non-flat dummy leaves areas measured by 2D images produced much larger errors than for flat dummy leaves (average relative errors of −8.61%

compared to −2.26%). However, in the case of flat dummy leaves, areas measured by TOF generated much larger errors than those measured by 2D images (average relative errors of 6.92% compared to −2.26%). But for non-flat dummy leaves, areas measured by TOF still produced more minor errors than those measured by 2D images (average relative errors of 5.24% compared to −8.61%).

For flat and non-flat dummy leaves, areas measured by dynamic SLS were one magnitude more accurate than 2D images and TOF (−0.35% and −0.38% for flat and non-flat dummy leave, respectively).

Table 1a. Summary of results for flat dummy leaves

	GT	2D	3D-TOF (Kinect DK)	3D-SLS (DST300)
Mean area (mm^2)	6123.8	5922.6	6587.5	6101.3
Min area (mm^2)	2500	2491.3	2400.4	2480.4
Max area (mm^2)	10000	9970.1	11225.7	9980.7
AVE errors #		−2.26%	6.92%	**−0.35%**
STD errors #		4.60%	7.37%	**0.74%**
Mean ABS errors #		3.75%	8.64%	**0.55%**

Table 1b. Summary of results for non-flat dummy leaves

	GT	2D	3D-TOF (Kinect DK)	3D-SLS (DST300)
Mean area (mm^2)	6123.8	5559.9	6518.0	6098.0
Min area (mm^2)	2500	2338.2	2402.3	2526.8
Max area (mm^2)	10000	8714.5	10972.4	9907.7
AVE errors #		−8.61%	5.24%	**−0.38%**
STD errors #		2.85%	4.31%	**0.99%**
Mean ABS errors #		8.61%	5.90%	**0.88%**

#: AVE error: average of errors in percentage.
STD error: standard deviation of errors in percentage.
Ave ABS error: average of absolute values of errors in percentage.

3.2 Real Plant Leaves

As shown in Table 2, for real plant leaves, the comparative area measurement accuracies were similar to those from non-flat dummy leaves. 2D images provided the least accurate results (average relative errors of −5.93%), and dynamic SLS produced the most accurate ones (average relative errors of 0.25%).

Table 2. Summary of results for real leaves

	GT	2D-IMG	3D-TOF	3D-SLS
Mean area (mm^2)	3417.0	3220.0	3495.6	3429.0
Min area (mm^2)	2239.9	2069.7	2247.7	2224.8
Max area (mm^2)	4741.6	4757.8	5311.8	4997.6
AVE errors #		−5.93%	1.99%	**0.25%**
STD errors #		3.51%	4.20%	**2.01%**
Mean ABS errors #		6.15%	3.52%	**1.44%**

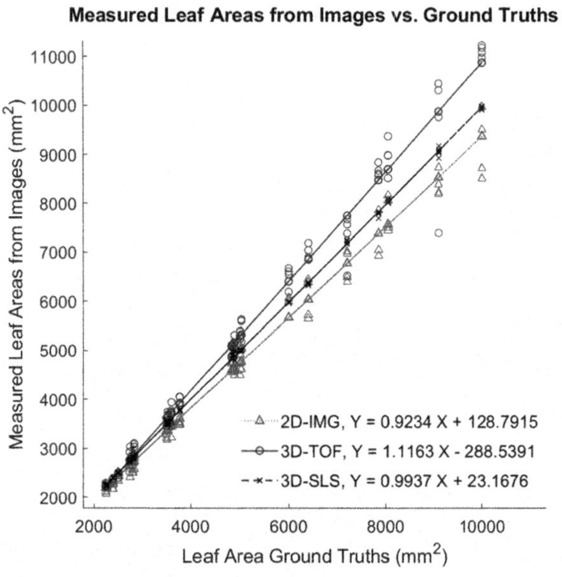

Fig. 4. Relationships between measured leaf areas and ground truths

Linear regression analyses were further done on measured non-flat dummy and natural leaves areas. The results are shown in Fig. 4. As expected, 2D images underestimated leaf areas, dynamic SLS estimated leaf areas accurately (the regression coefficient was very close to 1, and the offset was less than 1%). Still, TOF overestimated leaf areas as discussed above.

4 Discussions

As expected, except for flat dummy leaves, 3D imaging produced more accurate leaf areas than 2D images, as 2D images only captured a projection of the leaf surfaces, which often are not flat.

The surprising result was that in the case of flat dummy leaves, TOF 3D significantly overestimated areas and produced output less accurate than 2D images. The main underlying reason is that depth images from TOF imaging are often very noisy, and the noise characteristics are very different from 2D images and other 3D imaging modalities [16]. It should be noted that even with this overestimation shortcoming, TOF 3D still provides more accurate leaf areas than 2D images in non-flat dummy and natural leaves.

In all cases, dynamic SLS 3D gives the best leaf area measurements. The average of relative errors was no more than 0.25% as applied to real leaves, which was almost a magnitude better than that of TOF 3D at 1.99%, and its measurement variations were much more minor than those from TOF 3D as well (2.01% vs. 4.20%). This is among the most accurate leaf area measurements using image processing and computer vision.

As 3D imaging overcomes the shortcomings of using 2D images to compute leaf areas (non-flatness, dependence on measurement distance and orientations, etc.), 3D cameras can be mounted on mobile robots to conduct noncontact leaf area measurements regularly, for example, for the purpose of collect massive data to utilize machine learning methods to construct plat growth models given various environmental factors in the fast-growing field of facility agriculture [17].

5 Conclusion

This paper presents a joint point cloud segmentation and restoration method for leaf area measurement. This method combines an optical MEMS-based digital light projector and stereo vision to capture 3D leaf surface information through dynamic structured light modes. Using this method to perform leaf area measurements on both pseudo and real leaves, leaf area measurements were compared between an in-house constructed dynamic structured light stereo and a commercial TOF 3D camera (Azure Kinect DK, Microsoft), and it was found that the method proposed in this paper can accurately measure leaf area while reducing holes (missing pixels) and significant noise (flying pixels) in the point cloud effects.

Acknowledgments. This work was supported by the Natural Science Foundation of Guangdong Province of China (2020A1515010784) and Guang dong Youth Characteristic Innovation Project (2021KQNCX120), Natural Science Project of Guangdong University of Science and Technology (GKY-2021KYYBK-20).

References

1. Qiu, Z., Fang, H., Zhang, Y., He, Y.: Measurement of plant leaf area using imaging processing techniques. Proc. SPIE **6027**, 60273G (2006)

2. Lu, C., Ren, H., Zhang, Y., Shen, Y.: Leaf area measurement based on image processing. In: International Conference on Measuring Technology and Mechantronics Automation, pp 580–582 (2010)
3. Hartmann, A., et al.: HTPheno: an image analysis pipeline for high-throughput plant phenotyping. BMC Bioinf. **12**(148), 1–9 (2011)
4. Jansen, M., et al.: Simultaneous phenotyping of leaf growth and chlorophyll fluorescence via GROWSCREEN FLUORO allows detection of stress tolerance in Arabidopsis thaliana and other rosette plants. Funct. Plant Biol. **36**, 902–914 (2009)
5. Dornbusch, T., et al.: Measuring the diurnal pattern of leaf hyponasty and growth in Arabidopsis – a novel phenotyping approach using laser scanning. Funct. Plant Biol. **39**, 860–869 (2012)
6. Alenya, G., et al.: 3D modeling of leaves from color and ToF data for borotized plant measuring. In: IEEE International Conference on Robotics and Automation (ICRA) (2011)
7. Klose, R., et al.: Usability study of 3D time-of-flight cameras for automatic plant phenotyping. Bornimer Agrartechnische Berichte **69**, 93–105 (2009)
8. Andersen, H.J.: Geometric plant properties by relaxed stereo vision using simulated annealing. Comput. Electron. Agric. **49**, 219–232 (2005)
9. Golbach, F., et al.: Validation of plant part measurements using a 3D reconstruction method suitable for high-throughput seedling phenotyping. Mach. Vis. Appl. **27**, 663–680 (2016). https://doi.org/10.1007/s00138-015-0727-5
10. Geng, J.: Structured-light 3D surface imaging: a tutorial. Adv. Opt. Photon. **3**(2), 128–160 (2011)
11. Zhang, Z.: A flexible new technique for camera calibration. Microsoft Technical report MSR-TR-98-71 (1998)
12. Hirschmuller, H.: Accurate and efficient stereo processing by semi-global matching and mutual information. In: CVPR, pp. 807–814 (2005)
13. https://docs.microsoft.com/en-us/azure/Kinect-dk/
14. Shi, J., et al.: Normalized cut and image segmentation. IEEE Trans. Pattern Anal. Mach. Intell. **22**, 888–905 (2000)
15. Marcelo, B., et al.: Navier-stokes fluid dynamics, and image and video inpainting. In: IEEE International Conference on Computer Vision and Pattern Recognition (CVPR) (2001)
16. Falie, D., et al.: Noise characteristics of 3D time-of-flight cameras. In: 2007 International Symposium on Signals, Circuits and Systems (2007)
17. Li, G., et al.: Analysis on impact of facility agriculture on ecological function of modern agriculture. In: 2011 3rd International Conference on Environmental Science and Information Application Technology (ESIAT 2011)

Subgraph Matching Based on Path Adaptation for Large-Scale Graph

Xinmiao Hu, Sui Lin, Guangsi Xiong(✉), and Wenchao Jiang

School of Computer Science and Technology, Guangdong University of Technology, Guangzhou 510006, Guangdong, China
1106497528@qq.com

Abstract. To increase the accuracy and decrease the cost of subgraph querying in large-scale graph data, a subgraph matching method based on path adaptation is proposed. An index is built based on path RDF, and the query graph is decomposed into a set of paths to obtain a set of candidate paths for each path. Then, the candidate paths are concatenated together through K-Partition intersection. Experimental results show that the query accuracy is improved by 15% on average compared with SPATH and SPARRER when dealing with large-scale data.

Keywords: Social network · Knowledge discovery · Large-scale data graphs · Subgraph query · Subgraph matching

1 Introduction

RDF data is usually defined in the form of triple⟨S, P, O⟩, in which S (subject) represents subject, P (predict) represents predicate, O (object) represents object, and predicate represents semantic relationship between subject and object. RDF datasets are usually represented in the form of graphs, in which the vertices represent the subject and object, while predicates are mapped to directed edges connecting two vertices, which represent the semantic relationship between vertices. SPARQL is a query language developed for RDF, which can quickly find qualified results in large-scale RDF data graph. The core problem of SPARQL query is subgraph pattern matching [1, 2]. In other words, the process of pattern matching for RDF graph data is used to search for large-scale RDF data graph and find data subgraphs which are isomorphic to query graph. Therefore, this problem can also be called subgraph matching problem [3]. Subgraph matching is an important branch of graph mining. As a basic operation to realize efficient query on graph data, it is also widely used in social security, social network, biochemistry and other fields [4]. With the advent of the era of big data, the scale of RDF data is gradually increasing, the description of semantic relationship in RDF data model is more complex, the query process is more complex, and the query efficiency is lower. Therefore, the subgraph matching problem of large-scale graph data has become a challenge for academia and industry.

Y. Xu et al. (Eds.): ML4CS 2022, LNCS 13657, pp. 585–594, 2023.
https://doi.org/10.1007/978-3-031-20102-8_45

The subgraph matching problem on large-scale graph has been proved to be a NP problem. Ullmann [5] proposed the Ullmann algorithm to find isomorphic subgraphs by depth first search. Cordella [6] et al. Proposed VF2 algorithm, added pruning operation and search matching on the basis of Ullmann algorithm to improve the efficiency of the algorithm. Graphq [7] algorithm prunes according to the adjacency state and depth information to reduce the time cost. Gaddi [8] algorithm uses the method of constructing adjacency discrimination substructure distance when filtering candidate nodes, and uses backtracking method to get candidate subgraphs and complete subgraph matching. Zhang Shuo [9] proposed copesl algorithm, which uses the method of atlas compression to organize multiple graphs structurally. At the same time, an index feature generation method based on graph mining is given. In order to reduce the range of candidate nodes, TurboISO [10] constructs the query graph into NEC tree structure and matches it by depth first search. For small-scale single graph or atlas, these methods are more suitable, but can not meet the requirements of accuracy and efficiency of subgraph matching for large-scale data graph.

There are two subgraph matching method in RDF graph [11–22]. One is an accurate RDF graph matching algorithm based on subgraph isomorphism. Pattern Q is compared with all possible subgraphs in G and obtain all candidate subgraphs, then check the dominating relationship and return the best matching result. However, this method is inefficient in response time and may produce a lot of middle results. It needs a large number of subgraph isomorphism tests for Q and G, and its algorithm complexity is very high. Another method uses approximate matching strategy to reduce the time-consuming exhaustive search. This method appropriately reduces the rigid structure and label matching constraints of subgraph isomorphism. But the existing graph matching algorithms ignore lots of characteristics of RDF graph. For example, in RDF graph, these algorithms only consider the similarity between vertex and edge, and do not consider the structure between vertex and edge. It ignores the semantic relationship between resources, which is very important for subgraph matching in practical applications [11–22].

To solve these problems, we propose a subgraph matching algorithm based on path adaptation for large-scale graph. The path selected is not based on the matching vertex, but based on the path index to search the subgraph. An index is built based on path RDF, and the query graph is decomposed into a set of paths to obtain a set of candidate paths for each path. Then, the candidate paths are concatenated together through K-Partition intersection. Experiments are conducted to test the path index construction time and F-measure value on different datasets. Compared with Path algorithm and sparer algorithm, the algorithm has higher query accuracy and higher query efficiency.

2 Subgraph Matching Algorithm Based on Path Adaptation

2.1 Subgraph Matching

Define 1: Data graph of RDF [1, 2]

RDF data graph $G = (V_G, E_G, L_G)$, where V_G is a kind of finite vertices, $E_G \subset V \times V$ is a kind of directed edges, and L_G is a kind of labels corresponding to a kind of vertices.

Define 2: Query graph of RDF [1, 2]

Query graph $q = (V_Q, E_Q, L_Q)$, where V_Q is the kind of vertices in the query graph, E_Q is the kind of edges in the query graph, and L_Q is the kind of labels corresponding to vertices in the query graph.

Define 3: Graph path of RDF

In RDF graph, different paths represent various semantic among vertices. For RDF graph, its root vertex is a vertex with zero degree, and the target vertex is a point with zero degree of derivation. Let $g = (V, E, L)$ be an RDF graph. The directed path P in G is defined as a finite sequence $V_1, V_2, \ldots, V_n$ with different vertices $P = V$, where $V_i \in V$ and $(V_i, V_i + 1) \in E$ and $i \in [1, n - 1]$. Because there are not only vertices but also edges in the structure of RDF graph, the path expression for RDF graph can be interpreted as a sequence of "vertex edge" alternation.

Define 4: Matching of Sub graph

Given an RDF data graph G and a query graph Q, the subgraph matching query consists of element (vertex and edge) matching, structure matching and so on. The answer is a set of subgraphs m, which is similar to the query graph. As shown in Fig. 1, Fig. 1 (a) represents data graph G, and Fig. 1 (b) represents query graph Q. for query graph Q, the subgraph matching result of data graph G is (m1, m4, m3, m2,) [1, 2].

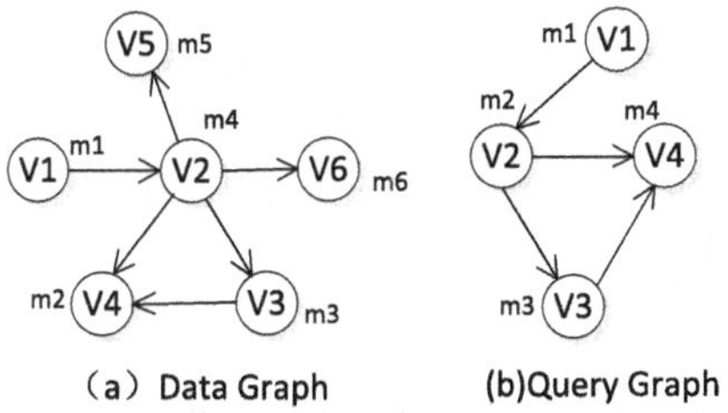

Fig. 1. Example of subgraph matching

Sub graph query is used to find occurrence times of it in RDF database graph. The query graph $q = (V_Q, E_Q, L_Q)$ is a graph of RDF in which each point $v \in V_Q$ is indexed with a label $l\ Q(V) \in \Sigma$. The query graph appoints the structure and semantic requirements that the subgraph of G must meet. That is: sub graph query takes query graph Q as input, searches data graph G containing or similar to query graph, and returns retrieved graph or new graph composed of retrieved graph.

2.2 Path Adaptation

Although trees and graphs can store more structural information, their potential huge scale and costly pruning expenses even transcend the advantages of search space pruning. Therefore, paths are more advantageous than trees and graphs as appropriate index patterns. In order to compare the data path with the input query path, and to determine that data path is most similar to the query path, a distance measure should be defined for the path, which is similar to using the edit operation to define the string. By defining the path to edit the distance, it is to change the path through the edit operation up to there is a path equal to the query path [23].

Define 5: Operations of Editing

Basic editing operations for an RDF path include: replacing an RDF entity or text, replacing an RDF attribute, removing an RDF example or text, removing an RDF attribute, inserting an RDF instance or text, and inserting an RDF attribute.

Define 6: Path of Edit

First, we give an RDF path P and an edit sequence $T = (\omega 1, \omega 2, \omega 3, \cdots \omega n)$, which $T(P) = \omega n(\cdots \omega 2(\omega 1(P)) \cdots\cdots)$. Then, each basic path editing operation ωi is distributed a specific cost C (ωi).The cost C (ωi) varies according to the type of editing operation and the properties of the RDF elements involved.

Define 7: Distance of Path Edit

The path editing distance between P and P′ is defined as $\text{dist}\left(P, P'\right) = \text{MinTi} \in T\{C(Ti)\}$, in which we give two paths P and P′. Ti is the sequence of path editing operations to convert P to P′.

2.3 Subgraph Matching Algorithm

When the editing distance of path between data path and input query path are getting smaller, they will be more similar. The graph similarity can be calculated by calculating the alignment on the path. The matching result of query graph Q on data graph G is the matching set of all paths of Q which constitute the connected component of G. In order to improve the accuracy and efficiency of subgraph matching in large-scale RDF data graph, a subgraph matching algorithm based on path adaptation is proposed.

(1) Data preprocessing: building graph index structure. The context aware path index is used to obtain the detailed information about the graph path, so as to realize the efficient retrieval of candidate matches. To get the set of all paths to a exist vertex v, breadth first search is used to explore G from root. The path expression from root to current vertex and the path expression of the vertex itself are output. The resource table can be used to locate the target vertex of each candidate path, so as to find the corresponding candidate path of the given vertex v in the query graph. To improve the efficiency of path based query processing, reverse path expression is used to omit the costly graph traversal.
(2) Query processing: query processing consists of 3 sub-stages: path decomposition, finding candidate paths and connecting candidate paths. Figure 2 shows the basic process of Q query on RDF graph G. The specific steps are as follows:

- Path decomposition. The query graph is divided into a group of paths $q = \{Q_1, Q_2, \ldots, Q_k\}$. In order to reconstruct the answer subgraph, intersection graph in k-partition used to save the structure information of query. In k-partition intersection graph, an edge (q_i, q_j) indicates that the paths q_i and q_j share at least one common vertex, that is, the paths q_i and q_j can be connected, and there is at least one intersection between them.

- Look for candidate paths. For each query path q ∈ Q, the edit distance dist (q, p) between paths is used to query the filtered matching set of path and candidate path.
- Splice candidate paths. The graph exploration algorithm is used to reconstruct the candidate paths to obtain the complete result matching. By message passing in the k-partition intersection graph, a group of approximate subgraphs contained in G is obtained. Then, the actual matching answers are sorted according to the path Edit distance.

(3) Graph matching processing

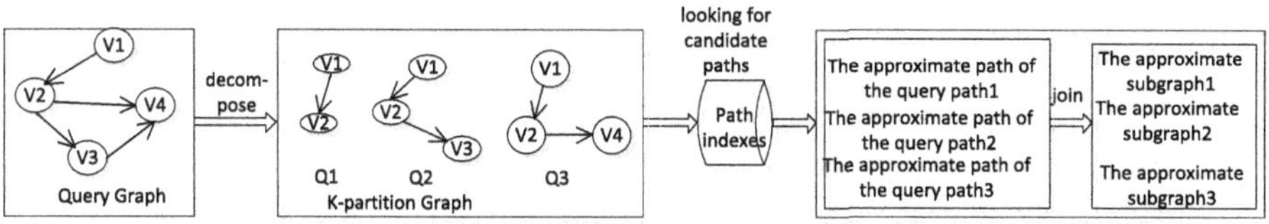

Fig. 2. Query processing phase diagram

By selecting the most relevant path and connecting it with the path with the lowest distance of each set, a complete query match is generated. The join condition is the number of join predicates between paths p and p′ is equal to the number of predicates between paths q and q′, wherein q and q′ are paths containing p and p′ respectively.

Through the above description, we can get the subgraph matching algorithm based on path adaptation

Input:Data graph G, k-partitionIntersection graph, the number of required answers K

Output:Top-k approximate answer set of query graph Q

The initial value of approximateanswersset is an empty set;

When | approximateanswersset | is always less than K and the candidate set

When the value is not empty, the output of ans is an empty set;

Assign max cardinality to q in k-partition graph;

Take Candidate Set.get(q) Assign to cn;

Take cn.dequeue Top() assigned to p;

Assign the set q to v;

The set q is added to ans, and the result is assigned to ans;

p, ans, candidate set, k-partition intersection graph, q, v Breadth first search;

Output approximate AnswersSet.put(ans);

Return to approximate answersset;

The breadth of p, ans, can didaser, k-partition interval graph (q, v) is excellent

The operation of the first search is as follows;

When (q, q') ∈ k-partiteinter section graph,

If q' ∈V so

cn =Candidate Set.get(q);

p = cn.dequeue Top();

If | L (p) ∩ L (p') | = | L (q) ∩ L (q') | then

ans = ans∪{p'};

$\pi[q'] = q$;

(p', ans, candidate set, k-partition intersection graph, q',5) Breadth first search;

V = V∪{q'};

In the matching process, starting from the matching of a path, the matching of connection paths is gradually increased. Once the candidate set is obtained, the graph search algorithm is executed by connecting the closest paths in the candidate set. First, the result set is initialized as an empty set. If no result is added in the connection process, the empty set is output. If K answers cannot be generated and the candidate set is not empty, the Top-k answers can be obtained by choosing and merging the paths with growing edit distance of each candidate set. Then the answer set is initialized, and the vertex q of k-partition intersection graph with the most overlapped vertices (connection predicates) of the existing path is selected. The complete answer is obtained by breadth first search traversal, as shown in the BFS visit function. Finally, the complete answer is included in the approximate answer set. By using this strategy, if K approximate answers of query graph Q cannot be found, the process stops.

3 Experimental Results and Analysis

The experimental configuration is windows 10 64 bit system, intel core (TM) i7-10710u CPU and 16 GB memory. The data set is a real subset from IMDB. The RDF data is used to construct a data graph, in which each triplet corresponds to an edge connecting two vertices, and each vertex is added a vertex label. By randomly selecting subgraphs from the data graph, some query collaboration graphs are artificially generated, and each query is associated with its requirements. Four query graph modes are shown in Fig. 3 which are chain query mode, star query mode, tree query mode and composite query mode. Figure 3 (a) is a chain query pattern with two paths, and Fig. 3 (b) is star query pattern with high selectivity. Figure 3 (c) is a tree query which can be decomposed into six paths from root vertex to leaf. Figure 3 (d) is a composite query that forms the query path from root to the target [23].

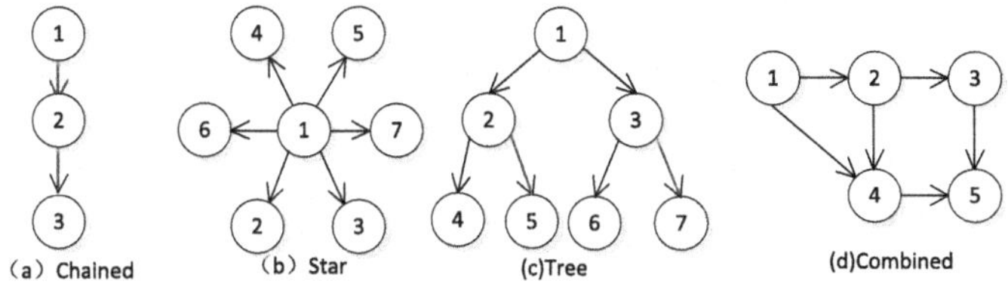

Fig. 3. Data set model diagram

Table 1. Index build comparison

#Triple (k)	1	5	10	30	60	500
Index time (MS)	289	536	782	932	1563	14689
Number of index paths	48761	84367	97653	124953	147265	2143674

Experimental tests are carried out for different RDF subsets to obtain the path based index construction time and the number of index paths in the whole data preprocessing stage, and we can see it in Table 1. As shown in Table 1 that the index building time and path number will change with the change of RDF data graph size, and the increase of index time is less than that of graph size. For example, the system constructs 147265 index paths with 1563 MS data graph created from three times the number of 60K. Although the 60K graph is six times larger than the 10K graph, the average index time increases by two times.

In order to prove the effectiveness of the algorithm. For each query: 1) precision (P) is the ratio of the returned related solutions to all solutions found by the system; 2) recall (R) is the ratio of the returned related solutions (in RS units) to all solutions; 3) F-measure (F-M) combines the results of precision and recall, which reflects the actual effect of the algorithm, that is to say $F - M = (2 \times P \times R)/(R + P)$.

By comparing the effectiveness of RDF graph path adaptation algorithm with sPath algorithm and sparer algorithm on the data set, and comparing the R value, P value and

F-M value of the three algorithms, the results can be seen in Table 2, and the F-M value histogram of the three algorithms is shown in Fig. 4.

Table 2. The path adaptation algorithm is compared with other algorithms

Data set	Path adaptation algorithm			SPATH			SPARRER		
	R	P	F-M	R	P	F-M	R	P	F-M
Chained	0.83	0.76	0.78	0.58	0.84	0.64	0.66	0.78	0.72
Star	0.79	0.70	0.76	0.40	0.81	0.56	0.61	0.64	0.62
Tree	0.68	0.72	0.74	0.58	0.72	0.64	0.58	0.68	0.60
Combined	0.47	0.58	0.58	0.38	0.68	0.50	0.44	0.58	0.50

According to the test data in Table 2 and Fig. 4, the algorithm in this paper is superior to the other two algorithms in terms of precision r value, recall p value and F-measure value, and can make better use of the F-measure value of structural information. At the same time, with the increase of path length, the search space for candidate paths will increase, which will lead to more intermediate matches.

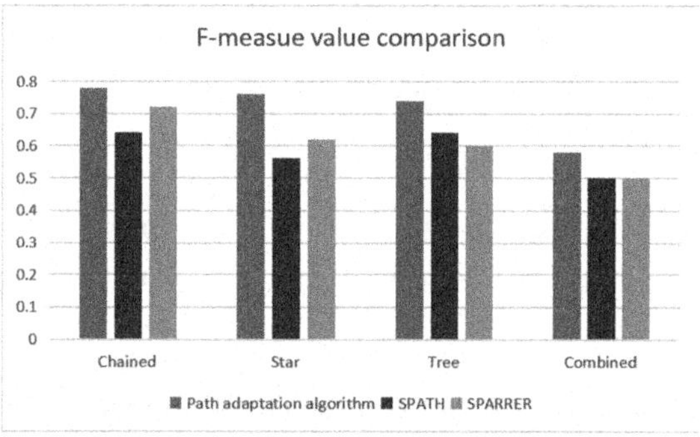

Fig. 4. Query performance on the dataset

4 Conclusion

A noval subgraph matching algorithm is proposed to improve the efficiency of subgraph querying on large-scale graph. This algorithm divides the query into multiple possible overlapping paths, finds the matching items of a single path, and selects the possible matching items with good selectivity according to the specific context conditions Subsets as candidates. The candidate paths are connected together to recover the query and finally complete the graph query processing. The experimental results compared with two algorithms on open datasets show that this method is better than others in path index construction and effectiveness.

References

1. Zhu, B., Li, G.Y., Zhao, L.: Efficient subgraph matching method based on Structure segmentation of RDF graph. J. Comput. Appl. **38**(7), 1898–1904, 1909 (2018)
2. Guan, H.Y., Zhu, B., Li, G.Y., Cai, Y.J.: Efficient subgraph matching method based on resource description frame-work graph segmentation and vertex selectivity. J. Comput. Appl. **39**(2), 360–369 (2019)
3. Zhou, Y.F., Zhang, X., Song, S.Y., et al.: Fast outlier detection algorithm based on local density. J. Comput. Appl. **37**(10), 2932–2937 (2017)
4. Ma, Z., Capretz, M.A., Yan, L.: Storing massive resource description framework (RDF) data; a survey. Knowl. Eng. Rev. **31**(4), 391–413 (2016)
5. Ullmann, J.R.: An algorithm for subgraph isomorphism. J. ACM **23**(1), 31–42 (1976)
6. Cordella, L.P., Foggia, P.: A(sub) graph isomorphism algorithm for matching large graphs. IEEE Trans. Pattern Anal. Mach. Intell. **26**(10), 1367–1372 (2004)
7. He, H., Singha, K.: Graphs-at-time: query language and access methods for graph databases. In: SIGMOD 2008: Proceedings of the 2008 ACM SIGMOD International Conference on Management of Data, pp. 405–418. ACM, New York (2008)
8. Zhang, S., Li, S., Yang J.: GADDI: distance index based subgraph matching in biological networks. In: Proceedings of the 12th International Conference on Extending Database Technology: Advances in Database Technology, pp. 192–203. ACM, New York (2009)
9. Zhang, S., Li, J.Z., Gao, H., et al.: A multi to-one subgraph isomorphism detection method. J. Softw. **21**(3), 401–414 (2010)
10. Han, W.S., Lee, J., Lee, J.H.: TurboISO: towards ultrafast and roubst subgraph isomorphism search in large graph database. In: ICMD 2013: Proceedings of the 2013 ACM SIGMOD International Conference on Management of Data, pp. 337–348. ACM, New York (2013)
11. Zou, L., Özsu, M.T.: Graph-based RDF data management. Data Sci. Eng. **2**, 56–70 (2017)
12. Zimmermann, N., Lopes, A., Polleres, U.: Straccia, a general framework for representing, reasoning and querying with annotated semanticweb data. J. Web Semant. **11**(3), 72–95 (2011)
13. Zhao, P., Han, J.: On graph query optimization in large networks. Proc. VLDB Endow. **3**(3), 340–351 (2010)
14. Zhang, D., Song, T., He, J., Shi, X., Dong, Y.: A similarity-oriented RDFgraph matching algorithm for ranking linked data. In: Proceedings of the 2012 E 12th International Conference on Computer and Information Technology, pp. 427–434 (2012)
15. Yan, L., Ma, R., Li, D., Cheng, J.: RDF approximate queries based on sesemantic similarity. Computing **99**(5), 481–491 (2017)
16. Yang, S., Wu, Y., Sun, H., Yan, X.: Schemaless and structureless graph querying. Proc. VLDB Endow. **7**(7), 565–576 (2014)
17. Shen, B., Zhao, M., Zhong, W., He, J.: An improved method for completely uncertain biological network alignment. BioMed Res. Int. **2015**, 1–11 (2015)
18. Shao, Y., Cui, B., Chen, L., Ma, L., Yao, J., Xu, N.: Parallel subgraph listing in a large-scale graph. In: ACM SIGMOD International Conference on Management of Data, pp. 625–636. ACM (2014)
19. Pivert, O., Slama, O., Thion, V.: An extension of SPARQL with fuzzy navigational capabilities for querying fuzzy RDF data. In: IEEE International Conference on Fuzzy Systems, pp. 2409–2416. IEEE (2016)
20. Moustafa, W.E., Kimmig, A., Deshpande, A., Getoor, L.: Subgraph pattern matching over uncertain graphs with identity linkage uncertainty. In: EEE, International Conference on Data Engineering, pp. 904–915. IEEE (2014)

21. Xu, W., Song, W.A., Fu, L.Z, Wei, L.V.: Distributed subgraph matching algorithm for large scale graph data. Comput. Sci. **04**(46) (2019)
22. Li, L., Dong, Y., Shi, W., Pan, J.: SQM: subgraph matching algorithm for single large-scale graph under Spark. J. Comput. Appl. **39**(1), 46–50 (2019)
23. Li, G., Yan, L., Ma, Z.: An approach for approximate subgraph matching in fuzzy RDF graph. J. Fuzzy Sets Syst. **376**, 106–126 (2019)

Photovoltaic Panel Intelligent Management and Identification Detection System Based on YOLOv5

Xueming Qiao[1], Dan Guo[1], Yuwen Li[1], Qi Xu[1], Baoning Gong[1], Yansheng Fu[2], Rongning Qu[3], Jingyuan Tan[2], Hongwei Zhao[4], and Dongjie Zhu[2](✉)

[1] State Grid Weihai Power Supply Company, No. 23, Kunming Road, Weihai, China
[2] School of Computer Science and Technology, Harbin Institute of Technology, Weihai 204209, China
zhudongjie@hit.edu.cn
[3] Department of Mathematics, Harbin Institute of Technology, Weihai 264209, China
[4] Shandong Baimeng Information Technology Co., Ltd., Weihai, China

Abstract. Photovoltaic power generation has significant energy, environmental protection and economic benefits. With the global attention to green energy, the development of photovoltaic power generation has become an inevitable trend. Photovoltaic panel assembly is a power generation device that generates direct current when exposed to sunlight, and is an important link in the photovoltaic power generation process. The geographic location of the photovoltaic panel, the user information to which the photovoltaic panel belongs, and the person in charge of the photovoltaic panel equipment are very important in the use of the photovoltaic panel, and need to be managed intelligently and efficiently. During the use of photovoltaic panels, photovoltaic panels need to undergo regular inspections to avoid affecting photovoltaic power generation output or causing safety accidents due to abnormal number and status of photovoltaic panel components. This paper builds a photovoltaic panel equipment intelligent management system to record photovoltaic equipment information in the power system. The system uses the YOLOv5 target detection model to realize image-based photovoltaic panel quantity identification and abnormality detection. The system compares with the equipment recorded information to give early warning of abnormal quantity and abnormal status. The advantage of the system proposed in this paper lies in the realization of efficient and intelligent management of photovoltaic panel information, high-precision identification of the number of photovoltaic panels, high-coverage detection of abnormal status, and real-time early warning of abnormal information.

Keywords: Photovoltaic panels · Object recognition · YOLOv5

1 Introduction

1.1 A Subsection Sample

Photovoltaic power generation is a new energy power supply method that meets the needs of policy and market demand. Countries around the world continue to deepen the

Y. Xu et al. (Eds.): ML4CS 2022, LNCS 13657, pp. 595–606, 2023.
https://doi.org/10.1007/978-3-031-20102-8_46

innovation of the entire photovoltaic power generation industry chain, and realize cost reduction through research and development covering all aspects of advanced materials, manufacturing and system applications. The focus of the photovoltaic power generation industry. In recent years, photovoltaic power generation has developed rapidly. In the first half of 2022, the newly installed photovoltaic power generation capacity in China has increased by 119% year-on-year. Among them, the cumulative installed capacity of distributed photovoltaic power generation has reached 130 million kilowatts, accounting for more than 1/3. However, there are some It is illegal for users to privately increase photovoltaic capacity for the purpose of defrauding the national power generation subsidy. From the user's point of view, this kind of behavior will cause the voltage in the home to exceed the maximum voltage of residential electricity, burn out electrical appliances, and even cause problems such as fire. If the user increases the capacity privately, it will bring security risks to the power grid transformers in the region and affect the quality of the power grid in the entire region. If the photovoltaic panels are damaged or foreign objects, the photovoltaic panels actually participating in power generation will decrease, resulting in the power generation of the photovoltaic panels. The actual power supply voltage drops, which in turn affects the user's normal demand for power supply. Therefore, it is necessary to regularly check the number and status of photovoltaic panels to avoid the reduction of photovoltaic power generation efficiency due to abnormal state of photovoltaic panel components or private expansion of photovoltaic panels by users, or even safety accidents such as electrical burnout and fire. The traditional photovoltaic panel detection method is to manually detect and count the photovoltaic panels one by one, and find abnormal photovoltaic panels through recording and comparison.

The manual inspection method of photovoltaic panels will consume a lot of labor costs, and because the inspection sites of photovoltaic panels are scattered, the photovoltaic power generation panels occupy a large area, and some photovoltaic power generation panels are located on the roof, glass curtain wall and high mountain areas, resulting in manual inspection methods not only the efficiency is low, and some photovoltaic panels cannot be manually inspected due to location problems. The collection and statistics of a large amount of photovoltaic panel information is prone to statistical errors due to fatigue of staff, and the statistical information is not easy to store and review and check troubles. Using traditional methods to survey will consume a lot of labor costs. Therefore, the photovoltaic power generation industry urgently needs a kind of a system and method for intelligent management, identification, and detection of photovoltaic panels.

This paper proposes a photovoltaic panel intelligent management and identification detection system based on YOLO series model [1–9]. The person in charge of the equipment can accurately know the number of photovoltaic panels in the area through the human-computer interaction interface provided by the system, and the system will detect the photovoltaic panel equipment in real-time and collect and record it. Information such as the specific location of the photovoltaic panel, when the photovoltaic panel is abnormal, the system will feedback the abnormal photovoltaic panel to the person in charge of the equipment in the form of an alarm, thereby realizing the intelligent management of the photovoltaic panel equipment. This system mainly uses YOLOv5 to identify photovoltaic panels, count the number of photovoltaic panels, and identify whether each photovoltaic panel has local occlusions that are difficult to find such as welding tape, silver paste and silver wire on the surface of the photovoltaic panel. It can detect whether there is serious ash accumulation on the board, and further feedback the fault situation of the photovoltaic panel to the man-machine interface, so as to realize the systematic management of the photovoltaic panel equipment.

2 Related Work

2.1 Object Detection

The artificial intelligence image recognition algorithm has been widely used in the power system, and the image recognition algorithm has been rapidly developed under the influence of the market. In 2014, the R-CNN algorithm proposed by Donahue et al. The integrated neural network extracts the features of the candidate regions, and then uses the SVM to classify the extracted features. This algorithm has achieved great performance improvements in detection speed and accuracy, but the R-CNN network has training time and processing speed. Disadvantages such as being slow and taking up a lot of disk space. Aiming at the computational redundancy problem of the R-CNN network due to the need to extract features for each candidate frame separately, He Kaiming et al. proposed the use of the feature space pyramid network SPP-Net to extract features from the entire image, and use multiple pipelines to extract features. Train and add a spatial pyramid pooling layer between the last convolutional layer and the fully connected layer to output a fixed-size feature vector to improve the detection accuracy of the network. Although the recognition accuracy has been improved, there are still high computational costs and training costs. Long time and large storage space. Then in 2015, Shaoqing Ren et al. proposed the Faster-RCNN [10] algorithm, which has faster recognition speed and less memory consumption than the R-CNN network. First, the RPN algorithm is used to generate anchor frames in the image, and the frame regression is used to identify the anchors. The frame is corrected to obtain a more accurate recommendation frame, and then the suggested window is input into the convolutional neural network for feature extraction, the suggested window is mapped to the last layer of convolution, and each suggested window is generated with a fixed size through the pooling layer. Finally, the classification probability and bounding box regression are jointly trained using softmax loss and smooth L1 loss. The network achieves an improvement in recognition accuracy by using RPN, but the use of a two-stage network results in slower network detection. In 2017, he et al. proposed the Mask R-CNN algorithm for the problem that the feature map does not match the original image area due to the error introduced by the use of RoI pooling for two integer quantization operations in the Faster R-CNN network. The defect of RoIAlign has been improved, and the bilinear interpolation method has greatly improved the accuracy of pixel positioning. Compared with the FasterR-CNN network, the running speed and detection accuracy have been improved, but the computational overhead has been increased, the detection speed of the algorithm does not meet the real-time requirements.

The SSD backbone network uses traditional convolutional structures such as VGG and ResNet, and then uses six feature maps of different scales to predict target objects of different sizes. The bottom layer detects small targets, and the high layer is responsible for detecting large targets. Multiple anchor boxes with different aspect ratios increase the number of trainable samples to improve the training effect of the network, but the SSD network has a general detection effect on small samples; the aspect ratio of the anchor box needs to be manually set, which is not universal. Strong; the underlying feature extraction is insufficient, etc.

2.2 YOLO Model

The YOLO series target detection network realizes real-time detection of target objects. Redmon et al. proposed the first-generation YOLO target detection network, which divides the input image into grids of equal size n*m, then extracts the corresponding candidate frame for each grid as a training sample, and finally judges each grid by judging each category of the network thus completes the detection of the target. However, YOLOv1 lacks the RPN mechanism, and the accuracy of the target detection results is low. In 2017, Redmon et al. replaced the backbone network of YOLO with Darknet19, and adopted the anchor box mechanism. Compared with the first generation, the recognition accuracy has been improved to a certain extent, but the accuracy is still It does not meet people's needs for real-time performance, so in 2018, the YOLOv3 network was proposed. The YOLOv3 network further replaced the backbone network with a deeper Darkent53 network, and adopted the feature pyramid network (Feature Pyramid Networks, FPN). The layer network and the high-level network are fused to detect target objects of different sizes through different detection frames. In order to further improve the performance of the network, in 2020, YOLOv4 adopts the CSPDarknet53 network to convert the changes of features into feature maps, further improving the feature recognition vision of the network, and the recognition accuracy of the network is further improved, but the recognition speed of the network needs to be promoted. In June 2020, YOLOv5 came out, which realized the real-time detection of video and webcam data, which is undoubtedly effective for the real-time detection of photovoltaic panels. Therefore, this paper adopts the YOLOv5 target detection network.

3 Design

3.1 Demand Module Description

The user groups of the photovoltaic panel intelligent management and identification detection system based on YOLOv5 are equipment testing employees and equipment management managers. Such users need to interact with the system on the mobile terminal and the PC terminal. The data processing in the system involves the type of photovoltaic panels, The geographic location of the photovoltaic panel and the user information to which the photovoltaic panel belongs. The functional module diagram of the system is shown in Fig. 1, and the specific functional requirements are described as follows:

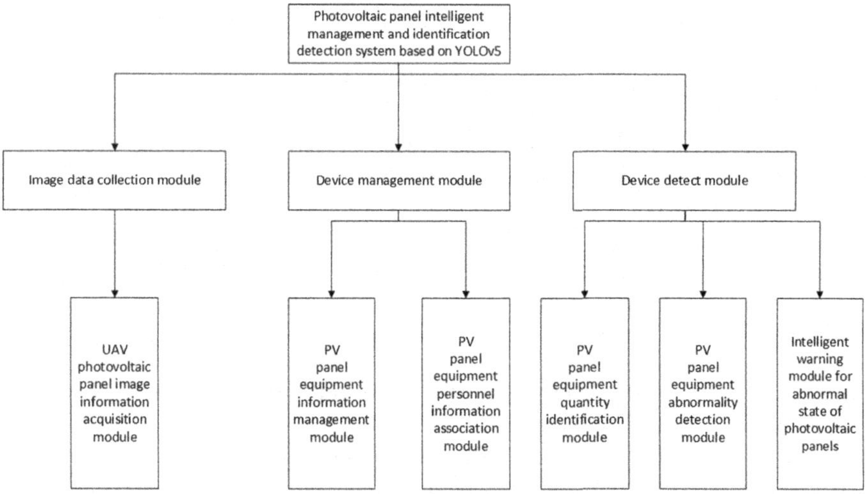

Fig. 1. The functional structure of the system.

UAV Photovoltaic Panel Image Information Acquisition Module. When the staff are working in the traditional photovoltaic panel image collection process, due to the need to carry a large number of testing equipment, safety accidents may occur during on-site operations. The layout of photovoltaic panels is generally high, and it is difficult for employees to collect photovoltaic panel pictures; and the geographical distribution of photovoltaic panels in a certain geographical area is relatively scattered, and employees will waste more time and labor costs in collection. This system integrates unmanned aerial vehicle technology, which can realize the efficient collection of photovoltaic panel images for the intelligent management and identification of subsequent photovoltaic panel equipment.

PV Panel Equipment Information Management Module. The photovoltaic panel equipment information management module stores the photovoltaic panel equipment in the power system, including the geographical location of the photovoltaic panel, the product model of the photovoltaic panel, the equipment status of the photovoltaic panel, and the staff to which the photovoltaic panel belongs. Using the intelligent system can clearly display the detailed information of photovoltaic panel equipment, which is convenient for the management of photovoltaic panel equipment.

PV Panel Equipment Personnel Information Association Module. The photovoltaic panel equipment personnel management module covers the account information of photovoltaic panel related construction employees and managers, and can add, delete, query and modify personnel information. The system assigns permissions to users based on the user's identity, and then realizes the operation of photovoltaic panels.

PV Panel Equipment Quantity Identification Module. The photovoltaic panel quantity identification module uses the image intelligent identification algorithm to identify the number and type of photovoltaic panels in the image based on the image content collected by the drone. By comparing the number and type of photovoltaic panels of the user with the identification results in the system database, it is judged whether there is any abnormality in the number and type of photovoltaic panels.

PV Panel Equipment Abnormality Detection Module. Based on the image content collected by the drone, the photovoltaic panel quantity identification module uses an image intelligent detection algorithm to identify whether the photovoltaic panels in the image are abnormal and the type of abnormality. By comparing the abnormal photovoltaic panel features in the system knowledge base with the identified result features, it is judged whether there is an abnormality in the photovoltaic panel and the type of the abnormality.

Intelligent Warning Module for Abnormal State of Photovoltaic Panels. According to the photovoltaic panel equipment identification and abnormal detection results of the image, the number and status of the equipment in the photovoltaic panel are given an early warning, and the abnormal information is submitted to the corresponding staff for processing.

3.2 System Structure

In the traditional Web development model, the page is directly generated on the server side, and the browser is only responsible for rendering the page, and partial changes of the page require the request and rendering of the entire page. There are many problems with this approach, such as inflexibility, single-page style, high technical route barriers, and so on.

The photovoltaic panel intelligent management and identification detection system based on YOLOv5 is developed using the C/S architecture [11] with the front and back ends separated. The back end uses the technical framework of Spring Boot [12] and SSM. The implementation of the data access interface uses the Hibernate framework. The logic layer (Service), the data persistence layer (Dao), and the model layer (Model) are reasonably separated. The front-end page uses Web and small programs for different user groups. Small programs are developed for ordinary users such as sales staff in sales offices. They are deployed through WeChat development tools; used for manager users such as sales managers Vue has developed a web background management system and deployed it on the cloud platform, which can be accessed directly through a browser. The architecture of the system is shown in Fig. 2, which can be divided into three layers.

The UI layer, the front end of the system, is located at the level of direct interaction with users. The applet end is developed and implemented using the WeChat applet development kit, and the Web background system uses the Vue framework for development and implementation. Page rendering, jumping, and User interaction processing, network requests, and data analysis are all controlled by the front-end.

The business layer, that is, the back end of the system. Most of the logic of the system is processed in the back end. The re-visit judgment of customers and the storage of face image information are realized through the Baidu face recognition API that is packaged twice, and the front end is transmitted the customer data is processed and associated, and at the same time it interacts with the data layer, and also queries the database through timed tasks to achieve the function of alarm.

The data access layer uses the ORM technology of the Hibernate framework to generate the entity classes corresponding to the database tables, and uses the MYSQL database to store data.

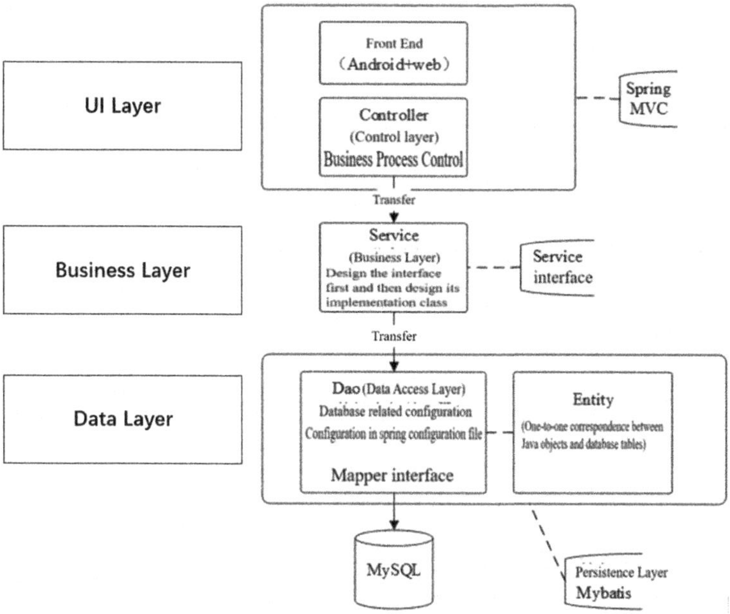

Fig. 2. The architecture of the system

4 Testing and Verification

4.1 Implementation Personnel Information Association Module

The personnel management interface is not the focus of the system. The main function of personnel management of the system is to manage the accounts of inspectors, that is, to manage app users. Managers are senior administrators of the system. After successfully entering the system, they can view the detailed information of the inspectors, modify or delete part of the information. In order to be more practical, we also added the function of batch import and export. This can add a large number of users in a short time, and it can also export the list in batches, which is convenient for checking attendance and so on. The personnel management interface is shown in Fig. 3.

Fig. 3. Personnel management interface diagram.

The staff adding interface is shown in Fig. 4.

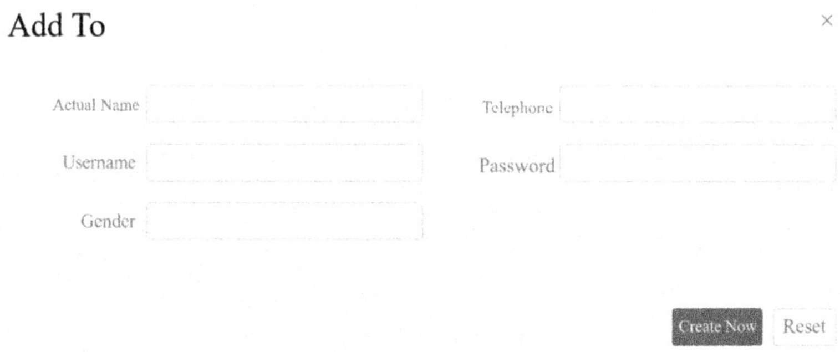

Fig. 4. Staff adding interface diagram.

The personnel deletion interface is shown in Fig. 5.

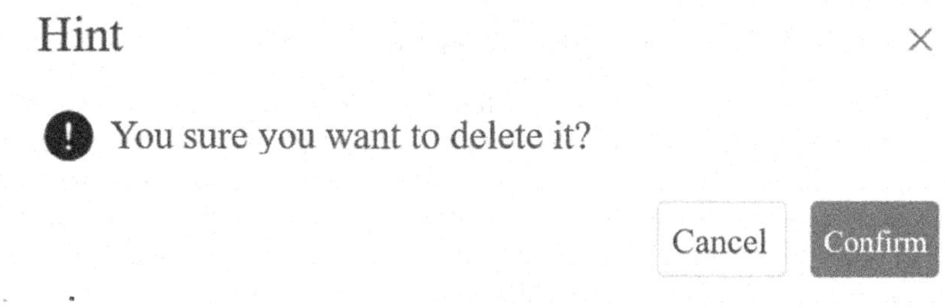

Fig. 5. Personnel deletion interface diagram

4.2 Implementation of Visiting Information Association Module

After obtaining images through drone inspection, employees log in to the system using mobile devices or PCs and enter the photovoltaic panel image recognition page. On the photovoltaic panel device identification page, you can choose to upload an image. The selected photovoltaic panel image is uploaded to the server deployed by the system via the mobile smart terminal or PC. The photovoltaic panel device identification page is shown in Fig. 6.

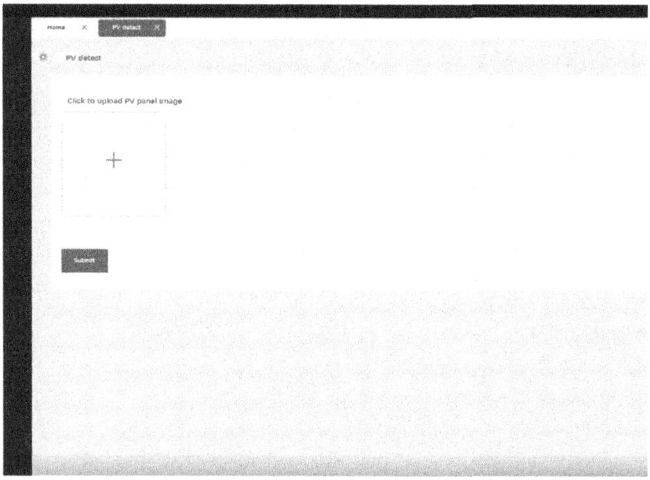

Fig. 6. The photovoltaic panel device identification page

The selected photovoltaic panel image will be uploaded to the data server deployed by the system, and the uploaded image will be displayed on the front end for the operator to compare, as shown in Fig. 7.

The image intelligent recognition model based on YOLOv5 training is called for the successfully uploaded photovoltaic panel image. The model can finally return the number of photovoltaic panels contained in the image by detecting and classifying the photovoltaic panels, as shown in Fig. 8.

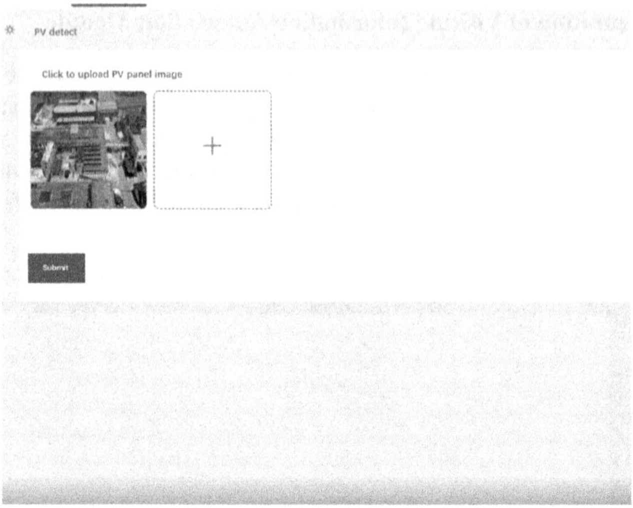

Fig. 7. Image upload success page

Fig. 8. Identification result of the number of photovoltaic panels

The system also supports batch processing of multiple images, as shown in Fig. 9.

This system supports the display of photovoltaic panel image recognition results using the method of visual comparison, as shown in Fig. 10. The display page includes the original image of the photovoltaic panel before image recognition and the image generated after the YOLOv5 model detection. In the generated image, the model will frame the identified photovoltaic panels, and make special annotations for abnormal photovoltaic panels. Relevant staff can efficiently detect the number and status of photovoltaic panels through the results of system image recognition, and deal with abnormal photovoltaic panels in time to avoid economic losses or safety accidents.

Fig. 9. Batch process image results

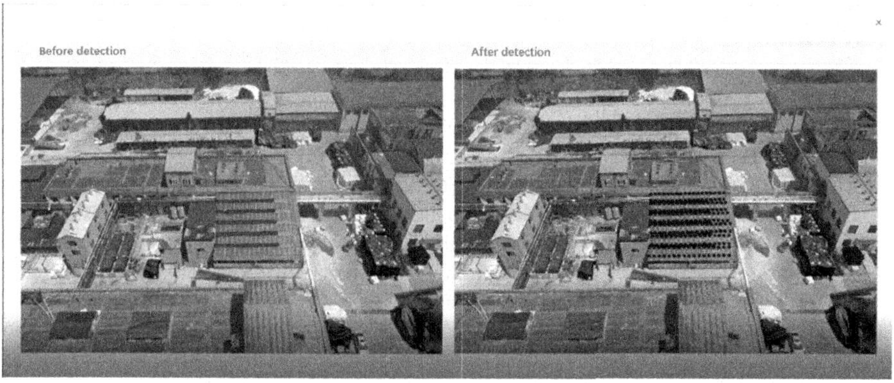

Fig. 10. Photovoltaic panel image recognition results comparison display

5 Conclusion

This paper introduces the design and implementation of a photovoltaic panel intelligent management and identification detection system based on YOLOv5. In the requirements analysis stage, the entire system is divided into modules, specific test cases are designed, and the system boundary is conceptually standardized. In this paper, the system is divided into photovoltaic panel equipment quantity identification module, photovoltaic panel equipment abnormality detection module, photovoltaic panel abnormality early warning module and photovoltaic panel information intelligent management module. The system realizes the use of YOLOv5 target detection network to count the number of photovoltaic panels, detects the state of photovoltaic panels through the features extracted by the model, determines whether there are obstructions on the surface of photovoltaic panels, and warns of abnormal conditions of photovoltaic panels. Not only that, the system realizes the informatization, intelligence and efficient management of photovoltaic panels by collecting information such as the geographical location of photovoltaic panels, user information to which photovoltaic panels belong, and the person in charge of photovoltaic panels.

Acknowledgement. The authors would like to thank the associate editor and the reviewers for their time and effort provided to review the manuscript.

Funding Statement. This work is supported by State Grid Shandong Electric Power Company Science and Technology Project Funding under Grant no. 62061320C007, SGS-DWH00YXJS2000127, the Fundamental Research Funds for the Central Universities (Grant No. HIT. NSRIF. 201714), Weihai Science and Technology Development Program (2016DX GJMS15), Weihai Scientific Research and Innovation Fund (2020) and Key Research and Development Program in Shandong Provincial (2017GGX90103).

Conflicts of Interest. The authors declare that they have no conflicts of interest to report regarding the present study.

References

1. Huang, R., Pedoeem, J., Chen, C.: YOLO-LITE: a real-time object detection algorithm optimized for non-GPU computers. In: 2018 IEEE International Conference on Big Data (Big Data), pp. 2503–2510. IEEE (2018)
2. Tian, Y., Yang, G., Wang, Z., et al.: Apple detection during different growth stages in orchards using the improved YOLO-V3 model. Comput. Electron. Agric. **157**, 417–426 (2019)
3. Laroca, R., Severo, E., Zanlorensi, L.A., et al.: A robust real-time automatic license plate recognition based on the YOLO detector. In: 2018 International Joint Conference on Neural Networks, pp. 1–10. IEEE (2018)
4. Redmon, J., Divvala, S., Girshick, R., et al.: You only look once: unified, real-time object detection. In: Proceedings of the IEEE Conference on Computer Vision and Pattern Recognition, pp. 779–788 (2016)
5. Redmon, J., Farhadi, A.: YOLO9000: better, faster, stronger. In: Proceedings of the IEEE Conference on Computer Vision and Pattern Recognition, pp. 7263–7271 (2017)
6. Redmon, J., Farhadi, A.: YOLOv3: an incremental improvement. arXiv preprint arXiv:1804.02767 (2018)
7. Bochkovskiy, A., Wang, C.Y., Liao, H.Y.M.: YOLOv4: optimal speed and accuracy of object detection. arXiv preprint arXiv:2004.10934 (2020)
8. Shafiee, M.J., Chywl, B., Li, F., et al.: Fast YOLO: a fast you only look once system for real-time embedded object detection in video. arXiv preprint arXiv:1709.05943 (2017)
9. Fang, W., Wang, L., Ren, P.: Tinier-YOLO: a real-time object detection method for constrained environments. IEEE Access **8**, 1935–1944 (2019)
10. Ren, S., He, K., Girshick, R., et al: Faster R-CNN: towards real-time object detection with region proposal networks. In: Advances in Neural Information Processing Systems 28 (2015)
11. Jiang, L., Guan, H., Xiang, Y.: Design of sales management system based on C/S mode. Sci. Technol. Eng. **09**, 608–611 (2005)
12. Lin, W.: Design and implementation of data synchronization system based on SPRING MVC architecture. Jilin University (2015)

Image Encryption Algorithm Based on a New Five-Dimensional Lorenz System

Xiujun Zhang[1(✉)], Xiaohong Zha[1], and Ke Luo[2]

[1] Center of Network Information, Nanchang Institute of Technology, Nanchang 330099, China
65656819@qq.com

[2] Department of Library, Shaoyang University, Shaoyang 422001, Hunan, China

Abstract. For the question of key space of image encryption algorithm based on the low dimension chaotic system is small and the safety is not high. On the basis of four-dimensional hyperchaotic Lorenz system, by adding the dimension of differential equations and adding a nonlinear term, this paper establishes a new five-dimensional hyperchaotic Lorenz system. And a digital image encryption algorithm based on this hyperchaotic system is proposed. First, we prove that the system is a hyperchaotic system, through the Lyapunov exponents calculation and simulation result of the trajectory and Chaotic attractor phase diagram. Then, a digital image encryption algorithm based on this hyperchaotic system is implemented. By analyzing the security performance of the algorithm, we found the algorithm is extremely sensitive to key, with very good diffusivity, and it can resist all kinds of attacks effectively such as brute force attack, chosen-plaintext attack and known-plaintext attack.

Keywords: Chaotic · Chaotic cryptography · Hyperchaotic system · Image encryption · Lyapunov exponents

1 Introduction

The rapid development of the Internet has facilitated the use of the network by unscrupulous elements to obtain unauthorized information. The core technology to guarantee information security is cryptographic means. Still, digital images have their own characteristics, such as strong correlation of adjacent pixel values and a large amount of information, thus making the traditional encryption algorithms IDEA, RSA, etc., unable to meet the image encryption needs. The properties of chaotic systems correspond well to the relevant characteristics required by cryptography, such as deterministic pseudo-randomness, attack complexity, diffusion, obfuscation, and key sensitivity, so the development of chaos theory provides a new direction for digital image encryption. However, low-dimensional chaotic systems have only one positive Lyapunov exponent, which can provide a too small a key space to resist current brute force attacks. Hyperchaotic systems have two positive Lyapunov exponents, which have stronger chaos and can provide a larger key space at the same time. Therefore, the study of hyperchaotic systems has become a current research hotspot [1, 2]. In this paper, a new variable is introduced on

Y. Xu et al. (Eds.): ML4CS 2022, LNCS 13657, pp. 607–618, 2023.
https://doi.org/10.1007/978-3-031-20102-8_47

the basis of the four-dimensional Lorenz system, and two nonlinear terms are introduced to increase the chaotic nature of the system motion, and a new differential equation is added to form a five-dimensional set of differential equations to construct a new five-dimensional hyperchaotic system. And based on this system, a digital image encryption algorithm is designed to adapt to the requirements of modern cryptographic systems.

2 New Five-Dimensional Hyperchaotic Lorenz System

In this paper, based on the four-dimensional hyperchaotic Lorenz system in the literature [3], a new variable and two nonlinear terms are introduced, and a differential equation is added to make a five-dimensional set of differential equations, in an attempt to construct a new five-dimensional hyperchaotic Lorenz system. The specific system is as follows.

System 1:

$$\begin{cases} \frac{\partial x}{\partial t} = a(y - x) + w + u \\ \frac{\partial y}{\partial t} = cx - y - 2xz \\ \frac{\partial z}{\partial t} = 2x^2 - bz \\ \frac{\partial w}{\partial t} = yz - dw \\ \frac{\partial u}{\partial t} = xy + yz \end{cases} \tag{1}$$

The values of a, b, c are the same as those of β, σ, ρ in the classical three-dimensional Lorenz system [4]. In this paper, we use the method of calculating the Lyaponov exponent of the differential equation system [5], when $a = 10; b = 8/3; c = 28; d = 2$, we solve the differential equation system Eq. 1 and obtain the Lyaponov exponent as: $L1 = 1.8639; L2 = 0.043589; L3 = -0.73393; L4 = -4.6126; L5 = -12.1176$; from $L1, L2$ greater than zero, we can see that the system has generated hyperchaotic motion. Further, the Lyapunov Exponents plot of the system is derived by experimental simulation in Fig. 1, which shows that there are two positive Lyapunov exponents, which are consistent with the hyperchaotic system based characteristics. Also, the motion trajectory of the simulated system and the phase diagram of the chaotic attractor in each plane further confirm that the system is hyperchaotic. The trajectory of the system when $a = 10;\ b = 8/3;\ c = 28;\ d = 2$ is shown in Fig. 2. From Figs. 2(a), 2(b), 2(c), 2(d), and 2(e), it is clear that each sequence value is deterministic and extremely sensitive to the initial value; at the same time, there exist the characteristics of randomness, and ergodicity in a certain range. Each subplot Figs. 3(a), 3(b), 3(c), 3(d), 3(e), 3(f), 3(g), 3(h), 3(i), 3(j) in Fig. 3 shows the phase simulation of the chaotic attractor of the system in the $x - y,\ x - z,\ x - w,\ y - w,\ y - z,\ z - w,\ x - y - z,\ y - z - w,\ x - y - w$ and $x - y - u$ planes.

The chaotic attractor of the system is obvious because the sequence values are randomly moving and ergodic within a certain range of values.

3 Digital Image Encryption Algorithm is Based on the New Five-Dimensional Hyperchaotic Lorenz System

In this paper, we design a digital image encryption algorithm based on the new five-dimensional hyperchaotic Lorenz system constructed in the previous section, and analyze the security of the encryption algorithm.

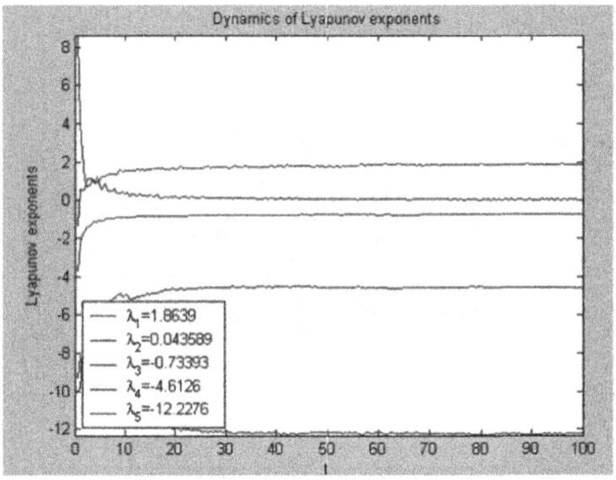

Fig. 1. Diagram of the Lyapunov Exponents corresponding to the system

The encryption algorithm is as follows:

Step1: Solve the new five-dimensional hyperchaotic Lorenz system to generate five sequences: *xi*, *yi*, *zi*, *wi*, *ui*.

Step2: Use m(j) = x(i), m(j + 1) = y(i), m(j + 2) = z(i), m(j + 3) = w(i), m(j + 4) = u(i), i = i + 1, j = j + 5 to take n (n = M * N) values after the sequence Q values to form M sequence. Q = 100000 in to this algorithm.

Step3: Expand the M sequence by a factor of K to obtain the H sequence. To ensure that the chaos of the chaotic sequence do not degenerate, K is generally taken to be greater than 100000.

Step4: $m = mod(H, 256)$. To improve the accuracy of H-sequence for encryption, reduce the computational error and prevent the large numbers from eating the small numbers, thus obtaining the chaotic sequence processed by the hyperchaotic system.

Step5: $e = m + x$. The original image value for the size.

Step6: $while(e > 255)$. e denotes the encrypted image value, this step is to ensure that the encrypted value of each pixel is between the valid values of $0 \sim 255$.

The combination of five initial values of $(x_0, y_0, z_0, w_0, u_0)$ is used as the key for this encryption algorithm.

4 Encryption Algorithm Security Analysis and Experimental Simulation

Security and effectiveness are the primary tasks to be considered in an encryption algorithm. In order to verify the effectiveness and security of the algorithm in this paper, the following experimental simulation and analysis are carried out using Matlab.

4.1 Histogram Analysis

A good cryptosystem should have good properties in terms of resistance to statistical attacks [6–8]. Figure 4(a) shows the original image statistical histogram and Fig. 4(b) shows the encrypted ciphertext image statistical histogram. Obviously, the ciphertext image statistical histogram has good statistical properties and uniform distribution, which

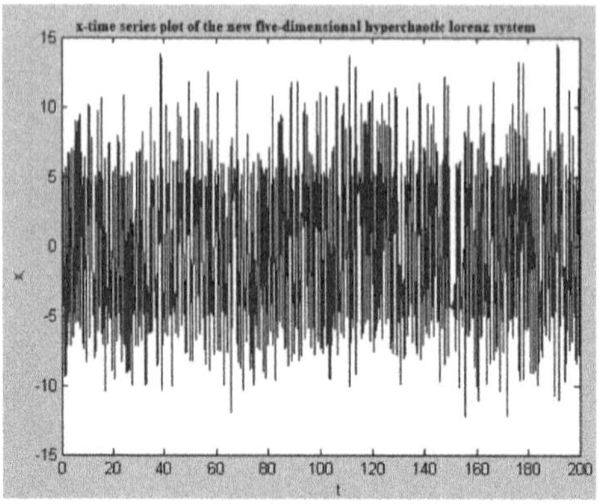

(a)

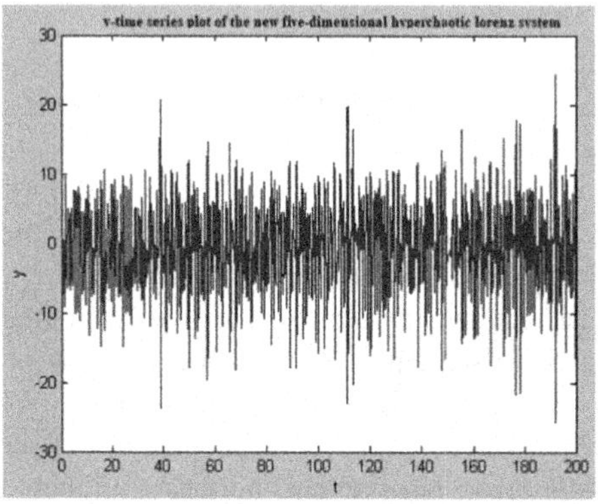

(b)

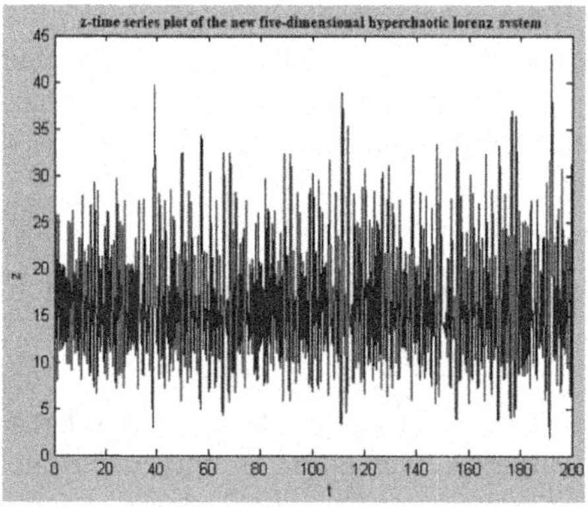

(c)

Fig. 2. (**a**) Sequential trajectory plot of x versus time t for the system (**b**) Sequential trajectory plot of y versus time t for system 1. (**c**) Sequential trajectory plot of z versus time t for system 1. (**d**) Sequential trajectory plot of w versus time t for system 1. (**e**) Sequential trajectory diagram of u versus time t for system 1.

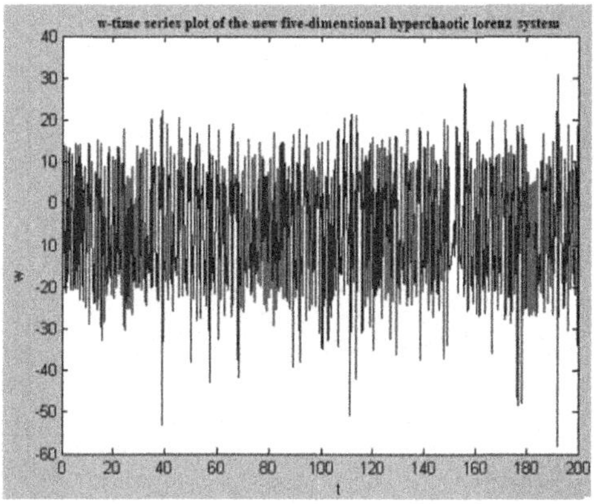

(d)

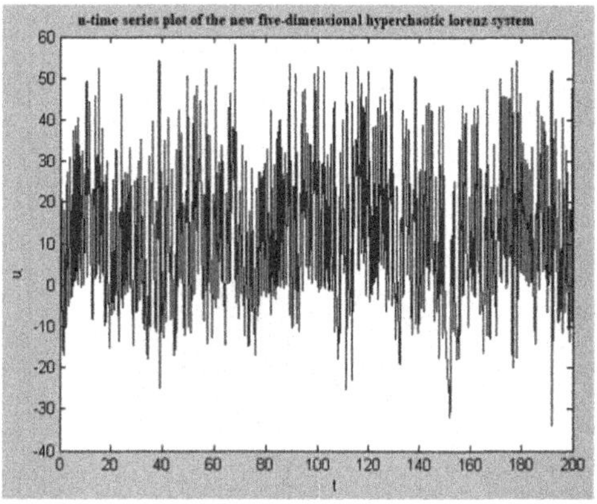

(e)

Fig. 2. *(continued)*

well perturbs the correlation of the original image. Therefore the algorithm can effectively resist the attacks on statistical aspects such as choosing tomorrow and known plaintexts.

4.2 Algorithm Key Sensitivity Testing and Analysis

In this paper, the five initial values x_0, y_0, z_0, w_0, u_0 are combined together to form the key of the algorithm. x_0, y_0, z_0, w_0, u_0 are real numbers and their optimal range of values is: $x_0 \in [-10, 10]$, $y_0 \in [-10, 10]$, $z_0 \in [5, 35]$. Set the initial key of the algorithm as follows:

$x_0 = 5.123456789123 42$; $y_0 = 6.12345678932164$; $z_0 = 10.98765432136987$; $w_0 = -10.74125896312345$; $u_0 = 20.12365478914723$. The cryptogram is generated after encryption by the algorithm steps, and then any of the initial values in the key x_0, y_0, z_0, w_0, u_0 is changed slightly and encrypted again to compare the number of different pixels corresponding to the two cryptograms. As seen in Table 1, even if one of the initial values of the key has 10^{-14} slightly changed, the resulting dense map has

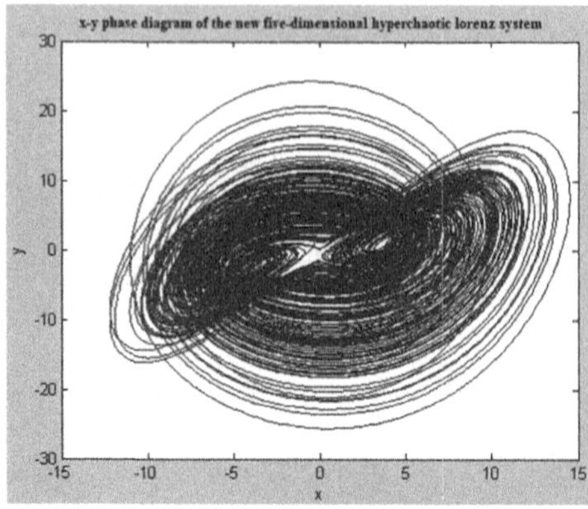

(a)

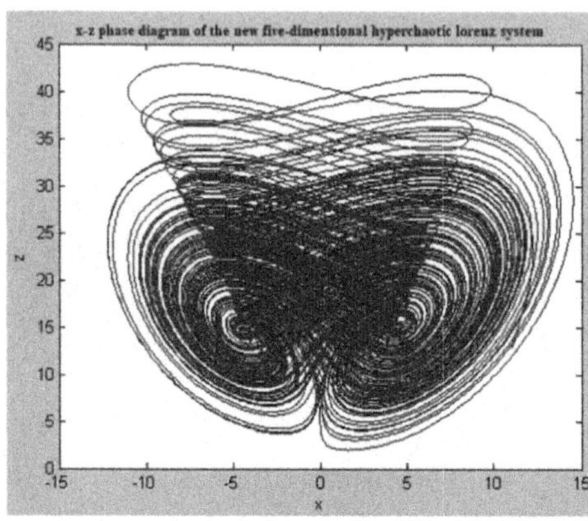

(b)

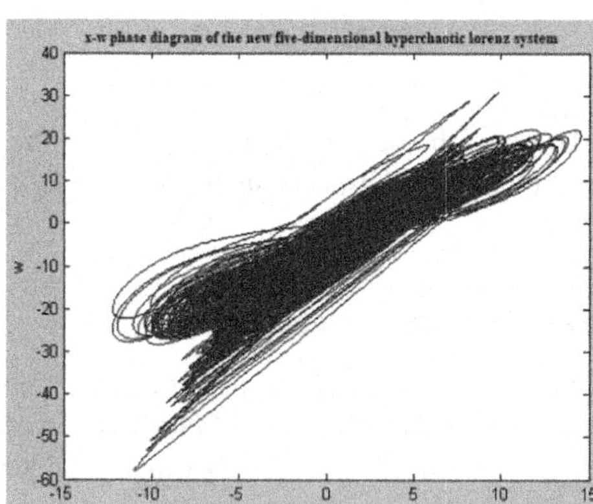

(c)

Fig. 3. (**a**) Projection of the chaotic attractor of system 1 in the x-y plane. (**b**) Projection of the chaotic attractor of system 1 in the x-z plane. (**c**) Projection of the chaotic attractor of system 1 in the x-w plane. (**d**) Projection of the chaotic attractor of system 1 in the y-z plane. (**e**) Projection of the chaotic attractor of system 1 in the z-w plane. (**f**) Projection of the chaotic attractor of system 1 in the y-w plane. (**g**) Projection of the chaotic attractor of system 1 in the x-y-z plane. (**h**) Projection of the chaotic attractor of system 1 in the y-z-w plane. (**i**) Projection of the chaotic attractor of system 1 in the x-y-w plane. (**j**) Projection of the chaotic attractor of system 1 in the x-y-u plane

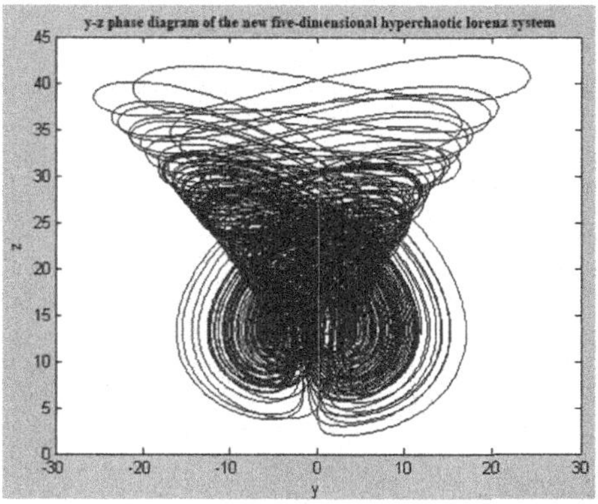

(d)

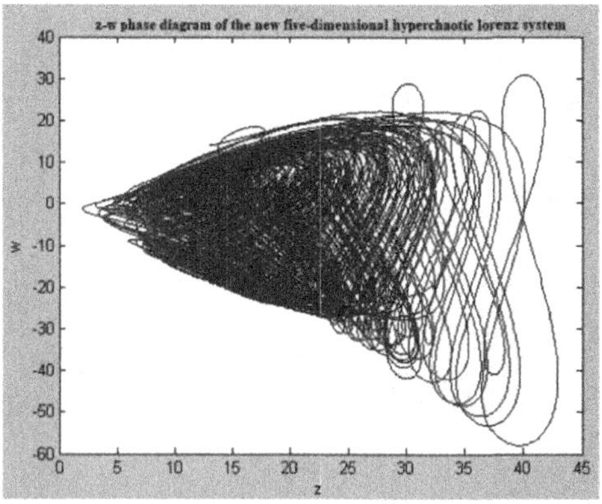

(e)

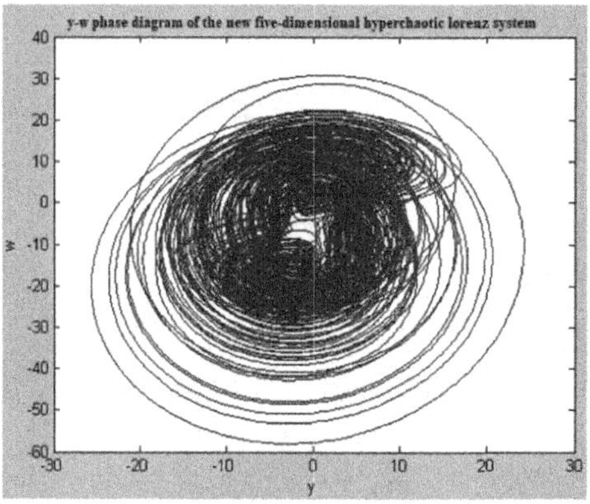

(f)

Fig. 3. (*continued*)

about 99.6% of different pixels. On the other hand, the encryption algorithm of Fig. 5 decrypts the encrypted *lena* image with an initial difference 10^{-14} from the key, and

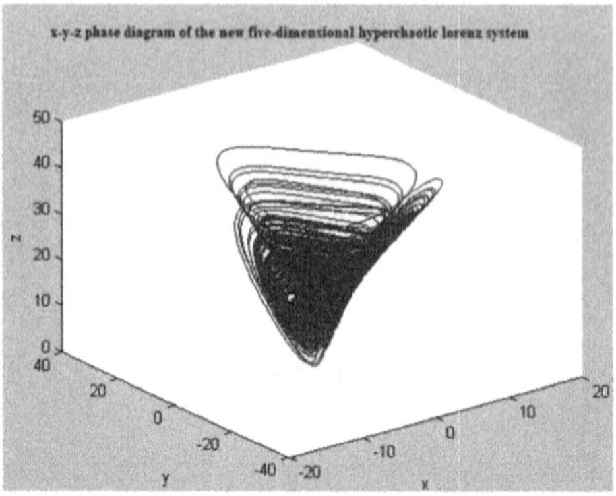

(g)

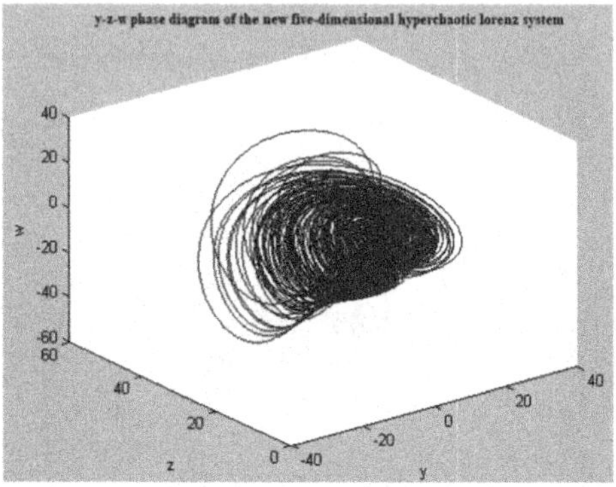

(h)

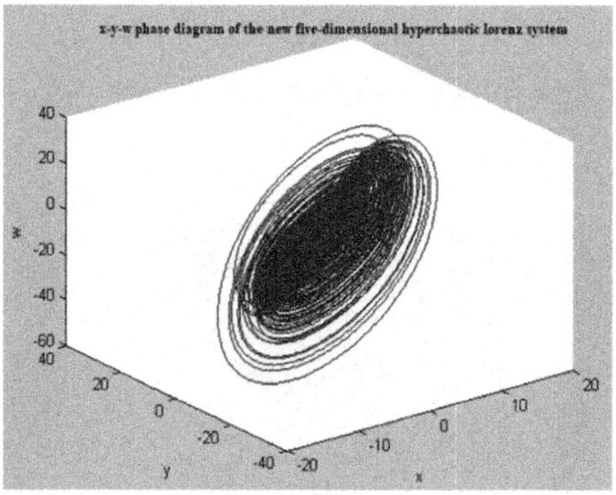

(i)

Fig. 3. (*continued*)

it turns out that it is completely unable to decrypt it correctly and does not reveal the original image information at all. Obviously, the encryption algorithm is very sensitive to the key.

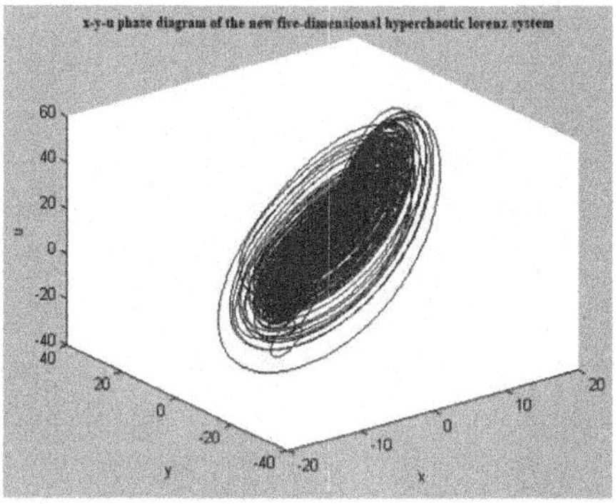

(j)

Fig. 3. *(continued)*

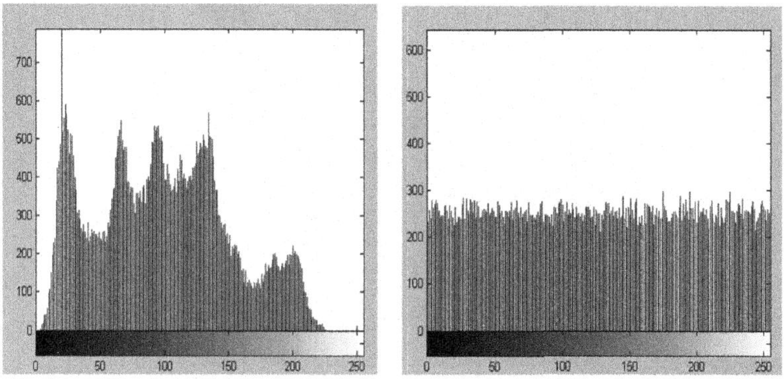

(a) (b)

Fig. 4. (**a**) Statistical histogram of the original image (**b**) Statistical histogram of the ciphertext image

4.3 Key Space Analysis

In this paper, the five initial values in the key are real numbers, which theoretically provide an infinite key space. It is assumed that the encryption system uses floating-point type with double precision and each initial value takes 15 valid digits. Then, the key space is $10^{15*5} = 10^{75} \approx 2100$. G. Alvarez and Shujun Li proposed that the key space κ should be larger than 2^{100} in order to be able to resist the brute force attack [9]. 2^{250} is much larger than 2^{100}, so the encryption algorithm designed in this paper has a large key space and can resist the current brute force attack.

4.4 Neighborhood Pixel Correlation Analysis

To measure the goodness of an encryption algorithm, we can also find the correlation between the neighboring pixels of the original image and the encrypted image respectively, and test whether the believed pixel correlation system number of the encrypted

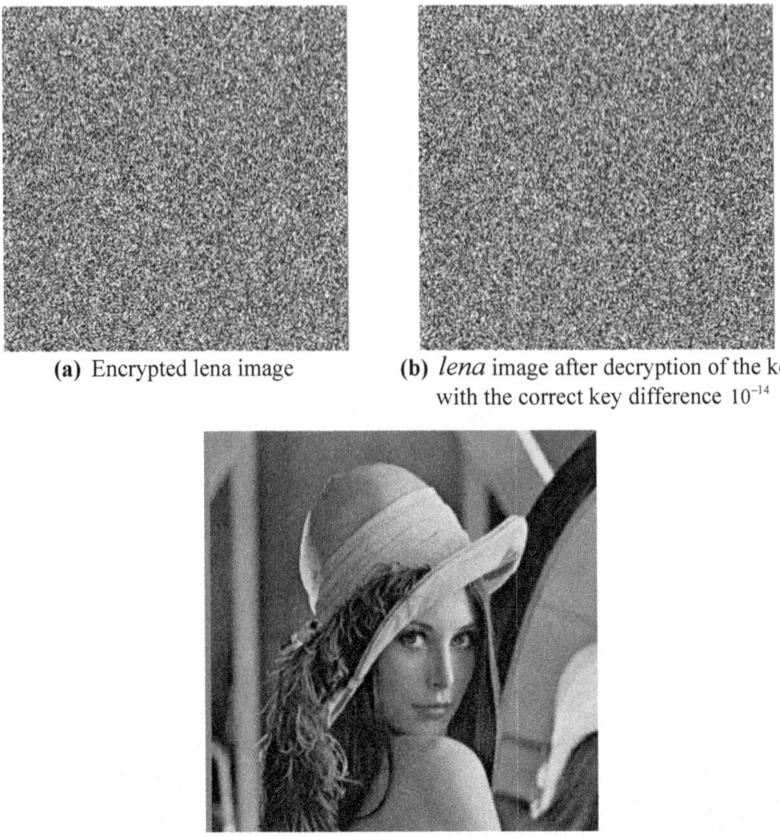

(a) Encrypted lena image

(b) *lena* image after decryption of the key with the correct key difference 10^{-14}

(c) *lena* image after decrypting the correct key

Fig. 5. Algorithm 1 key sensitivity test chart

dense image is small, If it is small and very close to zero, then the encryption algorithm is good.

Table 2 shows that in this paper, 1000 pixel pairs were randomly selected in the original and dense images, respectively, and then the pixel correlations in the horizontal and vertical directions and diagonal directions were tested, and the correlation coefficients in the three directions were calculated by applying the correlation coefficient formula in the literature [10]. From the table, we can see that the correlation coefficients of the original image in the three directions of vertical, horizontal and diagonal directions are all more than 0.9, while the correlation coefficients of the encrypted dense image in the three directions obviously drop significantly and even approach 0 in the horizontal and diagonal directions, indicating that the original adjacent pixel correlation of the image has been completely destroyed after the algorithm encryption. Therefore, the algorithm in this paper has good diffusivity.

Table 1. Ciphertext different pixel ratio

$(x_0, y_0, z_0, w_0, u_0)$ Initial value	Ciphertext different pixel ratio
$x_0 = 5.12345678912345$ $y_0 = 6.12345678932164$ $z_0 = 10.98765432136987$ $w_0 = -10.74125896312345$ $u_0 = 20.12365478914723$	99.58%
$x_0 = 5.12345678912342$ $y_0 = 6.12345678932165$ $z_0 = 10.98765432136987$ $w_0 = -10.74125896312345$ $u_0 = 20.12365478914723$	99.63%
$x_0 = 5.12345678912342$ $y_0 = 6.12345678932164$ $z_0 = 10.98765432136985$ $w_0 = -10.74125896312345$ $u_0 = 20.12365478914723$	99.66%
$x_0 = 5.12345678912342$ $y_0 = 6.12345678932164$ $z_0 = 10.98765432136987$ $w_0 = -10.74125896312347$ $u_0 = 20.12365478914723$	99.60%
$x_0 = 5.12345678912345$ $y_0 = 6.12345678932164$ $z_0 = 10.98765432136987$ $w_0 = -10.74125896312345$ $u_0 = 20.12365478914725$	99.58%

Table 2. Comparison of adjacent pixel correlation before and after algorithm 1 image encryption

Type	Vertical	Horizontal	Diagonal
Original image	0.96339	0.94719	0.91563
Encrypted image	0.018483	−0.0093376	0.00091402

5 Conclusion

This chapter first constructs a new five-dimensional hyperchaotic system based on the four-dimensional Lorenz system and proves its hyperchaotic nature; then proposes a digital image encryption algorithm based on the new five-dimensional hyperchaotic system and conducts the related simulation experiments; finally analyzes the security of the algorithm from four aspects. The simulation experiments and analysis results show that the algorithm in this paper can resist the current statistical attacks such as brute force attack, known plaintext attack and selective plaintext attack, and also has the features of good encryption effect, strong sensitivity to key and large key space, which meets the requirements of modern cryptography with high usability and security.

Acknowledgment. This paper is funded by *Education Department of Jiangxi Province of China* (GJJ181554), *Education Department of Hunan Province of China (21C0595),* Hunan Provincial Philosophy and Social Science fund project (21YBA179).

References

1. Sun, K.-H., Wang, Y., Wang, Y.: Hyperchaos behaviors and chaos synchronization of two unidirectional coupled simplified Lorenz systems. J. Cent. S. Univ. **21**(3), 948–955 (2014). https://doi.org/10.1007/s11771-014-2023-3
2. Zhuang, Z.-B., Li, J., Liu, J.-Y., Chen, S.-Q.: Image encryption algorithm based on new five-dimensional multi-ring multi-wing hyperchaotic system. Acta Physica Sinica **69**(4), 44–57 (2020)
3. Zhang, X., Wu, Z., Fang, Z.: A digital image encryption algorithm based on four-dimensional hyperchaotic system. Comput. Eng. **39**(8), 169–172 (2013)
4. Li, D., Lu, J., Wu, X.: Estimating the ultimate bound and positively invariant set for the Lorenz system and a unified chaotic system. J. Math. Anal. Appl. **323**(2), 844–853 (2006)
5. Ramasubramanian, K., Sriram, M.S.: A comparative study of computation of Lyapunov spectra with different algorithms. Physica D **139**, 72–86 (2000)
6. Tang, G., Liao, X.: Feistel-based chaotic cryptographic algorithm. J. Chongqing Univ. **28**(10), 54–58 (2005)
7. Qiu, S., Chen, Y., Wu, M., Ma, Z., Long, M., Liu, X.: A novel scheme of chaotic encryption system. J. Circuits Syst. **11**(1), 98–103 (2006)
8. Li, S., Dai, Y., Wang, X., Jia, X., Qin, Z.: New hybrid cryptosystem. J. Chin. Comput. Syst. **25**(6), 997–999 (2004)
9. Alvarez, G., Li, S.: Some basic cryptographic requirements for chaos-based cryptosystems. Int. J. Bifurc. Chaos **16**(8), 2129–2151 (2006)
10. Vinoskis, S.: The performance presumption. IEEE Internet Comput. **77**(4), 88–90 (2003)

Research on the Construction of an Accurate Procurement System for Library e-Resources in Foreign Language Under Dig Data Analysis

Ke Luo[1(✉)] and Xiujun Zhang[2]

[1] Department of Library, Shaoyang University, Shaoyang, Hunan, China
luoke00@qq.com
[2] Network Information Centre, Nanchang Institute of Technology, Nanchang, Jiangxi, China

Abstract. Due to the limited funds for the acquisition of university library resources, in order to improve the collection resource profitability and reduce the labor cost of libraries, a method of text classification using natural language processing is proposed to build an accurate procurement system for electronic book resources. Feature extraction is performed for the text information of the book collection, a feature vector matrix is established, and classification prediction is performed by machine learning algorithms. By optimizing the prediction model and evaluating the results with ten cross-validations, the accuracy of the LightGBM model testing reached 77.49%, so the acquisition system constructed based on this model can make effective decisions and thus optimize the structure of the collection resources.

Keywords: Artificial intelligence technology · Machine learning · TF-IDF · Text classification · Resource acquisition

1 Introduction

With the deepening of the construction of intelligent libraries in colleges and universities, the utilization rate of electronic resources has improved significantly compared with that of paper books, promoting the balance transfer between paper books and electronic books [1], and electronic resources have become an inevitable trend to replace paper books. According to the improvement of discipline construction and professional quality, more and more universities focus their library construction on developing foreign language electronic resources.

There are more than 400 large academic publishers in foreign countries, and more than 100,000 kinds of scholarly books are published every year [2]. If we still rely on the subjective will and experience of book interviewers, the quality of literature materials will undoubtedly be affected. Nowadays, the development and popularity of artificial intelligence have changed the traditional operation mode and ecosystem of various industries [3]. At the same time, it has put forward new thinkings for the innovation of book procurement mode and management mode of university libraries and pointed out the

Y. Xu et al. (Eds.): ML4CS 2022, LNCS 13657, pp. 619–630, 2023.
https://doi.org/10.1007/978-3-031-20102-8_48

direction for the construction of university libraries in the future [4]. In the future, book services, instead of simply catering to different readers, have become an essential element in the development of libraries, in addition to understanding the collections and how to meet the needs of readers.

Machine learning is a core and hot spot in the field of artificial intelligence, which can automatically identify patterns, discover rules and predict readers' borrowing behaviors based on massive data, thus meeting readers' personalized learning needs. To achieve maximum prediction accuracy and increase readers' downloads and visits, we utilize TF-IDF to feature engineer the text information of foreign book resources, use machine learning algorithms to forecast and classify them, and develop a set of correct purchase patterns.

2 Related Technologies

2.1 Machine Learning

The primary purpose of machine learning is to learn the input data through a selected model, extract valuable features or information from the data, and generalize a reasonable trend of change as a way to predict the data, which is a method that can readjust the parameters or structure in the model to improve the accuracy and reliability of the prediction after comparing the deviation of the predicted value with the actual value [5]. Machine learning can be classified into three main categories: supervised, unsupervised, and semi-supervised learning, depending on how the model is labeled with respect to the input data.

When analyzing massive amounts of data, different machine learning algorithms are often used because of the differences in research goals and objectives. Support Vector Machines (SVM), K-nearest neighbors (KNN), Decision Tree, Random Forest, Naive Bayes, and LightGBM are all applicable to classification problems. SVM achieves segmentation of samples by finding a hyperplane, but cannot handle multi-classification problems well, while K-nearest neighbors and random trees can achieve multi-classification, but both have the problem of low efficiency. Decision Tree and Naive Bayes algorithms are simple to use and easy to implement, but the former has some risk of overfitting, while the latter is very sensitive to the representation of the input data. Although random trees and neural networks are better for forecasting economic indicators, they are both "black boxes" and cannot be controlled by humans, so their interpretability is average. Based on the different machine learning algorithms, different machine learning algorithms have different advantages and disadvantages (as shown in Table 1), so the most suitable model can be selected according to different research objects in the specific analysis.

2.2 Text Classification

Text classification is an essential topic in the field of natural language processing, which involves binary or multiclass determination of text with a wide range of applications, including malicious email filtering, language recognition, sentiment analysis, etc.

Table 1. Comparison of machine learning methods

Methods	Advantages	Disadvantages	Applications
SVM	• High prediction accuracy • Non-random method • Rrobustness	Sensitive to parameter selection; difficult to solve multi-classification problems	Solving classification problems and predictions
KNN	• Non-linear effects • Easy to understand, no need to estimate a large number of parameters • No training required, high tolerance for outliers and noise	• Inefficient • Prone to dimensional disasters	Addressing classification issues and short-term liquidity predictions
Decision Tree	• Simple to use, able to handle categorical and continuous data; • Fast; • Less sensitive to missing values or omitted values in the dataset content	• General model accuracy • Prone to over-fitting problems	Solving classification problems and predicting
Random Forest	Integrated machine learning methods with smaller prediction errors can handle large amounts of data, are suitable for handling unbalanced data sets, and can balance the errors in selecting data	• "Black box" • Explaining the general performance	Solving classification problems and predicting
Naive Bayes	• Simple to calculate and use; • Few parameters to reduce the risk of data snooping	Sensitive to the representation of the input data and unable to consider the correlation between features	Solving classification problems
Logistic Regression	It can predict the probability between 0 and 1, and it is a good fit for data sets with linear relationship, and it is not limited to fractional values but also suitable for continuous values	Not easy to handle large amount of feature information, need to do transformation and dimensionality reduction first	Predicting

(*continued*)

Table 1. (*continued*)

Methods	Advantages	Disadvantages	Applications
LightGBM	Distributed, efficient, and faster training speed and efficiency	• High operational • Complexity and more memory usage	Learning multiple classifiers

The text classification process is divided into seven steps [6]. Firstly, the text dataset to be classified is collected, then the text is preprocessed with data, text features are extracted, and dimensionality is reduced, then the classifier is selected for training, and finally the performance of the classifier is evaluated, and the classifier with higher accuracy is selected for modeling.

Commonly used in fields such as text classification or text analysis is Term Frequency-Inverse Document Frequency[7] (TF-IDF), as a statistical method mainly used to evaluate the importance of a word in a dataset, corpus, as a reference for subsequent classification. The TF-IDF algorithm is made up of two major components: Term Frequency and Inverse Document Frequency.

Term Frequency (TF), evaluates the importance of all words in each text data, increasing with the frequency or number of occurrences in a single text data. Term frequency calculates the number of occurrences of a word in the target text data. $n_{i,j}$ represents the frequency of the ith word in document j, while $\sum_k n_{k,j}$ sums the frequency of all words in the target text data j, as shown in Eq. (1).

$$TF_{i,j} = \frac{n_{i,j}}{\sum_k n_{k,j}} \tag{1}$$

Inverse Document Frequency (IDF) is to evaluate the ratio of each word in the text database, when the word appears in more documents, the IDF will be smaller, also indicates that the word may be common words rather than important words, such as "the", "is" and other discontinued words. The IDF value is obtained by dividing the total number of documents|D| by the number containing the word in the database $|d_i \in D : t_i \in d_i|$, and then taking the logarithm of the result, as shown in Eq. (2).

$$IDF_{i,j} = log\frac{|D|}{|d_j \in D : t_j \in d_j|} \tag{2}$$

TF-IDF is defined as being calculated by multiplying TF and IDF, which is used to find keywords that frequently occur in the text database and are not commonly used words, as shown in Eq. (3).

$$TFIDF = TF \times IDF \tag{3}$$

2.3 Cross-Validation

Cross-validation [8] (CV) is a validation method that statistically partitions the data into smaller subsets, and is often used to evaluate models with generalization ability to new input data, suitable for solving overfitting problems caused by too few samples or improper parameter settings. The general cross-validation is K-fold cross-validation[9](K-fold CV) and leave-one-out cross-validation, while in this paper, we perform 10 times cross-validation with K-fold CV for the classification model, as shown in Fig. 1.

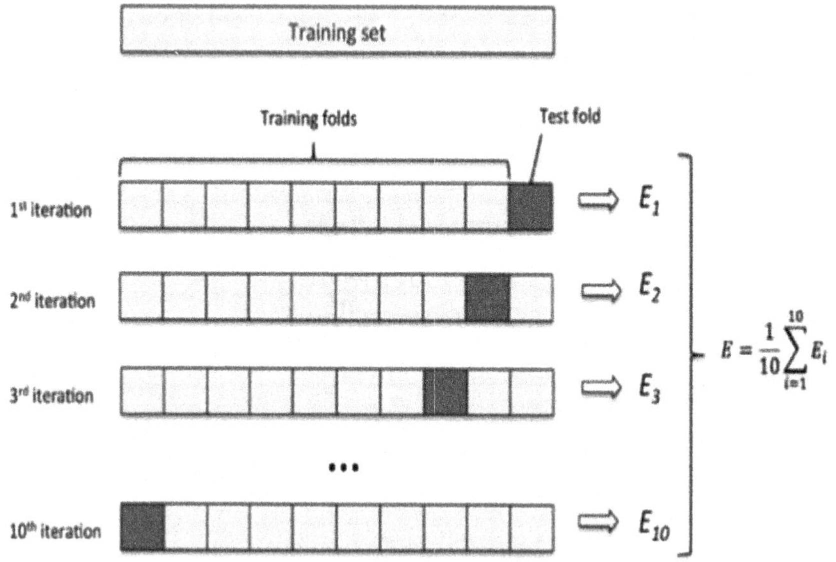

Fig. 1. 10-fold CV principle

K-fold CV is to divide the data set into K groups randomly and equally, then one group is used as the test data and $K-1$ group is used as the training data, and the above steps are repeated K times to finally obtain the accuracy of K groups and take the average value as the evaluation criterion.

2.4 Model Evaluation Criteria

The confusion matrix[10] for the binary classification problem is shown in Table 2, where negative indicates un-borrowed and positive indicates borrowed. Where: TN indicates that the book was correctly predicted to be borrowed, FN indicates that the book was incorrectly predicted to be borrowed, and FP indicates that it was incorrectly predicted to be un-borrowed; TP indicates that it was correctly predicted to be un-borrowed. Table 2 shows Confusion matrix of the dichotomous problem.

In the classification problem, the model can also extend several classification model metrics from the results obtained from the confusion matrix, including precision, recall, specificity and F1 scores combined evaluation metrics, with precision being the number of correct classifications evaluated as a proportion of all data points classified as correct. The specific meaning and calculation formula are shown in Table 3.

Table 2. Confusion matrix of 2-class

Confusion matrix		Predicted class	
		Un-borrowed samples	Borrowing samples
Actual class	Un-borrowed samples	TP	FN
	Borrowing samples	FP	TN

Table 3. Model evaluation metrics

Evaluation metrics	Formula
Precision	$precision = \frac{TP}{TP+FP}$
Recall	$Recall = \frac{TP}{TP+FN}$
Specificity	$Specificity = \frac{TN}{TN+FP}$
F1-Score	$F1 = \frac{2TP}{2TP+FR+FN}$
AUC	$AUC = \frac{1}{2}\sum_{i=2}^{m}(x_i - x_{i-1}) \cdot (y_i + y_{i-1})$
Accuracy	$Accuracy = \frac{TP+TN}{TP+FP+TN+FN}$

3 The Construction Process of Accurate Book Purchasing Model

In this paper, the access record data of the e-book platform of the university library is used as the research object, the correlation degree between the book texts are found by using TF-IDF, and the value is used as the independent variable of Random Forest, LightGBM, Naive Bayes and SVM models. Through parameter optimization and 10 times cross-validation, the classification model is finally evaluated for its effectiveness, and the prediction model is constructed based on the prediction results. The prediction model design process is shown in Fig. 2.

Step 1: Data cleaning of the raw data acquired by the platform. Data cleaning is the focus on the whole framework and the part with the largest workload. Its main contents include the removal of duplicate values, the filling of missing values, and the detection of outliers in the dataset.

Step 2: Merging the four parts of the dataset: book title, author, year of publication, publisher, and secondary processing such as punctuation and stop word cleaning.

Step 3: Processing the merged text with natural language for word separation, sentence breaking, keyword extraction, etc.

Step 4: The samples were randomly grouped 7:3 and divided into two groups, the training set, and the test set.

Step 5: Using the TF-IDF model, the training set and the test set are word vectorized separately, and a vector matrix is constructed.

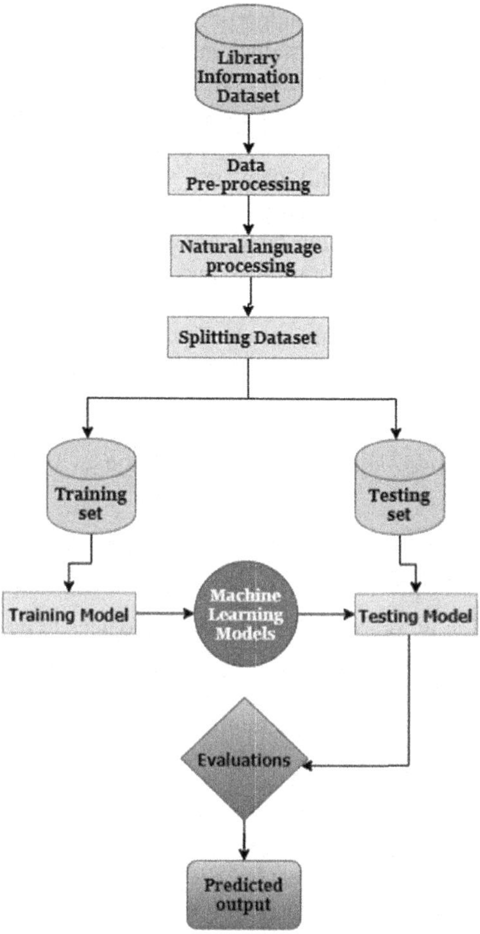

Fig. 2. Flowchart for building a precise book resource procurement model

Step 6: Based on the vector-matrix obtained in Step 5, a model was built using naive Bayes, LightGBM, Decision Tree and support vector machine, and the accuracy of the model and the classification model evaluated were derived by 10 cross-checks.

Step 7: The results of the predictions were used to evaluate the efficiency of the models and obtain the best model as an accurate purchasing decision system.

4 Experiments and Results Analysis

This experiment focuses on data mining for foreign language text data. A Lenovo desktop computer with NVIDIA GTX1070 VGA card and Intel(R) Pentium(R) CPU G645 was used. The programming language environment of Python 3.8 was built under Windows OS, and a machine learning prediction model was constructed using Scikit-Learn as the machine learning framework. Scikit-Learn is currently one of the most popular machine learning algorithm libraries, supporting a variety of tasks such as classification, regression, clustering, dimensionality reduction, and model selection.

The information used in this paper comes from the e-book data platform of university libraries, with the reading electronic materials of students and teachers from 2017 to 2021 as samples, and the format used for the dataset is CSV file, which is desensitized and anonymized data, including daily data such as library visits and downloads. The access process of electronic books usually includes three kinds of data tables: reader information table, access information table, and book information table. The data in each part contain a large number of attributes, and only important attributes that have an impact on the experimental results are retained, for example: reader information retains card number, gender, college, category, etc.; book information table selects book number, title, publisher, etc.; access flow data access time, logged-in user ID, IP number, card number, downloads, etc.

The experiments are divided into three major blocks, firstly data pre-processing, secondly feature extraction, and finally, the evaluation of the classification model's effectiveness.

4.1 Data Pre-processing

After the data collection is completed, the raw data also need to be data-organized, such as processing missing values, duplicates, and outliers, integrating and standardizing the data. If the raw data are used directly, the model validity may be reduced. Data pre-processing is a prerequisite for data mining, and only a good start can be made to continue the next work session.

4.1.1 Data Cleaning

Book sample data cleaning mainly reaches the objectives of standardization of data format, cleaning of abnormal data, correction of errors, and elimination of duplicate data, etc. The following measures are taken:

(1) Abnormal data values: the daily data volume of the e-book network platform is very huge, and data abnormalities will inevitably occur, which should be deleted when filtering text data are used to ensure subsequent feature engineering.
(2) Deactivated words: Deactivated words refer to words that occur frequently but meaningless, such as: of, in, is, have, and so on, retaining keywords, and the rest of the deactivated words should be deleted.
(3) Non-textual data: book information contains a large number of punctuation marks, accent marks, blank areas, non-English characters, and other non-textual data, which are not conducive to subsequent processing, such as word separation and should be deleted.

4.1.2 Data Integration

Data integration is the process of merging data from multiple files, and the main aspects involved are data selection, data conflicts, and inconsistency issues. In this paper, three data tables, reader information table, access information table and book information table, are integrated into one table, which mainly contains vertical appending of the same field attributes and horizontal merging with superposition of related attributes, etc. The attributes are some of the attributes retained in each table. When data are horizontally merged, it will lead to data redundancy because some attribute fields of the same object have different attribute names in different files, so eliminating data redundancy is an important work in data integration.

Since the attributes of the three different information data tables used in this paper are closely related to each other, the key attributes affecting readers' access are filtered by correlating the three data, such as: bibliographic system number, book title, author, year of publication, publisher, classification number, price, access IP number, the total number of accesses and other different types of fields. According to the total number of visits and downloads, a new lending status field is added as a feature marker, and the identification status of books without visits and downloads is 0. The lending status with visits and downloads is identified as 1, thus constructing the initial dataset of this paper.

4.2 Feature Engineering

The primary role of feature selection is to select the features that have the most practical value for outcome prediction from multiple features. After the initial data set is completed, it needs to be analyzed exploratively to explore the trends and relationships in the data. In general, the more prominent the link between attributes and demand is found i.e., the more prominent the attribute link is, the better the results are indicated. In this paper, the 13 extracted fields, such as bibliographic system number, book title, author, publication year, publisher, classification number, price, access IP number, and total number of visits, are used to realize the training session in building the machine learning model. Four fields, such as book title, author, publication year, and publisher, are found to be more relevant to book visits. Using the relationship between the features, the independent variable with the strongest relationship with the dependent variable was selected as the input feature. Finally, the dataset is segmented to create a training dataset and a test dataset. In this paper, we found that the most used methods to validate the model through statistical search of the literature are 10-fold cross-validation and 5-fold cross-validation.

4.3 Model Performance Evaluation

There are also differences in the prediction effects of different models for different data, so in the empirical analysis, the optimal model needs to be selected by comparing the values of relevant indicators, as shown in Table 5.

Model I is LightGBM: LightGBM is a gradient boosting model for machine learning, which has better efficiency and higher accuracy and is suitable for handling massive data. LightGBM has numerous parameters, and the optimal parameters can be obtained by using 10 cross-validations (Table 4), and its average accuracy can reach 77.49%.

Model II is SVC: SVC is a method used by SVM to deal with classification problems. SVM is a kind of supervised learning, which mainly finds a decision boundary on the hyperplane to maximize the boundary between two classifications and make them

Table 4. LightGBM parameter setting table

Parameter	Value	Parameter	Value
max_depth	−1	min_samples_split	gbdt
min_data_in_leaf	11	bagging_freq	0
feature_fraction	0.7	cat_smooth	0
bagging_fraction	1.0	min_split_gain	0.4
criterion	0.5	n_estimators	826
min_impurity_split	gini	min_impurity_decrease	0.0
objective	binary	metric	auc
n_jobs	−1	num_leaves	31
num_boost_round	1000	learning_rate	0.1

perfectly distinguishable. The larger the coefficient, the greater the penalty for classification errors, the higher the accuracy in the post-training test, but it is prone to overfitting. The model parameter C was set to 1.0, and the accuracy of the model was 75.06% by cross-validation and the SVC confusion matrix.

Model III is Logistic Regression: Logistic regression model, based on the concept of the regression model, is used to predict the likelihood of occurrence of binary category type variables, predicting that the text data belongs to that category is more likely. The model uses a sigmoid function, multiplying each text feature by a regression coefficient and summing the results, bringing them into this function to get a The model uses a sigmoid function that multiplies each text feature by a regression coefficient and sums the results into this function to obtain a value in the range between 0 and 1. The data to be classified are brought into the model and are classified into one category if they are greater than 0.5 and into another category if they are less than 0.5. The average accuracy of 67.92% was obtained by cross-validation.

Model IV is Naive Bayes: Naive Bayes model is mostly applied to text classification. In this study, we use a polynomial model to train the data, and after breaking the words using text data, we calculate the total number of words in the two classes divided by the total number of words in all of them, and we can get the prior probability; after calculating the number of words in each text data and +1 in the two classes respectively, we divide the total number of words represented by the two classes, that is the class conditional chance; bring in the text data to be classified and calculate how many chances the words account for in the two classes to judge as the class, and after cross-validation, the average accuracy is obtained as 64.43%.

Model V is Decision Tree: Decision Tree is commonly used for text classification, through which the model understands the meaning and rules of training results, and also applies to a large amount of text data. This study uses text features to build a model, in a top-down manner, where each node in the tree represents a feature attribute, and each tree represents the decision of which attribute is selected for the current node and extended down, in order to prevent overfitting. The pruning action is performed after the training is completed. After cross-validation, an average accuracy of 53.87% is obtained.

Model VI is KNN: The central idea of the K nearest neighbor algorithm is that a text data to be classified finds the K most similar neighbors in the text feature space, and most of the neighbors are classified into a certain class, then the text data to be classified is of that class. By cross-validation, the model parameter k value is set to 9, and the average accuracy of 55.21% is obtained.

Table 5. Classification model effectiveness evaluation table

Model	Accuracy	Precision	Recall	F1 scores
LightGBM	0.7749	0.7615	0.7697	0.7667
SVC	0.7506	0.7411	0.7345	0.7274
Logistic Regression	0.6792	0.6462	0.6088	0.6471
Naive Bayes	0.6443	0.6712	0.6771	0.6911
Decision Tree	0.5387	0.5717	0.6185	0.5771
KNN	0.5521	0.6185	0.5514	0.5252

5 Conclusion

In this paper, six refined machine learning methods are used to predict the borrowing of e-book visits provided by university libraries in the past five years, among which the prediction accuracy of the LightGBM model reaches 77.49%, and then proposes to construct a machine learning-based accurate purchasing model for foreign language e-book resources, which not only obtains high-quality data but also proposes valuable analysis decisions for e-book purchasing.

Acknowledgment. This paper is funded by Hunan Provincial Philosophy and Social Science fund project "Research on the Application of Artificial Intelligence Technology in Accurate Book Procurement in Universities under Smart Library" (21YBA179), and Education Department of Hunan Province of China (21C0595).

References

1. Latimer, K.: Redefining the library: current trends in library design. Art Libr. J. **35**(1), 28–34 (2010)
2. Huang, J.: Research on foreign language e-book acquisition mode. Libr. Dev. **S1**, 43–46 (2020)
3. Duan, Y., Edwards, J.S., Dwivedi, Y.K.: Artificial intelligence for decision making in the era of Big Data–evolution, challenges and research agenda. Int. J. Inf. Manag. **48**, 63–71 (2019)

4. Bai, G.: Research on the library intelligent resource procurement system based on big data. Res. Libr. Sci. **19**, 37–41 (2016)
5. Jordan, M.I., Mitchell, T.M.: Machine learning: trends, perspectives, and prospects. Science **349**(6245), 255–260 (2015)
6. Kadhim, A.I.: Survey on supervised machine learning techniques for automatic text classification. Artif. Intell. Rev. **52**, 273–292 (2019)
7. Kim, S.-W., Gil, J.-M.: Research paper classification systems based on TF-IDF and LDA schemes. HCIS **9**(1), 1–21 (2019). https://doi.org/10.1186/s13673-019-0192-7
8. Shao, J.: Linear model selection by cross-validation. J. Am. Stat. Assoc **88**(422), 486–494 (1993)
9. Liang, Z., Li, Z., Lai, K., Lin, Z., Li, T., Zhang, J.: Application of 10-fold cross-validation in the evaluation of generalization ability of prediction models and the realization. Chin. J. Hosp. Stat. **4**, 289–292 (2020)
10. Mi, A., Zhang, P.: A method of classifier selection based on confusion matric. J. Henan Polytech. Univ. (Nat. Sci.) **36**(2), 116–121 (2017)

Recognition Method of Wa Language Isolated Words Based on Convolutional Neural Network

Jinsheng Liu[1], Jianhou Gan[1,2(✉)], Ken Chen[1], Di Wu[1], and Wenlin Pan[3]

[1] Key Laboratory of Education Informatization for Nationalities, Yunnan Normal University, Ministry of Education, Kunming 650500, China
ganjh@ynnu.edu.cn

[2] Yunnan Key Laboratory of Smart Education, Yunnan Normal University, Kunming 650500, China

[3] School of Mathematics and Computer Science, Yunnan Minzu University, Kunming 650500, China

Abstract. Speech recognition technology is a popular research direction in artificial intelligence, especially with the development of deep learning technology, speech recognition gradually shifts from traditional recognition methods to end-to-end recognition based on deep learning. Most of the current speech recognition models have achieved high recognition accuracy for mainstream languages, but these models are relatively complex in structure and have many model parameters, which are not suitable for recognizing isolated words in low-resource languages. Based on the deep learning approach, we use a simple and effective model to recognize isolated words in Wa language of minority languages. The encoder includes a simplified deep convolutional neural network VGG and BiLSTM, where the VGG network is used to extract depth features of the audio signal and BiLSTM is further encoded. The decoder includes two decoding methods, CTC and Attention, which can be decoded individually or jointly, which is an end-to-end speech recognition model. We use this model to conduct experiments on our Wa isolated words speech dataset, and the experimental results show that the model has a good recognition effect. The WER is below 20% whether it is decoded alone or jointly.

Keywords: Wa language speech recognition · Isolated word · VGG · CTC · Attention

1 Introduction

China is a unified multi-ethnic country, and each nation has its own national language, among which the most used language is Chinese. From the current environment, the popularity of mandarin has affected the use and development of some minority languages, and even Chinese contains many Chinese dialects, and many local dialects are in danger of disappearing. Minority languages are an indispensable part of minority cultures, so it is very necessary to protect minority languages. Some Internet companies have made many contributions to the protection of dialects, and in 2017, iFLYTEK launched a dialect protection program using artificial intelligence techno-logy, inviting all people to

Y. Xu et al. (Eds.): ML4CS 2022, LNCS 13657, pp. 631–640, 2023.
https://doi.org/10.1007/978-3-031-20102-8_49

participate, so that everyone can do their part to protect the dialects of their hometowns. Nowadays, speech recognition technology provides a new approach to the preservation of minority languages and dialects, which is of great practical importance.

Speech recognition technology is mainly divided into traditional speech recognition methods and end-to-end models based on deep learning. Traditional speech recognition models contain acoustic, pronunciation dictionary and language models, each part of which has to be trained separately, and it is very difficult to build pronunciation dictionary if there is a lack of corresponding language knowledge. Early speech recognition was based on GMM-HMM, and with the development of deep neural network DNN, DNN was used instead of GMM, and DNN-HMM [1] recognition model was proposed with phoneme state as the modeling unit, and the recognition accuracy was significantly improved. The end-to-end model combines acoustic model, pronunciation dictionary and language model into a single model for unified training. The input audio feature information can directly generate corresponding natural language text information. The main end-to-end models are based on CTC [2], Encoder-Decoder [3] model based on Attention [4], joint CTC-Attention [5], and RNN Transducer [6]. And the end-to-end model further improves the recognition accuracy.

Most speech recognition models mainly recognize mainstream languages, although the recognition accuracy is high but the model is large and has many parameters, which may be less effective for recognizing our dataset. In order to improve the accuracy of recognizing isolated words in Wa, we use a simplified convolutional neural network based on VGG network [7] to build a model for recognizing isolated words in Wa.

2 Related Work

Due to the rich speech datasets of mainstream languages, many researchers have conducted in-depth studies on speech recognition of mainstream languages [8], and have been able to obtain high recognition accuracy. In recent years, the recognition of low-resource languages has also become a hot research topic, one of the purposes is to preserve these endangered low-resource languages. The speech datasets of low-resource languages are less available and few corpora, and the implementation of a model for recognizing low-resource languages usually requires a large amount of annotated audio data to ensure a good recognition accuracy, which is time-consuming and labor-intensive to obtain a large amount of effective annotated audio data for low-resource languages. In order to overcome the problem of low model recognition accuracy due to small effective labeled data set, many researchers have done related research work. Kuznetsova A et al. [9] introduced a difficulty measure called compression ratio as a scoring function for the original audio under various noise conditions. Yi J et al. [10] used adversarial transfer learning to make the shared layer of SHL-model learn more language-invariant features. Cho J et al. [11] first built a multilingual seq2seq model using multi-language data, and then migrated it to other low-resource languages. Xiao Y et al. [12] used a new adversarial meta-sampling method to address the situation where multilingual meta-learning may fail due to large differences in the size of data from different source languages. Schneider S et al. [13] used an unsupervised approach for training and pre-trained a multi-layer convolutional neural network in advance to reduce the use of labeled data while relying on a large amount of unlabeled audio data.

The above mentioned research work is based on the recognition of long speech sentences in low resource languages, but in low resource language recognition, there is another kind of isolated words recognition. Compared with collecting speech annotation data of mainstream languages, the collection of low-resource speech data is inherently time-consuming and labor-intensive, especially collecting long speech sequences, so many low-resource language datasets are based on isolated words, just like the Wa isolated word dataset we used, which are commonly used words in the life of the Wa people. For the speech recognition of isolated words, Gelin L et al. [14] considered that words spoken by children could be regarded as isolated words, they used rich adult speech data to train end-to-end model, and used transfer technology and a small amount of children's speech data to get a model to recognize children's speech with good results. Hu P et al. [15] mixed subwords and whole words of Uyghur language together to form hybrid words for language modeling and introduced difference LM to further improve the performance of the model. Li B et al. [16] recognized isolated words based on machine learning methods to extract different features and recognize words under different classifiers.

The dataset constructed in this paper is the word commonly used in the life of the Wa people. In order to better identify isolated words in Wa, we first extract the deep abstract features of the audio using a simplified VGG network, and input a speech signal into the convolutional network like a picture. Then BiLSTM was used to analyze the speech sequences with attention in the time dimension, and finally use CTC or Attention to get the output text and calculate the target loss to train the whole model.

We have collected a large number of Wa isolated words speech data, and used the deep learning method to recognize Wa words, which can achieve relatively high recognition accuracy. The research on Wa vocabulary recognition is beneficial to the protection and inheritance of minority culture. Next, we will carry out the research on related work, the use of model and ablation experiment.

3 Model

The speech recognition model we use includes three modules, the original speech feature extraction module, the encoder and the decoder. The encoder includes VGG network and BiLSTM layer, and the decoding layer includes CTC and Attention, and finally the difference between the predicted text and the real text is calculated using CTC or Attention. We introduce the extraction of Fbank features, deep convolutional network and CTC. Fig. 1 shows the model for recognizing isolated words speech in Wa.

3.1 Extraction of Fbank Features

Fbank features are common speech features in speech recognition field, and other common features are MFCC features. In contrast, Fbank is closer to the response characteristics of human ear, and there is obvious overlap between neighboring features with high correlation. MFCC can be obtained through discrete cosine transform, and the correlation between MFCC features will become smaller. We extract Fbank features by reading the original Wa isolated word audio files, and extract the audio feature vector

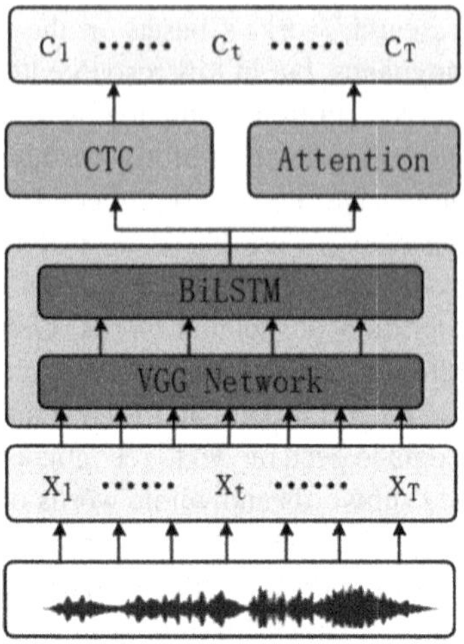

Fig. 1. Model for recognizing isolated words speech in Wa.

through a series of operations such as pre-emphasis, framing and windowing, discrete Fourier transform, and finally obtain 120-dimensional Fbank features. The window size of framing and windowing operation is 25ms and the frame shift is 10 ms. Before input to the decoding layer, the 2D features are expanded into 3D data for further extraction of deeper features in the VGG network layer.

3.2 Deep CNN

Zhang Y et al. [17] implemented end-to-end speech recognition using deep convolutional neural network as the feature extraction layer. At the same time, they used the idea of residual network [18] for reference to design residual convolution layer and residual LSTM layer [19] to solve the phenomenon of network degradation caused by too many network layers. Hori T et al. [5] refer to the VGG network using 6 layers of convolution and 2 layers of max pooling. The extracted feature networks we used are VGG networks with different depths to compare the speech recognition accuracy of networks with different layers.

3.3 CTC

In speech recognition tasks, it is usually necessary to align speech fragments and output labels, which increases the difficulty of training models. If we specify one character to correspond to several speech segments, due to the different speech speed of different people, it will lead to a large difference in recognition results for multiple people speaking the same sentence, which greatly reduces the model recognition effect. If we adopt manual alignment of each character corresponding to its position in the audio, the training effect is very good but time-consuming. The CTC method can automatically achieve the alignment of the length between the input speech and the output sequence, without considering the alignment of the training samples, and CTC introduces the blank character, which means the output label is empty. Define the input audio sequence $X = [x_1, x_2, \ldots\ldots, x_T]$, and the corresponding labeled text with symbol sequence $Y = [y_1, y_2, \ldots\ldots, y_U]$. The speech feature sequence X is input to the model, and CTC will calculate to get all the possible output distributions of Y. For example, the sequence to be output is $Y = [d, o, g]$, and Eq. (1) shows all the outputs related to Y obtained by CTC.

$$\left.\begin{array}{l} (d, o, g, -, -) \\ (d, d, o, g, -) \\ (d, -, d, o, g) \\ (-, d, o, g, -) \\ (-, d, o, o, g) \\ \ldots\ldots \\ (-, -, d, o, g) \end{array}\right\} = (d, o, g) \tag{1}$$

When getting each output path, the blank character is introduced, such as the '-' in the above figure, which means there is no corresponding character in Y. Simplifying all the outputs by removing duplicate characters and blank characters, the final Y sequence can be obtained for each output result. As shown in Eq. (2), the goal of CTC is to maximize the sum of the probability of all valid paths related to Y. $p(Y|X)$ can be derived, and the gradient training model is computed using the forward-backward calculation method.

$$p(Y|X) = \sum_{(X,Y)\in S} \prod_{t=1}^{T} p_t(a_t|X) \tag{2}$$

where $(X, Y) \in S$ is the training instance, X is the input speech feature sequence, Y is the labeled text sequence, t denotes each moment, a_t is the speech feature at each moment, and $pt\ (at\ |X)$ is the probability of characters in the output Y at each moment, using Eq. (3) to calculate the CTC loss.

$$L_{ctc} = -log\, p(Y|X) \tag{3}$$

Here we only introduce the decoding principle of speech recognition using CTC in detail.In the subsequent experiments, we will use CTC, Attention and the combined CTC-attention for comparative experiments. In the joint decoding, the loss will be calculated according to Eq. (4), where $0 \le \lambda \le 1$.

$$L_{all} = -\lambda log\, p_{ctc}(Y|X) - (1 - \lambda) log\, p_{att}(Y|X) \tag{4}$$

4 Experimental Results

4.1 Dataset

The Wa isolated words speech dataset we used was collected by our research team in Yanshuai Town, Canyuan Wa Autonomous County, Lincang City, Yunnan Province, with male and female pronouncers, age groups including primary school students, adults and the elderly, and recording environments including field recordings and studio recordings. We selected some of the corpus to train our model. The corpus contains 1860 common words, 11 speakers were selected. Each speaker was required to read the 1860 words 5 times, due to some uncertainties, some speakers read less than 1860 words, and some speakers may read a word less than 5 times or more than 5 times, ranging from 4 times to 7 times. After statistics, the final amount of speech data we can use is about 88,027 words. In order to better train the model, we divided the speech files of each pronouncer for each word into training set, validation set, and test set in a ratio of 3:1:1 to ensure that each dataset file contains the pronunciation data of each pronouncer for each word. Because of these uncertainties, the amount of data in each dataset may be different from the actual calculation amount when we divide the datasets, but the impact is not significant, and the amount of data in each part is shown in Table 1. The Wa vocabulary pronunciation dataset we used contains the pronunciation of Wa language and the corresponding Chinese translation, and some of the vocabulary data are compared as shown in Table 2.

Table 1. Data volume of training set, validation set, and test set.

Data type	Percentage/%	Data volume/bar
Training set	60	53319
Validation set	20	17354
Test set	20	17354

Table 2. Wa pronunciation and Chinese translation contrast.

Wa pronunciation	Chinese	Wa pronunciation	Chinese
si ngāix	Sun	rom glong	Creek
kix	Moon	rom ndūng	Pond
sim uing	Star	grax qē	Highway
hliex iag	Light rain	ma	Mountain
si yōng	Rainbow	gaeng	Water Field

4.2 Experiments

We conduct three sets of comparative experiments on the Wa isolated words speech dataset. The batch size used in all experiments is 32, and a total of 160K steps are trained and validated every 2K steps. The best model parameters and experimental results are saved at each validation, and the Adadelta algorithm is used as the optimizer. When using the VGG network, the 120-dimensional Fbank features are extracted first, and the

2D audio feature parameters are converted into 3D input to VGG network by referring to the method of image recognition, followed by a 5-layer BiLSTM, which is decoded by CTC or Attention alone or combined with CTC-Attention. The measure of the model is WER, and the calculation process is shown in Eq. (5), where S, D, and I are the number of words replaced, deleted, and inserted in the recognized sequence compared to the corresponding position of the real sequence, respectively, and N is the length of the real sequence, and the opposite accuracy is 100-WER%.

$$WER = 100 \cdot \frac{S + D + I}{N} \% \tag{5}$$

The first group of comparative experiments uses VGG networks of different depths as the network layers for extracting audio features in the encoding layer, including VGG(6) [5], VGG11, VGG13, and VGG16, while adding CNN and Conformer [20] in the encoding layer as a comparative experiment of the network layer for feature extraction, when using CNN, 2D audio features are directly input into the network for 1D convolution operations. This group of experiments uses Attention for decoding. The WER of the first experiment on the test set is shown in Table 3.

Table 3. The WER on the test set uses different encoders and the same Attention.

Model	WER[%]
VGG(6) + BiLSTM + Attention	18.47
VGG11 + BiLSTM + Attention	21.34
VGG13 + BiLSTM + Attention	51.9
VGG16 + BiLSTM + Attention	87.3
CNN + BiLSTM + Attention	19.88
Conformer + BiLSTM + Attention	54.1

It can be seen from Table 3 that when Attentiona is used, VGG(6) can reach 18.47% WER and CNN can reach 19.88% WER. With the use of deeper VGG or Conformer, the WER is very high, indicating that the recognition accuracy is not very ideal.

In the second experiment, CTC was used to replace Attention for decoding on the basis of the first experiment. The experimental results are shown in Table 4.

As can be seen from Table 4, the results are similar to those of the first group of experiments. The WER of 16.38%can be achieved by using VGG(6) and 16.49% can be achieved by using CNN. The deeper the network of feature extraction, the higher the WER and the lower the recognition accuracy.

In the third group, CTC-attention was used for joint decoding, where the value of λ was set as 0.5, with the same weight ratio between the two. The experimental results are shown in Table 5.

Firstly, it can be seen from Table 5 that the WER of the two are similar when joint decoding is used. Secondly, compared with the results obtained by using VGG(6), VGG11 and CNN alone, the results obtained by joint decoding are not very different,

Table 4. The WER on the test set uses different encoders and the same CTC.

Model	WER[%]
VGG(6) + BiLSTM + CTC	16.38
VGG11 + BiLSTM + CTC	19.33
VGG13 + BiLSTM + CTC	45.87
VGG16 + BiLSTM + CTC	82.44
CNN + BiLSTM + CTC	16.49
Conformer + BiLSTM + CTC	68.5

Table 5. The WER on the test set uses different encoders and the same CTC-Attention.

Model	WER[%]	
	Attention	CTC
VGG(6) + BiLSTM + Attention/CTC	16.79	16.86
VGG11 + BiLSTM + Attention/CTC	21.39	19.83
VGG13 + BiLSTM + Attention/CTC	15.27	15.07
VGG16 + BiLSTM + Attention/CTC	75.11	73.94
CNN + BiLSTM + Attention/CTC	16.33	16.19
Conformer + BiLSTM + Attention/CTC	42.04	42.52

but they are greatly improved for the three networks VGG13, VGG16 and Conformer. For example, VGG13 improved by around 40%, VGG16 by over 20%, and Conformer by between 10% and 30%.

From the above experimental results, we can conclude that compared with deep VGG and Conformer, the VGG(6) network model we used has a simple structure, fewer parameters during training, and a better recognition accuracy for Wa isolated word speech. Perhaps deep VGG and Conformer are more suitable for the recognition of continuous long speech. And the joint decoding can train the model better than the single decoding, so that the model converges faster and the recognition effect is better.

5 Conclusions

We use the end-to-end speech recognition model to train the Wa isolated words speech dataset we collected. The encoding part of the model is based on a simplified deep convolutional neural network VGG and BiLSTM. BiLSTM can better handle the dependencies between speech feature frames in the temporal dimension. The decoding part can be decoded separately and jointly with CTC or Attention. The experimental results on this dataset show that high recognition accuracy can be achieved using the end-to-end speech recognition model, but not higher than 90%,and the method is not scalable enough to be extended to other languages. We will subsequently investigate how to improve the structure of the model to enhance its performance, and try more other model structures in the encoding or decoding part, hoping to achieve better recognition results on the Wa isolated words dataset and try to extend it to other languages. At the same time, we also hope to lay the foundation for recognizing Wa continuous speech, and subsequently collect Wa continuous long speech with better speech quality and larger data volume, so that we can do our part to protect a low-resource language like Wa or a dying dialect.

Acknowledgements. This work is supported by Major Science and Technology Project of Yunnan Province (No. 202002AD080001), National New Liberal Arts Research and Reform Practice Project (No. 2021180030), Yunnan Innovation Team of Education Informatization for Nationalities, and Scientific Technology Innovation Team of Educational Big Data Application Technology in University of Yunnan Province.

References

1. Aung, M.A.A., Pa, W.P.: Time delay neural network for Myanmar automatic speech recognition. In: 2020 IEEE Conference on Computer Applications (ICCA), pp. 1–4. IEEE (2020)
2. Graves, A., Fernández, S., Gomez, F., et al.: Connectionist temporal classification: labelling unsegmented sequence data with recurrent neural networks. In: Proceedings of the 23rd International Conference on Machine Learning, pp. 369–376 (2006)
3. Chan, W., Jaitly, N., Le, Q., et al.: Listen, attend and spell: A neural network for large vocabulary conversational speech recognition. In: 2016 IEEE International Conference on Acoustics, Speech and Signal Processing (ICASSP), pp. 4960–4964. IEEE (2016)
4. Vaswani, A., Shazeer, N., Parmar, N., et al.: Attention is all you need. In: Advances in Neural Information Processing Systems, vol. 30 (2017)
5. Hori, T., Watanabe, S., Zhang, Y., et al.: Advances in joint CTC-attention based end-to-end speech recognition with a deep CNN encoder and RNN-LM. arXiv preprint arXiv:1706.02737 (2017)
6. Graves, A.: Sequence transduction with recurrent neural networks. arXiv preprint arXiv:1211.3711 (2012)
7. Simonyan, K., Zisserman, A.: Very deep convolutional networks for large-scale image recognition. arXiv preprint arXiv:1409.1556 (2014)
8. Zhang, B., Wu, D., Yao, Z., et al.: Unified streaming and non-streaming two-pass end-to-end model for speech recognition. arXiv preprint arXiv:2012.05481 (2020)
9. Kuznetsova, A., Kumar, A., Fox, J.D., et al.: Curriculum optimization for low-resource speech recognition. In: ICASSP 2022-2022 IEEE International Conference on Acoustics, Speech and Signal Processing (ICASSP), pp. 8187–8191. IEEE (2022)
10. Yi, J., Tao, J., Wen, Z., et al.: Language-adversarial transfer learning for low-resource speech recognition. IEEE/ACM Trans. Audio Speech Lang. Process. **27**(3), 621–630 (2018)
11. Cho, J., Baskar, M.K., Li, R., et al.: Multilingual sequence-to-sequence speech recognition: architecture, transfer learning, and language modelling. In: 2018 IEEE Spoken Language Technology Workshop (SLT), pp. 521–527. IEEE (2018)
12. Xiao, Y., Gong, K., Zhou, P., et al.: Adversarial meta sampling for multilingual low-resource speech recognition. arXiv preprint arXiv:2012.11896 (2020)
13. Schneider, S., Baevski, A., Collobert, R., et al.: wav2vec: unsupervised pre-training for speech recognition. arXiv preprint arXiv:1904.05862 (2019)

14. Gelin, L., Daniel, M., Pinquier, J., et al.: End-to-end acoustic modelling for phone recognition of young readers. Speech Commun. **134**, 71–84 (2021)
15. Hu, P., Huang, S., Lv, Z.: Investigating the use of mixed-units based modeling for improving uyghur speech recognition. In: SLTU, pp. 215–219 (2018)
16. Li, B., Wang, Y., Niu, Y., et al.: Research on isolated word recognition algorithm based on machine learning. In: 2020 IEEE 3rd International Conference on Information Systems and Computer Aided Education (ICISCAE), pp. 580–584. IEEE (2020)
17. Zhang, Y., Pezeshki, M., Brakel, P., et al.: Towards end-to-end speech recognition with deep convolutional neural networks. arXiv preprint arXiv:1701.02720 (2017)
18. He, K., Zhang, X., Ren, S., et al.: Deep residual learning for image recognition. In: Proceedings of the IEEE Conference on Computer Vision and Pattern Recognition, pp. 770–778 (2016)
19. Zhang, Y., Chan, W., Jaitly, N.: Very deep convolutional networks for end-to-end speech recognition. In: 2017 IEEE International Conference on Acoustics, Speech and Signal Processing (ICASSP), pp. 4845–4849. IEEE (2017)
20. Gulati, A., Qin, J., Chiu, C.C., et al.: Conformer: convolution-augmented transformer for speech recognition. arXiv preprint arXiv:2005.08100 (2020)

Binding Number and Fractional (k, m)-Covered Graph

Linli Zhu[1(✉)], Yu Pan[1], and Wei Gao[2]

[1] School of Computer Engineering, Jiangsu University of Technology, Changzhou 213001, China
zhulinli@jsut.edu.cn, ypan@jsut.edu.cn

[2] School of Information Science and Technology, Yunnan Normal University, Kunming 650500, China
gaowei@ynnu.edu.cn

Abstract. The stability of the network is an important factor considered during the network designing. Network engineers need to determine the structure of the network in advance and confirm that this structure has a certain degree of security. From the perspective of graph topology, the vulnerability of the corresponding network structure can be judged by calculating graph parameters. As an index to measure the stability of the network, the binding number is closely connected to the existence of the fractional factor. This article determines the binding number bounds for fractional (k, m)-covered graphs, and shows that this condition is the best. Then, we correct the counterexample which implies the sharpness of isolated toughness bound for the existence of fractional k-factor. Finally, the sun toughness conditions for a graph to be $(P_{\geq 2}, k)$- and $(P_{\geq 3}, k)$-factor critical covered are given, and we show that these sun toughness bounds are tight.

Keywords: Network · Binding number · Fractional factor · Fractional covered graph

1 Introduction

In the current era of highly developed internet, network security and personal privacy protection have become a hot topic in computer networks. After a network is built, only protection software upgrades and hardware upgrades and maintenance can be considered to ensure the security of the network. However, some networks are more likely to break defenses due to their own structural defects. For example, the star network has the advantage of being easy to control, but the disadvantage is obvious. Once the central vertex is breached, the entire network will be paralyzed. Therefore, network designers need to pay attention to the topology of the network in the design stage, and design a reasonable network structure to balance manufacturing costs and robustness.

Supported by organization x.

Y. Xu et al. (Eds.): ML4CS 2022, LNCS 13657, pp. 641–654, 2023.
https://doi.org/10.1007/978-3-031-20102-8_50

This article uses a graph structure to describe the network model, i.e., G is a graph consisting of a vertex set $V(G)$ to represent the stations and an edge set $E(G)$ to express the channels. Use $G[S]$ to express the subgraph induced by $S \subseteq V(G)$, and $G - S = G[V(G) \setminus S]$. For two disjoint vertex subsets S and T, we use $e_G(S,T)$ to denote the number of edges such that one end in S and another end in T. The distance $d_G(x,y)$ between two vertices x and y is the minimum length of paths between x and y in G. For graph G, G^p (here p is a positive integer) is denoted by

$$V(G^p) = V(G)$$

and

$$E(G^p) = \{xy|x, y \in V(G), d_G(x,y) \leq p\}.$$

All symbols and notations in the text use standard graph theory marks. For related content, please refer to [1]. In addition, this article only considers simple graphs, and does not consider the repeated edges and the direction of the edges in the network.

Binding number of graph G is denoted by $bind(G)$, introduced by Woodall [2]. It is a parameter with a long history and has attracted much attention from scholars in graph theory and computer science, which is formulated by

$$bind(G) = \min\left\{\frac{|N_G(X)|}{|X|} : \emptyset \neq X \subseteq V(G), N_G(X) \neq V(G)\right\}.$$

Let k be a positive integer and $h : E(G) \to [0,1]$. If $\sum_{x\sim e} h(e) = k$ holds for arbitrary $x \in V(G)$, then $G[F_h]$ is a fractional k-factor of G with indicator function h, where $F_h = \{e \in E(G)|h(e) > 0\}$. Yang and Kang [3] introduced the concept of fractional covered graph, i.e., a graph G is fractional covered if for any edge $e \in E(G)$, there is a fractional factor containing e. Li et al. [4] modified it as follows: a graph G is fractional covered if for any edge $e \in E(G)$, there is a fractional factor satisfying $h(e) = 1$. Liu [5] introduced the concept of fractional (g, f, m)-covered graph, i.e., a graph G is fractional (g, f, m)-covered if for each sub-graph H with m edges, there is a fractional (g, f)-factor with $h(e) = 1$ for any $e \in E(H)$. Here, fractional (g, f)-factor is an extension of fractional k-factors. Gao and Wang [6] determined the necessary and sufficient condition of a graph to be fractional (g, f, m)-covered. By setting $g(x) = f(x) = k$ for any $x \in V(G)$, we get the following lemma to characterize the fractional (g, f, m)-covered graphs.

Lemma 1. *Let G be a graph, $k \geq 2$ and $m \leq k$ be integers. Then G is a fractional (k,m)-covered graph if and only if for any $S \subseteq V(G)$,*

$$d_{G-S}(T) - k|T| + k|S| \geq \max_{H\subseteq G, |E(H)|=m} \{\sum_{x\in S} d_H(x) - e_H(T,S) + \Theta(S,T)\}, \quad (1)$$

where $T = \{x : x \in V(G) \setminus S, d_{G-S}(x) \leq k-1\}$ and

$$\Theta(S,T) = \sum_{1\leq d_{G\setminus E(H)-S}(x)-k+d_H(x)\leq e_H(x,S)-1, e_H(x,S)\geq 2} \{d_{G\setminus E(H)-S}(x)-k+d_H(x)\}.$$

This article considers the relationship between network stability parameters and the existence of fractional factors. The main contributions are manifested in the following.

Theorem 1. *Let $k \geq 2$ be an odd integer and $m \in \mathbb{N} \cup \{0\}$ with $2m \leq k+1$. Let G be a graph with n vertices such that $n > 4k+1-4\sqrt{k+1-2m}$. If*

$$bind(G) > \frac{(n-1)(2k-1)}{k(n-2)-2m+2},$$

then G is fractional (k, m)-covered.

Theorem 2. *Let $k \geq 2$ be an even integer and $m \in \mathbb{N} \cup \{0\}$ with $2m \leq k+2$. Let G be a graph with n vertices such that $n > 4k+1-4\sqrt{k+2-2m}$. If*

$$bind(G) > \frac{(n-1)(2k-1)}{k(n-2)-2m+3},$$

then G is fractional (k, m)-covered.

Obviously, both the arguments $2m \leq k+1$ in Theorem 1 and $2m \leq k+2$ in Theorem 2 imply $m \leq k$, and hence Lemma 1 can be used to prove the above two results.

2 Preliminary Results

The following lemmas are crucial to specific proof of Theorem 1 and Theorem 2.

Lemma 2. (Gao [7]) *Let a, b, c and m be integers such that $a \geq 2$, $2 \leq b \leq a-1$, $c \in \{0, 1, \cdots, 2m-1\}$ and $c \leq a$. Let t_1 and t_2 be non-negative integers. Assume that*

$$\frac{(a-b)t_2+c}{2a-b} \geq t_1 \tag{2}$$

and

$$\frac{(a-1)t_2+c}{2a-1}+1-b < t_1. \tag{3}$$

Then, $t_2 \leq 4a+1-4\sqrt{a-c}$.

Lemma 3. (Woodall [2]) *Let G be a graph with n vertices and $bind(G) > c$. Then $\delta(G) > n - \frac{n-1}{c}$.*

Suppose that graph G satisfies hypothesis of Theorem 1 and Theorem 2, but is not fractional (k, m)-covered. In terms of Lemma 1 and $\sum_{x \in S} d_H(x) - e_H(T, S) + \Theta(S, T) \leq 2m$, there exist $S \subseteq V(G)$ and $T = \{x : x \in V(G) \setminus S, d_{G-S}(x) \leq k-1\}$ such that

$$k|S| + \sum_{x \in T} d_{G-S}(x) - k|T| \leq 2m-1. \tag{4}$$

Clearly, $T \neq \emptyset$. Set

$$d_{min} = \min\{d_{G-S}(x) | x \in T\}.$$

The following lemmas describe the features of the counterexample.

Lemma 4. *For the counterexample G stated above, we have*

$$|S| \leq \frac{(k-d_{min})n+2m-1}{2k-d_{min}}.$$

Furthermore, if $k \equiv 0 (mod2)$, then

$$|S| \leq \frac{(k-d_{min})n+2m-2}{2k-d_{min}}.$$

Proof of Lemma 4. In terms of (4), we derive

$$k|S| + \sum_{x\in T}(d_{G-S}(x) - k) \leq 2m-1, \tag{5}$$

and

$$k|S| + (d_{min} - k)|T| \leq 2m-1. \tag{6}$$

According to $|T| \leq n - |S|$, (6) and the fact that $d_{G-S}(x) \leq k-1$ for all $x \in T$, we infer $|S| \leq \frac{(k-d_{min})n+2m-1}{2k-d_{min}}$.

Now, assume that $k \equiv 0(\text{mod}2)$. The following two subcases are divided according to the parity of d_{min}.

Case 1. $d_{min} \equiv 0(\text{mod}2)$.

In this circumstances, note that $k|S| + (d_{min} - k)|T| \equiv 0(\text{mod}2)$, and thus (6) becomes

$$k|S| + (d_{min} - k)|T| \leq 2m-2. \tag{7}$$

By means of $|T| \leq n - |S|$, (7) and the fact that $d_{G-S}(x) \leq k-1$ for all $x \in T$, we deduce $|S| \leq \frac{(k-d_{min})n+2m-2}{2k-d_{min}}$.

Case 2. $d_{min} \equiv 1(\text{mod}2)$.

In this situation, the following argument is separated into two cases in view of whether $V(G) - S - T$ is empty.

Case 2.1. $|V(G) - S - T| \geq 1$.

We obtain

$$|T| \leq n - |S| - 1. \tag{8}$$

Using (6), (8) and and the fact that $d_{G-S}(x) \leq k-1$ for all $x \in T$, we get $|S| \leq \frac{(k-d_{min})n+2m-2}{2k-d_{min}}$.

Case 2.2. $|V(G) - S - T| = 0$.

Case 2.2.1. There is vertex $x \in T$ satisfying $d_{G-S}(x) \geq d_{min} + 1$.

This assumption implies

$$\sum_{x\in T} d_{G-S}(x) \geq |T|d_{min} + 1. \tag{9}$$

In light of (5), (9), we yield $k|S| + (d_{min} - k)|T| \leq 2m-2$. Thus, using the same discussion as Case 1, we acquire $|S| \leq \frac{(k-d_{min})n+2m-2}{2k-d_{min}}$.

Case 2.2.2. All the vertices in T have degree d_{min} in $G - S$.

Hence, $d_T(x) = d_{min}$ for all $x \in T$. Since $d_{min} \equiv 1(\text{mod}2)$, we have $|T| \equiv 0(\text{mod}2)$ which reveals that $k|S| + (d_{min} - k)|T| \equiv 0(\text{mod}2)$. Using the same fashion as in Case 1, we get $|S| \leq \frac{(k-d_{min})n+2m-2}{2k-d_{min}}$. □

Lemma 5. $d_{min} \geq 1$.

Proof of Lemma 5. Note that $k \geq 2$. Suppose that $d_{min} = 0$ and set

$$\Omega = \{x \in T | d_{G-S} = 0\}.$$

Then, $|\Omega| \geq 1$ and $N_G(V(G) - S) \cap Z = \emptyset$. Thus, we determine

$$bind(G) \leq \frac{|N_G(V(G) - S)|}{|V(G) - S|} \leq \frac{n - |\Omega|}{n - |S|}.$$

In light of $\frac{(2k-1)(n-1)}{k(n-2)+2m-1} \leq \frac{n-|\Omega|}{n-|S|}$, we get

$$|S| + \frac{(n - |\Omega|)(k(n-2) + 2m - 1)}{(2k-1)(n-1)} \geq n. \tag{10}$$

Using (4), we verify

$$|S| \leq \frac{(k-1)n + |\Omega| + 2m - 1}{2k - 1}$$

which contradicts to (10). □

3 Proof of Main Theorems

The purpose here is to formally prove our main results.

3.1 Proof of Theorem 1

Suppose that k, m, G, n are defined as the hypothesis in Theorem 1. As the proof is followed by reduction to absurdity, we assume that G is not fractional (k, m)-covered, and S, T, d_{min} are defined as same as the last section. By means of $n > 4k + 1 - 4\sqrt{k + 1 - 2m}$ and $bind(G) > \frac{(n-1)(2k-1)}{k(n-2)-2m+2}$, we confirm that Lemma 4 and Lemma 5 are valid.

In terms of Lemma 4, we get

$$|S| \leq \frac{(k - d_{min})n + 2m - 1}{2k - d_{min}}. \tag{11}$$

Using Lemma 3, we obtain

$$\delta(G) > \frac{(k-1)n + 2m - 1}{2k - 1} + 1.$$

Combining with $\delta(G) \leq |S| + d_{min}$, we acquire

$$|S| > \frac{(k-1)n + 2m - 1}{2k - 1} + 1 - d_{min}. \tag{12}$$

According to Lemma 5 and the degree restricting in T, we deduce $1 \leq d_{min} \leq k-1$. If $d_{min} = 1$, then by means of (12), we obtain $|S| > \frac{(k-d_{min})n+2m-1}{2k-d_{min}}$, which contradicts to (11). Hence, we get $2 \leq d_{min} \leq k-1$. Using Lemma 2 with $a = k$, $b = d_{min}$, $c = 2m-1$, $t_1 = |S|$ and $t_2 = n$, we acquire $n \leq 4k+1-4\sqrt{k - 2m + 1}$, which conflicts to the hypothesis that $n > 4k + 1 - 4\sqrt{k - 2m + 1}$.

Therefore, Theorem 1 holds.

3.2 Proof of Theorem 2

Suppose that k, m, G, n are defined as the hypothesis in Theorem 2. As the proof is followed by reduction to absurdity, we assume that G is not fractional (k, m)-covered, and S, T, d_{min} are defined as same as the last section. By means of $n > 4k+1-4\sqrt{k+2-2m}$ and $bind(G) > \frac{(n-1)(2k-1)}{k(n-2)-2m+3}$, we confirm that Lemma 4 and Lemma 5 are valid.

In terms of Lemma 4, we get

$$|S| \leq \frac{(k-d_{min})n+2m-2}{2k-d_{min}}. \tag{13}$$

Using Lemma 3, we obtain

$$\delta(G) > \frac{(k-1)n+2m-2}{2k-1}+1.$$

Combining with $\delta(G) \leq |S| + d_{min}$, we acquire

$$|S| > \frac{(k-1)n+2m-2}{2k-1}+1-d_{min}. \tag{14}$$

According to Lemma 5 and the degree constraint of T, we deduce $1 \leq d_{min} \leq k-1$. If $d_{min}=1$, then by means of (14), we obtain $|S| > \frac{(k-d_{min})n+2m-2}{2k-d_{min}}$, which contradicts to (13). Hence, we get $2 \leq d_{min} \leq k-1$. Using Lemma 2 with $a=k$, $b=d_{min}$, $c=2m-2$, $t_1=|S|$ and $t_2=n$, we acquire $n \leq 4k+1-4\sqrt{k-2m+2}$, which contradicts to the hypothesis that $n > 4k+1-4\sqrt{k-2m+2}$.

In all, the proof of Theorem 2 is finished.

4 Sharpness

We first show that the vertex number n in Theorem 1 can't be reduced. Let p be a non-negative integer with $p \equiv 0 (\mathrm{mod} 2)$, $k = p^2+2m-1$ (large enough compared to m), and $n = 4p^2-4p+8m-3$. Consider

$$G = K_{2p^2-3p+4m-1} \vee C^{\frac{p}{2}}_{2p^2-p+4m-2},$$

then we verify

$$|V(G)| = n = 4k+1-4\sqrt{k-2m+1}$$

and

$$bind(G) = \frac{n-1}{n-(2p^2-3p+4m-1)-p} > \frac{(2k-1)(n-1)}{k(n-2)-2m+2}.$$

On the other hand, taking $S = V(K_{2p^2-3p+4m-1})$, then $T = V(C^{\frac{p}{2}}_{2p^2-p+4m-2})$. Clearly,

$$\max_{H \subseteq G, |E(H)|=m} \{\sum_{x \in S} d_H(x) - e_H(T,S) + \Theta(S,T)\} = 2m$$

and

$$\begin{aligned} &d_{G-S}(T) - k|T| + k|S| \\ &= p(2p^2 - p + 4m - 2) - k(2p^2 - p + 4m - 2) + k(2p^2 - 3p + 4m - 1) \\ &= 2m - 1 < 2m. \end{aligned}$$

Hence, G is not fractional (k, m)-covered, and the order of graph G in Theorem 1 is sharp.

For Theorem 2, we first show that the vertex number n can't be improved. Let p be a non-negative integer with $p \equiv 0(\text{mod}2)$, $k = p^2 + 2m - 2$ (large enough compared to m), and $n = 4p^2 - 4p + 8m - 7$. Consider

$$G = K_{2p^2-3p+4m-3} \vee C^{\frac{p}{2}}_{2p^2-p+4m-4},$$

then we verify

$$|V(G)| = n = 4k + 1 - 4\sqrt{k - 2m + 2}$$

and

$$bind(G) = \frac{n-1}{n - (2p^2 - 3p + 4m - 3) - p} > \frac{(2k-1)(n-1)}{k(n-2) - 2m + 3}.$$

On the other hand, taking $S = V(K_{2p^2-3p+4m-3})$, then $T = V(C^{\frac{p}{2}}_{2p^2-p+4m-4})$. Clearly,

$$\max_{H \subseteq G, |E(H)|=m} \{\sum_{x \in S} d_H(x) - e_H(T, S) + \Theta(S, T)\} = 2m$$

and

$$\begin{aligned} &d_{G-S}(T) - k|T| + k|S| \\ &= p(2p^2 - p + 4m - 4) - k(2p^2 - p + 4m - 4) + k(2p^2 - 3p + 4m - 3) \\ &= 2m - 2 < 2m. \end{aligned}$$

Hence, G is not fractional (k, m)-covered, and the order of G in Theorem 2 is sharp.

Next, we show that the binding number presented in Theorem 2 is best in some sense, i.e., $bind(G) > \frac{(n-1)(2k-1)}{k(n-2)-2m+3}$ can't be reduced by $bind(G) \geq \frac{(n-1)(2k-1)}{k(n-2)-2m+3}$. Let $k \geq 2$ and $0 \leq m \leq \frac{k+2}{2}$ be two integers such that $m \equiv 0(\text{mod}2)$ and $\frac{(k+1)m}{k} \equiv 0(\text{mod}2)$. Let $l = \frac{2k+m-2}{2}$ and $p = 2k - 4 + \frac{(k+1)m}{k}$. Thus, $n = p + 2l = 4k - 6 + \frac{(2k+1)m}{k}$. Consider $G = K_p \vee (lK_2)$. Then, we get

$$bind(G) = \frac{n-1}{2l-1} = \frac{n-1}{2k+m-3} = \frac{(2k-1)(n-1)}{k(n-2) - 2m + 3}.$$

Set $S = V(K_p)$, then $T = V(lK_2)$. We confirm that $|S| = p$, $|T| = 2l$ and

$$\max_{H \subseteq G, |E(H)|=m} \{\sum_{x \in S} d_H(x) - e_H(T, S) + \Theta(S, T)\} = 2m.$$

Therefore, we acquire

$$\begin{aligned} & d_{G-S}(T) - k|T| + k|S| \\ = & k|S| - k|T| + |T| = k|S| - (k-1)|T| \\ = & kp - 2(k-1)l \\ = & k(2k - 4 + \frac{(k+1)m}{k}) - (2k + m - 2)(k-1) \\ = & 2m - 2 < 2m. \end{aligned}$$

Therefore, G is not fractional (k, m)-covered, and the binding number in Theorem 2 is sharp.

5 Correct Counterexample in Ma and Liu [8]

The content of this section can be considered as a supplement to the main content of this paper. We point out that the counterexample given in Ma and Liu [8] for the optimal isolated toughness bound of fractional k-factor has loopholes, and thus revise this counterexample.

Beyond binding number, isolated toughness is another graph-based parameter to measure the vulnerability of the network. Let For a non-complete graph G, the isolated toughness of G is denoted by

$$I(G) = \min_{S \subset V(G), i(G-S) \geq 2} \left\{ \frac{|S|}{i(G-S)} \right\}$$

and $I(G) = +\infty$ if G is a complete graph, where $i(G-S)$ is the number of isolated vertices in $G - S$.

Ma and Liu [8] determined that a graph G has fractional k-factor if $\delta(G) \geq k$ and $I(G) \geq k$. Moreover, the authors proposed a counterexample to show that $I(G) \geq k$ can't be replaced by $I(G) \geq k - \varepsilon$, where ε is any positive real number. Their example is presented as follows. A graph G is obtained from K_{nk^2}, K_{k-1} and $(nk+1)K_1$, where

$$V(K_{nk^2}) = \{x_1, x_2, \cdots, x_{nk^2}\},$$

$$V((nk+1)K_1) = \{y_1, y_2, \cdots, y_{nk+1}\},$$

$$V(K_{k-1}) = \{z_1, z_2, \cdots, z_{k-1}\},$$

and n is a positive integer. Set

$$\begin{aligned} E(G) = & E(K_{nk^2}) \cup E(K_{k-1}) \cup \{\cup_{i=1}^{nk+1} x_i y_y\} \\ & \cup \{uv : u \in V(K_{k-1}), v \in V((nk+1)K_1)\}. \end{aligned}$$

Clearly, $\delta(G) \geq k$. Set $S = V(K_{k-1})$ and $T = V((nk+1)K_1)$, we have

$$k|S| - k|T| + \sum_{x \in T} d_{G-S}(x) < 0$$

which implies that G has no fractional k-factor. However, [8] stated that by setting $S = V(K_{nk^2}) \cup V(K_{k-1})$, it can be see that

$$I(G) = \frac{nk^2 + k - 1}{nk + 1} = k - \frac{1}{nk + 1} < k$$

and $\lim_{n \to +\infty} I(G) = k$, which explains the sharpness of isolated bound $\delta(G) \geq k$.

By analysing this counterexample, we found that the isolated toughness computation of G is not correct. In order to get $nk + 1$ isolated vertices, it is enough to delete $nk + 1$ vertices $x_1, x_2, \cdots, x_{nk+1}$ from $V(K_{nk^2})$. Hence, we yield

$$I(G) = \frac{(nk + 1) + (k - 1)}{nk + 1} = \frac{nk + k}{nk + 1}.$$

Therefore, this example can't explain the sharpness of isolated toughness condition $I(G) \geq k$.

Now, we show a correct counterexample which can reveal that $I(G) \geq k$ is tight. Consider $G = K_{n-1} \vee (nK_k)$ where $n \geq 2$ is a positive number, and we directly get

$$I(G) = \frac{(n - 1) + n(k - 1)}{n} = k - \frac{1}{n}$$

and $\lim_{n \to +\infty} I(G) = k$. On the other hand, set $S = V(K_{n-1})$ and $T = V(nK_k)$, we get

$$k|S| - k|T| + \sum_{x \in T} d_{G-S}(x) = k(n - 1) - nk = -k < 0,$$

where reveals that G has no fractional k-factor.

6 Sun Toughness and Path Factor Critical Covered Graphs

A graph R is factor-critical if any induced subgraph with order $|V(R)| - 1$ admitting a 1-factor. If H is K_1, or K_2 or the corona of a factor-critical graph R with $|V(R)| \geq 3$, then we call H as a sun, and the last case is called a big sun. Let $sun(G)$ be the number of sun components of G.

Zhou et al. [9] and Zhu et al. [10] introduced sun toughness $s(G)$ and $s'(G)$ which are stated as

$$s(G) = \min_{sun(G-S) \geq 2} \{\frac{|S|}{sun(G - S)}\}$$

and

$$s'(G) = \min_{sun(G-S) \geq 2} \{\frac{|S|}{sun(G - S) - 1}\}$$

respectively for non-complete graph. Moreover, $s(G) = s'(G) = +\infty$ if G is a complete graph.

A $P_{\geq n}$-factor covered graph was defined by Zhang and Zhou [11] which indicated that we can always find a $P_{\geq n}$-factor containing an arbitrary fixed edge e. So far, the existence rules for $P_{\geq n}$-factor covered graphs are determined in the special setting when $n \in \{2,3\}$.

Lemma 6. (Zhang and Zhou [11]) *Let G be a connected graph. Then G is $P_{\geq 2}$-factor covered if and only if $i(G-X) \leq 2|X| - \varepsilon_1$ for each $X \subseteq V(G)$, where*

$$\varepsilon_1 = \begin{cases} 2, & \text{if } X \text{ is not an independent set,} \\ 1, & X \text{ is independent and there exists a} \\ & \quad \text{nontrivial component of } G-X, \\ 0, & \text{otherwise,} \end{cases}$$

Lemma 7. (Zhang and Zhou [11]) *Assume G as a connected graph. Then G is $P_{\geq 3}$-factor covered if and only if $sun(G-X) \leq 2|X| - \varepsilon_2$ for each $X \subseteq V(G)$, where*

$$\varepsilon_2 = \begin{cases} 2, & \text{if } X \text{ is not an independent set,} \\ 1, & X \text{ is independent and there exists a} \\ & \quad \text{non-sun component of } G-X, \\ 0, & \text{otherwise,} \end{cases}$$

Furthermore, we call G is $(P_{\geq n}, k)$-factor critical covered if removing any k vertices from G, the obtained subgraph is $P_{\geq n}$-factor covered.

Theorem 3. *Let $k \in \mathbb{N} \cup \{0\}$ and G be a graph with $\kappa(G) \geq k+1$. If*

$$s(G) > \begin{cases} \frac{k+1}{2}, & \text{if } k \geq 1 \\ \frac{2}{3}, & \text{if } k = 0, \end{cases}$$

or $s'(G) > k+1$, then G is $(P_{\geq 2}, k)$-factor critical covered.

Proof. The theorem is clearly hold if G is a complete graph, and thus we consider the non-complete graph.

For arbitrary vertex subset U with k elements, let $G' = G - U$, and hence it is necessary to check G' is $P_{\geq 2}$-factor covered. Otherwise, suppose that G' is not $P_{\geq 2}$-factor covered, thus in view of Lemma 6, there is a $X \subseteq V(G')$ satisfying

$$i(G' - X) \geq 2|X| - \varepsilon_1 + 1. \tag{15}$$

If X is an empty set, then $\varepsilon_1 = 0$ and $i(G') \geq 1$ by means of (15), which contradicts to $\kappa(G) \geq k+1$. Hence, we infer that X is not empty. We consider three situations according to the value of ε_1.

Case 1. $\varepsilon_1 = 0$.

In this situation, we deduce $sun(G - U \cup X) \geq i(G' - X) \geq 2|X| + 1 \geq 3$. According to the definition of sun toughness, we get

$$\frac{k+1}{2} < s(G) \leq \frac{|X \cup U|}{sun(G - U \cup X)} \leq \frac{|X| + |U|}{i(G - U \cup X)}$$
$$\leq \frac{k + |X|}{2|X| + 1} = \frac{1}{2} + \frac{k - \frac{1}{2}}{2|X| + 1}.$$

If $k = 0$, then $\frac{2}{3} < s(G) \le \frac{1}{2} - \frac{1}{2(2|X|+1)} < \frac{1}{2}$, a contradiction. If $k \ge 1$, then

$$\frac{k+1}{2} < s(G) \le \frac{1}{2} + \frac{k-\frac{1}{2}}{2|X|+1} \le \frac{1}{2} + \frac{k-\frac{1}{2}}{2\times 1+1} = \frac{k+1}{3},$$

a contradiction.

For $s'(G)$, we obtain

$$k+1 < s'(G) \le \frac{|U \cup X|}{sun(G - U \cup X) - 1} \le \frac{|U| + |X|}{i(G - U \cup X) - 1}$$
$$\le \frac{k+|X|}{2|X|+1-1} = \frac{1}{2} + \frac{k}{2|X|} \le \frac{1}{2} + \frac{k}{2\times 1} = \frac{k+1}{2},$$

a contradiction.

Case 2. $\varepsilon_1 = 1$.

In this setting, we verify $sun(G - U \cup X) \ge i(G' - X) \ge 2|X| - \varepsilon_1 + 1 \ge 2$. According to the definition of sun toughness, we deduce

$$\frac{k+1}{2} < s(G) \le \frac{|U \cup X|}{sun(G - U \cup X)} \le \frac{|U| + |X|}{i(G - U \cup X)}$$
$$\le \frac{k+|X|}{2|X|} = \frac{1}{2} + \frac{k}{2|X|} \le \frac{1}{2} + \frac{k}{2\times 1} = \frac{k+1}{2}$$

or

$$k+1 < s'(G) \le \frac{|X \cup U|}{sun(G - X \cup U) - 1} \le \frac{|X| + |U|}{i(G - X \cup U) - 1}$$
$$\le \frac{k+|X|}{2|X|-1} = \frac{1}{2} + \frac{k+\frac{1}{2}}{2|X|-1} \le \frac{1}{2} + \frac{k+\frac{1}{2}}{2\times 1-1} = k+1,$$

a contradiction.

Case 3. $\varepsilon_1 = 2$.

We obtain that X is not an independent set (i.e., $|X| \ge 2$) and hence $sun(G - U \cup X) \ge i(G' - X) \ge 2|X| - \varepsilon_1 + 1 \ge 3$. In light of the definition of sun toughness, we get

$$\frac{k+1}{2} < s(G) \le \frac{|X \cup U|}{sun(G - X \cup U)} \le \frac{|X| + |U|}{i(G - U \cup X)}$$
$$\le \frac{k+|X|}{2|X|-1} = \frac{1}{2} + \frac{k+\frac{1}{2}}{2|X|-1} \le \frac{1}{2} + \frac{k+\frac{1}{2}}{2\times 2-1} = \frac{k+2}{3}$$

or

$$k+1 < s'(G) \le \frac{|U \cup X|}{sun(G - U \cup X) - 1} \le \frac{|U| + |X|}{i(G - U \cup X) - 1}$$
$$\le \frac{k+|X|}{2|X|-1-1} = \frac{1}{2} + \frac{k+1}{2|X|-2} \le \frac{1}{2} + \frac{k+1}{2\times 2-2} = \frac{k+2}{2},$$

a contradiction (in particular, when $k = 0$, we have $\frac{2}{3} < s(G) \le \frac{2}{3}$).

From what we discussed above, we conclude the result. □

Theorem 4. *Let $k \in \mathbb{N}$ and G be a graph with $|V(G)| \geq k+3$ and $\kappa(G) \geq k+1$. If $s(G) > \frac{k+1}{2}$ or $s'(G) > k+1$, then G is $(P_{\geq 3}, k)$-factor critical covered.*

Proof. The conclusion is obviously established if G is completed, and hence we discuss the non-complete graph.

For any vertex subset U with k vertices, let $G' = G - U$, and we need to prove that G' is $P_{\geq 3}$-factor covered. Otherwise, suppose that G' is not $P_{\geq 3}$-factor covered, hence in terms of Lemma 7, there exists a $X \subseteq V(G')$ satisfying

$$sun(G' - X) \geq 2|X| - \varepsilon_2 + 1. \tag{16}$$

If X is an empty set, then $\varepsilon_2 = 0$ and $sun(G') \geq 1$ by means of (16). Moreover, we confirm that G' is a big sun since $|V(G)| \geq k+3$ and $\kappa(G) \geq k+1$. Let R be the factor-critical of G' and $x \in V(R)$. Therefore, $|V(R)| \geq 3$ and

$$\begin{aligned} \frac{k+1}{2} < s(G) &\leq \frac{|U \cup (V(R) - \{x\})|}{sun(G - U - (V(R) - \{x\}))} = \frac{k + |V(R)| - 1}{|V(R)|} \\ &= \frac{k-1}{|V(R)|} + 1 \leq \frac{k-1}{3} + 1 = \frac{k+2}{3} \end{aligned}$$

or

$$\begin{aligned} k+1 < s'(G) &\leq \frac{|U \cup (V(R) - \{x\})|}{sun(G - U - (V(R) - \{x\})) - 1} = \frac{k + |V(R)| - 1}{|V(R)| - 1} \\ &= \frac{k}{|V(R)| - 1} + 1 \leq \frac{k}{2} + 1 = \frac{k+2}{2}, \end{aligned}$$

a contradiction. Thus, $|X| \geq 1$ and we discuss the following three cases by means of different values of ε_2.

Case 1. $\varepsilon_2 = 0$.

We yield $sun(G' - X) \geq 2|X| + 1 \geq 3$. According to the definition of sun toughness, we get

$$\begin{aligned} \frac{k+1}{2} < s(G) &\leq \frac{|U \cup X|}{sun(G - U \cup X)} \leq \frac{k + |X|}{2|X| + 1} \\ &= \frac{1}{2} + \frac{k - \frac{1}{2}}{2|X| + 1} \leq \frac{1}{2} + \frac{k - \frac{1}{2}}{2 \times 1 + 1} = \frac{k+1}{3} \end{aligned}$$

or

$$\begin{aligned} k+1 < s'(G) &\leq \frac{|U \cup X|}{sun(G - U \cup X) - 1} \leq \frac{k + |X|}{2|X| + 1 - 1} \\ &= \frac{1}{2} + \frac{k}{2|X|} \leq \frac{1}{2} + \frac{k}{2 \times 1} = \frac{k+1}{2}, \end{aligned}$$

a contradiction.

Case 2. $\varepsilon_2 = 1$.

We acquire $sun(G' - X) \geq 2|X| - \varepsilon_2 + 1 \geq 2$. Using the definition of sun toughness, we obtain

$$\frac{k+1}{2} < s(G) \leq \frac{|U \cup X|}{sun(G - U \cup X)} \leq \frac{k+|X|}{2|X|}$$
$$= \frac{1}{2} + \frac{k}{2|X|} \leq \frac{1}{2} + \frac{k}{2 \times 1} = \frac{k+1}{2}$$

or

$$k+1 < s'(G) \leq \frac{|U \cup X|}{sun(G - U \cup X) - 1} \leq \frac{k+|X|}{2|X|-1}$$
$$= \frac{1}{2} + \frac{k+\frac{1}{2}}{2|X|-1} \leq \frac{1}{2} + \frac{k+\frac{1}{2}}{2 \times 1 - 1} = k+1,$$

a contradiction.

Case 3. $\varepsilon_2 = 2$.

By the definition of ε_2, X is not an independent set and hence $sun(G' - X) \geq 2|X| - \varepsilon_2 + 1 \geq 3$. In light of the definition of sun toughness, we infer

$$\frac{k+1}{2} < s(G) \leq \frac{|X \cup U|}{sun(G - X \cup U)} \leq \frac{k+|X|}{2|X|-1}$$
$$= \frac{1}{2} + \frac{k+\frac{1}{2}}{2|X|-1} \leq \frac{1}{2} + \frac{k+\frac{1}{2}}{2 \times 2 - 1} = \frac{k+2}{3}$$

or

$$k+1 < s'(G) \leq \frac{|U \cup X|}{sun(G - U \cup X) - 1} \leq \frac{k+|X|}{2|X|-1-1}$$
$$= \frac{1}{2} + \frac{k+1}{2|X|-2} \leq \frac{1}{2} + \frac{k+1}{2 \times 2 - 2} = \frac{k+2}{2},$$

a contradiction.

In all, we finish the proof of Theorem 4. □

Note that $k = 0$ is not involved in Theorem 4. In fact, for the special setting of $k = 0$, Zhou et al. [9] determined that a connected graph with $|V(G)| \geq 3$ is P_3-factor covered if $s(G) \geq 1$, and also they verify that this bound is tight.

Next, we show that the sun toughness bounds in Theorem 3 and Theorem 4 are tight for $(P_{\geq 2}, k)$- and $(P_{\geq 3}, k)$-factor critical covered graphs. Let $G = K_{k+1} \vee (2K_1 \cup K_p)$ where p is a large integer number. We get $\kappa(G) = k+1$, $s(G) = \frac{k+1}{2}$ and $s'(G) = k+1$. Set G' as a sub-graph of G' which is given by removing k vertices from K_{k+1}, and X as a remaining vertex in G' which originally belongs to K_{k+1} in G. We get $\varepsilon_1 = \varepsilon_2 = 1$, $i(G' - X) = 2 > 1 = 2|X| - \varepsilon_1$ and $sun(G' - X) = 2 > 1 = 2|X| - \varepsilon_2$. By Lemma 6 and Lemma 7, G' is neither $P_{\geq 2}$-factor covered nor $P_{\geq 3}$-factor covered, and hence G is not $(P_{\geq 2}, k)$-factor critical covered and $(P_{\geq 3}, k)$-factor critical covered.

Finally, for a very special case, we show that $s(G) > \frac{2}{3}$ in Theorem 3 it sharp for a graph G to be $P_{\geq}$-factor covered. Considering $G = K_2 \vee (3K_1 \cup K_p)$ where

p is a large integer number. Obviously, $\kappa(G) = 2$ and $s(G) = \frac{2}{3}$. Let $S = V(K_2)$, and then we have $|S| = 2$, $\varepsilon_1 = 2$ and $i(G' - X) = 3 > 2 = 2|X| - \varepsilon_1$. In terms of Lemma 6, G is not $P_{\geq 2}$-factor covered.

7 Conclusion

The following questions can be used as topics for the research to continue.

- The conclusion obtained in this paper depends on the hypothesis that m is small enough. This assumption comes from the necessary and sufficient conditions presented in Gao and Wang [6] such that it is necessary to ensure $m \leq k$. However, in the Theorem 1 and Theorem 2, the corresponding constricts state that $m \leq \frac{k+1}{2}$ and $m \leq \frac{k+2}{2}$ respectively. Hence, there is still a gap that $\frac{k+1}{2} < m \leq k$ and $\frac{k+2}{2} < m \leq k$ should be considered in the future.
- In the specific network design stage, we need to achieve a balance between the satisfaction of the binding number condition and the reduction of the cost of network manufacturing. The specific design algorithm needs to be further studied.

References

1. Bondy, J.A., Murty, U.S.R.: Graph Theory. Springer, Berlin (2008)
2. Woodall, D.: The binding number of a graph and its Anderson number. J. Combin. Theory Ser. B **15**, 225–255 (1973)
3. Yang, J., Kang, W.: Fractional (g, f)-factor covered graph and deleted graph. In: Proceedings of the 6th Academic Exchange Conference of China Operations Research Society, pp. 450–454 (2000)
4. Li, Z., Yan, G., Zhang, X.: On fractional (g, f)-covered graphs. OR Trans. (China) **6**(4), 65–68 (2002)
5. Liu, S.: On fractional (g, f, m)-covered graphs. In: 2011 International Conference on Computers, Communications, Control and Automation (CCCA), pp. 246–248 (2011)
6. Gao, W., Wang, W.: On fractional (g, f, n', m)-critical covered graphs. J. Oper. Res. Soc. China (2022)
7. Gao, W.: Binding number of fractional (k, m)-deleted graphs for small m. J. Soochow Univ. (Nat. Sci. Ed.) **28**(1), 1–6 (2012)
8. Ma, Y., Liu, G.: Fractional factors and isolated toughness of graphs. Math. Appl. **19**(1), 188–194 (2006)
9. Zhou, S., Sun, Z., Liu, H.: Sun touthness and $P_{\geq 3}$-factors in graphs. Contrib. Discr. Math. **14**(1), 167–174 (2019)
10. Zhu, L., Baskonus, H.M., Gao, W.: A variant of sun toughness and the existence of path factors in networks. In: Chen, X., Yan, H., Yan, Q., Zhang, X. (eds.) ML4CS 2020. LNCS, vol. 12487, pp. 12–19. Springer, Cham (2020). https://doi.org/10.1007/978-3-030-62460-6_2
11. Zhang, H., Zhou, S.: Characterizations for $P_{\geq 2}$-factor and $P_{\geq 3}$-factor covered graphs. Discr. Math. **309**, 2067–2076 (2009)

Domination Based Federated Learning Algorithm

Yikuan Chen(✉), Liang Li, and Wei Gao

School of Information Science and Technology, Yunnan Normal University, Kunming 650500, China
342249994@qq.com, {liangli,gaowei}@ynnu.edu.cn

Abstract. Traditional centralized federated learning has only one server, which causes other clients to send their models to the server in order to participate in federated learning, no matter how far away they are. In this article, we design a novel domination based federated learning algorithm in terms of graph theory, where clients only need to send the model to the nearest neighbor. We give the execution steps of the specific algorithm.

Keywords: Federated learning · Domination · Decentralized model

1 Introduction

With the increase in the amount of data processing and the development of network technology, sharing data resources has become the mainstream. However, various companies and users are unwilling to disclose their data due to certain considerations, which finally leads to the emergence of data islands. In this context, federated learning was introduced. As a paradigm of distributed learning, it has received widespread attention in recent years (Fallah et al. [1], Ghosh et al. [2], Lam et al. [3], Collins et al. [4]).

The traditional federated learning model is centralized, which is composed of n clients and a server, and the corresponding graph structure is $K_{1,n}$ (see Fig. 1(a)). Specifically, after each client's update, the algorithm randomly selects the participating clients in this round according to a given fractional rate. The selected clients send the updated local models to the server, and the server sends the global model back to the designated clients after aggregation. Thus, after T iterations, the final global model is obtained.

The opposite of the centralized model is decentralized federated learning, for instance, cross-silo federated learning was introduced recently by Marfoq et al. [6]. In decentralized federated learning setting, the corresponding graph structure has no restrictions normally (see Fig. 1(b)), and the graph setting (undirected graph, directed graph, weighted graph, and fuzzy graph, ect) can be changed in light of the specific needs of the application.

Y. Xu et al. (Eds.): ML4CS 2022, LNCS 13657, pp. 655–662, 2023.
https://doi.org/10.1007/978-3-031-20102-8_51

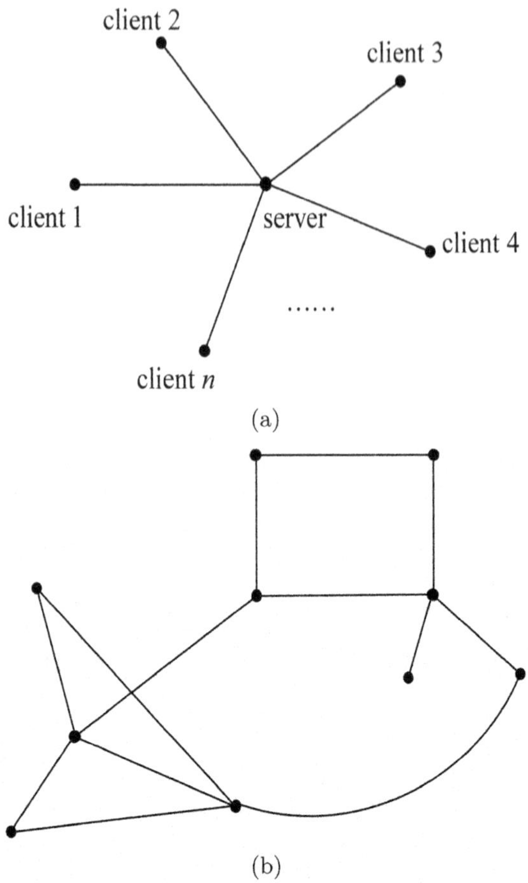

Fig. 1. Graph structure for centralized and decentralized federated learning.

In the actual application of the network, physical distance is a crucial factor to be considered. If the server is very far away from the client, it will lead to a long transmission time, which in turn affects the aggregation time. On the other hand, the transmission of models or encrypted data through multiple client vertices will increase the risk of leakage and bring security risks to the entire network. It always hopes that the server is very close to each client, while it turns out that the star network is the most vulnerable one. Under this background, decentralized models are becoming more and more popular. For example, in edge computing setting, the driver of each car always sends and receives information to the base station closest to him, and as the situation of the car changes, the base station that sends and receives information has to change again.

In this work, we raise a novel domination based federated learning which divides the vertex set of learning network into several dominating groups. In this way, the aggregation is executed in their neighborhood vertices. We give detailed processing tricks, as well as the complete execution steps of the entire algorithm.

2 Literature Review

Federated learning has received extensive attention and research both in theory and application, and has become a hot topic in distributed learning research in recent years. Hu et al. [5] proposed a privacy-preserving trick for learning effective personalized models on distributed user data while guaranteeing the differential privacy of user data. Kim et al. [8] introduced a blockchained federated learning formulation where local learning model updates are exchanged and verified. Zhu and Jin [7] optimized the neural network framewrok in federated learning in terms of a multi-objective evolutionary algorithm to simultaneously minimize the communication costs and the global model test errors. Nguyen et al. [9] raised a fast-convergent federated learning algorithm named FOLB and theoretically characterized a lower bound on its improvement. Amiri et al. [10] studied a global aggregation model for wireless edge devices with their own dataset.

Recent contributions in theoretical analysis of federated learning concern distinct angles. Hanzely et al. [15] proposed a lower bound on the communication complexity of personalized federated learning. Avdyukhin and Kasiviswanathan [16] showed that for smooth strongly convex and smooth nonconvex functions, asynchronous local SGD federated learning achieve convergence rates that match the synchronous setting which needs all clients to communicate simultaneously.

3 Setting

In this section, we manifest some basic concepts and notations which will be used in the next section.

3.1 Preliminary in Graph Theory

Let $G = (V, E)$ be a graph with vertex set V and edge set E. For $v \in V$, let $\mathcal{N}(v)$ be the open neighborhood of v and $d(v) = |\mathcal{N}(v)|$ be the degree of v. $D \subseteq V$ is a dominating set if for any vertex $v \in V - D$, there is a $y \in D$ such that $xy \in E$. Accordingly, the domination number of G is denoted by $\gamma(G)$ which is the minimum cardinality of all dominating sets of G, and the dominating set with cardinality $\gamma(G)$ is called the minimum dominating set. Usually, the minimum dominating set may not be unique, and any dominating set with minimum cardinality is minimum dominating set (for some recent contribution in this topic please see Kurita et al. [11], Galby et al. [12], Li et al. [13], and Oh [14]). For graphs with different settings, domination number and dominating set have different definitions:

- In directed graph setting, let $\mathcal{N}^-(v)$ and $\mathcal{N}^+(v)$ be the out-neighbourhood and in-neighbourhood of vertex v. $D \subseteq V$ is a dominating set if for any vertex $v \in V - D$, there is a $y \in D$ such that $x \in \mathcal{N}^+(y)$. Accordingly, the domination number of directed graph is the minimum cardinality of all dominating sets, and the minimum dominating set is a dominating set with minimum cardinality.

- In fuzzy graph setting, the minimum dominating set refers to the vertex subset which controls the all vertices via valid edges with minimum cumulative sum of edge membership function values (Gong et al. [17]).

3.2 Decentralized Federated Learning Framework

Let N be the number of clients in the whole federated learning network, l_i be the loss function of model in client i at sample ξ. The standard decentralized federated learning model can be formulated by

$$w_i^{t+1} = \begin{cases} \sum_{j \in \mathcal{N}_i^+ \cup \{i\}} \mathbf{A}_{i,j} w_j^t, & \text{if } t \equiv 0 (mod \tau) \\ w_i^t - \eta_i \frac{1}{k} \sum_{h=1}^{k} \nabla l_i(w_i^t, \xi_{i,h}^t), & \text{otherwise} \end{cases} \tag{1}$$

where k is the batch size, η_i is a step size, $\mathbf{A} \in \mathbb{R}^{N \times N}$ is a non-negative participate weight matrix, and τ is a parameter which determines how long the aggregation implement needs. The essence of this model assigns each vertex to the action of the server, which can aggregate the models from the vertices in the neighborhood, and does not need to send the aggregated model to the client like a centralized one.

4 Main Algorithm Description

If a vertex belongs to a final selected dominating set, then we call it a dominating vertex, and otherwise a non-dominating vertex. A non-dominating vertex associated with multiple dominating vertices is called a hesitate vertex (see Fig. 2). We call the client corresponding to dominating vertex, non-dominating vertex and hesitate vertex are dominating client, non-dominating client and hesitate client, respectively. For a hesitate client i, denote $\mathcal{N}_D(i) = \{j \in \mathcal{N}(i) \cap D\}$ as the dominating neighborhood of i, and hence $|\mathcal{N}_D(i)| \geq 2$. For a dominating client i, let $\mathcal{N}_h(i)$ be neighborhood of i consisting by hesitate vertices, and its neighborhood can be divided into two parts, i.e., $\mathcal{N}_1(i) = \{j | j \in \mathcal{N}(i) \cap D\}$, $\mathcal{N}_2(i) = \{j | j \in \mathcal{N}(i) - D - \mathcal{N}_h(i)\}$ and $\mathcal{N}_3(i) = \mathcal{N}(i) - \mathcal{N}_1(i) - \mathcal{N}_1(2)$ (neighborhood consists of hesitation vertices). Assume that each dominating vertex and its associated non-dominating vertices form a dominating group, so the number of dominating groups in the entire graph is exactly the cardinality of the dominating set. The first iteration step (i.e., function FIRSTROUND) says that after the dominating set is selected, for a hesitate vertex select a dominating group with the lowest degree of data heterogeneity, and start from the next iteration round (main algorithm), only aggregation with the selected dominating vertex in the fixed dominating group.

Domination based federated learning algorithm is presented in the following.

Algorithm 1. Domination based federated learning algorithm

Input: network graph G for federated learning with N vertices, T, η_i, w_i^0 $(1 \le i \le n)$, τ, k
Output: w_i^T for all clients i

D=Domination(G)
FIRSTROUND(G, D, η_i, w_i^0 $(1 \le i \le n)$, τ)
for $t = 0 \rightarrow T-1$ **do**
    for $r = 0 \rightarrow \tau - 1$ **do**
        $w_i^{t,r+1} \leftarrow w_i^{t,r} - \eta_i \frac{1}{k} \sum_{h=1}^{k} \nabla l_i(w_i^{t,r}, \xi_{i,h}^{t,r})$
    end for
    for i is a dominating client, in parallel **do**
        $w_i^{t+1} = \sum_{j \in \mathcal{N}_{exe}(i)} \mathbf{A}_{i,j} w_i^{t,\tau}$
        send w_i^{t+1} to neighborhood $\mathcal{N}_{exe}(i)$
    end for
end for

function DOMINATION(G)
    return a dominating set D with minimum cardinality of vertex number
end function

function FIRSTROUND(G, D, η_i, w_i^0 $(1 \le i \le n)$, τ,k (bitch number))
    $D = Domination(G)$
    for $i = 1 \rightarrow N$ in parallel **do**
        $t = 0$;
        while $t < \tau$ **do**
            $w_i^t - \eta_i \frac{1}{k} \sum_{h=1}^{k} \nabla l_i(w_i^t, \xi_{i,h}^t)$
        end while
    end for
    if i is a hesitate client **then**
        $x_i^{t+1} \leftarrow w_i^{t+1}$
    end if
    for $i \in D$ in parallel **do**
        $w_i^{t+1} = \sum_{j \in \mathcal{N}_2(i) \cup \mathcal{N}_3(i)} \mathbf{A}_{i,j} w_j^{t+1}$
        Dominating vertex i send w_i^{t+1} to non-dominating clients which associated to i
    end for
    if i is a non-dominating client **then**
        if i is a hesitate client **then**
            $j_{i*} = \arg\min_{j \in \mathcal{N}_D(i)} \|x_i^{t+1} - w_j^{t+1}\|$
            $w_i^{t+1} \leftarrow w_{j_{i*}}^{t+1}$
            update the local model using the newest w_i^{t+1} which is got from last step
            for $j \in \mathcal{N}_D(i)$ in parallel **do**
                $y(j_i) = \begin{cases} 1, \text{ if } j_i = j_{i*} \\ 0, \text{ otherwise} \end{cases}$
            end for
        else
            directly update the local model as w_i^{t+1} (which is send by dominting vertex)
        end if
    end if
    for i is a dominating client **do**
        $\mathcal{N}_{exe}(i) = \mathcal{N}_2(i) \cup \{j | y(j_i) = 1\}$
    end for
    for $i = 1 \rightarrow N$ **do**
        $w_i^0 \leftarrow w_i^{t+1}$
    end for
    return the updated w_i^0 for all clients i, and $\mathcal{N}_{exe}(i)$ if i is a dominating client
end function

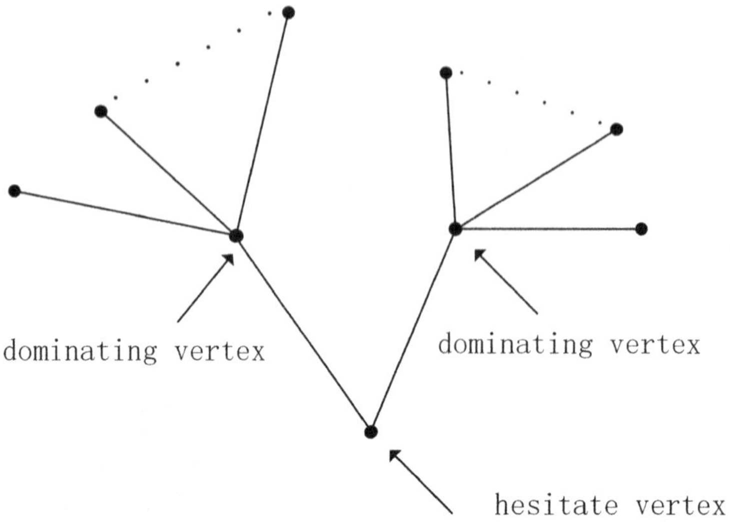

Fig. 2. A hesitate vertex.

For the above given domination based federated learning algorithm, the following explanations are supplemented.

(1) Even if the two dominating vertices are connected, there will be no aggregation each other.
(2) The client needs to receive and send information to the dominating vertex, so the corresponding graph model is an undirected graph. The setting of the directed graph in the traditional decentralized federated learning is not suitable for this calculation framework.
(3) Unlike vertex weight graph and fuzzy graph (where each vertex has a membership function value in interval [0,1]), the selection of the dominating set of the federated learning network graph in this algorithm follows from the traditional principle with the minimum number of vertices. Intuitively, under the framework of federated learning, vertices with small degrees of heterogeneity should be selected to be aggregated with each other. That is, the selection rule of the dominating set should be to find a set that minimizes the integration of the heterogeneity of each dominating group, but in fact this is not feasible. Imagine that if we choose a set of dominating vertices with a large number of vertices, then the maximum degree of each dominating group can be small, resulting in not enough vertices to aggregate. In the case of forcing clients who connect multiple dominating vertices to only select one dominating vertex for aggregation, it may happen that some dominating clients become data islands.

For instance, see Fig. 3, if the dominating set is selected as $\{v_1, \cdots, v_n, u_1, u_m\}$, where v is aggregation with v_1, u is aggregation with u_1, then

$v_2, \cdot, v_n, u_2, \cdots, u_m$ become data islands, i.e., no client sharing dominating global model with them.

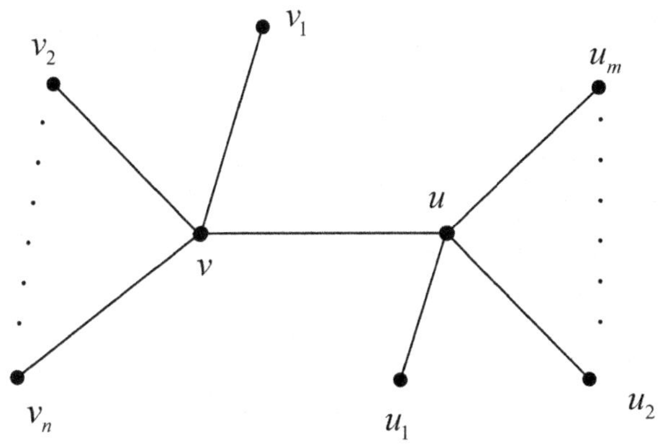

Fig. 3. A dominating set with vertices have small degrees.

5 Conclusion

In our article, we propose a new federated learning algorithm to avoid the far distance data transform and aggregation the model from neighborhood, and this trick from the domination in graph theory. Domination based federated learning is regarded as an algorithm between centralization and decentralization federated learning. It regards the selected dominating vertex as a local server, replacing the function of a single server in the classic federated learning, and distributing the updated dominating global model to the nearest clients by means of aggregation of its neighborhood in the same dominating group.

Acknowledgments. The authors thank the reviewers for their constructive comments in improving the quality of this paper. The research is partially supported by NSFC (no. 11761083).

Conflict of Interests. The authors declare that there is no conflict of interests regarding the publication of this paper.

References

1. Fallah, A., Mokhtari, A., Ozdaglar, A.: Personalized federated learning with theoretical guarantees: a model-agnostic meta-learning approach. In: 34th Conference on Neural Information Processing Systems (NeurIPS 2020), Vancouver, Canada (2020)
2. Ghosh, A., Chung, J., Yin, D., Ramchandran, K.: An efficient framework for clustered federated learning. In: 34th Conference on Neural Information Processing Systems (NeurIPS 2020), Vancouver, Canada (2020)

3. Lam, M., Wei, G., Brooks, D., Reddi, V.J., Mitzenmacher, M.: Gradient disaggregation breaking privacy in federated learning by reconstructing the user participant matrix. In: Proceedings of the 38th International Conference on Machine Learning, PMLR, vol. 139 (2021)
4. Collins, L., Hassani, H., Mokhtari, A., Shakkottai, S.: Exploiting shared representations for personalized federated learning. In: Proceedings of the 38th International Conference on Machine Learning, PMLR, vol. 139 (2021)
5. Hu, R., Guo, Y.X., Li, H.N., Pei, Q.Q., Gong, Y.M.: Personalized federated learning with differential privacy. IEEE Internet Things J. **7**(10), 9530–9539 (2020)
6. Marfoq, O., Xu, C., Neglia, G., Vidal, R.: Throughput-optimal topology design for cross-silo federated learning. In: 34th Conference on Neural Information Processing Systems (NeurIPS 2020), Vancouver, Canada (2020)
7. Zhu, H.Y., Jin, Y.C.: Multi-objective evolutionary federated learning. IEEE Trans. Neural Netw. Learn. Syst. **31**(4), 1310–1322 (2020)
8. Kim, H., Park, J., Bennis, M., Kim, S.L.: Blockchained on-device federated learning. IEEE Commun. Lett. **24**(6), 1279–1283 (2020)
9. Nguyen, H.T., Sehwag, V., Hosseinalipour, S., Brinton, C.G., Chiang, C.G., Poor, H.V.: Fast-convergent federated learning. IEEE J. Sel. Areas Commun. **39**(1), 201–218 (2021)
10. Amiri, M.M., Duman, T.M., Gunduz, D., Kulkarni, S.R., Poor, H.V.: Blind federated edge learning. IEEE Trans. Wirel. Commun. **20**(8), 5129–5143 (2021)
11. Kurita, K., Wasa, K., Arimura, H., Uno, T.: Efficient enumeration of dominating sets for sparse graphs. Discret. Appl. Math. **303**, 283–295 (2021)
12. Galby, E., Mann, F., Ries, B.: Blocking total dominating sets via edge contractions. Theoret. Comput. Sci. **877**, 18–35 (2021)
13. Li, R.Z., Wang, Y.P., Liu, H., Li, R.T., Hu, S.L., Yin, M.H.: A restart local search algorithm with Tabu method for the minimum weighted connected dominating set problem. J. Oper. Res. Soc. **73**, 2092–3103 (2021). https://doi.org/10.1080/01605682.2021.1952117
14. Oh, S.: Number of dominating sets in cylindric square grid graphs. Graphs Comb. **37**(4), 1357–1372 (2021)
15. Hanzely, F., Hanzely, S., Horváth, S., Richtárik, P.: Lower bounds and optimal algorithms for personalized federated learning. 34th Conference on Neural Information Processing Systems (NeurIPS 2020), Vancouver, Canada
16. Avdyukhin, D., Kasiviswanathan, S.P.: Federated learning under arbitrary communication patterns. In: Proceedings of the 38th International Conference on Machine Learning, PMLR 139 (2021)
17. Gong, S., Hua, G., Gao, W.: Domination of bipolar fuzzy graphs in various settings. Int. J. Comput. Intell. Syst. **14**(1), 1–14 (2021). https://doi.org/10.1007/s44196-021-00011-2

Structured Representation of Fuzzy Data by Bipolar Fuzzy Hypergraphs

Juanjuan Lu[1](✉), Linli Zhu[2], and Wei Gao[3]

[1] School of Chemical and Environmental Engineering, Jiangsu University of Technology, Changzhou 213001, China
ljj@jsut.edu.cn

[2] School of Computer Engineering, Jiangsu University of Technology, Changzhou 213001, China
zhulinli@jsut.edu.cn

[3] School of Information Science and Technology, Yunnan Normal University, Kunming 650500, China
gaowei@ynnu.edu.cn

Abstract. The main aim of the graph model is to implement the structured representation of data, and the hypergraph can be regarded as a promotion of graph which is used in a wider range of data representation scenarios. Bipolar fuzzy sets are employed to describe the uncertainty of the positive and negative of objectives, and fuzzy graphs are modelled to structure the description of uncertain data. In this work, for bipolar Pythagorean fuzzy set (BPFS) and bipolar intuitionistic fuzzy set (BIFS), the corresponding definitions of bipolar Pythagorean fuzzy hypergraph (BPFH) and bipolar intuitionistic fuzzy hypergraph (BIFH) are given, and they are described from the perspective of set theory. The characteristics under the bipolar hypergraph framework of this representation are discussed.

Keywords: Hypergraph · Fuzzy data · Data structured representation · Bipolar fuzzy set · Pythagorean fuzzy set · Intuitionistic fuzzy set · Bipolar Pythagorean fuzzy hypergraph · Bipolar intuitionistic fuzzy hypergraph

1 Introduction

As a tool for the structured representation of data, graphs are used in various fields of computer science. Therefore, the theory of graph representation of data has also become a hot topic for scholars. Hypergraph is a kind of generalization of graphs, used to represent the interrelationship between multiple data, and has a wide potential applications in various circumstances such as databases (several advances in hypergraph data representation can be referred to [1–4]).

Fuzzy data is used to describe the uncertainty of objective in light of the membership function, while the fuzzy graph is used to structure the fuzzy data. The vertex membership function (MF) is used to describe the uncertainty of the data itself, and the edge

Supported by Natural Science Foundation of Jiangsu Province, China (BK20191032) and University Philosophy and Social Science research projects of Jiangsu Province (2020SJA1195).

Y. Xu et al. (Eds.): ML4CS 2022, LNCS 13657, pp. 663–676, 2023.
https://doi.org/10.1007/978-3-031-20102-8_52

membership function is applied to describe the uncertainty of meta-relationship between the fuzzy data (see [5–7] for more details).

Although there have been some results on the hypergraph representation of fuzzy data, the fuzzy hypergraph theory is still open in most settings. This motivates us to do in-depth research on the structured representation of fuzzy data hypergraphs under a special framework. This article mainly studies BPFHs and BIFHs, and gives their definitions and some results in representation theory. The frame structure of this article is stated as follows: First, the existing definitions of BPFSs and BIFSs are introduced. Then, we extend them to the corresponding hypergraph models and present the framework in this setting.

2 Background

In the graph representation of fuzzy information, each vertex represents a record (or concept, or a piece) of information data. If there is a direct connection between two pieces of information, an edge is connected between the two vertices. The MF of the vertex is used to express the uncertainty of the concept or the information, and the MF of the edge is used to express the uncertainty of the binary relationship between two vertices. The biggest difference between a fuzzy hypergraph and a fuzzy graph lies in the edge set, where the relationship of fuzzy MFs is not defined on the binary set, but on the multivariate set. Specifically, let $H = (V, E)$ be a hypergraph, where $V = \{x_1, x_2, \cdots, x_n\}$ be a vertex set and $E = \{e_1, e_2, \cdots, e_m\}$ ($e_i \subseteq V(G)$ for $i \in \{1, \cdots, m\}$) be a hyperedge set.

For vertex set V and $A = \{(x, \xi_A^+, \xi_A^-) : x \in V\}$ where $\xi_A^+ : V \to [0, 1]$ is the positive MF and $\xi_A^- : V \to [-1, 0]$ is the negative MF defined on V respectively. Its support set is formulated by $\text{supp}(A) = \text{supp}^+(A) \cup \text{supp}^-(A)$ where $\text{supp}^+(A) = \{x \in V : \xi_A^+(x) > 0\}$ and $\text{supp}^-(A) = \{x \in V : \xi_A^-(x) < 0\}$ are positive support and negative support respectively. Denote the height and depth of A by $h(A) = \sup_{x\in V}\{\xi_A^+(x)\}$ and $d(A) = \inf_{x\in V}\{\xi_A^-(x)\}$ respectively. If $h(A) = 1$ and $d(A) = -1$, then the corresponding BFH is called normal.

A bipolar Pythagorean fuzzy set on V is denoted by $A = \{(x, \xi_A^+, \xi_A^-, \nu_A^+, \nu_A^-) : x \in V\}$, where $\xi_A^+, \nu_A^+ : V \to [0, 1]$ and $\xi_A^-, \nu_A^- : V \to [-1, 0]$ meet $(\xi_A^+)^2 + (\nu_A^+)^2 \in [0, 1]$ and $(\xi_A^-)^2 + (\nu_A^-)^2 \in [0, 1]$ for any $x \in V$. A mapping $B = (\xi_B^+, \xi_B^-, \nu_B^+, \nu_B^-) : V \times V \to ([0, 1] \times [-1, 0] \times [0, 1] \times [-1, 0])$ a bipolar Pythagorean fuzzy symmetry relation such that $\xi_B^+(x_i, x_j) \in [0, 1]$, $\xi_B^-(x_i, x_j) \in [-1, 0]$, $\nu_B^+(x_i, x_j) \in [0, 1]$, $\nu_B^-(x_i, x_j) \in [-1, 0]$ $(\xi_B^+(x_i, x_j))^2 + (\nu_B^+(x_i, x_j))^2 \in [0, 1]$ and $(\xi_B^-(x_i, x_j))^2 + (\nu_B^-(x_i, x_j))^2 \in [0, 1]$ for any $(x_i, x_j) \in V \times V$. A bipolar Pythagorean fuzzy graph $G = (V, A, B)$ with $A = (\xi_A^+, \xi_A^-, \nu_A^+, \nu_A^-)$ and $B = (\xi_B^+, \xi_B^-, \nu_B^+, \nu_B^-)$ satisfies the following relationships between vertex MF and edge MF:

$$\xi_B^+(x_i, x_j) \leq \xi_A^+(x_i) \wedge \xi_A^+(x_j), \tag{1}$$

$$\xi_B^-(x_i, x_j) \geq \xi_A^-(x_i) \vee \xi_A^-(x_j), \tag{2}$$

$$\nu_B^+(x_i, x_j) \geq \nu_A^+(x_i) \vee \nu_A^+(x_j), \tag{3}$$

$$\nu_B^-(x_i, x_j) \leq \nu_A^-(x_i) \wedge \nu_A^-(x_j). \tag{4}$$

Also, it is defined that $\xi_B^+ = \xi_B^- = \nu_B^+ = \nu_B^- = 0$ for any $(x_i, x_j) \in V \times V - E$. In bipolar Pythagorean fuzzy set, the height and depth are defined by $h(A) = (\sup_{x \in V} \xi_A^+(x), \inf_{x \in V} \nu_A^+(x))$ and $d(A) = (\inf_{x \in V} \xi_A^-(x), \sup_{x \in V} \nu_A^-(x))$ respectively.

A bipolar intuitionistic fuzzy set on V is defined as $A = \{(x, \xi_A^+, \xi_A^-, \nu_A^+, \nu_A^-) : x \in V\}$, where $\xi_A^+, \nu_A^+ : V \to [0, 1]$ and $\xi_A^-, \nu_A^- : V \to [-1, 0]$ satisfy $\xi_A^+ + \nu_A^+ \in [0, 1]$ and $\mu_A^- + \nu_A^- \in [-1, 0]$ for any $x \in V$. A mapping $B = (\xi_B^+, \xi_B^-, \nu_B^+, \nu_B^-) : V \times V \to ([0, 1] \times [-1, 0] \times [0, 1] \times [-1, 0])$ a bipolar intuitionistic fuzzy symmetry relation satisfies $\xi_B^+(x_i, x_j) \in [0, 1]$, $\xi_B^-(x_i, x_j) \in [-1, 0]$, $\nu_B^+(x_i, x_j) \in [0, 1]$, $\nu_B^-(x_i, x_j) \in [-1, 0]$, $\xi_B^+(x_i, x_j) + \nu_B^+(x_i, x_j) \in [0, 1]$ and $\xi_B^-(x_i, x_j) + \nu_B^-(x_i, x_j) \in [-1, 0]$ for any $(x_i, x_j) \in V \times V$. A bipolar intuitionistic fuzzy graph $G = (V, A, B)$ satisfies the above four relationship (1)–(4) between vertex and edge MFs. Note that $\xi_B^+ = \xi_B^- = \nu_B^+ = \nu_B^- = 0$ for any $(x_i, x_j) \in V \times V - E$. In bipolar intuitionistic fuzzy setting, the height and depth are defined by $h(A) = (\sup_{x \in V} \xi_A^+(x), \inf_{x \in V} \nu_A^+(x))$ and $d(A) = (\inf_{x \in V} \xi_A^-(x), \sup_{x \in V} \nu_A^-(x))$ respectively.

3 Bipolar Pythagorean Fuzzy Hypergraphs

We aim in current section to define BPFH and determine some characterizes on this data structure.

Definition 1. $H = (V, E)$ is a bipolar Pythagorean fuzzy hypergraph (in short, BPFH) if meets the following characteristics:

(i) $V = \{x_1, x_2, \cdots, x_n\}$ with $n < +\infty$ and $A = (\xi_A^+, \xi_A^-, \nu_A^+, \nu_A^-)$ is a bipolar Pythagorean MF defined on V satisfies $(\xi_A^+)^2 + (\nu_A^+)^2 \in [0, 1]$ and $(\xi_A^-)^2 + (\nu_A^-)^2 \in [0, 1]$ for any $x \in V$;

(ii) hypergraph set E is finite (with m hyperedges $\varsigma_1, \varsigma_2, \cdots, \varsigma_m$) family of bipolar Pythagorean fuzzy subsets ς_i ($i \in \{1, \cdots, m\}$);

(iii) $B = (\xi_B^+, \xi_B^-, \nu_B^+, \nu_B^-)$ is a bipolar Pythagorean fuzzy multiple relation on the hyperedges meet (let $\varsigma_i = \{x_{i_1}, x_{i_2}, \cdots, x_{i_{|\varsigma_i|}}\}$ for $1 \leq i \leq m$)

$$\xi_B^+(\varsigma_i) \leq min\{\xi_A^+(x_{i_1}), \xi_A^+(x_{i_2}), \cdots, \xi_A^+(x_{i_{|\varsigma_i|}})\}, \tag{5}$$

$$\xi_B^-(\varsigma_i) \geq \max\{\xi_A^-(x_{i_1}), \xi_A^-(x_{i_2}), \cdots, \xi_A^-(x_{i_{|\varsigma_i|}})\}, \tag{6}$$

$$\nu_B^+(\varsigma_i) \geq \max\{\nu_A^+(x_{i_1}), \nu_A^+(x_{i_2}), \cdots, \nu_A^+(x_{i_{|\varsigma_i|}})\}, \tag{7}$$

$$\nu_B^-(\varsigma_i) \leq \min\{\nu_A^-(x_{i_1}), \nu_A^-(x_{i_2}), \cdots, \nu_A^-(x_{i_{|\varsigma_i|}})\}; \tag{8}$$

(iv) $\bigcup_{i=1}^{m} \mathrm{supp}(\varsigma_i) = V$.

Furthermore, hypergraph $H = (V, E)$ is complete if " =" hold in Eqs. (5)–(8) for all hyperedges.

Example 1. Consider $H = (V, E)$ as depicted in Fig. 1 is a BPFH.

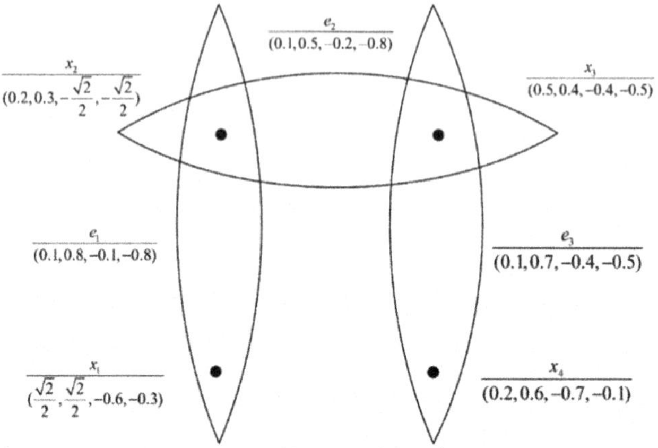

Fig. 1. A BPFH with four vertices and three hyperedges.

We have

$$\begin{gathered}
(\xi_A^+(x_1), \xi_A^-(x_1), \nu_A^+(x_1), \nu_A^-(x_1)) = (\sqrt{2}/2, \sqrt{2}/2, -0.6, -0.3),\\
(\xi_A^+(x_2), \xi_A^-(x_2), \nu_A^+(x_2), \nu_A^-(x_2)) = (0.2, 0.3, -\sqrt{2}/2, -\sqrt{2}/2),\\
(\xi_A^+(x_3), \xi_A^-(x_3), \nu_A^+(x_3), \nu_A^-(x_3)) = (0.5, 0.4, -0.4, -0.5),\\
(\xi_A^+(x_4), \xi_A^-(x_4), \nu_A^+(x_4), \nu_A^-(x_4)) = (0.2, 0.6, -0.7, -0.1).\\
e_1 = \{\frac{x_1}{(\sqrt{2}/2, \sqrt{2}/2, -0.6, -0.3)}, \frac{x_2}{(0.2, 0.3, -\sqrt{2}/2, -\sqrt{2}/2)}\},\\
e_2 = \{\frac{x_2}{(0.2, 0.3, -\sqrt{2}/2, -\sqrt{2}/2)}, \frac{x_3}{(0.5, 0.4, -0.4, -0.5)}\},\\
e_3 = \{\frac{x_3}{(0.5, 0.4, -0.4, -0.5)}, \frac{x_4}{(0.2, 0.6, -0.7, -0.1)}\},\\
(\xi_B^+(e_1) = 0.1, \xi_B^-(e_1) = 0.8, \nu_B^+(e_1) = -0.1, \nu_B^-(e_1) = -0.8),\\
(\xi_B^+(e_2) = 0.1, \xi_B^-(e_2) = 0.5, \nu_B^+(e_2) = -0.2, \nu_B^-(e_2) = -0.8),\\
(\xi_B^+(e_3) = 0.1, \xi_B^-(e_3) = 0.7, \nu_B^+(e_3) = -0.4, \nu_B^-(e_3) = -0.5).
\end{gathered}$$

Clearly, the BPFH presented in Fig. 1 is not a bipolar intuitionistic fuzzy hypergraph. Conversely, any BIFH is a BPFH.

Definition 2. A BPS $A = \{(x, \xi_A^+, \xi_A^-, \nu_A^+, \nu_A^-) : x \in V\} : V \to [0, 1] \times [0, 1] \times [-1, 0] \times [-1, 0]$ is an elementary bipolar Pythagorean fuzzy set if A is a single value on supp(A). A BPFH is elementary if its edge MF is elementary.

Theorem 1. Bipolar Pythagorean fuzzy graphs and bipolar Pythagorean fuzzy directed graphs are particular situations of BPFHs.

Definition 3. Let $H = (V, E)$ be a BPFH, $\alpha^+, \beta^+ \in [0, 1]$ be non-negative real numbers, and $\alpha^-, \beta^- \in [-1, 0]$ be non-positive real numbers. Let

- $A_{(\alpha^+,\beta^+,\alpha^-,\beta^-)} = \{x|\{\xi_A^+(x) \geq \alpha^+ \text{ or } \nu_A^+(x) \leq \beta^+\} \text{ and } \{\xi_A^-(x) \leq \alpha^- \text{ or } \nu_A^-(x) \geq \beta^-\}\}$;
- $E_{(\alpha^+,\beta^+,\alpha^-,\beta^-)} = \{A_{(\alpha^+,\beta^+,\alpha^-,\beta^-)}$, where A is four kinds of MF defined on $e_j \in E\}$;
- $V_{(\alpha^+,\beta^+,\alpha^-,\beta^-)} = \bigcup_A A_{(\alpha^+,\beta^+,\alpha^-,\beta^-)}$, where A has the same description in the previous item.

If $E_{(\alpha^+,\beta^+,\alpha^-,\beta^-)}$ is not empty, then the original hypergraph (without MF) $H_{(\alpha^+,\beta^+,\alpha^-,\beta^-)}$ (whose vertex set and hyperedge set are $V_{(\alpha^+,\beta^+,\alpha^-,\beta^-)}$ and $E_{(\alpha^+,\beta^+,\alpha^-,\beta^-)}$ respectively) is $(\alpha^+, \beta^+, \alpha^-, \beta^-)$-level hypergraph of H. Let X and Y be two families of sets with the following property: for any set belongs to X, there is another set belongs to Y such that the latter includes the former. We call Y absorbs X in this case.

Definition 4. Assume that $H = (V, E)$ is a BPFH, $(0, 0) < (\theta^+, \vartheta^+) \leq h(H)$ and $(0, 0) > (\theta^-, \vartheta^-) \geq d(H)$. Let $H_{(\theta^+,\vartheta^+,\theta^-,\vartheta^-)} = (V_{(\theta^+,\vartheta^+,\theta^-,\vartheta^-)}, E_{(\theta^+,\vartheta^+,\theta^-,\vartheta^-)})$ be $(\theta^+, \vartheta^+, \theta^-, \vartheta^-)$-level hypergraph of H. The real number sequence $\{(\theta_1^+, \vartheta_1^+, \theta_1^-, \vartheta_1^-), (\theta_2^+, \vartheta_2^+, \theta_2^-, \vartheta_2^-), \cdots, (\theta_n^+, \vartheta_n^+, \theta_n^-, \vartheta_n^-)\}$ with

$$0 < \theta_1^+ < \theta_2^+ < \cdots < \theta_n^+,$$

$$\vartheta_1^+ > \vartheta_2^+ > \cdots > \vartheta_n^+ > 0,$$

$$\theta_1^- > \theta_2^- > \cdots > \theta_n^- > -1,$$

$$-1 < \vartheta_1^- < \vartheta_2^- < \cdots < \vartheta_n^-,$$

where $(\theta_n^+, \vartheta_n^+) = h(A)$ and $(\theta_n^-, \vartheta_n^-) = d(A)$. If it meets the following two properties:

- if $\theta_i^+ < \alpha^+ \leq \theta_{i+1}^+$, $\vartheta_i^+ > \beta^+ \geq \vartheta_{i+1}^+$, $\theta_i^- > \alpha^- \geq \theta_{i+1}^-$ and $\vartheta_i^- < \beta^- \leq \vartheta_{i+1}^-$, then $E_{(\alpha^+,\beta^+,\alpha^-,\beta^-)} = E_{(\theta_{i+1}^+,\vartheta_{i+1}^+,\theta_{i+1}^-,\vartheta_{i+1}^-)}$;
- $E_{(\theta_{i+1}^+,\vartheta_{i+1}^+,\theta_{i+1}^-,\vartheta_{i+1}^-)}$ absorb $E_{(\theta_i^+,\vartheta_i^+,\theta_i^-,\vartheta_i^-)}$.

Then, we denote this sequence $\{(\theta_1^+, \vartheta_1^+, \theta_1^-, \vartheta_1^-), (\theta_2^+, \vartheta_2^+, \theta_2^-, \vartheta_2^-), \cdots, (\theta_n^+, \vartheta_n^+, \theta_n^-, \vartheta_n^-)\}$ by $F(H)$ which the fundamental sequence of H, and the set of $(\theta_i^+, \vartheta_i^+, \theta_i^-, \vartheta_i^-)$–level hypergraphs $\{H_{(\theta_1^+,\vartheta_1^+,\theta_1^-,\vartheta_1^-)}, H_{(\theta_2^+,\vartheta_2^+,\theta_2^-,\vartheta_2^-)}, \cdots, H_{(\theta_n^+,\vartheta_n^+,\theta_n^-,\vartheta_n^-)}\}$ is denoted by $C(H)$ which is the set of core BPFH of H (in short, the core of H).

Definition 5. Suppose $H = (V, E)$ is a BPFH with $F(H) = \{(\theta_1^+, \vartheta_1^+, \theta_1^-, \vartheta_1^-), (\theta_2^+, \vartheta_2^+, \theta_2^-, \vartheta_2^-), \cdots, (\theta_n^+, \vartheta_n^+, \theta_n^-, \vartheta_n^-)\}$ and $(\theta_{n+1}^+, \vartheta_{n+1}^+, \theta_{n+1}^-, \vartheta_{n+1}^-) = (0, 0, 0, 0)$. We say H is sectionally elementary if $E_{(\alpha^+, \beta^+, \alpha^-, \beta^-)} = E_{(\theta_i^+, \vartheta_i^+, \theta_i^-, \vartheta_i^-)}$ for all $(\alpha^+, \beta^+, \alpha^-, \beta^-) \in [(\theta_i^+, \vartheta_i^+, \theta_i^-, \vartheta_i^-), (\theta_{i+1}^+, \vartheta_{i+1}^+, \theta_{i+1}^-, \vartheta_{i+1}^-))$.

Definition 6. [8] A sequence of original hypergraph $H_i = (V_i, E_i)$ (here $1 \leq i \leq n$) is ordered if $H_i \subset H_{i+1}$ for $i \in \{1, \cdots, n-1\}$. The ordered sequence $H_i = (V_i, E_i)$ is simply ordered if $e \not\subset V_i$ for any $e \in E_{i+1} - E_i$.

Definition 7. A BPFH H is ordered (resp. simply ordered) if the corresponding $F(H)$ is ordered (resp. simply ordered).

Definition 8. The dual of a BPFH $H = (V, E)$ is a BPFH $H^D = (V^D, E^D)$ in which V^D is exactly the hyperedge set of H (keep the edgeMF, i.e., $(\xi_B^+, \xi_B^-, \nu_B^+, \nu_B^-)$ defined on the hyperedge set of H becomes $(\xi_A^+, \xi_A^-, \nu_A^+, \nu_A^-)$ defined on the vertex set of H^D) and hyperedge set E^D is exactly $V(H)$ (however, the MF on hyperedge set of should be redefined). Therefore, under this definition, the duality of the duality is no longer the original hypergraph.

Example 2. A BPFH $H = (V, E)$ is presented in Fig. 2.

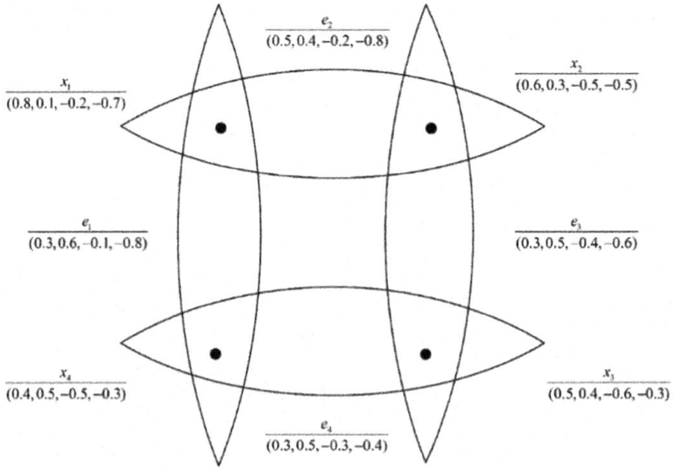

Fig. 2. The second example of BPFH $H = (V, E)$.

We deduce

$$(\xi_A^+(x_1), \xi_A^-(x_1), \nu_A^+(x_1), \nu_A^-(x_1)) = (0.8, 0.1, -0.2, -0.7),$$
$$(\xi_A^+(x_2), \xi_A^-(x_2), \nu_A^+(x_2), \nu_A^-(x_2)) = (0.6, 0.3, -0.5, -0.5),$$
$$(\xi_A^+(x_3), \xi_A^-(x_3), \nu_A^+(x_3), \nu_A^-(x_3)) = (0.5, 0.4, -0.6, -0.3),$$
$$(\xi_A^+(x_4), \xi_A^-(x_4), \nu_A^+(x_4), \nu_A^-(x_4)) = (0.4, 0.5, -0.5, -0.3).$$
$$e_1 = \{\frac{x_1}{(0.8,0.1,-0.2,-0.7)}, \frac{x_4}{(0.4,0.5,-0.5,-0.3)}\},$$
$$e_2 = \{\frac{x_1}{(0.8,0.1,-0.2,-0.7)}, \frac{x_2}{(0.6,0.3,-0.5,-0.5)}\},$$
$$e_3 = \{\frac{x_2}{(0.6,0.3,-0.5,-0.5)}, \frac{x_3}{(0.5,0.4,-0.6,-0.3)}\},$$
$$e_4 = \{\frac{x_3}{(0.5,0.4,-0.6,-0.3)}, \frac{x_4}{(0.4,0.5,-0.5,-0.3)}\},$$
$$(\xi_B^+(e_1) = 0.3, \xi_B^-(e_1) = 0.6, \nu_B^+(e_1) = -0.1, \nu_B^-(e_1) = -0.8),$$
$$(\xi_B^+(e_2) = 0.5, \xi_B^-(e_2) = 0.4, \nu_B^+(e_2) = -0.2, \nu_B^-(e_2) = -0.8),$$
$$(\xi_B^+(e_3) = 0.3, \xi_B^-(e_3) = 0.5, \nu_B^+(e_3) = -0.4, \nu_B^-(e_3) = -0.6),$$
$$(\xi_B^+(e_4) = 0.3, \xi_B^-(e_4) = 0.5, \nu_B^+(e_4) = -0.3, \nu_B^-(e_4) = -0.4).$$

Its dual BPFH is presented in Fig. 3.

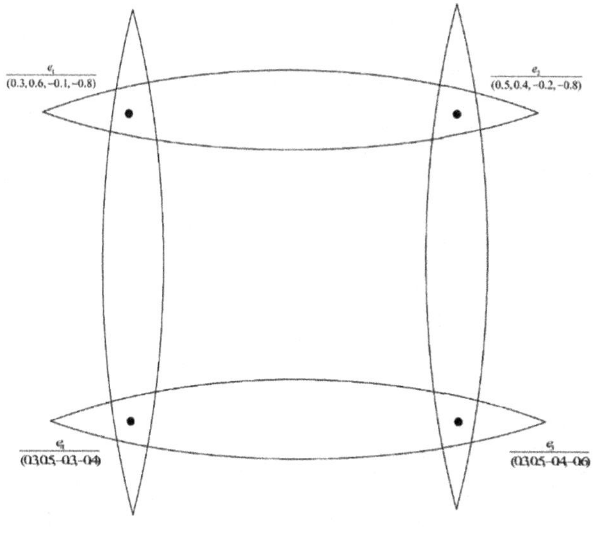

Fig. 3. Dual BPFH.

We infer.

$$
\begin{aligned}
(\xi_A^+(x_1), \xi_A^-(x_1), \nu_A^+(x_1), \nu_A^-(x_1)) &= (0.3, 0.6, -0.1, -0.8),\\
(\xi_A^+(x_2), \xi_A^-(x_2), \nu_A^+(x_2), \nu_A^-(x_2)) &= (0.5, 0.4, -0.2, -0.8)\\
(\xi_A^+(x_3), \xi_A^-(x_3), \nu_A^+(x_3), \nu_A^-(x_3)) &= (0.3, 0.5, -0.4, -0.6),\\
(\xi_A^+(x_4), \xi_A^-(x_4), \nu_A^+(x_4), \nu_A^-(x_4)) &= (0.3, 0.5, -0.3, -0.4).\\
e_1 &= \{\tfrac{x_1}{(0.3,0.6,-0.1,-0.8)}, \tfrac{x_2}{(0.5,0.4,-0.2,-0.8)}\},\\
e_2 &= \{\tfrac{x_2}{(0.5,0.4,-0.2,-0.8)}, \tfrac{x_3}{(0.3,0.5,-0.4,-0.6)}\},\\
e_3 &= \{\tfrac{x_3}{(0.3,0.5,-0.4,-0.6)}, \tfrac{x_4}{(0.3,0.5,-0.3,-0.4)}\},\\
e_4 &= \{\tfrac{x_4}{(0.3,0.5,-0.3,-0.4)}, \tfrac{x_1}{(0.3,0.6,-0.1,-0.8)}\}.
\end{aligned}
$$

Definition 9. The positive strength η^+ of a hyperedge e is denoted by the minimum positive membership ξ_A^+ and maximum positive non-membership ν_A^+ of vertices, i.e., let $e_i = \{x_{i_1}, x_{i_2}, \cdots, x_{i_{|e_i|}}\}$, then $\eta^+(e_i) = \{min\{\xi_A^+(x_{i_1}), \xi_A^+(x_{i_2}), \cdots, \xi_A^+(x_{i_{|e_i|}})\}$ or $\max\{\nu_A^+(x_{i_1}), \nu_A^+(x_{i_2}), \cdots, \nu_A^+(x_{i_{|e_i|}})\}\}$. The negative strength η^- of a hyperedge e is expressed as the maximum negative MF ξ_A^- and minimum negative non MF ν_A^- of vertices, then $\eta^-(e_i) = \{\max\{\xi_A^-(x_{i_1}), \xi_A^-(x_{i_2}), \cdots, \xi_A^-(x_{i_{|e_i|}})\}$ or $\min\{\nu_A^-(x_{i_1}), \nu_A^-(x_{i_2}),\cdots, \nu_A^-(x_{i_{|e_i|}})\}\}$ ..

For Definitions 1–9 in BPFH setting have the same statement as in BIFH setting, and we skip the details here. The following example is the explanation of BIFH.

Example 3. As depicted in Fig. 4, $H = (V, E)$ is a BIFH.

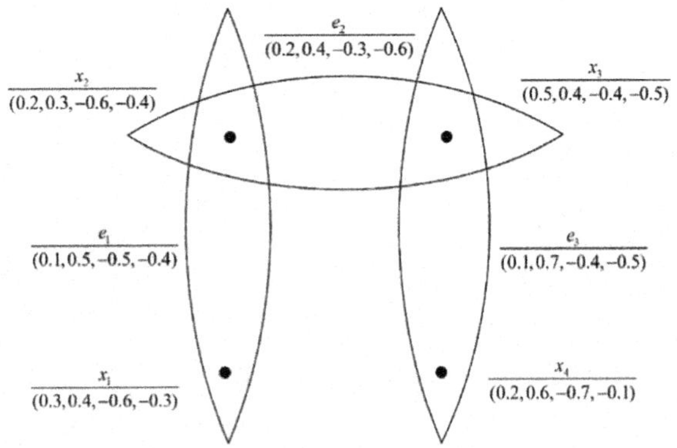

Fig. 4. A BIFH with four vertices and three hyperedges.

We have

$$(\xi_A^+(x_1), \xi_A^-(x_1), \nu_A^+(x_1), \nu_A^-(x_1)) = (0.3, 0.4, -0.6, -0.3),$$
$$(\xi_A^+(x_2), \xi_A^-(x_2), \nu_A^+(x_2), \nu_A^-(x_2)) = (0.2, 0.3, -0.6, -0.4),$$
$$(\xi_A^+(x_3), \xi_A^-(x_3), \nu_A^+(x_3), \nu_A^-(x_3)) = (0.5, 0.4, -0.4, -0.5),$$
$$(\xi_A^+(x_4), \xi_A^-(x_4), \nu_A^+(x_4), \nu_A^-(x_4)) = (0.2, 0.6, -0.7, -0.1).$$
$$e_1 = \{\frac{x_1}{(0.3,0.4,-0.6,-0.3)}, \frac{x_2}{(0.2,0.3,-0.6,-0.4)}\},$$
$$e_2 = \{\frac{x_2}{(0.2,0.3,-0.6,-0.4)}, \frac{x_3}{(0.5,0.4,-0.4,-0.5)}\},$$
$$e_3 = \{\frac{x_3}{(0.5,0.4,-0.4,-0.5)}, \frac{x_4}{(0.2,0.6,-0.7,-0.1)}\},$$
$$(\xi_B^+(e_1) = 0.1, \xi_B^-(e_1) = 0.5, \nu_B^+(e_1) = -0.5, \nu_B^-(e_1) = -0.4),$$
$$(\xi_B^+(e_2) = 0.2, \xi_B^-(e_2) = 0.4, \nu_B^+(e_2) = -0.3, \nu_B^-(e_2) = -0.6),$$
$$(\xi_B^+(e_3) = 0.1, \xi_B^-(e_3) = 0.7, \nu_B^+(e_3) = -0.4, \nu_B^-(e_3) = -0.5).$$

4 Examples

In this section, we show several instances to explain the representational concepts manifested in previous sections. The next instance is revised from Example 2.

Example 4. A complete BPFH $H = (V, E)$ is presented in Fig. 5.

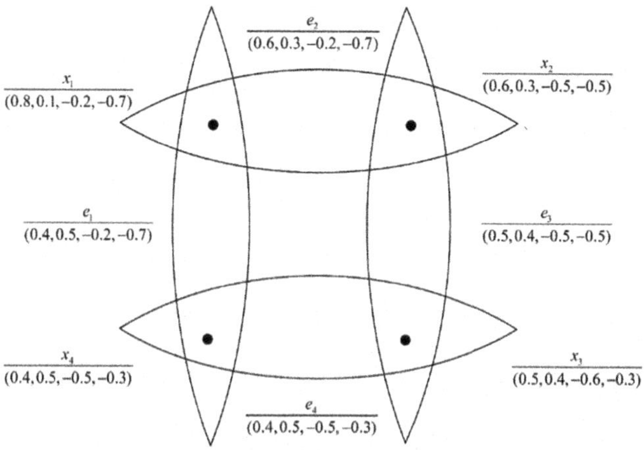

Fig. 5. A complete BPFH.

We deduce

$$(\xi_A^+(x_1), \xi_A^-(x_1), \nu_A^+(x_1), \nu_A^-(x_1)) = (0.8, 0.1, -0.2, -0.7),$$
$$(\xi_A^+(x_2), \xi_A^-(x_2), \nu_A^+(x_2), \nu_A^-(x_2)) = (0.6, 0.3, -0.5, -0.5),$$
$$(\xi_A^+(x_3), \xi_A^-(x_3), \nu_A^+(x_3), \nu_A^-(x_3)) = (0.5, 0.4, -0.6, -0.3),$$
$$(\xi_A^+(x_4), \xi_A^-(x_4), \nu_A^+(x_4), \nu_A^-(x_4)) = (0.4, 0.5, -0.5, -0.3).$$
$$e_1 = \{\frac{x_1}{(0.8,0.1,-0.2,-0.7)}, \frac{x_4}{(0.4,0.5,-0.5,-0.3)}\},$$
$$e_2 = \{\frac{x_1}{(0.8,0.1,-0.2,-0.7)}, \frac{x_2}{(0.6,0.3,-0.5,-0.5)}\},$$
$$e_3 = \{\frac{x_2}{(0.6,0.3,-0.5,-0.5)}, \frac{x_3}{(0.5,0.4,-0.6,-0.3)}\},$$
$$e_4 = \{\frac{x_3}{(0.5,0.4,-0.6,-0.3)}, \frac{x_4}{(0.4,0.5,-0.5,-0.3)}\},$$
$$(\xi_B^+(e_1) = 0.4, \xi_B^-(e_1) = 0.5, \nu_B^+(e_1) = -0.2, \nu_B^-(e_1) = -0.7),$$
$$(\xi_B^+(e_2) = 0.6, \xi_B^-(e_2) = 0.3, \nu_B^+(e_2) = -0.2, \nu_B^-(e_2) = -0.7),$$
$$(\xi_B^+(e_3) = 0.5, \xi_B^-(e_3) = 0.4, \nu_B^+(e_3) = -0.5, \nu_B^-(e_3) = -0.5),$$
$$(\xi_B^+(e_4) = 0.4, \xi_B^-(e_4) = 0.5, \nu_B^+(e_4) = -0.5, \nu_B^-(e_4) = -0.3).$$

It is not hard to check that " =" in Eqs. (5)–(8) hold for e_1–e_4, and hence H is complete.

Example 5. A BPFH is presented in Fig. 6. It is shown that $V = \{x_1, x_2, x_3, x_4, x_5, x_6\}$, $E = \{\varsigma_1, \varsigma_2, \varsigma_3, \varsigma_4\}$,

$$(\xi_A^+(x_1), \xi_A^-(x_1), \nu_A^+(x_1), \nu_A^-(x_1)) = (0.1, 0.9, -0.1, -0.9),$$
$$(\xi_A^+(x_2), \xi_A^-(x_2), \nu_A^+(x_2), \nu_A^-(x_2)) = (0.2, 0.8, -0.2, -0.8),$$
$$(\xi_A^+(x_3), \xi_A^-(x_3), \nu_A^+(x_3), \nu_A^-(x_3)) = (0.3, 0.7, -0.3, -0.7),$$
$$(\xi_A^+(x_4), \xi_A^-(x_4), \nu_A^+(x_4), \nu_A^-(x_4)) = (0.4, 0.6, -0.4, -0.6),$$
$$(\xi_A^+(x_5), \xi_A^-(x_5), \nu_A^+(x_5), \nu_A^-(x_5)) = (0.5, 0.5, -0.5, -0.5),$$
$$(\xi_A^+(x_6), \xi_A^-(x_6), \nu_A^+(x_6), \nu_A^-(x_6)) = (0.6, 0.4, -0.6, -0.4).$$
$$\varsigma_1 = \{\frac{x_1}{(0.1,0.9,-0.1,-0.9)}, \frac{x_2}{(0.2,0.8,-0.2,-0.8)}\},$$
$$\varsigma_2 = \{\frac{x_2}{(0.2,0.8,-0.2,-0.8)}, \frac{x_3}{(0.3,0.7,-0.3,-0.7)}, \frac{x_4}{(0.4,0.6,-0.4,-0.6)}\},$$
$$\varsigma_3 = \{\frac{x_1}{(0.1,0.9,-0.1,-0.9)}, \frac{x_4}{(0.4,0.6,-0.4,-0.6)}\},$$
$$\varsigma_4 = \{\frac{x_2}{(0.2,0.8,-0.2,-0.8)}, \frac{x_5}{(0.5,0.5,-0.5,-0.5)}, \frac{x_6}{(0.6,0.4,-0.6,-0.4)}\},$$
$$(\xi_B^+(\varsigma_1) = 0.1, \xi_B^-(\varsigma_1) = 0.9, \nu_B^+(\varsigma_1) = -0.1, \nu_B^-(\varsigma_1) = -0.9),$$
$$(\xi_B^+(\varsigma_2) = 0.2, \xi_B^-(\varsigma_2) = 0.8, \nu_B^+(\varsigma_2) = -0.2, \nu_B^-(\varsigma_2) = -0.8),$$
$$(\xi_B^+(\varsigma_3) = 0.1, \xi_B^-(\varsigma_3) = 0.9, \nu_B^+(\varsigma_3) = -0.1, \nu_B^-(\varsigma_3) = -0.9),$$
$$(\xi_B^+(\varsigma_4) = 0.2, \xi_B^-(\varsigma_4) = 0.8, \nu_B^+(\varsigma_4) = -0.2, \nu_B^-(\varsigma_4) = -0.8).$$

Take $(\theta_1^+, \vartheta_1^+, \theta_1^-, \vartheta_1^-) = (0.1, 0.9, -0.1, -0.9)$, $(\theta_2^+, \vartheta_2^+, \theta_2^-, \vartheta_2^-) = (0.2, 0.8, -0.2, -0.8)$, $(\theta_3^+, \vartheta_3^+, \theta_3^-, \vartheta_3^-) = (0.4, 0.6, -0.4, -0.6)$, and $(\theta_4^+, \vartheta_4^+, \theta_4^-, \vartheta_4^-) = (0.6, 0.4, -0.6, -0.4)$. Obviously, $\{(\theta_1^+, \vartheta_1^+, \theta_1^-, \vartheta_1^-), (\theta_2^+, \vartheta_2^+, \theta_2^-, \vartheta_2^-), (\theta_3^+, \vartheta_3^+, \theta_3^-, \vartheta_3^-), (\theta_4^+, \vartheta_4^+, \theta_4^-, \vartheta_4^-)\}$ is $F(H)$, and the set of $(\theta_i^+, \vartheta_i^+, \theta_i^-, \vartheta_i^-)$–level hypergraphs $\{H_{(\theta_1^+,\vartheta_1^+,\theta_1^-,\vartheta_1^-)}, H_{(\theta_2^+,\vartheta_2^+,\theta_2^-,\vartheta_2^-)}, H_{(\theta_3^+,\vartheta_3^+,\theta_3^-,\vartheta_3^-)}, H_{(\theta_4^+,\vartheta_4^+,\theta_4^-,\vartheta_4^-)}\}$ are depicted in Fig. 7.

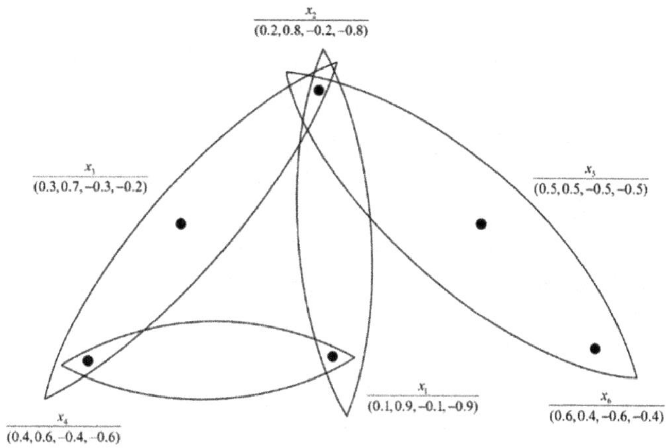

Fig. 6. A BPFH which is used to explain the fundamental sequence.

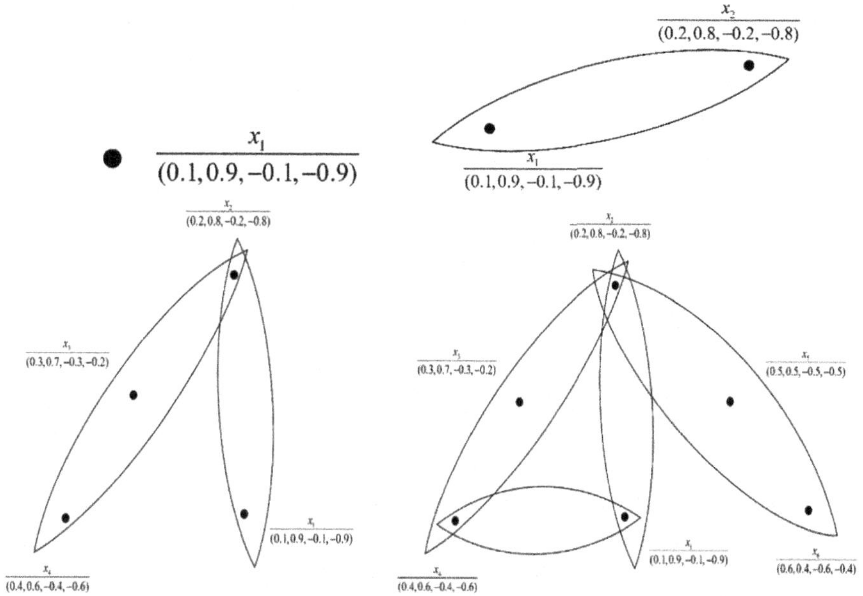

Fig. 7. The BPFH $H_{(\theta_1^+,\vartheta_1^+,\theta_1^-,\vartheta_1^-)}$, $H_{(\theta_2^+,\vartheta_2^+,\theta_2^-,\vartheta_2^-)}$, $H_{(\theta_3^+,\vartheta_3^+,\theta_3^-,\vartheta_3^-)}$ and $H_{(\theta_4^+,\vartheta_4^+,\theta_4^-,\vartheta_4^-)}$.

Example 6. This example uses campus ecology as an example to illustrate how to use hypergraph to build a model. In recent years, with the improvement of the quality of material life and the improvement of university campus hardware, more and more universities pay attention to ecological construction. Various plants have been planted on campus, and some ornamental animals, such as goldfish and swan, have been bred in campus lakes. The introduction of these animals has inevitably improved the ecological environment on the university campus. Wild cats, dogs, squirrels, frogs, lobsters, and birds have appeared. At the same time, some dangerous predators have appeared, such as snakes. As a result, a simple biological system and food chain are formed inside the university campus. According to the relationship between animals in the campus, we constructed the following hypergraph, where each vertex represents an animal, and if the attributes of the animals are the similar, then it constitutes a hyperedge. For example, the cats and dogs on campus are not necessarily all wild. They may be discarded pets, so they have a certain commonality. The MF of the vertex is used to describe the closeness of this animal to human beings, and the MF of the hypergraph is used to describe the closeness of the connection between this group of animals. The specific BPFH model can be seen in Fig. 8.

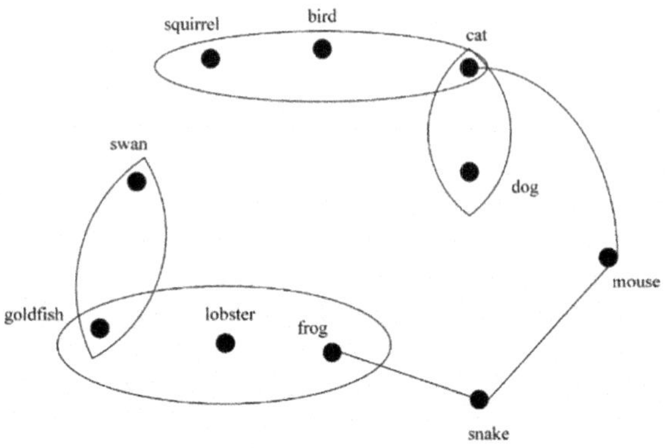

Fig. 8. The BPFH model of university campus ecosystem.

We infer $V = \{x_1 = \text{swan}, x_2 = \text{goldfish}, x_3 = \text{lobster}, x_4 = \text{frog}, x_5 = \text{snake}, x_6 = \text{mouse}, x_7 = \text{dog}, x_8 = \text{cat}, x_9 = \text{bird}, x_{10} = \text{squirrel}\}$, $E = \{\varsigma_1 = \{x_1, x_2\}, \varsigma_1 = \{x_2, x_3, x_4\}, \varsigma_3 = \{x_4, x_5\}, \varsigma_4 = \{x_5, x_6\}, \varsigma_5 = \{x_6, x_8\}, \varsigma_6 = \{x_7, x_8\},$

$\varsigma_7 = \{x_8, x_9, x_{10}\}\}$,

$$(\xi_A^+(x_1), \xi_A^-(x_1), \nu_A^+(x_1), \nu_A^-(x_1)) = (0.95, 0.05, -0.1, -0.9),$$
$$(\xi_A^+(x_2), \xi_A^-(x_2), \nu_A^+(x_2), \nu_A^-(x_2)) = (0.8, 0.15, -0.2, -0.7),$$
$$(\xi_A^+(x_3), \xi_A^-(x_3), \nu_A^+(x_3), \nu_A^-(x_3)) = (0.6, 0.4, -0.3, -0.6),$$
$$(\xi_A^+(x_4), \xi_A^-(x_4), \nu_A^+(x_4), \nu_A^-(x_4)) = (0.8, 0.1, -0.1, -0.7),$$
$$(\xi_A^+(x_5), \xi_A^-(x_5), \nu_A^+(x_5), \nu_A^-(x_5)) = (0.2, 0.7, -0.9, -0.1),$$
$$(\xi_A^+(x_6), \xi_A^-(x_6), \nu_A^+(x_6), \nu_A^-(x_6)) = (0.1, 0.9, -0.9, -0.1),$$
$$(\xi_A^+(x_7), \xi_A^-(x_7), \nu_A^+(x_7), \nu_A^-(x_7)) = (0.7, 0.3, -0.2, -0.7),$$
$$(\xi_A^+(x_8), \xi_A^-(x_8), \nu_A^+(x_8), \nu_A^-(x_8)) = (0.9, 0.1, -0.2, -0.8),$$
$$(\xi_A^+(x_9), \xi_A^-(x_9), \nu_A^+(x_9), \nu_A^-(x_9)) = (0.7, 0.2, -0.4, -0.5),$$
$$(\xi_A^+(x_6), \xi_A^-(x_6), \nu_A^+(x_6), \nu_A^-(x_6)) = (0.6, 0.4, -0.3, -0.6).$$
$$\varsigma_1 = \{\frac{x_1}{(0.95,0.05,-0.1,-0.9)}, \frac{x_2}{(0.8,0.15,-0.2,-0.7)}\},$$
$$\varsigma_2 = \{\frac{x_2}{(0.8,0.15,-0.2,-0.7)}, \frac{x_3}{(0.6,0.4,-0.3,-0.6)}, \frac{x_4}{(0.8,0.1,-0.1,-0.7)}\},$$
$$\varsigma_3 = \{\frac{x_4}{(0.8,0.1,-0.1,-0.7)}, \frac{x_5}{(0.2,0.7,-0.9,-0.1)}\},$$
$$\varsigma_4 = \{\frac{x_5}{(0.2,0.7,-0.9,-0.1)}, \frac{x_6}{(0.1,0.9,-0.9,-0.1)}\},$$
$$\varsigma_5 = \{\frac{x_6}{(0.1,0.9,-0.9,-0.1)}, \frac{x_8}{(0.9,0.1,-0.2,-0.8)}\},$$
$$\varsigma_6 = \{\frac{x_7}{(0.7,0.3,-0.2,-0.7)}, \frac{x_8}{(0.9,0.1,-0.2,-0.8)}\},$$
$$\varsigma_7 = \{\frac{x_8}{(0.9,0.1,-0.2,-0.8)}, \frac{x_9}{(0.7,0.2,-0.4,-0.5)}, \frac{x_{10}}{(0.6,0.4,-0.3,-0.6)}\}.$$
$$(\xi_B^+(\varsigma_1) = 0.8, \xi_B^-(\varsigma_1) = 0.15, \nu_B^+(\varsigma_1) = -0.1, \nu_B^-(\varsigma_1) = -0.9),$$
$$(\xi_B^+(\varsigma_2) = 0.5, \xi_B^-(\varsigma_2) = 0.5, \nu_B^+(\varsigma_2) = -0.1, \nu_B^-(\varsigma_2) = -0.8),$$
$$(\xi_B^+(\varsigma_3) = 0.1, \xi_B^-(\varsigma_3) = 0.9, \nu_B^+(\varsigma_3) = -0.2, \nu_B^-(\varsigma_3) = -0.8),$$
$$(\xi_B^+(\varsigma_4) = 0.1, \xi_B^-(\varsigma_4) = 0.9, \nu_B^+(\varsigma_4) = -0.9, \nu_B^-(\varsigma_4) = -0.1),$$
$$(\xi_B^+(\varsigma_5) = 0.1, \xi_B^-(\varsigma_5) = 0.9, \nu_B^+(\varsigma_5) = -0.2, \nu_B^-(\varsigma_5) = -0.8),$$
$$(\xi_B^+(\varsigma_6) = 0.6, \xi_B^-(\varsigma_6) = 0.3, \nu_B^+(\varsigma_6) = -0.1, \nu_B^-(\varsigma_6) = -0.8),$$
$$(\xi_B^+(\varsigma_7) = 0.5, \xi_B^-(\varsigma_7) = 0.4, \nu_B^+(\varsigma_7) = -0.1, \nu_B^-(\varsigma_7) = -0.9).$$

References

1. Ding, D.Q., Yang, X.G., Xia, F., Ma, T.F., Liu, H.Y., Tang, C.: Unsupervised feature selection via adaptive hypergraph regularized latent representation learning. Neurocomputing **378**, 79–97 (2020)
2. Bouhlel, N., Feki, G., Ben Ammar, A., Ben Amar, C.: Hypergraph learning with collaborative representation for image search reranking. Int. J. Multimedia Inf. Retr. **9**(3), 205–214 (2020). https://doi.org/10.1007/s13735-019-00191-w
3. Lv, X.Q., Wang, X., Wang, Q., Yu, J.Y.: 4D light field segmentation from light field super-pixel hypergraph representation. IEEE Trans. Vis. Comput. Graph. **27**(9), 3597–3610 (2021)
4. Eriksson, A., Edler, D., Rojas, A., de Domenico, M., Rosvall, M.: How choosing random-walk model and network representation matters for flow-based community detection in hypergraphs. Commun. Phys. **4**(1), 133 (2021). https://doi.org/10.1038/s42005-021-00634-z
5. Bai, J.J., Gong, B.A., Zhao, Y.N., Lei, F.Q., Yan, C.G., Gao, Y.: Multi-scale representation learning on hypergraph for 3D shape retrieval and recognition. IEEE Trans. Image Process. **30**, 5327–5338 (2021)

6. Mougouei, D., Powers, D.M.W.: Dependency-aware software requirements selection using fuzzy graphs and integer programming. Expert Syst. Appl. **167**, 113748 (2021). https://doi.org/10.1016/j.eswa.2020.113748
7. Binu, M., Mathew, S., Mordeson, J.N.: Cyclic connectivity index of fuzzy graphs. IEEE Trans. Fuzzy Syst. **29**(6), 1340–1349 (2021)
8. Akram, M., Dudek, W.A.: Intuitionistic fuzzy hypergraphs with applications. Inf. Sci. **218**, 182–193 (2013)

Deep Knowledge Tracing with GRU and Learning State Enhancement

Xiaoyu Han[1], Shu Zhang[1,2](✉), Juxiang Zhou[1,3], Zijie Li[1], and Jun Wang[1,3]

[1] Key Laboratory of Education Informatization for Nationalities, Ministry of Education, Yunnan Normal University, Kunming 650500, China
zhangshu@ynnu.edu.cn

[2] School of Information Science and Technology, Yunnan Normal University, Kunming 650500, China

[3] Yunnan Key Laboratory of Smart Education, Yunnan Normal University, Kunming 650500, China

Abstract. With the rapid development of artificial intelligence + education, knowledge tracing, as the core technology of adaptive education system, has gradually become a challenging research hotspot in the field of intelligent education. In recent years, the deep knowledge tracing model (DKT), which successfully applied neural network in knowledge tracing field for the first time, has made a great breakthrough in prediction accuracy, and has aroused the wave of knowledge tracing using neural network since then. In DKT, the recurrent neural network (RNN) stores the previous information of students in the hidden layer parameters. However, due to the continuous accumulation of hidden layer information, it is difficult to re-extract the important information at the earlier time, resulting in the deviation of prediction results. Meanwhile, the model does not consider the role of students' recent state. That often has a more important impact on students' current level of doing problems. Inspired by the above questions, we improved the DKT model and used the gate units of GRU model to determine the retention and forgetting of previous information, so as to solve the problem that the important information at the early time was difficult to use due to the continuous accumulation of hidden layer information. At the same time, the module of enhancing students' learning state is added in the model, and the recent learning information of students is effectively used to enhance students' recent learning state. The experimental results of the Assistment2009 and Assistment2017 public datasets show that the model proposed in this paper can effectively improve the accuracy of model prediction.

Keywords: Deep knowledge tracing · GRU model · Personalized learning

1 Introduction

In the teaching process, the individual needs of multiple students need to be met. Due to the limited attention and energy of teachers, students' learning state is constantly changing, so it is almost impossible for teachers to meet the personalized learning needs

Y. Xu et al. (Eds.): ML4CS 2022, LNCS 13657, pp. 677–686, 2023.
https://doi.org/10.1007/978-3-031-20102-8_53

of each student. Teachers generally judge students' mastery of knowledge points by their classroom performance and homework exercises. It is very complicated and time-consuming for teachers to mark students' homework exercises. If there are too many homework exercises to be marked, even if the teacher spends a lot of time, it is difficult to extract and summarize the knowledge points of each student's grasp of the situation. With the advent of the era of big data, the application of artificial intelligence in education is becoming more and more popular. The data generated by students in the learning process are stored in large quantities, and the ability of computers to process data is greatly strengthened. The development of educational data mining and educational data analysis has provided impetus for the development of learning forecasting. Knowledge tracing has become one of the important tools to meet students' individual needs.

Knowledge tracing refers to the computer modeling of relevant knowledge based on students' previous learning information, and the prediction of students' next answer performance based on students' previous problem-solving data [1]. To put it simply, the knowledge tracing task is to find a way to obtain the current knowledge state of students through the historical sequence data of students. Using the interactive information between students and questions, the purpose of predicting students' next answer performance is achieved.

Traditional knowledge tracing models include Bayesian knowledge tracing using Hidden Markov model [2] and PFA using Logistic regression model [3]. In 2015, neural network was successfully applied in the field of knowledge tracing for the first time, and it was named Deep Knowledge Tracing (DKT) [4]. DKT has made a great breakthrough in the prediction accuracy of knowledge tracing, which has aroused the wave of knowledge tracing by using neural network. For example, DKT+ model points out that there are two problems in DKT model. The model fails to reconstruct the observed input and the model fails to reconstruct the observed input, and add three regularization terms into the loss function to solve the above problems [5]. There are also models that use neural networks from different perspectives of students' learning as entry points, such as CKT model considering students' personalized differences [14]. AKT model using monotone attention mechanism to consider the connection between the current question and each question answered by learners in the past [7]. GKT model using graph neural network to model student proficiency [8] etc. All these methods contribute to the development of neural network in knowledge tracing.

DKT uses RNN [15] to learn the sequence of knowledge points with timing to predict students' future performance of knowledge points. In DKT, students' previous information is stored in the hidden layer parameters of RNN. However, with the continuous accumulation of hidden layer information, it is difficult to extract the important information at the earlier time, making it difficult to consider the important information at the earlier time in the current prediction, resulting in the deviation in prediction. The gate units of GRU model are used to determine the retention and forgetting of past information, in order to reduce the accumulation of unimportant information in hidden layer and solve the problem that RNN in DKT is difficult to predict with important information at earlier time. We found that students' recent learning state also has a certain impact on their current level of problem solving. If the student performs well in the previous problems, but performs poorly in the recent problems, it is highly likely that the student has problems in his recent learning state. And it is likely to affect the current performance of students. We use recent learning information to enhance students' recent learning state. The experiment proves that the above methods can make the model achieve better prediction effect.

Our main contributions are summarized as follows:

(1) We use GRU model to solve the problem that RNN in DKT is difficult to predict with important information at earlier time.
(2) We through recent learning information to enhance students' recent learning state. The accuracy of model prediction is improved effectively.

2 Related Work

Knowledge tracing is one of the important practices of artificial intelligence in education. In recent years, while improving the knowledge tracing method proposed earlier, the DKT based on RNN is also proposed, which is the first successful practice of deep neural network in the field of knowledge tracing. DKT is to build a model based on RNN to predict students' future performance through previous learning information. RNN is very effective for sequential data. It can mine temporal and semantic information in data. The ability of RNN can be used to predict students' future performance from their previous learning information.

In 1982, John Hopfield proposed the embryonic single layer feedback neural network of RNN. Although RNN at this time has the ability to process time sequence information, the defects of gradient vanishing and gradient explosion of RNN make it difficult to achieve good effects in some long-dependent scenes. In 1997, Hochreiter S and Schmidhuber J proposed Long Short Term Memory (LSTM) [16]. LSTM uses three gate units, namely forget gate, update gate and output gate. LSTM solves the problem of RNN training effectively through its gate units. Since then, various variations of LSTM have appeared [9–11]. GRU model [12] was proposed in 2014 and is one of the most famous transformations of LSTM. GRU and LSTM solve the same problems and also use gate units. The GRU uses two gate units: reset gate and update gate. In DKT, students' previous information is stored in the hidden layer parameters of RNN, but with the continuous accumulation of the hidden layer information, it is difficult to extract the important information at earlier moments, making it difficult to consider the important information at earlier moments in the current prediction. In order to solve this problem, we want to use the gate units of LSTM and GRU to determine the retention and forgetting of previous information, so as to reduce the accumulation of unimportant information in the hidden layer, and solve the problem that it is difficult to use the important information at earlier time to predict. Through experiments, we find that LSTM and GRU can achieve similar effects, but GRU has a simpler structure and easier training than LSTM. Therefore, we finally use GRU model to solve the problem that RNN in DKT is difficult to make use of important information at earlier time to predict.

In the field of knowledge tracing, scholars have made a lot of attempts to consider students' current learning state. Such as LPKT [6] simulates the learning process of students. The model is divided into three parts: learning module, forgetting module and prediction module. The model considers the current knowledge state of students through learning and forgetting. LFKT model [13] also considers students' learning and forgetting behaviors. LFKT model comprehensively considers four factors affecting knowledge forgetting, including knowledge repetition, knowledge learning interval, sequential learning interval and knowledge mastery degree. However, we found that students' recent performance also have a very important impact on their current learning state. For example, if a student gets three questions wrong in a row, there is a high probability that the student will also get the questions wrong at the current moment. Therefore, we added a module to enhance students' learning state in the model, using students' recent learning information to enhance students' recent learning state.

3 Model

3.1 Review of Deep Knowledge Tracing Model

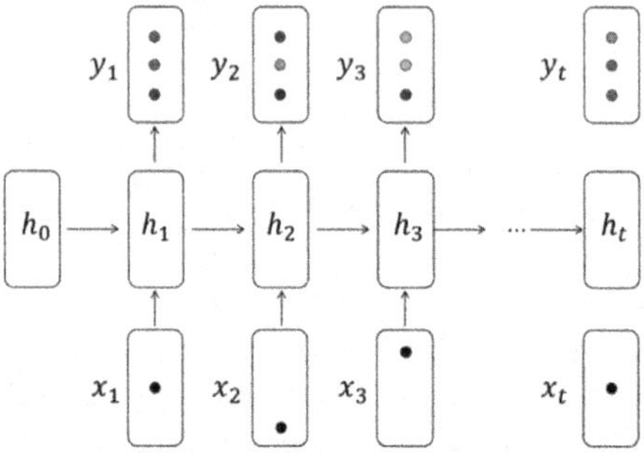

Fig. 1. DKT model schematic diagram.

Deep knowledge tracing is to predict students' future answer performance by using recurrent neural network (RNN) based on the relevant data of learners' knowledge point answers with time sequence and the relevant data of learners' correct or not answers to the knowledge point (as shown in Fig. 1). Where, x_t represents the data of students at time t, including information about knowledge points made by students at time t and information about correct or wrong answers. h_t represents the hidden layer state of recurrent neural network (RNN) at time t, and represents the comprehensive problem-solving information of students before time t. y_t represents the prediction of the students' performance in the next time. Because the model does not know which knowledge points the students will make next time by default, each prediction is the prediction of the correct probability of all the knowledge points the students will make next time.

The information transfer in the model can be simply described as follows: x_t will be put into the recurrent neural network to generate the original prediction data h_t (see Eq. 1). Then put the output of h_t through a fully connected layer into the activation function, control each element of the output between 0 and 1, and get the final prediction result (see Eq. 2, 3).

$$h_t = \tanh\left(W_x x_t + b_x + W_h h_{(t-1)} + b_h\right) \tag{1}$$

where, h_t is the hidden state at time t, x_t is the input at time t, and $h_{(t-1)}$ is the hidden state at time t − 1.

$$I = h_t A^T + b \tag{2}$$

where, h_t and I are the input and output of the linear layer, A is the weight, b is the bias.

$$\text{Sigmoid}(I) = \sigma(I) = \frac{1}{1 + \exp(-I)} \tag{3}$$

3.2 DKT Model Improvement Framework

We cut and onehot encoding the data of students, so that each information of students contains information about the skills they have done and the correct or incorrect information of students' answers, and there is a time sequence between the data. Form a sequence of students doing the exercises $\{x_1, x_2, x_3, x_4, \ldots, x_T\}$. Input students' problem-solving sequence into our model accordingly, and get the prediction of the model for students' next problem-solving performance. Our model schematic diagram is as shown in Fig. 2.

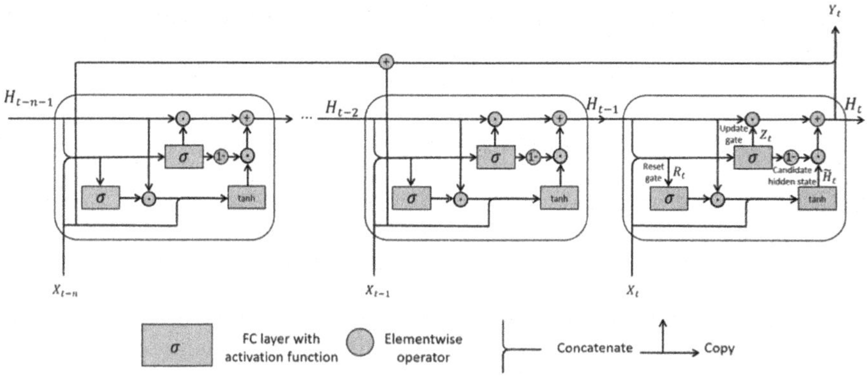

Fig. 2. Our model schematic diagram.

GRU Forms the Initial Forecast Data

The information of students' problem solving is input into our model as hidden layer information. Not all previous information is needed to predict current student performance. Therefore, we need reset gate and update gate, combined with the data of students doing questions at the current time X_t, to determine the hidden layer information needed to predict students' current answer performance. The information of the hidden layer is concated with the data of students doing the problem at the current moment. Through a fully connected layer, the vector with the same dimension as the hidden layer is obtained. Then, through the Sigmoid activation function, each element in the vector is controlled between 0–1. The reset gate and the update gate yield the same dimension as the hidden dimension R_t and Z_t, respectively (see Eqs. 4, 5). The update gate is used to control the degree to which the information of the previous moment is brought into the current state. The larger the value of the update gate, the more information of the previous moment is brought into the current state.

$$R_t = \sigma(X_t W_{xr} + H_{t-1} W_{hr} + b_r) \tag{4}$$

$$Z_t = \sigma(X_t W_{xz} + H_{t-1} W_{hz} + b_z) \tag{5}$$

The reset gate controls how much information from the previous state is written to the Candidate hidden state $\widetilde{H_t}$. The smaller the reset gate, the less information from the previous state is written. The reset gate yields a vector R_t with the same dimension as the hidden layer and each element being 0 to 1. The Candidate hidden state $\widetilde{H_t}$ is obtained by the initial processing of multiplying R_t by the elements of the hidden layer H_{t-1} (see Eq. 6). Because Candidate hidden state $\widetilde{H_t}$ is not directly output as the hidden state at time t, it is called Candidate hidden state. Update gate yields a vector Z_t with the same dimension as the hiddden layer and with each element value between 0 and 1. Multiply Z_t by the element of the last hidden state H_{t-1} to get the part of vector H_{t-1} that needs to remain in the current hidden state. Multiply $1 - Z_t$ by the candidate hidden state to get the part of the candidate hidden state that needs to be retained to the current hidden state. Add the two together to get the current hidden state, which is also the initial forecast data (see Eq. 7).

$$\widetilde{H_t} = \tanh\left(X_t W_{xh} + \left(R_t \odot H_{t-1}\right) W_{hh} + b_h\right) \tag{6}$$

$$H_t = Z_t \odot H_{t-1} + (1 - Z_t) \odot \widetilde{H_t} \tag{7}$$

Emphasis Students' Recent Learning State

$$Y_t = \sigma\left(\sum_{t-n}^{t-1} x_i W_{xy} + H_t W_{hy} + b_y\right) \tag{8}$$

where n is the number of recent problem-solving data of students that is needed to enhance their recent learning state, and H_t is the information of the hidden layer at time t.

If the student performs well in the previous problems, but performs poorly in the recent problems, it is highly likely that the student has problems in the recent learning state. And it is very likely to affect the current problem-solving performance. So if we use the recent learning information of students to enhance the students' recent learning state, the model will achieve better prediction results. The data of students' recent problem solving are spliced in the initial prediction result, and the final prediction of students' performance in the next problem solving is obtained through the full connection layer (see Eq. 8). The experiment proves that this method can make the model achieve better prediction effect.

4 Experiments

We use the Assistment2009 and Assistment2017 datasets to verify and illustrate the performance of the our model. This experiment is based on python3.8, PyTorch v1.9.1, cuda v11.1, and optimized using Adam optimizer. 70% of the data were taken as the training set and 30% as the verification set. The batch size was 64 and the number of training epochs was 70. The optimal value of 70 epochs was taken as the experimental result. The specific experimental results are shown in Table 1.

Table 1. The Assistment2009 and Assistment2017 datasets were used to test our model, and the AUC, ACC and RMSE changed with different models.

METRIC	ASSIST2009			ASSIST2017		
	AUC	ACC	RMSE	AUC	ACC	RMSE
DKT	0.8079	0.7648	0.4017	0.6917	0.6776	0.4547
OURS	0.8180	0.7693	0.3966	0.7084	0.6822	0.4520

According to the experimental data, our model performs well in the Assistment2009 and Assistment2017 datasets. In this task, it is feasible to use GRU model to solve the problem that RNN in DKT is difficult to predict with the important information at an earlier time, and to enhance students' recent learning state through students' recent learning information.

Experiments with Different Numbers of Questions

Table 2. When the size of hidden layer is 10 and the number of hidden layers is 1, the changes of AUC, ACC and RMSE of our model with the number of splicing questions.

METRIC	ASSIST2009			ASSIST2017		
	AUC	ACC	RMSE	AUC	ACC	RMSE
$Q_{num}=0$	0.8079	0.7648	0.4017	0.6885	0.6737	0.4571
$Q_{num}=1$	0.8115	0.7662	0.4006	0.6887	0.6738	0.4578
$Q_{num}=2$	0.8118	0.7665	0.4007	0.6882	0.6740	0.4583
$Q_{num}=3$	0.8098	0.7658	0.4016	0.6833	0.6724	0.4595
$Q_{num}=4$	0.8089	0.7631	0.4031	0.6867	0.6709	0.4591
$Q_{num}=5$	0.8056	0.7641	0.4025	0.6854	0.6702	0.4599

Where Q_{num} represents the number of student questions to be spliced.

As shown in Table 2, the prediction accuracy reached the highest when the original prediction results were combined with the recent two records of students. From the previous learning records to enhance the students' recent learning state, improve the prediction accuracy, indicating that the students' recent learning state has an impact on the current students' performance.

Experiments of Different Size of Hidden Layer

Table 3. Join together the previous two problem records of students, and when the number of hidden layers is 1, the AUC, ACC and RMSE changes with the size of hidden layer of GRU.

METRIC	ASSIST2009			ASSIST2017		
	AUC	ACC	RMSE	AUC	ACC	RMSE
H = 10	0.8140	0.7686	0.3987	0.6974	0.6780	0.4557
H = 20	0.8167	0.7700	0.3974	0.7038	0.6799	0.4535
H = 30	0.8171	0.7694	0.3967	0.7068	0.6805	0.4526
H = 40	0.8180	0.7693	0.3966	0.7084	0.6822	0.4520
H = 50	0.8165	0.7663	0.3997	0.7091	0.6823	0.4516

Where H is the size of the hidden layer.

The information of students' previous problem solving is stored in the hidden layer of GRU model. The larger the size of hidden layer, the more information is stored. But the bigger the size of hidden layer is not the better. The size of hidden layer can not be too large, also can not be too small. As shown in Table 3, when the size of the hidden layer is 40, the best prediction result can be achieved in the ASSIST2009 dataset. However, in the ASSIST2017 dataset, when the size of the hidden layer is 50, the best prediction results can be achieved in this task. After comprehensive consideration, the hidden layer size of 40 is adopted in the following experiment.

Experiments of Different Number of Hidden Layers

As shown in Table 4, the effect decreases when the number of layers increases in the ASSIST2009 dataset. But in the ASSIST2017 dataset, the effect increases with the number of layers in this task.

5 Conclusion

In this paper, we put forward two problems of DKT model: the problem that RNN in DKT is difficult to predict with the important information at earlier time, and the model cannot enhance the students' recent learning state. Experiments show that it is feasible to use GRU model to solve the problem that RNN in DKT is difficult to predict with important information at an earlier time, and to enhance students' recent learning state through recent learning information in this task. In the future, we will conduct more

Table 4. When the initial prediction data is combined with two records of students' previous exercises, and the size of hidden layer of GRU is 40, the AUC, ACC and RMSE changes with the number of hidden layers.

METRIC	ASSIST2009			ASSIST2017		
	AUC	ACC	RMSE	AUC	ACC	RMSE
L = 1	0.8180	0.7693	0.3966	0.7084	0.6822	0.4520
L = 2	0.8168	0.7667	0.3993	0.7112	0.6830	0.4511
L = 3	0.8158	0.7648	0.4007	0.7117	0.6833	0.4509
L = 4	0.8155	0.7665	0.4095	0.7121	0.6832	0.4510

Where L represents the number of hidden layers.

experiments to verify the improvement effect of other methods on DKT model. For example, the idea of residual neural network can be used to solve the problem that RNN cannot perform long-term memory. At the same time, convolution neural network can be used to extract students' problem-solving patterns (for example, if students make mistakes in question A, question B is highly likely to make mistakes).

Acknowledgment. This work is supported by National Natural Science Foundation of China (Grant No. 62166050), Yunnan Fundamental Research Projects (Grant No. 202201AS070021), Scientific research foundation of Yunnan Provincial Department of Education (Grant No. 2022Y180) Yunnan Innovation Team of Education Informatization for Nationalities, and Kunming Key Laboratory of Education Informatization.

References

1. Corbett, A.T., Anderson, J.R.: Knowledge tracing: Modeling the acquisition of procedural knowledge. User Model. User Adapt. Interact. **4**(4), 253–278 (1994)
2. Yudelson, M.V., Koedinger, K.R., Gordon, G.J.: Individualized Bayesian knowledge tracing models. In: Lane, H.C., Yacef, K., Mostow, J., Pavlik, P. (eds.) AIED 2013. LNCS, vol. 7926, pp. 171–180. Springer, Heidelberg (2013). https://doi.org/10.1007/978-3-642-39112-5_18
3. Pavlik Jr., P.I., Cen, H., Koedinger, K.R.: Performance factors analysis–a new alternative to knowledge tracing. Online Submission (2009)
4. Piech, C., Bassen, J., Huang, J., et al.: Deep knowledge tracing. In: Advances in Neural Information Processing Systems, 28 (2015)
5. Yeung, C.K., Yeung, D.Y.: Addressing two problems in deep knowledge tracing via prediction-consistent regularization. In: Proceedings of the Fifth Annual ACM Conference on Learning at Scale, pp. 1–10 (2018)
6. Shen, S., Liu, Q., Chen, E., et al.: Learning process-consistent knowledge tracing. In: Proceedings of the 27th ACM SIGKDD Conference on Knowledge Discovery & Data Mining, pp. 1452–1460 (2021)
7. Ghosh, A., Heffernan, N., Lan, A.S.: Context-aware attentive knowledge tracing. In: Proceedings of the 26th ACM SIGKDD International Conference on Knowledge Discovery & Data Mining, pp. 2330–2339 (2020)

8. Nakagawa, H., Iwasawa, Y., Matsuo, Y.: Graph-based knowledge tracing: modeling student proficiency using graph neural network. In: 2019 IEEE/WIC/ACM International Conference on Web Intelligence (WI), pp. 156–163 IEEE (2019)
9. Siami-Namini, S., Tavakoli, N., Namin, A.S.: The performance of LSTM and BiLSTM in forecasting time series. In: 2019 IEEE International Conference on Big Data (Big Data), pp. 3285–3292. IEEE (2019)
10. Tai, K.S., Socher, R., Manning, C.D.: Improved semantic representations from tree-structured long short-term memory networks. arXiv preprint arXiv:1503.00075 (2015)
11. Liang, X., Shen, X., Feng, J., Lin, L., Yan, S.: Semantic object parsing with graph LSTM. In: Leibe, B., Matas, J., Sebe, N., Welling, M. (eds) ECCV 2016. LNCS, vol. 9905, pp. 125–143. Springer, Cham (2016). https://doi.org/10.1007/978-3-319-46448-0_8
12. Dey, R., Salem, F.M.: Gate-variants of gated recurrent unit (GRU) neural networks. In: 2017 IEEE 60th International Midwest Symposium on Circuits and Systems (MWSCAS), pp. 1597–1600. IEEE (2017)
13. Li, X.G., Wei, S.Q., Zhang, X., Du, Y.F., Yu, G.: LFKT: deep knowledge tracing model with learning and forgetting behavior merging. Ruan Jian Xue Bao/J. Softw. **32**(3), 818–830 (2021). (in Chinese)
14. Shen, S., Liu, Q., Chen, E., et al.: Convolutional knowledge tracing: Modeling individualization in student learning process. In: Proceedings of the 43rd International ACM SIGIR Conference on Research and Development in Information Retrieval, pp. 1857–1860 (2020)
15. Sherstinsky, A.: Fundamentals of recurrent neural network (RNN) and long short-term memory (LSTM) network. Physica D **404**, 132306 (2020)
16. Hochreiter, S., Schmidhuber, J.: Long short-term memory. Neural Comput. **9**(8), 1735–1780 (1997)

Author Index

Printed in the United States
by Baker & Taylor Publisher Services